Criminal Justice

Second edition

Andrew Sanders LLB MA
Professor of Criminal Law and Criminology,
University of Manchester

Richard Young LLB PhD
Lecturer in Criminal Justice
Assistant Director, Centre for Criminological Research,
University of Oxford

Butterworths
London • Edinburgh • Dublin
2000

United Kingdom	Butterworths, a Division of Reed Elsevier (UK) Ltd, Halsbury House, 35 Chancery Lane, LONDON WC2A 1EL and 4 Hill Street, EDINBURGH EH2 3JZ
Australia	Butterworths, a Division of Reed International Books Australia Pty Ltd, CHATSWOOD, New South Wales
Canada	Butterworths Canada Ltd, MARKHAM, Ontario
Hong Kong	Butterworths Hong Kong, a division of Reed Elsevier (Greater China) Ltd, HONG KONG
India	Butterworths India, NEW DELHI
Ireland	Butterworth (Ireland) Ltd, DUBLIN
Malaysia	Malayan Law Journal Sdn Bhd, KUALA LUMPUR
New Zealand	Butterworths of New Zealand Ltd, WELLINGTON
Singapore	Butterworths Asia, SINGAPORE
South Africa	Butterworths Publishers (Pty) Ltd, DURBAN
USA	Lexis Law Publishing, CHARLOTTESVILLE, Virginia

© Reed Elsevier (UK) Ltd 2000

A CIP Catalogue record for this book is available from the British Library.

First edition   1994

ISBN 0 406 99989 9

Printed and bound in Great Britain by William Clowes Ltd, Beccles and London

Visit Butterworths LEXIS *direct* **at: http://www.butterworths.com**

Preface

'Even reviewers read a preface.' (Guedalla, 1929)

This book is primarily written for students of criminal justice or criminology at undergraduate and postgraduate level. It examines the various stages of the criminal process from the exercise of police powers on the street (stop-search and arrest) through to the final determination of guilt and innocence in the criminal courts, including appeals and reviews of miscarriages of justice.

Sentencing is discussed in the book only where it affects pre-trial and trial processes, such as plea bargaining. Sentencing and penal policy raise a number of related yet distinctive issues which merit separate treatment. We have, however, ventured forth into this territory in a number of places in this edition. This is particularly so in the first chapter where we consider the justifications for the coercion inherent in criminal justice.

Our approach is legal (in that we analyse the law), socio-legal (in that we consider how legal rules operate in practice) and sociological (in that we discuss why courts and criminal justice agencies operate in the way that they do). This book shows that both the effects of legal rules and the ways in which they are operated are central to understanding what those rules actually mean. The police are, for example, given a huge amount of discretion over how to exercise their powers as long as they act 'reasonably'. To understand what is 'reasonable' from the point of view of police officers, and from the point of view of the judiciary who are supposed to oversee the legality of police actions, we need to understand how the system really works. Further, the vacuum left by such vague standards as 'reasonableness' is often filled by Codes of Practice, government circulars and statements of policy. These various documents are therefore a form of law, and are certainly as important as court judgments and statutes.

We have concentrated on 'traditional' law enforcement as practised by the police and courts. But we have also paid attention to other strategies of law enforcement, as seen in the regulation of white collar crimes like fraud, tax evasion and pollution, alternative types of procedure such as restorative justice, and the increasing use of private police forces of various kinds. There remain some obvious gaps, such as the lack of a chapter on powers of entry, search and seizure. What we have done is to provide a framework of analysis, particularly in the first and final chapters, within which such issues can be explored by readers on their own.

We said in our original preface that the first edition (published in 1994) had been written during a period of apparently great change within the criminal justice system. The same is true now, in 2000. For example, the Human Rights Act 1998 and the Youth Justice and Criminal Evidence Act 1999 are about to come into effect even while we are still trying to assess the effect of such major pieces of legislation as the Crime and Disorder Act 1998 and the Criminal Justice and Public Order Act 1994. We commented in that original preface that, despite the great number of detailed changes taking place, and the controversy that some of them aroused, the government's legislative programme represented historical continuity rather than a break with tradition. Both editions of this book are arguments precisely to that effect. This is why we consider it is more important to grasp the sociological context within which the system operates than the minutiae of its legal rules. If we allow ourselves to be mesmerised by the ever-changing details we will be in danger of failing to see the nature and shape of the picture as a whole.

We think that the events of the six years since the first edition have confirmed this analysis. For example, many writers and practitioners believed that aspects of the Police and Criminal Evidence Act (eg the right to legal advice) would lead to greater safeguards in practice for suspects and significant restrictions on the police. We disagreed, partly because we had little belief in the power of the written rule to change policy and practice, and partly because we envisaged that there would be other changes to the criminal justice system to compensate for these changes. What we now see, six years on, is that the changes to the right of silence introduced in 1994, a largely permissive judicial attitude to police rule-breaking, and the increased use of proactive evidence-gathering have indeed undermined any increased protections that might have developed in the early 1990s.

We thus do not believe that 'the law' can be pinned down in the precise way that many law students would like, and many lawyers would claim. Also, taking a snapshot of the law at any one time is less instructive than assessing the way it is developing. The best thing about these intellectual arguments is that they let us off the hook of having to claim that the law is stated as at a certain date. If we were honest we would have to give a different date for each chapter, as the final revisions were made throughout the first eight months of 2000. Generally speaking, major developments up to the summer of 2000 are covered and, where possible, we are up-to-date as at October of this year.

This edition is different from the first edition in four important ways. First, there is the updating already mentioned, not just to incorporate the new legislation of which we have given examples, but also the usual torrent of infuriating case law and a vast amount of research and commentary. Second, it highlights two themes that were neglected in the first edition: victim-related issues and human rights. We now recognise, far more clearly than we did originally, that to understand many aspects of criminal justice we must consider these issues. Consequently, they are woven throughout the book, as well as having specific sections devoted to them in the first and final chapters. Third, it seeks to convey the experiences of the individuals and social groups who are targeted by the criminal justice system. If students and practitioners of criminal justice need to understand how the system appears to the police, it has to be equally important to understand the system from the viewpoint of suspects and defendants. This is another example of how 'contextual' material is part of the law itself. The European Convention on Human Rights prohibits 'inhuman or degrading' treatment, and the common law prohibits making suspects speak 'involuntarily'. But we only know what suspects find 'degrading', or what 'persuades' them to speak, if we understand how it feels to be in custody against one's will.

Perhaps the most important change in this edition it that it develops a new 'freedom model'. Our first edition used the crime control/due process models developed by the American academic, Herbert Packer. One of the problems of Packer's models is that they are not prescriptive. They can help clarify the implications of value choices, but cannot resolve clashes of competing values. Thus, if one is not 'for' the complete crime control approach (denying suspects and defendants most rights and protections) one had either to be 'for' due process (denying the police most powers) or end up advocating a messy and unprincipled compromise. When we came to write this edition we realised that we had to find a *normative* way of arguing a case for avoiding the extremes of crime control and due process. We do not think that the human rights approach, valuable though it is, is the best way to do this. Whether the 'freedom model' is any better will not be clear for some time.

Doubtless our model will be criticised for being philosophically vague and unrealistic in practice. We do not claim to be philosophers or practitioners and we must leave the details to others to work out. What we are trying to do in this book is build a coalition for change. Accordingly we identify practices and trends that should be unacceptable to anyone from the broad range of philosophical traditions consistent with the ideal of a democratic society founded on the rule of law. For pragmatic reasons,

Preface

we are clearer about what we are against, than precisely what we are for. That is why we describe the freedom model as having a core of indeterminancy and a penumbra of certainty. If people can use the freedom model to help understand both why the system works as it does, and how it might be improved, it will have served its purpose. We will welcome criticism, knowing that the reviews of our first bash at a textbook gave us the impetus to try harder this time.

Perhaps the least important change in this edition is that we have managed to reach agreement on the one footnote that saw us divided when the book first appeared. Although, in the process of writing, we remain each other's harshest critic, we resolved any differences of judgement without serious loss of blood. We have occasionally slipped a joke into the text, the origin of which was an attempt to cheer each other up as we laboured on into the small hours of another chilly morning. We left them in on the basis that students also need cheering up, faced, as they are, with overcrowded lecture theatres, declining staff-student ratios, inadequate grants, and the need to buy expensive textbooks.

We thank everyone who has helped us in this enterprise. We cannot name everyone, but would especially like to thank the people whose knowledge, good natures, and wallets we most shamelessly exploited. They are, in alphabetical order, Andrew Ashworth, Lois Bibbings, Ed Cape, Dave Cowan, Ben Goold, Steven Greer, Paddy Hillyard, Roger Hood and Carolyn Hoyle. The fact that the above surnames run from A-H gives rise to a reasonable suspicion that we have forgotten someone equally important, in which case our apologies. Wendy Brett helped get the manuscript in order, as did Hannah Young, Giselle Rosario and Rod Hill. The latter should also get a mention for pointing out that 'Police Complaints Authority' is an anagram of 'The lousy, impractical option'. Needless to say, all the many errors and omissions are not the fault of any of the above, but are due to overwork, messy lives and computer malfunction. All the best bits are by us.

Finally, we thank our families, partners, and dogs (Mutt and Jeff) who helped us in so many ways, and Butterworths for continuing to believe that we would produce this edition when not only our friends and colleagues, but we too, began to doubt it would ever happen. We conclude with another aphorism, one that sums up our approach to writing, and, perhaps, justifies the foul language that peppers this edition.

'It is desirable at times for ideas to possess a certain roughness, like drawings on heavy-grain paper. Thoughts having this quality are most likely to match the texture of actual experience.' (Rosenberg, 1973)

Andrew Sanders
The M56

Richard Young
Waterman's Arms

Contents

Contents

Chapter 3

Arrest   131

Chapter 4

Detention in the police station   187

Chapter 5

Police questioning   245

Chapter 6

Prosecutions   317

Chapter 7

The mass production of guilty pleas   395

Chapter 8

Summary justice in the magistrates' court   483

Chapter 9

Trial by judge and jury   551

Contents

Table of statutes

Table of statutes

Table of cases

Table of cases

R

S

The aims and values of 'criminal justice'

Criminal justice is endlessly fascinating, tragic, laced with the darkest of humour. Terrible, terrifying jokes are told by police officers and other participants as they try to cope with or give meaning to their work.[1] One purpose of this book is to explore the meaning of criminal justice from a variety of perspectives. In this chapter we will examine different theories about the aims and values of the criminal justice system - both what people think they are in practice and what they (and us) think they ideally should be. This will provide the framework within which the specific topics in the subsequent chapters (on police powers, courts, and so forth) will be discussed. By the end of the book you should be able to decide for yourself what you think the system is for, whether you agree with its goals, whether you think it achieves them, and what reforms you would like to see. Because the reality of criminal justice is so very far removed from its public image, we expect that you will be shocked by some of what you read. In coping with our subject matter we have ourselves resorted to dark humour on occasions. But whilst the study of criminal justice can be painfully funny, for those caught up in its operations there is little to smile about.

1. THE NATURE OF 'CRIMINAL JUSTICE'

Authors of a book with a title as vague as 'criminal justice' should begin by trying to define its subject matter. We all have our own ideas about what this term means. Each year during an introductory lecture one of us asks undergraduate law students to specify the main elements of criminal justice. The following are typically identified: the police, prosecutors, the

---

1   On the functions of police humour see C Hoyle, *Negotiating Domestic Violence* (Oxford: Clarendon, 1998) pp 74-82.

courts, and prisons. Defence lawyers are never mentioned. The image of criminal justice these students apparently have is of a system designed solely to apprehend and punish criminals. If that is all the system is for, then defence lawyers would naturally be marginal and easily overlooked.

In thinking about criminal justice we all have our own images, preconceptions and stereotypical assumptions. Part of the function of this chapter is to spell out our own values and explain the theoretical framework within which we think criminal justice can most usefully be understood and criticised. Our choice of framework inevitably affects the kinds of questions we ask about criminal justice. Such a choice cannot be avoided since even apparently atheoretical standpoints are based on some implicit notion of what criminal justice is about and how it works. So, for example, the students' view we mentioned above was based on an unarticulated theory that criminal justice exists to punish wrongdoers. Having adopted that theory, questions about the extent to which the criminal process produces miscarriages of justice and infringements of suspects' civil liberties do not readily spring to mind.

Our own image of the criminal justice system is one of a complex social institution which regulates potential, alleged and actual criminal activity within procedural limits supposed to protect citizens from wrongful treatment and wrongful conviction. This image draws heavily on that developed by Garland to understand aspects of modern society such as government, punishment, or education. He describes these social institutions as:

> 'established frameworks for the satisfaction of needs, the resolution of disputes and the regulation of life in a particular social sphere. Having developed as a means of managing tensions, arbitrating between conflicting forces, and getting certain necessary things done, social institutions typically contain within themselves traces of the contradictions and pluralities of interest which they seek to regulate.'[2]

As each social institution is geared towards managing its own set of conflicting goals and interests, each develops a distinctive identity through the emergence of specialised sub-institutions, processes, practices, and values. The institutional rationality or logic permeating each institution tends to frame and shape decision-making within it. No social institution, however, is entirely self-contained; each both affects and is affected by other institutions. So, for example, while the criminal justice system has a

2   D Garland, *Punishment and Modern Society* (Oxford: Clarendon Press, 1990) p 282.

developed history of its own, which explains much of what goes on v
it, the practice of criminal justice affects and is affected by the worlds of
education, politics, and government, by the forces of culture, economics
and technology, and by advances in such intellectual fields as criminology,
psychology, and sociology. Thus, whilst it makes analytical sense to treat
the institution of criminal justice as a definable object of study, we must
not lose sight of its relatedness with other societal institutions and
developments.

The complexity of social institutions arises not just from this aspect of
relatedness, however. Their complex nature also derives from the fact that
specific events or developments within them 'usually have a plurality of
causes which interact to shape their final form, a plurality of effects . . . and
a plurality of meanings which will vary with the actors and audiences
involved . . .'.[3] To give an example, the 'causes' of an arrest of a suspect
for domestic violence (and the form that arrest takes, eg, how much force
is used) may include: the perceived seriousness of the alleged assault, the
demeanour of the suspect, and the wishes of the victim; the attitudes of
the arresting officers towards domestic violence and to the legal and
procedural rules they are meant to observe in their work (ie, do these officers
believe in doing things 'by the book'?); the concerns the officers might
have about the possibility of being criticised, disciplined, sued or
prosecuted as a result of their actions; the technology available to them to
effect the arrest; the organisational structure and policies of the local police
force (eg, are arrests for domestic violence encouraged or discouraged);
the policing style that has developed locally and/or nationally (which might
range from 'zero tolerance' to seeking negotiated resolutions); and media
or political pressure on the police to target particular forms of criminal
activity. We will leave it to you to think about what the possible multiple
effects of an arrest might be, and what that arrest might mean to people
with different perspectives.[4]

If we are not to reduce analysis of criminal justice to a tedious list of all
possible causes, effects and meanings (imagine a whole book written like
the above paragraph!), we need to build on the fact that some factors and
outcomes are much more powerful than others. What are the *main*
conflicting goals and interests at stake? The very term 'criminal justice'
indicates that we are concerned with sub-institutions and practices charged
with regulating *criminal* behaviour and that, in so regulating, these
institutions and practices are meant to act *justly*. Let us consider the
problematic nature of the aims implied by these elements.

3   Garland (1990) p 280.
4   For our analysis of these issues see ch 3 on arrest.

2. CRIMINAL LAW AND CRIMINAL BEHAVIOUR

Criminal law represents and reflects socially determined judgments that some forms of behaviour should be authoritatively proscribed.[5] What is defined as criminal will vary from society to society and across time. There is nothing inevitable about what is, and is not, 'criminal'. Take England and Wales in the late twentieth century. Its criminal law is generally thought of as proscribing people and corporate bodies from culpably (ie, intentionally or recklessly) acting in particularly harmful or socially undesirable ways. However, much of such behaviour is not criminalised (racial discrimination, invasions of privacy, and the wasteful misuse of the earth's resources are possible examples) and many feel that much of what is criminalised should not be (examples might be smoking cannabis, brothel keeping and swearing by football fans). Moreover, the law criminalises many forms of behaviour where the actor has acted negligently or even, in the case of strict liability offences, where every care was taken to avoid harm. Decisions concerning which acts are to be criminalised are sometimes principled and consensual; more often they are the products of historical accident, political and administrative expedience, and shifting ideological notions of the appropriate reach of the criminal law.

Similar observations might be made about the way in which harmful behaviours are in practice identified as criminal and responded to as such. For example, some victims of domestic violence (including instances of marital rape) do not perceive that their partners have acted in a criminal fashion. And it may be that rowdy behaviour by unemployed scruffy youths will be interpreted in quite a different way to that engaged in by university graduates following their final examinations. One person's public disorder is another's youthful high spirits. These kinds of interpretative decisions are also influenced by shifts in ideology. Thus, for example, feminist writers and activists have over the last 20 years raised public awareness of domestic violence to the point where many more victims and police officers now interpret what takes place within the 'private' sphere of the home as criminal.

Since criminal laws and perceptions of criminality are social constructs it is not surprising that much criminal justice activity reflects the interests of powerful groups and actors. There are many more criminal laws and regulatory resources aimed at harmful behaviour by individuals than at harmful corporate activity, for example. And, as we shall see, tax fraud is prosecuted far less frequently than is benefits fraud. It is true that much of the criminal law (eg, the proscription of theft and inter-personal violence) expresses values which would find a high degree of consensual support

---

5   See H L A Hart, *Punishment and Responsibility* (Oxford: Clarendon Press, 1968) p 6.

within our society.[6] It would be odd if it were otherwise. Those in power generally find it politic to govern primarily by consent rather than by force, especially in a democracy based on universal suffrage. It is thus important that the criminal law be seen as in the interests of at least a majority of the electorate. Nonetheless, in a society in which power, status and wealth are unequally distributed along lines such as age, gender, race and class, much criminal justice activity will compound wider social divisions at the same time as important social values are upheld. Thus, for example, the prosecution and punishment of the poor for shoplifting upholds the value of private property whilst simultaneously reinforcing poverty.

In summary, the enforcement of the criminal law upholds social order for the benefit of all, reinforces a hierarchical form of social order which benefits some more than others, and, in an unequal society, is bound to be morally problematic. Consensus and conflict are thus likely to be interwoven in all attempts at 'maintaining order' and controlling crime. Even if crime control were the sole goal of the criminal justice system, as our students in section 1 of this chapter seemed to think, we would still have to: consider how much control, exercised against which offences and offenders, and to what extent; be aware of the unintended consequences of this control; and consider whether the benefits of, say, 'zero tolerance' of crime outweighs its direct costs and undesirable by-products.

3. JUSTICE OF PROCESS AND JUSTICE OF OUTCOME

The social institution with which this book is concerned is a 'criminal justice' system, not a 'criminal control' system. The terminology is important. Most criminal justice practices are inherently coercive. These practices, moreover, structure decisions about the allocation of state punishment, arguably the most coercive form of power the state wields. Since both the operation of the criminal process and the imposition of punishment infringe the liberty of individual citizens, criminal justice requires justification.[7]

The main divide in debates about the morality of punishment, at least in those societies committed to democratic values, is between liberalism and communitarianism.[8] The common ground in this debate is that the practice

---

6   See the discussion by J Braithwaite, *Crime, Shame and Reintegration* (Cambridge, CUP, 1989) pp 38-43.

7   N Lacey (ed), *A Reader on Criminal Justice* (Oxford: OUP, 1994) p 4.

8   The discussion here presents a simplified account of the differences between 'liberalism' and 'communitarianism' in order to highlight the distinctive underlying assumptions of each position and their implications for criminal justice. See further M Sandel (ed), *Liberalism and its Critics* (New York: New York UP, 1984) and S Mulhall and A Swift, *Liberals and Communitarians* 2nd edn (Oxford:

of punishment is seen as justified by the promotion of valued social goals. The division concerns the nature of the goals to be pursued.

Liberals are concerned with individual freedom, and see the purpose of the state as to provide individuals with a secure framework within which they can pursue their personal autonomy. Punishment is needed in order to protect this freedom from the threat of crime. Its function is to uphold the criminal law's norms of appropriate behaviour through censuring and attaching unpleasant consequences to those who are found to have breached those norms. The institution of punishment is meant to act as a general deterrent against future breaches of those norms as well as performing a socially educative function of declaring and reinforcing the idea that certain forms of social behaviour are particularly wrongful or immoral. The state's power to coerce individuals must, however, be strictly limited to that necessary to secure these aims of punishment, and this entails that punishment must be distributed in a way which appropriately marks the moral distinctions between different forms of criminal behaviour. This ideology lies behind the 'just deserts' model which heavily influenced sentencing reforms in both the United States and England from around the mid-1970s onwards. Punishment came to be seen as something that ought to consist of a fair or proportional amount of censure and retribution.[9]

Communitarian punishment theory values collective welfare at least as much as individual autonomy. It is based on the premise that people do not function autonomously in society but rather pursue their goals within webs of inter-dependency and social attachments.[10] Punishing an individual on the basis of their 'just deserts' may thus further rupture the social bonds already damaged by the offence, whilst imposing suffering on others who do not deserve it. 'Just deserts' thinking is also criticised on the basis that its premise of individual responsibility for crime and its belief in the deterrent and social educative efficacy of punishment ignores the extent to which aspects of social context and structure (poverty, mental capacity, gender relations, and so forth) shape the ability and willingness of individuals to

---

Blackwell, 1996). It is beyond the scope of this book to explore the vast literature on the philosophy of punishment and the often subtle distinctions between different theoretical positions - on which see A Duff and D Garland (eds), *A Reader on Punishment* (Oxford: OUP, 1994) and Matravers (ed), *Punishment and Political Theory* (Oxford: Hart, 1999).

9   The just deserts framework for sentencing was established by the Criminal Justice Act 1991. It was not free from internal contradiction and has been substantially modified subsequently. See generally A Ashworth, 'Sentencing' in M Maguire, R Morgan and R Reiner (eds), *The Oxford Handbook of Criminology* 2nd edn (Oxford: Clarendon Press, 1997).

10   See N Lacey, 'Community in Legal Theory: Idea, Ideal or Ideology' (1996) 15 Studies in Law, Politics and Society 105.

conform to the criminal law's requirements.[11] The aims of punishment should therefore prioritise the promotion of collective welfare through measures designed, for example, to reintegrate offenders into their 'communities' (with the intention of reducing the risk of re-offending and restoring social bonds) and to compensate victims.[12] Forms of welfarist sentencing have survived the ascendancy of the just deserts model, particularly in relation to offenders perceived to be so dangerous that they must be incapacitated for long periods in order to protect the public.[13] More recently, communitarians have agitated for those affected by an offence, including the offender, victim and their respective 'communities of care', to play a central role in deciding what the response to an offence should be.[14] We will look more closely at communitarian thinking on punishment when we examine below the issue of which models of criminal justice best serve the interests of victims.

The justification of the coercion involved in pre-trial and trial processes is linked to justifications for punishment. Both liberal and communitarian agree that the instrumental justification for having a system of investigation, arrest and prosecution is that it enables the state to pursue the same social goals as punishment. Many kinds of offence could not be detected unless special powers were provided to the police (and other law enforcement agencies) to enable them to do things which would otherwise constitute torts or even crimes. In recognition of this, the police are provided with various legal powers to stop and search citizens on the streets, to enter into their homes and seize their property, to detain them in police stations in order to question them, and to take body samples from them as by scraping saliva from inside the mouth. These powers clearly infringe the civil liberties that citizens are normally thought to possess and therefore require justification. The legal pre-condition that attaches to most of these powers is that the police must have 'reasonable suspicion' or 'reasonable belief' that evidence of crime will be obtained through exercising them. The question is whether this is an adequate justification for the exercise of such intrusive powers. This depends, at least in part, on whether we believe that the social benefits to be achieved by the use of police powers outweigh the disadvantages to individual suspects and other citizens. Inevitably, therefore, we must consider the social consequences of criminal justice practices. Granted that these practices infringe liberty, the question arises

11 See especially A Norrie, 'The Limits of Justice: Finding Fault in the Criminal Law' (1996) 59 MLR 540 who argues that the liberal and the communitarian conceptions of criminal justice both have value, and that achieving their synthesis is bound to be problematic.
12 Duff and Garland (1994) p 4.
13 Criminal Justice Act 1991, s 2(2)(b).
14 For a persuasive defence of this position see M Cavadino and J Dignan, 'Reparation, Retribution and Rights' (1997) 4 Int Rev Victimology 233.

of whether they infringe the liberty of some social groups more persistently or violently than others. We also have to see how effective they are at detecting or preventing crime, and whether alternative strategies of social control (such as creating conditions of fuller employment, or requiring car manufacturers to build better security into their products) might be preferable in some circumstances.

Criminal justice must also be concerned with controlling the use of police powers so as to ensure that they are not used for improper purposes, or in an unfairly discriminatory or overbearing fashion. This is important both to uphold the rule of law,[15] and as an expression of democratic ideals such as the equal worth of each citizen.[16] Thus, within criminal justice, we see various mechanisms ostensibly designed to constrain and shape the way in which the police exercise their powers. These include suspects' rights (such as the right to see a lawyer in the police station), and attempts to make the police accountable to the 'wider community' for the creation and implementation of force policies (for example, statutory consultative committees and the use of 'performance indicators'). These concerns about the provision, use and control of powers also apply to other state agencies involved in criminal justice, such as the prosecution and court services. Deciding whether to remand a defendant in custody or to withhold legal aid, for instance, can have a substantial impact on the liberty of the individual. Here too justifications are required if these processes are to be regarded as legitimate, and here too safeguards must be provided against abuses of power.

Liberals and communitarians would have no difficulty in agreeing that safeguards should be built into pre-conviction processes in order to ensure that the coercive harm inflicted through such processes does not 'outweigh' the ultimate social goods sought through invoking the criminal law. Where they would differ is in the precise arrangements that pre-trial justice could justifiably take. To a liberal, for example, the maintenance of the proper relationship between the state and the citizen requires that the individual suspect is treated with dignity and respect.[17] To help ensure that this is so the suspect must be provided with a battery of rights which state officials must observe. To a communitarian, by contrast, of as much importance as individual rights is the satisfaction of collective needs. Individual suspects

15   This is true regardless of one's preferred theory of the rule of law: P Craig, 'Formal and Substantive Conceptions of the Rule of Law: An Analytical Framework' (1997) PL 467 at p 478.

16   For a discussion of democratic values in the context of criminal justice see T Jones, T Newburn and D Smith, 'Policing and the Idea of Democracy' (1996) 36 BJ Crim 182.

17   See P Aranella, 'Rethinking the Functions of Criminal Procedure' reprinted in S Wasserstrom and C Snyder, A Criminal Procedure Anthology (Cincinnati: Anderson, 1996) at p 18.

might justifiably be given less rights if this would significantly advance collective welfare. Responsibilities and duties might be imposed as well as rights provided.[18]

Our discussion so far, focussing as it has on powers and the various mechanisms for controlling their use, has overlooked one crucial additional method by which power is legitimated in practice - consent. Lacey writes that: '. . . criminal justice is constantly at risk of being seen as cruel and oppressive, with consequent risks to the background support and compliance on which its stability and effectiveness depend. Whilst criminal justice power is ultimately coercive, its exercise depends at almost every level on many forms of cooperation and consensus.'[19] As we shall see in this book, consent has a double-edged quality in the operation of criminal justice. For whilst it enables criminal justice officials to achieve their goals without resorting to coercive legal powers, thus making criminal justice appear less repressive and more just, consent also enables those same officials to avoid the legal controls and safeguards which generally attach to those powers.

We have argued that it is impossible to evaluate criminal justice without keeping in mind the ultimate aims it is meant to secure. Since those aims are shaped by competing theories of political philosophy, and since no one theory dominates the law (either as expressed in books, or in action), we should expect to find tensions and contradictions at every level of criminal justice. One's view of how those contradictions should be resolved will also differ according to which political philosophy one prefers.

4. GUILT AND INNOCENCE

One point on which nearly everyone agrees, at least in theory, is that the pursuit of the ultimate social goals of criminal justice must be qualified by the goal of avoiding miscarriages of justice, ie, the conviction of the factually innocent. In order to legitimate a specific punishment 'a moral licence is required in the form of proof that the person punished broke the law. . .'.[20] But how compelling must this proof be? The higher the threshold we choose, the more difficult it will become to convict the guilty, thus impeding the pursuit of the ultimate social goals of punishment.

---

18 This approach is not necessarily inconsistent with a concern for human rights: M Cavadino, 'A Vindication of the Rights of Psychiatric Patients' (1997) 24 JLS 235 at p 237.

19 N Lacey, 'Introduction: Making Sense of Criminal Justice' in N Lacey (ed), *A Reader on Criminal Justice* (Oxford: OUP, 1994) pp 4-5.

20 H L A Hart, *Punishment and Responsibility* (Oxford: Clarendon Press, 1968) p 22. See also R M Dworkin, 'Principle, Policy, Procedure' in C Tapper (ed), *Crime, Proof and Punishment* (London: Butterworths, 1981).

The rhetoric of English criminal justice is that priority is given to protecting the factually innocent from wrongful conviction over bringing the factually guilty to justice. In *Hobson*,[1] decided in 1823, Holroyd J declared that 'it is a maxim of English law that 10 guilty men should escape rather than one innocent man should suffer.' Note that even at this rhetorical level the system does not offer any *guarantee* against miscarriages of justice occurring. The only way to ensure this would be not to prosecute anybody at all. But this cannot be countenanced, either from a liberal or a communitarian position. Therefore a compromise has to be struck between procedures which allow the effective prosecution of suspected offenders whilst reducing the risk of wrongful conviction to an acceptable level. Holroyd J did not suggest that it was better that 100, or 1,000 guilty persons went free in the effort to avoid a solitary conviction of an innocent. Protecting the innocent from conviction is not, and cannot be, the overriding consideration. This was recognised by the Court of Appeal in *Ward* when it said that criminal justice:

'. . . should be developed so as to reduce the risk of conviction of the innocent to an absolute minimum. At the same time we are very much alive to the fact that, although the avoidance of the conviction of the innocent must unquestionably be the primary consideration, the public interest would not be served by a multiplicity of rules which merely impede effective law enforcement.'[2]

This judgment, however, fudges two key issues. No-one in their right mind would advocate a multiplicity of rules which *merely* impeded effective law enforcement. Rules protecting suspects from harsh treatment or invasions of privacy often do impede 'effective' law enforcement, but, in a democracy, this price is seen as worth paying in order to protect the liberty and dignity of the individual suspect. Second, does the Court of Appeal really mean that the risk of miscarriages should be reduced to an 'absolute minimum'? That 10,000 guilty persons shall, if necessary to achieve this, go free? Leaving aside these rhetorical flourishes (or slips of the judicial typing finger), the judgment accepts the principle that protecting the innocent should be regarded as more important than convicting the guilty.

To what extent is the acquittal of the innocent defendant a priority of English criminal justice in fact? The main theoretical safeguard offered to suspects in the English system of criminal justice (and also under the European Convention of Human Rights) is the presumption of innocence. This presumption finds expression in the principle that guilt must be proved beyond reasonable doubt. There are two aspects to this principle; firstly it

1   1 Lew CC 261.
2   (1993) 96 Cr App Rep 1 at 52.

stipulates a high standard of proof, and, second, it places the burden of proof on the prosecution.

(a) The standard of proof

If a court was allowed to find a person guilty on the balance of probabilities (the standard of proof applied in civil cases) then many more factually guilty persons could be successfully prosecuted, but so too could many more who were factually innocent. If, on the other hand, it was required that guilt be proven beyond any doubt at all, whether reasonable or not, then few successful prosecutions could be brought. This would protect people who were actually innocent, but such a system would allow the vast majority of suspects who came to the notice of the police (and who were in fact guilty) to escape conviction. The standard of proof required (guilt beyond reasonable doubt) amounts to a compromise between two conflicting aims: to convict the guilty and acquit the innocent. The particular standard chosen expresses a preference for erroneous acquittals over erroneous convictions.

An analysis in the early 1980s of the practical operation of the criminal law showed that the high standard of proof requirement is often undermined by laws and practices which make conviction easier.[3] The Crime and Disorder Act 1998 provides a more recent example. Under s 1 either the police or local authority can apply to a magistrates' court for the making of an 'anti-social behaviour order'. The procedure involved is civil, not criminal. An order can be made if it is found on the balance of probabilities that a person had acted 'anti-socially', meaning in a manner which caused or was likely to cause harassment, alarm or distress. The order must be made for a minimum of two years and for the purpose of preventing further 'anti-social' acts by the defendant. The court has wide discretion to impose prohibitions such as curfews, or commands to avoid certain places or individuals. Doing anything in breach of the order (whether otherwise criminal or not), without reasonable excuse, is a criminal offence carrying a penalty of up to five years' imprisonment. To allow orders of such a penal character[4] to be made on the basis of the civil standard of proof does not suggest a strong commitment to avoiding miscarriages of justice. Imagine how you would feel if ordered to avoid frequenting any local pub for the next two years or risk imprisonment, because a magistrate had determined that you had *probably* behaved rowdily at closing time on some previous occasion.[5]

3   D McBarnet, *Conviction* (London: Macmillan, 1983).
4   See R Leng, R Taylor and M Wasik, *Blackstone's Guide to the Crime and Disorder Act 1998* (London: Blackstone, 1998) p 11.
5   See further A von Hirsch et al, 'Overtaking on the right' (1995) 145 NLJ 1501.

(b)   The burden of proof

Viscount Sankey LC described the burden of proof in *Woolmington v DPP* as the 'golden thread' which ran throughout criminal law.[6] 'No matter what the charge or where the trial, the principle that the prosecution must prove the guilt of the prisoner is part of the common law of England and no attempt to whittle it down can be entertained.'[7] In fact, however, the principle has been made subject to so many exceptions that one may question whether it is better thought of as a rule which applies only in certain residual situations.[8] Ashworth and Blake calculate that 219 out of the 540 indictable (ie serious) offences in common use involved a reversal of the burden of proof.[9] The Criminal Justice and Public Order Act 1994 created two new such offences in connection with terrorism, both carrying penalties of up to 10 years' imprisonment.[10] Thus it is now an offence for someone to possess any article giving rise to a reasonable suspicion that the article was possessed for a purpose connected with the commission, preparation or instigation of a terrorist act. Because articles that can be useful in terrorist activity include such otherwise innocuous items as rubber gloves, adhesive tape and nylon fishing line, the offence hinges on a 'reasonable suspicion' (of terrorist purpose), a concept which, as ch 2 will show, is both vague and relatively easy to establish. Once such a reasonable suspicion is aroused, the suspect can avoid conviction only by proving that the article was not possessed for such a purpose.[11]

At the less serious end of the criminal spectrum (ie summary offences), there are many more offences which similarly reverse the burden of proof. One important example is s 5 of the Public Order Act 1986. This provides

6   [1935] AC 462 at 481.
7   [1935] AC 462 at 481-2.
8   See A Ashworth, 'A threadbare principle' [1978] Crim LR 385, and 'Public Order and the Principles of English Criminal Law' [1987] Crim LR 153; and McBarnet (1983) pp 102-110.
9   A Ashworth and M Blake, 'The Presumption of Innocence in English Criminal Law' [1996] Crim L R 306.
10 Section 16A (possession of articles) and s 16B (collection of information) of the Prevention of Terrorism (Temporary Provisions) Act 1989, as inserted by s 82 of the 1994 Act. For discussion see A Hunt, 'Unravelling the golden thread - the prevention of terrorism and the presumption of innocence' (1994) Criminal Lawyer p 4.
11 See also the Criminal Justice (Terrorism and Conspiracy) Act 1998, rushed through Parliament in the wake of the Omagh atrocity in which 29 people were killed. The legislation makes admissible in evidence the unsubstantiated opinion of a senior police officer that a person has committed the offence of belonging to a proscribed organisation. Whilst such 'evidence' must be corroborated before conviction may follow, this corroboration may, under the Act, consist merely of a suspect's silence. This legislation effectively reverses the burden of proof - the suspect must refute the senior officer's opinion to avoid conviction.

that it is an offence to use threatening, abusive or insulting words or behaviour within the hearing or sight of a person likely to be caused harassment, alarm or distress thereby. If the prosecution proves these conduct elements (ie, that the defendant did do as alleged) accused persons may escape liability only if they can prove that their conduct was reasonable. Thus the prosecution does not have to prove that the defendant's behaviour was unreasonable to secure a conviction. The burden of proof is placed on the defendant. As we shall see in ch 3, in the common situation in which a suspect's behaviour may amount to any one of a number of overlapping offences, the police often prefer to make an arrest for this type of summary offence precisely because it is easier to prove.

The lesson to be drawn from this section is that, rather than be taken in by rhetorical flourishes concerning supposedly fundamental principles such as prioritising the protection of the innocent, one must consider in detail the actual rules and their operation. We must, in other words, be alive to the possibility that the rhetorical goals of criminal justice are not necessarily the same as the goals that are actually pursued.

5. ADVERSARIAL AND INQUISITORIAL THEORIES OF CRIMINAL JUSTICE

Evidence relating to guilt and innocence is not a ready-made objective body of facts. It has to be gathered, put in some coherent order and then presented. This is done in accordance with rules, principles and policies of criminal procedure and evidence. In the case of criminal justice systems there are two broad approaches to achieving the goal of rational fact-finding - the adversarial and the inquisitorial. The adversarial principle that it is for the prosecution to bring a case to court and prove guilt is a characteristic of the English system and of other common law systems such as Australia, Canada and the USA.[12] The major alternative to adversarial systems is that posed by civil law systems, such as France or Germany, based on inquisitorial principles.[13] In an inquisitorial system the dominant role in conducting a criminal inquiry is supposed to be played by the court. A

12 Although, as we saw in the previous section, whether this really is a principle is questionable. This serves as a further warning against accepting broad statements of principle at face value.
13 As we observed earlier, in developing their own identities and institutional rationalities complex social institutions are influenced by many other aspects of the society in which they are situated. The different cultural traditions of Scotland and England, for example, have produced quite different systems of criminal justice and a detailed consideration of the position north of the border is beyond the scope of this book.

dossier is prepared to enable the judge taking the case to master its details. The judge then makes decisions about which witnesses to call and examines them in person, with the prosecution and defence lawyers consigned to a subsidiary role. In some inquisitorial systems the dossier is prepared (in serious cases) by an examining magistrate, (*juge d'instruction*) with wide investigative powers, but more frequently this is done by the prosecutor and police.[14]

In the 'pure' adversarial system, by contrast, the burden of preparing the case for court falls on the parties themselves. The judge acts as an umpire, listening to the evidence produced by the parties, ensuring that the proceedings are conducted with procedural propriety, and announcing a decision at the conclusion of the case. If the parties choose not to call a certain witness, then however relevant that person's evidence might have been, there is nothing the court can do about it. The adversarial contest in court thus resembles a game in which truth might appear to be the loser.[15] Indeed, it is sometimes said that adversarial systems focus on proof, and inquisitorial systems on truth.[16] But this is too simplistic. Both systems are concerned with establishing the truth, but they differ on the best way of achieving that end.

Adversarial theory holds that 'truth is best discovered by powerful statements on both sides of the question'[17] which are then evaluated by a passive and impartial adjudicator. This recognises that the events leading up to a criminal offence, and the intentions or knowledge of the parties involved, are always open to interpretation and dispute. The danger in an inquisitorial system is that whoever conducts the investigation (whether the police, a prosecutor or an examining magistrate) will come to favour one particular view of the matter, and that this will influence the construction of the dossier. Material helpful to the accused may be excluded. There is also the danger that a trial judge, having formed an initial view of the case based on a reading of the dossier, will give too much weight to evidence adduced at the trial which is consistent with the pre-existing theory, and too little to that which conflicts with it.[18] Fuller is one writer

14   There are considerable differences between systems which are labelled 'inquisitorial': M Damaska, 'Evidentiary Barriers to Conviction and Two Models of Criminal Procedure: A Comparative Study' (1973) 121 U Penn LR 506.

15   See M E Frankel, 'The Search for the Truth: An Umpireal View' (1975) 123 U Penn LR 1031.

16   See the critique of the adversarial system by a Chief Constable, C Pollard, 'Public Safety, Accountability and the Courts' [1996] Crim LR 152, and the reply by A Ashworth, 'Crime, Community and Creeping Consequentialism' [1996] Crim LR 220.

17   *Ex p Lloyd* (1822) Mont 70, 72 n.

18   See the account of one inquisitorial trial by C Johnston, 'Trial by dossier' (1992) 142 NLJ 249.

who doubted the wisdom of adjudicators actively conducting inquiries in court:

'What starts as a preliminary diagnosis designed to direct the inquiry tends, quickly and imperceptibly, to become a fixed conclusion, as all that confirms this diagnosis makes a strong imprint on the mind, while all that runs counter to it is received with diverted attention.'[19]

Far better, according to the adversarial theory, that the judge remain impartial throughout and allow the parties to put forward their interpretations of the facts and law in the way most favourable to them.[20] By opening up a range of possible views, it is more likely that the 'real truth' will emerge. As Fuller put it:

'The arguments of counsel hold the case, as it were, in suspension between two opposing interpretations of it. While the proper classification of the case is thus kept unresolved, there is time to explore all of its peculiarities and nuances.'[1]

So, while inquisitorial systems are rightly portrayed as involving a preeminent commitment to search for the truth, the way in which that search is conducted can shape the 'truth' that is proclaimed in court. Adversarial systems, by contrast, with their emphasis on the parties proving their case, can lose sight of the truth for different reasons: one or both of the parties might deliberately suppress relevant evidence for tactical reasons, or one party (almost invariably the defendant) might lack adequate access to the resources or expertise needed to counterbalance the arguments of their opponent.[2]

The differences between adversarial and inquisitorial models extend well beyond the question of the best method to arrive at the truth. They also express different ideological conceptions of how power should be allocated in society.[3] These differences result in the adversarial model attaching less

19　L L Fuller, 'The Forms and Limits of Adjudication' (1978) 92 Harv LR 353 at p 383.
20　See the discussion by J Sprack, 'The Trial Process' in E Stockdale and S Casale (eds), *Criminal Justice Under Stress* (London: Blackstone Press, 1992) pp 67-70.
1　L L Fuller, 'The Forms and Limits of Adjudication' (1978) 92 Harv LR 353 at p 383.
2　See J McEwan, 'Adversarial and Inquisitorial Proceedings' in R Bull and D Carson (eds), *Handbook of Psychology in Legal Contexts* (Chichester: Wiley, 1995).
3　See M Damaska, *The Faces of Justice and State Authority* (New Haven: Yale, 1986) and the accessible discussion by J Jackson, 'Evidence: Legal Perspective' in R Bull and D Carson (eds), *Handbook of Psychology in Legal Contexts* (Chichester: Wiley, 1995).

Adversarial and inquisitorial theories of criminal justice

weight to the goal of reliable fact-finding than the inquisitorial model, not because that goal is seen as unimportant, but rather because of an acknowledgement that the pursuit of other important aims necessarily implies a reduced relative weighting for 'truth-discovery'.[4] The adversarial model asserts that the reality of any criminal matter is that the state is trying to prove a case against an individual citizen in order to fulfil its duty of enforcing the criminal law. In order to guard against the state abusing its powerful position, safeguards must be provided. One such safeguard is an expression of the constitutional doctrine of the separation of powers in that the state provides a forum in which one branch of government (the judicial, ie, the criminal courts) considers the case built and presented by another (the executive, ie, the police and the prosecution). The passivity of magistrates and judges required by adversarial theory can also be seen as an expression of this mistrust of official power, as can the use of lay people (juries and non-stipendiary magistrates) to deliver verdicts on guilt or innocence. These devices all seek, amongst other things, to guarantee the impartiality of adjudication.

The adversarial model is also sensitive to the need to provide safeguards against the abuse of power by the state's investigators and prosecutors. These safeguards seek to ensure that evidence is collected by fair and lawful means, which respect the dignity of individual citizens (including suspects), and which result in the presentation in a court of evidence which is both relevant and reliable. Thus, for example, defence lawyers are meant to play an active part at the investigative stage of a criminal case (advising the suspect, applying for bail, and so forth) and there are limits on the length of time suspects can be held by the police for questioning. The importance attached in an adversarial system to the integrity of the procedures followed in collecting evidence and proving guilt can also be seen in the development of a complex web of rules of evidence aimed at promoting both the fairness and reliability of verdicts pronounced by a court.[5]

In the inquisitorial system, by contrast, the underlying assumption is that the state can be (largely) trusted to conduct a neutral investigation into the truth. Therefore the need for safeguards such as passive adjudicators, a strict separation of investigative and adjudicative powers, rules of evidence and defence lawyers is seen as much reduced. It is not uncommon for suspects to be subjected to lengthy periods of pre-charge incarceration without access to legal advice. Leigh and Zedner have noted that 'while nothing in French law requires the over-use of detention, a tendency to do so seems deeply ingrained in the legal culture and doubtless derives from a desire not to release a suspect until the truth has been

4   See Damaska (1973) especially at pp 579–80 and n 197.
5   For a critical account of these rules see J McEwan, *Evidence and the Adversarial Process* 2nd edn (Oxford: Hart, 1998).

ascertained'.[6] All too often the supposed safeguard against oppressive police practices offered by judicial or prosecution control of the investigation process is a chimera. As Leigh and Zedner observe of the French system:

> 'by the time a suspect has been brought before the *juge d'instruction* he has already been in the hands of the police for 48 hours during which time he has been questioned vigorously. . . . We do not believe that the examining magistrate is a real protection against overbearing police practices save in rare cases where physical brutality is involved. Furthermore, despite the fact that only 10% of cases go before the *juge d'instruction*, the system is overburdened and works slowly.'[7]

The problem of abuse in the inquisitorial system, and doubts about the effectiveness of the juge d'instruction have led to their abolition in Germany in 1975. Corruption amongst investigative judges led to abolition in Italy in 1988. Whether adequate safeguards for suspects were put in place as a result of these changes seems doubtful.[8]

In order to avoid giving the impression that everything in the English adversarial garden is rosy we need now to overlay our account of the theoretical underpinnings of English criminal justice by saying something about its own weed-ridden history. We noted earlier that every complex social institution has its own history which is part of the key to understanding its present form. By summarising the particular form our adversarial system has taken over the last 20 years, we aim to throw into sharper relief the nature of its goals and values.

6. THE RECENT HISTORY OF ENGLISH CRIMINAL JUSTICE

In 1981, the Royal Commission on Criminal Procedure (the Philips Commission), originally set up because of the wrongful conviction of three youths for the murder of Maxwell Confait,[9] published its blueprint for a

6   L H Leigh and L Zedner, A Report on the Administration of Criminal Justice in the Pre-Trial phase in England and Germany (Royal Commission on Criminal Justice, Research Study no 1) (London: HMSO, 1992) p 53.
7   Leigh and Zedner (1992) at p 68.
8   See further N Jorg, S Field and C Brants, 'Are Inquisitorial and Adversarial Systems Converging?' in C Harding, P Fennell, N Jorg and B Swart, *Criminal Justice in Europe* (Oxford: Clarendon, 1995).
9   See the official inquiry into what became known as the 'Confait Affair': Report of an Inquiry into the Circumstances leading to the Trial of Three Persons on Charges arising out of the Death of Maxwell Confait and the Fire at 27 Doggett Road, London SE6 (HCP 90) (London: HMSO, 1977).

'fair, open, workable and efficient' system.[10] It recommended that there should be a 'fundamental balance' in criminal justice between the rights of suspects and the powers of the police.[11] Although not all of its proposals were accepted, the report of the Philips Commission led to the passing of the Police and Criminal Evidence Act 1984 (PACE) and the Prosecution of Offences Act 1985.

PACE, together with its associated Codes of Practice, provided, for the first time, a detailed legislative framework for the operation of police powers and suspects' rights. The 1985 Act created the Crown Prosecution Service to take over the prosecution function from the police. Lawyers, rather than the police, now have the final say on how cases should be brought to court. The aim was, in part, to try to ensure that a number of defects in criminal procedure exposed by the 'Confait Affair' - such as undue pressure on suspects to confess, the unavailability of legal advice for suspects in police stations, and the absence of an independent check on police decisions - would be eliminated, thereby reducing the risk of further miscarriages of justice.

However, since the mid-1980s, a string of similar cases have come to light including the 'Guildford Four', the 'Maguires', the 'Birmingham Six', Stefan Kiszko, Judith Ward, the 'Cardiff Three', the 'Tottenham Three', the Taylor sisters, and the 'Bridgewater Four'. Long terms of imprisonment were served by nearly all of the defendants in these cases. Paddy Nicholls, whose conviction was quashed on 12 June 1998, served 23 years for the 'murder' of someone later shown to have almost certainly died of natural causes.[12] The causes of the miscarriages of justice varied from case to case, but common features were the suppression by the police and prosecution agencies of evidence helpful to the defence, incriminating evidence (including false confessions) secured from suspects by the police use of psychological pressure and tricks, and the distortion, manipulation and occasional fabrication of prosecution evidence (again, including confession evidence).[13] By implication, a further cause was the inadequate resources available to the defence to guard against or uncover this wrongdoing prior to conviction. For all these reasons, the adversarial truth-discovery mechanism of hearing powerful arguments on both sides of the question had been undermined, and juries had understandably convicted on the basis of what had seemed in court to be overwhelming prosecution cases.

10 Royal Commission on Criminal Procedure (RCCP), Report (Cmnd 8092) (London: HMSO, 1981) para 10.1.
11 RCCP (1981) paras 1.11 to 1.35.
12 *The Guardian*, 13 June 1998.
13 For a useful account of some of the main cases see J Rozenberg, 'Miscarriages of Justice' in E Stockdale and S Casale (eds), *Criminal Justice under Stress* (London: Blackstone, 1992).

Some of the people involved in these cases were tried before the changes in the law ushered in by the Philips Commission, but others (such as the 'Cardiff Three', where three young men were wrongly accused of murdering a prostitute) were convicted under the new regime. Also, by July 1993, the convictions of 14 people had been quashed because of irregularities by one particular group of police officers (the West Midlands Serious Crime Squad), most of these being post-PACE cases.[14] The pressure created by these spectacular miscarriages led to the establishment of the Royal Commission on Criminal Justice (the Runciman Commission), which reported in 1993.[15] Never before had the protections for suspects against wrongful conviction appeared to require such urgent repair work. Yet the Runciman Commission advocated few major changes to the criminal process, arguing that there was no reason to believe that the 'great majority' of verdicts were 'not correct'.[16] Moreover, its recommendations taken overall favoured the interests of the police and prosecution agencies more than those of suspects.[17]

How can we explain this failure to strengthen the position of the defence relative to that of the prosecution? Most academic commentators have concluded that the root problem was that the Runciman Commission failed to develop an adequate evaluative framework to inform its work.[18] This failure was particularly evident in the Runciman Commission's approach to the theoretical basis of English criminal justice. It considered whether a shift to an inquisitorial mode of criminal procedure would reduce the risk of miscarriages of justice and concluded that it would not. Keeping the roles of police, prosecutor and judge separate from one another (as in the English adversarial system) was thought by the Commission to offer a better protection for innocent defendants than a system (such as the inquisitorial) which blurred investigative, prosecution and judicial functions.[19] It acknowledged, however, that some of its recommendations 'can fairly be interpreted as seeking to move the system in an inquisitorial direction, or

14   Many of these cases are discussed in T Kaye, 'Unsafe and Unsatisfactory?' Report of the Independent Inquiry into the working practices of the West Midlands Police Serious Crime Squad (London: Civil Liberties Trust, 1991).
15   Royal Commission on Criminal Justice (RCCJ), Report (Cm 2263) (London: HMSO, 1993).
16   RCCJ (1993) para 23.
17   For critiques see R Young and A Sanders, 'The Royal Commission on Criminal Justice: A Confidence Trick?' (1994) 15 OJLS 435; M McConville and L Bridges (eds), *Criminal Justice in Crisis* (Aldershot: Edward Elgar, 1994) and S Field and P Thomas (eds), *Justice and Efficiency? The Royal Commission on Criminal Justice* (London: Blackwell, 1994) (also published as (1994) 21 JLS no 1).
18   Its inept interpretation of empirical data, the poor quality of its arguments, and the feeble nature of many of its recommendations were other important factors: Young and Sanders (1994).
19   RCCJ (1993) para 14.

at least as seeking to minimise the danger of adversarial practices being taken too far.'[20] Thus the Runciman Commission advocated that the defence should be under greater obligations to disclose its arguments prior to trial, and that judges should be more interventionist in their management of trials, as by calling some witnesses themselves, and by preventing lawyers from engaging in 'unfair' cross-examination of vulnerable witnesses.

The difficulty with these proposals is that they were not grounded in a proper theoretical understanding of adversarial ideology - indeed the Runciman Commission seemed almost to congratulate itself on choosing instead to be 'guided by practical considerations' aimed at improving the criminal justice system's capacity to serve 'the interests of both justice and efficiency.'[1] It accordingly failed to resolve the contradiction, for example, between supporting both the adversarial ideal of the impartial passive judge and the inquisitorial ideal of the investigating interventionist judge.[2]

We shall see in later chapters how subsequent legislation based on the Runciman Commission's recommendations grafted important inquisitorial elements onto what remains an essentially adversarial structure. There is nothing new in such apparent contradiction. Many other mechanisms and accommodations have long been incorporated within it in the English context.[3] We have already seen, for example, how frequently the adversarial principle of the burden of proof lying on the prosecution is honoured only in the breach. The important point is that whatever goals are better secured by such accommodations, such as efficiency, undiluted truth-seeking, or a higher rate of convictions, are likely to be achievable only at the expense of the goals and values that adversarial ideology encompasses. Adversarial procedures as currently operated in this country are far from perfect. But reforms to those procedures which ignore their underlying rationality are likely to produce a system so weakened by its own internal contradictions that its claims to legitimacy will sound hollow.

A separate question raised by this sequence of events is whether the Runciman Commission was right to think that the new framework established by the 1984 and 1985 Acts was basically sound. Another view is that something more than mere tinkering was needed if suspects were to

20   RCCJ (1993) para 12.
1   RCCJ (1993) para 12. It is telling that whereas the Runciman Commission devoted a chapter to 'Prosecution', there is no equivalent chapter on defence.
2   See further J Jackson, 'The Royal Commission on Criminal Justice: (2) The Evidence Recommendations' [1993] Crim LR 817.
3   As is also true of the American system - see E Sward, 'Values, Ideology, and the Evolution of the Adversary System' (1989) 64 Indiana LJ 301. It is a commonplace to observe that no system of justice conforms exactly to an idealised adversarial or inquisitorial theory. For discussion of whether systems based on the different theories are 'converging' see Jorg et al (1995).

be adequately protected, as suggested by patterns of police malpractice and apparently (and actual) wrongful convictions that have come to light since the Commission reported.[4] An opposite view is that the mid-1980s legislation had already swung the pendulum so far in favour of safeguards for suspects that the ability of the police to bring criminals to justice had been unduly hampered, the occasional dramatic miscarriage or corruption case notwithstanding.

The latter view prevailed in the years immediately following the publication of the Runciman Commission's report. Taken together, the Criminal Justice and Public Order Act 1994, the Criminal Appeal Act 1995, the Criminal Procedure and Investigations Act 1996, the Police Act 1997, the Crime and Disorder Act 1998 and the Criminal Justice (Terrorism and Conspiracy) Act 1998 have provided the police and prosecution with important new powers and significantly reduced the rights and safeguards of suspects. But what exactly does it mean to claim that the police were 'unduly hampered' by PACE, or that suspects had been given 'too many' rights? Decisions about how much power to give the police and prosecution agencies cannot be factually determined but rather express value choices about the appropriate goals of criminal justice, the order in which they should be prioritised, and the appropriate means to achieve them. Is there any way of clarifying the implications of such choices and thus provide us with the normative material we need in order to come to a more rational decision about the appropriate means and ends of criminal justice?

These were the kinds of problem which, over 30 years ago, an American writer, Herbert Packer, tackled when he developed his two models of the criminal process: due process and crime control.[5] These models have been used by many commentators on criminal justice as useful tools of analysis, and you are likely to find frequent references to them when reading about criminal justice.[6] The models themselves have also been subjected to much

4 On miscarriages see the investigative journalism of Bob Woffinden in *The Guardian*, 6 December 1997 and (with Richard Webster) 9 May 1998; on police sexism, racism, cruelty and corruption see D Campbell's balanced analysis in the same newspaper, 14 December 1998; on quashed convictions since the RCCJ reported, see ch 10.

5 H L Packer, *The Limits of the Criminal Sanction* (Stanford: Stanford UP, 1968) ch 8.

6 See, for example, M McConville and J Baldwin, *Courts, Prosecution, and Conviction* (Oxford: Clarendon, 1981) pp 3-7; S H Bailey and M J Gunn, *Smith and Bailey on the English Legal System* 3rd edn (London: Sweet & Maxwell, 1996) pp 776-9; 912-5; and the first edition of this book. For refinements and other approaches see, for example, A E Bottoms and J D McClean, *Defendants in the Criminal Process* (London: Routledge, 1976) pp 226-232; M King, *The Framework of Criminal Justice* (London: Croom Helm, 1981) ch 2, A Norrie, '"Simulacra of Morality?" Beyond the Ideal/Actual Antinomies of Criminal Justice' in A Duff (ed), *Criminal Law: Principle and Critique* (New York: CUP, 1998), K Roach, 'Four models of the Criminal Process' (1999) 89 J Crim law and Criminology 671 and this edition of this book.

criticism. In the next section we explain the models, and comment on their strengths and weaknesses.

7. CRIME CONTROL AND DUE PROCESS

Packer developed his models in order to illuminate what he saw as the two conflicting value systems that competed for priority in the operation of the criminal process. Neither corresponded to reality, and neither was to be taken as the ideal. Rather, at each successive stage of the criminal process they represented extremes on a spectrum of possible ways of doing criminal justice. Use of the models would thus enable one to plot the position of current criminal justice practices at each stage, as well as to highlight the direction of actual and foreseeable trends along any given spectrum.

(a)   Crime control

In this model the repression of criminal conduct is viewed as by far the most important function to be performed by the criminal process. In the absence of such repression, a general disregard for the criminal law would develop and citizens would live in constant fear. In order to successfully uphold social freedom, the model must achieve a high rate of detection and conviction. But because crime levels are high and resources are very limited the model depends for success on speed and on minimising the opportunities for challenge. Formal fact-finding through examination and cross-examination in court is slow and wasteful. Speed can best be achieved by allowing the police to establish the facts through interrogation. To further guarantee speed, procedures must be uniform and routine, so that the model as a whole resembles a conveyor belt in its operation.

The quality control in this system is entrusted in large measure to the police. By the application of their expertise the probably innocent are quickly screened out of the process while the probably guilty are passed quickly through the remaining stages of the process. 'If there is confidence in the reliability of informal administrative fact-finding activities that take place in the early stages of the criminal process, the remaining stages of the process can be relatively perfunctory without any loss in operating efficiency.'[7] Indeed, the model goes further in claiming that the pre-trial administrative processes are more likely to produce reliable evidence of guilt than formal court procedures.

The ideal mechanism for truncating the judicial stage of the process is the guilty plea as then the need for lengthy and expensive trials is

---

7   Packer (1968) pp 160-161.

eliminated. The police will thus seek to extract confessions from those whom they presume to be guilty as this makes it very difficult for the suspect to do other than admit guilt at court. For as Packer concludes of the crime control model, 'when reduced to its barest essentials and operating at its most successful pitch, it offers two possibilities: an administrative fact-finding process leading (1) to exoneration of the suspect or (2) to the entry of a plea of guilty.'[8]

The crime control model accepts that some (but not many) mistakes will be made in identifying the probably guilty and the probably innocent, and is prepared to tolerate such mistakes for the sake of the overall goal of repressing crime efficiently. On the other hand, if too many guilty people escaped liability, or the system was perceived to be generally unreliable (as would be the case if it was shown that innocent people were being prosecuted on a large scale) then the deterrent efficacy of the criminal law would be weakened. Only in this situation does the reliability of decisions about guilt and innocence become a matter of independent concern within the crime control model. In other words, the wrongful conviction of the innocent is not seen as a problem per se. Safeguards against such miscarriages of justice are only accepted as necessary where a failure to provide them would jeopardise the overall goal of repressing crime. Otherwise, findings of guilt should be regarded as final.

While the crime control model can tolerate rules forbidding illegal arrests or coercive interrogations (since such rules might promote reliability) it strongly objects to those rules being enforced through the exclusion, in court, of illegally obtained evidence, or the quashing of convictions simply because the rules have been breached. From this perspective it is intolerable that credible evidence is ruled inadmissible merely because the methods used to obtain it were improper. To let the guilty go free on such a technicality undermines crime control. In the 'Dirty Harry' films, the eponymous hero played by Clint Eastwood is spurred into law-breaking action by the operation of just such a due process mechanism. For Harry, the ends - getting the bad guys - justify the means. The means used by the good and bad guys became identical and only the different ends sought enable us to tell which is which. 'Dirty Harry' is the personification of crime control ideology.

(b) Due process

The due process model lacks confidence in informal pre-trial fact-finding processes. The police will naturally hold a genuine belief that they have correctly apprehended the right suspect, but only in the movies are they

---

8   Packer (1968) pp 162-163.

invariably correct. Many factors may contribute to a mistaken belief in guilt which itself may become a force in the production of unreliable evidence against the suspect. For example, witnesses to disturbing events tend to make errors in recollecting details, or may be animated by a bias that the police either encourage or will not seek to discover. Similarly, confessions by suspects in police custody are as likely to signify psychological coercion as they are to demonstrate guilt. Due process therefore insists on formal, adjudicative, adversary fact-finding processes in which the case against the accused is tested before a public and impartial court.

Because of this concern with error, the due process model also rejects the crime control desire for finality. There must always be a possibility of a case being reopened to take account of some new fact that has come to light since the last public hearing. Unlike crime control, the due process model insists on the prevention and elimination of errors as an end in itself: 'The aim of the process is at least as much to protect the factually innocent as it is to convict the factually guilty.'[9]

As important as is its concern with reliability, the due process model upholds other values of more far-reaching effect. Chief amongst these is the primacy of the individual citizen, and thus the complementary need for limits on official power. Controls are needed to prevent state officials exercising their coercive powers in an oppressive manner. That such controls might impair the overall efficiency of the system is of minor concern to the due process model. The presumption of innocence can be seen as one such control, since it places the burden on the state to prove legal guilt in a procedurally proper manner.

In certain situations, the concern with abuse of power in the due process model takes precedence over reliability. Suppose, for example, that the police had illegally obtained evidence that established that a suspect had almost certainly committed a murder. The due process model would insist that the evidence be excluded at trial; if there was no other evidence of guilt, the suspect would walk free because of the procedural irregularity. It is only by demonstrating to officials that there is nothing to be gained by abusing power and breaking rules that adherence to them can be guaranteed.

The due process model is also concerned with the upholding of moral standards as a matter of principle. In the belief that an important way to encourage and affirm law-abiding behaviour is by example, unlawfully obtained evidence has to be excluded.[10] To do otherwise would be to undermine the moral condemnation which is meant to be conveyed by a finding of guilt.[11] An example of this kind of thinking is contained in

9   Packer (1968) p 165.
10   See Packer (1968) pp 231-232.
11   In his 'reconstruction' of Packer's models, Aranella (1996) p 21, points out that: 'A public trial, if fairly conducted, sends its own message about dignity, fairness, and justice that contributes to the moral force of the criminal sanction.'

Professor Michael Zander's note of dissent to the report of the Runciman Commission.[12] The dissent covered three points, one of which concerned the powers of the Court of Appeal when reviewing a conviction.[13] The majority view as expressed in the report proper was that, where there was sufficient reliable evidence of guilt, even the most serious misconduct by the prosecution should not result in the conviction being quashed: a classic crime control position. Zander's disagreement was fundamental:

'If the behaviour of the prosecution agencies has deprived a guilty verdict of its moral legitimacy the Court of Appeal must have a residual power to quash the verdict no matter how strong the evidence of guilt. The integrity of the criminal justice system is a higher objective than the conviction of any individual.'[14]

The due process model also upholds the ideal of equality - that everyone should be placed in the same position as regards the resources at their disposal to conduct an effective defence of a criminal charge. Thus, whenever the system affords a theoretical right for a lawyer to advise or represent a client, the due process model insists that substance be given to that right by providing public funds to those who cannot afford the costs of a lawyer unaided. Lawyers play a central part in this model since they are needed to bring into play the remedies and sanctions which due process offers as checks against the operation of the system.

Finally, the due process model is sceptical about the morality of the criminal sanction. It notes that in practice this sanction is used primarily against the psychologically and economically impaired. To seek to condemn and deter these people for their supposedly free-will decision to breach the criminal law smacks of cruel hypocrisy, particularly when there is a failure to provide for the individualised and humane rehabilitation of offenders. Adherents of this model are therefore generally in favour of limiting and restraining attempts to catch and punish alleged offenders. 'In short', as Packer puts it, 'doubts about the ends for which power is being exercised create pressure to limit the discretion with which that power is exercised.'[15]

At the risk of over-simplification, one can summarise the main conflict in values between the two models in the following way. Crime control values prioritise the conviction of the guilty, even at the risk of the conviction of some (fewer) innocents, and with the cost of infringing the liberties of suspects to achieve its goals; while due process values prioritise the

12   RCCJ (1993) p 221.
13   One other Commissioner lent her support to this aspect of Zander's dissent.
14   RCCJ (1993) p 235.
15   Packer (1968) p 171.

acquittal of the innocent, even if risking the frequent acquittal of the guilty, and giving high priority to the protection of civil liberties as an end in itself. Both models employ powerful arguments and Packer himself suggested that anyone who supported one model to the complete exclusion of the other 'would be rightly viewed as a fanatic'.[16]

In Packer's models it is common ground that the system has the potential to become an adversarial struggle in which the values of adversarial ideology would be honoured to the full. But whereas due process seeks to maximise this potential by introducing obstacles and hurdles for the prosecution to surmount at every stage, crime control seeks ways of ensuring that the adversarial contest never gets beyond the encounter between the police and the suspect in the police station. Due process and adversarial ideology thus can work harmoniously together, whereas crime control values tend to subvert adversarial procedures. Indeed, with its emphasis on trusting the police and prosecution to get at the truth in a reliable manner, the crime control model expresses some of the ideological elements which underpin the inquisitorial model.

(c)   What are the goals of crime control and due process?

In order to clarify the goals of Packer's two models we shall review briefly some important aspects of the debate which his work has stimulated. Some criticisms of Packer's analytical framework (and how it has been used) derive from a misunderstanding about the goals and values each model encompasses. Ashworth, for example, argues that Packer failed to give a clear explanation of the relationship between his two models, in as much as Packer conceded that their polarity was not absolute and that the ideology of due process was not the converse of that of crime control. Ashworth therefore suggests that the 'models might be reconstructed so as to suggest that crime control is the underlying purpose of the system, but that pursuit of this purpose should be qualified out of respect to due process.'[17] Similarly Smith argues that 'the Crime Control Model is concerned with the fundamental goal of the criminal justice system, whereas

16   Packer (1968) p 154.
17   A Ashworth, *The Criminal Process* 2nd edn (Oxford: OUP, 1998), p 27. See also his articles 'Criminal Justice and the Criminal Process' (1988) 28 BJ Crim 111 at p 117: 'crime control and due process may both be desirable objectives. . .' and 'Concepts of Criminal Justice' [1979] Crim LR 412 at 413 (fn 4). Ashworth's writing appears to assume that the two models only encompass one main aim each. In fact both models encompass an interest in protecting suspects and controlling crime but differ in their empirical assumptions (eg, *are* the police reliable fact-finders?) and their priorities and value choices (eg, how much weight *should* be given to individual dignity).

the Due Process Model is concerned with setting limits to the pursuit of that goal. Due Process is not a goal in itself.'[18]

These criticisms are misconceived. They place too much weight on the labels Packer applied to his models.[19] In particular, it is mistaken to regard the due process model as merely a negative model in which the aim is only to protect suspects. The two models share much common ground including the assumptions that the 'criminal process ordinarily ought to be invoked by those charged with the responsibility for doing so when it appears that a crime has been committed' and that 'a degree of scrutiny and control must be exercised with respect to the activities of law enforcement officers, ... the security and privacy of the individual may not be invaded at will.'[20] It thus follows that *both* models incorporate the belief that law enforcement is socially desirable[1] (because of its crime preventive effects) and *both* incorporate the belief that there must be some limits to the power of the government to pursue this underlying aim. The difference between the models, put simply, is that they represent very different points of view about what those limits should be.[2]

18   D Smith, 'Case Construction and the Goals of Criminal Process' (1998) 37 BJ Crim 319 at 335. See, to similar effect, Aranella (1996) p 19, and Damaska (1973) p 575.

19   Another criticism by Ashworth (1998) p 27 is that 'Packer assumed that the system of pre-trial justice is capable of affecting the crime rate, since he used the term Crime Control.' No such assumption was made. The crime control model represents a belief system, both a set of empirical beliefs (efficiently convicting the guilty will deter crime) and value commitments (civil liberties of suspects are less important than the repression of crime). All that Packer 'assumed' is that the belief that convicting the guilty efficiently could affect the crime rate was widespread enough to qualify as an important strand of thinking within one of his models of the criminal process. That is still surely the case. (Note that the due process model doubts the deterrent efficacy of punishment, thus illustrating that Packer (1968) p 170, 'assumed' that such scepticism was sufficiently widely held to count as another important strand of thinking within the criminal process.)

20   Packer (1968) pp 155-6.

1   Note the comment by Packer (1968) p 163 that the due process model 'does not rest on the idea that it is not socially desirable to repress crime, although critics of its application have been known to claim so.' See also P Duff, 'Crime Control, Due Process and "The Case for the Prosecution"' (1998) 38 BJ Crim 611.

2   See also M McConville, A Sanders and R Leng, 'Descriptive or Critical Sociology: The Choice is Yours' (1997) 37 BJ Crim 347 at 355-6. The rejoinder to this latter article, D Smith, 'Reform or Moral Outrage-The Choice is Yours' (1998) 38 BJ Crim 616, indicates that Smith has not grasped this point: 'There has to be a compromise [between the values of due process and crime control], because the crime control goal could not be pursued at all if the due process constraints were pressed to the limit of what is possible' (p 617). But while a system which adhered fully to the due process model would no doubt be 'inefficient' at producing convictions, it would still seek to convict some of the factually guilty - there would be 'quantitative output', not just 'quality control': Packer (1968) p 165.

Whereas Ashworth and Smith's criticisms are essentially theoretical, Choongh criticises Packer from an empirical standpoint, arguing that neither of his models adequately explains the experiences of a significant minority of those who are arrested and detained at the police station.[3] For these detainees there is never any intention by the police to invoke the criminal process:

> 'Arrest and detention is not, for this group of individuals, the stepping stone onto Packer's conveyor belt or the first stage of an obstacle course. It represents instead a self-contained policing system which makes use of a legal canopy to subordinate sections of society viewed as anti-police and innately criminal.'[4]

He argues that the police are here operating a 'social disciplinary' model, which encompasses the belief that:

> 'an acceptable and efficient way to police society is to identify classes of people who in various ways reject prevailing norms because it is amongst these classes that the threat of crime is at its most intense. . . the police are then justified in subjecting them to surveillance and subjugation, regardless of whether the individuals selected for this treatment are violating the criminal law at any given moment.'[5]

However, Packer was constructing models of the criminal process, not of policing; it is not surprising that 'social disciplining' was not central in his analysis. It is widely acknowledged that policing encompasses many aims: maintaining surveillance over public space, quelling disorder, responding to emergencies, rescuing pets, providing advice, directing traffic and so on.[6] Only some of these are associated with controlling crime and even fewer are necessarily related to the formal criminal process. What Choongh's work usefully does is highlight the way in which the police sometimes use resources provided by the criminal process (such as interrogation powers) to pursue some part of the broader police mission. Nonetheless, Packer was too astute an observer to have overlooked that police powers could be (indeed are) used to subject whole classes of people

3   S Choongh, 'Policing the Dross: A Social Disciplinary Model of Policing' (1998) 38 BJ Crim 623.
4   Choongh (1998) p 625.
5   Choongh (1998) p 627. The 'criminal classes' Choongh mentions are the lower-working class, ethnic minorities, travellers, gypsies and the homeless. See also S Choongh, *Policing as Social Discipline* (Oxford: Clarendon, 1997).
6   See the discussion in M Wasik, T Gibbons and M Redmayne, *Criminal Justice: Text and Materials* (Harlow: Longman, 1999) pp 111-120.

to surveillance and subordination.[7] Thus he noted that the crime control model rejected the due process idea that arrest should only be allowed when there was reason to believe that a specific individual had committed a specific crime.[8] Rather, 'people who are known to the police as previous offenders should be subject to arrest at any time for the limited purpose of determining whether they have been engaging in anti-social activities. . .'.[9] Secondly:

> 'anyone who behaves in a manner suggesting that he may be up to no good should be subject to arrest for investigation: it may turn out that he has committed an offence, but more importantly, the very fact of stopping him for questioning, either on the street or at the station house, may prevent the commission of a crime. As a third instance, those who make a living out of criminal activity should be made to realise that their presence in the community is unwanted if they persist in their criminal occupations; periodic checks of their activity, whether or not this involves an arrest, will help to bring that attitude home to them.'[10]

Packer clearly linked these forms of 'social disciplining' to the ultimate goal of controlling crime. So does Choongh, albeit unwittingly.[11] The type of 'social disciplining' documented in Choongh's work reflects an important strand of crime control ideology but does not justify the construction of a new model of the criminal process.

The main purpose of this chapter is, as we said at its start, to see what criminal justice is for. We have now clarified what adherents to crime control and due process models see as its purpose. Whether one believes the system is (or should be) governed predominantly by due process or crime control values, the purpose of the system would (or should) remain the same: to control crime, but with some protections for suspects. Where one locates an actual criminal process on the spectrum of possibilities represented by the two models depends largely on the nature and extent

---

7   Packer (1968) p 178, also noted that the criminal law itself might be so vaguely defined (eg, vagrancy and disorderly conduct laws) as to make 'social disciplining' lawful.

8   Packer (1968) p 176. Compare this with the mistaken assertion by Choongh (1998) pp 624-5 that both Packer's models assume that police behaviour at each stage of the criminal process anticipates a further 'legal step in the process to legal adjudication. Stop and search powers are activated because the police have reasonable suspicion that a crime has been, is or is about to be committed. . . [Arrest] is done with a view to charging him with an offence.'

9   Packer (1968) p 177. Compare with Choongh (1998) p 628: 'Having arrested individuals once, this in itself becomes reason for keeping them under surveillance . . . an individual becomes permanently suspect rather than a suspect for a particular offence.'

10   Packer (1968) p 177.

11   See Choongh (1998) pp 629 and 632 for example.

of those protections. By now you may have begun to think about which set of values you find the more attractive and this may have aroused your curiosity about where English criminal justice lies on Packer's spectrum. We will therefore provide a brief overview.

(d)   English criminal justice: due process or crime control?

The English criminal system, like the American, is usually characterised as one which emphasises adversarial procedures and due process safeguards. In terms of the formal structure we can observe these safeguards intensifying as a person's liberty is progressively constrained.[12] The least constraining exercise of police power is simple questioning on the street of someone who is merely a citizen, not a suspect. Since the questions are not aimed at incriminating the individual no due process protections are needed, but no compulsion can be exercised either. The police are here in a fact-finding or inquisitorial mode.

As soon as the police have any reason to suspect the individual an 'adversarial' relationship is formed; the citizen becomes a suspect. The police now have the task of collecting evidence of what they believe the suspect has done so that this can be proven to the satisfaction of the courts. To assist them in this task the law provides them with various powers and, in order to guard against the misuse of these powers, due process protections begin. Only if there is 'reasonable suspicion' can coercive powers be exercised to search or to arrest a suspect. On arrest the suspect is generally taken to a police station and detained. This requires further due process justification because civil liberties are further eroded by detention and its associated procedures such as interrogation, search of the suspect's home, and fingerprinting. Only if detention is adjudged to be 'necessary' (ie, in a broad sense of furthering the investigation) can it be authorised. If detention is authorised, further forms of due process protection come into play, such as the right to legal advice, a right not to be held incommunicado and other procedural safeguards. In order to charge and prosecute a detainee, further evidence is required and further protections are provided - vetting of the case by the Crown Prosecution Service and a grant of legal aid to prepare a defence. In order to convict there must be yet more evidence (proof beyond a reasonable doubt).

And so at each stage, as a citizen becomes in turn a suspect, a detainee, an accused, and a defendant, the due process requirements become more stringent. This is in accordance with Packer's portrayal of due process as an obstacle course with each successive stage presenting formidable impediments to carrying the citizen any further along the process. This

12   All the points made in this sub-section are discussed in later chapters, at which point supporting references are provided.

should mean that few factually innocent persons are found legally guilty, or are carried too far down the course, but it will also mean that many factually guilty persons will be ejected from the system for lack of the required standard of evidence.

If we look at the way the system actually operates, however, it displays certain features characteristic of a crime control model. Decisions to arrest and stop-search are often made on police instinct rather than reasonable suspicion, detention for the purpose of obtaining a confession is routinely and uniformly authorised, and incentives to plead guilty (such as sentence discounts) are routinely offered to suspects. Perhaps most telling is the fact that the great majority (over 90%) of defendants whose cases proceed to trial plead guilty and forego their right to initiate an adversarial battle. The prosecution evidence is not tested, and 'proof' beyond reasonable doubt is constituted by the plea itself. The probability in such a system is that many more factually innocent persons will be found legally guilty, and that many more factually guilty persons will be convicted, than if the system actually operated in the formal manner described above. In Packer's imagery, the system operates as a conveyor belt, moving suspects through a series of routinised procedures which lead, in the vast majority of those cases that reach court, to conviction.

Packer's conclusion in the American context was that the actual operation of the criminal process conformed closely to crime control, but that the law governing that process (as developed, in particular, by the Supreme Court) expressed due process ideology.[13] He identified a gap, in other words, between the law in books and the law in action. But as Packer himself pointed out, it was perfectly possible for the Supreme Court to change tack and develop case law which expressed crime control values.[14] If the rules themselves were in harmony with the crime control model, then there would be no need for the police to break them in order to achieve their central goal, (if such it is) of repressing crime efficiently. The only gap that would then exist would be between the law in books and due process ideology. McBarnet argued, in the early 1980s, that this was precisely the situation in Britain:

'the law governing the production, preparation and presentation of evidence does not live up to its own rhetoric. . . Police and court officials need not abuse the law to subvert the principles of justice; they need only use it.'[15]

13 Packer (1968) p 239.
14 Packer (1968) p 240.
15 McBarnet, at pp 154 and 156. Her analysis is, however, generally regarded as being too simplistic. See, for instance, McConville, Sanders, and Leng, *The Case for the Prosecution* (London: Routledge, 1991) chs 9–10 and Duff (1998) p 613.

The question of where on the spectrum between crime control and due process English criminal justice is today to be located must, therefore, take account of both the formal law as laid down in statutes and case law, and the actual operation of the system by officials operating within that legal framework. The first edition of this book, published in 1994, attempted to do this and concluded that the criminal process was far more oriented towards the crime control model than surface appearances might suggest, that there was a historical drift towards the crime control model, but that due process inspired safeguards remained, and would continue to remain, important.[16] Subsequent events have not caused us to revise that assessment. So where do we go from here? Does it matter which mix of crime control and due process values our system expresses, or that a shift away from the latter is occurring?

At this point it should be reiterated that Packer did not intend either of his models to be prescriptive.[17] Which value system one inclines towards is ultimately a matter of moral and political choice. This is not to say that one's choice is all just a matter of opinion, however. It is possible to make some evaluation of whether there is a need for more due process or more crime control simply by using Packer's framework. For example, the crime control model assumes that the police are reliable fact-finders, whereas the due process model rests, in part, on quite the contrary assumption. If it could be established that the police were not particularly reliable fact-finders then the argument in favour of more due process would be strengthened. On the other hand, if the evidence suggested that due process protections in a particular setting were thwarting the police from bringing most of the actually guilty to justice, the converse would be true. We begin to examine these issues in the next chapter, where we look at the first of the array of powers that PACE provides to police officers, the power to stop and search suspects. Ultimately, however, a preference for more crime control or more due process rests upon a value judgment rather than upon empirical evidence. All that analysis of the law in books and the law in action can provide is material to assist in the process of moral reasoning.

Critics have pointed out that Packer's models illuminate only some of the major conflicting interests at the heart of the criminal process. In particular, it has been noted by Ashworth that the models pay insufficient attention to issues relating to the efficient management of resources and to the victims of crime.[18] The importance of these dimensions has been

16   A Sanders and R Young, *Criminal Justice* (London: Butterworths, 1994) pp 460-1.

17   See Packer (1968) p 154.

18   Ashworth (1998) p 28. He also notes here that Packer saw a premium on speed as an aspect of the crime control model but seemed not to recognise that a properly developed notion of due process should insist that there be no unreasonable delay (as that can adversely affect defendants, eg, when they are remanded in custody prior to trial). But see Packer (1968) at pp 156 and 242-3.

increasingly recognised in recent years, and each is therefore reviewed below. Ashworth's main reason for not adopting Packer's models in his own analysis of the criminal process, however, is that they offer no way of definitively resolving conflicts in the criminal justice system between different sets of interests, such as those of suspects, victims, and society at large. He sets out to remedy this by seeking to establish definitive principles and goals for the operation of criminal justice.

8. THE PRINCIPLED (HUMAN) RIGHTS APPROACH

Ashworth argues that the 'balancing' of conflicting criminal justice aims and interests should not be driven by consequentialist calculations of which set of arrangements would produce the most overall benefit to society. Rather, individual rights must be assigned some special weight in the balancing process, particularly those enshrined as positive law in the European Convention on Human Rights (ECHR).[19] As this latter document is regarded as inadequate in a number of respects, Ashworth also considers, as a matter of principle, which interests ought to be protected through rights, and the extent of protection each right should be given. His main purpose is to develop a prescriptive theoretical framework: 'to locate a set or number of principles which have the authority or the persuasiveness to serve as goals for the criminal process or criteria by which to judge it.'[20]

He concedes that the protection of human rights is not the fundamental aim of the criminal process:

'Why do we process cases through the system towards a court appearance? Surely the answer to this question cannot be found in respect for human rights, whether in the form of the ECHR or any other declaration. We do not have a criminal process in order to show respect for human rights. We have a criminal process in order to assist in the conviction of the guilty and the acquittal of the innocent, in a way that respects the human rights of all individuals affected. The protection of human rights therefore needs to form part of the fundamental justification but it cannot be the sole or even the primary justification.'[1]

Ashworth clearly does not escape the pull of the language of due process and crime control. But his vision of the ideal criminal process differs from the type of process implied by Packer's models in that the goal of convicting the guilty would be authoritatively constrained by human rights principles

19   Ashworth (1998) pp 30-31.
20   Ashworth (1998) p 29.
1   Ashworth (1998) pp 65-66.

Chapter 1 — The aims and values of 'criminal justice'

instead of merely compromised to a varying extent by conflicting due process principles. We next consider the persuasiveness of this ideal.

(a) The prescriptive value of the principled approach

For Ashworth, the main principled priorities lie in protecting the rights of individuals caught up in the criminal process. These rights, such as the right of an innocent person not to be convicted, the right to be treated fairly and without discrimination, and the right to be presumed innocent, should be regarded as having special weight. Any derogations from them (based, say, on the claimed need to repress crime more effectively, or because of some national emergency) should be reasoned and minimal. However, he also recognises certain rights of victims as important too, such as the right to compensation and the right to respect in the criminal process. How does Ashworth suggest we resolve conflicts between different rights and between the protection of rights and the goal of controlling crime? Sometimes the problem is solved by the absolute status of one of the rights in conflict, as is the case with the prohibition by Art 3 of the ECHR of the use of torture or inhuman or degrading treatment or punishment. These methods of controlling crime are absolutely forbidden, regardless of what overall social benefits they might bring in a particular case or context.

Most of Ashworth's principles and rights, however, are 'fundamental' not 'absolute'. This is partly because of cost and partly because statements of rights cannot be allowed to stand in isolation from the overall justification for having a criminal process - to control crime. Both these concerns are well illustrated in Ashworth's discussion of why the principle that the innocent should be protected against wrongful conviction should be regarded as fundamental but not absolute.[2] First, he acknowledges that attempts to introduce ever-more elaborate safeguards against wrongful conviction could only be achieved by diverting resources from other important social needs, such as education, health, and social security. To put it bluntly, how many hospitals (and how many life-saving operations) are we prepared to sacrifice for the sake of achieving some marginal (and unquantifiable) increase in the protection of innocent people against wrongful conviction? Second, the more elaborate safeguards against wrongful conviction became, the more difficult it might be to convict the actually guilty. Ashworth's conclusion is that the criminal process should be organised in such a way as to render the risk of wrongful conviction 'acceptably low', and that this objective necessitates research both into the sources of error and the consequences of erecting safeguards against

2   Ashworth (1998) pp 50-52.

them.[3] That still leaves open the questions of what is to count as 'acceptably low', how much we are prepared to spend on achieving this, how much we are prepared to infringe the rights of victims in erecting such safeguards, and how we are to know when the actually guilty have been acquitted (and the innocent protected). As Ashworth acknowledges:

'It would be foolish to deny that conflicts will arise here, and equally foolish to deny that ultimately such conflicts will need to be resolved by means of some compromise or balancing. What is distinctive about the approach advocated here is that the process of resolving the conflicts should be securely based on facts established by research, and firmly grounded in a proper appreciation of the rights and interests of all relevant parties.'[4]

We agree that this is the correct approach to take. Indeed, we believe that the particular strength of Ashworth's framework is his method for seeking to resolve criminal justice issues. That method consists of balancing rights and interests only after:

'. . . a lengthy and careful process, whereby rights and interests are identified; arguments for including some and excluding others are set out; appropriate weights or priorities are assigned to particular rights and interests, either generally or in specific contexts; and so forth. Above all, this must be a properly researched, reasoned, and principled course of argument. . .'[5]

It is worth stressing, however, that there is no necessary reason at the moral level why anyone should adopt the rights framework advanced by Ashworth.[6] Utilitarians would adopt a completely different normative starting point and would therefore not weigh competing claims in the same way as does Ashworth. Similarly, communitarians and liberals would each attach different weights to the interests at stake. As will be seen below, we ourselves depart from Ashworth's prescriptive starting point. For we disagree with his assertion that the fundamental purpose of the criminal process is to assist in the conviction of the guilty and the acquittal of the

3   Ashworth (1998) p 51.
4   Ashworth (1998) p 52.
5   Ashworth (1998) p 31. For a more detailed analysis of Ashworth's approach see A Hunt and R Young, 'Criminal Justice and Academics: Publish and Be Ignored?' (1995) 17 Holds LR 193.
6   On the (perhaps insuperable) difficulties of establishing such a foundational reason see J Schwartz, 'Relativism, reflective equilibrium, and justice' (1997) 17 LS 128.

The principled (human) rights approach

innocent in a way that respects human rights. There is much more at stake than that.

Ashworth's framework, with its emphasis on procedural fairness, could be viewed as a principled defence of the key elements of Packer's due process model.[7] The defence is all the sounder for its sensitivity to other important factors including financial constraints, and the interests of victims, witnesses and the wider 'community'. In short, the framework alerts us to the complexity of the interests at stake within the criminal process, highlights and develops the (predominantly) liberal arguments for resolving issues in a particular manner, and provides us with a mode of argument which makes it easier to defend due process values (if that is what one wishes to do). However, it should by now be clear that a variety of more or less pro-suspect positions (for want of a better phrase) are consistent with his approach, and the approach itself is contestable from philosophical standpoints other than his own.

(b) The descriptive value of the principled approach

To what extent is it useful to examine the extent to which the criminal process conforms to human rights principles? There have in the past been no entrenched rights or principles governing the operation of criminal justice. Common law rights created by the judges and rights created by statute could be whittled away, amended, or removed altogether by the courts or by Parliament. Thus, for example, the Criminal Justice and Public Order Act 1994 severely limited a suspect's supposedly fundamental right to silence and we have already commented on how the presumption of innocence is often treated lightly.

However, since 1953 the UK has been bound at the international level by the ECHR.[8] This has meant that breaches of the fundamental rights set out in the Convention could be challenged, but only before the European Court of Human Rights in Strasbourg.[9] If the Court ruled that a breach had

7   That human rights norms effectively force one to adopt a due process rather than a crime control model is a point suggested by C Walker, *The Prevention of Terrorism in British Law* 2nd edn (Manchester: MUP, 1992) p 12.

8   In addition, criminal justice in this country is now subject in a growing number of areas to European Community law and, therefore, to judicial supervision from the European Court of Justice. See, eg, J Dine, 'European Community Criminal Law?' [1993] Crim LR 246; and E Baker, 'Taking European Criminal Law Seriously' [1998] Crim LR 361.

9   It should be noted that prior to the Human Rights Act 1998 our national courts sometimes did take into account the Convention in developing and construing national law, although the degree of enthusiasm with which they did so varied from case to case and over time. See Hunt (1998).

occurred the UK was obliged to amend the offending law or practice in order to give effect to our international obligations. The recognition that this procedure was cumbersome and slow eventually led to the passing of the Human Rights Act 1998. The legislation requires British courts to take account of the Convention and the decisions of the European Court. If a common law precedent is found to be inconsistent with the Convention, the latter must be followed. If, on the other hand, a court finds that a UK statute cannot be interpreted in accordance with the Convention, the court may make a 'declaration of incompatibility'. A new 'fast-track' procedure is provided for by the Act which will allow Parliament to amend the incompatible legislation.

Since signing the European Convention it may be said that Parliament has been bound to give effect to its provisions through its power to amend and make law binding in domestic courts. The principles and rights established through the jurisprudence of the European Court of Human Rights thus provide us with criteria with which to evaluate criminal justice. Laws and practices which undermine the positive rights established by the European Court may be seen as unethical, since they contravene our international obligations and are inconsistent with the rule of law. There are, however, a number of problems with using the human rights framework as a descriptive tool of analysis.

First, many of the rights and principles established in the Convention are couched in vague terms. This is so even of those that appear at first sight to be crystal clear. Thus, for example, Art 3 states that 'no one shall be subjected to torture or to inhuman or degrading treatment'. This apparent clarity, however, dissolves as soon as one starts to think about what would amount to inhuman or degrading treatment. Is it not degrading to be arrested in public, or to have saliva scraped from inside one's mouth, for example? This vagueness, is, of course, a quality of all legal rules, since they are inevitably 'open-textured' to a greater or lesser degree.[10] Rules always require interpretation and consideration of how they are to be applied in any given situation. One consequence of this is that no-one can simply ask the Court to review the compatibility of national laws with the Convention in the abstract. Rather, specific individuals have to make a case that their human rights were infringed by the way in which they were treated at the hands of state officials.[11] This means that judgments are sensitive to the facts of a particular case and may not provide definitive or indicative answers to the question of whether a law or legal practice in itself might be in breach of the Convention (in some or all circumstances).

10 H L A Hart, *The Concept of Law* (Oxford: Clarendon, 1961).
11 See the discussion by R Munday, 'Inferences from Silence and European Human Rights Law' [1996] Crim LR 370.

It can take much litigation before the exact parameters of human rights requirements become clear.

For example, a series of attempts has been made to test the validity of the provisions restricting the right to silence in the UK against those parts of the European Convention on Human Rights which declare a right to a 'fair and public hearing' (Art 6(1)) and that everyone 'shall be presumed innocent until proved guilty according to law' (Art 6(2)). The first such attempt was partially successful, in that the judgment of the European Court indicated that the application of these provisions might well infringe the Convention, and partially unsuccessful, in that the particular application of the provisions at issue in the proceedings was not regarded as having breached the Convention.[12]

A further problem with the Convention is that even its supporters recognise that in many respects the protection it offers to human rights is deficient.[13] Thus it makes virtually no special provision for the rights of vulnerable groups of suspects, such as juveniles or the mentally disordered, nor is there any explicit reference to the interests of victims or witnesses.[14] Some of the rights it does contain are subject to many broadly-drawn exceptions. For example no invasion of the right to privacy declared in Art 8 is allowed unless it is:

'in accordance with the law and is necessary in a democratic society in the interests of national security, public safety or the economic well-being of the country, for the prevention of disorder or crime, for the protection of health or morals, or for the protection of the rights and freedoms of others.'

It is true that the European Court sometimes interprets such exceptions strictly. But it is also true that the Court often allows considerable room for manoeuvre to member states through its 'margin of appreciation' doctrine. Under this doctrine a state's assessment of the need to invade rights is subjected to a relatively undemanding standard of judicial review. Moreover, Art 15 of the ECHR provides that at a time of 'public emergency threatening the life of the nation' the state can take measures derogating from its Convention obligations. Such measures must be 'strictly required by the exigencies of the situation', and there can be no derogation of the Art 2 right to life, or the Art 3 right to be free of torture and inhuman or degrading treatment. Nonetheless, state defences based on derogation are

12   *Murray* v *UK* (1996) 22 EHRR 29. This and subsequent cases are discussed in ch 5, section 2.
13   See Ashworth (1998) at pp 49-50 and at p 307: 'Its coverage of rights is incomplete and patchy.'
14   The European Court has indicated a willingness to make good some of these deficiencies when an opportunity presents itself: see further ch 9, section 3(b).

themselves subject to the margin of appreciation doctrine. This means that the ECtHR will not lightly interfere with the State's judgment that a 'public emergency' justifies interference with individual rights. In practice derogation provides another important way in which the provisions of the Convention Articles lose much of their apparent force.[15] Thus the UK entered a derogation in respect of the 'emergency' legislation prompted by the situation in Northern Ireland and its related breaches of the Art 5 criteria governing the legality of arrest and detention. The derogation has been adjudged valid by the European Court on successive occasions.[16]

None of this should be taken as implying that human rights are unimportant. They have for half a century provided a legal safety-net, precluding a jump by the state towards the kind of harsh and repressive criminal justice typical of extremely illiberal or totalitarian states. This has been particularly important at times when a weak government has been tempted to turn to populist 'tough on crime' measures in an attempt to revive its flagging political fortunes.[17] Thus, whilst Michael Howard's tenure at the Home Office in the mid-1990s might accurately be depicted in those terms, and whilst many despaired at the lurch towards the crime control model which he engineered, the European Convention set outer limits to what he could realistically do. The same is true of the Labour Home Secretary at the turn of the century, Jack Straw, whose respect for civil liberties appears to be no greater than that of his Tory predecessor. The influence of the Convention should be seen as much in what the state has *not* done in criminal justice over the last half-century as in particular developments of law and practice. Moreover, human rights jurisprudence has now developed to the point where it embodies an authoritative resolution of at least some of the conflicting interests at stake within criminal justice. Finally, as a result of the Human Rights Act 1998, human rights standards will in the near future play a much more influential role throughout the criminal process.[18] Never again will a Royal Commission be able to ignore human rights, as the Runciman Commission did. For all these reasons we believe that the protection of human rights must be considered in any modern analysis of criminal justice.

One final limitation of the human rights perspective is that it tends to offer highly individualistic remedies to abuses of power. Its core method

15 See S Marks, 'Civil Liberties at the Margin: the UK Derogation and the European Court of Human Rights' (1995) 15 OJLS 68.

16 *Ireland v UK* (1978) 2 EHRR 25; *Brannigan and McBride v UK* (1993) 17 EHRR 539.

17 See D Garland, 'The Limits of the Sovereign State: Strategies of Crime Control in Contemporary Society' (1996) 36 BJ Crim 445 at 462.

18 In the light of the English courts' track record of (mis)interpreting and 'under-applying' legal norms of non-domestic origin we should not, however, expect a transmogrification of domestic legal culture: see Hunt (1998) ch 8.

The principled (human) rights approach

of enforcement relies on somebody pursuing a complaint about the treatment they have suffered. This may not be appropriate where abuses of power are taking place against a disorganised and marginalised community as a whole, particularly where members of that community have no faith in law, lawyers or legal institutions. For in such a situation, no-one may be prepared to complain about what is happening, at least not until some considerable time has elapsed. Even then, an infringement might take years to establish; in the meantime, members of a whole community may continue to have their rights abused.

What is needed in addition to reactive remedies such as are offered under the ECHR is a proactive method of ensuring that systemic abuses are guarded against and checked. This is done, up to a point, by a committee established under the 1989 European Convention for the Prevention of Torture and Inhuman or Degrading Treatment or Punishment. The committee may visit the prisons and police stations of any member country and report on conditions which may be in breach of Art 3 of the European Convention on Human Rights. Thus, prisoners in England and Wales, a marginalised group if ever there was one, were found to be on the receiving end of practices that breached this Article.[19] This welcome proactive approach, however, far from covers all the rights supposedly protected by the European Convention.

In thinking about how else one might protect rights it is important to consider the potential of managerialism. To what extent can we expect or require the sub-institutions of criminal justice to manage their own affairs in such a way that they see respect for individual rights as part and parcel of their organisational goals?

9. MANAGERIALISM

Criminal justice is part of the public sector, financed by public revenue. As such, it has been much influenced by the 'new public management' promoted by successive Conservative governments from the early 1980s onwards.[20] The main motivating forces for this programme was an ideological preference for the disciplines of the market as a way of achieving value-for-money in the public sector, and a determination to bear down on

19   See further M Evans and R Morgan, 'The European Convention for the Prevention of Torture: Operational Practice' (1992) 41 ICLQ 590.
20   See N Lacey, 'Government as Manager, Citizen as Consumer: The Case of the Criminal Justice Act 1991' (1994) 57 MLR 534; E McLaughlin and K Murji, 'The end of public policing? Police reform and "the new managerialism"' in L Noaks, M Levi and M Maguire (eds), *Contemporary Issues in Criminology* (Cardiff: University of Wales Press, 1995).

public expenditure - a key element in the Conservative's political and economic programme.[1]

Efficiency, effectiveness and economy became the trinity which public sector officials were required to worship. Among the main mechanisms borrowed from the private sector in this programme were the fostering of 'consumer' power, the introduction of competition in the provision of services to those 'consumers', and the setting of clear objectives which would allow each service provider to be audited on their performance. Another key theme was that local 'managers' and local service-providers should be given greater autonomy, thus enabling them to be more responsive to consumer demand. Thus, for example, in education, quasi-consumers were created by providing parents with more information about schools (such as league tables based on tests and examinations) and more 'choice' in where to send their children. And head teachers suddenly found themselves responsible for handling a devolved budget, and thus for setting priorities for expenditure on their school.

The impact of new public management can be traced on all the sub-institutions of criminal justice dealt with in this book. Some of the more obvious manifestations are that the police force has become a consumer-oriented 'police service', the Crown Prosecution Service has been encouraged to think about the economics of its prosecution policies, the courts have had budgetary disciplines imposed on them and firms of defence solicitors have come under intense pressure to compete against one another for legal aid 'contracts'. Here, we will confine ourselves to a brief illustrative discussion of the impact of new public management on the police.[2]

The key impetus for 'what has become a persistent and high-profile pursuit of better value for money in police forces'[3] was Home Office Circular 114/1983. This called on chief police officers and local police authorities to formulate clear objectives and priorities for their force which reflected the wishes and needs of the public and took into account the views and experience of front-line officers. To ensure this was done, Her Majesty's Inspectors of Constabulary (HMIC) were required to report on how effectively chief police officers identified and responded to policing problems using these methods. Subsequently, increases in force establishments were made conditional on the police being able to demonstrate (for example, through 'output and performance measures')

1   See the discussion by S Savage and S Charman, 'Managing Change', in F Leishman, B Loveday and S Savage (eds), *Core Issues in Policing* (Harlow: Longman, 1996).
2   For essays concerned with contemporary trends in new public management as applied to the police see Leishman, Loveday and Savage (1996).
3   M Weatheritt, 'Measuring Police Performance: Accounting or Accountability' in R Reiner and S Spencer (eds), *Accountable Policing* (London: IPPR, 1993) p 26.

Managerialism

that objectives were being met. And since the late 1980s, the work of the Audit Commission, a body with a remit to undertake studies to promote economy, efficiency and effectiveness, has intensified the external scrutiny of policing.

One obvious effect of all this activity was the production of a mass of policing objectives, from generalised aims for police forces as a whole, down to area objectives intended to encourage junior officers to engage in purposeful activity. Of major significance was the publication in 1990 by the Association of Chief Police Officers (ACPO) of a statement of corporate values, to which every force has subsequently signed up. The statement reads:

'The purpose of the police service is to uphold the law fairly and firmly; to prevent crime; to pursue and bring to justice those who break the law; to keep the Queen's Peace; to protect, help and reassure the community; and to be seen to do this with integrity, common sense and sound judgment.

We must be compassionate, courteous and patient, acting without fear or favour or prejudice to the rights of others. We need to be professional, calm and restrained in the face of violence and apply only that force which is necessary to accomplish our lawful duty. We must strive to reduce the fears of the public and, so far as we can, to reflect their priorities in the action we take. We must respond to well founded criticism with a willingness to change.'

This statement incorporates due process values such as fairness, integrity and respecting the rights of others. On the other hand, it stresses that bringing to justice those who break the law is part of the purpose of policing whilst ignoring the dangers of convicting the innocent. In this, and in its emphasis on protecting the public and reflecting its priorities, the influence of crime control values can also clearly be seen. The protection of *human* rights is not mentioned at all.

The statement is at a high level of generality. In order better to appreciate how the values it expresses may be ranked in practice, and who is thus constructed as the key consumers of police services, it is necessary to examine the dozens of specific performance indicators drawn up by ACPO's Quality of Service Sub-Committee in 1992 in conjunction with HMIC and the Audit Commission.[4] The great majority of these indicators concern services provided to the general public and to victims of crime (eg how quickly 999 calls are answered and responded to), although some do relate to value-for-money and oppressive and discriminatory behaviour as well. Thus there are performance indicators on the number of complaints made

4   For a full list see Weatheritt (1993) pp 45-49.

against a police force and the number substantiated, and the rate of PACE stop/searches against the white population as compared with the ethnic minority population.

A difficulty with all such indicators, however, is that the police may be able to achieve 'good performance' simply by ensuring that any inefficient, oppressive or discriminatory practices are not caught by the measurements (for example, by carrying out stop/searches with 'consent' instead of using the PACE power - see ch 2). In recognition of this, many of the indicators require consumer opinions to be sought. However, suspects are rarely considered to be consumers whose opinions are thought worth measuring. As Weatheritt comments:

> '. . . the police service is well aware that its "consumers" are not a homogeneous category with clearly defined common interests. That is implied by the intention, in collecting consumer opinion, to concentrate on particular categories and sub-groups of users: people calling the police; victims of crime in general and victims of racial incidents and domestic violence in particular; and people reported for traffic violations (although this last represents the only category with whom the police come into adversarial contact whose views about police actions are to be sought). . . . An important omission is suspects - those enforced "consumers" of police attention, on whom virtually no national performance indicators are being collected.'[5]

The cynic might suggest that it is in relation to traffic violations that the police is most likely to encounter 'the respectable' suspect, and that this explains why it is only this group of suspects whose views are considered important.

On a more positive note we may note that managerialism has led to a renewed interest in the idea of police accountability to the community it serves. Thus, for example, the Audit Commission has emerged as a champion of local police authorities 'in line with its view that democratic responsiveness is one of the pre-conditions for effective performance.'[6]

Managerialism should not establish new substantive aims for criminal justice; rather it should prod the system into pursuing its own objectives more efficiently. In practice, however, it is arguable that the dominant managerial impetus has been the pursuit of ever more effective, efficient and economic crime control at the expense of the protection of due process values and human rights.[7] Those who would want to support this emphasis

5   Weatheritt (1993) pp 40-41.
6   Weatheritt (1993) p 35.
7   Compare the bleak assessment by C Jones, 'Auditing Criminal Justice' (1993) 33 BJ Crim 187 with the more optimistic analysis by Weatheritt (1993).

Managerialism

within managerialism would no doubt argue that crime control and the protection of human rights are in fact complementary in as much as deterring and censuring crime protects and upholds the human rights of victims. Is this all there is to say on the matter?

10. VICTIMS

We have noted that the due process and crime control models have little to say about the place of the victim within criminal justice. At the time Packer was writing in the late 1960s, the dominant concern of criminology concerned the treatment of suspected and convicted offenders. Subsequently there has been a rediscovery of the importance of victims to criminal justice. Surveys in the 1980s demonstrated their importance in reporting crime to the police, providing information on likely suspects, and acting as witnesses in prosecutions.[8] They also revealed that victims became increasingly dissatisfied with the criminal process over time.[9] Failures to keep them informed about the progress of 'their' case were felt particularly keenly. This is important from an instrumental standpoint as research also suggests that where victims perceive that the values and goals of the criminal process are insensitive or inimical to their interests, they are correspondingly less likely to come forward and participate in criminal justice.[10] This realisation has led to calls for reform in police practices, pre-trial procedures and in sentencing.

Criminal justice proved remarkably resistant to change.[11] The Victim's Charter, first published in 1990, represented a symbolically significant attempt to force the pace. It sets out the services a victim can expect from various criminal justice agencies. Experiments are under way to see how best to provide more systematic information to victims about 'their' cases and to provide sentencers with more systematic information about victims and the impact of the crime in question upon them.[12] But the Charter is

---

8   See, for example, M Hough and P Mayhew, Taking Account of Crime (Home Office Research Study no 111) (London: HMSO, 1985).

9   J Shapland, J Willmore and P Duff, *Victims in the Criminal Justice System* (Aldershot: Gower, 1985).

10   See J van Dijk, 'Implications of the International Crime Victims Survey for a Victim Perspective' in A Crawford and J Goodey (eds), *Integrating a Victim Perspective within Criminal Justice* (Aldershot: Ashgate, 2000).

11   See J Shapland, 'Fiefs and Peasants: Accomplishing Change for Victims in the Criminal Justice System' in M Maguire and J Pointing (eds), *Victims of Crime: A New Deal?* (Milton Keynes: Open UP, 1988).

12   See C Hoyle, R Morgan and A Sanders, The Victim's Charter: An Evaluation of Pilot Projects (Home Office Research Findings no 108) (London: Home Office, 1999) and A Sanders, C Hoyle, R Morgan and E Cape, 'Victim Statements: Don't Work, Can't Work' [2001] Crim LR (forthcoming).

vague and is notably short on enforceable commitments or rights.[13] Moreover, the managerialist-inspired auditing of criminal justice processes in the city of Milton Keynes has revealed that:

> '[t]he stage with by far the least resources. . . is recording crime and assisting victims. It is very clear from this audit that supporting victims (and helping them to help the criminal justice process) is *not* a criminal justice priority, *unless* those victims are child abuse victims.'[14]

This is partly because the adversarial system envisages a contest between the state, representing the public interest, and the individual suspect. This structure does not allow for a third party input such as that of the victim.

Let us pose the question of whether victims are better served by a due process or crime control model of adversarial justice. At first sight the crime control model appears to embody a greater concern for the victim. It offers the prospect of a higher rate of conviction of those accused of crime and, by aiming to dispose of cases expeditiously through encouraging defendants to plead guilty, it obviates the need for victims to come to court and give evidence. This latter feature is particularly important in cases involving violence, such as child abuse, sexual offences and other forms of assault, where the giving of evidence and the ordeal of cross-examination may prove highly distressing.[15] A clear example is rape, where the previous sexual history of the victim is still often treated by the courts as relevant to the issue of consent.[16] As McEwan puts it, 'There is little incentive for rape victims to come forward when the system which is supposed to protect the public from crime serves them up in court like laboratory specimens on a microscope slide.'[17]

But some victims may want to have 'their day in court' and some defendants may not be prepared to give in to pressures to plead guilty - especially if they are innocent. Pressure to make the trial experience less of an ordeal for victims has thus mounted. Sometimes inroads have been made

13   H Fenwick, 'Procedural "Rights" of Victims of Crime: Public or Private Ordering of the Criminal Justice Process?' (1997) 60 MLR 317.
14   J Shapland, J Hibbert, J l'Anson, A Sorsby and R Wild, Milton Keynes Criminal Justice Audit: Summary and Implications (Sheffield: University of Sheffield Institute for the Study of the Legal Profession, 1995) at p 23 (emphasis in original).
15   D Brereton, 'How Different are Rape Trials?: A Comparison of the Cross-Examination of Complainants in Rape and Assault Trials' (1997) 37 BJ Crim 242.
16   See J Temkin, 'Sexual History Evidence - the Ravishment of Section 2' [1993] Crim LR 3. The Youth Justice and Criminal Evidence Act 1999 is intended to change this: N Kibble, 'The Sexual History Provisions' [2000] Crim LR 274.
17   J McEwan, 'Documentary Hearsay Evidence - Refuge for the Vulnerable Witness?' [1989] Crim LR 629.

Victims

into the due process rights of the defendant in order better to protect the vulnerable victim. For example, the law now allows the admission of documentary (which includes videotaped) evidence in a limited range of cases, including where the statement is made to a police officer and the maker does not give oral evidence through fear.[18] But, like a see-saw, as trial procedures become more just or bearable for victims the defendant's ability to contest the prosecution case may become increasingly undermined. When evidence is admitted in documentary form the defence is given no opportunity to cross-examine the maker of the statement concerning its contents. This makes it less likely that defendants can win in court, and thus less likely that they will contest the matter in the first place. Crime control and concern for victims can thus be made to walk hand in hand.[19]

The benefits that the due process model offers victims are more subtle than those tendered by crime control. Typical crime control techniques employed to secure guilty pleas are offers of reduced charges or reduced sentences, as we shall explore in later chapters. To take the example of rape again, charge bargaining may result in victims learning to their horror that the legal process has labelled the act in question as some lesser wrong such as indecent assault, as happened to Jodie Foster's character in the 1988 film, 'The Accused'.[20] Of a sample of incidents recorded as rape in 1985 which resulted in conviction the proportion that were convicted of a less serious offence than rape or attempted rape was as high as 42%, and there was strong evidence that the motor for this downgrading of a case was charge bargaining.[1] In other cases where victims are vulnerable (eg where they have a learning disability) and in cases of domestic violence, too, reduced charges are often a source of anguish.[2] Similarly, sentence

---

18 See ss 23-26 of the Criminal Justice Act 1988. The Youth Justice and Criminal Evidence Act 1999 also aims to make the giving of evidence more bearable for some victims and witnesses. All these provisions are discussed in ch 9, sections 3 and 4.

19 See D Miers, 'The Responsibilities and the Rights of Victims of Crime' (1992) 55 MLR 482 at p 496.

20 On the same point see J Gregory and S Lees, 'Attrition in Rape and Sexual Assault Cases' (1996) 36 B J Crim 1 at p 10: '. . . interviews conducted with victims in the present study revealed how shocked and insulted many of them were at the lenient sentences frequently meted out to their attackers.'

1   S Grace, C Lloyd and L Smith, Rape: from Recording to Conviction (Research and Planning Unit Paper 71) (London: Home Office, 1992) pp 5 and 8. Also see J Harris and S Grace, A question of evidence? Investigating and prosecuting rape in the 1990s (Home Office Research Study no 196) (London: Home Office, 1999).

2   A Sanders, J Creaton, S Bird and L Weber, Victims with Learning Disabilities (Oxford: Centre for Criminological Research, 1997); A Cretney and G Davis, 'Prosecuting Domestic Assault: Victims Failing Courts or Courts Failing Victims?' (1997) 36 Howard JCJ 146.

discounts for pleas of guilty may result in convicted offenders receiving a more lenient penalty than victims consider just.[3] Due process, by contrast, opposes such strategies, which means that where a conviction occurs it is likely that the offence proved and the sentence imposed will more accurately reflect the victim's suffering.

More fundamentally, with the due process model's insistence on proof of (rather than belief in) guilt, it offers superior protection to that achieved by crime control against miscarriages of justice occurring. A wrongful conviction represents an injury to the victim (and to wider society), as well as to the defendant, because it means that 'their' offenders has not been correctly identified and convicted.[4] When Stefan Kiszko was cleared of the murder of Lesley Molseed after spending 16 years in prison, her father summed up the family's feelings, 'For us, it is just like Lesley had been murdered last week'. As counsel for Mr Kiszko put it:

'We acknowledge their pain in having to listen to some of the details surrounding their daughter's death and the new pain of learning that her killer has not, after all, been caught.'[5]

In addition, the lengthy campaigns usually needed to bring miscarriages of justice to light must make it nigh impossible for those victimised to put their experiences behind them.

But while systems in which crime control values predominate may convict more factually innocent persons than would due process-based systems, the former model is also capable of convicting far more factually guilty persons. Overall, more victims will be able to see 'their' offenders brought to justice, albeit of a flawed kind, in a system which rejects due process in favour of crime control. Thus, the dilemma that Packer highlighted through the use of his two models of criminal justice exists also in relation to arguments about the treatment of victims. The claims of victims must be weighed against the competing claims of efficiency, defendants, and the need to preserve the moral integrity of the criminal process. However, in weighing the social costs of 'wrongful' convictions and acquittals against each other, it is important to remember that the interests of victims do not fall solely onto one side of the scales.

3   H Fenwick, 'Charge Bargaining and Sentence Discount: the Victim's Perspective' (1997) 5 Int R Victimology 23.
4   D Dixon, *Law in Policing* (Oxford: Clarendon Press, 1997) p 283 observes that this 'is a glaring but often ignored lesson of the miscarriage cases.'
5   *The Guardian*, 18 February 1992. Similarly, when the three surviving members of the 'Bridgewater Four' had their convictions quashed after serving 19 years in prison, one of them observed: 'Not only have the police been devious and deceitful by getting innocent men in prison; far worse, after having a child killed the police have deceived Mr and Mrs Bridgewater': *The Guardian*, 22 February 1997.

It must also be recognised that people who report alleged crimes to the police are not always victims. Shop owners have been known to burn down their own premises in order to cash in on their insurance policies. Business people have sometimes staged robberies and burglaries for the same reason, or in order to cover up earlier asset losses through their own fraud or thieving. False allegations of rape are undoubtedly rare, but the risk of them occurring cannot be discounted.[6] Our natural sympathy for victims of crime should not blind us to the fact that one of the objects of the 'adversarial model' is to discover whether prosecution witnesses, including 'victims', are telling the truth or not. A system in which 'victims' were treated with kid gloves would be as indefensible as one which ritually humiliated them.[7]

In earlier sections we saw that conventional theoretical frameworks (including those of human rights and managerialism) see the main purpose of criminal justice as being to control crime, with due process restraints operating to a greater or lesser extent in a subsidiary fashion. Both purposes - crime control and restraints on power - can, as we have seen, work against the interests of victims. The interests of victims are furthered in conventional frameworks only as a by-product of their main goals.[8] Thus some interests of victims are not furthered at all within conventional frameworks. Some vulnerable victims find that, despite the types of protection discussed above, they cannot face continuing with proceedings. Many trials of rape and domestic violence, and where victims are otherwise vulnerable, collapse for this reason.[9] Other examples include a blackmail victim who found to his consternation that his identity was going to be revealed in the trial. He preferred to let the alleged blackmailers go free than let this happen.[10] On the other hand, some vulnerable victims are more concerned that their story be heard and that they be taken seriously than that they be protected from the rough and tumble of an adversarial trial. Many learning disabled victims, for instance, feel that it is important to have made their public accusation even if the poor memory or communication skills which are a result of their disability makes a conviction

6   See *Burnett* (7 April 2000, unreported) in which the Court of Appeal quashed convictions for rape and buggery on the ground that the complainant had made up the original allegations. The appellant spent 15 years in prison for crimes which had almost certainly never happened at all.

7   It is nonetheless true that there is much that can and is being done for victims without prejudicing the rights of defendants, such as providing them with counselling services, better information on the progress of prosecutions, and improved procedures for obtaining compensation. See generally, JUSTICE Committee on the role of the victim in criminal justice, Victims in Criminal Justice (London: JUSTICE, 1998).

8   See H Fenwick, 'Charge Bargaining and Sentence Discounts: The Victim's Perspective' (1997) 5 Int Rev of Victimology, p 23.

9   See Sanders et al (1997).

10   See *The Guardian*, 12 August 1993.

unlikely.[11] But under conventional frameworks these are illegitimate considerations - trials for these reasons both jeopardise due process considerations and fail to further crime control efficiently.

Only a 'victim centred' model of criminal justice would prioritise the interests of victims. As Cavadino and Dignan have noted, while such a model exists, (the 'civilian model') it does so only as a set of proposals which have never been implemented, even on an experimental basis.[12] The model argues for replacing adversarial justice in which the state prosecutes citizens in the name of the public interest with civil procedures which would be initiated by victims. Its obvious weakness 'is its failure to acknowledge that an offence may have broader social implications which go beyond the personal harm or loss experienced by the direct victim.'[13] This weakness is also evident in the 'victim/offender reparation model' which aims for state-initiated dialogue and reconciliation between offenders and victims, with some form of reparation as the usual outcome.[14] This explains why the many initiatives based on this model have remained as a marginal adjunct to the traditional adversarial model of justice, although, as we shall see, they have become increasingly important as a form of diversion from prosecution for, in particular, minor offences and juvenile offenders.

By contrast, the 'communitarian model' emphasises a wider set of interests. It has become the central element in New Zealand youth justice, an important strand in Australian justice, and looks likely to gain significant ground in England and Wales over the next few years.[15] It involves (at least in theory) a delegation of power from the state to members of the community to decide what the response to a detected offence should be. A conference is held to which are invited the victim, the offender and any other members of the community affected by the offence (in practice, this usually means those with close ties to the victim and offender, such as parents or spouses). The offender is encouraged to acknowledge the wrongfulness of the criminal behaviour and to engage in a process of negotiation aimed at achieving an agreement as to what should be done to put matters right which is acceptable to all. The coordinator of the conference (which in New Zealand is a youth justice worker and in Canberra,

11   See Sanders et al (1997).
12   J Dignan and M Cavadino, 'Towards a Framework for Conceptualising and Evaluating Models of Criminal Justice from a Victim's Perspective' (1996) 4 Int R Victimology 153 at p 165.
13   Dignan and Cavadino (1996) p 165.
14   The reparation model is also deficient from the victim's point of view inasmuch as it precludes public acknowledgement and condemnation of the wrong done: A Cretney and G Davis, *Punishing Violence* (London: Routledge, 1995) p 178.
15   See J Dignan, 'The Crime and Disorder Act and the Prospects for Restorative Justice' [1999] Crim LR 48 and C Ball, 'The Youth Justice and Criminal Evidence Act 1999: A significant move towards restorative justice, or a recipe for unintended consequences?' [2000] Crim LR 211.

Australia a police officer) has a duty to attend to the public interest, and, more specifically, any interests not actually represented at the conference - 'namely those "indirect" or "potential" victims who may be indignant at the breach of social norms involved in the offence.'[16] If an agreement emerges which is contrary to the public interest, the coordinator may veto it. If a satisfactory agreement cannot be reached then the case may be put before a criminal court for resolution in the traditional adversarial manner.

Difficult conflicts of interest arise in this, as with any, model of criminal justice. For example, what should be done when the public interest in discouraging offenders from further criminal behaviour points to a quite different solution to that sought by a particular victim? How much pressure should be put on offenders to accept obligations designed to turn them away from offending? And how can the power of coordinators to shape 'negotiations' at, and the outcomes of, community conferences, be adequately regulated?[17] Most importantly, the communitarian model has to be grounded in some wider political or moral theory. This need not necessarily be anti-liberal, but there is always the danger that 'the community' could be mobilised to support authoritarian approaches. This could be resisted if retributive principles could be reconciled with restorative or reparative justice. This is now the subject of much debate.[18]

For ourselves, we do not believe that the claims of victims, powerful though they are, should be allowed to over-ride all other considerations discussed in this chapter. At present, victim concerns are increasingly thrown into the pot indiscriminately, leading to an even more tangled web of irreconcilable demands and priorities than existed hitherto. The interests of victims do need to be taken into account but in a systematic fashion. To do this, an alternative framework is needed.

16   Dignan and Cavadino, p 173. For further discussion see R Young, 'Integrating a Multi-Victim Perspective into Criminal Justice Through Restorative Justice Conferences' in Crawford and Goodey (2000).
17   It would be foolish to ignore 'the lessons of history, which teach us how easily the parental ideology can be abused': Damaska (1973) p 572. It was in part the abuse of discretion under the rehabilitation theory of punishment that led to the rise of the just deserts model with its concern for limiting state power and consistency of treatment - see further A Norrie, 'The Limits of Justice: Finding Fault in the Criminal Law' (1996) 59 MLR 540.
18   A Ashworth, 'Some doubts about restorative justice' (1993) 4 Criminal Law Forum 277; L Zedner, 'Reparation and Retribution: are they reconcilable?' (1994) 57 MLR 228; and M Cavadino and J Dignan, 'Reparation, Retribution and Rights' (1997) 4 Int Rev Victimology 233.

11. AN ALTERNATIVE FRAMEWORK: THE ENHANCEMENT OF FREEDOM

We have seen that everyone recognises that there are many different values and interests at stake in criminal justice. The most important are:

- convicting the guilty
- protecting the innocent from wrongful conviction
- maintaining human rights: the protection of everyone (innocent and guilty) from arbitrary or oppressive treatment
- protecting victims
- maintaining order
- securing public confidence in, and cooperation with, policing and prosecution
- pursuing these goals efficiently and effectively without disproportionate cost and consequent harm to other public services.

Criminal justice is controversial, not because this list of goals is controversial, but because people differ over which are most important and which are to be given low priority. Many people, especially politicians, like to pretend that they are all equally achievable, but we have seen that this is dangerously misleading. One of the great virtues of Packer's models is that they alert us to the irreconcilability of many of these purposes. However, we have seen that both models are incomplete (they do not cater for the interests of victims, in particular) and neither is normatively acceptable in itself (ie neither model represents an ideal to aspire to). We saw that Ashworth's human rights perspective tries to overcome these two difficulties but the way in which he prioritises some rights and interests over others is itself controversial. Moreover, we are not convinced that a 'rights perspective' is the most fruitful way to critique criminal justice.

(a) Promoting freedom: the overriding purpose

Let us tackle the problem from a different angle and ask what is the point of protecting victims, offenders, and, indeed, anyone affected by the criminal justice system. In our view it is primarily to protect and enhance freedom. Why make it a crime to thieve or assault? Because the losses and hurts they cause are (among other things) losses of freedom - freedom to enjoy one's possessions, to walk the streets without fear, and so forth. We seek to convict thieves and violent offenders in the hope that the punishment or treatment consequent upon conviction will reduce their propensity to commit crime, and in the expectation that censuring their wrongdoing will reinforce everyone else's law-abiding instincts and behaviour. Either way the freedom of past and potential future victims should be enhanced through having their fear of crime reduced. In the same way, we can ask what is the point of protecting suspects and defendants, innocent or guilty. Again, protection is not a goal in itself, but a means to the end of promoting their freedom. And why do we insist that the police must obey the rule of law? Because their failure to do so undermines our sense that we live in a free society, where state officials cannot invade our lives in an arbitrary manner.

At first sight it may appear that we simply advocate a list of irreconcilable aims (protecting suspects, convicting the guilty, acquitting the innocent etc) in the same way that everyone else does. In a sense we do, for almost everyone agrees on what we want criminal justice to achieve. However, we see none of these objectives as goals in themselves. Instead we see them as means to achieving the overriding goal of freedom. This means that, in theory at least, the problem of allocating priority to conflicting goals is solved. All we have to do is to prioritise the goal that is likely to enhance freedom the most.[19]

What is most likely to enhance freedom will vary from circumstance to circumstance. Let us take a hypothetical example of a driver forced to brake suddenly by another driver speeding and driving carelessly. The irate victim reports the matter to the police. It is worth devoting some resources to catching and prosecuting the suspected offender, but not many. If the suspect claimed that her car was stolen on the day in question, and was then abandoned the next day near her home, would it be worth the expenditure involved in checking her alibis and looking for the (alleged) car thief? Would it be justifiable to hold her in custody and interrogate her? Those who share our implicit priorities would answer 'no' to both questions. Why? Because the freedom lost to the victims of this offence (both the irate complainant and future victims) by non-investigation is less than the freedom lost by the suspect if the police investigated the affair in the way that we would expect them to investigate a rape. And the expenditure involved would be out of all proportion to the benefits thereby gained. The police should be given better, more freedom enhancing, things to do with their limited time.

Because of shared implicit priorities and the simple nature of the example, the law and practice is at one with our analysis. The police are not normally permitted to arrest and interrogate for minor Road Traffic Act offences and they never devote substantial resources to single incidents like this. The real world is not so simple most of the time, of course; and our approach is not, most of the time, nearly so simple to put into practice as it is to state in theory. Take a couple of real-life examples. In the first, three lads were

19   See M Cavadino, 'A Vindication of the Rights of Psychiatric Patients' (1997) 24 J LS 235 for a similar approach (albeit expressed in the language of rights): 'what will the overall result of an action be for the amount of positive freedom enjoyed by those involved?'

involved in a dispute over a restaurant bill. They ended up refusing to pay. The police were called. The lads were arrested, detained, questioned and prosecuted. In the second example, the police had very good reason to believe that a house was being used for drug dealing. Following one particular short period of surveillance, during which a large number of people were seen entering and leaving the premises, the police raided the premises and detained all the occupants until they sorted out who was, and who was not, dealing in drugs.[20]

In the restaurant example the police's actions were justified in law.[1] In the second example the police had reasonable suspicion that *someone* in the house was dealing in drugs but they had no idea who. Legally, detention is allowed only of individuals who are specifically suspected of specific offences, and so the police were not legally justified in what they did. That restriction on the power to detain represents a typical legal compromise in our system between a crime control power and a due process constraint. However, that compromise fails to distinguish between minor and major crime, excepting the very broad-brush distinction between Road Traffic Act-type offences (where the police are allowed to detain briefly to look for evidence of a traffic offence) and most other crime (where evidence must precede detention). As can be seen from our examples, the police chose to arrest in both cases, but to do so they had to 'stretch' their power in the drugs case. The more rational approach might be to do as the police did in the drugs case, but not to arrest in the restaurant case - the opposite way to that indicated by the law. This would be rational because the victims of drugs offences suffer a lot more than the restaurant in the first example. And the relatively short detention at the house in the drugs case is less intrusive than the police station detention in the other case. In other words the freedom gained for victims by law enforcement has to be balanced against the freedom lost to suspects, and vice versa.

(b) Should the freedom of victims predominate?

To argue for these two measures of freedom to be balanced is one thing, but knowing how to do so is quite another. Crime control adherents would argue that suspects and offenders should have fewer rights than victims and that their freedoms should have a low weighting. We disagree for several reasons:

---

20 Both examples are drawn from field work notes collected during the research on which McConville et al (1991) is based.

1 Although the decision to prosecute probably failed to conform with government guidelines.

(i)   All applications of state power reduce freedom

While it is true that criminal acts reduce freedom, the inescapable fact is that once a crime is committed the harm it causes is usually irreversible; the application of State power may do nothing to redress the balance. Indeed, less than one-fifth of all stop-searches lead to arrest, and less than one-half of all arrests lead to caution or prosecution.[2] Unless stop-search and arrest has a deterrent effect in itself these are applications of power which reduce freedom in exchange for no gain whatsoever even if those who are apprehended but not prosecuted are guilty of offences. If they are innocent (and some will be) the loss of freedom will be all the more acutely felt. Our argument is that since society has a choice whether or not to allow the application of State power, it should only grant it if it is likely to enhance more freedom than it erodes. The use of power has therefore to be justified every time it is granted in principle (ie by law) and exercised in practice.[3]

(ii)   The application of state power is as damaging to the freedom of suspects and defendants as crime is to the freedom of victims

Even accepting the above, the crime control adherent would argue that it is worse to be a victim of crime than to be subjected to state coercion, and that the freedom of the suspect is more dispensable than that of the victim. Take another real-life example. One of our friends was walking alone late in the evening. Two men approached her and engaged her in unfriendly conversation against her will. Along with the fear of what they might do to her were her thoughts: what had she done to attract their attention? Was it the way she looked, something they knew about her, where she had been, her friends? She stood up for herself and they let her go. As she shook with fear and anger she wondered what might have happened had they not let her go, as she felt herself to be completely in their power.

We have just described what happened to our friend when she arrived at Birmingham airport, having just attended a Criminology conference in Belfast in 1997. Her encounter had been with (non-uniform) police, but it could equally have been with potential thugs. Now imagine her to be Irish.

2   See chs 2 and 3.
3   See Cavadino (1997) p 241 on how this might apply to detaining and compulsorily treating the mentally disordered: 'Potential victims of violence have a right to personal safety which comes into competition with the right to liberty of the potential detainee . . . But this does not mean that people may be justly deprived of their liberty . . . if there is any evidence of suspicion, however slight or unsubstantiated, that they might be dangerous to others. The nature of the risk to others must be assessed together with its likelihood of eventuating, and weighed against the undoubted diminution in the patient's freedom represented by the intervention.'

Perhaps this would happen every time she travelled between Belfast and Birmingham. She would begin to dread the journey and to fear looking anyone in the eye.[4] Or imagine someone living in the inner city, being subjected to this kind of treatment on the streets and in police stations, week after week.[5] But there are worse examples. Sometimes personal features of the suspect are deliberately used to increase the pressure of detention and questioning:

> 'I was just at customs . . . They had taken my cases away and the kids, they were one and two at the time and they were both in nappies, and they wouldn't let me get their nappies out of the cases . . . They took the children off me at the airport. The policewoman had to drag the youngest away from me. . . Then from Saturday to Tuesday they kept telling me that they had been put into care. . . It was terrible because they'd never been away . . . they'd never stayed with anyone.'

This woman was detained for three days and released without charge; her children had, in fact, been looked after by her parents and not been taken into care.[6]

In another case, Hillyard reports, the police read aloud the contents of a woman's diary: '. . . all sorts of ridiculous things, mostly to do with work - "see so-and-so at 7.30" - and things like "period"; because of PMT I would mark that in my diary.' In yet another the police examined a man's personal letters and photos, making such remarks as "Look at the size of the boobs on her . . . Did Shelagh screw?"[7] At other times, pressure is produced by insults - being called 'scum', 'losers', 'toe-rags' - or by being locked in a cell without being told what is likely to happen next.[8]

The distressing experience of arrest and detention need not be deliberate. One detainee reported the blankets in her cell smelling of vomit and the toilet being in the line of sight of the spy-hole in the door. Although the blankets were changed when she asked, and no-one actually looked at her sitting on the toilet, she felt vulnerable and dependent.[9] A businessman, arrested because a fellow diner overheard a conversation about bombings and shootings, was laid face down in the street, searched, handcuffed and escorted to a car with rifles pointing at him. Released, clothes filthy, five

4   See P Hillyard, *Suspect Community* (London: Pluto Press, 1993).
5   See S Choongh, *Policing as Social Discipline* (Oxford: Clarendon, 1997).
6   Hillyard (1993) p 50.
7   Hillyard (1993) pp 56-7.
8   S Singh, 'Understanding the long-term relationship between Police and Policed' in M McConville and L Bridges (eds), *Criminal Justice in Crisis* (Aldershot: Edward Elgar, 1994); M Young, *An Inside Job* (Oxford: Clarendon, 1991).
9   Hillyard (1993) p 99.

An alternative framework: the enhancement of freedom

hours later, his hand had begun turning blue and had a one-eighth inch ridge cut into it.[10]

Loss of freedom is not always a matter of individual incidents. Just as the suffering of the elderly person harassed by kids, or of the battered woman brutalised by her partner, can only be comprehended if the pattern of victimisation over time is taken into account, so the loss of freedom of suspects subjected to repeated stops and so forth is completely different to that suffered by a one-off victim (or a one-off suspect).

(iii)   Victims and offenders are not separate categories

So far in this book we have made an implicit assumption which is widely shared but is nonetheless erroneous: that victims and offenders are separate groups of people. In reality, just as most people are victims of crime at least once in their adult life, so most people also offend at some time in their lives, and many people do so many times. One third of all men in their 30s have been convicted of at least one non-Road Traffic Act offence.[11] Just think how many committed offences and got away with them, as only a minority of reported crimes end in conviction, and reported crimes are a minority of the total number of crimes committed. And who are the victims of crime? Disproportionately young working class men and members of ethnic minorities - the groups who are disproportionately represented among convicted offenders.[12] The very people who, as victims, crime control adherents would protect are those people whose freedom would be sacrificed the next day when they are, or are suspected of, offending.

(iv)   Most applications of state power fail to enhance freedom

It has been estimated that only about 7% of all crimes (about 20% of those reported to the police) are detected, and less than half of these lead to conviction or official caution.[13] When crimes are detected it is usually because of information provided by members of the public (very often the victim). This suggests, as we shall see further in later chapters, that most applications of state power - stop-search, arrest, and so forth - are not

---

10   Hillyard (1993) p 99.
11   R Morgan and T Newburn, *The Future of Policing* (Oxford: Clarendon, 1997) p 37.
12   Morgan and Newburn (1997) pp 26-7. See also J Hartless, J Ditton, G Nair and S Phillips, 'More Sinned Against than Sinning: A Study of Young Teenagers' Experience of Crime' (1995) 35 BJ Crim 114.
13   Morgan and Newburn (1997) p 35.

productive. In other words the pay-back for victims and the wider society from incursions on the freedom of suspects and offenders is small. Crime control adherents might argue that this is precisely because too much weighting is given to the rights of suspects and defendants. However, those against whom there is most evidence are currently most likely to be arrested, charged and convicted. If it became easier to arrest charge and convict, the proportion of guilty people against whom action would be taken would be lower even though the numbers would rise. Greater freedom for victims would be purchased at the expense of a disproportionately high freedom-cost to suspects.

There are also financial costs to increased law enforcement activity. Law enforcement is expensive. Police activity against suspects costs not only some of the freedom of those suspects, but community resources. Doing nothing saves money. If a given act of law enforcement had an identical effect on the freedom of victims and of offenders it should not take place, for it would cost money that could be used to enhance the lives (indeed, the positive freedom) of people through improved health, education, housing and so forth.

(v)   It is essential that victims, suspects and offenders respect the criminal justice system

Much successful policing depends on information and co-operation from the community. Without community support the police would be even less effective than they are now. But support is not guaranteed, and there is evidence that it is in decline. The proportion of the public who believe that the police do a 'very' or 'fairly' good job went down from 92% in 1982 to 82% in 1994, and those who thought they do a 'very good' job halved (from 43% to 24%).[14] Levels of satisfaction with the police are influenced by *how* the police do their job as well as by what they do and the results they get.[15] Thus the least favourable views of the police are held by ethnic minorities, black people in particular.[16] Tyler's empirical study found that people have a deeply ingrained sense of 'fairness' and justice' which enables them to accept results they regard as wrong if they feel the process by which they were achieved was fair.[17] That is one reason why it is so important that the police respect the rule of law.

14   T Bucke, Policing and the Public: Findings From the 1994 British Crime Survey (Home Office Research Findings no 28) (London: Home Office, 1995).
15   P Ekblom and K Heal, The police response to calls from the public (Home Office Research and Planning Unit Paper 9) (London: Home Office, 1982).
16   N Aye Maung, Young people, victimisation and the police (Home Office Research Study no 140) (London: HMSO, 1995).
17   T Tyler, *Why People Obey the Law* (New Haven: Yale University Press, 1990).

An alternative framework: the enhancement of freedom

If society divided neatly into offenders and the rest, the way offenders are treated by the police might not harm the way 'the rest' viewed the police, and their co-operation might not be jeopardised. As we have seen, however, very large numbers of people are both occasional offenders (and even more are occasional suspects) and occasional victims. The overlap between suspect-communities and victim-communities means that if the police needs to keep the victim-community on its side, it also needs to do the same for the suspect-community. Tyler's research suggests that treating suspects fairly is the best way to persuade them to respect, and thus cooperate with, the law in future. In other words, adherence to due process and the human rights of suspects and defendants can be of instrumental value in preventing and detecting crime as well as of value in itself.

(c)   What is 'freedom'?

We have so far used the term 'freedom' very loosely. As this is not a book of political philosophy we shall not attempt to define the term closely. We could spend much of this book defending our own preferred political philosophy and the set of reforms that would follow from it. But we prefer to concentrate instead on presenting a detailed analysis of how criminal justice actually works and providing some broadly drawn indications of how we think it should be reformed. We do this in the belief that a clear understanding of the reality of criminal justice is a necessary pre-condition of successful reform. And we are not convinced that it is either necessary or desirable in this book to tie our suggested reforms to a particular political philosophy. Instead, we believe that there is sufficient common ground between communitarians and liberals to make the vast majority of our suggestions for reform palatable to anyone who subscribes to democratic values and the rule of law. And from our perspective, it matters little that communitarians and liberals would differ in their responses to some of our ideas, because virtually any well thought out proposal for reform emanating from either of those political camps would be preferable to the current state of criminal justice.[18]

However, the types of freedom which we believe the criminal justice should enhance include those of the community at large. Thus the use of police powers against some communities more than others has to be taken

---

18   Our critique thus incorporates a prescriptive penumbra combined with a core of deliberate indeterminacy. A similar method is employed by J Schwartz, 'Relativism, reflective equilibrium, and justice' (1997) 17 LS 128 who writes that: 'If we can rule out domination as unjust, the remaining arbitrariness among emancipatory conceptions seems harmless. At any rate, to rule out conceptions that license domination would be progress' (p 153).

into account. As we shall see in later chapters, this is what happens with stop-search in relation to ethnic minorities, and the use of anti-terrorist powers in relation to people with Irish connections. Equally important is the propensity of some communities to be victimised in certain ways more than others. For instance, many poor communities are badly affected by drug-related crime. But if the police attempt to control crime in such communities by instilling more fear in its inhabitants than do the criminals the desirable ends will have been frustrated by the means. Poor communities also suffer from 'non-traditional' forms of crime too. Working class people are harmed far more by dangerous working conditions than they are by street attacks and pub fights. And we are all far more at risk from illegal driving practices than we are from those who we conventionally think of as criminal. It follows that we must question the differential powers provided by the law to police 'normal' crime, corporate crime and road traffic, to take just a few examples; and to question the different ways in which law enforcement bodies use those powers and the different experiences of people suspected of these different crimes.

We are concerned about the actual ability of people to exercise freedom, rather than a theoretical aspiration. This is why it makes no sense only to analyse the law without seeing how it actually works. To tell arrested suspects, for instance, that they can look up their rights in a law book to ensure that they are being treated fairly is a classic example of a theoretical right of zero practical value.[19] Law students (and academics!) have trouble understanding what the rights of suspects are after lengthy study, so what chance would most suspects have? Even if they did understand them, would it really make any difference? Asked by Choongh if the police had told him what his rights were, one detained suspect said bitterly:

'What rights? You wanna see your rights? Your rights is all on one piece of paper [suspect gets out the charge-sheet]. *That's* your rights, right here! . . . I'm gonna be here until the morning anyway, so there's no point is there.'[20]

And so we approach the enhancement of freedom through criminal justice by arguing that it be achieved by methods which take account of the real circumstances in which they operate. Due process mechanisms and crime control powers need to be sensitive to the context within which they operate. Searches of suspected drug-dealers which are carried out in such an oppressive, arbitrary and discriminatory way that they provoke

19   Under the Police and Criminal Evidence Act 1984, Code of Practice C, para 3.1 detained suspects have the right to consult the various codes of practice issued under that Act. See further ch 4.
20   Choongh (1997) p 178.

widespread rioting and long-term alienation of whole neighbourhoods from the police do not enlarge freedom but undermine it. The lawful use of arrest powers in a non-discriminatory manner which cannot be shown to detect or prevent a significant amount of crime does not enlarge freedom but undermines it. Due process mechanisms which result in little protection for suspects but cause humiliation to victims or impede the police from detecting serious crime do not enlarge freedom but undermine it. Layers of bureaucracy that add nothing to due process protections and which divert criminal justice officials from achieving legitimate goals do not enlarge freedom but undermine it. And in deciding how much power to give the police, how much due process to provide to suspects, it makes sense to consider, within the particular social context concerned, how powers are likely to be used and experienced in practice, how much (preferably serious) crime we might thereby detect or prevent, and how effective due process mechanisms are likely to be.

(d) Crime and social justice

If freedom is the goal of criminal justice, and the use of resources has to be taken into account, it follows that criminal justice should not be analysed in isolation from other aspects of society which encroach on freedom. This flows from our earlier analysis of the 'relatedness' of criminal justice to other social institutions. When considering the use of legal and financial resources to combat crime we should also consider other social needs in relation to, for instance, housing, employment, education, health, and so forth. Given the considerable evidence that many indices of poverty (such as housing and employment problems) are related to crime,[1] tackling these social problems might be more cost-effective than using the coercive powers of the State anyway.[2]

One way of ensuring that we do not see crime in isolation from other social problems, and of highlighting the importance of social crime *prevention* as well as individual crime *control* is to look at two divergent trends in social policy: those of social inclusion and social exclusion. The exclusionary approach is characterised by Faulkner as one whereby:

'Crime is to be prevented by efficiency of detection, certainty of conviction and severity of punishment... "Criminals" are to be seen as an "enemy" to be defeated and humiliated, in a "war" in which the police are seen as the "front line"'.

1 Morgan and Newburn (1997).
2 See, to similar effect, Ashworth (1998) p 316.

He contrasts this with Locke's view that 'the end of law is not to abolish or restrain but to preserve and enlarge freedom'. On this inclusionary approach:

> 'Authority will not be respected if it is simply imposed: it has to be accountable and it has to be legitimate in the sense that respect for it has to be earned and justified. Consideration for others and obedience to the law are learned by explanation, discussion, experience and example ... Solutions to the problem of crime have to be sought by inclusion within the community itself - among parents, in schools, by providing opportunities and hope for young people - and not by exclusion from it.'[3]

Greater fairness to all is possible without either undermining the ability of the system to bring the guilty to justice or to protect the innocent from wrongful conviction. This is because the criminal process as it currently operates shows strong exclusionary tendencies - failing to seek solutions from within the community, and failing to show adequate respect to individual citizens (whether in the roles of suspects, witnesses or victims). Thus the Milton Keynes Audit concluded that the lion's share of criminal justice resources were devoted to the effective and efficient processing of cases through a multi-layered, multi-institutional bureaucratic system. Attempting to ensure that this processing was done without abusing due process rights also took up a significant amount of time and resources. But few attempts were made to prevent re-offending and re-victimisation through work with defendants and victims, and through protecting the public from dangerous offenders. Nor were significant resources devoted to delivering a courteous, proper and effective service to victims, offenders and witnesses, so that their expectations of criminal justice were met.[4]

12. CONCLUSION

In this chapter we have shown that criminal justice can have several different purposes, many of which conflict with each other (and with social goals in other spheres of life) some or all of the time. While these conflicts will never be eradicated, it is important to have a way of prioritising the different purposes of criminal justice - not just in an abstract way, but in relation to specific problems. Only then can we hope to get near achieving the best possible solutions, in terms of maximum benefits for minimum

3   D Faulkner, *Darkness and Light: Justice, Crime and Management for Today* (London: Howard League, 1996) p 6.
4   Shapland et al (1995) p 32.

Conclusion

losses. Further, a rational system which applies consistent principles will be both fair and seen to be fair - which is a good thing in itself and has the added advantage of encouraging co-operation with the system and thus increasing the ability of criminal justice to control crime.

The previous section argued that a rational ordering of goals, which gives a clear steer to those carrying out the system's functions, is possible if we adopt freedom as the ultimate goal of criminal justice. This does not involve abandoning crime control, crime prevention, concern for the rights of suspects and victims, or cost-effectiveness. Instead it enables us to pursue all these goals to differing extents and in different ways according to the context in which one is operating. Of course Ashworthian weighting of competing goals, interests and rights will still be necessary under our framework, but adopting the language of freedom should help us to calculate the value of those weights in a persuasive way - in a common currency.[5] We might, for example, more effectively convince the police to respect suspects' rights if we highlight how these rights do not constrain but rather facilitate the achievement of the ultimate criminal justice goal of promoting freedom.

It should be clear that we are arguing normatively - that is, we are arguing that this is what the system should be aiming at. Throughout the book we shall contrast the way the system actually operates with the way we believe it should operate according to this framework. However, this will not always be a huge difference. We shall see that, much of the time, the system implicitly operates according to a 'freedom' framework anyway. So, for instance, in domestic violence cases much police work is context-sensitive and primarily aims to protect women victims; law enforcement per se is a secondary goal. 'Community policing', at its best, is another attempt to be context-sensitive. But because the freedom goal is never explicitly acknowledged, and sometimes other goals creep in, the system is frequently confused and lacks coherence. Our concern in the rest of the book will therefore be as much to describe the system analytically - to assess what it is trying to do and what it succeeds in doing - as it will be to advocate our normative position.

Another normative position, which we have shown is related to the 'freedom' objective, is that of an 'inclusive' society and, within it, an inclusive way of operating criminal justice. Again, we are as concerned to see the extent to which criminal justice is, or is not, inclusive as we are to argue for inclusiveness. Here we shall see that our normative goal and the harsh reality are farther away from each other than is the case in relation to the freedom objective. The social exclusionary tendencies of the criminal process reflects exclusionary tendencies within wider society. These tendencies were exacerbated, if not actually encouraged, under the

5   See, to similar effect, Cavadino (1997) p 239.

Conservative administrations in power from 1979 to 1997. But with the coming to power of a Labour administration avowedly committed to a more inclusionary political, economic and legal strategy, a more communitarian inclusionary approach within criminal justice seems now possible as well as desirable.

At the time of writing, however, it appears that the current Home Secretary, Jack Straw, is persisting with much of the 'tough on crime' rhetoric and policy that was formulated in opposition in an attempt to seal a perceived weak-spot in Labour's electoral armour.[6] We may have to wait for a new Home Secretary, free of personal crime control baggage, before the inclusionary philosophy is applied in full to criminal justice. In the meantime, it is important to sketch out the potential of an inclusionary approach. Raising awareness of the issues at stake may be one necessary step along the road to rational reform.

Packer's conclusion to his analysis of American criminal law and criminal process has received little subsequent attention. But his final words are as pertinent now as they were in the late 1960s: 'The criminal sanction is at once prime guarantor and prime threatener of human freedom. Used providently and humanely it is guarantor; used indiscriminately and coercively, it is threatener. The tensions that inhere in the criminal sanction can never be wholly resolved in favour of guaranty and against threat. But we can begin to try.'[7] It is time we tried here too.

---

6   See his statement to the House of Commons and the subsequent debate on 30 July 1997, Hansard, cols. 341-357. For critical analysis see J Fionda, 'New Labour, Old Hat: Youth Justice and the Crime and Disorder Act 1998' [1999] Crim LR 36 and A Sanders, 'What Principles Underlie Criminal Justice Policy in the 1990s?' (1998) 18 OJLS 533.
7   Packer (1968) p 366.

Chapter 2

Stop and search

I. STREET POLICING IN CONTEXT

'At 3.30 am I was patrolling with a uniformed officer who was driving an unmarked police car. A coloured man was walking slowly along the pavement of a well-lit major route. The officer slowed his car to walking pace and on two occasions passed the man at this speed, gazing at him as he passed. The officer commented, "These coloured people certainly ask for trouble from us. They seem to hang about and look suspicious."'[1]

(a) What do the police really do?

In a text book on criminal justice, it is natural to concentrate on the law enforcement role of the police. Thirty five years ago, however, Banton made the point that:

'The policeman on patrol is primarily a "peace officer" rather than a law officer. Relatively little of his time is spent enforcing the law in the sense of arresting offenders; far more is spent "keeping the peace" . . . the most striking thing about patrol work is the high proportion of cases in which policemen do not enforce the law.'[2]

If the police do not enforce the law most of the time, what do they do? In one study, it was found that only 18% of calls to a police station

1   S Holdaway, *Inside the British Police* (Oxford: Blackwell, 1983) p 90.
2   M Banton, *The Policeman in the Community* (London: Tavistock, 1964) p 127.

Street policing in context

concerned crime.[3] As Morgan and Newburn say, '. . . the police handle everything from unexpected childbirths, skid row alcoholics, drug addicts, emergency psychiatric cases, family fights, landlord-tenant disputes, and traffic violations, to occasional incidents of crime.'[4]. Of course, some of the disputes and fights (and all traffic violations) do break criminal laws. But whether and when this is so will often be a matter of judgment for the officers concerned. Since, in most of these cases, 'peace keeping' will be their main objective, the question is how best to keep the peace. If the peace can be kept between the disputants by consensus, as it often can, the law will only be enforced in serious cases: 'The police 'sort out' situations by listening patiently to endless stories about fancied slights, old grievances, new insults, mismatched expectations, indifference, infidelity, dishonesty and abuse. . . . Patient listening and gentle counselling are undoubtedly what patrol officers do most of their time.'[5] But if conflict continues or gets worse, the law can be invoked by the police. Fig 1 puts the law enforcement role of the police in perspective.

Fig 1 Outcome of calls to the police

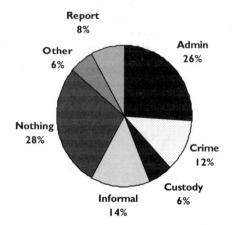

Source for Fig 1: P Waddington: *Calling the Police* (Aldershot, Avebury, 1993)

This shows that only 6% of calls from the public lead to arrests ('custody'). A crime report is completed in another 12%, so that the matter can be followed up later. In all the other cases the police judge that the incident is not criminal, or there is nothing formal they are able or willing to do.

3   P Ekblom and K Heal, The police response to calls from the public (Research and Planning Unit Paper no 9) (London: Home Office, 1982).
4   R Morgan and T Newburn, *The Future of Policing* (Oxford: OUP 1997) p 79.
5   D Bayley, *Police for the Future* (Oxford: OUP, 1994).

The fact that the police can choose whether or not to enforce the law underpins the way the criminal justice system works. Exactly the same is true of non-police agencies as well, which are discussed in detail in ch 6. This means, for instance, that the caseload of the courts is shaped not only by the way the law is enforced, but also by the way it is not enforced. In the rest of this section we will explore the range of factors which influence these discretionary enforcement decisions.

(b)   Proactive and reactive policing

Southgate and Ekblom estimate that, each year, around half of all adults have some contact with the police. Over 30% of those contacts (ie involving 16% of all adults) are adversarial, that is where the police suspect someone of something. Most adversarial encounters are stops of individuals either on foot or in vehicles.[6] More recent figures, from the 1996 British Crime Survey (BCS), are very similar.[7] So although there are many more neutral contacts than adversarial ones, a large proportion of people none the less are made aware of police suspicions about them. For some sections of the population this is particularly true: Southgate and Ekblom found that half of all 16–24-year-olds had experienced adversarial encounters, as had over one third of the unemployed of all ages. This disproportionate attention given to the young and unemployed was also confirmed by the BCS.

But at whose initiative are these adversarial contacts made? Lest the impression be given that the investigation of crime primarily revolves around classic detection methods such as fingerprinting, forensic science and the use of stop-search and arrest powers, we need to say some more about the nature of modern policing. In the decade or so following publication of Banton's book, policing became more technologically sophisticated. It was thought to be more efficient if, instead of officers patrolling the streets on foot looking for evidence of crime (a 'proactive' role in the police jargon), the police were able to react swiftly to reports of crime. The greater use of cars and personal radios in the late 1960s and 1970s switched the emphasis from 'proactive' to 'reactive' policing. Like the fire brigade, police officers (excluding the increasing numbers in support roles and in specialist sections such as juvenile liaison, fingerprints, and so forth) spent much of their time reacting to emergencies. This entailed visiting the scenes of crimes and interviewing victims (and witnesses, if any) and dealing with the subsequent paperwork. The volume of crime was such that little time was

6   P Southgate and P Ekblom, Contacts Between Police and Public (Home Office Research Study no 77) (London: HMSO, 1984) p 6.
7   C Mirrlees-Black and T Budd, Policing and the Public: Findings from the 1996 British Crime Survey (Home Office Research Findings no 60) (London: HMSO 1997). See, further, section 4(a) below.

Street policing in context

left actually to investigate, in the classical sense, except in very serious crimes.

'Fire brigade policing', as it became known, appeared to reduce the scope for the exercise of discretion by officers because they went where they were directed by victims and other members of the public. Research has found that civilians initiate police action or identify the suspect in well over half of all arrests.[8] Even those officers who act as 'detectives' rarely employ the classic detection methods we are all familiar with from television dramas and 'cop movies'.[9] Detectives actually spend most of their time:

'. . . gathering information from the public; locating suspects; interviewing and, on the basis of information derived from both the public and suspects, preparing cases for the prosecution.'[10]

This has led some writers to argue that police discretion to stop-search or arrest is unimportant and that most policing is done, in reality, by the public.[11] Although this body of work is a useful corrective to the view that the police do what they want, when they want, and in any way they want, it is just as one-sided. Regardless of changes in policing style, just because much policing is a response to the public, it does not follow that the nature of that response is predetermined. The police have to sift and interpret what they are told by the public, and they do so on the basis of their own views, experiences and priorities. This is acknowledged even by the 'policing by the public' school.[12] Although civilian knowledge of the offence starts off the investigation in over half of all arrests, civilians do not exercise such a decisive influence over most offence investigations. For most offences which come to the attention of the police do not lead to arrests. Usually the police investigate (or not) on their own initiative. This investigation is usually unproductive or leads to informal action only (see Fig 1 above). Indeed, officers responding to a call often have to decide there and then whether or not to classify the incident as a crime; if so, which specific crime; and whether to investigate it at all. Even if a suspected offender is identified, officers often discuss or negotiate an appropriate

8   M McConville, A Sanders and R Leng, *The Case for the Prosecution* (London: Routledge, 1991) p 19; J Burrows and R Tarling, Clearing up Crime (Home Office Research Study no 73) (London: HMSO, 1982); D Brown, Investigating Burglary (Home Office Research Study no 123) (London: HMSO, 1991).

9   See the studies discussed by R Reiner, *The Politics of the Police* (London: Harvester Wheatsheaf, 1992).

10   P Morris and K Heal, Crime Control and the Police (Home Office Research Study no 67) (London: HMSO, 1981).

11   See, in particular, J Shapland and J Vagg, *Policing by the Public* (London: Routledge, 1988) and D Steer, Uncovering Crime: The Police Role (Royal Commission on Criminal Procedure Research Study no 7) (London: HMSO, 1980).

12   See Shapland and Vagg, p 35.

response with the people involved in the incident. The outcome, however, whether arrest, a warning or no formal action at all, is largely in the hands of the officer.[13]

Where there is no suspected offender, decisions are almost entirely for the police. Although most police officers have apparently reactive roles, there have always been specialist groups of 'proactive' officers. For example, specialist drug, vice and serious crime squads are expected to take the lead in tackling particular spheres of criminal activity, and therefore stop-search and arrest very much on their own initiative.[14] Many non-specialist police officers get few opportunities to do this, or even to make any arrests at all. Thus when they get chances to make 'quality' arrests they grasp them enthusiastically. Indeed, promotion and the securing and retention of high status jobs (such as within CID) still depend partly on 'activity', as measured by stops and quality arrests.[15] As a general shift inspector put it: 'I would never demand a quota for arrests, but I do expect them to take an interest in crime, to investigate crime, and to show arrests wherever possible.'[16]

Even if the scope for exercising discretion did diminish when 'fire brigade policing' was at its height, the situation is changing again as policing continues to evolve. In the 1980s 'community policing' began to supplant 'fire brigade' policing, at least in the superficial sense of getting 'more bobbies back on the beat'. Most policing was still 'reactive', but, as a result of skilful advocacy on the part of 'community policing' lobbyists,[17] less

13 R Ericson, *Reproducing Order: A Study of Police Patrol Work* (Toronto: University of Toronto Press, 1982); C Kemp, C Norris and N Fielding, 'Legal Manoeuvres in Police Handling of Disputes' in D Farrington and S Walklate (eds), *Offenders and Victims, Theory and Policy* (London: British Society of Criminology, 1992).

14 See M Maguire and C Norris, The Conduct and Supervision of Criminal Investigations (Royal Commission on Criminal Justice Research Study no 5) (London: HMSO, 1992).

15 Maguire and Norris, ch 9; M McConville and D Shepherd, *Watching Police, Watching Communities* (London: Routledge, 1992) ch 7 and M Young, *An Inside Job* (Oxford: OUP, 1991). D Smith and J Gray, *Police and People in London* vol 4 (Policy Studies Institute) (Aldershot: Gower, 1983) suggest that 'activity' is not relevant for promotion (though it is for transfer to jobs such as CID). But note this acknowledgement, and implicit criticism, by the Royal Commission on Criminal Justice: 'We believe that police performance should be assessed on the basis of other factors besides arrest and conviction rates. . .', Report (Cm 2263) (London: HMSO, 1993) p 21. For a general discussion of 'performance culture', including detection rates in police forces, see B Loveday, 'The impact of performance culture on criminal justice agencies in England and Wales' (1999) 27 IJ Soc of Law 351.

16 N Fielding, *Community Policing* (Oxford: Clarendon, 1995) p 52.

17 Often police, or ex-police, officers themselves. For the most influential example, see J Alderson, *Policing Freedom* (Plymouth: Macdonald and Evans, 1979). There is now much scepticism about what 'community policing' really involves. See, for instance, McConville and Shepherd (1992).

so than was the case in the 1970s. Then in the early 1990s the Government decided that the 'peace-keeping' and community relations roles highlighted by Banton should no longer be prioritised as they use resources inefficiently. Police efficiency is now measured primarily in terms of crime-fighting, but instead of reactive policing, 'targeted' and 'intelligence-led' policing is encouraged.[18] This is highly proactive, in that specific offenders, offender-types, offences or geographical areas are targeted for police action on the basis of crime data, information from informants and so forth. Some of this work is done in partnership with local authorities and other local crime prevention agencies.[19] Part 1 of the Crime and Disorder Act 1998 (CDA) has put such partnerships on a statutory footing. In one remarkable example, Nottingham City Council 'hired' two police officers for an indefinite period to work solely on identifying the most troublesome youths on its 'problem' housing estates.[20] Traditional 'fire-brigade' responses will inevitably be displaced by these new forms of proactive policing, although we do not know to what extent. In 1993-4, before this latest change had got under way, a large sample of arrests found that at least 24% of all arrests were as a result of proactive policing (stop-searches, police-initiated inquiries, surveillance, and so forth).[1] Given that one chief constable could 'envisage a time when up to three quarters of all calls from the public to his force would no longer result in attendance by an officer',[2] we would expect proactive policing to account for a much higher percentage of arrests now. These new policing methods, which have serious implications for the ways in which police powers are exercised and for civil liberties in general, are sketched in the final chapter of this book. For the moment, the important point is that the influence of victims on the exercise of police discretion is decreasing again.

(c) Factors influencing the exercise of discretion

When officers see crimes, or suspected crimes, whether they exercise their discretion to stop-search or arrest depends partly on the probability that

18   See the Home Office White Paper, Police Reform (Cm 2281) (London: HMSO, 1993). Concrete proposals on these lines were made in Audit Commission, Helping with enquiries: tackling crime effectively (London: Audit Commission, 1993). A later report by the same body, Tackling crime effectively, vol 2 (London: Audit Commission, 1996) indicated that police forces were responding positively to these proposals.

19   See eg A Crawford, *The Local Governance of Crime* (Oxford: Clarendon, 1997).

20   'Council hires police gang-busters to crack down on young criminals' *The Guardian*, 11 January 2000.

1   C Phillips and D Brown, Entry into the Criminal Justice System - A Survey of Police Arrests and their Outcomes (Home Office Research Study no 185) (London: Home Office 1998) fig 2.1.

2   Morgan and Newburn, p 65.

a crime has been committed and partly on the probability that the suspect in question is responsible for that crime. Then there is the question of whether something is worth investigating or whether a person is worth arresting for that crime. To use the language of economics, the cost of investigating one crime is the opportunity lost to investigate others. Smith and Gray's study of the Metropolitan Police illustrates this well. A typical beat officer in London, they say:

> 'Walks past many illegally parked vehicles, drives behind speeding cars, walks past traders openly selling hard-core pornography, sees prostitutes soliciting, knows of many clubs selling liquor and providing gaming facilities without a licence, goes past unlicensed street traders, and so on, usually without taking any immediate action. Where he does take action over any one of these matters, this will usually occupy him for a considerable period, so that in the meantime he can do nothing about the others.'[3]

The myriad of crimes facing the police are not solely the relatively minor victimless crimes to which Smith and Gray refer. Every year in England and Wales alone, around four and a half million 'notifiable' offences (that is, the main non-traffic offences such as robbery, theft, burglary, violence and vandalism) are recorded by the police.[4] As if this were not staggering enough, the British Crime Survey regularly reveals that there is around three times as much domestic burglary, four times as much wounding, six times as much robbery and seven times as much vandalism as these official figures record. Overall, for the crimes where a direct comparison can be made, the BCS records around four times as many crimes as do the official police figures,[5] Although crimes abound almost everywhere, some are

3   D Smith and J Gray, *Police and People in London* vol 4 (Policy Studies Institute) (Aldershot: Gower, 1983) p 14.
4   D Povey and J Prime, Recorded Crime Statistics, England and Wales, April 1998-March 1999 (Home Office Statistical Bulletin 18/99) (London: Home Office, 1999).
5   C Mirrlees-Black, T Budd, S Partridge and P Mayhew, The 1998 British Crime Survey (Home Office Statistical Bulletin 21/98) (London: Home Office, 1998). This survey, relating in fact to 1997, is the latest, at the time of writing, of a series of regular surveys of 15,000 to 17,000 randomly selected people aged 16 or over. The primary aims are to assess the 'true' rate of victimisation in Britain and how levels of crime change over time. Previous surveys took place in 1982, 1984, 1988, 1992, 1994 and 1996. The discrepancy between actual rates of crime and the official figures stems both from the non-reporting of crimes to the police, and the non-recording by the police of reported offences. See generally A Bottomley and K Pease, *Crime and Punishment: Interpreting the Data* (Milton Keynes: Open UP, 1986); and M Maguire, 'Crime Statistics, Patterns and Trends' in M Maguire, R Morgan and R Reiner (eds), *Oxford Handbook of Criminology* 2nd edn (Oxford: Clarendon, 1997).

Street policing in context

easier to detect than others, and the amount and type of criminal activity varies with time and from place to place.

It follows that the police necessarily exercise discretion when deciding who to stop and who to arrest. Other things being equal, given the volume of crime, only the most serious offences and offenders will be selected. In this context, however, other things are rarely equal and a number of other important criteria govern the exercise of police discretion. In consequence, the police devote a large amount of resources to mundane crime and turn their backs on much serious crime. In a study of assault, Clarkson et al found no relationship between seriousness (except for the most extreme offences) and police investigation/court action.[6] The most important criteria influencing discretion are:[7]

– personal: where officers feel under pressure to make arrests in order to justify themselves and enhance job prospects, they may target simple cases (such as drunkenness and motoring offences);

– procedural: offenders who have the protection of the privacy of their home or office, for instance, are less vulnerable than people on the street or in public places, where no warrants are needed. This allows 'white collar' (ie business) crimes to be particularly well hidden. Tax evasion, pollution, unsafe working conditions and so forth—all as criminal as theft, assault and criminal damage—are conducted in private and are therefore protected by procedural safeguards;

– interpretational latitude: many substantive laws (eg offences against public order) are ambiguous, as are many police powers (eg arrest).[8] Such ambiguities may deter a police officer from acting or may, conversely, allow officers to act much as they wish;

– organisational constraints: some police forces adopt particular policies in relation to certain offences (eg a 'zero tolerance' campaign against drunken driving, vice or domestic violence; or a tolerance policy concerning the possession of 'soft' drugs);

– societal pressures: both the Police and Criminal Evidence Act 1984 (PACE) and the CDA 1998 require individual police forces to consult and work with local communities in relation to policing and crime reduction,[9] thus envisaging the shaping of policing by forces outside the police. Wider societal pressures occur from time to time in relation to particular offences such as robbery or, again, domestic violence.[10]

6   C Clarkson, A Cretney, G Davis and J Shepherd, 'Assaults: the relationship between seriousness, criminalisation and punishment' [1994] Crim LR 4, Table 2.

7   The following list is based loosely on A Bottomley, *Decisions in the Penal Process* (London: Martin Robertson, 1973) pp 37-43.

8   See below and ch 3.

9   PACE, s 106, CDA, ss 5 and 6

10   See, for instance, S Hall, C Critcher, T Jefferson, J Clarke and B Roberts, *Policing the Crisis* (London: Macmillan, 1978) for an analysis of, among other things, the 'mugging' scare of the 1970s.

It may be societal pressures, of course, which shape police organisational policies. In the United States, two towns with widely differing juvenile arrest rates were found to have similar juvenile crime rates. In the town with the low arrest rate, residents had exerted pressure on the police to avoid arrest wherever possible;[11]

- political pressures: as part of a campaign to secure more resources or powers for the police, police forces may deliberately allow the clear-up rate to fall.

The way in which some of these factors work is illustrated by a study by Walmsley of offences of 'indecency between males' between 1946 and 1976.[12] The Sexual Offences Act 1967 legalised many of these 'indecency' offences. If the level of homosexual activity remained constant, one would have expected the number of offences recorded by the police to decline, for a considerable amount of that homosexual behaviour would have been illegal before 1967 but legal afterwards. But Walmsley found the reverse. In 1967 there were 840 indecencies between males recorded by the police as offences, while between 1973 and 1976 the figure averaged just under 1,660—twice as much as in 1967. Walmsley also found the prosecution rate very much higher after 1967 than it was before.

It is most unlikely that there really were more crimes of this sort committed after 1967 than before. The more likely explanation is that the police were prosecuting in a higher proportion of suspected indecency cases than they had hitherto. It seems that the police, aware of society's ambivalent attitude to the criminalisation of homosexuality, had previously exercised discretion not to arrest and prosecute. When they sensed that clear lines had been drawn, in social attitudes as well as in the letter of the law, they responded by changing the way they exercised their discretion.[13] There are two general lessons here: firstly, that, whether the police act reactively or proactively, discretion still needs to be exercised and, secondly, that shifts in the way that discretion is operated can bring about dramatic changes in the apparent levels of crime.

(d) A typology of legal rules

It might be thought that police discretion is tightly constrained by legal rules. At times it is, but more frequently it is not. One reason for this is that while some rules constrain police action, there are few rules which require police action. When the police decide to act it is usually a policy which is at work, not a rule. Take, for example, PACE. Many of its provisions brought

11 See A Meehan, 'Internal Police Records and the Control of Juveniles' (1993) 33 BJ Crim 504.
12 R Walmsley, 'Indecencies Between Males' [1978] Crim LR 400.
13 Walmsley at p 405.

the law into line with police practice or police aspirations. Stop and search laws, for example, were extended by PACE from certain localities to the country as a whole, *allowing* the police to detain people they think are suspicious, but not *requiring* them to do so. In part, this enabled the police to operationalise their working assumptions more extensively than hitherto. Legal rules which respond to police aspirations may be termed 'enabling rules'. In part, it simply made legal what they were doing anyway. When the law is brought into line with pre-existing police practice the rules are 'legitimising'. As ch 4 will show, before 1984 many suspects used to 'help the police with their inquiries' before charge without being formally arrested; PACE now allows pre-charge detention in most cases for 24 hours, and longer in some serious cases. This legitimised their former practices, while also enabling them to extend detention where they really want this.

These examples demonstrate that many of the rules in PACE were not intended to control the police but rather were introduced to allow them more leeway. Bridges and Bunyan show that much of PACE was a product of 'the highly assertive evidence presented to the Royal Commission by various police spokesmen and pressure groups'.[14] It is no surprise to find that rules resulting from the initiative of the police generally embody more crime control values than due process values and run counter to the 'freedom' perspective presented in ch 1.

However, some of PACE has a freedom-enhancing due process character. These rules are intended to inhibit the police from following their working assumptions (or are intended to give that impression), especially where those working assumptions embody crime control values. If they succeed in this ostensible aim they are 'inhibitory rules'. If they do not (whether or not they were really intended to do so) they are 'presentational rules', which allow the police to follow their working assumptions (see Fig 2).[15] Presentational rules can thus be defined as those which appear to be inhibitory but in fact are not.

Few legal rules are as one-dimensional as this suggests, as most originate from mixed motives and/or messy compromises. For example, as soon as a rule legitimises a police practice (such as stop-search) it is likely to encourage greater use of that practice, and so has the effect of an enabling rule. Or, to take a different kind of example, some governments, especially from the early-1990s to the time of writing (2000), pass presentational legislation aimed at presenting them as hard-line even though they know

14 L Bridges and T Bunyan, 'Britain's new urban policing strategy - the Police and Criminal Evidence Bill in context' (1983) 10 JLS 85 at p 86. See also M McConville, A Sanders and R Leng, *The Case for the Prosecution* (London: Routledge, 1991) pp 173-8.

15 We have most humbly and gratefully borrowed - and re-worked - these terms from Smith and Gray (1993).

that these new laws will be largely ineffective: they give the impression of being more crime control oriented than in reality they are. However, despite these complications, the typology helps us to understand the major themes of the book. It is helpful to see this in diagrammatic form:

Fig 2: Types of legal rule and effect on police behaviour

	Rule expresses crime control values	*Rule expresses due process values*
Influence police	Enabling effect	Inhibitory effect
Do not influence police	Legitimising effect	Presentational effect

(e) Cop culture

We have seen that the purpose of some legal rules is to enable the police to do what they want. Some rules have the opposite purpose - to stop the police acting as they wish - but they do not always succeed in this objective. Moreover, many rules can be interpreted as the police want, as can other factors influencing discretion such as community pressures, and concepts such as 'seriousness'. The desires of local or wider communities (which are rarely expressed with one voice) need to be sifted and interpreted by the police. Similarly, offence 'seriousness' is not an objective category, and what is or is not 'insulting behaviour' under the Public Order Act 1986, for instance, will depend in part on one's view of the world. The police world outlook - which influences the way the police handle legal rules and non-legal influences - does not simply encapsulate that of society at large. It is moulded by 'cop culture'. This is

> 'rooted in constant problems which officers face in carrying out the role they are mandated to perform . . . Cop culture has developed as a patterned set of understandings which help to cope with and adjust to the pressures and tensions which confront the police.'[16]

Cop culture comprises a number of related elements. The most important is 'authority'. In Britain in particular, where the police rarely wield weapons,

16   R Reiner, *The Politics of the Police* (London: Harvester Wheatsheaf, 1992) p 109. For a discussion of the way in which cop culture affects the impact of rules on police discretion see A Goldsmith, 'Taking Police Culture Seriously: Police Discretion and the Limits of the Law' (1990) 1 Policing and Society 91.

they get people to do what they want without recourse to the law. Ordinarily, a request by an officer to stop or to answer questions is always underpinned by the unspoken threat of arrest or 'back-up', but this is only part of the *authority* of the officer. It is this authority which usually secures results without the need for coercion. Other related elements include a sense of 'danger', which is the officers' sense of the unpredictability of interactions with members of the public; the demand for deference from most members of the public, without which authority is undermined and order is threatened; the need, as we saw earlier, to produce 'results'; and a sense of mission to prevent 'them' from ruining things for 'us'.

This is a dichotomous view of society which sees a relatively small section of society perpetually on the verge of revolt against the respectable majority. The sense of impending chaos and the importance of the 'thin blue line' holding it at bay permeates cop culture. Only the police know what it is really like 'out there'. If the naive, well-meaning, respectable majority knew what it was like, they would not make police officers work with one hand tied behind their backs. Thus, though the police see their interests and values as being those of the majority, cop culture is impatient with that majority for not realising how much it needs the police and how impractical its due process values are.[17] The social isolation of officers from 'civilians' (both 'rough' and 'respectable') and the social solidarity among officers minimises the extent to which this view of the world is challenged. The negative effects of cop culture were recognised by the Runciman Commission, as in this reference to the effect of police solidarity on 'cover ups': 'There is a real risk that police officers and the civilian staff employed by police forces may be deterred by the prevailing culture from complaining openly about malpractice.'[18]

Cop culture leads to such descriptions of the police as being 'a race apart',[19] and a considerable body of research has tried to ascertain whether the intolerance and authoritarianism characteristic of the police is a product of socialisation after joining the service or a characteristic of the type of people who wish to become police officers.[20] One result is, as the rest of this chapter and later chapters will show, a very particular view of what constitutes 'suspicious' behaviour and impatience with any rules which get in the way of the 'fight against crime'. As Goldsmith points out, this

---

17   Reiner, ch 3, summarises the voluminous research literature. For a former police superintendent's critical account of cop culture see Young (1991).
18   Royal Commission on Criminal Justice, Report (Cm 2263) (London: HMSO, 1993) p 22.
19   See Banton (1964).
20   The research, which is inconclusive, is discussed by Reiner (1992) pp 125-128. Also see Young (1991).

means that legality is often sacrificed for efficiency.[1] Thus, cop culture acts as a powerful crime control engine at the heart of the machinery of criminal justice.

What we have said about 'cop culture' might lead one to believe that the police who subscribe to it see the world completely differently to the way others see it, and that cop culture never changes. This would be a mistake, though. There are differences within cop culture: between forces (eg between those which espouse community policing strongly and those which do not) and within forces (eg between 'management cops' and 'street cops', and between different types of squad). There are differences between aspects of modern cop culture and that of the 1960s (especially in relation to race, gender and sexual orientation). And the differences between cop culture and that of the wider society can be overstated. Impatience with rules which appear to impede the fight against crime is widespread through society.[2]

One reason why cop culture is generally thought to be completely distinct is that, when the police talk about what they do (and why they do it) they often exaggerate. Researchers, listening to what police officers say but not observing what they actually do, sometimes make the mistake of assuming that those officers are describing reality. In their talk, though, the police over-emphasise the danger of their job, the awfulness of the 'toe-rags' they deal with and their ethnic distinctiveness, and their own macho qualities. Hoyle, for instance, in research carried out in the early 1990s, found most officers expressing disparaging remarks about domestic disputes ('rubbish work') and most of the women victims of these disputes. But in reality she found that most officers handled these disputes sensitively.[3] Similarly, Smith and Gray found that police officers behaved in far less racist ways than their views would lead one to expect.[4] Hoyle therefore draws a distinction between 'canteen culture', which is the way they talk about their work and which incorporates in a strong form all the elements identified earlier, and the actual working rules of the police.

In view of this, it has been argued that we need not use the concept of 'cop culture'. Waddington, for instance, argues that the way that policing works and discretion is exercised depends on the demands of the job and the nature of society; canteen culture serves the role of relieving tension and justifying sometimes distasteful and distressing actions, and bears

1   Goldsmith (1990).
2   See J Chan, 'Changing Police Culture' (1996) 36 BJ Crim 109.
3   C Hoyle, *Negotiating Domestic Violence* (Oxford: Clarendon, 1998).
4   Smith and Gray (1983). Several other examples could be cited. See P A J Waddington, 'Police (Canteen) Sub-Culture: An Appreciation' (1999) 39 BJ Crim 286.

Street policing in context

no necessary relation to reality.[5] In our opinion, Waddington goes too far. If canteen culture were to become totally divorced from reality it could no longer serve the function of justifying what the police do. And, as we have said before, the demands of the job and the nature of society (and society's demands) can be interpreted in different ways. It follows that police culture will be a product in part of certain objective realities which change slowly (fundamental realities of policing, the way our society is structured, the hopeless situation in which many female victims of domestic violence find themselves and so forth), and in part a product of attitudes and perceptions specific to the police (attitudes to 'domestics' which fail to understand the predicament of the victims, to ethnic minorities, to discipline and so forth). Police culture can be seen as producing both 'canteen culture' on the one hand and, on the other, specific 'working rules' which are less extreme than implied by what the police say when eating their mixed grills. As for police practices, they are a product of the interaction of those working rules with countervailing social pressures (for instance from ethnic minority communities who resent aspects of police practices) and legal constraints. Chan quotes Bordieu, arguing that police officers follow 'the intuitions of a "logic of practice" which is the product of a lasting exposure to conditions similar to those in which [other officers] are placed.'[6] This can be represented diagrammatically (see Fig 3).

Figure 3 The effect of cop culture on police action

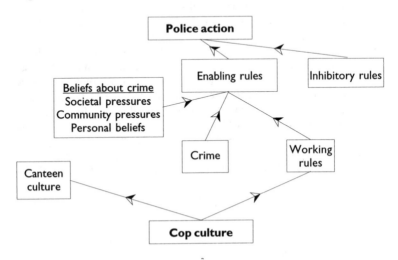

5   Waddington (1999).
6   Chan (1996) p 115.

In ch 1 we talked about the criminal justice system and its constituent sub-systems, such as the police, as social institutions which have their own history, internal logics and processes but which are also shaped by the specific society in which they operate. This discussion of police culture illustrates that in respect of the police. This is not just of academic interest. If, by the end of this book, you would like to change certain police practices you will have to consider how that can be done. You might advocate changing some legal rules, but you will first have to identify the conditions under which rules tend to become inhibitory or, by contrast, merely presentational. Or you might consider arguing for a change in police training or recruitment policy. But you will have to identify how that can be done without going against the grain of the structural realities of policing. It might not always be possible without changing elements of those structures such as class, race or gender differences.[7] The same kind of argument can be applied to other criminal justice sub-systems. Take non-police agencies, such as the Inland Revenue or the Factory Inspectorate, which enforce tax and health and safety laws. These agencies are also social institutions which have their own culture and logic which is also related to society. The specific criminal laws and offenders they deal with are, however, very different from those dealt with by the police. The result is a different culture, different working rules and different enforcement practices even though all these agencies deal with criminal laws, courts and punishments.

We said earlier that one effect of police culture is to elevate crime control concerns above those of due process in many situations. Few police officers welcome new due process rules. Another effect of police culture is to give priority to certain freedoms above others. Take police culture's exaggerated 'them' and 'us' attitudes. Less value is put on the freedom involved in activities (especially those of 'them') which impinge on the freedoms of others (especially those of 'us') than is put on 'our' freedoms to be undisturbed. As we shall see in ch 3, this typically results, for instance, in the police prioritising the maintenance of public order to an extent which is inconsistent with such democratic values as tolerance (of diversity and of peaceful protest) and the upholding of the rights of unpopular minorities. This leads to a tendency to over-police those who are perceived to be deviating from a 'respectable' norm. One way of changing police practices might be to inculcate a more democratic (or, to put it another way, more inclusive) set of values in officers. This could be done through, for example, changes in training, or by introducing new performance indicators. But the centrality of 'authority' in police culture, and in the deep structure of policing itself, limits how far this can take place; and if too much authority

---

7   See Chan (1996) for a discussion on these lines in relation to the reform of the police in Australia.

is taken from police officers they may have to rely more on overt coercion, with a net loss of freedom for us all. Further, to expect the police to be more tolerant of disorder and unpopular minorities than the rest of society is almost certainly unrealistic.[8] In the rest of this chapter we look at how the police as presently constituted operate the power to stop and search, and at some of their social consequences.

2. STOP AND SEARCH PRIOR TO PACE

The first power to which a police officer might wish to resort on the street is that of stopping and searching suspects. At the time of the Royal Commission on Criminal Procedure (Philips Commission) report in 1981, the law was confused and incoherent, having developed in an ad hoc manner. For example, whereas legislation on such matters as controlled drugs, firearms, and protected animals allowed stop and search for related crimes, there were no national stop and search powers for stolen goods or offensive weapons. On the other hand, local legislation for many big cities including London and Birmingham did allow stop and search for stolen goods.[9] It was irrational that the police had greater enforcement powers for some relatively minor offences than for some more important offences and that powers varied according to locality.

Most of these powers allowed the police to stop and search only if they 'reasonably suspected' a person of the offence in question. A major issue of concern in the 1970s and early 1980s was how far the police really were inhibited by the reasonable suspicion requirement. The early 1980s saw a number of riots in several inner-city areas where poverty and ethnic minority conflict with the police was (and still is) commonplace.[10] A massive stop-search operation, 'Swamp 81', in particular, was identified as one of the 'triggers' of the Brixton riot of 1981.[11] Described by some as 'saturation

---

8 Non-police agencies are discussed in detail in ch 6. Note that the opposite of what is said in this paragraph in respect of the police is true of most non-police agencies. The latter are very reluctant to encroach on the freedom of those whom they police. Clearly the job of law enforcement per se in an adversary system does not produce the distinctive elements which comprise 'cop culture'. It is worth thinking about why the police and other agencies differ from each other so much.

9 See Royal Commission on Criminal Procedure, The Investigation and Prosecution of Criminal Offences in England and Wales: The Law and Procedure (Cmnd 8092-1, app 1) or PACE Code of Practice A, Annex A, for a comprehensive list of stop and search powers.

10 For discussion, see E Cashmore and E McLaughlin (eds), Out of Order? (London: Routledge, 1991) p 113.

11 See further section 4 below. This was not the only civil disturbance 'triggered' by street confrontation: see Cashmore and McLaughlin (eds), (1991) p 149.

policing', stop-search on this scale was manifestly not on a 'reasonable suspicion' basis.[12]

There is no doubt that in some urban areas stop and search powers were used extensively: in 1981 there were over 700,000 recorded stops in London alone. Only 67,275 of these (that is, less than 10%) led to arrest, casting doubt on the level of suspicion in many of these cases. A survey in Moss Side (in Manchester) by Tuck and Southgate found that one third of males aged 16–35 reported being stopped, searched or arrested in 1979– 80, although the proportions were the same for blacks as for whites.[13] If minorities or the inhabitants of particular localities were disproportionately the subject of these powers, it is not surprising that resentment arose. Study after study in the 1970s, 1980s and 1990s discovered hostility to the police among young black people.[14] As Rex has noted more generally:

'While most white people in Britain feel that they can ultimately rely on the police to defend them, for many young blacks they seem an alien force or an occupying army.'[15]

The perception of unfairness, however, is not the same as actual unfairness. Whether or not legal rules were being breached, and whether or not police working practices were explicitly or implicitly racist, was a factual question which only empirical research could determine. The most important pieces of research, by Willis (for the Home Office) and by Smith and Gray (for the Policy Studies Institute), were carried out in the early 1980s with the co-operation of the Metropolitan Police in London.

The officers who Willis interviewed made a note of all the stops they made, and their reasons for them, during the research. She found that relatively few officers stopped and searched suspects for specific offences like theft or drugs. The most important single category of stops, according to police records, was 'movements'. Yet 'movements' does not constitute a valid reason for stopping. Indeed, when Willis interviewed police officers, she found 'that this category covered stops made on grounds which police

12   Sir L Scarman, The Brixton Disorders: 10-12 April 1981 (Cmnd 8427) (London: HMSO, 1981).

13   M Tuck and P Southgate, Ethnic Minorities, Crime and Policing (Home Office Research Study no 70) (London: HMSO, 1981).

14   See eg M McConville, 'Search of Persons and Premises: New Data from London' [1983] Crim LR 605; A Brogden, 'Sus is dead: what about "SaS"?' (1981) 9 New Community 44; G Gaskell, 'Black Youths and the Police' (1986) 2 Policing 26; T Jefferson, M Walker and M Seneviratne 'Ethnic Minorities, Crime and Criminal Justice: a study in a provincial city' in D Downes (ed), Unravelling Criminal Justice (London: Routledge, 1992) and P Southgate and D Crisp, Public Satisfaction with Police Services (Home Office Research and Planning Unit Paper no 73) (London: Home Office, 1993). The study by Tuck and Southgate (1981) is the only exception.

15   See J Rex, The Ghetto and the Underclass (Aldershot: Avebury, 1988) p 116.

officers find it hard to specify.'[16] If police officers find it hard to specify why they make a particular stop, it is difficult to say that their suspicion was 'reasonable'. The arrest rates for these 'movements' stops also suggest the absence of reasonable suspicion in most of them. Whilst there were many arrests of those stopped for offensive weapons and controlled drugs (between 30% and 100% of these stops), for 'movements' the arrest rates varied by police station from 1% to 6%. In other words, stops on grounds of movements were much less successful, which is not surprising if the police had little reason for making these stops in the first place. In many—perhaps most—of these stops, there was plainly no reasonable suspicion.

Willis' conclusions were bolstered by the PSI research. Smith and Gray categorised stops as follows: traffic offences (18%), reasonable suspicion of other offences (49%), and no good reason to stop (33%). Even these statistics flatter the police because the 'reasonable suspicion' criteria adopted by the PSI included 'running or moving quickly', 'hanging about, moving very slowly, especially at night' and 'being out on foot in the small hours of the morning'. Arguably such criteria artificially inflate the proportion of stops made on the basis of 'reasonable' suspicion, as the low arrest rate (similar to Willis') suggests. However, the PSI report did not conclude that stops were usually arbitrary. Rather, a distinct pattern of policing emerged:

'[Officers] strongly tend to choose young males, especially young black males. Other groups that they tend to single out are people who look scruffy or poor ("slag"), people who have long hair or unconventional dress (who, they think, may use drugs) and homosexuals. We observed two cases where men were stopped purely because they appeared to be homosexual. In a few cases there appeared to be no criteria at all and the stop is completely random; this happens especially in the early hours of the morning when police officers tend to be bored.'[17]

A similar point was made, in relation to stop and search for drugs of 'unconventional looking' youths, by the Advisory Committee on Drug Dependence,[18] and large numbers of stops observed by Southgate also appeared to be without reasonable suspicion.[19] Like the PSI, Willis also

---

16   C Willis, The Use, Effectiveness and Impact of Police Stop and Search Powers (Home Office Research and Planning Unit Paper no 15) (London: Home Office, 1983) p 15.

17   D Smith and J Gray, *Police and People in London* vol 4 (Policy Studies Institute) (Aldershot: Gower, 1983) p 233.

18   Report (1970) para 111.

19   P Southgate, Police-Public Encounters (Home Office Research Study no 90) (London: HMSO, 1986) app 1.

found that young black males were more likely to be stopped than whites, as did other studies such as the Islington Crime Survey where over half of the former had been stopped the previous year, as compared to less than one third of the latter.[20] While it is possible that young black people are out in the streets in the evening more than others, and are therefore more at risk of being stopped than others, their claims that the police picked on them disproportionately seemed powerful.

3. STOP AND SEARCH AFTER PACE

The Philips Commission knew that stop and search was difficult to control, and was aware of the damage which these powers could do to the relationship between police and black youth in particular. It recommended a single uniform power for the police to stop and search for stolen goods or 'articles which it is a criminal offence to possess', but it also believed that 'the exercise of the powers must be subject to strict safeguards.'[1] Along with many other of the Philips Commission's proposals, these recommendations were enacted in PACE. The bundle of laws and controls that resulted contained elements of all four of the types of rule we identified earlier: the extension of the powers nationwide legitimised pre-existing police working practices and, by cloaking officers with legal authority, enabled more intensive stop and search strategies in future. At the same time, inhibitory elements were incorporated (with limited success) in the form of 'safeguards'. In addition to these stop-search powers, we also need to consider similar powers provided by the Prevention of Terrorism (Temporary Provisions) Act 1989 and other legislation enacted since PACE. This will be considered in the course of the following discussion in subsection (b).

Section 1 of PACE is headed 'Power of constable to stop and search persons, vehicles, etc'. This power can best be understood as comprising three main elements: the 'reasonable suspicion' criterion, the offences to which stop and search is applicable, and the power itself. The safeguards which the Philips Commission thought were vital, now contained in ss 2 and 3, are a fourth element. A fifth element limits where stop and search may take place to any public place, any non-dwelling place to which the public have access, or a private place if the police officer is in that place lawfully (eg if invited in).[2]

20 T Jones, B McLean and J Young, The Islington Crime Survey (Aldershot: Gower, 1986).
1   Royal Commission on Criminal Procedure (RCCP), Report (Cmnd 8092) (London: HMSO, 1981) para 3.17.
2   For a more detailed account of the spatial limitation of the power to stop and search see V Bevan and K Lidstone, The Investigation of Crime: A Guide to Police Powers 2nd edn (London: Butterworths, 1996) pp 65-69.

(a) Reasonable suspicion

'Reasonable suspicion' is a widely used standard in English criminal justice: we shall see in later chapters that it governs many police powers such as arrest. This accords with the European Convention on Human Rights (ECHR), now incorporated into the Human Rights Act 1998, which also requires 'reasonable suspicion' where an offence is suspected.[3] If the criminal justice system applied 'due process' norms rigidly the police would not be allowed to exercise any powers of this kind without sufficient evidence to prosecute. On the other hand, if extreme 'crime control' values were applied the police would be allowed to apply coercive power if they had any suspicion. 'Reasonable suspicion' is an attempt to steer something of a middle course between these two polarities. It is aimed at inhibiting the police from stopping and searching indiscriminately—or, indeed, in discriminatory ways—without unduly fettering their ability to detect crime. It is a problematic standard by which to control and judge the police, as the Philips Commission recognised:

'We acknowledge the risk that the criterion could be loosely interpreted and have considered the possibility of trying to find some agreed standards which could form the grounds of reasonable suspicion and could be set out in a statute or in a code of practice. Like others before us we have concluded that the variety of circumstances that would have to be covered makes this impracticable. We have therefore looked for other means of ensuring that the criterion of reasonable suspicion is not devalued.'[4]

The Philips Commission thus recommended the retention of 'reasonable suspicion', despite its elasticity, and the government accepted this at the time. However, 'reasonable suspicion' has never been an element of all stop-search powers, and recent additions to these powers have not required it either. In the following discussion it should therefore be remembered that 'reasonable suspicion' is not required in anywhere near all stops, and that the law may therefore not be steering a middle course between due process and crime control after all. We shall return to this issue in subsection (b) when we examine the different offences in respect of which stops may be made.

Under s 1(3) of PACE, police officers may only stop and search if they have 'reasonable grounds for suspecting' that evidence of relevant offences will be found; and seizure may take place only of articles which, under s 1(7), the officer 'has reasonable grounds for suspecting' to be relevant. The few cases on reasonable suspicion do little to define it.

3   ECHR, Art 5(1)(c)
4   RCCP, Report, para 3.25.

According to the House of Lords in *Shaaban Bin Hussien v Chong Fook Kam*,[5] reasonable cause (which is synonymous with reasonable suspicion) is a lower standard than information sufficient to prove a prima facie case. Reasonable cause may take into account matters that could not be put in evidence at all, such as hearsay evidence,[6] or matters which although admissible would not on their own prove the case. Lord Devlin declared that:

> 'Suspicion arises at or near the starting point of an investigation of which the obtaining of prima facie proof is the end . . . Prima facie proof consists of admissible evidence. Suspicion can take into account matters that could not be put in evidence at all.'[7]

This definition, if such it is, fails to specify the nature of the thresholds between mere suspicion, reasonable suspicion and prima facie proof. Other cases are of little more help. In *King v Gardner*,[8] an officer heard a description over his radio of a suspect of a crime. Someone who was loitering nearby fitted this rather vague description so the officer asked for permission to search the large bag he was carrying. The suspect refused, assaulted the officer in an attempt to prevent the search and was arrested for assault in the execution of the officer's duty. The arrest could only be justifiable if the officer was right to carry out the search. This depended on him having reasonable suspicion (the Metropolitan Police byelaw in force at the time being similar to what is now PACE, s 1). It was held that the magistrates' court which heard the original case was entitled to conclude that there was no reasonable suspicion, as the description of the suspect was not sufficiently clear to create reasonable suspicion in relation to the person arrested, and his lingering around with a large bag did not create any additional suspicion.

This suggests a fairly high threshold of suspicion. However, in *Lodwick v Sanders*[9] a police officer stopped a lorry because it had no brake lights or tax disc. There was no initial suspicion of theft, but during discussion the officer asked the suspect if he owned the lorry, to which he answered: 'Maybe I do, maybe I don't. If you are going to do me, do me. If you're going to bollock me, bollock me and let me go. I'm in a hurry.' After further discussion the suspect tried to drive off, the officer tried to stop him, and the suspect assaulted the officer. As in *King v Gardner*, he was arrested for assaulting an officer in the execution of his duty. The question for the Divisional Court was whether the officer was acting in the execution of his

5   [1970] AC 942.
6   See eg *Erskine v Hollin* [1971] RTR 199.
7   [1970] AC 942 at 948-94.
8   (1979) 71 Cr App Rep 13.
9   [1985] 1WLR 382 (no relation).

duty in detaining the lorry driver in order to find out who owned the lorry. The suspect argued that there was no reasonable suspicion of theft, for the officer had found nothing out after making the stop that he did not know at the time of the stop. The Divisional Court, however, upheld the officer's decision.

Was it right to do so? At the time of the initial stop, all the officer reasonably suspected was that the lorry driver was committing various road traffic offences. All he found out following the stop was that the lorry driver refused to answer his questions about the possible theft of the lorry directly. Very little—if anything—was added to the officer's knowledge or understanding of the situation. Yet, for the Divisional Court, that very little seemed enough to create a reasonable suspicion. *King v Gardner* and *Lodwick v Sanders* are not easily reconcilable but this is as much a product of the vagueness of 'reasonable suspicion' as a concept than it is a criticism of the courts.[10] In the 10 years or so since the decision in *Lodwick v Sanders* there have been a few decisions of the Divisional Court in cases which raise similar issues, but they do no more to pin 'reasonable suspicion' down. In *Tomlinson*, for example, a man was wandering 'aimlessly' in Soho and going up to people but not talking to them. It was held on appeal that this behaviour, together with Soho's reputation for drugs, did not create a reasonable suspicion, as Tomlinson's behaviour could be accounted for in several innocent ways.[11] *Francis* was similar. Here, suspicion was created by the suspect driving in an area known for drugs, with a passenger. The last time the driver had been stopped her passenger (a different one) had been in possession of drugs. This, again, was held not to constitute 'reasonable suspicion'.[12] In *Slade*, on the other hand, the suspect's proximity to an address known for its drugs connections, noticing the officer and putting his hand in his pocket, and smiling 'smugly' was held to constitute reasonable suspicion.[13]

It would be difficult to slip a Rizla paper between the material facts of these 'reasonable suspicion' cases which nonetheless reach different conclusions. However, the 'reasonable suspicion' rule is not unique in its elasticity. Hart identified two elements in legal rules: a 'core' of settled meaning and a 'penumbra' of uncertainty.[14] All legal rules have both, he

10   See S H Bailey and D Birch, 'Recent Developments in the Law of Police Powers' [1982] Crim LR 475 for discussion of the few other cases prior to *Lodwick v Sanders*. These suggest that the courts have not applied their minds to this issue as rigorously as they might. Judging by *Castorina* (see ch 3 below), it seems that *Lodwick v Sanders* is more representative of the courts' thinking than is *King v Gardner*.

11   Reported in LAG Bulletin, May 1992, p 21.

12   LEXIS, CO/1434/91, June 1992.

13   LEXIS, CO/1678/96, October 1996. Also see *Lawrence* for a similar case: LEXIS CO/2775/94 May 1995.

14   See H Hart, *The Concept of Law* (Oxford: Clarendon, 1961).

argues, but some have more extensive penumbras than others. Reasonable suspicion, then, has a core meaning, encompassing such situations as someone trying to climb through a window at night (the fact that it could be a householder locked out does not affect the reasonableness of the suspicion). People hanging around with large bags, or people who answer questions evasively, fall within the penumbra of uncertainty. An alternative analysis is offered by Dworkin, who argues, in opposition to the legal positivists such as Hart, that law is not exclusively constituted by rules.[15] Underlying (and filling in the gaps between) the rules are principles which require continual interpretation and reinterpretation. Thus, the question of what constitutes reasonable suspicion is inevitably one that must be left to the courts to examine in an ethical and principled manner, since it is impossible for Parliament to lay down rigid rules in such a sensitive area. More radical accounts are offered by 'legal realists' and 'critical theorists' who come near to questioning the existence of legal rules altogether and who argue that courts interpret the wording of legal rules in the light of many factors (social, political, economic and so forth) rather than simply seeking their literal and grammatical meaning.[16] On this analysis, the court in *Lodwick v Sanders* may have been as much influenced by a desire to back police judgments and maintain police morale as by any canon of statutory interpretation.

These varied jurisprudential perspectives serve as warnings about the ability or willingness of courts and legislators to control the police (or any other agencies) through legal rules. On any of these analyses we should not be surprised by the impossibility of pinning down the meaning of 'reasonable suspicion'. We shall see the importance of the open-textured nature of much law, to use Hart's language, throughout the criminal justice system.[17]

An attempt to clarify the concept of 'reasonable suspicion' is contained in the PACE Code of Practice A (para 1.6) as follows:

'Whether a reasonable ground for suspicion exists will depend on the circumstances in each case, but there must be some objective basis for it. An officer will need to consider the nature of the article suspected of being carried in the context of other factors such as

---

15 R Dworkin, *Taking Rights Seriously* (London: Duckworth, 1977).
16 See R Cotterrell, *The Politics of Jurisprudence* (London: Butterworths, 1989) ch 7 (also chs 4 and 6 on Hart, Dworkin and other theorists).
17 Even apparently precise concepts such as the 'necessity' principle (s 37 of PACE), which governs the lawfulness of detaining suspects in police custody between arrest and charge, can be seen to lose certainty in the light of practice. See further ch 4, section 3(c).

the time and the place and the behaviour of the person concerned or those with him.'[18]

This still leaves scope to identify certain groups as more suspicious than others (as Willis and the PSI study showed the police did in the 1980s). This was acknowledged in the Code of Practice (para 1.7) in the following terms:

'Reasonable suspicion can never be supported on the basis of personal factors alone without supporting intelligence or information. For example, a person's colour, age, hairstyle or manner of dress, or the fact that he is known to have a previous conviction for possession of an unlawful article, cannot be used alone or in combination with each other as the sole basis on which to search that person. Nor may it be founded on the basis of stereotyped images of certain persons or groups as more likely to be committing offences.'

It is remarkable that a legislative code of practice directs, in effect, that people should not be stopped just because they are black. The provision is a rare example of the law attempting to take into account the social reality of policing on the streets. Recently, though, this cautionary note was undermined as a result of additions to the 1997 version of the Code as follows:

'1.6A . . . reasonable suspicion may be based upon reliable information or intelligence which indicates that members of a particular group or gang, or their associates, habitually carry knives unlawfully or weapons or controlled drugs.'

Carrying this further, para 1.7AA provides that where the police have such information about a particular gang, whose members 'wear a distinctive item of clothing or other means of identification. . .' simply being identifiable in that way constitutes reasonable suspicion of membership; and, by implication, reasonable suspicion of carrying those prohibited articles. These additions were ostensibly made because of concern about the

18   A number of Codes of Practice have been made by the Home Office under the authority of PACE. Codes of Practice are similar in effect to legislation, insofar as they must be taken into account by the courts, but they are brought into effect by statutory instrument. This makes them easy to amend in the light of experience. Code A was last amended in 1997. It applies not only to stop-search powers exercised under PACE, but also to those exercised under, for instance, the Prevention of Terrorism (Temporary Provisions) Act 1989 and the Criminal Justice and Public Order Act 1994.

habitual carrying of knives in public by many youths, but the wider suspicion relates to other weapons and drugs too.

The Code of Practice has, from the very start, raised as many questions as it answers. What, for instance, if a suspect does not simply refuse to answer questions put to him by an officer,[19] but refuses rudely and aggressively? Would this constitute 'behaviour of the person' creating reasonable suspicion?[20] As police officers themselves sometimes acknowledge, 'reasonable suspicion' can be very subjective.[1]

Lodwick v Sanders is rare among post-PACE appeals in that it turns upon the meaning of 'reasonable suspicion'. The paucity of cases is significant. If legal rules are, because of their due process content, in conflict with police working assumptions, the extent to which they are inhibitory will depend in part on their enforceability in the courts. The lack of reported court cases suggests that either the police are now adhering faithfully to the law or that the law is unenforceable. The vagueness of the reasonable suspicion test virtually rules out the possibility of strict adherence, and the evidence of research suggests that the paucity of legal cases is not due to the inhibitory qualities of the law.

Do PACE and the Codes of Practice restrain police discretion more than was the case when Willis and Smith and Gray did their research? A NACRO experiment in Tottenham in 1995 suggests not. The brainchild of the local MP and the local police commander, the police were required to give a leaflet to everyone stop-searched in the area which explained their rights. No new rules were introduced, although the use of stop-search as a performance indicator in the area was stopped, and the commitment of the area's senior police to non-racist policing was emphasised. In that year, the number of stop-searches was apparently halved, at a time when stop-searches in the Met in general continued to rise. Although the police themselves disputed the idea, it is likely that giving out a leaflet which set out the law concentrated the minds of officers on the rules and inhibited their use of the power.[2] Although we have to be cautious here, for both the police officers on the ground and the community itself thought that little had changed - giving rise to the suspicion that stop-searches may have continued in a more covert and 'consensual' manner - it does suggest that

---

19 Stated by the code of practice not to constitute reasonable suspicion (para 2.3).
20 See the arrest case of *Ricketts v Cox* (1981) 74 Cr App Rep 298, discussed in ch 3, below. There is evidence from Southgate (1986) that the demeanour of suspects influences police officers in this way but other research suggests that this is not universally so: see C Norris, N Fielding, C Kemp and J Fielding, 'Black and Blue: An Analysis of the Influence of Race on Being Stopped by the Police' (1992) 43 BJ Soc 207.
1   NACRO 'Policing Local Communities - The Tottenham Experiment' (London: NACRO, 1997) p 36.
2   NACRO (1997).

the police 'cross the line' into illegality much of the time in normal circumstances.

If the legal rules do little to constrain and structure police discretion, what does? Police officers often refer to 'instinct' and their 'experience'. As Fielding observes, experience is valued, whereas 'books' or theory are not.[3] The reality of the streets, not a legal text, is what police officers primarily respond to. In one of many similar cases discussed by McConville et al, the police checked the occupants of a parked car. Asked why, they said: 'it was just a matter of instinct . . . something indefinable.'[4] Another officer confided: 'When you get to know an area and see a villain about at two in the morning you will always stop him to see what he is about.'[5] Whether or not being a 'villain' walking around in the middle of the night qualifies as 'reasonable suspicion' in law, it is enough for many police officers. Dixon et al, for instance, report photographs of drug offenders being posted on police parade room walls with the note 'well worth a stop and search'.[6] All this is echoed by interviewees in the NACRO study who had been stop-searched. Although their comments - eg 'Stop acting on instinct all the time', 'The police should . . . not make assumptions about black people', 'why is a group of black people standing together on the street so suspicious?' - are not verifiable, as policing was not observed by the authors of the study, this is the constant refrain. Choongh, for instance, found many members of ethnic minorities and people with criminal records saying the same things:

'Once you got a record or anything they're always trying to catch you on something.'

'You walk the streets, yea? And the copper will say, "Where you come from?", "Why you running?" . . . Then they turn your pockets out.'

'If they see me on the street they come straight over, pull my jacket off and start searching me, being rough with me. They ask me a lot of questions about my mates, who I've been with, what's happening - "What can you tell me?"'[7]

3   N Fielding, *Joining Forces* (London: Routledge, 1988).
4   M McConville, A Sanders and R Leng, *The Case for the Prosecution* (London: Routledge, 1991) p 27.
5   McConville, Sanders and Leng, p 24.
6   D Dixon, A K Bottomley, C A Coleman, M Gill and D Wall, 'Reality and Rules in the Construction and Regulation of Police Suspicion' (1989) 17 IJ Sociology of Law 185 at 194.
7   S Choongh, *Policing as Social Discipline* (Oxford: Clarendon, 1997) p 45.

Being where one does not belong—incongruity—is particularly important: a scruffily dressed young male in a 'posh' area, for instance, or for that matter someone dressed in a dinner jacket driving around a decaying inner-city area. There is an even-handedness here which is more apparent than real. The rich may seem to be equally at risk of having police power exercised against them if they spend time in poor areas as are the poor in wealthy areas. But wealthy people are less likely to be in such areas, will not be offended if the police suggest that they do not 'belong', and generally possess fewer traits (race, previous convictions and so forth) which would, when added to incongruity, lead to suspiciousness. It is also far easier for the wealthy to avoid incongruity when out of their own area (by dressing scruffily) than it is for the poor.

Membership of an ethnic minority, especially if one is black and especially if one is in an area with few black people, is also important. Norris et al observed police stops in 1986-7 by accompanying police officers on patrol duty. In one London borough they observed 272 stops, of which 28% were of black people, even though black people constituted only 10% of the local population.[8] Each black person was stopped four times as often as each white person (Asians, incidentally, were stopped disproportionately infrequently).[9] As expected from the pre-PACE research, young males were also stopped disproportionately often. This meant that, in that area, between one-quarter and one-third of white males under 35 would be stopped in one year, while for black males under 35 the figure would be a remarkable 9 out of 10. This would be justifiable if black people were actually behaving disproportionately more criminally to this extent. Norris et al did not attempt to assess the justifiability of these stops under s 1. However, they divided the reasons for stops into 'tangible' and 'intangible' reasons, black people being more frequently stopped for 'intangible' reasons than were white people. An example, from a different research study, is given by Southgate, whereby a well-dressed black youth was carrying a bag but doing nothing suspicious. 'Let's give him a look. I want to see what's in that bag', said the officer.[10] The quote from Holdaway's research at the head of this chapter gives an insight into the

8   Norris et al (1992). The analysis of British Crime Survey data by W Skogan, The Police and Public in England and Wales (London: HMSO, 1990) also reveals disproportionate stops among young people and black people, and especially people who are both young and black. The same is true of the NACRO study and another study in North London: J Young, Policing the Streets - Stops and Search in North London (London: Islington Council, 1994).

9   Home Office research has produced similar findings: P Southgate and D Crisp, Public Satisfaction with Police Services (Home Office Research and Planning Unit Paper no 73) (London: Home Office, 1993). Again the findings of the NACRO (1997) and Young (1994) studies are similar.

10   P Southgate, Police-Public Encounters (Home Office Research Study no 90) (London: HMSO, 1986) app 1.

thinking behind this. Another is provided by police officers in the NACRO study. They told researchers that, for instance, they were 'guided by descriptions of suspects given by their control rooms and these were sometimes vague. In this area [an area of South London] the majority of victims identified suspects as black. Descriptions of white suspects tended to be fuller than descriptions of black suspects. . . . Given the higher rate of unemployment among young black men, they were more likely to be on the streets, and if a victim's description came close to what officers observed, then officers were obliged to carry out the search.'[11]

What comes out of this material, as well as much other research, pre- and post-PACE, and from Australia and the USA as well as the UK, is that much police discretion is based on stereotyping. This process enables rough and ready but very speedy judgements about a person's character (their 'master status') to be made on the basis of visible signs (known as 'auxiliary traits').[12] These auxiliary traits include age, scruffiness, attitude to the police, previous convictions and ethnic group. A classic example of stereotyping is provided by the 50-year-old Bishop of Stepney, who finally expressed his anger at being stopped by the police after being stopped eight times in eight years. When asked why he stopped the bishop's car, the officer simply said 'open the boot' : 'He asked me what I did, and I said, "I'm the Bishop of Stepney". He said "whoops", I revealed my dog collar and he looked as if he'd just seen a ghost.' The officer immediately told him he could go, refusing to say why he had stopped the bishop. The bishop commented,

'When you ask and somebody doesn't give a reason and they seem to be hiding behind a uniform . . . that creates a feeling that they are more powerful than you and can act in any way they want over you. I just felt as if I was being treated like a little boy.'[13]

The stereotyping in this case is clear. Middle-aged men normally have a respectable master-status in the eyes of the police. However, the bishop's black auxiliary trait trumped his middle-aged auxiliary trait, giving him a 'suspicious' master status. The black auxiliary trait was then trumped when

---

11   NACRO (1997) p 39. Police officers are actually hardly ever 'obliged' to exercise this kind of power.

12   The terminology is used by criminologists who adopt the 'social reaction' (or 'labelling') perspective. For American examples, see I Piliavin and S Briar, 'Police Encounters with Juveniles' (1964) 70 AJS 206, discussed in ch 3, section 4(b)(iii) below; and A Cicourel, *The Social Organisation of Juvenile Justice* (London: Heinemann, 1976). For an English example in this tradition see O Gill, 'Urban stereotypes and delinquent incidents' (1976) 16 BJ Crim 312. For an Australian example, see D Dixon, *Law in policing* (Oxford: Clarendon, 1997) ch 3.

13   *The Guardian*, 24 January 2000

his clerical collar was revealed, returning to him the 'respectable' master status he would have had, had he not been black.

Let us draw together the threads of this section so far. PACE requires reasonable suspicion in order to stop-search, but the courts allow this to be interpreted in ways that give police officers considerable latitude. Legal understandings of 'reasonable suspicion' play little part in the thought processes or decision making of police officers. This is not just because this concept is so hard to define. It is, more fundamentally, because it does not chime with the experience of police officers. The police generally stop those who they perceive to threaten order and authority, or who appear 'suspicious'. This is not a matter of individual police behaviour, but an ingrained institutional process - a feature of police culture and also a reaction to the official statistics of crime which disproportionately feature the young, black, manual/unemployed and male.

It is possible that PACE may slowly be bringing about a degree of cultural change. An officer quoted by McConville et al expressed concern 'that a lot of young coppers were being taught to act by the book and having instinctive policing trained out of them'.[14] To put this another way, as a police inspector did, 'there is a need to change police culture away from the negative stereotype image of a young black African-Caribbean as an offender.'[15] The experience of the NACRO experiment suggests that limited change can happen, but only with constant reinforcement, not only in relation to what the rules are, but also in relation to the effects of adhering to them (or not). This is a matter of both positive reinforcement (not rewarding, through performance indicators, stops simply on a volume basis) and negative reinforcement (the threat of disciplinary action for racism and rule-breaking, discussed in ch 11, and again illustrated by the police management attitude in Tottenham at the time of the experiment). Policing in general does not yet embody either form of reinforcement, and the watering down of 'reasonable suspicion' in the Code in 1997 in para 1.7AA is a move in the opposite direction. The conclusion of the authors of the NACRO study therefore hold good in the main: 'the guidance on reasonable suspicion in the PACE Code of Practice is not clearly understood, or remembered, or put into practice . . . The 'culture' on divisions [ie on the street] will have a stronger impact on probationary officers than classroom teaching can hope to achieve.'[16]

14 McConville et al (1991) p 24.
15 NACRO (1997) p 26.
16 NACRO (1997) p 41.

(b)   The offences

Under s 1(3) of PACE, a police officer may stop and search only if 'he has reasonable grounds for suspecting that he will find stolen or prohibited articles or any article to which subsection (8A) below applies.' 'Stolen articles' clearly include those stolen in contravention of s 1 of the Theft Act 1968. Whether they also include goods obtained by deception (s 15 Theft Act) or blackmail (s 21) is less clear. Bevan and Lidstone suggest that since s 24 of the Theft Act defines such articles as stolen goods, 'it must be assumed that 'stolen' bears the same meaning.'[17]. However, Levenson and Fairweather point out that s 24 specifically applies to the Theft Act alone. Arguing that it should apply to s 1 of PACE would not necessarily succeed in a criminal context, as the 'general rule of interpretation is that penal statutes are to be interpreted restrictively and therefore 'stolen' in the 1984 Act should have the narrower meaning.'[18]

Since both views have theoretical merit and there are no cases on the point, there can be no answer to the question (or, if one adopts an extreme positivist or Dworkinian position, the answer which exists has not yet been revealed to us). It is perhaps no wonder that the police pay so little attention to legal niceties when the law is so uncertain.

One case that has a bearing on what may be seized using the s 1 power is *DPP v Gomez*[19] where the House of Lords decided that 'appropriation' in theft could occur even when goods were taken with the fraudulently obtained consent of the owner. In making most offences of obtaining goods by deception also offences of theft, 'stolen' goods now undoubtedly include most goods obtained by deception. This is a good example of the way in which decisions which increase the scope of the substantive law may also increase police powers.

Here, however, the increase is more apparent than real. Even if the law were interpreted as not allowing searches for fraudulently obtained goods, it would make no difference to the reality of the police stop and search power. In the unlikely event of officers suspecting a person of carrying goods obtained by deception, as distinct from goods obtained by theft, they could simply not specify the exact offence in relation to which suspicion was held, or could (untruthfully) claim suspicion of theft. If fraudulently obtained goods were discovered, they could still be seized and the suspect arrested, for the fact that something was discovered other than that which was purportedly suspected does not preclude arrest and prosecution. Further, if the officers' suspicions were that precise, they would

17   Bevan and Lidstone (1996) p 51.
18   H Levenson and F Fairweather, *Police Powers, A Practitioner's Guide* (London: LAG, 1990) p 15.
19   [1993] AC 442.

undoubtedly have sufficient evidence on which to arrest (for the two powers have identical 'reasonable suspicion' thresholds).[20] The suspect could be searched and questioned when in custody without the need for prior stop and search. The significance of there being no cases on the point is not that no one has thought to litigate; it is that in the real world outside legal treatises there is no issue to litigate: the police can do as they wish in this respect regardless of the exact legal position. From this perspective we may say that, as far as stop and search powers are concerned, *Gomez* does not create an enabling rule but merely a legitimising one.

What is a 'prohibited article'? According to s 1(7) and (8), it is either (i) an offensive weapon or (ii) an article intended for use in burglary, theft, taking vehicles or obtaining property by deception. Section 1(8A) was added by the Criminal Justice Act 1988. It allows searches for articles which, under s 139 of that Act, are unlawful if carried without a good excuse. Such articles include anything with blades or sharp points, including penknives if the blade is over three inches long. This enlarges the already extensive notion of the offensive weapon. Any item can be classed as an offensive weapon so long as it can be shown that the person possessed it with intention to cause injury. Thus a stone[1] and a pepperpot[2] have been held to be offensive weapons, and such articles as steel combs, shoes with stiletto heels[3] or even pens might be considered offensive. Again we can see that the broadness of substantive criminal law impinges on the procedural power of the police. The Philips Commission recognised this but, by a majority, rejected the argument that the vagueness surrounding the offence of carrying an offensive weapon made it too dangerous to give the police a power to stop and search: 'If there is imprecision in the definition of the offence, the remedy for the difficulty . . . lies in removing that imprecision rather than in refusing the police the power to search.'[4] Similarly, a very wide range of articles could be intended for use in committing crimes of dishonesty. The purpose of a jemmy or set of skeleton keys may be fairly obvious, but one's own cheque book would be such an article if one set out intending to purchase goods with it, knowing or suspecting that it would 'bounce'.[5]

To sum up, under PACE the police may stop and search for offensive weapons or for goods which either are stolen or would be used to commit offences of dishonesty. Broad as these powers are, they represent additions to (rather than replacements for) the miscellaneous powers to

---

20 See ch 3, below for discussion of arrest powers.
1 *Harrison v Thornton* [1966] Crim LR 388.
2 *Parkins* (1956) 120 JP Jo 250, a report of a first instance decision.
3 *The Times*, 25 September 1964.
4 Royal Commission on Criminal Procedure, Report (Cmnd 8092) (London: HMSO, 1981) para 3.21.
5 *Metropolitan Police Comr v Charles* [1976] 3 All ER 112.

which we referred earlier. Thus, powers to search for narcotics under drugs legislation are still important.[6] Section 159 of the Road Traffic Act 1972 (now s 163, Road Traffic Act 1988) is also important. This provides police officers with the power to stop vehicles if they are believed (whether reasonably or not in this case)[7] to be committing road traffic offences, such as having faulty lights or no tax disc. If the police stop a car under this section, they do not have the right per se to search for stolen goods or prohibited articles. However, if in the course of the stop under s 159 police suspicion relating to, for instance, theft is aroused, then the police will be able to continue the stop and search for that second purpose, as in *Lodwick v Sanders*, discussed earlier. In fact, after observing 1,000 encounters between police and public, Southgate states that: 'It was sometimes unclear whether, when stopping a vehicle, it was a criminal or a traffic law violation the officer suspected.'[8]

Extra powers to stop and search vehicles and pedestrians were included in the Criminal Justice and Public Order Act 1994. Where the police wish to stop-search for guns, knives or other weapons as provided under PACE, s 1, but there is no reasonable suspicion, s 60 CJPO can be invoked by a senior officer. This originally allowed, for a period not normally exceeding 24 hours, the police to stop-search anyone where there is a reasonable belief that 'incidents involving serious violence may take place in [a particular] locality'.[9] The Knives Act 1997 extended this power where that officer (who now need only be an Inspector) has a reasonable belief that persons are carrying 'dangerous instruments or offensive weapons', again with no requirement of reasonable suspicion against any particular individuals.[10] The CDA extended it yet further by allowing police officers to remove and seize items designed to prevent the person's identity being revealed, whether or not offensive weapons are found.[11] These powers are backed up, most unusually, by the provision in s 60 that a citizen commits a crime by not submitting to a stop when these powers are invoked. Although this appears to give yet more power to the police, refusal to submit to a 'regular' stop-search could be seen as obstruction or conduct liable to cause a breach of the peace, and thus amount, on the face of it, to a crime. One might have thought that s 60 would be particularly applicable before, say, certain football matches where rivalries are particularly intense, but it can be (and frequently is) a condition of entry to such events that

6   Misuse of Drugs Act 1971, s 23.
7   *Chief Constable of Gwent v Dash* [1986] RTR 41.
8   Southgate (1986) p 13.
9   CJPO, s 60 (2). Also see Code A, para 1.8. See Bevan and Lidstone (1996) pp 58-
     61 for details.
10   Knives Act 1997, s 8, amending CJPO s 60. This also allows the 24 hour period
     to be extended by a further 24 hours.
11   CDA, s 25, amending CJPO, s 60.

spectators submit to searches anyway. Fans who are in the general locality who have not yet tried to enter the ground, or who have left and are hanging around, would, however, be caught by s 60 where the police might otherwise lack in search powers. The CJPO also contains powers to stop cars and direct them away from raves and trespassory assemblies (offences in relation to which were created by that legislation)[12]. This is in addition to provision for 'road checks' (ie road blocks) in PACE, s 4. Here, again, individual cars in relation to which there is no particular suspicion may be stopped, although only if there is reasonable suspicion that a serious arrestable offence (defined in ch 3) has been committed and that someone connected with it might be in the relevant area.[13]

Wide-ranging powers are also provided by the Prevention of Terrorism (Temporary Provisions) Act 1989 (PTA), as amended by the CJPO (s 81) and the Prevention of Terrorism (Additional Powers) Act 1996. According to the new s 13A and 13B of the PTA, police officers may stop any vehicle or person and make any 'search he thinks fit whether or not he has any grounds for suspecting that the vehicle or person is carrying articles [which could be used in terrorist activities]' (sub-s (4)). Like s 60 CJPO, the power is confined to a specified locality and is backed by the creation of a criminal offence of failure to comply. A greater safeguard than is provided in s 60 is a requirement that authorisation be made only by a very senior officer. On the other hand, there need be no reasonable belief that any crime is being, or is about to be, committed; and the period may last for 28 days. This is in addition to stop-search powers provided under s 15 PTA. The latter powers may be exercised in any situation where arrest may be made in relation to several of the offences created under this legislation. Although reasonable suspicion is needed, the offences for which, and circumstances under which, arrest may be made are vague (they include, for instance, 'involvement' in 'terrorism').

Finally, Sch 5 PTA provides that 'Any person who has arrived in, or is seeking to leave, Great Britain or Northern Ireland, by ship or aircraft may be examined by an examining officer for the purposes of determining 'a) whether that person appears to be a person who is or has been concerned in . . . acts of terrorism'; or (under b) and c)) whether there are grounds for suspecting that 'any such person' is subject to an order excluding them from the mainland (para 2(1)). This amounts to a stop-search power for use at designated ports and airports. 'Examining' means questioning, and to be questioned requires detention. Thus 'examining officers', who include police officers (usually Special Branch)[14], may stop someone in transit,

12 Section 65 in relation to raves, and ss 70 and 71, which amend the Public Order Act 1986 by adding s 14C to it. Details are given by Bevan and Lidstone (1996) pp 87-9.
13 For a detailed discussion see Bevan and Lidstone (1996) pp 81-6.
14 P Hillyard, *Suspect Community* (London: Pluto Press, 1993) p 18.

Stop and search after PACE

detain them (for up to 12 hours by para 2(1)), question them and search them (by para 4(2)) . Not only need there be no reasonable suspicion in relation to offences of terrorism, there need be no suspicion at all - as the extract from para 2(1) indicates, the purpose of the 'examination' is to see whether or not the person appears to be, or should be suspected of, something connected with terrorism. Thus any person in a 'category' which makes it reasonable to an investigator that he should be asked questions in relation to possible offences of terrorism can be stopped and 'examined', which is basically a process of potentially lengthy questioning in private[15]. As Hillyard points out, 'In other words, it is lawful for examining officers to stop and examine someone simply because they are Irish.'[16] These are stop-search powers in all but name, but of a particularly draconian kind. The stop is lengthy, and the search is for the contents of one's mind rather than one's pocket. Failure to comply, as with the other PTA and CJPO powers, is a crime[17].

In summary, the following two lists divide stop-search powers into those which do (list A), and those which do not (list B), require reasonable suspicion at the time of the stop-search:

A

s 1 PACE ('stolen' goods; articles for use in theft etc; offensive weapons; bladed objects without lawful excuse);
s 23 Misuse of Drugs Act 1971 (drugs)
s 15 PTA (terrorist offences)

B

s 159 RTA 1972 (RTA offences)
s 60 CJPO 1994 (offensive weapons/dangerous implements)
ss 13A and 13B PTA (articles for use in terrorist activities)
Sch 5 PTA (terrorist offences: examinations at ports and airports)
s 4 PACE (road checks in relation to serious arrestable offences)
ss 14 and 65 CJPO (raves and trespassory assemblies)

The fact that there are more powers in list B than in list A does not necessarily mean that more stop-searches take place under powers not requiring reasonable suspicion than under powers that do. However, so many stop-searches may now take place without reasonable suspicion that the police are left with the ability to stop-search almost whenever they

15 See for a detailed discussion, C Walker, *The Prevention of Terrorism in British Law* (Manchester: MUP, 1992) ch 8.
16 Hillyard (1993) p 19.
17 PTA 1989, Sch 5, para 11.

want. These are therefore enabling rules par excellence, lacking most of the due process elements one usually finds provided when police powers are extended by statute. One might think that rules like this would be contrary to the ECHR and thus contrary to the Human Rights Act. Article 5 (1) allows 'deprivation of liberty' only on certain specified grounds. One such ground is contained in Art 5(1)(c), which requires 'reasonable suspicion of having committed an offence'; this covers list A but not list B. However, (1)(b) allows detention 'in order to secure the fulfilment of any obligation prescribed by law.' The European Commission has held that examinations under Sch 5 PTA comply with this provision,[18] and so it is likely that all the other powers in list B would also comply. These powers clearly fail to comply with both due process and our 'freedom' perspective. If they are nonetheless not contrary to the ECHR, the Human Rights approach to criminal justice can be seen to be of little value, in this context at least, despite its espousal by many influential commentators.[19]

Although these powers are directed at specific activities (such as terrorism), arrests are often made for reasons unconnected with the ostensible reasons for the stop-search, as Table 2.1 shows.[20]

Table 2.1: Stop-searches and arrests: powers where no reasonable suspicion are needed

	Road Checks (PACE, s 4)				CJPO 1994,s 60			
Year	No of checks	No vehicles stopped	connected arrests	unconnected arrests	Year	No of searches	connected arrests	unconnected arrests
1992	445	31,500	29	83	-	-	-	-
1993	3,560	48,800	50	902	-	-	-	-
1994	3,003	25,100	17	518	-	-	-	-
1995	113	17,100	35	3	1996	7,019	132	371
1996	162	21,400	16	66	1996/7	7,970	129	329
1997/8	139	24,500	8	24	1997/8	7,979	103	332

18 See discussion of *McVeigh, O'Neill and Evans v UK* (1981) in ch 3, section 3(d).
19 A Ashworth, *Criminal Process* 2nd edn (Oxford: OUP, 1998). See R Morgan, 'The process is the rule and the punishment is the process' (1996) 59 MLR 306. This review article compares the 1st editions of this text and of Ashworth's text (both published in 1994), praising the latter for its human rights framework.
20 Source: G Wilkins and C Addicott, 'Operation of Certain Police Powers under PACE, England and Wales 1997/8' (Home Office Statistical Bulletin 2/99) (London: Home Office, 1999). In the previous bulletin (27/97), the authors note, without providing statistics, that 'the overwhelming majority' of arrests under s 13A and 13B of the PTA 1989 'were not in connection with terrorism' (p 7) ie were not in connection with the ostensible reason for the search.

Despite the great increases in police stop-search powers since PACE was enacted, it remains true that the police have no powers to stop-search simply because someone is thought to be in some general sense 'suspicious'. Either the individual has to be suspected of something in particular (eg PACE, s 1) or something in particular has to be suspected in that vicinity (eg PACE, s 4; CJPO, s 60), or someone has to belong to a category which is deemed 'suspicious' (eg PTA examinations). However, it will often not be possible to know why someone is looking or acting generally 'suspicious'. Only a conversation and/or search will reveal the knife, explosives, drugs, stolen credit card, love letters, anarchist literature or condoms about which the individual may be embarrassed. As the figures above show in relation to two powers, not only are such suspicions usually unfounded but they are indeed often unrelated to that which ostensibly triggered the stop. Is the requirement that suspicion relate to a particular offence simply a presentational rule? Let us return to *Lodwick v Sanders*. Although the Divisional Court decided that there was reasonable suspicion of theft in this case, it is hard to see what produced the officer's suspicion other than the suspect's obstructiveness and hostility - which could, after all, have equally reflected fear of discovery of drugs or offensive weapons. But many people are, regrettably, obstructive and hostile to the police. Even if it signifies likely criminality (which it does not) it is as likely to be criminality for which stop and search cannot be used (such as being wanted for assault) as, say, theft. If this is true of someone with whom the police are already in conversation, how much more true it must be of most people who the police simply observe in the street or in their cars. If someone is acting 'suspiciously', how can a police officer tell if that person is about to commit a burglary or to threaten someone with a weapon? In one of McConville et al's cases, a youth ran away when he saw the police, so he was chased and searched.[1] A Krugerrand was found, so he was arrested. It turned out that he had this lawfully, but that hardly matters. The police often stop, search and arrest people who run away when they see police officers. This is, by any standards, suspicious behaviour. But of what can one reasonably suspect such people? In this particular case, was it really reasonable suspicion of theft? As one would expect from the national statistics displayed above, the arrests which resulted from stops in this study were often unrelated to the reasons for the stops.

The way police-public encounters begin in relation to one issue and end in completely unrelated ways has been observed by others, before and after PACE.[2] Smith, however, suggests not just that unsuspected offences come to light following legitimate stops, but also that suspicion

1   M McConville, A Sanders and R Leng, *The Case for the Prosecution* (London: Routledge, 1991) p 28.
2   See eg Southgate (1986) p 8.

of an offence to which PACE, s 1 applies is sometimes used as a pretext when other offences are suspected:

'... observations at police stations suggest that police may often find illegal immigrants by carrying out stops and searches of black people in vehicles or on foot. There is no power to detain or search a person in the street on suspicion of immigration offences, but some other justification can be found for the original stop.'[3]

We can extrapolate from this as follows: that suspicion of an offence for which no reasonable suspicion need be present is often claimed as a pretext when some other offence is suspected in relation to which the officer should have (but lacks) reasonable suspicion before making a stop. If so, the success rate would be expected to be low - which is precisely what the above figures show. However, in some areas and in some contexts, there are simply numerous crimes waiting to be discovered. The fact that there is no specific reason to stop those particular individuals or cars does not alter the fact that statistically the officer is more likely to notch up a successful 'collar' by stopping them than by stopping people randomly, or by stopping respectable-looking people in affluent suburbs. Most stops are in inner-city areas, largely because they are inner-city areas. These areas are not necessarily more criminogenic than others, but the crimes which predominate in them (drugs, car theft, burglary and street violence) are more amenable than most to discovery by stop and search. Not surprisingly, the attempt of legislators in the early 1980s through PACE, s 1 to require specific suspicion of specific offences as a condition of using stop and search powers is proving unsuccessful. That this was of no concern to the Conservative governments of the late 1980s and 1990s is demonstrated by the fact that they created so many powers where reasonable suspicion was not needed. The approach of the Labour government elected in 1997 appears to be little different.[4]

(c) The power

When we talk about 'the power' to stop-search, we are actually referring to a bundle of powers. For example, PACE, s 1(2)(b) states that a police officer 'may detain a person or vehicle for the purpose of ... a search', and

---

3 D Smith, 'Origins of Black Hostility to the Police' (1991) 2 Policing and Society 6.

4 Note, for example, the extension of CJPO, s 60 by the Labour Government's CDA, s 25. The degree of continuity between the 1990s governments in penal and criminal justice policy in general is remarkable. See A Sanders, 'What principles underlie criminal justice policy in the 1990s?' (1998) 18 OJLS 533.

s 1(6) provides a power to seize certain property discovered in the course of this search. In addition, the police have an implicit power to question.[5] However, there is no obligation to answer these questions and so the power of an officer to question is slightly different to the other powers contained in s 1. Suspects must submit to search and detention (and indeed 'reasonable force' may be used if the suspect objects)[6], but they need not answer questions. Other stop-search powers discussed earlier, in the CJPO, PTA and elsewhere in PACE, also contain these powers to detain, question and seize as well as to stop and to search. Time limits are rarely provided for the length of detention. For s 1 searches, for example, the only guidance is provided in the Code of Practice:

> 'The length of time for which a person or vehicle may be detained will depend on the circumstances, but must in all circumstances be reasonable and not extend beyond the time taken for the search. Where the exercise of the power requires reasonable suspicion, the thoroughness and extent of a search must depend on what is suspected of being carried, and by whom.'[7]

These laws require citizens to stop and submit to searches. They provide no powers to ask this of citizens. This is because no such powers are needed. Legally, anyone can ask anything of anyone else, whether they be police officers or ordinary citizens. Of course, it would be remarkable if ordinary citizens did go around asking people to agree to be stopped and searched, and few people would assent to such an odd request. Police officers, however, often do ask people if they will consent to be stopped and searched, and consent is often given. The Code of Practice makes clear the lawfulness of stop and search with consent: 'Nothing in this Code affects . . . the ability of an officer to search a person in the street with his consent where no search power exists . . .'[8] Such consensual searches do not require the exercise of formal powers, and, as a corollary, none of the restrictions outlined earlier— such as reasonable suspicion of specific offences— apply. Nor do the other controls to be discussed in the next section.

---

5   *Daniel v Morrison* (1979) 70 Cr App Rep 142.
6   Code A, para 3.2.
7   See para 3.3. Limitations on searches involving the removal of outer clothing are made in para 3.5.
8   Note 1D(b). It follows that police officers may question any persons they wish prior to arrest, whether or not they are exercising these s 1 powers. As note 1B states: 'This Code does not affect the ability of an officer to speak to or question a person in the ordinary course of his duties (and in the absence of reasonable suspicion) without detaining him or exercising any element of compulsion.'

The research of both Dixon et al and McConville et al found most stops to be 'consensual'.[9] Most officers carried out 'consensual' stops, and few exercised their statutory powers. As one officer explained to Dixon et al 'I have never had any problems with anyone refusing to be searched . . . so I have never had to fall back on proving my reasonable suspicion.'[10] Similarly, an officer told McConville et al that 'I've always got their consent . . . I tell people, "Why make life difficult on yourself."'[11]

Thus the official figures provide no true indication of the level of stops carried out, because of 'consent' searches.[12] But what is consent in this context? As Dixon et al point out, when an officer asks someone on the street whether they would mind answering questions, this is usually perceived not to be a genuine request, admitting either 'yes' or 'no' as an answer, but a polite way of insisting. Officers rarely disabuse suspects of that perception. As one officer interviewed admitted, 'a lot of people are not quite certain that they have the right to say no and then we sort of bamboozle them into allowing us to search.'[13] We should not be surprised that officers can do this, given the central importance of 'authority' to policing and police culture (see section 1 above).

Dixon et al go on to say that many people assume that an officer who says 'what have you got in your pocket?' or 'let's have a look in your bag' has a power to search. When police officers were asked how often people who were stopped and searched knew their rights, 79% said rarely or never. The researchers concluded that 'such lack of knowledge must mean that their "consent" has little substance.'[14] It is true that the Code of Practice (Note 1E) tries to protect the most vulnerable members of society: 'Juveniles, people suffering from a mental handicap or mental disorder and others who appear not to be capable of giving an informed consent should not be subject to a voluntary search.' However, society does not dichotomise into the vulnerable, who cannot make an informed decision about consent, and the strong, who can: if the 'officially' vulnerable need protection, what about 'ordinary' people who are intimidated by officialdom? In any case, Note 1E is unlikely to be an inhibitory rule of great power, for if a search of a vulnerable person did produce a 'result' no-one will criticise the officer; and if it does not, no-one of any influence is ever likely to hear about it. Moreover, whereas the courts are obliged to take into account the

9   D Dixon, C Coleman and K Bottomley, 'Consent and the Legal Regulation of Policing' (1990) 17 JLS 345 at p 348; McConville, Sanders and Leng (1991) p 94.
10   Dixon et al (1990) p 349.
11   McConville, Sanders and Leng (1991) p 94.
12   See the discussion in section 4 below.
13   Dixon et al (1990) p 348.
14   Dixon et al (1990) p 348.

provisions of a PACE Code of Practice, this is not true of Notes to such Codes.

Thus the formal equivalence between consensual stops by officers and consensual stops by citizens is completely unreal. Most people do as officers ask, but not as other strangers ask. The identical treatment by the law of dissimilar social situations allows police officers often to avoid the legal constraints discussed in this chapter. The legal sanctioning of 'consensual' searches by police officers is an enabling rule which renders legal safeguards largely presentational.

The failure of the law to address the reality of policing is evident in another way too. Breaking stop and search down into discrete actions, as we did at the start of this section, takes no account of the social processes involved. In an encounter which begins with a consensual and innocuous conversation, suspicion may develop and the suspect may get impatient. The point at which consent is no longer present and formal powers are, or should be, invoked cannot be identified with precision. This allows the police to manipulate the rules and, equally important, makes those rules irrelevant to policing and thus marginal to the basis for police decision making. Their potentially inhibitory effects are reduced almost to vanishing point.

(d) Constraints and controls on police discretion

The Philips Commission was aware that the criterion of reasonable suspicion could become devalued in practice, and that random stops should be guarded against. Its solution was to introduce a battery of secondary controls:

> 'We consider that the notification of the reason for the search to the person who has been stopped, the recording of searches by officers, and the monitoring of the records by supervising officers would be the most effective and practical ways of reducing the risk.'[15]

Section 2 of PACE accordingly stipulates that a police officer must provide certain information to suspects before searching them, including the officer's name and police station, the object of the proposed search and the grounds for proposing to make it.[16] The officer must also tell the suspect,

---

15   Royal Commission on Criminal Procedure, Report (Cmnd 8092) (London: HMSO, 1981) para 3.25.
16   Section 2(1) provides that this provision, and those in s 3, apply to searches under all legislation, not just PACE. It therefore applies to the powers discussed in Section (b) above.

unless this is not practical, that he is making a record of the circumstances of the search and that the suspect is entitled to a copy of it.[17]

Officers must make the record of the search as soon as practical unless it is not practical to make one at all (s 3(1) and (2)). It will rarely be impractical to make a record. It is obviously not practical for an officer to make a record in the context of a violent arrest, but it can be made afterwards. Only if a large number of people are being searched could the making of records at some point be impractical. But, since 'reasonable suspicion' of individuals can hardly exist, by definition, in the context of a mass search, the problem can only legitimately arise when the powers in the CJPO or PTA are invoked. Indeed, this is one of the due process objections to those powers.[18] Section 3(6) provides that the record must state:

(1) the object of the search (ie stolen goods or prohibited articles);
(2) the grounds for making it (ie what has given rise to the suspicion);
(3) the time and date when it was made;
(4) the place where it was made;
(5) whether anything (and if so what) was found;
(6) whether any (and if so what) injury to a person or damage to property appears to the officer to have resulted from the search.

As we have said, suspects are entitled to copies of these records if they request them. One purpose of providing information before search, committing it to writing afterwards and providing suspects with those records is to enable suspects to hold police officers to account if they misuse their powers. This is intended to provide a remedy for those who are wrongly stopped, and the fear of complaints should produce more compliance in the first place.

There are a number of reasons to question the realism of this. Firstly, it only applies to searches. Many stops do not go this far, and remain unrecorded.[19] Secondly, it is no use having a right not to be stopped and searched unlawfully if people do not know what that right entails. The difficulties discussed above in defining reasonable suspicion mean that it is virtually impossible to know what a right not to be stopped and searched unlawfully means. Thirdly, it is no use having a record made if people do not know of its existence. This is why the police are obliged to inform suspects that they may see the record. Not to do so is, in relation to PACE, s 1 for example, a breach of PACE. However, if the officer fails to inform the suspect, then the suspect will remain unaware of the entitlement to see the

---

17 PACE Code of Practice A, para 2.6.
18 In situations where there is thought to be a pressing social need for mass searches, such as at a particular football ground where there are grounds for fearing an outbreak of violence, submitting to a search can be made a condition of entry, in which case it will be a consensual search to which ss 2 and 3 will not apply.
19 Prior to PACE, Willis (1983) p 22 found that searches took place in only around a quarter of all stops.

record so will not know that the officer breached the legal duty to explain this. As Dixon et al point out, one major reform which is needed if PACE is to be at all effective in relation to powers on the street is for citizens to be fully educated about their rights and, by implication, not to have to rely on the police for this knowledge.[20]

Sections 2 and 3 apply only to non-consensual searches, for when there is consent no statutory powers need be invoked and, therefore, the search is not subject to any statutory controls. Since there are more 'consensual' searches than there are compulsory searches, most searches will not have records.[1] A further problem is the dubious nature of the 'consent' given in many searches. If the 'consensual' nature of a stop were to be disputed, it would usually be only the suspect's word against the officer's. The written record which—if completed accurately—would show what really happened will not have been made, precisely because the police officer designated the stop as consensual for official purposes. Some police forces seek to resolve this impasse by urging their officers to make records for all stops where there is reasonable suspicion regardless of whether or not there is consent. This is not a complete solution to the problem since in situations where there is no reasonable suspicion no record would be expected, and the legality or otherwise of the stop would turn on whether or not consent is given, which cannot be determined without witnesses.

Whether consensual or not, very large numbers of searches are not recorded - over 60% in one survey and nearly 50% in another.[2] Dixon et al found the recording of searches to be so rare that many officers did not even bother to carry the stop and search forms with them.[3]

The most obvious problem with written records is that police officers may write accounts designed more to fit the statutory criteria than the actual events. Only the bravest (or most foolish) officers would complete written records in such ways as to reveal the unlawfulness of a stop. So if there were a challenge to a particular stop, it would again be the suspect's word against the officer's, just as if there were no written record. The record therefore may be more of a protection for the officer than it is for the suspect. Many officers told Dixon and his colleagues that they made a record only if they feared that there would be some sort of 'comeback'. If, for example, a middle class person who was aware of the law happened to be stopped

---

20 D Dixon, A Bottomley, C Coleman, M Gill and D Wall, 'Reality and Rules in the Construction and Regulation of Police Suspicion' (1989) 17 IJ Sociology of Law, 185 at p 203.

1 Dixon et al (1990) p 348.

2 A Crawford, T Jones, T Woodhouse and J Young, The Second Islington Crime Survey (Enfield: Centre for Criminology, Middlesex University, 1990); K Painter et al, The Hammersmith Crime Survey (Enfield: Centre for Criminology, Middlesex University, 1989).

3 Dixon et al (1990).

'you would probably revert to the standard opening speech procedure and complete a form.'[4]

One function of a written record is to allow supervision: to allow a supervisory officer to examine an officer's work without having to observe it at first hand. In many jobs, written records of work do form a basic supervision. This is fine when the essence of one's work is actual writing—such as a university lecturer whose product is supposed to be work in the form of books or articles. A police officer's job is different. It is not to write things down but to act in accordance with the law. When a supervisory officer scrutinises an officer's record of an event, the scrutiny is not of what the officer did or whether it was within the law but of the officer's account of what was done. It is rather like a university lecturer's output being assessed on the basis of the author's own account of its academic value. The lecturer is as unlikely to give a poor self-assessment as a police officer is to portray a stop search as anything other than lawful.

In any event, records are generally treated by officers as 'mere paperwork'. Dixon et al report that some forms were completed tautologically (grounds for search being stated as 'suspicious behaviour'), while most officers were 'concerned about saving on paperwork'. Only a quarter of police supervisory officers questioned by Dixon et al mentioned checking paperwork as a form of supervision. Over three quarters of the constables and sergeants interviewed said that their stops were not generally supervised.[5]

Dixon et al did their research soon after PACE came into operation, but it seems that little changed in the late 1980s and 1990s. The NACRO research referred to earlier analysed stop-search records and found that 'what did emerge very clearly was the uniformity and standard phrases given in the section on grounds for the search. Certain stock sentences were repeated frequently . . . it is clear that a standard method for completing these [forms] is instilled into officers.'[6] It goes on to say that, as the officers' supervising officers had initialled all these forms but not questioned them, the forms had no credibility as a form of accountability or for ensuring that stop-searches were carried out fairly.

Police stop and search is a classic example of low visibility work. It is no criticism of the law or of the police hierarchy to say that stop and search cannot, for this reason, be adequately supervised. What is open to criticism is the pretence that effective supervision is possible and that requiring officers to make written records of stop-searches amounts to an adequate check on the legality of their actions. One may also censure the police hierarchy for failing to encourage supervisory officers to take their

4   Dixon et al (1990) p 349.
5   Dixon et al (1989) pp 200-1.
6   NACRO (1997) p 12.

responsibilities seriously. Adequate supervision may not be possible, but better supervision certainly is: senior officers can hardly be unaware of photographs of criminals on parade room walls with notes urging stops simply because of their criminal records.[7] The problems inherent in attempts to control low visibility and discretionary police work are compounded by laxity in the law and by a policing culture which emphasises 'results' rather than procedural propriety.

(e) Remedies

Where a stop is legally questionable, what is the probability and likely consequence of a successful challenge? If a stop is unsuccessful, both officers and suspects are usually happy to forget the whole incident, and the absence of reasonable suspicion will rarely be an issue. If the stop is successful, in the sense of a crime being discovered, it will rarely be questioned because the initial illegality becomes overshadowed by the crime itself. In the unlikely event of a challenge being made to a stop and search, what actions or remedies are available?

It is striking that PACE, PTA, the CJPO and so forth are all silent on this point, neither making it a crime nor a tort to stop and search someone unlawfully, to fail to provide information before search, or to make a record of it afterwards.[8] It is a crime for a citizen not to stop when lawfully directed to under the new powers in the CJPO and PTA (see section 3 (b) above). One would have thought that, to simply hold a balance between crime control and due process, it would also be a crime to unlawfully stop someone in the purported exercise of these powers. That it is not a crime, nor even a tort (in and of itself), is a sign of the balance that is really struck between the two.

At common law, a failure by an officer to provide information prior to search renders the stop and search unlawful.[9] An unlawful stop-search

---

7   See the reference to this in section 3(a) above. The problems inherent in attempts to control low visibility and discretionary police work are compounded by laxity in the law and by a policing culture which emphasises 'results' rather than procedural propriety. For discussion of the lax supervisory arrangements generally in police investigations, see J Baldwin and T Moloney, Supervision of Police Investigations in Serious Criminal Cases (Royal Commission on Criminal Justice Research Study no 4) (London: HMSO, 1992); and M Maguire and C Norris, The Conduct and Supervision of Criminal Investigations (Royal Commission on Criminal Justice Research Study no 5) (London: HMSO, 1992).

8   PACE, s 67(10) provides that a failure on the part of a police officer to comply with the provisions of Code of Practice A 'shall not of itself render him liable to any criminal or civil proceedings'.

9   The pre-Act case of Pedro v Diss [1981] 2 All ER 59 held, following Christie v Leachinsky [1947] AC 573, that detention was unlawful if the reason for it was not provided.

can lawfully be resisted by the use of reasonable force, as illustrated by *Pedro v Diss*[10]. The suspect concerned had used force to free himself from an unlawful detention and was, in consequence, charged with assaulting an officer in the execution of his duty. It was held that the unlawfulness of the detention meant that the officer was not acting in the execution of his duty, and so the assault was not criminal. But a violent response to the exercise of police power is still fairly unusual. A stop and search which was unlawful—whether because inadequate reasons were provided or because inadequate reasons existed (such as no reasonable suspicion)— would be more likely to give rise to the possibility of an action in tort or, if charges followed the discovery of stolen or prohibited articles, a motion to exclude from court evidence discovered as a result of the stop and search.

If stops are challenged in court (in either of these ways), and the officers' accounts differ from those of the suspect what would or could the court do? If defining the absence of reasonable suspicion is difficult, proving it is virtually impossible: these are low visibility decisions where there are seldom other civilian witnesses and where—because those stopped are so often people with previous convictions and so forth—suspects are easily 'discredited'.[11]

If a stop were to be successfully challenged in a criminal case, there is the possibility of the evidence obtained as a result of the search being excluded from trial, as happened in *Fennelly*.[12] However, as a Crown Court case, this is a weak authority and, as ch 11 will show, it is not consistent with the courts' normal interpretation of the exclusionary provisions of PACE. The decision of the trial judge in *Fennelly* would be a logical response within a system committed to due process but amounts to something of an aberration within the system as it normally operates in this country.

An action in tort might lie on grounds of wrongful arrest or even assault.[13] However, there have been no reported cases of this, partly because such an action would be speculative, and partly, no doubt, because the loss or damages suffered as a result of an unlawful stop and search is limited. It is not clear whether not making a record renders a stop and search unlawful and thus an assault. There is no case law or statutory provision on this, although the government, in reply to an MP's question, did express the view when PACE was passing through Parliament that a failure to make a record would not render a stop and search unlawful.

Article 5 of the ECHR, which provides a 'right to liberty and security of the person', may lead to some judicial development of the existing remedies

10 [1981] 2 All ER 59.
11 See the discussion of discrediting in the context of complaints against the police in ch 11, below.
12 [1989] Crim LR 142.
13 See further ch 3, section 5.

for unlawful stop-search. Section 7 of the Human Rights Act 1998 (HRA) creates a right to bring proceedings under that Act against a public authority alleged to have acted in contravention of the ECHR. This could be used by the victim of an allegedly unlawful stop-search. Section 8(1) of the HRA authorises a court which has found a breach of a Convention right by a public authority to grant such relief or remedy within its powers as it considers just and appropriate.[14] Thus the High Court might, for example, issue a declaration that a particular stop-search was unlawful. Moreover, Article 5(5) of the ECHR, which is 'incorporated' into English law by the HRA, provides an enforceable right to compensation to anyone 'who has been the victim of arrest or detention in contravention of the provisions of this Article'. Stops and searches clearly amount to detention so it follows that a right to damages has been created for stop-searches that breach the Convention. However, as we saw in section 3(b), stop-searches which offend due process principles are allowed by both English law and the European Court of Human Rights. In other words, the HRA may have done little to enlarge the meaningful scope of remedies in relation to stop-search. We will have to wait for HRA case law to develop before we can reach any final view on this.

One other possible remedy is the making of a complaint against the police officer concerned. PACE, s 67(8) makes it a disciplinary offence to breach any of the provisions in Code of Practice A. The chances of having a complaint upheld are low. This is partly because of the difficulty of establishing that an officer lacked reasonable suspicion or failed to give information prior to search, and partly because of the failings or inadequacies of the police complaints machinery.[15]

4. THE IMPACT OF STOP-SEARCH POWERS

If we look at stop-search in terms of crime control and due process we can see that, just as the legal rules attempt a balance between due process and crime control, so do actual police practices. The rules are inhibitory to some extent. Were this not so we would not find the police so often calling for wider powers.[16] However, they are not as inhibitory as they may appear, for police officers' fear of the sanctions for their breach is rarely sufficient

---

14   The Act does not incorporate Art 13 of the European Convention on Human Rights, ie, the duty to afford an effective remedy for breach of a Convention right. See J Wadham and H Mountfield, *Blackstone's Guide to the Human Rights Act 1998* (London: Blackstone, 1999) p 45: 'The rationale seemed to be that the Act itself constituted compliance with art 13, and perhaps a nervousness about excessive judicial creative zeal.'

15   See ch 11 on remedies.

16   This is, for instance, reported by the authors of the NACRO (1997) study.

to outweigh the influence of police culture and the perceived demands of the job. Actual practice is therefore tilted further towards crime control than are the rules in PACE. Whether the wider powers provided in the CJPO and PTA, and the changes to the Code of Practice made in the 1990s, will have a legitimating effect (authorising the police to do what they already do) or an enabling effect (encouraging them to move even further towards crime control) remains to be seen. Useful though analysis is in these due process/crime control terms, we should also have regard, as we argued in ch 1, to the enhancement of freedom. We need to look at whether the freedom gained for 'society' by catching criminals using stop-search exceeds or is less than the freedom lost by the people who are subjected to stop-search. Freedom can be lost in quantitative terms (ie how often a person or group is stop-searched) and in qualitative terms (ie the way in which these powers are exercised and their effects). In this section we look first at the quantitative issue, then at the crime control value of stop-search, and then at the qualitative issues.

(a) Changes in the numbers of stops and searches

One effect of the combination of ss 1–3 of PACE should have been more discriminating (ie reduced) use of stop-search in areas where it had previously been used extensively (such as inner London), but more overall use in those (relatively thinly populated) areas where these powers were previously not available. A measure of the inhibitory effectiveness of PACE is whether there are now fewer stops than there were in the early 1980s.

In 1981, it will be recalled, there were over 700,000 recorded stops in London alone. Post-PACE figures for the whole of England and Wales are shown in Table 2.2 (see p 112).

There certainly are considerably fewer recorded stop-searches now than there were in the early 1980s. On the face of it, this suggests that, at the time that Willis and the PSI did their research, the police in London used stop-search powers much more extensively than they or any other police force do now - although the rate of increase in the use of these powers over the last few years is such that this may not be true by the time we write the next edition. Further, we need to add to the million recorded stop-searches in 1997/8 some 30,000 recorded stop-searches under PACE, s 4 (road checks) and s 60, CJPO (see section 3(b) above).

But these figures are misleading. Firstly, there is no requirement to record simple stops. Only searches need be recorded (s 3), and in only

---

17   Source: G Wilkins and C Addicott (1999). These figures largely relate to stop-search under PACE, s 1, but also to PTA s 15, and s 23 MDA 1971 and some other less important powers where 'reasonable suspicion' is required.

Table 2.2: Recorded stop-searches under PACE and 'success rates'[17]

Year	Stop/Searches	Arrests	% leading to arrests
1986	109,800	18,900	17.2
1987	118,300	19,600	16.6
1988	149,600	23,700	15.8
1989	202,800	32,800	16.2
1990	256,900	39,200	15.3
1991	303,800	46,200	15.2
1992	351,700	48,700	13.8
1993	442,800	55,900	12.6
1994	576,000	70,300	12.2
1995	690,300	81,000	11.7
1996	814,500	87,700	10.8
1996/7	871,500	91,106	10.5
1997/8	1,050,700	108,700	10.3

10% of vehicle stops and 22% of pedestrian stops do searches take place.[18] Since there were nearly 343,000 recorded stops in the Metropolitan Area in 1997/8[19], and most stops are vehicle stops, this would suggest, on a conservative estimate, at least 2,000,000 Metropolitan non-consent stops in 1997/8. Secondly, even searches need not be recorded if they are 'consensual'. Thirdly, officers are known to be reluctant to record searches of any kind. Finally, there is enormous variation in recorded stop-searches between police force areas: Kent and Dyfed-Powys, for instance, have around three times as many, per head of population, than do Humberside and Thames Valley. Significantly, the 1997/8 arrest rates (ie the proportion of recorded stop-searches that result in arrest) of the high stop-search forces (Kent: 7.7%; Dyfed-Powys: 7.2%) are much lower than those of the low stop-search forces (Humberside: 14.5%; Thames Valley: 12.7%).[20] This might be because some forces simply record unsuccessful stop-searches less often than do others. Or it might simply be that Kent really does do three times as many stops as the demographically similar Thames Valley, and that the lower arrest rate reflects the fact that the more often you perform a task, the less discriminating you tend to be.

18   W Skogan, The Police and Public in England and Wales (Home Office Research Study no 117) (London: HMSO, 1990) p 33.
19   Wilkins and Addicott (1999). This is around one-third of the national total.
20   The Metropolitan arrest rate, at around 11%, was close to the national average. All figures are derived from Wilkins and Addicott (1999) Fig 2 and Table 1.

These recording problems render the absolute figures of little value. A more accurate estimate of the level of stops is provided by the regular British Crime Surveys (BCS). Whereas the 1988 BCS[1] found that 15% of all adults (ie several million people) were stopped in 1987–8—which is remarkably similar to the estimate made by Southgate and Ekblom pre-PACE some years earlier[2] - the 1996 BCS found the figure to be 17%. Of these, 14% were traffic stops and 3% were pedestrian stops (with some people experiencing both).[3] It therefore appears that stop-searches are indeed rising, although not at the dramatic rate that the official figures suggest. Traffic stops would generally be Road Traffic Act 1974, not 'PACE', stops, but if even only half of the pedestrian stops were PACE stops this would still total some half a million pedestrian stops, in a year when less than 150,000 were recorded. It is not possible to estimate accurately the levels of stop-search. However, although stop-search may have declined immediately after the introduction of PACE, it is now probably at a similar level to the 1970s and early 1980s, pre-PACE, and rising. This is despite the ostensibly inhibitory controls in PACE, ss 2 and 3.

(b) 'Success' rates and crime control

How valuable are stop-search powers for the police? Table 2.2 (above) shows that only around 10% of recorded stop-searches now lead to arrest. Although this is a downward trend over the years since PACE was introduced, the number of stop-searches leading to arrest has actually increased - but not as fast as the increase in recorded stop-searches. According to the 1992 British Crime Survey, only about 3% of pedestrian stops and 7% of car stops led to a prosecution, many of the latter doubtless being for minor road traffic offences.[4]

Overall, arrests following stops constitute a fairly small percentage of all arrests: the most recent large research study found that they accounted for 11% of arrests.[5] Moreover, there is little reason to believe that, in the absence of stop-search powers, most of these crimes would remain

1   Skogan (1990) Table 6.
2   P Southgate and P Ekblom, Contacts Between Police and Public (Home Office Research Study no 77) (London: HMSO, 1984). See discussion in section 1, above.
3   C Mirrlees-Black and T Budd, 'Policing and the Public: Findings from the 1996 British Crime Survey (Home Office Research Findings no 60) (London: Home Office, 1997).
4   W Skogan, Contacts between Police and Public - Findings from the 1992 British Crime Survey (Home Office Research Study no 134) (London: Home Office, 1994).
5   C Phillips and D Brown, Entry into the Criminal Justice System - A Survey of Police Arrests and their Outcomes (Home Office Research Study no 185) (London: Home Office 1998) pp 34-5.

The impact of stop-search powers

undetected. Firstly, there is the opportunity to search with consent. Without the power to compel lying behind requests, of course, fewer people would consent than they do now, but less coercive policing could improve police-community relations over time, increasing the flow of information about crime to the police. In other words, fewer stop-searches might lead to the more effective use of time rather than the opposite.[6] Secondly, the police could arrest where they genuinely have reasonable suspicion. Again, they would do so less often than they currently stop and search, but since we could expect a more selective policy to be based on more evidence, the fall in the detection rate is unlikely to be as extensive as one might otherwise expect.

None the less, there is little escaping the probability that, at least in the short term, the more stop-searches carried out, the more detections there will be. Forces which carry out a large number of stop-searches, like Kent and Dyfed-Powis, may have a lower arrest rate than do forces like Humberside and Thames Valley, but they do make more arrests. From the crime control perspective, the loss of liberty involved for suspects (whether innocent or not) is a price worth paying for increased detections. From a due process perspective, the marginal utility of each extra arrest would probably not outweigh the loss of liberty involved. However, crime control adherents place considerable emphasis on the fact-finding ability of professionals. Low arrest rates tend both to undermine that confidence in relation to stop-search and to strengthen the argument for more due process. The logic of the crime control argument is to allow stops on the basis of any suspicion. This is what s 4 PACE (road checks) and s 60 CJPO (search for dangerous implements) allow in specified circumstances, and look at the 'success' rates in the figures given in Table 2.1: 5.5% for s 60 and 0.1% for s 4, even including arrests unconnected with the reasons for the search. Similarly, Sch 5 PTA, which also allows random stops ('examinations') has a negligible success rate, if judged by arrests or charges. The statistics are of little value, as they only record examinations lasting over one hour. There were less than 300 in 1991, but an official report in 1987 estimated that there must be literally millions of brief examinations every year. Of these, only eight resulted in a charge in 1991 (less than 0.001% of the total).[7]

That, however, is not the end of the matter, for the widespread use of stop-search powers may be effective in deterring potential offenders. Thus David Powis, in a book written as a manual for police officers when he was a deputy assistant commissioner in the Metropolitan Police, argues that 'young officers' should never be disappointed if stopping an innocent

---

6   This is the argument of advocates of 'community policing', mentioned in section 1, above.

7   Hillyard (1993) pp 30-1.

person leads to no arrest: 'who is to say that an apparently unsuccessful stop is not a crime prevented? Real effort will give your police area a reputation that it is a hot place . . .'[8]

The police service as a whole, in its evidence to the Philips Commission, stressed the role of stop and search as part of a wide array of powers to combat crime.[9] This classic crime control argument gets perilously close to arguing for stop-search without reasonable suspicion on deterrent grounds. Even leaving aside the due process objections, one may doubt the effectiveness of such a policy. The problem was highlighted by Swamp 81.[10] This massive operation, in which the police made 943 stops, saturated the streets of Brixton for several days and triggered a riot. Scarman observed that:

'. . . the evidence is not clear that a street saturation operation does diminish street crime: it may well only drive it elsewhere. And, after the operation has ended, street crime returns.'[11]

So stop and search may impact upon crime at one time and in one place, but otherwise allows crime to flourish. This 'displacement' phenomenon is common in relation to other areas of crime and policing, such as prostitution and crime prevention measures.[12] Some 'targeted policing' (discussed in section 1 of this chapter) is of 'Swamp 81' variety, and s 60 CJPO powers now allow the police to do what they were not strictly allowed to do in Brixton in 1981. Little seems to have been learnt from that experience.

Another way in which stop and search contributes to crime control is in augmenting 'criminal intelligence'. Police collators, for instance, build up computer databases of information about suspects and witnesses based on information derived from stops.[13] Written records in particular—ostensibly introduced as protections for suspects—provide the basis for systematic collation of information about suspects.[14] In some areas, more

8   D Powis, *The Signs of Crime* (London: McGraw-Hill, 1977) p 104.
9   See M Brogden, 'Stopping the People' in J Baxter and L Koffman (eds), *Police: The Constitution and the Community* (Abingdon: Professional Books, 1985).
10   Sir L Scarman, The Brixton Disorders: 10-12 April 1981 (Cmnd 8427) (London: HMSO, 1981) para 3.27, discussed in section 2, above.
11   Scarman, para 4.78.
12   See eg R Leng and A Sanders, 'The CLRC Report on Prostitution' [1983] Crim LR 644.
13   D Dixon, A Bottomley, C Coleman, M Gill and D Wall, 'Reality and Rules in the Construction and Regulation of Police Suspicion' (1989) 17 IJ Sociology of Law, 185 at p 189.
14   C Willis, The Use, Effectiveness and Impact of Police Stop and Search Powers (Home Office Research and Planning Unit Paper no 15) (London: Home Office, 1983) p 15 and see L Bridges and T Bunyan, 'Britain's New Urban Policing Strategy - the Police and Criminal Evidence Bill in Context' (1983) 10 JLS 85.

The impact of stop–search powers

stops lead to fewer arrests, precisely because the criminal intelligence normally gathered after arrest is collected on the street instead. Sometimes complex systems of data storage are thereby created, allowing certain target populations to be monitored.[15] This is certainly happening on a large scale in relation to the use of PTA to monitor the Irish population in Britain and Northern Ireland.[16] Yet another example is the use by the police of Road Traffic Act powers to stop vehicles to check for roadworthiness and so forth, who then hand the information about the nature of the car, ownership and so forth over to fraud investigators from the Benefits Agency to see if drivers and passengers are claiming benefits. In 1996 the occupants of some 10,000 vehicles were picked on in this way.[17]

Stop and search, then, has a limited impact in terms of specific arrests, but could have a wider impact in general crime control. Brogden goes further and argues that this is actually part of a wider social control function: that historically the police have been more concerned with social control of the streets than with detecting crime.[18] From medieval times, such laws 'to keep in order the unruly' or to apprehend 'rogues, vagabonds and other disorderly persons' were common. The Head Constable of Liverpool instructed his men in 1878, for instance, to watch 'vigilantly the movements of all suspected persons . . . For the purposes of seeing whether his suspicions are well founded, he may stop any person . . .'[19] Reasonable suspicion, as found in the legislation of the 1970s and 1980s, was in many instances an afterthought - one which, we have seen, was increasingly dispensed with in the 1990s. PACE and the CJPO, far from providing a different kind of power for the police armoury, represent historical continuity. It is the attempt to impose due process on street policing which is the (perhaps short-lived) novelty. Stop-search, and the street policing which stop-search facilitates, is precisely about monitoring and controlling groups of 'suspicious' people, rather than about detecting specific crimes and specific criminals. Choongh therefore argues that stop-search, along with much other policing, is about neither crime control nor due process, since he believes that both models presuppose that police discretion is always exercised with a view to a possible prosecution. He argues that police power (including stop-search) is exercised as a form of social

15   See A Meehan, 'Internal Police Records and the Control of Juveniles' (1993) 33 BJ Crim 504; R Ericson and K Haggerty, *Policing the Risk Society* (Oxford: Clarendon, 1997).
16   Hillyard (1993), especially ch 12.
17   *Observer*, 2 February 1997.
18   Brogden (1985); and see also M Brogden and A Brogden, 'From Henry III to Liverpool 8' (1984) 12 IJ Sociology of Law 37.
19   Brogden (1985) pp 106-107.

discipline in itself against the groups to which we have drawn attention[20].
So, when, for example, a senior officer was asked about the success or
otherwise of Swamp 81, he did not mention catching criminals. Instead he
said, 'Yes I thought it was successful. It motivated officers.'[1] If certain
groups feel they are special targets it is because they are. They, or other
groups which used to occupy their place in society, always have been.
Officers are not allowed to 'swamp' Knightsbridge or Henley in order to
enhance motivation, for the inhabitants of these areas are not targeted.

This is where we see the importance of stop-search being limited to
public places. For it is those at the bottom of the socio-economic heap
who tend to gather in such places and are thus, as a group, subjected to
stop-search most frequently. As Lord Scarman observed in his report on
the Brixton disorders of 1981, young unemployed black people had little
alternative but to make their lives on the streets:

> 'And living much of their lives on the streets, they are brought into
> contact with the police who appear to them as the visible symbols of
> the authority of a society which has failed to bring them its benefits
> or do them justice.'[2]

In this tense situation, it is easy to see how stop-search could become
employed by the police as much to assert their own authority on the streets
(which we have seen is a key element in 'cop culture') as to detect specific
crimes.

(c) The experience of being stopped and searched

One reason for our concern about stop-search is that it undermines the
freedom of those subjected to it, or who fear that they will be subjected to
it. Freedom is undermined not only by the frequency of stop-search, or its
duration, but also by its nature. How invasive can it be? Paragraph 3.1 of
the PACE Code of Practice A, which applies to all stop-search powers,
states that 'Every reasonable effort must be made to reduce to the minimum
the embarrassment that a person being searched may experience.' Further,
according to para 3.5:

---

20 S Choongh (1997) especially chs 2-3. We return to this argument, with which we
agree insofar as it is not taken to refer to all or even most policing, in later
chapters. However, as we explained in ch 1, section 7(c) 'social discipline' can
be seen as part of a broad crime control approach. See also Dixon (1997) chs 2-
3.

1   Quoted in M Keith, *Race, Riots and Policing* (London: UCL Press, 1993) p 132.

2   Scarman (1981) para 2.23.

- search in public should consist only of a superficial examination of outer clothing;
- when a search is in public the only clothes that can be compulsorily removed are coats/jackets and gloves; and,
- a search 'out of public view' such as in a police van may be made if a more thorough search (for example requiring removal of a shirt or hat) is sought on reasonable grounds. In this case the officer conducting the search must be of the same sex as the suspect, and no one of a different sex may be present unless requested by the suspect.

Useful though this guidance is, it does not stop some stop-searches being humiliating. One 16-year-old white youth commented that a PACE search was 'disgusting - my girl-friend was strip-searched as well'.[3] In section 3(a) we saw how the Bishop of Stepney felt 'demeaned' even though it was 'only' his car, and not himself, who the officer wanted to search.[4] And in a PTA example, a woman, seven months pregnant, had travelled from England (where she lived, although she was originally from Belfast) to Dublin where she had been researching for a book she was writing. She was stopped and questioned on her way back. She was treated lawfully and politely. But she was questioned closely about her work, her luggage was searched twice, she was confined to a small room, her personal correspondence was read, and she was anxious about her husband and child who were waiting for her without knowing what was going on. She feared that, if they were so suspicious of her, she might be excluded from England (the power of exclusion is another sweeping PTA power) and thus permanently separated from her husband and child.[5] Although well within the guidance given in the Code of Practice, this examination was clearly highly intrusive and upsetting. Yet, lasting as it did, 'only' 50 minutes it - and thousands like it - does not even appear in the statistics, let alone have to be justified.

Not all PTA examinations and PACE searches conform to the Code of Practice. Hillyard gives a number of examples where women, in particular, are humiliated by examining officers. One said that 'It felt like rape' when her diaries and letters were read in front of her, another was both distressed and outraged when two officers read her diary (including her noting of her periods) aloud to each other. These were probably breaches of para 3.1 of the Code of Practice. In a non-PTA case a black man was told to pull down his trousers and underpants, causing him to burst into tears of anger and humiliation, leading to the officers later being disciplined.[6] Here the breach was acknowledged, but one fears that this is less than usual.

3   NACRO (1997) p 43.
4   *The Guardian*, 24 January 2000.
5   All the PTA examples are from Hillyard (1993) ch 3. See ch 1, section 11(b) for other examples.
6   Institute of Race Relations, *Policing against Black People* (London: IRR, 1987) pp 15-16.

People who are stop-searched are often stop-searched repeatedly. In Young's survey, over 60% of people who were stop-searched were subjected to this twice or more in a year; indeed, 22% suffered it six times or more in one year.[7] Young black men are particularly subject to repeated stops. A stop-search which, in itself, is not highly invasive often feels like it is when it happens repeatedly, which probably accounts for much of the distress of the Bishop of Stepney. In another example, Choongh tells of a man who said that because he was homeless and 'walking the streets' he was constantly stopped, searched and questioned.[8] Or take Mrs B and her son. She kept a record of how often her son was stopped by the police after she had given him a moped for his 16th birthday: 'Within four days her son had been pulled up seven times . . . Two weeks later, Mrs B had recorded 23 abusive encounters between her son and the police.' [9] According to one young black man, 'I get stopped so regularly that I wonder if I should leave my house sometimes.'[10] Some people respond to this by behaving suspiciously or even illegally, as did Mr Diedrick, who said that he refused to stop his car, when asked, because he had been stopped three times in five days and was fed up with it. The police gave chase. When they eventually caught up with him he was arrested.[11]

Similarly, the invasion of liberty is felt more deeply if it is, or is perceived to be, a product of prejudice or racism. This perception is understandable if, as in one case, the police asked the suspect what country he was from[12] or if one is middle aged as in the case of the Bishop of Stepney. Another example is given by a black journalist, Paul Myers, who was stop-searched late one night because he was running (for the last bus), looking lost, with two bags in an area with an allegedly high incidence of burglary. The officer then insisted on seeing identification and checking his address and other details over the radio. No illegality or rudeness is alleged by Myers. The officer even offered 'futile niceties' when they parted. They were futile because, Myers wrote, 'I had been denigrated by a reluctance [on the part of the officer] to yield to the evidence that I just happened to be a black man telling the truth.'[13] The kind of resentment produced can sometimes be identified even from the reports of incidents which police officers write. Brown and Ellis give several examples of stop-searches of black people who, according to the police, reacted with verbal anger immediately. One, stopped for a minor traffic offence, got more 'irate' and shouted 'This is

7   J Young, Policing the Streets - Stops and Search in North London (London: Islington Council, 1994).
8   Choongh (1997) p 47.
9   Haringey Independent Police Committee, reported in Institute of Race Relations (1987) pp 12-13.
10   NACRO (1997) p 44.
11   Institute of Race Relations (1987) p 13.
12   NACRO (1997) p 48.
13   *The Guardian*, 23 September 1997.

not a free country if you're black - why are you harassing me?'. Another, stopped because of a report of a nearby burglary, shouted and swore, saying 'What are you trying to stitch me up with?' and 'harass someone else'. Both were arrested for public order offences.[14]

An example which captures much of what this chapter has tried to convey is given by Michael Keith from his observations while researching the police in the late 1980s in Brixton, an area with a large Afro-Caribbean community with historically bad relations with the police. Two black youths were reportedly seen trying to break into a flat. When the police car, with Keith inside it, arrived at the block of flats two black youths were seen to be walking from the block. The car stopped abruptly by them and one ran off. He was caught after a chase and detained, along with the other youth, while their names were checked over the radio to see if they had criminal records.

> 'One PC, in particular, made little effort to hide his contempt for the black youths, yet his questioning remained technically correct in every other respect and violence was never threatened. After 10 minutes of waiting it was discovered that one of the youths had a criminal record. A friend of his, who had appeared subsequently, protested the innocence of the two, and was nearly arrested for assault when his verbal abuse of the two police began to get out of hand. . . . Just as the two PCs decided there was nothing more they could do, a couple of bottles were thrown from the back of the crowd.'[15]

No arrests were made. Keith reports four similar incidents all on that one shift. He says that, throughout all his observations he never saw any deliberate or overt racism on the part of officers, but they generally dealt with young black men with:

> 'a degree of caution and expectation of trouble . . . Almost invariably correct and polite in every technical respect, this level of suspicion remained obvious to both the observer and the black individuals concerned. Virtually all such encounters passed off peacefully, yet the tension and hostility remained built into the 'micro-sociology' of the meeting . . . Such behaviour, not deliberately racist by intention, is manifestly racist in effect . . .'[16]

14 D Brown and T Ellis, Policing low level disorder: police use of section 5 of the Public Order Act 1986 (Home Office Research Study no 135) (London: Home Office, 1994) pp 31-2.
15 Keith (1993) pp 129-130.
16 Keith (1993) p 198.

The result of all this is that, while nearly one third of all people who are stopped on foot are dissatisfied with the way the police handled the stop, the level of dissatisfaction for Afro-Caribbeans is twice as high. Asked what improvements they would like to see, young people who had been stop-searched asked that the police 'Be more polite, less hostile, give reason . . .', 'Stop being racist' and 'If they were less aggressive and listened to what I say . . .'[17]. Dissatisfaction is higher than average for the young and unemployed too.[18] In other words, dissatisfaction among those who are stopped is directly related to membership of those groups which are disproportionately stopped. Either, stop for stop, the police treat members of these groups worse than they do others, or being in a group which believes itself to be targeted creates sensitivity - which is another way of saying that the stop is, or is perceived to be, a greater invasion of their freedom. In reality both of these explanatory factors are at work here. Thus increased use of the power has an exponential effect on the resentment it causes. In most of the examples given here, paras 3.1 and 3.5 of the Code of Practice were adhered to, but the encounters were nonetheless humiliating or aggravating. As Keith points out, adherence to legal procedures does not necessarily prevent stop-search from being both counterproductive and an invasion of freedom; in evaluating the impact and value of stop-search much more needs to be examined than how far the police follow the rules.

(d) Stop-search, race and police-community relations

We have made reference before to the notions of 'policing by consent' and 'community policing'. These concepts are not as straightforward as they may sound, and the assumptions on which they are based are questionable.[19] However, in so far as these notions are tenable and desirable, the negative impact on them of extensive use of stop and search needs to be considered.

There is no doubt that many local communities get intensely angry and feel harassed as a result of stop and search, especially when they perceive these powers to be exercised in a discriminatory way. Black people are, without doubt, disproportionately stopped. 33% of Afro-Caribbean males

17 NACRO (1997) pp 45-6.
18 T Bucke, Ethnicity and Contacts with the Police: Latest Findings from the British Crime Survey (Home Office Research Findings no 59) (London: Home Office, 1997).
19 There is a contradiction between the aspiration to foster community solidarity and the encouragement of an informant culture, which is increasingly the direction of 'proactive policing'. See McConville and Shepherd (1992) and P Gordon, 'Community Policing: Towards the Local Police State' in P Scraton (ed), Law Order and the Authoritarian State (Milton Keynes: Open UP, 1987).

report being stopped, as compared to 21% of white and Asian males. For 16–25-year-old Afro-Caribbean males the proportion is even higher (53%, although 16-25-year-old white males are not far behind, at 47%). Afro-Caribbeans were also more likely than whites and Asians to be searched once stopped, more likely to be arrested, and more likely to be repeatedly stopped.[20] We saw in section 1 of this chapter that a large minority of people continue to have adversarial encounters with the police, and that the unemployed and young are disproportionately represented.[1] Afro-Caribbeans are also disproportionately represented, 27% experiencing adversarial encounters.[2] Nearly 10% of PACE stop-searches are of black people, a great over-representation in terms of their percentage of the overall population, making them six times more likely to be stopped than white people.[3]

The perception of discrimination is given substance by the enormous variation in recorded stop rates from police force to police force and, within a given force, from one locality to another. In 1987 in London, there were approximately 7.6 stops per 1,000 people, while in West Yorkshire there were only 0.8. But over half of the stops in the six subdivisions in Leeds were in just one subdivision, bringing the stops per 1,000 people in that subdivision much nearer to that of London. Significantly, that subdivision is an ethnically mixed inner-city area, and two thirds of the stops were for drugs (something of which black people are disproportionately suspected).[4] The differential use of search after stop - blacks are searched four times as often as whites following traffic stops - is further suggestive of discriminatory policing.[5]

These statistics do not, in themselves prove that there is discrimination or other unfairness at work. But even if young working class men, especially if they are black, do commit more crime and/or behave in objectively more suspicious ways than other people, the perception of unfairness among socially marginal sections of society would still be understandable. As it is, the research evidence discussed in section 3 (a) and earlier in this section of this chapter, shows that very large numbers of stop-search decisions

20   Bucke (1997).
1   19% of adults, according to the 1994 BCS, experience adversarial encounters. This rises to 24% for the unemployed and 32% for adults under 30. See T Bucke, Policing and the Public: Findings from the 1994 British Crime Survey (Home Office Research Findings no 28) (London: Home Office, 1995). If the BCS had surveyed juveniles the figures would doubtless show young people to be disproportionately represented to a greater extent still; this is clear from the NACRO study (1997).
2   Bucke (1995).
3   Home Office, Statistics on Race and the Criminal Justice System (London: Home Office Research and Statistics Department, 1999).
4   Jefferson, Walker and Seneviratne (1992).
5   Skogan (1994) p 34. Later BCS reports have similar findings.

are based on crude stereotypes, and that PACE made little difference to this. Although racism or prejudice is probably rarely at work directly, these stereotypes focus on age, gender, class and race in ways which disadvantage young black males in particular[6].

The Conservative MP John Wheeler understandably warned that 'the principal casualty [of PACE's stop and search powers] is likely to be a worsening of police community relations',[7] a view which is supported by Home Office research.[8] Scarman blamed 'unimaginative and inflexible' tactics (culminating in stop and search sweeps such as Swamp 81) for the fact that relations in Brixton had 'been a tale of failure'.[9] Keith quotes a police officer who says of Brixton, 'The hatred on the streets is so awful that you have to conform to the views of the rest of the [police] group to survive.'[10] As Norris et al say, the perception by many black communities of 'police behaviour will remain unfavourable because blacks feel, for understandable reasons, that they are subject to excessive levels of police surveillance.'[11] The fact that relations between the police and black people (and, to some extent, young people) are poor is recognised by many police officers; although most believe that resentment to be unjustified, many still think that it is important to improve relations[12]. Some comments made by police officers to the authors of the NACRO research 'conjure up an image of near warfare in terms of how they perceive the policing of the local community.'[13] This is confirmed by the views expressed by many of the 'suspect community' in the areas studied. As one young black man put it: 'Some of the police are alright, so why do they think that all black people are criminals? We treat them as individuals but they treat us all the

---

6 Police research unanimously reports the widespread expression of racist views by police officers: eg Southgate (1986), McConville and Shepherd (1992). But such views do not necessarily influence police actions. Thus, although Norris et al (1992) found disproportionate stopping of black youths, the attitudes displayed to black suspects were no more hostile or provocative, on average, than those displayed to white suspects. On the uncertain relationship between police views and police action see section 1(e) above. The MacPherson Inquiry into the police investigation of the murder of Stephen Lawrence found that there was 'institutional racism' in the police: L Bridges, 'The Lawrence Inquiry - Incompetence, Corruption and Institutional Racism' (1999) 26 JLS 298. For a detailed discussion which does not duck the complexities, see T Jefferson, 'Race, Crime and Policing' (1988) 16 IJ Soc of Law 521.

7 Quoted in Brogden (1985) pp 99-100.

8 R Clarke and M Hough, Crime and Police Effectiveness (Home Office Research Study no 79) (London: HMSO, 1984).

9 Scarman (1981) para 4.43.

10 Keith (1993) p 130.

11 C Norris, N Fielding, C Kemp and J Fielding, 'Black and Blue: An Analysis of the Influence of Race on Being Stopped by the Police' (1992) 43 BJ Sociology 207.

12 NACRO (1997) ch 7.

13 NACRO (1997) p 41.

The impact of stop-search powers

same - no respect!'[14] But it goes both ways, as the analogy with 'war' suggests. In one case a black person was reported as saying 'Fuck off' to a police officer as he passed. He was warned, swore again, and - asked why he was swearing - replied, 'Because I don't like you. I don't like the police'. When he was eventually arrested for a public order offence, he said 'What is this, pick on a nigger week?'[15] The perception of unfairness generated by this arrest - technically justified though the arrest was - will doubtless increase the perception of unfairness which gave rise to the suspect's initial hostility. Poor police-community relations increase crime.

If people believe the police to be against them—whether or not this belief is justified—then they are far less likely to participate in community policing. In the 1980s Jefferson et al found that hostility to the police in the black community was unrelated to the specific number of times individuals were stopped: hostility to the police had become a feature of the whole community.[16] By the turn of the 21st century things appeared to be no better in poor areas.[17] The authors of the NACRO survey were therefore not surprised to find that the members of the community to whom they spoke who had been stop-searched at least once, and who were predominantly black, were in the main unwilling to help the police and would in many cases not even call the police if they needed help themselves. As one said: 'If the police want co-operation they must earn it. Lack of trust is a two-way street. If they don't trust us we don't trust them either.'[18]

What the police gain from stop and search, on the one hand, they may lose through lack of public co-operation, on the other. Consider the consequences of the type of incident reported by Keith and by Brown and Ellis, discussed earlier, multiplied thousands of times every year. This may be a problem if the police seek to detect crime through public co-operation, and survey after survey shows more unwillingness on the part of black people and the young, and to some extent the poor, to help the police than is true of most other sections of society. For example, in May 1997 an Old Bailey trial judge condemned youths for not helping the police investigate a murder. But, as Myers says, 'Maybe he'd [the judge] never been casually harassed and insulted.'[19]

Just as cop culture divides individuals into 'rough' and 'respectable', so it divides areas similarly. McConville and Shepherd were discussing

---

14 NACRO (1997) p 42.
15 Brown and Ellis (1994) p 33.
16 This point has been made countless times. See, for example, Brogden (1985). People who are young, black or male have far less confidence in the police than do older, white females: McConville and Shepherd (1992) pp 16-19.
17 See eg Jones et al, (1986), Crawford et al (1990), Painter et al (1989); Skogan, (1994); Bucke (1997); Young, (1994).
18 NACRO (1997) p 45.
19 *The Guardian*, 23 September 1997. Also see Choongh (1997).

with an officer a 'Neighbourhood Watch' scheme in a middle class area which was surrounded by working class communities. Asked whether the new scheme would spread into the surrounding areas the officer replied, 'No, it's them that the scheme is protecting members from.'[20] Dixon quotes an officer whose view could serve as a leitmotiv throughout this book: 'PACE was meant to protect decent people, but we don't deal with decent people.'[1] Loss of co-operation from those areas would not worry the police, who have low expectations of them in the first place. If keeping black people in check is an implicit objective of the police, then the absence of a cooperative relationship and of information that might lead to a detection is a subsidiary matter. Exactly the same could be said in relation to Irish people: the way the PTA provisions are used do little to detect terrorism offences. We do not know whether they do much to reduce or deter terrorism. But they certainly do a lot to alienate people with Irish connections. Police practices which exclude and humiliate socially marginal people and produce few of the crime control benefits claimed of them are plainly unjustifiable if the objective is to protect and enhance the freedom of all.

5. CONCLUSION

We have seen that ss 1–3 of PACE are not of great inhibitory effect and a number of reasons for this have been identified. Firstly, the main legal constraint—reasonable suspicion—is too vague to act as a standard by which most police actions can be judged. Secondly, the provisions for providing information and recording of searches are difficult to enforce. Thirdly, many stops—probably most—are in formal terms done with consent, enabling the legal constraints and controls to be evaded. Fourthly, these due process provisions envisage a model of policing which does not accord with 'cop culture', the modern reality of street policing, or its history. Indeed, at the same time that they are being urged to conform to due process ideals, the performance of police officers is judged in part on the numbers of searches carried out.[2] Fifthly, even when the police do exercise discretion in accordance with the rules, the attitudes and values which underlie their suspicions influence the manner in which stop-search is conducted. This exacerbates the invasion of privacy which is inherent to stop-search. Sixthly, the remedies for unlawful stop and search are uncertain in scope, inadequate in operation and insufficiently stringent in effect. Finally, there are several powers outside ss 1-3 PACE, many of which

20 McConville and Shepherd (1992) p 140.
1   Dixon (1997) p 104.
2   NACRO (1997) ch 10.

Conclusion

were created in the 1990s, which allow stop-search without even the nominal requirement that there be reasonable suspicion.

The result is that the police still primarily act according to working assumptions based on 'suspiciousness', ie hunch, incongruity and stereotyping on the basis of types of people, previous records and so forth. These are all crime control norms, rooted as they are in the world of professional experience and police culture. The police sometimes discover crime when acting upon their instincts, but such suspicion as they have is seldom in relation to any particular offence, and therefore rarely is it 'reasonable' in terms of the due process norms of s 1 of PACE. Stop and search in operation corresponds far more closely to the crime control model than the due process model to which the law is purportedly oriented, which means that s 1 of PACE is primarily presentational, legitimising and enabling. One important consequence of this is the over-representation of black people in stop-search (and hence arrest and prosecution) statistics.

It is clear that much police work around stop and search fails to satisfy due process ideals. Sometimes this is because the law itself is constituted by enabling and legitimising rules, such as those which allow consensual stops (in all circumstances), and also certain non-consensual stops, in the absence of reasonable suspicion. The police need not subvert such laws to breach due process, they need only use them.[3] Sometimes, however, the police breach due process rules which are in conflict with their working assumptions.

It might be argued that to require the police to claim that they have 'reasonable suspicion' in relation to a particular offence when in fact they are simply generally suspicious is to encourage them to treat the provisions of the law with contempt (while pretending otherwise to suspects and courts). This cannot be healthy either for the law in general or for the regard in which the police are held. Would it be better either to allow stops on grounds of general suspicion or not to allow stops at all? The former option is not attractive from a due process perspective. Laws such as these could be seen, like speed limits, as broadly inhibitory, whereby no one expects precise compliance, but blatant transgression is rare. Relaxing the limits might only encourage the police to overstep the mark once again. Policing on the streets might then be based on random stops rather than, as now, on general suspicion. Or, worse, 'general suspicion' could become the basis for non-random stops that are even more discriminatory than is usual now.

On the other hand, attempting to 'firm up' the law and make it more inhibitory might be both undesirable (if it reduced police effectiveness) and impossible. Police behaviour on the street is inherently fact finding— ie inquisitorial—and the skilful finding of facts requires streetwise knowledge, technique, and experience. Talking to people with their consent

---

3   D McBarnet, *Conviction* (London: Macmillan, 1983) p 157.

- the starting point for many stops and often the ending point too - can and should never be prevented. Imposing an adversarial due process structure onto this craft is an attempt to deny one of the key elements of what policing is about. If policing is more about general social control than detection of specific crimes, then this is all the more true. And if the new managerialist ethos identified in ch 1, section 9, continues to reward officers for their 'productivity' (including arrests arising from stops) this will be more true still.

In ch 1, section 11, we argued that the purpose of criminal justice is, or should be, to promote freedom, and that in this endeavour both due process and crime control values had to be utilised in a 'context-sensitive' manner. As far as stop-search is concerned, context-sensitive due process means not requiring 'reasonable suspicion' in relation to particular offences, not requiring records to be made, and not attempting to control consent searches, because these requirements are unrealistic if the powers are to exist at all. Context-sensitive crime control means not allowing prejudice or stereotyping to shape the exercise of discretion such that particular communities are, or feel, discriminated against, not to allow life-style choices in themselves (usually made from a very limited range) to trigger the use of police powers, and not to humiliate individuals.

This chapter has shown that the law allows many apparently formal due process powers to be exercised in a context-sensitive manner in practice, but it does not in practice ensure that the crime control motor underlying the use of these powers is generally context-sensitive. Thus the freedom of actual and potential victims is protected to some extent through the arrest, deterrent and information-gathering effects of stop-search. But the freedom of suspects is hugely violated on three levels: at the community level, certain groups in society disproportionately suffer from both the actual exercise of the power and the fear that it will be exercised when in public places; at the quantitative level, the chances of being repeatedly stop-searched are very high if one is a member of one or more of those groups; and at the qualitative level, the exercise of the power, especially when it is repeated, represents suffering for the suspect which, in its different way, is as real as the suffering of many a victim. Indeed in some ways the loss of freedom of suspects and victims is similar. In many cases both groups fear that the invasion will recur. Feelings of persecution and loss of control over one's life sometimes arise. Behaviour changes, in an effort to avoid recurrence. Further, when stop-search triggers offences as a reaction to it (as in the examples given in section 4 (c)) and leads to the alienation of the community (and hence less assistance with crime-solving) freedom which is gained by stop-search is lost in the crimes which are not solved and which are even created.

The Philips Commission recommended a national stop and search power because:

'. . . people in the street who have committed property offences or have in their possession articles which it is a criminal offence to possess should not be entirely protected from the possibility of being searched. The availability of powers to search is of use in the detection of crime and the arrest of offenders.'[4]

Although this statement has a beguiling quality, it actually contains a trite and misleading argument. It is like saying that known offenders should not be entirely protected from the process of law enforcement. Of course they should not. But the important question does not relate to known offenders, for if the police knew who all the offenders were, our crime problems would be minimal. In reality, the identities of most actual offenders are unknown and many suspects are not actual offenders. To say that actual criminals should not be protected from the possibility of search is to miss the point. The real issue is whether people suspected of being criminals (many of whom will in fact be innocent) should be so protected.

The confusion arises from a false dichotomy in the Philips Commission's terms of reference, which enjoined it to have 'regard both to the interests of the community in bringing offenders to justice and to the rights and liberties of persons suspected or accused of crime . . .'[5] In reality, persons 'suspected or accused' have as much interest as anyone else in bringing actual offenders to justice, and all members of the 'community' are potential suspects. The question which requires consideration is whether the community as a whole should be subject to the interference with liberty which these powers involve, especially bearing in mind that they are not exercised against all sections of the community equally.

Who is to weigh up the competing demands of detection versus liberty? Those in positions of power in this debate (the two Royal Commissions, members of Parliament and the government, Home Office officials, senior police officers etc) are not a representative cross-section of society. The law is reviewed, made and implemented primarily by the white, middle aged, middle classes, while those who are stopped and searched are primarily the marginalised elements of society: the young unemployed, the homeless, the mentally disordered, the Irish, black people, and all the other 'toe rags', 'scum' and 'losers' who attract the attention of the police. One section of society shapes the law (both in books and in action) which bears down on the other. It is easy for the decision-making community to decide that it is in 'society's' interests for suspects to have their liberty compromised, when those suspects are mainly drawn from the non-decision-making community. Indeed, if it is true that stop and search is part of a wider strategy of policing against certain communities, then the apparent dichotomy in the Philips

4   RCCP, Report, para 3.17.
5   RCCP, Report, p vi.

Commission's terms of reference was not false: the suspect communities and the non-suspect communities are indeed distinct. In an 'inclusion/exclusion' society, the suspect communities are excluded from structures of decision making and affluence, and the non-suspect communities are included. One fundamental question raised by stop and search in a divided society is how far police powers are used to help perpetuate existing structures of inequality and subordination.

Conclusion

Chapter 3

Arrest

I. INTRODUCTION

In *Lewis v Chief Constable of the South Wales Constabulary*[1] it was stated that:

> 'Arrest is a matter of fact; it is not a legal concept . . . Arrest is a situation . . . Whether a person has been arrested depends not on the legality of his arrest but on whether he has been deprived of his liberty to go where he pleases.'

This is as good a definition of arrest as we have.[2] Although accurate, this clinical statement fails to capture the way arrest often renders suspects powerless, humiliated or even terrified. The Philips Commission in the 1980s recognised this:

> 'Arrest represents a major disruption to a suspect's life . . . police officers are so involved with the process of arrest and detention that they fail at times to understand the sense of alarm and dismay felt by some of those who suffer such treatment.'[3]

Perhaps this is the sort of treatment Philips had in mind:

---

1   [1991] 1 All ER 206 at 209-10, confirming *Spicer v Holt* [1977] AC 987.
2   It was endorsed in *Dawes v DPP* [1995] 1 Cr App Rep 65. In this case, the offender broke into a car which had been set up by the police to lock automatically when the door was closed, trapping him. This was the point at which he was held to be arrested.
3   Royal Commission on Criminal Procedure (RCCP), Report (Cmnd 8092) (London: HMSO, 1981) para 3.75.

Natt: 'Why am I being arrested?'
PC: 'You're just a pain in the arse ain't yer?'
Natt: 'Oh, God.'
PC: 'Why don't you go and set fire to yourself or something?'
Natt: 'You carry on arresting me without reason. Why?'
PC: 'Because you are a shit.'
[later] Natt: 'Why beat me? Why?'
PC: 'Because I like it.'
Natt: 'You like to beat me?'
PC: 'I got no respect for someone like you.'

We know that this is an accurate report of what happened because Natt tape-recorded it, having been verbally abused when previously stopped by police officers.[4] We do not know whether this kind of treatment is frequent or not, or why it happens, but the power given to the police gives them the opportunity. But arrest can be terrifying without the police deliberately abusing their powers:

'Two of them turned to my husband and said, "We are arresting you under the Prevention of Terrorism Act." I'm not kidding you, I was glad I was sitting down because I could feel my stomach going down to my feet. The Birmingham Six flashed through my mind. This is how innocent people are picked up. Up to then I had thought that the police didn't pick up people who are completely innocent. . . .When I got to Harlow police station I was formally arrested and I was then checked in. I was put in this room and a doctor came. . . . You feel terrible because you feel she thinks you are a criminal.'[5]

In this chapter we shall look at how far the police are, and should be, allowed to infringe the freedom of the individual in these ways. In other words we will examine the legal rules and how effective they are in controlling the use of arrest. We will also look at what reasons for arrest are lawful. We shall see that arrest is used for many purposes, some more legitimate than others. As with stop-search, this means we have to understand the informal working rules which help to structure police discretion. The first section of ch 2 is as applicable to arrest as it is to stop-search.

---

4 A fuller extract is provided in S Holdaway, *The Racialisation of British Policing* (Houndmills: Macmillan, 1996).
5 P Hillyard, *Suspect Community* (London: Pluto Press, 1993) pp 111-3.

2. ARREST AND THE PURPOSES OF CRIMINAL JUSTICE

(a) Models of criminal justice

In thinking about what values should underpin the law and practice of arrest it is useful to consider the three models we discussed in ch 1.

(i) Due process

Under this model, no one should be arrested unless it is clear that they probably committed a specific offence. Normally such a determination should be made by a magistrate who would then issue a warrant authorising the police to arrest. In situations of necessity the model would accept that the police may act without prior authority, but only on hard evidence which would be subject to subsequent judicial scrutiny.

This model accepts that these standards would impair police efficiency, but that this is the price to be paid 'for a regime that fosters personal privacy and champions the dignity and inviolability of the individual.'[6] Moreover, if the police were to be given wider powers to arrest suspects for questioning, it is unlikely that all classes of society would suffer greater interference, since the outcry would be too great. Rather, police powers would 'be applied in a discriminatory fashion to precisely those elements in the population—the poor, the ignorant, the illiterate, the unpopular—who are least able to draw attention to their plight and to whose sufferings the vast majority of the population are the least responsive.'[7]

(ii) Crime control

The adherent of this model would argue that the police need broad powers of arrest. They need to be able to round up known offenders from time to time to see if they are responsible for crimes occurring in the locality. They also need the power to act on their instincts by stopping suspicious looking characters. It may be that no crime will be detected by these methods, but the very fact of arresting such persons may prevent a planned crime. Periodic infringements of the liberty of known criminals may be enough to persuade them to leave the area or desist from their illegal activities.

The innocent have nothing to fear from such broad arrest powers. In the rare case where they are arrested by mistake, release will quickly follow. The police should therefore be given powers to arrest citizens irrespective

6   H Packer, *The Limits of the Criminal Sanction* (Standford: Stanford UP, 1968) p 179.
7   Packer, p 180.

of whether they are reasonably suspected of committing a particular crime. The standard should be no more than that a police officer honestly thinks that an arrest will serve the goal of crime control. Alternatively, the substantive laws must be so broadly defined that the reasonable suspicion hurdle can be easily overcome. A combination of vague laws and lax standards is ideal.

(iii)   Freedom

Under this model, it will be recalled, due process and crime control considerations are both regarded as relevant, but only when applied in a 'context-sensitive' manner and only in relation to the greater goal of promoting freedom. The model cautions against wide powers of arrest, because every arrest which fails to prevent or solve a crime creates a twofold loss of freedom: the arrestee loses some liberty and privacy; and the time, money and resources wasted in the arrest will have not been used to protect potential victims (eg through street patrols) or to provide non-law enforcement public services.

This model would allow wide powers if they led to a potentially greater gain in freedom - for example, in relation to particularly serious crimes or where they would be more likely to solve a crime. In some situations it will be very likely that a crime has been committed and that the offender is one of a group of people. Without arresting them all it may not be possible to find out who is responsible. A classic example is where a child is abused by one or other parent, each of whom accuses the other. Another is where a house, shared by several people, is raided and drugs found, each occupant again disclaiming responsibility.

Strict due process would not allow any arrests in any of these situations as there is nothing to suggest that any one individual probably committed the crime in question. Crime control would allow them all to be arrested as one of the suspects in each situation is undoubtedly criminal. The freedom model would weigh the certain loss of freedom to the potential arrestees against the possible gain in freedom were the crimes to be solved. Whether arrest would be allowed or not would therefore depend in part on the seriousness of the crimes and on how many people fell within the group suspected. The arrest of the two parents would be more likely to be justifiable within the freedom model than would the arrest of the multiple occupants of the house with drugs. In the latter case, context-sensitivity would also require consideration of how dangerous the drugs are and community relations considerations of the kind discussed in ch 2, section 4.

We might think that we could best promote complete context-sensitivity if the police are given total discretion to take all these considerations into account on a case-by-case basis. However, this approach would ignore the discussion in the previous chapter of the structural and cultural biases which, we saw, affect the way discretion is exercised. Further, citizens want to know, and have a right to know, whether an arrest is lawful or not (and the same applies to other police powers such as stop-search, search of one's home, and so forth). Freedom is reduced when people fear arbitrary interventions in their lives, or experience what they believe are arbitrary interventions. We therefore need to create rules which allow context-sensitivity yet also establish clearly what the police can and cannot do both in general and in relation to exceptional situations. These rules would take into account offence seriousness, the probability of solving the offence through arrest, the number of people whose liberty would be infringed by arrest, and the amount of liberty that arrest would erode (that is, for how long, and how undermining of dignity it would be). The availability of other methods of crime detection would also be relevant, as the freedom model is concerned to both facilitate detection and discourage the erosion of liberty. We will return to these issues later in this chapter.

(b) The place of arrest in the criminal process

(i) Changes in the use of arrest

Up until the early part of the nineteenth century, it was for magistrates to determine whether or not to prosecute someone. They usually made their decisions on the basis of information provided to them by police officers, other enforcement agencies or private citizens. If they were satisfied by this evidence, they could issue a warrant for arrest or a summons to appear in court at a later time. Some people were arrested first and then immediately brought before the magistrates, who, again decided whether or not to prosecute.[8] So arrest used simply to be a mechanism for bringing offenders to court. This is no longer so. Arrest and prosecution are now entirely separate in both theory and practice. Anything can follow arrest: no action at all, an official warning, charge or, indeed, release followed by a summons to appear at court. Around 50% of all arrests lead to prosecution, although the exact figures vary according to offence type, police force, and even police station.[9] Arrest is now simply an exercise of police power which does not, in itself, determine the next stage in the process.

---

8   See A Sanders, 'Arrest, Charge and Prosecution' (1986) 6 LS 257.
9   M McConville, A Sanders and R Leng, *The Case for the Prosecution* (London: Routledge, 1991). C Phillips and D Brown, Entry into the Criminal Justice System (Home Office Research Study no 185) (London: Home Office, 1998) pp 81-3.

The place of arrest in the investigative process has changed over the years. At one time, the police or any other law enforcer used to investigate an offence and then arrest (or not) at the end of that investigation. This means that the investigation took place (in theory) before the police exercised coercive powers. In reality, certainly in more recent years, many people 'helped the police with their inquiries' in the police station, which means that they were not arrested but in an undefined state of detention. If, as a result of this 'help', the police secured enough evidence to prosecute, they would arrest and bring the suspect before the magistrates; if they did not have enough evidence, the suspect was (eventually) released. Gradually, being in detention came to be seen as being under arrest, and so arrest moved nearer to the beginning of the investigative process. This was formalised by the Criminal Law Act 1967, which created a wide range of 'arrestable offences', ie offences for which the police could arrest without obtaining a warrant from the magistrates. It follows from all this that many more people are now arrested than once happened. The officially recorded numbers are rising steadily, reaching 1.96m in 1997-8.[10] It is not known how many people are arrested each year, as some of the 1.96m arrests will be of people who are arrested more than once.

Readers may begin to be worried by now. In a population of little over 50m people there are at least 2m arrests per year, many of which are frightening for the arrestee. What of our liberties? It is important to recall from the previous chapter that the law is permissive. It allows the police to exercise all manner of powers, but does not require them to do so. In reality, the police decide not to arrest far more often than they decide to actually do so. This varies from offence to offence. Officers do not ignore bank robberies and rapes just because they are not obliged to arrest suspects. But in some situations certain types of offence are routinely ignored or dealt with informally. Waddington, for example, comments that in the early 1990s 50,000 supporters of the miners' union and 150,000 TUC demonstrators protested against pit closures without one arrest being made. 'On some occasions the police would have been lawfully entitled to make wholesale arrests, but they consciously chose not to do so.'[11] Similarly, it appears that the police rarely use the arrest powers provided under the CJPO 1994 in relation to 'raves' and 'trespass', although the

---

10 Home Office, S 95 Statistics on Race and the CJS, 1997-8 (London: Home Office, 1998). We refer to 'officially recorded numbers' because, as always, official figures understate the real numbers. This is particularly true of the Metropolitan Police in this respect: see P Hillyard and D Gordon, 'Arresting statistics: the drift to informal justice in England and Wales' (1999) 26 JLS 502. Also, as we will argue in section 2(b)(iii) below many (perhaps most) stop-searches are also arrests - but not so classified.

11 P A J Waddington, *Liberty and Order* (London: UCL Press, 1994) p 39.

threat to use these powers often seems effective.[12] It follows that much of what the police do is not coercive. They frequently use fewer powers than they are entitled to, being influenced by the general considerations examined in the first section of ch 2. The question for this chapter is what leads them to arrest one person, in one context, and not another person in a different context.

(ii) The purposes of arrest

There are several lawful purposes of arrest (with or without subsequent detention), some rather more traditional than others, and also several 'unofficial' purposes. The traditional purposes include holding someone in a place of safety, securing someone's appearance at court who has breached a court order or failed to answer a summons, as part of transit between court and prison, and holding someone in custody in order to charge them. Arrests for these reasons are all to facilitate prosecution. They pose no great problems of principle or practice, and we will not be dealing with them in this chapter.

The other traditional purposes of arrest are to prevent a crime (or a further crime) taking place, and to maintain public order. Arrests for these purposes are not always to facilitate prosecution, and there may not be enough evidence to prosecute at the time of arrest. The police have a new power along these lines to 'remove' school age children in certain circumstances from public places, and take them to their school or other appropriate place. The aim here is not to take police or court action, but to deal with truancy and the crime problems which sometimes accompany it.[13]

Many arrests, for a variety of offences, are made on the basis of suspicion, when there is insufficient evidence to charge. A less traditional purpose of arrest, then, developed in the late twentieth century, is in order to obtain or secure evidence. This evidence comes from a variety of sources, including interviews with witnesses, searches of property, collection of forensic evidence and questioning of the suspects themselves.[14] This is all possible only because of a relaxation of legal

---

12   T Bucke and Z James, *Trespass and Protest: Policing under the Criminal Justice and Public Order Act 1994*, (London: Home Office, 1998).

13   The power is created by the Crime and Disorder Act 1998, s 16. It amounts to an arrest power although it is not called that in the legislation. It can only be used when a number of conditions are met. See R Leng, R Taylor and M Wasik, *Blackstone's Guide to the Crime and Disorder Act 1998* (London: Blackstone, 1998) pp 37-9.

14   M McConville, Corroboration and Confessions: The Impact of a Rule Requiring that no Conviction can be Sustained on the Basis of Confession Evidence Alone (Royal Commission on Criminal Justice Research Study no 13) (London: HMSO, 1993) pp 24-36. This report includes a discussion of the levels of evidence possessed by the police at the time of arrest, and how 'weak' arrests are strengthened. Also see Philips and Brown (1998) pp 43-4.

Arrest and the purposes of criminal justice

controls on police questioning which took place in the latter half of this century. Whereas at one time pre-charge detention was something which could only be authorised by the magistrates, pre-charge detention and questioning is now authorised by the police themselves. This self-authorisation is a feature of the crime control model. As recently as 1969, the House of Lords found itself in *Shaaban Bin Hussien v Chong Fook Kam* criticising the police for making:

'a premature arrest rather than one that was unjustifiable from first to last. The police made the mistake of arresting before questioning; if they had questioned first and arrested afterwards, there would have been no case against them.'[15]

The law now makes it very difficult for the police to ask questions of suspects prior to arrest.[16] Questioning away from the police station has been restricted in order to protect suspects, but with the ironic result that many arrests are 'premature' in the *Shaaban* sense. Freedom is lost through unnecessary detention, but possibly gained through greater protection of suspects. Whether or not these changes have led to a net gain in freedom is unclear. What is clear is that they have led to an enormous increase in arrests. We said earlier that there are now nearly 2m 'official' arrests each year. This is a 54% increase since 1981, an increase which, moreover, has taken place largely since the Police and Criminal Evidence Act 1984 (PACE) came into operation, and which shows no sign of slowing down.[17]

Another way of looking at these changes is to see the position of suspects detained in custody as being regularised. In the 1960s and 1970s, pre-trial detention was secured unlawfully or quasi-lawfully through the mechanism of 'helping the police with their inquiries', but now it is secured openly and lawfully through the mechanism of arrest and detention. The legal rules which we shall be discussing are therefore legitimising rules (legitimising the 'helping the police with their inquiries' syndrome) and enabling rules (enabling the police to act as they wish to do without fear of legal repercussions). The extent to which they are also inhibitory, preventing abuse of power through restrictions on their use, will be a key issue in this chapter and the next two.[18]

By contrast, the United States has largely adhered to the original idea of arrest as the culmination of investigation and a prelude to prosecution. Thus pre-charge detention is very limited and release without charge is

15 [1970] AC 942 at 949, per Lord Devlin.
16 See discussion of the Police and Criminal Evidence Act 1984 (PACE) Code of Practice C in ch 5, section 3.
17 Hillyard and Gordon (1999).
18 See ch 2, section 1(d) for the meaning of 'legitimising', 'enabling', 'inhibitory' and 'presentational' rules.

(as it used to be in Britain) rare. Moreover, the threshold for arrest—
'probable cause'—is more stringent than 'reasonable suspicion'. Stop and
search is allowed on the basis of 'reasonable suspicion', and so the
American police can stop and search in situations where they cannot arrest
- which, we shall see, may not be so in Britain. The result is relatively more
sparing use of arrest and formal detention in the United States. However,
de facto arrest and detention is used instead, police officers persuading
suspects to attend the station 'voluntarily' in a similar fashion to our
'helping with inquiries'.[19]

The Royal Commission on Criminal Procedure (Philips Commission)
wanted to restrict the wide arrest powers introduced by the Criminal Law
Act 1967 in Britain.[20] This is because it sought to restrict the exercise of
coercive power to circumstances where it was necessary. The Philips
Commission believed that coercive powers like arrest were often used
unnecessarily, relying on a study by Gemmill and Morgan-Giles which
showed great regional variations between police forces in the use of arrest,
on the one hand, and summons, on the other.[1] In other words, it seemed
that similar offences in similar circumstances were subject to arrest,
detention and charge in some areas, where in other areas they would be
subject to a summons to appear in court on a specified date.

The Philips Commission accordingly advocated a 'necessity principle'.
Arrest and detention would only have been allowed if one of the following
conditions applied:
(a) the person concerned refused to reveal his or her identity so that a
    summons could be served;
(b) there was a need to prevent the continual repetition of the offence;
(c) there was a need to protect the arrested person or property;
(d) there was a need to secure or preserve evidence, or obtain it by
    questioning;
(e) it was likely that the person would fail to appear at court to answer the
    summons.
If none of these conditions applied, suspects should be interviewed,
processed and brought to court in a less coercive manner than arrest and
detention.

In this way, the Philips Commission proposed that the police be allowed
to exercise coercive powers only when they needed to for prosecution
purposes. This approach implicitly embodies the 'freedom' objective which

19 Practice varies considerably, however, from locality to locality. See A Meehan,
    'Internal Police Records and the Control of Juveniles' (1993) 33 BJ Crim 504.
20 Royal Commission on Criminal Procedure, Report (Cmnd 8092) (London:
    HMSO, 1981) paras 3.75-3.79.
1   R Gemmill and R Morgan-Giles, Arrest, Charge and Summons: Arrest Practice
    and Resource Implications (Royal Commission on Criminal Procedure, Research
    Study no 9) (London: HMSO, 1981).

Arrest and the purposes of criminal justice

we advocate. However, the Commission had a legalistic and myopic view of police activity, assuming that arrests are always geared to investigating specific offences of which the arrestees are reasonably suspected.

Arrest and detention often has an 'unofficial' purpose, something which was ignored by Philips (and indeed by the Runciman Commission). Some arrests are to secure evidence of offences unrelated to the offences for which arrests are ostensibly carried out, committed either by the arrestees or by others.[2] Another purpose is to put the 'frighteners' on arrestees - to warn them not to take certain action or to punish them for actions they are believed to have carried out. Here, there is no intention to prosecute. Arrest and detention is used as a form of 'social disciplining'[3] or summary justice. Another purpose is to control individuals and groups, especially in public order situations, again with no intention of prosecuting (see later discussion). We shall see that the English courts also fail to acknowledge these 'unofficial' purposes of arrest, reducing their ability to restrain the police.[4] Yet these 'unofficial' purposes appear to be gaining in significance, now that more arrests are being disposed of by the police without recourse to the courts than are going to court.[5]

(iii)   Relationship between arrest and stop-search

We have seen that arrest is a deprivation of liberty. There need be no explicit statement of arrest or detention; arrest occurs if it is made clear that the arrestee would be prevented from leaving.[6] It follows from this that a trivial restraint of an individual, by, say, tugging someone's sleeve to attract their attention, is not an arrest.[7] If we can only define arrest by reference to a temporary deprivation of liberty whereby one is not free to go as one pleases, there is no distinction between arrest and stop-search, especially as most of the circumstances in which suspects may be stopped and searched amount to offences for which suspects may be arrested. If in every circumstance that a suspect may be lawfully stopped and searched he or she may also be arrested—if, indeed, the stop is in essence an arrest—the need for specific stop and search powers which we queried in ch 2 is brought further into question. Instead of 'stopping', the police could 'arrest'. The

---

2   See, for example, *Chalkley and Jeffries* [1998] 2 Cr App Rep 79, discussed in section 4(b) below.

3   S Choongh, *Policing as Social Discipline* (Oxford: Clarendon, 1997).

4   See discussion of *Plange v Chief Constable of South Humberside* in section 4 (b) below.

5   Hillyard and Gordon (1999). This reflects the increase in arrests and decrease in prosecutions (both in absolute and relative terms) in the 1990s. See ch 6 for discussion of post-arrest dispositions.

6   *Shaaban Bin Hussien v Chong Fook Kam* [1970] AC 942 at 949.

7   *Mepstead v DPP* [1996] Crim LR 111.

argument that more arrests (instead of stop-search) would involve too much bureaucracy or too much deprivation of liberty is false. The law does not require that someone be taken to a police station immediately on arrest. As we have seen, the definition of arrest merely involves the temporary deprivation of liberty. The police can, perfectly lawfully, arrest, search and question and then release that person. Perhaps the reason for not doing so is that an arrest simply sounds more dramatic and would make people more reluctant than they are now to accept such treatment on the streets.

As the police can generally arrest lawfully when they can lawfully stop and search, it is difficult to understand why so few recorded stop-searches under PACE (around 11%)[8] lead to arrest and police station detention. The act of stop and search will sometimes dispel reasonable suspicion, rendering any subsequent arrest unlawful. But this is unlikely to account for the majority of stop-searches which do not lead to arrest. Is it likely that suspicions which are dispelled in nearly 9 out of 10 cases will usually be 'reasonable'? In many cases where there are inadequate grounds for reasonable suspicion, the police are probably prepared to stop and search but reluctant to take the major step of arrest. If stop-search were abolished this might lead to more suspects being formally arrested and taken to the police station, but many fewer than are currently stop-searched. Whether this would be a good or bad thing would depend primarily on how far the balance of freedom is currently affected by the use of stop-search powers (see previous chapter), and how far - if a freedom perspective became accepted in our system - the use of arrest and detention powers could be shifted in a liberty-enhancing direction.

3.   THE LEGAL BASIS FOR ARREST

(a)   With warrant

At one time, arrest was only lawful if backed by a judicial warrant. Now it is rare for the police to seek prior approval for an arrest. This is because the Criminal Law Act 1967 created the concept of the 'arrestable offence' for which the police may arrest without warrant.

The move away from arrest warrants, which is part of the general move away from judicial supervision of police powers, means that most arrests are now made by the police acting on their own knowledge and initiative rather than acting under the supervision of magistrates. It mirrors the decline in the use of summonses (issued by magistrates) and search warrants (also issued by magistrates). Nowadays, the police themselves

8   See ch 2, section 4(a), Table 2.1.

The legal basis for arrest

generally decide what powers they will exercise and when. This is a crime control approach.

Warrants are nowadays mainly used when a suspect fails to appear in court to answer a summons or to answer bail. In these circumstances, the police or prosecutor would apply to the magistrates for a warrant,[9] which would usually be granted straight away, authorising the arrest of that suspect. The suspect can be kept in custody if the warrant so provides, and then made to appear before the magistrates, who will decide whether or not that person should be bailed.

(b) Arrestable offences under PACE

The police may arrest anyone, subject to certain conditions, for an 'arrestable offence' without a prior warrant. This is by far the most common basis for arrest. Any offence punishable by a jail term of five years or more is arrestable (PACE, s 24(1)) as are miscellaneous other offences (PACE, s 24(2) and (3)). This broadly re-enacts the pre-PACE law as created by the 1967 Act. It covers a very wide range of offences, because most English legislation provides for maximum punishments much heavier than the normal punishments. Thus theft is punishable by seven years in jail even though very few people get jailed at all for simple theft, and certainly very rarely for five years or more. Most offences of dishonesty and violence are therefore arrestable.

Under PACE, s 24 the police may arrest any person whom they reasonably suspect to be about to commit, or who is committing, or who has committed, an arrestable offence. This section also provides that the police may arrest even when they have no reasonable suspicion if the arrested person had in fact committed an arrestable offence, or was in the course of doing so, or was about to do so (sub-ss (5)(a), (4)(a) and (7)(a) respectively.) This is a classic crime control norm since the ends are regarded as justifying the means. It does not matter that the arrest was arbitrarily made, so long as the suspect turns out to have been engaged in a crime. We saw in ch 2 that the police frequently stop people who appear to be generally 'suspicious' without necessarily having a specific offence in mind. This provision allows them to arrest on this basis and, if their suspicions turn out to be justified, the arrest is lawful under PACE. The police might, for instance, see a well-known burglar walking down the street and simply arrest him because they know he is usually up to something dishonest. If, in the police station, he confessed to a burglary, and, say, the police find the stolen goods in his home, his guilt would be clear and his arrest would be valid under PACE. However, Art 5 of the European

---

9   Under the Magistrates Court Act 1980, s 125, as amended by PACE, s 33.

Convention on Human Rights (ECHR) stipulates, in effect, that no-one shall be deprived of his or her liberty through arrest except 'on a reasonable suspicion of having committed an offence or when it is reasonably considered necessary to prevent his committing an offence. . .'

Now that the Human Rights Act 1998 (HRA) is in force late, the provisions of the ECHR are enforceable in the English courts where legislation can be interpreted in a way that is compatible with the Convention. The problem with s 24 (sub-ss (5)(a), (4)(a) and (7)(a)) is that these provisions directly contradict Art 5. The courts will be able to issue a 'declaration of incompatibility'[10] which enables the government to amend the law, so as to comply with the Convention, on a 'fast track' procedure. But arrests made in these circumstances will not be unlawful as such. Indeed, even under the Convention, and when (or if) the law is changed, it could be that the unlawful arrest would be transformed into a lawful arrest when the evidence on which the eventual conviction is based is elicited.

The courts can exclude evidence obtained unlawfully or unfairly - such as in this instance when an arrest is made without reasonable suspicion. However, whether courts will exclude evidence and refuse to convict the clearly guilty arrested in contravention of the Convention is impossible to predict.[11] From a freedom perspective one might say that the lack of reasonable suspicion for arrest should not matter if the person is guilty, as future victims will have their freedom enhanced by convicting such people. On the other hand, the protection of people from arbitrary interference also enhances freedom. The crucial point is that if the police are allowed to arrest without reasonable suspicion it is likely that many such people will not be guilty and will not be charged or convicted of anything. The police get away with this most of the time because it is difficult to secure redress.[12] A freedom perspective has to take account of the social reality of criminal justice - that if the police retain this power, many innocent people, as well as guilty people, will continue to be wrongfully arrested and continue to lose elements of their freedom. The best deterrent in practice is to cause the police to lose their cases if they fail to adhere to the law.

The breadth of all the powers in s 24 gives rise to other problems. In particular, the police are entitled to arrest someone who is about to commit an arrestable offence (sub-s (7)) but they are also entitled to arrest someone who is attempting to commit an arrestable offence, since under s 4(1) of

---

10   HRA, ss 4, 10, and Sch 2.
11   This is part of a broader question of when valid evidence is obtained unlawfully or unfairly. Even though Convention rights might be regarded as 'higher rights' - on a par with constitutional rights in jurisdictions with written Constitutions - English courts have not excluded evidence simply as a result of their breach. See *Khan* [1996] 3 All ER 289. On exclusion of evidence in general, see ch 11.
12   Remedies are discussed in section 5 below.

the Criminal Attempts Act 1981 an attempt carries the same punishment as the full offence. It seems, therefore, that they may arrest people who are about to commit attempts. But what is to be done with those people? There may be no crime with which they could be charged. Being about to commit a crime would sometimes be conduct liable to cause a breach of the peace, but this need not always be so. In *Geddes*, for example,[13] the police arrested a man who had been hiding in the toilets of a school and who had with him a rope, masking tape and a knife. There was good reason to believe that he had been planning to abduct a child, but his conviction for attempted false imprisonment was quashed because his acts were 'merely preparatory'.[14] Even if the arrest power would have allowed the police to escort Geddes from the school, he was clearly a dangerous man who the police would have to set free.

The problem here is that the due process element in the law is not context-sensitive. If a 'freedom' approach were adopted, whether the arrest and detention of people 'about to' commit an offence would be allowed would depend, not on the legal niceties of the law of attempt, but on how much danger the intended victims would be in without arrest and detention and on how clear it was that someone was about to commit an offence.

(c) Non-arrestable offences

According to s 24, the police may only arrest without a warrant if the offence is arrestable, implying that all other offences are not summarily arrestable. However, s 25 (and certain other sections) make non-arrestable offences arrestable under certain circumstances. First, the police must have reasonable grounds for suspecting that an offence has been, or is being, committed or attempted. However, they may not arrest someone who is about to commit a non-arrestable offence unless the suspect's behaviour amounts to a criminal attempt. Further, arrest for such an offence is allowed only if 'it appears . . . that service of a summons is impractical or inappropriate because any of the general arrest conditions is satisfied' (s 25(1)). The 'impracticality conditions' are that the police do not know the name of the suspect or a suitable address for service of a summons, or have reasonable grounds for doubting whether any name or address furnished by the suspect is correct. The conditions concerned with the inappropriateness of using a summons are that the police have reasonable grounds for believing that arrest is necessary to protect a child or other vulnerable person from the suspect or to prevent the suspect hurting

13   [1996] Crim LR 894.
14   Following the interpretation of s 1 Criminal Attempts Act in *Campbell* [1991] Crim LR 268.

anyone, suffering physical injury, causing loss of or damage to property, committing an offence against public decency, or causing an unlawful obstruction of the highway.

What the impracticality conditions are concerned with is the probability of a suspect answering a summons and being traced if he or she does not do so, for summons is the only way to proceed against someone who is not arrested. Section 25 allows the police to arrest, even for minor offences (such as motoring or litter offences), if this is the only way of getting an offender to court. It is not enough for the police to consider that it would be more convenient or efficient to arrest rather than summons. The inappropriateness conditions are concerned with the perceived need to arrest rather than to set free (and to later answer a summons) in order to prevent the suspect causing further harm. This opens the door to arrest for minor offences, particularly in public order contexts.

An arrest is only lawful if, as s 25(1) implies, the officers believe that one of the general arrest conditions is met. If they do not so believe, the arrest will be unlawful.[15] In addition to this subjective element, the officers must have 'reasonable grounds' for believing that a specific arrest condition applies. In *G v DPP*,[16] an officer arrested G for a non-arrestable offence even though G had readily given his name and address to that officer shortly before committing the offence. The officer considered that the general arrest condition in s 25(3)(b) was satisfied because, in his experience, people who committed offences did not give their correct names and addresses. Such reasoning should have been condemned by the Divisional Court in reviewing the legality of the arrest, since its logic is such that the police would always be able to arrest for non-arrestable offences. Unfortunately, the court appears to have overlooked this point, although the arrest was held to be unlawful on other grounds.[17] An opportunity to affirm the importance of the general arrest conditions as a due process hurdle for the police to overcome was thereby missed.

These conditions, and the principle on which they are based, will be familiar as being similar to, although broader than, the necessity principle which the Philips Commission wanted to provide in relation to all arrests. What PACE has provided is that the necessity principle applies not in relation to all offences (which would have been an inhibitory rule), but in relation to non-arrestable offences only. Thus arrests can be made for arrestable offences even where it is reasonably believed that a summons would have been both practicable and appropriate. As an extension of the law of arrest, this is an enabling rule. Had the Divisional Court in *G v DPP*

---

15 *Edwards v DPP* (1993) 97 Cr App Rep 301.
16 [1989] Crim LR 150. The sparse details given in this report are fleshed out by A Lawson, 'Whither the "General Arrest Conditions"?' [1993] Crim LR 567.
17 See Lawson [1993] for a critique of the Divisional Court's reasoning.

upheld the arrest, the arrest conditions would have been rendered entirely presentational, for since all arrests are of suspected offenders the proposition of the police in that case would have justified the arrest of any and every suspect. As it is, there remains at least some potential inhibitory element in s 25, preventing it from being limitlessly enabling.[18]

A system based on the 'freedom' approach would not countenance the enabling element of s 25 in this form. To allow arrest for any offence if, for instance, the offender is unlikely to answer a summons fails to balance the certain freedom lost by arrest with, first, the extent of the freedom lost to victims by allowing relatively minor offences to go unpunished; and, secondly, the possible loss of freedom involved when it is only feared (not known) that an offender will not answer a summons. The freedom approach, in other words, would allow arrest for some non-arrestable offences on the sort of grounds found in s 25, but only after balancing seriousness of offence and the degree of probability of what is feared actually occurring. The same approach would also be adopted, as the Philips Commission wanted, in relation to many offences which are currently arrestable under s 24.

(d) Other statutory powers of arrest

Section 26 of and Sch 2 to PACE preserve the summary arrest powers provided by 21 existing statutes. As in relation to stop and search, PACE adds to, but rarely takes away, police powers.[19] Thus, police power is continually being extended. There are a large number of statutes providing arrest powers for specific offences, including the Bail Act 1976 (s 7) allowing arrest of persons who breach bail conditions, the Street Offences Act 1959, allowing arrest for soliciting and loitering for prostitution, various statutory drunkenness and vagrancy offences, and the power to 'remove' truanting children provided by the Crime and Disorder Act (s 16).

There are two broad categories of particular importance. The first is public order. The use of the criminal law to restrict public activity has steadily increased over the years, as have the powers of the police to enforce it. The Public Order Act 1936 was replaced by a new Act (with additional offences) in 1986, and the Criminal Justice and Public Order Act 1994 has added further offences. The police may arrest for the offences created by this legislation on the same basis that they may arrest for arrestable offences under s 24.

The second category is terrorism. Under the 1979 Prevention of Terrorism Act (PTA) the police could arrest for various terrorist offences simply on 'suspicion' that a terrorist offence had been, or was about to be,

---

18 See ch 2, section 1(d) for the meaning of 'enabling' and 'inhibitory' rules.
19 Although s 26 did abolish powers of summary arrest not explicity preserved.

committed. In *Fox, Campbell and Hartley v UK*[20] it was held that the ECHR Art 5 (1) (c) requirement of 'reasonable suspicion' could not be dispensed with even in the exceptional circumstances of terrorism. The Government had already changed the law in anticipation of this, and now the PTA 1989, s 14 (1) requires reasonable suspicion. However, three concerns, in particular, remain. First, in addition to allowing the arrest of those reasonably suspected to be guilty of various offences under the Act, and of those subject to an 'exclusion order', an officer may also arrest 'a person who is or has been concerned in the commission, preparation, or instigation of an act of terrorism to which this section applies.'[1] Although 'terrorism' usually involves crimes of great seriousness, no specific crime need be suspected under s 14 (1) (b), yet Art 5 (1) (c) talks about reasonable suspicion of an 'offence'. In *Brogan* it was held by the European Court that 'terrorism' came within the Convention's notion of an offence, and so this provision remains lawful.[2]

Second, what is 'reasonable suspicion' in the terrorism context? In *Fox, Campbell and Hartley v UK*,[3] the Court said that 'What may be regarded as 'reasonable' will however depend on all the circumstances . . . in view of all the difficulties inherent in the investigation and prosecution of terrorist-type offences in Northern Ireland, the 'reasonableness' of the suspicion justifying such arrests cannot always be judged according to the same standards as are applied in dealing with conventional crime. Nevertheless, the exigencies of dealing with terrorist crime cannot justify stretching the notion of 'reasonableness' to the point where the essence of the safeguard secured by Art 5 para 1 (c) is impaired . . .' This meant that the government had to furnish some information which could lead the court to accept the reasonableness of the suspicion. In that particular case the only basis for suspicion was the convictions of the suspects for terrorist acts seven years previously, and so there was held to be a breach of Art 5.

Third, for what purposes may there be an arrest? Article 5(1)(b) requires that in the absence of reasonable suspicion arrest may be made only pursuant to a 'lawful order of a court or . . . any obligation prescribed by law' (excepting some other technical reasons of no relevance here). In *McVeigh, O'Neill and Evans v UK*[4] the applicants were arrested in Liverpool, when they arrived from Ireland, in order to be 'examined' (a procedure akin to extended stop, search and questioning specific to the terrorism legislation, discussed in ch 2, section 3). The European Commission on Human Rights (in a preliminary procedure to a Court hearing) decided that 'the existence of organised terrorism is a feature of modern

20 (1990) 13 EHRR 157.
1   PTA 1989, s 14(1)(b).
2   (1988) 11 EHRR 117.
3   (1990) 13 EHRR 157.
4   (1981) 25 DR 15.

life whose emergence since the Convention was drafted cannot be ignored any more than the changes in social conditions and moral opinion which have taken place in the same period . . . the Convention organs must always be alert to the danger in this sphere adverted to by the Court, of undermining or even destroying democracy on the ground of defending it'. However, '. . . some compromise between the requirements for defending democratic society and individual rights is inherent in the system of the Convention . . .' Applying that principle to the specific context of the case, the Commission decided that the requirement to be examined was a lawful obligation for the purposes of Art 5 (1) (b), but only because of the limited circumstances (travel across a border), the 'threat from organised terrorism', and the fact that arrest and detention was rarely used to secure examinations.

In these cases the European Court is adopting a 'context-sensitive' approach which is consistent with the 'freedom' approach outlined in ch 1. However, whether its sensitivity is accurate depends on whether its confidence in the government and its agencies, that these provisions are rarely abused, is justified. Hillyard estimates that, out of some 2,308 people arrested under this legislation between 1974 and 1981, 1,984 (86%) were released without any legal action being taken.[5] He argues that most of these arrests were information-gathering in purpose and that, with such a high no-action rate, it is not plausible that there was reasonable suspicion in most of these cases. He points out that after major events there are often mass arrests. After the Woolwich and Guildford bombings of 1974, for example, 76 people were arrested, but only four - the 'Guildford Four' - were charged. Could there really have been 'reasonable suspicion' against the other 72, or even the majority of them?

Another example of the Court's misplaced sense of context-sensitivity is its view that the Convention obligation to inform someone promptly of the reason for their arrest (discussed in section 5 later) is discharged if the reason for the arrest becomes apparent in the interview. Whilst this might be reasonable in terms of time-scale, it is of little value if the reason for the provision is to reduce the disorientation of the suspect. And it might be unrealistic when one considers how hostile many 'interviews' are (see ch 5).

(e) Common law breach of the peace

Police may arrest if a breach of a peace is occurring, is imminent, or has recently happened and is likely to recur.[6] This means that the powers of arrest for breach of the peace are rather more restricted than the powers of

---

5 Hillyard (1993) ch 4.
6 *Howell* [1981] 3 All ER 383.

arrest for arrestable offences. Judgment is required, not only in relation to whether the breach of the peace is occurring, but also in relation to the question of imminence and recurrence. The police have 'the right to take reasonable steps to make the person who is breaking or threatening to break the peace refrain from doing so; and those reasonable steps in appropriate cases will include detaining him against his will.'[7]

What constitutes a breach of the peace is not always obvious. In *Howell*[8] the Court of Appeal confirmed the view that a breach of the peace must be related to violence: a breach of the peace occurs when harm is done, is likely to be done, or if someone fears that violence may occur. Thus threatening, abusive or insulting behaviour does not in itself constitute a breach of the peace, although it would if a police officer reasonably regarded it as likely to cause imminent violence. Demonstrations, picketing, disputes between neighbours, street brawls and so forth are the usual context for this type of problem, although this does not mean that most demonstrations—any more than most disputes between neighbours —actually end in breach of the peace. The lack of precision here offends the freedom perspective, for it leaves citizens unclear about what they can and cannot do without risking a 'breach of the peace arrest'.[9] It could also cause these laws to fall foul of the ECHR's principles of legality and forseeability, although the conservatism of the Court's judgments in this area (and, in future, the likely conservatism of the English courts' interpretation of the ECHR under the HRA) makes this unlikely.[10]

Belief in the imminence of a breach of the peace is necessarily difficult to pin down. This was particularly evident in the miners' strike of the mid-1980s where there was a number of violent confrontations at pits where miners refused to strike. In *Moss v McLachlan*,[11] 60 miners were stopped by a police roadblock on the M1 motorway while on their way to picket some pits a few miles away. They carried banners and shouted abuse at a lorry driver who was passing the road block to break the strike. The men could only be arrested if it was suspected that a breach of the peace was

---

7 *Albert v Lavin* [1981] 3 All ER 878 at 880.
8 [1981] 3 All ER 383.
9 Note, however, that in *Bibby v Chief Constable of Essex* (2000) 164 JP 297, CA, the circumstances in which someone *not* acting unlawfully could be arrested to avert a breach of the peace were confirmed as very narrow. The court ruled that there must be: the clearest of circumstances and a sufficiently real and present threat to the peace to justify this extreme step; the threat must be coming from the person who was to be arrested; the conduct must clearly interfere with the rights of others; the natural consequence of the conduct must be violence from a third party; and the conduct of the person arrested must be unreasonable.
10 D Nicolson and K Reid, 'Arrest for Breach of the Peace and the European Convention on Human Rights' [1996] Crim LR 764.
11 [1985] IRLR 76.

likely to occur. Skinner J stated that, provided the police officers 'honestly and reasonably form the opinion that there is a real risk of a breach of the peace in the sense that it is in close proximity both in place and time then the conditions exist for reasonable preventive action including if necessary the measures taken in this case [that is to say arrest] . . . The possibility of a breach must be real to justify any preventive action. The imminence or immediacy of the threat to the peace determines what action is reasonable.'[12]

In this particular case, the miners were abusive and the pits to which they were travelling were nearby, so it may be that the police were justified in the roadblock and the arrest of the men on those grounds. However, in another miners' strike incident, the police established a roadblock at the Dartford Tunnel near London, over 100 miles from the area which some miners intended to picket. The miners were turned back on the same basis as in *Moss v McLachlan*, even though it could hardly be said that a breach of the peace was imminent or proximate in these circumstances.[13]

There were many other incidents where striking miners were stopped by the police and were told when and how they could travel in the vicinity of working mines. Sometimes these miners were on their way to picket, and arguably there was a risk of a breach of the peace. However, police invocation of the breach of the peace law against striking miners spilled over into general restrictions on the liberty of striking miners and other members of mining communities. As one present put it, 'There were no justifications, just the threat of arrest if we failed to comply.'[14] It seems that a lot of police action threatened the use of these arrest powers to prevent picketing, regardless of whether there was an imminent risk of breaches of the peace. At times, such as these, of crises of law and order, legalistic models of policing simply collapse.[15] Police powers are stretched to enable the police to fulfil wider functions than would be possible if due process principles prevailed. Many arrests were made in order to stop the picketers carrying out their objective, rather than to prosecute, which could be a breach of the ECHR Art 5(1) (c) and perhaps domestic law.[16] And the way those powers were used were often aggressive, sometimes to the point of violent. One chief constable commented that people '. . .saw police officers being injured, they saw police officers inflicting injuries . . .'.[17] One

---

12 [1985] IRLR at 78-79.

13 R East and P Thomas, 'Freedom of Movement: *Moss v McLachlan*' (1985) 12 JLS 77.

14 P Green, *The Enemy Without: Policing and Class Consciousness in the Miners' Strike* (Milton Keynes: Open UP, 1990) p 63.

15 See I Balbus, *The Dialectics of Legal Repression* (New York: Russell Sage, 1973); and R Vogler, 'Magistrates and Civil Disorder' (November 1982) LAG Bull, 12.

16 Nicolson and Reid [1996] pp 771-2; and see discussion of *Plange* in section 4(b)(ii) below.

17 R Reiner, *Chief Constables* (Oxford: OUP, 1991) p 183.

result, according to a police officer, is that 'You enjoy the power it gives to inflict the collective will of the job on to a large crowd of people. . . . You are part of a vast crowd and if the whole thing is wrong or illegal, it's not you who's going to be picked up for it. That sort of violence becomes addictive.'[18]

The issue of freedom is central here, as the miners' strike represented a clash between the freedom of strikers to pursue their objectives by encroaching on the freedom of working miners and their employers, and the freedom of working miners to pursue their objectives in ways that undermined the objectives of the strikers. However, this is essentially a political clash. The law - and certainly the criminal law - should therefore have little part to play unless the striking (or working) miners committed acts that would have been criminal in any context (such as assault and criminal damage). By using arrest powers in respect of breach of the peace to protect the working miners, the police and judiciary elevated the freedom of strike-breakers and their employers over that of the striking miners. Nicolson and Reid argue that this could be a breach of Arts 10 and 11 of the ECHR (the protection of freedom of expression, peaceful association and assembly).[19] Further, the police committed far more resources to 'upholding the law' than could be justified, in a freedom model, by the seriousness of the offences being prevented or committed. The excessive force in, and 'stretched' legal justification for, many of these arrests are also antithetical to the freedom model. Finally, as the last chapter showed in a less extreme form in relation to stop-search, this type of policing alienates the communities subject to this policing as well as other communities, groups and individuals sympathetic to those being policed in this way. That creates further losses of freedom: the police receive less co-operation from those they have already alienated, become more divided from the rest of society, and become brutalised, increasingly seeing coercion rather than co-operation as the most viable law enforcement strategy. As the officer quoted in the preceding paragraph put it, the use of direct power in these ways '. . . was slightly awesome but after a while it became easy.' And the chief constable also quoted there feared, as a result, '. . . that the whole perception of police-public relations has changed in people's minds.'[20]

(f) Citizen's arrest

Before 1829, there was no organised professional police force in England and Wales, and it was many years before the police operated across the

18   R Graef, 'A spiral of mutual mistrust' (1989) *Independent*, 12 May.
19   Nicolson and Reid [1996] pp 772-4.
20   See generally C Townshend, *Making the Peace: Public Order and Public Security in Modern Britain* (Oxford: OUP, 1993) ch 9.

whole country. Before the establishment of the modern police, all citizens had the power to arrest suspects, and police powers were originally no greater than those of ordinary citizens. Little or no distinction was made, in theory, between the two, and arrestees had to be taken before the magistrates immediately, no matter who arrested them. Thus we find the Royal Commission on Police Powers and Procedure of 1929 saying:

> 'The principle remains that a policeman, in the view of the common law, is only "a person paid to perform, as a matter of duty, acts which if he was so minded he might have done voluntarily."'[1]

However true this might once have been, the police are now in a completely different position to that of a citizen. In recent years in particular, police officers have been given considerably more power than ordinary citizens. The powers of arrest for the new offences mentioned in section (d) above in the CJPO 1994 and in the Prevention of Terrorism Acts, for example, are available to police officers only. And the main arrest power in PACE - s 24 - only partially applies to citizens. Under s 24, citizens may arrest without warrant persons who are committing or are reasonably suspected to be committing, an arrestable offence. Where such an offence has been committed, citizens may arrest anyone guilty, or reasonably suspected to be guilty, of the offence. This means that citizen's arrests may lawfully take place for past and present but not future offences; and, for past offences, the offence must have been committed. It is not enough that there be reasonable suspicion that an offence occurred.

The citizen thus faces procedural complications under s 24 of PACE that do not apply to police officers.[2] A case which illustrates this is *Self*,[3] in which the defendant was seen taking a box of chocolates out of a shop. After being followed, he was arrested for theft and for 'assault with intent to resist lawful arrest' (he hit the shop assistant who carried out the citizen's arrest). He was acquitted of theft but convicted of assault. On appeal, it was held that if he had not committed theft the arrest was unlawful, even though reasonable suspicion existed, and therefore the conviction for assault must be quashed, since it is not a crime to resist unlawful arrest.

A large number of arrests, especially for shoplifting, are made by citizens. In most of these cases, the initial arrest is carried out by a shop employee; either a store detective employed for that purpose, or a member of the

---

1   Cmd 3297. Quoted in Royal Commission on Criminal Procedure, The Investigation and Prosecution of Criminal Offences in England and Wales: The Law and Procedure (Cmnd 8092-1) (London: HMSO, 1981) p 2.

2   Although, like police officers, citizens amy lawfully arrest in relation to committed offences even if they lacked reasonable suspicion that an offence had been committed. As discussed in section 3(b) above, this is contrary to Art 5 of the ECHR.

3   [1992] 3 All ER 476.

management. These are ordinary citizens for the purposes of the law, so when they detain people until the police arrive, they make citizen's arrests.

It is also common for store detectives to call the police before arresting, and let the police arrest. This may appear safer for the store detective. If s/he simply conveys the information that led to suspicion to the police, then the arrest is that of the police and there is no responsibility on the store detective.[4] It has been suggested, however, that if the store detective asks the police to arrest and does not give enough information for them to evaluate whether the suspicion was based on reasonable grounds, then the arrest might be the responsibility of the detective.[5] If this is decided to be so, it would be odd. First, because constitutionally police officers are supposed to decide for themselves whether to exercise their powers: legal theory has it that even a senior officer cannot order another officer to arrest.[6] Second, because, in line with the first point, it has been decided that, where reasonable suspicion is needed for arrest, the officer actually carrying out the arrest must have that reasonable suspicion.[7] In other words, the idea that officers should arrest 'on instructions' should never arise.

The subject of a citizen's arrest must be placed in lawful custody as soon as is practicable. This is generally understood to mean either the custody of the police or (as used to be usual) that of a magistrate, but in some circumstances it might be better to take the suspect briefly elsewhere. This is not covered by PACE, and the common law is confused. *In John Lewis & Co Ltd v Tims*,[8] the defendant (D) was arrested by a store detective and brought before the store manager for questioning. Even though D was not brought before the police or magistrates, this was held to be valid on the grounds that the arrestor was acting for someone else. This is an artificial argument; after all, most police arrests are really on behalf of other people, namely the victims. But it would be far from helpful to arrestees had the law been decided otherwise; for the consequence of citizen's arrest would usually then be that the police be contacted immediately without the victim (or, more usually, a shop manager) considering whether such drastic action was desirable. Large stores often require their store detectives or employees to bring alleged thieves before the management to decide what should be done, and this can hardly be criticised.

A similar situation arose in *Brewin*,[9] where a child was arrested by an ordinary person, who brought him before his father. This was held to be

4   *Davidson v Chief Constable of North Wales* [1994] 2 All ER 597.
5   In *Davidson* [1994] the point was raised, but the Court of Appeal left the issue open as it was judged to be irrelevant.
6   *Fisher v Oldham Corpn* [1930] 2 KB 364.
7   *O'Hara v Chief Constable of the RUC* [1997] 1 All ER 129, discussed in section 4(a) below.
8   [1952] AC 676.
9   [1976] Crim LR 742.

an unlawful arrest, since the arrest was not made on behalf of the father and there was no firm intention to take the child to the police. As a Crown Court decision, this is not authoritative, but it does illustrate the problem. Perhaps legislation should provide for citizen's arrest something on the lines of the Crime and Disorder Act, s 16, which (in certain restricted circumstances) allows police officers to take truanting children from public places back to school. The danger is that something close to kidnapping could be legitimised if citizens were given this kind of power. What is clear, though, is that the current uncertainty and convoluted reasoning regulating the law on citizen's arrest is in no one's interest. This is because it is largely context-insensitive. A 'freedom' approach would authorise the arrestor to bring the arrestee before whoever could most sympathetically and usefully take the next step although, as discussed in section 2, a freedom approach also requires certainty in the law. Thus the type of person to whom the arrestee would be brought, the seriousness of the offence, and the period of time and conditions involved would all have to be specified by such a provision.

(g) Non-police agencies

A considerable body of criminal law is enforced by non-police agencies. For example, health and safety laws are enforced by the Factory Inspectorate, tax laws by Customs and Excise and the Inland Revenue, and pollution laws by the Pollution Inspectorate. These are commonly regarded as 'regulatory offences' rather than as 'real crimes'. They are not, however, always less serious than police-enforced laws. Tax frauds involve at least as much money as dishonesty offences enforced by the police. More people die through the negligence of employers in breach of health and safety laws than die as a result of pub brawls, muggings and street fights, and pollution is more of a threat to the public's safety than is drunkenness, prostitution and criminal damage.[10]

The criminal justice system does not seem to treat these offences with the seriousness one would expect in view of the harm they cause. More freedom is lost as a result of these offences than as a result of many offences for which the police have far more extensive freedom-taking powers. Non-police agencies do not have the arrest powers possessed by the police, so are in the position of private citizens in this respect; and these offences are rarely arrestable. Very few are subject to maximum custodial sentences of five years or more (and so fail to qualify as arrestable under s 24(1) of PACE) and neither do they have specific arrest powers attached to them.

10 See generally S Box, *Power, Crime and Mystification* (London: Tavistock, 1983) chs 1 and 2; G Slapper and S Tombs, *Corporate Crime* (Harlow: Longman, 1999).

Nor do stop and search powers apply. There is therefore no equivalent of 'street policing' for these offences. Investigation is either reactive, in response to a major incident, or routine, in which case appointments are made with the potential 'criminal' to inspect the premises concerned.[11] The result is that these offences have a low profile in the criminal justice system and in society at large, creating a vicious circle, whereby because they are little known, there is little concern about them, ensuring that maximum penalties remain low, ensuring that little remains known, and so on. This issue is followed up further in ch 6.

4. ARREST DISCRETION AND REASONABLE SUSPICION

(a) Reasonable suspicion

We have seen that the term 'reasonable suspicion' is used as a condition for most arrests just as it is for most acts of stop and search. Whether it actually means the same in these contexts is unclear in the light of the ECHR. Article 5 requires reasonable suspicion, but in *Murray v UK*,[12] in which Mrs Murray was held in her house for a short time under terrorism legislation, it was held by the European Court that 'The length of the deprivation of liberty at risk may also be material to the level of suspicion required.'[13] The logical conclusion of this is that the level of suspicion required for any arrest would be influenced by the length of time of (and perhaps level of distress created by) the arrest. Whilst these are relevant issues for a freedom perspective, the lack of certainty in the law thereby created is antithetical to a freedom perspective. Precisely how 'reasonable suspicion' will be interpreted in the future, and whether or not there will be one standard in all contexts is impossible to predict. It is, however, clear that reasonable suspicion is a lower standard than information sufficient to establish a prima facie case. To quote Lord Devlin in *Shaaban Bin Hussien v Chong Fook Kam*:

> 'Suspicion arises at or near the starting point of an investigation of which the obtaining of prima facie proof is the end . . . Prima facie proof consists of admissible evidence. Suspicion can take into account matters that could not be put in evidence at all.'[14]

11   K Lidstone, R Hogg and F Sutcliffe, Prosecutions by Private Individuals and Non-Police Agencies (Royal Commission on Criminal Procedure, Research Study no 10) (London: HMSO, 1980).
12   Series A, vol 300-A, (1994) 19 EHRR 193.
13   (1994) 19 EHRR 193, paras 55-56.
14   [1970] AC 942 at 948-949. See ch 2, section 3(a) for a related discussion in the context of stop and search powers.

This means that it is very difficult to control police discretion, although the courts have shown little inclination to exert such control. In *Castorina v Chief Constable of Surrey*,[15] for example, the police arrested a middle aged woman for burgling the firm from which she had previously been dismissed. The grounds of suspicion were that the burglary appeared to be 'an inside job', and she was presumed by the police to have a grudge. Against this, she had no criminal record, and even the victim thought that she was an unlikely culprit. None the less, the evidence was held sufficient to warrant reasonable suspicion. The court emphasised that it was not a pre-condition of a lawful arrest that the police believe a suspect to be guilty. The issue was whether, given the information the police had at the time of the arrest, their suspicion could be regarded as reasonable. The decision gives the police considerable freedom to follow crime control norms, in that it allows them to arrest on little hard evidence. As Clayton and Tomlinson put it:

'If the police are justified in arresting a middle aged woman of good character on such flimsy grounds, without even questioning her as to her alibi or possible motives, then the law provides very scant protection for those suspected of crime.'[16]

Arrests are frequently made by officers on the basis of briefings from senior officers. In *O'Hara v Chief Constable of the RUC*[17] an officer was told that O'Hara was suspected of a terrorist offence and that his house should therefore be raided and searched and he should be arrested. The officer did all this, and O'Hara sued for wrongful arrest, alleging the absence of 'reasonable suspicion', when it turned out that he was wrongly suspected. It is not known whether the arresting officer knew any more than that the officer who briefed him claimed to have reasonable suspicion, and the basis for that suspicion was not elicited in the trial. The House of Lords decided that the arresting officer did possess reasonable suspicion because, Lord Hope stated, 'For obvious practical reasons police officers must be able to rely on each other in taking decisions as to whom to arrest.'[18] Whilst this is a rational approach (in crime control terms) it begs the question of whether or not those officers upon whom the arresting officers rely should have to show the reasonable basis for their suspicion. As Lord Steyn said in the same case, an order from a senior officer should not be enough to constitute reasonable suspicion. Steyn's view is in line with both a due process interpretation of these provisions, and with the idea of

15 [1988] NLJR 180.
16 R Clayton and H Tomlinson, 'Arrest and Reasonable Grounds for Suspicion' (1988) LS Gaz, 7 September, 22 at p 26.
17 [1997] 1 All ER 129.
18 [1997] 1 All ER 129 at 142.

constabulary independence, but it is unclear whether the court as a whole shared this view. It was prepared to accept that there was 'scant' but sufficient evidence on the grounds that the senior officer had not been cross-examined on the basis for his belief - even though the onus of proof is on the defendant (ie the police). This undemanding interpretation of 'reasonable suspicion' fails to satisfy the demands of a freedom perspective.

It is not just police powers such as those in s 24 of PACE which give the police discretion, but also many substantive laws. Vague laws give the police considerable latitude in deciding for themselves what behaviour is or is not criminal and, therefore, arrestable. Ashworth singles out the Public Order Act 1986 (POA) for particular criticism. He points out that the essence of a public order offence might be thought to be that it engenders fear of violence and disorder among bystanders. Yet, as he says, the 1986 Act:

'goes so far as to include an expressed dispensation from proof that any member of the public was even at the scene, let alone put in fear—a dispensation which virtually undermines the rationale of the offence. These dispensations undoubtedly smooth the path of the prosecutor and make it correspondingly more difficult for defendants to obtain an acquittal . . . does it seem right to convict a person of a serious public order offence without the need to hear the evidence from a member of the public?'[19]

Ashworth's point here is that the police are enabled to prove that a public order offence occurred by virtue of what they alone saw and what they infer from what they saw. This gives the police enormous discretion in deciding what is a crime and therefore in deciding when they should or should not, and can or cannot, arrest. Thus a Home Office study found that some police officers use the most minor offence in the 1986 Act (s 5) to cover 'misbehaviour' that was not previously criminal, while other officers stated that this was unnecessary, as 'in the past, they would always have found a means to arrest if misbehaviour was sufficiently offensive.'[20] In one study of 60 disputes to which the police were called, there were six arrests. There was evidence to justify arrest on the grounds of the victims' complaints, such as criminal damage or assault, but the arrests were actually for breach of the peace, drunkenness or possession of an offensive weapon. This was because these public order charges:

19 A Ashworth, 'Defining Offences Without Harm' in P Smith (ed), *Criminal Law:Essays in Honour of J C Smith* (London: Butterworths, 1987) p 17.
20 D Brown and T Ellis, Policing Low level disorder: police use of section 5 of the Public Order Act 1986 (Home Office Research Study no 135) (London: Home Office, 1994) p 21.

'only required police evidence and, therefore, did not require the production of independent evidence from witnesses or victim statements . . . because of the permissiveness of public order legislation, they can figure out precisely how to charge a person after they have made the arrest.'[1]

The result is that police officers on the street can arrest in such a way as to make conviction much more likely. Their choice reduces the possibility that suspects will be able to challenge their actions and minimises the accountability of the police to the judiciary.

There is a parallel here with some non-police agencies. Health and safety and pollution laws require all 'practical' steps to be taken to prevent accidents, pollution and so forth. The enforcement agency decides what is, and what is not, 'practical'. This has the potential for working like public order laws, whereby evidence justifying enforcement action (failure to take practical steps to prevent the accident) also constitutes substantial evidence of guilt, just as public order laws enable arrest and conviction when an officer regards action as likely to engender fear in others. Despite the theoretical parallel there is a practical difference. Non-police agencies work out what is 'practical' with the firms against whom they are enforcing the law. This is like the police negotiating with Saturday night pub rowdies how many bottles they will be allowed to smash on the way home. Law enforcement is partly dictated by the law (in so far as, for instance, pollution inspectors have no arrest powers) but also partly by policies formulated by those agencies.[2]

(b)   Working rules

The imprecision of public order laws enable them to be used as a resource for the police. Enabling rules are contained within the law itself, allowing—but not requiring—arrest in a very wide spectrum of circumstances. But if the law does not dictate when and who the police arrest, what does? We saw in relation to stop-search that, in deciding when and how to exercise their powers, the police draw on their experience and institutional objectives, as mediated by cop culture. On this basis, McConville et al identified various 'working rules' which, they argued, structure police

1   C Kemp, C Norris and N Fielding, 'Legal Manoeuvres in Police Handling of Disputes' in D Farrington and S Walklate (eds), *Offenders and Victims: Theory and Policy* (London: British Society of Criminology, 1992) p 73.
2   See eg B Hutter, *The Reasonable Arm of the Law?* (Oxford: OUP, 1988) particularly at pp 132-133.

decision-making.[3] These apply to arrest just as they do to stop and search. What are these working rules? How far are they consistent with the reasonable suspicion criterion and legality in general?

(i) Disorder and police authority

Ever since the creation of the modern police in the early nineteenth century, the maintenance of public order has been its prime concern.[4] With no national riot squads and with very sparing use of armed forces in situations of disorder, the police have the lead role in these matters. Consequently, the maintenance of order is always a concern of the police, in general policy terms and at the street policing level.

The maintenance of police authority is linked to this. Since the police usually have little if anything by way of weapons, they rely on numbers and their moral and legal authority (as distinct from fear) to persuade people to do as they are told. This is particularly important when disorder is imminent (eg street fights and pub brawls) but also in 'straightforward' criminal situations such as theft and burglary. In order to maintain the authority of the police, people must believe that when police officers make requests or give orders they have a moral right to do so or that they can enforce compliance. Thus, as we saw in relation to 'consent' searches, the police often secure co-operation because people believe that they will have to do as requested anyway.

It follows that when there are challenges to police authority or outbreaks of disorder, the police feel the need to get on top of the situation quickly, preferably by securing voluntary submission. If this is secured, and if no serious offences have been committed, the police usually take no further action. Thus Shapland and Hobbs found that only 19–25% of 'disturbances' attended by the police led to arrest.[5] Kemp, Norris and Fielding found the police taking 'immediate authoritative action' (which includes arrest, but also removing suspects, reporting the incident and so forth) in just one-third of criminal disputes.[6] However, if submission is not voluntary, the

---

3   M McConville, A Sanders and R Leng, *The Case for the Prosecution* (London: Routledge, 1991) p 27. R Ericson uses the similar formulation of 'recipe rules' in *Making Crime: A Study of Detective Work* (London: Butterworths, 1981).
4   R Reiner, *The Politics of the Police* (London: Harvester Wheatsheaf, 1992).
5   J Shapland and R Hobbs, 'Policing Priorities on the Ground' in R Morgan and D Smith (eds), *Coming to Terms with Policing* (London: Routledge, 1989).
6   Kemp et al (1992). Also see C Clarkson, A Cretney, G Davis and J Shepherd, 'Assaults: the Relationship between Seriousness, Criminalisation and Punishment' [1994] Crim LR 4.

police will enforce it. Now that violence is unacceptable,[7] arrest is all that is left to the police. Arrests for 'contempt of cop' are fairly common. Thus McConville et al give examples of cases where the police arrested because, as the police told them in one case, 'you come to the point like a parent with a child where if you don't do something the others will all join in.'[8] In another case, the police officer explained that it 'would have been all right if he'd just gone away but he had to be Jack the Lad . . . I grabbed him and arrested him.'[9] Regarding a dispute over a restaurant bill, the arresting officer said:

> 'Had their attitude towards the police been different we could have dealt with it in a different way . . . but there were another five, perhaps six, customers in the restaurant . . . So far as I was concerned it had got to be taken away from there.'[10]

Further examples are given by Waddington, Choongh and Brown and Ellis. One officer, referring to a police Support Unit, said ' . . . these boys, they won't wear it [back-chat from 'undesirables'] . . . if they get any mouth, they'll drag 'em in.'[11] Another told Choongh that if someone swore at an officer he deserved to be arrested as 'We shouldn't have to take that kind of shit, and we won't take it.' This is why, he explained to Choongh, there were often arrests for seemingly trivial matters under s 4 and s 5 of POA 1986.[12] Brown and Ellis cite many examples throughout their report, concluding that the police view is that if those who abuse the police 'realise that they can get away with it, respect for the police will decline further, and they will be the targets of more abuse in the future . . . It is hard to believe that, given the apparent attitudes to the police of those involved and the circumstances of the offences, arrest does in fact serve those ends.'[13]

This is not to suggest that the police always arrest those that are abusive or not co-operative. The police have wider goals, as embodied in the working rules, in mind. So where one working rule (order, for example) is more powerful than another (authority, as undermined by swearing, for example), arrest is unlikely. Context is very important. Swearing in the context of a political or environmental protest is something the police are

7   That officers would habitually mete out 'street justice' in times gone by is well documented. See eg M. Brogden, *On the Mersey Beat* (Oxford: Oxford UP, 1991) pp 96-100.
8   McConville et al (1991) p 25.
9   McConville et al (1991) p 25.
10 McConville et al (1991) p 25.
11 Choongh (1997) p 68.
12 Choongh (1997) p 75. These legislative provisions are discussed in sub-section 4(a) above.
13 Brown and Ellis (1994) pp 42-3 and passim; also see, for one more example out of many, P Waddington, *Policing Citizens* (London: UCL Press, 1999) p 135.

more likely to understand and tolerate than when dealing with 'rough' youths in a city centre or on a problem estate.

What does all this tell us about how far 'reasonable suspicion' is an inhibitory rule? Firstly, the 'reasonable suspicion' element is often missing from public order arrests. The restaurant case was really a civil debt matter, and when asked the basis for the arrest of 'Jack the Lad', all the officer could say was 'it's Ways and Means, just to get him away, control the situation . . .'[14] As has frequently been pointed out,[15] where order or authority are jeopardised, arrest is a resource for the police. It is not so much a means of getting someone to court as a means of control. Not only is prosecution not the main concern, but sometimes it is not envisaged at all, and persons arrested in this way are frequently released without charge.[16] Indeed, Choongh argues that some sections of the population are subjected to 'social discipline' by the police precisely by arresting on flimsy or no legal grounds, humiliating them while in custody, then releasing them without ever having intended to charge them. The aim is to leave them in no doubt that they are 'police property', to be treated as the police wish.[17]

This argument is based on Choongh's observational study of the way the police deal with the 'rough' elements of society. But the same could be said more broadly in situations where the police seek to control rather than to prosecute. This is particularly common in demonstrations, often engaged in by 'respectable' people. For example, Waddington discusses a 'gay pride' demonstration which was about to disrupt a royal procession: '. . . .the protesters were arrested and . . . not charged, for the police purpose had been to maintain the dignity of the event by removing the protesters . . .'.[18] In most situations, the flexibility of public order-type laws discussed earlier makes it difficult to say that there was insufficient evidence to arrest, for little evidence is required by them. Thus Kemp et al found that the police took action in a lower proportion of disturbances where criminal laws were being broken than where they were being complied with.[19] As we have already noted, the few arrests that did occur were for public order offences, even though arrests for criminal damage or assault would have been equally or more appropriate.

14 McConville, Sanders and Leng (1991) pp 25-26. The wryly named (and fictitious) 'Ways and Means Act' is frequently invoked in the absence of more helpful legislation.
15 M Chatterton 'Police in Social Control' in J King (ed), *Control Without Custody* (Cambridge: Institute of Criminology, University of Cambridge, 1976); A Sanders, 'Prosecution Decisions and the Attorney-General's Guidelines' [1985] Crim LR 4.
16 Kemp et al (1992).
17 Choongh (1997).
18 Waddington (1994) p 184.
19 Kemp et al (1992).

162

The weak inhibitory quality of 'reasonable suspicion', combined with the overwhelming need of the police to maintain order and authority has powerful consequences. It means that arrestees tend to be those with an 'attitude problem'. This falls disproportionately on those who dislike the police—particularly young, socially marginalised, black males—whose dislike is thus compounded, increasing the probability of 'attitude problems' next time round. Stop-search, which we saw in the previous chapter is disproportionately used against these people, frequently adds another twist to this spiral of mistrust. For example, Home Office research on the use of the POA shows that many stops lead to abusive responses from suspects, and consequent arrests under s 5 rather than for the suspected offences for which they were ostensibly stopped.[20]

In the more politically charged atmosphere of major strikes, riots, confrontations with 'alternative' movements and so forth, the police—as upholders of order and the status quo—seek to arrest those who challenge their authority.[1] Again this tends to be young or socially marginalised males. However, the re-establishment of order frequently requires that the police take a longer view than simply arresting all and sundry: in order to re-take control of the streets in the 'riots' of 1981, for example, the police sometimes allowed a remarkably large number of offences to take place without arrest.[2] Arrests are often avoided during riots and demonstrations because they could cause trouble to escalate or draw attention to perhaps dubious police riot-control tactics.[3]

There is another parallel here with non-police agencies. Just as suspects are arrested or not in part on the basis of their perceived moral character (as displayed by their attitude to the police) so this is also true of regulatory offences. Carson, for instance, found that factory inspectors only took action against those who appeared to be cavalier and disrespectful.[4] It is not just the police, then, who insist on the upholding of order and authority. However, the fact that the 'clients' of non-police agencies are generally companies or middle class individuals who are respectful of authority may partly account for the lower level of enforcement of their crimes than of the crimes with which the police are concerned. And, of course, non-police agencies, unlike the police, do not deal with people who threaten political authority or the established social order.

20   Brown and Ellis (1994) pp 31-2.
1   See, on the miners' strike, Green (1990) ch 3 and B Fine and R Millar (eds), *Policing the Miners' Strike* (London: Lawrence and Wishart, 1985).
2   R Vogler, *Reading the Riot Act* (Milton Keynes, Open UP, 1991) ch 8; P Waddington, *The Strong Arm of the Law* (Oxford: Clarendon, 1991) ch 6.
3   Waddington (1994) pp 38-9.
4   W G Carson, 'White Collar Crime and the Enforcement of Factory Legislation' (1970) 10 BJ Crim 383.

(ii)   Order, authority and legality

What is the legality of arrests made without any intention to prosecute, or made because the police are concerned with order rather than specific offences? One might think that if there is reasonable suspicion, then - since statutes that provide powers of summary arrest require nothing further - the police need prove nothing more. However, we saw earlier that arrest is traditionally seen as a criminal justice mechanism: to either facilitate charge (or another legitimate disposition, such as a caution), or to facilitate the production of evidence relevant to the case. The case law on judicial review of executive action (including that of the police) requires that powers be exercised for a proper purpose and that irrelevant considerations be excluded from the minds of those exercising powers. In *Plange v Chief Constable of South Humberside*[5] Mr Plange was accused of assault by someone who then told the police that he no longer wished to pursue the complaint. The police nonetheless arrested Plange but did not charge him. Plange sued the police for unlawful imprisonment based on the claim that the arrest was unlawful as they did not anticipate, nor intend, prosecution. The judge ruled that there was no case to go before the jury, and dismissed Plange's action. On appeal, the Court of Appeal held - following the general public law principles referred to above - that, although there was no breach of PACE, s 24 (6) 'if it was proved that the arresting officer knew that there was no possibility of a charge, it must usually follow that he had acted upon some irrelevant consideration or improper purpose.'[6] On this basis, the case was returned to the court of first instance for a re-trial. This decision is consistent with the view expressed by the European Commission in *McVeigh*.[7] Arrest, it said 'must be for the purpose of securing [the] fulfilment [of an obligation prescribed by law] and not, for instance, punitive in character.'

This means that many unofficial purposes of arrest - such as to put the 'frighteners' on people, or to secure information about other people's crimes - appear to be unlawful, although many public order arrests which do not have prosecution in mind would be lawful if they were made on reasonable suspicion that a crime was about to be committed. Commendable from both a due process and freedom viewpoint though this may be, the court appears unaware of the large number of arrests which would be outlawed by this reasoning. A more effective way of securing freedom (if that is what the courts seek) might be to recognise the realities of policing and consider the most effective ways of regulating the use of arrest for non-prosecution purposes. This, however, is something that the government, not the courts, should do.

5   (1992) Times, 23 March.
6   (1992) Times, 23 March.
7   (1981) 25 DR 15, discussed in section 3(d) above.

In *Chalkley and Jeffries*[8] another common police practice was questioned. The defendants were arrested for a credit card fraud for which there was reasonable suspicion. The real reason for the arrest was, however, to give other officers time to install bugging equipment in their house in order to gather evidence of a far more serious conspiracy to rob. At trial the defendants applied for this evidence to be ruled inadmissible because it was, they said, obtained unfairly. The judge refused to do this. The defendants pleaded guilty because this evidence was so incriminating, but then appealed against the conviction, saying that the judge was wrong. The Court of Appeal said that 'holding charges' (that is, arrests for one purpose while gathering evidence of a more serious charge) were entirely proper if those arrests were lawful. Whether they were lawful or not depended on whether a prosecution was possible or not - and prosecution for the fraud was a possibility (unlike the prosecution for assault in *Plange*). It is not likely that the Human Rights Act will affect this. As noted in section 3(d) below, cases decided in the European Court on the Prevention of Terrorism Acts have allowed arrests for offences of which the suspects were reasonably suspected even though the main purpose of the arrest was in relation to terrorism. Although the Court interprets the ECHR in relation to the context (thus accepting that what is allowed in exceptional circumstances might not be acceptable in other circumstances) there is no reason to think that the situation in *Chalkley* would fall foul of the ECHR.

One might argue that what lies at the heart of the public law principles governing this area of law is not whether prosecution is a theoretical possibility, but what the real motive is of the police. However, from a freedom point of view the ruling in *Chalkley* might be acceptable on the ground that an arrest was made on lawful grounds, involving a small deprivation of liberty, in order to counter a more significant crime (the conspiracy to rob). This would have to be balanced against the value the 'freedom' perspective puts on honesty from the police in dealing with the public.

(iii) Suspiciousness and previous convictions

There is a line in the classic film 'Casablanca' when, following a serious crime, the police chief instructs his officers to 'round up the usual suspects'. These are, of course, people with relevant previous convictions. It does not usually happen quite like this, although it can if the police mount a major investigation.[9] Indeed, such investigations provide a good excuse for arresting local 'villains' to see what else they will 'cough' to. Many

8   [1998] 2 Cr App Rep 79.
9   McConville, Sanders and Leng, (1991) p 24.

people are arrested for serious offences because they are known to favour the modus operandi employed,[10] and many police officers spend time with arrestees in order to get to know their criminal character traits for future reference.[11]

'Previous' triggers arrest in three common ways. It is sometimes the first lead in a reported crime, the police arresting someone known to do this kind of thing or to have previously pestered the victim in question. Thus McConville et al cite examples where this was the totality of evidence; no further police action, not surprisingly, was the frequent result.[12] Secondly, knowledge of someone's previous convictions leads to that person being followed, thus allowing the officer sometimes to watch the suspect until he commits a crime.[13] Finally, as we saw in the previous chapter, just being a known criminal can be enough to prompt a stop and search; if this reveals, say, drugs then arrest will follow. The point in these second and third situations is not that arrest is per se wrong (although frequently there will be no reasonable suspicion for the stop, where it occurs, which preceded it), but that if such people had no 'previous', their offences would probably not have been discovered. Again, the pattern created is one which leaves 'respectable' people out of the criminal justice net and repeatedly enmeshes those with low status.

This is now being encouraged at the highest levels. The Audit Commission, for example, calls for a greater focus on criminals rather than crimes: 'Target the Criminal', it urges, by developing an 'intelligence strategy based on target criminals . . . build an element of proactivity into all detective duties . . . encourage the use of informants.'[14] This is part of the managerialist strategy discussed in ch 1 and the new form of proactive policing discussed in the first section of ch 2. Rather than being the neutral efficient strategy implied, the result is a skewed suspect population suffering frequent and disproportionate invasions of liberty.

Being 'known to the police' is only a special case of appearing 'suspicious', which we saw was a key working rule in relation to stop-search. Association with other criminals, such as sharing a house where drugs are dealt or being seen in public together, is particularly important. Some associates are arrested even when the police have no evidence at all of their guilt; here, arrest is used to secure witness statements and is entirely

---

10   See D Smith and J Gray, *Police and People in London* vol 4 (Policy Studies Institute) (Aldershot: Gower, 1983) p 345 and A Sanders and L Bridges, 'Access to Legal Advice and Police Malpractice' [1990] Crim LR 494.

11   McConville et al (1991) p 23.

12   McConville et al (1991) ch 2.

13   McConville et al (1991) p 24.

14   Audit Commission, Helping with Enquiries - Tackling Crime Efficiently (London: HMSO, 1993) exhibit 20.

without reasonable suspicion.[15] Other 'suspicious' characteristics include appearance and attitude to the police. Attitude is related to the question of authority, discussed above. Suspects who are not co-operative when apprehended are often formally arrested without more ado, allowing further investigation to determine whether or not they are likely to be the culprits. In cases like this, it is clear that arrest has moved to the start of the investigative stage—too early in many instances for reasonable suspicion to be formed, and much earlier in any event than used to be common.

Even where there is reasonable suspicion, whether arrest takes place depends on a combination—all other things being equal—of offence seriousness and offender seriousness. The police judge the latter, in the absence of information about 'previous', by the attitude displayed by the suspect. In a classic American study, Piliavin and Briar observed police decisions whether or not to arrest or warn juvenile offenders on the street: 25 juveniles were arrested or given official reprimands and 41 juveniles were released with no official action at all. These different dispositions had little to do with the juveniles' alleged offences, but had a lot to do with their demeanour. Most of the co-operative juveniles were released with no official action, while most of the uncooperative juveniles were arrested or given official reprimands. As Piliavin and Briar put it:

> 'Assessment of character—the distinction between serious delinquents, "good" boys, misguided youths, and so on—and the dispositions which followed . . . were based on youths' personal characteristics, and not their offences.'[16]

In other words, the police attempted to avoid rigidity by taking action only in 'deserving' cases, but they based that judgment on rather superficial personal characteristics. More recently in Britain, Southgate reported similar findings:

> 'Observers noticed cases where officers enforced the law "by the book" in response to difficult or hostile people, whereas they applied discretion to offenders of a similar kind who were more amenable.'[17]

15   These specific examples are taken from several others discussed by R Leng, The Right to Silence in Police Interrogation: A Study of Some of the Issues Underlying the Debate (Royal Commission on Criminal Justice Research Study no 10) (London: HMSO, 1993) p 25.
16   I Piliavin and S Briar, 'Police Encounters with Juveniles' (1964) 70 AJ Sociology 206.
17   P Southgate, Police-Public Encounters (Home Office Research Study no 90) (London: HMSO, 1986) p 47.

The result in Southgate's study was that official action (including arrest) was taken against 45% of 'rude, hostile' suspects, 22% of 'civil' suspects, 11% of 'friendly' suspects, and 5% of those who displayed 'particular deference'. As one officer said to the researcher, after finding that one driver had no car tax disc: 'If he had not been so unhelpful I might not have been so determined to prosecute him.'[18] The first named author vividly remembers being stopped one night when he might have been over the drink-drive limit. Remembering what he had written in the first edition of this book about the importance of deference to the police and being co-operative, he grovelled shamelessly and looked contrite. After allowing him to abase himself at length, the officers let him go without being breathalysed. The second author watched (with amusement) a similar performance by his own brother after he was pulled over by the motorway police after a series of sudden lane changes.

(iv) Taking account of the victim

Subject to other factors, a decision to arrest will in part depend on whether formal police action is desired by the victim. If the victim's evidence is essential to any consequent prosecution (which is by no means always the case) then there may seem to be little point making an arrest without his or her agreement. Reality is not, however, so straightforward.

First, the police themselves sometimes influence the wishes of victims. When the police attend the scene of an alleged assault, for example, they are expected to use their judgment to decide whether it would be better for the victim if official action were taken, to conciliate or just to warn the offender. They will often discuss these alternatives with the victim, who may have a preference but who will usually be open to advice. Officers who do not wish to arrest can easily make this appear to be an unattractive option, which it may indeed be.[19]

Secondly, the police always pursue grave offences. McConville et al report a serious rape case which led to mass arrests of a broad category of suspect, largely for purposes of elimination.[20] Clarkson et al examined nearly 100 assault cases. The police pursued five of the most serious cases (all meriting charges of inflicting grievous bodily harm) despite the reluctance and unreliability of the victims.[1]

Thirdly, some victims are more influential than others. Ignoring the views of some—local businessmen and politicians, for instance—would cause

18   Southgate (1986) p 101.
19   S Edwards, *Policing Domestic Violence* (London: Sage, 1989); Kemp et al (1992).
20   McConville et al (1991) ch 2.
1   C Clarkson, A Cretney, G Davis and J Shepherd, 'Assaults: the Relationship between Seriousness, Criminalisation and Punishment' [1994] Crim LR 4.

more trouble for the police than ignoring others. So Kemp et al comment that in civil disputes, such as trespass, where no criminality is involved:

> 'the police often take immediate action . . . to end the dispute, generally by ensuring the physical removal of the "offender" from the scene. For instance, all 11 requests made by publicans, security guards, shop/office managers, and private landlords in our 60 disputes were supported by the police.'[2]

Kemp et al point out that the police have no power to force individuals to leave, and that they could simply explain to the complainants their civil law rights. The important point for us, apart from demonstrating the willingness of the police to exercise authority even where they have no power to back it up, is that police authority is generally exercised in favour of powerful high status victims, rather than victims of low status. Thus Kemp et al discuss a 'domestic' assault where theft was also alleged but to no avail. They say in relation to this case, though it serves equally well as a general statement, that '. . . throughout the incident the wishes of the complainant become secondary to those of the officer.'[3] When the police did arrest: 'Victims' views were basically ignored and the offence and the offender became police property to be disposed of in the manner which most suited police rather than victim priorities.'[4] These priorities include police authority and public order.[5]

The police are perhaps the most influential victims of all. This was explored earlier, in the sense that threats to their authority make them victims. But it goes further than this. Brown and Ellis found that in many of the public order arrests they looked at, the police appeared to be the only victims, even though the POA is supposed to protect the public: ' . . . what is at issue in many of the cases . . . is the enforcement of respect for the police.'[6]

The police are acting entirely within the law in these examples, for there are no laws establishing rights for victims in relation to arrest, and the Victim's Charter[7] simply says, without referring to arrest, that victims will be able to explain how the crime has affected them and that this will be 'taken into account' by the police and other agencies. Exactly the same

2 Kemp et al (1992) p 65.
3 Kemp et al (1992) p 72.
4 Kemp et al (1992) p 73.
5 A Sanders, 'Personal Violence and Public Order' (1988) 16 IJ Sociology of Law 359. We shall see in section 4(c) that the situation regarding domestic violence had changed by the mid-late 1990s, as the Home Office and chief constables now recognise the dangers and contradictions of these practices, although the impact of official policy changes is limited.
6 Brown and Ellis (1994) p 42.
7 Issued by the Home Office: 2nd edn (1996). See ch 12.

findings have been made in the United States, suggesting that this is not a local or temporary phenomenon.[8] As with many aspects of the operation of police powers, it is not what was done, but who did it or who was the victim of it, that matters most.

(v) Other factors

The other main working rules give primacy to organisational factors, 'information received' from informants or co-suspects and workload. We examined the impact of organisational and societal factors on police discretion in general in the first section of ch 2. Arrests are as subject to such influences as any other aspect of policing. Periodic panics over vice, drugs, 'mugging' and so forth lead to surges in arrests for these offences. Sometimes individual communities or police forces adopt particular arrest policies, especially in the United States where there is more local control of policing than in the United Kingdom. In one study, the arrest rate in town A was over three times as high as in town B, giving the impression of a much lower crime rate in the latter. In reality, though, the crime rates were very similar. The true difference was that the affluent middle class residents of town B put enormous pressure on the police not to arrest their offspring.[9]

The police frequently arrest suspects purely on the strength of an allegation, or 'information received'. If the allegation coincides with 'previous', so much the better, as in a case cited by McConville et al: '. . . you have to react on what you hear initially . . . when we checked his form we thought there might be a chance; the name even rang a bell to the lads . . .'[10] Since this arrestee did not fit the description and absolutely nothing connected him with the offence, it would have been difficult for the police to claim that they had 'reasonable suspicion'.

Workload can have all sorts of effects. Police officers avoid arresting when they have too much to do, and look for arrests when they have too little to do.[11] The weather can also be important (when it is cold and wet, almost any excuse to get back to the station will do), as can a host of other trivial factors. Overriding it all, however, is the drive for 'figures' and 'quality figures' in particular. As Young says:

'In this [CID] world the detection rate is of vital concern, and a succession of poor returns in the monthly or quarterly detection

8   See E Buzawa and C Buzawa, 'The Impact of Arrest on Domestic Assault' (1993) 36 American Behavioural Scientist 558.
9   A Meehan, 'Internal Police Records and the Control of Juveniles' (1993) 33 BJ Crim 504.
10   McConville et al (1991) p 30.
11   Choongh (1997) pp 71-2.

figures can break the ambitious detective inspector . . . As a result, those calls for a change of emphasis to such matters as "crime prevention" have little or no chance of obtaining prominence . . .'[12]

Exactly the same point is made by Maguire and Norris, who observe that arrest and detection rates are still important promotion criteria; and by Choongh, who observes that uniformed branches, as well as the CID, are under pressure to arrest.[13] Since a charge (or a caution) counts as a detection regardless of the outcome (hence regardless of the evidence) the pressures to treat 'reasonable suspicion' lightly are difficult to resist. From a freedom perspective this is objectionable, because police power should be used only where it increases freedom - something that merely counting 'figures' cannot take into account. It is interesting to see that this view is voiced, in different terminology, by police officers themselves. Smith and Gray, for example, report many officers saying that they end up making 'pointless . . . unnecessary or unjustified arrests and stops.'[14] This is one instance where a move towards 'freedom' would not be resisted by the police - perhaps because the drive for 'figures' is pure window-dressing, and therefore no more about crime control than it is about due process or freedom.

The use of working rules to guide arrest very often leads to more of a crime control than a due process approach. This is not necessarily antithetical to a 'freedom' approach. If respect for the police, for instance, allows the police to continue as a largely unarmed force, then the use of arrest to enforce respect would be acceptable if it worked. Unfortunately, it generally has the same effect as stop-search - in other words it is counter-productive and leads to a double loss of freedom. In conclusion, we can see that when the police follow working rules they do not always follow the legal rules. This is because a) some working rules prescribe for the police unlawful purposes in some circumstances, and b) some working rules prescribe unlawful criteria for arrest in some circumstances. This conclusion has been framed in deliberately imprecise terms because the English case law is vague and still developing in unpredictable ways.

(c) Domestic violence and arrest

From a legalistic point of view, the use of arrest for domestic violence should be no different to its use for any other crime. Domestic violence is assault.

---

12   M Young, *An Inside Job* (Oxford: OUP, 1991) p 255.
13   M Maguire and C Norris, The Conduct and Supervision of Criminal Investigations (Royal Commission on Criminal Justice, Research Study no 5) (London: HMSO, 1992) ch 5; Choongh (1997) pp 69-72.
14   Smith and Gray (1983) p 60.

Whether it is a relatively minor common assault or a very serious GBH or attempted murder depends on the seriousness of the injuries inflicted, if any, and the intent of the violent partner. Normally, one would expect these factors (including the strength of the evidence of them), along perhaps with the wishes of the victim, to determine whether or not the suspect is arrested. However, until the early 1990s it was hardly treated as a criminal problem at all, except in the most severe cases. So the police generally arrested only when they both anticipated a successful prosecution and perceived the injuries and/or danger to the victim as very great. In a study carried out in London in the early 1980s, but which was probably representative of the general national situation, Edwards found only a 2% arrest rate.[15] Domestic violence (along with other inter-personal violence) was unusual in that victims withdrew their complaints against perpetrators more frequently than did victims of other offences, and the police usually took this to mean that a prosecution would fail. Thus not only were the police reluctant to arrest where the victim was ambivalent, but they were reluctant to arrest also where she did ask for strong action, because they anticipated her changing her mind and often encouraged her to do so.[16] This created a vicious circle, insofar as many women lost confidence in the police and so were reluctant to call them, or were easily persuaded to withdraw their complaints because they expected the police to do little or nothing. This reinforced police beliefs about the victims and their lack of resolve to see their partners prosecuted.

This unsatisfactory situation led the Home Office to issue a circular which urged the police to take a more interventionist approach, arresting wherever there was evidence.[17] Hoyle's evaluation of the effect of the new policy found that arrest was still infrequent, occurring in only 17% of incidents. Grace found similar results.[18] This is an interesting example of what happens when official policies (or, by extension, laws) are changed in an attempt to alter police attitudes and practices - some effect is discernable, but not as much as we would expect if only the 'normal' factors outlined in the previous paragraph were applied.[19] Hoyle found that 'cop culture' and 'working rules' still exerted a strong influence. The most important working rule, since 'suspiciousness' and 'order and authority' rarely applied, was the wishes of the victim. Whereas before the circular

---

15   Edwards (1989).
16   Edwards (1989).
17   Domestic Violence (Circular 66/90) (London: Home Office, 1990).
18   S Grace, Policing Domestic Violence in the 1990s (Home Office Research Study no 139) (London: Home Office, 1995); C Hoyle, *Negotiating Domestic Violence* (Oxford: Clarendon, 1998).
19   For a general discussion of the relationship between legal rules, policies and police action, see D Dixon, *Law in Policing*, (Oxford: Clarendon, 1997). For a more sceptical analysis, see the review of this book by A Sanders (1998) 25 JLS 443.

Arrest discretion and reasonable suspicion

the police rarely arrested even when the victim wished them to, the main effect of the circular was to persuade the police to arrest usually when the victim wanted, but still very rarely otherwise.

From a due process viewpoint, this might appear laudable. Arrests were usually based on a realistic assessment of the outcome of prosecution. But why did the police adopt this legalistic approach in domestic violence cases, and not in other cases? Why not arrest in order to put the 'frighteners' on perpetrators, or as a means of controlling their violence, as in other criminal contexts? Not only are the police inconsistent, but, from a 'freedom' perspective, they appear to have their priorities wrong. Hoyle, found, as have all other researchers, that most domestic violence victims suffer repeat victimisation.[20] In other words, their plight is far worse than might be suspected from any one incident to which the police are called. Arrest and, where appropriate, further action is therefore usually justifiable in terms of overall offence seriousness even if the specific offence to which the police are called is minor. Further, most women who call the police seek arrest even when they do not desire prosecution. They want the violence to stop, and time to consider their position.[1] Arrest provides this, and thus gives these victims far more freedom than is taken from perpetrators by arrest. While arrest on this basis (ie with, in many cases, reasonable suspicion but no intention or prospect of prosecution, let alone conviction) is justifiable on a freedom basis, and is common in other contexts, it would sometimes be difficult to reconcile with the law as stated in *Plange*.[2] In *Plange*, it will be recalled, the victim did not wish to testify, and - in the absence of other strong evidence - this meant that the case would not be prosecuted. This is precisely the situation in many domestic violence incidents, although if there was the danger of a further breach of the peace the arrest could be justified anyway.

It is therefore intriguing to find that the policy adopted in the 1990 circular is now being taken one step further. In the 1980s and 1990s US jurisdictions increasingly adopted 'mandatory arrest' policies for domestic violence cases: the police are instructed (not merely encouraged) to arrest, if there is sufficient evidence, regardless of the wishes of the victim or of the prospects of a successful prosecution. This is partly because attempts to encourage the police to change were only partially successful, like in the UK. It is also in order to take the initiative away from victims, in recognition of the intimidation and retaliation they suffer from many perpetrators who blame them for their arrest and (where it happens) prosecution. Mandatory or near mandatory arrest policies (known generically as 'pro-arrest' policies) are now becoming common in the UK too. Hoyle and Sanders found that

---

20   Hoyle (1998).

1   C Hoyle and A Sanders, 'Police Response to Domestic Violence: From Victim Choice to Victim Empowerment?' (2000) BJ Crim 40.

2   (1992) Times, 23 March, CA.

the police still did not fully operate the new policy, arrest rates in many areas being no higher than Hoyle had found them to be in the same areas when the 1990 circular operated.[3] Wright found the same in another area of the UK, and the same has been found in the USA.[4] Whilst it is, in theory, possible that police officers took on board the strictures of the Court of Appeal in *Plange* and perceive a conflict between the ratio decidendi of this case and the declared policy of their chief constables, the more likely explanation is that most officers either misunderstand the new policy or prefer to be guided by their own working rules. Victims of domestic violence are among the weakest groups in our society. Even though many are middle class professionals - domestic violence knows no class or ethnic boundaries - it is their abused status and self-image which makes them, in general, weak. The working rule relating to victims - that, in general, the views and interests of powerful victims only should be influential - remains in place.[5]

(d) Race, class and arrest

It is clear from the above that police working rules do not impact equally upon all sections of society. 'Cop culture' regards some social and racial groups as more criminogenic than others. This viewpoint finds no support in the research literature, although some groups probably do commit some types of crime more than do others. For example, young socially marginalised youths are almost certainly involved in more street drug dealing and robbery than are older people in regular work, but those older people commit other drugs offences and fraudulent crimes in large numbers instead. 'Targeting' may therefore be justified, but not in such a way that the offences which are primarily targeted are those which are, or are thought to be, committed by small sections of society.

The result of skewed targeting and the general operation of working rules based on police officers' cultural assumptions is a pattern of unjustified discrimination. For example, Stevens and Willis found that black people in deprived socio-economic conditions were no more likely to commit

3   Hoyle and Sanders (2000).
4   S Wright, 'Policing Domestic Violence: A Nottingham Case Study' (1998) 20 JSWFL 397. Regarding the USA, see, for instance, K Ferraro, 'Policing Woman Battering' (1989) 36 Social Problems 61. For a general discussion of pro-arrest policies, see R Morley and A Mullender, 'Hype or Hope? The Importation of Pro-Arrest Policies and Batterer's Programmes from North America to Britain as Key Measures for Preventing Violence Against Women in the Home' (1992) 6 IJLF 265.
5   The same kind of analysis could probably be made of black and Asian victims. The failure to investigate properly the murder of black teenager Stephen Lawrence has been taken by many to exemplify police attitudes towards ethnic minority victims of violence. See the Macpherson Report (1999).

crimes than were white people in those conditions.[6] Yet this study (pre-PACE) and post-PACE studies such as that by Jefferson and Walker, and Fitzgerald and Sibbitt[7] found disproportionate arrest rates among black people. Indeed, black people are five times more likely to be arrested than white people.[8] Although much of this is due to a higher proportion of black than white people in the general population being young and socially marginal, some of it is a product of proactive policing. Stevens and Willis found that black people were particularly liable to be arrested for offences such as preparatory and public order offences where 'there is considerable scope for selective perception of potential or actual offenders.'[9] Brown and Ellis, in more recent research, also found disproportionate arrests of black people for public order offences. Although they do not commit themselves to an explanation for this, they say that

'it may well be that black people are more likely to perceive s 5 warnings about their behaviour as provocation, leading to an escalation of the situation. Another possibility is that the police are more ready to react adversely where they receive abuse from black people.'[10]

Public order-type offences are classic products of proactive policing. They are, in other words, usually discovered as a result of police initiative, like other 'victimless' crimes (eg drugs, prostitution).

Around 75% of all arrests are for incidents reported to the police by the public.[11] It might be thought that this means that police bias through proactive policing would play only a small part in shaping the ethnic (and class) shape of the population of arrestees. However, just because the public report an incident, it does not follow that the public identifies the suspected offender. Phillips and Brown found that in 40% of arrests the main evidence was police evidence[12] - evidence which is often secured through the operation of working rules. That PACE has made little or no difference is evident from research by Norris et al. This found disproportionate stopping

6   P Stevens and C F Willis, Race, Crime and Arrests (HORS no 58) (London: HMSO, 1979).
7   T Jefferson and M Walker, 'Ethnic Minorities in the Criminal Justice System' [1992] Crim LR 83. M Fitzgerald and R Sibbitt, Ethnic Monitoring in Police Forces (Home Office Research Study no 173) (London: Home Office, 1997).
8   Home Office, s 95 Statistics on Race and the Criminal Justice System, 1997-8, HO 1998, Table 4.2. See discussion by P Hillyard and D Gordon (1999)
9   Stevens and Willis (1979) p 41.
10   Brown and Ellis (1994) p 33.
11   Phillips and Brown (1998) ch 2.
12   Phillips and Brown (1998) p 41.

(and disproportionate formal action[13] after stopping), of black people, even though their demeanour was similar to that of whites. The result is that, over one year, '. . . approximately one in three of the black male population under 35 would be involved in a stop resulting in formal police action in contrast to only one in ten of white males under 35.'[14]

It seems that just being black makes one suspicious and thus more liable to being arrested.[15] Fitzgerald and Sibbitt show this happening at a more general statistical level.[16] Being young and male, as well as black, is even more risky.[17] This is confirmed by the most recent research of all. Although, as Home Office researchers, Phillips and Brown are cautious in their interpretation of their figures, they show that not only are ethnic minorities over-represented among those who are arrested, but also that the evidence against ethnic minority arrestees is, on average, significantly weaker than against white arrestees. For example, in violent offences there was enough evidence to charge on arrest in 45% of white cases but only 37% and 17% respectively in cases involving black and Asian suspects, while for public order offences the corresponding figures were 84% (whites) 65% (blacks) and 64% (Asians).[18] The finding of the Official Inquiry into the failure to apprehend the murderers of black London teenager Stephen Lawrence, that the Metropolitan Police embodies 'institutional racism', fits in with our belief that simply being young and black increases the probability that one will attract police suspicion.[19] The extent to which this takes place is a matter of debate. But even Smith, who sets out to show that the massive over-representation of black people in prison is not due to bias, concedes that '. . . some bias against black people has been demonstrated at several stages of the process, and . . . some decision-making criteria clearly work to the disadvantage of black people. . .'[20] Or, as Holdaway puts it, 'It is not

13 This includes reports for summons and requirements to produce vehicle documents. There were too few arrests to make meaningful comparison of arrests alone.
14 C Norris et al, 'Black and Blue: An Analysis of the Influence of Race on being Stopped by the Police' (1992) 43 BJ Sociology 207 at 222.
15 The overall disproportionate arrest rates of blacks, as compared to whites, can only partially be explained in this way. The difference appears also to be due to the greater social deprivation of blacks and reporting and recording differences: Jefferson and Walker [1992]. Note that all these studies found that Asians were arrested disproportionately infrequently.
16 Fitzgerald and Sibbitt (1997).
17 M Fitzgerald, Ethnic Minorities and the Criminal Justice System (Royal Commission on Criminal Justice, Research Study no 20) (London: HMSO, 1993) p 16. This is all consistent with the American research. See Reiner (1992) pp 156-170 for a discussion of research findings from the UK and the USA.
18 Phillips and Brown (1998) p 45.
19 Sir William Macpherson of Cluny, The Stephen Lawrence Inquiry (Cm 4262-I) (London: SO, 1999).
20 D Smith, 'Ethnic Origins, Crime and Criminal Justice' in M Maguire, R Morgan and R Reiner (eds), Oxford Handbook of Criminology 2nd edn (Oxford: Clarendon, 1997) p 751.

either structural factors *or* police discrimination that lead to high crime rates for black youth but both.'[1]

Unemployed and low-paid people are also massively over-represented in the arrest statistics, even taking into account socio-economic conditions.[2] Only one-quarter of all the arrests in the most recent random sample were of employed people.[3] Hillyard and Gordon observe that arrest rates in the poorest areas of the UK are massively higher than in wealthier areas, reinforcing the 'north-south divide'.[4] In addition to community pressures and 'attitude' problems, these people are simply more vulnerable to being arrested. In 'Operation Major' in 1982, 283 people were arrested in one day and in one place on suspicion of fraud. Over 104 people were held for up to 10 hours before being released without charge. The suspiciousness which triggered their arrest was constituted by walking into a particular unemployment benefit office in Oxford. All people who walked into that office that day were, without exception, arrested. Some were accompanying claimants and not making a claim themselves, but were held anyway. This was not so much because they were disbelieved, for in some cases their innocence was obvious, but in order to prevent warnings being given to claimants due to arrive later in the day.[5] Clearly a large number of these arrests were made without 'reasonable suspicion'. Due process was completely sacrificed to crime control because of the nature of the suspects (claimants) and the victim (the government).

How can we explain the fact that many people are arrested on little or no evidence, in defiance of 'reasonable suspicion' laws, and that black people disproportionately suffer from this? We need to ask what the police want, and what they might fear, when they arrest. What they want is: to punish, by arrest and detention, those who fail to display respect; to maintain order and prevent further disorder or crime; or to secure evidence leading to prosecution and conviction. What they fear is adverse comeback if they 'mess up'. Arresting people on 'fishing expeditions' who may provide information, arresting people for the purpose of elimination, or arresting people to enforce order is therefore viable for the police if the arrestee is unlikely to sue, make a plausible complaint, or otherwise challenge their actions. This is true largely of low status people: those who are young,

1   S Holdaway, *The Racialisation of British Policing* (Houndmills: MacMillan, 1996) p 96. It should be borne in mind that the term 'high crime rates', in common use, relates to the recorded figures, which are a product of arrest practices as well as 'actual' crime. See pp 84-104 of Holdaway's book for a sophisticated discussion of race, crime and arrests.

2   Meehan (1993); A Sanders, 'Class Bias in Prosecutions' (1985) 24 Howard JCJ 76.

3   Philips and Brown (1998) p xii.

4   Hillyard and Gordon (1999).

5   R Franey, *Poor Law: the Mass Arrests of Homeless Claimants in Oxford* (London: CPAG, 1983).

black or working class (and especially of those who possess all three characteristics). Hence the pattern observed in relation to stop-search is repeated and amplified at the arrest stage. Patterns of bias are created through the following of police working rules which dictate who to select for arrest out of a much larger group of arrestable suspects. The rule that the police must act only when they have 'reasonable suspicion' is sometimes ignored in this process, but the flexibility of this requirement means that breach is often not necessary. It is therefore in part an enabling rule, allowing the police to use informal norms, and in part a presentational rule with little inhibitory effect.

(e) The experience of arrest

In this section of the chapter we have focussed on what 'reasonable suspicion' means in the context of arrest, how far arrest discretion actually adheres to this standard, and what the impact is on socially disadvantaged groups of the pattern of arrests. We did this because 'reasonable suspicion' is the key standard set out by law, and adherence to it ought to eliminate discrimination, or at least keep it to a minimum. However, it is not just the basis on which police power is exercised that is important, but also the way it is exercised. Tyler, for example, has found that most people can accept unjust results if they think the process by which those results were reached is fair.[6] If people are treated with respect and without unnecessary force when they are arrested, and detained for only as long as is necessary, their freedoms will be encroached on less than if their experience is unpleasant.[7] If we accept, as the Philips Commission did,[8] that arrest is intrinsically coercive, it follows that even a little overbearing behaviour on the part of the police encroaches significantly on the freedom of the suspect. The manner in which arrests are made is therefore of fundamental importance to a criminal justice system based on the freedom approach. And, as we saw in the previous chapter, the manner in which police powers are exerted is crucially important for police-citizen relations, which impact upon citizens' willingness to help clear up crime, which in turn impacts upon everyone's freedom.

In section 1 of this chapter, and in ch 1, we gave some examples of the way in which arrest can be humiliating or even terrifying. In another example, Choongh was told by a suspect that when he told police officers who stopped him on the street to 'leave me alone', they told him he was under arrest. When he objected 'he [an officer] punched me in the balls.'[9]

6　T Tyler, *Why People Obey the Law* (New Haven: Yale University Press, 1990).
7　See the discussion of the 'freedom' model in ch 1, section 11.
8　See section 1 above.
9　Choongh (1997) p 65.

Some readers might doubt the credibility of such a story. However, on one occasion, one of the authors saw outside his office that a store detective was struggling with a man who he had apprehended on suspicion of theft. The suspect's friend was remonstrating with the detective but did not physically intervene. Three officers arrived and arrested both men, dragging them to the police car. The friend, by now understandably protesting about his own innocence, was kneed in the groin to shut him up. Such examples often involve minority groups, such as black people or the Irish. In a prevention of terrorism example, 'out of nowhere, various plain clothes detectives pounced on us from behind and threw us up against the wall . . . they spread-eagled our legs. They told us not to turn around . . . One of them grabbed me by the throat and dragged me into one of the black Marias that had appeared from nowhere.'[10]

We suspect, but cannot prove, that socially marginal groups are treated disproportionately badly when arrested. We also suspect, but again cannot prove, that many arrests are unnecessarily violent, abusive or humiliating. We cannot demonstrate this because, even more than 'reasonable suspicion', the manner of arrest is almost unmeasurable. Further, it has hardly been studied and has never been the subject of litigation to our knowledge. The best possibility of control through the courts lies in Art 2 of the ECHR, under which 'No-one shall be subjected to torture or to inhuman or degrading treatment or punishment.' The examples we have referred to in this section of the chapter seem to us to amount to 'degrading treatment', although we have no idea whether the courts would agree.

None of this is intended to suggest that all or even most arrests are unnecessarily degrading. Sometimes the police make special efforts to arrest as clinically as possible. Waddington shows how when protests are arranged in advance, the policing strategy is also planned, usually with a view to minimising trouble for the police and disruption for the public. In an anti-poll tax riot, 'several people were arrested . . . the suspect was whisked away . . . what senior officers feared was the sight of officers struggling on the ground . . .'.[11] In this kind of situation, behaving badly to the suspect (in public at any rate) would conflict with police working rules. But sometimes behaving badly accords with such 'rules'. We need to question the idea that 'degrading' treatment on arrest is always 'unnecessary' in the sense that it is accidental or merely an expression of prejudice. We have seen that many arrests are made largely to effect control or assert authority. Sometimes the manner of arrest is intrinsic to this. Holdaway discusses how police officers often exercise powers intending 'education and punishment'. One example is where officers arrested some demonstrators who were sat in the road. An officer told him, 'There was a

10   Hilyard (1993) p 129.
11   Waddington (1994) p 56.

bloody great puddle by the side of the road, and when they were nicked they were swept right through this puddle.'[12]

We might therefore classify arrest-manner as follows: (i) normal, (ii) rude/aggressive (to further working rules), and (iii) rude/aggressive (due to spite or lack of sensitivity). We do not know the size of one group relative to another. Reducing the incidence of the third is realistic if police training and monitoring took these concerns seriously, but reducing the size of the second will be almost impossible whilst the police seek to 'discipline' large sections of society.

5. REMEDIES FOR WRONGFUL ARREST

What happens if the police arrest when they should not? Or in a way that they should not? We have seen in relation to stop-search (ch 2, section 3(e)) that the main problem suspects face in challenging police action is credibility. There are rarely independent witnesses to encounters on the street, and proving an absence of reasonable suspicion or reasonable belief is very difficult anyway. To these problems we can add the way the courts have interpreted the requirements of the law in such cases as *Castorina v Chief Constable of Surrey*[13] and those which we shall be examining later in this section.

Leaving such problems aside, what specific remedies are available? A complaint can be made to the Police Complaints Authority. This will be examined in ch 11. Exclusion in court of evidence obtained following wrongful arrest is another possibility, although this is a discretionary matter for the court even if the arrest is proved to be unlawful. The advantage of this remedy in relation to arrest is that it might deter the police from breaking the rules. However, it only operates when the police prosecute and would otherwise win the case. In other words, exclusion of evidence on the grounds of wrongful arrest only assists defendants if they are legally guilty, ie if the offences with which they are charged can be proved. Although arrest is lawful under PACE if the defendant 'is guilty of the offence', regardless of whether the police officer had reasonable suspicion or not, this is unlikely to be so when Art 5 of the ECHR takes effect.[14] Whether this would lead to exclusion of evidence cannot be predicted.

The main remedy available is to sue for wrongful arrest in the civil courts. Wrongful arrest is part of the general tort of false imprisonment, and

12   Holdaway (1983) p 10. See also Choongh (1997) for the argument that many arrests are made solely for these purposes, and that humiliation is central to this process.
13   [1988] NLJR 180, discussed in section 4(a) above.
14   See s 24(5)(a) of PACE, analysed in section 3(b) above, and the discussion there of Art 5.

damages can be awarded to compensate for loss.[15] Article 5(5) of the ECHR provides a right to compensation, but - as with unlawful stop-search - it is difficult to demonstrate a significant tangible loss from unlawful arrest. Juries had been increasingly awarding large sums, especially for exemplary damages. However, in 1997 the Court of Appeal decided that basic damages of only £500 per hour of liberty removed should be awarded, up to a maximum of £3,000 for a 24-hour period. Although extra could be awarded for aggravated and exemplary damages where the arrestee suffered particularly, the Court of Appeal limited this too.[16] Again, this is discussed more fully in ch 11.

Wrongful arrest occurs when the powers discussed in this chapter are exceeded. It also occurs when an arrest is 'unreasonable', even if no specific power is exceeded. This is because under administrative law principles of judicial review (known as Wednesbury principles) all arms of the executive are accountable to the courts for any unreasonable action. When using arrest powers, police officers must act in good faith, use the arrest powers for the purpose they were given, take into account relevant matters and disregard the irrelevant, and must not act in a way so unreasonable that no reasonable police officer could have so acted.[17] These principles, by their very nature, are capable of flexible application. It is thus crucial to examine the use the courts have made of them in this context.

Should an unnecessary arrest be treated as unreasonable? In a due process system, this would certainly be regarded as a wrongful arrest, but a crime control system would allow it if it enhanced police efficiency. We have seen that arrests need only be necessary if they are for non-arrestable offences (under s 25 of PACE) so it seems that, where arrestable offences are concerned, PACE gives priority to crime control considerations.

That this was also the pre-PACE common law position is demonstrated by the House of Lords decision in *Holgate-Mohammed v Duke*.[18] Stolen jewellery was sold to a shop by someone fitting the description of the suspect. There was therefore reasonable suspicion against the suspect. She was arrested and taken to the police station and questioned but not charged. She sued the police for wrongful arrest on the grounds that there was no need to arrest and detain her because she could have been questioned equally well at home or at work. The police conceded that she could have been questioned elsewhere and that she was not unco-operative, but they decided that she was more likely to confess if held in

---

15   For a fuller discussion of this topic see J Harrison and S Cragg, *Police Misconduct: Legal Remedies* 3rd edn (London: LAG, 1995) pp 134-147.

16   *Thompson v Metropolitan Police Comr, Hsu v Metropolitan Police Comr* [1997] 2 All ER 762

17   These principles derive from *Associated Provincial Picture Houses Ltd v Wednesbury Corpn* [1948] 1 KB 223.

18   [1984] 1 All ER 1054.

the police station. The arrest was not necessary, but from the police point of view it was desirable. The House of Lords declared that the question was whether the police had exercised their discretionary power to arrest in accordance with the Wednesbury principles. Their decision to arrest could be impugned only if they had taken into account some irrelevant factor that they should have excluded from their consideration. Since, the House of Lords decided, the greater likelihood of the suspect confessing if taken to the police station was a factor the police were entitled to take into account, it followed that they acted lawfully in exercising their power of arrest. This decision legitimised a police working rule which was then cemented into the fabric of PACE itself. The judges and Parliament thus seem to be agreed that the police should be encouraged to arrest whenever this would promote efficient crime control. This, again, appears to be consistent with the ECHR.

Similar considerations arise when considering whether the police have a duty to check a suspect's story on, or prior to, arrest. In Madden's case, a youth, who the police believed had been stealing, was stopped on the street.[19] They found on him a model car. Madden claimed that he had bought the car, telling the officers the name of the shop. Disbelieving him, the officers did not check the story. In the police station, he confessed to the crime but subsequently pleaded not guilty at his trial. He was acquitted, in part because he had a receipt to which the police had paid no attention. Given that his story could have been, but was not, checked, was this wrongful arrest? In other words, is there a duty on the police to seek evidence to dispel the suspicion which they may otherwise reasonably have, as one would expect if due process principles were applied? Or may the police do as they wish once a minimum threshold is reached, as in a crime control system? In *Castorina v Chief Constable of Surrey*,[20] the Court of Appeal faced the issue squarely, Purchas LJ stating that:

'There is ample authority for the proposition that courses of inquiry which may or may not be taken by an investigating police officer before arrest are not relevant to the consideration whether, on the information available to him at the time of the arrest, he had reasonable cause for suspicion. Of course, failure to follow an obvious course in exceptional circumstances may well be grounds for attacking the executive exercise of that power under Wednesbury principles.'[1]

Under this approach, the courts may only hold that the exercise of the discretionary power to arrest is unlawful in 'exceptional circumstances' and when the course of inquiry which was not pursued was 'obvious'.

19   See *The Guardian*, 9 March 1981.
20   [1988] NLJR 180 discussed in section 4(a) above.
1   [1988] NLJR at 181.

Note too that when these two conditions are satisfied, the arrest is not automatically unlawful since Purchas LJ went no further than saying that in such situations there 'may well be grounds' for challenging the exercise of the arrest power. The obligation to pursue a line of inquiry which might exculpate a suspect (so avoiding an unnecessary arrest) is clearly very limited. It is therefore debatable whether either Madden or, in the 'Confait Affair', [2] Latimore (who had a very strong alibi which was not checked by the police initially) were wrongfully arrested.[3]

The judges have considerable room for manouevre in deciding issues arising under the Wednesbury principles. The cases show that they have tended to adopt a crime control approach.[4] Judges have interpreted arrest rules in ways that enable the police to 'get on with the job', rather than seeking to inject inhibitory elements which would promote civil liberties and human rights.[5] This may be contrasted with a much more robust attitude to the actions of some other arms of the executive, where crime control considerations do not arise.[6] It is unlikely that incorporation of the ECHR will lead to a major shift in the thinking of English courts about the boundaries of lawful arrest. This is because in the cases of *Brogan* and *Murray*, discussed earlier, it was decided that it was not a breach of human rights to arrest someone on reasonable suspicion with a view to detaining them for interrogative purposes so long as the ultimate objective was to bring the person before a court to answer a criminal charge.

It is a clear case of wrongful arrest when an arrestee is not informed of the fact of, or the ground(s) of, his or her arrest as soon as it is reasonably practicable to do so. This has long been the case, according to the common law (see, for example, *Christie v Leachinsky*[7]), and the requirements to inform are now set out in PACE, s 28 and Art 5(2) of the ECHR. This is also consistent with the law on stop and search which requires that suspects be told why they are being stopped (see ch 2). Under the common law, this

2   See Sir Henry Fisher, Report of an Inquiry into the Circumstances leading to the Trial of Three Persons on Charges arising out of the Death of Maxwell Confait and the Fire at 27 Doggett Road, London SE6 (HCP 90) (London: HMSO, 1977).

3   Occasionally a suspect's 'alibi' is confirmed spontaneously by an independent bystander just prior to arrest, and this may lead a court to adjudge any arrest to have not been based on reasonable suspicion, as in *Conlan v Chief Constable of Northumbria* [2000] 6 CL 105.

4   See, for example, *Dumbell v Roberts* [1944] 1 All ER 326, *McCarrick v Oxford* [1983] RTR 117, and *Ward v Chief Constable of Avon and Somerset Constabulary* (1986) Times, 26 June, CA. See discussion in the 1st edn of this book at pp 100-1.

5   For an argument that judicial review based on the standard of Wednesbury unreasonableness provides inadequate protection for human rights, see R Singh, *The Future of Human Rights in the United Kingdom* (Oxford: Hart, 1997) pp 39-44.

6   The patterns of judicial control of discretionary powers are charted by J Griffiths, *The Politics of the Judiciary* 5th edn (London: Fontana, 1997).

7   [1947] AC 573.

information could be communicated by either words or action. In *Brosch*,[8] a citizen's arrest case discussed earlier, the manager had not told the arrestee that he was under arrest, or why, but since this was obvious it did not matter. PACE and the ECHR now oblige the police to give the reason for arrest explicitly, however obvious it may appear to be, as soon as practicable.[9] This imposes greater due process obligations on the police than did the common law.

Despite this, the police may not be subject to the degree of due process rigour that one might think from reading s 28. The first problem arises in relation to what is practicable. In *Murray v Minister of Defence*[10] (a Northern Ireland case), soldiers went to the defendant (M's) house at 7am, detained everyone and searched the premises. The soldier in charge remained with M. At 7.30am, he formally informed M of her arrest and took her to an army detention centre acting under a statute giving summary arrest powers similar to those in PACE, s 24. M's de facto arrest between 7am and 7.30am would appear to breach the common law and the equivalent of s 28. Following *Shaaban Bin Hussien v Chong Fook Kam*[11] (that, as in M's case, one is arrested if one is not allowed to leave the place in which one is kept) Lord Griffiths held that M was arrested at 7am (when her detention began) rather than at 7.30am when she was told that she was arrested. However, according to Lord Griffiths, 'If words of arrest are spoken as soon as the house is entered . . . there is a real risk that the alarm may be raised.'[12] It was therefore not practicable in his opinion to inform M of the fact of, and reasons for, her arrest immediately, and the arrest was therefore not unlawful. This seems to assume that the alarm was not raised when the group of armed soldiers entered the house, rounded everyone up, gave it a thorough search and did not even tell the occupants what was going to happen to them. The decision in this case does not alter the principle at stake but—unless 'terrorist' cases are being treated as special cases—it does suggest that drawing the line about when something is reasonably practicable is not easy. As it happens, as we saw in section 3(d), terrorist cases are treated differently, but where that leaves the obligation to inform 'as soon as it is reasonably practicable' is unclear.

The European Court is no more rigorous on this human rights point than the House of Lords, with whom it agreed.[13] It was even less so a few

8   [1988] Crim LR 743.
9   The reason(s) need not be a precise formulation of the law, however. See *Abbassy v Metropolitan Police Comr* [1990] 1 All ER 193, where the defendants were arrested for 'unlawful possession' of a car. There is no such offence, but as this encompassed all the criminal possibilities the officers had in mind, the Court of Appeal said that this was satisfactory.
10   [1988] 2 All ER 521.
11   [1970] AC 942.
12   [1988] 2 All ER 521 at p 527.
13   (1994) 19 EHRR 193.

years before in *Fox*.[14] The Court in both cases held that it became obvious in the interviews of what the suspects were suspected, and thus the actions of the police were held to comply with Art 5 (2).[15] In *Fox* there was a delay of seven hours, but the Court regarded this as complying with the ECHR's requirement of 'promptness'.

What if a court does hold that an arrest was unlawful because the arrest, or reason for it, was not communicated to the suspect? In *DPP v L*[16] the suspect was arrested for an alleged public order offence, but not told this. She was taken to the police station where she assaulted an officer. She argued that she was being held unlawfully, therefore her assault was of an officer *not* executing his duty. On appeal the Divisional Court held that her initially unlawful arrest did not prevent the arrest becoming lawful when, in the police station, proper procedures were adopted. Her acquittal was therefore held to be wrong.

The less demanding the judiciary is in interpreting statutory controls on the police, the greater the play allowed to crime control principles. Even when the legislature, as in s 28 of PACE, appears to be creating strong inhibitory rules, the judiciary still manages to draw their due process sting by rendering them largely presentational, and it does not seem that the incorporation of the ECHR into English law will change this.

6. CONCLUSION

The law of arrest has evolved to accommodate changes in police practice, although it has not legitimated all of these changes. The police can now use arrest to facilitate investigation, rather than just as a mechanism to bring alleged offenders before the courts. The courts, and now PACE, have allowed policing considerations instead of due process considerations to dictate the shape and content of the law. Crime control values underlie the law of arrest in several respects. Firstly, although the Philips Commission rightly saw arrest as intrinsically coercive and wanted to restrict it to situations where this was necessary, no such restriction is placed on the police in s 24 of PACE. Secondly, where the law was changed by PACE it was largely by providing arrest powers where they had not previously existed (allowing summary arrest, where 'necessary', in non-arrestable offences in s 25). Thirdly, whereas most executive agencies are increasingly subject to judicial review along Wednesbury lines, this remains exceptional

---

14   *Fox, Campbell and Hartley v UK* (1990) 13 EHRR 157.
15   An 'unacceptable dilution of a basic guarantee': D Harris, M O'Boyle and C Warbrick, *Law of the European Convention on Human Rights* (London: Butterworths, 1995) p 130.
16   [1999] Crim LR 752. Discussed further in ch 4, section 3(c).

in respect of arrest. Fourth, much that is a product of unlawful police action is held to be lawful, thus allowing the end to justify the means - eg where PACE, s 24 allows arrest without reasonable suspicion of 'anyone who is guilty', and where the courts allow an unlawful arrest to be turned into a lawful arrest. Finally, the substantive law in most public order offences and in common law breach of the peace is so vague that the police have even more freedom to arrest according to their own priorities than they would otherwise have.

The main due process element in arrest law is the 'reasonable suspicion' requirement, but this is such a low threshold that most arrests are based on weak evidence, and many are based on virtually no evidence. More investigation would be possible prior to most arrests, but this is not required by the law. The law offers little due process protection and, instead, provides wide boundaries within which the police operate according to their own working rules. Offence seriousness, the probability that the suspect has committed an arrestable offence and the views of the victim (although some victims more than others) all influence police decisions whether or not to arrest, but other police working rules are equally important. These are based on criteria of 'suspiciousness' and 'disorder' that—like stop and search—bear more heavily on some sections of society than others. Patterns of bias result which are a product only in part of police rule breaking. Some people are arrested as a punishment or enforcement mechanism in itself, or in order to gather information about the crimes of others, with no intention that they should ever be prosecuted. The leading cases, English as well as under the ECHR, can be read to mean that many of these arrests are unlawful, but it is so difficult to prove that the objectives of the police were unlawful that the prospects of changing police behaviour through the courts are slim. An equally great problem is that some sections of the population are constantly singled out when others are also likely to be guilty of many crimes. A skewed suspect population is constructed, which distorts the whole criminal process thereafter.

This problem can be observed on the broader socio-legal canvas when we consider non-police agencies. Though some of the criteria operated by these agencies are those used by the police (such as disrespect) the offenders are generally more 'respectable' and so application of identical criteria produces different results. In fields of employment and housing, this would be regarded as indirect and unacceptable discrimination.

However, it should not be thought that it is necessarily possible, or even desirable, to create due process-based arrest laws. As with stop-search, police-suspect interactions leading to arrest are fluid and unpredictable. As with stop-search, arrest is sometimes used in order to gather information, rather than as a prelude to court processes (thus limiting the accountability of the police to the law). Different arrest (and stop-search) patterns may not reflect different crime rates so much as different ways of securing criminal intelligence information.[17] Consequently, the police often arrest in ways that are abusive and humiliating, they do so in large numbers, and get poor results - 'poor' in the senses that detections are relatively few in number, generally for relatively minor offences, and discriminatory in the patterns they produce. The promotion of freedom is ill-served by this. For those of us who instinctively lean towards due process the response should not necessarily be to demand tighter definitions of 'reasonable suspicion', for this strategy is unlikely to work. Instead, we might take a leaf out of the book of the non-police agencies and require the police to arrest less and use summons more, as the Philips Commission recommended. This produces less coercion and less loss of freedom.

If we are to accept the necessity of crime control techniques, we might none the less seek a greater say in the crimes to be controlled. We might, for example, seek more public control over the types of situation for which arrest is and is not to be regarded as appropriate.[18] For example, during the miners' strike the police operated on the basis of political and social values not shared by many of the police authorities to which the police are nominally accountable.[19] By contrast, a stronger response to domestic violence, using mandatory arrest laws, might be sought, although we have seen that the police are adept at avoiding action—in this case, domestic violence arrests—which they do not favour. Adopting the 'freedom perspective' outlined in ch 1 should produce a more rational and less authoritarian approach to arrest even though traditional 'due process' standards would not always be adhered to. The use of brief periods of arrest in public order situations can protect the freedom of some citizens while impacting only marginally on the freedom of the arrestee. The same is true of mandatory arrest in domestic violence. Allowing arrests on the basis of 'briefings' is not contrary to 'freedom' if the briefer is called to account. Using arrest as a punishment, such as Choongh discusses, is, however, another matter entirely.

Finally, if we do accept the necessity of some methods of crime control in the interests of freedom, it does not follow that we should accept that model's assumptions about the reliability of administrative fact-finding. Instead, we should treat with scepticism police claims that, as professionals, they can be trusted not to make mistakes. No one with the amount of power the police possess should ever be trusted to that extent.

17   A Meehan, 'Internal Police Records and the Control of Juveniles' (1993) 33 BJ Crim 504.
18   This raises broad issues concerning police accountability. See further, R Reiner, *The Politics of the Police* (London: Harvester Wheatsheaf, 1992) pp 236-249 and R Reiner and S Spencer (eds), *Accountable Policing* (London: IPPR, 1993).
19   M Brake and C Hale, *Public Order and Private Lives* (London: Routledge, 1992) pp 44-58.

Chapter 4

Detention in the police station

A woman was arrested for theft. In the police station she spoke to her solicitor on the phone.

> Suspect (S) to the police custody officer (CO): 'He just said to tell you I've got nothing to say . . .'
> CO: 'But this constable wants to ask you some questions . . . whether or not you want to answer them . . . Are you willing to go into the interview without your solicitor present? If not, we'll have to . . . ask him to come down and then you'll have to wait, we'll have to lock you up.'

S decided not to wait. The interview took place without a solicitor present.

> S [After initially denying intent to steal]: 'I'm confused . . . You might as well put it all down as "yes". I did take them all.'
> Officer, 'With intent to steal?'
> S: 'Yes.'[1]

I. INTRODUCTION

When the police arrest suspects they usually take them to a police station, especially if they plan to subject those suspects to an intrusive investigation or to prosecute. It is only if they decide to release suspects immediately or (rarely) to report them for summons that they would not take this course of action.

---

1   A Sanders, L Bridges, A Mulvaney and G Crozier, Advice and Assistance at Police Stations and the 24 Hour Duty Solicitor Scheme (London: Lord Chancellor's Department, 1989) pp 123, 139.

Prior to the Police and Criminal Evidence Act 1984 (PACE), which came into force in 1985, the rights of suspects and powers of the police in the police station were governed largely by the Judges' Rules. Because of important gaps, their unclear status and their inconsistent enforcement by the courts, the situation had by the 1970s and 1980s become very confused. For example, the Judges' Rules were virtually silent on the permissible length of detention prior to charge. This led to the police routinely consigning suspects into the unsatisfactory limbo of 'helping the police with their inquiries'. The need to reform the law was clear to everyone, but the direction which reform should take was controversial. In the event, the government implemented the proposals of the Royal Commission on Criminal Procedure (the Philips Commission).[2]

In this chapter we assess some of the rights and powers provided in PACE, its associated Codes of Practice, and subsequent developments. In the next chapter we look at police questioning, most of which also takes place in police stations but which sometimes takes place elsewhere too. First we need to understand how the different models outlined in ch 1 approach the treatment of suspects in the police station.

In a crime control system, the police would have discretion to deal with arrested suspects as they thought fit in order to ascertain the truth. Suspects are most likely to co-operate with the police and reveal the truth if denied the opportunity to consult with friends, family or, in particular, a lawyer. Outside interference with the police-suspect encounter in the police station cannot be tolerated. The length of detention should be governed by considerations of efficiency alone. Suspects should be held for as long as it is thought that further questioning may provide useful information, but no longer.

In a due process system, the detention of suspects in police custody would be very tightly controlled, if it was allowed at all. Since the police should not arrest unless they first have sufficient information to prove guilt, it follows that there is no necessity to secure a confession from the suspect. Arrest should be followed by charge and judicial proceedings, not by administrative investigation.[3] Some interval of time must elapse between arresting suspects and bringing them before the courts, however. It may be in the suspect's interests to talk to the police during this period since the information provided may dispel suspicion and lead to earlier release. But this opportunity for dialogue may be abused, so safeguards must be provided. Suspects must be told that they are under no obligation to answer questions, that it will not be held against them at court if they

---

2   See I Bryan, *Interrogation and Confession* (Aldershot: Dartmouth, 1997) chs 7-9 for discussion of the Judges Rules and the pre-PACE situation.

3   See ch 3, section 2(a) above, for discussion of the place of arrest in due process and crime control systems.

maintain silence, that anything said may be used in evidence and that they are free to consult with a lawyer before answering questions.

The freedom perspective would be reluctant to allow police station detention on mere suspicion, even if it is reasonable. But the more evidence the police had, and the more serious the suspected crime, the more likely it would be that, under this approach, police station detention would be allowed. Also important would be whether the police could secure the evidence they needed by means which did not encroach on the freedom of the suspect, and on how alienating the experience of custody would be for the suspect.

We will see that the law steers something of a middle course between the polarities of crime control and due process, and even incorporates elements of the freedom approach, although this is not how it works out in reality. PACE allows detention for the purpose of questioning, but seeks to regulate the conditions under which questioning may take place. Police officers do not have complete discretion, but control or supervision is exercised by other (more senior) police officers. The intention of the Philips Commission was not so much to balance the rights of defendants with the rights of the police, or indeed to give priority to one over the other; rather, the philosophy was both to give the police more powers and also to provide more checks and controls on the use of those powers and to provide more safeguards and rights for suspects.

This approach is consistent with the European Convention on Human Rights (ECHR), which is now incorporated, as explained in ch 1, in the Human Rights Act (HRA). Article 5 allows arrest and detention on various grounds. The ones that concern us in this chapter and the next are

'1.(b) . . . to secure the fulfilment of any obligation prescribed by law;'

'1.(c) . . .for the purpose of bringing him before the competent legal authority on reasonable suspicion . . .'

One of the aims of this chapter and the next is to see how real the checks, controls and safeguards provided in PACE are. Another is to evaluate the probable effect of the ECHR and HRA.

2. THE POWERS AND DUTIES OF THE CUSTODY OFFICER

We saw in ch 3 that the police station has become the primary site of criminal investigation through changes in police practice. Changes in the law did not keep pace for most of the twentieth century, and institutions such as arrest changed their function without altering their form. The

'Confait' scandal[4] showed how important it was to recognise how much power the police held over detained suspects. This led to the acceptance, via the Philips Commission, that clear legal regulation of what goes on in the police station was necessary.

(a)   The custody officer

PACE created a new type of police officer named the 'custody officer'. Every 'designated' police station—that is, a police station which has the facilities to hold suspects for significant lengths of time—must have a custody officer available at all times.[5] Custody officers must be at least of the rank of sergeant,[6] but need have no particular training in order to carry out their duties. Any other officer may carry out their functions when they are not available.[7] The post is important, however, as it is on this officer that the main responsibility rests for the maintenance of the rights of suspects.

Custody officers are meant to be independent of any investigation in which a detained suspect is involved.[8] So, whilst acting as a custody officer, that individual must not be involved in the process of securing evidence from or about suspects. Although in some areas custody officers do that job and no other for lengthy periods, in others it is common to alternate this job with other duties. Brown et al found that these differing arrangements made no difference to the way in which custody officers performed their duties.[9] At root, a custody officer is still a police officer involved in normal policing. This creates role conflict for custody officers, requiring them to wear different hats, if not at the same time, then at least in close proximity to each other.

Arrested suspects are generally brought straight to a police station and immediately brought before the custody officer. The principle is that nothing may happen to that suspect after arrest prior to being 'logged in' by the custody officer. The custody officer fills in a 'custody record' form for

---

4   Sir Henry Fisher, Report of an Inquiry into the Circumstances leading to the Trial of Three Persons on Charges arising out of the Death of Maxwell Confait and the Fire at 27 Doggett Road, London SE6 (HCP 90) (London: HMSO, 1977). See J Baxter and L Koffman, 'The Confait Inheritance - Forgotten Lessons?' [1983] Cambrian LR 14.

5   PACE, s 36.

6   PACE, s 36(3).

7   PACE, s 36(4).

8   V Bevan and K Lidstone, *The Investigation of Crime* 2nd ed (London: Butterworths, 1996) pp 322-3.

9   D Brown, T Ellis and K Larcombe, Changing the Code: Police Detention under the Revised PACE Codes of Practice (Home Office Research Study no 129) (London: HMSO, 1992) p 34.

each suspect brought before him. Custody records vary from force to force but they all contain the same basic information. After some personal details (name, address and so forth) are taken down, the custody officer has to decide whether or not to detain the suspect and, if so, on what grounds, and whether or not to charge the suspect (and, again, on what grounds). This is all written on the form.

Custody officers have to decide whether the offence for which the person was arrested was a 'serious arrestable offence' or not. Serious arrestable offences (defined in s 116 of PACE) include murder, treason, rape, and various firearms offences.[10] Other arrestable offences can also be regarded as serious if their commission has led, or is intended to lead, to one of various consequences. These include serious harm to any person or serious financial gain to any person.[11] Serious harm or serious loss is defined as 'if, having regard to all the circumstances, it is serious for the person who suffers it.'[12] Thus a very poor person stealing a small amount might be regarded as making a substantial financial gain, where this would not be true if a rich person stole the same amount. And a relatively minor theft from a very poor person could be a serious arrestable offence, while the same value theft from a rich person would not be. Thus in *McIvor*[13] and *Smith*[14] thefts from a hunt of 28 dogs worth £800, and from a shop of goods worth £916 respectively, were not regarded as serious arrestable offences. The relativistic definition of 'serious arrestable offence' provides enormous scope for subjective interpretation. We shall see later what the consequences are of an offence being defined by a custody officer as 'serious'.

Now that an important purpose of arrest and detention is recognised to be to facilitate questioning, PACE has introduced a new regime for questioning aimed at eliminating the abuses which used sometimes to occur. The police may interrogate several times in any period of detention, subject to the rights of the suspect discussed later. But they may normally only do so in a room equipped for this purpose with tape recording facilities, in the presence of an appropriate adult (if the suspect is 'vulnerable') and in the presence of a legal advisor (if requested by the suspect). It is the responsibility of the custody officer to ensure that all these conditions are met. For example, as we shall see in ch 5, it is up to custody officers to ensure that police officers do not speak to suspects in their cell, in case unfair inducements or threats are made. Details of any visitors to suspects in their cells have to be recorded on the custody record.

10   See Sch 5 to PACE for a full list.
11   PACE, s 116.
12   PACE, s 116 (7).
13   [1987] Crim LR 409.
14   [1987] Crim LR 579.

The custody officer also has to decide whether to seek authorisation for further periods of detention (discussed later) and whether to allow other powers to be exercised. These include intimate and non-intimate searches of suspects, house searches, and the holding of identification parades. The custody officer decides whether or not suspects should be charged and prosecuted (discussed in ch 6) and, if so, whether they should be held in custody or released on bail (discussed later in this chapter). Again this is all noted on the custody record.

Code of Practice C (which sets out the rights of suspects in the police station and the powers of the police) also requires custody officers to ensure that suspects are treated properly in terms of food, sleep, warmth, sanitary conditions, medical treatment and so on. These provisions comply with Art 3 of the ECHR whereby no-one should be subject to torture or inhuman or degrading treatment. Although there are occasional abuses, no research has suggested that, since PACE was enacted, these provisions are frequently or systematically breached.[15] Clearly the custody officer role is of central importance but s/he is a relatively junior police officer. Throughout this and the next chapter we will see that, perhaps for this reason, custody officers do not carry out their protective role as one would expect from the wording of PACE and the Code of Practice. This raises the question of whether, if arrests on reasonable suspicion have to be justified by Art 5 1(c) of the ECHR (see section 1 above), a custody officer can be regarded as a 'competent legal authority' for this purpose.

(b) The rights of suspects[16]

Custody officers should immediately inform those suspects who are to be detained of their most important rights, both orally and by giving them a notice in writing. These include the right to consult a lawyer privately, which we will discuss in section 4 of this chapter. Other rights include having someone informed of one's arrest, consulting a copy of the PACE Code of Practice C and making a telephone call to anyone of their choice.

The right to have someone informed when arrested—otherwise known as 'intimation'—is described in the Code of Practice as the 'right not to be held incommunicado'.[17] Under s 56(1) of PACE, a suspect may have:

15 Although people detained under the Prevention of Terrorism Acts (PTA) in specially constructed or adapted cells do often complain about these matters. See P Hillyard, *Suspect Community* (London: Pluto Press, 1993) ch 7.

16 The outline provided here will not attempt to discuss comprehensively the rights of suspects. A good reference text is Bevan and Lidstone (1996).

17 Code of Practice C: The Detention, Treatment and Questioning of Persons by Police Officers (London: HMSO, 1995) para 5.

'One friend or relative or a person who is known to him or is likely to take an interest in his welfare told, as soon as is practicable except to the extent that delay is permitted by this section, that he has been arrested and is being detained . . .'

The police are not allowed to stop suspects exercising this right. They may delay its exercise, but only under very strict conditions.[18] The police applied their delaying power to around 1% of requests in 1988 but only 0.2% of requests in 1991.[19] However, Note D to para 5 of Code of Practice C provides that 'In some circumstances it may not be appropriate to use the telephone' in compliance with s 56. This means that the custody officer can require that intimation be made in a written form only.

The exercise by suspects of the separate right to a telephone call or to contact someone by letter[20] may be delayed on a similar basis to the right of intimation, except that here the power to delay is not restricted to serious arrestable offences. Suspects may also 'receive visits at the custody officer's discretion'.[1] Discretion is to be exercised in the light of the availability of sufficient manpower to supervise visits 'and any possible hindrance to the investigation'.[2] These last two 'rights' (to a phone call/ letter and to receive visits) need not be communicated orally to suspects by custody officers on reception, or indeed at any other time. The only way in which suspects who do not already know of these rights can find them out is by consulting Code of Practice C and (in the case of the phone call) the written notice. Not surprisingly, very few people ask for visits, and less than 10% of suspects ask for a phone call.[3] This may well be fewer than before PACE.[4]

Although intimation is formally delayed rarely, informal delay is more common. According to Dixon et al, informal delay in intimation 'may be deliberate, for example, when officers who wish to search premises wait to inform a suspect's family of arrest until they arrive to search his/her house'.[5] Dixon et al point out that informal delay is also often an unintentional product of pressure of work. It takes time for officers to get around to informing a relative or friend of someone's arrest. The result is that the provisions on intimation, while embodying due process values, are not fully adhered to. However, since s 56(1) merely provides that

18 The conditions are similar to those which apply to the delaying of a suspect's access to legal advice, discussed below, section 4(a).
19 Brown et al (1992) pp 54-56.
20 Code of Practice C, para 5.6.
1   Code of Practice C, para 5.4.
2   Code of Practice C, Note 5B.
3   Brown et al (1992) p 55.
4   D Dixon, K Bottomley, C Coleman, M Gill and D Wall, 'Safeguarding the Rights of Suspects in Police Custody' (1990) 1 Policing and Society at 118.
5   Dixon et al (1990) p 118.

The powers and duties of the custody officer

intimation should be done 'as soon as is practicable', it is difficult for suspects to demonstrate that the law has been broken. Thus there are no reported cases where delay of intimation or refusal to intimate was an issue.[6] Requests for phone calls also frequently appear to be informally delayed or ignored. Brown et al found that custody records recorded requests in 7–8% of cases, but they observed requests being made in 10–12% of cases.[7] Further, it is no use telling suspects what rights they have if they do not understand what they are being told. The police often made little or no effort to help suspects understand their rights when PACE was first enacted, and it appears that little had changed 10 years later.[8]

Suspects detained under the PTA 1989 have the same rights as other suspects, but the police are allowed to delay the granting of these rights on broader grounds than usual.[9] Nearly half of all PTA suspects request that someone be informed, and delay was imposed (often for more than 24 hours) in around three quarters of these cases.[10]

At first glance it might seem that whether these rights are granted or not, or whether they are delayed, is peripheral to the big issues - whether suspects are intimidated or not, whether suspects are legally detained or not, and so on. However, they can make a great difference to the *experience* of being in custody. We will see in section 3 (d) that, for the freedom perspective, this is crucial.

(c)   Vulnerable suspects

Some people have specific vulnerabilities, such as deafness or an inability to understand English. The custody officer must locate interpreters for such people.[11] Suspects who are 'generally' vulnerable—ie juveniles, the mentally handicapped and the mentally disordered—have special protections, in recognition of their greater welfare needs and susceptibility to coercion or suggestion. It is no accident that in the 'Confait Affair' two of the wrongly convicted youths were juveniles, while the 18-year-old had a mental age of 13.[12] In more recent years, a large number of 'miscarriage'

---

6   See P Mirfield, *Silence, Confessions and Improperly Obtained Evidence* (Oxford: Clarendon, 1997) p 185 for a discussion of the few cases where intimation was known to be delayed.

7   Brown et al (1992) p 55; similar findings are reported by S Choongh, *Policing as Social Discipline* (Oxford: Clarendon, 1997) ch 6.

8   On mid-1980s research see Sanders et al (1989) ch 4; for more recent research see Choongh (1997) ch 6.

9   C Walker, *The Prevention of Terrorism in British Law* 2nd edn (Manchester: MUP, 1992) pp 164-173.

10   Brown et al (1992).

11   Code of Practice C, para 3.6.

12   Baxter and Koffman (1983).

cases have concerned mentally disturbed or handicapped individuals (such as Judith Ward and Stefan Kiszko - see chapter 1 section 6). The police must inform an 'appropriate adult' of their detention and ask that person— usually a parent, guardian or social worker—to attend the station.[13] If mental disorder is suspected, or the suspect talks or acts oddly (other than through drunkenness) a police surgeon must also be called.[14]

Appropriate adults have several responsibilities: to see and advise the detainee in private, to request (if appropriate) a solicitor on the detainee's behalf and to attend interviews, offering advice as appropriate, ensuring fairness and facilitating communication. Interviews cannot take place without an appropriate adult except in the most extreme circumstances. Although there is some overlap with the role of a legal advisor (and in the early days of PACE, lawyers were frequently asked to fulfil the dual role) having an appropriate adult does not diminish the suspect's right to separate legal advice. However, in practice the police are reluctant to call a lawyer until the appropriate adult arrives, even though such a delay is a clear breach of Code of Practice C.[15] An appropriate adult is unlikely to arrive for an hour or more, by which time there is a major disincentive to further delay whilst waiting for a lawyer. The police know this, and sometimes exaggerate the likely delay in order to discourage requests for legal advice.[16]

Vulnerable suspects are by no means rare. In the most recent study, nearly one-fifth of all suspects were juveniles, and in some stations the percentage is far higher.[17] Whilst suspects with other vulnerabilities may appear to be few and far between, they are not always easy to identify. People with learning disabilities or other educational or social disadvantages often try to hide these problems, and thus learn to appear confident and capable.[18] Gudjonsson et al found that, in a sample of 156 adult detainees, the police only called appropriate adults in 4% of cases.[19] Yet clinical psychologists in the research team identified 15% of the

13   Code of Practice C, paras 3.6-3.14.
14   Code of Practice C, para 9.2.
15   Note 3G. See Brown et al (1992) p 62.
16   A Sanders and L Bridges, 'Access to Legal Advice and Police Malpractice' [1990] Crim LR 494; Brown et al (1992) pp 31-34.
17   T Bucke and D Brown, In Police Custody: Police Powers and Suspects' Rights Under the Revised Pace Codes of Practice (Home Office Research Study no 174) (London: Home Office, 1997) p 6.
18   Examples include the 'Tottenham Three' and 'Cardiff Three' cases: see ch 5, sections 3-4 for discussion of these cases.
19   Indeed, the percentage of suspects treated by the police as disordered or handicapped is generally far lower than this: only 2% in the large sample examined by Bucke and Brown (1997) p 7, and even less in the sample examined by T Nemitz and P Bean, 'The Use of the Appropriate Adult Scheme' (1994) 34 Med Sci and the Law 161.

The powers and duties of the custody officer

detainees as vulnerable after an interview of 10–15 minutes, and a further 5% after more extensive tests. This shows that, even if the police think that a suspect may be disordered or handicapped, the professional help they seek may not always identify the problem. Indeed, police surgeons (GPs who work part-time for the police) often have no psychiatric training at all. They therefore often fail to identify mental disorder.[20] Failure to identify people with a mental disability or disorder not only leads to treatment in breach of the Code of Practice and PACE, but can also lead to prosecution where diversion (see ch 6) would be more appropriate, and even to tragedy. In one case the police were concerned about a suspect, called a doctor, but then released him when the doctor pronounced him calm and 'perfectly logical'. He was in fact a paranoid schizophrenic who set himself on fire 12 hours later and died in hospital.[1]

Custody officers often try to process cases as quickly as possible. For these and other reasons they sometimes deliberately keep appropriate adults away from suspects with relatively mild disorders or disabilities. They also frequently do not call surgeons when suspects act strangely, and some surgeons advise custody officers on the phone and then do not attend the suspect.[2] For example, Palmer reports a custody officer speaking of a suspect who the police put in a paper suit without zips (for fear he would self-harm) yet for whom they did not call a doctor or appropriate adult because they did not consider him mentally ill.[3] These are all clear breaches of the Code.

Not only do the police not always recognise the need for an appropriate adult or doctor, or act accordingly when they do, but this help is not always secured even when it is sought. Bucke and Brown[4] found that 91% of all juveniles had an appropriate adult with them for all or some of their time in custody, but this was true for only two thirds of other vulnerable suspects. On average, the wait for an appropriate adult is a little over one hour.[5] As we shall see, a few hours' detention can be very stressful for even the most 'normal' people, so for vulnerable people this can be very serious indeed. *Aspinall*, where the suspect was a schizophrenic, is a typical case. Two police surgeons considered him fit to be interviewed, whilst confirming his mental illness. He was interviewed without an appropriate adult (a clear breach of Code C), and gave answers which undermined his credibility at

20   J Laing, 'The Mentally Disordered Suspect At the Police Station' [1995] Crim LR 371.
1   *The Guardian*, 30 November 1993. Cited in Laing [1995].
2   C Phillips and D Brown, Entry into the Criminal Justice System (Home Office Research Study no 185) (London: Home Office, 1998) pp 55-6; T Nemitz and Bean (1994).
3   C Palmer, 'Still Vulnerable After All These Years' [1996] Crim LR 633.
4   Bucke and Brown (1997).
5   Phillips and Brown (1998) p 56.

his trial. He was convicted of drugs offences, but won his appeal because the absence of an appropriate adult invalidated his interview.[6]

Social workers have dual 'welfare' and 'control' roles, and since they have to work closely with the police it is difficult for them to act as the suspect's advocate when acting as an appropriate adult. Many 'appropriate adults' misunderstand what is happening, fail to realise how an apparently innocent series of questions and answers can be incriminating, and are as intimidated as are the suspects.[7] Bucke and Brown report many family members acting as appropriate adults who clearly did not understand what had been happening, or who simply sat on the sidelines paying little attention.[8] This is true not just of family members, who may have little or no experience of dealing with the police. It includes professional social workers and nominees from local victim support volunteer groups who the police select precisely because, according to one officer, they are 'on our side - on the side of the victim.'[9] There is therefore often more of an illusion of protection than the reality. Thus Dixon et al say that some parents:

'are notoriously keen to help the police in obtaining confessions from their children. In one incident a mother promised to 'get my fist round his lug' (which she later did . . . much to the approval of the investigating officers).'[10]

Several years on, Bucke and Brown report similar conversations, such as the parents who asked the custody officer to give their 'lad the fright of his life'.[11] This partly reflects the contradictions in the Code of Practice about the role of the appropriate adult, which is, inter alia, 'to advise' and 'to facilitate communication'.[12] It may be proper to advise a suspect to remain silent (especially if no lawyer is present) but this cannot be said to facilitate communication. Hence not only parents, but also professional social workers, are left not understanding their proper role. Many professional social workers were horrified, after taking a training course for appropriate adults, to find that they had previously been failing to intervene in coercive interviews when they were entitled to do so.[13] The

---

6   [1999] Crim LR 741. On exclusion of evidence obtained in breach of PACE or the Codes, see ch 11.
7   Brown et al (1992) p 72.
8   Bucke and Brown (1997) pp 14-15.
9   Nemitz and Bean (1994).
10   Dixon et (1992) p 119.
11   Bucke and Brown (1997) p 14.
12   Code of Practice C, para 11.16.
13   Confidentiality can also be a problem: J Hodgson, 'Vulnerable Suspects and the Appropriate Adult' [1997] Crim LR 785.

police do not help here, often failing even to try to explain to suspects and appropriate adults what is expected of them,[14] despite the stipulation in Code of Practice C that they do so.[15]

Clearly at present only a minority of vulnerable suspects secure the help they need from responsible adults and doctors, and even with the best will in the world substantial numbers will always be missed in the absence of duty psychologists and doctors in all busy stations. Even then, to dichotomise 'vulnerable' and 'normal' people in this way is unrealistic. For when in police detention, most of us would be vulnerable to some extent, but often in unpredictable ways. The legal recognition of vulnerability raises major questions about detention, coercion and voluntariness, which we shall explore in ch 5.

(d) Police bail

Suspects who have no action taken against them or who are immediately cautioned (ie officially warned - discussed in ch 6) are released unconditionally from detention. In most other cases, custody officers have to decide whether or not to grant bail. Bail with the stipulation that the suspect return to the station on a given date is given when the police wish to make further inquiries or to consider whether or not to charge.[16] This is used for over 20% of juvenile suspects, and 10-20% of adults. The outcome is frequently a caution in juvenile cases, but no action at all (NFA) for nearly half of all adults.[17]

The main time when bail is considered is after suspects are charged with criminal offences.[18] The custody officer must order release, in most cases, unless certain conditions are satisfied, namely:
(a) if the suspect's name and address cannot be ascertained;
(b) if the suspect is regarded as unlikely to appear in court to answer the charge;
(c) if interference with witnesses or further investigation is likely; or
(d) if it is thought that the suspect would commit an offence if released.
If one of these conditions is satisfied, the custody officer may keep the suspect in custody until the next magistrates' court hearing.

14 Bucke and Brown (1997), ch 2; Nemitz and Bean (1994).
15 Code of Practice C, paras 3.12 and 11.16. See Brown et al (1992) p 72. Also see Palmer [1996]; and B Littlechild, 'Reassessing the Role of the 'Appropriate Adult", [1995] Crim LR 540.
16 PACE, s 34(5).
17 See Phillips and Brown (1998) pp 82-5; and Bucke and Brown (1997) ch 6.
18 PACE, s 38; Magistrates' Court Act 1980, s 43, as amended by PACE, s 47.

These provisions echo the general arrest conditions in s 25.[19] Most of them require custody officers to predict what might happen if the suspect is released. These predictions are based on what they are told by the arresting or investigating officers and what little may be known about a suspect's previous record of appearing at court, offending on bail and so forth. It is impossible for suspects to prove that they would not do something wrong if released. Essentially, decisions are taken quickly on the basis of inadequate information. Although this is done by custody officers, who should protect suspects from the possible partisanship of arresting officers, most of the information used will come from those very officers. Moreover, assessment of the quality of the information on which decision-making is based is almost impossible. Thus although custody officers are supposed to be objective, basing their decisions on reasonable grounds, subjectivism is inevitable, as is suggested by the wide disparity in bail rates from one police station to another.[20] Subjectivism and discretion allow the police to make decisions, when they occasionally wish to, which are wholly unrelated to the nature of the individual offence. Thus at times of riot (or disorder characterised as such) 'it appears that police bail was denied *en masse* as a matter of policy.'[1]

The decision to grant or withhold bail after charge is almost entirely one for the police. One reason why many suspects used to be denied bail is that the police often wanted conditions attached to bail—for instance, that the suspect not contact the victim or a particular witness. Conditions could be attached by a court[2] but not by the police. The Criminal Justice and Public Order Act 1994 (CJPO) gave the police the power to attach most of the conditions that a court can attach.[3] The drawback is that this gives the police considerable power to control the movements of released suspects or to operate conditions as informal punishments.[4] Most suspects are more concerned about securing bail than they are about being charged.[5] Not only is a night in the cells unpleasant, but it makes it more difficult to secure court bail, which, in turn, might reduce the chances of securing acquittal or a non-custodial sentence.[6] This makes bail an

---

19 See ch 3, section 3(b) above.
20 Phillips and Brown (1998) pp 115-8. Different offence and offender mixes will also affect bail rates.
1   R Vogler, *Reading the Riot Act* (Milton Keynes: Open UP, 1991) p 118.
2   See ch 8, below, where the principles regarding bail are discussed fully.
3   CJPO 1994, s 27. This amends PACE, s 47 and the Bail Act 1976, ss 3 and 5.
4   The dangers, as well as the benefits, of giving police this discretion are discussed by J Raine and M Willson, 'Just Bail at the Police Station?' (1995) 22 JLS 571.
5   A Sanders, L Bridges, A Mulvaney and G Crozier, Advice and Assistance at Police Stations and the 24 Hour Duty Solicitor Scheme (London: Lord Chancellor's Department, 1989) pp 72-73.
6   R Morgan and S Jones, 'Bail or Jail?' in E Stockdale and S Casale (eds), *Criminal Justice Under Stress* (London: Blackstone, 1992).

important bargaining counter, particularly in relation to confessions, as we shall see in ch 5. Legal advisors can make representations about bail to the police, but lawyers rarely remain until this decision is made.[7] Giving the police the power to make conditions provides them with a new stack of bargaining chips.[8]

Phillips and Brown found that, prior to the changes brought in by the CJPO, around 28% of those charged were refused bail by the police. Violent offences, including robbery, and burglary, less frequently attracted bail than other offences. Ethnic minority suspects were refused bail more often than white suspects, regardless of offence or any other factor that they could identify.[9] Bucke and Brown's research was done after the CJPO was introduced. In their sample fewer suspects were refused bail (20%), but only 63% were unconditionally bailed (as compared to 72% before). The other 17% were conditionally bailed. Again, black (though not Asian) suspects were detained disproportionately often, and the use of conditions varied greatly from station to station.[10] They, along with Raine and Willson (whose findings are similar),[11] conclude that many people who would previously have been granted unconditional bail are now only granted bail with conditions, although undoubtedly some who would previously have been detained are now given bail.

Offending when on police bail does not seem to have been reduced as a result of the use of conditions, perhaps because bail conditions are so difficult to enforce. But nor does the increase in bail, as a result of conditions, lead to more offending or more failure to appear in court: Brown found that 12% of those bailed by the police committed at least one offence while on bail, and 7% did not attend their first court appearance, but he considered it unlikely that the use of conditions affected these figures.[12]

Whether, overall, the CJPO has produced a net gain or net loss of freedom is difficult to determine. However, it seems that, as usual, the freedom of the most socially marginalised - in this case, black suspects - is valued less than that of others in the criminal justice system. No doubt, as discussed in the first section of ch 2, this is because of the effect of police culture on police discretion.

---

7   See section 4, below.

8   J Raine and M Willson, 'Police Bail with Conditions' (1997) 37 BJ Crim 593.

9   Phillips and Brown (1998) pp 115-8.

10   Bucke and Brown (1997) ch 7; variable use of conditions was also found by Raine and Willson (1997) and D Brown, Offending on Bail and Police Use of Conditional Bail (Home Office Research Findings no 72) (London: Home Office, 1998).

11   Raine and Willson (1997).

12   Brown (1998).

3. DETENTION WITHOUT CHARGE

(a) 'Helping the police with their inquiries'

According to s 29 of PACE, anyone who is at a police station voluntarily (ie not there under arrest):

> '(a) shall be entitled to leave at will unless he is placed under arrest;
> (b) shall be informed at once that he is under arrest if a decision is taken by a constable to prevent him leaving at will.'

This is at first sight an odd provision for all it is saying is that if someone is not under arrest—that is, not deprived of their liberty—then they are not to be deprived of their liberty. This tautology can only be understood in its historical context.

Historically the police have been reluctant to arrest suspects against whom they had not enough evidence to allow them to lay charges immediately. This is because, before 1964, a suspect normally had to be charged immediately following arrest and could not be questioned first. Arrest marked the end of the investigation, and its purpose was to enable the suspect to be brought to court. The solution for the police who needed extra evidence through, for instance, questioning was to put people in a situation where they could be questioned without formally arresting them. Even then, the fiction that the police did not interrogate was still maintained, through the mechanism of the 'voluntary statement' of confession. This might mean detaining someone at their home or another place, or in the police station. Many court cases turned on whether someone could be detained without being 'arrested'. The limbo in which such people were placed was known as 'helping the police with their inquiries', generally understood to mean people who were involuntarily detained but not formally arrested. A revision to the Judges Rules in 1964 made it easier for the police to interrogate following arrest but it was still common for suspects to 'help the police with their inquiries'.[13] Section 29 is designed to make it absolutely clear that this limbo is no longer allowed.

Taken on its own, s 29 appears to be an inhibitory rule providing more due process for suspects than had existed hitherto. However, we need to see how far it has really affected police practices, and how the other provisions of PACE affect detention before charge. McKenzie et al looked at three different police force areas, and found that in two of those areas very few people were in the police station voluntarily yet also under suspicion by the police. In the other area, however, about a third of all

---

13   The historical background is discussed by D Dixon, *Law in Policing* (Oxford: Clarendon, 1997) pp 126-147; I Bryan, *Interrogation and Confession* (Aldershot: Dartmouth, 1997) chs 6-8.

suspects were there as 'volunteers'—ie they were there 'helping the police with their inquiries'.[14] In a quarter of the police forces surveyed by McKenzie et al, there were formal arrangements for dealing with 'voluntary' attenders. Contrary to the words of s 29, 'voluntary' attenders are not generally free to leave. As a police inspector told McKenzie at al:

> 'The problem is whether the people actually believe they can leave. I think about 50% of them are convinced that they wouldn't be allowed to and the truth is they wouldn't.'[15]

That the police are guided more by their crime control 'needs' than by the due process values in the law is indicated by a Scottish study showing that after pre-charge detention of only six hours was introduced in Scotland, one third of all suspects (and in one area, over half) were 'volunteers' in 1981–84.[16] So when the police wish to process suspects as 'voluntary attenders', it appears that s 29 has little inhibitory effect. This renders it largely presentational, giving the appearance of due process whilst not affecting police behaviour in practice. That s 29 is not flouted more often (Brown, for example suggests that 'voluntary' attendance is now rare)[17] is due to the fact that the 24-hour detention time-limit which applies for most offences is usually more than adequate for police purposes. It is to these time-limits that we now turn.

(b)   Time limits for detention

Under s 41(1) of PACE, if the offence is not a serious arrestable offence then the suspect may be detained without charge for up to 24 hours after the 'relevant time'. For serious arrestable offences, s 42(1) provides that detention may be for up to 36 hours initially. The 'relevant time' is usually the time of arrival at the police station, but not for 'volunteers', for whom it is the time of arrest.[18] It is this provision that gives the police the incentive to maintain the 'helping with inquiries' fiction that McKenzie et al discovered. As a detective sergeant told the researchers: '. . . it's

14   J McKenzie, R Morgan and R Reiner, 'Helping the Police with their Enquiries' [1990] Crim LR 22.
15   McKenzie et al (1990) p 32.
16   J Curran and J Garnie, Detention or Voluntary Attendance?: Police Use of Detention under section 2 of the Criminal Justice (Scotland) Act 1980 (Scottish Office) (Edinburgh: HMSO, 1986).
17   D Brown, PACE Ten Years On (Home Office Research Study no 155) (London, Home Office 1997) pp 68-70.
18   Unusual circumstances can affect the operation of these rules, making it an extremely complicated area of law. See Bevan and Lidstone (1995) pp 352-7.

convenient because you set the time and . . . it avoids the time clock consideration. If arrest is necessary later, it doesn't count.'[19]

Detention has to be reviewed periodically. Firstly, a senior officer independent of the investigation (usually the custody officer) must review the detention 'not later than six hours after the detention was first authorised'.[20] The second review must be 'not later than nine hours after the first' and subsequent reviews must be at intervals of not more than nine hours.[1] To extend detention beyond 24 hours (in the case of serious arrestable offences) the review must be conducted by an officer of superintendent rank or above. Reviews may be postponed but only under exceptional circumstances and for as short a time as is practicable. The reviewing officer may only authorise continued detention if the original purpose of detention still holds good and if the investigation is being conducted 'diligently and expeditiously'.[2] The reviewing officer must take note of any representations against continued detention which the suspect may make.[3] In reality, though:

'the review procedure tends to be routinised and insubstantial, at least in its early stages; the opportunity to make representations can often consist merely of an inspector asking the suspect, "All right mate?" through the hatch in the cell door.'[4]

Indeed, reviews may take place over the telephone if the review officer is not at the station.[5] Rather than this being exceptional, as was doubtless intended, Dixon et al found this to be common. Moreover, custody record entries often failed to note this use of the telephone, giving the impression that the review was carried out in person. Frequently, they say, 'the inspector's role is purely presentational',[6] which could be said of the rules on reviews as a whole.

If the police wish to continue the detention beyond 36 hours (in the case of serious arrestable offences) this is possible, up to a maximum of a further 60 hours.[7] The same criteria apply as above, but authorisation must

19   McKenzie et al (1990).
20   PACE, s 40(3)(a).
1   PACE, s 40(3)(b)-(c).
2   PACE, s 42(1)(c).
3   PACE, s 40(12)-(14). It is not clear how wide are the purposes of reviews. See E Cape, 'Detention Without Charge: What Does "Sufficient Evidence To Charge" Mean?' [1999] Crim LR 874
4   D Dixon, K Bottomley, C Coleman, M Gill and D Wall, 'Safeguarding the Rights of Suspects in Police Custody' (1990) 1 Policing and Society 115, at pp 130-131.
5   Code of Practice C, Note 15C.
6   Dixon et al (1992) at 131.
7   PACE, ss 42-43.

Detention without charge

be by an officer of the rank of superintendent or above, and the police must apply to a magistrates' court for a 'warrant of further detention'.[8] This application must generally be made before the 36-hour period has expired but, in exceptional circumstances, there is some leeway. The criteria on which magistrates decide whether or not to grant such a warrant are broadly similar to the criteria which the superintendent must apply under s 42 in deciding whether to authorise continued detention in the first place. If the police still wish to detain a suspect without charge after the period of further detention has expired, they may apply to a magistrate again for an extension of the warrant for further detention. Such an extension may be granted by a magistrate under s 44 as long as that extension neither exceeds 36 hours nor ends later than 96 hours after the initial 'relevant time'.[9] This means that the police may apply for, and secure, two warrants of further detention following the initial 36-hour detention. But 96 hours is the overall maximum permissible length of detention without charge.

It is rare for the police to extend detention beyond 24 hours. In 1997/8 this applied to 674 suspects who were released without charge.[10] Warrants of further detention are sought even less frequently. In 1990, for instance, there were only 405 applications, and the numbers in subsequent years have ranged from 343 to 220. When warrants are requested they are almost invariably granted (only five were refused in 1997/8). This is to be expected, since the magistrates apply the same criteria as the police and on the basis of information which the police provide. While the suspect will usually be legally represented, there are few grounds on which defence arguments can be made for release. For instance, if there is little evidence against a suspect, this would scarcely ever justify release since the point of the extended detention is precisely to secure more evidence. The percentages of these suspects who are charged have varied over the years from 67% to 91%.[11]

The fact that detention beyond 24 hours is rare does not necessarily mean that the safeguards are adequate. The police usually have no reason to detain suspects once they consider that they have obtained full information from the suspect concerning the alleged offence. To detain any further would be inefficient. Occasionally, though, the police may wish to prolong detention, regardless of evidential or other legal considerations (as where they are seeking information on other suspects). The detention provisions, and the way in which legal duties are carried out by senior police officers, gives them the scope to do almost as they see fit in those few cases of such importance to them. Nonetheless, although Art 5 (3) of

8   PACE, s 43.
9   PACE, s 44(3).
10 G Wilkins and C Addicott, Operation of Certain Police Powers under PACE , 1997/8 (London: Home Office 1999).
11 Wilkins and Addicott (1999).

the ECHR provides that suspects in detention must be brought before a court 'promptly', detention for further investigation has been held not to violate the ECHR when the grounds for arrest are reasonable and when there is recourse after a reasonable period (as under PACE) to judicial oversight.[12]

Whether the offence is a serious arrestable offence or not, the suspect must be released when either the period of detention expires or when detention is no longer necessary because the original reason for detention no longer applies. Release is either unconditional, on bail to return to the police station pending further inquiries or (having been charged) on bail to appear in court. The only circumstances in which the suspect would not be released would be if he or she was charged and kept in custody pending the earliest available court hearing.[13] Suspects who are released because the time limit has been reached cannot be rearrested without warrant for the same offence unless new evidence is uncovered after release.[14]

When suspects are released on bail to return to the police station, further inquiries will have been made in the meantime. If those inquiries produce more evidence, the police are entitled to 'start the clock' where it had previously been 'stopped'. If they do not, the police should not (in principle) have any further cause to detain the suspect. However, PACE provides that the clock may be started again from the place it had reached at the time of release, even if further inquiries produced no new evidence.[15]

One of the purposes of this part of PACE was to shorten the length of detention, in the interests both of suspects and police efficiency. Because there were no proper records prior to PACE it is difficult to know whether PACE has succeeded in this objective or not. We know that, on average, suspects are held for around six and a half hours. As one might expect, the average detention length increases with the seriousness of the alleged offence, but not according to whether or not the suspect is charged. Detention is, on average, increased when a doctor, appropriate adult or lawyer is sought.[16] It seems that the overwhelming majority of arrestees are held for less than nine hours, and over half for less than six hours. Maguire concludes that PACE has probably led to longer detention lengths for people who would otherwise have been kept in for very short periods but quite possibly shorter periods of detention for those who would otherwise have been kept in for long periods of time.[17] In very few cases

12   (1988) 11 EHRR 117.
13   The question of police bail is discussed in section 2(d) above.
14   PACE, s 41(9).
15   PACE, s 47(5)-(6).
16   Phillips and Brown (1998) pp 109-111.
17   M Maguire, 'Effects of the PACE provisions on Detention and Questioning' (1988) 28 BJ Crim 19.

Detention without charge

is the 24-hour limit a problem, and so in serious cases the extra time is rarely needed either. The reason for these changed lengths of detention is partly because the police now avoid long periods of detention. Unless the offence is a 'serious arrestable', the 24-hour limit is absolute, and even the periodic reviews may concentrate investigating officers' minds. But few people are held for only a brief period partly because of the length of time it takes to complete the paperwork and partly because of the greater numbers seeking legal advice.

Under the PTA 1989 the police are able to detain suspected terrorists for up to 48 hours on their own authority (with periodic reviews by senior officers), and can apply to the Secretary of State for an extension of detention for a further five days. Unlike PACE, extended detention under the terrorist provisions does not have even the inadequate safeguard of a hearing before a magistrate. These provisions have been held to be breaches of the ECHR. Britain's response has not been to change the law to comply with human rights standards, but to 'derogate' from the ECHR.[18] The derogation was unsuccessfully challenged in *Brannigan and McBride v UK*.[19] The numbers detained under this legislation vary from year to year, from 34 to over 200. These variations reflect the frequent political changes concerning Northern Ireland. In 1996, for example, there were 84 detentions (not including 'examinations' of people entering or leaving Great Britain or Northern Ireland). Only two of these people were charged under the PTA, and 15 were charged with offences under other legislation. 23 of the 84 had their detention extended beyond 48 hours, of whom 10 were released without charge. Literally hundreds of people are 'examined' each year, of whom hardly any are charged with an offence.[20]

(c)   The purpose of detention

Now that we have examined the *mechanisms* for authorising and reviewing detention, we need to examine the *criteria* used to decide whether or not detention should be authorised or continued. Under s 37 of PACE:

'(1)   The custody officer. . . shall determine whether he has before him sufficient evidence to charge that person with the offence for which he was arrested and may detain him at the police station for such period as is necessary to enable him to do so.

(2)   If the custody officer determines that he does not have such evidence before him the person arrested shall be released either

18   Walker (1992) pp 164-185.
19   (1993) 17 EHRR 539.
20   Home Office, Statistics on the Operation of Prevention of Terrorism Legislation, (HO Stat Bull, 4/97) (London: Home Office, 1997).

on bail or without bail, unless the custody officer has reasonable grounds for believing that his detention without being charged is necessary to secure or preserve evidence relating to an offence for which he is under arrest or to obtain such evidence by questioning him.

(3) If the custody officer has reasonable grounds for so believing he may authorise the person arrested to be kept in police detention.'

These provisions broadly follow the Philips Commission's recommendations and embody its 'necessity principle'. We saw in the chapter on arrest that the Philips Commission believed that many suspects who were arrested and charged could be reported and summonsed instead. It wished to ensure that arrests which led to detention would only be made when necessary. Thus, the Commission stated: 'We do seek to alter the practice whereby the inevitable sequence on the creation of reasonable suspicion is arrest, followed by being taken to the station.'[1]

Similarly, the Commission wanted to see pre-charge detention for questioning kept to a necessary minimum. The necessity principle was not accepted by the government in relation to arrest but it was in relation to detention. This has created some tensions. At least half of all formally arrested suspects are detained for questioning.[2] In these cases, if the arrests were on reasonable grounds and there existed sufficient evidence to prosecute, arrest will be lawful but pre-charge detention following the arrest would be unlawful. This is because s 37 requires the custody officer to charge and then either release or detain (pending a court appearance) any suspect brought into the station against whom there is already sufficient evidence to prosecute (these rules are discussed in ch 5). But custody officers are rarely in a position to determine whether there is such evidence unless an arresting officer wishes them to know it, and it is not clear what duties custody officers have to seek to discover it.[3]

In practice, custody officers seem to act on the assumption that a determination of whether there is sufficient evidence to charge cannot be made one way or the other until after questioning has taken place. The law envisages, however, that custody officers must make their determination as soon as the arrestee comes to the head of the queue in front of the

1   Royal Commission on Criminal Procedure (RCCP), Report (Cmnd 8092-1) (London: HMSO, 1981) para 3.75.
2   Brown et al (1992) p 90. However, as we saw in ch 3, section 4, in public order situations in particular, many people are 'informally' arrested and then released without being taken to a police station.
3   E Cape, 'Detention Without Charge: What Does "Sufficient Evidence To Charge" Mean?' [1999] Crim LR 874. Officers may withhold knowledge that there is sufficient evidence to charge because they may have a variety of reasons for wanting to question suspects. See ch 5, section 1.

custody desk. The obvious solution to this dilemma is to couple a determination that there is insufficient evidence to charge with a decision under s 37 (2) that there are reasonable grounds for believing that detention without charge is 'necessary' in order to obtain evidence by questioning. But what does 'necessary' in this statutory context mean?

The then Home Secretary, Douglas Hurd, said in Parliament in 1984, that the question is whether 'this detention was necessary—not desirable, convenient or a good idea but necessary.'[4] A reasonable interpretation of a convenient or desirable detention would be one that was convenient in the sense that it increased the probability of confession and/or was the most cost-effective way of carrying out enquiries. A reasonable interpretation of a necessary detention would be one where there was no other practicable way of gathering, securing or preserving evidence in relation to the offence in question. If the latter interpretation was adopted by custody officers then there should be proportionately few authorisations of detention. A determination that there was insufficient evidence to charge would ordinarily be coupled with a decision that such evidence could be obtained in ways that did not require the detention of the arrestee. The presumption in s 37 (2) would then apply, and the custody officer would then be obliged to release the arrestee either on bail or unconditionally.

The scenario envisaged here—of large numbers of perfectly lawful arrests being negatived by custody officers refusing to authorise detention—is not a likely scenario, nor does it correspond with reality. Research has established that virtually all arresting officers are successful in having their suspects detained. Many of the custody officers interviewed by McConville et al expressed surprise that the detention decision could be anything other than automatic. Thus one, when pressed on whether he would ever refuse to authorise detention, replied: 'Probably not in practice, no'. Another said:

'Often the bloke's remonstrating saying "Not me, it wasn't me. I haven't done it, you've got the wrong man", but of course I have to take the policeman's word, so I accept him on what the policeman tells me.'[5]

As Dixon et al comment after finding not one refusal of detention in their research, 'reception into custody has become an essentially routinised process'.[6] Most custody officers simply write out the words of s 37 and

---

4   HC Official Report, SC E, 16 February 1984, col 1229.
5   M McConville, A Sanders and R Leng, *The Case for the Prosecution* (London: Routledge, 1991) p 44.
6   D Dixon, K Bottomley, C Coleman, M Gill and D Wall, 'Safeguarding the Rights of Suspects in Police Custody' (1990) 1 Policing and Society 115 at p 130.

some have even asked for a rubber stamp with these words already on it.[7] In *DPP v L* the Divisional Court accepted this to the extent of saying that custody officers need not inquire into the lawfulness of an arrest.[8] Here the arrest was unlawful because the suspect had not been informed of the reason for the arrest. The Divisional Court said that this did not invalidate her detention, because, *it assumed*, the custody officer gave her the reason when he 'booked her in'. Obviously the Divisional Court had not read the first edition of this book where we show that custody officers so routinise the detention process that this is not a reasonable assumption to make. So if you know any High Court judges, show them this passage, and ask them, with due respect, why they have been abdicating their responsibility to give the custody officer 'safeguard' some practical meaning.

We have seen that the function and place of arrest in relation to investigation has changed over time: whereas at one time arrests came at the end of an investigation and were the inevitable prelude to prosecution, arrest has gradually moved nearer to the beginning of the investigation. Arrest can be made on the basis of a bare reasonable suspicion, and it often is. Since that will not suffice to prosecute, the law now envisages that the police will frequently need to get more evidence in order to prosecute.[9] This development occurred gradually and along with this, of course, came the limbo of 'helping the police with their inquiries'. Section 37 of PACE formalises the process by recognising that suspects will be detained without charge following arrest when there is insufficient evidence to prosecute and that the main purpose of this detention is to secure that evidence.

This endorses the decision in *Holgate-Mohammed v Duke*,[10] where the House of Lords ruled that the greater likelihood of confession if a suspect was held at a police station was a legitimate reason for detention. This decision is entirely consistent with the crime control model. It is, however, entirely inconsistent with the supposed due process presumption in s 37 against detention. It is also inconsistent with the freedom model, for the freedom of those detained is traded in for the sake of police convenience. This is a bad bargain as the police could clear up crime in ways less costly to freedom. Securing evidence through questioning is rarely necessary, but it is considerably more convenient for the police than

7   I McKenzie, R Morgan and R Reiner, 'Helping the Police with their Enquiries' [1990] Crim LR 22 at p 24.

8   [1999] Crim LR 752. This case is also discussed in ch 3, section 5. The same position was adopted by the Court of Appeal in *Clarke v Chief Constable of North Wales Police* (5 April 2000, unreported).

9   This is in fact the reality: M McConville, Corroboration and Confessions: The Impact of a Rule that no Conviction can be Sustained on the Basis of Confession Evidence Alone (Royal Commission on Criminal Justice Research Study no 13) (London: HMSO, 1993).

10 [1984] AC 437, discussed in ch 3, section 5.

Detention without charge

securing evidence in most other ways. As investigation by questioning is envisaged in PACE and its Codes usually as taking place during detention (see ch 5), the authorisation of detention must be the norm.

Moreover, there is little to prevent pre-charge detention for questioning taking place even in cases where there is already sufficient evidence to charge. Arresting officers usually want to strengthen their cases against suspects regardless of whether there already exists sufficient evidence to charge or not. In practice, they know that a taped confession from the arrestee will make the case watertight and that to get such evidence they have to question the arrestee in custody prior to charge. As we will see in ch 5, they may also have other reasons for wanting to detain suspects for questioning, such as general intelligence-gathering or the imposition of authority. By not telling custody officers the full extent of the evidence already obtained against the suspect, it is easy for arresting officers to secure pre-charge detention in all cases. Thus Phillips and Brown note that in 61% of cases in their sample, arresting officers told the researcher that the evidence on arrest was sufficient to charge. The same study found that 'The reception of suspects into custody was found to be a routine matter and arresting officers were not typically asked to provide much information about the offence.'[11]

The presumption against detention in s 37 is thus entirely presentational since it goes against the crime control grain of the rest of the law and practice in this area. It seems then that—rather than the police carrying out the law as made by Parliament—Parliament makes laws aimed at legitimising existing police practice (as happened in successive revisions of the Judges' Rules). What was once part of a judicial process (arrest followed by the prosecution decision) is now part of an Executive process. Not only does this mean that the police make initial decisions relating to detention (as we have seen, up to 36 hours without judicial authority) but in nearly half of all cases this detention is not followed by any judicial proceedings.[12] The Royal Commission on Criminal Justice (Runciman Commission) appeared to be aware of this situation but simply recommended that proper figures be kept.[13] On the fundamental issues of the basis for authorisation of detention, voluntary attendance and reviews of detention, the Runciman Commission was silent.

11   Phillips and Brown (1998) p 43.
12   McConville et al (1991) p 104, found that only 58% of detained adults and 35% of detained juveniles were prosecuted. Since that study was carried out, in the late 1980s, the caution rate has continued to rise, leading to even smaller proportions being prosecuted in the 1990s (see ch 5).
13   Royal Commission on Criminal Justice (RCCJ), Report (Cm 2263) (London: HMSO, 1993) p 30.

(d) The experience of detention

Detention of less than six hours in most cases appears not to be excessive. But what do those six (or four, or eight) hours feel like? We all know the difference between three hours in a darkened cinema and only one in a tedious lecture. An excruciating one-hour lecture can feel even longer than a Celine Dion ballad. Imagine a period four times as long, with fear thrown in, and the worry that one might be in the cells overnight. The fact that length of detention (up to 24 hours) is in the hands of the police leads suspects to believe that the police 'can do anything they want. They can keep you in overnight if they want'.[14]

Police control is asserted from the moment the custody officer begins the 'booking in' procedure. Suspects are immediately deprived of autonomy, and the police demand deference and obedience. Those who do not provide it are often abused or laughed at. Take this example, of a suspect who was upset and who refused to speak, observed by Choongh:

> 'He was shouted at by both the CO [custody officer] and the arresting officers, eg "Come on Mickey, don't be a dick." When this failed to break his resistance, the CO shouted, "Alright! We can play it the hard way. Put him in the cell and he can stay there until he decides to be a good boy!"'[15]

Choongh observed some suspects, who responded with abuse or who refused to do what they were told, being dragged off to the cells where it sounded like they were being beaten. The fact that this was done while an academic researcher was observing, suggests that the police were unconcerned at this. Choongh emphasises that none of these suspects were physically threatening to the police. 'What each of them had done was to challenge the 'usual procedure': challenge the right of the police to treat them as inanimate objects.'[16] One of Choongh's interviewees understood what was happening in a way that only the experience of detention provides:

> 'The bottom line is that they've got the power, yea? Like one of them said to me out there, "You keep your mouth shut in here, because we can do whatever we want to you in here." And that's all it boils down to.'[17]

14 A Sanders, L Bridges, A Mulvaney and G Grozier, Advice and Assistance at Police Stations and the 24 Hour Duty Solicitor Scheme (London: Lord Chancellor's Department, 1989) p 77
15 S Choongh, *Policing as Social Discipline* (Oxford: Clarendon, 1997) p 89.
16 Choongh (1993) p 94.
17 S Choongh, *Policing as Social Discipline* (Oxford: Clarendon, 1997) p 87.

After being booked in, suspects are usually taken to a cell. Almost everything that happens next is in the hands of the police too. For drug addicts and alcoholics they control when the next 'fix' or drink becomes possible. They control food, drinks, heating and who (and what) one might share one's cell with. It may smell of the previous or co-occupant's urine or vomit. The co-occupant may look and sound violent or crazy. They even control when and if you are allowed to use the toilet - no joke if, as in one of Hillyard's cases, you're a woman arrested after an evening in the pub and the male custody officer makes you wait four hours.[18]

Crime control adherents argue that innocent people have nothing to worry about if they are arrested. Maybe it has never happened to them. Listen to someone to whom it did happen:

> 'There I was banged up in a jail and I hadn't done anything, and I was being taken away from my place of work, I'd been separated from my family... Here was a policeman telling me that I had nothing to fear from him and he couldn't see the stupidity of his statement.'[19]

Many suspects also have to endure much of what other suspects are going through in neighbouring cells. Irving reports an almost constant din of 'rhythmic banging and hammering, shouting and cursing, groaning, screaming and crying.'[20] Detention is not only boring, scary, unpleasant and uncertain. It can also be isolating, disorienting and humiliating. As we saw earlier, the police control visits, phone calls, and messages to the outside world. Also, personal possessions, including mobile phones, are taken away. At one and the same time one is isolated yet without privacy. Detainees are usually alone in their cells, often with no idea of the passing of time, yet able to be viewed by the police. Intimate bodily functions have to be announced to the world - the world shrinks to the police station - as one has to ask for toilet paper, for the toilet to be flushed or for sanitary towels. One may be fingerprinted and have 'intimate' and 'non-intimate' samples taken. Intimate samples include semen and blood. 'Non-intimate' sample taking includes having hairs plucked, fingernails scraped and your saliva examined. If someone put a gloved finger in your mouth in order to scrape out some saliva, would you see that as a 'non-intimate' act? That's how PACE sees it. Just being searched is invasive. The Philips Commission recognised this and recommended that searches should not be carried out on a routine basis,[1] but this has been ignored. For some very serious

---

18 P Hillyard, *Suspect Community* (London: Pluto Press, 1993) p 151. On the importance of police control, see R Leo, 'Police Interrogation and Social Control' (1994) 3 SLS 93.

19 Hillyard (1993) pp 186-7.

20 B Irving, Police Interrogation: A Study of Current Practice (Royal Commission Research Paper No 2) (London: HMSO, 1980) p 122.

1 RCCP (1981) para 3.117.

offences, some PTA detentions, or if drugs are suspected to be secreted away, suspects are strip-searched, have samples of body fluids taken, or are examined by a doctor. As Hillyard puts it:

'These processes are common to the initiation into many "total institutions" and Goffman has described them as "mortification processes" because the self is systematically, if often unintentionally, mortified through a series of debasements, degradations, and humiliations.'[2]

The insistence of Human Rights and Due Process theorists on 'rights' makes little sense in these conditions:

'Yea, I understood me rights, but do you get rights in here? The loo don't flush, it stinks. You get breakfast in a cardboard box and it's freezing cold . . . it's not the law, it's just the fucking conditions . . . no fags, nowhere to wash, you've no idea what time it is . . .'[3]

Choongh asked the suspects he interviewed how they felt when locked up. He classified the 72 replies as 'intolerable', 'distressing' or 'indifferent'. One quarter were indifferent to the experience, but one fifth found the experience 'intolerable'. A little over half found it 'distressing', using phrases like feeling 'trapped', 'powerless' and 'angry'.[4]

Detention is not awful for everyone. Occasionally the police have to detain people who they see as allies, not as threats, such as the well-dressed and well-spoken driver who had a little too much wine at lunchtime. Unlike most detainees, he did not have to 'buy' good treatment by being deferential and showing the police that they know who is in charge.[5] Choongh also found that large numbers of suspects had such low expectations of their treatment that they were indifferent to things that most people would find outrageous.

It is not surprising that even a short time in detention feels like a very long time, and that therefore the most important factor affecting suspects' decisions whether to ask for legal advice is the likely length of detention.[6] As one detainee in Choongh's research told him, when asked why he had not requested a solicitor, 'I'm happy I'm out, yea? That's the only thing I care about, I don't care what happens to me in court.'[7] Moreover, the

2   P Hillyard, *Suspect Community* (London: Pluto Press, 1993) p 151.
3   Choongh (1993) p 178.
4   Choongh (1993) pp 97-8.
5   Choongh (1993) pp 206-7
6   Sanders et al (1989) ch 4.
7   Choongh (1993) p 149. *Aspinall* [1999] Crim LR 741 (section 2(c) above) concerned a particularly vulnerable suspect who was prepared to say anything to get out after being isolated for over 13 hours.

Detention without charge

significance of detention lengths is not only the actual detention length but also the threat created by the 24-hour limit. Suspects do not know that the average detention lasts 'only' six hours or so, and rightly fear that the way they behave could lead to their being confined for longer anyway - or could affect whether they get out at all before being hauled off to court. The subjective experience of 'only' six hours detention, and of the threat of longer detention, is something which few legislators, judges, academics or university students are likely to have endured.

Looking at the experience of detention in the light of its purposes and time limits, we can see that crime control considerations clearly outweigh those of due process, particularly in relation to serious suspected offences. But it may be that under a 'freedom' perspective the detention of suspects in some circumstances where evidence is thin and detention not strictly necessary is justified - especially if the detention is for a short period and the offence serious. Britain adopts this approach only in a crude way by providing great power for suspected terrorism, less for 'serious arrestables' and less still for arrestables. But arrestable offences cover a very wide spectrum, and 24 hours is a very long time. A freedom perspective would demand more fine tuning, shorter detention periods, less isolation and degradation and more judicial supervision. Human rights perspectives, such as that of Ashworth, are of little use here, for only the most extreme behaviours documented in this section (beating and gross abuse) contravene the ECHR or the PACE Code of Practice.[8] Intimate body searches, for example, have been held to not contravene the Art 3 right not to be subjected to degrading treatment.[9] Most of this police behaviour is not illegal or even deliberately degrading - it is simply an inevitable product of involuntary detention and of the prioritisation of crime control over freedom.

4. THE RIGHT TO LEGAL ADVICE

Prior to PACE, access to legal advice was governed by the Judges' Rules. The preamble to the Rules stated the principle that a suspected person should be able to consult privately with a solicitor provided that it caused the police no unreasonable 'hindrance'. This principle was not easy to operate in practice. Firstly, the Judges' Rules were not 'law' in the sense of being common law or statute. No specific enforcement power was provided, so all that a suspect who was denied access to legal advice could do was to ask for the evidence obtained as a result to be excluded from

---

8   On beating and psychologically damaging interrogation techniques, see *Ireland v UK* (1978) 2 EHRR 25.
9   *McFeeley v UK* (Application No 8317/78, (1980) 20 DR 44).

trial, if there was one. The second problem was the proviso in the Rules which allowed denial of access if it would be likely to cause 'unreasonable hindrance'. What was or was not reasonable was never clearly established. Thirdly, as confirmed by the Fisher inquiry into the 'Confait Affair', many suspects (including the wrongly convicted youths in that case) did not know they had such a right. Elsewhere in the Judges Rules, one of the 'administrative directions' placed an obligation on the police to inform suspects of this right, but in the Fisher inquiry many police officers claimed not to know about this. Fisher quotes a deputy assistant commissioner of the Metropolitan Police saying that 'it has never been recognised by the police . . . as a duty to tell a prisoner . . . that he has the right to consult a solicitor'.[10]

Thus, few suspects were informed by officers of this right, fewer tried to exercise it and fewer still had their requests granted. There are no reliable estimates of the proportion of suspects who used to secure legal advice, but in Softley's study of four police stations, around 9% sought advice and around 7% actually secured it.[11] Even these figures are artificially high, for in one of these police stations the police were told (for the purposes of the research) that they had to inform all suspects of their right to a solicitor, whereas in the other three stations they were not so directed. In the station in which suspects were routinely informed of their rights, the numbers requesting and securing access were considerably higher than in the others. As one would expect, being told one's rights is vital. The Philips Commission recognised this, and its recommendations, which aimed to make the right to advice truly available to all, were implemented by the government in PACE.

(a)   The right to advice under PACE and the HRA

Section 58 of PACE states the right of access in the clearest possible terms:

'(1) A person arrested. . . shall be entitled, if he so requests, to consult a solicitor privately at any time . . .

---

10   Sir H Fisher, Report of an Inquiry into the Circumstances leading to the Trial of Three Persons on Charges arising out of the Death of Maxwell Confait and the Fire at 27 Doggett Road, London SE6 (HCP 90) (London: HMSO, 1977). It is now generally acknowledged by the police 'establishment' that the Judges' Rules were frequently broken by the police. See the speech by Sir John Woodcock (Chief Inspector of Constabulary), quoted in M Zander, 'Ethics and Criminal Investigation by the Police' (unpublished manuscript).
11   P Softley, Police Interrogation: An Observational Study in Four Police Stations (Royal Commission on Criminal Procedure Research Study no 4) (London: HMSO, 1980).

(4)   If a person makes such a request, he must be permitted to consult a solicitor as soon as is practicable except to the extent that delay is permitted by this section . . ..

(6)   Delay in compliance with a request is only permitted—
(a)   in the case of a person who is in police detention for a serious arrestable offence; and
(b)   if an officer of at least the rank of superintendent authorises it.'

This differs in a number of important respects from the formulation which used to exist in the Judges' Rules. The fact that this is a statutory provision makes it unequivocal, although there is still no clear remedy available to suspects who are denied this right (see section 5 below). Secondly, the exception provided in sub-s (6) to the right to advice is reasonably tightly drawn. Thirdly, even this exception does not allow advice to be refused but merely delayed. All suspects must be permitted, if they wish, to consult a solicitor within 36 hours (the period beyond which suspects cannot be held without the authorisation of a magistrate).[12] Section 58 applies only to arrested persons, thus excluding 'volunteers'. We have seen that many volunteers are in fact suspects and are in need of legal advice as arrested detainees. Since 'volunteers' are, technically, free to go, however, they are free to do as they please in any lawful way, including insisting on seeing a lawyer. Should the police prevent them from doing so, they would then be deemed to be under arrest.

The 'right to consult a solicitor privately at any time' is a powerful one. As we shall see, legal advice in the station is always provided free of charge. Suspects have the right to see a solicitor in person and not be overheard.[13] Suspects who initially decline a solicitor can demand one later, even in the middle of an interview. And they can require that the solicitor be present in the interview and may consult with that solicitor (publicly or privately) during it.[14] As part of the ECHR 'right to a fair trial', everyone 'charged with a criminal offence' has the right to legal assistance. Suspects are 'to be given it free when the interests of justice so require.'[15] Although this only seems to apply to people being prosecuted (ie charged), the European Court has held that it applies to suspects under arrest too if what happens when under arrest could affect the fairness of a subsequent trial: 'The concept of fairness enshrined in Art 6 requires that the accused had the

---

12   PACE, s 58(5).
13   The ECHR has also been interpreted to require this. See *S v Switzerland* (1991) 14 EHRR 670.
14   Code of Practice C, para 6.8 and PACE, s 58 (1).
15   Article 6, para 3 (c). On the meaning of 'the interests of justice', see A Ashworth, 'Human Rights, Legal Aid and Criminal Justice' in R Young and D Wall (eds), *Access to Criminal Justice* (London: Blackstone, 1996) and ch 8, section 2.

benefit of the assistance of a lawyer already at the initial stages of police interrogation.'[16] The Court held that a defendant could not have a fair trial if he had been interviewed while access to advice was being withheld, especially as adverse inferences could be made had he remained silent.[17]

There are obvious potential difficulties with the right of access. One is that the interview might be unduly delayed while waiting for a solicitor. If the consequences would be truly serious (bearing in mind the 24-hour limit in most cases) an officer of the rank of superintendent or above may authorise the interview in the solicitor's absence.[18] If a lawyer's advice and assistance in the interview is such that the police are 'unable properly to put questions to the suspect', the lawyer can be required to leave, but only if authorised by a superintendent, and an opportunity must be given to the suspect to be represented by a replacement lawyer.[19]

(i) Delaying access

Section 58(8) of PACE provides that (in cases of serious arrestable offences only):

> '. . . an officer may only authorise delay where he has reasonable grounds for believing that the exercise of the right . . .
> (a) will lead to interference with or harm to evidence . . .; or
> (b) will lead to the alerting of other persons suspected of having committed such an offence . . .; or
> (c) will hinder the recovery of any property obtained as a result of such an offence.'[20].

In the first few years of the operation of PACE, it was not clear how broad these delaying powers were. In *Re Walters,*[1] for instance, the defendant was suspected of a drugs offence and access was delayed because the police feared that co-conspirators might be alerted by using a solicitor as an innocent agent. Deciding that only manifestly unreasonable decisions should be interfered with by the courts, the delay was endorsed by the Divisional Court.

---

16 *Murray v UK* (1996) 22 EHRR 29. Quoted by E Cape, 'Sidelining Defence Lawyers: Police station advice after *Condron*' (1997) 1 IJ Evid and Proof 386 at p 398. In this case, access to a lawyer was delayed in accordance with the PTA 1989, s 14. This allows delay on similar, but less stringent grounds, to those of PACE, and for up to 48 hours.

17 See ch 5, section 2, for discussion of the right of silence.

18 Code of Practice C, para 6.6.

19 Code of Practice C, paras 6.9-6.10.

20 Section 58(8A) also provides for delay in relation to certain offences relating to drugs. Also see Annexe B of Code C.

1 [1987] Crim LR 577.

However, in *Samuel*[2] the situation changed. The defendant (D) asked for a solicitor, but access was delayed on the grounds that he had been arrested for a serious arrestable offence and that witnesses or evidence could be interfered with if D saw a solicitor. The police had no particular reason to fear this, but stated that it was possible. By the time D saw his solicitor, he had purportedly confessed. The concerns of the police about D seeing a solicitor in this case were particularly unfortunate, because the solicitor concerned had recently been appointed a Crown Court Recorder and imputations of dishonesty or incompetence would have been extremely hard to substantiate. The Court of Appeal took an unsympathetic view of the police's argument and held that in order to justify delay under s 58 the police would have to demonstrate some reason to believe that, in the particular case, access could lead to one of the specified consequences. The Court of Appeal went on to note that if, as in this case, the solicitor was a duty solicitor (ie not known to the suspect) this would be virtually impossible for the police to prove, since neither the police nor the suspect would know who that individual was until such time as he or she arrived at the police station. The Court of Appeal therefore held that the delay of access was unlawful.[3]

As we observed earlier in this chapter, 'serious arrestable offence' is a vague term which gave rise to great fear, prior to the enactment of PACE, that it would be abused. Cases like *Walters* gave some substance to this fear, but *Samuel* and the cases which followed it reversed that trend. In 1987, delay was authorised in around 1% of all cases,[4] but in research covering 12,500 cases conducted in the mid-1990s, no delays were authorised at all.[5] We shall see later on that the problem now is not formal delay of access but the informal delay which results from the police bending or breaking the rules. Delay under the Prevention of Terrorism Acts is still doubtless contemplated from time to time, but as we saw earlier, this is now very difficult to justify, given the way Art 6 of the ECHR is interpreted.[6]

(ii) Notification of the right to advice

As we saw before, not all suspects know their rights. Code of Practice C is intended to deal with this:

2   [1988] 2 All ER 135.
3   In *Alladice* (1988) 87 Cr App Rep 380 the (differently constituted) Court of Appeal regarded itself as bound by *Samuel* but was rather more sympathetic to the police. This led them to a different view of the consequences following on from unlawful delay of access: see ch 11, section 4(b) below.
4   D Brown, Detention at the Police Station under the Police and Criminal Evidence Act 1984 (Home Office Research Study no 104) (London: HMSO, 1989) p 68.
5   Bucke and Brown (1997) p 23.
6   See discussion of *Murray v UK* (1996) 22 EHRR 29 in section 4(a) above.

'3.1   When a person is brought to a police station under arrest or is arrested at the police station having attended there voluntarily, the custody officer must inform him clearly of the following rights and of the fact that they are continuing rights . . .
(i)   The right to have someone informed of his arrest . . .
(ii)   The right to consult privately with a solicitor and the fact that independent legal advice is available free of charge; and
(iii)   The right to consult these codes of practice.

3.2   In addition the custody officer must give the person a written notice setting out the above three rights . . . The notice must also explain the arrangements for obtaining legal advice . . .'

This should ensure that arrested suspects are told their rights (including that legal advice is free) orally and in a written form. But there are two important loopholes here. Firstly, volunteers 'helping with inquiries' need not be told their rights, unless the police caution them that they are under suspicion.[7] Secondly, the obligation begins only when the suspect is brought to the police station. Suspects who are arrested a long way from the place of the alleged crime are therefore in police custody for a long time (whilst being transported to the relevant police station) before they are informed of their rights other than the right to silence. This will not usually matter, since most questioning is prohibited before arrival at the station (discussed in ch 5). But illegal interviewing sometimes occurs anyway, and there is no prohibition on letting suspects incriminate themselves voluntarily—if that is an appropriate way of describing the actions of suspects in police custody. Thus in *Khan*[8] the defendant was arrested in Wales and driven to Birmingham by the police who alleged that he voluntarily confessed in the car.

The procedure to be adopted on arrival at the station is as follows. After authorising detention, custody officers must tell suspects of their rights. They will be asked specifically whether they want to consult a solicitor. If so, a solicitor must be contacted as soon as possible. Every step in this process must be recorded on the custody record. For this set of protections to work it is essential that the police operate the system in good faith, and that a solicitor be readily available.

7   Code C, para 3.15.
8   (CA: 1990, unreported). Discussed in T Kaye, 'Unsafe and Unsatisfactory?' Report of the Independent Inquiry into the Working Practices of the West Midlands Police Serious Crime Squad (London: Civil Liberties Trust, 1991).

The right to legal advice

(iii) The 24-hour duty solicitor scheme

It is one thing to provide suspects with a right to advice, but delivering the advice is another matter entirely. Solicitors are obviously not available around the clock and many suspects are arrested at night, weekends or other awkward times. Before PACE this was a major problem. In Softley's 1980 study, around one-quarter of all suspects who requested advice did not get any. This was sometimes because the police refused to let them see a solicitor, but often a solicitor simply could not be found. There was a clear need to provide some form of scheme which secured access within a reasonable amount of time for the sake of both the suspect and the police so that unreasonable delay was not caused. This was bound to cost a lot of money. To the government's credit, it undertook to provide such money as was required.

Suspects requesting legal advice may choose to speak to their 'own' lawyer (if they have one) or may choose from a list of local lawyers which the police provide. In either case the custody officer will phone the lawyer and ask him or her to speak to the suspect on the phone or to come to the station. If the suspect does not favour either of these alternatives, or if the chosen solicitor is unavailable, a duty solicitor can be requested. The country is divided into a number of legal aid regions, within each of which are several areas. Each area has, or should have, a duty solicitor scheme.[9]

When a duty solicitor is requested, the custody sergeant will not phone a solicitor directly. Instead, a telephone referral service is contacted. The service informs a duty solicitor of the suspect's request for legal advice. Local schemes are organised by local Law Societies, but there is no obligation on solicitors to participate. Although all police stations are now covered by schemes, some schemes have too few solicitors. Consequently, duty solicitors cannot always get to the police station quickly, and sometimes fail to get there at all.[10] All police station work, whether done on a private or duty solicitor basis, is paid for by the state on an hourly basis at no cost to the suspect. Article 6 ECHR, discussed earlier, only requires that free assistance be provided 'when the interests of justice so require' (ie when the cases is sufficiently serious or when the suspect is vulnerable), so PACE goes further than it needs to satisfy our human rights obligations.

9   These were originally established under s 59 of PACE. See now the Legal Aid Board 'Legal Advice and Assistance at Police Stations Register Arrangements 1995'.
10   A Sanders, L Bridges, A Mulvaney and G Crozier, *Advice and Assistance at Police Stations and the 24 Hour Duty Solicitor Scheme* (London: Lord Chancellor's Department, 1989).

(b) The takeup of advice by suspects

When solicitors are contacted, they phone the police station and speak to the suspect or come directly to the station or do both. But not all suspects who request advice actually secure it. Despite large increases in the request rate since 1988, only one-third of all suspects receive advice:

Table 4.1: Request and consultation rates, 1988-1996[11]

	Request rate (%)	Consultation rate (%)
1988	25	19
1991	32	25
1995-6	40	34

Within these general figures, there are considerable variations. For instance, advice is sought more often for serious than for minor offences, and advice is sought and received in over half of all cases involving offences tried in the Crown Court.[12] This is understandable, unlike the great variations which persist between different police stations.[13]

Despite the general increase, less than half of suspects exercise their right to advice, and fewer still actually secure it. This seems difficult to understand at first sight. Nearly all are in the police station involuntarily. Most will be frightened or apprehensive, unsure of their rights and worried about how long they will be detained. Many perceive the police to be 'against' them—as of course they are in an adversarial system. Against this intimidating backcloth they are being offered something for nothing: a lawyer, whose sole job whilst in the station will be to help that suspect, at precisely nil cost. Yet the response of the majority is to say 'no thanks'.

In the earliest study of PACE, Maguire observed that some suspects have a predisposition to seek advice while others do not, and some are very much easier to influence than are others.[14] Suspects arrested for trivial offences like drunkenness are entitled to advice but they correctly perceive that it would be of little use to them. There is a low elasticity of demand among these suspects. Other suspects who reject the idea of legal advice include those who are confident that they can handle the situation and, at the opposite end of the spectrum, fatalistic suspects who believe that nothing can help them at all. Needless to say, neither the confidence nor

11 Figures derived from Bucke and Brown (1997) ch 3.
12 Royal Commission on Criminal Justice (RCCJ), Report (Cm 2263) (London: HMSO, 1993) p 35.
13 Brown et al (1992). Bucke and Brown (1997) ch 3.
14 M Maguire, 'Effects of the PACE Provisions on Detention and Questioning' (1988) 28 BJ Crim 19.

the fatalism are always justified.[15] Some suspects simply trust the police to deal with them so fairly that they see no need for advice or help from anyone else, which will again be true only some of the time and, of course, begs the question of what is 'fair' in an adversary system.[16]

As we saw earlier, the main goal of many suspects is to get out of the station as soon as possible. These suspects refuse advice only because it might delay their departure. One-half of all suspects refusing advice would have requested it had a solicitor been in the station.[17] Some suspects plan ahead by leaving messages with parents or friends that a solicitor is to be secured if they are not home by a certain time.[18] These suspects make strategic decisions based on their past experience with police and solicitors. Sometimes their experiences with solicitors are so unsatisfactory that this is why they are reluctant to request them. Others have a low opinion of duty solicitors in particular, and so would see only their own solicitor, preferring to see no one rather than the duty solicitor: 'Duty solicitors are crap anyway, they work for the fucking police and the courts.'[19] Most suspects have no opportunity to plan ahead. The defendant in *Aspinall* requested a solicitor but, because of a mix-up, he did not see one. After 13 hours in custody he signed the custody record to say that he no longer wished to see a solicitor, 'the reason being I want to get home to my missus and kid.'[20]

Some suspects have an inflexible elasticity of demand because they always want a solicitor. Many of these are likely to be charged with serious offences, have long records or believe that a solicitor can do them no harm and may well do them some good. These suspects demand solicitors in almost any circumstances, and would do so even if the police did not have to inform them of their rights and to arrange advice for them.

Between these two groups, Maguire argued, there is a large group of suspects, accused of moderately serious crimes such as shoplifting, car theft, handling stolen goods, burglary and deception, who have a very high elasticity of demand.[1] Many of these suspects, when they do not

15 See Bucke and Brown (1997) p 22.
16 Discussed more fully in A Sanders and L Bridges, 'The right to legal advice', in C Walker and K Starmer (eds), *Miscarriages of Justice* (London: Blackstone, 1999); and in A Sanders, 'Access to Justice in the Police Station: An Elusive Dream?' in R Young and D Wall (eds), *Access to Criminal Justice* (London: Blackstone, 1996).
17 Brown et al (1992) p 53.
18 Sanders et al (1989).
19 Choongh (1993) p 149. Sanders et al also found suspects who believed this. This belief is understandable in view of the way many duty solicitors used to, and sometimes still do, behave. See section 4(d) below.
20 [1999] Crim LR 741. See sections 2(c) and 3 (d) above for discussion of this case.
1   Maguire (1988).

seek advice, say that this is because it is 'not worth it', or that they will wait to see what happens (very few later deciding to seek advice).[2] Decisions about whether or not to seek advice are influenced by a large number of factors. These include the attitudes and practices of the police and the availability and likely quality of the advice.

(c) The attitudes and practices of the police

Many suspects learn about their rights for the first time when told them by the custody officer. Others may know some of their rights but not crucial details (such as advice being free). Others may be afraid to ask for a lawyer. It follows that the way the police inform suspects of their rights—whether the choice is put as a 'question expecting the answer yes or the answer no'[3]—could be an important influence upon them. Sanders et al in the late-1980s observed the reception of suspects into custody in ten police stations and concluded that the police utilise 'ploys' to dissuade suspects from seeking advice in over 40% of all cases. Table 4.2 (see p 224) shows the great range of ploys used.[4]

It is likely that ploys are (or were) even more extensively used than this study detected, since, in this context, the presence of an observer inevitably affects the process being observed. In one example given by Sanders et al, two juveniles suspected of shoplifting from Mothercare were being processed by a custody officer. When the researcher walked into the custody area, he heard and saw the custody officer reading out the suspects' rights in an incomprehensible manner. The custody officer looked up, saw the researcher and said, 'Are you the chap from Mothercare?'. The researcher replied, 'No, I am the chap from Birmingham University', whereupon the custody officer went bright red, stopped, and started reading out the suspects rights very slowly and clearly from the beginning.[5]

Reading rights quickly and incomprehensibly and/or incompletely is the most frequently used ploy. In the somewhat contradictory words of a police officer:

> 'Now, under PACE, you read them their rights as quickly as you can—hit them with it so quick they can't take it in—say 'sign here, here and here' and there you are: nothing has changed. We all know that, though you wouldn't get any policeman to admit it to you.'[6]

2   See Bucke and Brown (1997) p 22.
3   Maguire (1988) p 31.
4   Source: Sanders et al (1989) p 59.
5   Sanders et al (1989) p 63.
6   Sanders et al (1989) p 58.

The right to legal advice

Table 4.2: Types of ploy

Ploy	Frequency (principal ploy only)	
	No	%
1. Rights told too quickly/incomprehensibly/ incompletely	142	42.9
2. Suspect query answered unhelpfully/incorrectly	5	1.5
3. Inability of suspect to name own solicitor	2	0.6
4. 'It's not a very serious charge'	1	0.3
5. 'You'll have to wait in the cells until the solicitor gets here'	13	3.9
6. 'You don't have to make your mind up now. You can have one later if you want to'	27	8.2
7. 'You're only going to be here a short time'	25	7.6
8. 'You're only here to be charged/interviewed'	14	4.2
9. [to juvenile] 'You'll have to [or 'do you want to'] wait until an adult gets here'	18	5.4
10. [to adult] '[Juvenile] has said he doesn't want one'	8	2.4
11. Combination of 9 and 10	4	1.2
12. 'We won't be able to get a solicitor at this time/ none of them will come out/he won't be in his office'	6	1.8
13. 'You don't need one for this type of offence'	2	0.6
14. 'Sign here, here and here' [no information given]	7	2.1
15. 'You don't have to have one'	4	1.2
16. 'You're being transferred to another station – wait until you get there'	6	1.8
17. Custody officer interprets indecision/silence as refusal	9	2.7
18. 'You're not going to be interviewed/charged'	1	0.3
19. 'You can go and see a solicitor when you get out/at court'	9	2.7
20. 'You're (probably) going to get bail'	6	1.8
21. Gives suspect *Solicitors' Directory* or list of solicitors without explanation/assistance	3	0.9
22. Other	19	5.7
Total	331	100.0

Comments such as 'you'll have to wait in the cells until a solicitor gets here' are a dire threat to those suspects for whom length of detention is a greater concern than whether or not they are charged. Whilst the warning is true it is also incomplete: it ignores the fact that most suspects are put in the cells until they are interrogated anyway.

It is difficult to establish a causal link between the use of police ploys and actual requests for advice by suspects. Sanders et al found that there was little correlation between the two but this may have been because the police use these ploys primarily against those suspects whom they thought would ask for a solicitor anyway, or for whom they particularly did not want a solicitor involved. Brown et al considers the lack of correlation to be evidence that custody officers are not deliberately trying to obstruct suspects. They argue that:

'. . . over-speedy and unclear expositions of rights may have occurred simply because custody officers were all too familiar with what they were saying and failed to appreciate that to some suspects the information was new and unfamiliar . . .'[7]

Similarly, Morgan et al found 'active discouragement, leading questions, or incomplete statement of rights' in 'only' about 14% of cases. In the rest, they say, rights were presented 'reasonably', but that 'few suspects are in a 'reasonable' frame of mind at the time. There is usually no attempt to make sure the statement has been understood.'[8]

In the early 1990s, Brown et al found that although the overwhelming majority of suspects recalled being informed of their rights in general, little over half were aware that advice would be free, and even fewer were aware that they could consult an independent solicitor in private.[9] Consistent with this, Clare and Gudjonsson found that only 40% of suspects could fully understand the written notice of rights provided to them.[10] It seems, then, that the police go through the motions of providing thoroughly due process-based rights to advice, but insufficient attention has been paid to ensuring that the message gets through to the vulnerable, the anxious and the less intelligent, who need them most. And it carries on, in part, because so few suspects realise that their rights are being inadequately communicated to them. Only 8% of suspects interviewed by Brown et al thought they misunderstood what the police told them, even though many

7   Brown et al (1992) p 29.
8   R Morgan, R Reiner and I McKenzie, Police Powers and Policy: A Study of the Work of Custody Officers (report to ESRC) (unpublished).
9   Brown et al (1992) pp 37-42.
10 I Clare and G Gudjonsson, Devising and Piloting an Experimental Version of the Notice to Detained Persons (Royal Commission on Criminal Justice, Research Study no 7) (London: HMSO, 1993).

more than this were unaware of important details, and Choongh's findings were similar.

In the most recent research, in the mid-1990s, different suspects were still found to be treated significantly differently by custody officers. Although we do not know to what extent or to what effect, one example is the classic ploy of stressing that advice could be requested later even if it is initially refused.[11] These researchers found that request rates varied between police stations and that this could not be explained according to the factors on which they collected systematic data - perhaps because they did not systematically document the ways in which suspects were treated.[12] Also a related study found that few suspects (almost none at all in two stations) were not asked why they refused legal advice, a clear breach of the latest version of the Code of Practice (para 6.5).[13]

Perhaps less important than whether the police deliberately obstruct suspects is how often their words or actions actually do so - which, it appears, is quite often. How far the police engage in 'ploys' remains a matter of debate, but some police manoeuvres are clear-cut. The notification provisions of Code of Practice C were breached, in the opinion of Brown's observers, in 16% of the cases observed prior to the revision of the PACE Codes of Practice in 1991, and in 26% of the cases observed after that revision, which required the police to give more information to suspects. Brown et al found that sometimes no information at all was provided. Occasionally, suspects were simply asked if they wanted a solicitor.[14]

Whether or not advice was originally requested, the police are supposed to remind suspects of their right to legal advice at the time of each review of detention and at the start of the interview.[15] This was not so under the original version of Code of Practice C, and although the police usually now do this they fail to do so in around one quarter of all cases. That the police do not encourage late requests is evident from the following extract from the transcript of a trial:[16]

> Q: [Defence Counsel]: 'At the end of that interview you offered the opportunity to have a lawyer?'
> A: [Officer]: 'That is correct.'

11 Phillips and Brown (1998) p 61. Also see Choongh (1993) ch 6 for similar findings.
12 Phillips and Brown (1998) Fig 4.1.
13 Bucke and Brown (1997) ch 3.
14 D Brown, T Ellis and K Larcombe, Changing the Code: Police Detention under the Revised PACE Codes of Practice (Home Office Research Study no 129) (London: HMSO, 1992) p 31. About 7-8% of suspects were warned about the likely delay if they requested a lawyer (though Brown et al (1992) p 42 do not interpret this as a 'ploy').
15 Code of Practice C, paras 15.3 and 11.2.
16 Letter from the trial judge, Judge Sanders - no relation - published at [1989] Crim LR 763.

Q: 'Why did you not do that at the beginning?'
A: 'Because he had already been offered the opportunity to have a solicitor. If he wanted a solicitor he was welcome to have one but I am not going to encourage it.'
Q: 'You did not offer him one for that reason?'
A: 'No, not at the beginning of the interview.'
Q: 'You suspected that if he did get a solicitor he would be advised to say nothing?'
A: 'Yes.'
Q: 'Which is why he was not offered one?'
A: 'Yes.'

It is clear that, whether by accident or design, many officers discourage recourse to legal advice much of the time. But it is equally clear that many suspects—those with relatively inelastic demand—increasingly persevere with their requests. The police usually accept this, and the request rate is consequently rising. However in some cases—presumably where the police are particularly keen to interrogate the suspect without a lawyer present—the police go to great lengths to block access. The first tactic is to employ numerous ploys.[17] The second is to trick suspects into signing the custody record in the wrong place. This has been officially acknowledged as a problem to the extent that the original Code of Practice was revised to incorporate a specific injunction against this:

'The custody officer shall ask the detained person whether . . . he would like legal advice. The person shall be asked to sign the custody record to confirm his decision. The custody officer is responsible for ensuring that in confirming any decision the person signs in the correct place.'[18]

Another abuse stems from the fact that after advice is requested it is up to the police to make the call. Sometimes the police do not call the lawyer at all, which is clearly unlawful. Sometimes the call is delayed, allowing time to persuade suspects to withdraw their requests for advice, to be interrogated before the lawyer arrives, or to be informally interviewed.[19] Dixon et al comment that solicitors frequently complain that on arrival at the station they are often 'informed by officers that the suspect has

17 Sanders et al (1989) p 57, found that in these cases the request rate is noticeably lower than average.
18 Paragraph 3.5.
19 A Sanders and L Bridges, 'Access to Legal Advice and Police Malpractice' [1990] Crim LR 494. All these abuses were also observed in the small-scale observational study by Choongh (1993) ch 6.

changed his mind, agreed to talk to them, and confessed.'[20] The suspicion is that the police play a large part in this volte face. Unfortunately, custody records give no reason for failure to secure advice in one quarter of all such cases, thus making it difficult to account for the gap between the numbers requesting advice and those actually securing it.[1]

It would appear that giving the police the job of 'triggering' legal advice is a major obstacle to the success of the scheme. If the scheme were modified to allow solicitors to be in the police station round the clock it would almost certainly increase the advice rate, although it would be difficult and expensive to organise. Alternatively, s 58 might be amended so that advice would be provided unless actively refused. This would at least ensure that all the confused suspects who currently do not secure advice would do so. The Runciman Commission recommended none of these solutions. Apart from some minor changes, it recommended that even suspects who refuse advice 'should then be given the opportunity of speaking to a duty solicitor on the telephone.'[2] But suspects are already entitled to do this. Runciman presumably has it in mind that suspects who refuse advice be asked again. In view of who will be doing the asking, this is unlikely to make any difference. Moreover, this proposal makes assumptions about the value of telephone advice which we shall see are unwarranted. If the police really want to help suspects, they could at present suggest that they speak to a solicitor on the phone. No delay would be incurred and the suspect would have nothing to lose. That this happens only rarely cannot be a mere oversight. The Runciman Commission could have taken this further, recommending that all suspects should automatically be put into telephone contact with a duty solicitor in order to discuss the question of legal advice. The only losers, apart from crime control adherents, would be the Treasury.

(d) The attitudes and practices of the legal profession

It would be misleading to give the impression that all, or even most, of the problems of securing legal advice in police stations are the fault of the police. Many suspects do not want legal advice because of their experiences with duty solicitors or even with lawyers in general. Delivering legal services to suspects in police custody has many difficulties.

---

20 D Dixon, K Bottomley, C Coleman, M Gill and D Wall, 'Safeguarding the Rights of Suspects in Police Custody' (1990) 1 Policing and Society 115 at 128.
1 Brown et al (1992) p 61.
2 RCCJ (1993) p 36.

(i) Unavailability and contact time

We have seen that not all suspects who request advice get any. This is sometimes due to cancellation of requests because suspects do not want to wait any longer for advice to be provided. In some cases an able and willing solicitor simply cannot be located. This is bound to happen when suspects want to speak to their own solicitors, and this is what most suspects want.[3] Duty solicitor schemes are supposed to provide a safety net, but they do not always require someone to be on duty.

There are three types of duty solicitor scheme: rota, panel or mixed rota/panel. In a rota scheme, there will always be one or more solicitors on duty, who are paid a retainer for this purpose and who are obliged to provide advice. In a panel scheme, no one is so obliged, but panel membership is an indication of a general willingness to advise. In a mixed system, a solicitor is on duty part of the time. Panel and mixed systems are generally located in small towns where there is relatively little demand. However, because of the difficulty of recruiting solicitors, sometimes there are panel schemes where there should be rotas, or only one solicitor on duty where there should be two or three.

Half of all contacts with solicitors are made within 30 minutes, and three-quarters within one hour.[4] Delay is sometimes unavoidable, especially at night or if a solicitor is already dealing with a client. However, solicitors are reluctant to attend a police station simply 'to hold a suspect's hand', so they usually delay attendance until the police are ready to interview. Although understandable from the solicitors' point of view, who argue that initial phone contact should provide all the reassurance suspects need, this ignores the frightening isolation of detention discussed earlier. As one more sensitive solicitor put it: '. . . I think the terror of being alone in the police station is such, it [contact with a solicitor] may have no legal value whatsoever, but the psychological value of speaking to a solicitor early is not inconsiderable.'[5]

If solicitors are overstretched, the service to suspects may suffer in quality and quantity. Regarding quantity, even duty solicitors were unavailable 20% of the time in the early days of the scheme. By 1991, the overall contact rate with solicitors was 87%, and for duty solicitors the rate was around 95%.[6] Some areas, probably where duty solicitor schemes

---

3   Phillips and Brown (1998) ch 4 found that about 65% of suspects seeking advice wanted their own solicitor.

4   Brown et al (1992) p 62.

5   L Bridges et al, 'Quality in Criminal Defence Services' (London: Legal Aid Board, 2000) pp 67-8.

6   Brown et al (1992) pp 59-60. Note that consultations only occurred in 90% of all cases in which contact was made - often because, by that time, the suspect had already been dealt with.

are particularly stretched, have great trouble putting suspects in contact with solicitors. One station in Brown et al's study had a consultation rate in relation to requests below 50% in 1990 and just 66% in 1991.

(ii) Solicitor or clerk

Of those suspects who do secure advice, a large number do not see a solicitor at all, but a solicitor's clerk or trainee solicitor. This was so in around 30% of cases observed by Sanders et al in the 1980s, the proportion being rather higher for 'own' solicitors (50%) than for duty solicitors (16%). Although the numbers fluctuate, a large minority of suspects continue to see non-solicitors.[7] This proportion is likely to rise again in the future now that all 'franchised' duty solicitors are allowed to use non-solicitors who are trained or in training, although a solicitor must first speak on the phone to the suspect before a non-solicitor is allowed to advise.[8]

There is nothing wrong with the use of trained paralegals or trainees, but in the 1980s and early 1990s many were not trained and there were terrible abuses.[9] Now, however, all non-solicitors have to be trained and to pass tests, or be in training. The aim of this 'accreditation' scheme is to ensure that suspects are not disadvantaged by being advised by non-solicitors, and it appears to be successful. Most accredited paralegals themselves, and researchers evaluating the scheme, consider that the training leads to better advice, more time spent with suspects, and a more adversarial approach in police interviews.[10] However, the level from which quality has been raised, and which was set by many qualified solicitors, was not very high, as we shall see. Further, some firms employ 'trainee' paralegals who are not being trained at all, then after six months replace them with other 'trainees'. Attempts are being made to prevent this evasion of training requirements.[11] If unqualified staff have to satisfy certain basic levels of competence, logic demands that the same be required of qualified staff. At the time of writing the Legal Aid Board (to be renamed the Legal

---

7   M McConville and J Hodgson, Custodial Legal Advice and the Right to Silence (Royal Commission on Criminal Justice Research Study no 16) (London: HMSO, 1993) p 17. Also see M McConville, J Hodgson, L Bridges and A Pavlovic, *Standing Accused* (Oxford: Clarendon, 1994). Phillips and Brown (1998) ch 4.

8   For details see E Cape, *Defending Suspects at Police Stations* 3rd edn (London: Legal Action Group, 1999) ch 1.

9   See, for example, discussion in the 1st edn of this book. Also see Sanders (1996) and M McConville, J Hodgson, L Bridges and A Pavlovic, *Standing Accused* (Oxford: Clarendon, 1994).

10   L Bridges and S Choongh, *Improving Police Station Legal Advice* (London: Law Society, 1998) ch 4.

11   Bridges and Choongh (1998); L Bridges et al, *Quality in Criminal Defence Services* (London: Legal Aid Board, 2000).

Services Commission) is considering extending accreditation requirements to all solicitors who wish to do police station work but it is not clear whether this will happen.[12]

If junior staff are to be used extensively it is important that they, and the quality of their work, be supervised. Traditionally this is done in an ad hoc way, if at all, in solicitors' firms. The Legal Aid Board now insists on supervision, usually in the form of reviews of completed cases, but ensuring firms do this is impossible. Research carried out in the late 1990s indicates that some firms do not take it seriously. As a senior member of a firm which had reviewed only one case in 10 months wrote to his colleagues, 'We must complete the periodic reviews . . . We cannot afford to leave it any longer. It will not take a minute to do it.'[13] Even firms that do appear to take it seriously identify very few of the flaws in case handling that the researchers identified, and remedial action where flaws are identified appear very rare.[14]

(iii)   Advice in person or over the telephone

Initial contact between suspects and lawyers is usually by telephone. About a fifth of all advice is over the phone alone.[15] There is considerable variation, however, as duty solicitors are less willing to attend the station than are 'own' solicitors, some stations are geographically less convenient than others for solicitors and advisors are more likely to attend the station for serious offences than for minor ones. Telephone advice is not necessarily inappropriate. The offence may be trivial and guilt not in doubt; the suspect may want advice on one specific thing only; the police may want to know something discrete and straightforward before, for instance, release on bail. Sometimes it will be clearly inappropriate; where, for instance:

(a)   the suspect is disputing, or unclear about, the allegations;
(b)   the offence is serious;
(c)   the suspect is vulnerable;
(d)   detention is likely to be lengthy; or,
(e)   there may have been police malpractice.

Solicitors are professionals who ought to be able to judge these matters. They have official guidance to assist them and, when in doubt, they should

12   E Cape, 'New Labour: New Criminal Justice?' (2000) Legal Action, February, p 6.
13   L Bridges et al, Quality in Criminal Defence Services (London: Legal Aid Board, 2000) p 99.
14   Bridges et al (2000) ch 6.
15   Phillips and Brown (1998) ch 4. Telephone advice used to be used even more. See Brown et al (1992) and Sanders et al (1989).

go to the station. Moreover, once at the station they should stay, in all but exceptional cases, for any interview that might take place.[16]

In reality, solicitors are often guided by considerations other than the needs of the suspect, and much telephone advice is unsatisfactory. Advice is sometimes given to remain silent, for instance. Although this tells suspects their rights, it does not actually help them to remain silent in the face of vigorous questioning. Sanders et al found that solicitors were wanted for many things other than the simple provision of legal advice— to witness what went on, to act as emotional supports, to secure bail, and to take action over alleged malpractice. As the legislation acknowledges, access to a solicitor is to provide not just advice but also assistance. Little assistance can be provided over the telephone.

Just as the police fail to adhere, in many cases, to their code of practice, so some solicitors fail to adhere to theirs. Around 14% of all suspects in 1988 saw a legal advisor in person. Of all interrogated suspects, about 22% saw a legal advisor in person, but only about 14% had a legal advisor with them in the interrogation, because many solicitors who attended the station did not attend the interrogation.[17] The result was that many suspects might as well not have received any advice for all the use their lawyer was to them. Many suspects will not be frank with an often unknown voice on the phone: they may not trust the person, and in any case the police sometimes listen to the conversation. As one suspect told Sanders et al: 'If you met him face to face you could talk'. Another, asked if she would have the same solicitor again, replied 'We've not really had him have we? For all I know it might not have been a solicitor!'[18] Cases were seen where suspects who told the solicitor that they had been assaulted were left to languish in the cells for half the weekend, and where suspects were told on the phone 'not to say anything' in the interview when it must have been known that for most suspects this advice would be impossible to follow.[19] As we have seen, many suspects are vulnerable (but not recognised as such) and many more are less than fully rational as a result of their predicament. Most of these people need the support of someone whose duty is to look after their interests.

As a result of these abuses the official guidance for solicitors on when to attend stations was tightened up in the 1990s, creating much clearer obligations for duty solicitors.[20] In 1995-6 a large research study found

16   For details of the guidance, see E Cape, *Defending Suspects at Police Stations* 3rd edn (London: Legal Action Group, 1999) pp 26-8.
17   Sanders et al, ch 6.
18   Sanders et al, pp 119-120.
19   Sanders et al, pp 117-126.
20   Cape (1999) pp 26-8. Until 2000 'own' solicitors could do as they wished, although the desire to keep their client led them to be more willing to give a good service than when they are when acting as duty solicitors. Pilot contracting in 1998

that 37% of suspects had an advisor with them in all their interviews.[1] Even so, around one-fifth of all suspects who secure advice still receive telephone advice alone.[2] A significant proportion of these should have police station attendance, and duty solicitors still give telephone advice far more often than do 'own' solicitors even though most duty solicitors are 'own' solicitors in some contexts and vice versa. It seems that the type of service given depends as much on the status of the client and the 'culture' of the law firm in question as the nature of the case, although solicitors deny this.[3] Many solicitors argue that, even if telephone advice is sometimes given inappropriately, this is all that can be expected of an under-remunerated profession under pressure.[4] To compound the problem, in most police stations suspects have to speak to their solicitors in the custody room.[5] Police officers are therefore able to listen to these conversations, sometimes on purpose but sometimes because they have to continue with their work within earshot. This has been held to breach s 58 (and, by implication, ECHR Art 6).[6]

(iv)   The quality of advice and assistance

In an adversarial system, solicitors would be expected to advise and assist suspects in the police station to the best of their abilities, regardless of how difficult this might make it for the police to secure evidence sufficient to prosecute. Under due process and freedom models, we would expect to find protections for suspects detained against their will, and would expect legal advisors to help suspects to use these protections. Thus in Britain there are rules which aim to prevent oppressive questioning and allow suspects to stay silent (albeit with a possible penalty - see ch 5), which solicitors should use to their clients' advantage. As the Code of Practice itself states, 'The solicitor's only role in the police station is to protect and advance the legal rights of his client.'[7]

required 'own' solicitors to adhere to the same rules as duty solicitors. (L Bridges et al, Quality in Criminal Defence Services (London: Legal Aid Board, 2000).

1   Bucke and Brown (1997) ch 4. Most suspects are interviewed only once. Bucke and Brown found that, in the minority of cases where there is more than one interview an advisor is normally, but not always, present for them all.

2   L Bridges, E Cape, A Abubaker and C Bennett, *Quality in Criminal Defence Services* (London: Legal Aid Board, 2000).

3   Sanders et al (1989) ch 6; Bridges et al (2000).

4   The 'pressure' argument is supported by Brown et al (1992) p 88, but rejected by McConville et al (1994) who point out that some firms, albeit a minority, provide a very good service without noticeable financial hardship. Also see J Hodgson, 'Adding Injury to Injustice: the Suspect At the Police Station' (1994) 21 JLS 85.

5   Phillips and Brown (1998) ch 4.

6   See the county court case of *Roques*, discussed in section 5 below.

7   Paragraph 6d.

What should legal advisors do? According to Cape, a leading practitioner/academic on this topic, they should:

- advise them as to their best interests;
- keep an accurate record of their consultations with their clients and of the police interview;
- ensure their clients act according to their best interests (subject to not knowingly lying or actively misleading);
- ensure the police act fairly and lawfully; and
- protect clients from unnecessary pressure and distress.[8]

What all this means in concrete terms will vary from case to case. If suspects who indicated they would remain silent start to answer they can be reminded of their right to silence and, if necessary, a private consultation can be demanded. If suspects' answers are unclear, or points that could help them are not brought out, the advisor can ask clarificatory questions or suggest that the suspect may want to add something. If questioning becomes hectoring or abusive, or a threatening manner or gestures are used, the advisor should intervene by, for example, objecting, asking for re-phrasing, asking for a break or advising silence. Advisors have to be careful that they do not contravene Code of Practice C.[9]

Early research into the work of legal advisors found that legal advisors did very little when they attended interrogations, frequently seeing their task as facilitating the process, rather than protecting the rights of their clients.[10] Baldwin, for example, described most legal advisors as 'essentially passive'.[11] However, Roberts pointed out that this does not mean that they fail to do their job in most cases:

> '. . . if the police interviewer was behaving professionally and the suspect did not need assistance, intervention on the part of the solicitor would be quite unnecessary.'[12]

Without matching the behaviour of the police and of the solicitor against Code of Practice C and the official guidance, we cannot know whether non-intervention was justified or not. Bridges and Choongh did this, finding that in around one quarter of interviews no intervention is called for.

8   E Cape, *Defending Suspects At Police Stations* 3rd edn (London, Legal Action Group, 1999) chs 3, 5, 7.

9   Discussed above, Code para 6.9. Also see Notes 6D and 6E. Practical advice is provided by Cape (1999) pp 275-302.

10   See Brown et al (1992) p 89, and McConville and Hodgson (1993). See also, for further examples, Sanders and Bridges (1993) at p 51 and D Dixon, 'Common Sense, Legal Advice, and the Right of Silence' [1991] PL 233 at p 242.

11   J Baldwin, The Role of Legal Representatives at the Police Station (Royal Commission on Criminal Justice Research Study no 3) (London: HMSO, 1993) Table 1.

12   D Roberts, 'Questioning the Suspect: the Solicitor's Role' [1993] Crim LR 369.

Advisors do intervene in most of those in which it is called for, but in over half of all such cases they do so less often than they should. This level of performance, while not brilliant, is better than it used to be. However, advisors rarely challenge police behaviour in interviews, such as objectionable police questioning.[13] This can be crucial, as the 'Cardiff Three' case shows.[14] In this case, three men were convicted of killing a woman after one 'confessed'. He challenged the confession in court, but the trial judge ruled it admissible. The tapes of questioning were played to the Court of Appeal, which condemned them as contrary to Code of Practice C, quashed the convictions and criticised the defendant's lawyer for sitting through these interrogations without objecting. Whilst this is just one case, it is illustrative of many others.

The problem is that, contrary to one's intuition, adversarialism is not a natural stance for most defence lawyers, particularly those who spend a lot of time advising suspects. To such lawyers, the police station is the workplace and the importance of maintaining good relations with work colleagues (ie the police) is an important consideration. Dixon quotes a solicitor who says:

> 'You've got to do the best for your client, but you've still got to live with the system many years on. So . . . most solicitors do their best for their clients, but they also . . . won't generally upset the police.'[15]

Even Roberts, the author of the original Law Society guidance for police station advisors, is not sure what the role of the advisor should be: 'Interviews run better if the solicitor is able to establish a working relationship with the interviewer based on mutual respect.'[16] Better for whom? And at what cost are those working relationships purchased? Advisors are in a position of role conflict on potentially hostile territory. No wonder many solicitors seek to avoid this work. And, given the nature of most custodial legal advice, it is not surprising that the police are less hostile to the provision of advice than they used to be, even though advice rates have risen. The police know that advice rarely gets in the way of their carrying out their adversarial role. Yet the response of the Runciman Commission to all this evidence—which it did not challenge—was simply to call for more and better training of solicitors and paralegals, and for more

13 L Bridges and S Choongh, Improving Police Station Legal Advice (London: Law Society, 1998) ch 8. This research, done in the mid-1990s, shows that, despite limitations in quality, there has been a big improvement since McConville and Hodgson (1993) carried out their research in the late 1980s.
14 Paris, Abdullahi and Miller (1993) 97 Cr App R 99.The case is briefly discussed by the Runicman Commission: Royal Commission on Criminal Justice, Report (Cm 2263) (London: HMSO, 1993) pp 58 and 62.
15 Dixon [1991] p 239. Also see Baldwin (1993) Table 1.
16 Roberts [1993] p 370.

monitoring.[17] As Baldwin, author of some of the research on which this recommendation was based, comments, this 'looks at best superficial'.[18]

Since PACE was passed in 1984 the numbers of suspects securing advice and assistance, and having an advisor with them in interviews, has risen dramatically. Training for advisors has improved, and they have been made increasingly aware of their adversarial role in defending their clients. This should have led to greatly improved protection for suspects, but the improvements are limited, for various reasons.

First, it is difficult to give good advice without knowing the police case against the suspect. But the police need tell suspects and their advisors nothing;[19] in order to get information from the police they usually need to give something back, unless the police have tactical reasons for disclosing elements of their case. That 'something' is usually information, as distinct from silence. The police are well aware of the hold they have over solicitors: 'One of the solicitors from Gutts and Co asked me why some CID officers were walking towards the cell blocks. Cheeky bastard! . . . He's getting no co-operation from me from now on - not until I get an apology.' (Custody officer).[20]

Second, remaining silent can, as a result of the CJPO 1994, lead to great disadvantages at trial, as we shall see in ch 5. Advisors have to make very difficult judgments. Silence alone is not enough to convict a defendant. So, if the police have no admissible evidence, a client would be well advised to remain silent; but since the police need not tell suspects and their advisors what evidence they have, it is often not possible to know whether such advice is good advice.[1] Thus, paradoxically, in many cases advisors can best help their clients by encouraging co-operation with the police, even though co-operation is the antithesis of adversarialism.[2]

A different kind of consideration is the development of franchising, contracting and fixed fee systems. The Access to Justice Act (AJA) 1999 provides for payment to 'franchised' firms on the basis of fixed fee contracts for most criminal legal aid work. The Act is due to be implemented over several years from late 2000 onwards. At the time of writing (mid 2000), its likely effects are not known, especially as contracting had not yet been implemented, but some of the pilot arrangements for police station legal

17 RCCJ (1993) pp 35-39. The recommendations have been partially implemented. See Bridges and Choongh (1998) and Bridges et al (2000).
18 J Baldwin, 'Power and Police Interviews' (1993) 143 NLJ 1194 at 1195.
19 *Imran and Hussain* [1997] Crim LR 754.
20 S Choongh, *Policing as Social Discipline* (Oxford: Clarendon, 1997) p 85.
1 For a good practical discussion see Cape (1999) pp 192-218.
2 For further discussion of these and other ways in which advisors need to negotiate with the police, albeit from a position of inequality, in order to serve their clients' interests, see A Sanders, 'Access to Justice in the Police Station: An Elusive Dream?' in R Young and D Wall (eds), *Access to Criminal Justice* (London: Blackstone, 1996). It does seem that the police do now disclose more to advisors than they used to. See Bridges and Choongh (1998).

advice have been evaluated by Bridges et al. Franchising sets standards for law firms who could lose their contracts if they fail to meet them. However, as observed earlier, the (very light) supervision requirements are of limited effectiveness. Bridges et al set a threshold whereby essential work should be carried out in at least 70% of all cases. 44% of firms in their research failed this test. 60% failed a more rigorous test of quality. Very few of these flaws in case handling are either identified or acted upon. Thus most firms have a long way to go in delivering legal advice of adequate quality.[3]

Further, under s 12 (1) AJA 1999, the Criminal Defence Service (CDS) (an arm of the Legal Services Commission - the LSC) will begin operations in April 2001. There are plans for the CDS to create a salaried public defender system, under which some defence solicitors will become part of the machinery of the criminal justice system and committed to fulfilling its objectives.[4] These include speedy justice, which sometimes conflicts with full justice.[5] This is likely to lead to further role confusion of the type suffered by Roberts.[6] As it is, solicitors tend to discourage suspects from pleading not guilty or failing to co-operate with the police. This is not just because, as noted earlier, of the pressure for reciprocal co-operation. It also stems from the non-adversarial character of the profession, the dim view many lawyers take of suspects, and (especially when acting as duty solicitors)[7] the limited effort lawyers will provide for a limited reward. An example of this is a lorry driver arrested for importing cannabis and ecstasy in his lorry. He declined a solicitor, and, when questioned, denied knowing anything about the drugs. He was then advised by the police to secure legal advice. The duty solicitor, without asking to hear his story, advised him that he would get six years if he pleaded guilty to knowingly importing cannabis but 12 years if he contested this and was convicted after a trial of importing both types of drug. Eventually he pleaded guilty to knowingly importing cannabis but changed his plea, citing the pressure put on him to plead guilty by the solicitor. When asked about this, the solicitor admitted not seeking the lorry driver's side of the case, saying that as a solicitor practising in Dover who had been a duty solicitor in many cases like this, he was 'only' giving his standard advice based on his experience that 99% of cases like this end in conviction.[8]

3   Bridges et al (2000) chs 5-6.
4   Lord Chancellor's Department, Modernising Justice: the Government's Plans for Reforming Legal Services and the Courts (Cm 4155) (London: SO, 1998). Contracting and franchising are further discussed in ch 8, section 2(d).
5   E Cape, 'New Labour: New Criminal Justice?' (2000) Legal Action, February, p 6.
6   Roberts [1993].
7   Choongh (1997) ch 6
8   Thanks to Ed Cape for details of this case. It is at the time of writing being heard by the Court of Appeal.

(e) Legal advice in the station: assistance for whom?

It seems that suspects are at nearly as much risk from the legal profession as from the police. Attempts to ensure that adequate standards are maintained include a regional network of committees to oversee local duty solicitors schemes, a national committee of the Legal Aid Board to oversee and regulate the operation of the duty solicitor scheme as a whole and, from 2000, contracting and franchising. Solicitors who breach the scheme or their contracts—who, for instance, are unavailable when on duty, fail to give advice at the station when they should, or fail to supervise paralegals—can lose their contracts. However, a lot of rule breaking is undiscovered (suspects either do not know they should receive a better service, do not know to whom to complain or are fatalistic about the chances of anything being done about it) and local and regional committees are reluctant to discipline their members.[9] Professional self-regulation is always problematic. Disciplinary action is therefore rare and lenient. Whether contracting and franchising will lead to tougher quality control remains to be seen, but it is unlikely if fixed fees are set at levels which squeeze lawyers financially. Solicitors' firms are businesses. They act according to the profit motive. The less they get paid for, the less they do.

Also, we have seen that the police station is police territory. When the whole purpose of due process rights is to protect suspects from the police, to make the police the main gatekeepers to these rights and to information and other needs of suspects is plainly illogical. The counter-argument would be that the purpose of the custody officer as an independent officer is precisely to stand between suspects, on the one hand, and investigating officers, on the other. Since custody officers have no specific interest in any one case, the custody officer will protect suspects by full enforcement of the rights in Code of Practice C, even if investigating officers object. This, however, relies on the rather formalistic distinction between a custody officer's duty and an investigating officer's duty. It does not take into account the shared outlook of different police officers. It also does not take into account the fact that an officer who wishes to secure the co-operation of fellow officers one day will not wish to 'get in their way' by acting out the custody officer role to perfection another day. Both custody officers and solicitors have to get on with other police officers in the latter's territory. 'Independent' operation under these conditions is hardly conceivable.

Suspects need protecting from police, lawyers and themselves. Voluntarism (consent) is completely misplaced when dealing with an

---

9   Sanders et al (1989) ch 8.

intrinsically coercive situation.[10] Just as it is nonsense to argue that most confessions are voluntary, the same is true of decisions about advice. Some suspects are asked by lawyers on the phone whether they want them to come to the station, when the whole point about suspects in detention is that they cannot be assumed to be able to make rational or informed decisions for themselves. The rules at present are operated contrary to the interests of suspects because their interests and the interests of the gatekeepers diverge.

To make the rules work it would be necessary to install gatekeepers with the same interests as suspects, perhaps by paying solicitors or trained paralegals for effective police station work, and locating them in police stations so that they can see suspects with no delay. This might appear to be a ludicrous and expensive idea. But in 1997 a government committee argued that police-CPS working methods could be improved by installing prosecutors in police stations.[11] This recommendation was speedily implemented without regard to cost or other factors (see ch 6).The Runciman Commission could have made recommendations on these lines for police station defence but did not do so. Clearly helping the police and CPS takes far higher priority than helping suspects. Commenting on the greater power of the police as compared to suspects, Baldwin says that Runciman's recommendations:

'do little, if anything, to modify this power base. It will be surprising if, in consequence, there is much change in existing police practice. The Commission's view seems to be that the status quo represents the best way forward.'[12]

In reality, the most significant power differential is between the police and the legal profession, on the one hand, and the suspect, on the other. But perhaps because of the Runciman Commission's complacency, that differential, and the practices which flow from it, have been largely unchanged. Thus, in summary, police station legal advice and assistance often provides the most bare protection because: the police are gatekeepers, allowing them to manipulate the rules and the situation to dissuade suspects from seeking advice; the law gives the police a dominant bargaining position vis-a-vis both suspect and lawyer; the financial incentives for solicitors to do a minimalist job are greater than for them to do a fully adversarial job; and the professional ideology of the majority of

10 See R Young and D Wall, 'Criminal Justice, Legal Aid and the Defence of Liberty' in R Young and D Wall (eds), *Access to Criminal Justice* (London: Blackstone, 1996).
11 Home Office (Narey Report), Review of Delay in the Criminal Justice System (London: Home Office, 1997).
12 Baldwin (1993) 'Power and Police Interviews' at p 1197.

The right to legal advice

solicitors, similar to that of the police, holds most suspects to be guilty and unworthy of a 'Rolls Royce' service.

5. REMEDIES

We saw in chapters 2 (section 3(e)) and 3 (section 5) that the new rights for suspects are rarely complemented by remedies where those rights are breached. We argued there that the new right to damages for breaches of the ECHR right to liberty and security of the person (Art 5) is unlikely to have enlarged a citizen's remedies in any meaningful way. For similar reasons, most notably the apparent compatibility of English law with Convention requirements, we think the same is true here. What of the position in home-grown domestic law?

When no specific remedies are attached to provisions creating due process safeguards, actions by aggrieved persons alleging a breach of a safeguard have to be fitted within an existing tort - in the case of wrongful arrest, for example, false imprisonment. Thus unlawful stops only have remedies available when they amount to unlawful arrests. The same is largely true where there are breaches of the rights covered in this chapter. Thus wrongful detention is also covered by the tort of false imprisonment. Since detention is always authorised, and in a 'rubber stamp' manner, one might have thought that many suspects would sue. In fact, there appear to be no reported cases challenging the initial decision to detain following a lawful arrest, and the one unreported case is distinctly discouraging of such challenges.[13] The police are universally assumed to have the right to detain in these circumstances.[14] The main circumstance where a suspect can sue for false imprisonment is where the time-limit, overall or at the end of a review period, expires. In one case a suspect whose review was held two hours' late was awarded £500 for false imprisonment of two hours.[15] Since the purpose of periodic reviews is to ascertain whether continued detention is justified, the failure to review was held to create a false imprisonment until a proper review was carried out.

As far as access to legal advice is concerned, denial of a solicitor is not a breach of contract. Nor is it a tort or a crime. No specific remedy was provided for breach of PACE, s 58, but there is a tort of breach of statutory

---

13   In *Clarke v Chief Constable of North Wales Police* (5 April 2000, unreported) the Court of Appeal held that a custody officer is entitled to assume that an arrest is lawfully effected, unless there is evidence to the contrary. It went on to say that an arrest which was lawful could not become unlawful simply because the custody officer failed to ascertain its basis or the manner of its execution.

14   The poor quality of many legal advisers (see sub-section (d)(iv) above) means that we might characterise this as an unthinking, or even self-serving, assumption.

15   *Roberts v Chief Constable of Cheshire Constabulary* [1999] 1 WLR 662.

duty. This is rarely invoked successfully[16] but in 1995 a suspect who had to speak to his solicitor on the phone while being overheard by a police officer was successful. Section 58, it will be remembered, provides a right to private consultation, which was denied in this case.[17] Although only a first instance county court decision, this is consistent with the ECHR, Art 6 of which provides a right to privacy, and Art 3 of which has been interpreted to provide a right to advice in private.[18] However, most of the rights discussed in this chapter - to be informed of one's rights, to a phone call, for vulnerable suspects and so forth - are contained in Code C. They are not part of PACE or the ECHR. Since a Code is not a statute, breach of it is not a breach of statutory duty, and no other remedies are provided.

The situation is similar in relation to questioning. Torture is a crime.[19] It is also, along with 'inhuman or degrading treatment', contrary to Art 3 of the ECHR. But it is very rare indeed for questioning to fall into these categories. We shall see in ch 5 that PACE provides that evidence obtained through oppressive or unfair questioning may, and sometimes has to be, excluded from trial. But this provides no formal right as such to suspects in relation to questioning. And trials are an endangered species in this country. Exclusionary devices can have no purchase when the vast majority of cases are disposed of by NFA, cautions, and guilty pleas. We shall also see that Code C provides numerous rights to contemporaneous recording, warnings and so forth, but - as with the other rights provided in the Code - these are not actionable.

The importance of the protection of suspects can be gauged by the fact that there are better remedies available for damage to reputation and trespass on one's land. All suspects whose police station 'rights' are breached can do most of the time is to either make an official complaint or seek to have evidence obtained in consequence of the breach of their rights excluded from trial. These are applicable to breach of other police powers, too, and will be discussed in ch 11. At this point we can simply note that these procedures have a limited deterrent effect on the police, making the rules as much presentational as inhibitory.

6. CONCLUSION

The treatment of suspects in the police station is central to criminal justice. This is agreed by adherents of due process and crime control alike. For the latter, important evidence can be secured in the police station. This is

16   See A Sanders, 'Rights, Remedies and the PACE Act' [1988] Crim LR 802.
17   *Roques v Metropolitan Police Comr* (1997) Legal Action, September, p 23.
18   See discussion in section 4 above.
19   Criminal Justice Act 1988, s 134.

precisely what worries due process adherents. Few would argue with the Runciman Commission that:

> 'The protection of suspects from unfair or unreasonable pressure is just as important to the criminal justice system as the thoroughness with which the police carry out their investigations.'[20]

Yet PACE allows the police to detain for a considerable period of time in order to let them investigate even though for many people this detention is coercive in itself. We have seen that especially vulnerable people are given special protection but that vulnerability is not always recognised by the police. Further, to allocate everyone into either a 'vulnerable' or 'normal' category is unrealistic. And the rights which apply to all suspects in detention, while an advance on what existed prior to PACE, have a limited protective effect. This is partly because of the way those rights work in practice, but also partly because of the legal rules themselves. These rules allow lawyers and police officers to behave in ways that dissuade many suspects from exercising their rights; allow police detention to be so unpleasant that many suspects are prepared to do almost anything, including waiving their rights, to get out as quickly as possible; and, especially since the changes to the right of silence in 1994, make it difficult for lawyers to give useful advice and assistance to suspects.

Perhaps suspects in police custody should be *told* that they will see a lawyer, not *asked* if they want one. It is true that, in normal circumstances, people do not have things foisted on them against their will simply because someone else thinks it will be good for them. But suspects are not in normal circumstances. If they can be held in stinking conditions against their will, their mouths and hair invaded against their will, and questioned against their will why shouldn't they be given something that does them some good against their will? Vulnerable suspects are given appropriate adults whether they like it or not. This is because they are vulnerable. But we have argued that, in police custody, many 'normal' people are also vulnerable.

The detention regime is as offensive to the freedom perspective as it is to due process. Yet the floor of rights provided by the ECHR is so minimal that PACE and the CJPO give more protection to suspects than our human rights obligations require. For example, the ECHR says nothing about vulnerable suspects, many specific rights to assistance (such as intimation and visitors) or police bail. Nor is the length of detention regulated except at the most extreme end.

---

20   RCCJ (1993) p 25.

The traditional way of protecting people's rights is by providing them with remedies when their rights are breached. But we have seen that the rights which we examined in this chapter are hardly protected in this way at all. The ostensible reason for this is that custody officers are supposed to safeguard the interests of suspects. Without police rule breaking, there would be no need to have custody officers. But custody officers are police officers. If suspects need protection from the police, then by what logic can custody officers be expected to provide that protection? The Runciman Commission recognised, to some extent, the failures of custody officers such as allowing cell visits by officers (see ch 5), rubber stamping detention, failing to provide clear information about rights and adopting ploys to avoid suspects receiving legal advice. Their performance, they say: '. . . still leaves something to be desired . . . it may also be unrealistic to expect a police officer to take an independent view of a case investigated by colleagues.'[1]

After considering the poor performance of custody officers, the Runciman Commission then discussed (very briefly) whether another body could do the job of the custody officer. They decided that all the pressures on them would also be on a replacement body without that body even having the authority, vis-a-vis the police, of a custody officer. This was a due process/crime control cross-roads. The Runciman Commission could either allow things to go on, more or less as now (with minor enhancement to the custody officer role) and accept the coercive nature of police station detention; or it could take police investigation out of the police station. It chose the former.[2] Once it is decided, as the Runciman Commission did, that the police station should be the focus of investigation, and that the police should be free to detain suspects for 24 hours or more in order to interrogate, the crime control framework is accepted.[3] The room for due process and freedom is thereby fundamentally circumscribed. To fully appreciate the real power this puts into the hands of the police, we need to examine questioning in detail. That is the subject of ch 5.

1   RCCJ (1993) p 31. Also see Choongh (1997) pp 172-7 for a catalogue of abuses allowed or perpetrated by custody officers.
2   RCCJ (1993) pp 31-34.
3   For further discussion see A Sanders and R Young, 'The Rule of Law, Due Process, and Pre-Trial Criminal Justice' (1994) 47 CLP 125.

Conclusion

Chapter 5

Police questioning

DI to suspect: ' . . . If you'd rather have six [burglary charges] than two that's a matter for you. . . . That's the only fucking deal I can strike with you. . . . I mean I could really fucking throw it on thick for you. . . You're either going to have six fucking charges or you're going to have two and the only fucking way you're having two is you start fucking talking to us.'[1]

1. WHY ARE THE POLICE ALLOWED TO QUESTION SUSPECTS?

In chapter 4 we saw that the Police and Criminal Evidence Act 1984 (PACE) allows the police to detain suspects in order to question them. Most of us take this for granted. But it is not self-evident that the police should have this power. The presumption of innocence is a basic human right: 'Everyone charged with a criminal offence shall be presumed innocent until proved guilty by law.'[2] It is a fundamental element of both the freedom and due process perspectives. This means that:

- no-one should be allowed to hold anyone else against their will unless this is authorised by a judge or magistrate;
- detention should be on the basis of substantial objective evidence against that person;
- suspects should not be required to give evidence of innocence or to answer the case for the prosecution;

1 This is an extract from a secretly recorded interrogation reported in M McConville, 'Videotaping Interrogations: Police Behaviour on and off camera' [1992] Crim LR 532. Discussed in section 4 below.
2 Article 6 (2) ECHR (now part of the Human Rights Act 1998). The term 'charged' is interpreted to include arrested even if not charged in the English sense of prosecution being initiated.

- the police should not be able to require suspects to answer questions; and,
- police methods of extracting purportedly voluntary confessions should be viewed sceptically.

We saw in ch 4 that 'voluntariness' and 'consent' are meaningless in situations where all the choices available to suspects are unpleasant. The law used to be based on these principles, and police questioning in custody was all but ruled out, at least in theory. The preface (by a judge) to one of the earliest guides to the police said that when an officer:

> 'has a person in custody for a crime, it is wrong to question such person touching the crime of which he is accused . . . There is, however, no objection to a constable listening to any mere voluntary statement which a prisoner desires to make . . . Never act unfairly to a prisoner by coaxing him by word or conduct to divulge anything. If you do, you will assuredly be severely handled at the trial, and it is not unlikely your evidence will be disbelieved.'[3]

This position was reflected in the original version of the Judges Rules in 1912, although this did allow the police to invite suspects to make voluntary statements. Persons making voluntary statements were not to be 'cross-examined' and only questions aimed at 'removing ambiguity' were to be asked. As the Judges Rules were transformed over the years, however, police *interrogation* became more acceptable. The final formulation of the Judges Rules (in force from 1964 until their replacement by PACE) no longer purported to discourage questioning but merely to regulate its methods. PACE and Code of Practice C (Note 1B) maintains the general rule that no one need talk to the police, but that the police may none the less interrogate suspects in order to persuade them to talk. This is one of several disadvantages which, for many years, suspects and defendants had been liable to suffer if they withheld from the police explanations and information. Now, since the Criminal Justice and Public Order Act 1994 (CJPO), silence can lead to yet more disadvantages. This is all discussed in detail in section 2 below.

It is clear from this that the criminal justice system has been steadily moving away from the purist due process position in existence at the end of the nineteenth century. But the extreme crime control position is not adopted either, otherwise the police would be allowed to hold suspects in order to question them if they had any suspicions about them. Suspects

3 Preface to Vincent's Police Code (1882). Reproduced in Royal Commission on Criminal Procedure (RCCP), The Investigation and Prosecution of Criminal Offences in England and Wales: The Law and Procedure (Cmnd 8092-1) (London: HMSO, 1981) app 13, pp 162-163. This position was confirmed in *Knight and Thayre* (1905) 20 Cox CC 711.

would not have the right to refuse to answer questions and the police would thus be allowed to exert extreme pressure on suspects to speak.

The freedom perspective would not necessarily adopt a purist due process approach. Whether detention for questioning would be allowed would depend in part on the degree of suspicion against the suspect, the seriousness of the offence suspected, and the necessity of securing evidence by questioning under custodial conditions.[4] These would be essential criteria within the freedom approach because of its recognition that custodial detention in itself deprives suspects of freedom. The approach would not countenance questioning which placed any more pressure on suspects than arose from detention itself.

It will be recalled that in *Holgate-Mohammed v Duke*[5] the police acknowledged that the reason they arrested the suspect and took her to the police station, rather than interviewing her at home, was because people are more likely to confess when interrogated under conditions of involuntary detention. After all, there are confessions and incriminating statements in at least 60% of all cases where there is an interrogation, and in around 80% of guilty pleas.[6] Confession evidence may not be the only way of securing conviction, but it is the easiest method. A clear and credible confession often eliminates the need to secure extra evidence (for example, from witnesses or by forensic analysis of blood or semen samples), enabling more cases to be cleared up, and cleared up more quickly, than would otherwise be so. The idea that suspects are not pressured to speak when interrogated, and that the system embodies due process principles, is clearly untenable.

Changes to the right of silence in 1994 take the system even further down the crime control path. Just how far down that path we have moved, and what would be needed to incorporate a freedom perspective, is the subject of this chapter.

We should start by acknowledging that the way in which most offences are constructed encourages interrogation. The most often prosecuted (non-Road Traffic Act) criminal offences in England require evidence of mens rea (intent or recklessness) in order to convict the defendant. Assault is only a crime if a person is hurt intentionally or recklessly as distinct from someone stumbling or being careless and hurting the victim accidentally.

4   This was the approach of the Phillips Commission, discussed in ch 4, section 1.
5   [1984] 1 All ER 1054 discussed in ch 3, section 5.
6   J Baldwin, 'Police Interview Techniques: Establishing Truth or Proof?' (1993) 33 BJ Crim 325, Table 2; C Phillips and D Brown, Entry into the Criminal Justice System: a Survey of Police Arrests and their Outcomes (Home Office Research Study no 185) (London: Home Office, 1998) ch 5; T Bucke and D Brown, 'In Police Custody: Police Powers and Suspects' Rights Under the Revised Pace Codes of Practice (Home Office Research Study no 174) (London: Home Office, 1997) ch 4.

Theft is not theft if another's goods are taken accidentally. But how are the police to prove that an item was taken or a person injured deliberately rather than accidentally? Sometimes there will be objective evidence of intent, such as the egging on of someone to do the crime or a written plan, but this is rare. Evidence of intent can best be obtained by the statement of the person doing the crime.[7] Much police interrogation is geared not to establishing the objective facts—who took the articles or injured the victim, about which there is often no dispute—but what the person intended by his or her actions.[8] It follows that, if guilt had to be secured by reference to objective facts alone, the pressure on the police to interrogate would be reduced.

There are, however, many functions of interrogation other than the securing of incriminating statements. Firstly, in the course of interrogation the police often secure valuable information unrelated to the offence in question, such as suspects' other possible offences. McConville and Baldwin found that 21% of all guilty pleaders gave information on their other offences. Suspects may also give information about their associates (7% of guilty pleaders in McConville and Baldwin's study did so).[9]

Secondly, we saw in ch 2 that policing is increasingly 'proactive'. That is, the police target certain suspects or locations, often acting on tip-offs or surveillance-based information. Over weeks, or sometimes months, the police secure sightings, film and so forth which may point to the involvement of certain suspects in particular crimes. Interrogation then is not so much to secure confessions, as to either catch offenders out in lies (such as denying being in a location where a crime was committed) or to secure silence about suspicious activities. Coupled with the adverse inferences that can now be drawn against both silence and failure to account for being somewhere suspicious (see section 2 below) silence or lies can be equally useful to the police.

Thirdly, information about past or planned crimes in which the suspect is not involved, or general 'criminal intelligence', is also often provided.[10] This is often part of a 'deal', the information being exchanged for bail, lesser

---

7   See also the related discussion in ch 9, section 4(b).

8   R Evans, The Conduct of Police Interviews with Juveniles (Royal Commission on Criminal Justice Research Study no 8) (London: HMSO, 1993) and McConville et al (1991) ch 4.

9   M McConville and J Baldwin, *Courts, Prosecution and Conviction* (Oxford: OUP, 1981) ch 8. Also see Phillips and Brown (1998) ch 5; Bucke and Brown (1997) ch 4.

10   M McConville, A Sanders and R Leng, *The Case for the Prosecution* (London: Routledge, 1991) ch 4; M Maguire and C Norris, The Conduct and Supervision of Criminal Investigations (Royal Commission on Criminal Justice, Research Study no 5) (London: HMSO, 1992) chs 5 and 7; S Choongh, *Policing as Social Discipline* (Oxford: Clarendon, 1997) p 175; P Hillyard, *Suspect Community* (London: Pluto, 1993) ch 8.

charges, no prosecution at all or money. As Banton pointed out in 1964,[11] and Hobbs more recently,[12] every suspect is a potential informant. Just as stop-search is used in a crime control or even a repressive fashion to facilitate the broadest policing role,[13] so this is true also of questioning. A few of the police officers interviewed by McConville et al claimed that the restrictions imposed by PACE prevented deals being done, but most said that they had found ways of continuing as before. As one said in relation to access to solicitors: 'You can't make deals with the solicitor present but you can when he's not there. It needs watching that, but you can still do it.'[14]

According to one CID officer, suspects are often keen to open negotiations: 'They [suspects] always want to deal. When they're arrested they're immediately in the game of damage limitation.'[15] Many are as keen as the police on excluding third parties from such negotiations. On one of the few occasions when Sanders et al were denied access to an interrogation, the suspect avowed, somewhat melodramatically, that he would be 'a dead man' if anyone except the officer was present at what was to ensue.[16] Deals are rarely struck 'cold'. Good bargaining is based on a trusting relationship, a hallmark of 'good' policing. These relationships are built and maintained through policing at every level—on the street, in the station, in court—preventing legal regulation from neatly demarcating separate steps of the process.

Finally, interrogation by, and confession to, the police is part of a wider exercise of social and political power. The influential writer, Michel Foucault, identified new forms of power in modern societies which had been added to the traditional armoury of overt coercion and control. These include the allocation of space (for example, where certain categories of people are, and are not, allowed to go without permission), the regulation of time (through, for example work and school) and surveillance (through street policing and its partial replacement, CCTV cameras). He also identifies specialist knowledge, in the professions and the police, as a form of power.[17] Foucault highlighted a 'power/knowledge nexus'. To simplify, power

11   M Banton, *The Policeman in the Community* (London: Tavistock, 1964).
12   D Hobbs, *Doing the Business* (Oxford: OUP, 1988).
13   See ch 2, section 4(b).
14   McConville et al (1991) p 62. The truth of this is evident from the interrogation extract reproduced at the head of this chapter.
15   Quoted by Maguire and Norris (1992) p 47.
16   A Sanders, L Bridges, A Mulvaney and G Crozier, *Advice and Assistance at Police Stations and the 24 Hour Duty Solicitor Scheme* (London: Lord Chancellor's Department, 1989).
17   M Foucault, *Discipline and Punish* (London: Allen Lane, 1977). See S Watson, 'Foucault and Social Policy', in G Lewis et al, *Rethinking Social Policy* (Milton Keynes, Open UP, 2000) for an accessible summary of Foucault's work. See also K Stenson, 'Crime Control, Social Policy and Liberalism' in the same volume.

provides the means to gain knowledge over a subject which in turn increases the power over the now better-known subject. A central element here is confessional statements.[18] Confession, usually as a result of questioning, intrudes on the most intimate aspects of personal and social life. Take, for example, those classic TV cop dramas, where the dogged detective turns up all manner of seedy goings-on by people who plead for these secrets to remain secrets, only to be told that this is either not possible or that non-revelation has a price.

Questioning and confession gives power to the questioner and takes power away from the confessor. The more the police, for example, are given powers to question, the more 'ordinary' people are in their power. Those 'ordinary' people are not, however, randomly selected. As we saw in chapters 2-4, the social distribution of suspects and defendants is skewed towards the most socially marginal. Nor are these suspects merely interrogated because they are believed to have committed a specific crime. As Choongh demonstrates, the police arrest and interrogate those belonging to social groups which are regarded as 'police property' precisely because this exercise of power is a form of discipline:

'Interrogation is something which the police can do to a suspect whether the suspect likes it or not . . . the police use the interview room as a forum to inform 'policed' communities that they can be asked any question, and in any manner, regardless of whether it relates to the original suspicion.'[19]

As the police gain extra powers their ability to discipline and control in this way increases. People in socially marginalised groups who do not obey the rules of time, space and social behaviour are subject to stop-search, arrest and interrogation, punishing them for their transgressions.

This discussion of discipline and confessions is not entirely in line with Foucault's governmentality thesis, that power is increasingly dispersed through society. For we are arguing that the traditional criminal justice system is developing in such a way as to concentrate power in the hands of the police, power which is mostly used against the socially marginalised.[20] Foucault's insights nonetheless alert us to the value to

18   M Foucault, *The History of Sexuality* vol 1 (London: Allen Lane, 1979).
19   Choongh (1997) pp 135-6. Also see Hillyard (1993) ch 8; P Waddington, *Policing Citizens* (London: UCL Press, 1999) especially ch 5; R Leo 'Police Interrogation and Social Control' (1994) 3 Social and Legal Studies 93. Drawing on Foucault, these writers show how police power is both a product and a pre-condition of their ability to interrogate.
20   We contend this is so notwithstanding the growing importance of such forms of dispersed power as private policing and the novel forms of regulatory activity which are shaping the global economy. J Braithwaite, 'The New Regulatory State

the powerful of being able to make those with less power account to them through questioning.

2. THE RIGHT OF SILENCE

The right of silence occurs at three stages in the criminal process. Firstly, there is a right to silence on the streets. People need not speak to police officers if they are stopped and questioned, whether or not s 1 stop-search powers are being exercised.[1] Silence is not obstruction, although refusal to answer questions could be if accompanied by abuse.[2] Further, under para 10.1 of Code of Practice C, suspects must, unless the questioning is carried out as part of the exercise of stop-search powers, be told that they need not answer questions:

> 'A person whom there are grounds to suspect of an offence must be cautioned before any questions about it (or further questions if it is his answers to previous questions that provide grounds for suspicion) are put to him for the purpose of obtaining evidence ...'

It follows that people who are not suspected of offences need not be cautioned. The caution begins: 'You do not have to say anything ...'. On arrest, suspects must be cautioned unless this is impracticable because of the condition or behaviour of the suspect or unless the suspect had been cautioned immediately before arrest. The second stage where the right of silence may be exercised is in the police station, which we shall deal with in this chapter. Thus suspects must be cautioned again at the start of any and every interrogation. Finally there is the right to silence in court, looked at in ch 9, section 4(a)(ii).

---

and the Transformation of Criminology' (2000) 40 BJ Crim 222 at p 299 argues that criminology, 'with its focus on the old state institutions of police-courts-prisons' is of 'limited relevance' given 'the crimes which pose the greatest risks to all of us' (on which see ch 6, section 5). This ignores that these 'old' state institutions are a) thriving and expanding, and, b) not just posing a 'risk' of intrusive interference with citizens' freedom, but severely (and ever more intensively) limiting that freedom for some, but certainly not 'all of us'. We think that documenting this is of more than 'limited relevance', at least to the interests of the most marginal groups in society.

1   For stop-search powers see ch 2, above.
2   *Ricketts v Cox* (1981) 74 Cr App Rep 298 and *Green v DPP* [1991] Crim LR 782.

(a) What is the right of silence?

According to Art 6 ECHR (now part of the Human Rights Act 1998) all defendants have the right to a fair trial and '. . . shall be presumed innocent until proven guilty according to law.' The European Court of Human Rights (ECtHR) has ruled that the right of silence 'lies at the heart' of these provisions but that it is not an absolute right.[3] This leaves governments and courts considerable room for manoeuvre over the extent to which this right—and the related 'privilege against self-incrimination'— should be preserved. It is here that due process and crime control principles clash most fundamentally. For the due process adherent, it is up to the prosecution to find its own evidence, and anything else negates the presumption of innocence. For the adherent to crime control, only the guilty have something to hide. Innocent people have nothing to fear by assisting the prosecution, and have much to gain. As Bentham infamously expressed this point: 'Innocence claims the right of speaking, as guilt invokes the privilege of silence.'[4]

The common law and early Judges' Rules adopted the classic due process position. As we have seen, this began to be modified some years ago.[5] Indeed some statutes adopt an extreme crime control position in order to deal with certain crimes where suspects have particular advantages. The best example is the investigation by such bodies as the Inland Revenue and Department of Trade and Industry of shady financial dealings. These agencies have the power to compel answers on pain of fines for silence. As a result of *Saunders v UK*[6] the Youth Justice and Criminal Evidence Act 1999[7] amends relevant legislation to prevent the admissibility in criminal proceedings of answers which are extracted in this way.

It might be said that suspects retain a right of silence as long as it is no crime to remain silent.[8] Even if one accepts this approach (which we believe is too simplistic) the privilege against self-incrimination is nonetheless eroded if suspects and defendants suffer as a result of silence. For many years this has been so, but more so now than ever as a result of the CJPO 1994. As Mirfield says: 'Attenuation may be all that has come about, but it is very substantial attenuation indeed.'[9]

3   *Condron v UK* [2000] Crim LR 679.
4   Quoted by S Greer, 'The Right to Silence: A Review of the Current Debate' (1990) 53 MLR 719.
5   See I Bryan, *Interrogation and Confession* (Aldershot: Avebury, 1997) chs 1-7 and S Easton, *The Case for the Right to Silence* (Aldershot: Ashgate, 1998) ch 1.
6   (1996) 23 EHRR 313.
7   Section 59 and Sch 3.
8   This was the view of the Lord Chief Justice in *Cowan* [1996] QB 373.
9   P Mirfield, *Silence, Confessions and Improperly Obtained Evidence* (Oxford: Clarendon, 1997) p 246. Also see D Dixon, *Law in Policing* (Oxford: Clarendon, 1997) ch 6.

(i) The Criminal Justice and Public Order Act 1994

Under the CJPO 1994, courts may draw inferences when defendants:

- rely upon facts in their defence which they did not mention to the police when they had a reasonable opportunity to do so prior to being charged (s 34);
- fail to testify in their own defence (s 35);
- fail to provide explanations for incriminating objects, substances or marks (s 36);
- fail to provide explanations for their presence near to the scene of crimes (s 37).

Thus the caution now says: 'You do not have to say anything. But it may harm your defence if you do not mention when questioned something which you later rely on in court. Anything you do say may be given in evidence.'[10] Previously, courts were not supposed to take into account a suspect or defendant's refusal to speak, nor the fact that the first mention of a particular defence might be in court.[11] The CJPO changes all that by eroding the right of silence in general in the police station (s 34) and in court (s 35) and in relation to certain types of circumstantial evidence (ss 36, 37). It may seem that the CJPO allows courts to convict people because they are silent, or because they answer some questions but not all. While this could sometimes be the effect of the CJPO in practice, this is not what the letter of the law says.

First, the CJPO itself states that no-one should have a case to answer or be convicted on the basis of adverse inferences alone.[12] Thus courts should not convict simply because of such silence or failures or delays in explanation, if there is no other prosecution evidence. This restriction has been tightened up as a result of the ECHR. In *Murray* it was held by the ECtHR (in relation to similar provisions in Northern Ireland) that a conviction must not be based 'solely or mainly' on the fact of silence.[13] Suppose, for example, that a defendant, accused of acting as a lookout while his friends were breaking into premises, claimed in court that he was merely waiting for his wife. If the defendant had not said this to the police the court would be entitled to infer that the claim in court was a lie, but in the absence of any direct evidence that he helped his friends he should

10 PACE Code of Practice C, para 10.4.
11 There were many statutory and common law incursions into this principle: see subsection (ii) below and ch 9, section 4(a)(ii).
12 Section 38(3).
13 (1996) 22 EHRR 29 at para 47. This decision led commentators to argue that the CJPO will result in breaches of Art 6 because it did not preclude conviction where silence is the main evidence: see, for example, R Munday, 'Inferences from Silence and European Human Rights Law' [1996] Crim LR 370 and A Ashworth, 'Art 6 and the Fairness of Trials' [1999] Crim LR 261. See also the discussion in subsection (e) below.

The right of silence

still not be convicted. To convict him on his silence, plus the circumstantial evidence that he happened to be in the same vicinity as his burglarious mates, would amount to finding him guilty 'mainly' due to his silence. The ECtHR also said that adverse inferences could properly be drawn from silence 'in situations which clearly call for an explanation', and that those inferences may then be taken into account 'in assessing the persuasiveness of the evidence adduced by the prosecution.'

The inferences drawn in *Murray* were under the Northern Ireland provisions equivalent to the CJPO, ss 37(2) and 35(2) (failure to provide explanation for presence near scene of crime and failure to testify at trial respectively). This left open the question of whether the ECtHR would regard a failure to answer questions during interrogation by the police as a situation which 'clearly called for an explanation'. The answer came in the ECtHR decision in *Condron*.[14] The Court ruled that adverse inferences could be drawn (under s 34, CJPO) from a suspect's silence in the face of police questioning, but that a jury must be told that they could do so only if that silence could 'sensibly' be attributed to the accused having no answer to the questions, or none that would stand up to cross-examination. In other words, the Court has found that silence in the face of police questions can, but does not necessarily, amount to a situation which so clearly called for an explanation that adverse inferences may be drawn. We examine in more detail below (sub-section (d)) the question of when silence can 'sensibly' be attributed to having no good answer to police questions.

Second, the CJPO (ss 36 and 37 in particular) originally eroded the right of silence on the street. However, the right to legal advice has been held to be implicit in the Art 6 right to a fair trial and presumption of innocence (see ch 4, section 4(a)). In *Murray*[15] the ECtHR interpreted this to mean that adverse inferences should only be drawn against silent suspects who had first had the opportunity to seek legal advice. This can only really occur after a suspect has been taken to a police station, as we saw in ch 4. Thus domestic legislation has had to be changed to make it Convention compatible.[16]

Third, inferences can only be drawn in relation to ss 36 and 37 if the police have first told the suspect what objects and so forth they believe are incriminating and that adverse inferences could be drawn from failure to account for them.[17]

14 See *Condron v UK* [2000] Crim LR 679 and accompanying commentary by Andrew Ashworth. See also A Jennings, 'Is Silence Still Golden?' (2000) Archbold News, 14 June p 5 and ch 9, section 4(a)(ii).
15 (1996) 22 EHRR 29.
16 The Youth Justice and Criminal Evidence Act 1999, s 58 amends the CJPO to this effect.
17 Code of Practice C, para 10.5B.

(ii) Other ways in which the right of silence is eroded

Silence (or delay in explaining) has for many years been used against suspects and defendants as a result of PACE, s 37. As ch 4 showed, this allows detention to be continued to obtain evidence by questioning. There is nothing a suspect can gain by saying to a custody officer: 'There is no point in you holding me for questioning, because I do not intend to answer any question.' Suspects who refuse to speak can be held until they do so, subject to the time limits. These are grim consequences. Lengthy detention, particularly overnight, is the most feared consequence of arrest for most suspects.[18] The modern crime control response, however, seems to be that:

'. . . all citizens may be required to submit to detention and questioning when the conditions set out in the PACE Act are fulfilled. Thus, where the silent suspect is further detained he is simply fulfilling this general social duty rather than suffering punishment for silence.'[19]

The fact that silent suspects end up fulfilling a more onerous 'social duty' than do suspects who confess is inescapable.

Second, it might be thought that suspects wishing to exercise their right to silence would not be pressured to change their minds. However, not only can silence lengthen detention, but in the words of Code of Practice C:

'This code does not affect the principle that all citizens have a duty to help police officers to prevent crime and discover offenders. This is a civic rather than a legal duty; but when a police officer is trying to discover when or by whom an offence has been committed he is entitled to question any person from whom he thinks useful information can be obtained, subject to the restrictions imposed by this code. A person's declaration that he is unwilling to reply does not alter this entitlement' (Note 1B).

Thus, in one of McConville and Hodgson's examples, the police response to a suspect exercising the right to silence was laced with quiet menace: 'Don't rely on anyone else and don't think we'll just let it go because in one interview you make no replies—we're just starting.'[20]

18   A Sanders and L Bridges, 'Access to Legal Advice and Police Malpractice' [1990] Crim LR 494; Choongh (1997) ch 6.
19   R Leng, The Right to Silence in Police Interrogation: A Study of Some of the Issues Underlying the Debate (Royal Commission on Criminal Justice Research Study no 10) (London: HMSO, 1993).
20   M McConville and J Hodgson, Custodial Legal Advice and the Right to Silence (Royal Commission on Criminal Justice Research Study no 16) (London: HMSO, 1993) p 124.

The right of silence

We have seen that questions aimed at persuading suspects to confess were once unlawful. Now, a variety of tactics are permissible,[1] and we shall see that many other, impermissible, tactics are commonly employed. In another of McConville and Hodgson's examples, the police repeatedly tried to find out where the suspect bought a 'dodgy' car, but he could not or would not say. Eventually his advisor intervened:

> Clerk: 'I think [my client] has given an explanation and you're putting the same question again and again.'
> Officer 1: 'We're giving him ample opportunity to explain the events and we're not satisfied with the answers.'
> Officer 2: 'We'll go over it again.'[2]

For suspects without a solicitor present, the situation is even worse. Sanders et al report a case where a woman was advised on the phone to remain silent. She informed the police of this, who said (entirely properly) that she would none the less be questioned. Despite her distress she was interrogated and 'confessed'.[3] None of this would have been allowed in 1912 when detention for questioning was unlawful. The result now is false confessions as in Kiszko and the 'Confait Affair', discussed in section 5 below.

Third, there have for years been various statutory exceptions to the principle that defendants can withhold the nature of their defence until trial. For example, defendants should generally give advance warning if they wish to provide expert evidence or evidence of an alibi.[4] This is so the police and prosecution can investigate the claims of the defence. It also gives the police the opportunity to adapt their case to get around such evidence, as in the Confait affair, where a pathologist was persuaded to change the estimated time of the victim's death in order to neutralise the suspect's alibi.[5]

Finally, prior to the introduction of the CJPO, in 80% of all Crown Court trials where defendants were silent under police questioning this became known to the jury.[6] Juries and magistrates probably took silence account even when they were not supposed to. As one police officer put it, '. . . in

---

1   *Holgate-Mohammed v Duke* [1984] AC 437.
2   McConville and Hodgson (1993) p 186.
3   The crucial interactions are quoted at the very beginning of ch 4.
4   On expert evidence see PACE, s 81 and Crown Court Rules 1987, SI 1087 No 716. On alibis see Criminal Justice Act 1967, s 11.
5   See Report of an Inquiry into the Circumstances leading to the Trial of Three Persons on Charges arising out of the Death of Maxwell Confait and the Fire at 27 Doggett Road, London SE6 (HCP 90) (London: HMSO, 1977).
6   M Zander and P Henderson, Crown Court Study (Royal Commission on Criminal Justice Research Study no 19) (London: HMSO, 1993).

the past you may have actually been happy for him to give a "no comment" interview, go to court, offer an explanation and let the jury sit and think: "This man has already been interviewed by the police, why didn't he answer the questions then?"[7] Certainly this is how many suspects think silence will be interpreted.[8] Thus the CJPO is just one of a series of obstacles placed in the way of suspects exercising their right to silence. If suspects and defendants suffer to this extreme because they are exercising their 'rights', in this case that of silence, can they really be said to be rights?

(b)   The extent of use of the 'right'

Just over half of all suspects who are interrogated fully confess or make incriminating statements to the police. These figures have been fairly consistent from before PACE to after the CJPO.[9] Around one-third of all suspects deny, with some sort of explanation, the offence(s) of which they are suspected. It appears that few suspects exercise the right of silence in totality, but no proper figures are kept and estimates from research vary wildly. Brown estimated that, between 1985 and 1994, between 5% and 9% of all interviewed suspects exercised total silence, and a similar number refused to answer some questions.[10] The rights provided to suspects in PACE as such do not appear to have led to more use of silence, although there was some increase in both the total and selective use of silence, especially in London, just before the introduction of the CJPO.[11]

In the most recent research, carried out after the introduction of the CJPO, refusal to answer all or some questions is back down to the 1985-1994 levels, almost certainly because lawyers advise silence less readily than previously.

---

7   T Bucke, R Street and D Brown, The Right of Silence: The Impact of the CJPO 1994 (Home Office Research Study no 199) (London: Home Office, 2000) pp 35-36.

8   Choongh (1997) ch 6.

9   See Bucke et al (2000) for the most recent research. See 1st ed of this book, p 194, fn 15-17 for details of earlier research, and for discussion of the problems of defining 'silence'.

10   D Brown, PACE Ten Years on - A Review of The Research (Home Office Research Study no 155) (London: HMSO; 1997). Brown reached this conclusion after examining the many different research studies available. Leng's (1993) analysis of the same studies concluded a somewhat lower figure for both. This is largely because Leng did not regard it as 'silence' if unanswered questions were legally irrelevant.

11   Phillips and Brown (1998).

Table 1: The use of the right of silence

	Refused all Q's	Refused some Q's	Answered All
Phillips and Brown (pre-CJPO)	10%	13%	77%
Bucke and Brown (post CJPO)	6%	10%	84%

Source: A Ashworth, *The Criminal Process* 2nd ed (Oxford: OUP, 1998) p 104, based on Home Office research.

Refusal is higher in London than elsewhere, and higher among black suspects than white and Asian suspects. Also, refusal is three times as high among those who had legal advice than those who did not.[12] Whether people are silent because of legal assistance, or are determined to seek assistance because they wish to remain silent, is not known. However, McConville and Hodgson (in the early 1990s) found few cases of suspects remaining silent because this was what they had been told by their advisors.[13] When silence was advised it was most often because advisors felt that they had insufficient information about the case and when they felt that suspects might wrongly incriminate themselves.

Concern is often expressed by senior police officers that professional criminals and persons suspected of serious offences exercise silence disproportionately often and thus escape prosecution or, if charged, conviction. There is next to nothing in the research to support this view. Moston and Williamson (in the early 1990s) found little association between silence and the seriousness of the charge or court verdict.[14] Leng, also in the early 1990s, also found that in only a tiny percentage of non-prosecuted cases and acquittals was silence exercised, and that these outcomes rarely seemed to be a product of silence.[15] Few 'ambush' defences (ie defences based on 'facts' not known to the police and not disclosed in interview) were mounted in court, and none successfully. In some cases, successful defences were based on points suspects attempted to raise in interviews but to which the police refused to listen. Leng concluded that there were as many cases where the police could have acted on what suspects told them, or attempted to tell them, as where suspects refused to tell them material things. Although anecdotal evidence post-CJPO suggests that

12   Bucke et al (2000) ch 3.
13   McConville and Hodgson (1993).
14   S Moston and T Williamson, 'The Extent of Silence in Police Stations' in S Greer and R Morgan (eds), The Right to Silence Debate: Proceedings of a Conference at the University of Bristol in March 1990 (Bristol: University of Bristol, 1990).
15   Leng (1993).

the few ambush defences that did exist has now gone down to a very low level indeed, it is not thought that the CJPO has affected the conviction rate.[16]

(c) The pros and cons of the right of silence

This remains a hotly debated issue. In 1972 the Criminal Law Revision Committee recommended abolition of the rule that no inference of guilt should be drawn from silence, but this was never implemented. The matter was reconsidered by the Royal Commission on Criminal Procedure (Philips Commission), which considered the merits of adopting compromise solutions which would erode the right in some respects but not destroy it absolutely. It decided that, to be practical, the right would either have to be retained in its entirety or abolished completely. The Commission was unwilling to erode due process to the extent of abolition, and so it recommended retention.[17] This was accepted by the government. Then in 1987 the matter was raised again by the Home Secretary following complaints by the police that 'their' conviction rate was being halved. Even the Lord Chief Justice joined in on the side of the police.[18] The Home Secretary announced in May 1988 that he intended to modify the right of silence and announced a Home Office working party to make recommendations. This led to a change in the law in Northern Ireland in 1989, but proposals for England were deferred pending the report of the Royal Commission on Criminal Justice (Runciman Commission) as a result of the Guildford Four and Birmingham Six cases.[19]

Various arguments for abolition were put to the Runciman Commission:
(i)   proper police interviewing seeks the truth and this is impossible if suspects refuse to answer questions;
(ii)   the need to prove mens rea elements places pressure on the police to secure confessions which would be alleviated if the court could draw inferences about guilt from silence;
(iii) suspects mount 'ambush' defences;
(iv)   it is experienced criminals, not vulnerable suspects, who benefit from the right;
(v)   the right of silence was necessary when suspects lacked proper safeguards, but now that PACE and Code of Practice C requires tape recording, regulates custodial treatment and provides for legal advice

16   Bucke et al (2000) ch 4.
17   Royal Commission on Criminal Procedure Report (RCCP) (Cmnd 8092) (London: HMSO, 1981) pp 80-91.
18   *Alladice* (1988) 87 Cr App Rep 380.
19   These events are chronicled by Greer (1990).

to be given where requested this is no longer true and the system has become unbalanced.[20]

These arguments can be met by evidence that:

(i) the current pressures on suspects leading to false confessions and misleading incriminating statements would be increased if suspects feared that they would prejudice their position in court if they were to remain silent when questioned;

(ii) the pressure on the police to seek confessions is self-imposed because of their reluctance to seek independent evidence and that they are not interested in neutral fact seeking;

(iii) ambush defences are rare;

(iv) it is vulnerable suspects, not suspects with serious criminal records, who will generally succumb to increased pressure created by changes to the right of silence;

(v) the safeguards in PACE and Code of Practice C are weak and used by a minority of suspects.

The Runciman Commission was split on whether to recommend that adverse inferences be drawn from silence. But the majority agreed with the Philips Commission that:

'It might put strong (and additional) psychological pressure upon some suspects . . . This in our view might well increase the risk of innocent people . . . making damaging statements.'[1]

The majority of the Runciman Commission also thought that erosion of the right of silence would have little effect on experienced criminals, whose conviction rate would therefore not be substantially increased. The Runciman Commission used an 'instrumental retentionist'[2] argument: little would be gained and much might be lost by abolition or change. Whilst we agree with this, the problem with it is that it gave ground to the crime control approach. If it were found that the innocent could be better protected than at present, and that those believed to be guilty were increasingly using silence to escape conviction, the argument would swing the other way. Would this matter, if the innocent were protected? 'Symbolic retentionists'[3] would say 'yes'. It is true, they argue, that silence can obstruct the prosecution but this is the whole point of due process. State power is great enough without increasing it further. The right of silence proclaims an ideology of innocence until proven guilty which is all the more necessary in the face of practices which proclaim an ideology of guilty

20   RCCP (1981) pp 80-91.
1   Royal Commission on Criminal Justice (RCCJ), Report (Cm 2263) (London: HMSO, 1993) p 55, quoting RCCP (1981) para 4.50.
2   See Greer (1990).
3   Greer (1990).

until proven innocent. Despite the views of Runciman, for which the government had deliberately waited before deciding what to do about the right of silence, the CJPO was enacted before most of the (pathetically weak) safeguards for suspects recommended by Runciman were enacted.

Another concern is that, when defences are disclosed to the police, their natural reaction in an adversarial system is to attempt to neutralise those defences. In the 'Confait Affair', the defendants' alibi was neutralised by 'adjusting' the time of death.[4] In the case of the Taylor sisters, an alibi witness was arrested at dawn and told that she would face a charge of conspiracy to murder if she did not change her story.[5] Since the CJPO was enacted, this problem now extends to all lines of defence, not just alibis.

McConville and Hodgson point to the increased use of arrest over the last 20 years or so. They argue that the traditional relationship between suspicion and arrest has, in many cases, been reversed:

'Instead of reasonable suspicion giving rise to an arrest, in these cases arrest occurs first, often without a suspicion which can be said to be reasonable. The result of this is that ensuing procedures relating to detention and interrogation, instead of being underpinned by legal justification, are used in order to prop up an otherwise precipitate and unlawful arrest.'[6]

Where this used to happen, the interrogation often collapsed and the suspect was released. Abolition of the right of silence could have led, in some of these cases, to suspects being charged and then convicted on the basis, in part, of their failure to answer groundless accusations; and in others to their being intimidated (by the prospect of an adverse inference) into incriminating themselves, perhaps misleadingly.

Retentionists argue that the right also has valuable side effects, or would have if suspects were not pressured so often into not exercising it. Firstly, it should lead to less emphasis on confessions and more on independent evidence. Secondly, it gives suspects a bargaining tool to secure immediate disclosure from police. Had the Runciman Commission's recommendation[7] that the police be obliged to inform legal advisors of the evidence against their clients been acted upon, this argument would have been undermined. As things stand, the police exercise silence when they wish and to the extent that they wish, so why should suspects not also do so? Thirdly, the police can now arrest on 'fishing expeditions' (ie without reasonable suspicion) even more than before. They can make accusations for which

---

4   This, and the failure to disclose the adjustment to the defence, was the main ground for the convictions being quashed.
5   *Observer*, 13 June 1993.
6   McConville and Hodgson (1993) p 198.
7   RCCJ (1993) p 36.

there might be little evidence and the silence of the accused can corroborate evidence which would otherwise be inadequate for conviction. Fourth, many suspects do not understand what is meant by 'adverse inferences', and even the police acknowledge that some think that the caution requires them to answer questions. Some police try to explain what the caution means, but others are discouraged from this.[8] Since only around one third of suspects get legal advice,[9] the police are the only source of advice most suspects have.

The Philips Commission (and PACE and Code of Practice C) was established to secure a 'balance' which included the right of silence, on one side, and increased powers to arrest, detain, stop-search and so forth, on the other. The government was satisfied with this 'balance' when it enacted these changes. The only thing that happened subsequently to 'upset' the balance was that many more suspects than previously (albeit a minority) actually began to exercise their rights. Despite this, it was the spate of miscarriages of justice of the late 1980s and early 1990s, not any perceived impotence on the part of the criminal justice system, that led to the Runciman Commission being appointed. Yet, despite that body's views, the government enacted the most fundamental erosion of suspects' rights which we have seen in decades. As with other changes in policy, such as police cautioning (see ch 6, section 4(a)), the CJPO was not a product of evidence and argument, but of rhetoric and politics.

(d)   'Sidelining' legal advice

One of the most important pieces of advice which legal advisers can give to suspects is that they need not answer questions and, in some circumstances, that it is not in their interests to do so. If, for example, the police have no objective basis for suspicion, silence should lead to release without charge, while answering questions could lead to enough evidence for charge even if the suspect is not guilty (if, for example, the suspect admitted being in the vicinity of the crime). One circumstance in which it may not be in the interests of the client to a..swer police questions is when the legal adviser and suspect know too little about the police case to answer it effectively. We saw in ch 4 (section 4(d)(iv)) that the police need not disclose anything about the case.[10] Legal advisers sometimes seek to

8   Bucke et al (2000) ch 3; B Tully and D Morgan, 'Fair warning?' (1997) Police Review (29 September) 24.

9   See ch 4, section 4(b).

10   Although we should reiterate here that inferences can only be drawn in relation to CJPO, ss 36 (incriminating marks or objects found on suspect) and 37 (presence in the vicinity of a crime) if the police have first told the suspect what objects and so forth they believe are incriminating and that adverse inferences could be drawn from failure to account for them: Code of Practice C, para 10.5B.

secure the disclosure of the police case by advising that the client remain silent until this information is provided. This bargaining chip has now been lost because of a combination of the CJPO and the case law erected on top of it.

In *Argent*[11], silence was advised until the nature of the case, if any, against the suspect was known. In court it was argued that there should be no adverse inference from silence a) because it was as a result of legal advice, and b) in the absence of an outline of the police evidence at that stage. The Court of Appeal rejected both arguments, saying that the test in the CJPO is whether it was reasonable to have mentioned the fact relied on (in the case, for example, of s 34) when questioned. Whether legal advice to stay silent made silence reasonable depended on what passed between lawyer and suspect. And police disclosure was relevant only if this was necessary in order for the suspect's silence to be regarded as unreasonable. Other appellate cases have adopted the same line.[12]

This makes it difficult for lawyers to advise silence and for suspects to know whether to follow that advice. As Cape says: 'It is somewhat bizarre for a person to exercise this fundamental right [to legal advice] and then to be penalised for acting on the very thing that the right is intended to secure.'[13] Some suspects doubtless rely on legal advice because they lack confidence in their own judgement in unfamiliar circumstances, but to convince a court of this they might have to reveal what passed between them and their lawyers. This amounts to a waiver of professional privilege, allowing the prosecution to expose all that passed between them, which might be against the wishes or interests of the suspects.[14] If it is reasonable for the State to pay for suspects to secure legal advice (as, we saw in ch 4, section 4(a), both the British Government and the ECtHR evidently think it is), is it not reasonable for suspects to rely on that advice without worrying whether or not a court or jury would agree?

The ECtHR came close, but not close enough, to saying this in *Condron v UK*[15] a case in which suspects had been advised by their solicitor not to answer police questions because they were suffering from the symptoms of heroin withdrawal. As noted above (section 2(a)(i)), the ECtHR said that if a defendant refuses to answer questions on the advice of a solicitor it

11   [1997] 2 Cr App Rep 27.
12   See *Roble* [1997] Crim LR 449; *Moshaid* [1998] Crim LR 420 and *Condron* [1997] 1 WLR 827 (not to be confused with the ECtHR decision: *Condron v UK* [2000] Crim LR 679).
13   E Cape, 'Sidelining Defence Lawyers: Police Station Advice After *Condron*' (1997) 1 IJ Evid and Proof 386 at p 398.
14   See *Roble* [1997] Crim LR 449 and the accompanying instructive commentary. If a defendant seeks to explain why a legal adviser advised silence this constitutes a waiver of privilege even if the legal adviser is not called to give evidence at the trial: *Bowden* [1999] 2 Cr App Rep 176.
15   [2000] Crim LR 679.

would be wrong to allow a jury to draw an adverse inference from that silence unless they were first told that they must not do so unless they believed that silence could only sensibly be attributed to the suspect having no good answer to the questions. This stops short of a clear judgment that advice to remain silent constitutes a reasonable explanation for that silence. It seems that the ECtHR is concerned that some (factually guilty) suspects may claim that they remained silent on legal advice in situations where they were determined to remain silent in any event in order to avoid incriminating themselves, or that lawyers may advise silence for other than a 'good reason'. The upshot is that legal advisers and suspects still cannot know for sure how a court will choose to interpret a decision, made following legal advice, to remain silent. Moreover, the court in *Condron* found nothing wrong with the fact that defendants may, because of the *Argent* decision, experience 'indirect compulsion'[16] to reveal the content of the advice received from a lawyer. The effect of *Argent* has thus been ameliorated, rather than neutralised, by *Condron*; the police have retained the whip hand in their dealings with legal advisers and suspects.

Despite the ruling in *Argent* there is some evidence to suggest that the police do disclose at least some of their case more readily now, knowing that this makes the drawing of adverse inferences more probable.[17] However, as always the police retain control. That is, *they* decide whether to disclose anything, what to disclose, and when to do so. Sometimes disclosure of part of a case can give a misleading impression. Although no adverse inferences should be drawn if the police actively misled the suspect, partial disclosure which had this effect is not necessarily construed as active deception.[18] Overall, in Cape's words: 'Custodial legal advice may be guaranteed by the ECHR, but its value as such is in danger of being seriously eroded.'[19]

(e)   Interpreting the CJPO: further problems

A major concern is that courts might convict defendants largely on the basis of what they did not tell the police, assuming (not necessarily rightly) that silence or lies are signs of a guilty conscience. As we saw in (a) above, under the ECHR the courts are only supposed to consider silence as some supporting evidence; it cannot form the main or sole basis for a conviction. The Court of Appeal in *Birchall* recognised that the CJPO, as it initially

---

16   At para 60 of the decision.
17   Bucke et al (2000) ch 3.
18   See, for example, *Imran and Hussain* [1997] Crim LR 754, discussed in section 4(b).
19   Cape (1997) at p 402.
20   *Murray v UK* (1996) 22 EHRR 29.

stood, facilitated breaches of the Convention (because it only precluded convictions based solely on silence).[1] The problem has been partially recognised by the judiciary. A model direction for juries states that jurors may take silence into account as 'some additional support' for the prosecution case.[2] But jurors and magistrates are given no indication as to the weight to give silence, and so in reality the danger of conviction when there is little concrete evidence has been increased by the CJPO. Moreover, the model direction allows juries to view silence as direct evidence of guilt, rather than simply as evidence that a claim made in court might be untrue. It has been argued that this is contrary to the ECHR.[3] In *Condron* the ECtHR itself said that silence should be taken into account - using 'caution' - only where the circumstances clearly call for an explanation and silence could only 'sensibly' be attributed to the defendant having no good answer to the questions put by the police.[4] The ECtHR did not explicitly touch on the question of whether in this situation the adverse inference could extend beyond the issue of the truthfulness of a claim made in court by the defendant to the central question of guilt itself. Its decision should, however, lead to a narrowing of the circumstances in which trial judges are at liberty to direct a jury that it may draw an adverse inference. Whether this will make much practical difference is more debatable, since we do not know whether juries (or magistrates) will in fact draw adverse inferences only in the situations that they are supposed to.[5] Moreover, the Court of Appeal has reacted to the ECtHR decision in *Condron* in its usual minimalist manner by stressing that a mis-direction (or lack of direction when one is required) by a trial judge on the issue of adverse inferences will not necessarily infringe the Art 6 right to a fair trial, nor render a conviction unsafe.[6]

Precisely what silence can be evidence *of* is a practical, as well as a theoretical, problem. In *Hart*, for example, the main evidence of drug smuggling by the defendant, which he did not explain, was possession of

1   *Birchall* [1999] Crim LR 311.The relevant ECHR provision is Art 6: the right to a fair trial. Similar fears are also expressed by some barristers: Bucke et al (2000) ch 4.
2   Approved by the Court of Appeal in *Cowan* [1996] QB 373 and reproduced by S Easton, 'Legal Advice, Common Sense and the Right of Silence' (1998) 2 IJ Evidence and Proof 109.
3   R Pattenden, 'Silence: Lord Taylor's Legacy' (1998) 2 IJ Evidence and Proof 141.
4   The ECtHR ruled that the defendants had been denied a fair trial because the Court of Appeal upheld the conviction even though the judge's direction to the jury on drawing inferences from silence was faulty (because it left the jury at liberty to draw an adverse inference even if they believed that the defendants had remained silent, for good reason, on the advice of their solicitor).
5   The quality of fact-finding by magistrates and juries is covered in chs 8 and 9 respectively.
6   See *Francom, Latif, Latif, Bevis and Harker* (CA: 31 July 2000, unreported).

an incriminating phone number. There was a bare prima facie case, and Hart was convicted.[7] He was lucky, because this was quashed on appeal, but (as explained in ch 10) it is very difficult to win appeals. This is an example of speculation (about the defendant's motives in remaining silent) masquerading as 'common sense'.[8] As Pattenden puts it, silence becomes 'evidential poly-filler for cracks in the wall of incriminating evidence which the prosecution has built around the accused.'[9] Much depends on whether the courts interpret the CJPO in ways that assist the defence or the prosecution. Pattenden, in line with most other commentators, states:

> 'The larger picture that emerges . . . is of a Court of Appeal so committed to crime control that at almost every turn - even when an interpretation favourable to the defence is plausible - the legislation has been construed in the prosecution's favour.'[10]

Subsequent cases serve largely to confirm her view. In *McGuinness*,[11] for example, the police had sufficient evidence to charge the defendant with handling stolen goods before he was interviewed. He was nonetheless interviewed, and gave a different explanation to the one he gave at trial. The jury was invited to draw an adverse inference from this under s 34 because he relied on alleged facts at trial that he did not mention to the police. He appealed against his conviction, arguing that he should have been charged prior to the interview, making the interview a breach of Code C, para 11.4 (discussed in section 3 (e) below). He therefore argued that the interview was invalid and that it should be excluded from evidence. This argument was rejected on the grounds that the police could never be sure if there was sufficient evidence to proceed until they had heard the suspect's story. The effect of this is to render para 11.4 almost meaningless, as all the police ever need do, however much evidence they have, is to say that they keep an open mind until they question the suspect. Clearly, the Court of Appeal thought it was worth creating this absurd situation in order to give the CJPO more 'bite' than it would otherwise have had, allowing adverse inferences to be drawn wherever possible. On the other hand, in *Mountford*[12] the Court of Appeal held that if the fact not disclosed at interview is the key fact in the case about which the jury have to decide, then the jury should not be invited to make an adverse inference. Although this decision is favourable to the defence it also shows just how complicated

---

7   Unreported, 23 April 1998 (CA). Discussed by D Birch, 'Suffering in Silence' [1999] Crim LR 769.
8   Cape (1997); Easton (1998).
9   R Pattenden, 'Inferences from Silence' [1995] Crim LR 602 at p 607.
10   Pattenden (1998) p 164.
11   [1999] Crim LR 318.
12   [1999] Crim LR 575.

and unpredictable the law now is, making the legal advisor's job all the harder.

Only a few years ago the police used to complain that they had to tell the defence everything (albeit only in the run-up to trial) and the defence had to say nothing. This, to the extent that it was true, was an inevitable result of the due process presumption of innocence.[13] Now the boot is on the other foot. The defence is punished if it does not tell the police anything at a time, in the station, when the police need reveal nothing. One way of partially getting round the problem advocated by Cape[14] is to hand to the police a short statement of facts and then to refuse to answer questions. It was held in *McGarry*[15] that this was a sufficient statement of facts to prevent adverse inferences being drawn from the defendant's refusal to answer questions. The police are nonetheless advantaged by this by comparison with the pre-CJPO situation. First, at the time of arrest, defendants may not know all the facts which they later rely upon. Second, this gives the police a preview of the defendant's defence which they can then prepare against (or seek to neutralise) in advance of the trial. Third, courts might see the device of supplying a written statement as itself suspicious, especially if it becomes accepted that such statements are most likely to be made by 'professional criminals', as some police officers and legal advisers have suggested is the case.[16]

If suspects and defendants are to suffer for not explaining themselves, it is hard to maintain that there is still a presumption of innocence (as required by Art 6 (2) of the ECHR). This is a reason for reverting to the pre-CJPO position in principle. Principles appear to be of little concern to Governments, Labour and Conservative, or their Royal Commissions, but there are good practical reasons, too, for this. First, the changes have caused more trouble for courts than they have resolved.[17] Second, they swung the balance too far to the police by sidelining police station legal advice (the main due process-based reform initiated by PACE). Third, they pressure vulnerable suspects into speaking against their will, but probably have little effect on professional criminals.[18]

There is no doubt that the erosion of the right of silence by the CJPO and the other developments discussed earlier offend against the freedom principle because they produced minimal gains to off-set significant losses. Despite this, the CJPO and associated developments are largely Human

13 The police view was a considerable over-statement of the legal reality (as opposed to the due process rhetoric). See further ch 9, section 4(a)(ii).
14 E Cape, *Defending Suspects at Police Stations* (London: LAG, 1999) pp 181 and 211.
15 [1998] 3 All ER 805.
16 Bucke et al (2000) pp 36-37.
17 Birch [1999].
18 Bucke et al (2000); see generally, Easton (1998).

The right of silence

Rights Act-proof, as a result of the approach of the ECtHR. It might have been thought, in the light of its decisions in *Funke*[19] and then *Saunders v UK*[20], that any abrogation of the right of silence breached Art 6 of the ECHR. The Court objected to defendants being 'compelled' to speak in these cases. The decisions in *Murray* and *Condron*[1], though, go in a different direction. The Court in *Condron* stated that: 'The fact that the issue of the applicant's silence was left to a jury cannot of itself be considered incompatible with the requirements of a fair trial.' We are left with the distinction drawn in *Murray* between 'improper' compulsion (what happened in *Funke* and in *Saunders*) and 'proper' compulsion (which includes, subject to the safeguards we have discussed, drawing adverse inferences). The basis of this distinction is obscure. One could hardly ever truly compel someone to speak, as even someone under torture makes a choice whether to speak or die. It is a coerced choice. On the other hand, most people who confess do so only because the police put them under pressure, which the CJPO is explicitly designed to increase. So, again, the decision to speak is a coerced choice. As Wasik et al say, the Court simply decided, on no principled basis ('ad hoc line drawing') that certain forms of compulsion are wrong.[2] The human rights perspective, once again, has nothing to say about these most worrying developments at the turn of the century.

3. REGULATING POLICE QUESTIONING

(a) When and where are the police allowed to question suspects?

The police question citizens in many types of situation and for many reasons. Their powers to stop and search, for example, discussed in ch 2, include the power to question suspects. This questioning sometimes confirms the initial suspicion. Another common situation is where the police think that a citizen could give them information about a suspect. The answers given, or not given, by someone not initially under suspicion sometimes create suspicion.[3] If so, the 'caution', 'You do not have to say anything . . .', must be given.[4] If there is 'reasonable suspicion', the police

19 *Funke v France* (1993) 16 EHRR 297.
20 (1997) 23 EHRR 313.
1 [2000] Crim LR 679.
2 M Wasik, T Gibbons and M Redmayne, *Criminal Justice: Text and Materials* (London: Longman, 1999) p 314; see also K Starmer and M Woolf, 'The Right to Silence' in C Walker and K Starmer (eds), *Miscarriages of Justice* (London: Blackstone, 1999).
3 An example is *James* [1996] Crim LR 650, discussed below.
4 PACE Code of Practice C, paras 10.1 and 10.4.

can arrest. If they do, questioning must cease temporarily, as we shall see. If there is no 'reasonable suspicion', the police cannot arrest, but questioning may continue wherever it began until the suspicions are either allayed or increased. In the latter case the suspect would usually be arrested. But even if the police develop very strong suspicions, there is no *obligation* to arrest and therefore they may carry on questioning. Much police questioning, both of suspects and non-suspects, therefore takes place outside the police station without (or prior to) arrest. This is a form of 'informal questioning' to be discussed in detail later (see section 4 (e) below).

Once the police decide to arrest, para 11.1 of Code of Practice C states that the suspect 'must not be interviewed about the relevant offence except at a police station. . .'[5] When a person is arrested, PACE s 30(1) states that the suspect 'shall be taken to a police station by a constable as soon as practicable after the arrest'. As so often with criminal justice, the phrase 'as soon as practicable' is of prime importance. And so, under s 30(10) the police can delay taking an arrestee to a police station 'if the presence of that person elsewhere is necessary in order to carry out such investigations as it is reasonable to carry out immediately.' The police can also simply release an arrestee instead of taking him/her to the station if 'there are no grounds for keeping him under arrest.'[6] As we saw in ch 3, this is quite common in public order situations in particular.

Thus, generally speaking, if people who are arrested are to be questioned, this must be only in a 'formal interview'. That is, they must be taken to a police station at once, checked in by the custody officer, offered their rights as set out in ch 4, and questioned only after that. But situations are envisaged where police officers can justifiably delay taking suspects to a police station after arrest. Why does this matter? There are dilemmas here which do not involve the clash of due process and crime control principles, but which create problems for due process itself and for the enhancement of freedom. The conveyance of arrested persons to a station immediately is desirable for several reasons. Firstly, it enables custody officers to decide whether or not arrests are justified and whether suspects are particularly vulnerable. Secondly, it allows as little time to elapse as possible after arrest before suspects have the opportunity to exercise their rights under ss 56 and 58 to consult a lawyer and to have their arrest made known to a relative or friend. Thirdly, it prevents police officers holding suspects incommunicado against their will, thus minimising the opportunity for interrogation in uncontrolled conditions and prior to securing legal advice. In *Kerawalla* the defendant was arrested in a hotel room and questioned there without being allowed to exercise his ss 56 and 58 rights.

5   There are some exceptions which (thankfully) need not concern us here.
6   PACE, s 30 (7).

The Court of Appeal held that they were not applicable to persons detained at premises other than a police station.[7]

On the other hand, we saw in ch 3 that it is undesirable to encourage peremptory arrest on bare reasonable suspicion if the suspect has a exonerating story. If the story can be checked by, for instance, going to the suspects' home to check documents,[8] to a shop where the suspect says he bought allegedly stolen goods[9] or to a place of work where an alibi could be confirmed, this must be better for the suspect than being held in custody while these investigations are made. Then there are suspects who feel, and often are, under less pressure if interrogated somewhere they feel comfortable, such as at home or in the office of their solicitor.[10]

The only way out of this dilemma would be for the police to arrest less often even when they have reasonable suspicion, as the Philips Commission advocated. Its preference was for the suspect to be reported for summons instead, and investigations continued without the suspect being in custody. This would not solve the problem of whether to allow questioning on the street, and it would not be practical in anywhere near all cases, but it would sometimes help. However we have seen that the government completely rejected this approach, that PACE actually extended arrest powers (allowing arrest for non-arrestable offences in certain circumstances) and the Runciman Commission did not even consider the issue.

The result in s 30 is a messy compromise. Its imprecision provides an opportunity for the operation of crime control working rules in relation to interrogation. So, despite its due process credentials, it is primarily an enabling rule. It enables the police to insist on immediate police station interrogation except when they determine that some other course of action is preferable. The suspect has no say in the matter. This enables the police to lengthen the time between arrest and police station detention, exacerbating another problem. If the police interrogate in the period between arrest and arrival at the station, or if information is voluntarily given, should the police and courts be able to use the information? A due process approach would say 'no', as would a freedom approach if the reason for the delay was in order to extract information under these conditions, ie without the protections which apply at the police station. But a crime control approach—concerned only with the truth of what the suspect told the police—would accept the information if it was reliable.

Section 30(10) does not in itself give permission to officers to interrogate other than in a police station. However, incriminating statements made to

7   [1991] Crim LR 451 and see the accompanying commentary which rightly criticises this decision as unnecessarily restrictive.

8   As in *McCarrick v Oxford* [1983] RTR 117, discussed in ch 3, section 5.

9   As in *Madden's* case, also discussed in ch 3, section 5.

10   A good example is *Holgate-Mohammed v Duke* [1984] AC 437.

the police prior to arrest, or en route to a police station or some other place envisaged in s 30(10) (such as the suspect's home or place of work), are not invalidated simply because the information was not given in the police station. This gives the police an incentive to seek a confession prior to arrival at the police station, and the Code of Practice gives the police permission to do this prior to arrest.

(b) What is a police interview?

Drawing a clear line between questioning (an interview) and a discussion or conversation can be very difficult. Yet it is vital to do so because s 30 of PACE and Code of Practice C, para 11.1, are only concerned with 'interviews'. If a mere 'conversation' takes place between a suspect and an officer, this is not regulated by s 30 or para 11.1, regardless of whether it produces useful information for the police. Further, the 'caution' that 'You do not have to say anything', which must be given before the start of an interview, need not be given prior to a 'conversation'.[11] According to para 11.1A of Code C:

'. . . an interview is the questioning of a person regarding his involvement or suspected involvement in a criminal offence or offences which, by virtue of para 10.1 of Code C, is required to be carried out under caution.'

This applies whether the interview is 'formal' or 'informal'. It is obvious that all post-arrest conversations about suspected offences should be regarded as interviews because an arrested person is, by definition, a suspect. Thus in *Absolam*,[12] the defendant was arrested for suspected drugs offences. He was questioned in the charge room and allegedly gave incriminating answers. Only then was he read his rights and cautioned. A record of the questions and his answers was made but not shown to him. If this was an 'interview', then what happened was unlawful because it took place before the suspect was read his rights and before he had had the opportunity to seek legal advice. If it was not an interview, then it was not unlawful and those protections were not applicable. The Court of Appeal held that this was an interview.[13] In *Miller*[14] one question asked in the charge room was held to be an interview.

11   Code of Practice C, paras 10.1 and 10.4.
12   (1988) 88 Cr App Rep 332.
13   Similarly, conversations in *Oransaye* [1993] Crim LR 772 (questioning at the custody officer's desk) and in *Goddard* [1994] Crim LR 46 (questioning prior to being taken to the police station) were held to be interviews.
14   [1998] Crim LR 209.

However, as we have seen, much police questioning begins as simple information seeking from possible witnesses who may or may not become suspects. It would be neither possible nor desirable to provide such witnesses with all the protections of Code of Practice C and PACE (and the accompanying coercion of police station custody) before the police were allowed to talk to them. It is therefore essential for the law to provide that, up to a certain point, question and answer sessions between police and citizens shall not be regarded as interviews for the purposes of PACE. The question is at what stage questions and answers should be regarded as 'interviews' and at what stage 'civilians' should become 'suspects'.

The courts have adopted several ways of distinguishing these two types of questioning. For some time it looked as though interviews were being defined as conversations which took place in police stations; anything which took place outside a police station was not an interview.[15] But allowing the place of the discussion to determine its legal status made little sense. Many genuine witnesses give evidence to the police in police stations and attend police stations to, for instance, identify possible criminals. Such witnesses do not (or, at least, should not) need the protection of PACE and Code of Practice C. Further, if the place of the conversation is to determine whether the protection of PACE and the Code of Practice is provided, the ability of the police to determine where the conversation takes place will distort what happens. The simple result would be that, rather than interviewing suspects inside police stations, the police would simply do more interviews outside.

Another approach is to examine the intention of the officers in question. But as Field points out, it is easy for officers to claim that it was their intention merely to seek information when in fact it was not.[16] The courts have been rather gullible in this respect. In *Maguire*[17] two youths, seen pushing open the door of a flat, were told on the way to the police car, 'You've both been caught. Now tell us the truth . . . It's for your own good.' This was held not to be an interview. Similarly, in *Pullen*,[18] the court believed that officers visited the defendant's cell 'with the object of relaxing him and . . . restoring some of his dignity', thus holding that only a conversation took place.[19] Some cases, such as *Younis*[20] where the conversation took place in a police car, have been decided on the basis that an exchange is not an interview if it is initiated by the suspect. This could only be relevant if the whole discussion was on the lines initiated by the suspect, which was not so in *Younis*. It is arguable, in any event, that whether someone

15 See, for example, *Maguire* (1989) 90 Cr App Rep 115 and *Younis* [1990] Crim LR 425.
16   S Field, 'Defining Interviews under PACE' (1993) 13 LS 254.
17 (1989) 90 Cr App Rep 115.
18 [1991] Crim LR 457.
19 Note, however, *Hunt* [1992] Crim LR 582, where the court was more sceptical.
20 [1990] Crim LR 425. Similar cases are discussed by Field (1993) at pp 261-263.

needs protection depends on the objective evidence against them and on the nature of the discussion, rather than on who initiated it or on the intention of the police.[1]

This seems to have been recognised in *Weekes*.[2] Here the Court of Appeal said that an 'understandable enquiry' became an 'interview' when the suspect started making admissions. But what good is this if the purpose of defining a conversation as an 'interview' is to prevent admissions being made without due process protections? This would be a helpful ruling only if it meant that whatever was said as a result of 'understandable enquiries' became unusable as a result of the exchange's transformation into an 'interview'.[3] This was not the line taken subsequently, however. In *James*,[4] for example, a man disappeared. His business partner was questioned without suspicion initially existing, but suspicion that he murdered the missing man grew in the course of discussions during which no caution was given. The Court of Appeal held that these were not interviews, even when they asked 'Have you killed David Martin?', that the police were not wrong to have given no caution, and that the evidence of the discussions could be used against James.

There is no obvious way of distinguishing 'conversations' and pre-arrest 'interviews'. Since all questioning is done with a view (perhaps among others) to securing incriminating statements, should the person being questioned be guilty, all questioning could be regarded as constituting an interview, and hence not lawful except in the police station under caution. But this would not be regarded by people who could exonerate themselves on the spot, let alone by the police, as desirable.

Police-citizen encounters away from the police station are usually characterised by their low visibility. This means that what went on (who initiated the conversation, what was being sought by it, what the intentions of the officers were and so forth) is only the officers' word against the suspect's. The whole point of PACE and Code of Practice C regulating formal 'interviews' was to eradicate this problem by being able to verify what was said and done objectively. It is precisely this objective verification which the police seek to avoid by so often trying to ensure that their discussions are not classified as interviews.

Field concludes that, no matter how the wording of Code of Practice C is altered, the problems discussed here will remain while the incentives to bargain and deal remain.[5] He has been shown to be correct, in that the 1995 version of Code C adopted a tougher definition of 'interview' than had previously been used (it is quoted at the start of this section) but that

1   See *Sparks* [1991] Crim LR 128.
2   (1993) 97 Cr App Rep 222.
3   See H Fenwick, 'Confessions, Recording Rules, and Miscarriages of Justice: A Mistaken Emphasis?' [1993] Crim LR 174.
4   [1996] Crim LR 650.
5   Field [1993] at 263.

did not stop the Court of Appeal deciding *James* similarly to *Weekes*. Equally, the incentive to secure, through informal questioning, confession evidence which can be used in court will still be there for as long as the rules of evidence allow it.[6] Maguire and Norris report that the utility of evidence in court is a major factor influencing whether police officers go out of their way to secure such evidence.[7] PACE, largely through s 30(1) and Code of Practice C, para 11.1, sought to protect suspects by moving interrogation into what was thought to be the controlled environment of the police station. The police responded by increasingly questioning 'informally', and Code of Practice C, para 11.1A, is an attempt to control this. This can be seen as a partially successful attempt to impose inhibitory due process rules on a body wedded to crime control-based working rules. However, it is not self-evident that suspects are protected by the movement of interviewing into the police station. We shall see that detention is experienced by most suspects as inherently coercive, producing pressures to say and do things, in order to secure release, which they would not normally do. Protection from unregulated police activity is increased in this way, but so is the pressure created by allowing lengthy police detention, to be discussed later.

(c)   Recording of interviews

Accurate recording of interviews is essential. Without knowing what was said and done, by both police officers and suspects, it is impossible to know what pressure was placed on suspects to confess or even whether they confessed at all. Prior to PACE, questions and answers were rarely tape recorded. Confessions and denials came in one of two forms. Firstly, 'verbals'; these were police officers' accounts of suspects' (supposedly) voluntary verbal statements, usually written down some time after they were made. Secondly, 'voluntary' written statements, written either by the suspect or, at the suspect's dictation, by a police officer. Both came to be challenged increasingly frequently. 'Verbals' were often said not to reflect accurately what suspects really said, and were sometimes alleged to be complete fabrications.[8] Similarly, voluntary written statements were often said to have been the work of the officers themselves. In an infamous scandal of the 1960s, Sergeant Challenor and several colleagues were eventually successfully prosecuted for these practices (and many instances of corruption and brutality) when it was found that statements made by

6   See ch 11 for discussion of the exclusion of unlawfully obtained evidence.
7   Maguire and Norris (1992) p 46.
8   The Royal Commissions of 1929 and 1962, as well as the Phillips Commission, were concerned about 'verbals'. See B Cox, *Civil Liberties in Britain* (Harmondsworth: Penguin, 1975) ch 4.

suspects he had arrested all used the same improbable phrases such as 'travelling in a northerly direction' and 'it's a fair cop guv, it was me wot done it'.[9]

Inaccuracy, commonly known as 'gilding the lily', took three forms. Firstly, there was alteration of the words used to create a different impression, either deliberately or inadvertently. As Lord Devlin put it in 1960, when he was a High Court judge, many statements use '. . . the stately language of the police station where, for example, people never eat but partake of refreshment and never quarrel but indulge in altercations.'[10] Police officers, like everyone else, have imperfect recall, and mistakes are made when conversations are reconstructed at a later time, especially when the purpose of the reconstruction is to prove a point.[11]

Secondly, there was the incomplete recording of what was said. It was common to only write down what suspects said 'when they start telling the truth', ie when they agreed with the allegations being put to them.[12] We shall see that police tactics can lead suspects to 'confess' against their will, and this is difficult to challenge if previous denials are not recorded. Thirdly, there is complete fabrication, as in at least some of Sergeant Challenor's cases. In the 'Confait Affair', allegedly voluntary statements were either written by the police entirely or consisted of words put into the suspects' mouths by the police.

The Philips Commission realised the dangers of all these forms of inaccuracy. It did not believe that all, or even most, alleged statements were false. But some were, as even police officers will admit.[13] The problem was in distinguishing the false from the true. In keeping with its general philosophy of keeping records of police-suspect encounters, the Philips Commission recommended that all exchanges be accurately written down so that the question of fabricated confessions did not arise. So, when PACE was introduced, Code of Practice C (para 11.5) required 'an accurate record' of interrogation to be made either 'during the course of the interview' (and to be a 'verbatim record') or, if this was not practicable, 'an account of the interview which adequately and accurately summarises it'.

9   Cox (1975).
10 P Devlin, *Criminal Prosecution in England* (OUP, 1960) p 39.
11 G Stephenson, 'Should Collaborative Testimony be Permitted in Courts of Law?' [1990] Crim LR 302.
12 A Sanders, 'Constructing the Case for the Prosecution' (1987) 14 JLS 229.
13 See McConville et al (1991) pp 84-87. In the wake of the sensational miscarriages of justices which came to light in the late 1980s, many senior officers admitted that 'noble cause' corruption had occurred but claimed that PACE had put a stop to it. See R Reiner, 'Policing and the Police' in M Maguire, R Morgan and R Reiner (eds) *Oxford Handbook of Criminology* (Oxford: OUP, 1997). The claim, but not the admission, was then retracted by the Metropolitan Police Commissioner, in the face of overwhelming evidence that corruption continued unabated: (*The Guardian*, 11 March 95). See further ch 6(3)(c).

Regulating police questioning

There were several problems with this. For the police, the labourious writing down of everything everyone said slowed the interview, gave suspects time to think, and inhibited the establishment of rapport. This was why the police found (or believed) PACE hampered them.[14] Also, just as before, what was written down might not be accurate or complete. The only difference was that the police would have to claim that it was written contemporaneously instead of afterwards, which is only a small safeguard. It was enough (eventually) in the 'Birmingham Six', 'Guildford Four', and 'Tottenham Three' cases. The convictions in all these cases were largely based on allegedly contemporaneously written confessions, but later scientific evidence proved them not to have been written at the time.[15] Finally, there was the problem of what happens outside the interrogation and when it was not 'practicable' to record contemporaneously. Because of the difficulties in establishing rapport while writing everything down, not wanting everything said and done to be recorded, not wanting a legal advisor present, and so forth, this problem grew in magnitude.[16]

The glaring nature of these problems led to many eminent figures asking, well before the Philips Commission reported, for the routine tape recording of interrogations.[17] This was initially resisted by the police, a classic police response being that:

'It would wreck the way we do interviews . . . You'd always say things like "Don't fuck me about" but you couldn't on tape which would be in front of a judge and jury really.'[18]

However, following the introduction of a new Code of Practice on Tape Recording in 1988 (Code of Practice E), the police adapted rapidly, and tape recording is now mandatory in all indictable and either-way cases except in exceptional circumstances. Quick-fire question and answer has returned, allowing the re-emergence of most of the old tactics. It is more difficult for the police to record proceedings selectively, and impossible for them to fabricate recordings, but the third problem, interrogation outside the

14 M Maguire, 'Effects of the PACE Provisions on Detention and Questioning' (1988) 28 BJ Crim 19.

15 See J Rozenberg, 'Miscarriages of Justice' in E Stockdale and S Casale (eds), *Criminal Justice Under Stress* (London: Blackstone, 1992), and C Walker, 'Miscarriages of Justice in Principle and Practice' in C Walker and K Starmer (eds) *Miscarriages of Justice* (London: Blackstone, 1999). Also see discussion in ch 6.

16 All these problems of writing down what was, or was not, said apply particularly to informal interviewing, which is discussed later. See, for example, *Miller* [1998] Crim LR 209.

17 See especially G Williams, 'The Authentication of Statements to the Police' [1979] Crim LR 6.

18 M McConville, A Sanders and R Leng, *The Case for the Prosecution* (London: Routledge, 1991) p 60.

interview room, remains.[19] Moston and Stephenson comment that it is rare to see general conversation appearing on taped interviews, even though conversation between suspect and interviewer at some point is usual. This, they say: '. . . confirms the inadequacy of tape recording inside the police station as a wholly adequate record of all relevant verbal exchanges between suspect and interviewer.'[20]

The PACE Codes of Practice now require interview rooms to have tamper-proof tape recording facilities, and once the interview begins everything said by all parties must be tape recorded, although there is an 'if practicable' escape clause (Code of Practice E, para 3.3) and an exception in relation to persons suspected of involvement in terrorism or espionage (Code of Practice E, para 3.2). As Fenwick notes, there is no good reason to exclude such cases, and every reason to include them since so many miscarriage of justice cases have concerned disputed confessions in terrorism cases.[21] Generally, a copy (which can be provided to the suspect) as well as a master copy will be made. If no tape recording is made, everything said and done must be written down accurately and fully, whether or not the interview takes place at a police station (Code of Practice C, para 11.5(a)). Under para 11.5(c), this must be done during the course of the interview:

'unless in the investigating officer's view this would not be practicable or would interfere with the conduct of the interview, and must constitute either a verbatim record of what has been said or, failing this, an account of the interview which adequately and accurately summarises it.'

Paragraph 11.7 provides that 'if an interview record is not made in the course of the interview it must be made as soon as practicable after its completion'. Further, 'unless it is impracticable the person interviewed shall be given the opportunity to read the interview record and sign it as correct or to indicate the respect in which he considers it inaccurate' (para 11.10).

This is to ensure that what actually was said is written down and that nothing that was not said is not written down. It is also to ensure that suspects who agree that everything has been written down fairly and accurately indicate that this is their view. If a solicitor is present and the suspect so indicates then it is almost impossible to challenge the accuracy

19   This is why video taping of interrogation, with which there have been several experiments, is of no substantial help. See McConville [1992].
20   S Moston and G Stephenson, The Questioning and Interviewing of Suspects Outside the Police Station (Royal Commission on Criminal Justice Research Study no 22) (HMSO, 1993) p 36.
21   Fenwick [1993].

Regulating police questioning

of the written record, thus reducing the number of cases where there is doubt about what was said. There are three problems. Firstly, even though suspects may sign what is written down, this does not mean that what was written down was accurate, for people frequently fail to read documents which they sign. This is not a problem in the majority of formal interviews now that they are tape recorded.

Secondly, although what is written down (or tape recorded) may be accurate, it may none the less be unreliable when suspects are induced to confess, are subjected to oppressive pressure or have words put into their mouths. Not only do these things sometimes happen on tape and with a lawyer present, but they also happen before or between interviews. It is true that: 'A written record should also be made of any comments made by a suspected person, including unsolicited comments, which are outside the context of an interview but which might be relevant to the offence' (Code of Practice C, para 11.13). But it need not be written at the time, and it need only be provided to the suspect for verification and signing 'where practicable'. If these comments were made as a result of unlawful pressure, the full exchange is not likely to be fully recorded by the police and, as with pre-PACE verbals, what was said (and why) often becomes simply a matter of who is believed.

The third problem is that these provisions are not mandatory: they all have 'if practicable' escape clauses. The net result is that interviews outside the station are hardly ever contemporaneously recorded. Moston and Stephenson found that the police admitted to failing to do this in nearly two-thirds of all such interviews, and suspects were asked to check the record in little over one quarter of such cases.[1]

When alleged confessions are not contemporaneously recorded the opportunities for dispute about what was really said are legion. The situation is back where it was in the days of Sergeant Challenor's 'verbals' and 'voluntary' statements. Thus in *Khan*,[2] for instance, one interview took place in the police car from Wales back to Birmingham, and one took place later in the police station. The defendant was alleged to have confessed to robbery during the journey, but he denied the offence in the police station and also denied making the earlier alleged confession. The police claimed that they took contemporaneous notes of the interview in the car (which were not shown to *Khan* at the time). This was accepted at trial at first instance, and he was convicted. It later became clear that the police officers did not write the notes in the car, casting doubt on whether he really did confess, and so his conviction was quashed on appeal.

1   Moston and Stephenson (1993).
2   (1990) unreported, CA. Discussed by T Kaye, 'Unsafe and Unsatisfactory?' Report of the Independent Inquiry into the Working Practices of the West Midlands Police Serious Crime Squad (London: Civil Liberties Trust, 1991).

Another example is *Dunn*.[3] The defendant was interviewed with his legal advisor present and denied criminal activity. At the end, while reading through the interview notes, the police claimed that he confessed. The police said that they wrote down this alleged confession, but they did not show the questions and answers to the suspect or to his legal advisor. The court none the less allowed the alleged confession to be used as evidence, as did the Court of Appeal, even though these were clear breaches of Code of Practice C. The courts are, however, unpredictable. In yet another case where, after the formal interview, it was claimed that admissions were made, no note was made of the alleged admissions and the Court of Appeal said that these should not have been used in evidence.[4]

These examples show that even when the police are proved to have broken these provisions of Code of Practice C for no good reason, the evidence secured as a result may still be accepted, sometimes with disastrous results for the suspect. They also illustrate the wide scope the police have for breaking them, and the opportunities thus provided simply to fabricate confessions and/or impose unlawful pressure on suspects to confess. For every instance where fabrication is proved there must be a dozen where it is alleged. As *Dunn* and *Khan* show, it is often impossible to establish who is telling the truth. Sometimes, and we will never know how often, the courts get it wrong. At other times the police fabricate confessions by people who really are guilty, but it is usually impossible to tell in which cases this is true.[5] These problems, and these mistakes, will continue for as long as confession evidence secured in the absence of an independent party remains admissible in court.

(d) Protections for suspects: legal advice and appropriate adults

All suspects in custody are entitled to legal advice, and all vulnerable suspects must be accompanied in formal interviews by an appropriate adult.[6] Because the right to legal advice is a continuing one, suspects are able to request a solicitor when an interview is about to take place, or even during one, as the Code of Practice C (para.11.2) acknowledges:

3   (1990) 91 Cr App Rep 237. Discussed in J Hodgson, 'Tipping the Scales of Justice' [1992] Crim LR 854. There are many other examples, such as *Canale* [1990] 2 All ER 187.
4   *Weerdesteyn* [1995] 1 Cr App Rep 405.
5   Even if it were possible to establish that a fabricated confession had been attributed to a person who was in fact guilty, the due process adherent would still argue for an acquittal. The need to uphold the integrity of the criminal process would be seen as more important than the securing of convictions in these cases.
6   These topics are discussed fully in ch 4, sections 2 and 4.

'Immediately prior to the commencement or re-commencement of any interview at a police station or other authorised place of detention, the interviewing officer should remind the suspect of his entitlement to free legal advice.'

Not only may suspects not be interviewed if they ask for solicitors who have yet to arrive,[7] but also interviews must stop when suspects request a solicitor. As is usually the case with due process safeguards 'in the nick', these provisions rely on the police informing suspects of a right which is designed to protect them against those very same police officers.

These provisions are subject to exceptions in special circumstances.[8] These include detention under the Prevention of Terrorism Acts. Also, interviews may take place even if legal advice has been requested but not yet received so long as the general delaying conditions apply.[9] If these provisions do not apply, the interview may none the less take place if an officer of the rank of superintendent or above has reasonable grounds for believing that delay will involve risk of harm to persons or serious loss or damage to property, or if waiting for a lawyer could lead to 'unreasonable delay to the process of investigation'. An inspector may authorise interviewing if no legal advisor can be found at all. Interviews may take place even when these conditions do not apply when suspects who had requested advice change their minds. In these circumstances, suspects must give their agreement, in writing or on tape, to being interviewed without legal advice and an officer of the rank of inspector or above must agree to this.

Given the rights of suspects to be accompanied by legal advisors (and, where applicable, appropriate adults) why is police questioning still a problem? Firstly, questioning in the absence of a legal advisor is not invalid if the above provisions are complied with. And even scrupulous compliance with all due process safeguards (including telling the suspect of their right to free legal advice) does not usually result in a lawyer attending for interview. We have seen that only a relatively small proportion of suspects who are interviewed by the police (little over one third) have a legal advisor present to support them. Even though some more suspects secure advice of some kind (eg, over the telephone, or from an 'appropriate adult') this does not wrest control of questioning from the police.[10] The police can rarely delay access lawfully, and now rarely try, but many suspects do not seek, or appear to change their minds about, lawyers.

7   Code of Practice C, para 6.6.
8   Code of Practice C, para 6.6.
9   These are set out in PACE, s 58 and discussed in ch 4, section 4(a). The police rarely try to delay access nowadays.
10   See ch 4, section 4 for discussion of how the right to legal advice operates in practice.

Secondly, many legal advisors, and most appropriate adults, are supine in the face of oppressive interrogation, as in the 'Cardiff Three' case and the more general research discussed earlier.[11] However, it has to be recognised that, even if legal advisors are minded to intervene, interrogation is controlled by the police, as in the following example:

Sol: '. . . the second clarification is the wallet.'
DC: 'We're not on trial here; we're asking the questions, not you; we don't have to clarify anything.'
Sol: 'I am entitled as any defence solicitor would be to ask for clarification—you don't need to give it, officer.'
DC: 'We're not clarifying things here, we're not on trial. You can ask these things later when it comes to court.'[12]

This illustrates a key problem for the argument that legal advice could be a safeguard if the police and legal profession changed their ways. Legal advisors can only intervene to prevent interrogation methods which fail to conform to the standards discussed below. But we will see that none of the key standards are clear. Not only does this give the police considerable leeway, but it would produce uncertainty in the mind of the most assertive solicitor, let alone the average unqualified clerk. Thus Ed Cape, in an authoritative guide for defence solicitors, drawing on his extensive experience as a solicitor and his academic expertise, says, when discussing bullying by interviewers: 'The lawyer should usually, therefore, intervene at an early stage, although the point of intervention requires careful judgement.'[13] So the good lawyer, far from being a caped crusader on behalf of the client, must hold back, be ponderous. Moreover, whilst the distinction between 'interviews' and 'conversations' remains, legal advisors and appropriate adults will continue to be excluded from informal 'conversations' which may be as important as formal interviews (discussed in section 4 below).

(e) When interviews must end

Paragraph 11.4 of Code of Practice C provides:

'As soon as a police officer who is making enquiries . . . believes that a prosecution should be brought against him and that there is sufficient evidence for it to succeed, he should ask the person if he

---

11 See ch 4, section 4.
12 McConville and Hodgson (1993) p 127. The authors note that the solicitor made no further attempt to interrupt the interrogation. Other examples are provided by Baldwin (1993).
13 Cape (1999), *Defending Suspects at Police Stations* p 296.

has anything further to say . . . the officer shall without delay cease to question him about that offence.'

This broadly continues the old common law which provided that once an officer believed that someone should be prosecuted and that there is sufficient evidence, it would be unfair to continue the interrogation.[14] Paragraph 11.4 also implies that suspects cannot be interrogated about a particular offence after being charged with that offence. This is confirmed (with some minor exceptions) in paragraph 16.5: 'Questions relating to an offence may not be put to a person after he has been charged with that offence or informed that he may be prosecuted for it . . .'

There are three main problems with these provisions. First, the police have a duty to divert offenders from prosecution where appropriate. It may therefore be important to get evidence of, for instance, the suspect's emotional state. This is addressed by the provision that questioning need end only when the officer 'believes that a prosecution should be brought'. But s 37(7) simply provides that:

'. . . if the custody officer determines that he has before him sufficient evidence to charge the person arrested with the offence for which he was arrested, the person arrested—
(a)   shall be charged; or
(b)   shall be released without charge . . .'

If evidence relating to diversion has not been secured, it would appear that PACE prevents it being secured through further questioning. The Code appears to contradict PACE, but this is not legally possible as it is subordinate to PACE.[15] Section 37(7) could inhibit the capacity of the police to secure the information they need to divert offenders from prosecution. In practice, the police interrogate routinely in any case where mens rea is required, even though they will often have sufficient evidence already, but they rarely attempt to secure evidence relevant to diversion.[16] As the police are anxious to secure an admission to the mens rea element of the crime, one can understand why they would not wish to prompt the suspect into claiming emotional instability, depression or dependency on tranquillisers. The last thing they want to hear is 'I was so upset that I didn't know what I was doing.'[17]

14   Also see s 37(7) and para 16.1, which provide that once there is sufficient evidence to charge, the suspect should be charged or released: either way, further interrogation is precluded.
15   E Cape, 'Detention Without Charge: What does 'Sufficient Evidence to Charge' Mean?' [1999] Crim LR 874.
16   McConville et al (1991).
17   See ch 6, section 3(c)(ii) for an illustration and further discussion.

The second problem is that 'sufficient evidence to charge' could mean a prima facie case, or alternatively the more demanding standard of 'reasonable prospect of conviction'. Although the latter is more sensible as it corresponds with the test applied by the CPS (as we shall see in ch 6) this is not consistent with a narrow interpretation of the legislation.[18] Finally, there is the provision that the interviewing officer 'should ask the person if he has anything further to say'. On the face of it, this is easy to comply with. But in some cases where interviewers have taken this opportunity to press their questions further, the courts have held that this is permissible. In *McGuiness*,[19] the Court of Appeal said that, without giving the suspect a full opportunity to explain himself, including questions and answers, the police would not know whether they should prosecute.[20]

From a freedom point of view it is wrong in many circumstances for the courts to allow the police to continue to question suspects once they have sufficient evidence to prosecute. For without a cut-off point, the police would be allowed to carry out indeterminate interrogations until the permissible period of detention had ended. This is because they would always be able to claim that further information might be forthcoming, but only under conditions of involuntary detention. This would lead to even greater infringement of suspects' liberty than already occurs. On the other hand, suspects who are innocent or who have strong mitigating circumstances might benefit from the police probing further. In these circumstances adherents of the freedom perspective might be tempted to advocate some relaxation of the test in s 37(7). Whether the police, as currently constituted, can be relied upon to operate in this discriminating freedom-enhancing manner is open to question. After all, the sensible freedom model adherent accepts that the police are not particularly good at distinguishing those who should be prosecuted from those who should not, and are not usually interested in uncovering exculpatory or mitigating evidence.

4. 'WE HAVE WAYS OF MAKING YOU TALK'

We have seen that, until the latter half of the twentieth century, compulsory custodial interviewing was greatly restricted. Involuntary detention and interrogation, particularly when not judicially authorised, was seen to undermine the right of silence and to be alien to the due process ideal - especially as everyone realised that there was enormous scope for abuse by the police of suspects. Consequently the Judges' Rules required that

18 Cape [1999] 'Detention Without Charge'.
19 Crim LR [1999] 318, discussed in section 2(e) above. *Odeyemi* [1999] Crim LR 828 was decided similarly.
20 See further, Cape [1999] 'Detention Without Charge'.

interviews be carried out in ways that were not 'oppressive' or otherwise liable to produce involuntary or unreliable confessions (as where, for example, 'inducements' to confess were offered). Confession evidence which was secured in breach of these rules was unusable in court.[1] This all remains true under PACE and Code of Practice C, but the legal meaning of these concepts has changed.

The Code of Practice provides for interrogation to take place under reasonable conditions, specifying adequate breaks for rest and refreshment (paras 12.2 and 12.7), adequate physical conditions (paras 12.4 and 12.5) and allowing the presence of a legal advisor (if requested). The purpose of all this is in part humanitarian but it is also to ensure that interrogations are conducted fairly and that confessions or other information secured is reliable and thus usable in court. However, acceptable methods of questioning and the number of interviews and their length are not specified. Interviewing may take place over the 24-hour period (or up to four days, for serious arrestable offences) of compulsory detention, which would have been regarded as oppressive per se a century ago. In 1882, it was regarded as unfair even to 'coax' a confession out of a suspect[2] although it is true that suspects now have many protections that did not exist 100 years ago.[3] By contrast Code of Practice C (para.11.3) now simply says:

> 'No police officer may try to obtain answers to questions or to elicit a statement by the use of oppression ... [or] ... shall indicate, except in answer to a direct question, what action will be taken on the part of the police if the person being interviewed answers questions, makes a statement or refuses to do either.'

Police interviews with suspects are not usually simple chats. In an accusatorial system they are often adversarial. Some suspects are happy to tell the police everything they know. They may be confident of their ability to establish their innocence or be anxious to clear their conscience by confessing. For many suspects, however, telling the police what they know gains them nothing and can lose them a lot. In the main, then, the interview is about negotiating release of information (in exchange for something worth gaining) and/or attempting to persuade suspects to provide information which they do not want to provide. Whatever the situation, police strategy is first directed to establishing control. The police control where, when and how interrogations take place, what is asked, what information is given to suspects, and what is said to suspects or solicitors outside the interrogation. This keeps suspects on the defensive, nervous,

---

1   Judges' Rules 1964, principle (e). See RCCP (1981) Law and Procedure p 154.
2   See section 1 above.
3   See ch 4.

less able to exercise their normal powers of judgment, and unsure of the applicability of any rights of which they may have knowledge.

This was recognised by the American Supreme Court in the famous *Miranda* ruling, saying that 'the very fact of custodial interrogation exerts a heavy toll on individual liberty and trades on the weaknesses of individuals.'[4] This is illustrated by a study conducted by Griffiths and Ayres of well-educated students who had been told their rights, had consulted lawyers, and had been warned of imminent interrogation.[5] Despite these favourable conditions, many talked to their interrogators despite initial declarations of their unwillingness to do so. Driver concludes his summary of the police science and social science literature on interrogation by describing all interrogation as inherently coercive and incapable of being equally balanced between police and suspect.[6] Police interrogation has to be coercive and imbalanced if it is to produce results in most cases, because, as we said before, the police have to try to induce suspects to talk about things that most do not want to talk about. As we saw in section 1, Code C (Note 1B) explicitly states that the police are entitled to question suspects who state that they do not wish to answer questions. The police *Guide to Interviewing* amplifies this, saying that officers should not be discouraged by suspects saying they will not answer questions or by initial 'no comment' answers. Officers should, it says, continue to ask 'all the relevant questions'.[7] The reason for this is to persuade suspects not to exercise their right to silence. It is also, since the passing of the CJPO provisions discussed in section 2, to enable courts to draw adverse inferences in respect of facts which might later be relied upon.

The police have enormous power when the suspect is in custody. At one time, before the forms of regulation discussed in the previous section were established, this power sometimes overflowed into actual violence. Examples include the 'Sheffield Rhino whip' scandal (in the 1960s), the notorious West Midlands Police 'Serious Crime Squad'[8] (in the 1970s), and even incidents following the enactment of PACE in the 1990s. We do not know how common this was, in part because there was even less control and monitoring of interrogations then than there is now. And, because violence is illegal and has always rendered confessions inadmissible, few officers admitted to it. Moreover, the threat of violence is as important as

4   D Dixon, 'Common Sense, Legal Advice, and the Right of Silence' [1991] PL 233.
5   J Griffiths and R Ayres, 'A postscript to the Miranda Project: Interrogation of Draft Protestors' (1967) 77 Yale LJ 300.
6   E Driver, 'Confessions and the Social Psychology of Coercion' (1968) 82 Harv LR 42.
7   Central Planning and Training Unit, Guide to Interviewing (London: HMSO, 1992) p 62. This *Guide* is discussed later in this section.
8   Aptly named in view of the serious crimes it committed. See further Kaye (1991).

'We have ways of making you talk'

the actual use of violence, if suspects know or fear that the police are prepared to use it. There is little doubt that violence, and the threat thereof, is now infrequent.[9] The police have had to develop non-violent 'tactics' which aim at the same results through legal means.[10]

(a)   Police interrogation tactics: legal standards

Nowhere does PACE or Code C specify what tactics are, and are not, lawful.[11] 'Torture' is a crime.[12] Otherwise, the standards imposed on the police arise solely through such law as there is regulating the acceptability or exclusion, at trial, of evidence. This is discussed further in ch 11. This means that breaches of these standards (and the protections, including that of legal advice, discussed in ch 4) only affect the police adversely if they prosecute the suspect(s) in question, and seek to use evidence obtained thereby. If, for example, the police interrogate largely to put the 'frighteners' on someone (as discussed in section 1 above), there is nothing to stop them breaching any or all of these standards.

(i)   The police must not offer 'inducements'

Paragraph 11.3 of PACE Code of Practice C (quoted above) implicitly prohibits the offering of 'inducements', such as bail or non-prosecution.[13] The problem with this is that 'deals' and 'bargains' are central to police-suspect relationships, and what is a deal other than an agreement that each side will accept the inducements offered by the other? As Dixon points out, interrogation is often as much a process of negotiation (over bail, charges and information about other offences and other suspects, etc) as confrontation.[14] Paragraph 11.3 has not changed this, and so it is largely a presentational rule.[15] This is particularly the case since the courts seek

---

9   But note that arrests are often violent (see ch 3, sections 3(e) and 4(e)) and this must create a fear of repetition in some suspects' minds.

10   This is true of many jurisdictions. On the USA, see Leo (1994). On Australia, see Dixon (1997) ch 5.

11   See A Sanders and R Young, 'The Legal Wilderness of Police Interrogation' in (1994) The Tom Sargant Memorial Lecture, pp 20-26.

12   Criminal Justice Act 1988, s 134.

13   See *Northam* (1967) 52 Cr App Rep 97 and *Howden-Simpson* [1991] Crim LR 49 (discussed in ch 11) where the inducement was an offer to refrain from interviewing the choirboys for whom the suspect was responsible.

14   D Dixon, 'Common Sense, Legal Advice, and the Right to Silence' [1991] PL 233.

15   See ch 2, section 1(d) for discussion of the nature of legal rules as presentational, legitimising, enabling or inhibitory.

a causal connection between the inducement and the confession. Thus in *Weeks*[16] for example, the police implied that the suspect would be held in custody until he told them what they wanted to hear. His partial confession was not excluded because the court did not believe that he was influenced by this. The gap between the law and reality could hardly be greater than it is here. The ban on inducements reflects a fear that people offered inducements may say whatever they think the police want to hear, regardless of whether or not it is true. The fear is entirely justified, but it cannot be simply legislated away. The only way to inhibit inducements to confess substantially would be to reduce or eliminate the value of confessions to the police.

(ii) Interrogation must not be 'unfair'

This is not mentioned in Code of Practice C, but it arises because PACE, s 78 allows any evidence to be excluded at trial (at the discretion of the judge) if it is obtained 'unfairly'. Examples arising out of the conduct of the interrogation include lies and deception (*Mason*[17]), failure to record suspects' statements contemporaneously (*Canale*[18]) and questioning juveniles without an appropriate adult (*Fogah*[19]). There are also countless other situations outside the interrogation in which s 78 has been invoked, such as *Samuel*[20] (denial of the right to a solicitor) and *Absolam*[1] (failure to advise of the right to legal advice). However, this standard inhibits the police only at the extreme end of what might ordinarily be regarded as 'unfair'. No modern case, for example, has ever regarded 'coaxing' as unfair, otherwise most interrogation would be pointless. Further, what a judge may regard as 'unfair' is something of a lottery, the Court of Appeal rarely interferes with this discretionary power of the trial judge (see ch 11), and if a legal representative is in the interrogation this is usually regarded as sufficient protection to blunt the unfairness.[2]

(iii) Interrogation must not be 'oppressive'

Section 76(8) states that oppression 'includes torture, inhuman or degrading treatment, and the use or threat of violence (whether or not

---

16   [1995] Crim LR 52.
17   [1988] 1 WLR 139.
18   [1990] 2 All ER 187.
19   [1989] Crim LR 141.
20   [1988] QB 615.
1   (1988) 88 Cr App Rep 332.
2   Cape (1999), *Defending Suspects at Police Stations* ch 13.

'We have ways of making you talk'

amounting to torture).' Confession evidence obtained in this way has to be excluded under s 76. In *Fulling*,[3] the defendant made incriminating statements after being told that her lover had been having an affair with the occupant of the next cell. The Court of Appeal adopted the dictionary definition of oppression, which is:

'Exercise of authority or power in a burdensome, harsh, or wrongful manner, unjust or cruel treatment of subjects, inferiors etc; the imposition of unreasonable or unjust burdens.'

This extremely wide definition was qualified with the view that this would normally have to include an 'impropriety' by the police. The courts do not view all 'improprieties' as oppressive.[4] Presumably this is why the police were held not to have acted 'oppressively' in this case, for the trick played on Fulling was undoubtedly 'cruel', although perhaps not what one would normally think of as oppressive. The recourse to the dictionary definition by Lord Lane CJ in *Fulling* was essentially rhetorical, and the courts have yet to clarify what is meant in law by oppression. This uncertainty can be useful for the police because it gives them latitude and enables them to shrug off responsibility if 'the wheel comes off'. By the same token, it means that, even if the police wanted to behave ethically, they cannot know quite how far they can go. For example, in a murder case where the trial judge refused to accept alleged confessions secured after the police wrongly told the defendant that they had identification evidence and 'pounded him with sexual allegations' the head of CID for the force concerned said 'It is a matter of interpretation as to what is oppressive . . . It is rather difficult to establish the truth by pussyfooting about.'[5] In reality, 'oppression' is argued in few cases, since the same result (exclusion of confessions) can be secured under the 'unfairness' provision of PACE, s 78.

(iv)   Answers and statements must be given 'voluntarily'

The Phillips Commission regarded everything which took place in police custody as being 'involuntary', for anything which a suspect might do voluntarily would not require compulsory detention in the first place. If the job of the police is to persuade people to speak when they do not wish

3   [1987] QB 426.
4   In *Davison* [1988] Crim LR 442, for instance (as in many other cases), unlawful denial of access to a solicitor was held not be to oppressive. Also see *Parker* [1995] Crim LR 233.
5   *The Guardian*,22 November 1993. This was the *Heron* case. See Dixon (1997) pp 169-177 for discussion of this and other cases illustrating the judicial approach to interrogation standards.

to speak, to regard their speaking as 'voluntary' is a nonsense. Philips regarded itself as faced with the choice between banning custodial interrogation (the due process option) or abandoning the voluntariness principle (the crime control option). It chose the latter. Perhaps regarding this logic as unpalatable, the government retained the voluntariness principle in the form of the caution (that no one need say anything unless they wish to do so) but undermined it by allowing the police to interrogate suspects who declare their unwillingness to speak.[6] The principle is explicitly stated nowhere in PACE or Code of Practice C. The law allows the police to persuade suspects to speak when they do not wish to do so, subject to the limits we have just discussed. This ambivalence in the law between the due process principle of voluntariness and the crime control principle of allowing the police latitude in how much pressure they may bring to bear on suspects creates uncertainty about the limits of police interrogation on which the law is largely silent.

(v) 'Unreliable' answers and statements

Under PACE, s 76(2)(b) confession evidence must be excluded if 'anything said or done' renders it 'unreliable'. This overlaps substantially with 'oppression', 'inducements' and lack of voluntariness, as the products of any of these things would often be regarded as unreliable. Occasionally unreliability can arise without any of these applying. An example is *Souter*.[7] A soldier suspected of rape was too distressed to be interviewed. A superior officer tried to calm him, whereupon Souter confessed. The Court of Appeal held that the trial judge had been wrong to allow the confession to be used as the circumstances made the confession unreliable.

(b) Traditional police questioning tactics

Legal standards exist ostensibly to prevent questioning falling below minimal human rights standards and to attempt to ensure that confessions and other information provided is reliable. Yet we have seen that police questioning is inherently coercive. As one suspect put it,

> 'You see, like, they tell you you don't have to talk, then they pressure you to talk. You say "no comment, no comment", and they keep asking you questions . . . It's nonsense innit?'[8]

---

6   Code of Practice C, Note 1B, quoted in section 1.
7   [1995] Crim LR 729.
8   C Adams, *Balance in Pre-Trial Criminal Justice* (unpublished PhD thesis, LSE) p 247.

It is to the nature of that pressure, steering a course between illegality and ineffectiveness, that we now turn.

(i)   Use of custodial conditions

Interrogation is nearly always on territory chosen by the police. This enables them to control suspects which is a key to successful interrogation.[9] The manipulation of custodial conditions is particularly important. Since this, along with several other tactics, was first identified by Irving,[10] several other researchers have endorsed his findings. Just being held for interview is a 'frightener',[11] and suspects are usually placed in the cells for a while prior to interview to 'soften them up' even if there is nothing to prevent the interview going ahead immediately.[12] Isolation, assertion of authority and control over details such as precise times of drinks, breaks and so forth all make the experience of detention intimidating.[13] In the interrogation itself police authority is crucial, eg 'I'll decide when the interview finishes', and '. . . don't think we'll just let it go just because in one interview you make no replies—we're just starting.'[14] Many forms of pressure can be applied. Here are two examples provided by suspects interviewed by Choongh:

'. . .they were really doing my head in, asking me silly questions, asking me things which had nothing to do with anything.'

'I felt they were trying to push me into a situation, which happens to a lot of people when you're frightened and you're bombarded with questions from two people, in that situation when you're scared you just think, well just say "yes", just to please the guy, anything to stop the pressure. . .'[15]

Recalcitrant suspects are often returned to the cells as a warning of how they will have to spend the rest of their 24-hour detention; a severe threat in view of the feelings of most suspects about detention. Thus Softley found that occasionally a confession was produced almost immediately

---

9   Leo (1994).

10   B Irving, Police Interrogation: A Study of Current Practice (Royal Commission on Criminal Procedure Research Paper No 2) (London: HMSO, 1980).

11   Evans (1993) p 25.

12   Sanders et al (1989).

13   See ch 4, section 3 (d). For examples see Choongh (1997) pp 109-110.

14   Both examples taken from McConville and Hodgson (1993) p 126. Also see Hillyard (1993) ch 8.

15   Choongh (1997) pp 119-120.

on return to the cells.[16] None of this is unlawful in most circumstances, as *Weeks* indicated, although this does depend on the causal connection between what the police do and say, and what the suspect does and says.[17] Cape gives an example of a young single parent whose baby had been left with a relative. She was distressed, and the officer repeatedly asked her what she would do about her baby if she was in police custody for much longer.[18] Cape regards this as an unlawful inducement to confess, although whether a court would agree remains to be seen.

(ii)   Police discretion

Sometimes the police allude (overtly or in a veiled manner) to their discretion in relation to bail, the level and number of charges to be preferred, other suspects to be investigated and so forth. Co-operation (or not) will influence the way that discretion is exercised. Examples include the police saying threateningly to a legal representative, in the presence of the suspect, 'We'll have to see about bail if he's not talking', and the police telling a legal representative that they would not charge his client if he confessed.[19] The interviews from one police station looked at by Baldwin contained a spate of inducements to confess on the promise that the offences would merely be 'taken into consideration' (TICd).[20] These are all examples of inducements and, as such, unlawful in the sense that confessions produced as a result could be excluded. Estimates vary regarding how frequently unlawful inducements are used. Irving and McKenzie found none,[1] whereas McConville and Hodgson found some, but not many.[2] It is possible that the police were less inhibited in front of

16   P Softley, Police Interrogation: An Observational Study in Four Police Stations (Royal Commission on Criminal Procedure Research Study no 4) (London: HMSO, 1980).
17   [1995] Crim LR 52, discussed in section 4(a)(i) above.
18   Cape (1999) p 292.
19   McConville and Hodgson (1993) pp 121-22. See also the extract from an informal interview quoted in subsection (e) below.
20   Baldwin (1993) pp 348-349. Offences taken into consideration are put before the court in abbreviated form at a normal hearing for some other offence. 'TICs' may influence sentencing, but the advantage to the defendant is that it allows the slate to be wiped clean. See also the extract from an informal interview in subsection (e) below.
1   B Irving and I McKenzie, Police Interrogation: The Effects of the Police and Criminal Evidence Act 1984 (London: Police Foundation, 1989).
2   McConville and Hodgson (1993). Note that they only observed cases in which there was a legal advisor present. If the legal representatives do inhibit the police, one would expect more breaches of Code of Practice C and PACE in cases not observed by them, especially as the presence of the researchers themselves could have exerted an inhibitory influence. See also Choongh (1997) pp 110-111.

'We have ways of making you talk'

McConville and Hodgson than in front of Irving and McKenzie because PACE was still new and untried when the latter did their research, but by the time the former did theirs (1991–92) the police felt more confident about bending the rules. How frequently unlawful inducements are offered when no researcher is watching cannot be known. Sometimes, however, the police are caught off-guard, as when they do not realise their behaviour is being watched by an outsider. On these occasions their actions can be so outrageous as to cause jaws to hit the floor.[3]

An entirely lawful use of discretion is the withholding, or drip-feeding, of selected items of information. As we saw in section 2 (above) the police need not tell suspects what they know or suspect, and so they often use information as a bargaining chip. This disorients suspects and undermines the efficacy of any legal advice they may have received. Choongh reports several suspects saying that they answered police questions in the hope that then they could discover of what they were suspected.[4] By withholding or drip-feeding information the police can engage in active or passive deception, of which the latter is entirely lawful (see sub-section (vi) below).

(iii)   Provision of expert knowledge

This is where the police play on their specialist knowledge of the legal system to suggest what the effect will be of their co-operation or otherwise on the attitude of the court, likely sentence, the chance of receiving expert help, and so forth.[5] In the 'Cardiff Three' case, one of the suspects attempted to retract earlier incriminating statements he had made, and was immediately told that 'you're looking at a life sentence if this goes wrong'. He thereupon continued to confess.[6]

(iv)   Consequences of confession

Persuasive interviewers can lead suspects to believe that confession will make them appear to be more worthy people and that non-co-operation is socially, emotionally and practically undesirable. For example, 'What's your girlfriend to think about you?', and 'sometime you'll have to stand up like

---

3   See the quote at the head of this ch and the explanatory footnote that accompanies it. Fuller quotes drawn from this illuminating case are set out in subsection (e) below.

4   Choongh (1997) pp 112-115.

5   The sentence discount offered to those who co-operate in their own conviction is discussed in ch 7.

6   *Paris, Abdullahi, Miller* (1992) 97 Cr App Rep 99. Also see Leo (1994).

a man . . .'[7] In some circumstances this could lead to confession being regarded as unreliable, as in *Souter*, where the (very distressed) soldier was told 'to stop crying, to be a soldier and to be a man.'[8] A guide for police officers written by an officer suggests that suspects be told 'If you admit it and plead guilty, chances are it'll all be over and done with very quickly', or 'Once you've admitted it, you'll be able to put all this lot behind you and turn over a new leaf.'[9] Some of these tactics might be regarded as inducements.

(v) No decision to be made

While the other tactics attempt to force suspects to make a decision, this tactic suggests that there is no decision to make. The suspect is led to understand that the police have sufficient evidence anyway, so that there is no point in non co-operation, as when an officer said: 'We've had a complaint saying you were there . . . There are five people to say you were there.'[10] This is lawful if the police are telling the truth, but not (in the sense that it is 'unfair' in terms of s 78 PACE) if it is untrue.[11] Where, as often happens, the strength of such evidence is misrepresented, the legality of this depends on how great was the misrepresentation, whether the police were acting in a bona fide way and so forth. Since the police do not have to disclose any of their evidence to suspects or their lawyers at the interrogation (see section 2 above) it will often not be known at that time whether such claims are true, untrue or exaggerated.

(vi) Deception

As we have seen, lying is generally regarded as 'unfair'. But there are other forms of deception, both active and passive, which the police often use, which are generally lawful. For example, one of the writers once asked a detective how he got a suspect to admit to a factory break-in. The officer replied that he had asked the works manager if anyone had a grudge against the factory. The suspect was named as being aggrieved about being sacked shortly before. He was arrested. In interview the suspect denied the break-in. So the detective told him that he might as well confess, since his fingerprints were all over the place: a classic example of the 'no decision to be made' tactic. He did confess, the writer commented that this was not surprising in the circumstances, and the detective fell about laughing, for

7   McConville and Hodgson (1993) pp 123-24.
8   Mirfield (1997) p 89, drawing on the transcript of *Souter* [1995] Crim LR 729.
9   J Walkley, *Police Interrogation* (1988) p 58.
10   McConville and Hodgson (1993) p 125.
11   *Mason* [1987] 3 All ER 481.

the writer had fallen for the same deception as the suspect: since the suspect had worked there, *of course* his fingerprints were all over the place, but this was not evidence that he had broken in.

An example of 'passive' deception occurred in *Imran and Hussain*[12]. The suspects had been videotaped, without their knowledge, going into a shop where there had been an attempted robbery. The police did not tell them this, and they did not admit going into the shop. At trial this left them vulnerable under the CJPO (discussed in section 2 above), and they contended that adverse inferences should not be drawn since the police had passively deceived them. They were convicted, and the Court of Appeal held that what the police had, and had not, said was entirely lawful. Another common example of passive deception is not telling suspects of what they are suspected. Arrestees must be cautioned and given a valid reason for arrest, although the police have a lot of room for manoeuvre if they judge there to be insufficient evidence to arrest (see section 3 above). But the police may give the impression that the arrest and interview is largely for one offence when in reality it is largely for another. The courts did not object to this in *Chalkley and Jeffries*,[13] where the arrest and interview were engineered simply to get the defendant out of his house while bugging equipment was installed. However, in *Williams*[14] a fight broke out on a bus, leading to a young man jumping out and dying. The men involved in the fight were arrested, cautioned and interviewed but thought that the police were only concerned with the man's death. Evidence from their interviews was used in order to charge them with public order offences, but was excluded under PACE, s 78 (as being 'unfair') by the trial judge, because of the suspects' misapprehension.

Williams is an interesting example of deceptive tactics, but the judge's decision is irreconcilable with *Imran and Hussain* and other cases where there was active deception. One such, albeit not in the context of a formal interview, was *Maclean and Kosten*,[15] discussed in (e) below. Cases decided similarly, albeit where confessions are not obtained through interviews, are those where suspects confess to each other without knowing that their cells are bugged.[16] As a Crown Court decision, *Williams* is of no precedential value, and is, in the crime control terms adopted in most cases, eccentric.[17]

---

12   [1997] Crim LR 754.
13   [1998] 2 Cr App Rep 79. See discussion in ch 3, section 4(b)(ii).
14   [1991] Crim LR 708.
15   [1993] Crim LR 687.
16   For example, *Bailey and Smith* (1993) 97 Cr App Rep 365; *Roberts* [1997] 1 Cr App Rep 217.
17   See the commentary at [1991] Crim LR 709. For a general discussion see A Ashworth, 'Should the police be allowed to use deceptive practices?' (1998) 114 LQR 108.

A tactic may be unlawful but it will still be employed if the police think they can get away with it. Waddington gives an example of a man suspected of a series of thefts from work. The last in the series was of money that had been treated with a chemical which was supposed to show up, under UV light, on the hands of anyone who touched it. The man's hands were passed under the light, the detectives commented on the clear chemical reflection, told the suspect they had enough evidence to charge him, and then turned to the other thefts, to which the suspect confessed. In fact, unknown to the suspect, the machine was faulty and had not picked out the chemical. Since the suspect was charged only with the crimes to which he confessed (and not to the one about which he had been deceived) the police may have got away with this if they had been challenged.[18] As a detective told an American researcher: 'Interrogation is essentially a cross between a chess game and poker: you have to carefully strategise and outsmart the suspect with each move you make, but a lot of it really comes down to how well you can bluff and deceive.'[19]

(vii) Now is the time to explain

This implies to suspects who divulge only a little information that failure to explain fully will lead to unspecified harmful consequences. For example, 'It's only fair to tell you that it's in your own interests and to your benefit to give your version of events.'[20]. The changes to the right of silence discussed earlier mean that this may well often be true, or that the suspect is likely to suffer whether s/he speaks or not. A similar tactic has been used by the police giving suspects leaflets on these lines: 'My position is one of impartiality. I am here to seek the truth. . . . Have you any information you can now furnish me with which would ultimately assist the CPS in making a decision not to prosecute in this matter?'[1]

(viii) Accusation or abuse

Examples include: 'Why are they [witnesses] lying? . . . I asked for a reason—there isn't one—why?', 'You, young man, are a liar basically . . .'[2]

---

18 Waddington (1999) pp 136-37. Such a challenge would be unlikely unless a solicitor had been present and would in any event be under s 78 PACE, whereby exclusion is a discretionary matter for the judge: ch 11.
19 Leo (1994) p 107.
20 McConville and Hodgson (1993) p 129; Leo (1994).
1   Extracted from a pro-forma used at one time by officers in Avon and Somerset. Cape (1999) p 274.
2   McConville and Hodgson (1993) p 128. Also see JUSTICE, Unreliable Evidence? Confessions and the Safety of Convictions (London: JUSTICE, 1994); Hillyard (1993) ch 8.

and the infamous 'Mr Nice and Mr Nasty' Mutt and Jeff routine. Most of the time, according to Cape,[3] none of this would be regarded as either oppressive or unfair.[4] All these tactics were used in the Cardiff Three case. Here, Miller - a young man with learning difficulties - was subjected to 14 hours of interrogation, over no less than 19 separate interrogations, held over a four-day period, much of which was extremely aggressive. After 300 denials (and 13 hours of interrogation) he eventually 'confessed'. As the Court of Appeal put it: 'The officers made it clear to Mr Miller that they would go on interviewing him until he agreed with the version of events they required.' He, and two associates, were convicted of murder. They appealed. When the Court of Appeal judges began hearing the interrogation tapes, they stopped the case and allowed the appeal of all three men on the grounds of oppression before they reached the end, so shocked were they at the behaviour of the police. According to the Lord Chief Justice:

'Miller was bullied and hectored. The officers . . . were not so much questioning him as shouting at him what they wanted him to say . . . It is impossible to convey on the printed page the pace, force, and menace of the officer's delivery.'[5]

The printed page is certainly no substitute for hearing the tapes, but one extract serves well enough to illustrate the hectoring that Miller endured when he tried to deny involvement in murder:

Police: 'How you could sit there and say that. You've been in that room—seen that girl there, in the state that she was in. And you're supposed to have had all this wonderful care for her. Seen her damned head hang off, and her arms cut, and stabbed to death, and you sit there and tell us that you know nothing at all about it, nothing at all about it.

Suspect: 'I wasn't there.'
Police: 'How you can ever . . .'
Suspect: 'I wasn't there.'
Police: 'I just don't know how you can sit there.'

Despite the high profile of this case, because three men were wrongly jailed for murder, the interrogation techniques employed in it may not have been unusual. Revealingly, the Chief Constable of South Wales said that, although he did not support oppressive interviewing, two High Court

3   Cape (1999) ch 7.
4   See, for example, *Emmerson* (1990) 92 Cr App Rep 284, where rude, discourteous questioning in a raised voice, and swearing, was held not to be oppressive.
5   *Paris, Abdullahi, Miller* (1992) 97 Cr App Rep 99.

judges had allowed the 'Cardiff Three' confession evidence and 'a full debate on what constituted oppressive questioning was now needed.'[6] Baldwin also provides examples. For example, at one point in a series of very aggressive interviews of a juvenile for murder, the officer—in an uncanny echo of the 'Cardiff Three' case—said:

> 'You can sit here, looking at the floor, crying and crying, but I am not going to walk out of that door; you are not going to leave here until I hear it from your own lips. Do you understand? Did you murder that boy?'[7]

These were not idle threats. Custodial interrogation lasted three days. For serious arrestable offences, the police do not only have ways of making you talk. They have days to make you talk too.

(c) 'Ethical' interviewing

In the early 1990s criticism of traditional police interrogation techniques spread from the 'usual suspects' (that is, academics like us, along with a few pressure groups and defence-oriented lawyers) to the courts, Home Office officials and even the police themselves.[8] The Runciman Commission complained that there is:

> '. . . an over-ready assumption on the part of some interviewing officers of the suspect's guilt and on occasion the exertion of undue pressure amounting to bullying or harassment . . . They entered the interview room with their minds made up and treated the suspect's explanation with unjustified scepticism.'

In 1992, whilst Runciman was deliberating, the Home Office issued a circular to the police setting out 'Principles of Investigative Interviewing'[9] These are:

Home Office Circular 22/1992 Principles of investigative interviewing
1) The role of investigative interviewing is to obtain accurate and reliable information from suspects, witnesses or victims in order to discover the truth about matters under police investigation.

---

6   *The Guardian*, 17 December 1992.
7   Baldwin (1993) p 347.
8   See, for example, the musings of a senior police officer: T Williamson, 'Reflections on Current Police Practice', in D Morgan and G Stephenson, *Suspicion and Silence* (London: Blackstone, 1994).
9   Home Office Circular 22/1992. This was enthusiastically endorsed by the Runciman Commission.

'We have ways of making you talk'

2) Investigative interviewing should be approached with an open mind. Information obtained from the person who is being interviewed should always be tested against what the interviewing officer already knows or what can reasonably be established.

3) When questioning anyone a police officer must act fairly in the circumstances of each individual case.

4) The police interviewer is not bound to accept the first answer given. Questioning is not unfair merely because it is persistent.

5) Even when the right of silence is exercised by a suspect, the police still have a right to put questions.

6) When conducting an interview, police officers are free to ask questions in order to establish the truth; except for interviews with child victims of sexual or violent abuse which are to be used in criminal proceedings, they are not constrained by the rules applied to lawyers in court.

7) Vulnerable people, whether victims, witnesses, or suspects, must be treated with particular consideration at all times.

A 'Guide to Interviewing' expands these principles, including that of the 'open mind', and sets out a PEACE model.[10] This advocates planning and preparation (P), in which the interviewers consider the objectives of the interview and what they wish to prove; engagement and explanation (E), in which interviewers establish relationships with suspects and explain their rights; account, clarification and challenge (A), in which the suspects' accounts are sought and, where appropriate, clarified and challenged; closure (C) of the interview; and evaluation (E), in which interviewers consider what more, if anything, needs to be done in the light of the interview. The *Guide* then sets out two approaches to interviewing, both of which can be used within PEACE. First, 'cognitive interviewing' encourages the interviewee to re-live the event in question and provide an account with minimal interference. However, although cognitive interviewing has been found to be valuable with willing participants (especially prosecution witnesses) it has not worked well with unwilling participants.[11] For this reason, no doubt, the *Guide* advocates the 'Management of Conversation' approach for most suspects. The interviewee provides an account of what happened. The interviewer then divides this account up, homing in on each element in turn; this is the 'A' section of the PEACE model.

10   Home Office, Central Planning and Training Unit, *Guide to Interviewing* (London: HMSO, 1992).

11   See J Cherryman and R Bull, 'Investigative Interviewing' in F Leishman, B Loveday and S Savage (eds), *Core Issues in Policing* (Harlow: Longman, 1996).

The 'Management of Conversation' approach conceals a fundamental conflict between the traditional approach, criticised by Runciman, and the 'Principles' which advocate an open mind. A suspects' account can be pursued and probed either with an open mind or with scepticism, in a friendly or in a bullying way. Newton, for example, comments: 'I have difficulty in recognising this package as an ethical framework for interviewing.'[12] The whole point of most interviews is to exert pressure. This is not usually out of a desire to humiliate suspects or 'fit them up'. It is a product, as one would expect in a crime control system, of a belief in the suspect's guilt and of resource and legal constraints which put a premium on confession evidence. As an officer told Choongh, ' . . . we certainly question on the basis that the person sitting in front of us is guilty - that's what we're paid to do, I mean we can't assume they're innocent, we'd never get the job done.'[13] The use of terms by Runciman like 'unjustified' and 'an over-ready assumption' is indicative of a failure to understand the nature of police interrogation. Runciman says that there is a need to inculcate those skills 'which are most likely to elicit the truth while at the same time ensuring that they are exercised within a clearly defined code of ethical conduct.'[14] There is no recognition that eliciting the truth and behaving ethically will often be mutually exclusive, or that eliciting the truth in most cases entails tactics which elicit untruths in others.[15]

Further, before any ethical or cognitive approach can supplant the traditional approach, officers need to be adequately trained and supervised, training needs to be related to practical policing problems, this approach needs to become part of the whole ethos of policing, and officers need to be rewarded for changing the way they do things. There is little evidence of significant progress on any of these points as yet, and little prospect of any in the foreseeable future.[16]

(d) The effectiveness of tactics

Some tactics will be more effective than others. According to McConville and Hodgson, the most common tactics are (in order of frequency of use)

12 T Newton, 'The Place of Ethics in Investigative Interviewing by Police Officers' (1998) Howard JCJ 52 at p 66.
13 Choongh (1997) p 124.
14 RCCJ (1993) p 13.
15 The Runciman Commission is far from alone in this. For another naive approach, see Cherryman and Bull (1996).
16 Newton (1998); A Memon et al, 'Improving the Quality of the Police Interview: Can Training in the Use of Cognitive Techniques help?' (1995) 5 Policing and Society 53; Choongh (1997) pp 128-130.

'We have ways of making you talk'

'no decision to make', 'accusation/abuse' and 'consequences'. With any one suspect, however, it may be difficult to guess what will be effective. It is not surprising to find that in the majority of cases more than one tactic is used. If one tactic does not work, the police move on to another.[17] Even then, tactics are thought to fail to elicit confessions as often as they succeed,[18] or even most of the time.[19] Police interrogation in general is described in most research reports as often ineffective, clumsy, rambling, repetitious and hit and miss.[20] Thus Maguire, for example, found that most interrogation was done by unsupervised junior officers whose approaches were individualistic and 'reactive' (ie reactive to the response of suspects).[1] Only rarely (usually when there is an immediate confession) is no tactic used.[2] Effectiveness may also be affected by the presence or absence of lawyers and appropriate adults, and so forth.

The vulnerability of the suspect is crucial. The essence of interrogation tactics is to locate a particular vulnerability and exploit it. In a sense all suspects are vulnerable, however. Twenty-four hours provides a lot of time to explore the vulnerabilities of the psyche. Indeed, Evans comments of juveniles that: 'The very fact that juveniles are arrested and detained for questioning by the police may render them psychologically vulnerable.'[3] Not surprisingly, tactics are most used where there is no ready confession and where the other evidence is weak or lacking in a crucial respect, such as intention.[4]

From the crime control perspective, tactics are crucial in securing vital information that would be otherwise unobtainable or obtainable only at considerable expense. From the due process perspective, tactics are to be condemned both because they excessively infringe and abuse the liberty of the individual and because they are likely to elicit self-incriminating statements in cases where suspects are factually innocent. The freedom viewpoint is close to that of due process, but puts more emphasis on the effect of tactics on the particular suspect and less on how far tactics adhere to 'objective' legal standards.

---

17   Hillyard (1993) ch 8.
18   Evans (1993) pp 44-46.
19   Baldwin (1993).
20   See Baldwin (1993) and S Moston and T Engelberg, 'Police Questioning Techniques in Tape Recorded Interviews with Criminal Suspects' (1993) 3 Policing and Society 223.
1   M Maguire, 'The Wrong Message at the Wrong Time?' in Morgan and Stephenson (1994).
2   McConville and Hodgson (1993) p 129 Table 7.1.
3   Evans (1993) p 26.
4   Evans (1993) p 31.

(e) Informal questioning

Questioning is 'informal' if, instead of taking place in a police station interview room, it is done in the street, in the car, at the custody officer's desk or in the cells; or if proper cautions and rights are not provided and if the proceedings are not recorded. In this section we do not classify neutral attempts to elicit information as 'questioning' for if the police are genuinely neutral then the person is not being questioned in an adversarial sense (although we saw in section 3 above that the police have, in practice a lot of room for manouevre). Nor do we include questioning during a stop-search, discussed in ch 2 (sections 3(a) and 4(c)).

There are many reasons why the police question suspects informally. Some of these reasons are lawful. We saw in section 3(a) that sometimes the police suspect an individual of a crime but have no 'reasonable suspicion'. The police therefore cannot arrest, but (after cautioning the individual) they can continue questioning. The suspect need not answer, but usually does. Also, informal interviews are sometimes initiated by suspects who wish to 'deal' confidentially. This makes it hard to disprove police claims that informal discussions began at the behest of the suspect as said in, for instance, *Younis*, *Khan*[5] and *Menard*.[6] Much informal questioning is unlawful (in the sense that the products of that questioning could be excluded from evidence at a trial). We saw in section 3(a) that if a suspect has been arrested, the police cannot question him/her until 'booked in' at the police station. The police may want to, though, as informal questioning is uncontrolled and unsupervised, there is no time clock running, no legal advisor will be present and there are no independent witnesses or checks on the tactics used to elicit incriminating material.

The important point about informal questioning is that, like all questioning, it is an encounter which the police set out to control. When the police choose to question informally, it is because the constraints on formal questioning which we have discussed in this section would limit their control. Informal questioning subverts the PACE framework of rules designed to protect the suspect. In an attempt to control it, PACE and Code of Practice C provide that 'interviews' may only take place outside police stations and police station interview rooms in exceptional circumstances. As with so many due process rules, these rules go against the grain of policing and, indeed, of normal social interaction. So, now that formal interviewing is restricted by regulations and protections for the suspect it is not surprising that informal questioning is common.

There is an almost infinite range of circumstances in which informal questioning takes place. In *Maclean and Kosten*,[7] for example, a customs

5   *Younis* and *Khan* are discussed in section 3 above.
6   [1995] 1 Cr App Rep 306
7   [1993] Crim LR 687

officer pretended to be a car salvage operator. By this ruse he secured incriminating statements over the phone from the defendant, who was not in custody, indicating that he had imported drugs in an impounded car. The Court of Appeal held that informal interviewing in this type of undercover operation was acceptable, because cautioning, arresting and formally interviewing the suspect would defeat the purpose of the operation. Whilst this is true, it illustrates the crime control/due process dilemma: to allow law enforcement bodies opportunities to secure powerful evidence, protections which are generally thought necessary to protect suspects have to be set aside.

The most obvious place to question informally is in the car on the way to the station. As a CID officer said to Maguire and Norris: 'You can't just sit in the car in silence.'[8] Talking is not, in itself, unlawful and it need not amount to an interview but, even without the ever-present prospect of a deal, it would be unnatural for conversation not to turn to the reason for the arrest. Since suspect-initiated conversations are no different in principle from police-initiated conversations,[9] both may easily become attempts to elicit relevant information. Maguire and Norris quote another officer who said that he 'would not be doing his job'[10] if he did not talk to prisoners, thus echoing the officer who told McConville et al that 'no policeman who did his job is going to say 'no' if a suspect wanted to talk 'off the record'.[11]

The longer the journey, the more likely it will be that informal questioning develops out of conversation, whether intended or not. Thus whether or not the defendant in *Khan* (see section 3 (c)) really did make admissions in the car, it was predictable that conversation would turn to his alleged offence on a long journey from Wales to Birmingham. Some journeys, however, are unnecessarily lengthened by taking the 'scenic route'.[12] This is a route which lasts as long as it takes to secure the admissions desired, and is clearly unlawful.[13] McConville and Morrel found that when experiments began with the tape recording of interviews in Scotland in the early 1980s, journey times to police stations got significantly longer: questioning which could no longer take place without scrutiny in police stations simply took place in police cars instead.[14] That this still happens is confirmed by Maguire and Norris. They were, however, unable to

8   Maguire and Norris (1992) p 46.
9   Notwithstanding the view of the Court of Appeal in, for instance, *Younis*, (see section 3).
10   Maguire and Norris (1992) p 46.
11   McConville et al (1991) p 58.
12   Sometimes prompted by an understandable desire to avoid Birmingham.
13   PACE, s 30(1), requires transfer to a police station as soon as reasonably practicable.
14   M McConville and P Morrell, 'Recording the Interrogation: Have the Police got it Taped?' [1983] Crim LR 158.

estimate the extent of informal interviewing either in its lawful or unlawful forms.[15]

An attempt was made to estimate frequency by Brown et al and by Moston and Stephenson.[16] In both studies, police officers making the arrests in the cases being researched were asked whether they asked suspects questions before arrival at the police station. In Brown et al's study, 19% said they did before the 1991 revision of Code of Practice C was introduced, and 10% afterwards. In a further 19% and 16% of cases respectively, the police said that unsolicited comments were made by the suspects.[17] Much, and possibly most, of this questioning, it seems, amounts to 'interviewing',[18] and a large minority of these suspects made admissions or incriminating statements. Moston and Stephenson asked police officers to complete questionnaires about the questioning and interviewing of suspects outside the station. Questioning was reported in 31% of all cases, and interviewing in 8.1% (in over half of which there was initial questioning too). One quarter of the latter were police car interviews. Full confessions were secured in over 40% of informal interviews, and damaging statements in a further one third. These are much higher rates than are usual for custodial interviewing. Is it that suspects prepared to talk under these circumstances are natural 'confessors'? Is it that the police can be more effective when not restricted? Or are the police simply reporting more of those cases where there clearly was interviewing (because of the recorded statements of the suspects) than those where it could be hidden? In neither study were the police asked whether the questioning or interviewing was lawful in terms of Code of Practice C, para 11.1.

Both studies are methodologically flawed to such an extent that their reliability is highly questionable. Firstly, neither were studies of informal interviewing, but were studies of police claims about informal interviewing. The police might be expected to be less than honest about this, and they were. Moston and Stephenson asked the police about non-offence related conversation. Such conversation is perfectly proper, yet in one-third of cases it was claimed that no conversation took place at all. The researchers comment:

'These figures are of interest, if only for the fact that police officers often claim to make what are colloquially called 'deaf and dumb' arrests . . . This appears to be merely a convenient fiction, at least in a significant proportion of cases.'[19]

15 Maguire and Norris (1992) p 46.
16 Moston and Stephenson (1993); D Brown, T Ellis and K Larcombe, *Changing the Code* (Home Office Research Study no 129) (London: HMSO, 1992).
17 Brown et al (1992) p 81.
18 See Brown et al (1992) p 82 Table 6.3.
19 Moston and Stephenson (1993) p 24.

'We have ways of making you talk'

Similarly, Brown et al report an instance where:

> 'CID officers were overheard discussing what had been said to them by the suspect in the car on the way to the station, but recorded on the form that no questions had been asked or unsolicited comments made.'[20]

If the police lie (or fail to record the truth) some of the time how can we be confident that they do not do so much of the time? Suspects could have been asked about this issue but they were not. This is lamentable, especially in relation to Brown's study, where suspects were asked about other aspects of the research on, for instance, legal advice. Choongh, by contrast, did ask suspects, 20% of whom said that there had been informal questioning.[1] Although this is no more reliable than findings based on what police officers told other researchers, it is no less reliable either, and in fact the findings are remarkably similar.

The second flaw in Moston and Stephenson and Brown et al's research is that they did not ask about informal interviewing inside the station. Officers were given an implicit opportunity to report this, but the low rate (less than 1%) could have been as much because they were not asked about it directly as because it happened rarely. Finally, the police were asked by Moston and Stephenson separately about 'questioning' and 'interviewing'. This is a distinction which has even defeated the Court of Appeal, so to draw conclusions from questionnaires making this distinction is worthless. Despite all this, a considerable amount of informal interviewing is admitted by the police.

Informal interviewing in the police station has also been found to be prevalent. Dixon et al, for instance, found 53% of officers admitting always or often 'clarifying' suspects' accounts before beginning the 'proper' interview.[2] Only 28% said they did so rarely or never. Choongh observed two officers hectoring and intimidating a suspect who they had just brought into the charge room who denied knowing the car he had been in was stolen. Poking his finger at the suspect, with his face very close, he repeatedly shouted: 'That's not the truth, is it? Is it?' The custody officer did not intervene.[3] Apart from its oppressive character, questioning of this kind, in the charge room, before legal advice was offered, breaches several provisions of the Code.

Many officers say that pre-interview questioning is important to establish a rapport, as might be expected given the importance of

---

20   Brown et al (1992) p 84.
1   Choongh (1997) p 169.
2   D Dixon, K Bottomley, C Coleman, M Gill and D Wall, 'Safeguarding the Rights of Suspects in Police Custody' (1990) 1 Policing and Society 115.
3   Choongh (1997) pp 170 & 175.

relationships and dealing. One officer said to McConville et al: 'I'd never go cold into an interview. I'd always have a run over first with the person, do an informal chat without taking notes.' This is particularly important for the police if the suspect wants a solicitor. Some custody officers, another officer told McConville et al, 'will just bend a little bit, if you want a quick word with [suspects] to see, you know, if somebody wants a solicitor and you haven't had a chance to chat and don't want him to have a solicitor yet.'[4] The co-operation of the custody officer in allowing 'off the record' access to suspects is not essential, however, since informal interviews can take place immediately prior to the tape recorded session. As an officer told Evans and Ferguson, 'I like to have a little chat to get things straight before I switch on the tape.'[5] This is unlawful, yet apparently frequent if we can judge by the number of times interviews appear to be 'little more than an attempt to validate what has already been rehearsed'.[6]

Cell visits are also prevalent. Sanders and Bridges, for instance, discuss a case where a CID officer admitted going to the cell of a suspect who refused to confess and secured a confession by being nice to him.[7] According to the custody record, the suspect had asked to see the officer. In the police area researched by Dixon et al, these visits are recorded as 'welfare visits', showing that custody officers allow custody records to be doctored to hide the truth.[8] As well as cell visits, informal interviews also occur at the end of the 'official' questioning, as when a detective inspector joined other officers and proceeded to threaten the suspect in an 'unpleasant, hectoring and abusive tone'.[9] In this case, microphones installed for the purpose of a TV documentary recorded the informal interview, providing us with an insight into the behaviour of police officers when they believe themselves to be 'off the record'. The defendant had been arrested on suspicion of several burglaries but denied involvement in any of them. Once the police tape recorder was switched off, the detective inspector slipped into 'informal' mode:

DI: '. . . I've told you what I'm gonna do. I ain't bullshitting you, I'm gonna charge you with six [offences]. If you want six fucking charges, you can have six charges—your barrister ain't got much of a fucking argument at the end of the day. I don't really

---

4   McConville et al (1991) pp 58-9. Examples are also given by A Sanders and L Bridges, 'Access to Legal Advice and Police Malpractice' [1990] Crim LR 494; and Choongh (1997) p 175.

5   R Evans and T Ferguson, Comparing Different Juvenile Cautioning Systems in One Police Force Area (Report to the Home Office Research and Planning Unit) (1991).

6   Baldwin (1993) p 347.

7   Sanders and Bridges (1990).

8   Dixon et al (1990).

9   McConville [1992] p 542.

want to charge you with six fucking charges: I'd rather charge you with a couple and you can have four TICs. You can rip the fucking TICs up once you get to court—I don't really give a shit. Do you understand what I am saying?'

Suspect: 'Mmm.'

. . .

DI: 'Now bullshit aside now, that's the deal I can offer. Quite simply you fucking take it or leave it. You know what's going to happen if you fucking leave it. I mean you ain't going to fucking lose nothing, you don't lose anything by saying "OK, I'll fucking take that." '

Another detective: 'Plus the fact that you've got a couple of charges, court in the morning, def the breach of curfew, "he's got two charges of burglary, he's helped us out." We won't oppose bail. Otherwise we get six charges, "he didn't wanna fucking know" and remand in custody.'

. . .

DI: 'As I say, we'd lay it on heavy or we come off fucking light, it's a matter for you. The most important thing is you've got a fucking decision to make. You're either going to have six fucking charges or you're going to have two and the only fucking way you're having two is you start fucking talking to us.'[10]

None of this exchange was discoverable from the official taped record of the formal questioning, and the custody officer knew nothing about the informal interview. The detective inspector's presence in the interview was not recorded on the custody sheet, and the custody officer made this note in the custody record: 'PACE codes of practice complied with.'[11] Records are rarely made of informal questioning which, officially, simply does not happen. Thus in *Conway*[12] it was accepted that officers visited the defendant's cell (allegedly at his request) even though this had not been recorded in the custody record. Informal questioning is usually officially acknowledged only when a confession is made or alleged by the police, as for example, in *Dunn*.[13]

Informal interviewing inside the station is usually a blatant breach of PACE and Code of Practice C, for it can rarely be impractical to turn an informal chat into a formal interview if one is already inside a police station. It often occurs between interviews precisely because the suspect in question does not want to talk. Since the aim of the informal chat is to

10   We have used only a relatively small, but representative, part of these officers' attempt to trigger a confession. The entire exchange is quoted by McConville [1992] pp 542-543.

11   McConville [1992] pp 544-545.

12   [1994] Crim LR 838.

13   (1990) 91 Cr App Rep 237. Discussed in section 3 (c) above.

change the minds of suspects, the dangers of coercion or unlawful inducements—precisely the dangers which the formal interviewing regime of PACE is ostensibly designed to combat—are obvious. Despite this, the products of these interviews are usable as evidence in court even when there is no independent verification of what was said and how what was allegedly said was obtained.

The wrongful conviction and jailing of *Khan* (see section 3 (c)) is an example of what can happen not only when crime control practices are followed, but also when legal rules—in this case, the rule that information freely volunteered may be written down and used—contain crime control values. Research has failed to provide reliable estimates of how frequent informal interviewing really is, whether unlawful or not. And we will never know how often alleged confessions made under these conditions are fabricated by the police. Yet every research project on questioning carried out since PACE was introduced, with one exception,[14] has found that it exists,[15] and many of the infamous miscarriages of the 1990–93 period involved fabricated confessions. In *Miller*[16] the defendant was alleged to drop a bag of Ecstasy tablets as he was being escorted to the custody room. The police officer claimed she said to him, 'I have just seen you drop this . . . Are these Ecstasy tablets?', to which he is alleged to have said 'Yes'. He denied dropping the tablets, having ever had them, and having the conversation. The Court of Appeal held that the judge had wrongly allowed this conversation to be used as evidence. For this was an interview held in breach of the Code and, one suspects from the Law Report, the Court was dubious about the veracity of the police.

Informal interviewing will never be eradicated. As Moston and Stephenson say: 'One central process, namely the general process of questioning and discussion leading to arrest, remains concealed from view, submerged in secrecy and obfuscation.'[17] All that can be done is to refuse to accept its products as evidence in court. The Runciman Commission, however, simply accepted that there was a considerable amount of questioning outside the station, and did not discuss informal interviewing inside the station. Although the Commission recommended that informal interviewing be reduced by encouraging police officers to use portable tape recorders 'because any breach of the code by police officers may be tape recorded', it also commented that 'many witnesses suggested to us that spontaneous remarks uttered on arrest are often the most truthful. We agree.'[18] No evidence or reasoning was given for their agreement with

14   Irving and McKenzie (1989).
15   This includes writers such as Dixon et al (1990) who distance themselves from the most harsh critics of the police.
16   [1998] Crim LR 209, discussed in section 3 above.
17   Moston and Stephenson (1993) p 43.
18   RCCJ (1993) pp 28 and p 61 respectively.

'We have ways of making you talk'

this suggestion. This attitude is likely to encourage police officers to provoke spontaneity on the part of arrestees or, at least, to claim that remarks were spontaneously made. The conclusion flowing from Runciman's approach is that courts should continue to accept evidence provided in such exchanges, whether tape recorded or not, otherwise 'some reliable confessions might be lost.'[19] The absence of concern that some *unreliable* confessions might also be lost betrays the crime control thinking of Runciman and its reluctance to impose inhibitory rules on the police.

5.   CONFESSIONS

(a)   False confessions

False confessions were one of the motors driving the Philips Commission and PACE. Although the Confait Affair was the cause celebre of the 1970s, other cases included that of Errol Madden,[20] who was accused of stealing a model car, and a man who 'confessed' to stealing money from his employer.[1] The claims in both cases that the confessions were false and made because of pressure from the police were verified by the fact that both the model car and the money turned out not to be stolen at all. The PACE framework of contemporaneous recording and interviewing in the station, together with the outlawing of oppressive treatment, was developed in order to prevent such cases. In the event, as we know from cases like the 'Cardiff Three'[2] and the 'Tottenham Three',[3] the new laws made little difference.

Usually, it is unclear whether confessions made under pressure are false or not. It is generally more difficult to establish conclusively that someone is innocent than to prove that they are guilty. But cases like Madden and the 'Confait Affair' illustrate that the police presumption of guilt, which leads them to apply intense pressure to confess, is sometimes demonstrably and wholly unfounded. One such case in the post-PACE era is that of David Blythe. He was arrested in 1987 for murder. He was questioned for hours without legal advice and 'confessed'. He was charged and kept in prison awaiting trial for 11 months. Shortly before the trial was due to commence, someone else was arrested for the murder about whose guilt there was no doubt at all. The prosecution dropped the case against Blythe. The police accepted that he was completely innocent, yet something had happened

19   RCCJ (1993) pp 60-61.
20   Discussed in ch 3, section 5.
1   Cox (1975) p 177.
2   *Paris, Abdullahi and Miller* (1992) 97 Cr App Rep 99
3   *Raghip, Silcott and Braithwaite* (1991) Times, 9 December.

when he was in custody to make him 'confess'.[4] Richard Buckland similarly confessed (to murder and rape) and was prosecuted. The case was dropped only when forensic evidence was shown to exonerate him, and the real murderer was convicted in 1988.[5]

From the due process and freedom perspectives, however, protections for suspects are justified in themselves and should not be dependent on whether or not oppressive behaviour or inducements really do lead to false confessions. However, all systems have some false confessions and some wrongful convictions (see the discussion in ch 1), so the fact that there are some false confessions does not automatically mean that the system must be changed. In order to eliminate false confessions, in line with due process, we would have to so fundamentally change the nature of police questioning that there would be many fewer convictions of guilty people. Crime control adherents would wish to maintain the processes which produce false confessions as long as they produce even greater numbers of reliable confessions and expeditious convictions. The freedom approach, however, would weigh up the loss of convictions of the guilty against the problems of false confessions and oppressive questioning and consider the cost-effectiveness of additions or alternatives to confession evidence.

In discussing false confessions we need to distinguish between innocent people who confess 'voluntarily'[6]; people whose innocence or otherwise is unknown who 'confess' through coercion; and people, again whose innocence is unknown, who allegedly confess but who in fact do not. The last category concerns fabricated confessions, and was discussed earlier (sections 3(c) and 4(e)). There are a number of reasons why people who are, or may be, innocent confess.[7]

(i) 'Coerced-compliant' confessions

Here the suspect knows that the confession is false, but is prepared to confess to escape pressure. This pressure will sometimes be the result of oppressive questioning tactics, or sometimes of the 'mere' experience of custody and questioning. Coerced-compliant confessions apparently happened in the 'Confait Affair' and probably in the 'Cardiff Three' case and several of the other infamous miscarriage cases. Many of these cases

4 *The Guardian*, 2 February 1988.
5 (1988) Times, 23 January. Discussed by Choongh (1997) p 128.
6 Occasionally people falsely confess even without police pressure, as recognised by Sir Peter Imbert, former Metropolitan Police Commissioner: *The Times*, 17 May 1994.
7 The developer of these first two categories provides a full discussion in G Gudjonsson, *The Psychology of Interrogations, Confessions, and Testimony* (Chichester: Wiley, 1992).

Confessions

involved vulnerable suspects, but people with average IQ and normal personality characteristics are also vulnerable to tactics of this type, as in a false murder confession discussed by Gudjonsson and Mackeith.[8] These confessions can also arise from strong inducements.

(ii) 'Coerced-internalised' confessions

Here, suspects begin to doubt their own memory. They temporarily believe in their own guilt because of disorientation. Carol Richardson, one of the 'Guildford Four' (imprisoned for terrorist offences for 14 years before having their convictions quashed), reported this experience after being told of the alleged confession of a fellow suspect.[9] Similarly, in the remarkable 'Kerry Babies' case, a whole family falsely confessed to murdering a baby as a result of the pressure to which they were subjected. One said, 'I didn't think my mind was my own . . . in the end I was convinced I had done it.'[10] In establishing control, interrogators frequently try to throw suspects off balance, creating the continual danger that the suspect will be completely unbalanced.

(iii) 'Coerced-passive' confession

Here questioning leads suspects to 'admit' to committing an offence without necessarily adopting or even understanding the substance of this admission. Given the extent to which much questioning centres on repetitive accusations, the pressure simply to agree is enormous. In one case discussed by McConville et al, it was accepted that the suspect broke a car windscreen in the course of an argument. The question was, why? The following exchange took place:

> Police: 'Did you intend to smash the windscreen?'
> Suspect: 'No.'
> Police: 'So you just swung your hand out in a reckless manner?'
> Suspect: 'Yes, that's it, just arguing . . . Just arguing, reckless, it wasn't intentional to break it.'[11]

8 G Gudjonsson and J Mackeith, 'A Proven Case of False Confession: Psychological Aspects of the Coerced-compliant Type' (1990) 30 Med Sci Law 187.

9 G Stephenson, *The Psychology of Criminal Justice* (Oxford: Blackwell, 1992) p 127.

10 This was an Irish case which happened in 1984 when there were no PACE-type protections. For an analysis of this fascinating case, see P O'Mahony, 'The Kerry babies case: Towards a Social Psychological Analysis' [1992] 13 Irish Jo Psychology 223.

11 McConville et al (1991) p 70.

Although the suspect probably did not understand this, here the interviewer was not offering a way 'out' of guilt but a way 'in' to an acceptance that the act was done with the mens rea required for criminal damage.[12] In other examples, suspects agreed that they 'stole' goods simply because they took them (not necessarily with intent permanently to deprive the owner), without understanding the legal implications of the term.

Sometimes the police will be confident that, if they can establish that a suspect committed the actus reus of the crime, no claim of lack of mens rea or justification will stand up in court. In such cases they may induce the suspect to admit to committing the act in question by suggesting that the suspect was justified in carrying it out (and thus would have a defence). A journalist who carried out an observational study of American homicide detectives saw many examples of suspects being offered such ways 'out' that were actually ways 'in'.[13] As he puts it:

> 'The majority of those who acknowledge their complicity in a killing must be baited by detectives with something more tempting than penitence. They must be made to believe that their crime is not really murder, that their excuse is both accepted and unique, that they will, with the help of the detective, be judged less evil than they really are . . . the detective must let the suspect know that his guilt is certain and easily established by the existing evidence. He must then offer the Out . . . "Look, bunk, I'm giving you a chance. He came at you right? You were scared. It was self-defense . . . He came at you right?" "Yeah, he came at me." The Out leads in.'

(iv) Interrogative suggestibility

This involves suspects receiving messages in ways which affect their subsequent response. This can occur in all three of the confession types discussed above. 'Vulnerable' suspects are particularly susceptible.[14] Stefan Kiszko had a mental age of 12, and was jailed for life in 1976 for murdering a schoolgirl. He had been interrogated repeatedly, and eventually 'confessed' after his sixth interrogation. In 1992, his conviction was quashed after it was found that the semen on the victim's body could not have been his. This evidence was available at the time of the trial but was not revealed.

---

12   See Criminal Damage Act, s 1, which provides that criminal damage can be committed either intentionally *or* recklessly.

13   D Simon, *Homicide: A Year on the Killing Streets* (London: Hodder & Stoughton, 1992) at pp 194-207.

14   B Littlechild, 'Reassessing the Role of the "Appropriate Adult"' [1995] Crim LR 540.

Kiszko died, aged 41, less than two years after his release. A family friend commented: 'After being released, Stefan could not rouse himself and never recovered from what happened . . . He could not face the world.'[15]

Vulnerable people now have the additional protection during questioning of an 'appropriate adult'. But as we have seen, the police often fail to identify vulnerable suspects. This was so in the 'Tottenham Three'[16] case, and lower profile examples include *Brine*[17] and *Miller*.[18] In the first two of these cases, confessions were rejected by the Court of Appeal because of the vulnerability of the defendants, but this was not the result in *Miller*. Further, neither appropriate adults nor legal advice prevent the police from placing on suspects the kinds of pressures faced by Kiszko. Indeed, the point of many police tactics is to identify and exploit vulnerabilities in 'ordinary' people. As the Runciman Commission said:

'. . . under certain circumstances individuals may confess to crimes they have not committed . . . it is more likely that they will do so in interviews conducted in police custody even when proper safeguards apply.'[19]

The dangers of interrogative suggestibility are enhanced by the types of question commonly asked. If questioning was primarily fact-finding, questions would generally be of an open kind ('what did you see?', 'what did you do?') where there would be few dangers of false confessions, if only because the criminal alone would be able to provide the correct details. It may be true, as Evans argues, that most questioning is like this.[20] In Evans' study, most suspects readily confessed. The important question is what happens in questioning where suspects do not readily confess? McConville and Hodgson argue that the questions then turn to admission seeking. The most important question forms of this type which they identify are, firstly, leading questions. These seek particular answers by foreclosing others (for example, 'You went down there to get the stuff and you assaulted her, didn't you?').[1] Secondly, there are statement questions (such as, 'You did it. You went there. There is no sign of entry, no force; whoever did it, did it by key.'); thirdly, there are legal closure questions ('So you stole the goods?'); fourthly, there are questions seeking the adoption of police

15 *The Guardian*, 24 December 1993.
16 *Raghip, Silcott and Braithwaite* (1991) Times, 9 December.
17 [1992] Crim LR 122, discussed in ch 11 below.
18 [1986] 1 WLR 1191, discussed in ch 11 below.
19 RCCJ (1993) p 64.
20 Evans (1993). Note, however, that his study was of juveniles only and, as he recognises, many formal interrogations were preceded by informal questioning, the content of which he was unaware.
1 McConville and Hodgson (1993) p 137.

opinions ('You are not innocent, you know what goes on.'). Finally, there are accusatory questions.[2]

In the process of 'asking' these questions, the police sometimes let information slip which suspects may incorporate into their answers.[3] And sometimes as the police ask for detail, and the innocent suspect gets it wrong, the suspect is contradicted until, by chance, the correct answer is produced. But in many cases the police seek little more than 'yes' and 'no' answers, particularly when the purpose of the questioning is primarily to demonstrate a 'guilty mind'.[4] Thus Baldwin comments that:

> 'Officers can be seen in many of these examples preoccupied with establishing relevant 'points to prove', albeit tackling the question mechanically and inexpertly, almost regardless of the suspects' responses.'[5]

What many researchers, including Baldwin, have described as inadequate interview technique[6] is, in reality, entirely adequate for the purposes of the police. It is the establishment of proof, regardless of truth. The same is true of hectoring, accusatorial questioning. Much of the time it is (as far as it is possible to judge) within the law, and it is consistent with the adversarial role of the police. Yet the Runciman Commission stated that: 'In our view the safeguards under PACE against false confessions are comprehensive and, while not foolproof, are substantially sound.'[7]

To say that the police should minimise false confessions by not interrogating in these ways is too simplistic. These ways are the only ways by which people who are reluctant to confess will do so. It is not possible, certainly on the basis of current knowledge and expertise, to reduce false confessions without reducing true ones. Only Runciman's failure to analyse adequately the nature of questioning could lead them to conclude that the police might be trained to develop interviewing techniques which were not aggressive and adversarial. The radical solution to such entrenched police practices is not to have custodial questioning, or at least not to rely on it so heavily. This raises the question of corroboration.

2   For an illustration, see the extract from the 'Cardiff Three' interviews, quoted in section 4 above.
3   'Would I be right in saying that it was cakes and chocolate?': see Baldwin (1993). This occurred in the 'Cardiff Three', case, above (the police 'fed' Miller with the idea that the reason he could not 'remember' being present at the murder was that he was under the influence of drugs at the time) as did numerous instances of all the admission-seeking questions detailed in the text.
4   See Evans (1993) p 38.
5   Baldwin (1993) p 340.
6   'A stubborn refusal to listen to a suspect's explanation (or even to allow a suspect to advance an explanation) is a critical failing . . .': Baldwin (1993) p 344.
7   RCCJ (1993) p 57.

(b) Corroboration

At present it is possible, and common, to convict on confession evidence alone. As with other evidence there is no need for independent evidence of guilt (corroboration). This reflects a crime control approach: that the police would not be prosecuting if they had no reliable belief in guilt, and that court proceedings exist in most cases merely to approve this prior determination of guilt. Adherents of this approach argue that there is usually other evidence of guilt anyway (for example, the defendant's criminal record) which cannot be revealed in court because of the rules of evidence,[8] and that there is no need to verify uncorroborated evidence because innocent suspects can present evidence of their innocence if they wish. This means that the occasional examples of false and fabricated confessions which do occur are nearly always exposed for what they are, and wrongful convictions are rare. The few that do slip through the net are usually corrected eventually, and they are a small price to pay for the greater number of convictions, and more effective use of resources, which conviction on uncorroborated confession evidence allows.[9]

Due process advocates of a corroboration rule are sceptical about police motives and ability to identify the guilty, and sceptical about the value of inadmissible evidence. For the due process adherent, corroboration would have several advantages. Firstly, it would reduce the number of evidentially weak prosecutions, either because cases prosecuted at present would not be prosecuted or because the police would secure corroborative evidence in weak cases, thereby strengthening them. Secondly, it would make convictions more certain and reliable. Although there might be fewer cases prosecuted, there would be less chance of cases being 'lost' and thus the overall level of convictions might be little changed. And there would certainly be fewer questionable convictions. Thirdly, it would shift the emphasis in police investigation away from questioning to other sources of evidence. The incentive to secure confessions through coercion, or to fabricate confessions, would be reduced.

In England and Wales at present, the police frequently fail to interview witnesses to crimes, to secure identification evidence and to do scientific tests on fingerprints, blood, hair samples and so forth. In one study, reasonable steps (not including scientific tests) were taken to secure additional evidence in around 80% of the cases, but available sources were, for no apparent reason, not checked in over 10%. In most of the rest, investigation stopped after a confession was obtained because a guilty

8   The extent to which this is true is discussed in ch 9, section 4(a)(iii).
9   The same arguments are applicable to other forms of contestable evidence, such as identification evidence. See Stephenson (1992).

plea was anticipated.[10] It is not that further investigation was impossible in most of these cases, but that it was simply unnecessary to go through these costly and time-consuming processes when the law allows conviction on confession evidence alone.

It is very difficult to predict what the exact consequences would be of a corroboration rule. Scotland has one, about which there appears to be little dissatisfaction, but it is in a weak form which does not require truly independent evidence.[11] Many different types of corroboration rule are conceivable, all of which would have different effects.[12] However, McConville found that at present, in most prosecution cases, where there is a confession there is also admissible independent evidence.[13] A Home Office study carried out for the Runciman Commission found even fewer cases dependent on confession evidence alone.[14] What of the remainder, which would have fallen foul of a corroboration rule? McConville found that in many of them independent evidence existed which could have been produced at court, and in many others it may have been possible to collect such evidence. About one third of the confession-only cases (about 3% of all prosecuted cases in which the police had interrogated) could not have satisfied a corroboration requirement. In some of these cases, this was because the confessions were so uncertain that they were incapable of being substantiated by reliable evidence. They ended in acquittal anyway. The others, which did end in conviction, would probably not have survived a corroboration rule (sometimes deservedly, given the dubious circumstances of the confessions) but were not particularly serious offences.

As McConville concludes, even the most stringent corroboration rule would affect relatively few cases and lead to few extra acquittals. However, the majority of the Runciman Commission (which was split on the issue) was concerned that the small percentage of cases which would be affected would amount to a large number in absolute terms, and that such a rule 'would not by itself prevent miscarriages of justice resulting from fabricated confessions and the production of supporting evidence obtained by

---

10   M McConville, Corroboration and Confessions: The Impact of a Rule Requiring that no Conviction can be Sustained on the Basis of Confession Evidence Alone (Royal Commission on Criminal Justice Research Study no 13) (London: HMSO, 1993) Table 5.1.

11   Sheriff I Macphail, 'Safeguards in the Scottish Criminal Justice System' [1992] Crim LR 144 at pp 148-152.

12   See McConville (1993) pp 50-58; R Pattenden, 'Should Confessions be Corroborated?' (1991) 107 LQR 319. For a general discussion which includes a review of the law in Scotland and Australia, see Mirfield (1997) pp 345-352.

13   This was true of 86.6% of the cases in his study: McConville (1993) p 61.

14   RCCJ (1993) p 65.

improper means.'[15] It was worried that a corroboration rule would lead to too many guilty defendants walking free, whilst offering negligible protection to the innocent. It was also concerned that the benefits to be derived from such a rule, if any, did not justify the cost of requiring the police to conduct more thorough investigations. Runciman recommended, instead, that judges give a 'corroboration warning' to juries. This would represent a timid step in the direction of due process but the government has not acted on this recommendation.

Runciman's reasoning is flawed. Firstly, it amounts to saying that a valid reason for not having a safeguard is that it might be abused by the police. In that case, we might as well do away with all safeguards for suspects, for, as we have seen, they are all abused to a lesser or greater degree. The real question is whether a safeguard would offer significant benefits to suspects, and this involves assessing the likelihood that it would be abused. It is one thing for police officers to coerce suspects into confessing or to 'gild the lily' and another deliberately to frame suspects. If, as the research suggests, police officers are often not aware of the pressures under which they place many suspects, there is no reason to believe that in many false confession cases the police would invent supporting evidence, as Runciman seems to be suggesting.[16] It follows that a corroboration rule probably would offer significant protection.

Secondly, there seems to be an inconsistency is saying that, under a corroboration rule, the police would frame the innocent but let the guilty walk free. If anything, one would imagine that it would be easier to frame the guilty, since there are likely to be more raw materials to work with in constructing a prosecution case if a person is actually guilty. If the police did set out to frame any suspects in such a crude fashion, the innocent would suffer no more than the guilty, and probably less so. The other side of the coin is that the innocent would stand to gain more from a corroboration rule than would the guilty, since it would be easier to corroborate a true confession than a false one. It is in this light that one must place Runciman's anxiety over the resource implications of corroboration. The main purpose of a corroboration rule would be to protect the victims of false and fabricated confessions. We know that there are such cases, we know that currently some such cases end in conviction and lengthy prison sentences, and that only luck leads to the eventual

---

15 RCCJ (1993) p 65. For general discussion, see I Dennis, 'Miscarriages of Justice and the Law of Confessions' [1993] PL 291 and J Jackson, 'Royal Commission on Criminal Justice: The Evidence Recommendations' [1993] Crim LR 817.

16 Undoubtedly, however, there is some risk of the police breaking the rules to this extent. In some cases dealt with by Sergeant Challenor (see section 3 above), suspects were 'fitted up' (evidence was planted on their person or property) and identification parades 'fixed' (witnesses were given cues regarding who to pick out). This still appears to happen from time to time in the post-PACE era: see eg the *Darvell* case (1992) unreported, CA and ch 6 (3)(c).

release of some (but who could say all?) of the defendants involved. No one would suggest that these cases form more than a tiny percentage of the hundreds of thousands of cases prosecuted each year. There may be only a few, perhaps a few dozen, each year. But if a corroboration rule led to the non-prosecution or the acquittal of at least some of these few then, to the adherent of due process or freedom, that rule would be worth its weight in gold. One can only conclude that the majority of the Runciman Commission were crime control adherents. That was their privilege. But we were entitled to expect a better argued case and a clearer articulation and defence of those values from a body set up in the wake of a string of spectacular miscarriages of justice.

6. CONCLUSION

One of the themes of this book is that the criminal justice system should explicitly subscribe to the freedom principle which already implicitly underlies it but which is often overshadowed by crime control and (less often) due process. The due process/crime control debate about police questioning usually revolves around the problem of false confessions and wrongful convictions. To a lesser extent it is about abuse of powers, regardless of the outcome. These are important matters, and civil libertarians advocating a due process approach have had some success in controlling the crime control tendencies of the police and government. This has led to the establishment of a set of standards, set out in PACE, its Codes, the ECHR and in the cases on all these provisions; and the protections analysed in ch 4, especially the right to legal advice and assistance. But this success is limited. First, we have seen that these standards are both vague and less stringent than were applied a hundred years ago. Second, the value of advice and assistance (especially intervention during questioning) is blunted by lawyers not knowing what standards the police should adhere to and by the effect of the CJPO. Third, excepting when ECHR rights are breached (in this context, Art 3, relating to inhuman and degrading treatment), suspects who suffer from breaches of these standards have no remedy apart from the capricious possibility of the exclusion of evidence (discussed in ch 11).

A more fundamental problem with the due process and human rights approaches is that they do not acknowledge the pain, suffering, humiliation and erosion of self-respect that police questioning - in the forms which we have seen it takes - creates. For the freedom perspective, the *quality* of police actions is as important as the form and quantity. As with stop-search, arrest and general police station detention, police questioning is punitive in itself. In the context of compulsory police station detention for lengthy periods, and bearing in mind its purposes, this is inevitable.

How did this come about? PACE and its associated codes of practice created a legal framework which deliberately shifted suspect-focused police investigation into the police station. In this respect, and in the detailed rules provided, the change followed an established trend rather than producing a radical break with the past. As McConville and Baldwin said in 1982, before PACE was even drafted:

'. . . the really crucial exchanges in the criminal process have shifted from courts into police interrogation rooms. It is these exchanges that, in a majority of cases, colour what happens at later stages in the criminal process. Indeed they often determine the outcome of cases at trial.'[17]

Detention and questioning post-arrest and pre-charge had become more common throughout this century, especially after 1964. Section 37 and ss 41–44 of PACE set time limits beyond which detention could not extend, explicitly allowing detention pre-charge up to these limits. Not only do these provisions *allow* the police to detain for questioning, but s 30 almost *obliges* them to detain if they wish to question, as do increasingly tighter definitions of 'interview'. This is both enabling and legitimising[18] of police norms, but ironically it is an unintended consequence of a policy designed to help suspects by attempting to regulate the pressures placed on them by the police. It enables the police to do their job, which is to carry out their adversarial role on crime control lines, because to act as neutral fact-finders would be a negation of what traditional policing is all about. Restricting the police to interviewing in the police station and nowhere else could only be regarded as a due process protection if the context of detention was governed by due process standards. The reality is that, since the police station is 'police territory', it cannot be wrested from police control. Hence due process safeguards for suspects in the police station are much weaker than they appear, and manifestly fail to 'balance' the powers of the police. Crime control laws tolerate barely restricted questioning, the use of police evidence of what was said in evidence and convictions based on that evidence even when it is contested and uncorroborated.

The police are no more impartial seekers after truth now than they ever were and it is difficult to imagine them being so in the future. As McBarnet argued in relation to the pre-PACE law, the fact that the police act as they do is not surprising, for the law, for the most part, enables them to act in this way.[19] It is the rhetoric of due process which is out of step. However, McBarnet's sweeping characterisation of *all* law as crime control in content is not accurate, certainly in the post-PACE world. But the laws which are

17   M McConville and J Baldwin, 'The Role of Interrogation in Crime Discovery and Conviction' (1982) 22 BJ Crim 165 at p 174.
18   For an explanation of these terms see ch 2, section 1(d).
19   D McBarnet, *Conviction* (London: Macmillan, 1983).

due process-oriented do not hinder the police unduly, for they are reasonably easy to evade or break when the police 'need' to do so. The crime control reality is hidden by the sanitised language of 'interviews' and 'questioning' but the police know very well what they are doing:

> 'It's not an interview, let's face it. I mean most people don't want to be in there, it's not pleasant for them. We know what we want out of it. It's an interrogation, that's what it is, we just don't use the word because it doesn't sound nice.'[20]

What about the shift in questioning techniques over the years from violence to manipulation?

> 'Contemporary interrogation strategies . . . penetrate beyond the control of individual behaviour to the control of human thought. In this process the suspect ends up, sometimes unwittingly, cooperating in the process of his own control.'[1]

Many, such as Leo, argue that this is a major improvement: manipulation is less harmful than violence; and manipulation, because it is lawful, is not hidden and is therefore amenable to legal control. It follows that, if the current situation is to be tolerated, the pretence that 'involuntariness', oppression and inducements are generally unlawful should be dropped. Standards for the conduct of questioning should then be prescribed. These would not eliminate oppression, but they would at least set clear limits to it, provide a yardstick for legal advisors, and provide remedies for suspects and defendants who can prove they are breached.

Whether governments wish to subject questioning to genuine legal control is another matter. For all the brave talk of 'ethical' interviewing for most of the 1990s, little has happened to implement it, and no legal obligations have been introduced. For the fact is that, unlike the shift from violence to manipulation, this new shift would lead to fewer confessions and less interrogation-produced evidence. Leo supports the manipulative techniques he analyses, on the grounds that they are 'more humane and civilised' than coercion and 'respect [suspects'] dignity',[2] but the fact that they satisfy human rights standards does not alter the fact that they are, by the standards of our freedom perspective, woefully lacking. Further, as Leo acknowledges, false confessions and wrongful convictions still occur.

20   Police sergeant, quoted by Choongh (1997) p 117.
1   Leo (1994) p 98.
2   Leo (1994) p 117. Similar arguments are advanced by Dixon, who positions himself between what he regards as the overly-critical views of the current writers and the complacent views of the police: D Dixon, *Law in Policing* (Oxford: Clarendon, 1997) esp ch 4. For a police-oriented view that interrogation in the UK is bounded by due process, see I McKenzie, 'Regulating Custodial Interviews: A Comparative Study' (1994) 22 IJ Sociology of Law 239.

For crime control adherents, but not the freedom perspective, these are a small price to pay.

Perhaps the most powerful obstacle to the widespread adoption of 'ethical interviewing' is that the humiliation of suspects is not simply a by-product of police questioning. It is often its *purpose*. When that is so, prosecution and conviction is often not sought, leaving the coercion and psychological brutality hidden, its perpetrators unaccountable, and remedies unavailable.

Neither the Philips Commission nor the Runciman Commission appeared to accept either that the system should operate in the ways we have characterised them (thus rejecting the crime control rhetoric of the police) or that it does so (thus rejecting the due process proposals of the critics). They preferred to believe that the police are capable of both being adversarial and impartial even with unco-operative suspects. The contradictions involved reach their peak in the person of the custody officer who, we have seen, offers scant protection for detainees.

Once it is decided, as the Runciman Commission did, that the police station should be the focus of investigation, and that (by rejecting a corroboration rule) confession evidence alone could form the sole basis for conviction, the crime control framework is accepted, and the room for due process is fundamentally circumscribed. But a pure due process system is not on the cards, and might not be in society's interest. A freedom-based approach would try to counter-balance police power effectively, as would be expected in a fully adversarial system. This means not making the rights of suspects dependent on custody officers, but making them either automatic or guaranteed by a genuine third party. Independent lawyers working in police stations might be a solution. Unlike most legal aid lawyers at present, however, they would need to attend all interrogations and possess an adversarial ethos. If they were based in law centres rotating with other law centre lawyers, they might not get 'captured' by the police ethos.[3] The law could provide that no questioning would be valid unless a defence lawyer was present. If that is too much for managerialists and crime control adherents to stomach, could we not at least have a rule that rendered confessions to the police inadmissible in evidence unless tape-recorded? Where a suspect wishes to impart confidential information to the police, this could be done informally but without the evidence being directly usable in court. Even limited reforms are inconceivable at present. Far from reducing the pressures on suspects in these ways, the government, by eroding the right of silence, increased them yet further.

3   See the related discussion in D O'Brien and J A Epp, 'Salaried Defenders and the Access to Justice Act 1999' (2000) 63 MLR 394, building on M McConville, J Hodgson, L Bridges and A Pavlovic, *Standing Accused* (Oxford: Clarendon Press, 1994) pp 296-97.

Chapter 6

Prosecutions

'[The police] don't get the offenders. And if they catch them they don't charge them. If I was to offend someone like this the police would harass me instead of turning a blind eye which is what I feel they do in case of white offenders. And the offenders feel they can do anything they like as they are always let off.' [Pakistani victim of a racial incident reported to the police][1]

I. INTRODUCTION

Before police forces were established in 1829 and for some years thereafter, neither local nor central government accepted responsibility for day-to-day law enforcement. Prosecutions could be initiated by anyone. Suspects were generally prosecuted, if at all, by the victim. Police powers of arrest, search and interrogation were originally no greater than those of ordinary citizens. Similarly, no special prosecution powers were provided. If the police, or anyone else, wished to prosecute, they had to 'lay an information' before the local magistrates. If the latter were satisfied that there was sufficient evidence they would issue a warrant for the suspect's arrest or a summons to appear in court.[2] Prosecution decisions were judicially controlled.

As police forces and police powers grew throughout the nineteenth and twentieth centuries, victims came to expect the police to initiate and conduct prosecutions for them. Extra arrest powers were provided to the police and they developed the practice of 'charging' suspects, whereby they took suspects before the magistrates without laying an information

1   Quoted by B Bowling, *Violent Racism* (Oxford: Clarendon, 1998) at p 237.
2   See ch 3, section 3(a) above.

in advance. The police thus began to take control of prosecution decisions away from the magistrates, but no specific prosecution powers or responsibilities were conferred on the police. Private prosecution remained the model on which police prosecutions were based, and the right of private prosecution has remained to this day.[3]

In the absence of specific laws to regulate their prosecutions, the police evolved their own system. They prosecuted most of their own cases in the magistrates' courts, some forces allocating specific officers to undertake this task. For Crown Court cases, they instructed solicitors who then instructed barristers.[4] Most forces used just a few local firms of solicitors, whom they also began to use for the more difficult magistrates' court cases. Gradually, and particularly in the 1960s and 1970s, the larger police forces began to employ their own solicitors, there being dozens of lawyers in the largest prosecuting solicitors departments.[5] Under the traditional solicitor-client relationship, solicitors had to carry out the instructions of the police.[6] If the police insisted on prosecuting a weak case to further their crime control goals, there was little or nothing the prosecutor could do about it.[7]

These arrangements for prosecution came under fire in the 'Confait Affair', where the prosecutor was found to have been either unable, or unwilling, to act independently. This may have been a contributory factor in the wrongful convictions in that unhappy episode.[8] The Royal Commission on Criminal Procedure (Philips Commission) proposed an independent prosecution service which would take over cases which the police had decided to prosecute. If the prosecutor did not agree with the police, the case could be dropped, the charges changed, or more evidence sought.[9] The government accepted the main thrust of the Commission's proposals.[10] The result was the establishment of the Crown Prosecution Service (CPS) by the Prosecution of Offences Act 1985.

3   See A Sanders, 'Arrest, Charge and Prosecution' (1986) 6 LS 257 and section 6(d) below for further discussion of private prosecutions.
4   See J Sigler, 'Public Prosecution in England and Wales' [1974] Crim LR 642 on the use of barristers, and for a general account of the system up to that time.
5   M Weatheritt, The Prosecution System: Survey of Prosecuting Solicitors' Departments (Royal Commission on Criminal Procedure, Research Study no 11) (London: HMSO, 1980).
6   See Sigler [1974] and Royal Commission on Criminal Procedure (RCCP), The Investigation of Criminal Offences in England and Wales: The Law and Procedure (Cmnd 8092-1) (London: HMSO, 1981) pp 49-52.
7   RCCP, Report (Cmnd 8092) (London: HMSO, 1981) para 6.27.
8   See Report of an Inquiry into the Circumstances leading to the Trial of Three Persons on Charges arising out of the Death of Maxwell Confait and the Fire at 27 Doggett Road, London SE6 (HCP 90) (London: HMSO, 1977).
9   RCCP (1981) Report, ch 7.
10 It did not accept the Commission's recommendations on accountability. See section 6 below.

The head of the CPS was to be the Director of Public Prosecutions (DPP). The DPP was first established in 1879 with the function of advising the police on criminal matters and handling particularly important cases. At the time of the establishment of the CPS, the Office of the DPP (which comprised around 70 lawyers) handled murders, other very serious cases, and prosecutions of police officers.[11] The sudden jump to a national service, with an initial establishment of over 1,500 lawyers, created severe organisational problems, including, in the early days, chronic under-staffing.[12]

Despite the national identity of the CPS, prosecutors are still based locally, the CPS being organised into areas which match police force areas. The area structure has been altered several times since 1986, reflecting conflicting and changing views about what the CPS is for and to who or what it should be accountable.[13] The direct effect on police procedures of the 1985 Act has been relatively small, for the police remain entitled to make initial decisions (whether to prosecute or not) in the same ways as previously. Only when the case is passed to the CPS is control relinquished. This was the first time since 1829 that the police lost a significant power, except in so far as PACE can be seen in this way. This chapter will examine whether the combination of laws, policies and procedures of different prosecuting and enforcement agencies leads to a justice process that is fair, effective and freedom-enhancing.

2.   DISCRETION

When the police are interviewing suspects, they have to stop doing so when they believe that 'a prosecution should be brought' and that 'there is sufficient evidence'.[14] This does not require them to prosecute, as this is a discretionary decision (like stop-search and arrest). When the police do not prosecute they may delay their decision (either releasing the suspect on bail to return at a later date or reporting the suspect with a view to a summons), they may release the suspect with a warning or they may take no further action (NFA) at all. The police have many different reasons for deciding not to prosecute: sometimes there is insufficient evidence, some cases are too trivial, sometimes there will be particularly extenuating circumstances, and sometimes immunity from prosecution is exchanged

11   See Sigler [1974] and RCCP (1981) Law and Procedure, paras 155-161.
12   See J Rozenberg, *The Case for the Crown* (Wellingborough: Equation, 1987).
13   See section 6 below.
14   PACE Code of Practice C, para 11.4. See *McGuinness* [1999] Crim LR 318 on the difficulties this can cause the police, and discussion in ch 4 sections 2(e) and 3(e).

for information about other offences and other offenders.[15] In this section we examine how these discretionary decisions are regulated.

(a) 'Legality' and 'opportunity'

It is usual to describe prosecution systems as falling into one of two types. The first is the 'legality system'. This is common among European countries of the inquisitorial type, such as Germany. Under the legality principle, the police must report all offences to the prosecutor, who must prosecute. In principle, there is no discretion, although the police sometimes screen out cases where there is no evidence.[16] Common law countries, on the other hand, such as Britain and the United States, tend to have 'opportunity systems' in which there is complete discretion. As a former Attorney-General, Lord Shawcross put it:

> 'It has never been the rule in this country—I hope it never will be— that suspected criminal offences must automatically be the subject of prosecution. Indeed the very first Regulations under which the Director of Public Prosecutions worked provided that he should . . . prosecute "wherever it appears that the effects or the circumstances of [a crime's] commission are of such character that a prosecution in respect thereof is required in the public interest." That is still the dominant consideration.'[17]

Opportunity and legality systems are clearly diametrically opposed principles. Legal systems do not, in reality, divide so neatly. Some (like Italy) are in a state of transition, while others (like France) combine elements of both.[18] Police discretion in England and Wales is usually exercised, in relation to adults at any rate, in favour of prosecuting. This is true of all police forces in opportunity-based legal systems. But it is not true of all law enforcement bodies within such systems. Thus discretion is usually exercised by *non*-police agencies (such as the Inland Revenue) *against* prosecution.[19] On the other hand, even in the most rigid legality-based

---

15 On the importance of 'deals' see ch 5, sections 1 and 4(a)(i).
16 See L Leigh and L Zedner, A Report on the Administration of Criminal Justice in France and Germany (Royal Commission on Criminal Justice Research Study no 1) (London: HMSO, 1992) pp 28-30.
17 Quoted approvingly in the Attorney-General's guidelines for prosecution, which apply to the police, and in para 6.1 of the Code for Crown Prosecutors (London: CPS, 1994).
18 Leigh and Zedner (1992); T Vander Becken (ed), *Prosecution Discretion in European Criminal Justice Systems* (forthcoming).
19 See section 5 below.

systems discretion is exercised more and more frequently. This is usually a product of specific provisions, especially for juveniles, in the laws of those countries. As in Britain, juveniles, old offenders and motoring offences tend to be given special consideration, and ordinary adults are increasingly diverted from prosecution.[20] In Sweden, for example, prosecution will often be waived if a fine would be the likely consequence of prosecution. This means that many small shoplifting cases and possession of soft drugs cases are not prosecuted.[1]

At first glance it seems that 'legality' and 'opportunity' systems of prosecution produce similar practical outcomes. Closer inspection reveals some important differences. Because diversion in a legality system is an exception to a general rule, non-prosecution decisions are relatively strictly controlled even if they are greater in number than in a system like that in England and Wales. The conditions under which those exceptions can be made are generally specified in the laws of those countries, and diversion decisions are usually made by prosecutors. In order to encourage consistency and adherence to official policy, there are relatively small numbers of senior decision-makers. In England and Wales, by contrast, discretion is not closely controlled. Neither the basis for the exercise of discretion nor the level of decision-maker is consistent throughout the system. As a result of the process of historical evolution discussed above, rather than through the establishment of any clear principles, neither prosecution nor non-prosecution is the legal responsibility of any one rank or part of the police force. Another difference is that, in major crimes, prosecutors (in Germany) or examining magistrates (in France) play an important part in the early stages of the investigation and prosecution process. These people are impartial, in theory at least, in a way that police forces are not and could never be. In Britain, where there is no equivalent of these officials, the prosecution system is the same no matter how serious the offence.

(b) 'Constabulary independence'

One consequence of the 'opportunity principle' in the United Kingdom is that no one has the authority to tell the police, or indeed other law enforcement agencies such as the Inland Revenue and Customs and Excise, how or when to use their powers.[2] This applies to powers such as arrest,

20 Leigh and Zedner (1992); Vander Becken (forthcoming).
1   See A Sanders, 'Diverting Offenders from Prosecution: Can we Learn from other Countries?' (1986) 150 JP 614.
2   It should be noted, however, that the decision not to prosecute in the *Treadaway* case was quashed as a result of a successful judicial review action. See ch 11, section 3 for discussion. Another non-prosecution decision was quashed in *DPP, ex p Jones* [2000] IRLR 373.

and to decisions such as whether or not to prosecute. This doctrine of 'constabulary independence' gives law enforcement agencies enormous amounts of discretion. In *Arrowsmith v Jenkins*, the defendant (D) spoke for 30 minutes at a public meeting which obstructed a highway. She was arrested for this offence and was convicted. She appealed on the basis that many meetings had been held in that place previously and that in the past the police had not prosecuted anyone for a criminal offence. D in effect asked 'Why pick on me?' The court's answer on appeal was: 'That, of course, has nothing to do with this court. The sole question here is whether the defendant had contravened s 121(1) of the Highways Act 1959.'[3] Similarly, in *IRC, ex p Mead*[4] the applicants, who were being prosecuted for tax offences, objected on the grounds that similar offenders were not being prosecuted. It was held that it was not necessarily wrong for apparently similar cases to be dealt with differently. Limits have, in principle, none the less been set to the doctrine of constabulary independence. In *Mead* itself, for example, the court stressed that agencies that prosecute selectively should ensure that all decisions should be in accordance with a stated policy.[5]

What of a policy not to prosecute certain offences at all? In *Metropolitan Police Comr, ex p Blackburn* the policy of the Metropolitan Police at that time not to prosecute certain establishments for illegal gambling was challenged. The police altered their policy in the course of the case thus removing the need for a judicial decision. Lord Denning, however, could not resist the chance to make an obiter statement (ie not binding on future courts):

'There are some policy decisions with which, I think, the court in a case can if necessary interfere. Suppose a Chief Constable were to issue a directive to his men that no person should be prosecuted for stealing any goods less than £100 in value. I should have thought that the court could countermand it. He would be failing in his duty to enforce the law.'[6]

This is powerful rhetoric, but to date, it appears that no one has successfully challenged decisions not to prosecute and not to exercise other powers under the obiter in *Blackburn*, despite several attempts to do so. For example, in *Chief Constable of Devon and Cornwall, ex p CEGB*[7] the police

3   [1963] 2 QB 561 at 566, per Lord Parker CJ.
4   [1993] 1 All ER 772.
5   For discussion see C Hilson, 'Discretion to Prosecute and Judicial Review' [1993] Crim LR 739. Also see *Chief Constable of the Kent Constabulary, ex p L* [1993] 1 All ER 756.
6   [1968] 2 QB 118 at 136.
7   [1981] 3 All ER 826.

refused to remove protesters from a field. The CEGB claimed that the protesters' behaviour was conduct liable to cause a breach of the peace. It asked the court to state that there is a duty on the police to enforce the law in such cases (and, if necessary, to prosecute) citing Denning's remarks in *Blackburn*. But the court regarded this as an individual case, refusing to see the police inaction as a part of a general policy even though it did stem from their general community policing strategy.[8] And in *Chief Constable of Sussex, ex p ITF Ltd*[9] animal rights protesters made it impossible for ITF to export live animals without police protection. The police gave protection only on certain days, citing competing pressures on police resources. ITF claimed that the police were wrong to exercise discretion by under-enforcing the law, but the House of Lords held that the police had to balance all the demands upon it and that full enforcement of the law was therefore impossible.[10]

The doctrine of constabulary independence is therefore virtually impregnable. The consequence is almost complete autonomy for law enforcement bodies in all enforcement and prosecution decisions. This protects them from interference from individuals and from local and central government. The doctrine of independence might have been appropriate in the days when a victim did not have to rely on only one enforcement agency (usually the police). But now that it is manifestly the job of the police (and other agencies) to enforce the law, we have to ask whether these agencies should be virtually the sole judges of when arrest and prosecution is, and is not, appropriate. No one is advocating political decisions about individual cases, but accountability for prosecution policies is entirely compatible with the rule of law. Indeed, Jefferson and Grimshaw argue that this is essential in a modern democracy.[11] Parliament and the government should formulate prosecution policy, and the job of the courts should be to make sure that enforcement and prosecution agencies stick to it.

At present, the Home Office does formulate policy for the police in relation to cautioning, but not in relation to the more general exercise of police prosecution powers. The CPS has a Code for Crown Prosecutors but this is formulated by the DPP. Both policies are published, but they are

8   See discussion of community policing in ch 2, section 1(a), above.
9   [1999] 1 All ER 129. Discussed in C Barnard and I Hare, 'Police Discretion and the Rule of Law: European Community Rights Versus Civil Rights' (2000) 63 MLR 581.
10 Also see *Metropolitan Police Comr, ex p P* (1995) 160 JP 367, discussed by R Evans, 'Is a police caution amenable to judicial review?' [1996] Crim LR 104.
11 T Jefferson and R Grimshaw, *Controlling the Constable: Police Accountability in England and Wales* (London: Muller, 1984). See ch 3, section 4, for a brief discussion of these issues in relation to the policing of industrial disputes and of domestic violence. See section 6 below for an extended discussion of accountability.

vague. The police and CPS have created for themselves more detailed guidelines for their own use which are not published. Against the argument for more openness, Hilson argues that if police and CPS prosecution policies—eg not to prosecute shoplifting of goods worth less than £1, or speeding offences where the limit is exceeded by less than 10 mph—became publicly available then this would be a green light to everyone to break the law up to these limits.[12] He argues that other agencies, such as the Inland Revenue, are able to publish their detailed policies without this happening because they have other ways of securing compliance. Given the level of tax evasion, this is debatable.[13] In so far as he is right, however, it would not be unreasonable to allow alternative sanctions to be operated by the police or, preferably, the CPS.[14] One such example would be the 'prosecutor fine' used in Scotland. This is used in minor cases as an alternative to prosecution.[15] Although this type of scheme is not without its adverse implications for due process, it seems that such prosecution policies can operate in a way which is both open and generous to suspects, without undermining whatever deterrent effect the law might have, thus potentially advancing the 'freedom' approach.

There appear to be three broad legal principles restraining the police and other prosecution agencies from following their informal crime control norms. Firstly, a prosecution must not be made in bad faith. If it is, the court may hold it to be an abuse of process and dismiss the case.[16] It may also be possible to sue for malicious prosecution, this being the only available tortious remedy for wrongful prosecution decisions. However, prosecution must have been malicious in the sense that false information was deliberately provided, and the prosecution must have been resolved in the defendant's favour (either through acquittal or discontinuance).[17] Here again we see the application of the crime control principle that the end justifies the means. No matter how malicious a prosecution might have been, a person would have no remedy if found guilty in the criminal courts.

Decisions not to prosecute which are taken in bad faith (eg for personal reasons) are not reviewable in these ways. There is no such thing as an action for malicious non-prosecution. A second principle, though, which applies to all prosecution decisions, positive or negative, is that they must

12 Hilson [1993] pp 743-747.
13 D Cook, *Rich Law, Poor Law* (Milton Keynes: Open UP, 1989); D Cook, *Poverty, Crime and Punishment* (London: CPAG, 1997).
14 See A Sanders, 'The Limits to Diversion from Prosecution' (1988) 28 BJ Crim 513.
15 See, for example, P Duff, 'The Prosecutor Fine and Social Control' (1993) 33 BJ Crim 481.
16 See Hilson [1993] and cases cited therein.
17 R Clayton and H Tomlinson, *Civil Actions Against the Police* 2nd edn (London: Sweet & Maxwell, 1992).

not be *Wednesbury* unreasonable.[18] One difficulty in challenging prosecution decisions is that there is no general duty to give reasons for decisions.[19] This makes it difficult to know whether grounds for challenge exist. Those grounds are, in any case, narrowly drawn. Courts will not interfere with the decision of the enforcement body in question unless the exercise of discretion was so offensive or incompetent that it was completely unreasonable. This is the same principle that operates in relation to unlawful arrest.[20] An example would be prosecuting a case where there was no prima facie evidence (ie where there would be insufficient evidence to convict even if the defence gave no evidence on its own behalf).

Finally, prosecution decisions must be taken only after consideration and application of a consistent policy. Thus in *Metropolitan Police Comr, ex p P*, a caution was successfully challenged on the grounds that government guidelines on cautioning were not followed.[1] And in *DPP, ex p C*[2] a decision to drop the prosecution of a man accused of non-consensual buggery of his wife was successfully challenged because the prosecutor had not considered all the possibilities laid down in the Code before the decision was taken.

We have seen that the courts exercise a light touch in the control of prosecution policy and practice. The judges are, quite rightly, not prepared to do the legislature's job of establishing prosecution policy. This does, however, leave a vacuum. Agencies establish their own policies and are allowed to implement them flexibly within the broad limits set by the courts. Legislation and case law can tell us little about prosecutions. It is therefore vital to examine prosecution policies, to see how they are implemented, and to question the consequent patterns of prosecution and non-prosecution. All agencies work within the broad framework established by the 'Attorney-General's Guidelines on Prosecution', whereby prosecution can only go ahead if, firstly, there is sufficient evidence; and, secondly, prosecution is in the 'public interest'.[3] 'If the case does not pass the evidential test, it must not go ahead, no matter how important or serious

18 This concept derives from *Associated Provincial Picture Houses Ltd v Wednesbury Corpn* [1948] 1 KB 223.

19 See *DPP, ex p Manning* [2000] 3 WLR 463: held no general duty in either English or ECHR law to give reasons for non-prosecution, although a duty could arise in exceptional circumstances. (On the facts of that case, where a coroner's jury had recorded a verdict of unlawful killing in relation to the death of a prisoner at the hands of a prison officer, the Court of Appeal ruled that there was a duty to give reasons for not prosecuting that officer.)

20 See ch 3, section 5.

1 (1995) 160 JP 367, discussed in section 4(a).

2 [1995] 1 Cr App Rep 136. Discussed by G Dingwall, 'Judicial Review and the DPP' (1995) 54 CLJ 265.

3 See A Sanders, 'Prosecution Decisions and the Attorney-General's Guidelines' [1985] Crim LR 4.

Discretion

it might be'.[4] In the next two sections we look at how the police and CPS work within the broad framework of these two tests, and then we look at the markedly different response of non-police agencies to the same tests.

3. EVIDENTIAL SUFFICIENCY

(a) Deciding that there is insufficient evidence

The police frequently decide that they have insufficient evidence to prosecute. Many arrests are of the 'wrong' suspect. Such arrests occur routinely when the police trawl large suspect populations in major crime enquiries. They also happen in more minor cases, such as drugs raids where people are arrested indiscriminately, and in cases where the police act on 'information received' which turns out to be mistaken.[5] Sometimes the police believe that they have the right suspect, but still consider that they have insufficient evidence to take the matter further. Sometimes the evidence cannot be secured, but in other cases the police decide that it is not worth investing the time and trouble to pursue the matter further. On occasion, further action could reveal matters which the police would rather conceal, such as a case where, as a police inspector put it, prosecution 'might prove embarrassing to the police' because of racist language used during the arrest.[6] In yet other cases a 'deal' is struck in which non-prosecution is traded for information from the suspect. There are also cases like 'domestics' in which the police traditionally showed little interest, although the situation is now changing, at least as far as domestic violence against women is concerned.[7]

Thus, large numbers of suspects are released from detention with no further action being taken (NFA). McConville et al [8] found that around one-quarter, and Phillips and Brown [9] one-fifth, of all arrests ended in NFA. Although this might seem surprising, it must be remembered that if an arrest is made on the basis of 'reasonable suspicion' alone, more evidence will be needed before the case becomes prosecutable, and little over half of all suspects make incriminating statements. Phillips and Brown found that around 30% of arresting officers considered that there was insufficient

---

4   Code for Crown Prosecutors, (London: CPS, 1994) para 4.1.
5   See ch 3, section 4(b) for a discussion of the working rules which shape patterns of arrest.
6   M McConville, A Sanders and R Leng, *The Case for the Prosecution* (London: Routledge, 1991) p 111.
7   See ch 3, section 4(c) and section 6 below.
8   McConville, Sanders and Leng (1991) p 104, Table 10.
9   C Phillips and D Brown, Entry into the criminal justice system: a survey of police arrests and their outcomes (Home Office Research Study no 185) (London: Home Office, 1998) p 83, Table 6.1. There are no official figures on this point.

evidence to charge at the time of arrest; the authors rightly believe this to be an under-estimate, particularly as 10% of the supposedly strong cases actually resulted in NFA.[10] Not only does arrest involve a significant curtailment of liberty, but it happens to many people who are factually innocent and many more who will remain legally innocent throughout their encounter with the criminal process.

There is nothing new in the police disposing of cases through NFA, but the scale has changed in recent years. Thus, Steer found an NFA rate of only 8.3% in 1974.[11] There have been two changes since then. Firstly, as a result of the Philips Commission finding that large numbers of weak cases were being prosecuted,[12] the Attorney-General's guidelines for prosecution were issued in 1983. The police previously used the 'prima facie case' test which allowed prosecutions even where the chances of conviction might be slim. Now they are supposed to use a 'realistic prospect of conviction' test, under which conviction has to be more likely than acquittal.

The new test does not require a belief in the innocence of a defendant in order for a case to be dropped, nor a belief in guilt for a case to be proceeded with; thus it has come under criticism. Williams argues that allegedly corrupt police officers are frequently not prosecuted because it is feared that juries will not accept the word of private citizens, especially if they have criminal records, against that of police officers. Similarly, the application of the test can mean that sophisticated fraudsters are not prosecuted on the ground that it would be difficult to get a jury to understand and convict on the complicated evidence involved.[13] To the extent that prosecutors act on such beliefs about juries,[14] we can see that the application of the same test to people of different status leads to different results, allowing high status fraudsters to avoid prosecution.[15] Williams argues that the test should not be whether a jury is likely to convict, but whether it ought to convict, given the admissible evidence available to the prosecutor. It is bad enough, he says, that someone believed to be guilty gets acquitted, but to spare them the anguish of the trial too is over-generous.

The 'realistic prospect' test creates a tougher threshold for the police to surmount than did the old prima facie test. One might have hoped for fewer weak arrests, but instead there appear to be more arrests without

10   Phillips and Brown (1998) pp 43-4; 89-90.
11   D Steer, Uncovering Crime: The Police Role (Royal Commission on Criminal Procedure Research Study no 7) (London: HMSO, 1980) Table 4.
12   RCCP (1981) Report, pp 130-131.
13   G Williams, 'Letting off the Guilty and Prosecuting the Innocent' [1985] Crim LR 115.
14   Little is known about the actual behaviour of juries and their reasons for acquittal: see ch 9, section 5.
15   For discussion of this point in the context of arrest, see ch 3, section 4(c).

prosecution. This has been facilitated by another development in the law: PACE. For s 37 allows suspects to be detained precisely in order to secure sufficient evidence to prosecute. Release without charge is explicitly recognised as a legitimate outcome should that evidence not be produced.

Allowing the police to arrest, collect evidence and weed out cases which they decide do not warrant judicial proceedings is a classic 'let the experts decide' crime control strategy. In practice, whether a case ends in NFA depends not just on police evaluations of evidential strength and offence seriousness but also on how much the police want to prosecute a particular case and a particular individual. This in turn shapes the thoroughness and creativity with which any investigation is carried out. In other words, the degree of interest shown by the police in any particular case or category of case is crucially affected by their own working rules. Just as some cases are prosecuted because the police wish them to be, so others are not because the police do not wish them to be. Still others are not prosecuted, or the prosecution collapses as in the Stephen Lawrence affair, because the police had insufficient interest or competence to investigate thoroughly.[16]

(b)   Police working rules and the custody officer

We have already seen that arrests can be used as a resource in street policing.[17] Arrest often suffices to impose police authority or control, rendering prosecution unnecessary. Often, though, prosecution will be a natural follow-through, especially when a complaint has been made against the officer,[18] or when the latter is assaulted.[19] A police officer justified one prosecution to McConville et al by pointing out that, 'We can't have people going round pushing police officers when they feel like it.'[20] Waddington discusses a case where the rowdiness of the arrestee was exaggerated in order to *legally* justify an arrest which the police thought was *morally* justifiable, and essential to maintain their authority.[1] The working rules examined in chapters 2 and 3 therefore continue to have force in the shaping of prosecution decisions, even when the evidence is weak. Conversely, where there is no public order issue in a clear-cut incident the police may regard prosecution as pointless unless they see the crime involved as

16   Sir William Macpherson of Cluny, The Stephen Lawrence Inquiry (Cm 4262-I) (London: SO, 1999). See section 6 below, and ch 3.
17   See ch 3, section 4(b).
18   See Sanders [1985]; and McConville et al (1991).
19   C Clarkson, A Cretney, G Davis and J Shepherd, 'Assaults: the relationship between seriousness, criminalisation and punishment' [1994] Crim LR 4.
20   McConville et al (1991), fieldnote.
1   P Waddington, *Policing Citizens* (London: UCL Press, 1999) p 135.

serious. This has been a particular problem in domestic violence cases, discussed in detail later.[2]

The Philips Commission was anxious to reduce the number of arrests and the number of weak cases prosecuted. Since arresting officers will often have strong reasons for prosecuting, it was obvious that the imposition of objective standards would be impossible without the decision to prosecute being made by someone independent. The Philips Commission resolved to remedy this through the 'arrest only when necessary' principle, the 'realistic prospect of conviction' test, the custody officer and the CPS. Under its proposals, in most cases in which the police wanted to prosecute, they would have had to report the suspect. The suspect would then have been considered for summons by a senior officer on the basis of a written file of evidence.

This is the system used for road traffic offences, most non-arrestable offences and a small proportion of minor arrestable thefts and assaults. Decisions take longer than with arrest and charge but they are based on a detached consideration of the evidence, and the coercive process of arrest is avoided. However, the 'arrest only when necessary' principle was not applied in PACE to arrestable offences.[3] The result has been that a much larger proportion of cases are processed by way of arrest and charge than the Philips Commission envisaged. Indeed, a far higher proportion of all prosecutions of non-summary offences are by way of arrest and charge now (92%) than was so in 1981.[4]

The safeguard offered by the Philips Commission for arrest and charge cases (enacted in PACE) was to replace the charge sergeant with the supposedly more independent custody officer. The problem with decisions taken by charge sergeants was that they were based only on the report of the arresting officer(s) together, perhaps, with that of the interviewing officer (often the same officer). Decisions usually had to be immediate, were based on what the officer(s) said was the evidence and in the presence of those officers. This all made dispassionate decision-making virtually impossible. Thus, the Prosecuting Solicitors' Society commented:

'the view of the charge sergeant ... must therefore be gained from what he is told by the investigating officer. As an independent check this must be almost without value.'[5]

2   See section 6.
3   See ch 3, section 3(c).
4   G Barclay and C Tavares (eds), Information on the Criminal Justice System in England and Wales: Digest 4 (London: Home Office, 1999) ch 4. See, for comparisons over time, McConville et al (1991) pp 38-40. Phillips and Brown (1998) p 86.
5   Evidence to the Philips Commission (1979) para 3.3. This was the message which also emerged from the research of the 1970s and early 1980s. See Sanders [1985].

Evidential sufficiency

The defect in this part of the Philips Commission's strategy is that custody officers are in exactly the same social, occupational and structural position as were the old charge sergeants. Chapter 4 showed that, in relation to the rights of suspects, the custody officer is no more independent than charge sergeants used to be. The same is true in relation to decisions to charge. One custody officer told McConville et al: 'I would go along with what the arresting officers have to say.' Another, when asked whether he had put questions to an arresting officer or the suspect to form his own view of an incident, replied: 'Not at all. I accept that [the officer's] got no cause to be telling lies and the [suspect] has.'[6] It is very rare for custody officers to caution or NFA when arresting officers want to charge, or vice versa. Like the charge sergeants of pre-PACE days, custody officers take information from arresting/interviewing officers alone, treating their version of events as inherently reliable and the suspect's, if listened to at all, as a tissue of self-interested lies. This dichotomous approach to the nature of truth ignores the sociological reality that most sets of facts can be interpreted in different ways, and that sometimes arresting officers do have cause to be telling lies.

Arresting officers can present cases to custody officers in ways that secure the results they want. Officers who want to slip dubious charges past possibly sceptical custody officers can make alleged offences seem particularly serious, or the evidence seem particularly strong. In practice, then, the realistic prospect of conviction test, if in the custody officer's mind at all, is easily overcome. Thus in one of McConville et al's cases there was, in what had been portrayed to the custody officer as a s 47 assault, virtually no injury. The charge had to be reduced in court to the charge of common assault (which would not normally be prosecuted by the police).[7]

A further point is that the custody officer follows the same working rules about order, authority and suspiciousness as do all other police officers. In one case discussed by McConville et al, the suspect had no previous convictions and was arrested for drunkenness. The arresting officer said that he had been getting on the custody officer's nerves because he had been 'mouthy', and so was prosecuted for being drunk and disorderly even though he had not actually been disorderly in public. The custody officer said:

'To be perfectly frank you make your decision on what you see in front of you. If he gives you a hard time, say verbally, then you think, "Oh yeah, he's obviously given the PC a hard time on the street and

6 McConville et al (1991) p 119. Note that even if the custody officer does wish to hear a suspect's story, the rules on interviewing would make this difficult: see ch 5, section 3. Once again, the attempt to secure due process tends towards an opposite effect.

7 McConville et al (1991) p 112.

he's obviously of a disorderly nature and therefore we'll send him to court." That's how I decide.'[8]

Have things changed between the research of McConville et al, done in the mid-1980s, and that of Phillips and Brown, done in the mid-1990s? Although Phillips and Brown do not discuss NFA decisions by custody officers they 'cast doubt on how searchingly custody officers do enquire into the evidence. The reception of suspects into custody was often found to be a routine matter. . .'[9] Similarly, research carried out in 1996 found that few custody officers or investigating officers sought CPS advice on charges, despite their sometimes inadequate grasp of the relevant facts or law in particular cases. In a striking echo of the pre-CPS situation, one custody officer told researchers, 'the investigators know the ins and outs of the case and I have to deal with the other prisoners.'[10] This gives us little confidence that custody officer decision-making has changed substantially over the last 20 years. Now that it has been shown that ethnic minority defendants are more likely to have their cases discontinued *and* to be acquitted in court,[11] it seems that the racist elements within cop culture still lead to disproportionate wrongful prosecutions which custody officers remain unable or unwilling to stop.

(c) Case construction, evidential sufficiency and the CPS

This section is primarily concerned with the initial decision to prosecute or not, and with the review of decisions to prosecute by the CPS. The CPS is supposed continually to review this decision until the case has finished, and so our discussion needs to include elements of the pre-trial and trial stages.[12] Article 6 of the European Convention on Human Rights (ECHR) provides the right to a 'fair trial'. Inherent in this is the principle of 'equality of arms'. In order to guard against breaches of Art 6, the CPS should exercise a 'Minister of Justice' role, ensuring, for example, that the defence is treated fairly and has access to all relevant information.

The first task of the CPS, like that of the custody officer, is to ensure that prosecution cases pass the test of evidential sufficiency. How well has this part of the Philips Commission's strategy to sieve weak cases out of the system at an early stage worked? Every case which the police decide

8   McConville et al (1991) p 114.
9   Phillips and Brown (1998) p 43.
10   J Baldwin and A Hunt, 'Prosecutors Advising in Police Stations' [1998] Crim LR 521 at p 529.
11   B Mhlanga, *Race and the CPS* (London: SO, 1999) summarised in: S 95 Findings no 1 (London: Home Office, 2000).
12   Fuller discussion of court processes is contained in chs 7-9.

Evidential sufficiency

should be prosecuted reaches the CPS prior to the first court hearing (although sometimes only immediately before it). The CPS is entitled to drop ('discontinue') the case either immediately or at any time thereafter.[13] What is the point of the police prosecuting weak cases when the CPS can simply drop them? The answer in part is that when this happens the officers involved can claim that the CPS exercised its judgment poorly. When crime rates rise, the CPS is a useful scapegoat for the wider failure of the crime control strategy. In police 'cop culture', the CPS, in dropping cases, lets the public (and the police) down,[14] and this argument has been reproduced by commentators in the wider public arena.[15] The CPS has even been dubbed by one wit in blue 'the Criminal Protection Society'. However, the reasons for the police pushing weak cases into the prosecution system run deeper than this.

The 'realistic prospect of conviction' test is a predictive rule. As Williams observed,[16] it does not relate to the likelihood of guilt but to the likelihood of conviction. It is, in other words, not a rule which asks officers to prosecute cases which are necessarily intrinsically stronger, but cases in which they think they can secure sufficient evidence. This may seem a pedantic distinction, but it is not. The rule encourages the police to strengthen cases which would otherwise be weak. So there may not be fewer prosecutions of weak cases, but simply prosecutions of the same cases in which the evidence has been strengthened. Although this may lead to more forensic investigation, bolstering those cases which would otherwise be likely to fail, it also encourages the stronger construction of cases, whereby weak cases remain weak, but are made to appear strong.

The CPS is in a similar position to that of the custody officer in having to rely on what they are told by police officers who may, and often do, have an interest in the case. The CPS position is not quite so dependent as is that of the custody officer. Firstly, there is no time pressure on the CPS: the suspect is not in the cells awaiting a decision. Secondly, the CPS makes decisions on the basis of written files in which obvious flaws will be more difficult to conceal. On the other hand, the CPS is not a decision taker but a decision confirmer or reverser. It is more difficult to reverse a decision of which one disapproves than it is to refuse to take it in the first place. The result is 'prosecution momentum': the continued prosecution of cases which perhaps should never have begun. We say 'perhaps' because the CPS will often, through no fault of its own, not know how weak or strong

13   Prosecution of Offences Act 1985, s 23.

14   See D Crisp and D Moxon, Case Screening by the CPS (Home Office Research Study no 137) (London: Home Office, 1994) pp 19-20 for examples of such criticisms.

15   See, for example, D Rose, *In the Name of the Law: The Collapse of Criminal Justice* (London: Jonathan Cape, 1996) especially chs 4 and 8.

16   See section 3(a) above.

a case is when it first sees the file if, for example, identification or scientific evidence (drugs analysis, fingerprints, and so forth) is still being processed.[17] Suppose the scientific evidence, when it arrives, is inconclusive. The problem is that it is even more difficult to reverse a decision to prosecute a case that has been on-going for weeks or months than it is to reverse it when it is first received from the police.

The proportion of cases discontinued by the CPS gradually rose in the first few years (to 13.5% of all cases in 1992–3) and then fell a little (to around 12% for most of the 1990s).[18] Nearly half of these are cases dropped for evidential insufficiency, while in another 17% of dropped cases the prosecution is unable to proceed because, for instance, material witnesses went missing or refused to give evidence.[19] This might suggest that the CPS is doing the job which Philips set out for it. However, between 1985 and 1997 the percentage of cases ending in conviction fell in the Crown Court (83% to 76%). Although these figures include discontinuances and cases where no evidence was offered, acquittals following a full trial rose significantly. In the magistrates' courts the conviction rate remains very high (only 1-2% being acquitted).[20]

How can we explain this? First, some cases can be seen to be evidentially weak from the outset, and these are usually dropped. Even then the CPS rarely flexes its muscles independently, as in most of these cases the police themselves—often supervising officers responsible for an area's prosecutions—point out these weaknesses to the CPS. If the CPS did not exist, the police would probably drop most of these cases anyway. The Lawrence case was such an example: the police did charge some of the five suspects, but when the CPS discontinued the case (in consultation with the police) this came as no surprise to the senior investigating officers, and the official enquiry report regarded the CPS decision as inevitable on the basis of the evidence collected by the police.[1] Then there are the cases which appear weak, which the police do not wish to drop and which the CPS do prosecute. Sometimes this is because the police working rules which led to the initial charges embody values shared by the CPS. As one prosecutor told McConville et al, when one suspect gets 'away with it . . .

17 A Ashworth and J Fionda, 'The New Code for Crown Prosecutors: Prosecution, Accountability and the Public Interest' [1994] Crim LR 894; and reply by R Daw, 'A Response' [1994] Crim LR 904.
18 Barclay and Tavares (1999) ch 4.
19 Crown Prosecution Service, Discontinuance Survey (November 1993) (unpublished).
20 M McConville and A Sanders, 'Weak Cases and the CPS' (1992) LS Gaz, 12 February, p 24. For figures for 1996 and 1997, see Sir Iain Glidewell, The Review of the Crown Prosecution Service: A Report (Cm 3960) (London: HMSO, 1998) ch 4 and Barclay and Tavares (1999) ch 4. The disparity between conviction rates in the two levels of court is discussed in ch 8 below.
1 Macpherson (1999).

it gets back to the others. You've got to get to know your territory—it's a bit of a policy decision.'[2] Sharing working rules need not always involve a cynical calculation of this sort. A commitment to do whatever is reasonably possible for vulnerable victims has also been found to lead to prosecutions continuing despite evidential weakness.[3] At other times there is a good chance of a guilty plea,[4] or the chance of a freak conviction.[5] In many cases, the CPS tell the police that the case will be dropped if the defendant pleads not guilty. In others, prosecutors do not evaluate the evidence rigorously because they assume the defendant will plead guilty anyway. Why give up the likelihood of a conviction for the certainty of a 'failure'? A 'realistic prospect of conviction' requires nothing other than a weighing of the odds.

This explanation is largely based on the research of McConville et al, which was carried out when the CPS was new. Some commentators question the continued validity of their findings in the light of revised versions of the Code for Crown Prosecutors and the general increased confidence that one might expect an organisation to develop over the years.[6] However, research carried out in the 1990s largely confirms the earlier findings. Baldwin, for example, argues that 'weak cases continue to be committed to the Crown Court because of a reluctance, even a disinclination, on the part of certain reviewing lawyers to make the tough decisions in serious cases required of them under the Code for Crown Prosecutors.'[7] Indeed, when Sanders et al found that the CPS often continued the prosecution of weak cases if vulnerable victims wished them to,[8] the CPS actually sought to publicise these findings. This was because in the mid-1990s many people and organisations were accusing the CPS of doing too little to help vulnerable victims.[9] The (admittedly impressionistic) finding of Hoyano et al, who specifically looked at the impact of revisions to the Code which became effective in 1994, was that its changes made little or no difference to prosecutors' decisions.[10] This is unsurprising, as the sharing of values

2   Quoted by McConville and Sanders (1992).
3   A Sanders, J Creaton, S Bird and L Weber, Victims with Learning Disabilities (Oxford: Centre for Criminological Research, 1997) summarised in Home Office Research Findings no 44, (London: HMSO, 1996); and see section 6 below.
4   See ch 7.
5   See chs 8-9.
6   See, in particular, Philips and Brown (1998) p 139.
7   J Baldwin, 'Understanding Judge Ordered and Directed Acquittals in the Crown Court' [1997] Crim LR 536 at p 547.
8   Sanders et al (1997).
9   Including academic commentators such as J Gregory and S Lees, 'Attrition in Rape and Sexual Assault Cases' (1996) 36 BJ Crim 1.
10   A Hoyano, L Hoyano, G Davis and S Goldie, 'A Study of the Impact of the Revised Code for Crown Prosecutors' [1997] Crim LR 556. This version of the Code (the third) is discussed by Ashworth and Fionda [1994] and Daw [1994].

by the police and the CPS, and the structurally weak position of the latter, are changed neither by different Codes nor by greater expertise and experience.

In any group of cases with a realistic prospect of conviction, we would expect some cases to end in acquittal, and some to end in conviction. It is impossible for the CPS to be sure which will fall into which category and so it is not surprising that there is a significant acquittal rate. This has been recognised for some years.[11] The real issue is whether the CPS is failing to identify cases that do not have a realistic prospect of conviction. In a study for the Runciman Commission, Block et al looked at 100 ordered and directed Crown Court acquittals. At least one-quarter of the acquittals were certainly foreseeable (ie manifestly more likely than not to fail) and another quarter were possibly foreseeable.[12] Baldwin's later study found foreseeable weakness evident in an even higher proportion of ordered and directed acquittals.[13] Similarly, in the Runciman Commission's Crown Court study around 20% of the contested cases were regarded by the barristers and judges involved as 'weak'. Around 80% of these cases ended in acquittal, but significant numbers ended in conviction.[14] To drop all cases predicted as possible acquittals would therefore lead to convictions as well as acquittals being reduced.[15] Had Block et al and Baldwin looked at 100 convictions, a large number of them would doubtless also have been foreseen as possible acquittals.[16]

The above argument does require one important modification. Some acquittals which are predictable will be so at an early stage by, at best, the police alone. This is because they are constructed to appear stronger than they 'really' are. To some extent, a case which is so constructed actually is strong. Facts do not exist in abstract, and who is to say what 'really' happened, or what was in a suspect's mind? Both sides of an adversarial system construct facts, because most facts are not neutral objective entities to be dispassionately evaluated.

When the police construct cases, they seek evidence which will prove their case and avoid or undermine evidence which goes against it. They may do this because they fear that the CPS will not share its view of the

---

11 See G Mansfield and J Peay, *The Director of Public Prosecutions* (London: Tavistock, 1987).

12 B Block, C Corbett, and J Peay, Ordered and Directed Acquittals in the Crown Court (Royal Commission on Criminal Justice Research Study no 15) (London: HMSO, 1993).

13 Baldwin [1997] p 536.

14 M Zander and P Henderson, Crown Court Study (Royal Commission on Criminal Justice Research Study no 19) (London: HMSO, 1993) pp 184-185.

15 See discussion in ch 9, section 1. See also P Lewis, 'The CPS and Acquittals by Judge: Finding the Balance' [1997] Crim LR 653, which - although a response by the CPS to Baldwin's research - does not challenge Baldwin's findings.

16 McConville et al (1991) ch 8 found that many results were impossible to predict.

importance of prosecuting a particular case. Alternatively, they may do it because they predict that although the CPS will support their decision to prosecute, the chances of success at court if the case is contested would otherwise be slim. A well-constructed case may induce a guilty plea from the defendant, and may even be strong enough to stand up to scrutiny in an adversarial trial.

There is nothing necessarily wrong with case construction. It is a natural part of the adversarial system. All law enforcement agencies do it.[17] It would be unobjectionable if the defence had similar resources and a similar approach, but they have neither.[18] Police constructions therefore tend to dominate prosecution and court processes, giving them enormous power in the process of determining guilt and innocence. Let us examine some of the ways in which the police construct cases.

(i) Fabrication of evidence

One way of constructing cases is by creating the facts. Occasionally this may be pure fabrication. This is what Sgt Challenor was notorious for,[19] and there was fabrication in many miscarriages of justice in the 1980s and 1990s. For example, in the 'Guildford Four' case, the police claimed to have taken a contemporaneous note of an interview with one of the defendants, Patrick Armstrong, and then had this typed up. Some 14 years after the interview took place, it was discovered that the typed notes contained deletions and additions, both typed and handwritten. Yet the supposedly contemporaneous handwritten note of the interview corresponded with the amended version of the typed notes. When the Court of Appeal was faced with these facts, it concluded that either the typed notes were a complete fabrication, subsequently copied out by hand so as to appear contemporaneously made, or the police had started with a contemporaneous note, typed it up, amended it to make it more effective as prosecution evidence, and then converted it back to a handwritten note. Either way, the police had lied. This proved vital to the success of the appeal for, as Lord Lane CJ put it: 'If they were prepared to tell this sort of lie, then the whole of their evidence became suspect.' None the less, it took 14 years to demolish this particular police construction.[20] Another way in which

17 See D Nelken, *The Limits of the Legal Process* (London: Academic Press, 1983) for a study of case construction by housing officials in relation to harassment cases.

18 M McConville, J Hodgson and L Bridges, *Standing Accused* (Oxford: Clarendon, 1994).

19 See ch 5 above.

20 See J Rozenberg, 'Miscarriages of Justice' in E Stockdale and S Casale (eds), *Criminal Justice Under Stress* (London: Blackstone, 1992) p 94.

the police can create prosecution evidence is by holding rigged witness identification parades. In *Kamara*[1] a witness picked out the defendant from a 'line-up' and this helped secure his conviction for murder, for which he received a sentence of life imprisonment. His identification was perhaps somewhat surprising given that the witness had previously described the suspect to the police in a way which differed from the defendant's appearance. One ground for quashing his conviction, some 19 years later, was that he had been placed on the identification parade wearing prison clothes! So, not such a surprising identification after all.

Every time a scandal like this erupts the police say that they have rooted out the corruption and law-breaking and tightened up procedures, or that the law has changed to prevent it happening again. We think they do protest too much. There is certainly no doubt that scandalous police behaviour has persisted in the aftermath of PACE 1984 and the creation of the CPS the following year. Drawing on research carried out in the 1980s and early 1990s, Keith quotes an officer saying: 'If you raid somewhere and there is this bloke, who you know pushes, standing in there and there's drugs all around him on the floor that he got rid of as you arrive, you've got a choice. Either you let him go away to spoil more lives or you say you saw him drop the bags on the floor or 'find' one of them in his pocket.'[2] This example, one of many we could give,[3] is often termed 'noble cause corruption', the existence of which the Metropolitan Police Commissioner himself has admitted.[4]

From a freedom perspective fabrication of evidence is an ignoble act done in an ignoble cause. It undermines the rule of law and amounts to a non-democratic arrogation of power by the police. And, of course, it leads to significant losses of freedom to those who should never have been convicted. To take a recent example, in July 2000 three men sentenced to 10 years each for armed robbery in 1995 were released by the Court of Appeal. The crucial evidence against them was a witness identification of one of them, and a palm print of one of the others at the scene of the crime together with the discovery in his flat of a stun gun allegedly used in the robbery; strong evidence indeed. Would you have convicted if you had sat as a juror on the original trial? Eventually it was discovered, because the officers involved had been subsequently convicted of a series of corruption offences, that the witness had been shown a photo of the suspect before the ID parade (another way to rig a line-up) the palm print

1   CA: 9 May 2000, unreported.
2   M Keith, *Race Riots and Policing* (London: UCL Press, 1993) p 138.
3   See, for example, P Waddington, *Policing Citizens* (London: UCL Press, 1999) pp 147-9, and the quashing in July 2000 of the convictions in 1990 of the 'M25 Three' (police found to have conspired with an informant to give perjured evidence in court): *Davis, Rowe and Johnson* (CA, 17 July 2000, unreported).
4   *The Guardian*, 11 March 1995. See Waddington (1999).

Evidential sufficiency

had failed to match on the first two occasions and so the final match was, in the euphemistic words of the courts 'unreliable', and the stun gun had probably been planted by the officers.[5]

(ii) Interrogation

The process of construction is more subtle when evidence is obtained through an 'interview'. Most suspects do not confess their crimes in an unprompted manner.[6] Confessions, and other self-incriminating statements, are usually the product of interrogation and must be distilled from a sequence of questions and answers. In this sense, then, even 'non-fabricated' confessions are created by the police (in conjunction with the suspect). The 'facts' pointing towards guilt are therefore, in large part, a product of police processes.

The way the police interrogate is important in constructing cases both in the questions asked and in those not asked. In one case examined by McConville et al, a store detective had asked a suspected shoplifter whether she had forgotten to pay. If she had indeed forgotten to pay, or raised a reasonable doubt about that at court, then she would be entitled to an acquittal on the grounds of no mens rea. The police decision-maker in the case advised the store detective not to ask this sort of question in future.[7] As we have seen, and as this example illustrates, the police are reluctant to uncover exonerating facts. The police do not seek all the evidence which might bear on the guilt or innocence of suspects, but only the evidence which will strengthen the case against them.

(iii) Summaries of interviews

It is standard for the police to prepare a summary of any tape recorded interview with a suspect. In practice, both defence and prosecution lawyers tend to rely on these summaries in order to save time and money.[8] For many years these particular police constructions have been known to be inaccurate,[9] and they continue to be so.[10] Their inaccuracy is, however,

5   *The Guardian*, 13 July 2000.
6   See ch 5.
7   McConville et al (1991) p 74.
8   See J Baldwin and J Bedward, 'Summarising Tape Recordings of Police Interviews' [1991] Crim LR 671 at 672.
9   See Baldwin and Bedward [1991]. See also A Sanders, 'Constructing the Case for the Prosecution' (1987) 14 JLS 229 and McConville et al (1991). A similar problem arises in summary proceedings, where disclosure often takes place by way of a summary of the prosecution case, again prepared by the police: J Baldwin and A Mulvaney, 'Advance Disclosure in the Magistrates' Courts: How useful are the Prosecution summaries?' [1987] Crim LR 805.

unidirectional. That is, summaries nearly always overstate, and rarely understate, the extent to which a full confession or an incriminating statement was made.[11] Prosecution files are therefore constructed to appear to be stronger than they 'really' are. In the rare event that a tape of an interview is listened to or the full transcript read, prosecution momentum will have developed. Sometimes it is only when cases are contested that different versions of the facts emerge. Thus in an offensive weapon case, a 'truncheon', as the police file described it, turned out to be a decorated rounders bat, a common souvenir from Spain.[12] The pressures on defendants not to contest cases are, however, intense.[13] Moreover, under new reforms aimed at reducing delay, many magistrates' court cases are disposed of the day after the defendant is charged.[14] In these 'fast-tracked' cases there is no time to transcribe interviews, and the police summary is necessarily relied upon. This violates the spirit of the 'equality of arms' principle which, as explained at the beginning of this sub-section, is inherent in Art 6 of the ECHR (the right to a fair trial) and, therefore, the Human Rights Act 1998. Whether it would be held by English courts to be literally contrary to that Act remains to be seen.

(iv) Forensic evidence

The importance of scientific evidence to prosecution cases has increased in recent years. One reason for this is that confession evidence has reduced slightly in importance as a consequence of the changes introduced by PACE.[15] Another explanatory factor is scientific innovations such as DNA testing and the computerised matching of fingerprint records. But even apparently 'hard' scientifically determined facts about times of death, the matching of materials at the scene of a crime, fingerprints, DNA and so forth may not add much strength to a prosecution case. It has been estimated that, in cases where it is used, scientific evidence is of conclusive value in 61% of cases, and of strong value in a further 14%. This means

---

10 J Baldwin, Preparing the Record of Taped Interview (Royal Commission on Criminal Justice Research Study no 2) (London: HMSO, 1992).
11 This point is further discussed in ch 7, section 3(c), below.
12 McConville et al (1991) pp 116-17.
13 See chs 7-8.
14 These innovations were proposed in M Narey, Review of Delay in the Criminal Justice System (London: Home Office, 1997). The Crime and Disorder Act 1998 contains measures aimed at implementing this strategy. See R Leng, R Taylor and M Wasik, *Blackstone's Guide to The Crime and Disorder Act 1998* (London: Blackstone, 1998) ch 5, and ch 8 below, for discussion.
15 See ch 5.

that it is of little or no value in around 25% of cases.[16] The number of cases in which scientific evidence was obtained but discarded as useless is not known. Like all evidence, it is susceptible to the processes of case construction: 'a forensic scientist conjures up the image of a man in a white coat working in a laboratory, approaching his task with cold neutrality, and dedicated only to the pursuit of the truth. It is a sombre thought that the reality is somewhat different.'[17] What is the reality?

First, unlike most scientists, forensic scientists have little or no control over the material which they are testing, and the conditions in which it was collected and stored. Usually they test material collected by police officers. They have to rely on those officers not to contaminate the evidence, and to report all the relevant conditions in which it was collected. The material itself may be only partially adequate for testing - for example, blood may have been contaminated by other substances before the police arrived at the crime scene. And the police sometimes forward for examination evidence that might help their case but not that which might undermine it.[18] In a complex investigation there may be hundreds of actual or potential items for examination, and so there often has to be some selectivity anyway.

Second, forensic examination does not take place in a vacuum: scientists are asked whether particular substances can be identified, or whether a sexual assault could have occurred. This is often unavoidable, for any one substance might contain an infinite number of constituents. Without knowing what to test for, some analyses might never end. And the police always have to decide how much it is worth spending on such tests in any given case. But pointing the scientist in a particular direction has its dangers: 'Forensic scientists may become partisan.'[19] This danger is all the greater as, since the mid-1990s, governments have attempted to cut costs by subjecting the Forensic Science Service to free market pressures.[20]

Third, scientists sometimes disagree on the interpretation of their findings: scientists prefer to make clear the limits of their ability to reach black and white conclusions, but the criminal process discourages shades of grey. Scientists have to report on their findings, but cannot report on everything seen and found. They report on what appears relevant, and relevance is frequently a creation of the initial premises on which an

---

16   House of Lords Select Committee on Science and Technology, Forensic Science, 1992-3, HL 24.

17   Glidewell LJ in *Ward* (1992) 96 Cr App Rep 1 at 51.

18   P Roberts and C Willmore, The Role of Forensic Science Evidence in Criminal Proceedings (Royal Commission on Criminal Justice Research Study no 11) (London: HMSO, 1993).

19   Glidewell LJ in *Ward* (1992) 96 Cr App Rep 1 at 51.

20   P Roberts, 'What Price a Free Market in Forensic Science?' (1996) 36 BJ Crim 37.

investigation is based. In the *Maguire* case there was no doubt that the defendants had a substance on their hands that *could* have derived from nitro-glycerine (an explosive). Only after the Maguires had spent several years in prison did it become clear that the forensic tests had not been sufficiently specific to justify accepting the scientists' opinion that this was a more likely source than many others, such as playing cards or plastic gloves.[1] Or take Danny McNamee, the 'Hyde Park bomber', jailed for life in 1987. His conviction was largely based on fingerprint evidence given by the police's own experts. But at his successful appeal, over 10 years later, 14 fingerprint experts gave evidence. According to the Court of Appeal: 'Remarkably, and worryingly, save for those who said the print was unreadable, there was no unanimity between them, and very substantial areas of disagreement.'[2]

All these issues were identified by Roberts and Willmore in their research for the Runciman Commission. They comment that 'At each stage of the pre-trial process, forensic science is utilised by prosecution agencies as a tool for case construction.'[3] The limitations of scientific evidence are not, however, as worrying as the limitations of most other forms of evidence. The problem lies in the weight to be attributed to the evidence of the prosecution scientist. In the 'Confait Affair' the inability to fix the time of death of Confait accurately allowed the obfuscation of the facts by the prosecution which led to the wrongful conviction of the three defendants.[4] As Glidewell LJ warned in *Ward*, it is vital to recognise the reality of forensic science. This includes DNA evidence, which suffers from the same problems of selection and interpretation as all other scientific evidence.[5] Scientific results have to be interpreted accordingly. Like prosecutors, scientists are faced with an inescapable dilemma. If they remain detached and relatively non-partisan they have such little control over the information they handle that their dependence upon the police becomes near-total. Alternatively, if they seek to reduce their dependence on the police by

1   See Sir John May: Report of the inquiry into the circumstances surrounding the convictions arising out of the bomb attacks in Guildford and Woolwich in 1974, Second Report (1992-3 HC 296).
2   Quoted in B Woffinden, 'Thumbs Down' *The Guardian*, 12 January 1999.
3   Roberts and Willmore (1993) p 26. Also see, for good general discussions: P Roberts, 'Science in the Criminal Process' (1994) 14 OJLS 469; C Walker and E Stockdale, 'Forensic Science and Miscarriages of Justice' (1995) 54 Camb LJ 69 and C Jones, *Expert Witnesses* (Oxford: OUP, 1994).
4   J Rozenberg, *The Case for the Crown* (Wellingborough: Equation, 1987). The quote from Glidewell LJ above in *Ward*, some 20 years after *Confait*, indicates that the problems in the latter case were neither unique nor only historical interest. Great doubt was cast on the validity of the scientific evidence in several of the 'Irish' convictions which were eventually overturned.
5   See, for example, M Redmayne, 'Doubts and Burdens: DNA Evidence, Probability and the Courts' [1995] Crim LR 464; M Redmayne, 'The DNA Database: Civil Liberty and Evidentiary Issues' [1998] Crim LR 437.

getting involved in the investigation (directing the samples to be examined for example), their partisanship will increase. In the search to blame individuals for the errors inherent in systems, scientists have frequently been blamed for taking one stance and then, only a short time later, for taking the other.[6]

For the scientist, as for the prosecutor, there is no solution to this dilemma. But for the criminal justice system, it is vital to recognise the problem in at least two ways. First, since science rarely provides *conclusive* proof, the *degree* of proof required should be high in order to minimise wrongful convictions. McNamee won his appeal because not one of the 14 fingerprint experts who testified could find more than 11 characteristics matching the fingerprint found at the scene of the crime with McNamee's fingerprints. This fell short of the agreed threshold, which was 16 matching characteristics. Now, however, this threshold is to be abolished,[7] which is yet another move in the crime control direction. Second, balance is needed by providing the defence with appropriate resources. That, in this instance, means access to adequate defence science facilities. Restrictions on legal aid funding prevent this in most cases. Even the largely complacent Runciman Commission was critical of this.[8] Many prosecution case constructions based on spuriously 'solid' forensic science therefore go unchallenged.[9] As with summaries of interviews to which the defence have no proper access, this lack of proper funding for the defence arguably violates the principle of 'equality of arms' and, therefore Art 6 of the ECHR.[10]

(v)   Non-disclosure of evidence

'Confait' and the 'Irish' cases illustrate another form of case construction. The failure of the police to disclose relevant information can not only make cases appear strong to prosecutors, but actually to be strong in court—often leading, as in those cases, to wrongful convictions.[11] Other wrongful

---

6   See Jones (1994) ch 10, which includes discussion of *Confait* and several of the 'Irish' miscarriages of justice.

7   B Woffinden, 'Thumbs Down' *The Guardian*, 12 January 1999.

8   Royal Commission on Criminal Justice (RCCJ), Report (Cm 2263) (London: HMSO, 1993) ch 9.

9   A Grosskurth, 'With Science on their Side' (1992) Legal Action, May, p 7; Walker and Stockdale (1995).

10   See A Ashworth, 'Legal Aid, Human Rights and Criminal Justice' in R Young and D Wall (eds), *Access to Criminal Justice* (London: Blackstone, 1996).

11   This is further discussed in ch 9, section 4(a)(i) below. Also see Jones (1994) ch 10.

convictions resulting from lack of disclosure include *Virag*,[12] *Judith Ward*,[13] the M25 Three[14] and the Bridgewater Four.[15] In *Ward*, the police hid certain evidence from the prosecution and the defence, and the prosecution hid other evidence from the defence. Government scientists had also deliberately suppressed material unhelpful to the Crown's case, and had created a distorted picture of the forensic evidence. The Court of Appeal laid down strict rules for disclosure in *Ward* which reduced the right of the prosecution to suppress evidence.

Ward represented the high-water mark of the trend towards due process in the law of disclosure. Subsequent cases[16] began a judicial retreat back towards crime control which was supported by the Runciman Commission. Decisions such as *Ward* 'created burdens for the prosecution that go beyond what is reasonable.'[17] Runciman proposed a new scheme, the general thrust of which was enacted in the Criminal Procedure and Investigations Act 1996 (hereafter CPIA). However, this is even more crime control-oriented than Runciman's proposal, although it was presented in terms of 'efficiency', adopting the language of managerialism which, we saw in ch 1, became in vogue in the 1990s.[18] The prosecution is under a duty in most cases to disclose the case which they plan to present to the court. The problem in such cases as *Ward* lies with material which they do *not* intend to present to the court. This might, for example, be knowledge of previous convictions of prosecution witnesses which could cast doubt on their honesty, witness statements which contradict or undermine witnesses whose statements incriminate the defendant(s), or initial failures to match fingerprint evidence with the accused.[19]

12 Unreported. Discussed in Sanders (1987) 'Constructing the Case for the Prosecution'.
13 [1993] 1 WLR 619.
14 Failure to disclose that a key prosecution witness was a police informant: *Davis, Rowe and Johnson* (CA, 17 July 2000, unreported).
15 In *Kamara* (CA 9 May 2000, unreported) convictions dating from 1981 (resulting in a sentence of life imprisonment) were quashed, in part, because of the non-disclosure by the DPP of 201 witness statements (which had been marked as 'non-material'). The Court of Appeal said that at least some of these statements could not be said to be 'of no real significance'.
16 For discussion of developments until the early 1990s see P O'Connor, 'Prosecution Disclosure' in C Walker and K Starmer (eds), *Justice in Error* (London: Blackstone, 1993).
17 RCCJ (1993) p 95.
18 M Redmayne, 'Process Gains and Process Values: the CPIA 1996' (1997) 60 MLR 79. We will only give the broadest outline of the law and its problems. For detailed discussions see, for example, J Sprack, 'The Criminal Procedure and Investigations Act 1996: The Duty of Disclosure' [1997] Crim LR 308; J Niblett, *Disclosure in Criminal Proceedings* (London: Blackstone, 1997).
19 This last point was crucial in a recently discovered miscarriage of justice: *The Guardian*, 13 July 2000.

Evidential sufficiency

Under the CPIA material must be disclosed if 'in the prosecutor's opinion [it] might undermine the case for the prosecution.'[20] This is a less onerous duty than was imposed in *Ward*, primarily because the material need only be that which might undermine the prosecution (as distinct from that which might bolster the defence). Further, the test is subjective, not objective: as long as the prosecutor holds the opinion that disclosure would *not* undermine the prosecution, disclosure is not mandated, no matter how unreasonable that opinion is. Disclosure which takes place at this stage is known as 'primary disclosure'. The defence is then obliged to make a reciprocal disclosure of its case.[1] If the prosecution has material, previously undisclosed, that might assist this case, it must then make a 'secondary disclosure'.[2] Thus material which might assist a defence not originally canvassed need not be disclosed. Moreover the whole scheme depends on the honesty and competence of the police, for the CPS can only disclose to the defence that which the police let the CPS know about. The DPP himself has accepted that this could lead to miscarriages of justice.[3]

There are now, therefore, fewer rather than more restrictions on the ability of the prosecution to construct cases through non-disclosure than there were in the past. Alarm at the injustices that might be caused is widespread: 'When I go to international conferences and explain this Act to lawyers from other countries they look at me in disbelief and wonder how we can have a legal framework that is so patently unfair.'[4] In France, for example, defence lawyers have access to the full prosecution dossier.[5]

Ashworth suggests that the CPIA scheme could breach the ECHR in two ways. First, under the 'fair trial' requirements of Art 6.1, the European Court has insisted on the principle of 'equality of arms', which includes giving the defence access to all relevant evidence held by the prosecution.[6] It remains unclear whether the CPIA regime, under which secondary

---

20   CPIA, s 3 (1)(a).

1   CPIA, s 5.

2   CPIA, s 7(2).

3   *The Guardian*, 15 July 1999.

4   Law Society representative quoted by B Woffinden, 'No, you can't see. It might help your client' *The Guardian*, 4 May 1999.

5   H Trouille, 'A Look at French Criminal Procedure' [1994] Crim LR 735.

6   A Ashworth, *The Criminal Process* 2nd edn (Oxford: OUP, 1998) n 192 and cases cited therein. This principle was recently confirmed by the ECtHR in *Rowe and Davis v UK* [2000] Crim LR 584 a case in which the prosecution had decided to withhold evidence on the grounds of 'public interest immunity' without informing either the trial judge or the defence. This was found to be in breach of the Convention duty on the prosecution to disclose 'all material evidence in their possession for or against the accused.' If, in this situation, the prosecution had applied to the trial judge in an ex parte hearing (ie, no defence present) for permission not to disclose the evidence, there would have been no breach of the Convention according to the (less than emphatic) ECtHR decision in *Jasper v UK; Fitt v UK* [2000] Crim LR 586.

disclosure by the prosecution occurs only in the event of defence disclosure, will be seen as allowing breaches of this duty. Second, the defence disclosure obligation could infringe the presumption of innocence enshrined in Art 6.2 because it requires the defence to assist the prosecution.[7] However, given the tendency of common law judges to interpret domestic law as already compatible with European norms, and the 'margin of appreciation' doctrine of the European Court of Human Rights, other commentators think it unlikely that a successful challenge to these two aspects of the CPIA could be mounted under either the Human Rights Act 1998 or by taking a case to Strasbourg.[8]

(d) Is the CPS police-dependent?

We have argued in this section that, despite appearances to the contrary, the CPS is a police-dependent, rather than an independent, institution. CPS dependence on the police is partly by choice, in so far as the ethos of the two institutions are similar. It is partly a product of the performance indicators—conviction rates, primarily—established for it as criteria of success. Since both the police and the CPS are prosecuting agencies, it could not be expected that either of these conditions be otherwise. Finally, the CPS is almost entirely dependent on the police for its information about cases. Since cases are made up of nothing other than information, cases themselves are police products, and CPS decisions are therefore driven by the police. It is this structural dependency which undermines the due process potential of the CPS duty to ensure that prosecution cases pass the evidential sufficiency test. Put another way, the duty of the CPS to ensure 'equality of arms' with the defence, as required by the HRA 1998, can only be carried out to the extent that the police make this possible. This is not to say that the CPS never discontinues cases that the police would have preferred to see prosecuted. Police constructions are sometimes clumsy or unconvincing and prosecutors may in these circumstances step in to terminate an obviously flawed case. Whilst this degree of independent action is welcome it is only made possible in the first place by shoddy case construction by the police. It is thus difficult to accept that the CPS can ever be a truly independent agency.

4. THE PUBLIC INTEREST

If, and only if, a case passes the 'evidential' test, the police and CPS have then to consider whether prosecution is in the 'public interest'. This is a

7 *DPP, ex p Lee* [1999] 2 All ER 737.
8 See S Sharpe, 'HRA 1998: Article 6 and the Disclosure of Evidence in Criminal Trials' [1999] Crim LR 273.

very flexible concept. What one does or does not perceive as in the public interest will vary according to one's political and social outlook and one's experiences. If most judges are incapable of escaping this subjectivism,[9] why should we expect objectivism of police officers, the DPP, or the Attorney-General? Whether or not to prosecute 'political' offences used to be particularly controversial.[10] Examples include killings by soldiers and police officers in Northern Ireland, and alleged offences by police officers in general.[11] More obvious examples include offences against the Official Secrets Acts, including the leaking of classified information harmful to ministers but, arguably, not to the public.[12] At least with allegedly biased prosecutions the issues can be aired in public. Allegedly biased decisions not to prosecute are of such low visibility that even speculation is difficult. Occasionally an exceptional case comes to light. A senior judge who crashed her car, causing severe injuries to a passenger was deemed by the police to be in need of a 'driver rectification scheme'. Despite this, she was not prosecuted for careless driving. The reasons are not known but the decision was taken, exceptionally, by an assistant chief constable.[13]

The majority of cases involving the 'public interest' concern the question of warning as an alternative to prosecution. Also known as 'diversion' (that is, diversion from the courts) warnings are part of the armoury of all law enforcement agencies.[14] Police warnings (often referred to as 'cautioning') attracted little public controversy for many years until their use became so frequent that government and police spokespeople in the early 1990s began to blame them for rising crime rates. In this section we will look behind the generous facade of cautioning to see how far it increases freedom, and how far recent developments continue or reverse this trend.

9   As J Griffith argues in *The Politics of the Judiciary* 5th edn (London: Fontana, 1997).

10   J Edwards, *The Attorney General, Politics and the Public Interest* (London: Sweet & Maxwell, 1984).

11   For several examples see S Greer, 'Miscarriages of Criminal Justice Reconsidered' (1994) 57 MLR 58 at pp 64-65. Prosecution of police officers is considered further in ch 11.

12   C Ponting, *The Right to Know, The Inside Story of the Belgrano Affair* (London: Sphere, 1985). This 'affair' concerned the sinking during the Falklands War of an Argentinian battle-cruiser (with the loss of hundreds of lives) at a time when, as secret documents revealed, the Government and the military knew that it was sailing away from British waters.

13   *The Guardian*, 12 November 1998.

14   For an extended discussion, see, G Dingwall and C Harding, *Diversion in the Criminal Process* (London: Sweet & Maxwell, 1998).

(a) Cautioning

(i) Cautioning rates

Cautioning, along with the prosecution of weak cases, was a concern of the Philips Commission.[15] At that time only 4% of adults were cautioned for non-road traffic offences. The cautioning of juveniles was much more extensive (see Table 6.1). This was a result of encouragement of its use in the Children and Young Persons Act 1969, although the practice had existed for many years before that.[16] The extent of cautioning varied greatly from police force to police force, and it still does, as Table 6.1 and subsequent findings[17] show. Forces do change their policies, however, as is clear from the adult Metropolitan (London) figures.

Table 6.1: Caution rates (per cent of all those found guilty or cautioned for indictable offences) - selected police areas

	Juveniles		Adults	
	1978	*1992*	*1978*	*1992*
Cheshire	46	82	1	24
Cumbria	44	74	3	12
Devon/Cornwall	69	86	15	36
Met	46	78	0	30
South Yorks	47	78	9	25
Average	49	78	4	24

Variation between forces is less a product of the offence profiles of each force and more a product of offender mix (high cautioning forces have more offenders with no criminal record) and police forces pursuing different cautioning policies.[18] It seemed unfair to Philips that whether or not one

15 RCCP (1981) Report, paras 6.40-6.41.
16 J Ditchfield, Police Cautioning (Home Office Research Study no 37) (London: HMSO, 1976).
17 R Evans and R Ellis, Police Cautioning in the 1990s (Home Office Research Findings no 52) (London: HMSO, 1997). The 1998 figures for offenders cautioned as a percentage of all offenders found guilty or cautioned for the forces listed in Table 6.1 are: Cheshire (35%); Cumbria (34%); Devon and Cornwall (37%); Met (46%), and South Yorkshire (25%). Thames Valley Police had the lowest rate at 22%, Gloucestershire the highest at 47%, and the average for England and Wales was 37%: Home Office, Criminal Statistics England and Wales 1998 (Cm 4649) (London: SO, 2000).
18 G Laycock and R Tarling, 'Police Force Cautioning: Policy and Practice' (1985) 24 Howard JCJ 81.

The public interest

was prosecuted depended more on where the offence was committed than on what the offence was or who did it. The government agreed, and issued caution guidelines in 1985, 1990, and yet again in 1994.[19] These all acknowledged the variations which existed both within and between police forces and exhorted police forces to achieve greater consistency. In passing, we might question what is the point of organising police forces on a local basis under local control if local variations are regarded as unacceptable. To put the problem the other way round, what is more important: local control or consistency? It is nigh impossible to achieve both.

The use of cautioning was encouraged by government as well as social workers for some years. The ostensible reasons are stated in the 1990 circular:

> 'There is widespread agreement that the courts should only be used as a last resort, particularly for juveniles and young adults; and that diversion from the courts by means of cautioning or other forms of action may reduce the likelihood of re-offending.'[20]

Prosecution was therefore seen as potentially harmful, largely because of its stigmatising effects. By the early 1990s, however, the equally plausible view, that cautioning erodes the deterrent effect of the law and thus tacitly encourages crime, was being voiced by government. There is no reliable evidence on this issue one way or the other.[1] In all probability, prosecution will harmfully stigmatise some people, while cautioning will tacitly encourage others, and many other factors, such as the manner in which prosecution or caution is administered and the developmental stage of the individual will also be important. In other words, it is almost impossible to know what is the best strategy for any one person, and what is the best aggregate strategy for society as a whole will always be contestable. The Conservative governments of the early-mid 1990s and the subsequent Labour government of the late 1990s decided that cautioning should be

---

19 R Evans and C Wilkinson, 'Variation in Police Cautioning Policy and Practice in England and Wales' (1990) 29 Howard JCJ 155.

20 Home Office, The cautioning of offenders (Home Office Circular 59/1990) para 7.

1 S Keith, 'The Criminal Histories of those Cautioned in 1985 and 1988' (1992) 32 Home Office Research Bulletin 44, examined the conviction rates of young adults cautioned in 1985. She found that they were no more likely to be convicted within two years of being cautioned than young adults who were prosecuted at the age of 19. The overall conviction rates (for offenders of all ages) within two years of being cautioned was about 13%. This might suggest that the deterrent effect of cautioning on further offending is similar to that of prosecution. On the other hand, studies of reconviction rates are not studies of reoffending and so figures of this kind should be used with the utmost caution (and so say both of us).

restricted, more on the basis of the electoral appeal of these policies than their basis in research.[2] As we shall see later, the 1994 guidelines discouraged the use of 'repeat cautions' and the Crime and Disorder Act 1998 carries that policy through into the new framework for delivering 'reprimands' and 'warnings' to 10-17-year-olds. As Table 6.2 shows, cautioning of both adults and juveniles rose sharply in the 1980s and early 1990s, and then levelled off and fell as a result of this change in government policy. Despite the recent fall, cautioning levels remain far higher now than there were when the Philips Commission reported in the early 1980s.

Table 6.2: Caution rates (per cent of all found guilty or cautioned for indictable offences)

	Males			Females		
	14-17	*18-20*	*21+*	*14-17*	*18-20*	*21+*
1982	38	3	4	65	6	12
1984	45	5	5	71	10	16
1986	44	9	10	70	18	26
1988	49	12	12	70	24	29
1990	58	19	16	77	34	34
1992	63	29	23	84	50	46
1994	60	34	25	81	50	44
1996	54	35	26	76	50	44
1997	52	35	26	72	48	42
1998	(nk)	34	24	(nk)	46	39

(Source: Home Office, Criminal Statistics England and Wales 1998, Cm 4649) (London: SO, 2000), Table 5.3. (London: SO, 2000), and Home Office Statistical Bulletin 21/99) (nk = not known).

A number of issues arise from these trends. Firstly, more cautioning does not necessarily mean more consistent cautioning. Nor does it necessarily mean the right people being cautioned for the right reasons. A more fundamental problem is that of the overall level of prosecution and cautioning. Police prosecution rates remain much higher than those of other law enforcement agencies, such as the Health and Safety Executive and the Inland Revenue. Are there any good reasons for this? Underlying these issues is the most intractable problem of all: the control of prosecution and cautioning.

2   R Evans, 'Cautioning: Counting the cost of retrenchment' [1994] Crim LR 566; A Sanders, 'What principles underlie criminal justice policy in the 1990s?' (1998) 18 OJLS 533.

(ii) The framework of cautioning

The pattern of cautioning is affected by the organisational structure within which decision making takes place. The process begins with the investigating officer's opinion regarding what action should be taken in a case. This is communicated to the custody officer in cases where the suspect is arrested. The custody officer must then decide whether to charge, to arrange or administer a caution immediately or to release the suspect and report to a senior officer to decide whether to recommend caution or summons. Immediate cautions and informal warnings are used in most police forces but usually only for juveniles and minor motoring matters.[3] Suspects who are not arrested are simply reported. In the past, when senior officers considered the cases of juvenile suspects who were reported in either of the above ways, they often used to pass them onto a multi-disciplinary juvenile liaison bureau (JLB) which would either recommend a disposition to the police or, occasionally, have the decision delegated to it by the police.[4] In a few areas, there was this type of arrangement for adults too, especially for young adults aged 18–21.[5]

Now, under the Crime and Disorder Act 1998, juvenile caution decisions are returned to the police. JLBs - dubbed 'juvenile let-off bureaux' by some police - were seen as too 'soft'. The Act establishes, for the first time, a statutory framework for cautioning under 18s. Instead of 'cautions' it refers to 'reprimands' for first warnings (if the offence is not too serious) and 'warnings' for offenders who have been 'reprimanded' once or who commit an offence which is too serious for a reprimand. No-one who has been previously reprimanded may be reprimanded again, and no-one who has been warned may be warned again (unless two years have elapsed since the first warning). Reprimands are intended to replace informal juvenile warnings.

For under 18s there are two pre-conditions to be met in order to reprimand or warn: sufficient evidence of the offender's guilt to give a realistic prospect of conviction; and admission of the offence by the offender. An 'appropriate adult' must be present if the offender is under 17.[6] For adults there are the same pre-conditions, plus the need for the

3 Evans and Ellis (1997); Dingwall and Harding (1998) ch 7.
4 For a description of such a bureau, see S Uglow, A Dart, A Bottomley and C Hale, 'Cautioning Juveniles - Multi-Agency Impotence' [1992] Crim LR 632.
5 For examples, see R Evans, 'Evaluating Young Adult Diversion Schemes in the Metropolitan Police District' [1993] Crim LR 490 and J Dignan, 'Repairing the Damage' (1992) 32 BJ Crim 453.
6 Crime and Disorder Act 1998 (CADA), s 65 (1) and (5). See ch 4, section 2(c) for discussion of 'appropriate adults'. On the CADA generally see R Leng, R Taylor and M Wasik, *Blackstone's Guide to the Crime and Disorder Act 1998* (London: Blackstone, 1998).

offender's informed consent.[7] These pre-conditions are intended to ensure that, because a caution is a statement of guilt (which can be cited in court), the offender really is guilty and would be convicted if prosecuted. They are due process safeguards, intended to inhibit the police from cautioning whenever they adjudge a suspect to be guilty but they cannot, or would rather not, collect sufficient evidence to support a prosecution.

As a mechanism for protecting innocent suspects from administrative determinations of guilt, the pre-conditions have been found wanting. Earlier guidelines with the same pre-conditions were found to be breached on occasion.[8] Indeed, Sanders found that some cautions were administered precisely because there was insufficient evidence, and sometimes in the absence of consent or an admission.[9] Nor is consent or an admission a safeguard in reality. Young found that juveniles were prepared to admit and consent to almost anything to escape from the 'coercive jaws' of the criminal process.[10] Evans found that 22% of juvenile cautions in his study were in cases where there was no clear admission of guilt (in many, there were in fact denials).[11] Dignan echoes this in relation to adults, observing that offenders were required to 'bargain in the shadow of the law'.[12] In *Metropolitan Police Comr, ex p Thompson*[13] the cautioning inspector admitted that he often offered a caution and then asked the alleged offender if he understood that this amounted to an admission of the offence, with the implicit threat that if the suspect did not agree to this, he or she would be prosecuted instead of cautioned. Although the Divisional Court held that cautions offered as an inducement to confess, such as happened here, are invalid, it clearly had been a common practice and is unlikely to have been eradicated as a result of this one case. Another caution was quashed by the Divisional Court after a juvenile was incorrectly told that what he did (watch his cousin shoplift) amounted to theft. It was on this basis that he admitted his 'guilt' and consented to be cautioned. But as there was insufficient evidence to prosecute, there was no informed consent.[14] The Crime and Disorder Act 1998 has now taken away the requirement that juveniles consent to a caution, which may further encourage the police to think that they can impose reprimands and warnings as they please.

7   Home Office, The Cautioning of Offenders (Home Office Circular 18/1994).
8   Dignan (1992).
9   Sanders (1998) 'The Limits to Diversion from Prosecution'.
10   R Young, 'The Sandwell Mediation and Reparation Scheme' (Birmingham: West Midlands Probation Service, 1987).
11   R Evans, The Conduct of Police Interviews with Juveniles (Royal Commission on Criminal Justice Research Study no 8) (London: HMSO, 1993) p 41.
12   Dignan (1992) p 465.
13   [1997] 1 WLR 1519.
14   *Metropolitan Police Comr, ex p P* (1995) 160 JP 367 discussed by Evans [1996].

As in other contexts, the attempt to impose due process standards on the police through rules to be enforced by the police themselves appears doomed to failure. The pre-conditions to cautioning, reprimanding and warning are largely presentational rules, giving the appearance of due process, but having little effect on the police. The courts will not intervene except in exceptional circumstances, as Simon Brown LJ made clear in *ex p P*:

'Nothing contained in my judgment is intended to offer any sort of general encouragement to those cautioned to challenge the legality of their cautions. I accept Mr Lewis' submission in broad terms. Police officers responsible for applying this circular must enjoy a wide margin of appreciation as to the nature of the case and whether the preconditions for a caution are satisfied. As Watkins LJ made clear in *ex p L*, one would only rarely expect those who have been cautioned to succeed in showing that the decision was fatally flawed by a clear breach of the guidelines.'[15]

Thus deciding whether or not to caution remains nearly always a matter for the police alone. Moreover, we shall see that investigating officers who favour prosecution against caution can, as with those who favour prosecution against NFA, have the individual charged with little chance of resistance from the custody officer. It is now clear from all the official guidance and legislation that, in every case where there is sufficient evidence, the desirability of prosecution (as against caution or NFA) should be considered rather than assumed. The former Attorney-General's statement of the opportunity principle, to the effect that prosecution should only take place if it is in the public interest, appears to create a presumption against prosecution. This contrasts with the decision-making structure described above, which gives enormous power to arresting officers to secure the decision they favour, and with the changed emphasis of the cautioning policies of 1994 and 1998.

(iii) Cautioning criteria

The 1994 guidelines state that, if the cautioning pre-conditions are met, the police should take into account the 'public interest' criteria set out in the Code for Crown Prosecutors. The Crime and Disorder Act 1998 (CADA) provides similarly for the under 18s.[16] These criteria include:

15   Quoted from LEXIS 9 May 1995.
16   CADA, s 65 (1).

- the nature of the offence;
- the likely penalty if the offender were to be convicted;
- the offender's age, state of health, previous criminal history and attitude towards the offence (including offers to compensate victims, and so forth);
- the impact of the offence on the victim.

Factors making prosecution more likely include premeditation, the involvement of a group of offenders, a discriminatory motive, or the suspect being under a court order such as bail. The 1994 guidelines embody similar, although less generous, criteria to those of the past so it is not surprising that they have not substantially reduced disparity. For in any one case many of these criteria pull in different directions. An offender may have a criminal record but commit a minor offence for which he has compensated the victim; or may commit a relatively serious offence but have no previous criminal history. The victim may favour or oppose prosecution, or simply be indifferent.

Guidelines such as these suffer many faults.[17] We mention but three here. Firstly, vagueness: how serious, for instance, is 'serious'? In the *Kent* case, the decision to prosecute was said by the court to be a 'harsh' one, but the seriousness of the offence (assault) made it acceptable.[18] Seriousness is a subjective matter. Secondly, they are manipulable by the police. Cases can be constructed to seem more or less serious, as we shall see in relation to the views of victims of domestic violence.[19] Finally, the cautioning criteria are non-prioritised. In other words, it is impossible to say whether a given decision is right or wrong if an offender 'scores' high on one criterion and low on another. The guidelines explicitly state that the victim's consent is not essential to caution, but no guidance is provided on how far the victim's views should outweigh other criteria. Thus countless pieces of research have found the police justifying non-prosecution of some cases by reference to the views of the victim, but at the same time prosecuting other cases where the victim did not want prosecution.[20] Only 'seriousness' is prioritised, as this is a crucial criterion for deciding whether or not a repeat warning can be given to a juvenile.

The Association of Chief Police Officers (ACPO) acknowledges this lack of prioritisation. It therefore issued a 'gravity factor' scale to accompany the 1994 guidelines which allocates scores to mitigating and aggravating factors. However, one-third of all forces do not use this scale, and even in forces that do, officers who wish to deviate from it can and

---

17   For a longer discussion, see A Ashworth, 'The "Public Interest" Element in Prosecutions' [1987] Crim LR 595.
18   *Chief Constable of the Kent Constabulary, ex p L* [1993] 1 All ER 756.
19   See Clarkson et al [1994].
20   See, for example, A Sanders, 'Personal Violence and Pubic Order' (1988) 16 IJ Soc L 359; Evans (1991); Clarskon et al [1994].

do.[1] Rather than the criteria in these guidelines guiding decision-making, they end up justifying it. Thus, Evans found that a 'caution consideration chart' given to custody officers to encourage them to caution higher proportions of young adults was known by custody officers as the 'justification to charge sheet'. He comments that: 'The most common use of the chart was not as an aid to decision-making but as a written justification of a decision that had already been made.'[2] As with the pre-conditions discussed under the previous subheading, the application of ostensibly inhibitory criteria is left to the very institution which they are supposed to inhibit. Not surprisingly, this renders the criteria largely presentational. This all seemed to be lost on the Runciman Commission, which did not address itself to the abuses and inconsistencies of the cautioning system and recommended that the police retain their current responsibilities.[3] It also seems to have been lost on the government, whose Crime and Disorder Act 1998 ends what little involvement by non-police agencies previously existed in diversion decisions.

(iv) Restorative police cautioning

There are, broadly speaking, four main responses to crime: *punitive*, where the object is to punish offenders and to deter others; *rehabilitative*, where the object is to encourage offenders to desist or teach them how to avoid the situations which lead to offending; *restorative*, where the object is to enable or order the offender to make good the damage caused to the victim and/or the community, and, finally, *doing nothing* in the belief that the offence was a 'one-off', that the offender will 'grow out of crime', that intervention of any kind will do more to encourage than to discourage crime, or that the offence was so trivial that any official response would be an over-reaction. These different ideas underlie not only sentencing but also the process of deciding whether or not to prosecute. Most prosecutions are undertaken on a punitive basis, although not necessarily only on this basis, given the possibility of rehabilitative or restorative sentencing. Most cautioning used to be on the 'do nothing' basis, as cautioning led to little or no further action.[4] Informal warnings, and now, for juveniles, 'reprimands' under the Crime and Disorder Act 1998 are likely to remain on this basis.

---

1   Evans and Ellis (1997).
2   R Evans, 'Evaluating Young Adult Diversion Schemes in the Metropolitan Police District' [1993] Crim LR 490 at p 494.
3   RCCJ, (1993) Report, p 82.
4   Although the small amount of research on the way cautioning is administered shows that it is sometimes highly punitive: M Lee, *Youth, Crime, and Police Work* (Basingstoke: Macmillan, 1998).

Juvenile 'warnings' under the Crime and Disorder Act 1998, however, are intended to be primarily shaped by rehabilitative and restorative ideals. Everyone 'warned' will be assessed by a 'youth offending team' for a rehabilitative programme. All offenders who are positively assessed will be referred to an appropriate programme. The programmes should vary according to types of offender and types of offence. But participation is neither a legal obligation, nor a condition of receiving a warning, although non-participation (and any reasons given for non-participation) will be recorded and can be cited in future court proceedings.[5]

It is too early to know how these rehabilitative arrangements will work in practice. But they build upon existing 'restorative' or 'caution-plus' practices. These developed on a small scale in the 1980s and 1990s in many police forces, usually in relation to juveniles.[6] At one time the ethos of such schemes was primarily rehabilitative. But increasingly the cautioning process is used to encourage offenders to acknowledge the harm caused by the offence and to make restorative gestures such as apology or compensation. Some schemes have built on Braithwaite's theory that deviant behaviour can best be reduced by responding to it with reintegrative shaming.[7] These schemes aim to make offenders ashamed of their behaviour in a way which promotes their reintegration into their community. In a leading innovative development, all reprimands, warnings and cautions in the Thames Valley area are now intended to be restorative in character, and many take the form of a restorative 'conference' in which offenders, victims and their respective 'supporters' are invited to participate. Offenders tell their 'story' and are asked what harm they think they caused. Victims and their supporters put their 'side', and the offenders' supporters are also asked how the offence affected them.[8] This model of cautioning is supported by the Youth Justice Board, which has funded the training of other police services by Thames Valley Police and its partners. In an exploratory evaluation of restorative cautioning practices in one Thames Valley Police area it was found that, although there was little of the punitiveness that Lee observed in traditional cautioning,[9] the police emphasised the 'last chance' nature of the caution and the supposedly dire consequences of re-offending. Young and Goold argue that this element of overkill where the offence is relatively minor could undermine the

5   CADA, s 66.
6   Evans and Ellis (1997). But for a discussion of a scheme catering for adults too, see G Hughes, A Pilkington and R Leistan, 'Diversion in a Culture of Severity' 37 (1998) Howard JCJ 16.
7   J Braithwaite, *Crime, Shame and Reintegration* (Cambridge: CUP, 1989).
8   See further R Young, 'Integrating a Multi-Victim Perspective into Criminal Justice Through Restorative Justice Conferences' in A Crawford and J Goodey (eds), *Integrating a Victim Perspective within Criminal Justice* (Aldershot: Ashgate, 2000).
9   Lee (1998).

legitimacy of the process.[10] Unfortunately, warnings administered under the Crime and Disorder Act 1998 will indeed be of a 'last chance' kind, and so the police will be right to continue to emphasise this, however misguided this policy is in respect of some incidents and some offenders.

The new youth justice framework and the practices taking place within it encompass an uneasy mix of penal philosophies, and many current 'restorative justice' initiatives are attempting to be both rehabilitative and directly victim-oriented.[11] These objectives are laudable but not always mutually compatible. This goes to the root of the problem of multiple objectives discussed in ch 1 which gave rise to our proposed 'freedom' perspective. Restorative justice projects need to calibrate the degrees of freedom given and taken away to both offenders and victims (both current and future) by these projects, taking into account the importance of securing the human rights of all concerned, in order to assess the way in which the greatest overall amount of freedom can be secured.

(b) Police working rules and cautioning

We argue above that the cautioning 'rules' do not inhibit the police in any significant fashion. The official public interest criteria are replaced in practice by the unofficial police interest criteria. These working criteria may, however, lead to undesirable patterns of decision-making: cautioning of those who should be NFAd, cautioning of those who should be prosecuted, and prosecution of those who should be cautioned or NFAd.

There are two types of suspect who are cautioned when they should be NFAd. There are those who, as we have already observed, do not meet the three pre-conditions, and there are those whose offences are so trivial that normally no action would have been taken against them. Caution is supposed to be an alternative to prosecution, not to no action. Yet there is evidence that at least some of the increase in cautioning represents more offenders being drawn into the system. This phenomenon—net widening—was warned against in the 1990 cautioning guidelines although this warning has been dropped in subsequent versions. Its existence is, however, undeniable.[12] Indeed, since it has also happened with Scottish

10   R Young and B Goold, 'Restorative Police Cautioning in Aylesbury' [1999] Crim LR 126.

11   See J Dignan, 'The Crime and Disorder Act and the prospects for restorative justice' [1999] Crim LR 48; A Morris and L Gelsthorpe, 'Something Old, Something Borrowed, Something Blue, But Something New? A Comment on the Prospects for Restorative Justice under the Crime and Disorder Act 1998' [2000] Crim LR 18 and A Sanders, Taking Account of Victims in the Criminal Justice System, (Edinburgh: Scottish Office, 1999) pp 14-16.

12   Ditchfield (1976); H Parker, M Casburn and D Turnbull, *Receiving Juvenile Justice* (Oxford: Basil Blackwell, 1981); Sanders (1988) 'The Limits to Diversion from Prosecution'; Dignan (1992).

'prosecutor fines', it appears to be an endemic feature of all (so-called) alternatives to prosecution.[13]

If net-widening in a particular case is desired by the victim then it may be defensible under restorative justice principles, but police motives are rarely determined by the wishes of the victim alone. As far as the police are concerned, cautions are often as useful as prosecutions and they avoid a considerable amount of paperwork. It makes it worth arresting where it might otherwise not be worthwhile and, of course, where there is insufficient evidence it secures some kind of 'result'. Moreover, if the caution is presented as a favour to the suspect, it provides, or maintains, the basis of a relationship on which future 'deals' can be built. What is certain is that suspects are never given the choice between NFA and caution, even in cases where, if the suspect did not agree to a caution, the police would simply take no further action. Instead, in these cases, the choice is presented to the suspect as either caution or prosecution, and this usually produces the result the police seek. If this is bargaining in the shadow of the law, the nature of the bargains struck will reflect the unequal status of the parties involved.

Cautioning those who should be prosecuted is advantageous for the suspects involved, but may not be for their victims or for the public at large. An officer can secure this result by constructing cases to seem trivial. Sometimes the offence is portrayed as 'petty', 'a domestic' or 'out of character'.[14] Assessment of what is in character, again as with stop-search and arrest, is fraught with difficulties. Middle class and white people in particular appear to benefit from social stereotyping which see some groups as less prone to offending than others.[15] Others are treated leniently because they are useful to the police. Informers, for example, are often given an informal warning or caution rather than prosecuted as part of maintaining a mutually beneficial relationship. It is no accident that control of cautioning remains largely with the investigating officer, for cautioning can be an adjunct of other aspects of policing.

Where policing considerations such as order and authority point the other way, offenders are prosecuted and not cautioned. In one of McConville et al's cases, there was a fight outside a club which was notorious for minor disorder. The arresting officer said that the defendant would normally have been cautioned for his part in the fight but 'the reason he was charged was because we are objecting to the licence at [the club] . . .

---

13   Duff (1993). Also see discussion in section 8.
14   See, for example, Bowling (1998) p 251.
15   See M Fitzgerald, Ethnic Minorities and the Criminal Justice System (Royal Commission on Criminal Justice, Research Study no 20) (London: HMSO, 1993); A Sanders, 'Class Bias in Prosecutions' (1985) 24 Howard JCJ 76 and McConville et al (1991) p 109.

The public interest

and the more charges we've got the better'.[16] Kemp et al observe that it is not so much what the victim wants but who the victim is that counts.[17] When business victims demand prosecution, they generally get their way, even when the police have reservations.[18] And just as assessment of character and attitude to the offence can work to the benefit of some groups of people, it works in the opposite direction for those with a 'bad attitude' or 'suspect character'. In one case examined by McConville et al, a youth with previous convictions had picked up a Mars bar and broken a piece off. Asked why they had charged rather than cautioned, the police described the defendant as a 'toe-rag' who had been suspected of shoplifting on several occasions but never caught.[19]

Research carried out in the 1980s found that large numbers of cautionable cases were prosecuted.[20] Now that caution rates are a lot higher, it is likely that far fewer cautionable cases are being prosecuted (although net widening doubtless also accounts for an unquantifiable proportion of the higher numbers cautioned). However, there is no reason to believe that much has changed in the cases where it is important for the police that a cautionable case be prosecuted. The same working rules that lead to the construction of 'suspiciousness' on the street, for example, still make prosecution more likely than caution for some types of suspect. Thus, the same patterns of race bias which can be observed in street policing seem to operate here.[1] Evans found Afro-Caribbean juveniles to be prosecuted far more often than white juveniles in a study of the Metropolitan Police. He comments that 'this cannot be explained in terms of any differences in offence patterns for different ethnic groups or differences in the proportions of first offenders.'[2] After reviewing several pieces of research carried out throughout the 1970s and 1980s (but not including the above study by Evans), Fitzgerald concludes that: 'Once arrested, Afro-Caribbeans are less likely to be cautioned than whites and may be less likely than Asians to have no further action taken against them.'[3] She pins the blame on indirect factors rather than racism. She notes

16   McConville et al (1991) p 112.

17   C Kemp, C Norris and N Fielding, 'Legal Manoeuvres in Police Handling of Disputes' in D Farrington and S Walklate (eds), *Offenders and Victims: Theory and Policy* (London: British Society of Criminology, 1992).

18   See the examples cited by McConville et al (1991) pp 113-14.

19   McConville, Sanders and Leng (1991) pp 113-14.

20   See eg R Evans, 'Police Cautioning and the Young Adult Offender' [1991] Crim LR 598 and McConville et al (1991) ch 7.

1   See ch 2, section 3(a), and ch 3, section 4(c), above, for related discussion in the context of street policing.

2   R Evans, 'Comparing Young Adult and Juvenile Cautioning in the Metropolitan Police District' [1993] Crim LR 572 at p 576.

3   Fitzgerald (1993) p 33. Phillips and Brown (1998) p 92 also found that both black and Asian suspects were less likely to be cautioned than were white suspects.

that Afro-Caribbeans are less likely to admit the offence (thus disqualifying themselves from a caution or warning), are more likely to be disadvantaged by the application of 'social' criteria (such as domestic circumstances) in an 'ethno-centric' way (resulting in prosecution being seen as in the public interest), and tend to have more previous convictions and cautions (possibly because of earlier biased decisions). Some doubt on Fitzgerald's view that direct discrimination is not responsible is raised by Philips and Brown's finding that a far higher proportion of black and Asian defendants have their cases discontinued by the CPS than do white defendants. In typically guarded Home Office-speak they say: 'The possibility must be considered that, where the defendant was from an ethnic minority group, the police were more likely to submit for prosecution cases in which the evidence was weaker than average or where the public interest was against prosecution.'[4]

The custody officer is supposed to be a protection here. But as with evidential issues, the custody officer either acts as a rubber stamp or empathises with the arresting officer. Most custody officers, like police officers in general, are against extensive cautioning for adults in particular.[5] One custody officer put it this way:

'When someone sits and looks at it in a file coldly the next morning it probably gives them a slightly different picture to what I see—the toe-rag coming in effing and blinding at all and sundry . . . Straight away you think "well yeah, okay, here we go", perhaps an independent would say no, no, NFA.'[6]

Moreover, custody officers rely on the arresting officer alone for their information about the suspect. As one told McConville et al, 'I'm dependent completely on what the officer says happened.'[7] As with evidential matters, what the arresting officer does and does not say determines the construction of the case as serious or trivial, and the construction of the suspect either as a public enemy or as a temporarily lapsed paragon.

It may well be that the relatively low cautioning rates of Afro-Caribbean, as compared to white, and poor, as compared to middle class, suspects are contrary to the principle of equality of treatment.[8] But the chances of any one member of a marginalised social group proving discrimination *in his or her case,* given the ability of the police to construct cases, would be vanishingly small except in particularly blatant cases.

4   Phillips and Brown (1998) p 148. See also Mhlanga (1999) summarised in: s 95 Findings no 1 (London: Home Office, 2000).
5   Evans [1993] p 577.
6   McConville et al (1991) p 115.
7   McConville et al (1991) p 122.
8   Art 14 ECHR.

The public interest

(c) Case construction, the public interest and the CPS

One of the functions of the CPS is to exercise control over the 'public interest' dimension of prosecutions, although it cannot, of course, do anything about cases which were cautioned when they should have been NFAd or prosecuted. Indeed, the police can even tie the hands of the CPS by promising that a case will be dropped. Although discontinuance is the prerogative of the CPS alone, it has been held to be an abuse of process for prosecution to be continued after a promise, even from the police, that it will be dropped.[9] In this case the 'deal' was discontinuance in exchange for the suspect giving evidence for the prosecution in a murder trial. This illustrates both the structurally weak position of the CPS as compared to the police, and the way the police use prosecution and non-prosecution in the 'public interest' as part of broader policing strategies. Although this is evidence of the power of the crime control perspective, it is not necessarily antithetical to the freedom perspective for prosecutions in relatively minor cases to be dropped in order to secure convictions in serious cases. The problem, however, is that the prosecution in the serious case may be fatally compromised once it becomes known that a key Crown witness received an inducement to give evidence. This provides the police with an incentive to suppress evidence of the 'deal'. Such deals are therefore not conducive to openness and fairness within the criminal process: a key hallmark of a free society. This illustrates the importance of not applying the freedom perspective in a crude short-term manner.

The CPS can, in principle, ensure that cautionable cases are not prosecuted by discontinuing them. As discussed in sub-section (a) above, the 'public interest' criteria in the 1994 version of the Code for Crown Prosecutors explicitly correspond with the criteria in the Home Office cautioning guidelines.[10] Thus the step back, in the latter, from the previous enthusiasm for cautioning, is reflected in the 1994 Code: 'In cases of any seriousness, a prosecution will usually take place unless there are public interest factors tending against prosecution which clearly outweigh those tending in favour.'[11] Given the research showing that many cautionable

9   *Rv Croydon Justices, ex p Dean* [1993] QB 769.
10 That the changes in prosecution policy embodied in the 1994 CPS Code of Practice were driven by the Government's issuing of new cautioning guidelines for the police casts further doubt on the 'independence' of the CPS. See the discussion in Ashworth and Fionda [1994].
11 Para 6.2. See Ashworth and Fionda [1994] and A Sanders, 'The Silent Code' (1994) 144 NLJ 946 for critical appraisals of this version of the Code. Note that the CPS Code has not yet caught up with the Crime and Disorder Act. Under the Code, prosecutors should consider dropping cases involving minor offences even though the police are prevented from giving repeated warnings. See R Leng, R Taylor and M Wasik, *Blackstone's Guide to the Crime and Disorder Act 1998* (London: Blackstone, 1998) pp 75-83.

cases are still being prosecuted we would nonetheless expect the discontinuance of at least some such cases. We saw earlier that discontinuances rose from the late 1980s to the mid-1990s.[12] Unfortunately, the official statistics do not make it possible to ascertain how many of these are cautionable cases. Some research findings help fill this gap in our knowledge. Home Office research by Crisp and Moxon, and by Phillips and Brown, looked at large samples of cases in the early and mid-1990s respectively.[13] Nearly one-third of the discontinuances were on 'public interest' grounds. However, in only 4% of cases in the research of Crisp and Moxon, and 8% in that of Phillips and Brown, did the CPS recommend that a caution be substituted. Given the propensity of the police to initiate prosecutions in cautionable cases these figures seem low. On the other hand, by the time the CPS discontinued cases it was sometimes too late to suggest a caution instead (because the matter had become 'stale'). A more realistic view of the proportion of cases discontinued by the CPS that should have been cautioned by the police on public interest grounds (rather than marked for prosecution) would be somewhere between around 6% and a third. Ultimately, it remains unclear whether all the cautionable cases are now being correctly identified by the CPS. We doubt that they are, for the reasons given below.

When McConville et al did their research, soon after the CPS was established, few cases were discontinued on grounds of cautionability. They found that, as with evidential sufficiency, there was little incentive for the CPS to drop cases on this basis. They also found that the CPS and the police had similar outlooks and evaluated cases in much the same way. In one case, where a prosecutor did want to discontinue, the police objected (they sought prosecution for deterrent purposes) and the prosecutor was overruled by his boss. Even lip service was rarely paid to the 'public interest'.[14] There is scant reason to think that the incentive structure and value system of the CPS has changed dramatically since that research was done.

The most important problem for the CPS, however, is that police construction makes it often difficult and sometimes impossible to identify cautionable cases. Factors which could point towards caution or other forms of diversion are downplayed in the file, or such facts are not brought out by the police because of failure to ask appropriate questions. Thus in one of McConville et al's cases, the file did not reveal the character of the victim, giving the erroneous impression that an assault on him was unprovoked. Some prosecutors recognise this problem, although most of

12 CPS, Annual Report 1990-1991 (London: HMSO, 1991) p 11 and CPS, Annual Report 1992-1993 (London: HMSO, 1993) p 18.
13 D Crisp and D Moxon, Case screening by the CPS (Home Office Research Study no 137) (London: HMSO, 1994); Phillips and Brown (1998).
14 M McConville and A Sanders, 'Fairness and the CPS' (1992) 142 NLJ 120.

Crisp's respondents appeared to be inappropriately—perhaps even irresponsibly—sanguine.[15] As a Scottish prosecutor told Moody and Tombs 'they [the police] usually don't do it deliberately but they can do it because they decide that the fiscal doesn't want to know that, doesn't need to know that.'[16] And, of course, there is exaggeration. Evans comments that when one digs:

'beneath the legal labels of offences to assess their true seriousness . . . a significant number of "trivial" offences are dealt with by the criminal justice system with legal labels attached that exaggerate their seriousness.'[17]

McConville et al argue that police construction of all these kinds is to be expected and that the CPS attitudes and practices uncovered by their research are entrenched features of an agency whose raison d'être is prosecution. As with the police, they argue, if one is concerned with the protection of the interests of suspects, the last place to seek that protection is in an agency with an adversarial relationship with those suspects which, moreover, depends for all of its information on another agency with an adversarial relationship with suspects.

Were they too pessimistic in assuming that the CPS was incapable or unwilling to fulfil its statutory obligations? While the CPS is undoubtedly discontinuing more cautionable cases now than it used to, the issue—as with police cautioning itself—is whether they are discontinuing as often as they should and when they should. It is unlikely that they are doing either. In 1988 the VERA Institute conducted an experiment in one court with the co-operation of police, CPS and probation services. Random samples of less serious adult cases were allocated to either an 'experimental' or a 'control' group. Probation officers took the experimental group cases and collected information relevant to cautionability which they passed onto the CPS. Before this intervention, the discontinuance rate in this court on 'public interest' grounds was 1%. This rose to 4% in the control group and 7% in the experimental group. In the month immediately following the intervention the rate fell to 2%.[18] After that, a few additional experimental

15   D Crisp, 'Standardising Prosecutions' (1993) 34 Home Office Research Bulletin 13.
16   S Moody and J Tombs, *Prosecution in the Public Interest* (Edinburgh: Scottish Academic Press, 1982) pp 47-48. See also L Gelsthorpe and H Giller, 'More Justice for Juveniles' [1990] Crim LR 153 and S Elliman, 'Independent Information for the CPS' (1990) 140 NLJ 812 and 864.
17   R Evans, 'Police Cautioning and the Young Adult Offender' [1991] Crim LR 598 at 605.
18   C Stone, Public Interest Case Assessment (London: Inner London Probation Service, 1989).

'public interest case assessment' (PICA) schemes, as they are known, were established, with similar results.[19] Unfortunately, the costs of running these schemes were, the Home Office researchers concluded, greater than the savings achieved through diversion of these cases from the courts. However, this is partly because, despite the extra information, the CPS still did not discontinue all the cases which they could have: many of the PICA cases that continued received a conditional discharge in court, suggesting sufficient non-seriousness to warrant discontinuance. It seems that, despite the CPS view that 'times have changed' since the research of McConville et al, the CPS mind-set is still that of a *prosecution* agency rather than, as in countries like Holland[20] a *criminal justice* agency.

PICA schemes show that just sensitising prosecutors to the issue leads to more (albeit insufficient) discontinuances. Thus discontinuances rose in both the 'control' and 'experimental' groups in the original VERA Institute study. More important, however, is the fact that the extra information provided by PICA schemes—which the police either do not collect or which they keep from the CPS—enables the CPS to make their own independent decisions. Clearly the independence of the CPS is a chimera without independent sources of information. Until schemes like this become widespread, the CPS will not be able, even if it is willing, to fulfil its statutory obligations.

How, then, is the rise in 'public interest' discontinuances to be explained? Crisp and Moxon, and Phillips and Brown, found that well over half of them were because a nominal penalty was expected, the defendant was charged with other serious offences or the offence was in some other way too trivial.[1] The Code for Crown Prosecutors requires prosecutors to consider whether a case is too trivial to warrant prosecution: 'particularly where the offence is triable on indictment when Crown Prosecutors should also weigh the likely penalty with the likely length and cost of the proceedings.'[2] One plausible explanation for the rise in discontinuances would be that, at a time of managerial-style constraints on public expenditure, Crown Prosecutors have become increasingly focused on issues of cost effectiveness in prosecutions. This leaves open the question of whether cautionability on other grounds (such as old age and mental disorder) is being spotted and acted upon as often as it should be.

In the absence of more detailed analyses of CPS practice in the 1990s, the Runciman Commission's judgment that the public interest 'part of the

19   D Crisp, C Whittaker and J Harris, Public Interest Case Assessment Schemes, (Home Office Research Study no 138) (London: Home Office, 1995).
20   C Brants and S Field, 'Discretion and Accountability in Prosecution', in C Harding, P Fennell, N Jorg and B Swart (eds), *Criminal Justice in Europe: A Comparative Study* (Oxford: Clarendon, 1995).
1   Crisp and Moxon (1994); Phillips and Brown (1998).
2   Para 8(i).

Code is being appropriately applied'[3] seems too hasty. As it is, the Home Office research to which it had access comments that 'prosecutors have no way of knowing what gaps there are in the information they receive'.[4] The Runciman Commission's recommendation that PICA schemes should be expanded 'across the country'[5] suggests that it too should have realised that the CPS is not applying the Code satisfactorily at present (otherwise there would be no need for PICA schemes). The main failure of the Runciman Commission in this respect, however, is its failure to consider whether the CPS is capable of working as intended, with or without PICA schemes, given the adversarial structure of the criminal justice system. Our argument here is the same as it is regarding the evidential test in section 3(d): that the CPS is largely police-dependent.

5. NON-POLICE PROSECUTION AGENCIES

Substantial numbers of prosecutions are brought by non-police agencies. Health and Safety offences are dealt with by the Health and Safety Executive (HSE), pollution offences by the Environment Agency, tax evasion by the Inland Revenue, TV licence evasion by the Television Licensing Authority (TVLA), Social Security fraud by the Department of Social Security (DSS), and other frauds by various agencies including the Department of Trade and Industry, and the Serious Fraud Office (SFO). Local authorities are responsible for all sorts of offences including harassment and unlawful eviction of tenants. The British 'opportunity' principle has enabled each body to develop its own prosecution policies and patterns which are often radically different to those of the police.[6]

Many of the 'suspects' dealt with by these agencies are companies. Their offences ought to be of major concern to policy makers and the public. For some 500 people die at work every year (by comparison, there are less than 1,000 'official' homicides each year), thousands die each year from occupational diseases (estimates vary wildly) and there are some 18,000 major work-related injuries annually.[7] The Health and Safety Executive estimates that in most of these incidents the employer was in breach of the

---

3   RCCJ (1993) Report, p 77.
4   Crisp (1993) p 15.
5   RCCJ (1993) Report, p 83.
6   K Lidstone, R Hogg, and F Sutcliffe, Prosecution by Private Individuals and Non-Police Agencies (Royal Commission on Criminal Procedure Research Study no 10) (London: HMSO, 1981).
7   F Pearce and S Tombs, 'Ideology, Hegemony and Empiricism: Compliance Theories of Regulation' (1990) 30 BJ Crim 423; C Wells, *Corporations and Criminal Responsibility* (Oxford: OUP, 1993); G Slapper and S Tombs, *Corporate Crime* (Harlow: Longman, 1999).

Health and Safety at Work Act 1974. Thus, most of these incidents give rise to potential criminal, as well as civil, liability. Fraud is equally serious, in a different way. Levi estimates that just a few major fraud cases equal in value all the theft and burglary cases prosecuted by the police each year.[8] The SFO has a case load of only the 60 or 70 most serious frauds at any one time, their aggregate 'value' being estimated, in some years, at more than £5 billion.[9] Doubtless the same is true of tax evasion, where the overwhelming majority of traders' accounts, for instance, understate profits.[10]

(a) Patterns of enforcement

Few non-police agencies possess arrest powers. When they do, it is for offences which are, or could be, enforced also by the police—Customs and Excise (drugs) and the Social Security Inspectorate (benefit fraud) are particularly good examples. With these offences, prosecution patterns and processes are similar to those of the police. But since non-police agencies cannot usually arrest, neither can they charge or detain suspects. Instead they report for summons. Prosecution decisions are always taken in the cold light of day, on the basis of a full written file, by senior officials. In principle, the approach of non-police agencies is the same as that of the police and the CPS. Take the HSE's official policy:

'Enforcing authorities must use discretion in deciding whether to initiate a prosecution. Other approaches to enforcement can often promote health and safety more effectively but, where the circumstances warrant it, prosecution without prior warning and recourse to alternative sanctions may be appropriate.'[11]

In practice, the decision-making structure of the non-police agencies produces a propensity not to prosecute.[12] Their prosecution decisions are controlled by the organisation, in contrast to the police, where prosecution decisions are controlled by individual officers on the ground. Moreover, since these offences usually take place in private rather than in public (drug offences and social security fraud again being exceptions) offences are not discovered by patrols or members of the public, and, in the absence of coercive detention, confessions are rare. Offences often

8   M Levi, The Investigation, Prosecution and Trial of Serious Fraud (Royal Commission on Criminal Justice Research Study no 14) (London: HMSO, 1993).
9   Slapper and Tombs (1999) p 61.
10   Cook (1989).
11   HSE, Statement on Enforcement Policy, 1995.
12   See Sanders (1985) 'Class Bias in Prosecutions'.

come to light because of accidents or routine inspections, which are sometimes arranged in advance with the 'suspect'.

This means that discovering offending without waiting for accidents to happen is difficult. The response has been to seek information from the 'suspects' themselves. This requires a very different attitude to that of the police on the streets. The result is the development of 'compliance' modes of working. Rather than treating their suspects as criminals, regulatory agencies seek to maintain continuing relationships with companies, to create 'a friendly working atmosphere',[13] to try to persuade them to comply with the law, and to avoid prosecution wherever possible. Non-police agencies and business criminals 'bargain and bluff' with each other.[14] As with cautioning, this is done 'in the shadow of the law'. The difference here, however, is that the relative bargaining powers are closer to being equal. Indeed, agencies are sometimes in a weaker bargaining position than the companies that they are regulating.[15] Thus Hutter comments that 'officers are to some extent dependent upon the co-operation of the regulated to comply with their demands.'[16]

When agencies discover offences, they usually warn the offenders informally. Enforcement notices (warning letters) are rare; prohibition notices (stopping work until the law is complied with) are rarer still; and prosecution is the last resort. The compliance approach inevitably leads to a reluctance to prosecute. A study of 96 Australian non-police agencies found that, over a three-year period, one-third had launched not one prosecution.[17] In Britain and the United States also, prosecutions by non-police agencies are rare.[18] This is justified on the grounds that most corporations are 'responsible' and not the 'amoral calculators' predisposed to take advantage of this 'persuasion first' policy.[19] Companies that do take advantage and hold the law in contempt are slightly more likely to be prosecuted.[20] Prosecutions are so rare that, in principle, a judicial review invoking the *Blackburn* principle[1] might be thought possible. However, there was no hint of criticism of what the court described as the

---

13 B Hutter, *The Reasonable Arm of the Law?* (Oxford: Clarendon, 1988) p 189.
14 K Hawkins, 'Bargain and Bluff' (1983) 5 L Pol Q 8.
15 G Richardson, with A Ogus, and P Burrows, *Policing Pollution: A Study of Regulation and Enforcement* (Oxford: Clarendon, 1983).
16 Hutter (1988) p 188.
17 Wells (1993) p 27.
18 See Dingwall and Harding (1998) ch 5 for a general discussion.
19 Pearce and Tombs (1990). Also see D Cowan and A Marsh, 'There's Regulatory Crime and then there's Landlord Crime: From Rachmanites to Partners' (2000) (unpublished).
20 W Carson, 'White-Collar Crime and the Enforcement of Factory Legislation' (1970) 10 BJ Crim 383.
1   See section 2(b) above.

Inland Revenue's 'selective enforcement' policy in *Mead*.[2] Thus not only does the HSE investigate little over 10% of all major injuries reported to it (even though it believes most of those reported to involve criminal offences), but it prosecutes only 10% of those it does investigate.[3]

The aim of the compliance strategy is prevention rather than deterrence and punishment. The strategy has been characterised as comprising a 'pyramid' of sanctions. At the base is informal pressure, followed, less frequently, by different forms of notice, then threats of prosecution and finally prosecution itself. This strategy, some argue, will usually be as effective a deterrent as a 'first-resort' prosecution strategy, but without its disadvantages.[4] Whether this is true or not will depend, in part, on the speed at which the pyramid is ascended and the size of its prosecution apex. It does mean, though, that both 'deterrence' and 'compliance' strategies are compatible with the pyramid idea, the difference between them depending on the way the pyramid is constructed and used. But there are three questions of principle: Is the compliance approach an effective method of crime prevention? Is it justifiable for this strategy to be adopted by non-police agencies but not by the police? Are the freedoms of all sections of society equally weighted by these different agencies?

Regarding effectiveness (and leaving the other issues to later), this is a relative matter. How effective would these agencies be if their energies were dissipated by court cases? The answer is dependent on their resources, which are minimal and growing smaller. In the 1980s, the Health and Safety Executive's inspectors, for instance, were reduced in number while the traditional 'law and order' budget rose.[5] In 1999-2000 the government finally boosted spending on the HSE in real terms, but resources still prevent the majority of non-fatal serious injuries from being investigated.[6] To take another example, it has been found that waste operators have been dumping tons of hazardous waste in unauthorised sites (including next to shopping centres) in order to evade tax. The Environment Agency, which is supposed to inspect sites, said 'We haven't got the resources to do it.'[7] The enforcement of 'regulatory' offences is not, it seems, a 'law and order' matter. Questions about the methods of these agencies thus cannot be divorced from political choices about the allocation of resources. The 'pyramid' idea can only work if agencies have the resources and political backing to use all its layers effectively. In general, as Snider says:

2   This case is also discussed in section 2(b).
3   *The Guardian*, 3 November 1999.
4   I Ayres and J Braithwaite, *Responsive regulation: Transcending the deregulation debate* (New York: OUP, 1992).
5   Wells (1993) p 24.
6   *The Guardian*, 23 February 1999.
7   *The Guardian*, 5 April 2000.

'States will do as little as possible to enforce health and safety laws. They will pass them only when forced to do so by public crisis or union agitation, strengthen them reluctantly, weaken them whenever possible, and enforce them in a manner calculated not to seriously impede profitability'[8]

Note that this is the mirror image of what takes place in 'traditional' criminal justice. Thus we have already seen in chapters 2-5 that the State does as little as possible to enforce due process protections for suspects. It creates these only when forced to do so by public crisis or international law, it strengthens them reluctantly, weakens them wherever possible, and enforces them in a manner calculated not to seriously impede the pursuit of police goals.

(b) Corporate manslaughter

Since companies have legal personality, they can, in principle, commit and be convicted of criminal offences. Proving mens rea can be difficult, if not impossible, but not all offences have mens rea requirements. Manslaughter by gross negligence is one such offence.[9] The theoretical possibility of convicting companies for manslaughter had been known for years, but none had succeeded until the OLL case in 1994 (discussed at the end of this sub-section). Between 1969 and 1993, 18,151 people were killed at work. Yet not one company was convicted of homicide in relation to these deaths.[10] Were the inadequate and unfortunate Stone and Dobinson[11] really more culpable than every one of the companies which broke the Health and Safety at Work Act in these cases? It seems unlikely. Slapper estimates that in 20% of work-place deaths there is a prima facie case of manslaughter.[12] In many cases foremen, managers and/or directors are also responsible for these deaths. Hundreds of people have died in disasters like the Kings Cross fire of 1987, the Piper Alpha oil rig fire of 1988, the sinking of the 'Marchioness' in 1989 and various train crashes.[13] There have been no prosecutions for manslaughter in any of these incidents,

8   L Snider, 'The regulatory dance: understanding reform process in corporate crime' (1991) 19 IJ Soc of Law 209.

9   *Adomako* [1993] 4 All ER 935.

10   G Slapper, 'Corporate Manslaughter' (1993) 2 Social and Legal Studies 423.

11   *Stone, Dobinson* [1977] 2 All ER 341. Stone and Dobinson were convicted of manslaughter after 'omitting' to adequately discharge their 'duty of care' by summoning help for someone living with them who was wasting away. That they had low I.Q, had walked to the next village to try to get medical help, and had mentioned their concerns to pub staff, did not save them.

12   *The Guardian*, 23 February 1999.

13   Slapper (1993) 'Corporate Manslaughter'.

apart from the 'Herald of Free Enterprise' disaster.[14] It is true that there is usually no deliberate law breaking in these cases (or, at least, no deliberate intention to cause injury), and these deaths occurred in the course of the perpetrators' attempts to do their legitimate jobs. But that is true also of the many surgeons and anaesthetists who have faced manslaughter charges.[15]

The virtual immunity of companies and individual managers from serious criminal charges is not inevitable in practice (as Dutch experience shows),[16] or in theory.[17] For example, the HSE has an agreed procedure with the police and CPS when there is a work-place death or incident endangering life. According to this, a senior police officer should attend the scene of the incident, and should make an initial assessment about whether the circumstances might justify a charge of manslaughter, or other serious general criminal offence. If there is prima facie evidence, the police should investigate. Although the police liaise with CPS and HSE, the decision whether to prosecute or not is, as with any other suspected crime, for the police. If they decide, whether before or after investigation, that there is insufficient evidence for a general prosecution, the case is returned to the HSE to consider prosecution under the Health and Safety at Work Act or other enforcement action.[18] This sounds fine, but take a typical example: the death of Simon Jones, a casual labourer who was crushed by a two-ton crane grab. Ten months after he died no-one had been prosecuted for any offence at all, let alone for manslaughter, even though the HSE had issued improvement and prohibition notices in order to change the company's procedures, showing that the company was clearly at fault.[19]

The substantive law, as developed by the judiciary, makes corporate manslaughter difficult to prove, especially where the defendant company is large. This is because fault has to be attributed to someone within the company who can be identified as its controlling mind. The Law Commission recognised the problems caused by this identification doctrine and in 1994 proposed changing the law.[20] Some commentators fear that

14 *P & O Ferries* (1990) 93 Cr App Rep 72.
15 Slapper (1993) 'Corporate Manslaughter'; M Childs, 'Medical Manslaughter and Corporate Liability' (1999) 19 Legal Studies 316.
16 S Field and N Jorg, 'Corporate Liability and Manslaughter: Should we be going Dutch?' [1991] Crim LR 156.
17 Wells (1993) pp 111-113.
18 HSE, Work-related Deaths: A Protocol for Liaison (HSE, 1998)
19 *The Guardian*, 23 February 1999. On 23 March 2000 the Divisional Court in *DPP, ex p Jones* [2000] IRLR 373 quashed the decision not to prosecute on the ground that irrelevant considerations had been taken into account, and a faulty interpretation of the law of manslaughter applied. The DPP was ordered to reconsider the decision concerning prosecution.
20 Law Commission, Involuntary Manslaughter (Report no 135) (London: HMSO, 1994).

the Commission's proposal for a separate corporate manslaughter offence could further marginalise corporate killing.[1] However, the Law Commission reiterated its support for a separate offence in 1996,[2] and the government in May 2000 announced its broad acceptance of the Law Commission's approach.[3] The test for the proposed new offence of 'corporate killing' will be whether a management failure by the corporation is the cause of death and whether that failure constitutes conduct falling far below what could be reasonably expected. The intention is to make this offence triable only in the Crown Court in order to mark its seriousness. If legislation follows this will be a significant step forward. Nonetheless the economic, political and social factors which make agencies and governments reluctant to press prosecutions against companies will remain in play. These are much more difficult to change.

By the late 1990s there were still very few corporate manslaughter prosecutions.[4] Only three had been successful at the time this chapter was finalised, and all of these were of small companies.[5] These cases are clearly of an exceptional nature. To emphasise this point, consider the OLL case in which the defendant company ran a small 'activity centre' for young people. Several children drowned in a canoe accident as a result of the absence of elementary safety precautions.[6] The dead were children, the failures of the company were gross, and its managing director (who was also convicted) knew the risks.[7] There is plenty of evidence to warrant manslaughter prosecutions against larger-scale corporations, as in the Southall and Paddington rail crashes.[8] Or, in a more typical case, against the small company whose negligence led to the death by electrocution of one of its employees. Here, there were prosecutions, but only in relation to

---

1   For example, C Clarkson, 'Kicking corporate bodies and damning their souls' (1996) 59 MLR 557; C Wells, 'Corporate killing' (1997) 148 NLJ 1467.

2   Law Commission, Involuntary Manslaughter (Report no 237) (London: HMSO, 1996).

3   Home Office, Reforming the Law on Involuntary Manslaughter (London: Home Office, 2000).

4   Between 1992 and 1998 there were only 18 manslaughter prosecutions for work-place deaths: B Ecclestone, 'Work related deaths' (1998) 148 NLJ 910. This was around 1% of work-place deaths in that period: C Wells, 'Work related deaths' (1998) 148 NLJ 1007.

5   See Home Office (2000) Reforming the Law on Involuntary Manslaughter, para 3.16.

6   This was the 'Lyme Bay' tragedy. See A Ridley and L Dunford, 'No Soul to be damned, no body to be kicked: responsibility, blame, and corporate punishment' (1996) 24 IJ Soc of Law 1.

7   S Tombs, 'Law, resistance and reform: Regulating safety crimes in the UK' (1995) 4 Social and Legal Studies 343. See also Slapper and Tombs (1999) p 33.

8   In the Southall case the train operator was indicted for manslaughter but the case foundered in the courts: A-G's Reference (No 2 of 1999) [2000] Crim LR 475. See also L Christian, 'Let Down by Lawyers' The Guardian, 15 May 2000.

the Health and Safety at Work Act, and a fine of £15,000 was levied on appeal.[9] The Director of Public Prosecution's reluctance to take risks in these cases contrasts sharply with the Crown Prosecution Service's usual willingness to interpret the evidential test broadly. It would be reassuring to think that this is why the Government proposes to give the HSE (and similar bodies) full responsibility for investigating and prosecuting the new manslaughter offence, but the HSE's track record suggests the opposite.

(c) Explaining different patterns of prosecution

To summarise the above, non-police agencies usually exercise their discretion not to prosecute rather than to prosecute, preferring to use a 'compliance' strategy. Their enforcement patterns form the mirror image of those of the police, who usually use a deterrent and punitive strategy. Why do such differences arise and how are they maintained in practice?[10]

(i) Do different crimes and criminals need different strategies?

A view one sometimes encounters is that the coercive methods characteristic of the police are not generally appropriate for people and crimes dealt with by non-police agencies. This sometimes takes the form of the argument that 'white collar' crime is 'self-regulating', ie that these criminals keep their crime levels as low as possible anyway. The evidence of higher levels of crime when enforcement is reduced or eliminated demonstrates that this is not so. Deterrence methods, whether straightforwardly coercive or of the 'pyramid' kind, often work better with these crimes than with street crimes. To take one example, the National Rivers Authority claims that its relatively vigorous prosecution policy in the 1990s has reduced pollution.[11] The reality, as might be expected, is that some people, and some organisations, behave more morally than others. Thus Haines, for example, examining work-place deaths in Australia, found that some companies responded to deaths by trying to eliminate future risk, while others confined themselves to changes aimed at limiting

9   *F Howe & Son (Engineers) Ltd* [1999] Crim LR 238.
10   There is a sharp debate between researchers who adhere to different positions. See Pearce and Tombs (1990) and the reply by K Hawkins, 'Compliance Strategy, Prosecution Policy, and Aunt Sally: A Comment on Pearce and Tombs' (1990) 30 BJ Crim 444.
11   Dingwall and Harding (1998) pp 81-83. And see generally F Pearce and S Tombs, 'Hazards, Law and Class: Contextualising the regulation of corporate crime' (1997) 6 Social and Legal Studies 79.

Non-police prosecution agencies

their legal liability.[12] However, this is not just a matter of individual or randomly-appearing morality. Haines found that 'virtuous' organisational cultures were made less virtuous by adverse economic and financial factors. Even the most moral business-people behave less morally when economic competition creates pressure to cut costs. Thus Thames Trains rejected plans to introduce an £8.2m safety system because it estimated that this would save only one life. Its valuation of a life at only £2.5m meant that the investment was thought uneconomic. In the event, 31 people died two years later when one of its trains went through a red light in an accident that the safety system would have prevented. In those two years £7.5 m was paid to shareholders.[13]

It is often said that these crimes and criminals are 'different' from those the police and CPS deal with. Significantly, non-police agencies are usually referred to as 'regulatory', and their law enforcement processes as 'regulation', neutral terms from which stigma and condemnation are removed. Where cause and effect lie here is difficult to say. Does a lack of social stigma lie behind the use of these terms, or do the terms contribute to the lack of stigma? Put this way, one can see that it is not a case of cause and effect at all, but rather of two causes operating on each other in a circular fashion. One result is that neither the public at large nor traditional text books treat 'regulatory offences' as 'real' crimes (mala in se). They are seen, instead, as *mala prohibita*—not things wrong in themselves, but merely things that society requires to be better regulated. It is sometimes said that the behaviour being controlled resembles acceptable business practice and hence is not mala in se. However, as Wells points out, this misses the point that it is businesspeople who construct the image of what practices are to be regarded as acceptable in their world. What many men regard as acceptable, by way of rape and violence, is no longer acceptable to the rest of us and nor should it be.[14] Letting criminals decide by what standards they should be judged tells us more about the sources of power in society than about the acceptability or harm of the behaviour in question.

(ii) Are different enforcement patterns the result of class bias and 'corporate capture'?

Explanations involving class may appear to be overly conspiratorial in nature and out-moded. But we have seen that much crime, of the conventional as well as corporate kind, imposes greater burdens on socially disadvantaged people, as does law enforcement. Class bias—like race

12 F Haines, *Corporate Regulation: Beyond 'Punish or Persuade'* (Oxford: Clarendon, 1997).
13 *The Times*, 12 May 2000. This was the Paddington rail crash of 1999.
14 Wells (1993) pp 23-26. Also see Slapper and Tombs (1999) ch 5.

bias—can arise indirectly through the application of criteria which bear more heavily on one section of society than another.[15] Thus Hawkins argues that, in the enforcement of 'regulatory' criminal laws, there is a 'need to preserve a fragile balance between the interests of economic activity on the one hand and the public welfare on the other.'[16] It is the unfortunate lot of the poor, the main target group for the police, that their economic activity has increasingly become non-existent through unemployment or replaceable through de-skilling.

Credence is given to this explanation by the fact that the only non-police agencies 'out of line' are those that deal with the poor and/or street criminals. First, there is the Department of Social Security fraud inspectorate which deals with social security claimants. Cook found that in 1986–87, for instance, 8,000 supplementary benefit fraudsters were prosecuted, as compared to 459 tax cheats.[17] This strategy makes sense only in ideological—rather than practical—terms. The ideologies relate to 'deserving' and 'undeserving' groups, to those who work and those who do not, and so forth. Second there is the Customs and Excise, which is particularly interesting as it deals with areas as diverse as drugs (classic street crime) and corporate VAT (classic suite crime). Drug offences are enforced and prosecuted by Customs and Excise in the way that the police use the law (ie, severely), while corporate VAT fraud is enforced in the way that the Inland Revenue enforce the law (ie, lightly). Third, there is the TVLA. This agency is owned by the Post Office, which collects TV licence fees for the BBC. It is an offence not to possess a current licence if one has a TV, and officially there is no way of negotiating one's way out of prosecution even though the Code for Crown Prosecutors is supposed to apply. Thousands of people - virtually all from the poorest sections of society and disproportionately women - are prosecuted every year, and literally hundreds are jailed for fine default. Yet the sums of money involved are similar to those which the Inland Revenue collects, without penalty, years after they are due.[18]

According to the related explanation of 'corporate capture', regulatory agencies become collusive as a result of their dependence on their 'suspects/ clients':

'A captured agency no longer mediates between the interests of the public, which is to be protected through regulation, and the interests

---

15 Sanders (1985) 'Class Bias in Prosecutions'; Slapper and Tombs (1999).
16 K Hawkins, *Environment and Enforcement* (Oxford: OUP, 1984) p 9.
17 Cook (1989).
18 C Walker and D Wall, 'Imprisoning the Poor: TV Licence Evaders and the Criminal Justice System' [1997] Crim LR 173; C Panatzis and D Gordon, 'Television Licence Evasion and the Criminalisation of Female Poverty' (1997) 36 Howard JCJ 170.

of the regulated industry. Instead it uses its discretion to advance the goals of regulation only so far as industry interests permit.'[19]

Thus corporations act according to capitalist laws of economic behaviour rather than laws of due process or social justice. If forced to comply with laws which make processes uneconomic (or, more realistically, less profitable) firms will simply scale down or move their business. Regulatory agencies which genuinely care about their true clients (the workers within the industry they regulate) are thus forced into choosing between two unpalatable alternatives: corporate law breaking or reduced economic activity.

(iii) Do compliance strategies work better than deterrent strategies?

Slapper and Tombs argue that not only do compliance strategies work poorly, but deterrent strategies can work well, as with the pollution example mentioned earlier. Companies and business-people are far more likely to 'hear' and evaluate deterrent messages than many of the low-level criminals whose thefts and robberies stem from chaotic lives. Corporate crime is usually rationally planned and continuing (rather than one-off), hence capable of being deterred if the likely costs exceed the likely gains. The death of Simon Jones, discussed above, provides one such example: months after the HSE issued improvement and prohibition notices (but no prosecutions) the company was still breaking the law, because the sloppy procedures that led to Simon's death were less costly of time and money than sticking to the law.[20] Is this what the HSE regards, in the words of its own enforcement policy, as 'a quick and effective response to flagrant breaches of the law and a discriminating and efficient approach to other breaches.'?[1] According to Slapper and Tombs, deterrent strategies should work well with most corporate crime because detection rates are potentially high (if sufficient investigative resources are provided). The reason for this is the continuing nature of the crime, and the fact that once a corporate crime is discovered the identity of the criminal is usually obvious.[2]

Slapper and Tombs acknowledge that, ultimately, it is not possible accurately to assess the effectiveness of either strategy. First, deterrent strategies are never used in this context, so no direct comparison is possible.

19 N Frank and M Lombness, *Controlling Corporate Illegality* (Cincinnati: Anderson, 1988) p 97. This is not always confined to non-police agencies. Police corruption, or even honest 'undercover' work, displays these elements too. See D Hobbs, *Doing the Business* (Oxford: OUP, 1988).
20 *The Guardian*, 23 February 1999.
1   HSE, Statement on Enforcement Policy, 1995.
2   Slapper and Tombs (1999) ch 8.

Second, the investigative resources necessary for a deterrent strategy are never provided. Third, since we do not know how much of this type of crime there is (partly because of inadequate investigative resources), we cannot assess the effect of enforcement (although the vast amount that we do know about is highly suggestive). Indeed, they note that advocates of compliance strategies do not make real claims for the success of these strategies, but simply focus on the limitations of deterrent strategies.[3] Snider, drawing on North American evidence, says, 'if there is evidence that criminalisation does not work (which there is) there is equally compelling evidence that co-operation does not work either.'[4] This is, however, too simplistic. First, whether any strategy works or not is a matter of degree, not a binary work/fail divide. Second, it ignores Haines' argument that regulatory strategies need to take account of the workplace culture to which they are applied.[5] What is needed is a context-sensitive use of the regulatory pyramid, allowing the use of whichever strategy is most appropriate in the circumstances.

(iv) Are different enforcement patterns the result of the range of non-prosecution sanctions?

Another reason for different enforcement patterns might be that there are fewer alternatives to prosecution available to the police/CPS than are available to non-police agencies.[6] Some credence is given to this if we consider developments in Scotland in the 1980s. When Moody and Tombs first researched prosecutions, the pattern was similar to the English pattern. By 1991, the non-prosecution rate (including motoring offences) was 47%—a six-fold increase in a decade. Tombs and Moody now argue that this is primarily a consequence of a vastly increased range of alternatives to prosecution, including fixed penalties, prosecutor fines and diversion to social work, mediation and so forth.[7]

It might appear that traditional sanctions (fine, probation or prison) are inappropriate for many corporate crimes in particular. But this is certainly not true of non-police offences such as tax evasion where prison might be

---

3   An exception is J Braithwaite, 'Restorative Justice: Assessing Optimistic and Pessimistic Accounts' (1999) 25 Crime and Justice: A Review of Research 1. Braithwaite criticises both deterrent strategies and laissez faire compliance strategies and favours a regulatory strategy based on reintegrative shaming.

4   L Snider, *Bad Business: Corporate Crime in Canada* (Toronto: University of Toronto Press, 1993) p 142.

5   Haines (1997).

6   See Sanders (1988), 'The Limits to Diversion from Prosecution'.

7   J Tombs and S Moody, 'Alternatives to Prosecution: The Public Interest Redefined' [1993] Crim LR 357. Note, however, that some of these 'alternative' dispositions will have been alternatives to NFA rather than to prosecution.

a very effective deterrent. Also, sentences similar to community service and probation could be devised for companies.[8] Equally important is the fact that diversionary measures could be used more by the police. One example is the well-publicised use in Birmingham's red-light district of letters warning 'kerb crawlers' that their car registrations have been noted and that, if seen in the district again, prosecution will follow. The arrival of the post during the family breakfast was reported to have struck fear into the heart of many a well-heeled Brummie for several weeks thereafter. This sort of thing, with appropriate safeguards, could be extended to many offences.

It appears, then, that progress will require the development of alternatives on Scottish lines, but whether the police or the CPS should be in charge of them is a difficult question. More fundamentally, thought needs to be given to what kinds of offending really are more worthy of prosecution and what kinds of offender are amenable to prosecution and alternatives to it. It is by no means obvious that the current pattern of policies and practices optimises freedom. But without government intervention to alter the economic factors at work, different prosecution policies for regulatory offences could do equal amounts of harm in unanticipated ways.

(d) Profit, freedom and working rules

It is sometimes in the economic interests of companies to be better regulated: improved safety, and thus fewer accidents, could save money in insurance and compensation and increase employee loyalty.[9] However, one effect of competition is that this will be true only if all companies in a particular sector have to comply equally. If one company is allowed to undercut the others by spending less on, for example, safety the others will be tempted to stop complying. This is not an argument against the 'pyramid' approach per se, but it does mean that approach has to both have a heavy deterrent 'clout', and be applied equally to all firms in any one sector. This is particularly difficult in a global economy.

We have seen in earlier chapters that the *way* in which criminal justice measures such as arrest are carried out can increase their freedom enhancing/reducing effects. The same is true in the prosecution context. It is hard to see what economic interests are served by applying diversionary measures in a way which humiliates social security fraudsters if at the same time tax cheats are treated with courtesy. Yet this is what happens.[10] If the object is to humiliate claimants to deter future fraud, why not do the same to tax evaders?

8 S Box, *Power, Crime and Mystification* (London: Tavistock, 1983) pp 67-74; Slapper and Tombs (1999) ch 9.
9 Tombs (1995).
10 Dingwall and Harding (1998) ch 5.

It is striking that non-police agencies, like the police, put their own working rules before legal rules. As Hutter puts it, 'on those occasions when the law is perceived as being discordant with popular, or individual, morality, it is morality rather than the law which takes priority.'[11] The difference is that whereas this works against the interests of suspects in the case of the police, it works in favour of suspects in the case of most non-police agencies. It seems, then, that the explanation for differential enforcement patterns lies more in the differences between different types of offender, and the different economic, political and cultural contexts of different offences, than in 'objective' differences between types of offence or agency. Not only have we seen that non-police agencies adopt police–style methods and enforcement patterns when dealing with poor offenders. But also, the police and CPS adopt the non-police approach when dealing with rich and/or corporate offenders (especially when the victims are poor). Take the most serious crime of all: homicide. We saw earlier that only some 1% of work-place deaths are prosecuted as manslaughter. Yet the police always investigate work-place deaths and, where they wish to, they involve the CPS too. When hundreds of people die at work every year, these are surely vulnerable victims. Yet the robust approach to evidential and public interest tests taken by the police and CPS in 'normal' circumstances (that is, when the offender is poor) is not taken here. Freedom (of some), it seems, is covertly traded for profit.

6. PROSECUTION ACCOUNTABILITY

(a) To whom should prosecutors be accountable?

Accountability is needed in order ensure the appropriateness of the enforcement policy of a given agency. Accountability is vital for any agency which employs 'strong' discretion - that is, discretion exercised on the basis of the agency's own criteria and working rules. All prosecution agencies do this. If the CPS is to divert more cases from courts than they do now, in line with other prosecution agencies and with similar agencies in many other countries, the arguments for clear accountability become all the stronger.[12] This was recognised by the 1981 (Philips) Commission even if not by the 1993 (Runciman) Commission. Yet the even greater need for accountability of other agencies, which exercise non-prosecution discretion to an even greater degree, is rarely acknowledged.

11 Hutter (1988) p 202.
12 For arguments drawing on the experience of other jurisdictions see C Brants and S Field, 'Discretion and Accountability in Prosecution' in P Fennell et al (eds), *Criminal Justice in Europe: A Comparative Study* (Oxford: Clarendon, 1995); G Di Federico, 'Prosecutorial Independence and the democratic requirement of accountability in Italy' (1998) 38 BJ Crim 371.

To whom should these agencies be accountable if the 'freedom' approach is to be pursued? A number of apparently competing interest groups might stake a claim here. The CPS, for example, takes, or is supposed to take, into account the interests of the police, of victims, of defendants, of taxpayers, and of wider society as embodied in the notion of the public interest. All prosecution agencies are forced to juggle competing considerations, and the difficulty of satisfying all their 'stakeholders' might appear insuperable. However, if we set the ultimate goal of these agencies as the promotion of freedom, competing goals and interest groups can all, in theory, be catered for in a rational manner. The key is to realise that accountability requires an agency to explain and justify its actions in terms that appear legitimate to the various 'stakeholders' - it does not require an agency to act at the behest of any one interest group.

The second role of accountability is to consider the appropriateness of the varied enforcement policies of different agencies. Hood et al believe that these variations are due in part to the 'mutuality deficit' (the failure of regulatory agencies to communicate with each other) and the 'oversight deficit' ('no-one-in-charge-government').[13] Hence, they consider it 'not surprising that coherent principles and practices tend to be conspicuously absent in regulation within government.'[14] The accountability of the police and the Crown Prosecution Service is an important element of criminal justice policy and practice, but the accountability of other enforcement agencies is discussed rarely, if ever. However, for administrative lawyers this is a crucial question of 'regulatory legitimacy', which every agency must secure if it is 'to merit and receive public approval'.[15] Harlow and Rawlings usefully outline five possible sources of legitimacy: legislative mandate, expertise, efficiency/effectiveness, oversight and due process.[16] Let us consider briefly each in turn in relation to prosecution agencies.

(i) Legislative mandate

An agency can claim its actions are legitimate to the extent that they are mandated by law passed in a democratic manner. The more discretion an

---

13   C Hood, O James, G Jones, C Scott and T Travers, *Regulation Inside Government* (Oxford: OUP, 1999) p 220.

14   Hood et al (1999) p 212. Neither they nor other administrative lawyers apply their work to the police/non-police enforcement agency problem. We do not know whether they would accept the argument of section 5 that explaining these variations requires consideration of underlying socio-economic forces in addition to the bureaucratic elements they identify.

15   R Baldwin, *Regulation in Question* (London: LSE, 1995).

16   C Harlow and R Rawlings, *Law and Administration* 2nd edn (London: Butterworths, 1997) ch 10.

agency has, however, the less its actions are *mandated*, so this source cannot render fully legitimate the activities of enforcement bodies, such as prosecution agencies, which exercise strong discretion.

(ii) Expertise

A proper level of expertise is a precondition of legitimacy, but it is insufficient alone. This is because prosecution discretion involves trade-offs between competing criteria and this is less a matter of expertise than of opinion and policy.

(iii) Efficiency and effectiveness

Agencies that achieve their set objectives efficiently are more likely to win public approval than those that do not. Even leaving aside different views of what 'effective' enforcement policies are, the levels of all types of crime prevent this being a prime source of legitimacy for prosecution agencies.

(iv) Oversight

The more an agency is enmeshed within webs of responsibility to other agencies, the more easily it can avoid the charge that it is acting as a 'law unto itself.' Accountability to external bodies can take one of three forms. First, 'obedience', whereby the external body controls some or all of the agency's activities. Second, 'consultative', where the external body offers its views. Finally, 'explanatory', which simply requires the agency to explain its activities to the external body. Enforcement agencies other than the police and CPS are subject to none of these other than in such weak forms as a requirement to submit an annual report to Parliament.

(v) Due process

Agencies can achieve greater legitimacy by adopting fair procedures, and by pursuing such values as consistency, equality of treatment, transparency and the participation of outside interests. We have seen these standards becoming more prevalent in the police and CPS but not other prosecution agencies. It is precisely because there is no consistency and equality in relation to the different groups dealt with by different prosecution agencies that greater accountability is needed.

The lack of accountability of regulatory agencies in general (not just those dealing with crime) lead Harlow and Rawlings to consider reforms

Prosecution accountability

such as a 'Regulatory Charter', in which: 'The Government should provide a clear statement of the principles governing regulation.'[17] This would require inconsistent application of those principles by different agencies to be changed if they could not be justified. Alternatively, one or more 'super agencies' could be established. This idea was put forward by the Labour Party before it came into government[18] but is not currently a priority.

As far as the police and CPS are concerned, the balance between prosecution and caution, and between prosecution and NFA, has always been weighted towards prosecution, despite the proportion cautioned rising substantially in the 1980s and early 1990s. This reflects crime control values. Whilst this might achieve freedom for future victims it will be at the expense of the freedom of defendants (many of whom are ultimately acquitted or convicted of only minor offences). As far as most other agencies are concerned, the balance is in the opposite direction, towards freedom for suspects and defendants at the expense of future victims. It is not obvious why high status corporate and individual offenders should have their freedom protected more than that of 'typical' offenders, when tax evasion, pollution and dangerous machinery all cause at least as much harm as do shoplifting, public disorder and burglary. There is no public debate about this because the absence of cross-agency accountability mechanisms allows the issue to be hidden. The issue of manslaughter, discussed in section 5, highlights a key problem created by the lack of accountability and the proliferation of prosecution agencies: the application of the law in the most grossly unequal ways.

(b) Organisation of the Crown Prosecution Service

In the introduction to this chapter we said a little about the development of the Crown Prosecution Service. We now need to examine this in more depth from the standpoint of accountability. The CPS was established as an *independent* prosecution agency. Independence from both the police and government was seen as important because it was agreed that suspects and defendants needed an extra layer of protection. The CPS was to be accountable, not to defendants, but to the law in a neutral fashion. The natural affinity of CPS thinking with police thinking makes this aspiration unrealistic, as we have seen. But an effort was nonetheless made to establish organisational independence. The Philips Commission recommended that for each police force area there be a Chief Crown Prosecutor, each with his/her own staff, and accountable to the local Police

17 Harlow and Rawlings (1997) quoting C Veljanovski, *The Future of Industry Regulation in the UK* (London: European Policy Forum, 1993) p 82.
18 P Hain, 'Regulating for the common good' (1994) Utilities Law Review 90.

Authority (to be re-named the Police and Prosecutions Authority). It was therefore envisaged that both agencies should respond to a local democratic voice. But the government opted for a different model of accountability. It established the CPS as a national agency under the DPP which was to be politically independent by virtue of being under the 'superintendance' of the Attorney-General. 31 CPS areas, each with a Chief Crown Prosecutor, were established to cover the work of one or two police forces, thus maintaining local links. These links were, however, with the local police rather than with the wider local community. After a few years, the number of areas was reduced to 13 in an attempt to increase consistency through greater central control, although a branch structure within the areas was created to correspond with groups of police divisions. As part of the assertion of independence by the CPS, offices were sited away from police stations, and meetings between the police and CPS lawyers in either police stations or CPS offices were discouraged. As a former DPP put it: 'Suddenly a steel curtain came down between the two services and this went a bit too far. People in both services, both the police force and ourselves, felt that we must keep our distance, we must not talk to each other, we must not communicate, the CPS is independent of the police and must be seen to be so.'[19]

The CPS therefore became increasingly bureaucratic, developing its own priorities, procedures and criteria for decision-making. Victims and the police expressed unhappiness at the remoteness of 'Fortress CPS', yet, as we have seen, there is no evidence that defendants were greatly protected by this inglorious isolation. Mounting concern eventually reached a head, and the government decided that, to bring prosecution decision making nearer to the police, there should be 42 CPS areas - one for each police force, and one for London as a whole. At the same time, a government report on delay in the criminal justice system recommended, among other things, that some CPS staff be stationed in police stations in order to process simple cases more speedily.[20] This was the practice in some areas prior to the establishment of the CPS and was an example of the chumminess which the CPS was supposed to have eradicated. Now the pendulum has swung back and the CPS is having to adjust to the government's enthusiasm for 'joined-up government'.

The government also established the Glidewell enquiry into the CPS, which reported in 1998. This review could have decided that if bureaucratic independence was undesirable, accountability to one or more of the following could be recommended: victims, police, local communities, or the wider society. Without explicitly debating the merits of each possibility,

19   Sir Allan Green, speaking in 1989 - quoted by Glidewell (1998) p 37.
20   Review of Delay in the Criminal Justice System (London: Home Office, 1997) - Narey Report. For an evaluation, see Baldwin and Hunt [1998].

Glidewell recommended 'closer and more effective co-operation between the agencies at local level, in response to local needs and conditions.'[1] These 'local needs and conditions' are not identified as stemming from local democratic processes, however, but from the police. Some prosecution processes are now carried out jointly by the police and CPS as a result of the Review's recommendations, which are in line with the Narey proposals.[2] Not long after the establishment of the CPS in 1986, local accountability for the police was attenuated by reducing the elected element in local police authorities. Thus not only is the CPS more tied into the police than it ever has been, but the influence of locally elected bodies on the police (and therefore on the CPS) has waned. The upshot is that the police now has more influence over prosecutions than it has had at any time since 1986.

Glidewell set out five objectives for the CPS. Four were concerned with efficiency and quality of decision-making (including fairness to the defendant) and the fifth with 'meeting the needs of victims and witnesses . . . under the Victim's Charter.'[3] While there is nothing wrong with these objectives the omission of the local democratic element is striking. Glidewell did recommend some 'local answerability', but explicitly rejected any involvement with local police authorities or police consultative committees.[4] The arrangements leave a gap which only the Home Office, the police and, to a limited extent, the victim, can fill.

Other enforcement agencies (such as the HSE) are in the position in which the CPS was heading until Glidewell reversed its trajectory. But while the CPS keeps its distance from defendants (and would see this as an integral part of its 'distance'), most other agencies pride themselves on their links with offenders. In contrast to the CPS, then, where the main influence is a crime control agency (the police), the main influence on these other agencies is due process or the freedom of the offender.

(c) Accountability to victims

We have seen that prosecution decisions are part of a continuous process of evaluation and construction, beginning with investigation and continuing after the initial decision to prosecute (or not) is taken by the police. The CPS is usually involved only at the end of this process. Victims are usually involved as witnesses at the start but hardly at all as victims

---

1   Glidewell (1998) p 118.
2   Glidewell (1998) ch 10.
3   Glidewell (1998) ch 7.
4   Glidewell (1998) pp 206-7.

per se at any stage. The only exception is that the initial decision for the police to prosecute or not, and for the CPS to endorse that decision or not, should 'take account' of the interests of the victim (this is not an obligation for other agencies where the victim is often less obvious). In any one case the problems that may arise are legion. There may be evidential and/or public interest reasons not to prosecute but the victim may seek prosecution. Or the evidential and/or public interest elements may point towards prosecution but the victim may not want this. Moreover, some victims may be judged to seek solutions that are not in their interest. Even leaving aside questions of probability of conviction, cost and the interests of the suspect, to whom should enforcement agencies be most accountable: future victims or the particular victim in any one case?

We saw in section 4 that the police take account of victims when this supports the action they want to take but do not necessarily do so when it does not. Just as the police construct a prime suspect out of various possible suspects they can construct 'ideal' victims when they wish to prosecute and 'unreliable' victims when they do not. This construction process will often not be apparent to the CPS for the reasons discussed earlier in this chapter. This process is particularly noticeable in violence cases where there is a high degree of moral and factual ambiguity. Many cases of violence will fail without the testimony of the victim. Clarkson, Cretney and Davis, in various publications, bemoan the failure of the 'offence against society' model of prosecution (because the sometimes unpredictable influence of victims leads to some serious cases not being prosecuted and some relatively minor cases being prosecuted) while also expressing concern that the interests of victims are not taken into account sufficiently.[5] It looks as if these researchers want it all ways, but this is not surprising. After all, victims do have a stake in 'their' crime. At the same time, violence should be discouraged in the interests of everyone. But if the victim is unlikely or unwilling to give evidence, who can blame the police and CPS for being unwilling to prosecute? Yet is it good enough to allow victims to let 'their' offenders get away with it when their reasons for not testifying about violence may be precisely their fear of more violence? The key, these researchers conclude, is to make it easier for victims to testify. The problem is more complex than this as we shall now show.

The greatest problem lies with vulnerable victims. Some victims are intrinsically vulnerable: the very young, very old, and mentally ill or impaired. They are unusually prey to exploitative offenders and less able

5   Clarkson [1994]; A Cretney G Davis, C Clarkson, and J Shepherd, 'Criminalising assault: the failure of the "offence against society" model' (1994) 34 BJ Crim 15, and A Cretney and G Davis, *Punishing Violence* (London: Routledge, 1995). Similarly, regarding sexual assaults, see Gregory and Lees (1996) 36 BJ Crim 1.

to give legally compelling evidence in court.[6] Other victims are vulnerable because of their social situations: victims of sexual offences, especially 'date rapes', often find their characters attacked in court and the chances of conviction low.[7] Victims of domestic violence usually remain in the relationships within which violence takes place during any potential court proceedings which makes them particularly vulnerable to further violence especially as court penalties for domestic violence tend to be mild.[8] And many workers in factories and building sites are vulnerable because they are in no economic position to leave their jobs or demand safer conditions.

To illustrate the problem, let us take the example of domestic violence, and revisit the discussion in ch 3, section 4(c). The traditional response of the police used to be to arrest only in the most extreme cases and to prosecute only rarely. In 1990 the Home Office encouraged the police to arrest more often. This also encouraged many forces to try to reduce the rates of NFA and 'no criming' which were far higher than average in domestic violence cases.[9] In Hoyle's research on the effect of the post-1990 policy in one police force area, she found that, out of 224 domestic violence arrests, 61% were refused charge and 27% charged. Most of the rest were cautioned. While the prosecution rate was higher than it had been in the past it remained at only about half the average rate for all arrests. Hoyle found that this was not because the police thought the offence trivial, the victim undeserving or the idea of prosecuting 'domestics' odd. It was nearly always because the victim either refused to make a statement against the offender or withdrew a statement made earlier. In other words, the police adopted a 'let the victim decide' approach. Where the injuries were serious the police sometimes tried to persuade victims to press the case, but still ultimately left it to the victim. In many cases this was in accordance with the evidential test, for without their evidence the case would not usually succeed. But in some cases such evidence would not have been needed, and it is legally possible to compel a witness to give evidence (or be in contempt of court if he or she refuses). Yet it rarely occurred to the police to override the wishes of the victim. The situation was similar at later stages of those cases which were prosecuted: when victims withdrew their statements their cases were dropped even if there would have been enough evidence to continue. The CPS is supposed to satisfy itself that victims in

6   Sanders et al (1997); Home Office, Speaking up for Justice, (London: Home Office, 1998); G Davis, L Hoyano, C Keenan, L Maitland and R Morgan, An Assessment of the Admissibility and Sufficiency of Evidence in Child Abuse Cases (London: Home Office 1999), and C Keenan, G Davis, L Hoyano and L Maitland, 'Interviewing Allegedly Abused Children with a View to Criminal Prosecution' [1999] Crim LR 863.
7   J Gregory and S Lees, 'Attrition in rape and sexual assault cases' (1996) 36 BJ Crim 1.
8   C Hoyle, Negotiating Domestic Violence (Oxford: OUP, 1998).
9   Hoyle (1998) ch 1.

this situation did not drop cases through pressure from perpetrators; it has rarely been found to do so.[10]

In recognition of the obvious downside of the 'let the victim decide' approach, pro-charge policies have developed in many police forces alongside 'pro-arrest' policies. In other words, all domestic violence arrests should lead to charges if they pass the evidential test. The idea is that the police would then not be able to manipulate victims into dropping their complaints and victims would not be exposed to the wrath of the violent perpetrator. To test these assumptions and to see what did influence the choice of victims, Hoyle and Sanders interviewed a sample of domestic violence victims.[11] They found that the police did not manipulate their choice, and many victims would not have welcomed the police deciding what was to happen. This was because most victims made decisions which were rational for them, given the very difficult circumstances in which they found themselves. If prosecution was likely to help them, they made and pressed their complaints, but if it was not (if, for example, they were still living with the perpetrator and did not wish to leave him) then they did not do this. Calling the police but not prosecuting was rational for women who wanted perpetrators to be taken away until their anger or drunkenness, for example, subsided. This was no guarantee that there would not be repeated violence in future - far from it. But prosecution provided no guarantee either. Acting against the wishes of victims, but in the supposed best interests of them or of society as a whole, would therefore often be counter-productive.[12]

Hoyle and Sanders concluded that the only solution was to ensure that victims were helped into situations where they did not have to choose between the violence of their partners or other degrading situations such as the hardship of single parenthood on benefits. Domestic violence victims need to be reassured that they can be re-housed, given adequate benefits, protected from further violence, and so forth. Under this 'victim empowerment' strategy more women would choose to prosecute than now. Some police domestic violence units embody this strategy in a small way but are hampered by not having power to directly help victims with housing and other non-criminal justice problems.

Just as not all domestic violence victims want their partners prosecuted under present arrangements, so not all would even under an 'empowerment'

10   See Hoyle (1998) pp 156-9 for a description of the CPS Statement of Policy in Domestic Violence cases, and for a discussion of what the CPS actually do. Similar findings are reported by Cretney and Davis, 'Prosecuting "Domestic" Assault' [1996] Crim LR 162.

11   C Hoyle and A Sanders, 'Police response to domestic violence: from victim choice to victim empowerment?' (2000) 40 BJ Crim 14.

12   See also A Cretney and G Davis, 'Prosecuting domestic assault: Victims failing courts or courts failing victims?' (1997) 36 Howard JCJ 146.

strategy. For, to return to the discussion in sections 4 and 5 about diversion, many women would rather adopt a rehabilitative than a punitive strategy. The 'do nothing' solution of cautioning would rarely be appropriate but 'domestic violence perpetrators programmes' are now developing and could be made part of a 'restorative cautioning' approach. What is needed is the type of imagination and drive that has gone into developing 'restorative justice' for juvenile offenders both as alternatives to prosecution and as part of the armoury of court dispositions in the Crime and Disorder Act 1998. The freedom of domestic violence victims (and, by extension other vulnerable victims) is surely at least as important as that of the victims of juvenile offenders - usually car, shop and home owners. Should their property losses really be regarded as worse erosions of freedom than the violence and fear suffered by millions of women, children, people with disabilities, and workers in unsafe environments?

The restrictive deployment of restorative justice principles in recent legislation is particularly striking in view of the real effort in the late 1990s which has gone into 'levelling the playing field' for vulnerable victims (that is, victims of rape, intimidated victims, and those who are vulnerable through age, illness or disability). Changes at the levels of legislation, policy and practice are now being made as a result of 'Speaking up for Justice'.[13] But the apparent accountability of the police and CPS to vulnerable victims is in fact very shallow. It means that these agencies defer to their choices when those victims do not seek to prosecute, but not when they do wish to prosecute. This is particularly unacceptable when the choices of the vulnerable are so constrained by disadvantageous economic, social and personal circumstances. If the freedom of vulnerable victims is to be taken as seriously as that of the more fortunate, the criminal justice system as a whole, in conjunction with non-criminal justice agencies, needs to be made more responsive to their needs - a nettle which 'Speaking up for Justice' did not grasp. As we saw in ch 1, the criminal justice system should not be analysed in isolation from other elements of the social structure, such as housing and welfare. Freedom from crime is not, in principle, any more important than freedom from poverty or illness. For many vulnerable victims freedom from the former will only be achieved when they are enabled to free themselves from the latter.

This discussion shows that the police and CPS are accountable to victims in respect of due process (in the sense set out in (a) above) to some extent, in that those outside interests are given some limited rights to participate. 'Oversight accountability' to victims has traditionally been very limited. However in recent years 'explanatory' and 'consultative' accountability

---

13 Home Office (1998). This report is bringing about change to police and CPS policy and practice regarding vulnerable victims, and led to the Youth Justice and Criminal Evidence Act 1999, discussed in ch 12.

has begun to develop. Following the recommendations of the Macpherson Report,[14] the CPS is now experimenting with explaining its prosecution decisions to victims, which is another, and welcome, step away from 'Fortress CPS'. As we shall argue in ch 12, the freedom of victims can be enhanced by treating their concerns seriously. This need not involve 'obedience' or even 'consultative' accountability, but it does require agencies to explain their actions to them. A clear commitment to explain is better than a luke-warm commitment to consult which is neither practised consistently nor legally enforceable. It hardly needs pointing out that non-police agencies are not engaged at all in this kind of exercise even though the victims of corporate crime suffer more 'physical, economic, political, social and human suffering and damage' than those of other crimes.[15] These victims are concentrated in the poorest and least powerful sections of society. It is no coincidence that their voices and interests are drowned out by the rustle of money-making, the hustle of profit-taking, the clink of wine glasses in corporate hospitality boxes.

(d) Accountability through private prosecutions?

Accountability of the criminal justice system as a whole to victims is sometimes said to be secured by the right of private prosecution. It will be recalled that, before the police became de facto national prosecutors in the mid-late nineteenth century, most prosecutions were private. The legal form of police/CPS prosecutions remains the same, and so victims (or indeed anyone else) may lay an information in order to seek a summons against anyone. If citizens are dissatisfied with police/CPS decisions not to prosecute, they may - with some   is is a form of accountability because   s or practices, thus putting pressure   ther defend or change them.

As with many aspects of Englis   een having a right in theory and bei   vate prosecutions in practice are only   that a public prosecution will not tak   ime may have elapsed, and too many   the police to prevent evidence from   sful private prosecution. This was highlighted in the *Stephen Lawrence* affair in which the police bungled the investigation into the murder of a young

---

14 Macpherson (1999). This was the enquiry into the Stephen Lawrence affair. Macpherson is here extending the logic of the elements of victim participation introduced by the Victims' Charter. See ch 12.
15 Slapper and Tombs (1999) p 84.

black man in 1993. As a result they had insufficient evidence to prosecute successfully the prime suspects and so the prosecution which was brought against some of them was dropped. A private prosecution of three of them in 1996 failed for the same reasons as the original prosecution.[16] The Hillsborough tragedy, in which 96 people died when the police lost control of a football crowd in 1989, was a different type of scandal. It took 10 years to mount private prosecutions against the officers who it is believed were most responsible. In July 1999 two were committed for trial when magistrates decided that there was sufficient evidence to prosecute.[17] These prosecutions were ultimately also unsuccessful (one of the officers was acquitted in July 2000, and the jury was 'hung' on the other). These cases illustrate two further functions of private prosecutions. One is symbolic, in that they can shame those responsible and highlight the suffering of the victims and their families. The second is that, as in these cases, they can become part of the campaign to do something about the wider social or political problems which led to the tragedies in the first place. But since private prosecutions are rarely possible (because of the money and energy required) this right does not fill the every-day 'accountability gap'.

The capacity of private prosecutions to hold enforcement agencies accountable in these ways is hampered in three other ways. First, there are many offences for which only designated prosecutors may prosecute. This includes most regulatory offences, closing off yet another way of holding non-police agencies accountable. Second, there is a variety of offences for which consent must be sought from the DPP or the law officers before they can be prosecuted. These tend to be political offences or obscure offences involving matters such as obscene publications. There is a danger here that the DPP may protect those that should be prosecuted (by refusing consent) or fail to protect those who should not be prosecuted (by granting consent). The House of Lords has ruled that the DPP's decision to consent to a prosecution is not amenable to judicial review unless tainted by dishonesty, bad faith or some other exceptional circumstance.[18] Potential private prosecutors who are thwarted by a DPP decision not to consent to a prosecution are thus unlikely to be able to have that decision over-turned.[19]

Third, there is the power of the DPP to take over any private prosecution and then either continue or discontinue.[20] The DPP can use any criteria in exercising this power that he or she wishes (subject to the 'Wednesbury'

---

16 Macpherson (1999). Discussed further in ch 3, section 4(d).
17 *The Guardian*, 21 July 99.
18 *DPP, ex p Kebelene* [1999] 3 WLR 972.
19 The Law Commission has proposed reducing the number of such offences on the basis of rational criteria: Law Commission, Consents to Prosecution (HC 1085) (Report no 255) (London: SO, 1998).
20 Prosecution of Offences Act, 1985, s 6 (2).

principles discussed in section 2 above). Thus in the Hillsborough case the police officers who were privately prosecuted unsuccessfully sought a judicial review of the DPP's decision not to take the case over even though it was (correctly) thought that prosecution would be unsuccessful.[1] This power is supposed to be exercised when private prosecutors behave vexatiously, which is consistent with the freedom approach. But there is nothing to stop the DPP doing this when the aim is to protect someone for social, political or economic reasons or with whom, perhaps, the police have struck a dubious 'deal'.[2] This is all contrary to the freedom approach. Currently it is often a matter of chance whether or not the DPP hears of a private prosecution. The Law Commission therefore recommends that magistrates' courts should have to report all such prosecutions to him, which can only increase the chances of ultimate failure.[3]

Accountability of enforcement agencies is anathema to the crime control approach because it fetters the discretion of 'the experts'. Neither the due process nor human rights approaches have much to say about accountability as they are concerned with individual rights in individual cases. But accountability is central to the freedom approach because this approach is as much concerned with socio-economic fairness and effective use of resources as it is with lawfulness. What we have seen in this section is that, in this respect, there is a long way to go to satisfy the freedom approach, particularly in relation to non-police agencies and their tremendous autonomy in comparison with the police and CPS.

7. CONCLUSION

One of the paradoxes of the criminal justice system is that the powers which ostensibly exist purely in order to facilitate prosecution - stop-search, arrest and so forth - are subject to more formal regulation than are the powers to prosecute themselves. Yet in reality those facilitative powers have much broader purposes and are inadequately regulated, while prosecution is subject to detailed guidelines and the supervision of the CPS and the courts. However, the police manage to minimise the impact of external scrutiny by these bodies: by case construction, by the use of arrest and immediate charge, and by cautioning, where this serves their purposes. The courts themselves, while asserting their theoretical right to review prosecution

---

1   *DPP, ex p Duckenfield* [1999] 2 All ER 873.
2   As happened in *Raymond v A-G* [1982] QB 839, for example. See A Sanders, 'An Independent Crown Prosecution Service?' [1986] Crim LR 16.
3   Law Commission (1998).

and non-prosecution decisions, largely opt out of this in practice.[4] Neither they nor government and Parliament care that different agencies adopt radically different approaches. The net result is a pattern of prosecution decisions which harmonise with economic imperatives but which, as a by-product, penalise the unfortunate and reward the powerful. The class and race differences created by stop-search and arrest practices are magnified by prosecution processes within the police and by separating police and non-police enforcement and prosecution.

None of this is to deny major changes in prosecution practices in the 1980s and 1990s. The CPS drops more weak and cautionable cases than the police used to. Some of the direct or indirect discrimination exercised by the police against ethnic minorities is blunted by CPS decision-making. The CPS and police are diverting more people who should not be prosecuted. Government guidelines do have some effect. But these rules, guidelines and controls are all only partially inhibitory. When the police want to, they generally secure cautions or prosecutions in breach of the rules. Little can be, or is, done about it. If these inhibitory rules are to be fully effective, they need to be backed up by effective sanctions—otherwise they are almost certain to become largely 'presentational'. There are no sanctions attached to the rules and guidelines discussed in this chapter.

Is prosecution policy about fairness and keeping criminalisation within bounds (freedom) or about balancing expediency with police working rules (crime control)? The retreat from widespread cautioning would suggest that we are moving back towards the latter. In any event, although cautioning is used for humanitarian reasons, it also: increases social control through net widening; saves money where there is little to be lost by not prosecuting; punishes those against whom there is insufficient evidence of guilt to justify this; and avoids prosecuting those people who could embarrass authority (at the micro (police) level and macro (state) level).

Many argue that cautioning is yet another example of reduced openness in government, with reduced opportunity for public control and scrutiny.[5] As part of other trends noted in this book, control over criminal justice is gradually passing from the judiciary to the police. The result is not just increased police control over the dispersal of stigma, but also increased control over the imposition of penalties. For it used to be common for juvenile offenders, in particular, to be given absolute or conditional discharges on first and sometimes second appearances in court as a 'warning shot'. Now this is rare, for the courts see the caution as that

---

4   Decisions not to prosecute police officers raise special problems. It has been held that judicial review does lie against such decisions: see ch 11, section 3, and the discussion of the *Treadaway* case.

5   See eg J Pratt, 'Diversion from the Juvenile Court' (1986) 26 B J Crim 212.

warning shot. Indeed, it is virtually forbidden under the Crime and Disorder Act 1998.[6] Not content with apprehending suspected offenders, the police have become triers of fact, deciders of guilt and innocence and dispensers of penalties. The trend towards inviting victims and others to take part in cautioning sessions in the name of restorative justice can only ever be a partial corrective to this increase in police power. Some writers have responded to the brute fact of this growing power by arguing against formal cautioning or, at least, against formal cautioning remaining in the hands of the police. Sadly, these debates were not even acknowledged as issues by the Runciman Commission or in the framing of legislation in the late 1990s.

The Commission did suggest that the CPS be given a greater role in diversion. In Scotland the CPS-equivalent (the procurator-fiscal service) can issue its own fines and conditionally divert to rehabilitation schemes (eg alcohol treatment schemes). In some other jurisdictions, such as Holland, prosecutors have yet greater powers.[7] In principle the Commission's suggestion is welcome, especially as so little diversion currently is rehabilitative in orientation: although juvenile warnings under the Crime and Disorder Act will have a rehabilitative element, most diversion in England and Wales is usually either punitive or 'do nothing' in orientation. However the CPS would remain as dependent on the police for information as they are now. Further, just as some police diversion is net-widening, the same is true of diversion by prosecutors.[8] The governments of the mid- and late-1990s, however, were concerned to reduce, not to increase, diversion and so even Runciman's proposals on this issue look too liberal to be implemented until there is another shift in government policy.

Just as the police cannot be expected to protect the rights of suspects, nor can we expect the CPS to do so. It is the job of defence lawyers to protect suspects' rights. But while expenditure on the CPS is rising, the legal aid budget is ever more tightly controlled.[9] The issue of summaries of taped interrogations exemplifies the problem. The police and CPS are castigated for producing and accepting these documents. But they have no interest in changing their practices. It should be the defence lawyers who check the accuracy of summaries. But without a remuneration structure that rewards this work, they have no interest either. And 'fast-tracking' of cases will not give them the opportunity. Similarly, the retreat from full disclosure and restrictions on legal aid for defence forensic science also prevent defence lawyers matching the power of the prosecution. The idea that the CPS exists to fulfil that function - of countering its own power

6   CADA, s 66 (4).
7   Dingwall and Harding (1998) pp 128-137.
8   Duff (1993).
9   On the latter point see D O'Brien and J A Epp, 'Salaried Defenders and the Access to Justice Act 1999' (2000) 63 MLR

- is as flawed in principle as we have shown it is half-hearted in practice. For example, even though the CPS does discontinue at least some cases which the police wish to be prosecuted to the bitter end, most are discontinued only after one or more court appearances.[10] This significantly reduces the freedom of defendants who, we should remember, are judged innocent in law and will often be innocent 'in fact'.

Would the CPS have prevented the infamous miscarriages of justice that gave rise to the Runciman Commission? It seems unlikely, for three reasons. Firstly, the police construct cases to appear to be strong and the job of the CPS is to pursue those cases with vigour. This they do. The fact that the miscarriage of justice cases were later shown to have all the strength of a house of cards does not alter the fact that they were seen as sufficiently impressive constructions to secure convictions in the first instance. Secondly, the CPS is hea   :uted the 'Birmingham Six', the 'Guil   iit Affair' and Stefan Kiszko. Third]   ontinued unabated into the 1990s. Th   f the CPS should be to prosecute. Wh   CPS of a 'Ministry of Justice' mentali   to regard such a changed mind-set as   is in any event unrealistic. What is   defence advocacy to counter-balance   ither side of the adversarial divide.

In this chapter we have foc   ther or not to prosecute: the evident   >th are central to the idea of 'freedom   :refore freedom by, for example, costin   erating stress. If the case is weak, the r   10 gain for society. If there are 'publi(ng, the gain in freedom of securing a c   loss of freedom entailed in securing 1   at law, policy and practice all implicitl   extent, and until the early 1990s the 1   hough the police remained largely in control of the process. Since 1994, not only have the police strengthened their grip on the process, allowing police priorities to supersede those of freedom, but also the 'public interest' is seen more and more as a matter of adopting a hard, anti-freedom, line. Although some commentators argue that there are progressive elements in Labour's approach, particularly the restorative justice elements in the Crime and Disorder Act, these elements suffer from confused thinking and

10   Phillips and Brown (1998) pp 145-6.

half-hearted support.[11] The risk of derailment in the face of a populist Conservative opposition will always be high. Moreover, the Labour government has committed itself to such populist causes as 'reducing crime' and 'protecting the public'. The management of 'risk' has become a major determinant of recent governmental policy in many western societies.[12] Minimising the risk of offending has come to be seen as necessarily outweighing the erosion of freedom inherent in the modern emphasis on 'community safety'. But some 'risks' (eg, posed by high status offenders) to some 'communities' (eg, the vulnerable) are clearly tolerated more than others. Those with economic, social or political power are regulated with a light touch, while for the rest our tolerance approaches zero.

---

11   Compare Dignan [1999] with A Morris and L Gelsthorpe, 'Something Old, Something Borrowed, Something Blue, but Something New? A Comment on the Prospects for Restorative Justice under the Crime and Disorder Act 1998' [2000] Crim LR 18.

12   See R Ericson and K Haggerty, *Policing the Risk Society* (Oxford: Clarendon Press, 1997) and J Braithwaite, 'The New Regulatory State and the Transformation of Criminology' (2000) 40 BJ Crim 222.

Chapter 7

The mass production of guilty pleas

[Defence] solicitor:	Will you drop the criminal damage?
Prosecutor:	But he's a pain in the arse.
Solicitor:	I know, but go on, he's pleading guilty to all the other stuff.
Prosecutor:	[Good humouredly] Oh, alright![1]

1. INTRODUCTION

Prosecutions take place either in the magistrates' courts (the lower courts) or the Crown Court. Where the prosecution takes place depends in large part on the legal classification of the offence. 'Summary' offences can be prosecuted only in the magistrates' court, offences triable only on indictment must be committed to the Crown Court, whilst 'either way' offences can be tried in either court. This classification is supposed to ensure that the Crown Court deals with the more serious cases. Crown Court judges are equipped with much greater sentencing powers than are possessed by magistrates. Various features of these courts are looked at in detail in chapters 8 and 9. Here we discuss a phenomenon that is common to both levels of court: the mass production of guilty pleas.

One of the most remarkable features of criminal justice in England and Wales is the very low proportion of prosecuted cases that result in contested trials. Usually defendants commit legal suicide by pleading guilty. It is difficult to be precise as to the guilty plea rate as official bodies collect and

---

1   This quote is taken from M McConville, J Hodgson, L Bridges and A Pavlovic, *Standing Accused* (Oxford: Clarendon, 1994) p 195.

present the relevant statistical information in different ways.[2] The figures can, however, be used to grasp the overall scale of the various ways in which prosecuted cases are terminated. The CPS 'completed' 1,359,100 cases in the magistrates' court in 1998. Of these 12% were discontinued (on evidential or public interest grounds),[3] 7% were written off (usually because the defendant failed to appear), 7% were committed to the Crown Court, 2% resulted in a bind over and 73% were heard in court. Of the 806,700 hearings in court, 82% of cases were concluded by a guilty plea, a further 12% were proved in the defendant's absence, 5% resulted in convictions following a trial and 2% resulted in acquittals. Thus of all cases which proceeded to a hearing, fully 98% resulted in a finding of guilt, in just 7% did a contested trial take place, and in over four-fifths the defendant simply threw in the towel by pleading guilty.[4]

In the Crown Court in 1998 60.6% of cases were terminated by a guilty plea, down from 69% in 1992.[5] These defendants either pleaded guilty to all charges or pleaded guilty to some and had pleas of not guilty to others accepted by the court without a jury being sworn in to hear the case.[6] 37,883 cases terminated in this way in 1999.[7] In recent years, nearly two-thirds of those defendants pleading not guilty to *all* counts have been acquitted.[8] In practice, most acquittals do not involve a consideration of the case by the jury following a contested trial. Instead, the judge simply directs or orders the jury to return a verdict of not guilty. In 1999, 67% of acquittals were of this nature.[9]

A particular feature of the Crown Court is 'cracked trials'. These are cases which are listed for a contested trial by jury but on the day of the trial the defendant is disposed of in some other way. There were 16,502 cracked trials in 1999. In three-quarters of these cases the defendant pleaded guilty to the original or some alternative count on the indictment, in a fifth the prosecution offered no evidence (resulting in an ordered acquittal) and

2   Home Office, Criminal Statistics England and Wales 1998 (Cm 4649) (London: SO, 2000) paras 6.8-6.9. It seems that the CPS figures are the most reliable for the cases in which it prosecutes. Because the CPS does not bring all prosecutions in the courts (see ch 6, section 5) we should bear in mind that its figures understate the number of court proceedings.
3   See ch 6, sections 3(c) and 4(c).
4   Home Office (2000) Table 6.2.
5   Lord Chancellor's Department, Judicial Statistics 1999 (Cm 4786) (London: SO, 2000) p 66 and Lord Chancellor's Department, Judicial Statistics 1992 (Cm 2268) (London: HMSO, 1993) Table 6.7, p 61 respectively.
6   Lord Chancellor's Department (2000) p 66. Note that the official statistics classify a case as disposed of by a guilty plea only if guilty pleas are entered by all co-defendants (if any).
7   Lord Chancellor's Department (2000) p 67.
8   The figure was 65% in 1999: Lord Chancellor's Department (2000) Table 6.9.
9   Lord Chancellor's Department (2000) Table 6.10. Directed and ordered acquittals are examined in ch 9, section 2.

the remainder were dealt with by way of a bind over.[10] The high rate of guilty pleas in the Crown Court raises two distinctive questions. Why is it that the great majority of those defendants who are presented directly with the chance to exercise the supposedly fundamental right of trial by jury choose not to do so? And why does the resolve of so many defendants to plead not guilty 'crack' at the doors of the Crown Court? We examine these puzzling questions below.

At first sight, the operation of the criminal courts appears to be consistent with the crime control model of criminal justice. The high rate of guilty pleas ensures that many of the most important due process protections which might apply in an adversarial system do not come into play.[11] Crucially, the prosecution is not obliged to prove its case beyond reasonable doubt before an impartial tribunal. Its evidence is not scrutinised, witnesses are not cross-examined, and no question as to the exclusion of evidence (on the grounds that it was obtained oppressively, unfairly, or in circumstances that might render it unreliable) can arise. The defendant stands condemned merely as a result of uttering the single word 'guilty' in open court. But is this absence of due process attributable to a free and informed decision by the defendant? Or does the criminal process itself encourage defendants to waive their due process rights by pleading guilty?

From the point of rational choice theory, whether or not a defendant pleads guilty is likely to depend on two crucial variables: firstly, the perceived likelihood of conviction, and second, the differential between the penalty likely to be imposed on a plea of guilty and that which would follow one of not guilty. This much is suggested by research. For example, on the basis of interviewing 282 convicted defendants in Crown Court Hedderman and Moxon concluded that: '. . . decisions to plead guilty were largely based on a realistic assessment of the chances of acquittal, and the potential benefits in terms of sentence severity.'[12] The researchers do not explain how they formed the view that the assessments made by defendants were 'realistic' although they do point to the crucial influence of legal advice in decisions regarding pleas. Thus, of those who changed their pleas, only one respondent said that this decision had been entirely his own; the rest said that they had been advised by their solicitor or barrister to plead guilty. It follows that in this chapter we need to look both at the systemic pressures on defendants to plead guilty, and the way that these are mediated in practice by lawyers (solicitors, barristers and, in the Crown Court, judges).

10   Lord Chancellor's Department (2000) p 66.
11   The crime control and due process models are discussed in ch 1, section 7.
12   C Hedderman and D Moxon, Magistrates' Court or Crown Court? Mode of Trial Decisions and Sentencing (Home Office Research Study no 125) (London: HMSO, 1992).

We need, in particular, to consider whether assessments of the chances of acquittal, and likely sentence if convicted, are 'realistic' or not.

There are three important features of the legal system which hold out the prospect of a lighter sentence to those pleading guilty: the sentence discount principle, the restrictions on the sentencing powers of magistrates, and charge bargaining.[13] We will look at each in turn.

2.   THE SENTENCE DISCOUNT PRINCIPLE

The most naked attempt to persuade defendants to plead guilty lies in the sentencing principle established by the Court of Appeal that defendants pleading guilty should receive a lighter sentence than those convicted after a contested trial. This principle has been loudly proclaimed, as in the case of *Cain* where Lord Widgery CJ affirmed that: 'Everyone knows that it is so and there is no doubt about it. Any accused person who does not know about it should know about it. The sooner he knows the better.'[14] It was said in *Boyd* in similarly robust terms that 'the court encourages pleas of guilty by knocking something off the sentence which would have been imposed if there had not been a plea of guilty.'[15] This principle has now been overlaid by some fairly weak statutory requirements. These are contained in s 48 of the Criminal Justice and Public Order Act 1994 (CJPO)[16], which provides:

'(1) In determining what sentence to pass on an offender who has pleaded guilty to an offence in proceedings before that or another court a court shall take into account-
(a)   the stage in the proceedings for the offence at which the offender indicated his intention to plead guilty, and
(b)   the circumstances in which this indication was given.
(2)   If, as a result of taking into account any matter mentioned in subsection (1) above, the court imposes a punishment on the offender

---

13   'Fact bargains' are another form of deal under which the prosecution and defence seek to agree a factual basis upon which a guilty plea would be acceptable to both sides. For example, the defendant might, in the hope of a lighter sentence, plead guilty to a charge of assault on the basis that the victim was 'slapped' rather than 'punched'. *Beswick* [1996] 1 Cr App Rep (S) 343 seeks to regulate such bargains. Space precludes further discussion here, but see Ashworth (1998) pp 275-276.
14   [1976] Crim LR 464.
15   (1980) 2 Cr App Rep (S) 234.
16   The Crime (Sentences) Act 1997 added a new sub-s (3) to CJPO s 48 but is unlikely to make any practical difference to sentencing (so is not discussed further here) for reasons explained by D A Thomas, 'The Crime (Sentences) Act 1997' [1998] Crim LR 83 at 90.

which is less severe than the punishment it would otherwise have imposed, it shall state in open court that it has done so.'[17]

Section 48(1) states that the timing of the indication to plead guilty, and the circumstances in which this indication was given shall be taken into account, but it does not demand that any discount in fact be given, nor does it say whether an early indication increases or decreases the chance of a discount. Similarly s 48(2) does not require a sentencer to refer to the discount principle in all circumstances, but only when a discount has in fact been given as a result of a guilty plea; even then the sentencer is not obliged to say how much has been 'knocked off' the convicted person's sentence. The section clearly assumes that sentencers must turn to the common law for an understanding of how the discount principle is meant to work in practice.

(a) Appellate decisions on the sentence discount principle

(i) The rationale of the principle

First, why do the courts seek to encourage guilty pleas? The obvious rationale lies in the time and expense that is saved when an accused agrees to plead guilty.[18] The drive to achieve 'efficiencies', in particular in the Crown Court, has underpinned most judicial thinking in this area. The average hearing time for a contested Crown Court trial is almost 10 hours compared with just over an hour for a guilty plea case.[19] The Home Office has estimated that, leaving aside the most serious offences, the average cost of a contested case in the Crown Court is £12,088 compared with £1,400 for a guilty plea case.[20] The savings involved in encouraging guilty pleas are clearly substantial and have grown as the workload of the Crown Court has increased. Since 1982 the annual number of cases committed for trial

---

17 A similar provision was introduced in Scotland by the Criminal Justice (Scotland) Act 1995, s 34. This should arouse more controversy than did CJPO, s 48 because Scottish judges had previously rejected the discount principle on the grounds that it amounted to punishing people for pleading not guilty and contravened the presumption of innocence: see A Ashworth, *The Criminal Process* 2nd edn (Oxford: OUP, 1998) p 287 and the sources cited there.

18 Cases in which this was explicitly recognised include *Boyd* (1980) 2 Cr App Rep (S) 234, *Hollington and Emmens* (1985) 7 Cr App Rep (S) 364, and *Buffrey* (1992) 14 Cr App Rep (S) 511.

19 Lord Chancellor's Department (2000) Table 6.21. The figures for 1992 were seven hours for contested trials and 54 minutes for guilty plea cases: Lord Chancellor's Department (1993) Table 6.20.

20 Home Office, Costs of the Criminal Justice System 1992, vol 1, p 16 (London: Home Office, 1992). For the most serious offences, such as murder and rape, no comparison is possible as nearly all defendants plead not guilty.

to the Crown Court showed an average growth rate of just over 4%, and reached a total of 100,994 cases in 1992.[1] Committals for trial subsequently declined to around 75,000 a year by the end of the decade. This apparent relief of pressure has been offset by the growth in committals to the Crown Court for sentence (up from 14,883 in 1992 to 31,928 in 1999). Thus, in 1999, the Crown Court received more cases than it disposed of, and its backlog of outstanding cases at the end of the year rose 3% to 24,624 cases.[2] The pressure to dispose of cases 'efficiently' remains a key factor underlying the sentence discount principle.

An important subsidiary factor is a recognition that by pleading guilty the defendant 'spares' any witnesses from having to attend court and from what may be the distressing experience of giving evidence.[3] If, for example, a defendant contests a charge of assault, the complainant will nearly always face lengthy cross-examination in an attempt to destroy his or her credibility as a witness.[4] The sentence discount principle thus operates as an inducement to the defendant to make life 'easier' for others. When defendants make life 'harder' for others by pleading not guilty, and particularly if this results in a complainant or witness having to endure intrusive cross-examination about intimate matters, the courts are most unlikely to exercise any leniency when sentencing.[5]

In *Buffrey*, in the context of a complicated fraud case, Lord Taylor CJ effectively summarised the official line on why a guilty plea should be rewarded with a reduction in sentence:

'Some reduction must be made, as frauds of this kind were so complex and took such a long time to unravel, that they became a burden to the criminal justice system. They were costly in time and money, and caused stress to jurors who had to try them, judges who had to try them, and to witnesses and the defendants themselves.'[6]

1   Lord Chancellor's Department (1993) Table 6.1.
2   Lord Chancellor's Department (2000) pp 63-64.
3   See *Barnes* (1983) 5 Cr App Rep (S) 368 (where a plea of guilt had spared the victim of an attempted rape from having to give evidence about the incident); *Sullivan* (1987) 9 Cr App Rep (S) 492, and *Burns* (28 July 2000, unreported), CA. See also *Billam* (1986) 82 Cr App Rep 347 which in laying down sentencing guidelines for those convicted of rape incorporated the discount principle on this basis.
4   See, for example, D Brereton, 'How Different are Rape Trials?: A Comparison of the Cross-Examination of Complaints in Rape and Assault Trials' (1997) 37 BJ Crim 242.
5   See, for example, *Lucas: Walsh* (15 February 2000, unreported), CA. A 72-year-old man was convicted of two offences (indecent assault on a male and indecency with a child) committed 20 years earlier. His sentence of five years' imprisonment was upheld, despite it being described as at the 'top end of the scale', largely because he had 'forced his victims to relive their experiences'.
6   (1992) 14 Cr App Rep (S) 511 at 515.

The argument that a plea of guilty should be rewarded because it evinces remorse is also occasionally referred to by the courts.[7] It is a singularly unconvincing rationale. The courts have no sure way of distinguishing between guilty pleas motivated by remorse and those entered simply in order to avoid a greater degree of punishment.

(ii) The variable size of the sentence discount

As the case of *Cain* (see p 398) shows, the courts are keen for a guilty plea to be entered at the earliest opportunity as that allows the maximum savings for the system to be made. At one time the earliest point at which a defendant could have formally indicated an intention to plead guilty to a count on a Crown Court indictment (ie, a formal accusation that the defendant committed a particular offence) would have been *after* the case was committed to that court. We will term the reduction in sentence available for such defendants as the 'standard' Crown Court discount. However, s 49 of the Criminal Procedure and Investigations Act 1996 introduced a new 'plea before venue' procedure for either way offences under which defendants are asked to indicate how they intend to plead *before* a decision is made as to 'mode of trial' (ie, which tier of court the case should be heard in). If an intention to plead guilty is indicated, the magistrates are obliged to 'try' the case in the magistrates' court there and then. The case may, however, still be committed to the Crown Court for sentence. It might have been thought that this earlier indication of plea should entitle the defendant to an additional discount over and above the standard discount for those pleading guilty as soon as they get to the Crown Court. But in *Rafferty*[8] the Court of Appeal said that in either way cases the standard discount should now be given to those who pleaded guilty in the magistrates' court as a result of the plea before venue procedure. Those who did not indicate such a plea when they had the opportunity to do so, and were subsequently committed to the Crown Court for trial or sentence, would henceforth get less than the old 'standard' Crown Court discount. The upshot is that the pressure to plead guilty has simply been shifted to an earlier point in the process.

In comparison with straightforward guilty plea cases, late pleas may involve considerable inconvenience and expense for the courts, for witnesses, for jurors and so on. The Court of Appeal has accordingly sought to discourage defendants from changing their pleas at a late stage in the court proceedings. This is illustrated by *Hollington and Emmens*. The defendant was in custody awaiting trial and, in order to keep certain

---

7   Eg, *Turner* [1970] QB 321; *Hastings* [1995] Crim LR 661.
8   [1998] Crim LR 433.

privileges allowed to remand prisoners maintaining their innocence, he initially entered a plea of not guilty. He changed his plea late in the proceedings. The Court of Appeal noted that such tactical pleas of not guilty caused a considerable waste of resources and continued:

'The sooner it was appreciated that defendants are not going to get full discount for pleas of guilty in these sort of circumstances, the better it will be for the administration of justice.'[9]

This was confirmed in the post CJPO case of *A and B,* in which the Court of Appeal went on to express a number of ways in which defendants could get extra discounts on top of the 'routine' discounts awarded for early pleas.[10] An 'enhanced discount' was available for those who cooperated with the police and prosecution authorities, as by agreeing to testify against a co-accused.[11] A 'further discount' should be given to those who helped the authorities in the suppression of serious crime (other than the one for which they had been arrested). The extent of this 'further discount' would depend on the quality and quantity of the help provided. The court suggested that a large 'further discount' should be given to those who, by supplying information to the authorities, put themselves or their families in personal jeopardy.[12] Finally, defendants who pleaded guilty and gave help to the authorities *after* conviction but before sentence was passed should be given 'credit' for this on top of the 'routine discount'. If the trial judge failed to do this, or assumed that the help was less valuable to the authorities than it later turned out to be, the Court of Appeal might reduce a sentence on appeal. Thus in this particular case the defendants were convicted of conspiring to import £2 million worth of Ecstasy tablets. The trial judge took into account their guilty pleas when imposing sentences of 13 and 14 years of imprisonment. After conviction the two had given assistance to the authorities said to have been of great value in investigating

9 (1985) 82 Cr App Rep 281 at 285.

10 [1998] Crim LR 757.

11 The judgment in *Hollington and Emmens* (1985) 82 Cr App Rep 281 similarly emphasised that an enhanced discount can be obtained by those who on arrest admit guilt and cooperate fully with the police. Defendants who would (probably) have escaped detection but for their voluntary decision to admit guilt are entitled to even more by way of a discount. See *Hoult* [1990] Crim LR 664 in which the Court of Appeal recognised that a defendant who had gone to a police station to give himself up three years after committing a robbery was entitled to a greater than usual discount.

12 For an example, see *Lee Albert Hammond* (23 February 2000, unreported), CA, in which a sentence was reduced from three years' imprisonment to 18 months because the defendant had revealed to the police from whom he had bought stolen antiques and, in consequence, needed police protection on his release from prison.

and prosecuting other serious crimes. The Court of Appeal felt that the trial judge had not reflected this adequately in the sentence and knocked a further two years off each sentence. With all this talk of 'credit', and of 'routine', 'further' and 'enhanced' discounts, it is a wonder that the Court of Appeal does not issue loyalty cards to the criminal courts' regular 'customers'.

While all these additional forms of discount are not strictly relevant to the principle of rewarding *guilty pleas* what should by now be clear is that this principle is part of a wider strategy of encouraging various forms of cooperation from suspects. That wider strategy in turn undoubtedly helps secure the mass production of guilty pleas, since it is difficult to see how a defendant who 'fully cooperates' with the police could realistically plead not guilty.

We have seen that the value of the guilty plea to the courts gradually reduces as time wears on and that the size of the discount is meant to be reduced correspondingly. This is in accordance with normal bargaining behaviour in that the largest discounts are only offered to those with something substantial to offer in return. The other side of the coin is that the courts have sometimes suggested that if an arrested person does not have much in the way of a defence to the charge then he or she cannot expect much by way of a discount for pleading guilty.[13] This position was reaffirmed in the post CJPO case of *Fearon*.[14] We may call this the 'caught red-handed' factor.

(iii) How large is the sentencing discount?

The appellate courts have been reluctant to specify a standard discount, arguing that sentencing is a subjective exercise which must be tailored to all the circumstances of each individual case.[15] This position was endorsed in *Buffrey* by Lord Taylor CJ:

> 'It would be quite wrong for us to suggest that there was any absolute rule as to what the discount should be. Each case must be assessed by the trial judge on its own facts and there will be considerable variance as between one case and another.'[16]

On the other hand, the Court of Appeal has been prepared to allow appeals against sentence on the ground that insufficient discount was given in

13 Eg, *Hollington and Emmens* (1985) 82 Cr App Rep 281.
14 [1996] 2 Cr App Rep (S) 25. See, to like effect, *Landy* (1995) 16 Cr App Rep 908.
15 See, for example, the case of *Williams* [1983] Crim LR 693.
16 (1992) 14 Cr App Rep (S) 511 at 515.

return for a plea of guilty.[17] This suggested to one eminent expert on sentencing that some convention or standard was operating in the 1980s to produce a discount of between a quarter and a third.[18] More recent cases suggest that it has become fairly well accepted that the 'standard discount' for an early guilty plea is a third.[19] More may be knocked off in special circumstances such as where the need for a particularly complex trial is obviated by a guilty plea or where the defendant was particularly helpful to the police.[20]

The principle that everything depends on the context and circumstances of each individual case was taken to its logical conclusion in *Costen*[1]. Here the Court of Appeal said that the sentencing discount could be withheld altogether if there had been a last-minute tactical change of plea or if the offender had been caught 'red-handed' and there was no possible defence to the charge.[2] Thus a sentencer may justifiably impose the maximum sentence allowed for in law despite the fact that the defendant pleaded guilty.[3] However, it is rare to withhold the discount completely, and in the post-CJPO case the Court of Appeal went so far as to say that the law required sentencing judges to give *some* discount for a guilty plea however strong the prosecution case may be.[4] To the extent that the sentencing discount principle is designed to maximise efficiency, this makes sense. If no discount was to be offered, defendants facing overwhelming

17 See, for instance, *Skilton and Blackham* (1982) 4 Cr App Rep (S) 339 and *Boyd* (1980) 2 Cr App Rep (S) 234. In *Buffrey* itself the prison sentence passed was reduced on appeal from 5 to 4 years.

18 See *Williams* [1983] Crim LR 693 and the accompanying commentary at 694.

19 See, for example, *Burns* (28 July 2000, unreported), CA.

20 See *Buffrey* (1992) 14 Cr App Rep (S) 511 where Lord Taylor CJ acknowledged that in complex cases, where great savings were produced by a guilty plea it might be proper to award a discount of one third to late plea changers. It follows that those pleading guilty from the outset in such cases should be rewarded by an even bigger discount. On helping the police, see *King* (1985) 7 Cr App Rep (S) 227. See also *Lowe* (1977) 66 Cr App Rep 122 where the suspect's cooperation with the police was said to have led to the breaking up of most of London's East End criminal gangs. The Court of Appeal reduced the sentence from 11.5 to 5 years.

1 (1989) 11 Cr App Rep (S) 182.

2 Following *Morris* (1988) 10 Cr App Rep (S) 216. Two further exceptions to the mitigating effect of a guilty plea were enumerated by Lord Lane CJ: where a long sentence, possibly the maximum sentence, was thought necessary to protect the public (following *Stabler* (1984) 6 Cr App Rep (S) 129); and where, as in *Costen*, the offender had been convicted on a 'specimen' count.

3 *Hastings* [1995] Crim LR 661. This case is impossible to reconcile with the earlier case of *Sharkey and Daniels* [1994] Crim LR 866 which held that a maximum sentence in such circumstances would be wrong in principle.

4 [1996] Crim LR 212. Similarly in *Murphy* (1993) 15 Cr App Rep (S) 329 it was ruled that in the case of a young offender the invariable practice should be to award some discount for a plea of guilty save in the most exceptional circumstances.

prosecution cases might think 'well, there's always a chance of a freak acquittal, I've nothing to lose by pleading not guilty, and at least this way I can go down fighting.' The Court of Appeal recognised this in *Davis*. Some bank robbers had been caught 'red-handed' and their subsequent pleas of guilty were accordingly treated as irrelevant to sentencing. On appeal, however, a different view was taken:

> '[T]he court bears in mind that these kinds of criminal will do anything at their trial to evade verdicts of guilty. They often do so by making attacks on police officers and by trying to beguile the jury into believing that in some way they have been treated unfairly. Fortunately they seldom succeed, but in the course of failing they waste much public time and money. They should be encouraged, as far as it is possible to encourage criminals, to stop these sort of tactics.'[5]

Because the defendants had chosen not to 'waste' the court's time in this way a modest discount was allowed, but the fact that this is not always the result of an appeal demonstrates that this area of 'law' is not rule-bound and hence arguably not law as conventionally understood at all. It seems that the Court of Appeal wants to have it both ways. It seeks to induce guilty pleas through discounts, so lays down a policy of requiring a discount for every guilty pleader. When faced with an 'undeserving' appellant, however, it sometimes cannot bring itself to meet its end of the bargain and introduces an exception to the policy so that a discount can be denied.[6] Faced with a more 'deserving' appellant (or a build up of pressure on the Crown Court) the exception to the policy is restricted or removed. This is the rule of officials, not law.

Some cases have examined whether the discount can change the nature as well as the quantum of the sentence.[7] The case of *Okinikan*[8] holds that a plea of guilty in combination with other mitigating factors may make the difference between an immediate prison sentence and a non-custodial disposal such as a fine or a community service order. The post-CJPO case of *Howells*[9] confirmed this by ruling that in deciding whether to impose a custodial sentence in borderline cases the sentencing court should 'ordinarily' take into account an offender's admission of responsibility, particularly if reflected in a guilty plea tendered at the earliest opportunity and accompanied by hard evidence of genuine remorse, as shown (for

5   (1980) 2 Cr App Rep (S) 168 at 170.
6   As in *Hastings* [1995] Crim LR 661.
7   See *Hollyman* (1979) 1 Cr App Rep (S) 289.
8   (1993) 14 Cr App Rep (S) 453.
9   [1998] Crim LR 836.

example) by an expression of regret to the victim and an offer of compensation.

The linkage between the guilty plea and other mitigating factors (and between a not guilty plea and aggravating factors) is what tends to intensify the pressures to plead guilty in practice. Those intending to plead not guilty are often advised by their lawyers of numerous *additional* disadvantages to this course of action should they be convicted, including: that any award of costs against them will be higher (because cases are so much more expensive if contested); that the facts which emerge during a contested trial will be damaging to the defendant; that it will then be difficult to mitigate on the basis that remorse is felt, and that the defendant will spend longer in the system awaiting trial. The likely overall impact of a guilty plea on the position of the defendant can thus be painted as very considerable indeed. The actual impact is rather different, as we shall now see.

(b) The impact of the discount principle on sentencing in the magistrates' court

The sentence discount principle was historically of little significance in the lower criminal courts, not least because appellate decisions were almost exclusively concerned with Crown Court sentencing. The sentencing guidelines issued by the Magistrates' Association as late as 1989 made no mention of the effect of a guilty plea, and magistrates publicly questioned the relevance of such a plea to sentence.[10] Research demonstrated that magistrates paid little attention to legal principle when sentencing, preferring to rely on their own intuitive sense of the right outcome.[11] One such study conducted in the early 1980s found that two-thirds of the 129 magistrates interviewed regarded a plea of guilty as of minor or no significance in mitigation.[12] The observational study by McConville et al conducted over a three-year period beginning in 1988 reported as follows:

> 'We found no evidence to support the idea that magistrates operate a discount system: this did not figure explicitly in lawyers' advice

---

10   See the discussion by M Wasik and A Turner, 'Sentencing Guidelines for the Magistrates' Courts' [1993] Crim LR 345 at p 355.

11   See R Tarling, Sentencing Practice in Magistrates' Courts (Home Office Research Study no 56) (London: HMSO, 1979) p 43; H Parker, M Sumner and G Jarvis, *Unmasking the Magistrates* (Milton Keynes: Open UP, 1989) p 84; and R Henham, *Sentencing Principles and Magistrates' Sentencing Behaviour* (Aldershot: Avebury, 1990) p 181.

12   Henham (1990) p 133.

over plea to defendants or in pleas of mitigation, and magistrates made little or no mention of it in sentencing.'[13]

The formal legal position changed in the mid-1990s. The 1993 version of the Magistrates' Association sentencing guidelines stated that 'a *timely* guilty plea may be regarded as a mitigating factor for which a sentencing discount of approximately one-third might be given.'[14] This version also incorporated the crime control principle that the weaker the evidence against an accused, the more inducement should be offered: 'An early admission of guilt where an offence would otherwise be undetected should attract a substantial discount, on the other hand, a last-minute plea when faced with witnesses may attract only a nominal discount'. New guidelines were issued in 1997, and these reflected the new statutory backing (ie, CJPO, s 48) for the sentence discount principle: 'The law requires that the court reduces the sentence for a timely guilty plea, but the provision should be used with judicial flexibility. A timely guilty plea may attract a sentence discount of up to one third but the precise amount of discount will depend on the facts of each case and a last-minute plea of guilty may attract only a nominal reduction.'[15]

What difference has all this made to actual sentencing practice? According to Flood-Page and Mackie, not much. They studied the sentencing of 3,000 defendants at 25 magistrates' courts in the mid-1990s. Looking just at defendants who received custodial sentences, they found that those who pleaded guilty had an average sentence length of 3.7 months compared with 3.8 months for those pleading not guilty. But, since there were only 30 contested cases that resulted in a prison sentence in their sample, the authors concede that they were unable to make any statistically reliable assessment of the impact of plea on sentence length. In other words, the difference in average sentence length may have been due to other factors, such as the possibility that contested cases more often involved more serious charges.[16] The authors do not discuss what influence plea had on the severity of other sentences, such as fines. There was some evidence, however, that the broad strategy of inducing cooperation with the police (or, to put it another way, penalising a lack of cooperation) did influence magisterial thinking. Thus sentencers treated as an aggravating

13 McConville et al (1994) p 188. Note that their own study suggests that the discount principle was not without some influence in the magistrates' courts (see at pp 167 and 205).
14 Magistrates' Association, Sentencing Guidelines (London: Magistrates' Association, 1993) p 3. Emphasis in original.
15 Magistrates' Association, Sentencing Guidelines (London: Magistrates' Association, 1997) para 2.4.
16 C Flood-Page and A Mackie, Sentencing Practice: an examination of decisions in magistrates' courts and the Crown Court in the mid-1990s (Home Office Research Study no 180) (London: Home Office, 1998) p 34.

factor aggressive or non-cooperative behaviour towards the police at the point of arrest; this was linked with a reduced likelihood of a fine and an increased likelihood of custody.[17] To the extent that magistrates were giving sentence discounts, white defendants benefited from the policy more often than ethnic minority defendants. This is because the latter pleaded not guilty more frequently than the former, thus disqualifying themselves from the possibility of a discounted sentence.[18] More generally, the study concluded that 'the attempts to predict sentences on the basis of case factors were not particularly successful . . . [which] suggests wide differences in the way these sentences are used . . .'[19] In other words, sentencing is still all over the place. The magistracy is an overwhelmingly white, middle-aged and middle-class institution which displays strong pro-authority attitudes and various forms of bias in all its decision-making.[20] For example, one magistrate told Flood-Page and Mackie that:

> 'We all resent having to fine people very low amounts for no insurance. We're all sitting in court, having paid our dues, and they are taking a chance and getting away with it. If they are on income support, how can they afford to own a car?'[1]

It is difficult to imagine this magistrate awarding a sentence discount to someone so obviously perceived to be 'undeserving'.[2]

Henham carried out a different type of study of this issue in Leicester and Nottingham magistrates' court in April 1998. Unfortunately the methods used in the study, and the way in which the results are reported,

---

17 Flood-Page and Mackie (1998) pp 22 and 47-8. The observational study by McConville et al (1994) pp 204-205 found that one of the standard ways in which defence solicitors seek to mitigate sentence is by stressing to the bench that their client was helpful to the police.
18 Flood-Page and Mackie (1998) p 117.
19 Flood-Page and Mackie (1998) p 129. Their conclusion encompassed sentencing in the Crown Court as well.
20 See the discussion in ch 8, section 5(a) and, for the impact of middle-class values on sentencing, see McConville et al (1994) pp 203-204.
1 Quoted in Flood-Page and Mackie (1998) pp 51-52.
2 Note that one effect of the plea before venue procedure, discussed in section 2(a)(ii) above, should have been that magistrates viewed fewer cases as requiring committal to the Crown Court for sentencing. The early guilty plea, with the large reduction in punishment it is supposed to earn, should have brought at least some of the cases that were previously committed to the Crown Court for trial within the magistrates' limited sentencing powers. (Magistrates must take into account the sentence discount when considering committal for sentence following the plea before venue procedure: *Warley Magistrates' Court, ex p DPP* [1998] 2 Cr App Rep 307.) That this has not happened provides indirect evidence of the failure by magistrates to apply the discount principle consistently. See L Bridges, 'False Starts and Unrealistic Expectations' (1999) Legal Action, October, 6 at pp 6-7.

limits the inferences we can draw from the findings. Henham relied on sentencers completing and returning a short questionnaire immediately after each guilty plea case had been finalised. This questionnaire prompted them directly to say what effect the guilty plea had on the sentence passed. A total of 210 questionnaires were returned. Henham does not indicate any non-response rate, so it is unclear how representative is his sample of cases.[3] A more serious problem, however, is that his research method relies on magistrates stating accurately how much discount (if any) they allowed for a guilty plea. He acknowledges that his respondents may have 'exaggerated, rationalised or characterised their responses inappropriately', but he does not provide us with any way of knowing to what extent such distortion occurred.[4] Given that his own research method sensitised the magistrates to the very issue he was hoping to collect valid information on, there is reason to believe that the extent of such distortion was great. Henham's study, therefore, is a study of *claims* made by magistrates about the influence of the sentence discount principle, and those claims were made in the knowledge that a researcher was assessing the extent to which magistrates were complying with the law by at least considering the award of a discount.

We also have some doubts about the assumptions made by Henham about what the law requires in this area, and, therefore, the critical judgments he makes about the supposed lack of fit between sentencers' practice and the law. One example is where he states that 'those Court of Appeal decisions which appear to sanction *no* discount in so-called "dead-bang" cases, are contrary to the clearly expressed intention of the legislature in s 48 to encourage and reward early guilty pleas.'[5] But there is no such clear expression in s 48. As we noted at the beginning of section 2, the wording is permissive rather than mandatory, and assumes that existing common law principles will continue to govern this area. It would have been easy enough for Parliament to say that some discount must always be given for a guilty plea, however small. It did not do so.

3   All we are told is that in one of the courts the less serious traffic offences were excluded altogether, as were prosecutions for not having a television licence, and those brought by the Vehicle Inspectorate. R Henham, 'Reconciling Process and Policy: Sentence Discounts in the Magistrates' Courts' [2000] Crim LR 436 at 442 n 37.

4   Henham [2000] at 442, fn 36. Although he states here that the 'problem of reliability is dealt with below' there is no further discussion of this issue in his article.

5   Henham [2000] pp 443-444. His citation of the commentary that accompanies *Hastings* [1995] Crim LR 661 (by D A Thomas) in support of this claim is equally unconvincing. Thomas, whilst speculating that to deny a discount in 'caught red-handed' cases 'might be seen to run contrary to the legislative policy of encouraging an early indication of the intention to plead guilty' notes, with more certainty, that 'a continuation of the present practice would not be inconsistent with the wording of the section'.

For what it is worth, Henham's main findings were as follows. In 90% of cases sentencers indicated that the guilty plea had at least some impact on the sentence. Similarly 86.2% of sentencers claimed that they had attached at least some importance to the stage at which the guilty plea was entered. A third of cases were said to have resulted in a sentence discount of more than one-third and around a fifth of cases less than a third; about 1 in 20 cases were claimed to have attracted no discount at all. The reason given by magistrates for giving less than a third discount included: 'caught red-handed' (25.8%); strength of prosecution case (13%); late plea of guilt (22.6%), and 'other' (38.7%).[6]

Henham's conclusion is that 'section 48 has done little to regulate the pragmatic nature of decision-making on sentence discounts';[7] in other words, magistrates have remained something of a law unto themselves. But, if we regard Henham's study as effectively one based on interviews with magistrates, the more significant conclusion is that magistrates are far more likely to claim that they are influenced by the sentencing discount principle than they were in the 1980s. To what extent this is due to the sensitising impact of the method used in Henham's study is unclear.

(c) The impact of the discount principle on sentencing in the Crown Court

In view of the apparent uncertainty displayed by the relatively small number of Court of Appeal judges about the nature and size of the guilty plea discount, it is not surprising to find even more uncertainty, and hence disparity, among Crown Court sentencers. Crown Court judges are pragmatists and have been found to display a measure of ignorance of, or resistance to, principles established by the Court of Appeal.[8] The way in which the discount principle was applied in practice prior to the CJPO was examined in three separate studies by Hood, Moxon, and Baldwin and

---

6   Henham [2000] p 445, Table 2. Although Henham gives the impression that Table 2 includes cases in which no discount was given (by referring to the Table as including details of 43 cases, and labelling Table 2 'Reasons where less than one-third discount') in fact the Table only includes details on 31 cases, and excludes the 12 in which no discount were given. It is unclear what reasons, or lack of them, are encompassed in the category 'other' in this Table.

7   Henham [2000] p 450.

8   Dissatisfaction with and ignorance of Court of Appeal sentencing principles amongst Crown Court judges is reported by Ashworth et al (1984) p 49. See also M Hunter, 'Judicial discretion: s 78 in practice' [1994] Crim LR 558 at 562, discussed in ch 11, section 5(c).

McConville.[9] The latter study, carried out in the 1970s, reported a spectrum of views on the discount principle:

> 'Some judges regard a reduction of perhaps a quarter or a third of whatever sentence is to be imposed as a fair reward in most cases for a guilty plea; others view any reduction in sentence as being solely conditional upon evidence of contrition on the part of the defendant which is recognised as a fairly exceptional occurrence.'[10]

However, all three studies suggested that Crown Court sentencing was consistent with the overall pattern of Court of Appeal judgments in a number of respects: firstly, discounts were generally being awarded for pleas of guilty; second, as expected, sentence lengths were being affected by guilty pleas; third, the type of sentence itself was often determined by whether or not someone pleaded guilty. This last point is crucial as the pressure exerted on defendants to plead guilty by the sentencing discount is obviously much greater if the plea can make the difference between a custodial and non-custodial sentence. Although few appellate cases have dealt with the question of whether such a large sentencing differential is justified, this body of research suggested that Crown Court judges were prepared to grant these large discounts.

One aspect of judicial practice was not consistent with the legal position, however. Late plea changers should, in legal theory, be receiving smaller discounts than those who pleaded guilty at an early stage. Yet despite the fact that the latter undoubtedly contributed more to the efficient administration of justice by the timing of their pleas of guilty, they received less of a reward than the late plea changers in both Baldwin and McConville's study and, to a lesser extent, in that conducted by Moxon. This is consistent with a model of bargaining in which last-minute concessions are offered by or wrung out of judges when it is clear that the defendant will otherwise stick with a plea of not guilty.

The research by Hood was the most sophisticated of these studies in that it rigorously took into account all measurable factors that might affect sentence length other than plea (eg, previous record). Only three months of the 10 months aggregate difference in sentence length between guilty pleaders and those contesting their cases was found to be attributable to the plea itself.[11] Hood also discovered that Afro-Caribbeans tend to plead

9   R Hood, *Race and Sentencing* (Oxford: OUP, 1992) p 87; D Moxon, Sentencing Practice in the Crown Court (Home Office Research Study no 103) (London: HMSO, 1988); and J Baldwin and M McConville, 'The Influence of the Sentencing Discount in Inducing Guilty Pleas' in J Baldwin and A Bottomley (eds), *Criminal Justice: Selected Readings* (Oxford: Martin Robertson, 1978) p 119.
10 Baldwin and McConville (1978) p 119.
11 Hood (1992) p 125.

The sentence discount principle

not guilty more frequently than whites and so are more often denied the benefit of the sentence discount principle.[12] As we have seen, Flood-Page and Mackie discovered a similar phenomenon in the magistrates' courts. In their Crown Court study, where the stakes are higher, the proportion of defendants pleading guilty by ethnic group was as follows: whites, 75%; blacks 66%, and Asians, 65%.[13] This clearly calls for further critical comment and you will not be surprised to learn that we are going to supply it (see subsection (e) below). First, however, we need to look more closely at the post CJPO studies of the operation of the sentence discount in the Crown Court by Flood-Page and Mackie, and by Henham.

The former study examined the sentencing of 1,777 defendants from 18 Crown Court centres over the period September 1995 to January 1996. Except for drug offences, plea did not appear to influence the choice between a custodial and non-custodial sentence. For those sent to prison, guilty pleaders on average got one third less than those who pleaded not guilty. Remarkably, the authors do not comment on the finding that for certain offences (robbery and theft and handling) those pleading guilty received *longer* sentences on average than those pleading not guilty.[14] All these findings are of little use because the researchers, on this issue, did not attempt to control for factors such as offence seriousness and previous record. They are thus unable, notwithstanding their claims to be measuring the 'impact of plea' to identify what effect (if any) the guilty plea was having on sentence.[15]

Their results also suggested that it was no longer true that defendants who pleaded guilty at the last moment received bigger discounts than those pleading guilty from the outset. The average length of prison sentence received was 21.8 months for the early guilty pleaders and 24.6 months for the late guilty pleaders.[16] The much more striking finding, however, is that those pleading not guilty who were convicted got 36.4 months on average.

12   Hood (1992) pp 202-203
13   Flood-Page and Mackie (1998) p 119.
14   Ashworth (1998) p 278 points out that the official criminal statistics show a similar counter-intuitive pattern (ie, of greater punishment for guilty pleaders than for those pleading not guilty) for the offences of indecent assault on a female and causing death by dangerous driving. Some of this pattern might be explained by the effects of charge-bargaining. Thus rapes may be downgraded to indecent assaults as a result of an agreement by the defendant to plead guilty. This might make the guilty plea cases within the latter offence category considerably more serious in nature than the not guilty plea cases. But this explanation has no purchase for robbery.
15   The points made in this paragraph are based on the presentation of results by Flood-Page and Mackie (1998) at pp 90-91.
16   This is such a small difference that it must be doubted whether, once all other factors are controlled for (eg previous record), there is really any difference at all. Practitioners have suggested that courts do not always reward early pleas in the way that they are supposed to, for example Sunman [1998] p 800.

The apparent incentive to plead guilty at an early stage pales into insignificance when compared with the disincentive to stick to a plea of not guilty. Of those fined, on average guilty pleaders were stung for £548 compared with £835 for those pleading not guilty. There was no significant difference in the length of a community service order, or probation order by plea. But all these findings are affected by the same fundamental flaw referred to in the preceding paragraph, so we should not give them much weight.[17] Overall, the research represents a missed opportunity to study the real impact of the guilty plea.

Henham examined 310 guilty plea cases from six Crown Court centres. He did not examine the effect of a guilty plea on sentencing except in an indirect manner. Transcripts of the judge's sentencing comments were examined to monitor the extent of 'compliance' with s 48 CJPO. Unfortunately, Henham chooses to treat an absence of sentencing comments on the effect of the guilty plea on sentence as 'non-compliance', even though he himself acknowledges that sentencers are not obliged by s 48 to make such comments if in fact they have not given any discount for a guilty plea. He made this choice on the basis that in only six of the 145 cases where no such comments were made did the sentencer explicitly say that no discount had been awarded for the guilty plea, drawing from this the 'reasonable' conclusion that 'that the remainder of those 145 cases where there was a failure to state the fact that a sentence discount had been given were in reality cases where a sentence discount *was* allowed.'[18] But this is speculation and arguably not the most reasonable conclusion to draw. It seems more likely that there were at least some cases where no discount was given for the guilty plea and the sentencer, under no obligation to explain this, confined his or her remarks to the various other matters where comment *is* obligatory. Why point out to the defendant that the system has failed to keep its side of the bargain (which it itself sought to induce) when this could threaten judicial legitimacy?

This raises the question of why no discount might be given in guilty plea cases. Perhaps Crown Court judges are like magistrates and the appellate judiciary in wanting to have it both ways. They like guilty pleas, but they do not like giving discounts to the 'undeserving'. Thus Henham found, in relation to sentencers' general approach to the discount principle in fixing sentence, that 'as many as 34.5% of sentencers considered the guilty plea as either "not particularly important" or "not important at all".' He finds this 'surprising'. We find it predictable. In a system which plays dirty with suspect's 'rights' at every stage in the process why should the

17   The points made in this paragraph are based on the presentation of results by Flood-Page and Mackie (1998) at pp 91-92.
18   R Henham, 'Bargain Justice or Justice Denied? Sentence Discounts and the Criminal Process' (1999) 63 MLR 515 at 527.

'right' to a sentence discount be any different?[19] By the same token, how can we be sure, on the basis of Henham's study, that all the Crown Court judges who said they were awarding a discount for a guilty plea actually did so? In the absence of some attempt to control for all other factors that might have influenced the sentence (particularly the seriousness of the offence and previous record of the offender) there is simply no way we can be confident about this. A policy of announcing that a discount had been given but not actually making any reduction would allow Crown Court judges to have the best of what would be a particularly bad 'bargain' for defendants. For all these reasons we doubt that Henham is correct in his implicit conclusion that in only six out of the 310 cases he looked at was a discount denied to a guilty pleader. The processes at work in the Crown Court are far more fluid than that. Crown Court judges are even more socially unrepresentative than are magistrates and we should not be surprised if this results in some defendants being denied a sentence discount. The fact that they are trained lawyers does not mean that their decisions will be free of bias. Indeed, Hood found evidence consistent with *direct* racial discrimination in one of the four Crown Court centres he studied.[20]

One reason why Crown Court judges may not feel the need in every case to reinforce *openly* the policy of inducing guilty pleas (ie, by announcing the award of discounts when sentencing) is that there are sufficient alternative *covert* ways of communicating this policy to defendants. As we shall now explore, these involve court clerks, the defendant's own legal adviser as well as backstage negotiations with the judges themselves.

(d) The communication of the discount to the defendant

The prospect of obtaining a reduction in sentence by pleading guilty influenced 65% of those pleading guilty in the Hedderman and Moxon study.[1] A study of Crown Court cases conducted by Zander and Henderson for the Royal Commission on Criminal Justice (Runciman Commission) also pointed to the importance of sentence reduction in decisions to plead guilty.[2] There is clearly widespread knowledge about the discount principle amongst defendants. In this section we explore how this is achieved.

19 See, in particular, chs 2-5 on the extent of police compliance with suspects' rights.
20 Hood (1992).
1   Hedderman and Moxon (1992).
2   Zander and Henderson (1993) p 146. Note that this study relied on questionnaires being returned by defendants, lawyers and other participants in Crown Court proceedings. As the response rate for defendants was only 19%, the study's findings on the views of defendants must be treated with great caution.

(i) The role of defence lawyers

The defence lawyer has a duty to the client 'to promote and protect fearlessly and by all proper and lawful means his [sic] lay client's best interests.'[3] In a system which operates a sentence discount principle this means that a defence lawyer is ethically obliged to point out the pros and cons of pleading guilty.[4] As Lord Parker CJ put it in the leading case of *Turner*:

> 'Counsel must be completely free to do what is his duty, namely to give the accused the best advice he can and, if need be, advice in strong terms. This will often include advice that a plea of guilty, showing an element of remorse, is a mitigating factor which may well enable the court to give a lesser sentence than would otherwise be the case.'[5]

Although Lord Parker went on to say that the defendant, 'having considered counsel's advice, must have a complete freedom of choice whether to plead guilty or not guilty',[6] one may question whether such freedom can co-exist with strong advice from counsel to plead guilty.

McConville et al carried out their observational research study in the magistrates' court at a time when the sentencing discount principle had yet to take firm root there.[7] There can be little doubt, however, that defence lawyers are increasingly communicating the fact of the discount 'in strong terms' now that the CJPO has given statutory backing for that principle. We assume this is so because of McConville et al's finding that most defence lawyers generally seek to persuade their clients to plead guilty. They argue (we think convincingly) that while there are many factors behind this unethical preference for trial-avoidance, the main factors are a presumption that the client is guilty, and a belief that the client is unworthy, and undeserving of a contested trial.[8] Where a client wishes to maintain innocence, the solicitor will emphasise (and usually exaggerate) the perils

---

3   General Council of the Bar, Code of Conduct for Barristers (1990) (with updating in 1997) para 203(a). The Law Society's Code for Advocacy (laying down professional standards for solicitors) contains equivalent wording.

4   See M Blake and A Ashworth, 'Some Ethical Issues in Prosecuting and Defending Criminal Cases' [1998] Crim LR 16 at pp 25-26.

5   [1970] 2 WLR 1093 at 1097.

6   [1970] 2 WLR 1093 at 1097.

7   Although McConville et al (1994) p 188 say that they found no evidence that the discount principle was at work in the operation of the magistrates' courts, they do give examples which suggest the contrary, as at p 167.

8   McConville et al (1994) ch 8. This argument finds support in A Mulcahy, 'The Justifications of Justice: Legal Practitioners' Accounts of Negotiated Case Settlements in Magistrates' Courts' (1994) 34 BJ Crim 411.

of pleading not guilty. In one assault case they observed, for example, the client had maintained from the outset that he had struck the complainant in self-defence. On the day set for his trial, the solicitor spoke to the client at the doors of the court:

Solicitor: All of the witnesses are here - are you still going to plead not guilty?

Client: Yes, why shouldn't I?

Solicitor: Well - I've prepared your case, but self-defence is a hard one to run and it's a very tough bench today.

Client: Are you saying I should plead guilty?

Solicitor: No, not at all - I'm just saying that there are two ways of handling this: you can plead not guilty, have a trial - you'll be cross-examined and the prosecution (and remember they have three witnesses) will say that you merely stuck one on him, that he hadn't got his fists raised.

Client: Yes, but. . . .

Solicitor: Let me finish - or, you can take the *other* course - whereby they won't even have a say and I can speak on your behalf I can say that he'd already hit George . . . it's much better mitigation.

Client: *I've* got a witness as well.

Solicitor: I know - but unfortunately your witness is well known in these courts.

Client: I know. Well, you're the expert and you say that the bench is tough, shall I plead guilty then?

Solicitor: That's entirely your decision.

Client: . . . and it would save a lot of time if I plead guilty wouldn't it?

Solicitor: Yes it would - if you have a trial you'll be here until at least lunchtime, probably after that - whereas if you decide to plead guilty you will be out of here within the hour - but time isn't really the issue.

Client: What do you think I'd get?

Solicitor: A hefty fine I should think.

Client: Thanks a lot.

Solicitor: But it won't be as great as if you were convicted after a trial, because the court costs would amount to more.

Client: I think I *will* be convicted, don't you?

Solicitor: I think so to be honest - even though none of the witnesses are police officers - you see, the chairman of the bench today is *very* prosecution minded.

Client: I'll plead guilty - because, as you say, it's a hard bench.

Solicitor:	It is, but it's your decision.
Client:	I know what these people are like . . . there are other things, like the people on the bench - and you're the expert, you have inside information about things like that, you know things about the bench and the prosecution that I don't know, so I've listened to you - and I'll plead guilty - but you *will* speak for me?
Solicitor:	Yes I will.[9]

Here we can see the solicitor stressing the savings in time and money to be obtained through pleading guilty, saying nothing of the possible advantages of pleading not guilty, and effectively ignoring the client's claim of innocence. Solicitors committed to trial avoidance, as most are, are sure to see the sentence discount principle as providing a useful additional pressure that they can bring to bear on defendants. It will dovetail nicely with their practice of seeking to mitigate on the basis that the defendant had cooperated with the needs of crime control, as in this example: 'I ask you to give my client credit for his plea. He was also co-operative with the police.'[10]

From November 2000 there will be a new opportunity to press upon defendants the advantages of an *early* plea of guilt. Under the Narey reforms[11] defendants will appear before the magistrates' courts within days of charge, either at early first hearings (EFHs)[12] or at early administrative hearings (EAHs). Cases will be assigned to EFHs by the police and prosecution on the basis that they are 'straightforward guilty pleas' and the intention is that the magistrates will convict at the EFH and proceed to sentencing as fast as possible. As Bridges notes, this seems to undermine the presumption of innocence and might cause unfair prejudice against defendants amongst the magistrates at these hearings.[13] Just over two-thirds of defendants in the courts which piloted this new mechanism pleaded guilty at the EFH,[14] no doubt with the active and unethical encouragement of their defence lawyers in many cases. EAHs are ostensibly held to determine the defendant's entitlement to legal aid but with the expectation that court clerks will engineer guilty pleas by explaining the implications of contesting the charge.[15] Duty solicitors can appear for

9   McConville et al (1994) pp 195-196 (emphasis in original).
10   McConville et al (1994) p 205.
11   Martin Narey was the chair of the inter-agency group set up to identify managerial devices which could 'speed up justice': Home Office, Review of Delay in the Criminal Justice System: a Report (London: Home Office, 1997).
12   See also ch 8, section 5(b).
13   Bridges (1999) p 8.
14   Bridges (1999) p 8.
15   See ch 8, section 3 for further discussion of EAHs and their case settlement function.

the defendant at an EAH but are as likely to join in with the project of persuading the client to plead guilty as they are to promote the client's true interests.[16]

Is the position any different in the Crown Court, where barristers rather than solicitors hold sway? Baldwin and McConville's study in the 1970s of late plea changers revealed that 40% of defendants had changed their plea as a result of pressure exerted by their barristers, in over half of which 'the advice counsel gave was of such a nature that no reasonable person could say that it was fair or proper or that the final decision to plead guilty was made voluntarily.'[17] The policy of offering large sentence discounts for guilty pleas provided barristers who wished to settle cases with powerful ammunition to fire at defendants. As one explained:

'The barrister then said, "If you're found guilty you will get about 10 or 15 years but if you plead guilty you will get 4 or 5 years." I was really shocked. I was so scared, sweating and nervous and he frightened me with this 10-15 years stuff and saying I had no chance. . . . I agreed to plead guilty but it wasn't my decision; I had no choice about it.'[18]

The study by McConville et al, conducted some 15 years later, showed that little had changed. They observed pre-trial conferences between counsel and client, held at court in order to settle the plea, and found that half the defendants involved were persuaded to enter guilty pleas immediately by their barristers 'with the remainder having to go through the same ordeal on a future occasion after their cases were adjourned without a plea.'[19] One might ask why these barristers had not advised these defendants to plead guilty at an earlier stage in the proceedings in order to earn the maximum discount on offer. The chance to press this advice is presented at pre-court conferences, but McConville et al found that any pressure applied in that setting tended to be subtle, and designed to sap the defendant's determination to go to trial rather than undermine it completely there and then. Even when the instructing solicitor told a barrister to give the client 'a talking to . . . You'll have to give him a hard time' the barrister chose not to give the client an ear-wigging, justifying this afterwards by saying: 'If you get too tough at the start, they sack you!'[20]

16 See ch 8, section 2(b) for a discussion of court duty solicitor schemes.
17 J Baldwin and M McConville, *Negotiated Justice* (London: Martin Robertson, 1977) p 45.
18 Baldwin and McConville (1977) pp 49-50.
19 McConville et al (1994) p 261.
20 McConville et al (1994) pp 253-254. The motivations of defence barristers are further explored in section 4(b)(i) below.

From the barrister's point of view, it makes economic sense to crack the trial at the doors of the court rather than well in advance, and the fact that it might be in the client's best interests to enter an *early* plea of guilt hardly seems to register. The sentence discount for a guilty plea did, however, feature in barristers' advice to clients in pre-court and court conferences alike, as in the following example:

> 'If you contest this and are convicted, you will definitely go to prison and it's just a question of the length of time. There would be no mitigation then because you have denied everything.'[1]

It must be stressed that even defendants represented by barristers of the highest possible integrity will come under pressure to plead guilty. That pressure will not be exerted by the barrister directly, but by a sentencing principle the operation of which effectively undermines due process rights. 'Bad' barristers merely exacerbate the problem.

A new duty to bring home the advantages of pleading guilty was created by the introduction of Plea and Directions Hearings (PDH) in all Crown Court proceedings in 1995. In this pre-trial forum the defendant is asked to indicate plea, and, if pleading guilty, the judge is meant to proceed to sentencing wherever possible. Otherwise, the judge seeks to identify the key issues in the case with the help of counsel and issues any directions necessary to ensure the smooth handling of the trial. Counsel for the defence must in every case complete a 'Judge's Questionnaire', question 1(b) of which asks if the defendant's attention has been drawn to s 48 of the CJPO.[2] Like the plea before venue system in the magistrates' court, one effect of this new procedure is the intensification of pressure on defendants to plead guilty as soon as possible, as seems to be reflected in the declining proportion of cracked trials amongst guilty plea cases.[3]

(ii) The role of sentencers

Since the CJPO 1994, s 48(2) came into force, one of the ways in which the sentence discount principle should be communicated is by the sentencer explaining that a discount has been given for the guilty plea. Thus we have seen that such remarks were made in 165 of the 310 Crown Court guilty plea cases examined by Henham.[4] Whilst the sentence discount principle

---

1   McConville et al (1994) p 254.
2   The questionnaire is reproduced by Sprack (2000) p 514.
3   Henham (1999) p 524.
4   Henham (1999); see subsection (c) above. In *Fearon* (1995) 2 Cr App Rep (S) 25 the Court of Appeal emphasised that it was highly desirable that sentencers should invariably make reference to a plea of guilty in their sentencing remarks

has long featured in some sentencers' comments, the effect of s 48(2) is likely to have increased the frequency with which this happens. This will have helped spread knowledge of the principle, especially amongst the courts' regular clientele.[5] But when facing a decision over plea what clients arguably need is *advance* notice of what discount will be forthcoming should they plead guilty. They can only get this from the sentencer, or, failing that, from their own lawyer's informed judgment about the likely discount.

We have seen that sentencing is a highly discretionary business, and that the size, nature, and even existence of the guilty plea discount is always uncertain. It depends as much upon the sentencer as on the facts of the case. This makes it difficult for ethically-minded defence lawyers to provide their clients with accurate advice about likely sentence depending on plea. Sentencers may have their own reasons, such as a desire to manage a burgeoning case load, for wanting to crack a trial. Should the law permit sentencers to indicate to defendants (or their lawyers) in advance what view they take of the alleged offence and what discount they would be prepared to give if a guilty plea was entered? The advantage of this would be that defendants would know exactly where they stood (although this assumes fair dealing on the part of the sentencer). The disadvantage would be that the impartiality of the court would be brought into question by such communications. It might seem as if the court were seeking to assist the prosecution in obtaining a conviction, thus placing even more pressure on the defendant to plead guilty.

The incentive for the defence and the sentencer to conduct a back-stage discussion of sentencing is not great in the magistrates' court. This is because the costs of summary contested trials are relatively small and the penalties relatively light. Moreover, there is little opportunity for informal relations to build up for, as McConville et al note, the bench of magistrates is detached from the activities of the lawyers.[6] The situation is quite different in the Crown Court, where barristers and judges (who are mostly ex-barristers) form a close-knit workgroup with shared values. Here it is common for judges and counsel to meet privately before or during the trial, and the Court of Appeal has been forced to try to regulate these meetings by the unethical nature of some of these encounters.

---

so that a defendant (and the Court of Appeal) would know that it had been taken into consideration. The research by Henham was conducted after this case was decided and his results suggest that a large proportion of sentencers are ignoring this injunction and/or that they consider it has no application where no discount is awarded.

5   In the early 1990s it was found that 62% of defendants in the Crown Court knew of the sentence discount principle: M Zander and P Henderson, The Crown Court Study, Royal Commission on Criminal Justice Research Study no 19 (London: HMSO, 1993) p 145.

6   McConville et al (1994) p 186.

In *Inns*, for example, the judge had sent for counsel before the trial began. There was a dispute as to what had been said in this private discussion, but the result was that the defendant had been advised by counsel that if he contested the case against him and lost an immediate custodial sentence would be imposed. As Lawton LJ, allowing the appeal, put it, 'he crumpled and took the view that contesting the case was not worth the risk.'[7] He pleaded guilty, was convicted and received a conditional discharge. On appeal, his conviction was quashed and a new trial ordered. Lawton LJ stressed in his judgment that:

> ' . . . the law attaches so much importance to a plea of guilty in open court that no further proof is required of the accused's guilt. When the accused is making a plea of guilty under pressure and threats, he does not make a free plea and the trial starts without there being a proper plea at all. All that follows thereafter is, in our judgment, a nullity.'[8]

This decision appears to be motivated by due process considerations in that it inhibits judges from exerting pressure on defendants to plead guilty. On the other hand, the discount principle itself exerts such pressure and the advice offered by counsel on this subject can be expressed, to use the language of *Turner*, 'in strong terms' if need be. The courts have sought to resolve this apparent contradiction by holding that strong advice from counsel does not nullify a plea. According to Lord Parker's judgment in *Turner*, any argument that defence counsel went so far in pressing upon a defendant the advantages of pleading guilty that a free choice of plea was denied is likely to fail: 'The Court would like to say that it is a very extravagant proposition, and one which would only be acceded to in a very extreme case.'[9] The law thus represents an uneasy compromise between due process and crime control values. A concern with due process appears to lie behind the prohibition on trial judges exerting pressure on defendants directly. The influence of the crime control model can be seen in the discount principle itself and in the leeway allowed to counsel in pressing the merits of pleading guilty on a defendant. That such latitude is granted suggests that the decision in *Inns* was motivated more by the need to preserve the appearance of an impartial judiciary than by any real concern with protecting the right of a defendant to put the prosecution to proof.

Turner remains to this day the leading case regulating what judges may say and do as regards sentencing and the discount principle prior to conviction. Lord Parker ruled that:

7   (1974) 60 Cr App Rep 231 at 233.
8   (1974) 60 Cr App Rep 231 at 233.
9   [1970] 2 WLR 1093 at 1096. Only someone completely unaware of, or callously indifferent to, the degree of pressure felt by defendants, as discussed above, could regard this as an 'extravagant proposition'.

'There must be freedom of access between counsel and judge. . . . This freedom of access is important because there may be matters calling for communication or discussion, which are of such a nature that counsel cannot in the interests of his client mention them in open court . . . counsel on both sides may wish to discuss with the judge whether it would be proper, in a particular case, for the prosecution to accept a plea to a lesser offence. . . .

The judge should, subject to the one exception referred to hereafter, never indicate the sentence which he is minded to impose. A statement that on a plea of guilty he would impose one sentence but that on a conviction following a plea of not guilty he would impose a severer sentence is one which should never be made. This could be taken to be undue pressure on the accused, thus depriving him of that complete freedom of choice which is essential. Such cases, however, are in the experience of the court happily rare. What on occasions does appear to happen however is that a judge will tell counsel that, having read the depositions and the antecedents, he can safely say that on a plea of guilty he will, for instance, make a probation order, something which may be helpful to counsel in advising the accused. The judge in such a case is no doubt careful not to mention what he would do if the accused were convicted following a plea of not guilty. Even so, the accused may well get the impression that the judge is intimating that in that event a severer sentence, maybe a custodial sentence, would result, so that again he may feel under pressure. This accordingly must also not be done. The only exception to this rule is that it should be permissible for a judge to say, if it be the case, that whatever happens, whether the accused pleads guilty or not guilty, the sentence will or will not take a particular form, eg a probation order or a fine, or a custodial sentence.

Finally, where such discussion on sentence has taken place between judge and counsel, counsel for the defence should disclose this to the accused and inform him of what took place.'[10]

Under the *Turner* rules a judge can give an indication that, irrespective of plea, a non-custodial sentence will be imposed. There thus remains a considerable incentive for defence counsel to see the judge in private. The only reason a defendant might be unwilling to plead guilty is the fear of receiving an immediate custodial sentence. If a judge can say that however the defendant pleads the penalty imposed will be a fine then defence counsel may find it much easier to persuade a client to plead guilty. This,

10   [1970] 2 WLR 1093 at 1097-8.

no doubt, is why it was seen as important in *Turner* to leave this option open to the judge.

Yet, by permitting limited discussions to take place about sentencing, the law has opened the door for misunderstandings to arise and for abuse to occur. It seems that many of those operating in the criminal courts have concluded that it is artificial and unrealistic for the law to encourage guilty pleas through the sentence discount whilst simultaneously denying defendants the opportunity to discover exactly what is on offer in the case at hand. In practice, both defence counsel and judges have abused their right to meet in private in order to engage in sentence bargaining.

(iii) Sentence bargaining in the Crown Court

Negotiations between judges and counsel, in which the former indicate what reduction in sentence an accused might secure by pleading guilty, are, as we have just established, contrary to law. As a corollary, the extent to which they take place is difficult to assess. One indication of the prevalence of sentence bargaining is the frequency with which cases on the matter have been heard by the Court of Appeal. In the late 1970s, for example, the Court of Appeal had to continually reaffirm the *Turner* rules in the face of appeals, 'all too many in number'.[11] Judgment in as many as seven plea bargaining cases was given by the Court of Appeal within the space of a year, with four of them being decided over an eight-day period in December 1977.[12]

A further spate of cases in the late 1980s suggests that Crown Court judges have retained their enthusiasm for sentence bargaining.[13] In *Smith* Russell LJ found it 'disturbing that despite frequent observations made in this Court discouraging unnecessary visits to the judge's room, they appear to continue up and down the country.'[14] This sentiment was echoed by Lord Lane CJ in the subsequent case of *Pitman*. 'There is it seems', he reflected wearily, 'a steady flow of appeals to this court arising from visits by counsel to the judge in his private room. No amount of criticism and no amount of warnings and no amount of exhortation seems to be able to prevent this happening.'[15] In the reported cases, defence counsel and

11 *Llewellyn* (1978) 67 Cr App Rep 149 at 151 per Roskill LJ.
12 The four being: *Howell* [1978] Crim LR 239; *Bird* (1977) 67 Cr App Rep 203; *Atkinson* (1978) 67 Cr App Rep 200, and *Ryan* (1978) 67 Cr App Rep 177. The other three cases were *Grice* (1978) 66 Cr App Rep 167; *Llewellyn* (1978) 67 Cr App Rep 149; and *Eccles* [1978] Crim LR 757.
13 See *Cullen* (1984) 81 Cr App Rep 17; *Keily* (1989) 11 Cr App Rep (S) 273; *Smith* [1990] 1 WLR 1311; and *Pitman* [1991] 1 All ER 468.
14 [1990] 1 WLR 1311 at 1314.
15 [1991] 1 All ER 468 at 470. See also *Preston* (1993) 98 Cr App Rep 405 at 425-26.

Crown Court judges seem to be equally implicated in sentence bargaining. Sometimes defence counsel takes the initiative by going to see the judge in private,[16] but often the judge summons counsel to initiate discussions over sentence.[17]

That sentence bargaining is an endemic and entrenched phenomenon in the Crown Court is further indicated by the evidence given by judges and counsel as part of these appeals. In *Plimmer*,[18] for example, the trial judge revealed that it was his standard practice to indicate what sentence he would give if a guilty plea were entered. In *Grice* the defendant pleaded not guilty to charges of having unlawful sexual intercourse with his adopted daughter. According to the judge himself:

> 'a "plea bargain" [was] offered, via Grice's defending counsel, that if he wished to plead guilty to the offences, and so spare the girl the ordeal of giving evidence, we would suspend the sentence. In other words, that the sentence of imprisonment would not come into operation providing Grice behaved himself.'[19]

In *Coward* defence counsel had 'submitted that it was a common practice for members of the Bar defending in criminal cases to ask to see the judge for the purpose of finding out what sort of sentence the judge would pass if there was a plea of guilty.'[20]

Research confirms the impression given by the reported cases that sentence bargaining is rife in the Crown Court. Around one in five of the late plea changers in Baldwin and McConville's study claimed to have given in to pressure by their barristers and accepted a sentence bargain, while in others barristers gave defendants a 'nod and a wink' that the ground had been prepared for a bargain.[1] The Court of Appeal's attempt to inhibit this practice has met with only limited success. McConville et al quote a senior solicitor as saying:

---

16 *Turner* [1970] QB 321; *Plimmer* (1975) 61 Cr App Rep 264; *Quartey* [1975] Crim LR 592; *Coward* (1979) 70 Cr App Rep 70; *Ryan* (1978) 67 Cr App Rep 177; and *Smith* [1990] 1 WLR 1311.

17 *Inns* (1974) 60 Cr App Rep 231; *Cain* [1976] Crim LR 464; *Bird* (1977) 67 Cr App Rep 203; *Atkinson* (1978) 67 Cr App Rep 200 (in this case the discussion took place at a pre-trial review); *Llewellyn* (1978) 67 Cr App Rep 149; *Grice* (1977) 66 Cr App Rep 167; *Eccles* [1978] Crim LR 757; *Winterflood* [1979] Crim LR 263; *Cullen* (1984) 81 Cr App Rep 17; *Keily* (1989) 11 Cr App Rep (S) 273; *James* [1990] Crim LR 815; and *Pitman* [1991] 1 All ER 468. In *Cullen* the Court of Appeal said 'We disapprove of a judge himself taking the initiative in sending for counsel.'

18 (1975) 61 Cr App Rep 264.

19 (1977) 66 Cr App Rep 167 at 170.

20 (1979) 70 Cr App Rep 70 at 75-6.

1 Baldwin and McConville (1977) pp 29-35.

'I don't browbeat clients into pleading guilty. But counsel often have their own ideas about what's going to happen that don't relate to the client. You see, they have something we don't - access to the Judge. So it's all discussed beforehand and the client is virtually told what to do.'[2]

Morison and Leith report that in some of the court centres they studied the practice of visiting the judge in private was frowned upon and did not appear to be employed. In others, however, 'it was commonplace for counsel to visit the judge's chambers before a case was heard to discuss what was to follow.'[3] The Crown Court survey conducted for the Runciman Commission provides one explanation for this flouting of the law: neither barristers nor trial judges appear to agree with the position adopted in *Turner*. On being asked, 'Do you think that *Turner* should be reformed to permit full and realistic discussion between counsel and the judge about plea and especially sentence?', the vast majority of barristers and two-thirds of the judges answered in the affirmative.[4] All of this suggests that lawyers and judges in the Crown Court, just like the police, habitually follow their own working assumptions rather than adhering to the legal rules.

The senior judiciary, however, have signalled their determination to stamp out sentence bargaining. Whereas the *Turner* rules stressed the need for freedom of access between counsel and the judge, subsequent case law has tended to emphasise that private out-of-court meetings should only be held where absolutely necessary.[5] It appears from the cases, however, that the Court of Appeal has been more concerned that private discussions are apt to produce 'embarrassing situations'[6] and 'unseemly disputes'[7] concerning the terms of any deal struck rather than because they violate due process principles of openness and impartiality. The Court has repeatedly emphasised that if private discussions do take place, a record

---

2   McConville et al (1994) p 253.
3   J Morison and P Leith, *The Barrister's World* (Milton Keynes: Open UP, 1992) p 135. See also J Plotnikoff and R Woolfson, From Committal to Trial: Delay at the Crown Court (London: Law Society, 1993) pp 67-68.
4   Zander and Henderson (1993) p 145. Fourteen examples of private discussions with the judge are to be found within a sub-sample of 43 cases drawn from this study, for which details are provided in M Zander, 'The "innocent" (?) who plead guilty' (1993) 143 NLJ 85.
5   See *Plimmer* (1975) 61 Cr App Rep 264; *Grice* (1977) 66 Cr App Rep 167; *Winterflood* [1979] Crim LR 263; and, more generally, *Harper-Taylor and Bakker* [1988] NLJR 80. See also P Curran, 'Discussions in the Judge's Private Room' [1991] Crim LR 79.
6   *Plimmer* (1975) 61 Cr App Rep 264.
7   *Smith* [1990] 1 WLR 1311.

must be made of what is said.[8] But this requirement might simply force Crown Court judges to adopt more subtle tactics. Just as the police are able to circumvent the controls that surround formal interviews at the police station, judges may be able to indicate by gestures (a nod and a wink perhaps?) as much as by words what sentencing deal is on offer. One Crown Court judge told us in an informal conversation that he sometimes transmits coded messages regarding the sentencing discount by calling in counsel to discuss how much longer a trial is expected to last. Morison and Leith comment: 'Knowing which judges to approach and how to interpret their signals is a difficult skill to master which depends on using personal knowledge about particular conditions.'[9]

An example of the problems that this delicate situation produces is provided by the case of *Coward*.[10] Defence counsel had asked the judge if he could give any indication as to sentence if his client changed his plea to guilty as part of a charge bargain agreed with the prosecution.[11] The judge firmly declined to do so. Counsel persisted by saying that he would be in difficulties in advising his client as to what to do, and mentioned the possibility that he would have to make an application to have the case transferred to another court. The judge said: 'You can trust me.' Defence counsel took this to mean that upon the entering of an acceptable plea of guilty a non-custodial sentence would follow. The judge, however, had meant only that defence counsel would have to trust his judgment. In the event a custodial sentence was imposed prompting yet another appeal.

Another problem is how far discussions with the judge should be confidential. The Court of Appeal has expressed conflicting views on whether defendants should be told of the judge's views,[12] but defence barristers will usually be happy to preserve the confidentiality of a private discussion. By only hinting that a sentence bargain has been struck they can make a defendant's decision to plead guilty more appeal-proof. To make a decision to plead guilty absolutely appeal-proof, the barrister need only assert that the advice given is based on previous experience of the trial judge's sentencing patterns rather than on any private discussion relating to the instant case. In either case the prediction of sentence is likely both to have a powerful effect and to be proven correct. In any event,

---

8   The need for some record to be made of any discussions regarding sentence was emphasised in *Llewellyn* (1978) 67 Cr App Rep 149; *Cullen* (1984) 81 Cr App Rep 17; *Keily* (1989) 11 Cr App Rep (S) 273; and *Smith* [1990] 1 WLR 1311.
9   Morison and Leith (1992) p 135.
10 (1979) 70 Cr App Rep 70.
11 There was no authoritative record of the discussion, but the various recollections were recognised by the Court of Appeal as differing not so much in substance as in emphasis. The details given in the text are drawn from the prosecuting counsel's notes on the basis that it is the most even-handed and plausible account.
12 Contrast *Turner* [1970] 2 QB 321 and *Bird* (1977) 67 Cr App Rep 203 with *Cain* [1976] Crim LR 464 and *Pitman* [1991] 1 All ER 468.

where barristers have taken the initiative in striking sentence bargains it is inconceivable that they will advise defendants that their behaviour was unlawful and that an appeal would be worthwhile. It is most unlikely that any reliable note of the 'discussion' between the barrister and the client will have been taken,[13] so even if a convicted person instructed a new lawyer to look into the matter it would be very difficult to establish any procedural malpractice. The relative isolation of the Crown Court judges from the Court of Appeal combined with the low probability of convicted offenders appealing means that the many barristers and judges disposed to do so can continue to follow their crime control working assumptions with little fear of being brought to account for their actions.

(e) What is wrong with sentence discounts?

(i) Due process objections

For the due process adherent, sentence discounts represent a marked departure from acceptable values. By encouraging defendants to convict themselves through a guilty plea, its effect is to undermine the principle that the burden of proof rests on the prosecution. The prosecution of cases involving no more than vague allegations and other potential misuses of state prosecutorial power may be left unchecked. Moreover, the high guilty plea rate to which the sentence discount contributes means that there is little incentive for the prosecuting authorities to ensure that only properly prepared cases are brought to trial. The number of weak cases prosecuted is likely to increase, as is the number of innocent persons wrongly convicted.

Take *Fearon,* and the caught red-handed factor for example.[14] Those facing strong prosecution evidence are presumed by the Court of Appeal to have little option but to plead guilty and, therefore, that it would be inappropriate to provide them with much of a reward for doing so. By contrast, a reward *is* regarded as appropriate for those who plead guilty in the face of weak prosecution cases. But we should be clear that this means that defendants are not merely *rewarded* for their noble decisions to own up to their wrongdoing, they are also being *induced* to waive their right to put the prosecution to proof. The reasoning in cases such as *Fearon* comes close to saying that the weaker the prosecution case, the more likely it is

13 One might have expected such a note to be taken by the instructing solicitor, but McConville et al (1994) p 242 found that 'practically all work connected with attending conferences with counsel, pre-trial discussions and actual court appearances is undertaken by non-qualified staff, many of whom have little or no experience of the legal system.'

14 [1996] 2 Cr App Rep (S) 25; discussed at the end of section 2(a)(ii) above.

that the defendant will put the prosecution to proof and the greater the sentencing discount will need to be to induce the defendant to plead guilty.[15] The risk of miscarriages of justice is obvious. That risk is exacerbated by the enhanced inducements offered to suspects to testify against their co-accused or to help the police suppress serious crime.[16] This is because of the temptation to provide perjured testimony and to make unfounded allegations in order to further their own interests.[17] From a freedom perspective we might also want to question whether it is right for the Court of Appeal to induce defendants to cooperate with the police to such an extent that they put their own safety and that of their families in jeopardy.[18]

A further problem is that the discount principle penalises those who stand on their right to put the prosecution to proof. This is an elementary point and yet many would dispute it. The argument put forward by the judiciary and supported by a number of commentators is that those pleading guilty are rewarded for so doing rather than those pleading not guilty being punished for contesting their case.[19] In the case of *Harper* the trial judge had commented in critical terms on the way in which the defendant, through his counsel, had conducted his case. The Court of Appeal reduced the sentence from five years' to three years' imprisonment. Its reasons were given by Lord Parker CJ:

> 'this court feels that there is a real danger . . . that the appellant was being given what was undoubtedly a serious sentence because he had pleaded not guilty and had run his defence in the way indicated by the recorder. This court feels it is quite improper to use language which may convey that an accused is being sentenced because he has pleaded not guilty, or because he has run his defence in a particular way. It is, however, of course proper to give a man a lesser sentence if he has shown genuine remorse, amongst other things by pleading guilty.'[20]

---

15   Note that the defendant is, in effect, being induced to confess, a point developed later in this subsection.
16   See the discussion of the principles laid down in *A and B* [1998] Crim LR 757 in section 2(a)(ii) above.
17   See C Walker, 'The Agenda of Miscarriages of Justice' in C Walker and K Starmer (eds) *Miscarriages of Justice* (London: Blackstone, 1999) at p 6 and references cited there.
18   See *A and B* [1998] Crim LR 757, discussed in section 2(a)(ii) above.
19   See, for example, E Stockdale and K Devlin, *Sentencing* (Waterlow, 1987) p 50 and J Sprack in E Stockdale and S Casale (eds), *Criminal Justice Under Stress* (London: Blackstone, 1992) p 86.
20   [1968] 2 QB 108 at 110.

This judgment seems more concerned with the language of sentencing than its substance. To characterise a guilty plea as mitigation rather than a not guilty plea as aggravation is simply hypocritical. The inescapable consequence of the sentence discount is that a significant price may have to be paid for putting the prosecution to proof, something which the defendants interviewed by Baldwin and McConville well understood:

> ' . . . it is easy to see why defendants often regard this sort of reasoning as meaningless. As far as we can tell, the sentencing differential is viewed by virtually all defendants as a penalty imposed on those who unsuccessfully contest their case.'[1]

The tension between the requirements of due process and crime control becomes acute in cases involving co-defendants facing identical charges where one pleads guilty and one not guilty. If a discount is given for a plea of guilty in this situation it will be immediately apparent to all that the defendant pleading not guilty has received a harsher punishment for doing so regardless of what the judge might say. The Court of Appeal has been prepared to sanction difference of treatment in cases where the discount has merely resulted in a shorter custodial sentence for the defendant pleading guilty, but has equivocated where the disparity has been greater. In *Hollyman*[2] three defendants were convicted on an identical charge. One received three months' immediate imprisonment and the others two months' imprisonment suspended for two years. The Court of Appeal ruled that it was sufficient justification for the different sentences that the latter pleaded guilty whilst the former contested the case. In *Tonks,*[3] by contrast, the Court of Appeal said that such a course of action would leave the imprisoned offender with a legitimate sense of grievance. The cases are irreconcilable. The trend, however, is towards a bare-faced acknowledgment that two virtually identical cases can be treated very differently simply because of some mitigating factor personal to one of the offenders involved (such as a guilty plea).

A further form of judicial hypocrisy is to be found in the disjunction between the sentence discount, and the rules we looked at in ch 5 (section 4(a)(i)) that ban the police from inducing suspects to confess by offering to drop charges or grant bail. For what is the effect of the principles set out in the case of *A and B* other than to offer an inducement to suspects to

---

1   J Baldwin and M McConville, 'The Influence of the Sentencing Discount in Inducing Guilty Pleas', in J Baldwin and A Bottomley (eds), *Criminal Justice: Selected Readings,* (Martin Robertson, 1978) p 119.
2   (1979) 1 Cr App Rep (S) 289.
3   [1980] Crim LR 59.

The sentence discount principle

confess?[4] If inducements by the police are thought to raise too great a risk of false confessions, why is this not so with sentence discounts? It seems that the judges want to have it both ways. They support the operation of a principle derived from crime control considerations of efficiency and expediency while denying that its practical operation undermines the due process right to put the prosecution to proof. They also conveniently ignore the danger that it will result in innocent people pleading guilty.

Another problem wrought by the discount principle is the intensification of the pressure to plead guilty at the earliest possible stage. We saw above, for example, how *Rafferty*[5] decided that the standard Crown Court discount should only be given to those who indicated their plea at the plea before venue stage. The danger of this is that the defendant may not by then have received adequate disclosure of the prosecution case.[6] The defendant may thus either feel pressurised into pleading guilty to something the prosecution could not have proved, or be penalised for refusing to indicate a guilty plea until more was known about the prosecution case. In *Rafferty* itself the court acknowledged that there might be a 'proper' reason for delaying the guilty plea until arrival in the Crown Court, in which case the standard discount might still be given. But one eminent commentator has interpreted *Rafferty* to mean that even those defendants with *good* reasons for delay, such as 'inadequate disclosure of the prosecution case, or inadequate opportunity to obtain considered legal advice', should get less discount than those indicating guilt at plea before venue stage.[7] If this is a mistaken interpretation, we think it one that many sentencers are likely to make too. We return to this problem of incomplete information on which to make the plea decision in section 5.

To the extent that the sentence discount can be conceptualised as a 'right', the due process adherent would also object to the capricious way in which the system operates. We showed in subsections (b) and (c) that sentencing in all criminal courts is marked by such inconsistency and forms of bias that many of those pleading guilty are denied their right to a discount. The sentencers remain unaccountable because there are so few 'standard' sentences for crimes which can function as a baseline below or above which cases with mitigating or aggravating characteristics can be evaluated. Thus, whether a discount has actually been awarded or not cannot easily be ascertained. Ashworth et al examined the sentencing practices of two judges and found that neither was aware of his own pattern of sentencing.

4   This case is discussed in section 2(a)(ii) above.
5   [1998] Crim LR 433, discussed in section 2(a)(ii) above.
6   See the discussion of this point in D Sunman, 'Advancing Disclosure: Can the Rules for Advance Information in the Magistrates' Courts be Improved?' [1998] Crim LR 798 at 800-01.
7   [1998] Crim LR 433 at 434 (commentary by D A Thomas).

In one drugs case, for example, the judge said the offence merited 21 months, but that the sentence would only be 15 months because of mitigating factors; in reality his average sentence for the weight of cannabis involved was 12 months. The authors of the study concluded that:

> ' ... this lack of self-awareness seemed to stem from the absence of a fixed point from which to make a reduction for mitigating factors . . . when a judge states in court (and himself believes) that he is passing a lower sentence so as to take account of a mitigating factor, he may not actually be making that reduction. The judge may feel that he is being merciful ... and the offender may believe that he has been fortunate, but the judge's unawareness of his own sentencing practices may mean that none of this is so.'[8]

This is not to say that all sentencing is arbitrary but it is certainly not a mechanical exercise the outcome of which is capable of exact prediction. The Court of Appeal has done little to discourage inconsistency in sentencing. In *Taylor and Rutherford*[9] for example, the defendant appealed against a sentence on the ground that it was longer than that imposed in a similar case.[10] The Court of Appeal rejected the appeal observing that there could be no fixed tariff on any sentencing matter. In its view, previous sentencing decisions were not to be treated as binding precedents, although they could provide guidance on an appropriate sentence. This begs the question of what is the appropriate sentence and allows such disparities that it is often impossible to clarify 'standard' sentences for particular offences.[11]

The research we have reviewed has also highlighted the potential of the principle to work racial injustice. Is it acceptable that those from ethnic minorities receive longer custodial sentences than whites simply because they exercise the right to put the prosecution to proof? To the crime control adherent this pattern of sentencing would be regarded as the product of the need for efficiency, it being mere coincidence that it happens to impinge more on blacks than whites. From the due process perspective, however, it is predictable that blacks would plead not guilty more often than whites, as one would expect them more often to be at the receiving end of abuses

8   A Ashworth, E Genders, G Mansfield, J Peay, and E Player, Sentencing in the Crown Court (Occasional Paper no 10) (Oxford Centre for Criminological Research, 1984) p 49.
9   [1983] Crim LR 692.
10 *Sequeira* (1982) 4 Cr App Rep (S) 65.
11 See the discussion by M Wasik, 'Sentencing: A Fresh Look at Aims and Objectives', in E Stockdale and S Casale (eds), *Criminal Justice Under Stress* (London: Blackstone, 1992).

The sentence discount principle

of police and prosecutorial power.[12] Faced, as they are on average, with cases based on weaker evidence or evidence so tainted by unfairness that a reasonable argument can be made for excluding it, it is no surprise that blacks have a higher rate of pleading not guilty. The sentence discount principle, by discouraging them from contesting these cases, thus works indirect racial discrimination.

(ii) The human rights perspective

There are a number of human rights arguments that can be mounted against the sentence discount principle, many of which mirror the due process objections.[13] Article 6(2) of the European Convention on Human Rights (ECHR) states that 'everyone charged with a criminal offence shall be presumed innocent until proved guilty according to law'. It is not contrary to that presumption for a defendant to make a free and informed decision to waive their right to a trial; the entry of a guilty plea can clearly be one way of proving guilt according to law. But it does appear contrary to that presumption for the state to seek to *induce* defendants to enter guilty pleas on the assumption that they are guilty, especially when the inducements are so large. If the state were to offer a defendant £10,000 to induce them to plead guilty to a theft we would rightly be appalled at this attempt to negate someone's rights. But this is exactly how the sentence discount principle works in practice.[14]

It is also arguable that the principle breaches what has been recognised by the ECtHR as the 'right of anyone charged with a criminal offence to remain silent and not to incriminate himself.'[15] Our system recognises that the police must not offer induce suspects to confess and if inducements are offered the resulting confession is likely to be ruled inadmissible on the ground of reliability.[16] Failing also to ban the considerable inducement of the sentence discount goes beyond mere hypocrisy; it sanctions a practice which is aimed at undermining the human right not to incriminate oneself.

Article 14 of the ECHR requires that the rights in the Convention 'shall be secured without discrimination on any ground such as sex, race,

---

12 On the processes by which black people become over-represented within the criminal justice system see: ch 2, sections 3(a) and 4(d) (stop-search); ch 3, section 4(d) (arrest); ch 4, section 2(d) (police bail); ch 5, section 1 (interrogation) and ch 6, section 4(b) (prosecution).

13 For a fuller discussion see Ashworth (1998) pp 286-92.

14 For the relative costs of contested cases and guilty plea cases see section 2(a)(i).

15 *Funke v France* (1993) 16 EHRR 297.

16 The ban on inducements is discussed in ch 5 (section 4(a)(i)), and the exclusion of unreliable evidence in ch 11, section 5.

colour ...'. We saw in the preceding subsection that the sentence discount principle creates an indirect form of racial discrimination.

Finally, the discount principle and the sentencing bargaining that accompanies it may contravene the Art 6(1) right to a fair and public hearing. Crucial 'negotiations' over plea (between lawyer and client, and between barrister and judge) are conducted in private. The defendant in the Crown Court is not necessarily told exactly what the judge has said to counsel.[17] These practices can hardly be called 'fair' or 'public'.

Whether the European Court of Human Rights (ECtHR) will accept that the sentence discount principle is contrary to the ECHR is unclear. It may be that it will fall back on the 'margin of appreciation' doctrine, thereby leaving it to the domestic courts to assess the human rights implications of English and Welsh practices. If this were to happen the prospects for judicially inspired reform would be bleak.

(iii)   Crime control and managerialism

From the crime control perspective, the only problem with sentence discounts is that they do not always operate as efficiently as they should. The fact that some 16,000 people did not plead guilty until the date set for Crown Court trial in 1999 is a key example of such inefficiency.[18] This was the perspective adopted by the Runciman Commission and it accordingly supported the sentencing discount principles developed by the Court of Appeal. In particular, it saw value in giving the greatest discounts for those pleading guilty at an early stage, but agreed that judges must retain their discretion to fix the discount according to the circumstances of the individual case.[19] It recommended that the principle that an early plea of guilty merits the largest discount should be more clearly articulated so as to have greater effect.[20] This immediately raises the question, effect on whom? The Runciman Commission accepted that it would be 'naive to suppose that innocent persons never plead guilty because of the prospect of the sentence discount'[1] but chose to place greater weight on the value to the system of encouraging the guilty to plead guilty. It rejected the possibility that clearer articulation of the discount principle would increase the risk that defendants may plead guilty to offences which they did not

17   An illustration will be found in section 4(b)(iv) below (the case in which the judge wanted to avoid any delay to his holiday).
18   See section 1 above.
19   Royal Commission on Criminal Justice (RCCJ), Report (Cm 2263) (London: HMSO, 1993), pp 111-112
20   Section 48 of the CJPO implemented this recommendation.
1   Ibid, p 110.

commit.[2] Thus it has also followed the Court of Appeal in its self-serving assumption that one can increase the pressure on the guilty to plead guilty without increasing the pressure on the innocent to do the same. No consideration was given to the argument that early pleas of guilty undermine the due process principle that it is for the prosecution to prove guilt. Indeed, no mention was made of the ECHR full stop.

That the Runciman Commission was wedded to crime control is also indicated by its deplorable treatment of Hood's research which had established that the discount principle works racial injustice. Its reaction was to express support for 'the recommendation made by Hood that the policy of offering sentence discounts should be kept under review.'[3] It was disingenuous (ie, dishonest) of the Runciman Commission to imply that Hood had merely called for this policy to be kept under review. What Professor Hood actually said was that 'it is time to consider all the implications of a policy which favours so strongly those who plead guilty, when ethnic minorities are less willing to forego their right to challenge a prosecution.'[4] What is a Royal Commission for if not to consider such implications? As Ashworth observes, 'the Commission was wrong to procrastinate on such an important issue.'[5] It is difficult to avoid the conclusion that the Runciman Commission here adopted the crime control position of placing greatest weight on the need for efficiency within the criminal process, and turned a myopic eye towards the evidence of the injustice both produced and compounded by the discount principle.

The Runciman Commission also recommended the introduction of a 'plea canvas' so that judges could be asked by the defence to indicate the maximum sentence that would be imposed should a guilty plea be entered at that stage in the proceedings. It did so despite its acceptance that 'to face defendants with a choice between what they might get on an immediate plea of guilty and what they might get if found guilty by the jury does amount to unacceptable pressure.'[6] Yet this is exactly what the plea canvas would achieve because counsel would be ethically obliged to explain to the defendant the additional penalty that would be added to the judge's declared 'maximum sentence' should conviction follow a not guilty plea. This recommendation would have overturned one of the *Turner* rules (reviewed in section 2(d)(ii) above) and effectively legitimised sentence bargaining. The Runciman Commission also wanted the precise amount of discount to be declared at the point of sentencing. These two recommendations remain unimplemented. Ashworth suggests that the judges 'are traditionally sensitive about making their sentence calculations

2   RCCJ (1993) p 112.
3   RCCJ (1993) p 114.
4   Hood (1992) p 182.
5   A Ashworth, 'Plea, Venue and Discontinuance' [1993] Crim LR 830 at p 838.
6   RCCJ (1993) para 7.50.

explicit, and probably resisted [the latter] proposal on the "thin end of the wedge" argument'.[7] We think a more powerful explanatory factor is concern amongst the appellate judiciary that to become more openly implicated in the brow-beating of defendants would threaten the legitimacy of the courts.

Henham's analysis of the sentence discount is largely inspired by the crime control model. Thus he is concerned that magistrates and judges do not always give the discounts they should and laments the savings on 'penal system resources' that are thereby lost.[8] But Henham does not consider whether much greater savings of such resources could be achieved by doing away with the discount principle altogether. Every time someone innocent pleads guilty due to the pressure exerted by this principle a needless punishment is imposed, adding to the strain on those who must administer it, such as the probation or prison service. Yet, whilst not blind to the arguments of principle against discounting sentences, Henham prefers to advocate 'short-term' reforms for more information to be made available to defendants on the implications of the choices they make. Thus he offers a redrafted version of CJPO, s 48 which would 'force' sentencers to explain exactly why a discount had, or had not, been awarded for a guilty plea, and explain the effect of their decision to the offender in ordinary language.[9] This might intensify the practical effect of the sentence discount principle, but whether it would result in defendants securing their 'right' to a 'fair' discount is more debatable. Those sentencers who are opposed to the discount principle, either generally or in its application to an 'undeserving' defendant before them, would find it easy to circumvent Henham's proposed redraft of s 48. An obvious method is case construction; that is, just like the police, judges could select, interpret and present 'the facts' in such a way that their sentencing remarks justified or disguised their preferred decision.[10] For example, the prosecution case could be referred to as 'overwhelming' in order to justify no discount.

A slightly riskier way of circumventing the Henham scheme would be to ignore it. As we saw with stop-search, where there is no expectation of effective supervision, and no effective remedy for malpractice, front-line officials tend to ignore procedural safeguards.[11] Henham includes no remedy in his draft scheme, and no penalty for judges who ignore it. The general principle is that failure to comply with a statutory duty to make a statement of some kind when passing a particular form of sentence does

7   Ashworth (1998) p 285.
8   Henham [2000] p 444.
9   Henham (1999) pp 536-537.
10 See, in particular, ch 6, sections 3(c) and 4(c) for police case construction techniques. See also ch 2, section 3(c) for an analysis in the context of stop-search of why written reasons for decisions do not provide an effective safeguard.
11 See ch 2, section 3, subsections (d) and (e).

not render the sentence invalid.[12] There is the possibility that the Court of Appeal will infer from a failure to mention some relevant sentencing criterion that the criterion was not taken into account when arriving at the sentence.[13] But appeals are infrequent,[14] and in any case the worst that can happen from the trial judge's point of view is some respectfully worded rebuke from the appellate judiciary coupled with some amendment to the sentence originally passed. This does not constitute effective supervision. The past track record of the courts in giving reasons for decisions when required to do so by legislation puts Henham's proposal into further doubt. The Criminal Justice Act 1988 contains an absolute requirement to state in open court the reasons for not making a compensation order in favour of the victim. Flood-Page and Mackie found that this was not done in 71% of magistrates' courts sentences and 60% of Crown Court sentences.[15]

One could argue that, when all the findings of the various studies reviewed in this section are taken together, a practice of awarding discounts for guilty pleas can be detected, but that the principles involved are applied in a way that is working indirect racial discrimination and disadvantaging those who conform to social stereotypes of the 'undeserving'. The discount principle is clearly working very effectively as an inducement to plead guilty yet the sentencing framework is so open-ended and permissive that magistrates and judges are able to avoid giving the legally required discounts with little risk of sanction. If this is a form of bargaining or negotiation, it is clear that advantage is being taken of the structurally weak position of defendants. Large numbers of them are, in short, getting ripped off.[16]

3. SENTENCING POWERS AND JURISDICTIONAL PRESSURES

There are various ways in which a plea of guilty can affect the *jurisdiction* of the criminal courts to try and sentence an offence. We will focus here on two particularly important examples which concern the threshold

---

12 See *Baverstock* (1992) 14 Cr App Rep (S) 471.
13 This happened in *Fearon* [1996] 2 Cr App Rep (S) 25 but in *Bishop* [2000] Crim LR 60 the Court of Appeal refused to make any reduction despite the trial judge's absence of comment about the guilty plea. See also *Aroride* [1999] 2 Cr App Rep (S) 406.
14 Appeals against conviction are examined in ch 10; most of the various procedural hurdles discussed there apply also to appeals against sentence.
15 Flood-Page and Mackie (1998) pp 61 and 111.
16 For a victim-centred analysis of 'plea bargaining' see ch 1 section 10. The freedom model's approach to these issues will be explored in the conclusion to this chapter.

between non-court disposals and the magistrates' court, and the magistrates' court and the Crown Court.[17]

(a) Pleading guilty in order to avoid the criminal courts

We saw in chapter 6, section 4(a)(ii) that youths and adults alike often accept a police caution (now known as reprimands and warnings in the case of youths) in order to avoid prosecution. Some admit to offences which they clearly did not commit, and many more to offences which the prosecution could not have proved. This 'bargaining in the shadow of the law' resulted in these offenders getting (or adding to) a criminal record, but they did not result in guilty pleas because pleas are only taken in court.[18] However, s 1(1) of the Youth Justice and Criminal Evidence Act 1999 (YJCEA) introduced a new procedure under which a plea of guilty in court will result in the case being diverted back out of the court for 'sentencing' purposes. These 'referral orders' are available to offenders who are prosecuted for the first time, who plead guilty, and for whom the magistrates consider that neither a custodial sentence nor an absolute discharge is warranted. The Youth Court is obliged, following conviction, to refer these 'offenders' to a 'youth offender panel' made up of trained volunteers. These panels will seek to involve offenders, their 'supporters', their victims and youth justice workers in agreeing an enforceable 'contract' designed to achieve reparation and the rehabilitation of the offender.[19] If a contract is complied with the Youth Court conviction will be regarded as 'spent' under the provisions of the Rehabilitation of Offenders Act 1974, thus removing many of the disadvantages of a criminal record.

The principle of introducing these discursive panels as an adjunct to the 'current sterile structures and procedures of the youth court'[20] have

17 Space precludes discussion of how the prosecution can, by charging an offence which carries either a longer than commensurate sentence (ie protective sentencing under the Criminal Justice Act 1991, s 2) or a mandatory sentence under the Crime Sentences Act 1997, exert enormous pressure on defendants to plead guilty to a lesser offence so as to preclude such consequences. For an example, see *Stephens* [2000] 2 Cr App Rep (S) 320, CA.

18 Another form of pressure to accept guilt (in effect) is an 'offer' by the prosecution (usually engineered by the defence solicitor) to drop charges in exchange for an agreement by the defendant to be bound-over by the court. Since such 'bind-over deals' do not result in a guilty plea we say no more about them here, but see J Baldwin, *Pre-Trial Justice* (Oxford: Basil Blackwell, 1985) pp 79-85 and McConville et al (1994) pp 196-198.

19 The contractual language used in the Act should not blind us to the coercive elements in this scheme: C Wonnacott, 'The counterfeit contract - reform, pretence and muddled principles in the new referral order' (1999) 11 Child and Fam LQ 209.

20 C Ball, 'A significant move towards restorative justice, or a recipe for unintended consequences?' [2000] Crim LR 211 at 215.

been welcomed in principle by commentators, although concerns have been raised about many of the details.[1] But little attention has been paid to the injustice that is likely to result from this new diversionary mechanism. Suppose a young girl with a clean record is arrested for a bike theft that she did not commit. If she refuses to accept guilt she will be ineligible for a reprimand, a warning and a referral to a Youth Offender Panel. The progressive nature of the 'tariff' for those admitting guilt, which is designed to restrain the punitive response of the system for the non-persistent offender, will be replaced by being thrown straight into the deep end of the Youth Court. This seems to us to be likely to increase the pressure to accept guilt so that a reprimand can be secured and the risk of a court sentence avoided. For those who have already been warned, the choice will be between (a) accepting guilt, thereby avoiding a court sentence and (following contract compliance) the full effects of a criminal conviction, and (b) denying guilt, thus running the risk of conviction and the consequent (non-discounted) sentence and full criminal record. Ball considers that this dilemma will result in guilty young people pleading not-guilty in order to avoid the greater intervention in their lives demanded by referral to the youth offender panel.[2] But this is to ignore the influence of lawyers who, as we have seen, are largely committed to trial avoidance, believe their clients to be guilty, and will no doubt stress the advantages of the youth offender panels and downplay their disadvantages.[3] Whereas Ball speculates that the effect of the 1999 Act will be more contested trials, we anticipate an increase in the guilty plea rate for young people prosecuted for the first time, and an increase in miscarriages of justice.

(b) Accepting guilt in order to avoid the Crown Court

The two-tier nature of criminal courts in this country puts pressure on adult defendants to plead guilty. As Heberling notes, 'the basic strategy in English guilty plea representation lies in keeping trial of the case at the magistrates' court level.'[4] The advantage to the defence of having the trial heard in the magistrates' court is that the sentencing powers of the

1   See Ball [2000]; Wonnacott (1999) and M Cavadino, I Crow and J Dignan, *Criminal Justice 2000* (Winchester: Waterside, 1999) pp 198-200.
2   Ball [2000] 216.
3   Note too that under s 2(2) of the YJCEA there is *discretion* to make a referral order in respect of an offender who is being dealt with by the court for the first time who pleads guilty to at least one offence but not guilty to others. We predict that defence lawyers acting for clients facing multiple charges will often encourage a guilty plea to at least one charge in order to keep the referral order option open.
4   J Heberling, 'Plea Negotiation in England' in Baldwin and Bottomley (1978) p 97.

magistrates are limited. Regardless of the statutory maxima prescribed for offences, the maximum penalty which magistrates can impose on summary conviction for an offence triable either way is six months' imprisonment and/or a fine of £5,000 (an aggregate of one year and/or £5,000 per offence on conviction of two or more either way offences).[5] The maximum penalty when sentencing for summary offences is set at six months' imprisonment or that prescribed by the statute creating the offence, whichever is the less.[6]

But even leaving aside the fact that magistrates' sentencing powers are limited, a de facto sentence discount can be achieved by having a case disposed of at the lower level. This is due to the fact that magistrates on average sentence more leniently than do Crown Court judges. Clear evidence that this was so was first produced by Hedderman and Moxon in a Home Office study of mode of trial decisions and sentencing published in 1992. In an attempt to ensure that like was compared with like the researchers identified cases dealt with in the magistrates' courts that matched those where the defendant had elected to go to the Crown Court as regards the features that could be expected to affect sentence. This exercise revealed that:

'. . . custody was used almost three times as often and sentences were, on average, about two and a half times longer in elected cases than in comparable cases at magistrates' courts. In other words, the Crown Court imposes more than seven times as much custody as do magistrates' courts for cases having similar characteristics.'[7]

Bridges has contended that this research failed adequately to take account of differences between cases tried at each level and thus overstates the sentencing differential at work.[8] Flood-Page and Mackie seem to accept that their study of sentencing did not find the considerable differences in the tariffs applied by magistrates' courts and the Crown Court found by earlier research, and that case factors (such as previous record, or breach of trust) pull in the same direction for all sentencers.[9] But they also note that factors which influenced Crown Court decisions to imprison featured

5   For the complex legal provisions regulating magistrates' sentencing powers for either way offences see J Sprack, *Emmins on Criminal Procedure* 8th edn (London: Blackstone, 2000) pp 168-69.
6   Magistrates' Courts Act 1980, s 31(1). The maximum level of a fine for a summary offence is currently £5,000. For the law governing sentencing for summary offences see Sprack (2000) pp 154-155 and 388-389.
7   C Hedderman and D Moxon, Magistrates' court or Crown Court? Mode of trial decisions and sentencing (Home Office Research Study no 125) (London: HMSO, 1992) p 37.
8   Bridges (1999).
9   Flood-Page and Mackie (1998) p 125.

in cases attracting community disposals in the magistrates' courts. The true position is probably that the Crown Court is somewhat more punitive than the magistrates' court and that the extent of the differential is over-estimated by some who work within the system, and deliberately exaggerated by others when this suits their purposes.

Thus McConville et al observed one lawyer making much of the likely sentencing differential between the two levels of court in 'advising' a defendant charged with shop theft. His solicitor, having decided he was guilty on the basis of his prior criminal record, had not bothered to view the CCTV footage from the shop's security cameras (which the prosecution intended to use as evidence). The solicitor was angered by the client's claim that the theft was committed by his girlfriend, and adopted a bullying tone in setting out the dire consequences of opting for a Crown Court contested trial:

'Solicitor: With your record, you can't afford to mess about. [He looks at the record] Oh, last dishonest 15 months ago. You say you had no idea what she was doing - that's a bit hard to swallow isn't it? What are you going to do?

Client: Plead not guilty.

Solicitor: [shouting] Cut the crap! And grow up! You're on film. You'll go down the steps [ie to custody] if you have a trial. I don't care what you plead. I enjoy trials. I don't know what the evidence is against you - you do because you were there. [Your co-defendant] will be a witness against you. It's on film. It's your neck. If you have a trial, do you want to go to Crown Court? And have a judge?

Client: [extremely distressed by now] No.

After more exchanges, the client agreed to plead guilty.'[10]

How, though, does a guilty plea help to ensure that a case is kept in the magistrates' courts? One way is through a charge bargain (see section 5) in which the prosecution drops an either way charge in return for a plea of guilty to a summary charge. Another way of boosting the number of summary trials was created by the 'plea before venue' procedure discussed in section 2(a)(ii) above. As noted there, for 'either way' offences, magistrates must now enquire what the defendant's plea is likely to be before deciding on whether the venue for trial should be the magistrates' court or the Crown Court. If defendants indicate an intention to plead guilty then the magistrates must proceed immediately to summary trial and record a conviction. Only if defendants indicate a likely not guilty plea can the

10 McConville et al (1994) p 193.

magistrates move on to the mode of trial hearing, decide that summary trial is unsuitable and commit the case to the Crown Court.

We should note, however, the important power of the magistrates to commit the defendant to Crown Court for sentencing following a summary trial of an either way offence if they feel that their own sentencing powers are inadequate.[11] A guilty plea, however, because it is meant to attract a sentence discount, should result in more cases being regarded by magistrates as within their sentencing powers.[12] But a much more certain way of convincing magistrates that their sentencing powers are adequate is for the defence to achieve a re-labelling of the charge as something less serious. This provides another crucial incentive for the practice of charge-bargaining. In the next section we examine this practice and its importance for the classification of offences and mode of trial decisions.

4. CHARGE BARGAINING

Charge bargaining typically involves the defendant agreeing to plead guilty in exchange for the prosecution proceeding on a less serious charge. For example, theft may be substituted for the original charge of burglary, or assault with intent replaced by simple assault. Alternatively, where the defendant is facing multiple charges, an agreement to plead guilty to at least one may result in the dropping of others. Unlike the sentence discount principle, where it is the law itself which exerts pressure to plead guilty, charge bargaining relies on advocates on each side of the adversarial divide reaching an agreement. In the magistrates' court charge bargaining takes place between crown prosecutors and solicitors, whereas in the Crown Court prosecution and defence barristers take centre stage. The dynamics in each setting are somewhat different and we shall look at each in turn.

(a) Charge bargaining in the magistrates' courts

(i) The role of the crown prosecutor

The law places little constraint on the ability of crown prosecutors to charge bargain. Under the Prosecution of Offences Act 1985 crown prosecutors

11 The main relevant legislative provision is the Magistrates' Court Act 1980, s 38. See Sprack (2000) pp 168-174 for a general overview, including discussion of the much more limited power of magistrates to commit to the Crown Court for sentencing defendants convicted of summary offences. For example, committal is possible where the summary offence is imprisonable and a defendant is already serving a suspended sentence.

12 As noted in section 2(b), the evidence suggests that, as regards guilty pleas secured through the plea before venue procedure, magistrates are not taking this factor into account in the way that they should: Bridges (1999).

have the power to make additions, deletions or alterations to the charges, and can terminate proceedings altogether. Even on the day of the trial itself the prosecutor can secure the dismissal of the case by offering no evidence. There are strong incentives for the police to 'over-charge' suspects[13] and this provides the CPS with the means and a motive to bargain with the defence. It is true that the Code for Crown Prosecutors states that prosecutors should not proceed with multiple charges, or more serious charges, simply in order to encourage the defendant to accept a charge bargain. But the prosecution momentum that develops following the laying of charges entails that the CPS generally does not downgrade charges except within the context of court proceedings.[14] In stressing 'the resource advantages both to the Service and the courts generally' of charge bargaining, the Code for Crown Prosecutors (para 11) makes it clear that such deals are not merely tolerated but encouraged and expected.[15] Where a deal cannot be struck, it is not unknown for the CPS to substitute a summary charge for an either way charge, so as to ensure that the defendant cannot opt for an expensive jury trial, and this practice has been held to be lawful.[16]

Crown prosecutors have another bargaining chip in their apparent influence over mode of trial decisions. The procedure to be applied at a mode of trial hearing is prescribed by the Magistrates' Courts Act 1980. At this hearing the prosecution and the defence are invited to make representations in turn about whether the offence is more suitable for summary trial or trial on indictment. Following on from this, the magistrates must determine whether the case is serious enough to justify trial on indictment.[17] If they conclude that it is then the case will be committed to the Crown Court irrespective of the accused's wishes. If the magistrates decide that summary trial is appropriate the court explains this to the accused and that the accused may either consent to a summary trial or opt for trial by jury. The choice, in this circumstance, is the accused's alone. Riley and Vennard, in a study conducted by the Home Office, found that magistrates' mode of trial decisions were in line with prosecution preferences in 96% of

---

13   See E Genders, 'Reform of the Offences Against the Person Act: Lessons from the Law in Action' [1999] Crim LR 689 at pp 692-693.

14   Genders [1999] p 691. On prosecution momentum and the inadequate safeguard against wrongful prosecutions provided by office-based review of cases by the CPS, see ch 6, section 3(c).

15   We follow Ashworth (1998) p 272 in citing the 1992 version of this Code (unless we state otherwise), and for the reason he gives, ie, that the streamlined 1994 version removed some revealing policy statements from public view.

16   *Canterbury and St Augustine Justices, ex p Klisiak* [1982] QB 398. See also ch 8, section 5(c).

17   See s 19 of the Magistrates' Courts Act 1980 for a list of the factors to be taken into account by magistrates when taking their decision.

cases.[18] Whatever the reasons for the correlation between the views of prosecutors and magistrates,[19] pre-trial negotiation may leave the defence in no doubt that the prosecution intend to press for a Crown Court trial in the event of a not guilty plea. Whilst this is sometimes what the defence wants anyway, this is not always so, as can be seen by the 'cut the crap' quote set out in section 3(b) above.

One thing a prosecutor may not do is hold out a promise of a particular sentence. In the English system the sentence is a matter for the judge not the prosecutor and the latter never recommends a particular sentence on a charge being proved.[20] Any sentence bargaining must accordingly take place between the defence lawyer and the judge. As we saw in section 2, sentence bargaining does take place in the Crown Court, but is frowned upon by the senior judiciary and is unheard of in the magistrates' courts.

(ii)   The regulation of pre-trial negotiation in the magistrates' courts

As discussed in section 2(e) above, the law's encouragement of guilty pleas is difficult, if not impossible, to reconcile with adversarial principle and the priority supposedly given to acquitting the innocent in legal rhetoric. How has the legal system attempted to manage this gap between due process rhetoric and crime control reality where charge bargaining is concerned? One method has been to employ language which glosses over awkward contradictions. A good example is that part of the code for Crown Prosecutors (para 11) which deals with charge bargaining:

'The over-riding consideration will be to ensure that the court is never left in the position of being unable to pass a proper sentence consistent with the gravity of the defendant's actions . . . Administrative convenience in the form of a rapid guilty plea should not take precedence over the interests of justice, but where the court is able to deal adequately with an offender on the basis of a plea which represents a criminal involvement not inconsistent with the alleged facts, the resource advantages both to the Service and the courts generally will be an important consideration.'

18   D Riley and J Vennard, Triable-either-way cases: Crown Court or Magistrates' Court? (Home Office Research Study no 98) (London: HMSO, 1988).
19   For discussion see Hedderman and Moxon (1992) pp 14-15.
20   See the comments of Scarman LJ in *Atkinson* (1978) 67 Cr App Rep 200. The prosecution may be under a duty to point out that a sentence proposed by a trial judge as a way of settling a case under the *Turner* rules (see section 2(d)(ii) above) is contrary to authority: *A-G's Reference (Nos 80 and 81 of 1999)* [2000] Crim LR 398.

This passage illustrates well the tension between principles of justice and the encouragement of pre-trial negotiation. For how can a court pass a sentence 'consistent with the gravity of the defendant's actions' if the prosecution accepts a plea of guilty to a charge which represents a degree of conduct less serious than that originally alleged? It is no answer to say an apt sentence is possible so long as the sentencing ranges for the original charge and the bargained for charge overlap sufficiently. The courts must sentence on the basis that only the lesser offence was actually committed.[1] Thus a wounding with intent charge which is bargained down to a charge of wounding will be sentenced as if the defendant had only committed a wounding. The slippery use of language is exemplified by the encouragement given to prosecutors to accept a plea 'which represents a criminal involvement not inconsistent with the alleged facts'. Presumably the double negative was used because of the difficulty involved in suggesting that a charge bargain might involve the case proceeding on a basis which was consistent with the alleged facts. These passages could only make sense if the original charge overstated what the defendant had done, in which case it would be wrong to extract a guilty plea as the price for reducing the charge.

A charge bargain involves the prosecution transforming the nature of the allegation so that a different legal label can be affixed to the case. Burglary becomes theft, wounding with intent to cause grievous bodily harm becomes simple wounding, rape becomes indecent assault, and so on. This is possible because when cases are disposed of by way of guilty pleas it is the lawyers rather than the courts who effectively construct truth and determine guilt and innocence. At one time the appellate courts discouraged the magistrates' courts from accepting jurisdiction for serious cases made to look like trivial either way cases through this kind of re-labelling.[2] But the modern trend has been to entreat magistrates to accept jurisdiction in a broader band of cases than hitherto. While mode of trial guidelines issued by the Court of Appeal state that the magistrates' court should never make its decision on the grounds of convenience or expedition, they contain a presumption in favour of summary trial: 'In general, except where otherwise stated, either way offences should be tried summarily unless the court considers that the particular case has one or more of the features set out below *and* that its sentencing powers are insufficient.'[3] The guidelines go on to list the aggravating features for a number of commonly occurring offences (burglary, theft, criminal damage

---

1   *Stewart* (1990) 12 Cr App Rep (S) 15.
2   See *Bodmin Justices, ex p McEwen* [1947] KB 321 at 324; *Coe* [1968] 1 WLR 1950 at 1953; and *King's Lynn Justices, ex p Carter* [1969] 1 QB 488.
3   · *Practice Note (Mode of Trial: Guidelines)* [1990] 1 WLR 1439. The guidelines are reproduced by Sprack (2000) pp 501-504.

and so on). If none of these are present then magistrates are, in effect, exhorted to try the case summarily even though they consider their sentencing powers to be inadequate. The Code for Crown Prosecutors goes further still. It advises that representations to the court at mode of trial hearings should focus on those matters to which the court is obliged to have regard but then adds:

> 'The prosecutor may also have regard to such factors as delay in the administration of justice, the additional cost and possible effects on witnesses of having the case heard in the Crown Court.'

This gives official endorsement to prosecutors taking into account both convenience and expedition when making representations to magistrates on mode of trial. There thus appears to be a drift towards crime control values in this part of the criminal process. This drift was accelerated by the introduction of the plea before venue procedure which requires magistrates to accept jurisdiction in any either way case where the defendant indicates an intention to plead guilty. This innovation stems in part from official concern expressed in recent years at the fact that the Crown Court more often than not passes sentences on cases committed by magistrates which would have been within the powers of the lower court.[4] In other words, whereas magistrates used to be berated for allowing the lawyers to redefine 'serious' cases as 'trivial', now they are criticised for treating 'trivial' cases as 'serious' on the ground that this incurs needless expenditure. In a recent case the Divisional Court has recognised that charge bargains are commonplace and that the integrity of criminal proceedings required that they should be adhered to. Thus it refused to interfere with a magistrates' court decision that the reinstatement of a charge by the CPS which had been dropped as part of a charge bargain was an abuse of process.[5] The conclusion must be that modern legal culture is decisively in favour of charge bargaining and other methods of cost-cutting achieved by 'defining deviance down'.[6]

4   This phenomenon can be seen even more starkly in the outcomes of committals for sentence. Flood-Mackie and Page (1998) p 89 report that 62% of defendants committed for sentence received a penalty which could have been imposed by the magistrates, the same proportion as found in the research by Hedderman and Moxon (1992).
5   *Crown Prosecution Service v Deborah Anne Edgar* (DC, 21 February 2000, unreported). See, to like effect, *Attorney-General's Reference No 44 of 2000* (16 October 2000, unreported), CA.
6   See D Garland, 'The Limits of the Sovereign State: Strategies of Crime Control in Contemporary Society' (1996) 36 BJ Crim 445.

(iii)   Lawyers' behaviour: manoeuvring, negotiating and pre-trial reviews

It might be thought that, given professional codes and ethical standards, defence lawyers could be relied upon to ensure that innocent persons do not accept the offer from the prosecution of a charge bargain and that prosecutors would only seek such bargains in cases where the evidence was strong in relation to the original charge.[7] What does research reveal?

An immediate difficulty is that, by definition, pre-trial manoeuvring and negotiation is not subject to public scrutiny. Lawyers freely admit, however, that wheeling and dealing is an integral part of their trade, and last-minute negotiations can be observed taking place on a daily basis in court buildings.[8] In the early 1980s a dozen or so magistrates' courts experimented with a more systematic approach to these negotiations. Pre-trial reviews were introduced for cases likely to be contested. Meetings between the opposing lawyers would be arranged by court clerks who would also be in attendance to make a note of any deals done. This formalisation of pre-trial negotiating allowed researchers to more easily study the types of exchange that occur between prosecutors and defence solicitors.

Before examining the research evidence, it is important to understand the importance of the disclosure of evidence to pre-trial bargaining. Since an adversarial system can only function properly if there is at least rough equivalence in the resources available to the defence and prosecution, it follows that the fruits of the police investigation should be disclosed to the defence regardless of whether or not they favour the prosecution. Moreover, fairness to the accused (who is presumed innocent) requires that the prosecution case is disclosed so that a defence may be prepared. These principles are broadly accepted in the Crown Court, but only gained a firm foothold in the magistrates' courts in 1985.

In theory, this meant that before then a key variable in a defendant's decision on plea, the strength of the prosecution case, was unknown. Similarly, there was, and remains, no general requirement that the defence disclose its case.[9] The prosecution would, therefore, be unsure as to the strength of its own case and whether it might be worth cutting its losses by striking a deal with the defence. In practice, informal exchanges between prosecution and defence solicitors enabled information to be traded and bargains to be struck. Pre-trial reviews encouraged the more routine

---

7   For a discussion of the relevant ethical standards, see Blake and Ashworth [1998].

8   This includes the Youth Court: see H Parker, M Casburn and D Turnbull, *Receiving Juvenile Justice* (Oxford: Basil Blackwell, 1981) pp 50-55.

9   Under the Criminal Procedure and Investigations Act 1996, s 6, the defence may tender a formal defence statement in order to trigger prosecution 'secondary disclosure' but the disadvantages of defence disclosure are likely to deter the defence from opting into this scheme: Sprack (2000) p 132. The position is different in relation to trial on indictment, on which see ch 6, section 3(v).

disclosure of evidence, partly in order to enable the issues in dispute to be clarified, but also in order to facilitate case settlement.

A study of pre-trial reviews conducted prior to 1985 by Baldwin discovered that defence solicitors were willing to trade information and favours with prosecutors.[10] A summary of this research concluded that:

'. . . the criminal courts, at least the lower courts, are based to a much greater extent on compromise and accommodation than on combat and confrontation. Few of these lawyers could be said to relish the thought of fighting cases in court if some acceptable "arrangement" of pleas seemed a possibility . . . Although the textbooks may be written on the assumption that adversarial attitudes will prevail, many solicitors have developed their own practices in which case settlement on an amicable basis is strongly favoured.'[11]

That defence lawyers were prepared to routinely disclose details of their clients' cases is indicative of their lack of concern for basic tenets concerning the rights of suspects supposedly central to English justice. It is, after all, for the prosecution to prove its case and it is not for the defence to assist in that process. In the magistrates' courts, however, defence solicitors appeared more concerned to 'play fair' with the prosecution.

The dynamics of pre-trial negotiations should have been altered by the introduction of rules in 1985 directing the prosecution to provide advance disclosure in at least summary form for cases triable either way that were to be heard in the magistrates' courts.[12] Although this development appeared to remove much of the incentive for defence solicitors to disclose details of their cases, the study by Baldwin suggested that no such incentive was needed. While some courts have abandoned or placed less emphasis upon pre-trial reviews, many more courts have taken their place. A survey by Mulcahy, Brownlee and Walker in the early 1990s found that of 218 respondent courts, 43 operated a formal pre-trial review system. A further 30 magistrates' courts conducted such reviews on an ad hoc basis whilst 21 other courts were considering introducing this mechanism.[13] The Narey reforms will, when fully implemented, institutionalise new forms of

---

10   Baldwin (1985) *Pre-Trial Justice*. For a summary of the Nottingham research see J Baldwin, 'Pre-Trial Settlement in the Magistrates' Courts' (1985) 24 Howard JCJ 108.

11   J Baldwin and F Feeney, 'Defence Disclosure in the Magistrates' Courts' (1986) 49 MLR 593 at pp 604-605.

12   Magistrates' Courts (Advance Information) Rules 1985, SI 1985 No 601.

13   A Mulcahy, I Brownlee and C Walker, 'An Evaluation of Pre-Trial Reviews in Leeds and Bradford Magistrates' Courts' (1993) 33 Home Office Research Bulletin 10.

pre-trial review in all magistrates' courts, in the shape of early first hearings and early administrative hearings.[14]

Opinions differ as to the value of pre-trial reviews, although the consensus in this country appears to be that they offer gains in terms of procedural efficiency.[15] According to Baldwin issues of real importance were resolved at nearly half of the reviews he recorded,[16] and Mulcahy et al argue that their data show that pre-trial reviews are cost-effective. The important question, however, is whether a practice which appears to so undermine the adversarial system of justice is defensible in principle. Baldwin argues that bargaining is endemic in the magistrates' courts and will take place whether or not pre-trial reviews are held. This leads him to the conclusion that:

> 'Though there are dangers in the extreme informality and flexibility of some of the arrangements that have been adopted, the pre-trial review at least provides a forum which is open to outside scrutiny, and the furtive business of plea negotiation in court corridors is replaced by discussions which are at once more ordered and more seemly.'[17]

If plea-trial reviews are to be accepted as the lesser of two unavoidable evils, what does 'outside scrutiny' reveal? Baldwin, found that 'the participants aimed to ensure that deals and compromises about charges tallied with the gravity of the offence as revealed in the evidence . . . the present writer did not observe a single case in which a bargain could fairly be described as improper.'[18]

There are two main flaws in this argument. One is that Baldwin did not observe how this 'proper bargain' was presented to the client, nor how the client reacted to it. The other is that the material on which the parties base their negotiations is at best partial and at worst thoroughly misleading. Taking the second point first, from May 1985 it became standard practice to disclose the prosecution case in summary form in either way cases.[19] A study of 200 such summaries (which were prepared by police officers) found that about a half did not provide a satisfactory precis of the prosecution's evidence and in about a third of all cases the summary was inaccurate or

14 The Narey reforms are discussed in section 2(d)(i) above.
15 For a short review of the American literature see Baldwin *Pre-Trial Justice* (1985) pp 6-10.
16 Baldwin *Pre-Trial Justice* (1985) p 40.
17 Baldwin *Pre-Trial Justice* (1985) pp 164-165.
18 Baldwin *Pre-Trial Justice* (1985) p 97.
19 See J Baldwin and A Mulvaney, 'Advance Disclosure in Magistrates' Courts: The Workings of Section 48' (1987) 151 JP 409, and, by the same authors, 'Advance Disclosure in the Magistrates' Courts: Two Cheers for Section 48' [1987] Crim LR 315.

misleading.[20] As the authors of the study noted, 'it is too often the prosecution's version of events (sometimes embellished by a certain amount of wishful thinking) that is represented in the summary'.[1] A further study by Baldwin for the Runciman Commission demonstrated that the problem persists: most summaries of police interviews were found to be unreliable and/or partial. The study indicates that the problem is not soluble by technical means or better training, which is not surprising if one sees the police as following their own working rules in an adversarial manner.[2]

The Crown Prosecution Service has placed less emphasis on case summaries in the last decade and introduced a system of disclosure of all witness statements in either way cases.[3] This provides defence solicitors with useful additional material. The new system has not, however, eradicated the use of prosecution summaries.[4] It is also important to note that there is only a limited statutory obligation placed upon prosecutors to disclose any evidence at all on a summary charge.[5] This is despite there being no good reason for the different treatment of this category of case.[6] But even when fuller disclosure of the prosecution case is made, a misleading impression may be given of the likelihood of conviction. There may be failures by the police, by forensic experts and by crown prosecutors to comply with the obligation of disclosure in respect of material helpful to the defence.[7] Furthermore, as we saw in chapter 5, police interviewing techniques result in statements of evidence being stripped of possible

---

20 J Baldwin and A Mulvaney, 'Advance Disclosure in the Magistrates' Courts: How useful are the prosecution summaries?' [1987] Crim LR 805 at p 808.
1   Baldwin and Mulvaney [1987] 'Advance Disclosure in the Magistrates' Courts: How useful are the prosecution summaries?' p 813.
2   J Baldwin, Preparing the Record of Taped Interview (Royal Commission on Criminal Justice Research Study no 2) (London: HMSO, 1992).
3   The new practice is based on a recommendation of the Working Group on Pre-Trial Issues, which reported in November 1990.
4   See Sunman [1998].
5   Under the Criminal Procedure and Investigations Act 1996, s 1(1), if a defendant pleads not guilty, prosecutors have a duty to disclose material which they do not intend to use at trial if it would, in their opinion, undermine the case for the prosecution. This puts the prosecutor in a powerful position, and can leave the defence in the dark. See, for example, the facts in South West Surrey Magistrates' Court, ex p James [2000] Crim LR 690. The CPS declined to provide the defence with a copy of the interview tape in which it was alleged that the defendant had made admissions. The defendant pleaded not guilty and after two further adjournments the Crown discontinued proceedings following the withdrawal by the complainant of her allegation of common assault. It was only when an application was made for defence costs to be awarded that the CPS disclosed the 'contents' of the interview by reading out a summary, the accuracy of which the defendant then disputed.
6   See generally C J Emmins, 'Why No Advance Information for Summary Offences?', [1987] Crim LR 608.
7   See ch 6, section 3(c)(v).

ambiguities and exculpatory statements by suspects. In the impartial setting of the courtroom, where evidence is given on oath and is subject to cross-examination, the case may take on a very different complexion. One obvious due process objection to pre-trial bargaining is thus that the lawyers are not negotiating on the basis of 'evidence' at all since the summaries and statements in the prosecution file are merely indications (or rather, one-sided versions) of what witnesses will say in court.

A system which encourages charge bargains not only allows the prosecution to secure convictions in weak cases that would not have stood up in court but may also lead to an increase in the number of such weak cases being prosecuted. Where a high guilty plea rate is achieved through such inducements there is little need for the prosecuting authorities to ensure that only properly prepared cases are brought to trial. It is interesting to note that when one United States jurisdiction 'banned' various forms of plea bargaining one effect was that prosecutors refused to proceed with weak cases and this, in turn, forced the police to investigate crimes more carefully and thoroughly from the outset.[8] From this perspective, charge bargains are per se improper.

It is true that prosecutors are directed by their Code to discontinue cases in which the evidence is weak and this provides a theoretical safeguard for defendants. However, the due process model warns us that the prosecutor cannot be trusted to screen out weak cases any more than the police can.[9] The research by McConville et al of prosecution practices provides empirical grounds for such distrust. They found that crown prosecutors, for a variety of reasons, rarely take the initiative in dropping cases. As they explain:

'Dropping cases on grounds of weakness will antagonize the police and may lose a successful conviction, since, as all participants in the system understand, the great majority of cases, weak or strong, are disposed of by guilty pleas. If, on the other hand, there is a weakness in the case which the defence intends to exploit, a decision to drop it, or amend the charges or drop charges in return for a bind over, may always be made once the defence have signalled their intent to contest the case ...'[10]

Their sample produced cases in which prosecutors had continued with weak cases in order to persuade defendants to withdraw complaints against

8   T W Carns and J Kruse, 'A Re-Evaluation of Alaska's Plea Bargaining Ban' (1981) 8 *Alaska Law Review* p 27.
9   H Packer, *The Limits of the Criminal Sanction* (Stanford: Stanford UP, 1969) p 207.
10   M McConville, A Sanders and R Leng, *The Case for the Prosecution* (London: Routledge, 1991) p 146.

the police,[11] or to secure a bind over,[12] or on the basis that the case would be dropped if the defendant pleaded not guilty.[13] They conclude that 'what the CPS seek is not a plea to what they can *prove*, but to what they can bluff or "arm-twist" defendants into.'[14]

Where it appears that such cases are to be contested, prosecutors are likely to seek some form of compromise, and in this they often see defence solicitors as their allies rather than their opponents. A good example is provided by the following exchange at a pre-trial review tape-recorded by Baldwin:

Prosecuting solicitor:	If Mr Hill will be bound over, everything else will be dismissed.
Defence solicitor:	That sounds reasonable, though I can't guarantee it. If he doesn't agree, I'd like to reconstitute the PTR.
Prosecuting solicitor:	I think I can tell you that no evidence will be offered even if he is not bound over. I think I ought to tell you that.
Defence solicitor:	Are you saying you're offering no evidence.
Prosecuting solicitor:	I would like a bind over in this case. And I'm asking you to go to your client and have a genuine interview with him, Peter, and ask him.
Defence solicitor:	OK. I'll have a genuine interview with him.
Prosecuting solicitor:	And say, 'The prosecution are asking you to be bound over', will you?
Defence solicitor:	You're not saying to me that I can't tell my client, 'Look, they've indicated to me that, even if you're not bound over, they're going to offer no evidence'?
Prosecuting solicitor:	No. You can tell him that, obviously, but I leave it to you as the way you do it.
Defence solicitor:	OK.
Prosecuting solicitor:	I don't like the look of this chap at all, quite frankly, because there are some awful offences being committed. He and his mates have been involved with knives and axes but

11   McConville, Sanders and Leng (1991) at p 144.
12   McConville, Sanders and Leng (1991) p 159. See also L Christian, 'Restriction without Conviction' in B Fine and R Millar (eds), *Policing the Miners' Strike* (London: Lawrence and Wishart, 1985) pp 132-133.
13   McConville, Sanders and Leng (1991) p 158.
14   McConville, Sanders and Leng (1991) p 166.

Charge bargaining

we can't identify who exactly is responsible. And he's the only one charged with any offence.[15]
[emphasis added]

The extent to which defence lawyers are prepared at pre-trial reviews to assist the prosecution by disclosing details of their clients' defence and by engaging in plea negotiation suggests that their commitment to adversarial due process is, at best, tenuous. Some writers have gone so far as to argue that 'defence lawyers opt into the crime control system. This is because they are *part of*, rather than challengers to, the apparatus of criminal justice.'[16] On this analysis, the common professional training and class culture that defence lawyers share with Crown Prosecutors is stressed, as is their shared allegiance to the court and its demand for efficiency in the administration of 'justice'. That defence lawyers may regard continuing relationships with prosecutors and court staff as overriding loyalty to defendants is well recognised.[17] More recently the very existence of any supposed loyalty has been brought into doubt by research into lawyers' attitudes which found that most clients are seen as guilty and morally undeserving of a trial.[18] Yet the rhetorical position of the defence lawyer as the champion of the defendant makes it easy for lawyers to persuade their clients to plead guilty. All lawyers need do is convince defendants that they will be convicted if they plead not guilty, and that there is a material advantage to be gained by pleading guilty. The legal system ensures that such advantages are there for the taking whilst prosecution disclosure provides the defence lawyer with ample material on which to base advice to defendants that their best interests lie in pleading guilty. Consider, for example, another of the exchanges tape-recorded by Baldwin, which occurred at the outset of the pre-trial review:

Defence solicitor: I want some ammunition . . . What we want is really, if you could supply it, some information about whether to lean on [the defendant]. Have you got lots of nice verbals?

Prosecuting solicitor: Right - I don't know about particularly nice verbals.
[He then reads out the statements of two police officer witnesses and gives the defence

15 Baldwin *Pre-Trial Justice* (1985) pp 81-82.
16 McConville, Sanders and Leng (1991) p 167.
17 See, for example, Baldwin *Pre-Trial Justice* (1995) at pp 89-90.
18 See McConville et al (1994) ch 8 and Mulcahy (1994). See also section 2(d)(i) above, and the opening quote to this chapter.

	solicitor a copy of the defendant's statement to the police.]
Prosecuting solicitor:	I think that should give you some of the necessary information to go back to him . . . Do you think you've now got sufficient to get a plea?
Defence solicitor:	Yes.
Prosecuting solicitor:	Great! Another all-day not guilty [case] bites the dust.[19]

We must now return to the point that Baldwin was wrong, in the absence of any direct observation of how the matter was presented to the defendant, to conclude that the negotiations he observed resulted in 'no improper bargains'. McConville et al (1994) adopted a research method which allowed them to observe virtually all the key interactions between defence solicitor and client. We quoted one of these interactions in section 3(b) above, in which a solicitor shouted at the client to 'cut the crap' and plead guilty, even though he had not examined the prosecution evidence. More generally McConville et al conclude that most bargains:

'. . . are not struck under pressure from, or even at the suggestion of, the prosecution. It is usually the defence solicitor who decides to press the matter. Trials are overbooked and under-prepared in the expectation that clients will plead guilty on the day - an expectation that solicitors ensure is fulfilled. Clients rarely put up any resistance to suggestions to plead guilty, and accept the advice of their lawyer - the expert - even where there is no clear admission of guilt.'[20]

'Bargains' arrived at under these circumstances do not strike us as proper. Baldwin may be right, however, to argue that pre-trial reviews are preferable to less visible forms of bargaining.[1] Their use has allowed researchers to learn a good deal more about the behaviour of lawyers in the lower courts. But what has been learnt should make us wary of concluding that pre-trial bargaining is conducted according to principles of propriety and fairness. From a crime control perspective it is possible to argue that prosecution and defence lawyers are simply acting in a realistic and pragmatic fashion and doing the public a service in helping to maintain a high rate of conviction at a relatively low cost. Most prosecutions brought by the police

19 Baldwin *Pre-Trial Justice* (1995) p 88.
20 McConville et al (1994) p 198.
1   As against this, one might argue that pre-trial reviews create an expectation that lawyers should negotiate (even where one or both sides may be reluctant to do so) whereas informal bargaining relies on the parties initiating the bargaining process themselves. For an illustration of the normative pressure to deal exerted by the pre-trial review see Baldwin *Pre-Trial Justice* (1995) pp 42-44.

are, after all, undoubtedly fully justified and, for summary offences in particular, the defendant's guilt can rarely be seriously in doubt. Or so the crime control adherent believes.

From a due process point of view, however, one might argue that there is a large proportion of prosecutions that are far from fully justified[2] and that, in any case, it is incumbent on defence lawyers to take seriously such ideals as the presumption of innocence and the right of silence. These are important protections not just for the minority of defendants who are in fact innocent, but also against the entrenchment of practices that encourage the state to exercise prosecutorial power in an unconstrained manner. Any form of pre-trial bargaining aimed at short-circuiting the court process results in an undermining of these protections. From this perspective, pre-trial reviews may be the lesser of two evils, but they remain an evil.

Is it possible to regulate pre-trial negotiation so as to adequately protect the defendant's interests?[3] Baldwin argues that, with adequate provision for the disclosure of the prosecution case and other safeguards (such as giving defendants a right to attend), pre-trial reviews need represent 'no affront to basic values enshrined in English criminal procedure'.[4] We have suggested that even full disclosure of all prosecution cases (including those for summary offences) would not necessarily work to the advantage of the defendant. Furthermore, the inhibiting effect of having defendants present during pre-trial reviews is likely only to displace the main bargaining encounters into less visible settings.[5] Whilst it is possible that the Crown Prosecution Service may achieve higher standards of case screening in future, it would make little sense in an adversarial system to rely upon prosecutorial propriety as a sufficient safeguard for defendants.

Another possibility would be some form of supervision of PTRs by a supposedly neutral official such as a magistrate or a court clerk. Sometimes PTRs take place in open court but any magistrates present tend to remain passive and aloof, leaving it to the court clerks to run the show.[6] As we discuss in chapter 8, section 3, court clerks support the crime control values PTRs advance. Thus clerks attending these reviews (whether in open court or not) will, if negotiations between the lawyers run into difficulty, actively encourage defence disclosure and case settlement.[7]

2   See ch 6, sections 3(c) and 4(c).
3   For a general discussion, see D Galligan, 'Regulating Pre-Trial Decisions', in I Dennis (ed), *Criminal Law and Justice* (London: Sweet & Maxwell, 1987).
4   Baldwin *Pre-Trial Justice* (1985) p 168.
5   As was observed to happen at the Leeds magistrates' court by Baldwin *Pre-Trial Justice* (1985) pp 111-112. This inhibiting effect is also noted by Mulcahy (1994) p 416.
6   See, for example, Mulcahy (1994) p 411.
7   See, for example, Baldwin *Pre-Trial Justice* (1985) p 43, and J Baldwin and A Mulvaney, Pre-Trial Settlement of Criminal Cases in Magistrates' Courts (Birmingham: University of Birmingham, 1987) p 15.

For pre-trial negotiation to give greater priority to due process values would seem to require, at the very least, the transformation of the ideology and culture of defence lawyers. This might be achieved, for example, by setting up 'criminal defence centres' to promote and support principled and truly adversarial criminal defence services.[8] Whether such a transformation is possible without wider cultural and structural changes in the legal system and in society itself remains an open question.

(b) Charge bargaining in the Crown Court

In the Crown Court, just as in the magistrates' court, charge bargaining is rife. 29% of the Hedderman and Moxon sample claimed to have pleaded guilty as a result of a charge bargain and the authors found plenty of evidence consistent with these claims. This was particularly so where the offence charged fell within the Offences Against the Person Act 1861. For example, across the five Crown Court centres studied, between 20 and 37% of the s 47 offences of causing actual bodily harm had originally been charged as s 20 offences of causing grievous bodily harm. Similarly, between one half and three quarters of the s 20 cases had originally been charged as more serious s 18 offences where an intention to inflict grievous bodily harm must be proved.[9] Numerous studies conducted in the 1990s support this conclusion.[10]

In one of the first studies of this phenomenon, McCabe and Purves examined the cases of 112 defendants who changed their plea to guilty at a late stage, 64 of whom were involved in some form of charge bargain.[11] The study emphasised the crucial role of lawyers in such decisions and was critical of the process involved:

'. . . it seems fair to say that in most, if not all, cases [a change of plea] followed after the defendant received 'certain good advice' from his legal representatives. This is especially the case with late or last-minute changes of plea where counsel, after reviewing his brief and assessing the evidence, speaks urgently to solicitor and defendant in a conference held, in all too many cases, immediately before the trial is due to start. . . . A feature of nearly all cases of plea-changing is the speed and urgency with which conferences, discussions and

---

8   See the proposals to this effect in McConville et al (1994) ch 11; and in Howard League, The Dynamics of Justice (Report of the Working Party on Criminal Justice Administration) (London: Howard League, 1993).
9   Hedderman and Moxon (1992) p 10.
10   Eg, Genders [1998]; McConville et al (1994) and L Bridges, 'Taking Liberties' (2000) Legal Action, July, p 6.
11   S McCabe and R Purves, By-passing the Jury (Oxford: Basil Blackwell, 1972).

negotiations are conducted . . . it gives rise to an impression that critical negotiations are conducted with furtiveness and without full consideration of matters such as the background of the defendant, the details of the offence, and the explanation to the defendant of his rights.'[12]

Somewhat paradoxically, McCabe and Purves were convinced that no substantial injustice resulted from such plea bargaining, arguing, on the basis of their scrutiny of the prosecution papers, that 'changes of plea are the result of a realistic and practical approach adopted by police, defence and prosecution lawyers, judges, and often, the defendants themselves.'[13] Since McCabe and Purves did not talk to defendants as part of their study their conclusion that changes of plea were based on a realistic and independent assessment by defendants of their bargaining position (rather than simply relying on the advice of their legal representatives) requires further consideration. Two further studies in the 1970s which were based largely on interviews with defendants help us build up a more accurate picture of the charge bargaining process. Bottoms and McClean found that most late plea changers were advised to plead guilty by their lawyers, and that few welcomed this advice. As they explained:

'. . . these defendants have for many weeks expected to plead not guilty. This intention has been supported by their solicitor - after all, a trained professional. Then, out of nowhere appears a barrister, usually on the morning of the trial, strongly suggesting a change of plea. It is hardly surprising if defendants acquiesce, faced with this predicament; it is also hardly surprising if some of them subsequently resent having acquiesced to last-minute pressure.'[14]

Exactly the same point was made by Baldwin and McConville in their study of late plea-changers, one of whom is quoted below:

'I was pleading not guilty all the way through - I was so adamant in my own mind that I'd be found not guilty. I didn't decide to plead guilty. It was decided for me from what the barrister said to me. He said, "This is going to drag on for days because they [the prosecution] won't drop these other offences. If you plead guilty to one, they'll drop these other offences. If you continue to plead not guilty, you'll only antagonise the judge." He said he'd go and see the judge, something which I don't readily agree with. He said "My

12   McCabe and Purves (1972) pp 9-10.
13   McCabe and Purves (1972) p 26.
14   A Bottoms and J McLean, *Defendants in the Criminal Process* (London: Routledge and Kegan Paul, 1976) p 130.

job is wheeling and dealing" and he went to see the judge and said "He's told me that we'll knock so many offences off and you'll get done for one." What could I do? I'd been told that the judge had made his findings even before I went into court. The barrister told me even what the judge was going to do [ie impose a fine].'[15]

These later studies revealed that legal advice was crucial in persuading defendants to plead guilty. That the cracked-trial is a barrister-centred phenomenon has been more recently confirmed by Bredar:

'This is a drama that usually unfolds in the corridors outside of court, in the barristers' robing rooms, and in the court cells. What generally happens is that prosecuting and defending counsel compare views on the strengths and weaknesses of their respective cases, and, in an indirect way, discuss what it would take from each side to get the case to "crack." Counsel come to a unified view about what would be an appropriate settlement of the matter, and generally that involves dismissal of one or more charges outstanding against the defendant, and guilty pleas to all the remaining charges, or to amended charges. . . . Defending counsel discusses the option with his client and instructing solicitors, with an eye towards gaining acceptance.'[16]

In view of this, it is important to examine in more detail the respective roles played by defence and prosecution counsel.

(i) The role of the defence barrister

The organisation of the legal profession into two distinct branches, solicitors and barristers, has an important bearing on charge bargaining. In most cases a solicitor representing a defendant must hand over the conduct of the case in the Crown Court to a member of the Bar. A defence barrister, on reading the brief prepared by the solicitor, may take a different view of the prospect of winning a case. Indeed, one of the advantages claimed for the split profession is that a barrister, with no direct relationship with the client, is able to be more objective about the prospects of winning a case in court. The introduction of a barrister into the case following committal to the Crown Court may thus lead to a change of plea being advised.[17]

15 Baldwin and McConville (1977) p 31.
16 J Bredar, 'Moving Up the Day of Reckoning: strategies for attacking the "cracked trials" problem' [1992] Crim LR 153 at p 155.
17 See further, Morison and Leith (1992) pp 67-69.

It is unlikely that a defence solicitor will dissent from counsel's opinion. The barrister, after all, is the acknowledged expert in the Crown Court arena. Furthermore, as we have seen, most defence solicitors operating in the magistrates' courts seem more interested in settling than contesting cases.[18] It is true that it is because of their advice that many defendants decide to elect trial by jury and plead not guilty. But this may not reflect any genuine commitment to adversarial due process values. Solicitors may have made tactical use of a not guilty plea to strengthen a defendant's bargaining position vis-a-vis the prosecution, to increase the chances of legal aid being granted and so on. In many instances, particularly where conferences are held on the day of the trial, the solicitor will not even be present when counsel advises a client to plead guilty, having sent one of the firm's clerks instead.[19] Ultimately, the high rate of guilty pleas and late plea changing by defendants indicates that many defence solicitors (and their representatives at court) are happy to allow barristers to fulfil their hired gun role of settling cases.[20]

Barristers are self-employed but group together in chambers, sharing office overheads and paying a percentage of their fees to a barristers' clerk. The latter is a pivotal figure whose functions include attracting work from solicitors, allocating briefs within chambers in cases where the solicitor has not specified a particular barrister, and negotiating the brief fee. Barristers, like all criminal lawyers, tend to accept 'too much' work in the expectation that many cases will be settled out of court.[1] This, in itself, provides them with an incentive to try and settle cases through negotiation. But barristers may not wish to achieve a settlement until the day of trial. Under the legal aid scheme the fee chargeable for a straightforward guilty plea case is much smaller than the trial fee obtainable if a case cracks at the last moment. Economic incentives such as this clearly influence the behaviour of lawyers.[2] According to Bredar, barristers deny deliberately avoiding early settlement but admit 'that their attention naturally is more focused on their cases which are at the trial (and thus more remunerative) stage, knowing that their cases which are at the earlier, plea review stage

18   See section 2(d)(i) above.
19   See Baldwin and McConville (1977) pp 46 and 55. The Crown Court study noted the significant involvement of unqualified staff in Crown Court work, and that 18% of defence respondents had become involved in the case as late as the day before or on the day of the trial itself: Zander and Henderson (1993) pp 194-195. See generally McConville et al (1994) for a dissection of the discontinuous nature of legal representation provided for defendants and the extensive use of unqualified staff at all stages of case processing.
20   Morison and Leith (1992) pp 67-69.
1   Morison and Leith (1992) p 64. See also section 4(a)(ii) above for similar findings by McConville et al (1994) regarding solicitors.
2   See the discussion in A Gray, P Fenn, and N Rickman, 'Controlling Lawyers' Costs through Standard Fees: An Economic Analysis' in R Young and D Wall (eds), *Access to Criminal Justice* (London: Blackstone, 1996).

will ripen with time.'[3] The observational study by McConville et al (1994) suggests that the avoidance of early settlement is often, in fact, quite deliberate.[4] By the same token, if a decent trial fee can be obtained by persuading a client to make a last-minute decision to plead guilty there is little financial incentive to fight a case. As one barrister interviewed by Morison and Leith put it, 'some barristers . . . take the view that if they get paid the same for doing a plea as for doing a trial they will accept . . . the plea and go home by 11.00 o'clock in the morning.'[5]

If, as often happens, barristers find that they cannot conduct a case at all due to pressure of work then briefs have to be returned to solicitors and another barrister found to handle the case. This happens in nearly half of all contested cases.[6] As barristers are self-employed, a returned brief represents lost income. Barristers who are double-booked commonly wait until the last possible moment before returning a brief. As one barrister has put it: 'You say to yourself, "Well, if something happens to the other case I'll be able to do this one, whereas if I pass it now and something happens to the other case next week I'll be unemployed."'[7] The problem is compounded by the intermediary role played by the barristers' clerks since they have a direct financial interest in keeping a brief within their chambers. One practising barrister has revealed that frequently:

'. . . barristers' clerks . . . hang on to a brief even when they know well in advance that the barrister originally instructed will be committed elsewhere. The clerk's aim is to keep the brief within chambers by only informing the solicitor of the difficulty at the eleventh hour, so that he will have no time to try and brief someone else, and will more easily settle for a substitute from the same set of chambers. Often this will be a barrister whom the solicitor does not know, and who is a person of less experience; furthermore because the switch is not made until the last moment the substitute has little time in which to prepare a brief.'[8]

3   Bredar [1992] p 157. See to like effect, J Plotnikoff and R Woolfson, From Committal to Trial: Delay at the Crown Court (London: Law Society, 1993) pp 62-65.
4   McConville et al (1994) pp 253-254 and see section 2(d)(i) above.
5   Morison and Leith (1992) p 132. The introduction in 1997 of a graduated fee scheme for barristers altered the structure of financial incentives but its effect on counsels' behaviour is unclear.
6   Zander and Henderson (1993) p 32.
7   Morison and Leith (1992) p 64.
8   J Caplan, 'The Criminal Bar' in R Hazell (ed), The Bar on Trial (London: Quartet, 1978). See also Royal Commission on Criminal Justice; Submission of Evidence by the Crown Prosecution Service, vol 1 Evidence, at pp 177-8. For a direct quote of one last-minute negotiation with a barrister's clerk, see P Rock, The Social World of an English Crown Court (Oxford: Clarendon, 1993) p 272.

This last-minute horse-trading is also attributable to the fact that the Crown Court issues a definitive list of the day's business it intends to transact as late as 4pm the previous day.[9] It is thus not surprising that in contested cases a third of defence barristers say that they receive the brief on the day before the hearing or on the day itself.[10] In consequence, barristers commonly arrive at court ill-prepared and ill-disposed to fight on a defendant's behalf, and their conferences with defendants are often hurried last-minute affairs.[11] Defendants do not see their barrister until the day of the trial in over half of all contested and 'cracked' cases.[12]

Most Crown Court work is funded by the state at a relatively low level and standard fees cover most of the cases handled. As in the magistrates' courts, practitioners say that the only way to make criminal work pay is to turn over a high volume of cases in a relatively standardised fashion.[13] There are some able barristers who have a genuine commitment to defence work. In addition, barristers of ability may, because of discrimination on the grounds of race, gender or class, find it impossible to break into the more lucrative areas of the Bar and, therefore, develop a criminal practice almost by default. Nonetheless, it remains true that the most able (as well as the best connected) young barristers will tend to gravitate towards privately funded commercial work, leaving the inexperienced and the less able to eke out a living by settling cases wherever possible so as to be able to move on to the next brief.

Perhaps of equal importance to these organisational factors, however, is the role allotted to defence counsel in the legal system. It is emphatically not the case that barristers are expected to use every resource at their disposal to secure an acquittal for persons accused of crime. The professional duties of defending counsel are set out in the Code of Conduct for the Bar of England and Wales (5th edn), para 202 of which states that:

> 'A practising barrister has an overriding duty to the court to ensure in the public interest that the proper and efficient administration of justice is achieved: he must assist the court in the administration of justice and must not deceive or knowingly or recklessly mislead the court.'

---

9   Rock (1993) pp 271-273.
10   Zander and Henderson (1993) p 30.
11   Defence barristers commonly claim that despite the late receipt of instructions they have sufficient time to prepare the case: Zander and Henderson (1993). This raises the question of what defence barristers regard as 'adequate' preparation, and for what purpose.
12   Zander and Henderson (1993) p 62.
13   Morison and Leith (1992) pp 43-44.

Thus, the barrister owes a duty first and foremost to the court, and should seek to ensure that justice is administered efficiently. A charge bargain represents an efficient disposal of a case, at least in comparison with the costs of a contested trial. But the Code also refers to the proper administration of justice. Paragraph 203 expands on what is meant by this:

'A practising barrister . . . must promote and protect fearlessly and by all proper and lawful means his lay client's best interests and do so without regard to his own interests or to any consequences to himself or to any other person (including his professional client or fellow members of the legal profession) . . .'

While it is the barrister's job to promote the client's best interests, this is not necessarily to be achieved by fighting the case to the finish.[14] That defence counsel have a duty to impress upon defendants the advantages that may be secured by agreeing to a charge bargain was stressed by Lord Parker CJ in *Hall*. The appellant claimed that he had been pressurised into pleading guilty by his counsel. In dismissing the appeal Lord Parker stated that:

'What the Court is looking to see is whether a prisoner in these circumstances has a free choice; the election must be his, the responsibility his, to plead Guilty or Not Guilty. At the same time, it is the clear duty of any counsel representing a client to assist the client to make up his mind by putting forward the pros and cons, if need be in strong language, to impress upon the client what the likely results are of certain courses of conduct.'[15]

In other words, barristers are obliged by law to make plain to defendants the considerable advantages to be gained through pleading guilty as part of a charge bargain. But the fact that a negotiated plea generally coincides with a barrister's self interest should make us wary of the proposition that a charge bargain will only be struck when that is in the client's best interests.

There are wide yet consistent variations in guilty plea rates across the circuits into which the Crown Court is organised. Thus, London has had the lowest guilty plea rate in the country for 30 years, while the Midland

14 For a general discussion of how ethical duties may conflict see Ashworth [1998]. For a deeper analysis, which argues that the function of ethical codes of practice is to legitimise the repressive role of criminal courts as increasingly expressed through the encouragement of plea bargaining, see M McConville, 'Plea Bargaining: Ethics and Politics' (1998) 25 JLS 562.

15 (1968) 52 Cr App Rep 528 at 534-535.

and Oxford, and North Eastern circuits have had the highest.[16] This suggests that some local bars may have developed a powerful culture in which the priority given to settling rather than fighting cases is particularly marked. In short, the claim of the Bar that it always puts the interests of its clients first simply beggars belief.[17]

(ii) The role of prosecuting counsel

Since the Crown Prosecution Service currently lacks rights of audience in the higher criminal courts it is obliged to brief barristers in private practice. A barrister may be defending one day and prosecuting the next. The Bar claims that this arrangement is advantageous since it puts the conduct of both sides of a criminal case into the hands of professional and independent lawyers with no psychological commitment to either prosecution or defence. As one barrister interviewed by Morison and Leith expressed it:

'We're independent . . . we get papers - defending or prosecuting - we take a totally objective view and if the client is totally up a gum tree or being stupid I can advise him so . . . By the same token, the prosecution service may be obsessed with the guilt of an individual even though there's bugger all evidence against him and I, by looking at it afresh from an objective standpoint, can advise them to the contrary.'[18]

This suggests that in the higher courts a defendant is better protected from 'unfair' charge bargaining than in the magistrates' courts because prosecuting counsel are not so concerned with achieving 'a result'. Whereas a Crown Prosecutor might seek to get a result even in a weak case through a charge bargain, a more objective barrister would simply drop the case altogether. Conversely, where a Crown Prosecutor might give too much weight to the bureaucratic demand for efficiency and case settlement, prosecuting counsel would follow the path of justice by prosecuting the case in accordance with the evidence.

16 See M Zander, 'What the Annual Statistics Tell Us About Pleas and Acquittals' [1991] Crim LR 252 and, for the most recent figures displaying the same pattern: Lord Chancellor's Department (2000) Table 6.8.

17 As regards summary justice the differences in guilty plea rates between magistrates' courts are less easy to discern as there are so few contested trials there and routine statistics on this issue are not collected. There is, however, plenty of research evidence indicating that magistrates' courts develop distinctive working cultures and that these have an effect on rates at which, for example, bail or legal aid is granted (see further ch 8).

18 Morison and Leith (1992) p 67.

The claim to objectivity needs to be seen in the light of how prosecuting and defence work is allocated and conducted in practice. Many barristers become type-cast as either defenders or prosecutors. The Crown Prosecution Service, for example, maintains a panel of barristers to whom as a matter of course briefs will be sent. These barristers may well become 'prosecution-minded' and in any event would be anxious not to jeopardise an important source of business by ignoring the wishes of their institutional client. Baldwin's interviews with barristers, for example, revealed a self-interested reluctance to suggest to the CPS that weak cases should be discontinued. In explaining this reluctance one said that he would be 'too terrified of the demi-gods at the CPS, particularly in these days of preferred chambers' while another revealed that 'there are some cases - the ones that are borderline - where, for my own position (as someone who is acceptable to the CPS), I would run it because I don't want to make enemies out of these people.'[19] Baldwin concludes that 'it is only on the day of the trial itself, when minds are more keenly focused than hitherto on the real issues in the case, when a decision might finally be taken to abandon a prosecution.'[20] That conclusion was reached in the context of a study of discontinued cases. But if one took a sample of all 'weak' cases one would no doubt find that prosecuting counsel prefer a last-minute charge bargain to discontinuance, as this secures 'a result' for their divine pay-masters. Even such bargains require the blessing of the boss. According to Bredar, once counsel have reached a 'unified view' of the appropriate settlement of the case:

> 'Prosecuting counsel then communicates this view to a CPS law clerk or lawyer, cautiously advising in favour of the proposal. . . . CPS law clerks, often in consultation with CPS lawyers over the telephone, seem to be the critical decision-makers: ie once they 'bless' the arrangement, the trial quickly "cracks."'[1]

This scarcely accords with the official image of the fearless independent barrister projected by the Bar. Prosecuting counsel have much the same financial and practical interest in driving charge bargains as do their defence counterparts.[2] Briefs are passed on by prosecuting counsel in around three-

19 J Baldwin, 'Understanding Judge Ordered and Directed Acquittals in the Crown Court' [1997] Crim LR 536 at 552-553. Baldwin adds that 'several barristers expressed concern about moves by the CPS to allocate work to sets of preferred chambers' (p 553, fn 31).

20 Baldwin (1999) p 554.

1   Bredar [1992] p 155.

2   Some have sought to resist the recent moves towards a salaried defender scheme, heralded by the Access to Justice Act 1999 (see ch 8, section 2(d)) by arguing that it will 'lead' to a culture of negotiated justice. But that culture is already with

Charge bargaining

fifths of contested cases and half of prosecuting barristers receive their brief either on the day before the hearing or on the day itself.[3] One barrister interviewed by Morison and Leith complained that:

> '. . . the public purse is very carefully monitored these days . . . most of the cases I do are standard fee cases where you get the same fee for prosecuting whether it's a plea or a trial . . . That is why so many cases go short, because certain members of my profession like to earn as much money for as little effort.'[4]

As with defence barristers, however, it would be misleading to portray a prosecuting barrister engaging in charge bargaining as having deviated from a legal duty to fight cases. According to the Court of Appeal in *Herbert*[5] the practice whereby counsel indicated that the Crown would be prepared to accept pleas of guilty to lesser offences than those charged, or to certain only of the charges, had long been accepted as properly part of counsel's duty. This duty involved satisfying the public interest in prosecuting serious wrongdoing while, on the other hand, not necessarily pursuing every charge regardless of the public purse. The decision confirms that charge bargaining is part of a prosecuting barrister's duty, not a deviation from it.[6] Consistent with this, the 'Judge's Questionnaire', now a standard part of the pre-trial 'Plea and Directions Hearing', contains the question: 'Will the prosecution accept part guilty or alternative pleas?'.[7] The institutional expectation is that cases should be prepared for settlement rather than for trial.

(iii) Keeping the customer satisfied

The implications of this discussion of the role of barristers in the Crown Court may now be spelled out. Counsel, whether defending or prosecuting, are expected to bargain over charges. The organisation of the courts and

---

us. As Lord Bach said in the House of Lords during the passing of this Act: 'one only needs to visit any robing room in any Crown Court in this country to know that bargaining takes place between an independent prosecuting barrister and an independent defence barrister. Sometimes it is for the convenience of the offender; sometimes it is not.' Quoted by O'Brien and Epp (2000) p 397, fn 30.

3   Zander and Henderson (1993) pp 30-32. See also Royal Commission on Criminal Justice; Submission of Evidence by the Crown Prosecution Service, vol 1 Evidence, at p 177, footnote 66.

4   Morison and Leith (1992) p 44.

5   (1991) 94 Cr App Rep 230.

6   On the ethical dimensions of this duty see Blake and Ashworth [1998] p 28.

7   The Plea and Directions Hearing is discussed in section 2(d)(i) above. The Judge's Questionnaire is reproduced in Sprack (2000) p 514.

the Bar means that such negotiations tend to take place at a late stage between parties pre-disposed to compromise. The close-knit social world of a local Bar means that the negotiating parties will, in all likelihood, have concluded many similar agreements in the past and that a relationship of trust will have built up between them. This is important, for, as Moody and Tombs noted in their study of charge bargaining in Scotland, the 'degree to which either party is prepared to negotiate with the other depends very much on a mutual exchange of respect and understanding.'[8] Agreement is facilitated by the fact that both sides are bound by the same code of professional ethics and owe a duty to the court to pursue the efficient administration of justice.

The interest in maintaining good relations with other barristers (and with judges seeking to manage a heavy caseload) may come to assume more importance than the interests of an individual defendant who will probably never be encountered again. As Galanter succinctly expresses it: 'Loyalty is often deflected from the one-time client to the forum or opposite party with whom the lawyer has continuing relations.'[9] In this situation, it is both tempting and easy for barristers to convince clients that their best interests lie in pleading guilty when this is not in fact so. The defence barrister's habit of lowering a defendant's expectations while creating a good impression of the legal service being offered is noted by Morison and Leith.[10] As one barrister told them:

'You always give the client the worst prognosis . . . there is not a barrister at the criminal bar who has not learned that lesson by under estimating what the client would get and then getting the shock of his life . . .'[11]

It is in this context that one must place the finding of the Crown Court survey that the great majority of defendants expressed satisfaction with the service provided by their legal representatives.[12] Most defence barristers are skilled advocates and it is no real surprise to find that defendants are persuaded into believing that their interests have been well served. The stark conclusion reached by Moody and Tombs suggests that the defendants' perceptions are often mistaken:

8   S Moody and J Tombs, 'Plea Negotiations in Scotland' [1983] Crim LR 297 at p 305.
9   M Galanter, 'Mega-Law and Mega-Lawyering in the Contemporary United States' in R Dingwall and P Lewis (eds), *The Sociology of the Professions* (London: Macmillan, 1983) p 159.
10   Morison and Leith (1992) p 70.
11   Morison and Leith (1992) pp 136-137.
12   Zander and Henderson (1993) p 67.

Charge bargaining

'there are constant factors which must be present if prosecution and defence are to agree. These centre round the notion of trust resulting in a co-alignment of interests and co-operation between traditional adversaries, while the accused, in the vast majority of cases where pleas are negotiated, stands to gain very little in material terms.'[13]

A decade later McConville et al observed case conferences between defence counsel and client held at court on the date fixed for settling plea. They report that the 'common denominator of court conferences is the determination of counsel to secure a guilty plea to some or all of the charges .... To secure this result, barristers deploy a range of techniques some of which are designed to stress the advantages of a prosecution offer and the bleakness of any alternative, and others of which are designed to encourage the client to hand the decision over to the barrister as an expert.'[14] Thus client satisfaction was sought by describing offers of a charge-bargain as 'excellent', 'the best that can be achieved' and 'better than we could have hoped for', and as something to be accepted rapidly whilst it was still on the table.[15] Most defence counsel pressed this kind of advice without having first tested whether the evidence would justify either the original charge or that now on offer. The potential for injustice is obvious.

(iv) Judicial supervision of charge bargaining in the Crown Court

If anyone could be expected to monitor the propriety of charge bargains it would surely be the judge. The judiciary's role as professional dispensers of justice would seem to mark them out as especially fitted for this task. According to McCabe and Purves, every one of the charge bargains they identified had been expressly endorsed by the judge.[16] Zander too argues that judicial supervision provides a safeguard in this area, citing in support the 'Yorkshire Ripper' case in 1981.[17] Here, the trial judge refused to endorse the prosecution's acceptance of Peter Sutcliffe's plea of guilty to manslaughter, insisting that the original murder charge be proceeded with.

At one time, the appellate courts required that the charge brought should correspond to the facts alleged. In *Coe*,[18] for instance, the court deprecated

---

13   Moody and Tombs (1983) p 307.
14   McConville et al (1994) pp 256-257. This was a large-scale study: 54 defendants were observed in these conferences.
15   McConville et al (1994) p 257.
16   McCabe and Purves (1972) p 29. See also Bredar [1992] p 155.
17   M Zander, *Cases and Materials on the English Legal System* 6th edn (London: Weidenfeld and Nicolson, 1992) p 293.
18   (1969) 53 Cr App Rep 66. This echoed the earlier case of *Soanes* (1948) 32 Cr App Rep 136.

charge reduction in the interests of convenience and ruled that the over-riding consideration must always be the proper administration of justice. This attitude has since been replaced by a recognition of the advantages of charge bargaining and the dangers of judicial involvement. We have already seen that in *Herbert*[19] the Court of Appeal accepted that it was proper for prosecuting counsel to take into account the savings in public expenditure that a charge bargain could achieve. The Court of Appeal in *Grafton*[20] subsequently decided that the trial judge is powerless to prevent Counsel dropping or reducing any charges except where the latter seeks the seal of judicial approval for a proposed deal. This rule (and its exception) is an incentive for counsel to keep judges out of charge bargaining altogether. Thus, if a case similar to that of Peter Sutcliffe were to go before the courts today, prosecuting counsel would be free to accept a plea of guilty to manslaughter so long as no express sanction was sought from the judge.

Should one classify *Grafton* as laying down a crime control *enabling* rule - encouraging counsel to pursue charge bargaining free of judicial interference? Or is it merely a rule which *legitimises* a long-established practice?[1] The answer depends on how far trial judges had previously ensured that charge bargains were based, as far as they can be, on considerations of justice rather than merely convenience and efficiency. What is the evidence on this point? The Peter Sutcliffe case provides an example of due process inspired judicial control (no doubt prompted by the high profile of that case) but there are many other cases which tend to show that trial judges are just as likely to encourage as restrict the practice of charge bargaining, and that the appellate judiciary welcome this. In *Winterflood*[2] the judge had sent for counsel after four days of the trial and asked if the defendant would plead guilty to handling stolen property if a robbery charge was dropped. The defendant agreed to this but appealed against the sentence imposed. In dismissing the appeal, the Court of Appeal stressed that private discussions before or during a trial were undesirable but that there was no reason why the discussion in this case should not have taken place, in the absence of the jury, in open court. Similarly, in *Llewellyn*[3] the Court of Appeal emphasised that trial judges should not feel inhibited from taking part in pre-trial reviews to discuss such matters as the correct way of proceeding with the charges brought.

The great majority of Crown Court judges are recruited from the ranks of the practising Bar. Many hold part-time appointments only, spending

19   (1991) 94 Cr App Rep 230.
20   [1993] QB 101.
1   For a discussion of the different nature of legal rules as legitimising, enabling, inhibitory or presentational, see ch 2, section 1(d).
2   [1979] Crim LR 263.
3   (1978) 67 Cr App Rep 149.

most of their time as barristers rather than judges. Prosecution and defence counsel have little to fear in seeking the approval of a judge for a charge bargain since all of the parties involved share a common outlook, all stand to gain from short-circuiting the formal trial process, and all are encouraged to enter into negotiations by the Court of Appeal. Sometimes judges, by indicating their desire for a speedy resolution of the case, exert much indirect pressure on their fellow lawyers to cut a deal. In an example given by McConville et al, defence counsel had been called to see the judge privately just before a trial listed for three days was due to begin. The judge said he wanted the jury to be able to retire to consider their verdict by 11am the following morning because he was going on 'his holidays' in the afternoon of that day. This led counsel to try to persuade the client that it would be tactically astute to agree to the trial being truncated because the judge 'is a fast judge . . . he likes the bare bones of a case . . .' (The judge's desire to pack his case and rest his bones in the sun was not conveyed to the client.) The client resisted, which prompted counsel to depict the preference for a full trial as 'complete madness' and 'bloody crazy!'. The client responded:

> 'You're not the one who might go away [to prison] at the end of the day. I've lost my family and now I might lose my liberty. I want to do it properly, it *must* be done right; I don't want to rush it now.'[4]

It is a pity that more of those working in the criminal courts do not share this freedom perspective or this concern for procedural propriety.

The appellate courts proclaim that charge bargains should represent a proper, not merely an inexpensive, outcome to a case, but is this mere lip-service to the interests of justice? The point, after all, of these bargains is to circumvent the very safeguards and procedural protections designed to discover the truth and to produce justice. To take just one example, the rationale for the rule that a jury should not be told of an accused's previous convictions is that the prejudicial effect of this knowledge would outweigh any probative value. Yet barristers engaged in charge bargaining act in full knowledge of any previous record that an accused might have. It is easy to see how a presumption of guilt might arise in these circumstances. The judge, whose independence is supposed to protect defendants against improper pressure, is merely an interested spectator (and potential dealer) at the market place of justice.

5. THE PROSPECT OF CONVICTION

The advantages to be gained by pleading guilty explain why defendants who think they will be convicted following trial decide to plead guilty. But

4   McConville et al (1994) p 265 (emphasis in original).

why do they expect to be found guilty? This expectation may be influenced by information received directly or indirectly from the court officials or from the prosecution and defence lawyers (or their staff).

(a) Predictions of conviction from the bench

Nothing is more likely to cause a defendant to abandon a not guilty plea than the official(s) conducting the trial expressing a view that the defendant is guilty, will be found guilty, and is wasting the court's time by pleading not guilty. The defendant can hardly expect a fair trial in such circumstances. With the dice so heavily loaded, all the defendant then has to decide is whether to opt for a more lenient sentence by pleading guilty. In other words, there is no longer a meaningful decision to be made. The problem of a bench communicating its prejudices in this way seems largely confined to the Crown Court where judges and barristers form a close-knit work group. There is less opportunity for magistrates to convey their views on the strength of the case to the parties. There is less incentive too, as contested cases form such a small proportion of magistrates' courts cases and do not take long to dispose of in any case.

The Court of Appeal has made it clear that it is improper for a judge to comment on the strength of the prosecution case as a way of persuading the defendant to enter a plea of guilty. A blatant case is *Barnes* in which the judge harangued the defendant and his barrister:

'I think it right I should tell you in the presence and hearing of your client that I take a very serious view indeed of hopeless cases, without the shadow of a defence, being contested at public expense. ... I am not going to mince matters. It is absolutely outrageous that other people are waiting for their trials because of behaviour like this.'[5]

The Court of Appeal expressed some sympathy with the trial judge's concerns but pointed out that the defendant was simply exercising his right to put the prosecution to proof. The appearance of a fair trial before an impartial judge had been completely destroyed by the trial judge's outburst and the conviction was accordingly quashed. However, the problem persists. Some of Baldwin and McConville's respondents claimed that they had been compelled to plead guilty by the judge, as in the following example:

'The barrister came back from seeing the judge and said, "Well, the judge says we can argue as long as you like but you'll be found guilty anyway." ... I think I was more forced into it [pleading guilty]

5   (1970) 55 Cr App Rep 100 at 104-105.

The prospect of conviction

than anything, personally. I was flogging a dead horse. I mean the judge had made up his mind before I even walked through the door.'[6]

Some cases reveal an astonishing level of judicial interference into the conduct of a trial supposed to be conducted on adversarial principles of due process. In *Pitman*[7] (a case of causing death by reckless driving) the judge sent for counsel and indicated that in his view there was no defence to the charge. Defence counsel said that he had advised a plea of not guilty as it was arguable that recklessness would not be made out by the prosecution. The judge replied pointedly that the defendant's plea was not a matter for counsel to determine.[8]

So long as trial judges continue to engage in sentence bargaining the likelihood is that they will either volunteer (or become drawn into giving) their views on the likely outcome of the case. And to a defendant offered a sentence discount in return for pleading guilty, it may seem as if the judge has already decided that a conviction is not in doubt and that all that remains to be determined is the appropriate sentence.

(b) Information from the prosecution

In order for the defence to assess the prospects of conviction it is obviously essential they have advance notice of the prosecution case and of any 'unused material' held by prosecution agencies which might help bolster the defence. As noted in section 4(a)(ii) the provisions for disclosure in the magistrates' courts are manifestly inadequate. Although advance disclosure of the prosecution case is more firmly established for trials on indictment, much depends on prosecutors exercising their discretion and their duties in a fair and proper manner, and gaps remain.[9] One gap was created by the English courts deciding that, if 'unused material' relates to informants or the work of undercover police officers, the prosecution can make an ex parte application to the court for permission not to disclose such material and the defence need not be told of this application.[10] The ECtHR has recently ruled that this procedure breached the Art 6 right to a

6   Baldwin and McConville (1977) p 33.
7   [1991] 1 All ER 468.
8   The obvious retort is that the defendant's plea was not a matter for the judge either. See also *James* [1990] Crim LR 815.
9   Our main discussion of the rules governing disclosure is in ch 6, section 3(c)(v) and see references cited there for more detail.
10   *Davis, Johnson and Rowe* [1993] 1 WLR 613. The Runciman Commission gave their blessing to this decision and recommended that further restrictions on the prosecution's duty to disclose should be introduced: RCCJ (1993) pp 95-96. This was achieved by the Criminal Procedure and Investigations Act 1996, discussed in ch 6, section 3(c)(v).

fair trial, a right which includes a duty on the prosecution to disclose all relevant evidence.[11] But in a case decided on the same day the ECtHR ruled that Art 6 was not breached in a situation where the defence was notified of an ex parte application for an order permitting non-disclosure of material evidence and where the trial judge had given the defence as much information as possible about that evidence without revealing what it was, and had allowed the defence to outline their case for requiring full prosecution disclosure.[12] These two decisions are not in conflict because they both accept that the prosecution duty of disclosure is not absolute, but must take into account competing interests such as the safety of prosecution witnesses. It follows, however, that defendants may decide to plead guilty in ignorance of evidence withheld (quite lawfully) by the prosecution that would have helped to establish innocence.

A more frequent problem is that the prosecution fails to comply with the duty to disclose. A failure to disclose evidence helpful to the defence has lain at the heart of most of the spectacular miscarriages of justice that have come to light in recent years. Such a failure occurred, for example, in all four of the now infamous 'terrorist' trials heard from 1974-1976.[13] It is not safe to assume that the framework of suspects' rights introduced by the Police and Criminal Evidence Act has engendered a new culture of disclosure within prosecution agencies. In July 1992 Michelle and Lisa Taylor were sentenced to life imprisonment for murder. The conviction was subsequently quashed, in part because the police had deliberately suppressed evidence that would have been helpful to the defence.[14] There have been many other post PACE cases of a similar nature.[15]

A failure to disclose evidence should not be seen as an occasional aberration, the understandable product, perhaps, of the pressure the police come under to achieve 'a result' in murder inquiries. The post PACE research by McConville et al shows that the police habitually construct the case for the prosecution in a way that strips it of any material helpful to the defence.[16] They also show how the police are adept at presenting positive 'facts' in a way that maximises the probability of prosecution and eventual conviction.[17] With certain offences under the Public Order Act 1986, for example, it must be proved that behaviour was 'threatening', 'abusive' or

11 *Rowe and Davis v UK* [2000] Crim LR 584.
12 *Jasper v UK; Fitt v UK* [2000] Crim LR 586, and see the accompanying critical commentary.
13 The 'Guildford Four', 'Birmingham Six', the 'Maguires' and Judith Ward cases.
14 *The Guardian*, 12 June 1993.
15 See ch 6, section 3(c)(v).
16 McConville, Sanders, and Leng (1991). Case construction is discussed in detail in ch 6, sections 3(c) and 4(c).
17 Forensic scientists are sometimes just as guilty of presenting their findings in a highly misleading fashion: *Ward* (1993) 96 Cr App Rep 1 provides a good example of this, and see further ch 6, section 3(c)(iv).

'insulting' or that others were likely to be caused 'alarm', 'harassment' or 'distress' by such behaviour. These are vague standards, which were found to provide ample scope for case construction:

> 'In the large number of cases in our sample in which it was alleged that a public order offence was committed in the presence of police officers, the key evidence was supplied by that officer's characterization of the suspect's behaviour and the assessment of its effects on other people. Because the officer anticipates review of the case for evidential sufficiency and having to prove the offence in court, the relevant behaviour of the accused is described in the exact terms of the offence. Generally evidence of this sort is inscrutable short of cross-examination in court.'[18]

There will be no cross-examination, however, if a defendant is persuaded to plead guilty on the strength of the prosecution case as it exists on paper. That case, far from allowing defendants to make a realistic assessment of their prospects of acquittal, paints a systematically distorted portrait of 'the facts' which may mislead a defendant into believing that there is no option but to plead guilty.

(c)   Advice from the defence barrister

It has been argued in this chapter that defence lawyers arrive at court pre-disposed to settle cases for organisational and ideological reasons, and that the law provides them with the raw materials with which to fashion a negotiated settlement. A further issue is whether lawyers provide proper advice on the prospect of acquittal.[19] Research suggests that they adopt an unduly pessimistic view of the likelihood of acquittal in order to increase the pressure on defendants to plead guilty. In most cases the client is simply presumed guilty and there is little attempt made to scrutinise the evidence or its relationship to legal categories of offence.[20]

Some barristers in the Baldwin and McConville study were consistently described, by different defendants in different cases, as either good or bad. The latter were 'seen very commonly as hurried, dismissive or in other ways unsatisfactory.'[1] We saw above how 'bad' lawyers may engage in charge

18   McConville, Sanders and Leng (1991) p 134.
19   Although we do not deal here with the part played by rules of evidence and procedure to assessments of the prospect of conviction, their importance should not be underestimated. See further ch 9, section 4(a) and, for more detailed analysis D McBarnet, *Conviction* (London: Macmillan, 1983).
20   See, in particular, McConville et al (1994) p 188 and pp 267-269
1   Baldwin and McConville (1977) p 42.

bargaining or make use of the sentencing discount principle in order to pressurise defendants into pleading guilty. The defendants interviewed by Baldwin and McConville claimed that barristers commonly backed up this pressure by stating that there was little or no chance of being acquitted if the trial proceeded. Protestations of innocence were often brushed aside as irrelevant to this question, as in the following example:

'My barrister pleaded guilty for me. I told him that I was innocent but he said I was a bloody nuisance and that nobody would believe me. He said, "The judge and the others will never believe what you say in court; they will always believe the police."'[2]

More recently the observational study by McConville et al has confirmed that a substantial proportion of both solicitors and barristers (and the unqualified staff they commonly use throughout the life of a case) continue to treat prosecution evidence uncritically, ignore protestations of innocence, and advise that the defendant has 'no choice' but to plead guilty.[3] This advice would clearly be contrary to the *Turner*[4] rules under which barristers are supposed to tell clients that they must only plead guilty if they accept that they are guilty. That some barristers were prepared to tell clients that they stood no chance of acquittal notwithstanding their claims of innocence stands as a warning that defendants may not receive objective advice as regards the strength of their position. It also has a critical bearing on the question we pose in the next section.

6. DO THE INNOCENT PLEAD GUILTY?

Many people would perhaps be prepared to tolerate charge bargaining, sentence discounts and sentence bargains if the net result was more convictions of the guilty and no corresponding increase in convictions of the innocent. The ends would be sufficiently desirable to render the means acceptable. This half-way house between due process and crime control may appear attractive, but in practice no guarantee can be given that the innocent will not be made to suffer as a result of striking such a compromise. This is despite the ostensible concern of the appellate courts to ensure that the innocent are not induced to plead guilty by charge bargains and the sentencing discount. Thus in the leading case of *Turner* Lord Parker CJ was at pains to stress that counsel 'of course will emphasize that the

2   Baldwin and McConville (1977) p 53.
3   McConville et al (1994) chs 7-10.
4   [1970] 2 QB 321.

accused must not plead guilty unless he has committed the acts constituting the offence charged.'[5]

The difficulty here is that a defence lawyer will not know if a particular client is innocent or not and indeed may be anxious not to find out. Barristers to whom confessions of guilt are made, for example, are subject to strict restrictions in how they may conduct a defence. Certain things they may still do, such as challenge the admissibility of prosecution evidence, but, according to the Code of Conduct for the Bar of England and Wales:

> '. . . a barrister must not assert as true that which he knows to be false. He must not connive at, much less attempt to substantiate a fraud. He must not set up an affirmative case inconsistent with the confession.'[6]

Thus in one interaction observed by McConville et al, counsel, on being told by a client that he had committed the offence of stealing a television as charged, feigned deafness, saying 'I don't hear so good when people make admissions.'[7]

Advice on charge bargains and the sentencing discount will thus be given to all clients, guilty or not. The court in *Turner* implicitly recognises this in insisting that barristers stress that no one should plead guilty unless they are guilty. There would be no need for such an exhortation if only the guilty were to receive advice on the advantages of pleading guilty. Many innocent persons will thus inevitably face advice from their barristers to the effect that they would derive considerable advantage from pleading guilty.

Having considered the options, the *Turner* rules state that the final choice of plea is the accused's alone. Nothing prevents accused persons from proclaiming innocence to their lawyers yet insisting on entering a guilty plea in court. In such a situation it might seem as if a defence lawyer would be contributing to a deception of the court, yet there is no due process requirement that the lawyer reveals the accused's true state of mind. Whereas barristers may not assert that defendants are innocent when they believe them to be guilty, they may conduct a case on the basis of a guilty plea while believing the defendant concerned to be innocent. As para 2.5 of the Bar's Code of Conduct explains:

> 'Where a defendant tells his counsel that he did not commit the offence with which [he] is charged but nevertheless insists on

5   [1970] 2 WLR 1093 at 1097.
6   See the discussion by Blake and Ashworth [1998] pp 19-21.
7   McConville et al (1994) p 251.

pleading guilty to it for reasons of his own, counsel must continue to represent him, but only after he has advised what the consequences will be and that what can be submitted in mitigation can only be on the basis that the client is guilty.'

The criminal justice system appears to be prepared to tolerate some frauds more than others.

The danger that the factually innocent will be induced to plead guilty is exacerbated by the law providing that the weaker the evidence against a defendant the greater the discount given for a plea of guilty should be.[8] One would expect that it would be harder for the police to construct strong cases against the innocent than against the guilty. The option of contesting a case should thus be more attractive to the innocent since they stand a better chance of success before a jury. Yet the effect of this aspect of the discount principle is to make that option less attractive to the innocent since the costs of failure before a jury are, in effect, increased. They have more discount to lose than the guilty in contesting their cases.

To some, it might seem as if the strongest 'safeguard' against miscarriages of justice arising out of plea bargaining and related practices is the axiomatic truth that no innocent person would ever claim guilt. But just as innocent people sometimes 'confess' to the police under interrogation, so too, it seems, (and often in consequence of having 'confessed' at an earlier stage) do innocent people plead guilty.[9] Nearly half of the late plea changers in Baldwin and McConville's study made substantial and credible claims of innocence.[10] According to one:

'The barrister turned round and says, "If I were you, I'd forget my pride. I know you think you're innocent but if you're proved guilty, I think you'll go down - I can't guarantee it but I think you will." Then I said, "I don't want to do bloody time for something I haven't done" . . . in the end, I turned round and said "Well, I'm here for your advice, I'll also accept it." He was very nice - he didn't try to force me, it was just his advice. I mean if you've got somebody like that as your counsel, you're a mug not to take their advice. That's the way I looked upon it, so I pleaded guilty."[11]

Baldwin and McConville acknowledged that they had no way of telling whether defendants were in fact innocent or not. But in a substantial number of these guilty plea cases independent assessors judged the

8   *Hollington and Emmens* (1986) 82 Cr App Rep 281 and see generally section 2, subsections (a)(ii) and (e)(i) above.
9   The phenomenon of false confession is discussed in ch 5, section 5.
10   Baldwin and McConville (1977) pp 62-63.
11   Baldwin and McConville (1977) p 66.

Do the innocent plead guilty?

evidence against the defendant to be weak.[12] The more recent study by McConville et al details numerous examples of legal advisers ignoring clients' protestations of innocence. In one example an unqualified clerk failed to get the prosecutor to agree that a case of driving without a licence could be adjourned so that evidence that the client had a licence could be obtained. The client was told that the case would most likely go ahead that day, which led to the following exchange:

Client:	Well, what does that mean for me?
Clerk (firmly):	It means you will have to plead guilty I'm afraid.
Client (indignantly):	But I'm not guilty!
Clerk (fatalistically):	I know, but you see, we haven't got any proof have we? We've got nothing to go on, nothing to fight with.
Client:	What if I had witnesses?
Clerk:	Well, it depends what they've witnessed. It's not enough for them to have just seen a driving licence in your hand . . . As it is, I think if you plead guilty the magistrates will only fine you.
Client (outraged):	That's not the point - it's not right is it?
Clerk:	Well, no - but if you plead not guilty and then they find you guilty you'll get a heftier fine. I know what you're saying - it's not right, but what can we do?[13]

At the other end of the legal status spectrum, barristers were similarly observed to sometimes fail in their legal duty to emphasise to clients that they should not plead guilty unless they were guilty. They also went on to assert in court things that they knew to be false in order to maximise the mitigating effects of the plea of guilty. McConville et al write:

'Thus, in a case in which the client was pressurised into a guilty plea - saying in conference that "it makes me feel sick because I didn't do it", an observation never pursued by the barrister - counsel told the court that it was a "spur of the moment offence" for which the client should be given credit because he had "the courage to plead guilty today." Similarly, in another case in which the accused asserted complete innocence but buckled after extensive pressure to accept an offer of a plea to a trivial charge . . . the barrister told the court that "this is not an artificial plea at all", thereby conveying the impression

12 Baldwin and McConville (1977) p 74.
13 McConville et al (1994) p 167.

that the plea was both voluntary and accurately reflected the extent of the defendant's involvement in the affair.'[14]

As to the overall scale of 'artificial pleading', the Crown Court study by Zander and Henderson included a number of 'cracked trials' in which the CPS said that, had they gone to trial, the defendant would have stood a 'good' or 'fairly good' chance of acquittal. On an annual basis, this would total over 600 cracked trials where the defendant would have stood a good chance of acquittal and over 2,000 such cases with a fairly good chance of acquittal.[15] Whilst it does not follow that defendants in these cases were all factually innocent, they may well have emerged from a contested trial legally innocent. The Crown Court study also found that 11% of defendants pleading guilty claimed to be innocent,[16] and that 6% of defence barristers were concerned that their clients had pleaded guilty despite being innocent - amounting to some 1,400 cases a year.[17]

7. CONCLUSION

The pre-trial processes in the criminal courts exhibit many of the hallmarks of the crime control model. In a system in which all the participants understand that the majority of cases will be disposed of by guilty pleas, attention is naturally focused on case settlement rather than preparing for a fight in court. The system itself is geared towards the routine production of guilty pleas, as can be seen in the legal aid fee structure, the organisation of the legal profession, the sentence discount principle and so on. The wholesale adoption of crime control ideology by solicitors, barristers and judges up and down the country further oils the conveyor belt moving defendants inexorably towards conviction. It is undeniable that elements within the legal profession remain committed to due process, but they provide the exception to the rule of crime control. That some defendants insist on trial by jury is in some ways the most remarkable feature of the criminal justice process.

14 McConville et al (1994) p 262.
15 Zander and Henderson (1993) p 157.
16 Zander and Henderson (1993) p 139. It should be borne in mind that the response rate of defendants was too low to be statistically reliable.
17 Zander and Henderson (1993) pp 138-139. The weight to be attached to this latter figure in view of the methodological weaknesses of the Crown Court survey has been much debated. M Zander, 'The "innocent" (?) who plead guilty' (1993) 143 NLJ 85 and M McConville and L Bridges, 'Pleading guilty whilst maintaining innocence' (1993) 143 NLJ 160. For further exchanges see (1993) 143 NLJ at pp 192, 228 and 276.

The possibility of regulating or even eradicating charge bargaining has been explored by a number of domestic writers,[18] and has been attempted, with some well-documented success, in one American jurisdiction.[19] There are good principled reasons why we should attempt such an eradication here. The due process and human rights arguments discussed in relation to the sentence discount (see section 2(e)) apply with much the same force to the practice of charge bargaining. To these we can add the victim-centred arguments against all forms of plea bargaining that were discussed in ch 1, section 10.[20]

As for the freedom model, whilst not blind to the considerable resource advantages of guilty pleas, it would not accept that sentence discounts and charge bargains are the most cost-effective and freedom-enhancing way of doing justice. It seems unlikely that all, or even a majority of, defendants would plead not guilty if we left the system as it is but eliminated discounts and bargains. For a start that should encourage the police and prosecutors to ensure that an appropriate charge is brought in the first place and that cases only come to court that satisfy the necessary evidential and public interest tests. Even under the current system many defendants readily accept their guilt and see no point in putting an unarguable case before the court.[1] The proportion of defendants who felt this way should increase under a reformed system which demanded ethical charging and prosecution practices. Many more defendants would plead guilty because of the considerable incentives to do so even in a land without plea bargaining. These incentives include less time spent inside the system (as more time is needed to prepare a contested case than a guilty plea), less time spent in court (it takes longer to fight a case than to concede it), lower court costs, the chance to mitigate on the basis of remorse, sparing any defence witnesses (such as friends or family) the ordeal of testifying, sparing oneself the ordeal of cross-examination, and so on.[2] Some are no doubt altruistic enough (or sufficiently remorseful) to want to spare victims and other prosecution witnesses the bother of testifying. It might take some time for our system to adjust to a regime of non-bargain justice[3] but that

---

18 See D Galligan, 'Regulating Pre-Trial Decisions', in I Dennis (ed), *Criminal Law and Justice* (London: Sweet & Maxwell, 1987); and A Bottomley, 'Sentencing reform and the structuring of pre-trial discretion' in M Wasik and K Pease (eds), *Sentencing Reform*, (Manchester: MUP, 1987).

19 Carns and Kruse. See also Ashworth (1998) p 293 for discussion of jurisdictions which shun sentence discounts.

20 See generally H Fenwick, 'Charge Bargaining and Sentence Discount: the Victim's Perspective' (1997) 5 Int R Victimology 23.

1 See McConville et al (1994) pp 182-185 for supporting references and for a careful discussion of the extent to which this point can be pressed.

2 Thus we saw in section 2(d)(i) how one solicitor stressed many benefits of pleading guilty that had nothing to do with sentence discounts or charge bargains.

3 We should not underestimate the extent to which plea bargaining has become an

fact has never stopped governments from implementing radical reform when they favour the prosecution, as was the case with the effective abolition of the right to silence. The fact that the elimination of bargain justice is in the interests of victims, defendants, and the promotion of human rights might yet convince a government that this strategy is worth pursuing.[4]

The strategy of simply eliminating bargain justice would represent progress, but it still leaves in place so many incentives to plead guilty that one might argue that the presumption of innocence would still effectively be undermined. A more radical proposal would be to do away with the concept of a guilty plea altogether, or to do so for Crown Court cases at least. Inquisitorial jurisdictions have traditionally functioned without a reliance on this concept.[5] Under this proposal there would in every case that fell within the no-plea regime a degree of judicial scrutiny of the prosecution case, so as to ensure that convictions were always based on sufficient, reliable, admissible and fairly obtained evidence. Defendants could be given a choice of trial by jury and judge, or trial by judge alone. Those not actively contesting guilt would be funnelled towards the latter option, whilst others could be given a more open choice.[6] Schulhofer has estimated that abolishing all systemic incentives to plead guilty in this way and replacing the guilty plea system with bench trials by judges sitting alone would increase the trial rate by some 650% but with only a 20% increase needed in judicial resources at the adjudication stage.[7] That seems a small price to pay for a more victim-centred system that better protects human rights and innocent defendants.[8]

An even more radical proposal would be to replace our current system of punishment with that of restorative justice in which offenders would be

entrenched feature of the criminal justice landscape, nor forget that it has supported the growth of institutions (such as state funded defence services) which serve its cause: G Fisher, 'Plea Bargaining's Triumph' (2000) 109 Yale LJ 857. One implication of Fisher's painstaking historical analysis is that to dismantle plea bargaining will require a fundamental reappraisal and reshaping of many other aspects of the criminal justice system.

4   We should note that the state has an interest in retaining plea bargaining, not just as a repressive tool, but also so as to be able to 'cut deals' with police informers, particularly where a not guilty plea could lead to embarrassing revelations about the state's collusion with those involved in organised crime, or in paramilitary activity in Northern Ireland: *The Guardian* 30 September 2000. On the corrupting effect of using informers, see further ch 12, section 3.

5   Although more recently they have begun to succumb to the temptation to bargain away this part of their legal heritage. See Ashworth (1998) pp 267-268 and the sources cited there.

6   See S Doran and J Jackson, 'The Case for Jury Waiver' [1997] Crim LR 155.

7   S Schulhofer, 'Plea bargaining as disaster' (1992) 101 Yale LJ 1979.

8   The extent to which innocent defendants are better protected under a non-bargain system is, we should acknowledge, a matter of controversy: see R Scott and W J Stuntz, 'A Reply: Imperfect Bargains, Imperfect Trials and Innocent Defendants' (1992) 101 YLJ 2011.

Conclusion

held accountable to victims for the harm done to them, usually through a process of mediation. This would entail a shift away from the 'battle' model of adversarial justice (whether due process or crime control oriented) towards the kind of 'family model' that was advocated by Griffiths in his largely overlooked critique of Packer's models.[9] In the family model it is assumed that state officials can be trusted to carry out their duties in good faith and using their best judgment, that those found to have offended should not be stigmatised or exiled but rather censured and reintegrated into society, and that everyone should be treated with respect.[10] The fact that the interests of those found to have offended would be promoted should mean that defendants and defence lawyers would not seek to turn the criminal process into an obstacle course save in those cases where guilt was in question. Instead, offenders would much more readily accept responsibility and the real issue would concern what needed to be done to put things right. Although Griffiths did not discuss the position of victims, it is apparent that his model would promote communitarian conceptions of punishment administered by and through the mechanism of a 'community conference'.[11] This model could therefore satisfy victims' interests in public vindication, in participation, and in repair. Fenwick, who looks at plea-bargaining from the victim's perspective, has expressed tentative support for this idea.[12] It would be stupid, however, to see the 'family model' as the holy grail of criminal justice reform. Griffiths had little to say on the content of criminal procedure in cases where guilt was contested. Others have noted, however, that the assumptions of the family model are consistent with an inquisitorial mode of procedure.[13] We noted in chapter 1 that the inquisitorial model has many weaknesses of its own, whilst the implication of subsequent chapters is that state officials have not yet shown themselves worthy of the kind of trust the family model calls for. There is also a danger that community conference outcomes between victims and offenders will turn out to be inadequately regulated by state officials and just as contrary to the public interest as the plea bargains they might replace.

So what is to be done? We have raised in this conclusion the kind of thorny questions best tackled by Royal Commissions, or at least so one might think. Yet the report of the Runciman Commission dealt with the subject of charge bargaining in a single sentence: 'We see no objection to such discussions, but the earlier they take place the better; consultation

9   J Griffith, 'Ideology in Criminal Procedure or a Third "Model" of the Criminal Process' (1970) 79 Yale LJ 359.
10   See also J Braithwaite, *Crime, Shame and Reintegration* (Cambridge: CUP, 1989).
11   See ch 1, section 10.
12   Fenwick (1997) pp 23-24 and 34-35.
13   M Damaska, 'Evidentiary Barriers to Conviction and Two Models of Criminal Procedure: A Comparative Study' (1973) 121 U Penn LR 506 at pp 570-573. For further discussion of the issues raised in this para see ch 1, section 10.

between counsel before the trial would often avoid the need for the case to be listed as a contested trial.'[14] On this subject, as on many others, the Runciman Commission failed to cite any evidence or marshal any supporting arguments to justify its preference for more crime control.[15] The Runciman Commission thus represents a missed opportunity to reassess the fundamentals of our system of criminal justice and nothing has happened since to indicate that any of the reforms mooted above might find favour with policy-makers. In drawing this chapter to a close we want to reflect for a moment on this dismal episode in the formulation of criminal justice policy.

As the Runciman Commission was set up in the wake of the freeing of the Birmingham Six it was widely expected that it would focus on the safeguards and reforms needed to better protect against miscarriages of justice. That these expectations proved false is partly attributable to the way in which the government set its terms of reference. These required the Runciman Commission 'to examine the effectiveness of the criminal justice system in England and Wales in securing the conviction of those guilty of criminal offences and the acquittal of those who are innocent, having regard to the efficient use of resources'.[16] It would have been open to the Runciman Commission to reject the implication in these terms of reference that all three of these matters are of equal weight. Instead it embraced this notion wholeheartedly. Thus, for example, it saw 'miscarriages of justice' as comprising both the conviction of the innocent and the acquittal of the guilty.[17] Because it regarded these matters of equal concern it saw no problem in recommending changes to the system which would both undermine the adversarial system and substantially increase the likelihood of innocent persons being convicted. For the Runciman Commission, these costs were more than offset by the prospect of convicting more of the guilty at a 'value for money'[18] price. It is this crude cost-benefit analysis that lay behind its proposals to abolish a defendant's right in either way cases to elect trial by jury[19] and to encourage greater use of all forms of plea bargaining.

To some extent, then, the Runciman Commission simply made a value choice, expressing a preference for more crime control and less due process.

---

14 RCCJ (1993) p 114. Many of its recommendations were designed to guarantee earlier communication between opposing counsel. For example, a requirement that the defence disclose its case in outline was supported, in part, because this might result in 'an earlier resolution through a plea of guilty' (p 97) and see also pp 101-108 on encouraging 'pre-trial preparation'.

15 Note that none of the 22 research studies funded by the Runciman Commission was on plea bargaining.

16 RCCJ (1993) p i.

17 RCCJ (1993) p 2.

18 See RCCJ (1993) pp 4-5.

19 Discussed in chapter 8.

But as we pointed out at the start of this book, empirical evidence should play a central part in informing one's choice of values. Certainly the Runciman Commission expressed beliefs about how the system works, but its views were based on stereotypes and prejudices as much as on hard evidence. Thus, it declares its conviction, without any supporting evidence or argument, that clearer articulation of the sentence discount principle would not increase the risks of the innocent pleading guilty.[20] Again, while the Runciman Commission found it 'odd' that most of those electing trial by jury eventually pleaded guilty it was not interested in exploring the reasons for this.[1] It was simply assumed that defendants were wasting everybody's time and money by delaying their pleas of guilty until the last moment. The current Home Secretary has expressed exactly the same lazy self-serving belief in pushing ahead with his plans to abolish the right to elect trial by jury.[2] He has ignored research evidence suggesting that the problem lies with the failure of the CPS to scrutinise their evidence at an early stage, and adjust charges accordingly, in many cases.[3] In the new politics of criminal justice,[4] the great mass of criminal defendants is constructed as 'undeserving' of due process, presumed guilty, and portrayed in public as cynical manipulators of the system who warrant swifter punishment. Moreover, the process by which punishment is legitimated should spare 'innocent victims' as much further 'ordeal' as possible. Summary trial serves these ends better than Crown Court trial, but a guilty plea better still.

This crime control line of reasoning, that guilty persons will take advantage of due process protections in order to further their own interests and in seeking to avoid their just deserts, is not borne out by research findings on the operation of the criminal process. Thus, for example, late plea changing in the Crown Court is predominantly the product of a system that simultaneously proclaims the right of defendants to call upon the prosecution to prove its case before judge and jury whilst doing its utmost to ensure that the vast majority waive that right. The mass production of guilty pleas has become a systemic imperative in the criminal courts. Defendants do not commonly play the system; the system plays with them, their rights, and their freedom.

20   RCCJ (1993) p 112.
1   See RCCJ (1993) p 86.
2   Quoted in P Duff, 'The Defendant's Right to Trial by Jury: A Neighbour's View' [2000] Crim LR 85. The Mode of Trial Bill, rejected again by the House of Lords in September 2000, is discussed in ch 8, section 5(c).
3   See discussion of mode of trial decisions in ch 8, section 5(c).
4   See McConville (1998).

Chapter 8

Summary justice in the magistrates' court

'Just before going into court, a solicitor suddenly caught sight of the defendant who had just arrived for trial and spoke to him in the following terms:

Solicitor: Zip your jacket up. You should be doing better than a string vest for court. How much gold do you have on? Take some of that off - I don't want you looking flashy. [The client takes off neck chain and bracelet.] And when you're in court, I don't want you looking like you have an attitude problem; so keep your fucking mouth shut and let me do the talking.

Client: Yeah, yeah, I know.'[1]

I. INTRODUCTION

In England and Wales, trials are held either in the magistrates' courts or the Crown Court. There are around 460 magistrates' courts, located in most large towns and cities. All criminal prosecutions begin in one of them, but the ultimate disposal of a case depends on its classification and the age of the defendant. Defendants charged with motoring offences (eg, driving whilst disqualified, excess alcohol or lack of due care and attention) or other summary offences (eg common assault, drunk and disorderly or soliciting) have their cases heard in the magistrates' courts. Defendants charged with offences triable only on indictment, such as murder, wounding with intent to cause grievous bodily harm and rape, are tried in the Crown Court. In

---

1   M McConville, J Hodgson, L Bridges and A Pavlovic, *Standing Accused* (Oxford: Clarendon Press, 1994) p 228.

Introduction

between there is a large band of offences which are triable either way; that is, they may be tried either summarily in the magistrates' courts or on indictment in the Crown Court. Examples of 'either way' offences are theft, burglary and assaults causing actual or grievous bodily harm.[2] At one time, if an indictable or either way case was to go to the Crown Court the magistrates had to decide whether there was a case to answer before 'committing' it to the Crown Court. Over the years this became a formality in most cases, and indictable-only cases are now sent to the Crown Court immediately after the defendant's first appearance without any scrutiny at all.[3]

Children and young persons aged between 10[4] and 17 (inclusive) are generally tried summarily in juvenile courts, renamed youth courts in October 1992.[5] The main exceptions include cases in which adult defendants are also involved. Thus, youths must be proceeded against in the adult magistrates' courts if they are jointly charged with an adult and may be so dealt with if different charges are made against an adult arising out of connected circumstances or where either the adult or youth faces accomplice liability in respect of the other's alleged offence.[6] Where a youth is proceeded against in the adult court under any of these circumstances, unless the offence is summary, the possibility then arises of the case being transferred to the Crown Court for trial.[7]

The other main exception to the norm of youth court trial concerns offences carrying particularly long sentences of imprisonment. Cases of murder and manslaughter must be transferred to the Crown Court, while offences where the defendant is over 14, and which carry a penalty for an adult of 14 or more years' imprisonment, may be so transferred.[8] This became a controversial matter in the *Bulger* case. Two 11-year-olds were tried and convicted of the murder of a toddler (Jamie Bulger) in 1993. The European Court held that holding their trial in the Crown Court was a violation of the European Convention on Human Rights (ECHR), Art 6 (the

2   This threefold classification was introduced by the Criminal Law Act 1977 and re-enacted by ss 17-25 Magistrates Courts Act 1980.
3   Crime and Disorder Act 1998, s 51. See R Leng, R Taylor and M Wasik, *Blackstone's Guide to the Crime and Disorder Act 1998* (London: Blackstone, 1998) pp 91-95.
4   Those under 10 cannot be prosecuted as it is conclusively presumed that they cannot be held criminally responsible for any offence: Children and Young Persons Act (CYPA)1933, s 50, as amended by the CYPA 1963 Act, s 16(1).
5   Criminal Justice Act 1991, s 70. For the sake of convenience, those between the ages of 10 and 17 (inclusive) will be referred to as youths in the text.
6   CYPA 1933, s 46 as extended by the CYPA 1963, s 18. Now see s 51, Crime and Disorder Act 1998.
7   Magistrates' Courts Act 1980, s 24, as amended.
8   For much fuller analysis of the complex jurisdictional position established by statute and case law see C Ball, K McCormac and N Stone, *Young Offenders* (London: Sweet & Maxwell, 1995) ch 5.

right to a fair trial), as 'the formality and ritual of the Crown Court must at times have seemed incomprehensible and intimidating for a child of 11.'[9] This will lead to changes in the rules applicable to young children, but not necessarily for older children who, it could be argued, can cope with Crown Court procedures as well (or as badly) as adults.

Youth courts are presided over by magistrates, and usually take place in magistrates' court buildings. Like the magistrates' courts, youth courts are criminal courts of inferior jurisdiction, offering a summary form of justice. Most of the issues to be discussed in this chapter are common to both forms of magisterial jurisdiction. References to the magistrates' courts in this chapter should be taken as including the youth court unless otherwise stated. The powers and procedures that apply differ in a number of important respects from those of the adult courts, however. In particular, proceedings in the youth court are not open to the public[10] and, although journalists may attend, there are strict limits concerning what they may report.[11]

The magistrates' court is the workhorse of the system. In 1997, for example, proceedings were begun against about 1.92 million defendants in the magistrates' courts. This is a fall from the 2.03 million prosecuted in 1992, reflecting a fall in recorded crime in the mid 1990s and an increase in the proportion of offenders diverted from prosecution. A quarter of these proceedings were in respect of indictable and either way offences, 45% concerned motoring offences, whilst the remaining 30% related to other types of summary offence. These figures do not include nearly 4 million parking tickets and 3.4 million fixed penalty notices issued for other motoring offences every year. Roughly 91,000 defendants (under 5% of the 1.92 million prosecuted) were committed to the Crown Court for trial.[12] Over 80% of those facing either way charges have their case heard in the magistrates' courts. The 'mode of trial' hearing held in either way cases determines not just where but how the case should be tried. The essence of summary justice is a speedy procedure, uncluttered with elaborate judicial rituals. To try a case summarily in the magistrates' courts is to try it without many of the formalities required by the common law.[13] As we shall see, the

9   *T and V v UK* [2000] 2 All ER 1024n.
10   CYPA 1933, s 47 as amended by the CYPA 1963, s 17(2).
11   CYPA 1933, s 49 as substituted by the Criminal Justice and Public Order Act 1994 (CJPO), s 49. See M Wasik and R Taylor, *Blackstone's Guide to the Criminal Justice and Public Order Act 1994* (London: Blackstone, 1999) pp 15-16. Section 45 of the Crime (Sentences) Act 1997 now allows a youth court to set aside the prohibition on the media identifying a child or young person where they have been convicted of an offence if the court is satisfied that it is in the public interest to do so.
12   G Barclay and C Tavares, Information on the Criminal Justice System in England and Wales: Digest No 4 (London: Home Office, 1999).
13   See D McBarnet, *Conviction* (London: Macmillan, 1983) pp 138-143.

'formalities' absent from magistrates' courts include juries and (in most cases) professional judges, for most magistrates are unpaid, part-time amateurs.

The question of who may represent the prosecution and the defence also depends on the level of court. Barristers in private practice (lawyers who specialise in court-based negotiation and advocacy, and the drafting of legal advice) may appear at either level to prosecute or defend whereas solicitors in private practice (traditionally regarded as the junior branch of the legal profession) have historically lacked rights of audience in the Crown Court. Whilst rights of audience were granted in principle to such solicitors as from 8 December 1993, under a procedure and according to criteria established by the Courts and Legal Services Act 1990, a 'Higher Courts Qualification' must be obtained by any solicitor wishing to exercise this right. The normal route to such a qualification is through the possession of extensive experience in criminal court advocacy and the passing of a special course run by the Law Society.[14] It thus seems likely that the Crown Court will remain largely the preserve of lawyers who specialise in court-based work (albeit that an increasing number will now be solicitor-advocates). By contrast, solicitors who appear in the magistrates' courts range from those who specialise in court-based work to those for whom a summary trial represents an occasional day out of the office.[15] Skilful advocacy in a contested adversarial trial can itself increase greatly the length and formality of the proceedings, and it is clear from the above that, in proportional terms, this is more likely (at least in theory) to be found in the Crown Court.

The lowly status of the magistrates' courts is also reflected in the more limited rights of audience that salaried/employed lawyers possess. This particularly affects Crown Prosecutors (whether qualified as barristers or solicitors), who may only appear in the magistrates' courts. The rationale for this denial of rights of audience in the Crown Court is that lawyers subject to an employer's bidding may find it less easy to exercise independent professional judgment. Leaving aside the merits or weaknesses of this position,[16] it rests on a belief that such professionalism and independence is not so important before the lower criminal courts. This belief also underpins the decision to allow non-legally qualified members of the CPS

14 See the Law Society's Higher Courts Qualification Regulations 1992. Rights of audience have been extended further by the Access to Justice Act 1999 (AJA), Part III.

15 See L Bridges, 'The professionalisation of criminal justice' (1992) Legal Action, August p 7. Note that solicitors' firms with the highest caseloads do not necessarily offer the best service to their clients: McConville et al (1994).

16 See J Rozenberg, *The Search for Justice* (London: Hodder & Stoughton, 1994) pp 153-162.

to appear as 'lay presenters' in the magistrates' courts for bail applications and guilty plea cases.[17]

The summary nature of magistrates' courts justice is reflected, as one might expect from the above description, in lower running costs. It has been estimated that the average cost of an uncontested Crown Court case is seven times, and that of a contested Crown Court case is 57 times, that of a typical either way case in the magistrates' courts.[18] But is there an adequate justification for the difference in treatment meted out to defendants according to how the offence with which they are charged is classified? One argument would be that since the sentencing powers of magistrates are limited to twelve months' imprisonment or a £5,000 fine, there is less of a need for due process safeguards to apply than in the Crown Court, where a defendant may face life imprisonment on conviction.[19] Another would be that summary offences involve straightforward issues, the determination of which do not require other than a straightforward procedure. This is certainly true, for example, of many motoring offences. As nearly half of the magistrates' workload is made up of such offences, observers in these courts might be forgiven for thinking that 'real crime' and courtroom drama were to be found elsewhere. Often, there are no observers. Journalists and curious members of the public tend to prefer the 'juicier' cases in the Crown Court.

The lack of public scrutiny of these magistrates' courts is particularly helpful for white collar offenders anxious to avoid any damaging publicity. We drew attention in ch 6, section 5, to the presumption against formal action operated by most regulatory agencies. On the rare occasion when white collar criminals are prosecuted, proceedings are virtually always kept in the magistrates' courts and often relegated to a special sitting away from the main work of the day. Thus, even when formal action is taken against business offenders, the visibility of their misdeeds remains low. This helps them play down the seriousness of their actions, and does nothing to challenge the common perception that the crimes they have committed are merely 'technical' in nature.[20]

17   Crime and Disorder Act 1998, s 53.
18   The average cost in 1997/8 of proceedings (including case preparation by police and CPS) in the magistrates' courts was £550, while in the Crown Court it was £8,600: Barclay and Tavares (1999). However, this is a misleading comparison since most magistrates' court cases are relatively simple and only a small proportion are contested. A better comparison is in relation to people pleading guilty to either way offences. The average cost of such a case in 1992 was about £210 in the magistrates' courts, and £1,400 in the Crown Court: Costs of the Criminal Justice System 1992, vol 1 (London: Home Office, 1992) pp 15-16.
19   For the complex legal provisions regulating magistrates' sentencing powers see J Sprack, *Emmins on Criminal Procedure* 8th edn (London: Blackstone, 2000) pp 168-69.
20   See the discussion by H Croall, 'Mistakes, Accidents and Someone Else's Fault: The Trading Offender in Court' (1988) 15 JLS 293.

The ideology of triviality that permeates the magistrates' courts is fuelled by the high proportion of defendants pleading guilty. According to the CPS, in 1997, of those cases which proceeded to a final conclusion, 81% pleaded guilty and 12% were decided in the absence of the defendant. Of the 7% who contested their cases, less than 2% (ie less than one-quarter of the not guilty pleaders) were acquitted. Thus around 98% of cases proceeding to a hearing resulted in conviction. Although this sounds remarkable, we should remember that the CPS discontinues about 12% of the cases it receives, many defendants who plead not guilty opt for a jury trial, and around 7% of cases are written off for a variety of reasons (such as the defendant disappearing).[1] Magistrates sometimes exaggerate the impression that their courts only deal with simple matters. A colleague of one of the authors was also a practising barrister in Yorkshire. In a rural court one day she sought to argue a point of law by reference to a leading House of Lords judgment. She was stopped before she had finished and informed that, as she was appearing before the Bogsworth magistrates, not the House of Lords, could she please get to the point?[2]

To summarise, the signals given off by magistrates' courts are that they deal with trivial matters in which the issues are straightforward, defendants willingly accept their guilt and the consequences for defendants of conviction are slight. In truth, however, magistrates are responsible for decisions of far-reaching importance. They decide whether defendants should be released on bail or should lose their liberty pending trial. In 1998, for example, they remanded 98,000 defendants in prison at some stage during the court proceedings.[3] It is for magistrates, together with their clerks, to determine whether defendants should receive legal aid to pay for representation. They can direct that either way contested cases should be heard in the Crown Court (or, soon, that they should stay in the magistrates' court), notwithstanding any objections from the defendant. They also have a role to play in supervising the work of other agencies. For example, as we have already seen,[4] the lower courts exercise a measure of supervision over the police in relation to such matters as periods of pre-charge detention of suspects and warrants allowing entry, search and seizure. Finally, magistrates have the ultimate power of depriving convicted defendants of part of their property or part of their liberty. In 1992, magistrates sent 22,000

---

1   Barclay and Tavares (1999). See ch 6, section 3(c) for discussion of discontinuances by the CPS.
2   See McConville et al (1994) p 225: '. . . magistrates' court cases are not argued on legal issues, which are usually assumed to be inappropriate in such a forum.'
3   Home Office, Criminal Statistics for England and Wales 1998 (Cm 4649) (London: SO, 2000) p 192.
4   For example, see ch 4, section 3(b).

offenders to prison, but this had more than doubled by 1998.[5] If they feel their sentencing powers are inadequate, they can commit defendants convicted of either way offences to the Crown Court for sentence. This was the fate of 17,632 people in 1998, 11,712 of whom were given an immediate custodial sentence.[6] One way or another, a large proportion of the prison population is there as a result of the decisions of magistrates.

The operation of the magistrates' courts appears to be consistent with the crime control model of criminal justice. We saw in ch 7 that the high rate of guilty pleas ensures that many of the most important due process protections which might apply in an adversarial system do not come into play. This chapter will show that the antipathy towards due process values in the lower courts is deep-rooted.

2. LEGAL AID AND LEGAL REPRESENTATION

Legal representation is central to the functioning of the freedom, due process and human rights models, since it should guarantee that defendants are made aware of their rights and that the remedies available for any abuses of those rights are secured. The principle of equality requires that wherever the criminal process affords a theoretical right to legal representation the means should be made available to enable defendants to exercise that right. To do otherwise would place the poor and those of modest means in an unequal position with the rich. These principles appear at first sight to be enshrined in the ECHR (and, therefore, the Human Rights Act 1998). Article 6.1 guarantees the right to a fair trial, and Art 6.3 guarantees every defendant the right '. . . to defend himself in person or through legal assistance of his own choosing or, if he has not sufficient means to pay for legal assistance, to be given it free when the interests of justice so require'.

For suspects detained for questioning in the police station, these due process principles are broadly accepted. As we saw in ch 4, section 4, the government provides funds so that all defendants, rich or poor, can have access to a lawyer, regardless of the type of offence with which they are suspected. The machinations of the police combined with the inadequate level of service provided by the legal profession may prevent the scheme from working as effectively as it might, but it nonetheless secures important freedom gains.

This may be contrasted with the position in the magistrates' courts, where legal representation may be characterised as a privilege rather than

---

5   Home Office, Criminal Statistics England and Wales 1992 (Cm 2410) (London: HMSO, 1993) p 145, para 7.27. For 1998 figures, see S Sisson, Cautions, Court Proceedings, and Sentencing: England and Wales, 1998 (London: Home Office, 1999).

6   Home Office (1999) Table 7.13.

as a right. This is compatible with the letter (but perhaps not the spirit) of the ECHR because of the proviso in Art 6.3 concerning 'the interests of justice'. Three types of publicly funded services are available: 'green form' advice and assistance, court-based duty solicitor schemes and criminal legal aid. From October 2000 only 'franchised' firms are able to provide these services, and from April 2001 these firms will, in their criminal work, be part of a new Criminal Defence Service. In the medium and long term this may transform criminal defence services but at the time of writing the nature of this change is difficult to estimate.[7]

(a) The green form scheme

Initial advice may be given by a solicitor under the 'green form' scheme.[8] Bureaucratic control of the operation of the scheme is minimal—all the solicitor needs to do is administer a simple means test.[9] The scheme can be used to cover the cost of preparing a case for court by, for example, taking statements from the defendant and other witnesses. The initial limit of two hours' work can be extended on obtaining authorisation from a legal aid area committee. In practice, the scheme is used by solicitors to cover the costs of an initial interview with a defendant and the making of a full application for legal aid.[10] Just over an hour and a quarter, on average, was spent on each criminal green form matter in 1998–9.[11] The main drawbacks of the scheme from a due process perspective are that it does not cover representation in court, it allows solicitors only a limited period of preparation time (subject to the possibility of extensions) and it is means-tested. The means test has been tightened significantly throughout the 1990s. The weekly disposable income limit is now (August 2000) just £84 for a person without dependants, and the disposable capital limit is just £1,000.

7   See ch 4(4)(d) for a brief discussion, and also D O'Brien and J A Epp, 'Salaried Defenders and the Access to Justice Act 1999' (2000) 63 MLR 394.
8   The statutory framework for the scheme is provided by Pt III of the Legal Aid Act 1988. Payment for legal services provided is claimed on a form which is . green in colour.
9   See further J Baldwin, 'The Green Form: Use or Abuse?' (1988) 138 NLJ 631.
10 For discussion of how solicitors use the green form scheme, see J Baldwin and S Hill, The Operation of the Green Form Scheme in England and Wales (London: Lord Chancellor's Department, 1988) pp 27-28.
11 See Legal Aid Board, Annual Reports 1998-99 (HC 537) (London: SO, 1999) p 121.

(b) Court-based duty solicitor schemes

Those who arrive at court unrepresented may receive advice from a duty solicitor. These schemes, originally operated by the legal profession on a voluntary basis, are now governed by the Legal Aid Act 1988 and regulations made thereunder.[12] Duty solicitors agree to be present at the court on a rota basis. Over one quarter of a million defendants receive assistance from a duty solicitor each year.[13] In around 100,000 of these cases each year the case is dealt with at that one hearing. Duty solicitor schemes rely on there being enough local firms to make a rota work. Sometimes schemes collapse, but in 1998-9 only one court was not covered.

No means test is applied, but the scheme is subject to a number of restrictions.[14] A duty solicitor may not provide representation in committal proceedings nor on a not guilty plea, nor, save in exceptional circumstances, may advice or representation be offered to defendants in connection with a non-imprisonable offence. These rules prevent duty solicitors from acting in the most complex or serious proceedings and also in relatively trivial cases. In the former, a grant of full criminal legal aid will usually be forthcoming, whilst in the latter it is apparently thought reasonable for defendants to be left unrepresented in court. Nor may duty solicitors act for a defendant who has already received advice from a duty solicitor on an earlier occasion in the same proceedings.[15] This last rule was designed to allay the fears of solicitors that courts might use the existence of a duty solicitor scheme as a reason for refusing the grant of full legal aid and also prevents duty solicitors from mopping up too much legal business.

The overall effect of these schemes has been mixed. Their development in the 1970s undoubtedly represented, in formal terms, a move towards greater due process in the summary courts. A duty solicitor could not be expected, however, to do more than argue a case for bail, or make a speech in mitigation in a straightforward guilty plea case. For more complicated cases, the objective would be to secure an adjournment in order for an application for full legal aid to be made, so that a solicitor could prepare the case properly.[16] One piece of research suggested that a duty solicitor

---

12 The origin of these schemes is explored in G Mungham and P Thomas, 'Solicitors and Clients: Altruism of Self-interest?' in R Dingwall and P Lewis (eds), *The Sociology of the Professions* (London: Macmillan, 1983).

13 Legal Aid Board (1999) p 114.

14 As laid down in the non-statutory Legal Aid Board Duty Solicitor Arrangements 1990.

15 This is subject to exceptions: (i) advice and representation may be given to such a defendant who is at risk of imprisonment for failing to pay a fine or to obey an order of the court; (ii) duty solicitors can appear at two 'early first hearings', regarding which see section 5(b).

16 See H Johnson, 'Court Duty Solicitors' (1992) Legal Action, May p 11, for an account of how the scheme works (or should work) in practice.

Legal aid and legal representation

scheme advanced due process values in that more defendants were released on bail and more defendants were granted legal aid.[17] By contrast, other research implied that duty solicitors were providing an inferior level of service compared with solicitors not acting under the scheme in that the former more often advised defendants to plead guilty at their first appearance in court. The reasons for this were complex, but the researchers concluded that, 'our evidence suggests that when dealing with their "established" clients, as opposed to what are often seen as "one-off" duty solicitor cases, solicitors may be less willing to proceed with the matter on the same day.'[18] One experienced duty solicitor has conceded that clients continue to see the service provided as second class.[19] A second-class service, however, is generally better than none at all. It seems incontrovertible that courts with duty solicitor schemes will adhere more closely overall to the due process model than those without.[20]

(c) Criminal legal aid

However one sees duty solicitor schemes, it is clear that they are no substitute for the proper funding of the full costs of preparing and mounting a defence. The most comprehensive form of help available is the criminal legal aid certificate.[1] To obtain a certificate, a defendant must make an application to the magistrates' court.[2] This form of legal aid is currently subject both to a means test and a merits test.

17 M King, The Effects of a Duty Solicitor Scheme: An Assessment of the Impact upon a Magistrates' Court (London: Cobden Trust, 1977). The study by R Young, T Moloney and A Sanders, In the Interests of Justice? (London: Legal Aid Board, 1992) paras 4.12-4.13 tended to confirm that where duty solicitors are active, more legal aid applications will be made, although the relationship is not a strong one. McConville et al (1994) p 5 point out that 'the evidence of the 1970s was that duty solicitor schemes, although coincidental with the rise in legal representation and legal aid in magistrates' courts, were not a direct cause of it, as shown by the fact that grants of legal aid increased sharply even in courts without such schemes.'

18 L Bridges, J Carter, and S Gorbing, 'The Impact of Duty Solicitor Schemes in Six Magistrates' Courts' (1992) LAG Bull, July, at p 14.

19 Johnson (1992).

20 See ch 4, section 4(d) for discussion of attempts to improve the quality of duty solicitors in general in the 1990s.

1   Criminal legal aid is governed by Pt V of the Legal Aid Act 1988 and the AJA 1999.

2   The process of applying for criminal legal aid has been speeded up (or truncated, depending on one's point of view) by the introduction of early administrative hearings under s 50 of the Crime and Disorder Act 1998. See further section 3 below.

(i) The means test

The proportion of the population eligible for non-contributory criminal legal aid fell sharply in 1993 when the means test was brought in line with that applied to income support claimants. The number of legal aid applicants who passed the means test did not decrease much, however, since so many of those appearing in the magistrates' courts are in receipt of income support. None the less, from a due process standpoint, it is objectionable that currently (August 2000) anyone with a disposable income of more than £53 a week has to pay a hefty contribution to their own defence (£1 for every £3 above £53).

The means test is not only unfair, but also expensive to administer. Fewer than 1% of applicants fail it. Another 5% are required to pay a contribution. But the total value of contributions collected is barely enough to pay for running the means testing system, and there are also hidden costs as when legal advisers get paid under the Green Form scheme for their work in collecting and presenting a client's financial circumstances on the legal aid application form.[3] Consequently the test will no longer be applied to magistrates' court cases, although contributions will be levied, where appropriate, in Crown Court cases.[4]

(ii) The merits test

Section 21(2) of the Legal Aid Act 1988 provides that legal aid may be granted where it appears desirable 'in the interests of justice' to do so, and s 22 specifies a number of factors which must be taken into account in determining this matter. Some of these criteria concern the seriousness of the consequences to the defendant of a conviction. If a defendant is facing loss of liberty, livelihood or reputation, more favourable consideration should be given to granting legal aid.[5] The remaining criteria concern the inability of the defendant adequately to conduct a case in person. Thus a grant of legal aid is more likely (at least in theory) if the case requires the tracing and interviewing of witnesses, consideration of a substantial question of law or expert cross-examination, or if the defendant has

---

3   Lord Chancellor's Department, Modernising Justice (Cm 4155) (London, SO, 1998) para 6.26.
4   AJA 1999, s 17.
5   In certain 'loss of liberty' situations, the defendant must be granted legal aid: where the person is applying for bail having been kept in custody following a remand hearing at which they were unrepresented (Legal Aid Act 1988, s 21(3)(c)), where the person is before the court for sentencing only and is to be kept in custody whilst inquiries or reports are prepared (s 21(3)(d)) and where youths are to be sentenced to custody (Criminal Justice Act 1982, s 2).

inadequate knowledge of English or suffers from some mental or physical disability. One final factor to be taken into account is whether it is in the interests of another that the accused be represented. This covers situations where it might lead to difficulties if the accused had to cross-examine witnesses in person, such as in child abuse cases. This is an area in which more due process for the accused can lead to better protection for victims.

These criteria are not exclusive—other factors may be taken into account.[6] Furthermore, s 21(7) of the 1988 Act stipulates that where a doubt arises as to whether legal aid should be granted to a person, 'the doubt shall be resolved in that person's favour'. On the other hand, the mere fact that the circumstances of a case fall squarely within one or more of the statutory criteria does not mean that a grant of legal aid must follow. The Divisional Court in a series of cases has made it plain that those taking decisions on legal aid have a very wide discretion when applying the interests of justice test.[7] Thus, save where the legislature has provided otherwise, no charge of any offence can be regarded as so serious that it leads to an automatic grant of legal aid.[8] Similarly, a legal aid application may be refused notwithstanding that the case involves difficult points of fact or law or that there is a need for expert cross-examination.[9]

The merits test was last fully reviewed in 1966 by the Widgery Committee which decisively rejected the due process equality principle in the following terms:

'It might be held that wherever there is a right to legal representation, the State has a duty, as a kind of social insurance, to provide it for anyone who cannot afford to provide it himself. We do not accept this view; legal representation cannot be said to be a necessary condition for the effective defence of every criminal charge. We had also to bear in mind the practical consideration that there is a limit both to the number of practitioners who can provide legal assistance and to the funds that the State can reasonably be expected to make available. Our conclusions therefore were . . . that the object of the system should be to secure that injustice does not arise through an accused person being prevented by lack of means from bringing

---

6   This is implicit in the wording of the section, and was acknowledged in *Liverpool City Magistrates, ex p McGhee* [1993] Crim LR 609.

7   See, in particular, *Macclesfield Justices, ex p Greenhalgh* (1979) 144 JP 142; *Crown Court at Cambridge, ex p Hagi* (1979) 144 JP 145 and *Havering Juvenile Court, ex p Buckley* (LEXIS 554 1983).

8   See *Highgate Justices, ex p Lewis* (1977) 142 JP 78. The legislature has singled out murder alone as a charge warranting an automatic grant of legal aid: s 21(3)(a) of the Legal Aid Act 1988.

9   See *Crown Court at Cambridge, ex p Hagi* (1979) 144 JP 145 and *Stratford Magistrates Court, ex p Gorman* (LEXIS 687 1989).

effectively before the court matters which may constitute a defence to the charge or mitigate the gravity of the offence.'[10]

Much, then, relies on the correct identification of those cases where injustice would arise if legal aid was refused. How much care is exercised in legal aid decision-making?

Applications for legal aid may be made orally in open court, or, as happens much more frequently, to the justices' clerk or other designated court officer on a standard form. This form is divided into sections relating to each of the statutory criteria in turn and is generally completed by a legal adviser acting under the 'green form' scheme described above. Research by Young et al into the determination of legal aid applications found that these forms were frequently completed by unqualified staff using standard wording which often exaggerated the case for granting legal aid.[11] In turn, court clerks were found to give little weight to the statutory criteria but applied a crude rule of thumb in determining an application. Defendants perceived to be charged with a 'serious' offence would almost automatically be granted legal aid, whereas those charged with a 'trivial' offence would similarly be refused. In the middle lay a grey area, which differed from court to court, wherein the chances of obtaining legal aid would depend on how well the legal aid application was argued.[12] Accidents of geography might therefore have a crucial bearing on whether an application is granted. Although around 90% of all applications are successful, some courts grant virtually all applications, whereas others refuse as many as one in four. Such a rough and ready process does not inspire confidence that the need for legal representation is being correctly identified.[13]

Whilst variation in grant rates between magistrates' courts is directly attributable to the somewhat idiosyncratic legal aid policies pursued by court clerks, at root the problem lies in the law itself. In allowing court clerks discretion in deciding which defendants should receive legal aid, the law condones the subversion of adversarial procedures. An adversarial system cannot work properly if there is an inequality of resources available to the prosecution and the defence. At the time of the Widgery Report, police officers often prosecuted in person, but prosecutions today are conducted

10   Report of the Departmental Committee on Legal Aid in Criminal Proceedings (Cmnd 2934) (London: HMSO, 1966) para 56. This document will be referred to hereafter as the Widgery Report.

11   Young et al (1992) at pp 62-86. See also D Wall, 'Keyholders to Criminal Justice' in R Young and D Wall (eds), *Access to Criminal Justice* (London: Blackstone, 1996).

12   Young et al (1992) pp 25-39.

13   Young et al (1992) For summaries of some of the main findings of this report see R Young, 'The Merits of Legal Aid in the Magistrates' Courts' [1993] Crim LR 336 and R Young 'Will Widgery Do?' in Young and Wall (eds) (1996).

by the Crown Prosecution Service (CPS). The case for making a grant of legal aid automatic has thus become all the stronger.[14] The arguments against this advanced by the Widgery Committee are unconvincing. Market forces will ensure that an increased demand for legal services will be met by an increased supply of lawyers willing to do the work. The argument concerning resources is one-sided, as the government has readily provided the funds to ensure that the prosecution is legally represented in every case, however 'trivial' or 'straightforward' it might be. And, because of the way cases are constructed by the prosecution to appear strong on paper,[15] it cannot safely be predicted in advance which cases might lead to injustice if representation was not provided. Good legal representation can: lead to the emergence of previously hidden aspects of the case; render problematic the prosecution version of events, and raise questions about the integrity of the procedures followed. It is impossible to estimate the proportion of cases in which legal aid is currently refused (or not applied for) that would benefit from legal representation. The proportion may be small, but if the system is to give priority to acquitting the innocent and other due process values, the argument for making legal aid much more widely available is hard to resist.

Unfortunately the Human Rights Act is unlikely to come to the rescue. It will be recalled that the 'fair trial' obligation to provide legal aid to poor people was limited in two respects. First, it applies only to those without 'sufficient means', which will no longer be an issue now that the Government has decided to abandon the legal aid means test for magistrates' court proceedings. Second, it applies only when it is 'in the interests of justice'. Ashworth observes that the ECHR test is the same as that in our domestic law, so only the most extraordinarily restrictive interpretation would fall foul of the European Court.[16] But as the Court has upheld a French claim where a man who faced a very large fine was denied free legal aid,[17] showing that loss of liberty is not the only criterion, it may be that those clerks who rely too heavily on a 'likely imprisonment' test will be acting unlawfully. The lower the likely sentence, the greater the loss of another kind of freedom (eg reputation) would be required unless

14 Forbes J in *Havering Juvenile Court, ex p Buckley* (LEXIS 554 1983) noted that the fact that the prosecution was legally represented was something that magistrates could properly take into account, while stressing that it did not follow that such representation meant that a bench was bound to grant legal aid. Note that in ostensibly simple guilty pleas, unqualified CPS employees may now prosecute (see section 5(b) below).

15 See M McConville, A Sanders and R Leng, *The Case for the Prosecution* (London: Routledge, 1991).

16 A Ashworth, 'Legal Aid, Human Rights, and Criminal Justice', in Young and Wall (eds) (1996).

17 *Pham Hoang v France* (1992) 16 EHRR 53, discussed by Ashworth (1996).

the case was unusually complex. Magistrates' cases can be complex, but the 'ideology of triviality' usually hides this successfully.

Some important due process protections have been built into the decision-making process. An application which has been refused can be renewed to the court or clerk at any time. On a renewal, a court clerk cannot refuse an application a second time, but must either grant it or refer it to the court for determination. The court retains the full power to grant or refuse. This enables the defence to have the application put before a different decision-maker, although, since the magistrates are used to relying on the advice of their clerk (who will be present in court when the application is renewed) the value of this 'second bite of the cherry' is not as great as it might be. Of greater importance is the right, introduced in 1982, to have a refusal of legal aid reviewed by an area committee of the Legal Aid Board. Courts and Area Committees now have to give reasons for their decisions.[18] The average grant rate of reviewed applications is 67%.[19] Whether this high success rate reflects over-restrictiveness on the part of courts and court clerks or well-chosen applications for review by solicitors is hard to say, not least because much fuller information is required by area committees than is normally supplied on the initial application to the court. Thus one would expect a high grant rate on review.[20] Only around 10% of all initial refusals are, however, put up for review. Many such refusals are in fact ineligible for review. This is because the power to review exists only if the refusal was on merits (rather than on means) and if the applicant is charged with an indictable or either way offence.[1] This provides an illustration of how defendants charged with summary offences are afforded few due process safeguards. The freedom of present and future victims, whose interests are broadly represented by the police and CPS who prosecute in virtually every case, is clearly more greatly valued than that of defendants - whose presumption of innocence is supposedly guaranteed by the ECHR.

(iii) The cost of legal aid

The introduction of a right of appeal to an area committee (alongside other developments such as duty solicitor schemes) undoubtedly contributed to an enormous rise in the proportion of defendants who are legally

---

18   Legal Aid in Criminal and Care Proceedings (General) Regulations 1995 (SI 542).
19   A Wood, 'Administrative Justice Within the Legal Aid Board', in Young and Wall (eds) (1996) at p 171.
20   Wood (1996) pp 178-79.
1   Since the power to review exists only on a first refusal by the court or clerk, applicants would be well advised to seek a review by an area committee prior to renewing an application to the court.

represented in the magistrates' court. In 1964, the overall ratio of grants of legal aid to the total number of defendants proceeded against on indictable matters was only one to nine.[2] By 1990, for every 100 defendants charged with indictable offences in the magistrates' courts, 105.4 legal aid certificates were issued, indicating that legal aid was being granted for at least some summary matters as well as for the great majority of indictable cases.[3]

The explosion in legal representation has been mirrored in the mounting cost of criminal legal aid. Between 1984 and 1994, annual criminal legal aid expenditure rose by 300% to £519 m.[4] By 1998 the annual cost was £733m. These increases are very much higher than inflation.[5] It was the dramatic increase in criminal legal aid costs in the early 1990s, particularly for magistrates' court work, that prompted the government to slash eligibility for green form advice and legal aid. Rates of remuneration for solicitors have also come under attack. In the White Paper which led to the Legal Aid Act 1988, the government declared that it did not consider that rates for legally aided work should match those applied in the private sector.[6] The 1988 Act duly failed to incorporate the long-standing principle that legal aid work should attract reasonable remuneration.[7] Another attempt to control legal aid expenditure came in June 1993 with the introduction of a system of payment giving solicitors a fixed fee to cover much of the work involved in a case.[8] Fees now fall into three bands, each of which has three categories (covering guilty pleas, contested cases and committals/transfers to the Crown Court). In 1998-9 80% of criminal legal aid expenditure was for work in the lowest band.[9]

The Law Society has argued that rates of remuneration are so low that legal aid work has become uneconomic and that many firms are giving up criminal legal aid work altogether. Remuneration is also a vital issue for the handful of firms of scientific experts who conduct forensic work for the defence. In Roberts and Willmore's study for the Royal Commission on Criminal Justice (Runciman Commission) defence experts:

2 See Bridges (1992). See also T Goriely, 'The Development of Criminal Legal Aid in England and Wales', in Young and Wall (eds) (1996).
3 See Young et al (1992) pp 9-10.
4 Lord Chancellor's Department, Legal Aid - Targeting Need: The Future of Publicly Funded Help in Solving Legal Problems and Disputes in England and Wales (Cm 2854) (London: HMSO, 1995).
5 Lord Chancellor's Department (1998) para 6.6. This is the White Paper on which the AJA 1999 is based.
6 Lord Chancellor's Department, Legal Aid in England and Wales: A New Framework (Cm 118) (London: Lord Chancellor's Department, 1987) para 48.
7 Legal Aid Act 1974, s 39(3). This aspect of the Parliamentary debate on the Legal Aid Act 1988 is reviewed in D Matheson, Legal Aid: The New Framework (London: Butterworths, 1988) pp 101-104.
8 See L Bridges, 'The Fixed Fees Battle' (1992) Legal Action, November, p 7.
9 Legal Aid Board (1999) App 2.3.

'pointed out that criminal legal aid work was not nearly as lucrative as civil litigation and that the ponderous and arbitrary means of payment made legal aid work an ever less attractive proposition.'[10]

The danger that market forces could shrink the pool of solicitors willing to do this work has now, however, been overtaken by the developments of the late 1990s. The Legal Aid Board is now the 'Legal Services Commission' (LSC); criminal legal aid will, from April 2001, be handled by an arm of the LSC to be called the 'Criminal Defence Service' (CDS); all firms of solicitors which wish to undertake legal aid work will have to enter into contracts with the CDS and be franchised; and, in the medium term, a salaried defender service will be established within the CDS.[11] This is in part a *deliberate* policy of restricting legal aid work to fewer firms. Ostensibly the aim is to increase both efficiency and quality, and it may well have this effect to some extent in relation to the worst firms. It will also reduce choice and quality-competition, which could lead to a reduced quality of service for defendants who would have been lucky enough to be represented by the better firms. When one bears in mind the dramatic rise in imprisonment rates in magistrates' courts in the late 1990s referred to earlier, it can be argued that there is now *more* need for high-quality criminal legal aid services than there used to be, not less.

A further development is contracting, which will gradually replace the fixed fee system, according to the White Paper. When firms contract with the CDS they will do so on the basis of a price for every type of service provided - such as attending a police station interview, advising a client on bail, taking a statement, making a bail application, presenting a speech in mitigation, and so on. The cheaper the price at which these services are offered, the more 'slots' firms will get in duty solicitor rotas (in police station and court schemes). Since duty solicitor schemes generate 'own client' business as well as being relatively lucrative in themselves, firms will have an incentive to offer their services cheaply.[12] But will they have a sufficient incentive to offer quality?

10   P Roberts and C Willmore, The Role of Forensic Science Evidence in Criminal Proceedings (Royal Commission on Criminal Justice Research Study no 11) (London: HMSO, 1993) p 73. To the Runciman Commission it was 'unacceptable that, where scientific work is commissioned by the defence in a case, either the solicitor or the scientist is left unpaid for long periods (sometimes for a year or more)': Royal Commission on Criminal Justice (RCCJ), Report (Cm 2263) (London: HMSO, 1993) p 155. See also R Stockdale and C Walker, 'Forensic Evidence' in C Walker and K Starmer (eds), *Miscarriages of Justice* (London: Blackstone, 1999).

11   AJA 1999, ss 1 and 12. Also see Lord Chancellor's Department (1998) ch 6. For critical discussion see O'Brien and Epp (2000).

12   Lord Chancellor's Department (1998) para 6.22.

Legal aid and legal representation

(d) The quality of defence work under legal aid

Has criminal defence work, in the light of depressing income levels produced by such devices as low-rate standard fees, become a second-rate service? An obvious point is that low paid (and thus low status) legal aid work may deter the best of newly qualified lawyers (and forensic scientists) from specialising in criminal defence. It also leads to experienced criminal practitioners seeking to achieve greater financial security and status by switching to more lucrative types of legal activity such as corporate and commercial work.[13] These are only general tendencies of course but it would be surprising if criminal lawyers as a group were as highly qualified and experienced as those operating in, say, commercial practice.

Traditionally, the majority of solicitors' offices undertaking criminal defence work used not to specialise in this area and were responsible for little more than one court appearance per month. As Bridges observes, standards slipped in many offices through lack of practice.[14] At the other end of the scale, a small minority of offices do a disproportionately large amount of defence work. The organisation of these specialist criminal practices is a key determinant of the quality of defence work.[15] The essential point here is that solicitors are business people. Either they make a profit (or at least break even) or they go out of business. Many solicitors claim that the only way to make legal aid pay is to handle large numbers of cases in a streamlined and bureaucratic fashion. Profits can be maximised by the routine allocation of legally aided work to unqualified staff. As we have already seen in ch 4, section 4(d), the use of such staff to attend at police stations is extensive. This affects the quality of service unless training and supervision is stringent. Unqualified staff are also widely employed in carrying out initial interviews with defendants and applying for legal aid.[16] Research by McConville et al revealed that 66% of the 389 client interviews they monitored were carried out not by qualified lawyers but trainees, legal executives and former police officers.[17] The defendant will often meet a solicitor only on the morning of the court hearing. McConville et al who observed such meetings report that 'Several solicitors did not even know their clients by sight, let alone any details of their case . . .'[18] Where a

13 See R Smith, 'Resolving the Legal Aid Crisis' (1991) LS Gaz, 27 February, p 17. This is true also of defence experts: Roberts and Willmore (1993) p 74.

14 Bridges (1992) 'The Professionalisation of Criminal Justice' p 9.

15 See the insightful analysis of legal aid practices by M King, *The Framework of Criminal Justice* (London: Croom Helm, 1981) pp 68-75, and the empirical study by McConville et al (1994).

16 See McConville et al (1994) and Young, Molony and Sanders (1992) pp 81-86.

17 McConville et al (1994) pp 133-34.

18 McConville et al (1994) p 168.

solicitor briefs a barrister (or a solicitor advocate) to handle the case, the defendant becomes one step further removed from his or her legal representative.[19]

Criminal legal aid representation can therefore be characterised by *routinisation*, *delegation*, and *discontinuous representation*. Contracting makes this more and more inevitable, and franchising takes it for granted in order that criminal legal aid be efficient and cost-effective.[20] But whether it can at the same time be 'justice-effective' is another matter. The ideal of a close client-lawyer relationship in which the lawyer conducts the case in person from the police station right through to the courts is only rarely realised in practice.

A further problem is that a legal aid certificate may not cover all the work that the solicitor thinks is necessary in preparing the defence. In assessing claims for payment for legal services not covered by a fixed fee or contract price, the Legal Aid Board is supposed to 'allow a reasonable amount in respect of all work actually and reasonably done.'[1] In practice this means that solicitors often find themselves wrangling with Board officials over the correct level of payment to be made, or, indeed, over whether any payment at all should be forthcoming. Some solicitors have simply stopped carrying out certain preparatory steps in their cases, such as tracing and interviewing witnesses, for fear that they will not receive payment for such work.[2]

One way around this problem is to apply for prior authority to incur specified costs.[3] For example, if the defence wishes to obtain an expert report, they may first apply to the Legal Aid Board for authority to incur the additional expenditure involved. The delay and bureaucracy involved in this process (which can result in the defendant spending a further period remanded in custody) appears to deter solicitors from making applications for prior authority except in serious cases or where the need for an expert report is manifest.[4] None the less, the number of applications rises each year. There were 38,919 applications in 1998-9, of which nearly 6,000 (15.3%) were refused.[5] If the application is refused, the costs involved in

---

19   Solicitor-advocates (specialising, like barristers, in advocacy) are attracting an increasing market share of magistrates' courts work as they are more economic to 'brief' than barristers and operate more flexible working practices. The distinctive problems presented by the divided legal profession and the organisation of the Bar are explored in detail in ch 7.

20   L Bridges, E Cape, A Abubaker and C Bennett, Quality in Criminal Defence Services (London: Legal Aid Board, 2000) ch 1.

1   Legal Aid in Criminal and Care Proceedings (Costs) Regulations 1989, reg 4.

2   See Young, Moloney and Sanders (1992) pp 75-76 for instance.

3   Under reg 54 of the Legal Aid in Criminal and Care Proceedings (General) Regulations 1989.

4   Roberts and Willmore (1993) pp 78-81.

5   Legal Aid Board, Annual Reports 1998-9 (London, SO, 1999) p 112.

obtaining an expert report might still be allowed when the final bill is submitted for scrutiny, but, having received a shot across the bows, it is unlikely that a solicitor will take that risk.[6] Applications which are granted are nearly always limited to a specific sum, and if the need arises to exceed this sum further bureaucratic obstacles must be overcome. No such external controls apply to the police when they are conducting an investigation (although they may sometimes be deterred from commissioning expert reports by the cost involved).[7] The Runciman Commission's solution to the problems caused by the need to apply for prior authority for forensic science tests was to recommend the laying down of clear rules as to what defence solicitors could commission by way of expert reports without waiting for approval from the Legal Aid Board.[8] It did not, however, tackle the thornier question of what those rules should be, nor did it express any clear view on whether the rules needed to be more generous to the defence.

This unequal treatment of the prosecution and defence should be seen in the light of the revelations in cases such as the 'Birmingham Six',[9] *Maguire*[10] and *Ward*[11] that scientists acting for the police had misled the courts as to the reliability of the results they had obtained from forensic samples.[12] Steventon's study for the Runciman Commission demonstrated a continuing need for scrutiny of prosecution expert evidence—38% of defence lawyers who had obtained an independent analysis of DNA evidence found that the conclusions drawn by the expert differed from that drawn by the prosecution experts.[13] A broader Runciman Commission study of the use of forensic science evidence in run of the mill cases stressed the need to regard all scientific evidence with caution.[14]

The levels of remuneration obtained under legal aid, together with the way in which bills are assessed, combine to produce a situation in which many lawyers aim to spend as little time as possible on a case. Once standard procedures have been developed for unqualified staff to follow, it becomes almost inevitable that cases will be prepared in a standardised

6   A similar dilemma for the defence concerns the costs of an expert attending at court, for which no prior authority can be granted. The costs may not be allowed, if allowed may be reduced, and payment may not be forthcoming for several months. See B Steventon, The Ability to Challenge DNA Evidence (Royal Commission on Criminal Justice Research Study no 9) (London: HMSO, 1993) p 28.

7   For discussion of police decision-making in this respect, see Roberts and Willmore (1993) pp 14-18.

8   RCCJ (1993) pp 118 & 155.

9   (1991) 93 Cr App Rep 287 at 295-300.

10 (1992) 94 Cr App Rep 133 at 147-8.

11 (1993) 96 Cr App Rep 1 at 45-52.

12 For a discussion of these cases, see J Rozenberg, 'Miscarriages of Justice' in E Stockdale, and S Casale (eds), *Criminal Justice Under Stress* (London: Blackstone, 1992).

13 Steventon (1993) p 42.

14 Roberts and Willmore (1993) p 143.

manner. Fixed fees and contracting have probably reinforced bad practice. Under fixed fees systems, lawyers receive the same payment for a category of case whether they spend one hour or two hours preparing it. Only where cases can be presented as sufficiently complex to justify a higher level fee within a category will there be a financial incentive to do more than the bare minimum of preparation.[15] This makes it more likely that no attempt will be made to explore weaknesses in the prosecution case or possible defences to the charge.[16] It follows that, in terms of standardising cases to maximise profitability, defendants who can be persuaded to plead guilty hold a special attraction.[17]

The government's answer to this is that franchising sets standards which solicitors have to meet, on pain of losing their contracts. This is so only up to a point. For research carried out for the Legal Aid Board on pilot franchising schemes expressed little confidence that this system would ensure quality, although it did appear to bring very low performers up to a minimum level of competence.[18] It is true that in many areas there will be several firms contracted with the CDS. Defendants will be able to choose their firms, so that the firms with the best service (or, at any rate, which are the most popular) get the most business, regardless of price. Delivering the best quality services at the lowest prices is the objective. Whether this circle can be squared so easily remains to be seen. One problem is that in most small towns there is unlikely to be much choice of firm, as small firms are likely to be driven out of this business because of their uncompetitive working practices. The loss of small firms to criminal work is worrying in another way too. There are several small 'niche' firms which specialise in such issues as deaths in police custody, miscarriages of justice, complaints against the police, and so forth. Without campaigning solicitors such as Gareth Pierce, half the miscarriages uncovered in the 1980s and 1990s would remain hidden. This work is vital to the health of a legal system. As Bridges et al say, it must not be left to chance whether or not market forces will leave a place for these specialists.[19]

15   For discussion of lawyers' adaptations to a standard fee system, see A Gray, P Fenn and N Rickman, 'Controlling Lawyers' Costs through Standard Fees: An Economic Analysis' in Young and Wall (eds) (1996).

16   Worse still, research by Bridges et al (2000) ch 7 found that quality work is not necessarily secured just because a firm spends a long time on a case.

17   In a Scottish case, *Procurator Fiscal (Fort William) v Mclean and Mclean* (15 June 2000, unreported) the High Court of Justiciary held that a fixed fee system, because it provided an incentive for legal advisers to keep work done to a minimum, could, but did not necessarily, lead to a breach of the ECHR Art 6 right to a fair trial.

18   Bridges et al (2000). See discussion in ch 4, section 4.

19   Bridges et al (2000) ch 8. For an excellent critique of the concept of franchising, which argues that this introduces greater state control and cost cutting through the back door, see H Sommerlad, 'Criminal Legal Aid Reforms and the Restructuring of Legal Professionalism' in R Young and D Wall (eds) (1996).

Legal aid and legal representation

Further competition is planned through the creation of a salaried public defender system. It might seem that such a system, by removing the profit motive from defence work, would lead to improved standards. For this to be achieved, however, the salaried service would need to be set appropriate aims and given proper funding. The development of public defender systems in the United States does not bode well in this respect,[20] although other jurisdictions such as Canada have introduced such systems with greater success.[1] Clearly, much depends on the preferences of those responsible for setting up and funding salaried defenders. A pilot scheme is currently running in Scotland but we do not yet know how well it is working. Judging by the White Paper, quality of service is not likely to be much of a consideration for the government. A public defender system, it says:

'will produce better value for money for the taxpayer, because the two systems [public and private] will, in effect, both complement and compete against one another. The cost of the salaried service will provide a benchmark, which the CDS can use to assess whether the prices charged by private lawyers are reasonable.'[2]

The poor will always be dependent on the state to fund their defence regardless of whether legal services are based on private sector provision or salaried defenders. Either way, the state tends to draw the purse strings much tighter in relation to defence work than it does in sponsoring prosecutions. Criminal legal aid made up little over 7% of the overall total expenditure on the criminal justice system in 1999/2000. Legal aid costs of £900 million are dwarfed by the estimated £7,500 million spent on the police.[3] The experience on both sides of the Atlantic suggests that the state is more interested in cut-price efficient crime control than in expensive adversarial due process. There is a political dimension to this preference. Whereas cuts in spending on the police and prosecution services might be perceived as an indication that the government had gone 'soft' on crime, the due process rights of suspects present an easier target for cuts. Put crudely, there are currently more votes in crime control than in due process. The implications for the quality of a salaried defence service in particular, and adversarial justice in the magistrates' courts in general, are obvious.

20 See eg M McConville and C Mirsky, 'The State, the Legal Profession, and the Defence of the Poor' (1988) 15 JLS 342.
1   See O'Brien and Epp (2000). On the dangers of making cross-jurisdictional comparisons see C Tata, 'Comparing Legal Aid Spending' in F Regan, A Paterson, T Goriely and D Fleming (eds), *The Transformation of Legal Aid* (Oxford: OUP, 1999).
2   Lord Chancellor's Department (1998) para 6.19.
3   Barclay and Tavares (1999).

In its essentials, the legal aid scheme has the effect of nudging defence lawyers into a crime control mode of operation. From a freedom perspective, the due process argument for near-universal high quality criminal aid has to be balanced against competing demands on financial resources from other sectors of society (such as education and health, as discussed in chapter 1, section 11). It is relevant to ask whether the money is being spent properly. It is often said that much of the increase in the criminal legal aid bill is down to solicitors and defendants incurring unnecessary expenditure.[4] But as even the previous government's Green Paper accepted, 'demand is determined by the state' in the sense that if people were not arrested and prosecuted they would not seek criminal legal aid.[5] As Bridges points out, not only have arrests and prosecutions risen greatly over the last 30 years, but PACE in the mid-1980s authorised more police station detention than hitherto, and the CJPO in the mid-1990s further increased the need for lengthy police station attendances from legal representatives because the implications of the CJPO for each suspect are so difficult to foresee.[6] In other words, if the state is concerned about rising legal aid expenditure (as it should be) then the state should take responsibility for at least a part of the problem and alter its behaviour accordingly.

3. JUSTICES' CLERKS: LIBERAL BUREAUCRATS?

All magistrates belong to a bench, also known as a petty sessional division (PSD), of which there are currently 460. There is a bench for every court-house. Each PSD, or group of small PSDs, is advised by a justices clerk. Currently there are some 200 justices clerks. They are all qualified lawyers with specialist training. They have a staff of court clerks with more limited legal training who advise the magistrate(s) throughout each sitting. The provision of advice is essential, as most magistrates are part-time amateurs (see section 5 below). The justices clerk is responsible for case management, but the courts themselves are run by local chief executives[7].

Justices' clerks and their staff fulfil many functions in the magistrates' courts. They are responsible for training magistrates and they are also responsible for advising them on law, procedure and sentencing.[8] Through

---

4 See, for example, G Bevan, T Holland and M Partington, Organising Cost-Effective Access to Justice (London: Social Market Foundation, 1994); and Lord Chancellor's Department (1998) para 6.7.
5 Lord Chancellor's Department (1995) p 30.
6 L Bridges, 'The Reform of Criminal Legal Aid' in Young and Wall (eds) (1996).
7 Justices of the Peace Act, 1997, Part IV. See Lord Chancellor's Department, The Future Role of the Justices' Clerk: A Strategic Steer (London: LCD, 2000).
8 This latter aspect of their role is covered by a *Practice Direction* [1981] 2 All ER 831. And see Justices of the Peace Act, 1997, s 45.

pursuing a more or less conscious policy on the determination of legal aid applications, they can influence the level of legal representation. They are meant to assist unrepresented defendants in court. Finally, they shape the conduct of proceedings in court through their role in managing the court's business. Thus, they handle many pre-trial proceedings aimed at reducing delays in processing cases and they determine listing policies which might, for example, aim to dispose of as many cases in a single sitting of the court as possible. In carrying out these tasks, are clerks influenced by, and do they seek to advance, due process or crime control values?

As we have seen, court clerks have a fairly rough and ready approach to granting legal aid applications. The research by Young et al showed that some court clerks had a positive due process attitude towards legal representation whilst others were much less inclined to see the value of granting legal aid, particularly for guilty plea cases and for defendants charged with summary offences.[9] One common argument amongst the more restrictive court clerks was that, save in cases of particular difficulty or complexity, either a duty solicitor or they themselves could adequately protect a defendant's interests.

One study has suggested that court clerks distinctly prefer defendants to be represented by duty solicitors than by solicitors acting under a legal aid certificate.[10] The advantage to court clerks of directing legal work towards duty solicitors is that cases may be disposed of more expeditiously than if a legal aid certificate is granted. Duty solicitors can only act on the day, whereas legally aided solicitors might seek adjournments in order to prepare a case more thoroughly. One clerk interviewed by Young et al explained his reasons for refusing a particular application as follows:

'I think this is a duty solicitor job myself. I think with a bit of sensible advice that would be a plea. So, because in real terms the duty solicitor would get him to plead, we would refuse that one. I'm doing these from a practical point of view you realise.'[11]

This is a typical crime control line of thinking. The clerk is making a decision that the defendant is guilty based on scanty information. Because he has faith in his ability to distinguish between the clearly guilty and the possibly innocent, he decides to refuse legal aid, knowing that his decision is likely to produce the result that he considers the correct one. There is little difference in nature between this and the way in which the police set out to construct evidence against suspects. In both instances, a preference is

9   Young et al (1992) pp 34-39.
10   H Astor, 'The Unrepresented Defendant Revisited: A Consideration of the Role of the Clerk in Magistrates' Courts' (1986) 13 JLS 225 at p 234.
11   Young et al (1992) p 53.

being expressed for informal administrative fact-finding procedures over court-based adversarial proceedings as a means of disposing of the case.

The role of the clerk in assisting unrepresented defendants has been examined by Darbyshire and Astor in separate studies. Darbyshire found that some clerks were helpful and patient whilst others were brusque and intimidating.[12] Astor also noted varying standards of help on offer from clerks but made the important point that the 'allegiance of the clerks was ultimately not to the defendants, but to the rules—their insistence was that the court be run 'properly', not necessarily that the defendant understood what was going on.'[13] She argues that court clerks have a genuine interest in due process, since as the magistrates' courts' legal advisors they must ensure that the legitimacy of the court is not called into question. At the same time, she acknowledges, they have a strong bureaucratic interest in efficiency and saving court time. She accordingly follows Bottoms and McClean in arguing that the model of the criminal justice process which most accurately described the values 'typically held by humane and enlightened clerks'[14] was neither crime control nor due process, but the liberal bureaucratic model.[15]

According to Bottoms and McClean, the liberal bureaucratic model differs from crime control in that the need for justice to be done and seen to be done is accepted as ultimately overriding the importance of repressing criminal conduct. Priority must be given to protecting the innocent and the importance of formal adjudicative procedures is recognised. Thus far, this sounds like a fair account of the due process model. Bottoms and McClean argue, however, that the liberal bureaucrat has a strong interest in the efficient throughput of cases. Thus, due process protections must be limited. As they put it:

'If it were not so, then the whole system of criminal justice, with its ultimate value to the community in the form of liberal and humane crime control, would collapse. Moreover, it is right to build in sanctions to deter those who might otherwise use their "Due Process" rights frivolously, or to "try it on"; an administrative system at State expense should not exist for this kind of time-wasting.'[16]

---

12 See P Darbyshire, *The Magistrates' Clerk* (Chichester: Barry Rose, 1984). She outlines her research findings in 'The Role of the Magistrates' Clerk in Summary Proceedings' (1980) 144 JP 186, 201, 219, and 233.
13 Astor (1986) p 232.
14 A E Bottoms and J D McClean, *Defendants in the Criminal Process* (London: Routledge & Kegan Paul, 1976) p 228.
15 For a full appraisal of the due process and crime control models see ch 1, section 7.
16 Bottoms and McClean (1976) p 229.

They go on to note how the pressures on defendants to elect summary trial—in particular, the fear of a heavier sentence at the Crown Court—and the pressures on defendants to plead guilty all help to smooth the administrative operation of the system. They conclude that:

'despite the superficially apparent similarity of the value-systems underlying the Liberal Bureaucratic and Due Process Models, in practice the Liberal Bureaucratic Model offers much stronger support to the aims of the Crime Control Model than the Due Process Model.'[17]

Bottoms and McClean contradict themselves here by claiming that 'humane and enlightened' court clerks are genuinely concerned about protecting the innocent and upholding formal adjudicative procedures, at the same time as suggesting that they support rules and sanctions designed to deter defendants from exercising their due process rights. Such rules and sanctions are, after all, quintessential to the crime control model. The essential point to grasp here is that the crime control model represents one end of a spectrum of possible criminal justice systems, at the other end of which lies the due process model. By setting up these two opposing models, Packer hoped to illuminate the competing claims and tensions within criminal justice.[18] By contrast, the so-called liberal bureaucratic model is simply a factual description of the operation of the courts. This description reveals that court procedures display elements of the due process model in that contested trials do occur (albeit rarely), legal aid is (usually) available, court clerks will (on occasion) assist unrepresented defendants and so forth. However, the predominance of guilty plea cases, and the pressures on defendants to refrain from pushing the available due process levers, means that the magistrates' courts correspond much more closely to the crime control model than its polar opposite.

To return to Astor's work, while she is undoubtedly correct in suggesting that court clerks are anxious to see the rules followed, what is overlooked is that these rules themselves often incorporate crime control values. A denial of due process can accordingly be achieved without breaking the rules and without any undermining of the court's legitimacy. Thus, the discretion given to court clerks in determining legal aid applications means that they can, by refusing legal aid, deliver defendants into the arms of duty solicitors, knowing that this will aid efficiency and make a guilty plea more likely.

---

17 Bottoms and McClean (1976) p 232.
18 H L Packer, *The Limits of the Criminal Sanction* (Stanford: Stanford UP, 1968). See our discussion in ch 1, section 7.

An illustration of this is provided by the court clerk's role at the pre-trial stage. As the business managers of the magistrates' courts, clerks played a leading role in developing pre-trial reviews (discussed in ch 7). The Crime and Disorder Act 1998, s 50, has now introduced 'early administrative hearings' (EAHs) in cases where not guilty pleas are anticipated. These hearings, shortly after charge, at which legal aid and other case management issues can be dealt with, can be conducted by a single justice *or* the justices' clerk *or* their staff. This provision, only one of several similar in the Crime and Disorder Act,[19] grants to clerks powers previously reserved to magistrates. It arguably blurs the advisory and judicial line between justices' clerks and magistrates. It also gives extensive powers to staff who may not be professionally qualified.[20] EAHs, along with other new measures discussed later, are a product of attempts to reduce delays recommended by the Narey Report.[1] Providing clerks with extra powers of this kind is also an example of the managerialism discussed in ch 1, section 9. As in the pre-trial reviews of the 1980s and 1990s (which will continue to operate where courts wish them to) court clerks will in EAHs be expected actively to encourage defence disclosure and case settlement.[2] Indeed, defence disclosure is built into the very nature of the EAH since defendants must explain why they think their case merits a grant of legal aid.[3] As for case settlement, the Narey Report observed (with approval) that experimental EAH schemes had been set up in some courts:

'. . . so that the defendant can hear what the court expects from him in terms of obtaining legal representation and supplying evidence to enable the court to consider a legal aid application. The clerk . . . explains to the defendant the nature of the forthcoming proceedings and the implications of the charge against him. In some cases this prompts a guilty plea . . .'[4]

The enthusiasm of clerks for wheeling and dealing in informal settings, such as immediately prior to a youth court hearing,[5] is inconsistent with the liberal bureaucrat's supposed concern for justice to be done and to be

19 See, for example, s 49.
20 P Darbyshire, 'A Comment on the Powers of Magistrates' Clerks' [1999] Crim LR 377.
1   Home Office (Narey Report), Review of Delay in the Criminal Justice System: A Report (London: Home Office, 1997).
2   See eg J Baldwin, *Pre-Trial Justice* (Oxford: Basil Blackwell, 1985) p 43 and J Baldwin and A Mulvaney, Pre-Trial Settlement of Criminal Cases in Magistrates' Courts (Birmingham: University of Birmingham, 1987) p 15.
3   For discussion of the merits test see section 2(c)(ii) above.
4   Home Office (1997) Narey Report, ch 5.
5   See H Parker, M Casburn and D Turnbull, *Receiving Juvenile Justice* (Oxford: Basil Blackwell, 1981) pp 50-55.

seen to be done.[6] It is, however, consistent with the law and with managerial policy.

New funding methods for courts and performance-related pay for clerks, dependent on the throughput of cases, introduced in the early 1990s are another example of this managerialism. Cases handled are allocated a number of points based on such things as the seriousness of the offence, the number of defendants involved and so forth. The higher the points scored overall, the higher a court's grant (and clerks' pay) will be. Significantly, the points value of a case is not affected by whether it is disposed of by a guilty plea or following a full trial lasting several hours or days.[7] The government is calling on clerks to pipe a guilty plea tune.

4. SUMMONS, BAIL OR JAIL

Should defendants awaiting trial (or sentencing) be imprisoned? Imprisonment without trial has three obvious attractions for adherents to the crime control model: firstly, it secures the attendance of defendants at court; secondly, it impairs the ability of defendants to interfere with prosecution witnesses; and, thirdly, it prevents defendants from committing further offences whilst awaiting trial. That imprisoned defendants might not have committed any offence in the first place hardly arises due to the factual presumption of guilt at work in this model. Contrast this with the due process model. The normative presumption of innocence is antithetical to pre-trial custody.[8] Preserving the freedom of the innocent and guarding against abuses of state power should be priorities. Pre-trial imprisonment may result in an undermining of the defendant's ability or willingness to contest the case and unwarranted or excessive punishment. Punishment will be unwarranted for innocent persons and this is so regardless of whether they are ultimately acquitted or convicted on a guilty plea entered under pressure. It will be excessive for those who are guilty but who face charges which would normally attract a non-custodial or short custodial penalty.

To this the crime control adherent can retort that it is all to the good that defendants' willingness and ability to contest cases is undermined by pre-trial detention. The vast majority of defendants are factually guilty and it would put an intolerable strain on the system if they all contested that fact. Moreover, the obvious conclusion to draw from the argument

---

6   See Bottoms and McClean (1976) p 229.
7   Lord Chancellor's Department, A New Framework for Local Justice (Cm 1829) (London: LCD, 1992).
8   Especially as custodial remands can be for months: see subsection (f) below. Also see U N Raifeartaigh, 'Reconciling Bail Law with the Presumption of Innocence' (1997) 17 Ox JLS 1.

that pre-trial detention may involve punishment which exceeds that likely to be imposed by a court on conviction is that sentencers are too lenient. As Packer puts it, 'For many such persons, a short period spent in jail awaiting trial is not only a useful reminder that crime does not pay but also the only reminder they are likely to get.'[9] The model nevertheless accepts that it would be counter-productive to crime control to overload police cells and the prison system with minor offenders. It maintains, however, that any limits to pre-trial detention should be governed by this consideration of crime control efficiency, rather than by any abstract notion of a right to pre-trial liberty.

The freedom model shares most of the suppositions of the due process model, but would not ignore the interests of victims and witnesses in being protected from intimidation and 'further' harm by those defendants who manifest a clear and present danger of committing serious offences. It would also give weight to the fact that imprisoning people before trial does not stop them committing offences. There are plenty of opportunities for that within prison.[10] Other prisoners (whether convicted or not) deserve to have their interest in being protected from suspected 'dangerous' offenders taken into account too. In other words, this model would seek to maximise the freedom of all involved, but in a principled way.

We shall argue in this section that crime control values are more influential than those of the other models. People charged with minor offences are usually summonsed to appear on a particular date and no further restriction on their liberty is imposed. With more serious charges, the courts typically proceed by way of a series of remand hearings. The purpose of these hearings is to determine what degree of liberty defendants should be permitted to retain pending trial. Defendants may either be remanded in custody or remanded on bail. Since 1991 magistrates have been empowered to remand defendants for extended periods in custody of up to 28 days in duration.[11]

About 55% of persons proceeded against at magistrates' courts in 1998 were summonsed, 38% were arrested and bailed by the police, and 7% (143,000 people) were remanded in custody by the police pending first court appearance. The magistrates, for their part, remanded 98,000 people in custody during the court proceedings, about 15% of all those it remanded.[12] By comparison, in 1992 10% of defendants remanded by magistrates were remanded in custody (nearly 49,000 in total).[13] Thus, although the *proportion* of defendants who are remanded in custody is relatively small,

9   Packer (1968) p 212.
10   See, for example, I O'Donnell and K Edgar (1998) 'Routine Victimisation in Prisons', 37 Howard JCJ 266.
11   Magistrates' Courts (Remand in Custody) Order 1991, SI 1991 No 2667.
12   Home Office (2000) pp 191-92.
13   Home Office (1993) p 183.

the numbers involved are large and rising. Untried prisoners on remand make up around one fifth of the prison population, and therefore contribute greatly to prison overcrowding. Conditions for defendants held on remand are amongst the worst that exist within the prison system—in one institution prisoners have spent 18.5 hours a day in small cells lacking integral sanitation. Remand prisoners have played an active role in the sporadic outbreaks of rioting that have left some establishments (most notably Strangeways in April 1990) in smouldering ruins.[14] Keeping unconvicted defendants in stinking conditions might not conflict with the letter of the law, but if the concept of human rights is to mean more than a mere sign-up to an international treaty the least we could do is to keep remand prisoners in non-prison conditions.[15]

(a) The principles of bail law

As we saw in ch 5, sections 1-2, Art 6(2) ECHR affirms the presumption of innocence. Although the provision that allows arrest and detention in order to bring a suspect before a court (discussed in ch 4, section 3) clearly also allows pre-trial remands in custody, this may be done only 'when it is reasonably considered necessary to prevent his committing an offence or fleeing after having done so' (Art 5(1)(c)). This is qualified by Art 5(3):

'Everyone arrested or detained . . . shall be brought promptly before a judge . . . and shall be entitled to trial within a reasonable time or to release pending trial. Release may be conditioned by guarantees to appear for trial.'

To comply with the ECHR (and thus the HRA 1998), then, it seems that the law:
(i)   must allow remands in custody only when reasonably considered necessary;
(ii) can allow conditions to be set for bail;
(iii) must minimise delay for defendants remanded in custody.
English law is largely governed by the Bail Act 1976, along with some important later additions. Section 4(1) provides that a defendant 'shall be

14   See R Morgan and S Jones, 'Bail or Jail?' in E Stockdale and S Casale (eds), *Criminal Justice Under Stress* (London: Blackstone, 1992).
15   See, for example, Lord Windlesham, 'Punishment and Prevention: The Inappropriate Prisoners' [1988] Crim LR 140; and Lord Woolf, Prison Disturbances, April 1990: Report of an Inquiry (Cm 1456) (London: HMSO, 1991), discussed by Morgan and Jones (1992).

granted bail except as provided in Sch 1 to this Act'.[16] This creates a due process presumption in favour of bail (a right to bail) although the strength of that presumption depends on the nature of the exceptions set out in Sch 1. On the face of it, this complies with the ECHR, but we shall see that English law does not, or may not do so (depending on how the courts apply it) in some important respects. Another important due process protection which is part of the English and Welsh system is the right of appeal against adverse bail decisions. In the rest of this section we will examine each of these issues in turn, seeing how far the law corresponds with the reality, and how valuable the human rights approach is in protecting the freedom of defendants.

(b) Criteria for withholding bail: the law

For defendants charged with non-imprisonable (ie very trivial) offences, bail need not be granted if there has been a previous failure to answer bail and the court believes that there would be a further failure to appear on this occasion. The restrictiveness of this test is welcome but its practical impact is slight because such defendants would generally be proceeded against by way of summons from the outset.

For defendants charged with imprisonable offences, the grounds for refusing bail are much wider.[17] Bail need not be granted if the court is satisfied that there are 'substantial grounds' for believing that the defendant, if released on bail, would either fail to appear, commit an offence or interfere with witnesses or otherwise obstruct the course of justice. Nor need bail be granted if a court is satisfied that the defendant has previously failed to answer bail for the offence or ought to be kept in custody for his or her own 'protection' or 'welfare', or where there has been insufficient time to obtain enough information about the person for the court. In determining whether there are substantial grounds for believing that a defendant would fail to appear, commit an offence or obstruct the course of justice, Sch 1 to the Bail Act 1976 provides that the court is to have regard to, firstly, the nature and seriousness of the offence; secondly, the character, previous convictions, associations and community ties of the person; thirdly, the person's record in regard to any previous grant of bail; and finally, the strength of the evidence against the person.[18]

The due process model would object to most of the grounds for detention laid down in the 1976 Act. Whether the freedom model would

16   For an excellent account of the genesis and (limited) impact of the Bail Act 1976, see King (1981) pp 130-37.
17   Bail Act 1976, Sch 1, Pt 1 paras 2-6.
18   Bail Act 1976, Sch 1, Pt 1 para 9.

object would depend on how discriminating the courts were in making use of them, and on the nature of the offences to which they were applied. We will examine here the three main grounds for refusing bail.

(i) Obstructing the course of justice

To detain someone because they might interfere with a prosecution witness is manifestly unsatisfactory, since it penalises the defendant for a supposed disposition. Other ways of reducing the risk of interference can be employed, such as offering police protection to particularly vulnerable witnesses, making bail conditional on the defendant keeping well away from such persons, or making it a crime to intimidate witnesses.[19] However, there is undoubtedly some witness intimidation,[20] and this reduces the freedom of victims and witnesses. From a freedom perspective, it would only be proper to remand in custody on this ground if there is evidence that a person has manifested a clear intent to obstruct the course of justice if left at liberty. The level of proof required for that evidence would need careful consideration.

(ii) Committing an offence

A similar objection lies against the ground that the defendant will commit an offence if released. Under this ground too, someone may be deprived of liberty because of a supposed disposition. The objection is stronger here, however, since a prediction that someone will commit an offence if released rests on the assumption that the defendant committed the offence with which he or she is currently charged. The law thus allows a factual presumption of guilt to override the normative presumption of innocence. Nor should we forget that putting someone behind bars pending trial does not stop them committing offences; ' routine victimisation' takes place in prisons.[1]

The issue of 'dangerousness' as a ground for detaining persons not yet convicted of crime, or for extending (perhaps indefinitely) the period of detention for those who have been convicted, has been much debated in the context of sentencing and parole, and a similar dilemma applies to

---

19   As it now is, under CJPO 1994, s 51.
20   Home Office, Speaking up for Justice, Report of the Interdepartmental Working Group on the treatment of Vulnerable or Intimidated Witnesses in the Criminal Justice System, (London: Home Office, 1998) ch 4.
1   O'Donnell and Edgar (1998).

the bail decision.[2] The due process model would argue that the defendants' interests should in every case be given special weight. Ashworth seems to agree, citing an Irish case which held that this objection to bail is a form of preventive justice 'alien to the true purpose of bail'.[3] But it would be an affront to common sense to say that a suspected serial killer or pathological rapist should automatically be released on bail. There is also the particular problem of people charged with offences committed while already on bail.[4]

This is where the freedom approach offers a way of reconciling conflicting interests. Under that approach it is legitimate to weigh the risk of future victimisation (as with future intimidation as discussed above) against the freedom lost to remanded defendants. The freedom perspective also alerts us to the fact that the alternatives to a remand in custody might be more corrosive of freedom. Not all of us would accept the seal of approval that Ashworth implicitly gives to the Irish Supreme Court's preferred 'combination of police surveillance, speedy trial and deterrent sentences.'[5] However, since the freedom lost by remand is certain, and that to future victims only a possibility, strong safeguards are necessary. In particular, proper standards are needed to determine who may be presumed sufficiently dangerous to warrant a departure from the normative position that no one should be imprisoned until convicted. By allowing this ground to be applied in all offences which are merely imprisonable (rather than ones in which long terms of imprisonment are likely or virtually certain), and on the basis of little hard information, the Bail Act singularly fails this test.

(iii) Failure to answer bail

To detain defendants because of a fear that they might not attend voluntarily to answer the charges against them has greater merit, since the presumption of pre-trial liberty would quickly fall into disrepute if defendants absconded in large numbers. This fear should be properly grounded, however, and much depends on how magistrates make their predictions as to who is likely to abscond if granted bail and what level of

2   For a discussion of the 'dangerousness debate' see N Padfield, 'Bailing and Sentencing the Dangerous' in N Walker (ed), *Dangerous People* (London: Blackstone, 1996). For a recent study of risk based decision-making see R Hood and S Shute, The Parole System at Work (Home Office Research Study no 202) (London: Home Office, 2000).
3   *People (A-G) v Callaghan* [1966] IR 426 at 516; cited by A Ashworth, *The Criminal Process* 2nd edn (Oxford: OUP, 1998) p 211. Note that the ECHR Art 5 accepts this as a valid ground of detention, as long as there is a 'real' risk of a serious offence: Law Commission, Bail and the Human Rights Act, 1998 (Consultation Paper no 157) (London: SO, 1999) para 5.14.
4   See ss 25 and 26 CJPO 1994, discussed below.
5   *Ryan v DPP* [1989] IR 399 at 407; cited by Ashworth (1998) p 211.

risk they are prepared to tolerate. The factors that they are required to take account of, such as the seriousness of the offence and previous bail record, while clearly bearing on the risk of a defendant absconding, are open to wide interpretation.

For decision-making on this ground to conform to the freedom model, three things are necessary. First, the offence needs to be sufficiently serious for the loss of freedom of the detained defendant to be outweighed by the interests of the state in securing a conviction (if guilt is proved). To remand in custody for, say, several weeks, someone accused of minor criminal damage for which a fine would be imposed would be disproportionate. Second, mechanisms to achieve attendance short of detention should be used wherever possible. Section 6 of the 1976 Act makes it an offence punishable by imprisonment and/or a fine to fail to answer to bail without reasonable cause. This threat should be enough to guarantee the attendance of the great majority of those facing less serious charges. In addition, s 3(6) allows for persons to be released on bail subject to conditions (examined next). Finally, decision-making needs to be consistent, principled and based on high quality information (examined thereafter).

(c) Conditional bail

Section 3(6) of the 1976 Act allows for persons to be released on bail subject to such conditions as appear to the court to be necessary to secure that the defendant surrenders to the court at the appropriate time, does not commit an offence on bail or obstruct the course of justice and is available for the purpose of enabling a court report to be prepared to assist in sentencing. Defendants released on conditional bail typically have to report to the police at periodic intervals, or must reside at a specified address (such as a bail hostel) or must keep away from certain places or people. The government has sought to encourage a greater use of conditional bail for defendants thought to pose too great a risk if released unconditionally. Thus over 2,000 places are provided in bail hostels and other forms of supervised accommodation. Around half of all bail is conditional. Courts vary considerably in their use of conditions, and some use them in ways contrary to the Bail Act, such as imposing a requirement to report to the police station the day before the next court appearance so that the defendant can be reminded about that appearance.[6] This practice fits so well with the dominant managerial ethos that it can only be a matter of time before a law is passed to legitimise it. A 'precedent', should one be thought

---

6   A Hucklesby, 'The Use and Abuse of Conditional Bail' (1994) 33 Howard JCJ 258; J Raine and M Willson, 'The Imposition of Conditions in Bail Decisions' (1996) 35 Howard JCJ 256.

necessary, is s 54(2) of the Crime and Disorder Act 1998, which allows a condition to be attached to a grant of bail requiring a defendant to attend an interview with a legal adviser. Combined with the new device of the early administrative hearing (see section 3 above) s 54(2) is designed to ensure that defendants can be 'processed' by the court as fast as possible.

There are many difficulties with bail conditions. One is that they may impose excessive restrictions on the liberty of defendants whose alleged offences are 'political'. This is particularly so as one of the grounds for imposing a condition is to neutralise the fear that a defendant will commit an offence (any offence) if bailed. The breadth and vagueness of many criminal laws entails that highly restrictive conditions may lawfully be imposed. Thus in *Mansfield Justices, ex p Sharkey*,[7] the Divisional Court upheld the legality of a condition that defendants facing charges arising out of picketing did not take part in any further demonstration connected with the trade dispute between striking miners and the National Coal Board. The court's reasoning was that those attempting to prevent miners going to work by force of numbers and threats of violence would have been guilty of at least the public order offence of threatening behaviour. Anyone attending such a demonstration must be regarded as knowingly taking part in that threatening behaviour. To guard against the risk of the defendants committing offences on bail, it was, the court argued, necessary to prevent them from picketing. However, Percy-Smith and Hillyard argue that the widespread policy of imposing this form of conditional bail on striking miners was motivated by a desire not to control crime, but to hamper legitimate protest.[8] Similarly, Vogler, who analysed mass custodial remands in the 'riots' of 1981, found that in Manchester, for example, curfews were used almost en masse. Many defendants charged with minor offences such as obstruction of the highway (maximum penalty: £50 fine) were being subjected to stringent restrictions for as much as four months.[9] When laws are drawn in broad crime control terms there is the clear potential for them to be used in a repressive manner for political reasons.[10]

The second difficulty with bail conditions is that they are sometimes unrelated to the objection to bail voiced by the CPS. For example, curfews should be used for defendants thought to pose a risk of offending, but they are sometimes used when the objection is that the defendant may abscond. This sometimes happens when solicitors offer any conditions to

---

7   [1985] 1 All ER 193.
8   J Percy-Smith and P Hillyard, 'Miners in the Arms of the Law: A Statistical Analysis' (1985) 12 JLS 345. See to like effect N Blake, 'Picketing, Justice and the Law' in B Fine and R Millar (eds), *Policing the Miners' Strike* (London: Lawrence and Wishart, 1985).
9   R Vogler, *Reading the Riot Act* (Milton Keynes: Open UP, 1991) p 153.
10   See our earlier discussion of this in the context of stop-search powers in ch 2, section 3(b).

bolster their application for bail, or when courts simply attach conditions indiscriminately.[11] It also happens when conditions are imposed as a form of 'summary punishment' - for example, imposing a condition of residence to stop a defendant going on holiday or visiting friends.[12]

Third, conditions are imposed on some defendants who would otherwise have received unconditional bail, rather than those who were genuinely at risk of a custodial remand. The evidence on this point is somewhat unsatisfactory and equivocal in nature although it seems that some 'net widening' has taken place.[13] Raine and Willson, for example, found that many defence solicitors routinely offer bail conditions to the court in cases where they might have secured unconditional bail. And sometimes a defence solicitor and a prosecutor will strike a 'deal' that the latter will not oppose bail if the former does not oppose conditions.[14]

Although breach of a condition of bail is not an offence, it may lead to defendants being brought back before the court for reconsideration of their remand status. Indeed, defendants can be arrested if the police have 'reasonable grounds' to believe that they have broken, *or 'are likely to break'*, any of their conditions.[15] Under any of these circumstances 'the defendant need not be granted bail'.[16] Conditions often operate in arbitrary and discriminatory ways. Financial conditions weigh far more heavily on poor people than on others, and sometimes lead to remands in custody.[17] Residence conditions similarly operate unfairly on the homeless and rootless. Most other conditions are largely unenforceable. When curfews, for example, are breached, the only defendants at any risk at all of being caught are those who the police recognise. These will usually be defendants who are 'known to the police' or who stand out - such as members of ethnic minorities in largely-white areas.[18] The opportunity for the discriminatory use of discretion discussed in chapters 2 and 3 is obvious here, especially as arrest can be on suspicion that a defendant might break a condition.

11 Hucklesby (1994).
12 Raine and Willson (1996).
13 Consider eg the debate concerning whether bail hostels are being used to accommodate persons who would otherwise have been remanded in custody: K White and S Brody, 'The Use of Bail Hostels' [1980] Crim LR 420; J Pratt and K Bray, 'Bail Hostels - Alternatives to Custody?' (1985) 25 BJ Crim 160; and H Lewis and G Mair, Bail and Probation Work II: the use of London Bail Hostels for Bailees (Home Office Research and Planning Unit Paper no 50) (London: Home Office, 1989). Also see Hucklesby (1994).
14 A Hucklesby, 'Remand Decision Makers' [1997] Crim LR 269.
15 Bail Act 1976, s 7.
16 Bail Act 1976, s 4. Concern has been expressed that might breach the ECHR: Law Commission (1999) para 8.9. The Law Commission's report is summarised in: Editorial, 'Bail and Human Rights' [2000] Crim LR 69.
17 P Cavadino and B Gibson, *Bail: The Law, Best Practice and the Debate* (Winchester: Waterside Press, 1993) p 170.
18 Hucklesby (1994); Raine and Willson (1996).

Anyone who can disprove this is likely to be using their brain in ways that are far more profitable than minor crime.

(d) Criteria for withholding bail: the decision-making process

We have seen that about 15% of all defendants who are arrested and charged (as distinct from summonsed) are remanded in custody. The custody remand rate varies considerably between different courts. Hucklesby, for example, found custody rates of 9% in two of the courts she studied, but 25% in the other court, even though the case mix was substantially the same in all three. Even in the two apparently similar courts, similar cases were treated dissimilarly. Variations between courts in the way criteria are evaluated therefore produce a 'justice by geography' effect[19] : what happens to a defendant in a borderline case depends as much on the court as on the case, just as with other aspects of magistrates' decision-making such as legal aid and sentencing. This is due largely to different 'court cultures'. One element in a court's culture is whether or not it includes a stipendiary (who, Hucklesby found, granted bail less often).[20] Nonetheless, despite the *differences* between courts, the features which are *common* to all courts are more important.

(i) The absence of adversarialism

The ECHR and the Bail Act 1976 appear to require bail to be granted, in normal circumstances, unless there is clear evidence to substantiate a belief that one of the evils envisaged by Sch 1 will occur if the defendant is released. Most remand hearings are uncontested. Hucklesby's study of 1,524 remand hearings found that in around 85% of cases the CPS did not request a remand in custody. And in only just over a half of all cases where the CPS requested a remand in custody was this opposed by the defence. It is very rare for magistrates to question these agreed proposals.[1] Hucklesby therefore argues that the real decision-makers are the police (who make recommendations to the CPS), the CPS and defence lawyers.

---

19 Similar to the effect of local police decision-making leading to cautioning variations - see ch 6, section 4(a).
20 A Hucklesby, 'Court Culture: An Explanation of Variations in the Use of Bail by Magistrates Courts' (1997) 36 Howard JCJ 129. The differences between lay and stipendiary magistrates are discussed in section 5(a) below. For another example showing differences between courts, see F Paterson and C Whittaker, *Operating Bail* (Edinburgh: Scottish Office, 1994).
1 Hucklesby [1997] 'Remand Decision Makers' p 271.

She found that in virtually every case where unconditional bail was recommended by CPS, this was granted; in virtually every case where conditional bail was recommended by CPS, this was also granted; and in 86% of cases where custody was requested by CPS, this was granted too. And although police or prosecution objections to bail are not invariably upheld by magistrates, *un*conditional bail is hardly ever granted when bail is opposed.[2] In one respect the analysis by Hucklesby is thin. When she argues that the lack of adversarialism indicates that magistrates are less active in decision-making than are police, CPS and lawyers, she does not refer to her own findings elsewhere that these professionals know their local courts and tailor their applications accordingly. In other words, CPS will apply for remands in custody in certain types of borderline case in some courts but not others, and defence solicitors will oppose this more in some courts than others.[3]

In only a small proportion of remand hearings, then, is bail contested - less than 10%. The low percentage of cases in which the defence challenges CPS recommendations for custody has to be seen in the context of s 154 of the Criminal Justice Act 1988. This provides that, once a defendant has been refused bail, any argument may be used to support an application at the next remand hearing whether or not it has been used previously but thereafter 'the court need not hear arguments as to fact or law which it has heard previously'. Courts often interpret this as a licence to hear a maximum of two applications.[4] Thus Hucklesby found that where bail was opposed by CPS, defence lawyers usually applied for bail at the first appearance (in 85% of these cases) but did so in less than half of subsequent appearances. The lack of adversarialism also reflects the evaluation that many defence lawyers make - rightly or wrongly - of their clients' cases. Put bluntly, they do not want to lose credibility with the court, and often put that consideration above the interests of their clients.[5] Both Hucklesby and McConville et al found that when lawyers are instructed, contrary to their professional advice, to apply for bail, they let the court know that they do not have their heart in it by using coded language such as 'I am instructed

---

2   Hucklesby [1997] 'Remand Decision Makers' Table 1.
3   Hucklesby (1997) 'Court Culture'. This happens in Scotland too: Paterson and Whittaker (1994).
4   It seems that many advocates, magistrates and court clerks close their minds to the possibility of a renewed bail application: See M Hinchcliffe, 'Beating the Bail Bandits' (1992) LS Gaz 1 July 19 at 20; N Corre, 'Three Frequent Questions on the Bail Act' [1989] Crim LR 493 at 496-497; and the letter, (1991) JP 771. See also *Blyth Juvenile Court, ex p G* [1991] Crim LR 693 and *Dover and East Kent Justices, ex p Dean* (1991) 156 JP 357.
5   Hucklesby [1997] 'Remand Decision Makers'; McConville et al (1994). The same is true of the CPS, but arguably their duty to the police is different to that of defence lawyers to their clients.

to say that ...'. Sometimes the code is not difficult to crack, as with the following lawyer's culinary comments to the bench:

'He tells me - and I know you will take this with a pinch of salt, but I am instructed to say it so I shall say it - that he intended to surrender to the warrant. As I say, you may take that with a pinch of salt but I have said what I was instructed to say by my client'.[6]

As Brink and Stone comment on the basis of research with similar findings:

'Such an attitude is hardly unique to criminal solicitors in this country, but wherever it is found it is generally regarded as a corruption of the adversary system of justice. Lawyers, as officers of the court, have an obligation to serve the cause of justice, but in an adversary system justice is served by the strongest possible arguments being put in every case.'[7]

Brink and Stone's findings are all the more striking given that their research focussed on solicitors who were identified by the London Criminal Courts Solicitors' Association as 'highly qualified, experienced and respected.'[8]

(ii) The information on which bail decisions are made

The Bail Act's presumption in favour of bail fits with the ECHR's stipulation that bail decisions be based on *evidence* (not 'speculation') and that the burden of proof be on the prosecution.[9] But Hucklesby found that bail was granted in less than 1 in 3 contested bail applications, partly because defence solicitors are seen by magistrates as less objective than the CPS. Consequently, challenging the police version of events, as put forward by the CPS, is usually unsuccessful, despite the fact that strength of evidence is supposed to be a consideration under the Bail Act.[10] Clearly defendants have an uphill struggle to overcome CPS objections to the 'right to bail'.

But how, in reality, could it be otherwise? Terms like 'prediction' and 'risk' are virtual synonyms for 'speculation', so how could it ever be *proved* that someone will abscond or commit 'further' offences? Moreover, how could it be proved *beyond reasonable doubt* as some ECHR cases seem

6   McConville et al (1994) p 181.
7   B Brink and C Stone, 'Defendants who do not ask for Bail' [1988] Crim LR 152.
8   Brink and Stone [1988] p 153.
9   *W v Switzerland* (1993) 17 EHRR 60.
10   A Hucklesby, 'Bail or Jail? The Practical Operation of the Bail Act 1976' (1996) 23 JLS 213.

to suggest?[11] The rhetoric is here at odds with the law, as well as the practice. As Hayes, a magistrate and academic points out:

> 'the bail decision is a matter of guesswork, of hunches, not capable of precise explanation. Will he turn up, will he do it again? Each magistrate will apply his own criteria and his own values to his decision.'[12]

The complexity of the Bail Act's provisions and the importance of what is at stake might lead one to think that bail hearings are painstaking affairs. Go and visit your local magistrates' court and you will see for yourself the whirlwind reality. Bail decision-making is speedy. In Zander's study of London courts, the amount of time spent discussing whether defendants should retain their liberty was five minutes or less in 86% of the 261 remand cases observed.[13] Even where a remand in custody is sought, proceedings are rapid. As many as 60% of such decisions in Zander's study were reached within five minutes.[14] Another indication that bail decision making is cursory, if not slipshod, is that in at least some courts defendants have been convicted of the non-existent offence of breaching bail conditions.[15] Magistrates courts were castigated in the Woolf Report on prison disturbances for giving insufficient status to the bail decision.[16]

Doherty and East identify the main reason for the speed with which bail decisions are taken as being the heavy workload of the magistrates' courts. The participants in the proceedings are all well known to each other and are aware that they are expected to assist in the speedy disposal of business:

11 See cases cited in J Burrow, 'Bail and the Human Rights Act 1998' (2000) 150 NLJ 677. The same problem arises concerning defendants 'likely' to breach bail conditions.

12 M Hayes, 'Where Now the Right to Bail?' [1981] Crim LR 20 at p 22. The 'values' of magistrates, and of the legal framework they operate within, may result in some women getting a raw deal: M Eaton, 'The Question of Bail' in P Carlen and A Worrall (eds), *Gender, Crime and Justice* (Milton Keynes: Open UP, 1987).

13 M Zander, 'Operation of the Bail Act in London Magistrates' Courts' (1979) 129 NLJ 108.

14 Zander (1979).

15 See N Cameron, 'Bail Act 1976: Two Inconsistencies and an Imaginary Offence' (1980) 130 NLJ 382.

16 See Prison Disturbances April 1990, Report of an Inquiry by The Rt Hon Lord Justice Woolf (Parts I and II) and His Honour Judge Stephen Tumim (Part II) (Cm 1456) (HMSO, 1991): 'All too often, remands are dealt with by a single Magistrate or two Magistrates rather than a full Court. They can be dealt with hurriedly on a Saturday morning' (para 10.80).

'In these circumstances it is probably inevitable that a camaraderie develops between the participants, and this no doubt partially explains why so few of the hearings attended were markedly adversarial in character . . . In a situation where there is an expectation that cases are dealt with quickly, often in a non-adversarial fashion, it is perhaps not surprising that only limited information of a low quality is made available to the courts.'[17]

In addition to the limited information given to the courts, most information comes from the police. Just as the police 'construct' cases for prosecution, making cases appear stronger (or weaker) than they might otherwise appear,[18] so they can do this with remand applications. The police also often make recommendations to the CPS on whether or not to seek a remand in custody or conditional bail. Phillips and Brown found that in 85% of such cases the CPS followed the police recommendation.[19] Research has also shown that a police decision to either bail a suspect from the police station or remand to next court appearance is an important factor in determining whether the CPS and the court will favour bail or remand.[20] This is something akin to prosecution momentum, which we looked at in ch 6, section 3(c). Magistrates, with their concern for upholding authority, are naturally disinclined to 'overturn' a police decision to hold someone in custody pending trial. The police thus exert a strong influence over bail processes.

Bail information schemes, which in 1996 operated in 193 of the 450 courts and in 38 prisons, go some way towards remedying these problems.[1] These schemes involve the probation service providing verified information to the CPS in cases where the police indicate an objection to bail. It appears that such schemes are successful in persuading prosecutors and magistrates to adopt a more liberal attitude to the grant of bail without leading to more offending on bail or absconding.[2] The majority of courts

---

17   M J Doherty and R East, 'Bail Decisions in Magistrates' Courts' (1985) 25 BJ Crim 251 at p 263.

18   McConville et al (1991); case construction is discussed in ch 6, section 3(c) in particular.

19   C Phillips and D Brown, Entry into the Criminal Justice System (Home Office Research Study no 185) (London: Home Office, 1998); B Mhlanga, Race and the CPS (London, SO, 1999) pp 134-35.

20   J Burrows, P Henderson and P Morgan, Improving Bail Decisions: the bail process project, phase 1 (Research and Planning Unit Paper 90) (London: Home Office, 1994).

1   G Mair and C Lloyd, 'Policy and Progress in the Development of Bail Schemes in England and Wales' in F Paterson (ed), Understanding Bail in Britain (Edinburgh: Scottish Office, 1996).

2   Mair and Lloyd (1996). The same is true of Scotland where similar schemes have been established: G McIvor, 'The Impact of Bail Services in Scotland' in Paterson (1996).

(albeit the smaller ones) currently operate without bail information schemes, however, so many magistrates have little on which to base their decisions. And since the proportion remanded in custody is going up, not down, it is clear that the effect of these schemes is limited.

(iii) Breach of bail

The police often complain that too many defendants are released on bail. In the early 1990s they highlighted the 'growing problem' of 'bail bandits', ie persons offending while on bail.[3] The research evidence tends to suggest that in fact there has been little change in the rate of known offending on bail over the last 15-20 years. Around 10%-17% of those bailed are known to commit an offence.[4] Many regard this as unacceptable, but it is exceptionally difficult to identify who will, and who will not, offend while on bail. The greater the number of defendants remanded in custody because of fears of offending, the more remands in custody there will be of defendants who would *not* offend while on bail.[5] Indeed, a Scottish study found that offending on bail was hardly higher in the court with the highest bail rate than in the court with the lowest rate.[6]

Despite this, the government in 1992 announced a number of proposals aimed at tackling 'bail banditry'.[7] One gave the prosecution for the first time the right to appeal against a grant of bail (see sub-section (e) below). Another initiative was contained in s 26 of the Criminal Justice and Public Order Act 1994 (CJPO). This states that anybody charged with an indictable or either way offence committed whilst already on bail, 'need not be granted bail', thus introducing another exception to the ever-diminishing 'right to bail.' However, since alleged offending on bail could always have been used as a reason for refusing bail (constituting, as it does, compelling evidence of a risk of the offender committing an offence if released on bail), this provision has made little difference to bail rates.[8] In addition to the

---

3   See the articles in (1991) Police Review, 19 July and 6 September, which summarise the results of studies carried out by the Avon and Somerset and Northumbria police, respectively. For a critique, see A Hucklesby, 'The Problem with Bail Bandits' (1992) 142 NLJ 558. And what of the politically invisible 'Remand Bandits' (remand prisoners committing crimes against other remand prisoners or prison staff)?

4   A Hucklesby and E Marshall, 'Tackling Offending on Bail' (2000) 39 Howard JCJ 150. Also see D Brown, Offending on Bail and Police Use of Conditional Bail (Research Findings no 72) (London: Home Office, 1998); P Morgan and P Henderson, Remand Decisions and Offending on Bail (Home Office Research Study no 184) (London: Home Office, 1998).

5   Hucklesby and Marshall (2000).

6   Paterson and Whittaker (1994).

7   Hucklesby and Marshall (2000).

8   Hucklesby and Marshall (2000).

problem of some defendants offending on bail, about 12% of those bailed by magistrates' courts in 1998 failed to appear, this being a rise of a few percentage points over the rate in the early 1990s.[9]

All such bare statistics must be treated with caution. For example, statistics on absconding may overstate the problem in that there may be good reasons why defendants fail to appear at court (eg, illness or death). Statistics of offending on bail may understate the problem, in that much offending on bail no doubt remains undetected, or may overstate it in that they take no account of the possible triviality of the offences in question or the fact that increasing delays in prosecuting cases are likely to lead to an increased offending on bail rate.[10] That people 'abscond' or offend on bail is not necessarily a sign that the remand decision was wrong.

(iv) Wrongful denial of bail

It is similarly impossible to estimate the number of defendants who are wrongly denied bail. There are three broad categories. First, in 1998, 22% of all defendants remanded in custody were acquitted or not proceeded against. Second, a further 36% were given non-custodial sentences. In total, less than half of all defendants in custody before trial are put in custody afterwards.[11] This is, on the face of it, a gross denial of due process and freedom standards. However, the fact that many persons denied bail are not subsequently convicted may be testimony to the fairness of the courts.[12] In other words, adjudicators seem able in at least some cases to overcome the prejudicial effect created by the sight of an accused being brought up from the cells under the courtroom. Similarly, the high proportionate use of non-custodial sentences for those denied bail and subsequently convicted does not prove that the remand decision was incorrect.[13] Defendants may, for example, have been remanded for their own protection or because it was feared that they would not answer to bail.[14] Some defendants will have been judged to have suffered enough and not be given the custodial sentences that they might otherwise have got. Perhaps we should be more worried about the positive correlation between denial of bail on the one hand and conviction and custodial sentences on the other, in so far as the former may partially explain the latter.

9   Home Office (2000) p 193 and Home Office (1993) p 193, Table 8.11 respectively.
10   On the latter point, see Hucklesby (1992) p 560.
11   Home Office (2000) p 192.
12   Morgan and Jones (1992) pp 38-9.
13   Morgan and Jones (1992) p 39.
14   On this, see the letters from two judges: [1993] Crim LR 324.

A third category of defendants wrongly denied bail is those who would not have breached their bail. This is even more difficult to quantify. The enormous disparities in the rates at which different courts refuse bail discussed earlier shows that some, without good reason, remand more than others.[15] Moreover, bail information schemes have confirmed that many remands in custody where such schemes do not operate are unwarranted and that the standard of decision-making can be improved.[16] As is so often the case in the criminal process, certain groups suffer more than others as a result of the law allowing a large element of discretion to those taking decisions. Hood, for example, found that black defendants had a greater likelihood of being remanded in custody than white defendants, even when all factors legally relevant to the bail decision were taken into account.[17] The framework created by the Bail Act clearly does little to prevent bad, arbitrary or even racist decision-making.[18]

Court clerks are obliged to record a court's reasons for refusing bail or imposing or varying conditions.[19] In addition, the defendant must be informed as to the reasons for any refusal of bail. These requirements are supposed to ensure that magistrates keep within the terms of the Act. But as White has observed:

> 'it would be a poor clerk who could not formulate a reason falling within the terms of the Act and it would be a foolish magistrate who insisted on recording a personal prejudice as the reason for the decision.'[20]

Further, reasons are often given by way of a pro forma which fails to explain why defence arguments were rejected. This procedure could fall foul of the ECHR.[1]

---

15 See Hucklesby (1997) 'Court Culture'; Paterson and Whittaker (1994).
16 The original experiment from which these schemes developed showed that the increase in granting bail resulting from the provision of better information on defendants did not result in an increase in the failure rate, whether measured as offending on bail, breach of bail conditions or non-attendance at court. See C Stone, Bail Information for the Crown Prosecution Service (New York: VERA Institute of Justice, 1988).
17 R Hood, Race and Sentencing (Oxford: Clarendon Press, 1992) pp 146-149. The treatment of women is discussed in Eaton (1987).
18 Compare this with the situation applying in countries which have fundamental rights enshrined in constitutional charters. See eg N Padfield, 'The Right to Bail: a Canadian Perspective' [1993] Crim LR 510.
19 Bail Act 1976, s 5.
20 R C White, The Administration of Justice (Oxford: Basil Blackwell, 1985) p 84.
1   Law Commission (1999) para 4.21.

(e) Appeals against bail decisions

An appeal against a refusal of bail may be made to the Crown Court under a procedure introduced in 1983, and solicitors enjoy a right of audience for this purpose.[2] Unrepresented defendants of limited means are at a distinct disadvantage here because, although this step lies within the scope of an existing legal aid certificate, legal aid may not be granted solely for the purpose of this type of bail application. For those not on legal aid, the Official Solicitor—a government lawyer whose duties include safeguarding the rights of prisoners—may act. An alternative procedure is to apply to a High Court judge in chambers.[3] Legal aid is theoretically available but the legal aid authorities would require compelling reasons why a defendant should be given access to the High Court in preference to the (cheaper) Crown Court. One such reason would be the need to challenge the conditions attached to a grant of bail, since these cannot be contested in the Crown Court. Again, the Official Solicitor may act for those denied legal aid, although for most defendants such a safety net provides cold comfort. Under the Official Solicitor procedure, a paper application is simply forwarded to the judge and there is no oral argument. The success rate for Official Solicitor applications in 1980 was 9%, compared with 69% for those privately represented.[4] Generally, it seems that lawyers are wary of making use of these various appeal procedures, on the ground that an unsuccessful outcome might prejudice any subsequent attempt to persuade magistrates to reconsider the question of bail.[5]

The converse of defendants appealing against the refusal of bail is the prosecution appealing against its grant. The Bail (Amendment) Act 1993, gives the prosecution for the first time the right to appeal against a grant of bail. An appeal lies to a judge in chambers where the defendant stands charged with a crime carrying at least five years' imprisonment.[6] A defendant must be remanded in custody pending the outcome of the appeal which must take place within 48 hours. This gives the prosecution the power, in effect, to override (albeit temporarily) a judicial decision to release on bail which can be seen as 'a potentially dangerous departure from constitutional principle.'[7] The Divisional Court, however, seems not to

---

2   Criminal Justice Act 1982, s 60.
3   Criminal Justice Act 1982, s 22.
4   Official Report HC written answers, 6th Series, vol 13, cols 274-275, 23 November 1981. See also N Bases and M Smith, 'A Study of Bail Applications Through the Official Solicitor to the Judge in Chambers by Brixton Prisoners in 1974' [1976] Crim LR 541.
5   See A Hall, 'Bail: Appeals' (1984) LAG Bull December 145.
6   Additional offences expressly included by the Act are those of taking a conveyance without authority and aggravated vehicle taking ('joyriding'), ss 12 and 12A of the Theft Act 1968 respectively.
7   See the comments by A Samuels (1993) Magistrate, November, 183.

share this sense of danger, as is indicated by its lax interpretation of the 1993 Act's procedural safeguards for defendants.[8]

(f) Time spent on remand

There are legislative time limits where defendants are in custody trial, but courts can, and usually do, grant extensions.[9] In 1990 the usual wait in custody for a Crown Court trial was 17 weeks, but only three weeks for a magistrates' court trial. By the mid-1990s the average wait for the Crown Court was down to less than 10 weeks but for magistrates it was up to seven weeks.[10] Two to four months may seem a long time to wait in prison for a trial at the conclusion of which there is an even chance of an acquittal or non-custodial sentence, but this pales into insignificance by comparison with some other countries. Although the ECHR has held that a delay of over five years breached Art 5(3)[11] it held in another case that a delay of four years did not.[12] So unconvicted prisoners in the UK can expect little help from the HRA when it is implemented.[13]

(g) A right to bail?

For most defendants the presumption in favour of bail is uncontested. But most defendants are charged with minor offences and given non-custodial sentences anyway. The situation is different when the police and CPS consider that a defendant should be remanded in custody. In these cases the crime control presumption of guilt, which operates not only on the courts but also on defence solicitors much of the time, is more powerful than legal rules and Human Rights principles. At times of stress, such as 'riots' and industrial strife, there is what Vogler describes as an 'almost complete surrender of the magistrates to policing rather than judicial priorities ...'[14] When the police seek curfew conditions, the magistrates comply. Remands in custody are similarly 'rubber stamped'. Even committed defence lawyers know that there is no point resisting these joint

---

8   See the discussion of *Crown Court at Isleworth, ex p Clarke* [1998] 1 Cr App Rep 257 by D Tucker, 'The Prosecutor on the Starting Block: The Mechanics of the Bail (Amendment) Act 1993' [1998] Crim LR 728.

9   Prosecution of Offences Act 1985 as amended. For details, see A Samuels 'Custody Time Limits' [1997] Crim LR 260.

10 Ashworth (1998) p 219.

11 *Tomasi v France* (1992) 15 EHRR 1.

12 Referred to by Ashworth (1998) p 208.

13 Law Commission (1999) para 12.19.

14 Vogler (1991) p 144.

strategies. Vogler found that the Merseyside police 'flooded' the courts with defendants in the first week of the 1981 Liverpool 'riot':

> 'In these circumstances, the presumption regarding bail became reversed, and the major, most severe single punishment inflicted by the court became the custodial remand rather than the post-conviction sentence.'[15]

At a more obviously political level, the governments of the late 1980s and 1990s responded similarly to populist panics. We have seen that, most notably, the CJPO 1994, ss 25 and 26 altered bail law for high profile defendants. According to s 26, defendants charged with offences allegedly committed while on bail 'need not' be presumed to be entitled to bail. And s 25 banned bail for anyone charged with rape or homicide offences (or attempts) who had a previous conviction for such an offence. The fact that courts hardly needed reminding that such defendants (especially in the s 25 category) would need a particularly persuasive argument if they were to secure bail was irrelevant: appearing 'tough' was more important than human rights or matters of principle. Section 25 was amended by s 56 of the Crime and Disorder Act 1998 so that now in such cases there is a rebuttable presumption against bail. This was done in anticipation of s 25 falling foul of the ECHR, which it duly did.[16] Whether the amendment, which arguably violates the presumption of innocence because it places the burden of proof onto the defendant, will pass muster will depend on whether courts operate with a presumption of bail. As the Law Commission says: 'It is liable to be . . . applied in a way which would violate the Convention.'[17]

The Labour Home Secretary, Jack Straw, is no exception to the list of populist Home Secretaries who seek to have it all ways. In July 2000, two months before implementation of the HRA 1998, he announced plans to encourage magistrates to deny bail to more defendants falling into the s 26 category. The existing presumption in favour of granting bail to all defendants might need to be re-examined, he told the annual conference of the Association of Chief Police Officers.[18] His justification for this was the 'frustration' felt by police officers at seeing the 'prolific offenders' they catch being released on bail. Once more we see courts (and governments) being put at the service of what the *police* identify as problems and solutions.

15   Vogler (1991) p 143.
16   *CC v UK* [1999] Crim LR 228; *Caballero v UK* [2000] Crim LR 587. See P Leach, 'Automatic Denial of Bail and the European Convention' [1999] Crim LR 300.
17   Law Commission (1999) para 9.30. Note a similar warning regarding s 26: para 6.14.
18   *Daily Mail*, 6 July 2000.

Incorporation of the ECHR into English law is likely to have more effect through the operation of Art 5(5) than through changes to laws aimed at regulating the betes noires of bail bandits and second-time murderers. Article 5(5) gives everyone deprived of their Art 5 rights a right to compensation. The reluctance of British governments to accept liberal bail laws which are urged on them in the name of principle is likely to crumble very quickly if its stance becomes a financial liability. Nonetheless it is ironic that the effect of the ECHR will largely be confined to prompting changes to laws, like CJPO, ss 25 and 26, which have made little or no practical difference to bail rates and practices. The Convention will make absolutely no difference to those thousands of people remanded in custody each year under laws which conform to the ECHR but through court practices which in reality reverse the presumption of a right to bail.

5.   THE QUALITY AND FAIRNESS OF SUMMARY JUSTICE

When most people think of criminal prosecutions they think of jury trials. But only the Crown Court has jury trials. The most serious cases have what is assumed to be the best system, and the one that commands the most public support.[19] Leaving aside the issue of cost, the reason for magistrates' courts not having juries can therefore be only because *either* the nature of magistrates' court cases makes jury trial unsuitable; *or* the relative triviality of magistrates' court cases makes jury trial unnecessary. The former is untenable. As far as triviality is concerned we know that this is the *ideology* surrounding magistrates' work, but that it is not the reality. Consequently, we should strive to bring as many elements of judge-and-jury trial as is reasonably possible to the magistrates' courts. Doran and Glenn suggest that courts should embody three basic principles: fairness, efficiency, and accountability (including commanding public confidence).[20] These principles are central to our freedom perspective, and Crown Court trials satisfy these criteria, albeit imperfectly.[1] First, the jury embodies 'social' fairness (in terms of independent fact-finding and the application of societal morality) because it is made up of ordinary people without an institutional stake in 'either side' of the criminal justice system. Juries also

19   L Bridges, S Choongh and M McConville, Ethnic Minority Defendants and the Right to Elect Jury Trial (London: Commission for Racial Equality, 2000) A Sanders, The Future of Magistrates' Courts and the Magistracy in England and Wales (London: IPPR, 2000).

20   S Doran and R Glenn, Lay Involvement in Adjudication: Review of the Criminal Justice System in Northern Ireland (Criminal Justice Review Research Report no 11) (Belfast: SO, 2000).

1   See generally ch 9, where various exceptions and caveats to the points we make here are discussed.

embody fairness because they make decisions after group discussions and cannot find anyone guilty unless an overwhelming majority are in favour. The judge embodies 'legal' fairness in the sense of the dispassionate application of the rule of law. Judges explain the relevant law to juries, who then adjudicate between competing factual claims. Second, the jury commands public confidence and, by its existence, makes (a small part of) the criminal justice system accountable to the community. Finally, the judge's professionalism and knowledge assists efficiency. In this section we assess the extent to which magistrates and magistrates' courts give effect to these principles by being adequate substitutes for judge-and-jury trial. This is important, as there are around four times as many magistrates' court trials as there are Crown Court trials.

(a) The magistrates

For the last two to three hundred years, magistrates' courts have been largely presided over by lay magistrates. The exception has been Inner London, where stipendiary magistrates (full-time judges who have been practising lawyers or qualified court clerks) have traditionally heard a high proportion of cases. The AJA has now renamed stipendiaries 'District Judges (Magistrates Courts)' and we shall use both terms in the following analysis.

The complex separation of function and mixture of professional expertise and lay involvement in the Crown Court is in contrast with magistrates' courts proceedings. Questions of both law and fact are there decided upon by a bench of three (sometimes two) lay magistrates, or by a stipendiary magistrate sitting alone.[2] Lay magistrates rely upon the court clerk for legal advice. There are around 30,000 lay magistrates and 100 full time stipendiary magistrates, along with about 150 part-timers, based mainly in large urban centres.[3] Half of the stipendiaries are now based outside London, a 300% increase over the last 10 years. This means that a very substantial minority of cases in cities outside Inner London, and around half of cases in Inner London, are handled by stipendiaries. There is no differentiation between the work done by stipendiaries and that done by lay justices, except that the occasional very long trial is generally given to stipendiaries. Government policy has been to resist calls to allocate lay justices one type of work and stipendiaries another because of a belief that lay justices would

2   Building on earlier provisions, the Crime and Disorder Act, 1998, ss 49, 50 allows JPs sitting alone to make certain decisions, such as at EAHs (see section 3 above).
3   P Seago, C Walker and D Wall, 'The Development of the Professional Magistracy in England and Wales' [2000] Crim LR 631.

resent being deprived of the whole range of work.[4] The effect of this policy is that whether decisions on bail, guilt and sentencing are taken by a professional or by a group of amateurs is essentially a matter of chance. Should not some more principled basis for allocating cases be established?

Many common law based jurisdictions have lay justices. But there are few, if any, which give lay justices sentencing powers as extensive as exist in England and Wales.[5] In Scotland, for example, where lay justices in district courts handle one-third of all cases, lay justices have the power to imprison for up to 60 days, and they use this power sparingly. On the other hand, professional judges sitting alone are also rarely given the power that stipendiaries have here. Stipendiaries are now even allowed to sit alone in the youth court.[6] This is surprising because, even in jurisdictions where lay magistrates are little used, it is generally thought valuable to involve lay people and/or experts in child development as well as lawyers when dealing with young people.[7] At least, under 'referral orders', youth offender panels (which will have a varied membership) will do much of the sentencing work of the youth court, going some way towards ameliorating this development.[8]

How well do magistrates embody the three basic principles of fairness, efficiency, and accountability that we have identified? Anyone may apply to become a lay magistrate, but most people do not know that, and appointments are made on the recommendation of local advisory committees which are largely made up of local JPs. Even the magistrates association has described this committee system as 'a self-perpetuating oligarchy'.[9] Although the lay magistracy is now more representative of the community than it used to be, successive surveys of its membership shows that it remains predominantly white, middle aged and middle class.[10] A typical magistrate's response to this type of point was that: 'If a person's

4   See Seago et al [2000].

5   See, for a range of jurisdictions, Sir T Skyrme, *History of the Justices of the Peace* (Chichester: Barry Rose, 1994).

6   Crime and Disorder Act 1998, s 48; AJA 1999, Sch 11.

7   On Northern Ireland, see Doran and Glenn (2000); in Scotland most juvenile justice is diverted to 'Children's Hearings' which are quasi-judicial and include non-lawyers.

8   Youth Justice and Criminal Evidence Act 1999, s 1. There are dangers in the use of 'citizens' sentencing panels': see C Ball, 'A significant move towards restorative justice, or a recipe for unintended consequences?' [2000] Crim LR 211.

9   P Darbyshire, 'For the New Lord Chancellor: Some Causes for Concern About Magistrates' [1997] Crim LR 861.

10 For example, J Baldwin, 'The Social Composition of the Magistracy' (1975) 16 BJ Crim 171; E Burney *Magistrate, Court and Community* (London: Hutchinson, 1979); M King and C May, *Black Magistrates* (London: Cobden Trust, 1985); J Dignan and A Whynne, 'A Microcosm of the Local Community? Reflections on the Composition of the Magistracy in a Petty Sessional Division in the North Midlands' (1997) 37 BJ Crim 184.

still on the shop floor when they're of an age to be appointed then they probably haven't got what it takes to be a magistrate.'[11] Brown found that juvenile court magistrates in the late 1980s judged the families of the juveniles appearing before them by standards that were 'deeply gender and class biased.'[12] In a striking echo of what we know of the world-view of the police (discussed in ch 2, section 1(e)), she concluded that magistrates 'perceived themselves as representatives of the upright conscience. . . . The 'threat' of disorder posed by the judged to the judges, is a threat of all the other undisciplined young 'out there'.'[13] No wonder the defence solicitor quoted at the beginning of this chapter was concerned about clients not looking 'too flashy'.

Magistrates have an undue respect for, and trust in, authority. The typical view, expressed to Hucklesby regarding bail, was: 'I think for the protection of the public you've got to come down on the side of the CPS or the police who say "we want this person in custody".'[14] We saw in section 4 that in politically charged situations, in particular, magistrates effectively put themselves at the disposal of police and government. They value authority, and identify with other institutions (such as the police and CPS) which wield it. There may be a lack of understanding on the bench as to why a defendant might resist arrest, or refuse to answer police questions, dissemble or make a false confession. Magistrates may have standards of behaviour which are unrepresentative of the wider community and this may be of importance in applying the law. For example, in property offences the test for whether an action is dishonest is whether ordinary people would regard the act as dishonest and whether the defendant was aware that the act would be so regarded.[15] But magistrates are not representative of ordinary people. If charged with a crime of violence you can escape liability if you acted in reasonable self-defence. Views on what would be reasonable resistance if wrongfully arrested in the presence of one's family, friends or workmates might depend on whether one has ever experienced something similar. But magistrates have seldom had adversarial contacts with the police. Juries are less susceptible to these forms of unconscious class bias.

Not only are lay magistrates less representative than juries, they are also 'insiders'. Although lay justices are unpaid part-time volunteers, they are quite different from unprepared and predominantly once-in-a-lifetime jurors. Magistrates may be only lightly trained compared to professional judges, but they serve substantial apprenticeships. Most of them sit in court once-a-week, some sit twice a week, and all sit at least once a

11   Darbyshire [1997] 'For the New Lord Chancellor'.
12   S Brown, *Magistrates at Work* (Buckingham: Open UP, 1991) p 41.
13   Brown (1991) pp 112-3.
14   Hucklesby, 'Remand Decision Makers' [1997] p 276.
15   *Ghosh* [1982] 2 All ER 689.

The quality and fairness of summary justice

fortnight. These magistrates may be lay in the sense that they not legally qualified, but they are not untutored amateurs. By contrast, juries come fresh to the criminal courts, hear one or more cases, then leave again to return to their normal occupations. It must be difficult for magistrates to treat each case on its individual merits when they have heard the same stories countless times before. Moreover, every magistrates' court seems to have its fair share of 'regulars', defendants well known to the bench. When asked if magistrates' familiarity with the regulars was a problem, the Chief Executive of Nottingham magistrates' court replied:

> 'If your name is Bane or Pain in Nottingham, then you're notorious. Some of them have changed their name by deed poll. The Banes and the Pains provide a lot of work for this court and everybody knows them. If it's a problem at this court, the biggest Bench in the country, with over 450 justices, then it could be a problem anywhere.'[16]

So not only do magistrates (and their clerks) hear the same stories all the time, they hear them in relation to the same people. As one magistrate acknowledged to Darbyshire: 'Oh, yes. Whenever we see a certain solicitor we always know we've got Doris Day up before us and she always pleads not guilty.'[17] This level of familiarity must sometimes induce in defendants (or their solicitors) feelings of the 'que sera, sera' variety, as appears to have been the case in the following fatalistic exchange observed by McConville et al:

> Solicitor: 'I'll suggest conditional bail, I'll see. The Chairman's not bad but the clerk's a cow - you had her last time . . .'
> Client: 'If I get bail, I'll be surprised!'[18]

Particular problems may be faced by unrepresented defendants. The work of Carlen suggests that magistrates (and their clerks) have a greater interest in maintaining social control in their courtrooms than in giving free rein to defendants to challenge authority by contesting the prosecution version of events or by, for example, raising awkward questions about behind the scenes negotiations regarding bail or plea.[19]

16 Quoted by P Darbyshire, 'Previous Misconduct and Magistrates' Courts: Some Tales from the Real World' [1997] Crim LR 105 at p 107. Darbyshire is herself at pains to point out that she substituted fake names for the real ones given to her, and that any similarity to the names of real defendants at Nottingham is purely coincidental.
17 Darbyshire [1997] 'Previous Misconduct and Magistrates' Courts' at p 107. We assume this name was changed too.
18 McConville et al (1994) p 174.
19 P Carlen, 'Remedial Routines for the Maintenance of Control in Magistrates' Courts' (1974) 1 BJ Law & Soc 101 and P Carlen, *Magistrates' Justice* (London: Martin Robertson, 1976).

Further, since juries are 'outsiders', lawyers have to explain things in everyday language in Crown Court trials, ensuring that justice is public in substance as well as in form, and giving defendants, victims and others a fair chance of understanding what is going on. Because magistrates are 'insiders', none of this is true. Defendants are often bewildered by magistrates' courts hearings.[20]

On the test of 'social fairness', lay magistrates are clearly a poor substitute for the jury. But stipendiaries are even less satisfactory. If we need juries to bring the world of social fairness into the Crown Court because judges are professionally and socially elite then the same applies when a district judge (magistrates' court) presides. At least a bench of lay magistrates is likely to have one person under 40 and/or one person with an average income. In areas with a large ethnic minority population, ethnic minorities are represented too, although not proportionately to their population. None of this is true of stipendiaries. Further, lay justices make most of their decisions in panels of three after group discussion, unlike lone stipendiaries.

Nor do magistrates serve to make the criminal justice system accountable to the community in the way that juries do. They are insufficiently representative of the communities they supposedly serve to be able to fulfil this function. It is true that lay magistrates stress their 'local' character, but it is not clear why 'localness' should be a virtue of justice.[1] In any case, few magistrates live in the same locales as prosecuted offenders. What is true of lay justices regarding accountability is even more true of stipendiaries, who often do not even have the dubious virtue of being 'local'.

On the test of 'legal fairness' and efficiency, stipendiaries are doubtless a good substitute for Crown Court judges, but lay magistrates are, by definition, not legally qualified. Their clerks are supposed to make up for their deficit, in the same way that judges advise juries on the relevant law. But stipendiaries are, as one would expect, much more efficient than are lay justices if we define 'efficient' as 'quick'.[2] They are also thought to adjourn cases less readily, to stand up more robustly to prosecution and defence lawyers alike, and to be better at case management.[3]

In conclusion, it seems undeniable that magistrates are a poor substitute for judge-and-jury.[4] This will be a particularly acute problem if, as is likely,

20   Carlen (1976); McBarnet (1983).
1   Seago et al [2000] Crim LR 631.
2   Seago et al [2000] Table 4.
3   See the Home Office (1997) Narey Report.
4   See Z Bankowski, N Hutton, and J McManus *Lay Justice?* (Edinburgh: Clark, 1987) ch 9 for a discussion of the analogy between juries and lay magistrates. This is also a good discussion of the Scottish system. Note that we are talking in terms of judge-and-*jury*, and *trials*, rather than the whole range of court

the defendant's right to choose jury trial in 'either way' cases is removed (see subsection (c) below). Magistrates' court trials embody two (fairness and accountability) of the three basic principles far less well than do Crown Court trials. However, lay justices embody these principles better than do stipendiaries. Yet we are seeing more work being done by stipendiaries, rather than less. The 'efficiency' principle is implicitly being prioritised over the principles of fairness and accountability: a move away from 'freedom' towards 'crime control'. Short of introducing jury trial into magistrates' court - a utopian idea in view of current moves to reduce the use of juries - what can be done?

It has been suggested that there is no need for lay magistrates' involvement in the most minor guilty pleas. Stipendiaries could handle these. For contested cases and cases of medium-seriousness, a stipendiary could sit with two lay justices.[5] This would mean much less need for lay justices than now and less need for training on their part as they would sit with a judge. Lay justices could therefore be drawn from a wider cross section of the community than now, perhaps sitting only a handful of times per year, for a limited term of, say, five years. They would have fewer 'insider' characteristics than lay justices do currently. In this way they could be a better jury-substitute than now. It is possible that lay 'wingers' could be overawed by a professional judge, but mixed panels of this kind are common in European criminal systems, and wingers are, though marginal to some extent, by no means uninfluential.[6] Any objection to the mixed panel idea on the basis that it represents some dangerous foreign device that could never take root in domestic soil can easily be countered. Mixed panels already exist within our system. As we shall detail in ch 10, section 2(a), convicted persons who appeal to the Crown Court are entitled to a complete rehearing before a professional judge flanked by lay magistrates. Unfortunately, they have been so neglected in the criminal justice literature that we have little idea how they work.

This is something that could be looked at by Auld LJ, who has been tasked by the Home Secretary with carrying out a condensed inquiry into the criminal justice system.[7] Whether it will grasp this democratic nettle

proceedings, because juries are not involved in Crown Court sentencing. It is not obvious that they should be left out. If the 'community' element embodied in lay justices is thought valuable for sentencing in magistrates' courts, why not similarly involve juries in the Crown Court? See Sanders (2000).

5   P Darbyshire 'An Essay on the Importance and Neglect of the Magistracy' (1997) Crim LR 627; Association of Justices Chief Executives and Justices Clerks Society, Criminal Courts Review: Response to LJ Auld (July 2000) (unpublished); Sanders (2000).

6   Darbyshire 'An Essay on the Importance and Neglect of the Magistracy' [1997]; Doran and Glenn (2000); Sanders (2000).

7   M Zander, 'What on Earth is Lord Justice Auld Supposed to Do?' [2000] Crim LR 419.

remains to be seen. In the meantime defendants will continue to have their fates decided by either a trio of 'half-baked professionals'[8] or a lone professional at the bottom of the judicial hierarchy.

(b) Acquittals and convictions

Many defendants do not expect justice to be done in the magistrates' court. Typically, they regard the Crown Court as fairer and more thorough in its approach and offering a better chance of acquittal. By contrast, magistrates' courts are seen as amateurish and pro-police, but speedier and offering the prospect of a more lenient sentence.[9] There is evidence to suggest that their perceptions are accurate.[10] Vennard's study of contested cases in the magistrates' courts found that there was a tendency for magistrates to accept the accuracy of police eye witness evidence and their interpretation of events as against the defendant's denial of the alleged conduct or a claim that the act did not constitute a crime. This is consistent with what we know of contested bail applications, discussed in section 4 above, where they generally prefer to believe the police and CPS rather than the defence, turning the burden of proof on its head. Vennard found that, even where defendants' credibility was not directly impugned and there was no confession the majority of cases ended in conviction.[11] A further study by Vennard concluded that for contested either way cases, the chances of acquittal were substantially higher in the Crown Court (57%) than in the magistrates' courts (30%).[12] More recent research, by Bridges et al (discussed in subsection (c) below) lends support to the belief that, case-for-case, acquittal is far less likely in the magistrates' courts than in the Crown Court.

We might hope that times have changed since 1974, when the chairman of the bench said in one case: 'My principle in such cases [when the evidence of a police officer and a citizen conflicts] has always been to believe the

8   Burney (1979) p 216.
9   See Bottoms and McClean (1976) pp 87-100; J Gregory, Crown Court or Magistrates' Court? (Office of Population Censuses and Surveys) (London: HMSO, 1976) and D Riley and J Vennard, Triable-Either-Way Cases: Crown Court or Magistrates' Court? (Home Office Research Study, no 98) (London: HMSO, 1988) pp 16-18.
10 On sentencing, see ch 7.
11 J Vennard, Contested Trials in Magistrates' Courts (Home Office Research Study no 71) (London: HMSO, 1981) p 21.
12 J Vennard, 'The Outcome of Contested Trials' in D Moxon (ed), *Managing Criminal Justice* (London: HMSO, 1985). A Ashworth, 'Plea, Venue and Discontinuance' [1993] Crim LR 830, who does not cite the Vennard (1981) study, argues for caution in interpreting this finding.

evidence of the police officer ...'[13] But neither Darbyshire nor the research we have cited gives us reason to believe this. Darbyshire comments: 'Magistrates astonished me by supporting this statement in recent conversations.'[14] This helps to explain the lower acquittal rate in magistrates' courts than in the Crown Court that we observed at the start of this chapter. The high success rate of appeal to the Crown Court is further evidence of poor decision-making in the magistrates' courts, as we argue in detail in ch 10, section 2(a).

There are a number of possible explanations for the higher acquittal rate in the Crown Court. The first is that the magistracy and juries are, as we have seen, very different. We might expect case hardened 'insiders' with little experience of the conditions to which many defendants are subjected to be sceptical of what defendants say and to be over-ready to believe the police. A defence solicitor made this telling remark:

'We sometimes wonder [at the magistrates' court] who has to prove guilt or innocence. Certainly, sometimes I've felt that I'm the one who's having to do all the work - whereas really it should be the prosecution who are proving all the elements, rather than the defence having to disprove the elements of the offence.'[15]

The second is simply numerical. At the Crown Court, the prosecution has to convince at least 10 out of the 12 jurors that the defendant is guilty.[16] In the magistrates' court, it is enough to convince two out of the three lay magistrates, or even just one stipendiary magistrate. As one defendant recently put it:

' . . . when you go to a magistrates' court, there is only one thing - you are guilty . . . at the Crown Court, you've got a better chance because you've got 12 people and at the magistrates' court, you've got either one or three people to decide.'[17]

Finally, the procedures in the lower courts place defendants at a distinct disadvantage. The prosecution need not disclose its case in advance to

13 *Bingham Justices, ex p Jowitt* (1974) Times, 3 July.

14 Darbyshire [1997] 'For the New Lord Chancellor'.

15 T Bucke, R Street and D Brown, The right of silence: the impact of the Criminal Justice and Public Order Act 1994 (Home Office Research Study no 199) (London: Home Office, 2000) p 47. See also McConville et al (1994) pp 226-27.

16 Until 1967 the jury's decision had to be unanimous. Now, under the Criminal Justice Act 1967, s 13(3), the court is not supposed to consider the possibility of a majority verdict until at least two hours have elapsed since the jury retired.

17 Quoted by L Bridges 'Taking Liberties' (2000) Legal Action, July, 6 at p 8.

defendants charged with summary offences[18] and legal aid is less freely available than in the Crown Court. Furthermore, magistrates, unlike jurors, are privy to much inadmissible evidence. This is because the admissibility of evidence is a question of law which can be decided by the judge in the absence of the jury in the Crown Court. Magistrates, by contrast, determine both questions of fact and law. Even if they decide, for example, that a disputed confession is inadmissible, they may still be prejudiced by the knowledge that an alleged confession exists.[19] For this reason this procedure could fall foul of Art 6 ECHR. A 'mixed panel' system, such as that suggested earlier, could ameliorate this problem, as the professional chair could hear the legal arguments in the absence of the lay 'wingers'. There is also some evidence that justices' clerks may occasionally, whether in private or in whispers, transmit opinions, prejudices and hearsay information to magistrates.[20] Magistrates' courts are also less accountable in that their proceedings are not recorded in full. If the defence wish to appeal on a point of law to the Divisional Court the magistrates draw up a statement of the facts, the cases cited and their decision. This gives justices' clerks ample opportunity to cover their tracks.[1]

In its drive to increase 'efficiency', the government has implemented several 'Narey reforms' aimed at reducing delay. These include 'early administrative hearings' (EAHs) (see section 3 above) and 'early first hearings' (EFH). Under the EFH 'fast-track' procedure for anticipated guilty pleas in 'simple' cases, hearings are intended to be within 24 hours of charge where possible,[2] and magistrates are encouraged to sentence immediately. It follows that applications to adjourn are viewed negatively, even though many defendants will arrive without having had legal advice, and advance information (disclosure) from the prosecution will not have occurred.[3] Court duty solicitors are available, but have little time to take instructions, and will not be able to see every one due to appear in a session. 'Lay presenters'

18 See D Sunman, 'Advancing Disclosure: Can the Rules for Advance Information in the Magistrates' Courts be Improved?' [1998] Crim LR 798 at 800. Only once a defendant has pleaded not guilty does the Criminal Procedure and Investigations Act 1996 require the prosecutor to make 'primary disclosure'. For an account of the complexities involved here see Sprack (2000) (London: Blackstone, 2000) pp 132-33.
19 See further M Wasik, 'Magistrates: Knowledge of Previous Convictions' [1996] Crim LR 851. A similar problem exists in relation to the Diplock Courts of Northern Ireland, in which a professional judge determines the case without a jury: J Jackson and S Doran, *Judge Without Jury* (Oxford: Clarendon, 1995) pp 243-250. Diplock courts are discussed further in ch 10, section 6.
20 See H McLaughlin, 'Court Clerks: Advisers or Decision-Makers' (1990) 30 BJ Crim 358 at 364.
1   For fuller discussion see I A Heaton-Armstrong, 'The Verdict of the Court ... and its Clerk?' (1986) 150 JP 340, 342, 357-359.
2   As required by s 46 of the Crime and Disorder Act 1998.
3   See Sunman [1998].

appear for the CPS.[4] This means that in some cases there will be not a single qualified lawyer in the court room to ensure that justice is done. To structure proceedings so that the police and CPS decide whether cases are, from the defendant's point of view, contestable, complex or far reaching in their consequences undermines the presumption of innocence.[5] This managerialism gone mad is completely incompatible with the freedom approach.

(c) Mode of trial

In 'either way' cases adult defendants have (at the time of writing) the 'right' to elect a jury trial in the Crown Court. Youths have no such right; they are prosecuted in the youth court, which is essentially the magistrates' court in (supposedly) more paternalistic guise.[6] Although little remarked upon in the literature, this is actually a major restriction on trial by jury. Close to 50,000 'youths' were sentenced for non-summary offences in 1998.[7] Vast numbers of citizens enter 'adulthood' with convictions for such serious offences as theft or fairly serious violence, without ever having had the chance to contest their guilt before the 'community' as embodied by the jury. And by 'youths' we should remember that we are talking about those aged 17 and under. In 1998 nearly 40,000 persons aged between 15 and 17 (inclusive) were convicted in the youth court of non-summary criminal offences.[8] One can have sex and get married at 16, drive a car at 17, yet not be entitled to what is generally regarded as a superior form of justice until 18. Even those aged 18 can find themselves tried and convicted in a youth court so long as the court had considered the mode of trial issue at a point in the proceedings when they were still 17.[9] Youth Court is often thought of as a liberal measure, deigned to spare 'kids' the trauma of a judicial setting designed for adults. But it also results in young adults being funnelled into the conviction sausage-machine that is the magistrates' court. Once convicted, they can be committed to the Crown Court for sentence if the magistrates consider their sentencing powers to be inadequate. This was the fate of 800 'youths' in 1998.[10] So young adults

4   Crime and Disorder Act 1998, s 53.
5   L Bridges, 'False starts and unrealistic expectations' (1999) Legal Action, 6 October, p 6.
6   As noted in section 1, 'youths' can only be tried in the Crown Court if charged with a grave crime, or if they are to be co-tried with adult defendants.
7   This estimate is based on Home Office (2000) Tables 7.8-7.10.
8   This estimate is based on Home Office (2000) Table 7.10.
9   For a recent example, see *West London Justices, ex p Siley-Winditt* (DC, 13 July 2000, unreported).
10 Home Office (2000) Table 6.7.

can get justice for kids and sentencing for adults. This puts the supposed liberality of the youth court mechanism in a rather different light. We will have more to say about the power of magistrates to commit for sentence below.

Not surprisingly, in view of our discussion in the preceding subsection, many adults exercise their right to trial by jury if they intend pleading not guilty. Adults intending to plead guilty usually prefer to stay in the magistrates' court as its sentencing powers are restricted to six months' prison. This is not such a restriction as it might seem as magistrates can, as with youths, send the case to the Crown Court for sentencing following a conviction regardless of the defendant's wishes. Sometimes adult defendants want to plead not guilty in the magistrates' court but are prevented from doing so by the magistrates declining jurisdiction and committing the case for Crown Court trial. In these circumstances, the 'right' to jury trial becomes almost a duty (which can only be escaped by pleading guilty on arrival in the Crown Court). The magistrates used also to have the power to decline jurisdiction even in cases where an adult defendant was minded to plead guilty, although this has recently changed as we discuss below.

Hedderman and Moxon found that the perception that the Crown Court offered a fairer hearing even influenced some adult defendants who were not planning to contest their cases. Just over a quarter of defendants in their study who elected Crown Court trial did so intending to plead guilty.[11] Hedderman and Moxon also discovered that a majority of defendants who elected Crown Court trial (including some of those who intended to plead guilty), together with over a third of the solicitors interviewed, were apparently labouring under the false impression that Crown Court judges imposed lighter sentences than magistrates.[12]

The proportion of either way cases committed to the Crown Court has grown in recent years and this has led to increased costs for the courts, the CPS, the probation service, the legal aid fund and the prison system. It has also been a major factor in fuelling prison overcrowding, both because defendants remanded in custody have longer to wait if committed to the

---

11 C Hedderman and D Moxon, Magistrates' Court or Crown Court?: Mode of Trial Decisions and Sentencing (Home Office Research Study, no 125) (London: HMSO, 1992) p 23.

12 Hedderman and Moxon (1992) p 20. This finding departs from the pattern found by other studies. Whether this should be taken as evidence of a widespread misconception of recent origin about sentencing patterns or rather attributed to a methodological flaw in the way in which comparisons were made between sentencing at the two levels of court is not clear. See further L Bridges, 'The Right to Jury Trial: How the Royal Commission Got it Wrong' (1993) 143 NLJ 1542 and Bridges (2000) 'Taking Liberties'.

Crown Court,[13] and because Crown Court judges make much more use of custodial sentences than do magistrates.[14]

On the face of it, there appear to be two types of Crown Court adult defendant in either way cases. There are the defendants who plead guilty in the Crown Court and who could have been dealt with identically (but more quickly and cheaply) in the magistrates' courts. And there are the defendants who opt for the Crown Court because they think they are more likely to be acquitted. From a freedom perspective the option chosen by the latter group of defendants is perfectly understandable, whereas the former group's preferences are more questionable. For the crime control adherent, however, defendants who are acquitted in the Crown Court are seen to have cheated the system, whereas either way defendants who are convicted (whether following a contested trial or not) are perceived to have wasted the time and money that would have been saved had they stayed in the lower courts. Various attempts underpinned by these crime control assumptions have been made to restrict the flow of cases committed from the magistrates' courts. Unfortunately these attempts have not separated out the different reasons for opting for the Crown Court and so have ended up penalising those who wish to plead not guilty before a jury as well as the committed guilty pleaders.

The crudest way of reducing the numbers of Crown Court cases of all kinds is simply to reclassify either way offences as summary only. Thus, s 15 of the Criminal Law Act 1977 made a number of public order offences and drink-driving offences purely summary. Similarly, the Criminal Justice Act 1988 (ss 37 and 39) reclassified the offences of taking a motor vehicle, driving whilst disqualified and common assault as summary offences. A more subtle approach has been to encourage magistrates to accept jurisdiction in a higher proportion of cases, and to exhort CPS lawyers to suggest this to them, most notably through 'mode of trial guidelines'.[15] This has not been a successful strategy. In 1998 72% of triable either way cases tried at the Crown Court were committed because magistrates declined jurisdiction, rather than because defendants elected to be tried at that court, a proportion that has increased steadily from 63% in 1992.[16]

Another strategy has been to encourage the charging of offences which are summary only in preference to those that are triable either way. 'Charging standards', introduced in 1994 following agreement by the police and CPS, set out principles and lists of physical harms to guide decisions

---

13   See Morgan and Jones (1992) p 38.
14   See Hedderman and Moxon (1992) p 37.
15   The 1995 guidelines are reproduced in M Wasik, T Gibbons and M Redmayne, Criminal Justice (London: Longman, 1999) pp 368-69. Also see S White, 'The Antecedents of the Mode of Trial Guidelines' [1996] Crim LR 471.
16   Home Office (2000) p 133.

about which charge to bring in offences of violence.[17] While such standards have been welcomed as a step towards achieving consistency, they also have effectively broadened the band of criminal behaviour that can fall within the summary only offences.[18] Moreover, the CPS is frequently accused of charging summary offences instead of either way offences (eg minor assaults instead of s 47 assaults), or even altering the charges to this effect once the case is under way, to keep the case in the magistrates' courts, thus depriving defendants of a Crown Court trial.[19]

Since 1997, adult defendants have had to indicate their plea before the trial court is decided. If they indicate a guilty plea in an 'either way' case, the magistrates have to deal with it themselves.[20] While these measures have led to a drop in the numbers of cases sent to the Crown Court for trial by magistrates, this is more than compensated for by a sharp rise in the numbers sent to the Crown Court for sentence.[1] Nonetheless, there are likely to have been some cost savings as Crown Court contested trials are far more expensive than Crown Court sentencing proceedings. On the other hand, the plea before venue procedure, by advancing the moment at which defendants are asked to indicate their plea, has increased the pressure to plead guilty. This is because the sentence discount principle (discussed in ch 7) works by offering the greatest discounts to those that plead guilty at the earliest opportunity.

We should note that these crime control approaches are frequently at odds with the wishes, and sometimes the interests, of victims. Many victims, especially of sexual offences, seek charges, procedures and sentences that fit what they believe to be the seriousness of the crime.[2]

The Runciman Commission also advocated the keeping of more cases in the magistrates' court, but by an even more radical step than those we have already documented. It argued that current procedures waste resources. This contention was based on Hedderman and Moxon's finding that, whilst the majority of those electing Crown Court trial did so in the expectation of a fairer trial, the great bulk of them (82% it believed) ended up pleading guilty anyway. It recommended that defendants should no longer enjoy the right to elect trial by jury. In either way cases where the

17 See now Crown Prosecution Service, Offences Against the Person Charging Standard Agreed by the Police and Crown Prosecution Service (London: CPS, 1996).
18 For discussion see A Ashworth and J Fionda, 'The New Code for Crown Prosecutors: Prosecution, Accountability and the Public Interest' [1994] Crim LR 894.
19 See discussion by A Ashworth, The Criminal Process 2nd edn (Oxford: OUP, 1998) pp 250-55.
20 See Criminal Procedure and Investigations Act 1996 s 49 for this 'plea before venue' procedure.
1   Bridges (1999).
2   See H Fenwick, 'Charge Bargaining and Sentence Discount: the Victim's Perspective' (1997) 5 Int R Victimology 23.

The quality and fairness of summary justice

prosecution and defence could not agree on the appropriate venue for trial, the decision should be left to the magistrates alone. Its declared motive for making this controversial recommendation was that the savings produced by keeping more cases in the magistrates' courts 'would enable more resources to be devoted to ensuring that the more serious cases going to the Crown Court are not only better prepared but more quickly heard.'[3] The cynic might reply that any resources saved might just as easily be devoted to funding fuel tax cuts or bailing out the Millennium Dome or some other pet project. A principled, rather than cynical, response came from Tony Blair, the Labour Shadow Home Secretary, who said in 1993:

'We disagree with the curtailment of the right to a jury trial . . . It is totally unsatisfactory to leave the decision on the right to a jury trial to magistrates . . . Fundamental rights to justice cannot be driven by administrative convenience. If we are to speed up and improve court efficiency, there are better ways to do it.'[4]

Yet in 1999 the (now) Labour Government, headed by the same Tony Blair, introduced a Bill into the House of Lords to enact Runciman's recommendations.[5] It was lost because there was so much opposition to it. Undaunted, the government re-introduced it into the House of Commons in 2000 but was defeated for the second time by the House of Lords.[6] Even if we could be sure that any savings obtained by abolishing the right to elect jury trial were applied to improve the quality of justice in the Crown Court, the strategy of allocating more cases to the magistrates' courts remains questionable. The Runciman Commission was well aware of the evidence that the chances of acquittal are better for defendants in the Crown Court, but said:

'We do not think that defendants should be able to choose their court of trial solely on the basis that they think that they will get a fairer hearing at one level than the other. Magistrates' courts conduct over 93% of all criminal cases and should be trusted to try cases fairly.'[7]

3 Royal Commission on Criminal Justice, Report (Cm 2263) (London: HMSO, 1993) p 88.
4 *The Guardian,* 7 July 1993.
5 We apologise for succumbing to the temptation to erect and dismantle this particular man of straw.
6 Criminal Justice (Mode of Trial) Bill 2000. The Government has indicated that it will try again in the event that the Labour Party win the next election.
7 Royal Commission on Criminal Justice, Report (Cm 2263) (London: HMSO, 1993) p 88.

Since the Runciman Commission failed to commission any research on magistrates' courts (despite the fact that they conduct over 93% of all criminal cases) it is unclear why we should trust magistrates to try cases fairly. The evidence which we have examined suggests that we should not.

The Runciman Commission also overlooked the fact that Hedderman and Moxon's study was of convicted defendants only and that, since just under half of those pleading not guilty in the Crown Court are eventually acquitted, their figures significantly understate the number of defendants who maintain not guilty pleas following election.[8] None the less, it is clearly the case that substantial numbers of defendants do change their plea to guilty following committal. This, however, leads to another criticism of the Runciman Commission. Instead of regarding extensive plea changing as a puzzling phenomenon to be explored, it took the view that 'the facts speak for themselves'[9] and that there was self-evidently a waste of resources that ought to be eliminated. But unless we understand why plea changing occurs, we cannot rationally decide what the appropriate response should be.[10] The Government has similarly, and equally wilfully, buried its head in the sand. It seems that no official body wants to countenance the possibility that it is not defendants who are abusing the system, but the system that is abusing defendants.[11]

Finally, one might criticise the Runciman Commission for concentrating its fire on the wrong target. Since most either way cases are committed at the direction of magistrates rather than on an election by a defendant,[12] why did not the Runciman Commission recommend (or even give some thought to the possibility) that in either way cases it should be solely the right of the defendant to choose the venue for trial? Of course one can enter into lengthy discussions about whether such a choice deserves the status of a 'right'.[13] Certainly it is not a human right, as the ECHR focuses on the right to a fair trial (Art 6) rather than stipulating the composition of the tribunal that must provide this. It has become fashionable to point to other jurisdictions, such as Scotland, which do not give defendants any right to choose their trial venue. Duff does this, noting that 'this has not caused any controversy or problems.' In an eerie echo of the Runciman Commission's complacent comment about magistrates' courts, he says of the proposal to give magistrates the power to determine where either way

8   Hedderman and Moxon (1992) p 11. A point made also by Bridges (1993).
9   Here, we are quoting Michael Zander, a member of the Royal Commission, giving a presentation at the British Society of Criminology Conference held in Cardiff on 29 July 1993.
10   For our analysis of the main reasons for changes of plea see ch 7.
11   See ch 7 and Bridges (2000) 'Taking Liberties'.
12   See, for example, the figures reproduced by Bridges (1999).
13   See the discussion by A Ashworth, *The Criminal Process* 2nd edn (Oxford: OUP, 1998) pp 257-58.

cases should be heard that 'there is no reason to suspect that the courts cannot be trusted to fulfil this role in a just manner.'[14] As we have shown in this chapter, there is in fact every reason to suspect this. Duff also fails to give sufficient weight to the fact that cases which are ordered to remain in the lower courts in Scotland remain there for sentencing too.[15] In other words defendants kept in the lower courts of Scotland for trial are not at risk of lengthy sentences of imprisonment. That might explain why there has been no 'controversy' about mode of trial decisions north of the border.[16]

By contrast, in England and Wales, if the Mode of Trial Bill is enacted, the State will have it both ways. Adult defendants will be deprived of the right to choose trial venue, but the State will not be deprived of the right to send defendants to the Crown Court for sentencing following conviction in the magistrates' court. Cases which are deemed to be insufficiently serious to warrant jury trial can nonetheless be deemed too serious to be sentenced by magistrates. If the right of defendants to Crown Court trial in either way cases is lost, not only should the right of the state to Crown Court sentencing in cases tried summarily be lost, but jury-like characteristics must be introduced into the magistrates' court process (see subsection (a) above).

More fundamentally, there is no need to erode further the due process right of defendants charged with either way offences to elect trial by jury in order to relieve pressure on the Crown Court. For if magistrates lost their power to commit cases to the Crown Court for sentence, many more defendants might voluntarily elect for trial in the lower courts,[17] especially if the fairness of those trials was enhanced. Removing the right of magistrates to decline jurisdiction in either way cases would also relieve much pressure on the Crown Court. The suspicion must be that the Government's attempt to abolish the right to elect jury trial is motivated by other concerns, such as increasing the rates of guilty pleas and convictions, almost regardless of whether this is justified by the strength of the prosecution evidence.

14   P Duff, 'The Defendant's Right to Trial by Jury: A Neighbour's View' [2000] Crim LR 85 at p 94.

15   This point was made in a letter by L Bridges [2000] Crim LR 512 in response to Duff [2000].

16   It is, in any case, naive to infer from a lack of controversy that all is well. For example, other jurisdictions often have much less well developed empirical and critical research traditions than exist in England and Wales and, in consequence, much injustice may remain undetected and politically invisible.

17   See Legal Action Group, Preventing Miscarriages of Justice (London: LAG Education and Service Trust Ltd, 1993) p 5.

Research by Bridges et al in the mid/late 1990s fills some of the gaps left by the 'Royal Omission on Criminal Justice'.[18] They looked at the reasons for electing jury trial in a sample of defendants. They found that the defendants fell into two main groups. First, there were those that denied the charges, pleaded not guilty and were either tried by a jury or had the case dropped. Second, were defendants who contested one or more of the (often several) charges against them or the seriousness of the charge(s). Most of this group pleaded guilty to lesser charges when these were offered by the prosecution, or contested the charges they disagreed with. In most cases in the second group the 'deals' could have been done without going to the Crown Court, but it was the unwillingness of the CPS, not the defence, to alter its position that led to the unnecessary Crown Court appearances. Often, it was only moving 'up' to a court with a 'proper' judge (and, perhaps, having to instruct an independent barrister to prosecute) that prompted the CPS to scrutinise its case sufficiently to let itself 'deal'. In many of these cases, it must be remembered, pressure to drop or reduce charges comes from the judge who has read the committal papers, so this is not simply a matter of the CPS having no stomach for a fight. If the Mode of Trial Bill is enacted, taking away the defendant's right to a Crown Court trial, it is not just the chances of acquittal that will be reduced for many defendants, but the pressure to negotiate. Who knows what would have happened if the cases in which the CPS dropped or reduced charges had gone to trial before less independently minded magistrates? When Bridges et al looked at the cases in their sample which were tried in the magistrates' court they found that only one (out of 14) ended in acquittal.[19]

The loss of the right to choose Crown Court trial will not impact evenly across all types of adult defendant. Cases with ethnic minority defendants are disproportionately discontinued, dismissed and acquitted. This makes up, to some extent, for their disproportionate presence in the stop-search, arrest and charge statistics. It seems that when the CPS, juries and (to a lesser extent) magistrates are put to the test, they see the flaws in many weak cases and act accordingly. This benefits ethnic minority defendants, the prosecution cases against whom are disproportionately weak.[20] What Bridges et al show is that, much of the time, it is election for Crown Court trial that puts the rest of the criminal justice system to the test. Keeping

18 The joke is by Darbyshire [1997] 'An Essay on the Importance and Neglect of the Magistracy'.
19 Bridges et al (2000). Summarised in Bridges (2000) 'Taking Liberties'. This work will provide a useful starting point for the larger-scale investigation into the treatment of ethnic minority defendants that the Lord Chancellor's Department has funded the Oxford Centre for Criminological Research to carry out. That this funding has been provided indicates that not all parts of the Government are insensitive to this issue.
20 Phillips and Brown (1998).

cases in the magistrates' courts will reduce the ability of the defence to put pressure on the CPS, and this will have a disproportionately adverse impact on ethnic minority defendants. In contrast to the theoretically weak and empirically duff arguments advanced in support of the Mode of Trial Bill, Bridges' conclusions are compelling and chilling:

'There comes a point when the constant repetition of half-truths and the refusal to acknowledge or engage with contrary evidence becomes a lie; and when turning a blind eye to the effects of policies in sustaining patterns of discrimination in the criminal justice system, and undermining ethnic minorities' rights to defend themselves against such practice through legitimate channels, itself becomes racist. The government, in its relentless pursuit of the Mode of Trial Bill, is close to reaching both of these points.'[1]

6. CONCLUSION

It is no exaggeration to say that magistrates' courts are crime control courts overlaid with a thin layer of due process icing. At every twist and turn in the process, defendants are saddled with handicaps which undermine their willingness or ability to stand on their rights in court. Some are denied legal aid, some are denied bail and a majority do not receive proper assistance and advice from their legal advisers. Some will not receive advance disclosure of the prosecution case and many more will receive inadequate or misleading disclosure.[2] Some defendants will be offered tempting oven-ready deals prepared by prosecutors and served up by legal advisers.[3] Many adult defendants will be told that longer delays and a higher sentence can be expected if they elect trial by jury but that the prospects of acquittal before the magistrates are bleak. Many will already know this from previous experience. Youths who would like to contest their guilt before a jury have no choice but to lump magistrates' court trial.

For defendants, the process must seem like an obstacle course which presents formidable impediments to them continuing to maintain their innocence. Meanwhile managerialist reforms hurry and harry the defendant on to the ever-more smooth path of least resistance, the guilty plea. Some will end up pleading guilty to crimes they did not commit, others will plead guilty to crimes that the prosecution could not have proved beyond reasonable doubt and still others will be found guilty in either or both of these situations.

1   Bridges [2000] p 8.
2   For a discussion of inadequate disclosure see ch 6, section (c)(iii).
3   See ch 7.

These miscarriages of justice are not the stuff of headline news. The possibility that innocent people will plead guilty is even now little recognised and excites little concern. Appreciation of the role that more due process could play in protecting us against the abuse of police and prosecutorial power is very limited, but this is to be expected. For it tends to be marginalised groups (black people, the unemployed and the poor) who suffer most from whatever abuse of power takes place. It is easy for the rest of us to turn a blind eye to this as we gratefully focus instead on the high conviction rate that our courts achieve in seeking to repress crime on our behalf.

This is all done in the name of 'efficiency'. Efficiency is consistent with the freedom perspective, but not at any cost. The cost appears small because these low-profile courts appear to deal with trivia. But in reality they deal with a vast amount of serious issues.[4] The processes and sentencing outcomes in many cases are enormously intrusive, yet most adjudication is done by either a bench of case-hardened lay magistrates or a similarly case-hardened lone professional judge - chosen, in any one case, at random. Doris Day, and other 'regular' defendants, will continue to be caught between an all too familiar rock and a hard place, with diminishing prospects of being allowed to take their case before a jury. One might have hoped that a government boastful of having brought ECHR 'rights home' would have sought to bolster the fairness of trial by magistrates, especially in view of its desire to keep more cases in these courts. Instead, it has combined an attack on trial by jury with a programme of managerial reforms that have reduced the jury-like qualities of the magistracy. We are told by the Government that with rights come responsibilities. It seems that it is less interested in the right to a fair trial than it is in the responsibility of defendants to plead guilty and the responsibility of magistrates' courts to convict.

Conclusion

4   Darbyshire [1997] 'An Essay on the Importance and Neglect of the Magistracy'.

Chapter 9

Trial by judge and jury

Trials by jury can be sharply contested affairs in which the case construction techniques used at earlier stages of the criminal process (see chs 1-6) are exposed to 12 members of the public. These dozen jurors have to choose who to believe, and their choice may depend to a large extent on their backgrounds and prior experiences, as well as the mores, prejudices and panics of the wider society in which they live. Sometimes it comes down to little more than whether people have faith in the police or not. What, for example, do you make of the following cross-examination concerning the initial encounter between the police and the defendant which led to his arrest?:

Prosecutor: 'You agree that you were talking loudly?'

Defendant: 'I was not talking loud. I couldn't have been because I knew that it was late.'

Prosecutor: 'You were talking at the top of your voice and one of the officers asked you to lower your voice, did he not and you replied "I haven't fucking done anything".'

Defendant: 'One asked me to lower my voice but I didn't say that. I must have said something similar but I am sure I didn't use the word "fucking"'.

Prosecutor: 'You signed the written statement of the interview you had with the police at the police station, did you not' [the prosecutor read it out. The word "fucking" was abbreviated thus: F]?'

Defendant: 'The police must have added "F" to suit themselves.'

Prosecutor: 'Two officers could not have been lying about you talking very loudly when people were trying to get some sleep and being abusive when you were asked to lower your voice. They were on duty keeping the peace. Why would they tell lies about your behaviour on that morning?'

Defendant: 'It is not impossible, after all they are mates.'[1]

Citizens with little adversarial contact with the police may find the defendant's story incredible. Those drawn from 'suspect communities' (or who happen to have read this book) may be less sure. The *second* most distinctive feature about trial by jury is that it subjects the constructions of the crime control professionals to a measure of true external scrutiny. The *most* distinctive feature is how rarely this happens. Statistically, jury trial is something of an irrelevance.

Of all defendants proceeded against in the criminal courts, less than 1% have their fate determined by a jury.[2] The vast majority of criminal proceedings (over 95%) are concluded in the magistrates' courts. Even of those committed to the Crown Court for trial, only around a third plead not guilty to all counts.[3] In recent years, nearly two-thirds of those defendants pleading not guilty to all counts have been acquitted.[4] In practice, most such cases are terminated without the jury being required to assess the question of guilt. The judge simply directs or orders the jury to return a verdict of not guilty. In 1999, 67% of acquittals were of this nature.[5]

The pattern of acquittals is but one pointer to the importance of the trial judge in the Crown Court. Even where it is left to the jury to decide whether the prosecution has proved guilt beyond reasonable doubt, judges often exert a strong influence on the outcome and are far from being the passive impartial referee as depicted in adversarial theory.[6] Trial by jury may be thought of as 'a cornerstone of our system of criminal justice'[7] but the title of this chapter more accurately reflects what takes place in the Crown Court.

1   Quoted in A Kalunta-Krumpton, 'The Prosecution and Defence of Black Defendants in Drug Trials' (1998) 38 BJ Crim 561 at 581.
2   Close to two million defendants are proceeded against each year in the magistrates' courts: Criminal Statistics England and Wales 1998 (Cm 4649) (London: Stationery Office, 1999), p 131. 15,820 defendants experienced jury trial in 1999: Judicial Statistics 1999 (Cm 4786) (London: SO, 2000) Tables 6.10 and 6.11.
3   In 1999, 26,031 defendants pleaded not guilty to all counts, 3,537 not guilty to some counts and guilty to the others, and 47,452 pleaded guilty to all counts: Judicial Statistics (1999) Table 6.9.
4   The figure was 65% in 1999: Judicial Statistics (1999) Table 6.9.
5   Judicial Statistics (1999) Table 6.10.
6   See further J Jackson and S Doran, *Judge Without Jury* (Oxford: Clarendon, 1995) pp 99-110.
7   Home Office, Juries in Serious Fraud Trials (London: Home Office Communication Directorate, 1998) para 2.2.

1. DIRECTED AND ORDERED ACQUITTALS - WEAK CASES?

The formal distinction between directed and ordered acquittals is not difficult to grasp, although, as we shall see, the position in practice is more complex. If the prosecution indicates that it will not be offering evidence at trial, the judge orders the jury to acquit. A directed acquittal, by contrast, occurs on the instigation of the prosecutor, the defence or the judge, after the trial has begun. The proper approach to be taken in deciding whether to direct an acquittal was laid down in *Galbraith* where Lord Lane CJ ruled that 'Where the judge comes to the conclusion that the prosecution evidence, taken at the highest, is such that a jury properly directed could not properly convict upon it, it is his duty, upon a submission being made, to stop the case.'[8]

In 1999, out of a total of 16,947 acquittals of defendants pleading not guilty to all counts, 8,800 were judge-ordered acquittals and a further 2,484 were judge-directed.[9] The proportion of Crown Court proceedings which result in non-jury acquittals has been rising steadily since the creation of the Crown Prosecution Service (CPS) in the mid-1980s, although the reasons for this are a matter of dispute.[10] Certainly, the level of directed and ordered acquittals raises the question of whether the prosecution is adequately discharging its duty to continue only with those cases where a court is more likely than not to convict.[11] Research for the Royal Commission on Criminal Justice (Runciman Commission) by Block, Corbett and Peay found that nearly half of the directed and ordered acquittals examined were 'unforeseeable' - in just over half of these either the victim or a witness went missing or refused to testify.[12] Other cases became (unforeseeably) weak for a variety of reasons such as where changes in the law defining the offence charged meant that the evidence no longer justified the prosecution in proceeding.

In 55% of the cases studied by Block et al, however, the acquittal was considered one which the prosecution either could or should have foreseen.

8   [1981] 1 WLR 1039 at 1042.
9   Judicial Statistics (1999) Table 6.10.
10   See J Baldwin, 'Understanding Judge Ordered and Directed Acquittals in the Crown Court' [1997] Crim LR 536 at p 537 and P E Lewis, 'The CPS and Acquittals by Judge: Finding the Balance' [1997] Crim LR 653.
11   This duty is set out in Crown Prosecution Service, Code for Crown Prosecutors (London: CPS, 1994) paras 3-5.
12   B Block, C Corbett and J Peay, Ordered and Directed Acquittals in the Crown Court, (Royal Commission on Criminal Justice, Research Study no 15) (London: HMSO, 1993). The results are summarised by the authors in 'Ordered and Directed Acquittals in the Crown Court: A Time of Change?' [1993] Crim LR p 95. Baldwin [1997] p 539 notes that crucial witnesses failed to appear at court, retracted statements or wished the prosecution dropped in 44.4% of the ordered acquittals in his sample.

In some instances the prosecution spotted the weakness only after committal and, lacking the legal power to discontinue, properly sought an ordered acquittal.[13] But in 43% of all the sampled cases the prosecution had failed to spot or act upon weaknesses in the case in a timely fashion, if at all. In 15% of all cases the weakness was foreseeable even before committal, while in some weak cases the prosecution was prepared to offer evidence at trial, prompting Block et al to comment:

> 'it is an indictment of the CPS that these cases were not converted into ordered acquittals by earlier CPS action, or prevented from becoming acquittals at all by even earlier discontinuance.'[14]

In a subsequent study of a sample of CPS files, supplemented by interviews with prosecutors, Baldwin found that 'early warning signs about the likelihood of the prosecution ending in acquittal were noted [in the CPS file] in no fewer than 87.3% of judge ordered acquittals [and] 73.1% of judge directed acquittals.'[15] He observes that CPS lawyers rarely attempted in any significant way to strengthen these cases and that some were disinclined to discontinue weak cases, particular where the alleged crime was particularly serious.[16] These studies support the argument developed in earlier chapters, that the prosecution duty to discontinue weak cases does not provide an adequate due process safeguard for defendants.[17] Should one attribute wrongful failures to discontinue to unsatisfactory bureaucratic procedures and professional misjudgment as Block et al appear to do? No doubt this provides one explanatory factor, but other research shows that the prosecution are often fully aware of weaknesses in their case but proceed in the hope that defendants will throw in their hands and plead guilty.[18] If a defendant calls the prosecution's bluff by insisting on trial by jury, one natural response is to drop the case by offering no evidence.

13 Under s 23 of the Prosecution of Offences Act 1985, a Crown Court case can only be discontinued prior to committal by the magistrates' court. The Runciman Commission recommended that the CPS be given the power to discontinue proceedings up to the beginning of a Crown Court trial: Report (Cm 2263) (London: HMSO, 1993) p 77.

14 Block et al, 'A Time of Change?' (1993) p 101.

15 Baldwin [1997] p 541. But note that Baldwin's sample over-represents cases likely to cause prosecutors' difficulty: Lewis [1997].

16 A similar blurring of the supposedly separate evidential and public interest tests was detected by A Hoyano, L Hoyano, G Davis and S Goldie, 'A Study of the Impact of the Revised Code for Crown Prosecutors' [1997] Crim LR 556 at 562.

17 See, in particular, ch 6 section 3(c) and the discussion by the Royal Commission on Criminal Justice (RCCJ), Report (Cm 2263) (London: HMSO, 1993) pp 74-79.

18 See M McConville, A Sanders and R Leng, The Case for the Prosecution (London: Routledge, 1991) ch 8; Baldwin [1997] p 548.

Block et al also noted that around half of the directed acquittals occurred before the end of the prosecution case at the intervention of the judge. There were also cases in which the judge pressured the prosecution into offering no evidence by revealing that the result of the case would be a bind over whether or not the prosecution went ahead.[19] In the researchers' view, the seriousness of the offence and the strength of the evidence in many such instances was such that the case should have been left to the jury to decide.

How might one explain the high proportion of acquittals which are ordered or directed by Crown Court judges? One would expect such activity in a system based on due process values since it suggests that officials, in weeding out weak cases, are giving priority to protecting the innocent against wrongful conviction. Some directed and ordered acquittals are undoubtedly attributable to such concerns in that it is known, for example, that some prosecutors have more of a due process orientation than others.[20] Yet against the due process analysis providing a wholly satisfactory explanation is the fact that some prosecutors knowingly allow flimsy cases to proceed through the system until the point of trial itself, and judges appear prepared on occasion to terminate proceedings where the prosecution has a reasonable prospect of success.

From a crime control point of view, jury trial is an expensive charade and a chronically inefficient method by which to repress crime. Every effort is therefore made to short-circuit the trial process by inducing a high guilty plea rate. This leaves open the question of what to do in that small minority of cases in which defendants maintain their innocence. Confidence in the system would be sapped if prosecutions in very serious cases, such as murder, armed robbery and serial rape, were not pursued. But in cases involving less serious offences, such as assault, theft or burglary, the arguments for devoting further precious resources to securing a conviction are weaker, particularly where the defendant has opted for Crown Court trial. As Hedderman and Moxon's study of mode-of-trial decisions noted:

'some respondents (justices' clerks and magistrates as well as Chief Crown Prosecutors) questioned the logic of allowing defendants the automatic right to take to the Crown Court matters which were so trivial that judges and prosecutors felt they could not sensibly be pursued there.'[1]

19 The bind over is best described as a 'suspended fine' and may be imposed on anyone involved in court proceedings, whether found guilty of an offence or not.
20 Baldwin [1997] p 554.
1   C Hedderman and D Moxon, Magistrates' Court or Crown Court? (Home Office Research Study no 125) (London: HMSO, 1992) p 16. See, to like effect, Hoyano et al [1997] p 563.

Where the prosecution evidence is not overwhelming (or the matter is perceived to be other than very serious) either the judge or the CPS (or prosecution counsel) may step in to prevent the case continuing. On this analysis, directed and ordered acquittals may be as much a product of crime control as due process concerns. That still leaves unexplained why Crown Court judges were found by Block et al to be terminating some evidentially strong cases of serious crime. Seriousness and strength of evidence are both, however, factors that are open to interpretation and some trial judges may simply be taking a different view to prosecutors, police or researchers as to what counts as an important enough case to justify the resources involved in a Crown Court contest. They may also be less susceptible to the pressure that the police and CPS have come under in recent years to pursue cases involving vulnerable victims (eg, rape, domestic violence and child abuse).[2]

The study by Block et al raises further questions about the propriety of defence solicitor or counsel advising defendants that, given the 'strength' of the prosecution case, they should plead guilty.[3] The strength of the case on paper will often not be reflected in court should the defence decide to fight. It should be noted, however, that the Block et al study was not one of weak cases per se, but of cases that ended in an ordered or directed acquittal (some of which were in fact strong). It would be erroneous to assume that all weak cases end in acquittal. Some end in conviction. In the Crown Court study conducted by Zander and Henderson, judges, defence barristers, and prosecution barristers agreed that around one-fifth of all contested cases were based on a weak prosecution case. Although the great majority of these cases ended in acquittal, the respondents reported that between 4-8% ended in conviction.[4] Conversely, strong cases do not always end in conviction - the acquittal rate in such cases was between 21 and 27% according to barristers and judges.[5]

This evidence suggests that the outcome of contested cases is often uncertain. This helps explain why the CPS prosecutes so many weak cases. Where the CPS drop a case, a conviction is lost, whereas one which is continued may result in conviction, notwithstanding its apparent weakness. The police know this, and also know that most cases will, in any event, terminate with a guilty plea. To attempt to secure more evidence in order to 'firm up' a prosecution case, or to clarify ambiguous statements

2   The influence on the police of changing public attitudes to offences involving vulnerable victims is discussed in J Gregory and S Lees, 'Attrition in Rape and Sexual Assault Cases' (1996) 36 BJ Crim 1 at pp 2-8. For the attitude of prosecutors see Baldwin [1997] p 543.
3   See ch 7 on plea bargaining.
4   M Zander and P Henderson, Crown Court Study (Royal Commission on Criminal Justice, Research Study no 19) (London: HMSO, 1993) pp 184-185.
5   Zander and Henderson (1993) p 185.

made by witnesses, 'would often be, from the police point of view, wasted effort'.[6] Baldwin found the same attitude among some of the CPS lawyers he interviewed.[7] McConville et al conclude that:

> 'Many [not guilty] verdicts, even when judge-directed, were impossible to predict. Indeed, most contests, and many non-contested cases, represent intrinsically ambiguous situations or situations in which the "facts" were simply incomplete in vital ways. These were cases which the police may have been able to clarify but did not, cases in which clarification was not possible or potentially strong cases which - because of their relative or absolute triviality - the police and/or CPS could not be bothered to fight over . . . The idea that the pattern of acquittals and convictions reflects either real situations "out there" or the product of the obstacle course of Due Process just does not stand up to scrutiny.'[8]

The outcome of cases is also dependant on the level of preparatory work carried out by the prosecution and the defence. In reality the defence rarely does more than respond to the prosecution case, and it is the level of care and effort that the police commit to a case that is the crucial factor in determining outcome. As earlier chapters have shown, police commitment is more a product of their own informal working rules and assumptions than officially sanctioned criteria such as the seriousness of the case.[9] As a corollary, the minority of Crown Court cases that go before a jury for determination range from the trivial to the very serious, from the evidentially weak to those in which the prosecution appears to hold all the aces. It is important to keep this point in mind when we consider (in sections 4 and 5 below) the various attempts that have been made to evaluate the performance of the jury and whether the acquittal rate by the jury is 'too high'.

We have suggested that current practice in this area is influenced by both due process and crime control values. These models do not help us determine how these tensions should be resolved and they leave out of consideration the interests of victims. From a freedom perspective, however, we can accept the importance of ensuring that evidentially weak cases are either discontinued or strengthened, regardless of whether or not the victim is vulnerable. It is not acceptable to have defendants run the risk of conviction, particularly in a serious case, where the evidence is weak. But because resources are limited, this perspective contends that strengthening would be the better option in cases of seriousness, and discontinuing the

6   McConville, Sanders and Leng (1991) p 160.
7   Baldwin [1997] at p 548.
8   McConville, Sanders and Leng (1991) p 171.
9   See ch 6 in particular.

better option in relatively trivial matters. But subject as they are to the increasing pressures introduced by managerialism, Crown Prosecutors consider that, even if they were inclined to do so, they do not have the time or resources (legal, financial, and organisational) to review cases thoroughly or to arrange for their strengthening.[10] It is unrealistic to expect the CPS to be able to re-orient itself towards the freedom model in the absence of support for that model amongst the political and legal elites which determine the goals and resources of such public agencies. So whilst we should, in principle, support trial judges who order and direct acquittals in evidentially weak cases, we should not forget that the better option in some of these cases is likely to have been strengthening at an earlier stage in the life of the case.[11]

The freedom model would also demand that vulnerable victims are empowered so that, for example, they felt able to attend court and give evidence if that is what they wished to do.[12] It is too easy to assume that the retraction of a witness statement or the failure of a prosecution witness to appear at court is 'unforeseeable' and thus nobody's fault. Decisions by witnesses are not taken in a vacuum but are crucially affected by socio-economic factors and the shadow of the law and legal processes.[13] For example, one of us worked on the Baldwin study of non-jury acquittals (discussed above) and saw from a reading of CPS files how vulnerable witnesses sometimes braved a court appearance[14] only to find that the case was adjourned by the trial judge at the last minute. One can imagine the anxiety, inconvenience and frustration this may have caused. Not surprisingly these witnesses sometimes failed to appear subsequently. The time and convenience of civilian witnesses ranks low in the priorities of those operating the Crown Court.[15] If the rules of criminal procedure and evidence, and the practices of trial judges and court administrators, were more sensitive to the problems of vulnerable witnesses, without prejudicing

10   See Baldwin [1997] p 547. Managerialism is discussed in ch 1, section 9.
11   A further alternative is to remove the relatively non-serious cases from the expensive setting of the Crown Court and handle them in the magistrates' court instead. As we saw in ch 8, this approach seems to prioritise economic considerations over those of justice.
12   See ch 6, section 6(c) for a discussion of victim empowerment, and ch 12 for discussion of the provisions of the Youth Justice and Criminal Evidence Act 1999 designed to support vulnerable witnesses.
13   See the discussion by Gregory and Lees (1996).
14   In a national survey it was found that 97% of Crown Court centres had experienced at least some intimidation of victims and witnesses: J Shapland and E Bell, 'Victims in the Magistrates' Courts and Crown Court' [1998] Crim LR 537 at p 543.
15   See P Rock, *The Social World of an English Crown Court* (Oxford: Clarendon, 1993) ch 7. While victim-awareness and facilities for witnesses have shown marked improvement over the last 15 years there are still many 'blind spots' such as inadequate arrangements for child care and patchy provision of separate waiting rooms, information points and so forth: Shapland and Bell (1998).

the right of the defendant to a fair trial, the level of ordered and directed acquittals could be reduced in a freedom-enhancing way. As matters stand, trial judges must bear some responsibility for creating the conditions which cause potentially freedom-enhancing prosecutions to result in directed and ordered acquittals.

2. THE COMPOSITION OF THE JURY

For centuries eligibility to serve on a jury was tied to a property qualification. Following the Juries Act 1974 (as amended), a person is eligible for jury service if aged between 18 and 70, included on the electoral register and resident in the UK for at least five years since the age of thirteen. Many of those falling within these parameters are nonetheless ineligible, disqualified or excusable from service. The ineligible include those who might have an undue influence on a jury's deliberations, such as lawyers, judges and the police, and those who are seen as unsuited for a judgmental role, such as nuns, monks and the clergy. The disqualified include anyone who has received a sentence of imprisonment or community service in the preceding 10 years[16] or anyone placed on probation in the last five years. Members of Parliament, the armed services and the medical profession have the right to be excused if summoned, while any person may be excused service if they can show good cause.

Jury trial is the public face of the criminal justice system, the image with which we are all familiar from countless news reports and fictionalised accounts. Some have argued that the jury's symbolic or legitimising function far outweighs its practical significance in that the great bulk of defendants are dealt with in the magistrates' courts or by way of a guilty plea, and that the elaborate ritual of a Crown Court contested trial distracts our attention from the lack of due process in pre-trial and post-trial procedures.[17] All of this is true. Nonetheless, the jury is a key battleground for the due process and crime control models. This is so because jury trial is employed in the most grave cases such as murder, rape, and terrorism. A high rate of guilty verdicts is thus essential to the strategy of effective crime control. The deterrent aim of the system would be undermined if in 'too high' a proportion of these widely publicised cases the defendants were allowed to walk free from the court. Similarly, the very authority of the state might be called into question if juries acquitted too readily,

---

16   Those who have received a custodial sentence of five years or more are ineligible for jury service for the rest of their life.

17   See in particular P Darbyshire, 'The Lamp That Shows That Freedom Lives - Is it Worth the Candle?' [1991] Crim LR 740 and, by the same author, 'An Essay on the Importance and Neglect of the Magistracy' [1997] Crim LR 627.

especially in obviously political cases concerning official secrets, terrorist activities and so forth.

A particular problem for crime control adherents is created by the jury's power to acquit in cases where they have no doubt as to the legal guilt of the defendant but consider the prosecution to be oppressive, the law broken to be unjust or the punishment threatened to be excessive.[18] All three factors were probably at work, for example, in the acquittal of Clive Ponting for offences against the Official Secrets Act (leaking papers containing evidence of Government duplicity during the Falklands War).[19] The exercise of such 'jury equity' sabotages crime control in the immediate case and may provoke calls for more due process in pre-trial procedures in future. Ways must therefore be found to ensure that juries will both trust the police and prosecution agencies to correctly identify the guilty, and back the use of state power against the particular defendant before them. This problem became critical in the early 1970s with the widening of the jury franchise. Juries were no longer guaranteed to be 'predominantly male, middle-aged, middle-minded and middle-class'[20] and so could not be relied upon to instinctively lean towards upholding the exercise of state authority. As we shall see, efforts to regulate and restrict jury power have intensified since the jury franchise was widened.

The influence of crime control thought can be seen in the long history of attempts to rig the composition of the jury.[1] Selection from the pool of eligible jurors is supposed to be random so as to produce a jury which is (reasonably) representative of the wider community. As Lord Denning put it in *Crown Court at Sheffield, ex p Brownlow*:[2] 'We believe that 12 persons selected at random are likely to be a cross-section of the people as a whole and thus represent the view of the common man.' Cutting against the principle of random selection is the preliminary investigation of potential jurors by the prosecution in some cases. Information obtained by such 'jury vetting' may be used by the prosecution to 'stand by' (ie exclude) jurors before the trial begins.[3] The practice came to light in modern times in the 1978 'ABC trial' of a soldier and two journalists for offences under

---

18   As has occurred in a number of celebrated cases throughout legal history: W Cornish, *The Jury* (London: Penguin, 1968) ch 5 and M Freeman, 'The Jury on Trial' (1981) CLP 65 at pp 90-93. For an elegant defence of such 'jury equity' see P Devlin, 'The Conscience of the Jury' (1991) 107 LQR 398.

19   C Ponting, *The Right to Know, The Inside Story of the Belgrano Affair* (London: Sphere, 1985). The next such case is likely to be that of David Shayler, the ex-MI5 officer who disclosed 'state secrets' and was arrested in August 2000.

20   P Devlin, *Trial by Jury* (London: Stevens & Sons, 1956) p 20.

1   See Freeman (1981) pp 75-76 for examples drawn from the eighteenth and nineteenth centuries.

2   [1980] QB 530 at 541.

3   On the right to stand by see J McEldowney, 'Stand by for the Crown - An Historical Analysis' [1979] Crim LR 272.

the Official Secrets Act. As a result of a secret prosecution application to the judge, an 82 member panel from which a jury was to be chosen was vetted for 'loyalty'. Defence objections to this process were strengthened when it was discovered that the prosecution had failed to act on information that two members of the jury so selected had signed the Official Secrets Act and that the foreman was an ex-member of the SAS (Special Air Services regiment). As a result of the public outcry which followed, the Attorney-General published the guidelines for the vetting of jury panels which had existed as a 'restricted document' for three years previously.[4] It was admitted in Parliament that jury vetting had been going on 'at least since 1948, and probably since a great deal earlier than that.'[5]

In a civil case decided soon after, the Court of Appeal opined that jury vetting was unconstitutional,[6] but when the point arose for decision in a criminal appeal, *Mason*,[7] a differently constituted Court of Appeal upheld the practice of routine Criminal Records Office checks. There would be no objection to this if the purpose of the check was merely to establish whether any juror fell foul of the disqualification provisions in the Juries Act 1974. But the Court went on to say that the prosecution could justifiably exclude a juror with a criminal conviction not serious enough to trigger a statutory disqualification.[8]

The Court of Appeal refrained from commenting on jury vetting which went beyond checking criminal records, but the latest redraft of the Attorney-General guidelines states that additional checks may be made with the security services and the police special branch in security and terrorist cases. This is to counter the perceived 'danger that a juror's political beliefs are so biased as to go beyond normally reflecting the broad spectrum of views and interests in the community to reflect the extreme views of sectarian interest or pressure groups to a degree which might interfere with his fair assessment of the facts of the case or lead him to exert improper pressure on his fellow jurors'.[9] Since 'extreme views' is a term capable of wide interpretation there is clearly scope for abuse here.[10]

4   The guidelines were published in *The Times* on 11 October 1978.
5   HC Deb 5th Series, vol 958, col 28, 13 November 1978.
6   *Crown Court at Sheffield, ex p Brownlow* [1980] QB 530 at 542 and 545. One can only speculate as to whether the Court was influenced by the fact that in this case it was the defence which was seeking to vet the jury.
7   [1981] QB 881.
8   The Runciman Commission supported the routine screening of jurors for criminal convictions but failed to tackle the question of whether details of non-disqualifying convictions should be passed to the prosecution: RCCJ (1993) p 133.
9   Attorney-General's Guidelines on the Exercise of the Crown of its Right of Stand-by (1988) 88 Cr App Rep 123, para 5. The Attorney-General must authorise each request for such additional checks.
10 See, for example, R East, 'Jury Packing: A Thing of the Past' (1985) 48 MLR 518 at 527-8. J Sprack, *Emmins on Criminal Procedure* (London: Blackstone Press, 2000) p 262 states that the Attorney-General authorises inquiries going

Whether authorised or unauthorised jury vetting is widespread or takes place only in cases which are particularly important or sensitive is impossible to know. The secrecy surrounding the practice is itself a denial of due process values. A further problem is that the prosecution is placed under no duty to 'stand by' jurors when checks suggest that they might be biased against the defendant. Instead the guidelines provide that in such a situation:

> 'the defence should be given, at least, an indication of why that potential juror may be inimical to their interests; but because of its nature and source it may not be possible to give the defence more than a general indication.'[11]

This falls a long way short of mandating full disclosure to the defence. Moreover, the Association of Chief Police Officers has recommended that the police should only make checks on behalf of the defence if requested to do so by the Director of Public Prosecutions.[12] There is no law which stops the defence from vetting a jury panel itself, although it might have difficulty in securing the names sufficiently in advance. The problem is money. Unlike the prosecution, most defendants do not have abundant resources and the Criminal Defence Service[13] would not pay for a vetting exercise. The evidence suggests that the state authorities are more concerned with ensuring a 'fair' hearing for the prosecution than for the defendant.[14]

Other restrictions on the ability of the defence to influence the composition of the jury support this conclusion. The defence have traditionally been allowed to exclude prospective jurors without the need

---

beyond checks on convictions 'only in a handful of cases' but gives no source for this assertion. In any case, the focus of any critical scrutiny should not merely be on the frequency with which authorisation is given, but also on the nature of the cases which trigger the procedure, the reliability of the information held or gathered by the security services, and the impact on jury selection.

11 (1988) 88 Cr App Rep 123 at para 11.
12 The recommendations are published as an annex to the Attorney-General's guidelines: (1989) 88 Cr App Rep 123.
13 The Criminal Defence Service administers criminal legal aid under the auspices of the Legal Services Commission, both bodies created by the Access to Justice Act 1999. They replace the Legal Aid Board.
14 It should also be noted that if the defence discover after the trial that certain jurors could have been challenged for cause, the common law and s 18 of the Juries Act 1974 virtually preclude the quashing of a conviction on the ground that the jury may have been biased against the defendant. Thus the Court of Appeal in *Box* [1964] 1 QB 430 refused to quash a conviction where the jury foreman knew that the appellants were ex-burglars and 'villains' and had been heard to say that he 'did not need to hear the evidence' and 'would get them 10 years'. See further Sprack (2000) pp 263-65.

to give any reason. The number of such 'peremptory challenges' allowed was reduced from 20 to seven in 1948 and to three (per defendant) in 1977 before being abolished by s 118 of the Criminal Justice Act 1987. In the White Paper which preceded the 1987 Act the Government accepted that peremptory challenge might be used for proper reasons such as to adjust the age, sex or race balance on the jury, but contended that the defence sometimes abused the right so as to remove jurors thought to have too much respect for the law.[15] If the system was serious about prioritising the acquittal of the innocent, one might think that the occasional 'abuse' of the right of peremptory challenge would be regarded as a price worth paying for more representative juries. At the very least one would expect that the right of peremptory challenge in proper circumstances (as described in the White Paper) would be preserved in any reform of the law. Yet despite the timely publication of research showing that peremptory challenges had no discernible impact on the likelihood of acquittal,[16] the Government successfully pressed through its plan to abolish this defence right in its entirety.[17] By contrast, the Government resisted the powerful argument that fairness demanded that the prosecution should simultaneously lose its equivalent right to 'stand by' (ie, exclude) jurors without cause. Instead the Attorney-General issued yet more guidelines exhorting, but not requiring, prosecutors to exercise this right more sparingly in future.[18]

The defence continues to share with the prosecution the right to challenge any juror 'for cause', but this is of little practical use since jurors may not be questioned about their beliefs or background unless counsel knows of facts to justify such questioning.[19] Where the fruits of a prosecution vetting are passed on to the defence, the generality of the information supplied (see above) may not be enough to support a challenge

15 Criminal Justice, Plans for Legislation (Cmnd 9658) (London: Home Office, 1986) para 33.
16 See J Vennard and D Riley, 'The Use of Peremptory Challenge and Stand By of Jurors and Their Relationship to Final Outcome' [1988] Crim LR p 731.
17 For fierce criticism see J Gobert, 'The Peremptory Challenge - An Obituary' [1989] Crim LR p 528.
18 The guidelines are to be found at (1988) 88 Cr App Rep 123.
19 See *Chandler (No 2)* [1964] 1 All ER 761. See further R Buxton, 'Challenging and Discharging Jurors' [1990] Crim LR p 225. If there is prejudicial publicity in advance of the trial, the judge may direct that the jury should answer a questionnaire to test for bias, but this will only be done in fairly extreme cases: see *Andrews (Tracey)* [1999] Crim LR 156 and accompanying commentary. Compare this with the position in the United States where questioning of prospective jurors is standard practice: R May, 'Jury Selection in the United States: Are there lessons to be learned?' [1998] Crim LR 270. See also the consultation paper issued by the Home Office, Juries in Serious Fraud Trials (London: Home Office Communication Directorate, 1998) para 4.4 of which states that prosecution and defence counsel have in 'some recent fraud trials' devised a questionnaire for potential jurors to test for personal hardship grounds for excusal and knowledge of, or bias against, the defendants.

for cause. Usually defence counsel know no more than a juror's name and address.[20]

The defence can form a visual impression as to the racial, class, and age balance on the jury, and this raises the question of whether challenges can be made for cause to achieve a more mixed jury. A Practice Note issued in 1973 stressed that it would be wrong to allow the exclusion of jurors on such 'general' grounds as race, religion, political beliefs or occupation.[1] The Court of Appeal subsequently followed this up by declaring in *Ford*[2] that a judge had no discretion to discharge a juror in order to secure a racially-mixed jury nor otherwise to influence the overall composition of the jury. For the Court, '"fairness" is achieved by the principle of random selection.'[3] Whereas the Government had suggested in its 1987 White Paper that it would be proper to peremptorily challenge so as to achieve a socially mixed jury, the courts subsequently denied the defence the ability to challenge for cause on just this basis. Again, the fear seems to be that the defence will seek to 'rig' the jury in its favour. Yet little concern is evident that random selection from the available pool of jurors is unlikely to produce a representative jury. Some groups, such as ethnic minorities and the young, are under-represented on the electoral register, and local councils do not always ensure that the courts have the most complete or recent register to work from.[4] Moreover, *random* selection can never guarantee a *representative* jury. Suppose that 1 in 12 of the eligible population within a court catchment area was black. A random selection process which selected 12 people for jury service would not guarantee at least one black juror. Sometimes it would result in juries with one or more black jurors, sometimes not.

Put all the above factors together and the upshot is that an all-white jury may hear a criminal case against a black defendant even though such a jury might be wholly unrepresentative of the local community.[5] As Bohlander observes:

20 Details of occupation were removed from jury lists in 1983 by order of the Lord Chancellor. A challenge for cause would have been difficult to ground on a juror's occupation, but, prior to the Criminal Justice Act 1987, jurors whose occupations suggested a pro-prosecution outlook might have been peremptorily challenged.

1 [1973] 1 All ER 240.

2 [1989] 3 All ER 445; followed in *Tarrant* [1998] Crim LR 342 where a conviction was quashed on the basis that the judge was wrong to discharge a jury on the basis that 11 out of 12 of them came from the same postal district, and wrong to direct that the new jury should be drawn from a panel brought in from outside the court's normal catchment area.

3 [1989] 3 All ER 445 at 449.

4 See *The Law Magazine*, 30 October 1987, p 20; P Robertshaw, S Cox and N Van Hoen, 'Jury Populations and Jury Verdicts' 20 IJ Sociology of Law 271.

5 For an illustration of the dangers involved see J Robbins, 'Who said anything about law?' (1990) 140 NLJ 1275. For an empirical study of the racialised nature of trials involving black defendants see Kalunta-Krumpton (1998).

'As a result there exists . . . the distinct possibility that the different life style, mentality and experience arising from membership of an ethnic minority will not be taken sufficiently into account in trials where members of such a minority are the defendants.'[6]

In high-profile cases heard by all white juries it is not just ethnic minority defendants who may feel a sense of injustice, but also the community from which they are drawn. An extreme example of the dangers involved is the Rodney King case in which a jury with no African-American jurors failed to convict Los Angeles police officers of misconduct even though they had been video-taped kicking and beating an African-American suspect as he lay on the ground. This 'triggered the worst race riot in American history, two days of violence that cost 58 lives and nearly one billion pounds in property damage.'[7] Whilst the fraught history of unjust race-relations in the United States provided the tinder box for this conflagration, it would be naive to think that England and Wales could never experience such problems.[8] As we have seen in earlier chapters, ethnic minorities often suffer disproportionately from the exercise of police powers and pre-trial discretion, and damage has been done to police-community relations as a result. There is a sense of racial injustice amongst some communities in this country that could be dangerously exacerbated by convictions delivered by all-white juries.

The Runciman Commission was aware that two-thirds of all jury trials are heard by white juries, and that the area of concern about jury composition most frequently mentioned by defence barristers was racial mix.[9] Its response was to recommend that the judge be allowed to engineer a racially mixed jury (on application from the defendant), but only in cases with 'unusual and special features'. The Runciman Commission illustrated its proposal by continuing:

'a black defendant charged with burglary would be unlikely to succeed in such an application. But black people accused of violence against a member of an extremist organisation who they said had been making racial taunts against them and their friends might well succeed.'[10]

Cases with such features are likely to be rare. The recommendation is based on the false premise that race is only a relevant factor within criminal justice

6   M Bohlander, '". . . By a jury of his peers" - The issue of multi-racial juries in a poly-ethnic society' [1992] XIV(1) Liverpool Law Review 67.
7   A Alschuler, 'The all-white American jury' (1995) 145 NLJ 1005.
8   See further P Herbert, 'Racism, impartiality and juries' (1995) 145 NLJ 1138. For some evidence of racial prejudice affecting juries see section 5(b) below.
9   See Zander and Henderson (1993) p 241.
10   RCCJ (1993) pp 133-134.

when the alleged offence itself has some inter-racial characteristic. It ignores the evidence that race plays a much broader role within the operation of the criminal process than this, as, for example, in the patterns of law enforcement. Thus one might imagine that an all-white jury would be less likely to exercise 'jury equity' on the behalf of a black victim of an oppressive prosecution than would a racially mixed jury. Despite the timid nature of the Runciman recommendations, it has been totally ignored.

The incorporation through the Human Rights Act of the European Convention on Human Rights (ECHR) will not result in any great change in English law and practice concerning jury selection. Whilst Art 6 gives defendants the right to a fair trial by an independent and impartial tribunal, the European Court of Human Rights (ECtHR) presumes that members of a tribunal are impartial unless there is evidence to the contrary.[11] The argument that it is nigh impossible to produce such evidence in the British context, where juries do not give reasons for their decision, and that therefore the subjective presumption should not apply, was rejected by the ECtHR in *Pullar v UK*.[12] The Court accepts, however, that if an objective observer would have any ground for a legitimate doubt about a tribunal's impartiality that this is sufficient for a violation.[13] Would an all-white jury trying a black defendant give rise to such a doubt? It seems not. In *Gregory v UK*[14] the black defendant was convicted of robbery on a majority verdict and sentenced to six years' imprisonment. One hour after the jury had retired to consider its verdict, one juror sent a note to the judge reading 'jury showing racial overtones, one member to be excused'. The judge recalled the jury and told them that 'any thoughts of prejudice of one form or another, for or against anybody, must be put out of your minds' and that they must decide the case on the evidence alone. The ECtHR held that this redirection was sufficiently forceful to dispel any objectively held misgivings about the impartiality of the jury. Do you think Mr Gregory will have seen it that way? If you were one of his friends would you not have wanted the judge to identify the jurors showing 'racial overtones' and to have discharged them?[15] Given the judgment that a violation of the Convention did not occur in this case, it is simply inconceivable that a violation would be found on the sole ground that an all-white jury had determined the fate of an ethnic minority defendant.

11   See the discussion by C Ovey, 'The European Convention on Human Rights and the Criminal Lawyer: An Introduction' [1998] Crim LR 4 at p 9.
12   (1996) 22 EHRR 391.
13   Ovey [1998] p 9.
14   (1997) 25 EHRR 577; but see now *Sanders v UK* [2000] Crim LR 767 in which the ECtHR (by 4 votes to 3) found a breach of Art 6 in fairly similar circumstances.
15   The Juries Act, s 16 allows a jury to continue to hear a case with as few as nine members. Under s 17 a nine member jury must be unanimous, whereas juries with 10 or 11 members can bring in verdicts so long as there is not more than one dissentient.

Jury vetting presents a dilemma for the state. It cannot be seen to interfere with the composition of the jury too readily as this will undermine the useful legitimising effect of jury trial on the criminal process as a whole.[16] On the other hand, the desire to influence the outcome of a particular trial is sometimes very strong. The law both reflects this tension and provides for its resolution by enabling interference to take place on a covert basis. The prosecution may simply stand by a juror without giving any reason and the defence need not be told that jury vetting has taken place. The prosecution's duties and powers are governed by broadly-drawn administrative directions and guidelines which provide no sanctions for breach. In stark contrast, the defence has to state reasons for challenging jurors, and may not seek to change the overall balance of the jury. Furthermore, its more limited powers are governed by restrictive case law. The different treatment of prosecution and defence by the state authorities (including Parliament, the government and the courts) is revealing as to the dominant values in our political and legal culture.

3. THE VERDICT OF THE JURY

As we shall now explore, efforts to influence the jury's verdict in the direction of conviction have extended beyond the design and implementation of the selection procedures.

(a) Majority verdicts

For centuries jury verdicts had to be unanimous but the Criminal Justice Act 1967 permitted a majority of not less than ten out of twelve. This change has been seen by some critics as undermining the requirement that the prosecution proves guilt beyond reasonable doubt. As Freeman puts it, 'If one or two jurymen conscientiously feel strong enough to dissent from the majority view that demonstrates to my satisfaction that there is reasonable doubt as to the guilt of the accused.'[17] Others have seen majority verdicts as merely a means to prevent extremists blocking convictions: 'it would enable the racist views of a member of an extreme right wing political party to be discounted in the jury's decision-making.'[18] The rationale for the 1967 reform was ostensibly to prevent professional criminals escaping conviction by the expedient of bribing or intimidating individual jurors. That this occasionally happens is undeniable. But the

16 P Duff and M Findlay, 'Jury vetting - The jury under attack' (1983) 3 LS 159 at pp 171-173.
17 Freeman (1981) p 69.
18 R White, *The Administration of Justice* (Oxford: Basil Blackwell, 1991) p 126.

question remains of whether the majority verdict is the correct response to that problem.

In answering, one must consider the effect of the change. The introduction of majority verdicts led to a trebling of the rate at which juries fail to reach unanimity,[19] and over one in five guilty verdicts are now by majority.[20] As Freeman explains:

> 'juries when told by judges that they may consider a non-unanimous verdict simply stop deliberating when they reach the requisite majority. This may save time and money and it may be "convenient" but how relevant should these considerations be? When managerial efficiency becomes the dominant consideration, justice can soon take a back seat.'[1]

Majority verdicts have thus prodded jury trial in the direction of crime control. The argument that this was necessary in order to guard against 'jury nobbling' is similar to that used to deny bail to defendants on the ground that they might otherwise interfere with prosecution witnesses.[2] In both cases the argument appears to give greater weight to the conviction of the guilty at the expense of the acquittal of the innocent. In both cases there is a more appropriate response, which is to safeguard the administration of justice by other means, such as more effective protection for witnesses and jurors. The judge can, for example, make a jury protection order, under which the police will provide protection for members of the jury during the course of the trial.[3] The vast majority of trials do not involve professional criminals and so the risk of 'jury nobbling' is low. The solution adopted, allowing (in all cases) the views of one-sixth of the jury to be dismissed as 'unreasonable', appears grossly disproportionate to the supposed problem. Moreover, the determined big-time 'nobbler' can evade the supposed safeguard by the simple expedient of intimidating three or more jurors.

It is interesting to note the legislative innovations in the mid-1990s designed to deter and perhaps remedy intimidation of jurors. While there has long been a common law offence of perverting the course of justice,

---

19   See Freeman (1981) p 70.

20   Judicial Statistics (1999) Table 6.11. In 1992 the figure was nearer one in eight: Judicial Statistics 1992 (Cm 2268) (London: HMSO, 1993) p 62, Table 6.10.

1   Freeman (1981) p 70. See also P Darbyshire, 'Notes of a Lawyer Juror' (1990) 140 NLJ 1264 at p 1266.

2   On bail, see ch 8, section 3.

3   The potential prejudice or fear this might cause in the minds of the jury should be addressed by some explanatory remarks by the trial judge: *Comerford* [1998] 1 Cr App Rep 235. The same case decides that a trial judge may take the precautionary step of having the members of the jury referred to by numbers instead of the more usual procedure of stating their names in open court as they are sworn in.

Parliament created a new offence of intimidating witnesses and jurors by s 51(1) of the Criminal Justice and Public Order Act 1994. Two years later it went further by enacting a new procedure for re-opening acquittals allegedly tainted by interference with the administration of justice.[4] Whilst these complex provisions are unlikely to be used with any frequency, 'from a constitutional perspective they represent a major inroad into the fundamental rule against double jeopardy.'[5] Nor did the creation of these new 'safeguards' against jury nobbling lead to any re-assessment by the Government of the 'need' for majority verdicts. As in other areas of the criminal process, once a due process safeguard is dismantled or weakened, the chances of it being resurrected are slim indeed.

The argument that majority verdicts allow the views of extremists to be neutralised is defective. By definition, people of extreme views are in a minority in the populace at large. Most juries will have no such jurors and so the problem will rarely arise. Moreover, the views of an extremist will seldom have a bearing on the decision-making process: if a white defendant is alleged to have burgled a shop run by white owners, would not the racist be as open-minded as the next person on the question of guilt? The danger of an extremist very occasionally blocking a justifiable conviction (or acquittal) has to be weighed against the overall due process cost of allowing a majority verdict to be returned in any and every criminal case.

In so far as the 'extremist' argument is used to justify majority verdicts, there is a double-standard at work. Like the argument for jury vetting, it claims that the random selection principle cannot be trusted in cases where fierce ethnic or political conflicts are involved. There is some truth in this and that is precisely why ethnic minorities demand some black people on juries when racial hostility is an element. Yet this has been rejected by the Government and the courts. In short, the argument that random selection is defective is accepted when this serves prosecution interests, but not otherwise.

In Scotland, where juries are 15-strong, it is possible to convict on a simple majority of eight jurors voting for a guilty verdict. Although this suggests that Scots law has even less regard for the presumption of innocence than English law, the comparison is misleading. Scotland has other means of safeguarding defendants which have no parallel in England, such as a general requirement of corroboration of prosecution evidence.[6] Moreover, if a Scottish jury cannot achieve the requisite majority for conviction, the defendant is entitled to an acquittal.[7] In England, by

4   Criminal Procedure and Investigations Act 1996, ss 54 to 57.
5   R Leng and R Taylor, *Blackstone's Guide to the Criminal Procedure and Investigations Act 1996* (London: Blackstone, 1996) at p 91.
6   See generally Sheriff I D Macphail QC, 'Safeguards in the Scottish Criminal Justice System' [1992] Crim LR 144.
7   In which case the verdict will either be 'not guilty' or 'not proven'. See G Maher, 'Jury verdicts and the presumption of innocence' (1983) 3 LS 146.

contrast, the defendant is acquitted only if at least 10 out of 12 jurors vote for a verdict of not guilty. Otherwise, the jury is said to be 'hung' and the prosecution may opt for a re-trial. This symmetry with the requirement for a guilty verdict is impossible to reconcile with the presumption of innocence.[8] For whenever between three and nine jurors vote for acquittal, the prosecution has failed to prove guilt and the presumption of innocence would demand that the defendant be acquitted. Instead, the English system allows guilt or innocence to remain an open question pending a retrial. Statistics on this issue are not published as a matter of course although it is known that some 370 re-trials of hung cases were heard in 1981.[9] Re-trials for this reason also seem somewhat inconsistent with the principle of double jeopardy – that no-one should stand trial on the same charge twice.

(b) The conduct of the trial by the judge

It is well recognised that judges may have a powerful influence on jury verdicts. Historically juries were commonly told by judges what verdicts to return and, although juries had the right in legal theory to rebel, they seldom did so. The advent of defence lawyers in the eighteenth century broke up this cosy relationship between judge and jury and caused the criminal trial to move much closer to the adversarial ideal of a passive and impartial judge.[10] The judgment by Lord Denning in *Jones v National Coal Board* is generally regarded as the classic statement of the modern position:

'The judge's part in [an adversarial trial] is to hearken to the evidence, only himself asking questions of witnesses when it is necessary to clear up any point that has been overlooked or left obscure; to see that the advocates behave themselves seemly and keep to the rules laid down by law; to exclude irrelevancies and discourage repetition; to make sure by wise intervention that he follows the points the advocates are making and can assess their worth; . . . If he goes beyond this, he drops the mantle of a judge and assumes the robe of an advocate . . .'[11]

8   Maher (1983) p 151.
9   S Butler, Acquittal Rates (Home Office Research and Planning Unit Paper 16) (London: HMSO, 1983) p 7.
10 J Langbein, 'The Criminal Trial Before Lawyers' (1978) 45 U Ch LR 263 at p 314.
11 [1957] 2 QB 55 at 64.

Moreover, it is now clear law that a judge may not direct a jury to convict, however strong the prosecution case may be.[12] At one level, that judges may direct an acquittal but not a conviction is evidence that the law on this point reflects the due process stance that wrongful convictions are a greater evil than wrongful acquittals. The same position underlies the duty of the judge to put before the jury any defence which arises from the evidence even if not explicitly raised by defence counsel.[13] But other aspects of the legal framework governing trials reveals that conviction-minded judges are given ample scope to parade their views and prejudices before the jury.

The judgment in *Jones v National Coal Board* accepts that judges may properly ask some questions and make some interventions, but its tone suggests that these should be limited in number and scope. The reality is that the Court of Appeal has allowed judges a large degree of freedom in conducting trials.[14] In *Gunning*[15] a conviction was quashed where the judge had asked 165 questions compared with 172 from counsel. But in *Matthews*[16] a conviction was upheld even though it was conceded that the number of judicial interventions and questions were excessive. The judge had asked 524 questions to counsel's 538, but the Court of Appeal concluded that counsel had not been diverted from his own line of questioning. The issue should not be whether such a diversion occurred, however, but whether the degree of intervention from the bench compromised the appearance or substance of judicial impartiality. The appellate courts seem unable or unwilling to grasp this point. The Court of Appeal ruled in *Ptohopoulos*[17] that gross discourtesy to counsel cannot in itself be sufficient to justify quashing a conviction. In *Hircock*[18] the trial judge had muttered 'Oh God', and groaned and sighed throughout defending counsel's closing speech. One would have thought that such gross discourtesy impinged on the fairness of the trial. The Court of Appeal decided, however, that the judge's behaviour did not reflect any view of the defendant's case, but was simply implicit criticism of the conduct of the case by defence counsel. One cannot help wondering whether the jury appreciated this subtle distinction. It is further worth noting that the

---

12 *DPP v Stonehouse* [1978] AC 55. A possible exception to the principle that a judge may not direct a conviction is where the defence is based on a point of law and the judge rules against the defence on that point: *Hill and Hall* (1988) 89 Cr App Rep 74. This, however, seems irreconcilable with the concept of jury equity.

13 See S Doran, 'Alternative Defences: the "invisible" burden on the trial judge' [1991] Crim LR 878.

14 For reviews of the case law, see S Doran, 'Descent to Avernus' (1989) 139 NLJ 1147, and Jackson and Doran, *Judge Without Jury* (1995) pp 104-110.

15 [1980] Crim LR 592.

16 [1983] Crim LR 683. See, similarly, *Webb; Simpson* (23 October 2000, unreported), CA.

17 [1968] Crim LR 52.

18 [1969] 1 All ER 47.

appellate judiciary are unable to criticise or remedy excessive interventions by the trial judge which result in an acquittal. This is because there is generally no appeal from an acquittal.[19] Thus it is open to a trial judge to harangue or undermine prosecution lawyers and witnesses with little fear that the case will result in an appeal.

The appellate cases just discussed give an indication of the scope for judicial intervention and provide some extreme examples of behaviour by trial judges. By their nature they cannot, however, tell us the frequency with which trial judges *typically* question witnesses or interrupt counsel, the nature of those interventions, or whether such interventions are welcomed by other participants. What little research evidence there is makes it clear that there is considerable variation between judges. Jackson and Doran studied 17 jury trials in Northern Ireland presided over by nine different judges. They found that of the 77 judicial objections to counsel's questioning, two-thirds (54) were made by just two judges in three of the trials. By contrast, four of the judges made no more than one objection per trial they heard.[20] This study also found that one judicial question was asked every 5.5 minutes during the taking of oral evidence from witnesses.[1] Much of this questioning was legitimate in that it was designed to clarify evidence, but 14% of defence witnesses (compared with 6% of prosecution witnesses) were subjected to inquisitorial questioning designed to elicit new information.[2] In other words, the judges often did take on the robe of an advocate. The authors were unable to settle upon an explanation for this greater tendency to probe defence witnesses but note that it may have been that the judges observed were simply more disposed to believe the prosecution evidence. Not surprisingly, they found that 'prosecution counsel were generally happier about judicial questioning than defence counsel.'[3] In England and Wales, the Crown Court survey carried out for the Runciman Commission found no support from either prosecuting or defence counsel for more 'robust interventions' from the judge. Where judges had intervened in trials, the interruptions favoured the prosecution much more frequently than they did the defence.[4]

The Runciman Commission advocated that judges should be more interventionist in conducting trials in order to save time and money and because shorter trials would make it easier for jurors to recall the essential facts. It also wanted judges to prevent witnesses being 'subjected to

---

19 For one exception see section 3(a) above. See also ch 10, section 2(b).
20 J Jackson and S Doran, *Judge Without Jury* (Oxford: Clarendon, 1995) p 122 Table 5.4.
1 Jackson and Doran (1995) p 132.
2 Jackson and Doran (1995) p 154 Table 6.10.
3 Jackson and Doran (1995) pp 160-62.
4 M Zander and P Henderson, Crown Court Study (Royal Commission on Criminal Justice, Research Study no 19) (London: HMSO, 1993) pp 137-38.

bullying and intimidatory tactics by counsel or to deliberately and unnecessarily prolonged cross-examination.'[5] It brushed aside the suggestion that such interventions might give the 'impression of bias' and failed to acknowledge the violence that its proposals would do to the adversarial theory of justice which asserts that the production' and presentation of evidence must be left to the parties in dispute.[6] Moreover, its proposals evince a degree of trust in judicial impartiality which scarcely seems justified on the track record of the courts.[7]

The Court of Appeal reacted enthusiastically to the Runciman recommendation. It drew on it in *Whybrow and Saunders*[8] where Lord Taylor CJ supported greater judicial intervention to prevent trials becoming protracted. However, the Court also reiterated that a trial judge must act like an umpire rather than an advocate for one side or the other. This acknowledged the inevitable clash that exists here between such values as efficiency, procedural fairness and crime control. This is not just a simple clash between due process and crime control principles, however. Neither model adequately caters for victims and other witnesses.[9] When the conduct of the case is left to defence and prosecution lawyers, victims often suffer.[10] Concern at the treatment of rape victims in court, in particular, leads naturally to the position adopted by the Runciman Commission.[11]

From a freedom perspective we would want arguments and policy decisions about judicial intervention to be grounded in clear principles which take into account the various interests at stake. The European Court on Human Rights has provided an important lead here. One of the deficiencies of the European Convention for Human Rights is that it does not spell out the rights of victims or witnesses.[12] But in *Doorson v Netherlands* the Court noted that while Art 6 (right to a fair trial) did not explicitly require consideration of the interests of witnesses and victims called upon to testify, a duty to protect those interests could be supported by reference to Arts 2 (right to life), 5 (liberty and security) and 8 (right to respect for private life). It thus concluded that the 'principles of fair trial

---

5   RCCJ (1993) p 122.
6   See ch 1, section 5 for discussion.
7   It is telling that the Runciman Commission made no reference to its own Crown Court survey on this point.
8   [1994] NLJR 124.
9   See ch 1, sections 7 and 10.
10 See D Brereton, 'How Different are Rape Trials? A Comparison of the Cross-Examination of Complainants in Rape and Assault Trials' (1997) 37 BJ Crim 242, and P Rock, *The Social World of an English Crown Court* (Oxford: Clarendon, 1993) ch 2.
11 See the discussion by L Ellison, 'Cross-Examination in Rape Trials' [1998] Crim LR 605.
12 A Ashworth, 'Victims' Rights, Defendants' Rights and Criminal Procedure' in A Crawford and J Goodey (eds), *Integrating a Victim Perspective within Criminal Justice* (Aldershot: Ashgate, 2000) at p 189.

also require that in appropriate cases the interests of the defence are balanced against those of witnesses or victims called upon to testify.'[13] In similar vein the Court of Appeal has recently ruled in *Brown (Milton Anthony)*[14] that: 'It is the clear duty of the trial judge to do everything he can, consistently with giving the defendant a fair trial, to minimise the trauma suffered by other participants . . .' Parliament, through the Youth Justice and Criminal Evidence Act 1999, has provided trial judges with various new 'special measures' and devices designed to encourage them to safeguard the interests of fearful or vulnerable witnesses in court.[15] Thus, for example, trial judges will be able to authorise the giving of evidence by live link, by video-recorded evidence-in-chief or *in camera,* and will be able to prohibit cross-examination by the defendant in person.

Whilst this legislative concern for victims and witnesses is welcome, there remain some troubling aspects to these developments. First, the new Act overlooks the fact that trial judges are sometimes directly responsible through their own questioning for the 'trauma' suffered by witnesses in court. Second, there has been no recognition by criminal justice policy makers that some trial judges can and do exhibit bias, more often than not against the defence, through their interventions during a trial. As we have seen such behaviour is inadequately regulated by the senior judiciary. Third, the accused is specifically excluded from the new 'special measures' introduced by the Youth Justice and Criminal Evidence Act. Yet this overlooks that defendants can be vulnerable or fearful in the same way as victims. They may find the experience of cross-examination by the prosecution just as humiliating or offensive as complainants find cross-examination by the defence.[16] The legislation also seems to be based on the faulty assumption that defendants and victims are distinct groups of people.[17] Both these deficiencies are captured in the scenario depicted by Birch: 'If A and B are equally [learning] disabled, and B's answer to a complaint of sexual assault made by A is that A was the aggressor and he the victim, why should A be the only one to benefit from special measures because it has been decided to prosecute B?'[18] In showing concern for

13   (1996) 23 EHRR 330 at 358. See also *Van Mechelen v Netherlands* (1998) 25 EHRR 647.
14   [1998] 2 Cr App Rep 364 at 391.
15   See D Birch, 'A Better Deal for Vulnerable Witnesses?' [2000] Crim LR 223.
16   As where racial stereotypes are invoked against black defendants: Kalunta-Krumpton (1998).
17   For a critique of this assumption see ch 1, section 11(b)(iii).
18   Birch [2000] pp 242-43. The decision of the ECtHR in *T v UK and V v UK* [2000] Crim LR 187, that the two young defendants tried for the murder of Jamie Bulger were unable to participate effectively in the Crown Court proceedings, has prompted a new practice direction, and may prompt amendment of the Youth Justice and Criminal Evidence Act 1999, at least in relation to young defendants. See further A Gillespie, 'Practice direction on child defendants and the case of *T v UK*' (2000) 150 NLJ 320.

victims it is important not to lose sight of the need to address the conduct (and powers) of the trial judge in relation to the defence case in general, and the defendant in particular. The new legislation advances the freedom of victims and most other witnesses but it has turned a blind eye to the plight of defendants in court. This is discussed further in the concluding chapter.

(c) Summing up by the judge

The last word in a contested trial before the jury retires to consider its verdict is always that of the judge. The judge explains the law to the jury and provides them with a summary of the evidence.[19] This gives judges an opportunity to influence the outcome of the trial, and some famous miscarriages of justice have resulted. Thus in the case of Derek Bentley (hanged in 1953) the eminent trial judge (Lord Goddard CJ) suggested in his summary of the evidence that, as witnesses, the police were likely to be accurate and reliable, and defendants inaccurate and unreliable.[20] The most notorious modern example of such an attempt was in the trial of the 'Birmingham Six', where Bridge J over a three-day summing-up skilfully led the jury by the nose to a verdict of guilty.[1] He began by telling the jury that 'however hard a judge tries to be impartial, inevitably his presentation of the evidence is bound to be coloured by his own view.' He then left them in no doubt as to what that view might be.[2] For example, he sought to depict the defence contention that the police had fabricated evidence and lied in court as far-fetched:

'If the defendants are giving you honest and substantially accurate evidence, there is no escape from the fact that the police are involved in a conspiracy to commit a variety of crimes which must be unprecedented in the annals of British criminal history.'

Other defence witnesses were similarly discredited, such as the prison doctor who gave evidence of injuries to the accused and their probable infliction by the police:

19 On the extent of this judicial obligation see *Amado-Taylor* [2000] Crim LR 618 and accompanying commentary.
20 *Bentley* [1999] Crim LR 330.
1   Excerpts from the transcript of the trial are reproduced (with critical commentary) by J Wood in C Walker and K Starmer (eds), *Miscarriages of Justice* (London: Blackstone, 1999) p 226. See also in this book the discussion by J Jackson, 'Trial Procedures' (at p 199) on the summing up in the Carl Bridgewater case.
2   After the jury convicted, the judge commented that the evidence in the case was the clearest and most overwhelming he had ever heard.

'. . . can you believe one single word of what Dr Harwood says? There are inescapably many perjurers who have given evidence. If Dr Harwood is one of them, is he not the worst?'

Mr Justice Bridge made this performance appeal-proof, however, by continually reminding the jurors that it was for them, not him, to decide where the truth lay.[3] Where this formalistic incantation is omitted, the Court of Appeal has sometimes intervened. Thus in *Berrada*[4] the judge observed that the defendant's allegations of police misconduct were 'really monstrous and wicked'. The Court of Appeal rebuked the judge, declaring that her duty was to sum up impartially without seeking to inflate evidence by 'sarcastic and extravagant comment'.[5] More temperate language from the judge is all that the law requires, however. The senior judiciary have declared that trial judges are entitled to express their opinions on the facts in robust and confident terms,[6] and may even observe that the defendant's story is a remarkable one.[7]

One danger in giving judges such freedom of manoeuvre is that they are privy to much inadmissible evidence, including the defendant's previous convictions (if any), and may therefore be biased against the defendant. Zander and Henderson found that in cases where judges summed up for conviction and where the defendant had a previous record the summation was in line with the evidence as often as it was against the weight of the evidence.[8] On this basis, they argue that judges do not appear to be influenced by knowledge of prior convictions. This is a crude analysis, however. One would need to control for all factors that might lead to a judge summing up for conviction (such as race, class or sex of the defendant, political/media pressures to clamp down on particular crimes,

---

3   In the third (and successful) appeal by the Birmingham Six the Court of Appeal acknowledged the forceful nature of the summing up by Bridge J, but did not accept that this had vitiated the proceedings. As Lloyd LJ put it, 'the judge also made it clear throughout the summing-up that it was for the jury, and not for him, to determine where the truth lay': *McIlkenny* (1991) 93 Cr App Rep 287 at 293.

4   (1989) 91 Cr App Rep 131n.

5   See also *Osborne-Odelli* [1998] Crim LR 902 and *Gibbons and Winterburn* (22 June 1993) in which convictions were quashed because of an unfair summing up by the trial judge. Amongst many other prejudicial comments the trial judge in the latter case had referred to the defendant as an 'an old lag trying to go straight'. See the discussion by P Robertshaw, *Summary Justice* (London: Cassell, 1998) pp 26-28.

6   See per Channel J in *Cohen* (1909) 2 Cr App Rep 197 at 208.

7   Per Lord Reading CJ in *O'Donnell* (1917) 12 Cr App Rep 219 at 221. See also the speeches by Lord Salmon and Lord Edmund-Davies in *DPP v Stonehouse* [1978] AC 55. The former said, for example, that it would be in order for a judge to sum up to the jury 'in such a way as to make it plain that he considers the accused is guilty and should be convicted' (at p 80).

8   Zander and Henderson (1993) p 135.

and so on) in order to establish whether knowledge of a defendant's previous record played a part. Also, if judges sum up for conviction against the evidence they are plainly prejudiced - whether by knowledge of previous record or not is hardly important! On the other hand, judges sometimes make plain in their summary of the evidence that they think an acquittal the right result, as in the Stephen Waldorf case in which the two police officers on trial had shot and pistol-whipped an innocent man by mistake.[9] In general, judges simply get case-hardened and sceptical about defendants, particularly when they are not seen as respectable characters. As we saw in ch 8, section 5(b), in relation to magistrates, this is one of the central arguments for employing a jury to decide questions of fact. Extensive judicial intervention introduces into trials the very problem that the use of juries is meant to avoid - prejudice.

The Runciman Commission was adamant that judges should be 'wholly neutral in any comment that they make on the credibility of the evidence . . . it is inappropriate for judges to intrude their own views of whether or not a witness is to be believed.'[10] Its clear stance on this issue was undermined, however, by the failure to discuss either the extent to which judges do sum up in a biased fashion, or the extent to which case law allows them to do so. Notably, it failed to make any formal recommendation on the matter, which suggests that either it mistakenly believed that the behaviour of trial judges and the law conformed to its view of the ideal, or that it thought the issue a trivial one which raised few problems in practice. Yet its own Crown Court study suggested that trial judges commonly display bias. According to prosecutors, in over 1,000 cases in 1992 the judge summed up against the weight of the evidence, while the figure was more than 2,000 (nearly 10% of all cases tried by jury) according to defence barristers. Prosecuting barristers tended to think that where the summing up was against the weight of the evidence, it favoured an acquittal. According to defence barristers, however, in 92% of the cases where the summing up was identified as biased in this sense, the bias was towards conviction.[11] In half of these cases the jury convicted.[12]

The Court of Appeal defends trial judges making comments 'one way or the other' on the basis that juries 'are more robust than people often

9   See *The Times*, 19 October 1983.
10 See RCCJ (1993) p 124.
11 Note that this does not mean that prosecution and defence counsel were disagreeing about where the bias lay in particular cases, since they may well have been talking about different cases. Prosecutors will tend to be alive to bias against their interests but not notice when the bias runs in their favour, and the same is true of defence lawyers. Zander and Henderson (1993) p 131, presented evidence of the extent of agreement as to which side was favoured in the judge's summation, but did not do this for cases where the summation not only favoured one side or the other, but was against the weight of the evidence.
12 See Zander and Henderson (1993) pp 135-6.

give them credit for.'[13] How can we know that juries ignore biased comments in the absence of any research evidence? Theoretically, one would expect there to be at least some influence. First, the summaries are clearly intended to influence the jury else there would be no point in making them. Second, as Robertshaw points out, members of the jury are symbolically and physically constructed as passive and silent observers from the side-lines during the trial. By contrast, the judge is raised up on high, centre stage, and given the 'superior status indicators of wig and robes . . . All procedural moves and sequences pass through the judge, to whom deferential behaviour and speech forms are routine . . . . The role-expectation for the jury throughout the trial is one of dependence on the judge.'[14] This dependency is exacerbated by the practice in England and Wales of providing jurors in advance of the trial with only a rather perfunctory oral explanation of their role, delivered by the jury bailiff, supplemented by a short video film prepared by the Lord Chancellor's Department.[15]

In the United States, an historical distrust of officialdom is reflected in the rule in most state jurisdictions that the judge in a criminal trial must express no opinion on the weight or credibility of the testimony of a witness, or on the merits of either side of the case.[16] In some continental jurisdictions, such as France, the other extreme of the argument may be seen, in that judges are allowed to retire with juries in order to determine the verdict. The evidence suggests that this co-decision model produces a much lower acquittal rate than when matters are left in the hands of the jury alone.[17] A model nearer to hand is that of Scotland which limits trial judges to directing on the law and explaining how the evidence is relevant to the legal ingredients of each charge. This seems to ensure greater respect for the jury's role as fact-finder and ultimate determiner of guilt.[18] If we think it important that our long-term freedom should not be taken away by a process effectively dominated by state-paid professionals then there is much to be said for the Scottish approach.

13   *Spencer (John)* (1994) Times, 13 July, discussed in Robertshaw (1998) pp 32-3.
14   Robertshaw (1998) p 15 (see also at pp 192-3).
15   See (1992) 142 NLJ 1031. By contrast, jurors in France receive from the judge up to half a day's training in court procedures and in their role, and defence and prosecuting lawyers may attend this session if they wish: R Munday, 'What do the French think of their jury?' (1995) 15 LS 65 at pp 73-76.
16   See D Wolchover, 'Should Judges Sum up on the Facts?' [1989] Crim LR 781.
17   See R Munday, 'Jury trial, continental style' (1993) 13 LS 204 at p 216 in particular.
18   Robertshaw (1998) pp 23-5 and 179-93.

4. TRIAL: PROCEDURE, EVIDENCE AND LAW

(a) Procedure and evidence

In an adversarial system the decision-makers are meant to be passive. It is not part of the jury's role to investigate matters for itself away from the courtroom.[19] Jurors can ask questions of witnesses in court but rarely do so.[20] Any question is meant to be passed in writing to the judge who will then relay it to a witness if appropriate. The artificiality of this procedure undoubtedly deters jurors from a more proactive role in the trial and they receive little encouragement to assert themselves.[1] It follows that juries must reach their verdicts on the material that is placed before them by counsel for the prosecution and defence. This material is itself shaped by the rules of criminal procedure and evidence. This body of law accordingly forms yet another battleground for Packer's two models of the criminal process.

The clarion call for the crime control model was sounded by the then Commissioner of the Metropolitan Police, Sir Robert Mark, in his Dimbleby Lecture of 1973. Mark was the first high-profile police officer to seek openly to influence criminal justice policy-making.[2] The impact of his intervention continues to resonate today. Arguing that the jury acquits an unacceptably high proportion of those whom the police believe to be guilty, Mark pinned the blame on procedural rules and crooked lawyers:

'It is, of course, right that in a serious criminal case the burden of proof should be on the prosecution. But in trying to discharge that burden the prosecution has to act within a complicated framework of rules which were designed to give every advantage to the defence. The prosecution has to give the defence advance notice of the whole of its case, but the accused, unless he wants to raise an alibi, can keep his a secret until the actual trial. When the police interrogate a suspect or charge him they have to keep reminding him that he need not say anything. If he has a criminal record the jury are not ordinarily allowed to know about it . . . The criminal and his lawyers take every advantage of these technical rules . . . Because of its technicality and its uncertainty, the criminal trial has come to be regarded as a

19   To do so may amount to a serious irregularity vitiating any subsequent conviction. See *Davis, Rowe and Johnson* (17 July 2000, unreported), CA.

20   In the Crown Court study, under half of jurors had wanted to ask a question and less than a fifth of this number had actually done so: Zander and Henderson (1993) p 213.

1   Nearly a third of jurors in the Crown Court study had not been informed at any stage that they could ask questions: Zander and Henderson (1993) p 213.

2   For an account of the police in the political arena see R Reiner, *The Politics of the Police* 2nd edn (London: Harvester Wheatsheaf, 1992) pp 91-96.

game of skill and chance in which the rules are binding on one side only.'[3]

Much of the academic response to Mark was concerned with demonstrating that the acquittal rate by juries was not 'too high',[4] that professional criminals were not frequently escaping justice by exploiting the rules,[5] and that there was little evidence to support the 'bent lawyers' thesis.[6] Less attention was paid to whether the rules of criminal procedure and evidence did indeed unduly favour the defence. Let us examine Mark's three examples of such 'technical' rules.

(i) Advance disclosure of prosecution evidence

The requirement that the prosecution give notice of its case to the defence is intended to redress an imbalance between the parties to the case. As was noted by Lloyd LJ in the successful Birmingham Six appeal, a 'disadvantage of the adversarial system may be that the parties are not evenly matched in resources . . . But the inequality of resources is ameliorated by the obligation on the part of the prosecution to make available all material which may prove helpful to the defence.'[7] The resources of the police and prosecution far outweigh those available to the defence.[8] Moreover, the police are involved in the case from the outset, whereas the defence will not begin to operate until a suspect is arrested. In these circumstances, it is not possible for the defence to carry out an adequate independent investigation of an offence. Advance prosecution disclosure should not be seen as advantaging the defence, but as a means of attempting to redress a structural disadvantage. Indeed, unless accused persons are told what the details of allegations against them are, they cannot prepare a defence.

3 R Mark, *Minority Verdict* The 1973 Dimbleby Lecture (London: BBC, 1973). The core of the lecture is reproduced in M Zander, *Cases and Materials on the English Legal System* (London: Weidenfeld and Nicolson, 1992) pp 471-475.

4 Commentators typically pointed out that most Crown Court defendants plead guilty and that of those found not guilty by the jury most are acquitted on the order or directi_. of the judge, a pattern that holds true today (see section 1).

5 Limited support for Mark's thesis was provided by J A Mack, 'Full-time Major Criminals and the Courts' (1976) 39 MLR 241, but see the response by A Sanders, 'Does Professional Crime Pay? - A Critical Comment on Mack' (1977) 40 MLR 553. See also J Baldwin and M McConville, *Jury Trials* (Oxford: OUP, 1979) pp 110-12.

6 See Baldwin and McConville (1979) p 118, and, by the same authors, 'Allegations Against Lawyers' [1978] Crim LR p 744.

7 *McIlkenny* (1991) 93 Cr App Rep 287 at 312.

8 See G Barclay and C Tavares, Information on the criminal justice system in England and Wales: Digest 4 (London: Home Office, 1999) ch 8.

The duty to disclose was by no means as absolute in 1973 as Mark implied, and the police, the CPS and other prosecution agencies often failed to meet its requirements.[9] The common law regime has since been replaced by the Criminal Procedure and Investigation Act 1996 following continuing police complaints that their duty to disclose evidence was too onerous.[10] Under this Act the prosecution duty to disclose has been cut back at the same time as a new defence duty to disclose its 'case' has been introduced.[11] As discussed in ch 6, section 3, it seems unlikely that the central elements of the new regime will be found to infringe the European Convention on Human Rights. The police, despite the weakness of the arguments deployed by Sir Robert Mark and others, have got their way. Disclosure rules are no longer binding only on the prosecution, so no longer do they fulfil their old function of helping to redress the structural imbalance within the adversarial system. Indeed, one could reasonably argue that they now unduly favour the prosecution. And where disclosure is perhaps most needed, by the police in advance of their interrogation of the suspect, no duty to disclose exists.[12] This was true at the time Mark made his claims and it remains true today. What has changed since Mark's time is that, if suspects remain silent when questioned by the police, the odds of adverse inferences being drawn against them at trial have shot up. The 'rules' on disclosure are now indeed somewhat one-sided - in favour of the police.

(ii)   The right of silence

Mark acknowledged the inroad made into the right of silence by s 11 of the Criminal Justice Act 1967 which requires alibi defences to be notified to the police in advance of the trial, so that they may be 'checked'. What he failed to mention was the limited extent to which the right of silence was respected by the courts.[13] The Court of Appeal in *Gerard*[14] declined to

---

9   See P O'Connor, 'Prosecution Disclosure: Principle, Practice and Justice' in C Walker and K Starmer (eds), *Justice in Error* (London: Blackstone, 1993) and our discussion of disclosure at ch 6 section 3(c) in particular.

10   See, for example, the views expressed by the current Chief Constable of Thames Valley Police, C Pollard, 'A Case for Disclosure' [1994] Crim LR 42.

11   See the assessment by B Fitzpatrick, 'Disclosure: Principles, Processes and Politics' in C Walker and K Starmer (eds), *Miscarriages of Justice* (London: Blackstone, 1999).

12   See ch 5, sections (d) and (e).

13   For a full review of the relevant case law, see the four-part article by D Wolchover (1989) 139 NLJ at 396, 428, 484 and 501, and also K Starmer and M Woolf, 'The Right to Silence' in C Walker and K Starmer (eds), *Miscarriages of Justice* (London: Blackstone, 1999) pp 100-102.

14   (1948) 32 Cr App Rep 132.

intervene when a trial judge commented that an accused's silence before charge might appear 'perhaps a little curious' and 'a little odd'. In *Chandler*[15] the Court of Appeal ruled that where an accused and an accuser were on equal terms it would be in order to invite the jury to consider whether silence in the face of an accusation or question amounted to an acceptance of what had been said. This equal terms doctrine was in accordance with earlier cases such as *Parkes v R*[16] but the new departure was to assert that suspects might be adjudged as on level or even superior terms vis-a-vis police officers. Thus in *Chandler*, a police officer was held to be on equal terms with a suspect because the latter had his solicitor present during questioning.[17] None of this seems consistent with the view of Mark that procedural rules developed so as to give every advantage to the defence.

Since Mark wrote there have been two major statutory developments.[18] The Criminal Procedure and Investigations Act 1996 placed a positive duty on the defence to disclose its 'case' prior to trial (see ch 6, section 3). This is a clear departure from the right to silence. Two years earlier, the Criminal Justice and Public Order Act 1994 had brought about a major attenuation of the right to silence and this now supplements the effect of the 1996 Act. The most significant aspects of the 1994 Act were analysed in depth in ch 5, section 2. That is where the reader should turn for our discussion of the principles involved, and the evidence that bears on the costs and benefits of the right to silence. Our focus there was on those sections of the 1994 Act which allow the jury to draw adverse inferences against suspects if they remain silent *during the investigation* of the alleged crime. Here we look briefly at the sections which allow the jury to draw adverse inferences against accused persons who decline to give evidence *in court*, and which allow the prosecutor to make adverse comment if a defendant remains silent.[19]

Section 35(2) imposes a duty on the court, at the end of the prosecution case, to make accused persons aware of the possibility of the drawing of adverse inferences if they choose not to give evidence or refuse to answer any question on giving evidence. Section 38(2) sets out some restrictions on this new crime control power by stipulating that a person shall not have a case to answer or be convicted of an offence 'solely' through an adverse inference. This section must now be read in the light of subsequent judicial

---

15   [1976] 1 WLR 585.

16   (1976) 64 Cr App Rep 25.

17   See also the case of *Horne* [1990] Crim LR 188 where the equal terms doctrine was applied to silence in response to a victim's accusation made in the presence of police officers.

18   There were many other statutory inroads into the right to silence, particularly from the 1980s onwards: see ch 5, section 2 for discussion.

19   See the analysis by M Wasik and R Taylor, *Blackstone's Guide to the Criminal Justice and Public Order Act 1994* (London: Blackstone, 1995) pp 62-68.

interpretation. In the leading case the Court of Appeal in *Cowan*[20] set out five points which a trial judge must convey to the jury before an adverse inference can be drawn under s 35:

(i)   the burden of proof remains on the prosecution at all times;
(ii) the defendant is entitled to remain silent;
(iii) an inference from failure to give evidence cannot on its own prove guilt;
(iv) the jury must be satisfied that the prosecution established a case to answer before drawing any adverse inferences from the defendant's silence;
(v)   the jury may draw an adverse inference if it concludes that the silence can only sensibly be attributed to the accused having no good answer to the prosecution case.

The Court of Appeal also indicated that there might be other circumstances in which a trial judge might think it right to direct or advise against drawing an adverse inference. Whether this interpretation of s 35 is sufficient to avoid violations of the 'fair trial' provisions (Art 6) of the European Convention on Human Rights is questionable. In *Murray v UK*[1] the European Court examined a conviction obtained under similar legislation in Northern Ireland. Whilst confining its attention to the facts of the case, it held that in situations which clearly called for an explanation from accused persons, their silence could be taken into account in assessing the persuasiveness of the prosecution case. In other words, the ECtHR accepted that there was no absolute right to not have adverse inferences drawn from silence. But it also held that it was incompatible with the immunity from self-incrimination to base a conviction 'solely or mainly' on a refusal to give evidence at trial. This may go further than s 35 which only expressly prevents a conviction which is based 'solely' on such a refusal.[2] What may make s 35 'Convention proof' is the fourth *Cowan* requirement. This requires a jury to believe that there is a case for the defendant to answer before they consider whether to *add* to that prosecution case by drawing an adverse inference from the defendant's silence in court. It is at least arguable that this requirement of an independent prima facie case means that a conviction will not be based either solely *or mainly* on silence. In the subsequent case of *Birchall*[3] the Court of Appeal took the view that, in the absence of careful directions to juries on what adverse inferences they could draw, the application of s 35 could lead to successful challenges under the ECHR. It therefore ruled that it was essential that the fourth condition in *Cowan* formed part of the direction to juries, and that a failure to include it rendered a conviction unsafe. It may be that the Convention

---

20   [1996] QB 373.
1   (1996) 22 EHRR 29
2   As confirmed by *Cowan*: see point (iii) in the preceding paragraph.
3   [1999] Crim LR 311.

Chapter 9 Trial by judge and jury

has softened the crime control impact of the 1994 Act. Nonetheless, whereas at one time, as Mark put it, the police had to keep reminding suspects that they need not say anything, nowadays police, prosecutors and trial judges may or must remind suspects that they need to say something if they want to avoid seriously damaging the chances of acquittal.

(iii) The jury's ignorance of the defendant's criminal record

The rationale for the principle that juries should not ordinarily be told of a defendant's previous convictions (or otherwise be informed that the defendant is of bad character) is that the prejudicial impact of this information outweighs its probative value.[4] Some empirical support for such a prejudicial effect was provided by research done for the Law Commission by Sally Lloyd-Bostock, the results of which were published in 1996.[5] Using mock juries Lloyd-Bostock found that knowledge of previous convictions similar to the offence charged increased the perceived probability of guilt. It also indicated that convictions for offences which provoke an all-round negative evaluation of the perpetrator, such as indecent assault on a child, are likely to be particularly prejudicial to a defendant whatever the current offence charged. Given the level of hysteria[6] and vigilante violence against sex offenders 'named and shamed' by the tabloid press in summer 2000, we might indeed doubt whether anyone known to have previously been convicted of a sexual offence involving a child could receive a fair trial for any offence. This is a good example of the need to situate analyses of criminal justice within a wider social context (see ch 1, section 1). We can hardly expect juries to be unprejudiced if drawn from a society consumed with such hatred and fear.

Whether one sees the principle of not admitting previous convictions into evidence as unduly favouring the defendant depends, in part, on a judgment as to how reliable the police are at identifying the probably guilty in the first place. As we have shown in earlier chapters, the police tend to focus their attention upon 'known criminals'.[7] Statistically, this strategy may be effective in increasing the number of guilty persons detected, but, by giving insufficient attention to independent evidence of guilt, it also increases the risk that innocent people will be drawn into the criminal process. From a due process perspective, this insight would strengthen

4   See *Selvey v DPP* [1968] 2 All ER 497.
5   Law Commission, Evidence in Criminal Proceedings: Previous Misconduct of a Defendant, Consultation Paper no 141 (London: HMSO, 1996), Appendix D. Also reported in S Lloyd-Bostock 'The Effects of Hearing About the Defendant's Previous Criminal Record: A Simulation Study' [2000] Crim LR 734.
6   On 30 August 2000, BBC News 24 reported that vigilantes had vandalised the home of a paediatrician under the mistaken belief that this is the label applied to sex offenders.
7   See ch 2, section 3(a) and, especially, ch 3(b)(iii).

the argument for keeping the defendant's past record from the jury. Denied this knowledge, the jury is forced to focus on the essential issue - is there sufficient evidence that the defendant committed the offence as charged?

As Mark himself recognised, this rule is not applied rigidly, and there are a number of exceptions to it. Firstly, where defendants assert that they are of good character,[8] the prosecution may rebut this by introducing evidence of previous convictions. This seems at first sight a reasonable exception: defendants can hardly complain at the unfairness of the jury being told of a past record of theft if they have claimed to be honest and trustworthy. On the other hand, the courts have adopted a broad definition of what counts as asserting good character. For example, in *Coulman*[9] the defence was held to have led evidence of good character by establishing that the defendant was married, had a family and was in regular employment.[10]

Second, if the facts alleged are similar to the facts of previous incidents involving the defendant then the jury may be told of the latter.[11] This rule is sometimes expressed as though there need be some 'striking' similarity. But in the leading case of *DPP v P*[12] the House of Lords ruled that it was not essential to show that the similarities were striking or that the circumstances were unusual. All that was necessary is that in the judge's view the probative force of the evidence of previous misconduct was sufficiently great as to make it just to admit it notwithstanding that it was prejudicial to the accused. This seems to leave defendants with convictions for a similar offence to that with which they are now charged at considerable risk of having their record put before a jury.[13] In the case of handling stolen goods the Theft Act 1968 puts the matter beyond doubt. Section 27(3) provides that once the prosecution has adduced evidence that the defendant committed the actus reus of the offence (handling) previous convictions for theft or handling are admissible for the purpose of proving mens rea (knowledge or belief that the goods were stolen).[14] This all means that juries are invited to find someone guilty on the same crime control basis that underpinned the defendant's initial arrest by the police.[15]

8   On which see *Stronach* [1988] Crim LR 48.
9   (1927) 20 Cr App Rep 106.
10 See the discussion by D McBarnet, *Conviction* (London: Macmillan, 1983) pp 112-113.
11 Even if these previous incidents were the subject of acquittals: *Z* [2000] 3 All ER 385, HL, overturning *Z* [2000] Crim LR 293, CA.
12 [1991] 2 AC 447.
13 For further discussion, see A Zuckerman, 'Similar Fact Evidence: The Unobservable Rule' (1987) 104 LQR 187.
14 The effect of this rule has been tempered by the due process inspired decision given in *Herron* [1967] 1 QB 107 that the judge retains a discretion not to admit evidence of previous theft/handling convictions where its prejudicial effect would outweigh its probative value.
15 See ch 3, section 4(b) on the importance of 'previous' to arrests.

The third exception is that where one co-accused gives evidence against another co-accused, the latter can cross-examine the former about his previous convictions.[16] Roberts notes how the courts have developed the law on this point so that 'any accused who in any way harms the defence of a co-accused automatically loses his character shield, even if the defendant's "attack" was a necessary ingredient of his defence and/or the effect on his co-accused's case would be negligible in comparison to the grave prejudice that will probably result to the defendant from having his record revealed to the jury.'[17] In other words, the courts have demonstrated a strong preference for crime control values.

The fourth exception is also the most controversial. The Criminal Evidence Act 1898, s 1(f) permits the introduction of previous convictions where 'the nature or conduct of the defence is such as to involve imputations on the character of the . . . witnesses for the prosecution.'[18] This 'tit for tat' rule typically comes into play where the defendant alleges that the police have fabricated or planted incriminating evidence. Since such fabrication undoubtedly occurs from time to time the question arises of whether it can be right to have a rule which will penalize at least some defendants for making wholly justified attacks on the character of police witnesses. Another common situation is where the defendant asserts self-defence or provocation as justification or excuse for an assault. This can be interpreted as an implicit attack on the character of the (alleged) victim. The trial judge retains a discretion not to allow the defendant's bad character to be put before the jury if it would be seriously prejudicial to do so. But the Court of Appeal allows judges wide latitude here, as in *Wainwright*[19] where it upheld the decision to admit into evidence the previous conviction of the defendant for attempted murder in the course of a murder trial in which the defence argued self-defence. As Ormerod notes, 'there can be only a slim chance that the jury relied on this evidence solely in assessing credibility, despite instructions [from the trial judge] to do so.'[20]

16 See further, R Munday, 'The Wilder Permutations of s 1(f) of the Criminal Evidence Act 1898' (1987) 7 LS 137.
17 P Roberts, 'All the Usual Suspects: A Critical Appraisal of Law Commission Consultation Paper No 141' [1997] Crim LR 75 at p 83.
18 For guidelines on how judges should exercise their discretion under s 1(f) see *Britzman and Hall* [1983] 1 All ER 371.
19 [1998] Crim LR 665.
20 [1998] Crim LR 668. If the Court of Appeal wishes to interfere with the trial outcome, one way it can do so is by holding that the defence's cross-examination of prosecution witnesses amounts only to an 'emphatic denial' of the charge, rather than an 'imputation'. It has done this even where, as it itself acknowledged, the emphatic denial necessarily entailed an accusation that the witness is lying under oath: *Desmond* [1999] Crim LR 313. As in other areas of appellate practice (see ch 10, sections 3(e) and 4(d)), the Court of Appeal has left itself plenty of room for manoeuvre so that it can 'do justice' according to its own lights.

The rationale for the rule seems to be that knowledge of a defendant's previous convictions will assist the jury in deciding who is telling the truth, the police or the defendant. But if evidence of past misconduct is generally thought to be too prejudicial, it seems anomalous that it is not so regarded in this situation also. If previous convictions are meant to be indicative of the defendant's dishonesty, why are they not routinely admitted in evidence in cases such as where the defendant admits taking goods from a store without payment but denies that this was done intentionally? The principled argument against the rule is that it is wrong to penalise the defence for testing the prosecution evidence and that the penalty is in any case too harsh as the prejudicial effect of the jury hearing of the previous convictions far outweighs any probative value they might have.[1]

The impact of this rule of evidence can be seen in Baldwin and McConville's study of late plea changers discussed in ch 7. 40% of their sample alleged in interview that the police had falsely attributed to them verbal admissions, and a third of those claiming to be innocent made such allegations.[2] But their counsel had almost invariably advised that any challenge to the police evidence would be foolish since it would rebound on them, the police evidence would be preferred anyway, and the judge might be sufficiently annoyed by the defence tactics to impose a heavier sentence.[3] At the same time if no challenge were made conviction was inevitable. Faced with such advice it is not surprising that these defendants changed their plea to guilty. As one defendant interviewed by Baldwin and McConville put it:

> 'My barrister kept saying I had no chance and that it would be bad if I fought it in court. . . . I said, "No way, I'm not having it; this copper has made up verbals." The barrister said, "If you stick to your plea of not guilty, it seems to me there is going to be some right mud-slinging towards the police. If you do get found guilty, as you will on something, the judge is going to say, "You don't like the police - our blokes - and all these allegations were made to try and cover yourself up for striking this poor [victim]," and you'll get done very heavily."'[4]

Interestingly, this kind of advice was pressed upon defendants with no previous convictions as well as upon recidivists. This suggests that the

1   See further Roberts (1997) pp 90-91. A contrary position is taken by J McEwan, 'Law Commission Dodges the Nettles in Consultation Paper No 141' [1997] Crim LR 93.
2   J Baldwin and M McConville, *Negotiated Justice* (London: Martin Robertson, 1977) p 68.
3   Baldwin and McConville (1977) p 69.
4   Baldwin and McConville (1977) p 47.

real rationale for the tit-for-tat rule is the perceived need to deter attacks on the integrity of the state authorities which might undermine public confidence in the criminal justice system. Where defendants lack previous records, it appears that other mechanisms (such as the threat of stiffer sentences) are employed to deter them from challenging the prosecution version of events. Defence lawyers seem often to co-opt themselves into this project of minimising such challenges, as we also saw in ch 7.

It is important to stress that the controls and safeguards introduced by the Police and Criminal Evidence Act[5] since the Baldwin and McConville study was conducted have not altered the position in any significant way. It is still open to the prosecution to adduce evidence of an alleged verbal confession, which in turn makes it desirable, but, given the tit-for-tat rule, not necessarily sensible, for the defence to challenge the veracity of prosecution witnesses. McConville et al's post-PACE study found many examples of defence lawyers advising their clients not to challenge 'the veracity of statements made in custody which the defendant alleged were, in some measure, the product of police malpractice.' The advice from lawyers to their clients was blunt: 'If we say they're lying, they can call in your character and then there will be only one result.'[6] The due process objections to the tit-for-tat rule - that it increases the risk that the innocent will plead or be found guilty and that it encourages the police to fabricate evidence - should be borne in mind in evaluating Mark's view that the rules of the adversarial 'game' bind and hamper only the prosecution.

What is the overall impact of the four exceptions to the principle that juries are not told of an accused's prior criminal record? Zander and Henderson found that a defendant had previous convictions in 77% of all Crown Court cases tried over a two week period in 1992, and that the jury was told of these convictions in a fifth of the relevant cases.[7] In how many more cases guilty pleas were entered (and trial by jury thereby waived) because of the chilling effect of the evidence rules reviewed above is unknown.

(iv)   Other rules of evidence

We have shown above that Mark's three examples of rules that favour the defence are neither so absolute nor so one-sided as he contended. There

---

5   See chs 4-5 in particular.

6   M McConville, J Hodgson, L Bridges and A Pavlovic, *Standing Accused* (Oxford: Clarendon, 1994) p 217.

7   Zander and Henderson (1993) paras 4.6.1-4.6.8. For the position in the lower courts see M Wasik, 'Magistrates: Knowledge of Previous Convictions' [1996] Crim LR 851, and P Darbyshire, 'Previous Misconduct and Magistrates' Courts - Some Tales from the Real World' [1997] Crim LR 105.

are many other important procedural and evidential rules that favour the prosecution rather than the defence. For instance, there is no requirement that the prosecution produce evidence to corroborate the evidence of a witness, or the confession of an accused. The jury used to be warned that it was dangerous to convict on the unsupported statement of certain types of witness (children, accomplices and complainants in sexual cases) but this neither amounted to requiring corroboration, nor did it preclude a conviction. The law seemed to accept that its own rules could give rise to convictions of an unsatisfactory nature. The warning may have even made things worse as research with mock juries suggested that conviction was more likely if a corroboration warning was given,[8] perhaps because the warning served to highlight a key plank in the prosecution case.[9] The former requirement to give a warning was abolished by s 34 of the Criminal Justice Act 1988 as far as the evidence of children is concerned, and by ss 32-33 of the Criminal Justice and Public Order Act 1994 in relation to the evidence of accomplices and complainants. It remains within the trial judge's discretion to comment on the strength of the prosecution case when summing up, and this might include a warning about convicting in the absence of any independent evidence supporting the testimony of a particular witness.[10] Finally, it should be noted that no corroboration warning is required where the only evidence is an alleged confession, yet, as ch 5, section 5, demonstrated, extreme caution in this area is vital.

Where the evidence against the accused rests substantially on identification evidence the case of *Turnbull*[11] requires that the judge should direct an acquittal if the quality of the evidence is poor, but otherwise should warn the jury of the need for caution before convicting on such evidence.[12] Arguably these guidelines do not go far enough in protecting accused persons from wrongful conviction given the inherently unreliable nature of identification evidence, and the role such evidence is known to have played in miscarriages of justice.[13] Furthermore, the senior judiciary are not consistent in their stipulations concerning when this due process safeguard is needed. Jackson noted in 1999 that earlier cases like *Curry*[14] confined the impact of *Turnbull* to 'fleeting glimpse' sightings, but that 'it is now clear that the cases in which the warning can be dispensed with are

8   L Sealy and W Cornish, 'Juries and the Rules of Evidence' [1973] Crim LR 208.
9   R Leng and R Taylor, *Blackstone's Guide to the Criminal Procedure and Investigations Act 1996* (London: Blackstone, 1996) at p 47.
10 See, for example, *L* [1999] Crim LR 489.
11 [1977] QB 224.
12 For the position regarding voice identification see *Roberts* [2000] Crim LR 183 and accompanying commentary.
13 See further, J Jackson, 'The Insufficiency of Identification Evidence Based on Personal Impression' [1986] Crim LR 203.
14 [1983] Crim LR 737.

"wholly exceptional"'.[15] Since then the Court of Appeal has re-heated *Curry* by holding[16] that *Turnbull* was intended primarily to deal with cases of fleeting encounters. Trying to derive clarity from case law is liable to give you indigestion.

The rules prohibiting the admission of hearsay evidence (already subject to many exceptions) were weakened considerably by s 23 of the Criminal Justice Act 1988. This allows first-hand documentary evidence to be admitted if the maker is dead, ill, cannot be located and brought to court, or if the statement is made to a police officer and the maker does not give oral evidence through fear or because the authorities deem it important to keep the witness out of the public arena. This cuts against the traditional emphasis in criminal procedure on the importance of evidence being given orally in open court so that it may be subject to cross-examination. In the Court of Appeal, May LJ has pointed out that 'you cannot conduct an argument with, nor ask questions of, a piece of paper.'[17] That Court has policed the boundaries of s 23, for example by discouraging judges from allowing juries to speculate that the reason a person does not give oral evidence is fear of the defendant.[18] Nonetheless, as Jackson notes, s 23 'has increased the ability of the prosecution to submit dubious documentary evidence against the accused.'[19]

Article 6(3)(d) of the European Convention sets out the minimum right of everyone charged with a criminal offence 'to examine or have examined witnesses against him'. At first sight the s 23 device seems liable to produce breaches of this right, but the Court of Appeal has held that s 23 is not in itself contrary to Art 6.[20] From the European Court of Human Rights' perspective, the question of whether evidence admitted under s 23 produces breaches of the Convention is likely to turn on the strength of the rest of the prosecution case, and the provision of compensating safeguards for defendants, such as the warning provided to juries about the danger of relying on statements not subjected to cross-examination.[1]

The Runciman Commission approach to the law of evidence was somewhat contradictory. On the one hand it proposed changes which would increase the due process protection of suspects from wrongful

---

15   Jackson (1999) p 195, citing *Shand v R* [1996] 1 All ER 511.

16   *Beckles and Montague* [1999] Crim LR 148.

17   *Radak, Adjei, Butler-Rees and Meghjee* [1999] Crim LR 223.

18   See *Wood and Fitzsimmons* [1998] Crim LR 213. Trial judges are also meant to warn the jury of the dangers of accepting witness evidence not subject to cross-examination, but the warning need not take any specific form: *Batt and Batt* [1995] Crim LR 240.

19   J Jackson, 'Trial Procedures', in C Walker and K Starmer (eds), *Justice in Error* (London: Blackstone, 1993) p 139.

20   *Thomas, Flannagan, Thomas and Smith* [1998] Crim LR 887.

1   See A Ashworth, 'Article 6 and the Fairness of Trials' [1999] Crim LR 261 at 268-69.

conviction. One example is the recommendation that an attack on the character of a witness for the prosecution which is central to the defence should not expose the accused to the risk of cross-examination concerning previous convictions.[2] Thus, if the defence rested on an allegation that the police had fabricated a confession the police could be accused of having lied without fear of the tit-for-tat rule coming into play. Another example is its recommendation that judges should be required to warn juries of the dangers of convicting on the basis of confession evidence alone.[3] It also recommended retention of the right to silence, albeit in modified form. None of these recommendations was accepted by the Government.

On the other hand, a somewhat larger number of recommendations were designed to make it easier for the prosecution to secure a conviction. For example, the Runciman Commission wanted the rules on hearsay evidence to be relaxed still further. It also recommended that where the accused admits committing the actus reus of the crime but denies acting with intent, knowledge or recklessness (as the case may be) previous convictions for a similar offence should be admissible. And, by a majority, it turned its back on the much canvassed proposal that convictions based on confession evidence should not be tolerated in the absence of corroboration.[4] In his review of this aspect of the Runciman Commissions' work Jackson concludes that 'it is difficult to feel confident that its recommendations do enough to restore faith in the system's ability to avert miscarriages of justice. . .'.[5] Subsequent legislation, such as the Criminal Justice and Public Order Act 1994 (abolition of right to silence and of corroboration warnings) and the Youth Justice and Criminal Evidence Act 1999 (introduction of further protective devices for vulnerable witnesses *other* than the defendant)[6], indicates that successive governments have been more interested in enhancing the ability of the system to efficiently produce convictions.

We conclude by recalling that Sir Robert Mark argued that jury trials were lopsided affairs in which the prosecution was bound by rules whilst the defence could play dirty. In the interests of even-handed analysis let us record that the prosecution authorities are not above foul play themselves. We saw in earlier chapters how these authorities seek to construct cases so as to ensure the outcome they seek, and that this can involve such unethical practices as fabricating and tampering with

---

2   RCCJ (1993) p 127. A similar position was subsequently taken by the Law
     Commission. See Roberts [1997].
3   RCCJ (1993) p 68.
4   See RCCJ (1993) at pp 127, 126 and 68 respectively. The corroboration issue is
     discussed more fully in ch 5, section 5(b).
5   J Jackson, 'The Evidence Recommendations' [1993] Crim LR p 817 at 828.
6   See section 3(b) above.

evidence.[7] Two cases which came to light in the 1990s show that it would be wrong to assume that they would not dare 'tamper' with the jury itself. In *Kaul*[8] the police improperly took away from the court a rucksack already admitted into evidence and even more improperly placed items in it which were prejudicial to the defendant, returning it to court the following day. This only came to light because the jury, having taken the rucksack with them when retiring to consider their verdict, sent a note to the judge querying why the contents of the rucksack had not been mentioned during the trial. The Court of Appeal in quashing the conviction referred to its earlier unreported decision in *Ellis* (10 June 1991) in which 'documents which should not have been shown to the jury were "accidentally" given to them, allegedly by a police witness.'[9] In one sense it is understandable that the police stoop to such tactics. As we saw in section 1 of this chapter, despite all the supposed safeguards, weak cases do end up in front of the jury. The police are naturally sometimes tempted to strengthen them through a last minute piece of case construction.

(b) Substantive law and the definition of offences

In understanding how juries came to be convinced of guilt beyond reasonable doubt it is also necessary to look at the structure of substantive criminal law. We can do no more than scratch the surface of this issue here, but the links between criminal law and criminal justice are too important to ignore.[10] We commented in earlier chapters on how the breadth of the criminal law has implications for police powers of arrest and stop and search, and the implications are no less important at the trial stage. The essential point is that the fewer the elements that have to be proved by the prosecution, and the easier the law makes it to prove those elements, the more likely it is that juries will convict. All-encompassing offence definitions are antithetical to due process since they cover a variety of acts and states of mind ranging from the venal to the virtuous. To be presumed innocent is of little significance if the prosecution need do little to prove guilt. This is precisely what makes such definitions attractive to crime control adherents, since they assist in curtailing inefficient and pointless adversarial trials. Moreover, they may deter defendants from opting for trial in the first place and thus contribute to maintaining a high guilty plea rate.

7   See especially ch 6, section 3(c).
8   [1998] Crim LR 135.
9   Commentary to *Kaul* [1998] Crim LR 135 at p 137.
10 For an insightful treatment of this theme see N Lacey, 'Criminology, Criminal Law and Criminalization' in M Maguire, R Morgan and R Reiner (eds), *Oxford Handbook of Criminology* 2nd edn (Oxford: Clarendon, 1997).

Many examples of broadly drawn offences could be given. McBarnet has pointed out that crimes such as theft and assault cover a much wider range of behaviour than the lay person generally realises.[11] Under the Theft Act 1968, the actus reus of theft is the appropriation of property belonging to another, and any assumption of any one right of the owner amounts to an appropriation.[12] Moreover, the House of Lords has held in *Gomez*[13] that it is an appropriation notwithstanding that the owner authorises the taking or moving of property. Thus simply taking down a bottle of whisky from a supermarket shelf amounts to an appropriation and if there is, in addition, evidence of dishonesty and an intention to permanently deprive the supermarket of the whisky, then a conviction for theft could follow. As the only evidence of a defendant's state of mind in this situation is likely to be a confession, it is dangerous to reduce the conduct element of the crime of theft to this minimum. As we saw in ch 5, the risk of false confessions is great and it would be more in accordance with due process principles to require that the defendant did some act which was strongly corroborative of a criminal purpose (such as concealing the whisky under a coat).

General principles of liability further extend the prodigious reach of the criminal law. For example, s 1(1) of the Criminal Attempts Act 1981 makes it an offence to do an act which is more than merely preparatory to the commission of an indictable offence if done with intent to commit such offence. To take our earlier example, merely reaching to pick up the bottle of whisky from the shelf may be classified as a criminal attempt.

The law concerning the mental element in crime is also often broadly drawn, as in the case of 'Caldwell recklessness'. Prior to the case of *Caldwell*[14] decisions of the Court of Appeal had established that 'recklessness' (the mental element required in offences such as assault, criminal damage, and one of the variants of manslaughter) meant the state of mind of one who was consciously aware of the risk that an action would bring about certain consequences.[15] In *Caldwell*, a case of criminal damage, the House of Lords held by a narrow majority that the term also encompassed persons who failed to consider whether such a risk existed when that risk would have been obvious to a reasonable person. There are sound policy arguments for extending the scope of recklessness in this way - the moral culpability of someone who cannot be bothered to address his or her mind to the possibility of risk may be no less than one who consciously takes risks but exercises a degree of care in doing so.[16] But

11   See D McBarnet, *Conviction* (London: Macmillan, 1983) pp 13-14.
12   *Morris* [1984] AC 320.
13   [1993] 1 All ER 1.
14   [1981] 1 All ER 961.
15   See, in particular, *Cunningham* [1957] 2 QB 396, and *Stephenson* [1979] QB 695.
16   See S Gardner, 'Recklessness refined' (1993) 109 LQR 21.

while Lord Diplock, speaking for the majority, justified the development of the law on such moral grounds, it is striking that he was much influenced by the supposed difficulties juries would have in distinguishing those who appreciated the risks in their actions and those who did not.[17] In the subsequent case of *Reid* Lord Keith reiterated this point, arguing that it would be impossible for a juror to be satisfied beyond reasonable doubt that a defendant was aware of a risk rather than having merely failed to advert to the possibility of risk. 'So logically', he continued, 'if only the first state of mind constituted the relevant mens rea, it would be impossible ever to get a conviction.'[18]

We are dealing here with entirely bogus logic. The appellate courts, after some equivocation, confined the impact of *Caldwell* to offences of criminal damage. They refused to apply its broader definition of recklessness to rape,[19] assault[20] and statutorily defined offences against the person which require the act to be performed 'maliciously'.[1] In these latter cases the courts have been content that juries will be able to draw practical distinctions between the two states of mind referred to by Lord Keith. What is certainly true is that the decision in *Caldwell* extends the ambit of liability in criminal damage cases so as to make it more likely that defendants will plead guilty or that juries will convict. As well as increasing the conviction rate, this saves time as it is no longer necessary for the prosecution to adduce evidence of the defendant's state of mind - only the objective circumstances need be put before the jury.[2]

How does the law deal with the alternative situation where the prosecution must establish intent or foresight of risk? How can the prosecution make the jury sure beyond reasonable doubt of a defendant's state of mind? The defendant, after all, cannot be compelled to answer questions about this matter. In reality, as we have seen, many defendants do answer police questions designed to elicit evidence of the requisite state of mind.[3] Where there is no confession, some other device must be

17   [1981] 1 All ER 961 at 965. As a result of a series of legislative interventions, the most recent of which is s 46 of the Criminal Justice and Public Order Act 1994, criminal damage offences are only triable before a jury if the property loss is at least £5,000. Two thousand such cases were tried in the Crown Court in 1998: Criminal Statistics 1998 (Cm 4649) (London: SO, 2000) Table 6C.
18   [1992] 3 All ER 673.
19   *Satnam and Kewal* (1983) 78 Cr App Rep 149.
20   *Spratt* [1990] 1 WLR 1073.
1   See *Savage* [1991] 4 All ER 698.
2   Thus in *Lawrence* [1982] AC 510 at 527 Lord Diplock observed that: 'if satisfied that an obvious and serious risk was created by the manner of the defendant's driving, the jury are entitled to infer that he was in one or other of the states of mind required to constitute the offence and will probably do so; but regard must be given to any explanation he gives as to his state of mind which may displace the inference.'
3   See ch 5, sections 4-5.

found if the jury is to be convinced of guilt. One is the adverse inference that can be drawn from a defendant's silence. Another is the advice which may be given to the jury that the question of what a reasonable person would have intended or foreseen in identical circumstances is something to be considered in reaching its verdict. As the Court of Appeal put it in a pre-*Caldwell* criminal damage case, *Stephenson*:[4]

> 'A man is reckless when he carries out [a] deliberate act appreciating that there is a risk that damage to property may result from his act .... Proof of the requisite state of knowledge in the mind of the defendant will in most cases present little difficulty. The fact that the risk of some damage would have been obvious to anyone in his right mind in the position of the defendant is not conclusive proof of the defendant's knowledge, but it may well be and in many cases doubtless will be a matter which will drive the jury to the conclusion that the defendant himself must have appreciated the risk.'

Trial judges can accordingly reassure juries that the state of a defendant's mind, far from being virtually unknowable in the absence of a confession, can be established from objective circumstances 'in most cases [with] little difficulty.'

We may also note that the criminal law generally ignores the defendant's motive in defining what counts as a guilty state of mind.[5] Defendants charged with theft of food will not be heard to say in their defence that they were hungry, nor will those who enter a boarded-up building as trespassers, intending to chop up floorboards for firewood, be allowed to defend a charge of burglary by arguing that they were cold and homeless. Juries are enjoined to do justice according to law, but the law incorporates a particular kind of justice which skates over awkward problems arising from gross inequalities in society.[6] In this way too, the issues to be debated at trial are narrowed and the potential for adversarial challenge is reduced.

Finally, we should not forget the discussion in ch 1, section 4, regarding the burden of proof. As noted there, in 1996 it was calculated that 219 out of the 540 indictable (ie triable in the Crown Court) offences then in common use involved a reversal of the burden of proof.[7] A good illustration of an

---

4   [1979] QB 695 at 703.
5   See the discussion by A Norrie, *Crime, Reason and History* (London: Weidenfeld and Nicolson, 1993) pp 36-47.
6   There is a striking contrast here with non-police agencies. Immunity from prosecution (and hence conviction) for crimes which are a product of the economic facts of life is almost universally accepted. See ch 6, section 5 for further discussion.
7   A Ashworth and M Blake, 'The Presumption of Innocence in English Criminal Law' [1996] Crim L R 306.

offence which involves such a reversal is that of 'living off immoral earnings'. Section 30(2) of the Sexual Offences Act 1956, provides:

> 'for the purposes of this section a man who lives with or is habitually in the company of a prostitute, or who exercises control, direction or influence over a prostitute's movements in a way which shows he is aiding, abetting or compelling her prostitution with others shall be presumed to be knowingly living on the earnings of prostitution, unless he proves to the contrary.'

Thus, once the objective circumstances have been established by the prosecution, which can amount to no more than living with a prostitute, the offence is presumed. It becomes for the defence to prove innocence rather than the prosecution to prove guilt. When offences are defined in this way, the presumption of innocence and the right to silence have little content or force. It might be thought that convincing a jury of guilt will become more difficult following the reception into English law through the Human Rights Act of the ECHR. Article 6(2) provides that 'everyone charged with a criminal offence shall be presumed innocent until proved guilty according to law'. But the presumption of innocence at the European level seems to have little more positive content than is the case in England and Wales. Thus the ECtHR held in the leading case of *Salabiaku v France*[8] that conviction could be based upon a 'simple or objective fact as such, irrespective of whether it results from criminal intent or negligence'. It further held, however, that presumptions of fact or law within the criminal law must be confined 'within reasonable limits which take into account the importance of what is at stake and maintain the rights of the defence.' Quite what those reasonable limits are is a matter of some debate,[9] but they appear to be fairly broadly drawn. For example, the 'living off immoral earnings' provision quoted above was found by the European Commission not to offend the ECHR.[10] Overall it seems unlikely that any radical reappraisal of the criminal law will be required.[11] That is certainly the view of the Court of

---

8   (1988) 13 EHRR 379.

9   Compare R Buxton, 'The Human Rights Act and the Substantive Criminal Law' [2000] Crim LR 331 with A Ashworth, 'The Human Rights Act and the Substantive Criminal Law: A Non-Minimalist View' [2000] Crim LR 564 and P Lewis, 'The Human Rights Act 1998: Shifting the Burden' [2000] Crim LR 667.

10 *RP v UK* Application no 5124/71, 42 CD 135, 1972.

11 Whilst space precludes analysis of whether the ECHR would outlaw some of the more vague or general catch-all criminal offences contained within statute and common law, our conclusion would be the same. For opposing views see Buxton [2000] and Ashworth [2000] 'The Human Rights Act and the Substantive Criminal Law: A Non-Minimalist View'.

Appeal as expressed in the recent case of *Lambert, Ali and Jordan*.[12] All of this further undermines Sir Robert Mark's implicit claim, set out at the start of this section, that the burden of proof lay only on the prosecution and that the rules 'were designed to give every advantage to the defence'.

5. EVALUATING THE JURY'S PERFORMANCE

It was argued in ch 8 that magistrates are more likely than jurors to embrace crime control ideology. This is largely because jurors are outsiders, free of the administrative concerns of dealing speedily with a large caseload. Moreover, unlike magistrates, jurors bear no direct responsibility for sentencing,[13] and are accordingly less likely to see themselves as instruments for upholding law and order. As jury service is statistically a less than once in a lifetime opportunity, it seems unlikely that in such circumstances jurors will in general subscribe to the crime control view that their task is to trust the prosecution evidence and convict without more ado. On the other hand, one must not simply assume that the jury operates according to due process principles. This is all the more so when we recall the concerns we raised in section 2 about the pro-prosecution bias in the law and practice of jury selection. Rather, we must question whether juries in practice set aside their prejudices, seek hard evidence of guilt, and apply the appropriate standard of proof.

An immediate problem is that juries are not required to articulate reasons for the conclusions they reach at the end of a case. They deliberate in private and, on their return to the court, merely give a general verdict of 'guilty' or 'not guilty'.[14] Moreover, a stifling and all-embracing concern to protect the secrecy of the jury has prevented any systematic study based on direct observation or recording of its deliberations. For many years the exact legal position was unclear on this point, although a convention of jury secrecy was maintained. But s 8 of the Contempt of Court Act 1981 made it a contempt to 'obtain, disclose or solicit any particulars of statements made, opinions expressed, arguments advanced or votes cast by members of a jury in the course of their deliberation.' It is sometimes said that such a

---

12　[2000] 35 LS Gaz R 36. The Lord Chief Justice gave judgment holding that neither the defences in ss 5(4) and 28 of the Misuse of Drugs Act 1971 nor s 2(2) Homicide Act 1957, each of which placed the burden of proof on the balance of probabilities on criminal defendants, violated Art 6 of the European Convention on Human Rights because neither was concerned with the ingredients of the offence.

13　In some jurisdictions jurors do bear some responsibility for sentencing: see Munday (1995). See further ch 8, section 5(a).

14　In the case of a 'guilty' verdict the jury foreman will be asked to state the number of jurors voting for and against conviction. To avoid 'second-rate acquittals', this question is not put if a 'not guilty' verdict is returned.

rule is necessary to protect individual jurors from reprisals or to preserve the finality of jury verdicts, although closer analysis suggests that the purpose of s 8 was to 'maintain the authority of particular verdicts, and indeed of jury trial in general, in the eyes of the public.'[15]

Do juries deserve public confidence? The answer to this can only be equivocal since the existing studies are either anecdotal, or based on the impressions of judges, lawyers and police officers, or on simulations with 'shadow' or 'mock' juries.[16] To this motley collection can be added the Runciman Commission's Crown Court survey of views on the jury. We will look at each type of evidence in turn.

(a) General impressions

Individual jurors have published their recollections of their period of service both before and after the Contempt of Court Act 1981. Some have been disillusioned or even dismayed by their experiences while others have reported broad satisfaction with the jury process.[17] As such experiences are unlikely to be typical we do not dwell upon them here. For the same reason we do not dwell upon the oddities revealed by case law.[18]

The large-scale Crown Court survey carried out for the Runciman Commission found that 80% of jurors rated trial by jury as a good or very good system and only 5% rated it as poor or worse.[19] Jurors typically claimed that they had little difficulty in understanding or remembering the evidence, in coping with legalistic language or in following directions on the law from the judge.[20] The judges surveyed thought the jury system was good or very good in terms of 'generally getting a sensible result' in

---

15 J Jaconelli, 'Some thoughts on jury secrecy' (1990) 10 LS 91 at p 99. Thus if a foreman wrongly declares the verdict of guilty to be 'unanimous' the Court of Appeal will refuse to inquire into the matter: *Hart* [1998] Crim LR 417; *Millward* [1999] Crim LR 164. See also the survey by I Bing, 'Curing Bias in Criminal Trials - the consequences of *R v Gough*' [1998] Crim LR 148. Whether the courts should have a wider power to inquire into the verdict is discussed in J C Smith, 'Is Ignorance Bliss? Could Jury Trials Survive Investigation?' (1998) 38 Med Sci Law 98.

16 For a summary of recent research in New Zealand, see C Dyer, 'Anyone know what the judge is on about?' *The Guardian*, 17 July 2000, supplement pp 14-15.

17 See, for example, the five accounts published in (1990) 140 NLJ 1264-1276.

18 Such as: the foreman who, after the jury retired, produced his own list of the defendant's previous convictions (*Thompson* (1961) 46 Cr App Rep 72); the profoundly deaf jury member who missed half of the evidence and all of the summing up (*Chapman and Lauday* (1976) 63 Cr App Rep 75); and the members of a jury who consulted a 'ouija board' for help in reaching their verdict (*Young (Stephen Andrew)* [1995] 2 Cr App Rep 379).

19 Zander and Henderson (1993) p 232.

20 See Zander and Henderson (1993) at pp 206, 208, 212, and 216 respectively.

79% of cases, the prosecution barristers in 82% and defence barristers in 91%. The survey found that 8% of judges rated the system as poor or very poor, compared with 4% of prosecuting barristers and 2% of defence barristers.[1] While such ratings of trial by jury as 'good' or 'bad' are somewhat crude and subjective, the findings of this survey nonetheless reveal a high level of support for this institution.

(b) Professional disagreement with juries

A number of studies have examined the extent of disagreement with jury verdicts in particular cases. In the USA, Kalven and Zeisel examined 3,576 trials and found that judges agreed with the decision reached by the jury in 75% of cases.[2] As Stephenson has pointed out, this is not a particularly high level of agreement. On his analysis, the most striking finding of this study is that judges, as well as agreeing with nearly all jury decisions to convict, would also have convicted 57% of the 1,083 persons whom the jury acquitted.[3] Judges attributed the disagreement between themselves and the juries they instructed to a range of factors. In nearly a third of cases they thought juries had been swayed by their dislike for the law and had exercised jury equity. In 15% of cases they acquitted, in the judge's view, because either the defendant or defence counsel had made a favourable impression upon them. In 54% of cases the judge thought that the jury had taken a different approach to the evidence.[4]

The early English studies that measured the extent of agreement amongst lawyers and police officers with jury verdicts concluded that these groups for the most part had no quarrel with the jury's decision.[5] The most substantial study of this type, conducted by Baldwin and McConville in the mid-1970s, painted a more critical picture. Of 370 randomly selected cases heard in one Crown Court centre, 114 ended in acquittal. Of the latter, serious doubts were expressed about the jury's verdict by the judge in 32% of cases, by the police in 44%, by prosecuting solicitors in 26% and by defence solicitors in 10% of cases.[6] Baldwin and McConville defined a 'questionable acquittal' as one where the judge and at least one other respondent thought the acquittal was not justified. They considered

1   Zander and Henderson (1993) pp 172-73.
2   H Kalven and H Zeisel, *The American Jury* (Boston: Little Brown, 1966).
3   G Stephenson, *The Psychology of Criminal Justice* (Oxford: Basil Blackwell, 1992) pp 180-81.
4   Kalven and Zeisel (1966) p 115.
5   See S McCabe and R Purves, *The Jury at Work*, (Oxford: Basil Blackwell, 1972) and M Zander, 'Are Too Many Professional Criminals Avoiding Conviction ?' (1974) 37 MLR 28. For a critique of such research, see Freeman (1981) pp 85-97.
6   Baldwin and McConville (1979) pp 45-47.

Evaluating the jury's performance

whether jury equity explained the high incidence of questionable acquittals (36% of all acquittals), but concluded that it did not. As they put it:

'The number of defendants who seem to us to have been acquitted in questionable circumstances, without any apparent equitable justification save in a handful of cases, suggests that trial by jury is a relatively crude instrument for establishing the truth.'[7]

The proportion of convictions that were questioned was much smaller, but in fifteen cases (6% of all convictions) two or more of the parties to the case had serious doubts about the jury's verdict. Whereas the judge had reservations in eight of these cases, it is striking that the police doubted the verdict in all but two instances. The researchers considered that the most likely explanation for these doubtful convictions was that the jury had failed to appreciate the high standard of proof required in criminal cases and that it had lacked comprehension of the issues involved.[8] There was also evidence to suggest that in some of these cases the jury might have been swayed by racial prejudice.[9] This, from a due process point of view, is the flip side of 'jury equity' and it must be taken into account by those who find attractive the idea of a jury following 'its conscience' rather than the law.[10] Overall, the authors concluded that:

'the performance of the jury did not always appear to accord with the principle underlying the trial system in England that it is better to acquit those who are probably guilty than to convict any who are possibly innocent. On the contrary, the jury appeared on occasion to be over-ready to acquit those who were probably guilty and insufficiently prepared to protect the possibly innocent.'[11]

Two points need to be made concerning Baldwin and McConville's work. The first is that their methods for assessing questionable jury acquittals is itself highly questionable. Of the four parties to the case whose views they sought, two (prosecuting solicitor and police) are clearly conviction minded, one (the judge) is, as this chapter has argued, very often pro-conviction, and only one is likely to be pro-acquittal (defence solicitor). Note that

7   Baldwin and McConville (1979) pp 66-67.
8   Baldwin and McConville (1979) p 76.
9   Baldwin and McConville (1979) pp 80-81.This could be addressed by ensuring a more representative racial mix on the jury: see section 2 above.
10   See also, J Gordon, 'Juries as Judges of the Law' (1992) 108 LQR 272 at 278.
11   Baldwin and McConville (1979) p 128. See also Zander and Henderson (1993) pp 162-172, for the reactions of lawyers, police officers and judges to particular jury verdicts. As with Baldwin and McConville, 'problematic' acquittals were found to be more prevalent than problematic convictions.

whereas defence solicitors had serious doubts about acquittals in 10% of all acquittal cases, the other three groups had such doubts in much larger proportions ranging from 26% to 44%. By defining a questionable acquittal as one in which the judge and one other party to the case thought the jury's verdict to be wrong, Baldwin and McConville built into their measurements an inherent prosecution bias. That juries were found to be acquittal-prone by the standards of state officials and representatives is not surprising given the state's commitment to crime control values.

The second point is to ask what meaning to attribute to evidence of disagreement between professionals and lay jurors. If juries always reached verdicts of which judges approved one might legitimately question the value of having a jury at all. One of the strongest arguments for retaining trial by jury is to avoid leaving the fate of defendants to be determined by professionals, applying professional standards. Thus, Bankowski and Mungham contend that since there is no consensus about what constitutes a 'good' jury decision, and because the lawyer's view of a case is not the only sensible or rational interpretation, professional disagreement with jury verdicts tells us nothing meaningful about jury competence.[12] Baldwin and McConville attempt to deal with this critique by arguing as follows:

> 'A verdict is not invalidated simply because the lawyers do not agree with it; equally it is not validated by the mere fact that they approve of it. On the other hand, determining whether a verdict accords with the law provides one starting-point for locating the extent of jury departure from legal rules.'[13]

But it does not follow from the fact that lawyers (including judges) disagree with a verdict that the jury has departed from the legal rules. If one accepts that law is not an absolute but must always be interpreted and applied in specific contexts and circumstances it follows that jurors may take a different view of what the law requires in a particular case to that adopted by lawyers. The institution of the jury represents a policy preference for the process by which this judgment is to be reached to be left ultimately in the hands of lay people rather than professionals. This injection of a lay element into the administering of justice does not have to be justified on the ground that the jury is more reliable or efficient as a finder of fact than a professional judge. Rather, one can argue that lay involvement is necessary in order to allow jury equity to be exercised (if we think this to be desirable) and also to ensure that law and justice do not become

12   G Mungham and Z Bankowski, 'The jury in the legal system' in P Carlen (ed), *The Sociology of Law* (Keele: University of Keele, 1976) p 209. See also M Freeman (1981) pp 85-88 and 95-97 in particular.
13   Baldwin and McConville (1979) p 18.

monopolised by professionals.[14] From a freedom perspective, there are good reasons why professional expertise should be challenged and laid bare before the community as represented by the 12 individuals on the jury. This seems consistent with the current Government's encouragement of 'active citizenship' and its oft-repeated view that 'with rights come responsibilities'. There is evidence that serving on a jury can lead to a sense of pride in the accomplishment of an important civic duty and the awakening of a more general interest in the administration of justice.[15] Lay participation in criminal justice, whether in the form of lay magistrates or the jury, is an element of democracy.[16] Jury service, by furthering transparency and accountability within criminal justice, is a safeguard of a free society.

(c) Shadow juries

An obvious difficulty with all studies measuring professional disagreement with verdicts is that they are based on indirect measurements of the jury's work. It is possible that observation of the jury's deliberations would have indicated to Baldwin and McConville a satisfactory explanation (whether of an evidential or equitable nature) for many of the verdicts they classified as questionable.

Direct observation of 'shadow' juries - where a panel of people observe or listen to trials in tandem with the real jury, and then retire to consider their 'verdict' - have provided some insight into the dynamics of the jury room.[17] All such studies show a fairly high level of correspondence between the verdicts of the real and the shadow juries, suggesting that the latter approach their simulated task in a reasonably realistic manner. In a study of 30 cases, McCabe and Purves concluded that:

'The "shadow" juries showed considerable determination in looking for evidence upon which convictions could be based; when it seemed

---

14   See Mungham and Bankowski (1976) and Freeman (1981) for extended treatment of this theme. See also ch 8, section 5, where we illustrate how juries, when compared with social elites, such as magistrates or lawyers, may reach a different (and, arguably, better) view of what the law requires.

15   Munday (1995) at pp 68-71.

16   J Gobert, *Justice, Democracy and the Jury* (Aldershot: Dartmouth, 1997); Z Bankowski, N Hutton and J McManus, *Lay Justice?* (Edinburgh: T & T Clark, 1987) chs 1, 9.

17   Another kind of research involves 'mock juries' in which panels of people observe and then deliberate on mock trials. This research tends to be rather artificial but can shed some light on issues such as whether jurors are likely to be prejudiced by hearing of a defendant's previous convictions. The Lloyd-Bostock research was of this type: see section 4(a)(iii) above. See also the study by Honess, Levi and Charman discussed in section 6 below.

inadequate, they were not prepared to allow their own "hunch" that the defendant was involved in some way in the offence that was charged to stand in the way of an acquittal . . . There was little evidence of perversity in the final decisions of these thirty groups. One acquittal only showed that sympathy and impatience with the triviality of the case so influenced the "shadow" jurors' view of the evidence that they refused to convict.'[18]

Another study, also conducted in the early 1970s, concluded to like effect that juries approach the task of determining guilt as a serious responsibility.[19] More recently, McConville has reported on a televised study of five real cases heard by a shadow jury. Striking a decidedly more positive tone than in his earlier work on juries with Baldwin, he writes that:

'Although not dealing with the fate of actual defendants, the shadow jury's deliberations have an authentic ring, marked by fierce debate, acute analysis, common sense, personal experience, stubbornness and occasional whiffs of prejudice . . . Overall, the quality and power of the argument within the shadow jury room, and the high level of correspondence between the verdicts of the real and shadow juries, suggests that confidence in the jury is well-placed.'[20]

(d) Jury research in context

Criminal justice has undergone a series of fundamental changes over the last 15 years. Notable amongst these are PACE, the inception of the Crown Prosecution Service, and amongst the many other recent 'reforms' to the law of evidence, the major attenuation of the right to silence. The impact of all this on the workings of jury trials has yet to be charted properly. The weight of the evidence to date suggests, however, that juries do conform much more closely to due process values than to crime control ideology. But since, as demonstrated earlier, it is not the jury, but the judge, who is the central directing figure in a trial, and since judges commonly adopt crime control positions, juries are in reality unlikely to base decisions on anything like a pure due process approach.

Juries do not act in a vacuum, nor do they act as finders of the truth.[1] They simply decide 'a case'. The case that is presented to the jury is shaped by rules of evidence, procedure and substantive law, the presentation skills

18 S McCabe and R Purves, *The Shadow Jury at Work* (Oxford: Basil Blackwell, 1974).
19 L Sealy and W Cornish, 'Juries and the Rules of Evidence' [1973] Crim LR 208.
20 M McConville, 'Shadowing the jury' (1991) 141 NLJ 1588 at pp 1588 and 1595.
1 See Mungham and Bankowski (1976) p 206 and pp 212-13.

of opposing counsel, the preparatory work by the police, the influence of the judge and a host of other factors. We have argued throughout this book that all pre-trial and trial processes are imbued, to a greater or lesser degree, with crime control values. No matter how due process oriented juries might be, they cannot be relied upon to spot the crime control workmanship that went into building the case put before them. To expect the jury to deconstruct the case and re-examine it under a due process microscope is simply unrealistic. The fact that every major miscarriage of justice case that has come to light in recent years was preceded by a guilty verdict from a jury is evidence of this. Having said that, judges are no different to juries in this respect. They too can only deal with the case as presented. And that will have been shaped by the processes covered in chs 2-6 of this book. This is a point worth bearing in mind when we consider, in the next section, the value of 'Diplock courts'.

6.   NARROWING THE JURY'S DOMAIN

As we have seen throughout this chapter, the prevailing attitude of the State seems to be that juries are costly and too prone to acquit. This attitude has repeatedly found expression in moves to restrict juries from hearing certain categories of case altogether. The reality is that so few contested Crown Court trials now take place that a person's chances of doing jury service between the eligible ages of 18-70 'have been whittled down to one in six'.[2] Here we review briefly the trend *away* from trial by jury and consider some of the broader implications of the move *towards* other modes of trial.

Since 1973, defendants in Northern Ireland charged with offences deemed to be terrorist-related are tried by a single judge sitting without a jury.[3] The introduction of these 'Diplock courts' was justified on the grounds that firstly, the circumstances of that province left jurors exposed to intimidation and, second, that jurors were likely to return perverse verdicts borne of partisanship.[4] However, the thrust of the report which proposed these courts was to dismantle a series of procedural rights and

2   P Darbyshire, 'Strengthening the Argument in Favour of the Defendant's Right to Elect' [1997] Crim LR 911.
3   See the Northern Ireland (Emergency Provisions) Act 1973. The criteria and methods for directing cases to single judge courts are rough-and-ready and have resulted in the diversion of many cases lacking a terrorist connection away from juries: see J Jackson and S Doran, 'Diplock and the Presumption Against Jury Trial: a critique' [1992] Crim LR 755.
4   Report of the Commission to consider legal procedures to deal with terrorist activities in Northern Ireland (Cmnd 5185) (London: HMSO, 1972). The Commission was chaired by Lord Diplock.

safeguards for suspects so as to ease the path towards a conviction.[5] As no empirical evidence existed to justify the supposed concerns about jury trials, the suspicion must be that the change was in reality part of the strategy to secure more guilty verdicts. The annual number of cases heard in Diplock courts is small, falling from over 1,000 in the mid 1970s to around 400 in the 1990s[6] but they represent an area of criminal activity in which, for obvious reasons, the state is particularly keen to secure a high conviction rate.

Some have argued that the Diplock judges have become increasingly prone to accepting police and prosecution evidence in preference to that of the defence and that this 'case-hardening' has led to a decline in the acquittal rate since the Diplock courts were created.[7] The evidence regarding whether there has been such a decline, and whether it is produced by case-hardening, is not clear-cut.[8] Jackson and Doran highlight a perhaps more important point, which is that trial by jury produces a higher average acquittal rate than does Diplock trial.[9] Their own comparison of Diplock trials with jury trials suggests one reason for this is that they found that Diplock judges confined their consideration of the case to the strict legal issue of guilt or innocence. In other words, these judges eschewed the broader jury role of considering the merits (or morality) of prosecuting and punishing a particular defendant.[10] That role tends to work in the defendant's favour, but does not invariably do so as juries may wish to punish certain individuals even though the legal elements of the offence may not be made out. Counsel interviewed by Jackson and Doran claimed that sexual cases were particularly difficult to defend before juries. As one put it: 'It would suit me nearly as well not to have a jury at all because I would rather the case was dealt with in a colder, unemotional fashion because there's enough emotion to start with.'[11] This chimes with our earlier comments in section 4(a)(iii) about the dangers of jury trial for individuals who are liable to be stereotyped or stigmatised during the proceedings. Doran and Jackson suggest that one solution would be the introduction of a new right to waive trial by jury. Instead trial would be by a professional judge.[12] We think this a promising idea but it has been advanced in a

---

5   See P Hillyard, 'The Normalization of Special Powers: from Northern Ireland to Britain' in P Scraton (ed), *Law, Order and the Authoritarian State* (Milton Keynes: Open UP, 1987) at pp 285-86.
6   Jackson and Doran (1995) p 19.
7   Jackson and Doran (1995) p 294. See also B Dickson, 'Northern Ireland's Emergency Legislation - The Wrong Medicine?' [1992] PL 592 at pp 609-10.
8   Jackson and Doran (1995) pp 33-36.
9   Jackson and Doran (1995) p 34.
10   Jackson and Doran (1995) pp 291-94.
11   See J Jackson and S Doran, 'Judge and Jury: Towards a New Division of Labour in Criminal Trials' (1997) 60 MLR 759 at pp 764-65.
12   S Doran and J Jackson, 'The Case for Jury Waiver' [1997] Crim LR 155.

climate deeply hostile to the creation of new rights for defendants. The Government is set on taking away a defendant's right to opt for Crown Court trial in either way cases (see below). It is highly unlikely that it would favour giving defendants who are tried in the Crown Court any right to opt for the mode of trial they thought gave them the best chance of an acquittal.

In England and Wales no attempt has yet been made to remove terrorist-related or other very serious kinds of offences from the province of the jury. There has been much debate, however, about the wisdom of asking lay juries to act as fact-finders in complex fraud trials. In 1986 the Roskill Committee recommended that complex fraud cases might better be heard by a special tribunal.[13] The Runciman Commission also looked at this issue and concluded that, in the absence of research evidence on the workings of jury trials, there was no basis on which to recommend dispensing with juries for complex frauds or other lengthy cases.[14] The difficulty of achieving or sustaining convictions in these cases has kept this issue alive. From a freedom perspective we welcome this as we would not wish to see powerful fraudsters granted effective immunity from conviction. There is some basis for questioning whether ordinary juries can, as matters stand, return fair and accurate verdicts on matters as complex as insider trading, bond-washing and so forth. In 1998 the Government published a consultation document which canvassed various options for change, such as screening potential jurors for competence, judge-only trials, or a mixed judge and lay member tribunal.[15] It also noted the continuing lack of empirical information on whether and to what degree juries failed to grasp the evidence and issues in complex fraud trials. Research subsequently published by Honess, Levi and Charman, based on a simulation of the trial of Kevin Maxwell, found that 'with some screening and more focused help for the jury, non-specialist jurors are sufficiently competent to understand and deal with the information relevant to their verdicts.'[16] Given the importance of lay involvement in criminal justice we hope that heed is taken of this research. What it suggests is needed is a re-appraisal of the way jurors are selected and then treated during the trial. Jackson and Doran, on the basis of their comparative study of jury and non-jury trial, have similarly argued that if juries are to maximise their fact-finding potential they should be encouraged to engage in more active inquiry during the trial.[17] In this way any areas of potential confusion, prejudice or misunderstanding on

13   Report of the Departmental Committee on Fraud Trials (London: HMSO, 1986).
14   RCCJ (1993) p 136.
15   Juries in Serious Fraud Trials (London: Home Office, 1998).
16   T M Honess, M Levi and E A Charman, 'Juror Competence in Processing Complex Information: Implications from a Simulation of the Maxwell Trial' [1998] Crim LR 763 at p 773.
17   J Jackson and S Doran, 'Judge and Jury: Towards a New Division of Labour in Criminal Trials' (1997) 60 MLR 759 at pp 775-778.

their part could be exposed and addressed, thus allowing the jury to make better sense of the case as it develops and to reach more justifiable verdicts. This strategy is at least worth a try. To jump immediately to the option of dispensing with the jury in complex fraud cases is likely to set a precedent which will make it harder to resist further whittling away in future.

In this context, however, it is as well to remember that while the most serious cases in the criminal calendar remain within the domain of the jury, some fairly serious offences (such as assault on a police constable) have been redirected to the magistrates' courts. Parliament has reclassified many previously 'either way' offences as summary only in order to remove them from the province of the jury and the current Government has determined to go further by ending the right of defendants in 'either way' offences the right to choose jury trial.[18]

This latest attack on the jury's role seems primarily to be driven by cost-cutting but a useful side-effect, from the crime control point of view, is that magistrates are more likely to convict in these cases.[19] This may be particularly important in public order situations where legitimate protest (picketing, anti-racist marches, demonstrations against capitalism or visits by heads of totalitarian states, and so forth) spills over (allegedly) into criminal acts. Such threats to public order, like terrorist offences, amount to threats to the authority of the state itself. Usually the prosecution evidence in such cases consists entirely of police accounts. A not guilty verdict by a jury would, therefore, both call into question the integrity of the police and undermine the moral authority of the state. Small wonder then that the state ensures that the vast majority of public order offences are heard in the magistrates' courts.

7. CONCLUSION

The one recommendation of the Runciman Commission that received unequivocal support from the academic community is that s 8 of the Contempt of Court Act 1981 should be amended so as to permit proper research into jury decision-making.[20] For while the evidence available suggests that juries conform more to due process principles than other components of the criminal justice system, that evidence is neither so satisfactory, nor so unequivocal, as to be conclusive. Such research would, however, have to be clear about what was being tested. As we have argued, assessing whether professional lawyers agree with jury verdicts is an

18 See ch 8, section 5(c).
19 See ch 8, section 5(c). For further discussion see A Sanders, 'The Erosion of Jury Trial' (1980) 5 Holds LR 21.
20 See RCCJ (1993) p 2.

inherently unsatisfactory approach to this issue. In our view, an examination of the process by which juries arrive at their verdicts is likely to provide more meaningful insights. But any such research must recognise that jury decision-making cannot be divorced from the overall context of the criminal justice system.

Moreover, research should not be confined to an examination of the workings of the jury. Rather, a comparison should be attempted between different possible modes of trial, including: trial by lay magistrates; by a stipendiary magistrate sitting with or without lay colleagues (see ch 8, section 5); by a Crown Court judge sitting with lay magistrates (see ch 10, section 2(a)) and by Diplock courts. For while jury trial undoubtedly has its faults, the real question is whether other modes of trial are, or could be made to be, any better. Where comparisons have been attempted they have tended to flatter jury trial.[1] We noted in ch 8, section 5, that research by Vennard suggests that juries approach prosecution evidence with more circumspection than do magistrates.[2] The empirical evidence concerning the gathering and presentation of evidence by the police and the CPS (reviewed in chs 2-6) shows that a degree of wariness is justified. This may convince some of the force of due process arguments in favour of the jury, but the committed crime control adherent may still prefer to see priority given to maintaining a high conviction rate at low cost. As we stressed in ch 1, arguments about the future development of the criminal justice system should be informed by hard facts, but can rarely be resolved by them.

Finally, one should bear in mind that for the vast majority of defendants, arguments about modes of trial are essentially meaningless. The 'mode of trial' most often employed in this country is the simple guilty plea. The great majority of defendants in both the magistrates' courts and the Crown Court waive their right to put the prosecution to proof, waive their right to a trial. Thus, perhaps the single most important reform of the system would be to require that magistrates and judges should not accept a plea of guilty (and police officers should not caution) without first examining closely the adequacy of the prosecution case.[3] Such a reform could scarcely be effective, however, given the current absence of a cultural commitment to due process amongst legislators, the appeal courts, trial judges, lawyers and the police. From this perspective, the jury's injection of due process into a predominantly crime control system might appear to be little more than a placebo. Nevertheless, from a freedom perspective that 'little more' is well worth preserving both for symbolic and practical reasons.

1   This is certainly our reading of Jackson and Doran (1995), the best such comparative study within a domestic setting.
2   See J Vennard, *Contested Trials in Magistrates' Courts* (Home Office Research Study no 71) (London: HMSO, 1981) p 21.
3   See Jackson and Doran (1995) p 301.

Chapter 10

Appeals against conviction

Gerry Conlon, one of the Guildford Four, wrote a book about the miscarriage of justice that led to him losing 15 years of freedom. This is what he had to say about his initial appeal against conviction, heard in 1977:

> '. . . we were knocked back to gaol. It took about an hour to read out the judgment in that cold, hard way they do it. The last sentences of the judgment were: "In the end we are all of the clear opinion that there are no possible grounds for doubting the justice of any of these four convictions or for ordering retrials. We therefore propose to dispose of all those applications for leave to appeal by refusing them."
> Carole was crying. Disbelief was written all over Paul's and Paddy's faces. But somehow we had to face it - the judges couldn't see the wood for the trees. Or, more likely, they couldn't admit - even to themselves - there might have been an almighty miscarriage of justice.'

Twelve years later the Guildford Four secured a fresh appeal at which the Crown, in the light of evidence of gross investigative malpractice by the police, no longer sought to uphold their convictions:

> 'We held carnations, the symbols of innocence . . . Then the Lord Chief Justice pronounced his judgment. He looked like he was eating a scalded cat and was barely getting the words out. I don't remember much of the detail, but I was hanging on his every word, because there was one I was waiting for. He came towards his conclusion, telling the court that for all these reasons their Lordships no longer felt the verdicts were safe, and it was therefore his duty to pronounce them -

In this very moment I jumped up and tossed my carnation high into the well of the court, and it was followed by the flowers of the others.

And then he said it - QUASHED.

We were in the Old Bailey's Court Number Two. In 1975 the verdicts of guilt over the Guildford Four had been pronounced here. In 1977 the appeal of the Guildford Four had been lost here. In 1989 it was third time lucky. Justice had finally been done.'[1]

I. WHAT VALUES SHOULD UNDERPIN APPELLATE PROCEDURES?

Appeals procedures allow the decisions of trial courts to be reviewed. Appeals can fulfil a number of functions, and express a variety of values. In this introduction we will use Packer's models to begin exploring the various possibilities, and adopt the freedom perspective to help us choose amongst them. Part of the common ground that exists between the crime control and due process models is that the criminal system's potential for error necessitates some form of appellate review. The two models differ sharply as to the desirable scope of such review.

(a) Crime control

The crime control model rests on the assumption that the administrative procedures operated by police and prosecutors reliably screen out the probably innocent at an early stage. That the vast majority of those processed through the system plead guilty is testimony to this essential fact. Where defendants plead not guilty, any remaining doubts about guilt should be resolved by the court of first instance. Thus, as Packer puts it, in the crime control model:

'the role of an appellate review system is highly marginal: it is available to correct those occasional slips in which the trier of fact either makes a plain error about factual guilt or makes so gross a procedural mistake that the reliability of the guilt-determining process is called into question.'[2]

---

1   G Conlon, *Proved Innocent* (London: Penguin, 1990) pp 168 and 228-9.
2   H L Packer, *The Limits of the Criminal Sanction* (Stanford: Stanford UP, 1968) p 228.

The aim of ensuring certainty and finality within the criminal process would be undermined if convicted persons could delay the imposition of punishment. Appeals should therefore be so discouraged that only those with the clearest grounds for complaint will pursue the matter. No financial assistance should be given to the appellant until the case has been screened and determined to be of sufficient merit. Moreover, as the quote above suggests, the grounds for appeal should be narrow. Only when the appellate tribunal finds that no reasonable trier of fact could have convicted on the evidence presented should a conviction be quashed. It would not be enough for the appellate court to consider that it would have acquitted or that most juries would have acquitted. Procedural errors, such as biased summaries of evidence by trial judges, should likewise not justify the quashing of a conviction unless it is determined that, had the error not occurred, an acquittal would have been probable. Above all else, if on a review of the evidence, the appellate court concludes that the accused's factual guilt was adequately established at trial, the conviction must be upheld regardless of the fairness of the proceedings. Any procedural error such as the admission at trial of evidence produced by oppressive questioning by the police should be the subject of remedies that operate independently of the criminal trial (for example, disciplinary action or re-training). This model therefore focuses exclusively on the accuracy of the determination of factual guilt by the court of trial.

(b) Due process

The demand for finality is very low in this model. It should remain possible to re-open a case whenever there is an allegation of factual error that has not received an adjudicative hearing in a fact-finding context. Appellate review is also seen as a crucial means of upholding the moral integrity of the criminal process. Abuses of official power, whether by the police, prosecutors or trial judges, must be corrected and deterred. Any infringement of the basic rights of an accused person, such as unlawful arrests, oppressive interrogation or the wrongful admission of evidence at trial, should suffice for the quashing of a conviction, regardless of the strength of the evidence against the appellant. Even minor infringements of procedural rules may justify this course if their cumulative effect is significant. As Packer puts it:

> 'The reversal of a criminal conviction is a small price to pay for an affirmation of proper values and a deterrent example of what will happen when those values are slighted. When an appellate court finds it necessary to castigate the conduct of the police, the

prosecutor, or the trial court, but fails to reverse a conviction, it simply breeds disrespect for the very standards it is trying to affirm.'[3]

Moreover, the further elaboration of due process rights depends upon a steady flow of appeals to the higher courts. The raw material for these appeals is plentiful, given this model's assumption that frequent mistakes about factual guilt are made at earlier stages of the process. There must, therefore, be unrestricted access to appellate review. Preliminary screening of appeals to assess their worth should be seen for what it is—a second-rate form of appellate review. Finally, but of fundamental importance, legal aid must be available to underwrite the cost of appealing. If convicted persons are unable to afford legal advice and representation the chances are that they will neither appreciate whether grounds for appeal exist nor be able to present their case effectively.

(c) Freedom

Considering how freedom can be maximised should help us determine the weight which should be given to conflicting values such as the crime control need for finality and the due process facilitation of further challenge.

The main way in which crime control claims to promote freedom is by general deterrence: apprehending and punishing a reasonably high percentage of the guilty ensures extensive compliance with the norms of the criminal law. But it seems doubtful that this deterrent effect would be significantly undermined by allowing convicted persons to appeal. Because the presumption of innocence is displaced by a finding of guilt, the trial court will be able to publicly censure the offending behaviour through its sentence and any remarks that sentencers choose to make. The reporting of the sentence and accompanying remarks is what produces most of any general deterrent effect. Indeed, even if a conviction is ultimately quashed on appeal, the sentence and denunciation delivered at trial will still be effective in so far as it reinforced general perceptions of the wrongfulness of the type of offending behaviour at stake.[4]

The crime control objective of general deterrence could, however, be obstructed if a large number of convicted people successfully appeal. Post-conviction denunciation will lose its immediate power if the frequent or expected response is that it will be challenged. But if large numbers of convicted people successfully appeal there would be something badly wrong with the earlier stages of the criminal process. If those stages are

---

3   Packer (1968) p 232.
4   For a more sophisticated analysis of mechanisms of deterrence than is possible here, see A von Hirsch, A Bottoms, E Burney and P-O Wilkstrom, *Criminal Deterrence and Sentence Severity* (Oxford: Hart, 1999).

working properly there should usually be clear evidence of guilt established in a fair manner by the time defendants reach court. We can expect most defendants to plead guilty when faced with such evidence - if only to get the case over with as quickly as possible. Similarly, we can expect that only a minority of those who are convicted following a not guilty plea will appeal. This will be all the more true if punishment is designed to censure and reintegrate rather than stigmatise and exclude. It follows that while the punishment of some convicted persons may be delayed by a system of appeal, the general practice of punishment following swiftly after conviction will continue for the great majority.

Crime control - and our own freedom perspective - is also concerned about resources. All things being equal, both perspectives would seek to discourage large numbers of appeals when the resources they consume could be better spent elsewhere. There is thus justification for filtering out appeals which are clearly without merit.

Overall it seems that the social freedom to be achieved by affording only minimal rights of appeal is largely speculative and relatively slight. By contrast the freedom lost to people who are factually innocent but convicted is tangible and significant. There may be losses of reputation, job prospects, actual employment, money (where one is fined), or freedom to determine one's own actions (as where one is imprisoned or ordered to perform community service). The families of these people often suffer too. To deny a right of appeal would be to ensure that such wrongful losses of freedom could not be redressed or at least minimised. Moreover, it would virtually guarantee that the criminal 'case' remained closed, thus insulating any person who in fact committed the crime from investigation and apprehension.

What of 'the victim'? It is true that an appeal may cause difficulties for victims, such as delaying their sense of 'closure' and perhaps requiring them to submit to further stressful courtroom experiences.[5] But a wrongful conviction which cannot be corrected virtually ensures that victims will never see 'their' offender brought to justice. That offender will remain at large, and in some cases may even prey on the same victim again. Moreover, as we pointed out in ch 1, defendants and victims are not separate groups of people. Thus, even if we were to concede that providing appeal rights favoured 'defendants' more than 'victims' we would not be privileging one group of people over another - rather we would be determining that, *in the long run*, the promotion of freedom is best achieved *for everyone* by allowing liberally framed rights of appeal.

---

5   See also ch 1, section 10, on the anguish caused to the relatives of murder victims when it emerges that those originally convicted for the offence are themselves victims of miscarriages of justice.

So far we have only dealt with the issue of convictions which are wrong in the sense that a factually innocent person has been convicted. What of the due process argument that procedural errors and malpractice might justify the quashing of a conviction irrespective of whether factual guilt has been established beyond reasonable doubt? Here the considerations differ little from those that apply in relation to the power to exclude unfairly obtained evidence contained in s 78 of PACE.[6] To quash a reliable conviction on the ground that the procedures which led to it were tainted by unfairness leaves someone who has offended at large, causing important losses of freedom, not least to victims. On the other hand, the occasional quashing of convictions on the ground of procedural unfairness should have no more impact on the general deterrence achieved through the practices of conviction, denunciation and punishment than the quashing of convictions on any other ground. This is so even leaving aside the point that the moral message communicated by a verdict of guilty may be weakened or destroyed where it was produced in an unfair way.[7]

By contrast, quashing a reliable but unfair conviction may make a significant difference to the respect shown by the police, prosecutors, magistrates, judges and others to the rules and principles of criminal procedure. For while criminal justice actors know that most defendants will not seek to put their guilt in dispute or overturn their convictions, they cannot know for sure which few defendants will contest these matters. The safe option is therefore to keep to the rules, just in case. For the quashing of a conviction in these circumstances will not only lead to a guilty person walking free, but might lead to scrutiny and criticism of the practices that led to this happening. What does the quashing of unfairly obtained convictions achieve in terms of freedom? It helps ensure that invasions of liberty which take place within criminal justice processes do so within the rule of law. The freedom of everyone (including victims) is enhanced if we know that officials will not ignore our rights when it suits them or otherwise invade our liberty in an arbitrary fashion. That is surely a truer mark of a free society than one which has a lower than average crime rate. And, by definition, other remedies for unfairness within the criminal process (eg, civil actions, disciplinary procedures, prosecution of corrupt police officers) are not sufficient deterrents to malpractice. If they were, we would not be discussing the need to quash a conviction on the ground of procedural unfairness. If the police and other criminal justice actors want to avoid the quashing of reliable convictions all they have to do is abide by the rules. Our broad brush conclusion is that freedom is best served by affording broadly drawn appeal rights in which the grounds for quashing a conviction include procedural unfairness.

6   See ch 11.
7   See von Hirsch et al (1999) p 40.

2. APPEALS FROM THE MAGISTRATES' COURTS

There are three channels of appellate or supervisory review for those convicted in the magistrates' courts: a rehearing in the Crown Court; an appeal by way of case stated to the Divisional Court, or judicial review.

(a) Rehearings in the Crown Court

The Crown Court hears far more appeals than does the Court of Appeal.[8] In 1999, 6,313 appeals against a magistrates' court conviction were heard at the Crown Court,[9] compared with 551 appeals heard by the Court of Appeal against a Crown Court conviction.[10] The rights of appeal in the English system differ markedly according to whether the defendant was convicted in the magistrates' court[11] or the Crown Court.[12] Partly as a result of historical accident, and partly due to the unsatisfactory nature of summary justice, magistrates' courts convictions are subject to more extensive forms of appellate review.[13] No leave is required for an appeal from this court to the Crown Court, and the appeal takes the form of a complete rehearing of the case before a professional judge and two or more magistrates who took no part in the original trial.[14] The grounds for appeal are unrestricted and therefore do not need to be stated,[15] and fresh evidence will be admitted. The Royal Commission on Criminal Justice (Runciman Commission) was careful to draw attention to this up-market 'second bite of the cherry' for 'aggrieved defendants' in its report. It did so to pre-empt criticisms of its proposal to increase the proportion of defendants tried in the magistrates' courts by removing the right to elect trial by jury in either

---

8   All figures given in the text include appeals against either conviction or conviction and sentence, but, unless otherwise specified, exclude appeals against sentence only.

9   Judicial Statistics 1999, Cm 4786, Table 10.4 (London: Lord Chancellor's Department, 2000).

10 Judicial Statistics (1999) Table 1.8. Although the Home Office calculates the figures differently the broad patterns concerning the relative throughput of the two appellate processes and overall appeal trends are similar. See J Mattinson, *Criminal Appeals England and Wales, 1995 and 1996* (Research and Statistical Bulletin 3/98) (London: Home Office, 1998), n 2.

11 Young persons convicted by magistrates when sitting as a youth court have the same rights of appeal as adult defendants.

12 For a comprehensive account see R Pattenden, *English Criminal Appeals 1844-1994* (Oxford: Clarendon Press, 1996).

13 See I Scott, 'Criminal Procedure: Appeals to Quarter Sessions' (1970) 134 JP and G Rev 843.

14 Supreme Court Act 1981, s 74; Crown Court Rules 1982, r 5. In exceptional circumstances a judge may sit with just one magistrate: Crown Court Rules 1982, r 4; *Crown Court at Knutsford, ex p Jones* (1985) 7 Cr App Rep (S) 448.

15 Save in exceptional circumstances: Crown Court Rules 1982, Pt III, Sch. 3.

way offences.[16] The implication was that any unfairness arising in the magistrates' courts could always be put right on appeal. But this form of appellate review is neither so generous nor so effective as the Runciman Commission implied.

To begin with, an appeal against conviction does not lie to the Crown Court if the defendant pleaded guilty.[17] This automatically excludes over four-fifths of all defendants tried in the lower courts from the appeal system.[18] Many such defendants may be very much aggrieved by the circumstances of the police investigation, the conduct of the prosecution and the behaviour of the magistrates' court itself, yet have felt themselves to have had little option but to plead guilty.[19] Only if the plea of guilty can be said to have been entered equivocally or under duress can a complaint be made to the Crown Court.[20] If the complaint is found to have substance the Court must remit the case back to the magistrates' court so that a full trial can take place there.[1] Of course, the degree of pressure on a defendant to plead guilty which would qualify as 'duress' is much more narrowly defined in a system which operates on crime control lines than one in which due process principles prevail. The Court of Appeal insists, for example, that while defendants who plead guilty as a result of a charge bargain may face difficult choices between unpalatable alternatives, that is no ground for arguing that the plea of guilty was not freely made.[2] Not surprisingly, few defendants convicted on a guilty plea in the magistrates' courts mount successful challenges.[3] Moreover, the Crown Court cannot hear an appeal by a defendant who unequivocally pleaded guilty even if subsequently discovered evidence reveals them to be innocent.[4] By contrast the Court of Appeal can hear appeals from persons convicted in the Crown Court in like circumstances.

---

16   Royal Commission on Criminal Justice (RCCJ), Report (Cm 2263) (London: HMSO, 1993) p 88. Now see the Criminal Justice (Mode of Trial) Bill, discussed in ch 8.

17   Magistrates' Courts Act 1980, s 108; *Crown Court at Birmingham, ex p Sharma* [1988] Crim L R 741.

18   From 1993-1998 81-82% of cases involving the Crown Prosecution Service which proceeded to a hearing were disposed of by a guilty plea: Criminal Statistics, England and Wales 1998, Cm 4649 (London: Home Office, 2000) Table 6.2.

19   For discussion, see ch 7.

20   See S Seabrooke and J Sprack, *Criminal Evidence and Procedure* 2nd edn (London: Blackstone Press: 1999) pp 281-2.

1   *Crown Court at Huntingdon, ex p Jordan* [1981] QB 857.

2   *Herbert* (1991) 94 Cr App Rep 230.

3   Only 35 appeals to the Crown Court were remitted to the magistrates' courts in 1996: Mattinson (1998) Table 4.

4   Pattenden (1996) p 229.

An appeal to the Crown Court must be commenced within 21 days of the conclusion of the proceedings in the magistrates' courts.[5] Defendants who were legally aided in the magistrates' courts may receive preliminary advice, at public expense, on whether they have grounds for appeal.[6] Those who were not legally aided may receive advice under the 'green form' scheme.[7] In all cases, however, a grant of full legal aid for appellate proceedings is subject to the application of a means test and a merits test. Virtually all applications for legal aid for this purpose are granted but a majority of those appealing against conviction do not make an application.[8] The reasons for this are unclear. Some of those not legally aided are wealthy enough to fund their own representation while others appear unrepresented. Presumably others abandon all thoughts of an appeal on being advised that if they were to apply for legal aid they would be unable to meet either the means or the merits test. Since the wealthy can fund their appeals regardless of the merits of the case, the legal aid rules breach the due process equality principle.[9] These rules provide a screening device in all but name for all but the rich.

The re-hearing itself is a relatively perfunctory affair. The average hearing time for an appeal is just under an hour, compared with almost 10 hours for a normal Crown Court trial.[10] The absence of a jury is one obvious factor lying behind this speed. Another is likely to be the lack of enthusiasm of legally aided lawyers to argue the case as fully as they perhaps should. Given that they are paid a fixed fee for this work, economics dictate that the faster they can dispose of the matter the better.[11] Moreover, this type of work is routinely allocated to inexperienced barristers, preparation on both sides tends to be minimal and prosecution disclosure of fresh evidence is almost unknown.[12] Where the appellant is unrepresented, there is no legally qualified court clerk to offer any help (unlike in the magistrates' court) and no duty solicitor (or barrister) scheme either. Imagine a lay-person trying to counter the arguments of a prosecution barrister in an oak panelled courtroom presided over by a bewigged judge.

---

5 Crown Court Rules 1982, r 7. This rule allows an applicant to seek an extension of this time limit but there is no right to an oral hearing or to reasons for a refusal to grant an extension: *Crown Court at Croydon, ex p Smith* (1983) 77 Cr App Rep 277.
6 Legal Aid Act 1988, s 19(2).
7 See ch 8, section 2, above.
8 Of the 6,313 appellants appearing in the Crown Court in 1999, only 2,742 were represented on legal aid: Judicial Statistics (1999) Table 10.4.
9 See ch 8, section 2, above.
10 Judicial Statistics (1999) Table 6.21 (this table, unfortunately, aggregates appeals against sentence with those against conviction).
11 D Nation, 'He can always appeal' (1992) 156 JP 521.
12 Pattenden (1996) p 242.

A further off-putting feature of these appeals is the wide power of the Crown Court to vary the decision appealed, remit the matter back to the magistrates with their opinion or make such other order as the court thinks just.[13] In one recent case the Crown Court ordered the appellant to pay £28,000 in costs, which included an element for the costs incurred by the prosecutor in the magistrates' court. This was despite the fact that the magistrates' court had already made its own costs order (of £260). This power to re-open the initial costs decision was upheld by the Divisional Court in *Hamilton-Johnson v RSPCA*.[14] The Court went on to provide the prosecutors with a deterrent mechanism by observing that if a prosecutor respondent proposed to ask the Crown Court to vary in his or her favour a costs order made in the court below, detailed notice in writing should be given to the appellant so that the appellant's mind could be directed to the possible consequences of any decision to pursue an appeal. Another possible consequence is a higher sentence. Unlike the Court of Appeal, which has no power to change a sentence on hearing an appeal against conviction, it is open to the Crown Court to impose a severer sentence than that imposed by the magistrates.[15] Ashworth argues that this can be justified on the basis that the fresh evidence introduced at the rehearing might make the offence seem more serious.[16] Against that should be weighed the chilling effect on a convicted person considering whether to appeal. How can such a person be sure that the Crown Court will not impose a stiffer punishment to mark its disapproval of what it sees as a 'frivolous' request for a rehearing?[17] In a system which is organised around the principle of penalising defendants for resisting conviction (as expressed through sentence discounts for those pleading guilty) it is easy to understand a prospective appellant's fears. The uncertainty of outcome and the possibility of being punished (in effect) for appealing may dissuade the aggrieved defendant from taking matters further, notwithstanding that in reality the Crown Court rarely increases a sentence on an appeal against conviction.[18] No doubt the various problematic aspects of the appeal

13 Supreme Court Act 1981, s 48. Remission back to the magistrates' court occurs in practice only in cases where the original conviction is found to have been based on a guilty plea which was equivocal or made under duress.
14 4 April 2000, unreported.
15 Supreme Court Act 1981, s 48(4). Any new sentence must be within the sentencing limits which apply to the magistrates' court.
16 A Ashworth, 'Prosecution and Procedure in Criminal Justice' [1979] Crim L R 490.
17 Pattenden (1996) p 219, states that the power to increase a sentence is 'intended as a deterrent to frivolous appeals.' J Sprack, *Emmins on Criminal Procedure* (London: Blackstone, 2000) p 448 takes the same view.
18 For discussion, see I Scott, 'Appeals to the Crown Court following Summary Conviction' (paper delivered to SPTL Criminal Law Group) (1977) pp 17–19. In 1996, 112 of those appealing to the Crown Court were given an increased sentence of the same type: Mattinson (1998) Table 4. A further 989 appellants

process discussed above also helps to explain the fact that about a fifth of those who do decide to challenge their convictions later abandon their appeals.[19]

Notwithstanding the procedural difficulties outlined above, the appeal rate is quite high, despite initial appearances to the contrary. In 1996, the number of defendants convicted in the magistrates' court was 1,368,900 according to CPS figures,[20] yet there were only some 10,441 appeals against conviction in that year,[1] giving an appeal rate of 0.76%. But seven-eighths of the cases completed by the CPS in the magistrates' courts were terminated by a guilty plea, thus disqualifying the defendants in those cases from appealing.[2] Thus 10,441 appeals were produced by the 150,200 cases where the convictions did not follow a guilty plea, giving an appeal rate of 7%. In other words, around 1 in 14 of those defendants who are eligible for an appeal opt for a rehearing in the Crown Court.[3] That more do not do so should not be taken as a sign of satisfaction with summary trial procedures. As the James Committee noted, delay, expense, a reluctance to face the ordeal of a rehearing, a wish for finality and the possibility of receiving a stiffer sentence all provide disincentives to appealing.[4] In 1999, the average waiting time from lodging an appeal to the start of the rehearing in the Crown Court was roughly two months and about a tenth of defendants waited 16 weeks or more.[5]

The proportion of appeals against conviction to the Crown Court that were successful grew steadily from about a quarter in the mid-1980s to over 40% a decade later. In 1996 a new power introduced by the Criminal Appeal Act 1995 enabled magistrates to re-open cases to correct obvious mistakes more easily. This resulted in several thousand fewer appeals and a corresponding decline in the success rate to 33%.[6] Since the great majority of appeals assert simply that the original conviction was 'against the weight of the evidence',[7] the still large number of successful appeals (3,494 in 1996) raises further doubts about the quality of justice in the magistrates'

---

had their sentences 'varied' through the imposition of a different (usually less serious) type of sentence: Tables 4 and 9.

19 See Mattinson (1998) Table 4.
20 Criminal Statistics (1998) Table 6.3.
1   Mattinson (1998) Table 1.
2   Criminal Statistics: England and Wales (1998) Table 6.2.
3   Given the inconsistent and incomplete ways the figures are presented in official sources this figure is necessarily an estimate.
4   Report of the Interdepartmental Committee on The Distribution of Criminal Business between the Crown Court and Magistrates' Courts (Cmnd 6323) (London: HMSO, 1975) Table 7B p 139.
5   Judicial Statistics (1999) Table 6.20 (this Table aggregates appeals against conviction with those against sentence).
6   Mattinson (1998) Table 1.
7   Scott (1977) p 10.

courts. It is a pity that the Runciman Commission did not look at magistrates' courts in this way, adopt the James Committee's approach, and fund research on the issue. As it is, we can say little about the adequacy of appellate review by the Crown Court. Nearly all of the literature in this area concerns itself with the more glamorous matter of appeals to the Court of Appeal following trials on indictment.[8] Yet miscarriages of justice are not confined to cases serious enough to find their way to the senior judiciary, but are routinely produced by magistrates' courts up and down the country on a daily basis. Indeed, wrongful convictions occur on a widespread basis at the less serious end of the offence spectrum dealt with by the magistrates' courts. One indication of this is that rehearings relating to motor insurance offences make up the largest number of appeals (1,451 in 1996) and that just over half are successful. Another is that appeals against summary motoring convictions make up over half of all appeals to the Crown Court, appeals against summary non-motoring convictions over a quarter, with appeals against convictions for indictable offences contributing just a sixth of the total.[9]

In two significant ways the Government proved itself less complacent on this issue than the Runciman Commission. Firstly, it extended the powers of magistrates' courts to re-open cases to rectify mistakes.[10] This has allowed obvious and straightforward miscarriages of justice to be remedied relatively swiftly and cheaply. Secondly, s 11 of the Act permits the newly created Criminal Cases Review Commission (CCRC) to refer suspect convictions produced by the magistrates' courts - regardless of whether the defendant pleaded guilty or not. This is a due process safety net. Whereas the Runciman Commission recommended that the new review body should refer suspect Crown Court convictions back to the Court of Appeal, it said nothing about faulty convictions generated by the magistrates' courts. The extension of the CCRC net to all types of conviction is an important recognition that miscarriages of justice must not only be *seen* to be undone (ie, as in the high-profile cases such as the Birmingham Six, all of which originated in the Crown Court) but must also *be* undone in situations of low visibility. Whether the CCRC provides effective redress for low-level miscarriages of justice will be examined later in this chapter.

8   For example, in M Zander, *Cases and Materials on the English Legal System*, 8th edn (London: Butterworths, 1999) the material on appeals to the Crown Court (scattered throughout the 68-page chapter on appeals) is scarcely enough to fill a single page.
9   Mattinson (1998) Table 6.
10   Criminal Appeal Act 1995, s 24(1) amending Magistrates' Courts Act 1980, s 142.

(b) Appeals by way of case stated to the High Court

An appeal lies to the Divisional Court where it is claimed that the decision of the magistrates' court was in excess of jurisdiction or wrong in law.[11] Since no record of proceedings is kept in the magistrates' court, the clerk to the justices is required to state the details of the case including the question(s) for determination by the Divisional Court. The latter Court hears only legal argument and no evidence.

In principle this procedure gives defendants convicted of relatively trivial crimes access to the senior judiciary, thus allowing high quality supervision of some aspects of summary justice. Due process inspired rulings on the law by eminent judges will not only determine the case in question but also create binding precedents for the future. In practice, many difficulties attend this procedure from the perspective of a convicted person. The applicant must ask the magistrates' court to state a case within 21 days of the final determination of the case.[12] Although leave to appeal is not required, the justices may refuse to state a case if they consider the application 'frivolous'.[13] A further potential barrier is that the magistrates' court may require the prospective appellant to enter into a means-related recognisance to pay any costs ultimately awarded against him.[14] There is anecdotal evidence that magistrates' courts sometimes seek to deter prospective appellants still further by requiring a recognisance well in excess of any fines imposed by the court as its sentence.[15] Civil legal aid is available for this type of appeal but is subject to the usual means and merit tests.[16] There is a backlog of cases waiting to be heard by the Divisional Court and thus a delay of several months faces the appellant.[17] The court itself is almost invariably made up of a Lord Justice of Appeal and another High Court judge; limited judicial resources make it rare for more than two judges to hear the appeal.[18] The appeal fails in a two-judge court if the bench is divided.[19] If the appellant does persuade both judges that an error of law has occurred it is open to the Divisional Court to order a retrial in the magistrates' court,[20] although this should not be done if a

11 Magistrates' Courts Act 1980, s 111; Supreme Court Act 1981, s 28.
12 Magistrates' Courts Act 1980, s 111(2).
13 Magistrates' Courts Act 1980, s 111(4).
14 Magistrates' Courts Act 1980, s 114; *Newcastle-upon-Tyne Justices, ex p Skinner* [1987] 1 All ER 349.
15 J Backhouse, 'Rights of Appeal by Way of Case Stated - Should it be Simplified?' (1992) JPN 310.
16 Legal Aid Act 1988, Sch 2, pt 1.
17 Pattenden (1996) p 223.
18 Pattenden (1996) p 221.
19 *Flannagan v Shaw* [1920] 3 KB 96.
20 See, eg, *Jeffrey v Black* [1978] 1 All ER 555.

rehearing would be oppressive (eg, where a fair trial was no longer possible) or inappropriate (eg, the offence in question is trivial).[1]

The prosecution has the same right to appeal as does the defence, thus providing an exception to the usual rule that the prosecution cannot appeal against an acquittal.[2] The Divisional Court may dispose of the case in various ways, including remitting the case to the magistrates' court with a direction to convict. It appears that the appellate courts do not regard the concept of 'jury equity' as having any application in the magistrates' courts.[3] Magistrates may be dictated to in a way that juries may not.

Appeal by way of case stated is of little practical significance to the average person convicted in the magistrates' courts. About 150 such appeals are heard each year, of which less than half are successful. Some of these concern the civil jurisdiction of the magistrates' court (eg, licensing matters), others are prosecution appeals, and the typical defendant-initiated appeal probably concerns allegations of white collar crime.[4] Business people and corporations convicted of the latter type of crime can afford to pursue the matter and will be more concerned than the average defendant to establish a precedent that their routine activities are not against the criminal law.

(c) Judicial review

Applications for judicial review provide an alternative way of mounting a challenge to a magistrates' court decision in the Divisional Court. The purpose of such an action is to obtain a ruling that the proceedings in the lower court were tainted by illegality and to secure an appropriate remedy. For example, where the rules of natural justice have been breached, the Divisional Court may use the remedy of certiorari to quash the magistrates' decision. In hearing applications for judicial review the Divisional Court is not acting in an appellate capacity. Instead it is supervising an inferior

---

1   *Griffith v Jenkins* [1992] 1 All ER 65. Where the Divisional Court decision entails the innocence of the appellant the conviction will usually be quashed forthwith: Pattenden (1996) p 224.

2   As with so many 'fundamental' due process norms, this rule has numerous exceptions with more in the offing. For example, where an acquittal is 'tainted' because of interference with, or intimidation of, jurors or witnesses the defendant may face a second trial on the same charge: Criminal Procedure and Investigations Act 1996, ss 54-57. For other exceptions and provisional proposals for new prosecution rights of appeal, see Law Commission, Prosecution Appeals Against Judges' Rulings (Consultation Paper 158) (July 2000). For discussion of prosecution appeals see M Wasik, T Gibbons and M Redmayne, *Criminal Justice* (London: Longman, 1999) pp 557-62.

3   Jury equity was discussed in ch 9, sections 2 and 5.

4   Pattenden (1996) p 223.

court to ensure that it remains within the limits of its powers. In consequence the effect of quashing a conviction by certiorari is to render the proceedings before the magistrates' courts void. In theory this means that the defendant was never at any risk of a valid conviction and so the rule against double jeopardy (which holds that someone should not be exposed to the risk of conviction more than once for the same offence) is regarded as inapplicable.[5] It would thus be open to the Crown to re-prosecute the case although a leading treatise on criminal procedure considers this 'most unlikely' in practice.[6]

As with the appellate mechanisms already discussed, a number of procedural hurdles face the potential judicial review applicant. The application must be initiated promptly - normally within three months of the time at which the grounds for judicial review arose.[7] Civil legal aid is available to help with the costs of mounting a judicial review application but this is subject to both a means and merits test.[8] Permission to apply must always be obtained from the Divisional Court and in practice about two-thirds of applicants are denied this and are thus weeded out of the system. A single judge of the Court initially determines whether permission should be granted and this is usually done on the papers. In the event of a negative decision, the application may be renewed orally before the full Court. The Divisional Court is supposed to grant permission if on a quick perusal of the material presented it thinks that it discloses what might on further consideration turn out to be an arguable case in favour of granting the relief sought.[9] However, it seems that the Court in practice often applies a more stringent test in order to ensure that judicial workloads remain 'manageable').[10] There is no appeal against a decision by the full Court to refuse permission.

Obtaining permission places the applicant half way down the obstacle course but not yet in sight of the finishing line. A delay of between four and eight months in having the case heard can be expected.[11] Furthermore, the remedies available through this procedure are discretionary. This means that a convicted person may 'win' the argument but be denied a remedy because of some perceived broader interest of fairness or due administration of justice. An example is *Peterborough Justices, ex p Dowler*[12] in which

5   *Kent Justices, ex p Machin* [1952] 2 QB 355.
6   Sprack (2000) p 457.
7   Rules of Supreme Court, Ord 53 r 4(1).
8   Legal Aid Act 1988, s 15(2).
9   *IRC, ex p National Federation of Self-Employed and Small Businesses Ltd* [1982] AC 617.
10 See A Le Sueur and M Sunkin, 'Applications for Judicial Review: The Requirement of Leave' [1992] PL 102, and the discussion by C Harlow and R Rawlings, *Law and Administration*, 2nd edn (London: Butterworths, 1997) pp 530-536.
11 Pattenden (1996) p 227.
12 [1996] 2 Cr App Rep 561.

the Divisional Court decided that, because a procedurally unfair conviction might be remedied through an appeal by way of a rehearing in the Crown Court, certiorari would not issue.

There are somewhat fewer applications for judicial review each year than there are appeals by way of case stated. There is clearly an overlap between the two procedures as both are concerned with errors of law. Generally speaking the Divisional Court encourages the use of the appeal by way of case stated as this procedure enables the facts as found by the magistrates, as well as the legal determinations based on those facts, to be set out clearly.[13] On the other hand, if the rules of natural justice are breached (eg, the defence was not allowed a fair opportunity to present its case) this would not emerge from a case stated so judicial review should be pursued instead. Similarly, a refusal by a magistrates' court to state a case could by definition only be challenged by way of judicial review.[14]

At one time, the judicial view seemed to be that judicial review might only be employed to correct defects or irregularities in the trial itself.[15] A broader approach was established in *Leyland Justices, ex p Hawthorn*[16] where, following conviction, it emerged that the police had not told the defence of two witnesses whose statements were helpful to the defendant. This omission had prevented the court from giving the defendant a fair trial, so the conviction was quashed. Given the importance of pre-trial procedure in settling the fate of the defendant, this decision represented a significant shift towards due process values.

Subsequent cases suggest, however, that the Divisional Court will not quash a conviction simply because the prosecution failed in its duty to bring all material evidence before the court. Rather that failure must have resulted in an 'unjust or potentially unjust decision'.[17] This is in line with the general stance of the senior judiciary to unlawful police or prosecutor behaviour, since the focus is primarily on the factual accuracy of the conviction rather than the fairness of the procedures followed. This point is best explored in our review below of the way in which the Court of Appeal approaches its work. Before we reach that, let us pause to pull together the threads of the above discussion.

13   See *Morpeth Justices, ex p Ward* (1992) 95 Cr App R 215 at 222.
14   For further discussion of the complex question of which 'appellate' procedure should be pursued in a given circumstance see Pattenden (1996) pp 229-239 and Sprack (2000) pp 463-464.
15   See *West Sussex Quarter Sessions, ex p Albert and Maud Johnson Trust Ltd* [1974] QB 24, per Orr LJ.
16   [1979] 1 All ER 209.
17   See *Crown Court at Liverpool , ex p Roberts* [1986] Crim LR 622. For discussion of the case law, see J Spencer, 'Judicial Review of Criminal Proceedings' [1991] Crim LR 259 and Sprack (2000) pp 454-462.

(d) Evaluating the appeals procedures open to those convicted in the magistrates' court

We have argued that the right to a rehearing in the Crown Court is not so generous as it might appear. In particular, the legal aid rules discourage those of moderate means from challenging their convictions, whilst the bar against challenging a conviction following a guilty plea denies the vast majority of defendants any hope of redress. The appeal by way of case stated and the judicial review procedure are similarly of little practical significance to the vast majority of defendants. So few summary cases enter these two channels that senior judicial oversight of the quality of magistrates' courts justice is necessarily piecemeal. Moreover, the overlap between the three different procedures is a source of complexity and technicality of a degree sufficient to deter or ensnare all but the most determined or well represented appellant.

Various steps could be taken to improve this situation. For example, a low threshold filter for all three procedures of 'an arguable case' could be introduced alongside a uniform period within which to launch an appeal of three months (extendable if special circumstances arose). Legal aid should be granted in order to enable counsel to make an application to the relevant court for leave to appeal. If permission is granted, legal aid should automatically be made available for the conduct of the appeal (subject to a more generous means test than currently exists). Decisions concerning the appropriate appellate procedure should be governed by legislation rather than being left to judicial whim. Discretion regarding remedies should similarly be better structured through statutory criteria. These reforms would remove much complexity and uncertainty, put the relatively poor on a more equal footing with the rich, filter out some unmeritorious appeals which currently may contribute to delays in the Crown Court, and encourage a greater flow of appeals to the Divisional Court and thus a more comprehensive oversight of summary justice. The latter should help raise the standards of magisterial justice. The costs of any increase in the number of appeals could be more than offset by the benefits of a reduction in the number of unfair trials. Indeed, it is possible that the pool of unfair trials will shrink sufficiently to lead to an overall decline over time in the number of appeals.

Are such reforms at all likely? If one takes a historical perspective the answer must be that they are at least possible. In 1915, for example, the right to an appeal by way of a rehearing was described in a textbook as 'purely illusory' due to the costs and procedural technicalities involved.[18] Lord Atkin in an address to the Magistrates' Association in 1930 observed that:

18 Cited in Pattenden (1996) p 214.

'The truth of the matter is that it is only relatively rich men who can appeal at all from the justices. The poor are incapacitated from doing so; they are tied up by regulations which are sometimes so technically administered as to amount to a perfect scandal.'[19]

Half a million summary convictions generated just 314 appeals by way of rehearing in that year. Judicial review and appeal by way of case stated were similarly remedies available in practice only to the rich. In 1930 a busy Midlands court was reported to have stated just three cases since the First World War, all in licensing matters. In two instances the appellants were brewers, in the third an Earl.[20]

No doubt the spread of car ownership and consequential appearance of the middle classes in the dock for motoring offences is one factor behind the subsequent improvements in appeal procedures. The greater availability of legal aid and much higher levels of professional representation in the magistrates' courts are other linked factors. Any remaining deficiencies in the appeal procedures are nowadays less obvious. Further reforms are unlikely in the absence of better information about the social consequences of the present arrangements. Research is needed to uncover the factors influencing decisions concerning whether or not to appeal, how people experience the appeal procedures in practice, and whether some social groups (eg, ethnic minorities, women, the young, the poor) encounter greater difficulties than others in pursuing an appeal. Above all, light needs to be shed on the impact of appeal processes and decisions on the quality of magistrates' justice.

3. APPEALS FROM THE CROWN COURT TO THE COURT OF APPEAL

We turn now to appeals against conviction following a trial on indictment in the Crown Court. An appeal lies to the Court of Appeal but only on the ground that the conviction was 'unsafe'. Those convicted on indictment do not have the right to a rehearing. Instead, the Court of Appeal's role is essentially that of reviewing the fairness or accuracy of the result produced by the trial. Leave to appeal must be sought (within 28 days of conviction) from a single High Court judge, who determines the matter on the papers submitted by the putative appellant.[1] If an application for leave is refused,

---

19   Cited in Pattenden (1996) pp 214-215 and reproduced in Parl Deb HC, 3 Mar 1933, c 727.
20   Pattenden (1996) p 215.
1   Leave is not required in the rare cases which are certified as suitable for appeal by the trial judge under the power given by the Criminal Appeal Act 1968, s 1(2)(a). The Court of Appeal has actively discouraged trial judges from using this power: Pattenden (1996) pp 95-96. In doing so it has tightened its control over the level of its own workload.

it may be renewed (within 14 days) to the full Court of Appeal which will consider the matter afresh. Oral argument at this stage is unusual as legal aid is rarely available to cover the costs of a renewed application for leave. If the Court of Appeal decides to grant leave, the full appeal will then be heard. These various preliminary filters are supposed to weed out 'weak' appeals. As we shall now see, however, 'weakness' may be the product of the legal and social processes through which an appeal is funnelled rather than an objective quality.

(a) Financial considerations: legal aid and costs

Subject to a means test, it is standard for legal aid to be granted to cover representation for trials on indictment. This legal aid order extends to cover the cost of counsel advising on the prospect of a successful appeal against conviction. If counsel advises that there are grounds for appeal, then legal aid also funds the professional drafting of these grounds in support of the application to the single judge. If that application is successful, legal aid may (and, subject to the means test, invariably will) be granted by the Court of Appeal itself to cover the costs of the full appeal.[2] On the other hand, if counsel's initial advice is that there are no grounds for appeal, or if the application to the single judge is unsuccessful, then legal aid is terminated and the appellant must either pay for legal assistance privately or try to pursue an appeal unassisted. Initial advice from counsel that grounds for appeal do not exist can thus operate as an additional filter, since many convicted persons may be deterred from pursuing an appeal if denied access to legal assistance,[3] or may fail in an application to the single judge (or a renewed application to the Court of Appeal) purely because they lacked professional help in preparing the legal paperwork.[4] Since the rich can afford the legal costs of applications for leave to appeal to single judges and renewed applications to the Court of Appeal, regardless of the strength or weakness of the particular case, the legal aid rules once again breach the due process principle of equality of access to justice. This might be defensible if the filters in operation succeeded in weeding out only unarguable cases but, as we shall see, this is not so.

2   Legal Aid Act 1988, s 20(2).
3   In one study, approximately half of the prisoners who did not appeal gave as one of their reasons the fact that a lawyer had advised them not to appeal: J Plotnikoff and R Woolfson, Information and Advice for Prisoners about Grounds for Appeal and the Appeals Process (Royal Commission on Criminal Justice, Research Study no 18) (HMSO, 1993) p 78.
4   See the discussion by K Malleson, Review of the Appeal Process (Royal Commission on Criminal Justice, Research Study no 17) (London: HMSO, 1993) pp 29–30.

Another aspect of the appeals process which is shaped by the legal aid rules is the type and amount of work which lawyers will undertake in preparing appeals. As with legal aid generally, claims made for work done may be reduced or even refused if considered unreasonable. In one study, between a quarter and a third of solicitors and barristers complained that they had lost money in this way. It was claimed by 20% of solicitors that they no longer bothered to charge for work done in the 28 days following conviction, but this does not necessarily mean that they provided a proper service to clients. Others were clearly offering what they themselves regarded as a sub-standard service in order to stay within the legal aid rules:

'Many lawyers talked of a policy on the part of determining officers of reducing claims without reason or explanation and a total lack of understanding of the amount of work involved in properly serving the interests of one's client . . . Despite the obligation to communicate with their client, many solicitors said that the costs of visiting a prison to discuss an appeal were never allowed and some now refused to make such visits for this reason.'[5]

The frequent refusal by those administering legal aid to fund meetings between counsel and client results in the practical exclusion of appellants from the appeals process. That convicted persons do not always receive adequate legal assistance cannot be attributed solely to the legal aid rules, however, as the next section will demonstrate.

Finally, it is worth noting that an unsuccessful appellant may be ordered to pay whatever costs the Court of Appeal considers 'just and reasonable'.[6] Whilst a costs order is rarely made, it is one more discouraging factor.

(b) The quality of legal advice

There has long been concern at the quality of advice provided to convicted persons. The Criminal Justice Act 1967 entitled all legally aided defendants to legal advice on whether grounds for appeal existed. Zander's study in the early 1970s found that as many as one in ten of legally aided prisoners claimed not to have received such advice, and in at least 25% of cases where an appeal had been advised, no help was provided in drafting the

---

5 Plotnikoff and Woolfson (1993) p 83.
6 Prosecution of Offences Act 1985, s 18(2).

grounds.[7] Publication of these findings was followed by a flurry of pamphlets and good practice guides, as well as a practice note issued by the Lord Chief Justice,[8] all designed to emphasise counsel's obligations of advice and assistance to convicted persons.

Plotnikoff and Woolfson's research for the Runciman Commission established, however, that the legal profession is still failing its clients. Whereas a solicitor is supposed to attend the client in the court cells following conviction, 65% of solicitors indicated that unqualified staff carried out this function. A third of prisoners claimed that the question of an appeal was not discussed with them, as it should have been, immediately after conviction and the majority of these (comprising a quarter of all respondents) stated that they did not receive advice on appealing at any point during the 28 days following conviction. Sprack's view that the 'fairly strict enforcement of the 28-day limit for giving notice ought not to lead to injustice' because a legal adviser will 'normally see him after the verdict and sentence' is thus difficult to accept.[9] Although counsel should provide a client in the court cells with a written statement on whether grounds for appeal exist, almost 90% of solicitors and barristers said that clients were never given anything in writing during a cell visit.[10] The quality of advice offered was often poor, with solicitors most at fault. For example, half of those responding said that they gave the erroneous advice to clients that their sentences might be increased if their appeal was unsuccessful. Whilst the Crown Court can increase a sentence following an appeal from the magistrates' court, the Court of Appeal has no such power.[11] Yet the fear of an increased sentence was a major factor in decisions taken by prisoners convicted in the Crown Court not to appeal.[12] The researchers concluded that there was, amongst the legal profession, 'widespread ignorance both of some aspects of the law on appeals and of the guidelines to good practice on the responsibilities of legal advisers . . .'[13]

A safeguard for convicted persons given a custodial sentence is provided by each prison designating one of its staff as a 'legal aid officer',

7 M Zander, 'Legal Advice and Criminal Appeals: A Survey of Prisoners, Prisons and Lawyers' [1972] Crim LR p 132. Strong dissatisfaction amongst defendants with the level of attention received from lawyers following conviction was also detected by A Bottoms and J McClean, *Defendants in the Criminal Process* (London: Routledge & Kegan Paul, 1976) p 184.
8 [1974] 2 All ER 805.
9 Sprack (2000) p 425.
10 Plotnikoff and Woolfson (1993) p 73.
11 Whilst the loss of time rules (discussed later in the text) might reasonably (if somewhat misleadingly) be portrayed by legal advisers as a de facto power to increase sentence they are rarely applied in practice and could not in any case result in a substantially 'increased sentence'.
12 Plotnikoff and Woolfson (1993) p 82.
13 Plotnikoff and Woolfson (1993) p 115.

with responsibility to advise on appeals. In practice, however, this safety net is somewhat threadbare, largely because these prison officers are diverted by other demands on their time. As Plotnikoff and Woolfson conclude:

'These problems are reflected in the fact that only 32% of inmates claimed to have received advice on appeals from the prison and in the widespread ignorance of the appeals process demonstrated by prisoners in their responses.'[14]

Bottoms and McClean report that many of the convicted persons they interviewed saw the appeals process 'as a somewhat remote affair, a lawyer's procedure where they essentially had to rely on the professionals'.[15] A major determinant of the low appeals rate (discussed below) is that legal advice, when offered at all, is predominantly against appealing. Counsel are particularly unlikely to advise that their own negligent conduct of the defence at trial might provide grounds for an appeal. As Pattenden wryly observes: 'Grounds of appeal drafted by counsel very rarely allege error by the applicant's lawyers in marked contrast to applications drafted by convicted persons.'[16] Even where legal representatives concede that there might be merit in an appeal, their overestimation of the risks involved tends to deter all but the most committed of convicted persons from taking any further action.

(c) Temporal factors: time limits, delays and the loss of time 'rules'

The four-week time-limit for lodging an appeal causes difficulties for some appellants, especially those that do not receive legal advice after their trial ends in conviction. It can be waived following a special application to a single judge (with recourse to the full court on a refusal) but in practice a waiver is unlikely unless the proposed appeal has obvious merit. Historically, the Court of Appeal has been unsympathetic to applicants who have tried to excuse their failure to meet the 28-day deadline by

14 Plotnikoff and Woolfson (1993) p 118. This does not necessarily mean that prisoners did not receive adequate information and advice, although it does suggest that (in so far as they did) it was not communicated effectively. No independent research is available to test the claim (Interim Government Response, Royal Commission on Criminal Justice, February 1994, pp 36-37) that arrangements for providing appeals assistance to prisoners were improved in the aftermath of the Runciman Report.
15 Bottoms and Maclean (1976) p 178.
16 Pattenden (1996) pp 105-106.

reference to financial difficulties[17] or to a barrister's (perhaps bad) advice against appealing.[18] Sometimes the common law is 'clarified' in such a way as to entail that convictions based on the old understanding of the law were wrongful. The Court has refused to allow such convictions to be re-opened by an out-of-time appeal, even in the case of an applicant whose 28-day period had only just expired.[19] The 14-day limit for seeking to overturn a single judge's refusal to grant leave to appeal is even less likely to be extended. Generally, it is clear that the Court of Appeal places great weight on the value of finality when considering requests for out-of-time appeals, particularly when those requests originate from those seen as morally undeserving.[20] There is something of a lottery here, however.[1]

The incentive to appeal is much reduced for those imprisoned citizens who are due to be released before the appeal can be heard.[2] Delays in hearing cases will therefore be one determinant of the overall level of appeals. The defendant who is wrongly convicted of a serious crime can expect to spend at least a year in prison awaiting the chance to have his legal innocence established.[3] Whereas the prospective appellant is forced to act quickly to initiate the appeals process neither the single judge nor the Court of Appeal are required by Parliament to respond to either an application for leave or an appeal with similar expedition; time limits do not cut both ways. This is not to say that members of the Court of Appeal currently twiddle and fiddle their time away. Pattenden describes their collective case load as 'crushing', with evenings and weekends used to catch up on paperwork.[4] One judge has conceded that the speed with which individual appeals are heard may leave appellants with the perception that justice was not done to their case.[5] It would be counter-productive to impose time-limits on the Court of Appeal unless sufficient judges were in place to enable fairness as well as expedition in the handling of appeals.

17 *Moore* (1923) 17 Cr App Rep 155; *Cullum* (1942) 28 Cr App Rep 150.
18 *Burnett* [1964] Crim LR 404.
19 See *Ramsden* [1972] Crim LR 547. For discussion of the post Criminal Appeals Act case law on this point see K Kerrigan, 'Unlocking the Human Rights Floodgates' [2000] Crim LR 71 at 76-7.
20 For a recent example see *Richardson* [1999] Crim LR 563 where the Court refused an application for leave to appeal out of time even though it conceded that the delay was not the applicant's fault and that his conviction was undoubtedly 'unsafe'.
1 *Mullen* [1999] Crim LR 561 illustrates that not every 'morally undeserving' applicant for a late appeal is rebuffed.
2 11% of those deciding not to appeal gave this as one of their reasons in the study by Plotnikoff and Woolfson (1993) p 104.
3 Appellants can be granted bail but this is done only in exceptional circumstances: See generally Pattenden (1996) p 55 and pp 111-112.
4 Pattenden (1996) p 56.
5 Cited by Pattenden (1996) p 56.

A further off-putting feature of the appeals process is the loss of time 'rule', under which the Court of Appeal may order that some or all of the time spent appealing will not count towards a sentence of imprisonment. This is likely to have the greatest deterrent effect on those serving short sentences. For someone sentenced to life imprisonment the threat of an additional three months is unlikely to register. The rather arbitrary nature of the rule is still more starkly revealed when its inapplicability to those receiving a non-custodial sentence is borne in mind.

The loss of time rule is a classic crime control device aimed at deterring prisoners from exercising their 'right' of appeal. In 1966, a change in the law made it easier for convictions to be quashed, and this, together with the loss of the Court of Appeal's power to increase sentences and the demise of automatic loss of time provisions (dating back to 1907), resulted in a quadrupling of applications to the Court of Appeal. The Lord Chief Justice responded by announcing that in future single judges hearing applications for leave deemed 'frivolous' could, and should, order loss of time.[6] This warning proved effective: the number of applications was instantly halved and remained at the lower figure of around 6,000 a year for several years. A subsequent affirmation of this judicial policy gave a stern warning to those contemplating an appeal without professional assistance:

'It may be expected that such a [loss of time] direction will normally be made unless the grounds are not only settled and signed by counsel, but also supported by the written opinion of counsel.'[7]

This makes it still more unlikely that convicted persons whose lawyers advise against an appeal (or fail to give any advice at all) will pursue the matter. Denied legal aid, and faced with the potent threat of loss of time, the prospect of launching an appeal is scarcely an enticing one. One might seek to justify this from a freedom perspective by arguing that deterring 'frivolous' appeals enables the court to devote more resources to expediting the appeals of other appellants with stronger cases. But we cannot assume that appeals which are not supported by counsel are inherently weak. As we have seen, legal advice can be difficult to obtain and, when provided, may simply be wrong. Moreover, the difficulty of separating out the frivolous cases from the arguable is shown by the disagreement rate on questions of leave (which in some recent years has approached 20%) between the single judges and the full Court. As Pattenden notes: 'If the single judge can get it wrong that often, so presumably can counsel.'[8]

6 *Practice Note* [1970] 1 WLR 663.
7 *Practice Note* [1980] 1 All ER 555.
8 Pattenden (1996) p 115. See also at p 99 where she highlights that there is considerable variation in the frequency with which leave is granted between single judges.

Even those who are advised that they do have grounds for appeal may be deterred by the loss of time rules. Appellants denied leave to appeal by the single judge are warned that on a renewal of the application to the full court the risk of losing time is increased, 'since the appellant' (as the official guidance laconically puts it) 'will have the advantage of the single judge's view of the merits of his case'.[9] Single judges typically are required to determine applications for leave to appeal in batches of six in their spare time, usually in the evening after a day in court.[10] The criteria governing the granting of leave are somewhat murky, there is considerable variation amongst judges in their willingness to grant leave, and some habitually give scant reasons for refusing leave.[11] Is it appropriate that decisions made in this way should carry such ramifications for the application of the rules governing both legal aid and loss of time?

What most lawyers fail to point out to their clients is that loss of time orders are nowadays rare and, when made, do not exceed 28 days.[12] Malleson's examination of 65 renewed applications for leave to appeal (made in 1990 following refusal of leave by the single judge) found that the time loss rules were never mentioned, still less applied. This was so even though some of these applications were obviously regarded by the Court of Appeal as groundless, being described in such terms as 'disgraceful', 'a tissue of lies' or a 'cock and bull story'.[13]

The gap between the formal time loss rules and the practice of the court is not hard to explain. The court is able to have it both ways: its rules are so effective in keeping down its workload that, by almost never applying the rules in individual cases, it can give the appearance of adhering to due process values. This resolution of the conflict between the ideological demands of due process and crime control is highly functional for the criminal system. Indeed, one of the pervasive themes of this book has been to argue that the criminal system deflects criticism by projecting an image of due process whilst, behind the scenes, crime control engineering ensures that the reality is quite different.

There seems little prospect of getting rid of the loss of time rules. They chime with the managerial ethos that has become so prominent within the courts and a challenge to them on the basis that they infringe the European Convention on Human Rights has failed.[14]

---

9   A Guide to Proceedings in the Court of Appeal Criminal Division, (Criminal Appeals Office, 1990) para 9.2.
10 K Malleson, 'Miscarriages of Justice and the Accessibility of the Court of Appeal' [1991] Crim LR 323 at 331.
11 Pattenden (1996) pp 98-99.
12 See Plotnikoff and Woolfson (1993) p 79. By a convention established in 1966 the maximum loss of time that will be ordered is 90 days.
13 Malleson (1993) p 15.
14 *Monnell and Morris v United Kingdom* (1987) 10 EHRR 205.

(d) Appeal rates in context

Figures supplied to the Runciman Commission revealed that, in 1992, 14,661 persons were convicted in the Crown Court following a not guilty plea. Two-thirds of the 1,552 persons applying for leave to appeal in that year to the single judge had their application rejected. Some 40% persevered by renewing their application to the full Court but, of these, only 12% were successful. In total, 64% of those seeking leave to appeal had their applications refused. Of those who finally secured a full hearing, 299 (45%) succeeded in their appeal against conviction. So the appeal rate of those convicted in the Crown Court after pleading not guilty is about 1 in 10, and the overall rate at which convictions following not guilty pleas are overturned through an appeal is about 1 in 50.

The pattern of filtering out a majority of appeals has persisted since the Runciman Report. In 1999, for example, there were 2,104 applications for leave to appeal against conviction, of which just 480 were granted by the single judge and a further 123 by the full Court on a renewal of the application.[15] In that year, 551 appeals were heard and 171 were allowed.[16] Clearly the modern pattern of appeals does not represent much of a challenge to the dominant value of finality. Walker, relying on Home Office figures, suggests that there was a relatively short-lived rise in both applications to the Court of Appeal and 'especially of quashings around the time of the major Irish miscarriage of justice cases' in the early 1990s.[17] Figures from the Lord Chancellor's Department are calculated differently but tend to confirm this suggestion.[18] Thus it seems that the Court of Appeal became more sensitive to due process values when public concern about miscarriages of justice was at its height.

Those who reach the court are not a representative group of appellants, nor are they necessarily the appellants with the strongest cases. As Malleson notes, serious offences attracting long custodial sentences, relatively rare in the Crown Court, are the staple diet of the Court of Appeal.[19] Since more run of the mill cases are allocated to less experienced Crown Court judges (under whom miscarriages of justice might be expected to occur more frequently) it appears that the system operates so as to exclude the majority of potential appeals. As Malleson observes:

---

15 Judicial Statistics (1999) Table 1.7.
16 Judicial Statistics (1999) Table 1.8.
17 C Walker, 'The Judiciary' in C Walker and K Starmer (eds), *Miscarriages of Justice* (London: Blackstone, 1999) p 221.
18 Judicial Statistics (1999) Tables 1.7 and 1.8.
19 Malleson (1991) p 325. This is confirmed by more recent statistics: Mattinson (1998) Table 14.

'The appeal process can be likened to an obstacle race: only the determined, strong and well prepared will reach the end—and they are likely to be found in the higher reaches of the offence and sentence scale.'[20]

The true function of the various filters within the appeal system is not so much to weed out weak appeals as to deter all but the most committed from challenging their conviction. The strength of this commitment will depend as much on such factors as the availability of legal advice and legal aid, the quality of legal advice, sentence length, and the fear of loss of time, as on the merits of the case or the intensity of grievance nursed.

(e) The grounds for appeal

The Court of Appeal operates a quite different form of appellate review to that performed by the Crown Court. Whereas the latter rehears cases tried in the magistrates' courts from scratch, historically the Court of Appeal has defined its primary role as to review the procedures followed and decision reached in the trial court. A further factor dissuading convicted persons from challenging convictions is the historically restrictive approach of the Court of Appeal to the appeals that come before it. A significant change to its jurisdiction appeared to have been effected by the Criminal Appeal Act 1995 although the law is currently in a state of flux. In explaining why we cannot be more certain about the effect of this Act it is necessary to say something about the pre-existing law.

(i) Fairness and reliability: the meaning of an unsafe conviction

Section 2(1) of the Criminal Appeal Act 1968 used to provide as follows:

'. . . the Court of Appeal shall allow an appeal against conviction if they think:
(a) that the [conviction] of the jury should be set aside on the ground that under all the circumstances of the case it is unsafe and unsatisfactory; or
(b) that the judgment of the court of trial should be set aside on the ground of a wrong decision of any question of law; or
(c) that there was a material irregularity in the course of the trial, and in any other case shall dismiss the appeal:
Provided that the court may, notwithstanding that they are of opinion that the point raised in the appeal might be decided in favour of the

20   Malleson (1991) p 328.

appellant, dismiss the appeal if they consider that no miscarriage of justice has actually occurred.'[1]

The last sentence set out what became known as 'the proviso'—a device which allowed the upholding of a conviction even in the face of a material irregularity or a wrong decision on a question of law. This discouraged the Court of Appeal from adopting a pure due process posture in which the integrity of procedural justice must be upheld at virtually any cost. Rather it was prodded into the crime control approach of focussing ultimately on the appellant's factual guilt. But since the proviso merely gave the court the freedom to overlook procedural errors rather than mandating that it should do so,[2] the Court of Appeal was left to chart its own course between the poles of due process and crime control. Let us briefly review its navigational tendencies.

An extensive analysis of criminal appeals by Knight published in 1970 demonstrated that the proviso was frequently applied even in cases where there were serious errors at trial.[3] Knight's analysis did, however, uncover the occasional case in which a serious fault resulted in the quashing of a 'factually accurate' conviction,[4] and commentators have identified other such cases in more recent times.[5] In line with Knight's findings, Malleson's survey for the Runciman Commission found no consistent pattern in the use of the proviso.[6] Generally, it seems that a serious error or instance of malpractice at or before the trial was a necessary but not a sufficient condition for declining to exercise the proviso. We think that there is a plausible explanation for this apparently arbitrary pattern of discretion. The default position of the senior judiciary throughout the twentieth century was to use the device of the proviso to prevent the factually guilty from escaping justice 'on a technicality'.[7] But where the conduct of a trial was

---

1   For the sake of completeness we should here mention that a further appeal may lie (with leave) to the House of Lords but only if the Court of Appeal is prepared to certify that a point of law of general public importance is involved. Proceedings in the Crown Court are also subject to judicial review, in the same manner as are proceedings in the magistrates' courts.

2   A point either missed or underplayed by R Nobles and D Schiff, 'Miscarriages of Justice: A Systems Approach' (1995) 58 MLR 299, and by the same authors in 'Criminal Appeal Act 1995: The Semantics of Jurisdiction' (1996) 59 MLR 573 at 576-77.

3   M Knight, *Criminal Appeals* (London: Stevens, 1970) pp 15–21.

4   Knight (1970) pp 30–37.

5   See, for example, A Clarke, 'Safety or Supervision? The Unified Ground of Appeal and its Consequences in the Law of Abuse of Process and Exclusion of Evidence' [1999] Crim LR 108.

6   Malleson (1993).

7   Whereas the senior judiciary resisted the introduction of an appeal against conviction on the facts in 1907, the device of the proviso was welcomed: Pattenden (1996) p 182.

blatantly unfair, especially where this might or did become public knowledge, the court might decline to apply the proviso in order to avoid bringing the criminal justice system into disrepute.

What has been the effect of the Criminal Appeal Act 1995? Section 2 abolishes the proviso and substitutes for the three pre-existing grounds of appeal the single ground that the Court of Appeal thinks the conviction 'is unsafe'. But unsafe in what sense? The Act does not say. At first sight it appears that the 1995 Act has significantly curtailed the grounds on which an appeal can succeed. No longer can an 'unsatisfactory' verdict, a material irregularity in the conduct of the trial, or a wrong decision by the trial judge justify the quashing of a conviction. Rather it seems that the Court will now have to dismiss an appeal if in no doubt that an appellant is guilty of the offence committed, regardless of any procedural errors or malpractice associated with the prosecution and trial. This apparent shift to a pure crime control model was not acknowledged in Parliament during the passing of the legislation, however. Ministers asserted that the new law merely restated the existing practice of the Court of Appeal and that the senior judiciary were of the same view.[8] Accordingly, soon after the passing of the legislation Smith argued that any attempt to argue that the grounds of appeal had been narrowed 'would seem doomed to failure from the outset. . . the Court will continue to reach the same results as it has in the past.'[9]

If Professor Smith is a fan of 'The Simpsons' we imagine he has subsequently exclaimed 'Doh!' in frustration at his miscalculation.[10] It is true that some of the earliest post-Act case law did take the line he had anticipated.[11] But in *Chalkley and Jeffries*[12] the Court of Appeal changed tack by interpreting s 2 as meaning that the Court could not overturn a reliable guilty verdict however unfair the trial might have been. The same position was taken in other cases.[13] Moreover, in the case of *McDonald*[14] Auld LJ expressed his doubts that the jurisdiction to quash a conviction where the trial was adjudged to be not merely unfair but an abuse of process[15] had survived the change in the law brought about by the Criminal Appeal Act 1995.

8   See the discussion by J Smith, 'The Criminal Appeal Act 1995: (1) Appeals Against Conviction' [1995] Crim LR 920 at p 923.
9   Smith [1995] pp 923-924.
10 For his public (and more refined) reaction to post Criminal Appeal Act 1995 case law see his commentaries to the cases of *Simpson* (!) and *Kennedy* at [1998] Crim LR 482 and 740 respectively; and to the case of *Rajcoomar* [1999] Crim LR 729.
11 See, for example, *Hickmet* [1996] Crim LR 588.
12 [1998] 2 All ER 155. This case is also examined in ch 3 (arrest) and in ch 11 (in discussing exclusion of evidence).
13 *Kennedy* [1998] Crim LR 739; *Mills* [1997] 3 All ER 780.
14 Transcript no 97/273/X5. For a discussion of this case and the issues it raises see Clarke (1999).
15 *Horseferry Road Magistrates' Court, ex p Bennett* [1993] 3 All ER 138.

One commentator suggested that Auld LJ's judgment showed that he was 'troubled' by the restriction in the Court of Appeal's powers brought about by the 1995 Act, and that it suggested 'a court belatedly coming to terms with a radical diminution of its power.'[16] But can this be right given that the senior judiciary commented during the Act's passing that it represented no change to their existing practice? In doing so the appellate judges were acknowledging that their existing practice was overwhelmingly based on crime control values. In particular, the Court of Appeal has throughout its history consistently championed the value of finality over that of procedural fairness.[17] Nonetheless, an interpretation of the Criminal Appeals Act which ruled out any possibility of quashing a factually reliable conviction, even when the trial had been tainted by blatant unfairness, *would* mark a break with the past. It would also pose a threat to the legitimacy of the courts. No wonder some of the senior judiciary were 'troubled'.

In the subsequent case of *Mullen*[18] the Court of Appeal changed tack again by re-visiting the question of whether abuse of process rendered a conviction 'unsafe'. It opted for an examination of the Parliamentary history of the new legislation and determined that the intention of Parliament had been to restate the existing practice of the Court. On that basis it concluded that 'unsafe' did include a conviction achieved through an abuse of process.

This is one area in which the growing influence of the human rights perspective can be detected. Article 6 of the European Convention secures to an accused the right to a 'fair' trial. If unfairness at a trial could not lead in itself to the quashing of a conviction, the Court of Appeal would be failing to protect a fundamental human right. The denial of a fair trial and the failure of the appellate courts to cure this defect could then lead to an adverse finding against the UK by the European Court of Human Rights. This is exactly what occurred in *Condron v UK*[19] in which the European Court opined that 'the question whether or not the rights of the defence guaranteed to an accused under Art 6 of the Convention were secured in any given case cannot be assimilated to a finding that his conviction was safe in the absence of any enquiry into the issue of fairness.' Acknowledging that ruling, and preferring the approach of *Mullen* to that of *Chalkley and Jeffries*, the Court of Appeal in *Davis, Rowe and Johnson*[20]

16   Clarke (1999) pp 114-115.
17   See generally K Malleson, 'Appeals against Conviction and the Principle of Finality' (1994) 21 JLS 151; Nobles and Schiff (1995). For a critique of Nobles and Schiff's position see C Walker, 'Miscarriages of Justice in Principle and Practice' in C Walker and K Starmer (eds), *Miscarriages of Justice* (London: Blackstone, 1999) pp 42-43.
18   [1999] 2 Cr App Rep 143.
19   [2000] Crim LR 679.
20   See Archbold News, August 2000.

has now unequivocally accepted that a conviction may be unsafe even where there was no doubt about guilt.[1] However, the Court noted that 'the effect of any unfairness upon the safety of the conviction will vary according to its nature and degree' and rejected the argument that a breach of Art 6 would inexorably lead to a conviction being quashed. In short, the Court's view is that only when *it* takes the view that *serious* procedural unfairness has occurred will otherwise reliable convictions become 'unsafe'.

It is deplorable that there should have been such judicial vacillation for several years over a matter as important as this. Parliament should also bear some of the blame for its failure to spell out what an 'unsafe' conviction might be. Nobles and Schiff rightly argue that the Court of Appeal has always resisted being tied to statutory formulae, responding as much to their own perceptions and experience of 'justice', and to pressures on them, as to any 'literal' interpretation of statutory language.[2] Nonetheless, it would have been difficult for the Court to ignore a clear direction from Parliament to quash reliable convictions obtained unfairly. No such clarity was achieved in the 1995 Act. Perhaps the Government feared associating itself with an explicit statement that the 'obviously guilty' must go free when this is necessary to uphold the value of procedural fairness. It remains to be seen whether *Johnson, Rowe and Davis* marks the beginning of a new more due-process oriented approach by the Court of Appeal. If the Court upholds reliable convictions other than in cases of blatant and very serious procedural injustice then there will be little change from its pre-1995 practice except to the extent that such change is demanded by the European Court of Human Rights.[3]

(ii)   Reviewing 'mistakes' by juries

Another basis on which a conviction might be regarded as 'unsafe' is where the jury is thought to have reached the wrong conclusion. It was not until the Criminal Appeal Act 1907 that convicted persons were given the opportunity to appeal on the basis that a factual mistake about their guilt had been made by a jury. The grounds for an appeal were stated in s 4(1)

---

1   In doing so it also drew on the cases of *Smith (Patrick)* (1999) Times, 31 May and *Weir* (29 May 2000, unreported) which both expressed a preference for this broader approach to the interpretation of the Criminal Appeal Act 1995.

2   R Nobles and D Schiff, *Understanding Miscarriages of Justice* (Oxford: OUP, 2000) ch 3.

3   The extent to which the European Court of Human Rights will make such demands remains unclear. See *Khan (Sultan) v UK* [2000] Crim LR 684 and accompanying commentary.

in broad terms. The Court of Appeal was directed to allow an appeal if it thought the verdict of the jury was 'unreasonable' or could not be supported 'having regard to the evidence' or that 'on any ground there was a miscarriage of justice'. The Court chose to interpret these powers in the narrowest possible way. Prior to the mid-1960s, it refused to overturn the verdict of the jury unless it was one which no reasonable jury could have arrived at. The fact that members of the court thought that they themselves would have returned a different verdict was, according to the judgment in *Hopkins-Husson*, 'no ground for refusing to accept the verdict of the jury, which is the constitutional method of trial in this country.'[4] The value of finality was clearly paramount.

This stance had a certain logic to it given that the Court of Appeal took the view that it had not been set up to rehear cases.[5] Whereas the jury sees the witnesses and exhibits, and hears oral evidence, the Court of Appeal usually does no more than review the conduct of the trial as recorded in writing at the time. The jury might thus appear to be in a better position to assess the issue of guilt. On the other hand a concern with protecting the innocent might justify giving the benefit of any appellate doubt about guilt to a convicted person. It seems that it was the latter approach that Parliament sought to encourage in passing the 1907 Act.[6] The Court of Appeal preferred to act as if it had been given much narrower powers. Parliament eventually tried again by passing the Criminal Appeal Act 1966 which directed the Court to quash a conviction which was 'unsafe or unsatisfactory'. At first it seemed that the Court under Lord Chief Justice Widgery had taken heed. Its response to the new statutory formula was the introduction of the 'lurking doubt' test in *Cooper*:

> 'the court must in the end ask itself a subjective question, whether we are content to let the matter stand as it is, or whether there is not some lurking doubt in our minds which makes us wonder whether an injustice has been done.'[7]

In *Cooper*, there was no complaint about the way in which the case had been put in court—it was simply asserted that the jury had come to the wrong verdict. At first blush it would seem that the lurking doubt test hoisted the value of avoiding wrongful convictions above that of finality. However, relatively few convictions (less than one a year on average) have

---

4   (1949) 34 Cr App Rep 47, per Lord Goddard CJ. Note that jury trial is in fact used in relatively few criminal cases: ch 9.

5   Pattenden (1996) p 141.

6   Pattenden (1996) p 141.

7   [1969] 1 QB 267 at 271.

ever been quashed on this basis.[8] Whatever the rhetorical significance of *Cooper*, it was crime control business as usual for the Court of Appeal in the decades that followed. The Criminal Appeal Act 1995 does nothing to encourage more frequent quashings under the lurking doubt test.[9] Indeed, the propriety of ever using that test following the 1995 Act has been doubted by the Court of Appeal.[10]

We may conclude that the Court of Appeal's practice in this area has always exhibited a restrictive interpretation of its legislatively granted powers. Indeed, in an eerie echo of the reception of the Criminal Appeal Act 1995, Lord Chief Justice Widgery had claimed during a debate on the 1966 legislation that the new power to quash 'unsafe or unsatisfactory' convictions merely codified and legitimised the existing practice of the Court.[11] As the French might say, the more things have changed, the more they have stayed the same.

(iii) The admission of fresh evidence at appeal

When the Court of Appeal was set up in 1907 it was given the power to go beyond merely reviewing the papers relating to the original trial. Under s 9 it could order the production of any document, exhibit or other thing connected with the proceedings and order that witnesses attend for examination either before the Court or a commissioner appointed by the court. It could also refer questions to a special commissioner for reports, and appoint expert assessors. Parliament's intention was to allow the Court ample power to reopen a case and get at the truth. The Court of Appeal interpreted these powers restrictively and refused to admit new evidence on appeal except in very narrow circumstances. Most notably, the Court imposed a requirement that the evidence which an appellant wished to call must not have been available (in the sense that it could have been produced with reasonable diligence) at the trial.[12] The Court was thus expressing a preference for acting as a review body rather than one which would rehear the case. It was also seeking to protect the notion that the constitutional responsibility for convicting persons of serious crime rested with juries, not appellate judges.

Parliament responded in 1964 by introducing a new power which would allow the Court to order a retrial after the admission on appeal of fresh

---

8   Malleson (1993) p 24; Pattenden (1996) pp 146-147.
9   See the discussion by K Malleson, 'The Criminal Cases Review Commission: How Will It Work?' [1995] Crim LR 929 at 934-6.
10   *F* [1999] Crim LR 306, but see the doubts expressed about this case by Professor Smith in his accompanying commentary.
11   See Pattenden (1996) p 146.
12   Pattenden (1996) pp 130-132.

evidence.[13] This signalled to the Court that the legislature did not want it to treat the original jury's verdict as virtually sacrosanct. But the Court's restrictive approach to the reception of fresh evidence was maintained.[14] So Parliament tried again. It imposed a duty on the Court to admit credible evidence which would have been admissible at trial whenever there was a reasonable explanation for the failure to adduce it earlier.[15] In practice, however, the Court remained steadfast in its reluctance to step outside what it conceived to be its narrow review function by admitting fresh evidence. Certainly where the failure to adduce evidence at the original trial was attributable to a mistake on the part of the defendant's lawyers, the court rarely permitted that evidence, however cogent, to be heard on appeal.

In the infamous 1972 case of Luke Dougherty, a veritable busload of witnesses could have provided the defendant with a cast-iron alibi on a shoplifting charge, but only two were called at trial:[16] one was Dougherty's girlfriend and the other had previous convictions. The jury believed neither and convicted. Dougherty faced a 15-month prison sentence for a crime he plainly did not commit.[17] Leave to appeal was refused by the single judge, who ruled that the fresh evidence from others who went on the same bus trip as Dougherty could not be heard. The Court of Appeal subsequently confirmed that the single judge's stance was correct. It was only when the case was referred back to the Court of Appeal by the Home Secretary that the alibi witnesses were heard and the conviction quashed. But by this time Dougherty had already spent nine months in prison.

The Court has occasionally received new evidence of matters arising subsequent to the trial. As such evidence, by definition, could not have been adduced at trial, its reception amounts to an implicit acknowledgement that the Court's function goes beyond reviewing the propriety of what happened in the lower courts. But the grudging nature of the Court's stance in this regard belies any commitment to protecting the innocent from wrongful conviction. Witnesses who wish to retract their trial testimony should not expect to be welcomed by the Court as converts to the pursuit of truth and justice. As a judgment in 1990 put it: 'the mere fact that a prosecution witness chooses to come forward after the trial to assert that his evidence at trial was perjured will rarely provide a basis for permitting him to give evidence or for interfering with the conviction.'[18]

13 Criminal Appeal Act 1964, s 1.
14 Pattenden (1996) p 137.
15 Criminal Appeal Act 1966, s 5. The fresh evidence provisions were subsequently reenacted in the Criminal Appeal Act 1968, s 23.
16 The case is discussed at length in ch 2 of the Report of the Departmental Committee on Evidence of Identification in Criminal Cases, HCP 338 (1976).
17 The sentence for shoplifting was six months' imprisonment, and the judge activated a nine-month suspended sentence to run consecutively with this.
18 *Turner*, cited in Malleson (1993) p 10.

Malleson's study for the Runciman Commission demonstrated a continuing judicial distaste for fresh evidence: 'Only in very limited circumstances will such evidence be admitted and if admitted form the basis for a successful appeal.'[19] This broader approach is most likely where the case is grave and the fresh evidence of innocence overwhelming. It is difficult to avoid the conclusion that what chiefly influences the Court in these matters is whether it is likely to attract criticism for failing to reopen a case that has aroused public concern.[20] Otherwise, the value of finality is likely to dominate its thinking and the inaccuracy of the original verdict will be of subsidiary concern.

The Criminal Appeal Act 1995 is likely to entrench this ordering of values. Section 4 abolishes the rarely used power to rehear evidence presented at the trial, as well as the duty to admit fresh evidence in the circumstances laid down in the mid-1960s legislation. Parliament is evidently no longer interested in encouraging the reopening of more cases on appeal. The Court of Appeal is left with a discretion to admit fresh evidence having regard to factors which are worded similarly to those which it has long applied.[1] The main difference, if such it is, is that the Court should no longer have regard to whether the evidence is 'likely to be believed' but rather ask itself whether it is 'capable of belief'. The new wording originates from the Runciman Commission which believed it would encourage a more liberal approach to the reception of fresh evidence, a belief which the Government claimed to share. Academic commentators think, by contrast, that the new wording either makes no difference[2] or, if anything, encourages a more restrictive approach.[3] The Court of Appeal has recently reviewed its own practices as revealed in decided cases. It concluded that all applications to adduce fresh evidence turned on their own peculiar facts, adding that 'judicial reactions, being human, are not uniform.'[4] In other words, appellants should not regard cases where fresh evidence was admitted as establishing binding precedents. This reflects the judges' distaste for, and discouragement of, fresh evidence cases. The typical appeal continues to consist of no more than legal argument between opposing counsel.[5] The Court of Appeal remains, by stubborn inclination, a reviewing court.

19 Malleson (1993) p 11. See also P O'Connor, 'The Court of Appeal: Re-Trials and Tribulations' [1990] Crim LR 615 at 619.
20 See the discussion of the case law in Pattenden (1996) p 135.
1   The factors are the credibility, admissibility and relevance of the evidence and whether there is a reasonable explanation for the failure to adduce the evidence at trial: Criminal Appeal Act, 1968 s 23(2). See further *Trevor* [1998] Crim LR 652, *Cairns* [2000] Crim LR 473 and the commentaries to these case reports.
2   Pattenden (1996) p 138.
3   J Smith, 'Criminal Appeals and the Criminal Cases Review Commission - 2' (1995) NLJ 572 at 573.
4   See *Criminal Cases Review Commission, ex p Pearson* [1999] Crim LR 732 and accompanying commentary.
5   Seabrooke and Sprack (1999) p 356.

(iv) Retrials

The final power of the Court of Appeal which merits attention here is that provided by s 7(1) of the Criminal Appeal Act 1968 of ordering a retrial, 'where the interests of justice so require', following a decision to allow an appeal. The power used to apply only where an appeal was allowed on the basis of fresh evidence but by s 43 of the Criminal Justice Act 1988 this restriction was removed. Thus, s 7(1) gave the court an alternative to upholding a conviction by applying 'the proviso' (see section 3(e)(i) above) in cases where, although there had been some procedural error affecting the fairness of the trial, the Court concluded that the appellant was probably guilty. It might also encourage the Court to allow more appeals in the first place. If these were the effects of s 7(1), due process values would be advanced. But the subsection might also be used as an alternative to simply quashing a conviction in cases where the court has concluded that so serious a procedural error occurred at the original trial that the proviso should not be applied. If it were used in the latter way an important opportunity for affirming fundamental due process values would be lost. Section 7(1) merely provides that a retrial may be ordered if 'it appears to the court that the interests of justice so require', but gives no guidance as to whether the definition of those interests should be inspired by due process or crime control values. Again, then, we must examine the actual practice of the court in ordering retrials.

Historically, the Court of Appeal proved very reluctant to exercise its power to order retrials in fresh evidence cases.[6] This was partly because of the decision of the House of Lords in *Stafford v DPP*[7] that the task of the Court of Appeal in such cases was to decide whether it thought the verdict unsafe and unsatisfactory rather than open up the question of what a jury might think of the new evidence. Thus under *Stafford* the Court of Appeal may not quash a conviction simply because it thinks the fresh evidence might have caused the jury to acquit. This position is left unaltered by the Criminal Appeals Act 1995.[8] We saw above that the Court of Appeal is reluctant to admit fresh evidence of innocence on the basis that jury trial is the proper place for hearing and weighing evidence.[9] This works against appellants' interests. But if fresh evidence *is* admitted, how a jury might have reacted to that evidence becomes, at best, a matter to which the court may have regard. This also works against defendants' interests. Whereas a jury at a retrial would not know of the quashed conviction, of the defendant's previous convictions, and so forth, the Court of Appeal is

6   There have been exceptions such as *Cairns* [2000] Crim LR 473.
7   [1974] AC 878.
8   See *Trevor* [1998] Crim LR 652; *Cairns* [2000] Crim LR 473; *O' Brien* [2000] Crim LR 676, and the commentaries that accompany these case reports.
9   See section 3(e)(iii) above.

privy to such prejudicial material. Given the Court's historical stance of not ordering retrials in fresh evidence cases, the next best option from an appellant's point of view is for the judges to put themselves in an imaginary jury's shoes. Instead the judges have decided that they will decide the matter from their own point of view. It seems that the jury's role of determining guilt or innocence is regarded as constitutionally sacrosanct only when that works against the interests of appellants.[10]

The *Stafford* decision has no application to appeals not involving fresh evidence, however, and it seems that the Court of Appeal is more willing to order retrials in such cases. From 1985 to 1990, the number of retrials ordered per annum fluctuated from nought to three, but once the Criminal Justice Act 1988 amendment to s 7 came into force, the number jumped, to 15 in 1991.[11] The number of retrials then increased throughout the 1990s, reaching 73 in 1998 and 70 in 1999.[12] These figures represent a considerable change in practice but the reason for it is unclear. Since the abolition of the proviso by the Criminal Appeal Act 1995 the Court of Appeal's only way of securing the ultimate conviction of those who appear 'actually' guilty, but whose trials were so unfair as to render the initial conviction 'unsafe', is to order a retrial. But while this may have encouraged the ordering of more retrials it is apparent that the upwards trend pre-dated the Criminal Appeal Act 1995. It is difficult to determine whether the Court's modern practice is, on balance, expressing due process or crime control values. This is because the judgments of the Court of Appeal give little clue as to why retrials are thought appropriate in some cases but not others. The conventional textbook position is that the Court will take into account the period which has elapsed since the original trial, whether or not the appellant has been in custody, and the apparent strength of the case.[13] What is clear is that the court sometimes orders retrials even when there has been a flagrant breach of due process values at the original trial. An example is the case of *King* in which the Court denounced the trial judge's summing up for the jury in trenchant language: 'We have read this summing-up with dismay . . . we hope that we never again see a summing-up which is as unfair and unbalanced as this.'[14] Despite the ferocity of its criticism, the court ordered a retrial, thus, in Packer's phrasing, breeding disrespect for the very values it was professing to affirm. For why should the police, the prosecution or the trial judge remain faithful to the dictates of due process

---

10   This observation supports our view (developed further below) that Malleson (1994) p 156 errs in suggesting that what motivates appellate judges in interpreting their powers restrictively is respect for trial by jury.

11   For comment on this step-jump see Malleson (1993) p 25 and RCCJ (1993) p 175.

12   Judicial Statistics (1999) Table 1.8.

13   Seabrooke and Sprack (1999) p 359.

14   Cited in Malleson (1993) p 26.

if the worse that can happen in the event of infidelity is that the initial adversarial fight is declared void and a rematch ordered?

(v) Evaluating the appeal procedures open to those convicted in the Crown Court

From a freedom perspective it is evident that a number of obstacles to appealing against a Crown Court conviction need to be removed. First, legal services need to be made more readily available to those convicted, and especially to those imprisoned. The defendant's own legal representatives should have their legal aid bills cut by a large percentage in any case in which they failed to comply with their duty to advise in writing, immediately following conviction, on the prospects of an appeal. To ensure compliance, no legal aid bill should be paid unless a copy of counsel's written advice on this matter was attached to the claim for payment. But because legal advice is sometimes wrong, and because defendant's own legal representatives may be unable or unwilling to identify their own mistakes, it is important that convicted persons are provided with the means to get a second opinion. For this to be an effective right for those imprisoned, something along the lines of the police station duty solicitor scheme is needed. One possibility is for each prison to be visited by a duty barrister once a month in order to give general advice about appeal rights and offer specific advice to those interested in taking the matter further. This should encourage some barristers to become expert in appellate law and practice and thus lead to high-quality provision of advice. Their work could be supported in each prison by the prison officer designated as 'legal aid officer'. That support could encompass such matters as publicising the duty barrister scheme, ensuring that reference books are kept up to date, and helping with the administration of the scheme.

Second, the legal aid rules should be changed so that they place less weight on the advice of the defendant's original legal representatives and the views of the single judge. If a barrister giving a 'second opinion' takes the view that there is an arguable case, legal aid should be granted for the making of the application to the single judge. If the single judge refuses the application, that should not result in the termination of legal aid if counsel, having considered the single judge's reasons, forms the opinion that the case is still an arguable one.

Third, as with appeals from the magistrates' courts, we would argue for a more generous time limit of three months within which to initiate an appeal. This is crucial if our proposed duty barrister scheme is to work.

Fourth, there should be a more relaxed leave test which would filter out only 'unarguable' cases. The loss of time rules should be abolished. As they stand, they are likely to deter not only the 'frivolous' time-wasting appeal but also many worthwhile ones. They are also arbitrary in their application in that, as Sprack puts it, 'those who have not received custodial sentences may appeal with impunity, whereas those who are serving custodial sentences and, prima facie, have more urgent reasons for appealing, are liable to possible sanctions if they do so.'[15] It should be regarded as a sufficient filter that leave to appeal can be refused in any case that is plainly unarguable, and a sufficient deterrent to 'frivolous appeals' that unsuccessful appellants run the risk of an order for costs being made against them. Beyond that the disadvantages of applying more stringent filtering and deterrent mechanisms outweigh the possible benefits.

Of course these reforms would tend to increase the flow of appeals and this is unlikely to be popular with an already overworked judiciary. However, the solution is not to choke off appeals by erecting new procedural hurdles but rather for the judges to demand more resources from Parliament.[16] Whether they will make such demands is likely to depend in part on their own underlying value systems. As their patterns of discretionary decision-making, as reviewed above, suggest a preference for crime control values, it is unrealistic to expect these demands to be made with sufficient frequency to achieve any significant expansion of resources.[17] There is similarly little point in stimulating more appeals if the judges remain so reluctant to quash convictions. The passing of the Human Rights Act might cause a shift within the senior judiciary towards the due process and freedom models, as might changes in the selection, training and monitoring of judges.[18] Perhaps most promising of all, however, is the work of the Criminal Cases Review Commission in uncovering miscarriages of justice. This should at least prod the Court of Appeal into recognising that such miscarriages remain a frequent occurrence.

15   Sprack (2000) p 429.
16   Malleson (1994) p 162.
17   Malleson (1994) p 156 argues that the factors which influence the Court of Appeal's reluctance to quash convictions include due process concerns such as respect for jury verdicts, the need for speedy justice, and the fear that juries would, if they knew that an appellant had a generous right of appeal, deliberate less carefully and convict on weaker evidence. This is to misunderstand the due process model, at least as developed by Packer. The due process model would prefer the protection of an individual's right against wrongful conviction to upholding 'respect for the jury', and would prefer extensive appeal rights to the 'need' for a speedy post-conviction resolution of the case. As for the 'fear' that juries would become too conviction-prone, Malleson accepts too readily that this factor actually motivates judges rather than being a rhetorical smoke-screen designed to disguise the true reasons for restricting appeal rights.
18   See Walker (1999) 'The Judiciary' pp 213-215 for discussion of selection, training and monitoring.

4. POST-APPEAL REVIEW - THE CRIMINAL CASES REVIEW COMMISSION

A convicted person may only appeal once through the normal judicial channel.[19] A second appeal is not allowed even if the matter to be raised at the second appeal would have been quite different from that dealt with at the first. But once the standard appeal channels have been exhausted there remains the possibility of the case being referred back to the Court of Appeal through a non-judicial route. Since the Criminal Appeal Act 1995, the gatekeeper of this route has been the newly created Criminal Cases Review Commission. Prior to then, the Home Secretary had a statutory power to refer cases back to the Court of Appeal. In order to appreciate the significance of this change, it is necessary to say something about the pre-Act position.

(a) References by the Home Secretary to the Court of Appeal (prior to 1997)

On average, the Home Office received some 700–800 requests each year to reopen cases in this way, but very few references were made as a result of these petitions. The number of references increased in the years 1989–92, but still amounted to only seven cases per annum.[20] There were a number of interrelated factors behind this low success rate.

Legal aid was not available for the preparation of petitions and, in consequence, many were ill-conceived or poorly presented. Yet petitions needed to be detailed and convincingly argued to stand a chance of success. This is partly because they were considered by a small number of legally unqualified civil servants (based in 'C3' within the Home Office) who lacked the resources to carry out further investigation and research into particular grievances. These civil servants occasionally asked the police to re-examine evidence but critics argued that the police were more likely to cover-up their own wrongdoing than root it out.[1] More fundamentally, the Home Office was reluctant to refer many cases to the Court of Appeal for fear of being seen as interfering with the judicial function. Moreover, the Home Office had potentially conflicting roles, since it was responsible for the police and the maintenance of law and order. In practice the few cases it referred were those in which there was fresh evidence or some other new consideration of substance that had yet to be put before the court.

19 *Pinfold* [1988] QB 462.
20 See RCCJ (1993) p 181.
1   M Mansfield and N Taylor, 'Post-Conviction Procedures' in C Walker and K Starmer (eds), *Justice in Error* (London: Blackstone, 1993) p 164.

From the appellants' point of view, the unavailability of legal aid made it almost essential to enlist the aid of lawyers prepared to act on a voluntary basis and, better still, public figures, bodies or campaigning journalists prepared to fight their corner. How else was fresh evidence to be found when the convicted person remained incarcerated in prison, and how else could the Home Office be persuaded to act in this sensitive area? Luke Dougherty (discussed in section 3(e)(iii) above) would not have achieved even the limited degree of success that he did were it not for the campaigning group 'Justice' taking up the case on his behalf. A House of Commons select committee noted in 1982 that in practice the 'chances of a petition being ultimately successful might sometimes depend less on its intrinsic merits than on the amount of external support and publicity it was able to attract.'[2] Mansfield and Taylor similarly observe that:

'there was an air of inevitability about the release of the Guildford Four when, by late 1988, they had the endorsement of such worthies as Cardinal Basil Hume, Archbishop Runcie, two former Home Secretaries (Roy Jenkins and Merlyn Rees) and two former Law Lords (Lords Devlin and Scarman).'[3]

The Birmingham Six did not have such distinguished supporters. Lord Denning MR, in terminating the civil action brought by the 'Birmingham Six' for assault against the police, said:

'If the six men win, it will mean that the police were guilty of perjury, that they were guilty of violence and threats, and the confessions were involuntary and were improperly admitted in evidence and that the convictions were erroneous. That would mean the Home Secretary would either have to recommend that they be pardoned or he would have to remit the case to the Court of Appeal. This is such an appalling vista that every sensible person in the land would say: It cannot be right these actions should go further.'[4]

In Lord Denning's world view, it is evidently more important that the criminal justice system preserve its good name (even if undeserved) than that possibly innocent persons are given the chance to regain theirs.

In the event, the Home Office did, years later, remit the case to the Court of Appeal. The latter's distaste for the reference procedure was clear from the closing remarks of Lord Lane CJ:

'As has happened before in references by the Home Secretary to this court under s 17 of the Criminal Appeal Act 1968, the longer this

2   Home Affairs Committee, Report on Miscarriages of Justice, (HC 421) (1981-82) para 10.
3   Mansfield and Taylor (1993) p 166.
4   *McIlkenny v Chief Constable of the West Midlands* [1980] 2 WLR 689 at 706.

hearing has gone on the more convinced this court has become that the verdict of the jury was correct. We have no doubt that these convictions were both safe and satisfactory.'[5]

As Rozenberg puts it: 'Not only was Lord Lane saying Douglas Hurd had been wrong to send this case back to the Court of Appeal, he was suggesting that the Home Office was too ready to refer other hopeless cases.'[6] The 'Birmingham Six' remained in prison for 11 years after Lord Denning had refused to contemplate the 'awful' possibility that their story might be true, and for three years after Lord Lane dismissed their appeal in 1988. Only after a further reference from the Home Secretary were their convictions finally quashed, by which time they had collectively lost 96 years of freedom.

(b) The creation of the Criminal Cases Review Commission

The restrictive approach of the Court of Appeal, combined with the caution shown by the Home Office in dealing with petitions, led to repeated calls for reform. Many commentators and official reports argued for the creation of some extra-judicial tribunal or commission to be set up to consider alleged miscarriages of justice. Such proposals were deflected or rejected by successive governments over a period of some 25 years. It was almost inevitable that the idea would be taken up by the Runciman Commission given that the late 1980s and early 1990s had witnessed an unprecedented number of miscarriages of justice, many of which - like the Birmingham Six - had initially not been recognised as such by the Home Secretary and Court of Appeal. Its recommendation was that a 'Criminal Cases Review Authority' should be set up to consider alleged miscarriages of justice and to refer appropriate cases back to the Court of Appeal.

The Runciman Commission was taken to task by commentators for the conservative nature of its proposal.[7] Some of the main flaws identified were that the new body would rely on the police to carry out any necessary investigations, that it should not have to disclose the report produced for it by the police, that its decisions should not be subject to appeal or judicial review and that legal aid should not normally be made available during the period in which the Authority is investigating a case. Furthermore, it would lack the power to take cases of its own motion, and, when referring cases

---

5 Quoted by J Rozenberg, 'Miscarriages of Justice' in E Stockdale and S Casale (eds), *Criminal Justice Under Stress* (London: Blackstone, 1992) p 104.

6 Rozenberg (1992) p 104.

7 See, in particular, P Thornton, 'Miscarriages of Justice: A Lost Opportunity' [1993] Crim LR 926.

to the Court of Appeal, would have no power to make any recommendation as to outcome. Small wonder that Thornton was driven to the conclusion that 'Apart from being independent of the executive, the proposed body looks remarkably like C3.'[8] One may go further and question whether such independence would be more apparent than real, in the light of the Runciman Commission's recommendation that the members of the Authority be appointed by the government.[9] The parallels with the Police Complaints Authority (see ch 11) are all too obvious. Not surprisingly, the Conservative Government was content to accept the Runciman Commission's conservative blueprint more or less as it stood and made provision for the new Criminal Cases Review Commission (CCRC) in the Criminal Appeal Act 1995.

Our prediction in the 1994 edition of this book was that, unless provided with generous resources (which we thought unlikely) the review body would be forced into a sifting process almost as rigorous as that previously operated by the Home Secretary. We foresaw that applications to the reviewing body would still depend for their success on being professionally presented and argued. If legal aid was not made freely available (which we thought unlikely) a convicted person's chances of success would continue to be determined largely by whether they could persuade lawyers or campaigning bodies to act voluntarily on their behalf. Our overall prediction was that the reviewing body would deal mainly with high profile cases in which lengthy prison sentences were imposed. Mundane miscarriages of justice would, we believed, continue to be swept under the carpet. Were we right to be so pessimistic?

(c) The Criminal Cases Review Commission in action

The Commission assumed responsibility for referring cases to the Court of Appeal on 31 March 1997. In its first three years of operation it received 3,193 applications, consisting of 279 transferred from the Home Office, 1,105 new cases in 1997-98, 1,035 in 1998-99, and 774 in 1999-2000.[10] Thus, following an initial surge in applications, the average annual intake may now be settling down to roughly the same level as that the Home Office

8   Thornton [1993] p 929.
9   Under the Criminal Appeal Act 1995, appointments are made by the Crown on the recommendation of the Prime Minister. The selection procedure was run by the Home Office. Half of the first body of Commissioners to be appointed came from business, prosecution or police backgrounds whilst none came from a background of campaigning to root out miscarriages of justice: Taylor with Mansfield, 'Post-conviction procedures' in C Walker and K Starmer (eds), *Miscarriages of Justice* (London: Blackstone, 1999) pp 235-36.
10   Criminal Cases Review Commission, Annual Report 1999-2000, p 17.

dealt with. In the same period the Commission referred 80 cases to the Court of Appeal. It has thus shown itself more ready to refer cases than the Home Office used to be. But it is also clear that the vast majority of applications do not result in a referral. By 30 June 2000 some 2,000 applications had been rejected compared with just 90 referrals.[11] In other words an applicant to the Commission has less than a 1 in 20 chance of success. Below we explore what has led to this overwhelming pattern of failure.

The Commission may only refer cases in the restricted circumstances set out in s 13 of the Criminal Appeals Act 1995. It may not refer cases unless it considers that there is a 'real possibility' that the Court of Appeal will not uphold the conviction or sentence.[12] The framework within which appeals will be heard following a CCRC referral is no different from the legal framework governing the initial appeal.[13] It follows that the CCRC is obliged to take into account the narrow way in which the Court of Appeal interprets its own powers.[14] In other words, the Court of Appeal and the CCRC are applying the same criteria. So it is not surprising that the CCRC mirrors the Court of Appeal's practice of weeding out most putative appellants. Moreover, applicants must already have exhausted their appeal rights, and the Commission must consider that the case involves some argument or evidence not previously put forward at the trial or the appeal stage. These last two conditions do not apply only if the Commission considers there are 'exceptional circumstances' justifying the making of a referral.[15] Generally, then, it is clear that the CCRC provides a means by which the applicant may bring further appeals but only when there is something new *and* legally relevant to say. This is no different from the position that previously obtained under the old Home Office referral route. Without fresh evidence or new legal arguments the applicant to the CCRC is almost doomed to fail. Applicants who simply assert that the jury 'got it wrong' or that the CCRC should refer the case on the basis of a 'lurking doubt' make little headway.[16]

As we predicted, no provision for legal aid was made in the legislation setting up the CCRC. Thus another point of continuity with the old Home

---

11 See the CCRC's web-site at http://www.ccrc.gov.uk. Seven of these referrals were in respect of sentence only.

12 Although a CCRC referral of a magistrates' court conviction can be made to the Crown Court we will concentrate in the text on referrals of Crown Court convictions to the Court of Appeal. (Only one referral of a magistrates' court conviction has occurred to date.)

13 Criminal Appeals Act 1995, s 9(1).

14 As confirmed by *Criminal Cases Review Commission, ex p Pearson* [1999] 3 All ER 498.

15 An example would be where an applicant has not exhausted appeal rights but the CCRC has already decided to refer a related case involving a co-defendant: CCRC, Annual Report 1999-2000, p 8.

16 See further Malleson (1995).

Office procedure is that the only help available is through the 'Green Form' scheme. This allows legal advisers to be paid for up to two hours of advice and assistance before they must apply for an extension. The Government argued that this would be adequate as a lawyer would not be needed once the Commission began its investigations.[17] The CCRC has designed a clear application form that provides helpful guidance on its completion. But as commentators have pointed out, an effective application will be one based on an understanding of how the CCRC chooses to prioritise the cases it receives.[18] A more fundamental point is that the CCRC may only refer cases to the Court of Appeal if it considers that the Court of Appeal will interpret its powers in such a way as to give rise to a 'real possibility' that the conviction will be quashed. As a corollary, applicants must do more than merely assert their innocence. They must address themselves to the very legal points that would arise if their case was referred to the Court of Appeal. That is likely to take more than two hours of 'Green Form' advice and assistance to achieve. Finally, there is the argument that even once the CCRC has begun its investigation an applicant would benefit from having a solicitor ready to clarify or respond to any points troubling the CCRC.[19]

What have been the consequences of the lack of legal aid? In its first annual report (1997-98) the CCRC reported that only about 10% of the new applicants added to its case load that year were legally represented and then commonly by lawyers acting pro bono (ie, for free).[20] About a fifth of the 1,380 applications that year were deemed ineligible within a few weeks of receipt, usually because applicants had not exhausted their appeal rights.[1] This suggests that many of these applications were simply hopeless. The CCRC observed that legal representation for applicants was desirable. A year later the CCRC was expressing itself in much more forceful terms:

> 'Legal advisers can greatly assist applicants to identify relevant issues, to marshal information, and to develop submissions, eg by interviewing witnesses or obtaining expert reports. They are able to advise applicants on the Commission's case review process and to identify those issues that have already been dealt with at trial and cannot be taken further by the Commission. Unfortunately there is still only limited awareness within the legal profession, in advisory

---

17   See Taylor with Mansfield (1999) p 232.
18   Taylor with Mansfield (1999) p 232. For confirmation of this prescient remark, see CCRC, Annual Report 1999-2000, p 22: 'In 1999-2000, 291 requests for priority were received and 61 were accepted.'
19   Taylor with Mansfield (1999) p 233.
20   CCRC, Annual Report 1997-98, p 18.
1   CCRC, Annual Report 1997-98, p 17 and p 22.

agencies and in prisons, of the scope for securing legal advice, and legal aid to support legal representation of applicants. . . . The Commission has compiled a list of solicitors who have said that they are willing to advise on applications and to visit clients in prison. This list is sent on request to applicants who are not represented with strong encouragement to obtain legal advice and representation.'[2]

One can infer from this passage a desire by the CCRC for lawyers to help it carry out its work in three key ways: first, by taking on some of the investigative work that the CCRC would otherwise have to do; second, by filtering out hopeless applications before they reach the Commission; and, third, by making it easier for the Commission to grasp quickly the essential issues in those applications it does receive. This desire is unsurprising when one takes into account that after only two years in full operation the CCRC had a backlog of cases which it estimated would take it between three and four years to clear.[3] A continuing tide of hopeless applications and an enormous backlog of work had clearly concentrated the mind of the CCRC on the problems caused by the lack of legal representation. In its third Annual Report the CCRC reported its continuing efforts to disseminate information about the possibility and benefits of legal representation and noted that the percentage of applicants so represented had increased from 10% in 1997-98 to 30% in 1999-2000. It also noted that the decline in cases received that year was likely to have been influenced by the role of lawyers in deterring applications that had no prospect of success. Nonetheless, about a third of cases were screened out as ineligible shortly after receipt, and in the vast majority of cases proceeding past that stage the ultimate decision was not to refer.[4] Clearly, the chances of having a case referred to the Court of Appeal still depend on finding a lawyer or campaigning journalist willing to act for little financial reward. Justice remains a national lottery.

In one respect the CCRC represents a clear break from the past. It has chosen to investigate all cases considered prima facie eligible, and which raise significant new evidence or argument, with a thoroughness that is heartening from a freedom perspective. It proceeds by assembling the primary materials (exhibits, court transcripts and so forth), interviewing witnesses, and obtaining expert advice. The Commission usually elects to interview witnesses itself rather than relying on the police to do this - another welcome change. However, the first 13 *external* investigating officers appointed by the Commission were all police officers.

2   CCRC, Annual Report 1998-99, p 10.
3   CCRC, Annual Report 1998-99, p 12.
4   CCRC, Annual Report 1999-2000, pp 17-20.

Commentators have recorded their disappointment at this replication of Home Office practices and at the fact that the CCRC tends to draw external investigating officers from the same police force which initiated the original prosecution.[5] On the other hand, the CCRC reports that where it has turned to the police for help it 'has been well satisfied by the depth and thoroughness of the investigations that it has commissioned.'[6] Whether that satisfaction is warranted is unclear in the absence of independent research on the matter. Research is also needed in order to determine the fairness of the initial screening out of cases on the basis that they are ineligible or raise no new matters. Those lacking legal representation may be relying on the CCRC launching an investigation so as to discover the very new matters which the CCRC looks for before accepting a case for investigation. As Malleson observes, this is a Catch-22 situation.[7]

The capacity of the CCRC to investigate cases is limited by lack of adequate resources. The CCRC does not have enough case workers in post to process the case load in a thorough *and* timely manner. The result has been the build-up of the backlog noted above. The average delays within the CCRC for those with prima facie eligible cases can now be counted in years rather than months. The CCRC could have reacted to this either by cutting corners or by lobbying for more resources. Its main strategy has been the latter. In January 1998 it asked the Home Office to fund an increase in case workers from 27 to 60. After an initial refusal the Home Secretary agreed in February 1999 to fund an increase to 40 case workers.[8] The CCRC welcomed this but asserted that 'substantially more is needed'.[9] It also rejected the view of the Home Affairs Committee that the CCRC ought to be able to process more cases with greater speed by identifying at an early stage the most critical issues and concentrating on them.[10] Referring to this as a 'counsel of perfection', the CCRC responded that:

'. . . superficially attractive though it may be to skimp on thoroughness, the costs of mistakes leading to resubmission of cases, judicial review and diminished public confidence in the professional competence of the Commission, are likely to be overwhelmingly greater. . . . Not referring cases that should be referred, for lack of thoroughness in the review, perpetuates miscarriages of justice.'[11]

5   See A James, N Taylor and C Walker, 'The Criminal Cases Review Commission: Economy, Effectiveness and Justice' [2000] Crim LR 140 at p 145.
6   CCRC, Annual Report 1999-2000, p 15.
7   Malleson (1995) p 933.
8   James et al (2000) p 142.
9   CCRC, Annual Report 1998-99, p 5.
10   Home Affairs Committee, The Work of the Criminal Cases Review Commission, (1998-99 HC 569). For a fuller critique of this report see James et al (2000).
11   CCRC, Annual Report 1998-99, p 7 and p 15.

Chapter 10 Appeals against conviction

It continued to press for more resources and the Home Secretary eventually agreed to fund an increase to 50 case workers during the 2000-01 financial year.[12] This still falls short of what the CCRC considers it needs to reduce its backlog and the consequent delays it entails for applicants. It has made it clear that 'unless there is a very substantial reduction in the queueing time, there is a serious risk that applicants will be discouraged from applying to the Commission.'[13] This may be another factor behind the drop in applications in 1999-2000. The position may get worse if the implementation of the Human Rights Act 1998 on 2 October 2000 leads to a flood of new applications.[14]

We also need to consider the implications of the CCRC backlog for the patterns of application and referrals. In its first Annual Report 1997-98 the CCRC revealed (p 18) that a substantial majority of applicants had been convicted in the Crown Court and were seeking review of their convictions. Two-thirds of applicants were in custody at the date of application, of whom over-three quarters were serving sentences of six years or more. The 'over-representation' of those in custody serving long sentences is likely to have increased since then as a result of the CCRC's growing backlog. Those serving shorter prison sentences will increasingly think the game not worth the candle. From their point of view what matters most is how quickly the conviction can be quashed. Thus, to the delays within the CCRC must be added judicial delays on receipt of referrals. The Court of Appeal took an average of 185 working days from receipt to judgment in the referred cases concluded by 31 March 2000. The overall average will be close to a year given that the average delay at the Court of Appeal for the 45 referrals not concluded by that date was already 188 working days.[15] The CCRC affords priority to 'in-custody' cases over 'at-liberty' cases.[16] Even so, those sentenced to terms of imprisonment of less than five years are unlikely to see the CCRC as of much relevance. By the time they have exhausted their normal appeal rights, secured a referral from the CCRC, and had their referred case heard, they are likely to be at liberty again anyway. If a prisoner is due to be released before a fresh appeal is likely to be heard the incentive to pursue the matter is much reduced. While some will still want to 'clear their names', those with previous convictions of a similar type will presumably not see much point in doing this. The priority given by the CCRC to in-custody cases means that those wrongfully convicted in the

12 CCRC, Annual Report 1999-2000, p 5.
13 CCRC, Annual Report 1998-99, p 12.
14 See on this point K Kerrigan, 'Unlocking the Human Rights Floodgates' [2000] Crim LR 71.
15 CCRC, Annual Report 1999-2000, p 18. James et al (2000) p 146 note that several referrals have been pending for well over a year.
16 CCRC, Annual Report 1999-2000, p 22.

magistrates' courts receive from the CCRC least attention of all.[17] Two other aspects of the order in which the CCRC deals with cases are also worthy of mention. First, the CCRC chose to prioritise the cases it inherited from the Home Office, many of which were very old but high-profile in nature. Thus eight of the first 54 cases to be referred involved deceased convicted persons, including Derek Bentley, who was hanged in 1952.[18] Second, the CCRC has said that it will assign priority to cases that it believes 'to be of particular significance to the criminal justice system.'[19] It is unclear what it means by this. The intention might be to prioritise cases that could bring the Court of Appeal's attention to systemic defects within criminal justice and thus prevent future miscarriages. Less commendably, the CCRC's intention might be to push through those cases supported by the mass media or national figures such as ex-Home Secretaries. These cases could be seen of significance to the criminal justice system because if applicants with popular support are kept waiting for several years, public confidence in the CCRC and the wider criminal justice system might diminish. Our overall assessment is that, on the pattern to date, we were right to predict that the CCRC would deal mainly in high-profile cases involving those sentenced to long periods of imprisonment. Mundane miscarriages of justice, if brought to the CCRC's attention at all, are doomed to remain in the 'slow-pend' tray for years on end.

(d) The response of the Court of Appeal to the new referral process

Of the 38 appellants involved in cases referred back to the Court of Appeal in 1989–91, 37 had their convictions quashed.[20] There is little doubt that the uncovering of a string of sensational miscarriages of justice in the late 1980s and early 1990s amounted to both a cause and an effect of the Court of Appeal's greater willingness in recent years to contemplate 'appalling vistas' of police and prosecution malpractice. The strongly worded judgment in the *Judith Ward*[1] case, in which the Court of Appeal laid down clear rules governing the prosecution duty to disclose, is one example of this. Another example is the decision in *Edwards*[2] in the aftermath of the disbanding of the West Midlands Serious Crimes Squad in 1989 because

---

17   Of the first 80 referrals back to the appellate courts, only one was made to the Crown Court: CCRC, Annual Report 1999-2000, p 18.
18   For critical discussion see James et al (2000) pp 149-50.
19   CCRC, Annual Report 1999-2000, p 22.
20   Two of these were ordered to be retried and were subsequently acquitted: see RCCJ (1993) p 181.
1   [1993] 1 WLR 619.
2   [1991] 2 All ER 266.

of mounting allegations that its officers were fabricating evidence. The Court of Appeal here ruled that the prosecution had a duty to disclose a police officer's disciplinary record to the defence. It also said that the defence could put before the jury the fact that any police witnesses in the case had previously been disbelieved by juries in earlier trials.[3] The development of due process principles in cases such as these showed that the judiciary was no longer blind to the possibility of systematic malpractice by the police and prosecution agencies. Has this greater readiness to act on referrals carried on under the new system?

The signs are, on the whole, encouraging. In the very first case referred the Court of Appeal acknowledged that 'the Criminal Cases Review Commission is a necessary and welcome body, without whose work the injustice in this case might never have been identified.'[4] The presiding judge in the Court of Appeal added his stamp of approval in *Criminal Cases Review Commission, ex p Pearson*.[5] Lord Bingham CJ declared that: 'It is essential to the health and proper functioning of a modern democracy that the citizen accused of crime should be fairly tried and adequately protected against the risk and consequences of wrongful conviction.'[6] Although the CCRC does not have the power to make any recommendation to the appellate courts, its Statement of Reasons for making the reference have been cited in judgments 'and have clearly been of material assistance in many of the appeals.'[7]

The statistics bear out this picture of a warm reception for the new kid on the block. As at 30 June 2000 the appellate courts had heard 39 appeals as a result of a referral from the CCRC, of which 27 resulted in the quashing of the relevant conviction or sentence, and nine in the dismissal of the appeal. In the remaining three the Court of Appeal had reserved judgment. This is a high success rate, albeit not so high as that obtaining in the period 1989-91. The difference may not reflect a judicial hardening of attitude, however, so much as a policy by the CCRC to test the boundaries of the Court's willingness to reopen cases through the referral process. Thus, for example, it has referred cases where the law has developed since the time of the original trial, presumably with a view to testing whether convictions can become vulnerable in the light of more modern standards

---

3   This decision has nonetheless be seen as placing undue limits on the defence's ability to cast doubt on a police officer's credibility. See R Pattenden, 'Evidence of Previous Malpractice by Police Witnesses and *Edwards*' [1992] Crim LR 549 and the critical commentary accompanying *Twitchell* [2000] Crim LR 468.

4   *Mattan* (1998) Times, 5 March. The identified injustice could not be adequately remedied as Mr Mattan was hanged in 1952.

5   [1999] 3 All ER 498.

6   This position has also been forcefully articulated by Lord Steyn in *Secretary of State for the Home Department, ex p Simms* [1999] 3 All ER 400.

7   CCRC, Annual Report 1999-2000, p 18.

of due process.[8] The Court of Appeal has sent out contradictory signals on this point.[9]

The CCRC is bound to take notice of such signals given that it may only refer convictions where it considers there is a real possibility that the Court will quash them. Thus one would expect the 'success rate' of referrals to increase as the Court of Appeal lays down clearer norms in this area. But perhaps this is to expect too much. At present the CCRC's view is that too 'few referrals have been determined . . . for the Commission to discern any significant patterns or trends in these judgments.'[10] Will the rule of law be found at the end of the case law rainbow? We doubt it. The more one studies appellate judgments the less one expects to find clear norms which are consistently applied. Consider again the case law vacillation over such crucial jurisdictional points as whether a reliable conviction can nevertheless be so tainted by unfairness as to be unsafe. The difficulty of the CCRC's position then becomes evident. If the Court of Appeal continues to tack between the poles of due process and crime control, the CCRC will have no choice but to follow queasily in its wake.

5. CONCLUSION

The major miscarriage of justice cases show why the crime control demand for finality within the criminal process needs to be resisted. The Maguires, for example, had been convicted at trial in 1976 and had failed to have their convictions overturned through the normal appeal channel in 1977. An attempt to have the case referred back to the Court of Appeal foundered in 1987. The Home Office took the view that there was insufficient evidence to cast doubt on the validity of the prosecution's forensic evidence which suggested that the Maguires had handled explosives. The Home Office refused to set up a committee of scientists to reconsider that evidence. But when the 'Guildford Four' were released in 1989, Sir John May was asked by the Home Office to inquire into the circumstances of the convictions of the related Maguires' case. At last, adequate resources were committed to testing theories which might undermine the prosecution case. Sir John May's inquiry duly found that the Maguires need not have handled explosives at all; they could simply have picked up traces of nitro-glycerine from drying their hands on a towel. This finding led directly to the quashing of the Maguires' convictions. It also led to the forensic evidence in the 'Birmingham Six' case being scientifically reviewed. The

---

8   See James et al (2000) pp 143-44 for discussion of this line of referrals.
9   See (in chronological order) *Bentley* [1999] Crim LR 330; *Gerald* [1999] Crim LR 315; and *O'Brien* [2000] Crim LR 676. The Human Rights Act 1998 is also likely to have a bearing on this issue: see Kerrigan [2000].
10   CCRC, Annual Report 1999-2000, p 18.

Conclusion

findings this time were even more remarkable. It now appeared that tests which the prosecution had relied upon as demonstrating that the men had handled nitro-glycerine were thoroughly unreliable. The 'positive results' could equally well have been attributed to the soap used to wash the laboratory dishes prior to samples being tested or to the fact that the men smoked cigarettes.[11] In other cases, it has been a matter of sheer good luck that evidence of fabricated confessions, in the form of supposedly contemporaneous notes of interview, have not been destroyed or misplaced.

It follows that prosecution cases which appear to the trial court and the Court of Appeal as unshakeable at first, second and even third sight may be merely artful constructions built on foundations of sand.[12] In the 1988 appeal of the 'Birmingham Six', Lord Lane CJ said that fresh evidence had made the court sure that one of the men had had nitro-glycerine on his hand, 'for which there is and can be no innocent explanation.'[13] Three years later, the Court was forced to admit that a number of innocent and plausible explanations could be advanced to account for this fresh evidence. In 1988, the court had concluded that they were 'certain' that the superintendent in charge of the inquiry into the pub bombings in Birmingham, who the 'Birmingham Six' accused of fabricating evidence and perjury, had not sought to deceive them. In 1991 the Court said, 'On the evidence now before us, Superintendent Reade deceived the court.'[14] There could be few better illustrations of the point that the courts are not dealing in moral certainties and truth but in degrees of proof. An awareness of the realities of case construction by police and prosecution agencies strengthens the argument for always leaving open the possibility of a further challenge to the *factual* basis for a conviction.

From our freedom perspective we argued above that challenges should also be permissible to the *moral* basis for a conviction. Where convictions are tainted by unfairness there are strong arguments for quashing them regardless of how reliable they might be. The crime control arguments against this position are not without all force, however. It is important in particular to look for ways to reduce the frequency with which convictions of factually guilty persons have to be quashed on the ground of procedural unfairness. One way would be to say that only procedural errors made in 'bad faith' or which were 'significant' or which 'prejudiced the defendant' should lead to the loss of a conviction. But as we will see in our discussion of s 78 of PACE (in ch 11), such a strategy allows the courts too much latitude to overlook breaches of the rule of law. We would not favour going

11 For a fuller account of this sequence of events see Rozenberg (1992).
12 See ch 6 for a discussion of how prosecutions are 'constructed' to appear strong, as distinct from simply being an assemblage of 'facts'.
13 Quoted in Rozenberg (1992) p 104.
14 Rozenberg (1992) p 106.

much beyond allowing the courts to apply their usual policy of condoning trivial breaches of legal norms as expressed in the maxim: 'the law takes no account of trifles'.

A more productive strategy would be to improve the system of alternative 'remedies' for such unfairness (eg, civil actions) so that they exert as much deterrent influence as possible. Better still, we might persuade the police and other criminal justice actors that the end of conviction can never justify breaking the law (even if minor procedural errors might be excusable). Breaking adherence to crime control values will not be easy, but couching our exhortations in the language of freedom rather than in the non-goal oriented language of due process may help. We can go further in buttressing our arguments. The law gives suspects and defendants rights to certain forms of 'fair' treatment. These rights are sometimes bound to impair the efficient pursuit of the truth and the conviction of the guilty. There is a trade-off in values here which is a deliberate choice of public policy.[15] It follows that it would be fundamentally undemocratic for criminal justice officials 'to take the law into their own hands' by imposing their own views of a 'just' allocation of power and 'rights' as between the state and individual citizens. Upholding convictions where the police have, for example, bamboozled suspects into 'signing away their rights' undermines democracy as well as freedom.

Achieving a freedom-oriented appellate system will not be easy. In one of the earliest studies of the appeals process, Bottoms and McClean highlighted the conflict that exists between fairness and justice, on the one hand, and the demands of efficient administration, on the other. The central issue for them was the status of the appeals process. Was an appeal to be a general right for all defendants, or a special procedure designed to correct the occasional wrong? The history of the Court of Appeal suggests that it is the latter that was intended from the outset.

In the nineteenth century the law provided no means for correcting the errors of juries in criminal trials. This was in marked contrast to the position in civil trials, which were tried by the same judges and juries. Since the mid-seventeenth century it was open to dissatisfied litigants to move for a new trial on the grounds of fresh evidence or insufficiency of evidence to support the original verdict. In her painstaking review of the historical evidence Pattenden comments:

'It is difficult to explain this discrepancy except as nineteenth century proponents of reform did - as reflecting a greater concern for property than life or liberty.'[16]

15　See also Nobles and Schiff (1995) and, by the same authors, 'The Never Ending Story: Disguising Tragic Choices in Criminal Justice' (1997) 60 MLR 293.
16　Pattenden (1996) p 6.

This was not some abstract preference divorced from the material realities of the stratified society of that time. Only a wealthy minority had much property to speak of, and the life or liberty of those typically subjected to criminal proceedings did not concern those with the power to change the law. In consequence, 30 Bills designed to create a right of criminal appeal failed in Parliament between 1844 and 1906. The judiciary and Parliament refused to accept, or care, that innocent persons could be wrongly convicted. In addition there were problems of costs, no accurate record of trials, and insufficient judges to cope with the anticipated level of appeals. But as Pattenden notes:

'These difficulties might not have been regarded as insuperable if members of the legislature and their friends had been of the class of persons who frequently became liable to prosecution but. . . they were not. Most defendants belonged to the "criminal class", who were seen as a threat to the stability of the social order and the sanctity of private property . . . The Law Times observed in 1881 that, although precisely the same considerations required an appeal in criminal as in civil cases, "the offending classes found all the forces of society directed towards their suppression; and, as the law makers were stronger than the law breakers, the former had it all their own way."'[17]

The Court of Appeal was eventually created in 1907 in response to an outcry over a particularly gross miscarriage of justice, the Adolf Beck case. Following misidentification and serious errors by the original trial judge, Beck was wrongfully convicted on two occasions for crimes committed by another man. The Home Office rejected 16 attempts by him to have his case re-examined by use of prerogative powers. After the miscarriage came to light the press became so critical of the standards of criminal justice that public confidence in the courts was feared to be in jeopardy. Only now was the case for proper appellate machinery accepted. As Malleson convincingly argues:

'The original purpose of the Court of Criminal Appeal was therefore bound up with the desire of the judiciary to provide a mechanism to sift out and put right such serious and rare cases which generated public concern and brought the Criminal Justice System into disrepute . . . The present design of the system, the limited and narrow powers of the Court and the hazardous path to that institution are not accidental or a mistake but persist because there has never been

17   Malleson (1993) p 19.

the will or intention to have a system the size and scope of which is determined by the numbers of miscarriages of justice occurring.'[18]

Nobles and Schiff also argue that appeal reforms throughout the twentieth century were designed to mollify public (especially media) opinion, rather than to solve the underlying problems. However, they argue that these problems are insoluble anyway, dooming the efforts of 'reformists' to failure. This is because the only thorough appeal process is one that puts the investigation and court processes themselves on trial. The scope for uncovering error is infinite.[19] Whilst this is true, it is a valid criticism only of a purist due process position. The freedom perspective would not seek infinite appeals or infinite thoroughness because it holds that the scarcity of resources is a legitimate concern. This does not prevent us from critiquing the current appeal system.

The English system of appellate review is moulded by what can be seen as its crime control heritage. The crime control model is reluctant to concede that its procedures are likely to produce miscarriages of justice. From this perspective every acquittal and every successful appeal serves to sap public confidence in the reliability of the system in distinguishing the innocent from the guilty. This undermines the deterrent efficacy of the criminal law and threatens the entire crime control project. But public confidence might drain away altogether if the system failed to right its mistakes in a timely fashion. However, the processes of case construction and evidential constraints (such as the reluctance on appeal to admit fresh evidence) ensures that, although errors are legion, few become obvious. Even then, it is only when major public campaigns are mounted that the public takes an interest in the fate of convicted persons. The Court of Appeal exists to ensure that convictions in such high-profile cases are either quashed or given the seal of approval by the senior judiciary. Because miscarriages of justice occurring in more run of the mill cases attract minimal public interest, there is no need to ensure that they are subject to appellate review and much to be said for suppressing appeals. We hope, but do not anticipate, that the coming into force of the Human Rights Act 1998 will prompt a major reassessment of core appellate values.

---

18 Malleson [1991] p 331.
19 Nobles and Schiff (2000).

Chapter 11

Remedying police malpractice

'Althea Burnett, a blind mother of three, was playing with her children one Sunday afternoon in July 1996 when there was a knock at the front door of her South London home. She was surprised to be confronted by a man and a woman who identified themselves as police officers. "The woman said that somebody had taken a taxi from my address the previous day and left without paying," she says. The police were reluctant to believe her when she said she was unable to identify the woman whom she had met only once . . . "I was getting frightened. The children were also getting frightened," says Burnett. "I told the police I was blind and couldn't see what the woman looked like, but they kept asking me to identify her." Burnett began to shut the door. As she did so, it flew open and "my arm was grabbed for what felt like a long time". . .

Burnett says that by now she could hear many more police and she was dragged into the street without her shoes, while her children were screaming. Both Burnett and her mother repeatedly told the police she was blind but she claims she was given no guide as she was manhandled to a police van. "I was pleading with them to let go and for someone to guide me."

She was detained for more than an hour before being released without charge. She was given a warning for what the police claim was an assault on one of their officers but she denies any offence, saying that the supposed assault occurred when she put her arm out as the police grabbed her.

Since the incident, she has been diagnosed as suffering from chronic post-traumatic stress disorder. She has had bars put on the windows and is nervous of opening the door. "My children are still upset and my son doesn't want to go to school."

The Crown Prosecution Service wrote to her solicitor admitting that "the arrest was unlawful and therefore constituted an assault and false imprisonment." But after two years no police officer had been charged with an offence or disciplined. A CPS letter in April [1998] . . . says: "We concluded that these offences were somewhat of a technical nature . . . A criminal court was unlikely to impose more than a very small penalty . . . the loss of liberty lasting in total one hour and a quarter." '[1]

I. INTRODUCTION

In criminal justice, as in other systems, a balance has to be struck between guarding against error and injustice on the one hand, and facilitating efficiency on the other. The way that balance is and should be struck has been an important theme of this book. The imposition of controls on the police (such as restrictions on the use of powers, supervision by senior officers and the recording of events) and the provision of rights to suspects and defendants (such as legal aid) are, at least in part, attempts to guard against error and injustice. Since these attempts will never be entirely successful, it follows also that error and injustice have to be anticipated and procedures have to be established for their identification, correction and compensation.

This is recognised by the European Convention on Human Rights (ECHR), *most* of which has now (in effect) been incorporated into English law by the Human Rights Act 1998 (HRA). One key remedial provision is Art 5(5) of the ECHR, which provides an enforceable right to compensation to anyone 'who has been the victim of arrest or detention in contravention of the provisions of this Article'.[2] But the more general catch-all provision in Art 13, which requires that states provide an 'effective' remedy for a breach of any Convention right, has not been incorporated. This omission may reflect the fact that English law has, as we shall see, been deficient in providing effective remedies. For the moment, Art 13 binds the UK only at the international level.

Chapter 10 looked at appeal procedures. These are concerned with wrongful convictions, some (but by no means the majority) of which are a result of police malpractice. Exposing miscarriages of justice can expose malpractice, helping to prevent future abuses, but they do nothing directly to deal with the police at fault or to compensate the defendant. Then there are the cases in which conviction was not wrong - the defendant may even have pleaded guilty - but in which the defendants' rights were in some way abused, as where they are assaulted, or denied a solicitor. Finally, there are many cases of malpractice where the defendant was not even

---

1   *The Guardian*, June 1998.
2   See ch 2, section 3(e) for discussion.

prosecuted, and so the idea of appealing as a way of exposing an abuse does not arise. For all these cases, remedies are needed.

The role of remedial procedures is very different in different models. Due process is sceptical about the reliability of administrative fact-finding processes and therefore expects errors and injustices to be legion. The model accepts that maintaining public confidence in the system is important, but argues that the way to achieve this is for the system to demonstrate its willingness to own up to, and to correct, error and injustice. The exclusionary remedy, which operates at the trial stage, can serve this purpose. Errors that affect the reliability of evidence (such as uncorroborated confessions obtained through oppressive interrogations) must be corrected by the trial judge ruling that evidence inadmissible. But even where the evidence obtained unlawfully is shown to be reliable, exclusion must still follow, since only in this way can the system uphold its own integrity and remove the incentive for the police to break the rules. If the collapse of prosecution cases following exclusion adversely affects the morale of the police, the answer lies in their hands, since if they kept to the rules they would not lose convictions in this way. Other remedies must also be provided, however, since exclusionary rules can only affect that tiny percentage of criminal cases which are both prosecuted and contested, and may, in any case, be ineffective in punishing and deterring the particular police officers responsible for malpractice. Causes of action must therefore be provided to citizens so that they can sue such officers in the civil courts, and disciplinary mechanisms must be set up to investigate and punish wrongdoing. Criminal prosecution may be justified in some cases. A strong system of remedies is bound to impair police efficiency and reduce the conviction rate, but these are prices worth paying for enhancing fairness, individual liberty, and the protection of the factually innocent.

The crime control model concedes that error and injustice will occur but not on the scale envisaged by the due process adherent. Only errors which undermine confidence in the reliability of the evidence put before the court and the accuracy of the finding of guilt require an exclusionary remedy. It would be intolerable to allow a guilty person to go free because of some technical procedural error. To do so would undermine both police morale and public confidence in the system, whilst having little effect on police practices. By making remedies difficult to operate and available only in narrowly defined circumstances, crime control ensures that only those with genuine grievances will complain. The best way to tackle police malpractice is through disciplinary mechanisms which focus on how to make individual officers more efficient in future. Efficiency is generally best served by requiring police officers to keep to the rules regarding the treatment of suspects. In a crime control system, the primary aim of these rules is not to protect suspects but simply to ensure that any evidence obtained from them is reliable. Some police officers break them. If any evidence obtained as a result can be verified from other sources, all well and good. If not, the officer concerned may well have lost the opportunity to obtain a confession that would have been regarded as reliable. Officers who are unable to judge accurately when it is rational to break the rules in the search for the truth should be regarded as terminally inefficient and dismissed.

The approach of the freedom model is close to that of due process, but less extreme in its effects. The test is whether the freedom lost to the suspect by the malpractice (and which will be lost to future suspects if the malpractice is allowed to continue) is greater or less than the loss of freedom created by punishing and preventing the malpractice. Since most malpractice is simply a short-cut for the police, and is uncertain in its crime control effects anyway, in most cases the balance will come down in favour of using whatever remedies best eradicate the malpractice. But there is a difference between, say, psychologically assaulting a suspect in custody and using DNA evidence that should have been destroyed to detect a crime for which it was not collected. Both breach accepted standards of behaviour. But the former causes significant loss of freedom to the suspect while the latter does not. Rules concerning DNA evidence should be upheld (or, if they are bad rules, changed by legislation). But they do not necessarily have to be upheld by excluding conclusive evidence or by dismissing the officer responsible.

A major difference between the freedom model and the others is that the former takes account of what it *feels like* to be on the receiving end of malpractice. Loss of freedom, in this context like all others, is a qualitative as well as quantitative matter. This has the further implication that if malpractice consists of a suspect being treated with contempt, for example, remedies which provide monetary compensation, or exclusion of evidence, may not provide what the suspect is looking for. An apology and admission of poor behaviour, if genuine, can sometimes count for a lot more.

It can be seen that all three models accept that errors may be dealt with in many different ways but differ on what the purpose of a remedy should be. In reality, any one remedy may serve a variety of purposes, including apology, punishment, deterrence and righting the wrong. These are all remedies for individual victims of malpractice. In theory, provision of *individual* remedies should reduce malpractice in general, which is something which all the models aspire to (although some, freedom especially, with greater urgency than others). However, it would be wrong to assume that any of them are much use in this respect. We therefore need to think about why malpractice occurs and what can be done at an *organisational* level to reduce it. In this chapter we try to identify where our system of remedies lies between the polarities of due process and crime control, to determine what changes are needed to promote the freedom perspective, and give some thought to how different remedies impact on police processes in general.

2. PROSECUTIONS

The most obvious way to punish or deter the police from breaking the law is to prosecute them when they are believed to have done so. Breaches of the criminal law (for instance, assault, perjury and corruption) are sometimes prosecuted, as happened to three of the detectives accused of fabricating evidence in the 'Guildford Four' case.[3] This is rare, however, the DPP prosecuting in only about 1.5% of the cases of alleged police malpractice referred to him or her.[4] There were 38 convictions of police officers for non-traffic offences in 1998/9.[5] The evidential and public interest tests we discussed in chapter 6 should be applied when processing these cases. The difficulty of proving a case (where it is usually one citizen's word against that of one or more police officers) weighs heavily against prosecution. From a due process perspective, it is right that police officers are protected from prosecution when the case against them is weak. However, according to the then-Metropolitan Police Commissioner Paul Condon in 1997, corrupt police officers know the law so well that they can usually cover their tracks to ensure that the case against them is weak.[6] In other words, the same type of construction technique that the police use against 'normal' suspects to make a weak case strong is used (by the 'suspect' police officer at risk of prosecution) to make what could be a strong case weak.[7]

In so far as non-prosecution follows the application of 'public interest' criteria, one presumes that the need (as defined in the crime control model) to maintain police morale and public confidence in the criminal justice system are the operative factors. Unfortunately, the weak accountability for prosecution decisions at the level of prosecution policy means that these matters are rarely openly discussed even in principle, let alone in respect of individual cases.[8]

This makes it difficult to assess whether decisions not to prosecute police officers are shaped by due process or crime control considerations.

---

3   See J Rozenberg, 'Miscarriages of Justice' in E Stockdale and S Casale (eds), *Criminal Justice Under Stress* (London: Blackstone, 1992). The three detectives were acquitted following their trial in 1993. The judge ordered the jury to acquit because in his opinion the publicity prevented them receiving a fair trial. This does not mean that they were factually innocent, any more than it means that the 'Guildford Four' were factually guilty.

4   K Hyder, 'Cause for Complaint' (1990) New Statesman and Society, 12 January.

5   Home Office, Police Complaints and Discipline, Statistical Bulletin, 1998-9 (London: Home Office, 1999).

6   *The Guardian*, 5 December 1997.

7   Case construction techniques are discussed, in particular, in ch 6, sections 3 and 4.

8   See ch 6, section 6 for a discussion of prosecution accountability.

But the pattern of non-prosecutions is pervasive. Take the notorious West Midlands Police Serious Crime Squad. The inquiry in the early 1990s into its alleged fraud, perjury, corruption, fabrication of evidence and assault cost £4m. At least 15 people convicted on evidence produced by the squad were released by the Court of Appeal. Not one police officer has been prosecuted, despite the West Yorkshire police investigation into the squad recommending some prosecutions.[9] Even the judiciary is occasionally concerned. In *DPP, ex p Treadaway*[10] the Divisional Court ordered the DPP to reconsider the decision not to prosecute four of these officers, said by the High Court judge in his civil action *five years earlier* to have 'tortured' Treadaway. The judge awarded Treadaway £50,000 in compensation for having a plastic bag put over his head to encourage him to confess. The DPP admitted that she had not fully considered the High Court decision and therefore had not carried out her duty to apply the evidential test properly.[11]

Another serious concern over the years has been deaths in police custody. Like deaths at work, it is a reasonable prima facie assumption that these deaths occur because of a breach of duty on the part of the police (or, in the case of deaths at work, the employer). Manslaughter by omission (ie gross negligence manslaughter) should be prosecuted if death or GBH is reasonably foreseeable. If the death is caused by an unlawful act, say an assault, then constructive manslaughter, whereby only some harm need be foreseeable, should be prosecuted. Like deaths at work, it hardly ever happens. Occasionally, though, a particularly disturbing case comes to light. In 1997 two inquest juries found that Oluwashhijibomi Lapite and Richard O'Brien had been 'unlawfully killed' while in police custody. Lapite had 45 injuries. An officer admitted kicking him in the head as hard as he could, claiming that he was the most violent prisoner he had ever encountered, but the officers involved had only superficial injuries. O'Brien had 31 injuries. The last words his wife heard him say were: 'I can't breathe, let me up, you win.'[12] The DPP nonetheless decided not to prosecute in either case. Only when these decisions were, like that of *Treadaway*, judicially reviewed, did the DPP concede that she had made an error of law regarding manslaughter, and would reconsider her decision.[13] Three

9   *The Guardian*, 28 July 1994; House of Commons, Home Affairs Select Committee, Police Disciplinary and Complaints Procedure, 1st Report (HC 258-1, 1998), paras 24, 91.
10   Legal Action, October 1997, p 15.
11   See G Smith, 'The DPP and prosecutions of police officers' (1997) 147 NLJ, 8 August.
12   Statewatch (1997) July-Oct, p 19; Smith (1997).
13   Legal Action, October 1997, p 15.

officers were eventually prosecuted for the death of O'Brien but then acquitted.[14]

None of this changed the DPP's basic policy, insofar as anyone knows what that is. Alan Manning, a black remand prisoner, died from asphyxiation when prison officers used 'unreasonable restraint' methods on him. Three years after his death an inquest ruled that he had been unlawfully killed, but the DPP did not prosecute. Two years later, in a re-run of *Treadaway*, Manning's family succeeded in their application to judicially review this decision of the DPP.[15] In a similar case, Christopher Alder - another black man - was arrested and dumped half-naked and handcuffed onto a police station floor. As he lay dying, gasping for breath as blood blocked his air passages, he was accused by an officer of 'faking it'. Four other officers also watched, and only took action - too late - to save his life after he stopped breathing. For once we know the truth, as did the DPP, because all this was caught on a 12-minute police video. But the DPP only decided to review the decision not to prosecute for manslaughter after an inquest decided that he had been unlawfully killed.[16] Individual prosecutions, inquests and judicial reviews are blunt instruments which are no better at controlling police crime than 'normal' prosecutions are at controlling 'normal' crime. At a *systemic level*, we might hope that judicial reviews, inquests and prosecutions would be used by the DPP and police to investigate the sources of criminal malpractice and to create policies and practices to reduce them. But little or no opportunity appears to be taken at the organisational level to learn from these bitter lessons.

The Lapite and O'Brien deaths in custody were the subject of an official report by former Judge, Gerald Butler. The report's findings are also unlikely to change the DPP's policy. Butler was critical of the way the DPP's office organises its consideration of this type of case. But he decided that there was no pro-police bias and that there was no police-CPS conspiracy.[17] As Smith observes, this misses the point.[18] Investigations into deaths in

14 D Coles and F Murphy, 'O'Brien: Another Death in Police Custody' (1999) Legal Action, Nov, p 6. Although the authors do not use the term, their discussion of the case illustrates the 'construction' point made above in the context of the Metropolitan Police Commissioner's remarks about the difficulty of successfully prosecuting police officers. The DPP re-affirmed the decision not to prosecute the officers in the *Lapite* case: M Burton, 'Reviewing CPS decisions not to prosecute' [2001] Crim LR (forthcoming).
15 *DPP, ex p Manning* [2000] 3 WLR 463.
16 *The Guardian*, 25 August 2000. Alder received the injuries which led to his death before being arrested. On inquests into deaths in custody, see P Scraton and K Chadwick, *In the Arms of the Law: Coroners Inquests and Deaths in Custody* (London: Pluto, 1987).
17 G Butler, Inquiry into CPS Decision Making in relation to deaths in custody and related matters (London: SO, 1999).
18 G Smith, 'The Butler Report: an opportunity missed?' (1999) 149 NLJ 20 August.

dy and allegations of police and prison officer criminality are carried ᴏy the police as part of the general arrangements for inquiring into ᴊce wrongdoing (see section 4 below). As with all CPS prosecution decision-making, the CPS is dependent on the police investigation. What we are seeing is police constructions of cases as weak, leading to decisions not to prosecute, and, occasionally, enough independent evidence coming to the fore to convince a civil court or inquest that the weak police construction is faulty. For the same reasons, the incorporation of (most of) the ECHR into the HRA is likely to make little difference. It is true that states have positive obligations to investigate crimes and prosecute offenders where appropriate.[19] But what is, or is not 'appropriate', is for each state to determine within very broad limits, and the effect of police constructions to make cases appear weak would make a court acting under the HRA 1998 as powerless as the CPS is now. Butler's view that the DPP give reasons for not prosecuting where an inquest jury decided that there had been an unlawful killing (and perhaps in other cases) is welcome, provided that enough information is given to help the family of victims to pursue lines of enquiry that the police may have neglected.[20]

Thus while the Butler inquiry did indeed miss an opportunity to explore fully how deaths in police custody are investigated, it could not have done this without opening up the much thornier question of the investigation of malpractice in general (which we do in section 4 below).[1] Butler did not serve us well here. Inquiries always have to draw the line somewhere, so we might forgive the judge for steering clear of such a prickly topic. However, what was unpardonable was Butler's colour-blindness on the issue. Around one fifth of people who die in police custody are from ethnic minorities.[2] Butler stated that he could discern no bias against 'any section of the community' in the way the cases were dealt with, but did not express concern that police stations are disproportionately dangerous for ethnic minorities as compared to white people.

However, the most important reason why most malpractice and law-breaking is not prosecuted is because it is not contrary to the criminal law. This might seem a *non sequiter*. After all, there are all sorts of things that we might like to be criminal but which are not, like the humiliation of

---

19 *Aksoy v Turkey* (1996) 23 EHRR 553; *Kaya v Turkey* (1998) 28 EHRR 1. Discussed by G Smith, 'Police complaints and criminal prosecutions', paper presented to SPTL Annual Conference, 19 September 2000 (cited with the permission of the author).

20 This is now required in law following *DPP, ex p Manning* [2000] 3 WLR 463. For further discussion, see Burton [2001]. Also see ch 12, section 4, for discussion of the rights of victims in general to be informed or consulted.

1   For a critical discussion, see Amnesty International, Deaths in Police Custody: Lack of Police Accountability (London: AI, 2000).

2   12 out of 67 in 1998-9: Home Office, Statistics on Deaths in Police Custody, 1998-9 (London: Home Office, 1999).

students by egotistical academics in tutorials. But what the police do is different because of their power. 'Normal' people cannot make you stop and explain yourself time after time. The police can through their powers to stop and search.[3] Doing it wrongly breaks the law, but it does not break the criminal law. The same applies to detaining you when it is not 'necessary', exiling you to a cell between interrogations, exerting improper pressure on you for information when your solicitor is not there to protect you, not telling your family why you have disappeared and that you are (relatively) safe, denying you bail so you spend another night in the cells stinking of vomit and urine, and putting you through the prosecution mill only to drop the case weeks or months later.[4] In an age when it is a crime to drop a crisp packet, to swear at a football match, or to forget to buy a TV licence, but not a crime to abuse people in these ways, it looks like the freedom perspective is yet to be recognised by modern governments.

3. CIVIL ACTIONS

(a) Causes of action

Earlier chapters showed that the Police and Criminal Evidence Act 1984 (PACE) and later legislation defines, and sets limits to, a large number of police powers and rights for suspects. But no specific enforcement mechanisms or civil remedies are provided. As regards the codes of practice, s 67(10) of PACE provides that a failure on the part of a police officer to comply with any of their provisions 'shall not of itself render him liable to any criminal or civil proceedings.' Existing tortious remedies, developed many years before police forces and modern investigative techniques were created, have to be applied to the PACE framework of rights and powers, in so far as that is possible. There are several torts which are applicable.

(i) False imprisonment

The tort of false imprisonment applies to unlawful police detention. This would include detention in breach of the 'necessity' rule in s 37 of PACE (see chapter 4, section 3) although there are no reported cases on this. It also includes detention after the time at which a review (under PACE s 40) should be held. In *Roberts v Chief Constable of Cheshire Police*[5] a suspect was lawfully detained initially but the review of detention took place two

3   See ch 2.
4   See chs 4-6.
5   [1999] 1 WLR 662.

hours too late. Even though detention was confirmed, and so he would have been in custody for the two hours concerned anyway, the Court of Appeal held that since he had been falsely imprisoned for those two hours he should be compensated.[6] In the light of this, the courts' decisions that unlawful detention conditions do not make the detention itself unlawful, are bizarre: breaches of PACE Code of Practice C, for example, such as denying suspects refreshment or sleep, have been held not to form the basis of this action.[7] Compensating someone who has not suffered but not compensating someone who has, even though both types of loss are at the hands of the police in police stations, is a result of a formalistic application of legal rules and the absence of appropriate remedies. No thought is given by government or the courts to compensation for loss in proportion to the real loss of freedom.

False imprisonment also applies to wrongful arrest.[8] This is because the tort involves the unlawful infliction of bodily restraint.[9] Bodily restraint is the essence of both arrest and police station detention. It is also, of course, the essence of stop-search under PACE, s 1, for, as we argued in chapter 3 (section 2(b)(iii)), stop-search is a form of arrest. It should therefore follow that unlawful stop-search be subject to the tort of false imprisonment, but, once again, there are no reported cases on this. There is, otherwise, no specific civil action available in relation to stop-search. As we saw in ch 3, section 5, wrongful arrest can be established in a variety of ways, including arrests made without reasonable suspicion (so long as the suspect is not ultimately convicted) and a failure to inform the suspect of the reason for arrest.

(ii) Trespass

If the police enter property without lawful authority, an action for trespass may follow. This can occur when an arrest warrant is invalid, or in the purported exercising of other police powers, such as search and/or seizure of property (powers to enter property, search the premises and seize certain types of property are provided, in certain circumstances, by PACE, ss 8–22).[10]

6   He had been awarded £500 by the trial judge.
7   See eg *Williams v Home Office (No 2)* [1981] 1 All ER 1151.
8   See eg *Wershof v Metropolitan Police Comr* [1978] 3 All ER 540, discussed in subsection (c) below.
9   For details of all the torts discussed here see: J Harrison and S Cragg, *Police Misconduct: Legal Remedies* 3rd edn (London: LAG, 1995); R Clayton and R Tomlinson, *Civil Actions Against the Police* 3rd edn (London: Sweet & Maxwell, 1999).
10 Apologies to those of our readers who might reasonably have expected to see us cover entry, search and seizure properly in this edition. We intend to remedy this defect, life crises permitting, on our third bite of the cherry.

(iii) Assault and intimidation

Assault and intimidation are further torts which sometimes occur in the course of arrest. Anything in excess of 'reasonable force' to effect an arrest is an assault, and the threat of an unlawful act (for example, unreasonable use of force) is intimidation.[11] This may also occur if the police try to secure a confession through threats.[12]

(iv) Malicious prosecution

If a prosecution is initiated both without prima facie evidence and maliciously, the defendant may sue for malicious prosecution. The prosecution has, however, to have been resolved in the defendant's favour either through discontinuance or acquittal.[13] This is an application of the crime control principle that the end justifies the means. No matter how malicious a prosecution might have been, a person would have no remedy if convicted.

(v) Breach of statutory duty

This cause of action arises where no other remedy is available. However, it is unclear whether this action will lie in respect of all or even any breaches of PACE, and it certainly does not apply to rights found in the codes of practice only (such as the right to be informed of one's rights and the right not to be held incommunicado) as the latter are not statutes. If there have been any attempts to use this tort in relation to PACE, they have not been reported.

(b) Rights but what remedies?

We saw in section 2 that the biggest obstacle in the way of prosecuting the police is that much malpractice which would be criminal if done by 'normal' people is not criminal when done by the police. Some of those things, like wrongful arrest, can be the subject of actions in tort. But an awful lot of malpractice is not. No civil actions are possible in respect of much of the subject matter of this book, such as the right to legal advice, not to be kept incommunicado, and to be informed of one's rights; and the

---

11 See eg *Allen v Metropolitan Police Comr* [1980] Crim LR 441.
12 See, for example, the case of George Lewis, discussed in subsection (b) below.
13 See, for example, *Martin v Watson* [1996] AC 74.

duties of the police to interrogate fairly,[14] to do so under the formal conditions laid down in Code of Practice C, and to record all questions and answers. These provisions are supposedly the centre piece of the 'balance' struck by the Royal Commission on Criminal Procedure (Philips Commission) which it regarded as a quid pro quo for increasing police powers (regarding stop-search and pre-charge detention, for example). It was supposedly because these safeguards were so powerful that the right of silence had to go.[15] As against this, we should note that the government did not think to provide a remedy for suspects who suffer from the breach of these supposedly fundamental safeguards.[16] Loss of reputation can be compensated by suing for libel. Homeless travellers can be ejected from one's holiday cottage, development land or empty office block and sued for the owner's loss of amenity. But there is no such remedy if one is isolated from a lawyer and/or induced into a false confession through lies or deception. This is also true in relation to the abuse of other police powers not covered in this book, such as those concerning roadblocks and identification parades.

It is possible to provide compensation for wrongful conviction, but only where there has been a miscarriage of justice. A dramatic recent example was that of George Lewis, who was arrested by the notorious West Midlands Police Serious Crime Squad in 1987. He was head-butted, punched, racially abused and threatened with a syringe unless he signed blank sheets of interview notes. Police officers said he confessed in the car. He was convicted of armed robbery and spent over five years in jail until the Court of Appeal ordered a retrial (which the CPS abandoned). Eventually, in 1998, he received £200,000 compensation.[17] But if a wrongful conviction is quashed as a result of normal appeal procedures, then no compensation is payable.

What does the ECHR have to say about this? As noted in section 1, Art 5(5) provides that: 'Everyone who has been the victim of arrest or detention in contravention of the provisions of [Art 5] shall have an enforceable right to compensation.' However, Art 5 only provides that arrest and detention be carried out on the basis of reasonable suspicion, that the reason for arrest be given, and that the lawfulness of detention be decided promptly by a court of law, rights which are already provided for in the law of tort. Most of the rights discussed in, for example, chapter 4 (eg to legal

---

14 This duty is only implicit, but arises because the courts have a discretion under s 78 of PACE to exclude evidence which would have an adverse effect on the fairness of the proceedings if admitted. See ch 5.

15 This is an over-simplification: see ch 6, section 2.

16 A Sanders, 'Rights, Remedies and the Police and Criminal Evidence Act' [1988] Crim LR 802.

17 *The Guardian*, 20 January 1998.

advice) are covered by other parts of the ECHR (that of legal advice is covered by Art 6), and are therefore *not* the subject of obligatory remedies.[18]

Thus there is simply no civil remedy available in respect of many of the rights provided in PACE and the codes of practice. The inadequate protection of these rights indicates a lack of commitment to due process values and freedom, and the human rights perspective has little to say about this.[19] But the problem may stem more from a fundamental misunderstanding of how the criminal justice system works than a lack of commitment. The Royal Commission on Criminal Procedure (Philips Commission) considered that there was no need for new civil or criminal remedies to enforce the rights of suspects. Its view was that the new controls it advocated, such as the custody officer, combined with enhancements to the police complaints system, would provide sufficient protection. It is commendable that the Philips Commission, unlike the Royal Commission on Criminal Justice, considered the matter.[20] Although we know that relying on custody officers to stop malpractice is a flawed strategy, to say the least,[1] the Philips Commission was right to consider the need for police organisational controls to deal with malpractice. In the absence of these, how well do civil remedies work at the general level of deterring or controlling malpractice?

The basic principle of awards in tort is that 'damages' are supposed to compensate the plaintiff for loss. Torts are not crimes so punishment and deterrence are not the main objectives. But torts are *wrongs* and the civil law has recognised that there is sometimes a need to include elements of punishment and deterrence in awards of damages. For many years it has been possible to award 'punitive' or 'exemplary' damages in certain situations. They can be awarded against private defendants, as in the classic American *Ford Pinto* case. Huge punitive damages were awarded against the Ford Motor Corporation because it knew that the Pinto had a dangerous design fault, but calculated that it would be cheaper to pay the occasional fatal damages claim than to change the design. 'Punitive damages are, in effect, a fine payable to the plaintiff rather than the State.'[2] Punitive damages can also be awarded against public bodies in relation to 'oppressive, arbitrary or unconstitutional action by the servants of

18   As noted in section 1, Art 13, which requires an 'effective' remedy for breach of *any* Convention right, was not incorporated by the HRA.
19   A Ashworth, *The Criminal Process* 2nd edn (Oxford: OUP, 1998) a book the first edition of which blazed the trail for the human rights perspective on criminal justice in this country, does not even discuss the issue.
20   Royal Commission on Criminal Procedure (RCCP), Report (Cmnd 8092) (London: HMSO, 1981) paras 4.121-4.122.
1   For discussion of the role of the custody officer, see chs 4 and 5, above; for the police complaints system, see section 4, below.
2   P Cane, *Tort Law and Economic Interests* (Oxford: OUP, 1996) p 300.

Civil actions

government.'³ This is where 'the official acted intentionally or maliciously
. . .with a reckless disregard for its legality.'⁴ The purpose of this is
doubtless partly to punish the wrongdoer, but also to deter future
malpractice. When the police lose an action it is not the individual officers
who pay the damages but the police organisation. If punitive damages are
to realise their full potential they should deter the police hierarchy from
allowing or facilitating malpractice by individual officers, or, to put it more
positively, they should encourage the police to establish mechanisms or
cultures which discourage such action. They therefore have a potential to
act at a *systemic level* as well as remedying individual wrongs for
individuals. Actions for damages against the Metropolitan Police in
particular had been increasing in the early 1990s (see subsection (c) below)
and frequently large amounts of exemplary damages had been awarded.

Matters came to a head in *Thompson v Metropolitan Police Comr, Hsu
v Metropolitan Police Comr.*⁵ In these two separate cases Miss
Thompson was lawfully arrested for drink-driving. She was found to have
been assaulted by four or five officers after they decided to put her in a
cell, to which she objected. She was charged with assault, kept in custody
and prosecuted. She subsequently brought a civil action and was awarded
damages for assault, false imprisonment and malicious prosecution. In Mr
Hsu's case, two officers demanded entry to his home because of a complaint
by a former lodger of Hsu's that he had some of her belongings and would
not let her collect them. Hsu refused to let them in as they had no search
warrant. They attempted to force their way in. When Hsu tried to stop them
they assaulted him several times (including a kick that caused internal
injuries), racially abused him, arrested and detained him in the police station
for over an hour and refused to take him home even though he had no
shoes on. The jury awarded Hsu £220,000, £200,000 of which was punitive
damages, and awarded lesser amounts to Thompson.

The Court of Appeal reduced Hsu's punitive damages to £15,000 and
said that Thompson should only have received £25,000. This followed from
its decision that there should be an absolute limit for sums of punitive
damages in cases against the police of £50,000, but even that should be
awarded only in exceptional cases. Its reasoning was that:

> 'the person responsible for meeting [an award against the police] is
> not the wrongdoer, but his "employer". While it is possible that a
> chief constable could bear a responsibility for what has happened,

---

3   *Rookes v Barnard* [1964] AC 1129 at 1226. Now also see *Holden v Chief Constable
     of Lancashire* [1987] QB 380.
4   Cane (1996) p 301.
5   [1997] 2 All ER 762.

due to his failure to exercise proper control, the instances when this is alleged to have occurred should not be frequent.'[6]

This is a lost opportunity. The Court is denying the organisation a role in preventing malpractice as a justification for limiting punitive damages. In fact it should be doing the reverse, that is, ascribing to the organisation a role in preventing malpractice and backing this up by inflating punitive damages.[7] The Court's argument, that there is no point in awarding large amounts of punitive damages because the organisation which has to pay is not the individual that does the wrongdoing, could be used by large private organisations like Ford too. The idea of an upper limit does not apply where defendants are not the police, which is significant in itself. But judges generally dislike the idea of punitive damages because they result in the plaintiff receiving a windfall gain. This would not happen if the money were paid, as in a 'real' fine, to the state. This serves to illustrate part of the problem; in these cases civil actions are substitutes for prosecutions. The civil juries in these cases decided that the police officers committed crimes and so naturally people feel a need for elements of deterrence and punishment. That need would be better served through prosecutions, but we have already seen how rare this is, and the officers in these cases were not prosecuted. A more vigorous prosecution policy would enable civil actions to focus on the issue of compensation. As it is, we have a lackadaisical prosecution policy and an increasingly strait-jacketed civil regime.

(c) Pursuing civil actions

Having the right to sue does not mean that one is always able to sue. The main difficulty is establishing a case on the balance of probabilities (the civil standard of proof) when it is usually just one person's word against another's. Proving one's case is a major hurdle. Another factor is cost. A large proportion of people cannot afford the cost of their own lawyers, let alone those hired by the police. Fighting an appeal can be financially crippling and this may deter many, uncertain of their prospects of winning a case, from taking the gamble. Suspects are drawn from the poorest sections of society, so very few indeed can afford to sue. Legal aid is, in principle, available for those who cannot afford to sue. However, the means

6 [1997] 2 All ER 762 at 772.
7 A more positive view of this case is that the Court rejected the police's view that no punitive damages should be awarded at all because police complaints procedures were a more appropriate way of dealing with malpractice. See B Dixon and G Smith, 'Laying Down the Law: The Police, the Courts and Legal Accountability' (1998) 26 IJ Soc of Law 419.

test has been steadily tightened up in the 1980s and 1990s, making an ever smaller proportion of the population eligible for legal aid.[8]

There is also a 'merits' test. Legal aid is generally only granted if the action would be worth bringing were it to be privately funded. The issue here is partly one of likelihood of success.[9] It is also one of cost in relation to the likely level of damages.[10] As we saw earlier, two hours' unlawful detention where the suspect would have been detained anyway was held to be worth £500 in the late 1990s.[11] The Court of Appeal in *Hsu* and *Thompson*[12] set out 'starting points' for non-punitive damages. These were (in the late 1990s): £500 for each hour of unlawful detention on a reducing scale, with about £3,000 for a 24-hour period. Presumably, then, a wrongful stop-search or arrest which did not lead to police station detention would attract far less than £500. Such a brief detention, even if accompanied by an assault not causing injury, would not attract significant damages even if a claim of assault was upheld, so legal aid would generally not be provided.[13] Malicious prosecution would be a different matter. The Court of Appeal in *Hsu* and *Thompson*[14] decided that damages for malicious prosecution should begin at £2,000 because the suffering is drawn-out while fighting one's case. For a Crown Court case, which could last two years, £10,000 was suggested.

Serious malpractice can attract significant damages. In *Hsu* and *Thompson* the Court of Appeal decided that each plaintiff should receive £20,000 in non-punitive damages. Opinions of whether that was sufficient compensation for the degrading and unlawful actions of the police might legitimately differ. But we should acknowledge that it may be hard for us to understand the psychological impact of such treatment if we have not experienced it ourselves. Perhaps we can try to put ourselves in the shoes of Mr and Mrs White, for we all know what it is like to feel relaxed and secure in one's own home at night. This middle aged West Indian couple were dragged from their beds by the police. Their understandable resistance to such a shocking intrusion was met with overpowering violence. They

---

8   O Hansen, 'A Future for Legal Aid?' (1992) 19 JLS 85. See *Legal Action*, April 2000, p 34 for the up-to-date limits at the time of writing.

9   An applicant for legal aid must satisfy the legal aid authorities that there are 'reasonable grounds for taking . . . proceedings': Legal Aid Act 1988, s 15(2).

10   Under s 15(3) of the Legal Aid Act 1988, the legal aid authorities can refuse legal aid if it appears to the Board 'unreasonable' to grant it. The normal criterion is whether the financial benefit to be gained from bringing the action outweighs the cost involved.

11   *Roberts v Chief Constable of Cheshire Police* [1999] 1 WLR 662.

12   [1997] 2 All ER 762.

13   However, legal aid can be granted where the applicant's status, reputation or dignity was particularly harmed even if the monetary amount is small. See C Blake, 'Legal Aid: Past, Present and Future' (2000) Legal Action, Jan, p 6.

14   [1997] 2 All ER 762.

were held in custody, in their night clothes, for several hours. The final insult was to be charged with assaulting the arresting officers. At trial they were acquitted. They sued the police who, the judge said, 'showed no regard to human dignity' and were 'monstrously wicked'. Defendants who behave in 'monstrously wicked' ways usually get lengthy prison sentences. By contrast, one of the Whites was awarded £4,500 and the other £6,500 for assault, false imprisonment and malicious prosecution. They were also awarded £20,000 each exemplary damages.[15] Was that sufficient punishment for the police?

Exemplary damages are not awarded if the police are provoked by the plaintiff. Thus in *O'Connor v Hewitson*,[16] the arrested plaintiff was violent and unco-operative. The police hit him once or twice unnecessarily, for which he was awarded only £125. Nor are exemplary damages awarded if the police make a genuine mistake. In *Wershof v Metropolitan Police Comr*,[17] a solicitor was arrested in a shop. He was put in a 'half-nelson', marched down a crowded street, and detained in the police station for an hour. For assault and false imprisonment he was awarded £1,000. His behaviour, the judge commented, lacked 'discretion' (he forcefully asserted his rights). The class issue can be important here. People with reputations and salaries to lose would command relatively high levels of damages, but these people are rarely arrested, let alone wrongly. Wershof was an exception, and had he been an unemployed labourer he would have received far less than £1,000. In one case, a lecturer held incommunicado for 21 hours was awarded £600, perhaps illustrating the modern status of academics.[18]

In the mid-1990s it was decided that solicitors should be allowed to take cases on a 'no-win, no-fee' basis.[19] This has the advantage for victims of malpractice that they do not need to try to secure legal aid if a solicitor will take their case on this basis. This can help people whose damages would be low. But there is a lower limit, for if the claim is too low, the solicitor's share will not cover the *overhead* costs even though the losing side pays the costs of the action itself. The fundamental problem remains, that someone who is judged to have a less than evens chance of winning is most unlikely to find a solicitor willing to take the case, for this is too much of a risk when no win means no fee.

Most cases are settled out of court. As one might expect, settlement involves compromise; the plaintiff generally accepts a lower level of damages but avoids the delay involved in pursuing court proceedings and

15 (1982) Guardian, 24 April.
16 [1979] Crim LR 46.
17 [1978] 3 All ER 540.
18 See the cases discussed by J Robbilliard and J McEwan, *Police Powers and the Individual* (Oxford: Basil Blackwell, 1986) pp 254-255.
19 See, for discussion of Conditional Fees Agreements, Legal Action, March 2000, p 17.

the risk of losing. When civil cases are settled out of court, the remedy has served one of its purposes in that the individual citizen has obtained redress for a wrong. But the opportunity that a public court hearing would have provided for bringing police officers to account is diminished. When police forces settle they make no admission of liability and the shame of a public hearing and adjudication is avoided. The corollary of the high rate of case settlement is that most civil actions do not serve the purposes of punishment and deterrence as effectively as they might. They often also do not succeed in genuinely compensating for the suffering. Take Leslie Burnett, who in 1988 was stopped by two officers who said they saw him tampering with a car. When they began to use force on him, he resisted. One said: 'You black bastard, you're going to get it now.' More police arrived. He was handcuffed so tightly that his wrists bled. He was kicked and stamped on. A witness described the scene as, 'like birds of prey picking at a carcass.' At the police station he was racially abused. Mr Burnett was to say later, 'They all came to look at me like I was an exhibit in a zoo. They were all looking at me and laughing.' A doctor said he should be taken to hospital. Charged with assaulting the police, he was acquitted. In 1991 the Metropolitan Police settled out-of-court, awarding him £40,000 plus costs. But the police did not admit liability nor apologise to him. Mr Burnett said: 'I feel very bitter. Both my parents are ministers and they say I should forgive them but how can I? I see the officers in the street and they laugh at me. Why are they still in the police?'[20]

Overall, tens of millions of pounds have been paid to victims of malpractice over the last 20 years.[1] Despite all of the obstacles strewn in the path of those wanting to sue the police, the number of actions continues to grow. The number of successful actions (including out-of court-settlements) against the Metropolitan Police alone went up from 127 in 1991/2 to 389 in 1997/8.[2] So there must be well over 1,000 successful cases against the police as a whole each year. Examples include Daniel Goswell, who won £302,000 for being hit with a truncheon while being handcuffed, and Trevor Gerald who was awarded £125,000 for assault, false imprisonment and malicious prosecution (all awarded before the *Hsu* case restrained the level of damages). From the due process viewpoint a growth in successful civil actions represents justice, and no more need be said. But from both crime control and freedom perspectives there is a question of whether the money could be better spent on more positive aspects of policing. The crime control adherent would act, as the Court of Appeal did in *Hsu*, to reduce the amount of money paid out. For us, the answer is to tackle the problem at source by reducing the amount of malpractice so that

20   *The Guardian*, 2 July 1991.
1   For example, in the 7 years from 1991 to 1998, the Metropolitan Police has paid out some £12.4m. See Metropolitan Police Commissioner, Annual Reports.
2   See Metropolitan Police Commissioner, Annual Reports.

there are fewer victims and less money paid out. This means creating organisational structures and cultures which discourage malpractice. For cases like Leslie Burnett's are unlikely to have done anything either to change police behaviour or to protect Mr Burnett's freedom. Clearly civil actions do not succeed well in deterring malpractice, otherwise the number and value of civil claims would be going down, not up. The next question to ask is whether the police complaints system, the other remedy with the potential to put individual police officers on the spot, serves any of these purposes any better.

4. COMPLAINTS AGAINST THE POLICE

Most bureaucracies and public agencies maintain some form of grievance procedure for handling complaints by citizens of shoddy treatment. The 1964 Police Act introduced a uniform system for the investigation of complaints against the police. It provided for all complaints to be recorded and investigated by either a senior officer from the force or, where complaints were particularly serious, from a different force. Reports of the investigation went to the deputy chief constable (or, in certain cases, the Police Authority)[3], who decided whether or not there was evidence of:
(a) a criminal offence, in which case the file was sent to the Director of Public Prosecutions, who decided whether or not to prosecute;
(b) a disciplinary offence (including abuse of police power or the rights of suspects), in which case a disciplinary hearing was arranged; or
(c) no offence at all, in which case no action was taken.
The spectacle of the police investigating themselves, deciding whether or not the investigations revealed grounds for complaint, and then (in non-criminal allegations) deciding whether or not the complaint was proven, led to sharp criticism. In response, the Police Act 1976 established a civilian Police Complaints Board (PCB). All procedures remained as before except that where the police decided that there was no evidence for any proceedings, the file was passed onto the Board. In the nine years of its existence (1976–1985), the Board recommended charges in just 210 cases. Not surprisingly, it failed to enhance public confidence.[4] The opportunity was taken in PACE to modify the system yet again.

3   Each police force is loosely accountable to a police authority currently made up of local magistrates and councillors. The Metropolitan Police Force was an exceptional case, as it was accountable directly to the Home Secretary. See L Lustgarten, *The Governance of Police* (London: Sweet & Maxwell, 1986). This is set to change in 2000.
4   For discussion and chronicling of the events of the 1970s and early 1980s see Robbilliard and McEwan (1986) pp 227-233. D Brown, Police Complaints Procedure (Home Office Research Study no 93) (London: HMSO, 1987) is an interesting survey of complainants' views under the pre-PACE system.

Complaints against the police

The PCB was replaced by the Police Complaints Authority (PCA).[5] Like the PCB, this is a body of the 'great and the good', but some of its members are full-time and it has a substantial staff. As far as the majority of complaints are concerned, the system is almost unchanged. Investigation is by a senior officer who presents the investigation to the appropriate assistant or deputy chief constable. Where no action is proposed, and where the file is not sent to the DPP for consideration of criminal proceedings, the file is passed to the Police Complaints Authority (which can, if it considers it appropriate, order disciplinary proceedings or even send the file to the DPP for possible criminal proceedings).[6] The difference lies largely in respect of very serious and relatively minor complaints. The latter may now be dealt with informally, and are discussed below. The former are still investigated by the police, but under the supervision of the PCA.

Serious complaints include allegations of corruption or 'serious arrestable offences'[7] or conduct leading to death or serious injury. In such cases, the police must refer the complaint to the Police Complaints Authority to begin with. The police may also refer any other complaints to the Authority if they wish, and any other conduct by an officer which might be indicative of a serious criminal or disciplinary offence. In addition, the PCA can insist on any complaint being referred to it at any time, even if it does not come into the above categories.[8] Where the Police Complaints Authority is involved in any of these ways, it supervises the investigation, thus introducing, for the first time, an independent element into the complaints investigation process. The way in which the police investigate complaints is, however, still the key to the process.

By the late 1980s, so many serious allegations had been levelled against the police that nearly every force in the country was involved in complaints investigation, either as investigator of another force or as the subject of investigation by another force. In 1989–90, out of the 43 police forces, at least 17 had been investigated by another force, and at least 22 had carried out an investigation. Indeed, at least 10 forces had both been investigated and conducted an investigation. Investigations covered such allegations as incompetence (for example, in the Hillsborough tragedy), bribery and corruption, the planting of evidence, assault and the fabrication of confessions.[9]

Concern about the lack of public confidence in the system and a growing belief that the lack of confidence was justified continued to be expressed

---

5   PACE, s 83.
6   PACE, ss 92, 93.
7   See, for definition, ch 4, section 2.
8   PACE, ss 87-89.
9   See T Kaye, 'Unsafe and Unsatisfactory?' Report of the Independent Inquiry into the Working Practices of the West Midlands Police Serious Crime Squad (London: Civil Liberties Trust, 1991) app A.

in most quarters throughout the 1990s. Public confidence in the system is low, and falling. Until 1996 the PCA commissioned its own public attitude surveys. In 1996, for the first time, more people did not trust the police to investigate themselves (40%) than did trust them (37%). Moreover, the percentage believing the PCA to be independent and impartial was 39% and 37% respectively.[10] Even the Police Federation's survey, conducted in 1997, produced similar results: 59% said they would have the greatest confidence in a system of independent investigation, 16% opted for police investigation and 20% said they would have equal confidence in either.[11] That the lack of confidence is particularly marked in black communities added to this concern, especially in the wake of the *Stephen Lawrence* scandal.[12] Commentators also drew attention to a drop in complaints[13] being mirrored by a rise in civil actions, it thus appearing that the civil courts were filling a gap that the complaints system should fill.[14] Even before this report, the Conservative Government of the mid-1990s had planned to make some changes, but these were lost with the change of government in 1997. It then took two years for the new government to introduce new rules to reduce the obstacles in the way of complainants.[15] In the meantime, more reports came out recommending more fundamental change. Even the police now favour this, and the Home Office issued a consultation document early in 2000. At the time of writing (mid-2000) we still have the police investigating themselves, supervised (sometimes) by the PCA, but it is almost certainly only a matter of time before a genuinely independent system is brought in to supplement or replace the current system.[16] First we will discuss the current system and its flaws. At the end of this section we will examine the main proposals for reform.

10   Police Complaints Authority, Annual Report, 1995/6 (London: SO, 1996).
11   House of Commons, Home Affairs Select Committee, Police Disciplinary and Complaints Procedure, 1st Report (HC 258-1, 1998), p 194. All these surveys are discussed in J Harrison and M Cuneen, An Independent Police Complaints Commission (London: Liberty, 2000).
12   Sir William Macpherson of Cluny, The Stephen Lawrence Inquiry (Cm 4262-I) (London: SO, 1999). This was also found by the PCA's surveys. The Macpherson Report, further discussed in chs 3 and 6, was one of many in the 1980s and 1990s to recommend an independent complaints investigation system.
13   That is, the number of complaint cases, as distinct from the number of complaints. In many cases there are several complaints.
14   Dixon and Smith (1998).
15   The recent history is discussed by G Smith, 'Double Trouble' (1999) 149 NLJ 1223.
16   Although there is the possibility that the current Government will run out of fuel and lose the next election, which might result in further delay of reform.

(a) Investigation of complaints

The Police Complaints Authority neither investigates complaints itself nor has a body of investigators under its own control. 'Supervision' is at a distance, and only applies to a small proportion of complaints (around 5%).[17] This is largely an artefact of limited resources, as reflected in the fact that the PCA declines to supervise 70–80% of the cases referred to it by the police.[18] Even when the infamous West Midlands Police Serious Crime Squad affair erupted, the Authority initially avoided involvement. In one of the early cases, that of Paul Dandy, the police were alleged to have forged a confession. It was not until five months after the prosecution had dropped the charges against him, and following repeated calls for its involvement in the investigation of his complaints against the police, that the PCA expressed an interest.[19] The squad was disbanded over one year later, following the failure of several more of its cases and some barbed judicial criticism. Having taken this dramatic step, the West Midlands Police Chief Constable went further by asking the Police Complaints Authority to supervise an investigation into the squad's past activities. At last the PCA stirred itself. Dozens of cases, going back several years, were investigated by several officers from West Yorkshire working full-time over several months. Even so, PCA supervision amounted to just one member of the Authority, responsible for many other cases as well, meeting regularly with those officers.[20] Although some officers have been disciplined, including some dismissals, there have been no prosecutions (see section 2 above).

Maguire and Corbett studied the operation of the police complaints system in 1986–88. They identified three different ways in which complaints investigation may be 'supervised'. Initially the Police Complaints Authority receives basic documentation (for example, the custody record, if the complainant was arrested) and can decide which officer should investigate (whether from the force being investigated or from an outside force). It will also be given regular progress reports (at least monthly) by investigating officers. Where this is all that supervision involves (and 60% of Maguire and Corbett's sample involved little or no discussion between the PCA

17 In 1998-9, 761 complaint cases were supervised by the PCA, along with 192 non-complaint cases (eg all deaths in custody): PCA Annual Report, 1998-9 (London: SO, 2000). See generally, M Maguire and C Corbett, A Study of the Police Complaints System (London: HMSO, 1991).
18 Maguire and Corbett (1991) p 12.
19 See Kaye (1991) for discussion of this affair in general and Dandy's case in particular.
20 It is estimated that each member of the Authority has a caseload of 50-60 cases: B Loveday, 'Recent Developments in Police Complaints Procedure' (1989) Local Gov Studies, May/June, p 25.

and the investigating officer) it can be termed 'passive'.[1] 'Active' supervision entails substantive discussion of the progress of investigations and occasional observation of interviews with witnesses, and comprised around 30% of their sample. In 10% or less was supervision 'directive', in the sense that investigating officers were formally requested to pursue particular lines of inquiry.

The report of the investigation is sent to the Police Complaints Authority, not the police, in the first instance. Frequently the PCA requests more information or further interviews. When the supervising member of the PCA thinks that little more is to be gained from further investigation it accepts the report, which is then transmitted to the police. What action, if any, should follow from the investigation is considered by other PCA members separately. Maguire and Corbett found that at this stage members frequently 'noted a lack of thoroughness' in investigation by which time nothing could be done about it.[2]

This study also found that most complainants whose investigations were supervised by the PCA were dissatisfied with the process, had less faith in the complaints system than before they started and asserted that they had been kept badly informed throughout. This was despite the majority originally feeling more confident when they heard that the PCA would be involved.[3] Although complaints are more often 'successful' when they are supervised by the PCA than when they are not, this could be due simply to the fact that one criterion used in selecting cases for supervision is the likelihood of success.

The judiciary are sometimes critical of the performance of the Police Complaints Authority. In one case, the Court of Appeal quashed two convictions because of what the Lord Chief Justice called the 'tainted evidence' of several police officers. The circumstances of this case were being reviewed as part of a PCA investigation into one particular police station which had been proceeding for two years. The Lord Chief Justice said that 'dynamite' should be put behind the PCA.[4]

Even if all the investigation of all cases were supervised, and if that supervision were not so inadequate, the notion of investigation by the police would still be fundamentally flawed. This is because the Police Complaints Authority (like the PCB before it and, indeed, like the deputy chief constable) is in a similar position to that of the CPS. None of these bodies assesses the facts of the incidents complained of, except in those few cases where supervision is directive. What they assess are reports of the facts, compiled by investigators whose job is to present a case. Since those investigators are police officers, the case they are generally

1   Maguire and Corbett (1991) p 136.
2   See Maguire and Corbett (1991) p 143.
3   Maguire and Corbett (1991) pp 147-148.
4   *The Guardian*, 15 December 1993.

Complaints against the police

predisposed to present will be that there is insufficient evidence to proceed. For although investigating officers are investigating alleged wrongdoing by other officers, much of this wrongdoing is part of everyday policing, is consistent with police working rules and will have been engaged in by themselves and/or their close colleagues. Writing in 1975, Box and Russell argued that the police psychologically neutralise the apparently deviant nature of their rule breaking by using 'techniques of neutralisation' common to all occupational and cultural groups.[5] These techniques include 'condemning the condemners' and 'denying the victim', ie either blaming the complainant or disputing a crucial alleged fact about the complainant's injuries or loss. Such techniques enable the police to shrug off most complaints with a clear conscience.

Complaints investigation, which is akin to case construction in prosecution decisions (see chapter 6), is described by Box and Russell as a process of 'discrediting' based on neutralisation techniques. Just as cases against ordinary suspects can be constructed to justify prosecution, cases against police suspects can be constructed to justify no further action. Arrest and/or prosecution of the complainant is one method of discrediting. The White case, along with many others discussed in section 3 above, involved an attempt to discredit the Whites' complaints of assault by charging them with assaulting the arresting officers and resisting arrest.[6] Arrest and/or prosecution transforms the identity of the complainant from 'good citizen' to 'criminal suspect'. This makes denial by the police of the allegations more plausible and provides an explanation for what is claimed to be a false complaint (ie a complainant is said to be trying to use the complaints system to justify their own (alleged) violent resistance to arrest). Previous criminal record, a past record of mental illness and alleged drunkenness are other 'facts' used to discredit complainants.

The result is not just a generally low rate of substantiation, but a particularly low rate for those people whose complaints can be easily discredited. In Box and Russell's sample, 32% had two or more 'discredits' against them. None of their complaints was substantiated. One in ten of those with one discredit, but four in ten of those with no discredits, had their complaints substantiated. One result of this was that working class people had little success (8% of their complaints were substantiated, as against 28% of the complaints of middle class people).[7] It is, of course,

5   S Box and K Russell, 'The Politics of Discreditability: Disarming Complaints Against the Police' (1975) 23 Soc Rev 315.

6   For other examples, see A Sanders, 'Prosecution Decisions and the Attorney-General's Guidelines' [1985] Crim LR 4. See also ch 6, section 3(b) above.

7   Box and Russell (1975) also discuss other class attributes, such as lower educational levels, which could adversely affect the success of their complaints.

possible that drunks, criminals and the mentally ill really do make more false complaints than do other people. But the failure of the complaints mechanism in notorious cases such as Madden's case[8] and the 'Confait Affair'[9] leads one to suspect that, however true this may be in part, the investigative process is intrinsically faulty.

The more recent research by Maguire and Corbett suggests that the advent of the Police Complaints Authority has made little difference to the substance of the investigative process as described by Box and Russell. They detected 'a certain amount of "stereotyping" by police (including investigating) officers—for instance, a belief that almost all complaints by certain kinds of people are made purely in order to cause trouble for the police, or a tendency to treat complainants as either "deserving" or "non-deserving" of serious attention, depending on their background and character.'[10] Investigating officers, in other words, are steeped in 'cop culture' (see chapter 2, section 1) and are unable to avoid viewing policing and rule breaking through the eyes of that culture:

'What a police officer may honestly (and perhaps justifiably) regard as totally "reasonable force" to manoeuvre an intoxicated person quickly and effectively into a police van, may appear to the person—or to bystanders—as totally unreasonable force.'[11]

Sometimes these attitudes are noticed by the Police Complaints Authority, and commented upon adversely, but the PCA can do nothing about this, short of demanding a new investigation.

(b) Adjudication and discipline

Table 9.1 shows the number of complaints made in various years between 1986 and 1999 and the results of the investigations into them.[12]

---

8   *Police Complaints Board, ex p Madden* [1983] 2 All ER 353.
9   See J Baxter and L Koffman, 'The Confait inheritance - Forgotten Lessons?' [1983] Cambrian LR 14.
10   Box and Russell (1975) p 130.
11   M Maguire, 'Complaints against the Police: Where Now?' (unpublished manuscript).
12   Source: J Cotton and D Povey, Police Complaints and Discipline, 1998-9 (Statistical Bulletin 17/99) (London: Home Office 1999) (NK = not known).

Table 9.1: Complaints against the police and outcomes in selected years

	1986	1991	1995/6	1998/9
Total complaints	29,178	35,346	35,840	31,653
Complaints investigated	13,805	12,142	8,653	9,202
	(47%)	(34%)	(24%)	(29%)
Complaints withdrawn (including cases 'dispensed with')	11,335	14,224	15,535	11,423
	(39%)	(40%)	(43%)	(36%)
Informally resolved	4,038	8,980	11,652	11,028
	(14%)	(25%)	(33%)	(35%)
Substantiated	1,129	813	749	745
Prosecuted (non-RTA)	(NK)	(NK)	10	38
Disciplined	(NK)	(NK)	162	122
Dealt with 'by other means'	(NK)	(NK)	577	585

You can see that around a third of all complaints are withdrawn or 'dispensed with', the latter being when, for a variety of reasons, cases cannot be investigated. A similar number are dealt with by conciliation procedures. Both are discussed later. It is also striking that both the substantiation rate and the percentage of complaints in which there are charges is remarkably low. Look at the figures for 1998-9: there were 160 prosecutions and discipline charges taken together. These were:

0.5% of all complaints made;
0.8% of all complaints minus those informally resolved;
1.7% of all complaints investigated;
21.5% of all complaints substantiated.

Or we could look at the substantiation rate. In 1998-9, this was:

2.3% of all complaints made;
3.6% of all complaints minus those informally resolved;
8.1% of all complaints investigated.

The gap between substantiated complaints and those where action was taken (ie those dealt with 'by other means') is dramatic. In part this is due to early retirements by the officers complained against, and informal 'admonishments' or 'advice', and so forth. But this does not account for the very low substantiation rate. The low charge rate also reflects the fact that these figures are of complaints (not complainants). Nonetheless, there were some 20,000 complainants in 1998-9 (nearly 5,000 fewer than in 1994, and part of the general trend of falling complaint levels). So, including informal resolution and withdrawals, the charge rate *per complainant* was less than 1%, and the substantiation rate was less than 4%. Looking only at complaints investigated the rates were less than 3% and 12% respectively.

The impact of the Police Complaints Authority appears to be minimal. The overwhelming majority of disciplinary charges are the decisions of the police themselves. The PCA recommends charges in an additional 20-30 cases per year.[13] This, and the adjudication figures in general, is little different to the pre-PACE situation before the PCA replaced the PCB.

Lest it be thought that complaints are generally trivial, let us look at the case of Leroy McDowell and Wayne Taylor, black men in their early 30s. They were stopped and searched late one night because they were in a 'drugs-related area'. No drugs were found. They complained about being stopped, and were arrested and accused of threatening behaviour. They asked for medical help, because they suffer from sickle cell anaemia, but were instead locked in a cell. They were offered a caution which they refused. They were prosecuted and acquitted in 1995. They brought civil actions for wrongful arrest, malicious prosecution, trespass and (in relation to the medical issue) negligence. They each settled for £19,000 and the police did not accept liability. And the police officers? The arresting officers were 'admonished' and the custody officer 'given advice'.[14]

Of those complaints which were substantiated in 1998-9, 30% were for oppressive behaviour (of which more than half were assault), and 7% for malpractice. The more serious the complaint, the less likely to be successful it is. Thus nine times as many 'neglect of duty' complaints are successful as assault complaints.[15] However, 'dissatisfaction' with the process is not confined to unsuccessful complaints. Maguire and Corbett found that even successful complainants were unhappy at the time taken, the lack of apology and the lack of information provided (for example, about what the investigation found and about disciplinary proceedings). Poor communication is almost as much of a problem as the nature and quality of the investigation and subsequent decisions about disciplinary or criminal proceedings.

There are many reasons for the low rate of substantiation of complaints. Firstly, there is the process of case construction and discrediting, discussed earlier. Secondly, there is the closing of ranks by police officers who might have witnessed the events complained of and the inherent difficulty that people mistreated in police custody have in finding independent witnesses.

13 See eg A Hall, 'Police Complaints: Time for a Change' (1990) Legal Action, August, p 7.
14 *The Guardian*, 22 November 1997.
15 Maguire and Corbett (1991) ch 3.

'Cop culture', in other words, creates evidential problems.[16] A stark illustration of this is the 'Holloway Road transit case' in which five boys aged 13–16 were brutally beaten by a van load of police officers. It was established that the attack must have been carried out by officers patrolling in one of three specific police vans, but it was not known which. The police involved broke further criminal laws by covering up the truth. Many of those questioned exercised their right to silence. For over two years, investigation followed investigation, with no charges, because no officer was prepared to 'inform'. Only when immunity was promised to any officer not directly involved in the assault was the 'wall of silence' breached, leading eventually to the successful prosecution and jailing of five officers.[17] Dramatic though this case is, it is not unique. The 'Manchester case' in March 1985 involved nearly as much unprovoked brutality by police officers, but the identity of the officers could not be established.[18] Of the officers Maguire and Corbett interviewed, 60% 'admitted the existence of something like a "Code of Silence" among junior officers.'[19] As Loveday says, 'Breaking through the "blue curtain" has in practice proved as difficult for the PCA as for its predecessor body, the PCB.'[19]

These problems have been exacerbated by the evidential threshold. Until April 1999 this was the same standard of proof, beyond reasonable doubt, as is used in criminal proceedings. In every other occupation the civil standard (balance of probabilities) is used in disciplinary proceedings. The uniquely high standard for police disciplinary proceedings had the consequence that officers who were prosecuted and acquitted would be likely to escape if disciplined too. It also meant that if, as often happens, there is no evidence for or against the complaint other than the word of the officer(s) against the word of the complainant, what might have been provable on the balance of probabilities would fail to reach the higher threshold. The PCA itself has pointed out some of the consequences of this. For example, in 1998-9, according to the PCA's annual report, it was impossible to tell where the truth lay in 193 out of 203 complaints of 'racially discriminatory behaviour', which were therefore not upheld. In April 1999 this changed, as recommended by the Runciman Commission fully six years

16   See Lustgarten (1986).
17   The case is discussed by R East, 'Police Brutality: Lessons of the Holloway Road Assault' (1987) 137 NLJ 1010 and by B Hilliard, 'Holloway Road - Unfinished Business' (1987) 137 NLJ 1035.
18   Loveday (1989).
19   Loveday (1989) p 29. Individual police officers have occasionally yanked down this curtain and rooted out the misconduct of their colleagues. For example, a detective inspector in the Avon and Somerset force deserves significant credit for uncovering the malpractice by Surrey officers which led to the conviction of the 'Guildford Four'. She was acting for an inquiry ordered by the Home Office, rather than under the supervision of the PCA. See Rozenberg (1992).

earlier.[20] Now a charge need only be proven on the balance of probabilities.[1]

Further protection was provided by the double jeopardy rule, which prevented officers from being charged with disciplinary offences which are 'in substance the same' as criminal offences with which they had been charged and acquitted.[2] On one occasion, an innocent and unarmed man, Steven Waldorf, was mistaken for a dangerous criminal and shot several times by police officers. The officers who shot him were tried for attempted murder and inflicting grievous bodily harm, but were acquitted on the ground that they had acted in self-defence (mistakenly believing themselves to be under attack). This then made it impossible to bring disciplinary charges against them.[3] This rule was also the subject of a recommendation by the Runciman Commission, and was finally abolished in 1999.[4] At the time of writing (mid-2000) it is not yet known what effect these changes will have. Both should lead to a higher rate of substantiation and discipline because cases which are unsuccessfully prosecuted can now be subject to discipline charges (abolition of the double jeopardy rule) and with a greater chance of success (because of the altered level of proof needed). They should also lead to more prosecutions. One reason for the low prosecution rate until now has been concern that if the prosecution failed then nothing could be done. Now that it is possible to have two bites of the cherry the authorities need be less cautious. However, the fundamentals of the system remain unchanged. In particular, the DPP's prosecution decisions and the PCA's discipline decisions are made on the basis of police investigations. Only when this investigation system is radically reformed (discussed in subsection (e) below) will we see the dramatic changes that are needed.

Officers under investigation often take early retirement or resign for 'medical' reasons.[5] This is a form of plea bargain: from the police force's point of view the problem is dealt with easily and speedily, while the officers concerned lose their jobs but protect their record and pension rights. While the difficulties of proof doubtless strengthen the hands of police officers, the attractions of this type of bargain for both sides (but not complainants)

20 Royal Commission on Criminal Justice (RCCJ), Report (Cm 2263) (London: HMSO, 1993) p 48.
1   Police (Conduct) Regulations 1999, pursuant to Police Act 1996, ss 83, 87. Discussed in (1999) Legal Action, Dec, p 8.
2   PACE, s 104 (1).
3   M Tregilgas-Davey, 'The Police and Accountability' (1990) 140 NLJ 697. Note, however, that officers who are convicted of criminal offences are automatically guilty of the disciplinary offence of committing a crime: *Secretary of State for Home Department, ex p Thornton* [1986] 2 All ER 641. See s 104(2) of PACE.
4   This was done by activating a provision of the Police and Magistrates Court Act 1994. See Smith (1999) 'Double Trouble'.
5   See Hall (1990).

Complaints against the police

will never disappear. For the fact is that the police simply do not wish to discipline officers in many cases. This is sometimes because of sympathy with the officers, but more often because of fear of adverse publicity and the cans of worms (57 varieties) which might be opened.

If the police reject proceedings but the Police Complaints Authority insist on them—a rare but occasional event—the Authority may also insist on a disciplinary tribunal instead of the usual disciplinary proceedings conducted by a chief officer alone. The tribunal is chaired by a senior officer of the force which decided against proceedings (flanked by two PCA members) and the 'prosecution' is presented by another member of that force. In successive years, the Police Complaints Authority criticised police forces for presenting cases with such a lack of 'clarity and vigour' that they failed.[6] Even if the tribunal decides against the officer, the police chairperson or chief officer decides the punishment.[7] This is also true of the majority of discipline proceedings (which the police themselves decide to hold) where the PCA has no involvement at all. Fitting the punishment of police officers to the offence is a matter for the police alone.

Examination of the effects on the complaints and discipline process of proceedings in the ordinary courts is revealing. Over the five years 1988–92 inclusive, 80% of the Metropolitan Police officers involved in civil actions where over £10,000 was paid in damages or settlements had no disciplinary action taken against them.[8] The Runciman Commission was concerned that action was frequently not taken in this situation, nor where 'police malpractice has contributed to a miscarriage of justice', nor 'where a prosecution has been dismissed because of a more than technical breach of PACE or its codes and the actions of the police have been publicly criticised by the judge.'[9] Runciman found that the police had no mechanism for noting and acting upon judicial criticism of officers. A key element of the rule of law is that the police (along with all other arms of government) should be accountable to 'the law'. The reality, in this context, clearly falls well short of the rhetoric.

(c) Conciliation

One source of dissatisfaction among complainants discovered by Brown[10] was that making a complaint was 'all or nothing' regardless of the

6   Hall (1990).
7   PACE, s 94(7).
8   *The Guardian*, 15 April 1993.
9   RCCJ (1993) p 48. Also see House of Commons, Home Affairs Select Committee, Police Disciplinary and Complaints Procedure, 1st Report (HC 258-1, 1998) paras 25-6.
10 D Brown, Police Complaints Procedure (Home Office Research Study no 93) (London: HMSO, 1987).

seriousness of the incident. Many of them wanted nothing more than an apology and a recognition of how they felt about their treatment by the police. This was catered for by s 85 of PACE which allows the 'informal resolution' (conciliation) of complaints if this is the wish of both chief officer and complainant, and if the matter would be insufficiently serious for it to be dealt with through disciplinary proceedings even if proven.[11] Note that the officer complained of need not consent. Conciliation appears popular, being used by around one third of all complainants. However, research has shown that although most complainants using it do so voluntarily, some say that they are 'nudged' into it, or even presented with a fait accompli.[12] Conciliation is not the same as an officer being 'advised' or 'admonished', for conciliation involves no formal admission of guilt and is not noted on the officers' records.

The frequency of the use of conciliation indicates the relatively trivial nature of many complaints in objective terms, although they may not seem trivial to the complainants. Different forces interpret the seriousness threshold in diverse ways. Some reserve conciliation for incivility, while others also use it for harassment, neglect of duty (for example, not providing a party to a car accident with promised details of the other driver) and unlawful disclosure of information, such as informing an employer that an employee was a robbery suspect.[13] Some of these complaints end with explanations by the police (such as blaming civilian employees for information not being transmitted) and sometimes with simple apologies by the officer. Occasionally the outcome is more dramatic, as where an investigating officer gave the officer complained of what can only be described as a 'roasting' designed to intimidate him.[14] While most complainants were happy with the outcome, some were dissatisfied with it, feeling that the conciliatory spirit was lacking. Some wished to meet the officer complained against, but this was arranged only rarely. When the officer refuses to be conciliatory, the process should be regarded as having failed. This would leave the complainant either to withdraw the complaint or to pursue it formally. In practice, however, these options do not seem to be offered to complainants.

The flaws in the conciliation process make one wary about encouraging its wider use. However, Corbett found that some assault allegations, which are automatically classified as too serious for conciliation, might have been dealt with effectively in this way. In one, for example, the complainant admitted that he had struggled on arrest, and only wanted it acknowledged

11 Section 85 PACE has now been replaced by s 69 Police Act 1996, but there has been no material change.
12 C Corbett, 'Complaints Against the Police: The New Procedure of Informal Resolution' (1991) 2 Policing and Society 47; Maguire and Corbett (1991).
13 Corbett (1991).
14 Corbett (1991).

that the officer was 'a bit out of order'. Corbett concludes that, as it provides a rare opportunity for members of the police force and members of the public to understand each other's behaviour, its advantages outweigh its disadvantages.[15] Its speed and relatively high level of 'success' for the complainant are also important advantages (57% of these complainants were satisfied, compared with 10% whose complaints were fully investigated formally),[16] but this perhaps tells us more about the flaws in the formal procedures than the virtues of conciliation.

(d) Withdrawn complaints

The low level of substantiation of complaints against the police could reflect a high level of bogus complaints as much as unfair investigation processes. Were this so, one would expect most people with a grudge against the police—whether justified or not—to complain wherever possible. If anything, however, the reverse is true. Like the 'hidden figure' of unreported crime, there is a 'hidden figure' of unreported complaints. Tuck and Southgate found, prior to the creation of the Police Complaints Authority, that over 10% of their sample wished to complain, but only 1% actually took steps to do so and none actually completed the process.[17] The 1988 British Crime Survey found that little had changed after the creation of the PCA. 20% of the sample were 'really annoyed' by at least one officer over the previous five years; half of these (ie 10%) wished to complain, and 20% (ie 2%) took steps to do so, but it is not known how many pursued their complaints to a conclusion.[18]

Whatever the merits of a particular complaint, pursuing it is clearly not something done lightly.[19] The drop off rate of those who initiate a complaint but fail to complete it is important. Although complainants may complain directly to the Police Complaints Authority, callers are generally advised to contact their local police station—which is often the location of the incident being complained about. Once there, many are dissuaded from continuing by the police. Those who continue are interviewed by an investigating officer, after which around one-third of complainants withdraw their complaints.

15 Corbett (1991). See also Maguire (undated), for a discussion of the problem of complaints procedures being, in part, a matter of communication, perception and different experiences.

16 Maguire and Corbett (1991) Table 7.

17 M Tuck and P Southgate, Ethnic Minorities Crime and Policing (Home Office Research Study no 70) (London: HMSO, 1981).

18 P Mayhew, D Elliott and L Dowds, The 1988 British Crime Survey (Home Office Research Study no 111) (London: HMSO, 1989).

19 Contrast this with the belief of most police officers that most complaints are malicious and/or time wasting: Maguire and Corbett (1991) ch 5.

Many of those who persevered with their complaint told Maguire and Corbett that this was despite police pressure to withdraw. Pressure can take the form of inducements (for example, an offer to drop charges), charm (as when apologies or compensation is offered), threat (as where the possibility of charges against the complainant or associates is raised), dissuasion (explaining that success is very unlikely) or moral pressure (asking the complainant to consider the likely impact on the officer's career). Sometimes what is said satisfies complainants, who then withdraw, but most feel pressured into giving up. A higher proportion of assault complaints (60%) are withdrawn than average. Officers do not dispute the fact that they often advise withdrawal but, of course, they generally claim that they do this only where appropriate. Like most police work, interviews between investigating officers and complainants are hidden from view, making what the police do largely unaccountable. Even the thin protection of the PCA is not provided where complaints are withdrawn. As long as the police remain responsible for complaints investigation, this situation will continue. Police working rules will continue to dominate the complaints process. The weakness of the legal framework for handling complaints enables the police to continue breaking the PACE rules (for example, denying a suspect access to legal advice) with little fear of being disciplined for doing so. We may therefore conclude that that legal framework is essentially presentational, providing an appearance of due process whilst changing police behaviour very little.[20]

(e) Proposals for reform

Despite several major changes in the system over the past 30 years or so, the complaints system is still unsatisfactory—except as a way of preserving the freedom of the police to follow their own informal norms. This is partly because investigating deviance by anyone (including criminals) is intrinsically difficult and likely to fail in the majority of cases.[1] It is also because processes requiring articulate argument, polite persistence and so forth favour middle class people. Since most complainants are working class, they are less likely to succeed in their complaints.[2]

Little can be done about the above problems. However, what could be altered are the other most important features of the system: the way it deals with complainants and the investigation of the police by the police. It is

20 These kinds of problems have been observed in many other jurisdictions, and not just in Britain. See A Goldsmith, 'External Review and Self-Regulation' in A Goldsmith (ed), *Complaints Against the Police: the Trend to External Review* (Oxford: OUP, 1991).

1   See Goldsmith (1991).

2   Box and Russell (1975).

common for complaints about professions to be investigated by those professions. This form of 'self-regulation' is used for doctors and lawyers, for example. However, the police are different in many ways. First, while self-regulation is by no means ever perfect, the record of police complaints investigation is particularly lamentable (although not just in the UK). Second, the police have uniquely coercive powers, giving them greater opportunity for malpractice of a kind that carries very serious consequences for the individual citizen. Third, there is usually some element of choice on the part of people using doctors, lawyers, accountants and so forth, which is not true of suspects. If one is dissatisfied with one's doctor or lawyer one will generally not use them again, but citizens cannot choose their police officers or when those officers make contact. Finally, the police have a greater capacity to hide malpractice than other professions because of their greater power and their capacity to choose the time, place, and manner of their interaction with citizens.

In the words of the government's Consultation Paper: 'There is now something close to a consensus that the present system, however good or otherwise it may be in reaching the right result when a complaint against the police is investigated, does not enjoy full public confidence.'[3] As the Paper acknowledges, this has been stated by countless official inquiries as well as the PCA (and PCB before it) and other critics.[4] Even the European Committee for the Prevention of Torture and Inhuman or Degrading Treatment or Punishment criticised the fact that 'the police themselves maintain a firm grip upon the handling of complaints against them.' It doubted whether, in view of this, the PCA could command public confidence even if it did adequately supervise investigation, and recommended an independent investigating agency.[5] The Committee's view was based, in part, on its examination of Metropolitan Police files in several cases where the police settled cases where suspects were injured in police custody but where there had been no prosecutions or disciplinary proceedings. We cannot make an independent assessment of whether the Committee's conclusions were justified, for the government censored these sections, the report now having blank spaces on four separate pages.[6]

---

3   Home Office, Complaints against the Police: A Consultation Paper (London: Home Office, 2000) para 1. Also see the government's response to Home Affairs Select Committee, Police Discipline and Complaints Procedures, 2nd Special Report (HC 683) (London: SO, 1998).

4   See, for example, Sir L Scarman, The Brixton Disorders: 10-12 April 1981 (Cmnd 8427) (London: HMSO, 1981); MacPherson (1999), and Home Affairs Select Committee (1998). Also see Police Complaints Board, Triennial Report (London: HMSO, 1980), discussed by Loveday (1989).

5   Quoted in Harrison and Cuneen (2000) p 1.

6   The Guardian, 13 January 2000.

The Consultation Paper states the Government's 'sympathy for the concept of a more independent police complaints system'[7] but leaves open how it should be provided. It also enters a caveat that cost will prevent such a system operating for most complaints. In other words it could be 'no change' for the majority of investigations. If so, the new system could violate the ECHR (and, therefore, the HRA 1998). In *Khan* the applicant's house was bugged, and the evidence obtained thereby contributed to the evidence that led to his conviction for drugs offences. The bugging was unlawful, but Khan was unsuccessful in having the evidence excluded (discussed in section 5 below). He took his case to the European Court on Human Rights (ECtHR), which decided that although his right to privacy had been violated, it was for the English courts to determine what to do with the resultant evidence. Under Art 13 everyone has a right to seek an effective remedy against allegedly unlawful actions. The English police complaints system did not provide this, according to the ECtHR, because it is not sufficiently independent.[8]

Independent investigation by 'civilian' investigators or civilian review boards is not a new or untested idea. In some jurisdictions, such as Toronto and several American cities, these solutions appears to be more successful than our own. They are, however, fraught with new difficulties. These include obstruction of investigators by the police, civilian investigators over-identifying with the problems of the police, the creation of cumbersome procedures to protect officers from the new outside body, and a lack of understanding of policing on the part of civilians.[9] This last problem both impedes investigators in finding out what really happened, as officers can erect smoke-screens more easily and pull the wool over the eyes of novices, and could lead to lack of understanding of why certain malpractice takes place, reducing the possibility of effective punishment and prevention measures.[10] It is also said that civilians who have not experienced 'the street' could 'not easily tell the difference between an officer "trying honestly to do his job, but perhaps making mistakes", and a truly deviant officer "who should not be in uniform".'[11] Many of the problems can be summed up as those of breaking into police culture, which, as we saw in chapter 2, is very powerful. Nonetheless, many people argue

7   Home Office (2000) p 1.
8   *Khan (Sultan) v United Kingdom* [2000] Crim LR 684.
9   For good surveys, see Loveday (1989) and M McMahon, 'Police Accountability: the Situation of Complaints in Toronto' (1988) 12 Contemporary Crises 301. Also see A Goldsmith and S Farson, 'Complaints against the Police in Canada: A New Approach' [1987] Crim LR 615; Goldsmith (ed) (1991), and Harrison and Cuneen (2000).
10   D Bayley, 'Getting serious about police brutality' in P Stenning (ed), *Accountability for Criminal Justice* (Toronto: University of Toronto Press, 1995).
11   Maguire (undated) (quoting police officers).

that where 'external' involvement in investigation is more than merely supervisory its impact can be considerable.[12]

The treatment of complainants is a separate issue from who investigates. Unlike in a civil case, complainants have no rights in the investigation process, such as to ensure that their witnesses are interviewed. Complainants may attend the disciplinary hearing or tribunal (if there is one) but not until they give evidence. They cannot stay for the verdict or punishment (if any) and may never find it out. Some complaints take a year or more to investigate and then a hearing may take as long again. Again, complainants have no right to know the causes of the delay and have no power to question it. Complainants have no right to the investigation file or to know its contents. Indeed, under s 98 of PACE, it is a criminal offence for anything other than a summary of an investigation to be disclosed except for the purpose of disciplinary or legal proceedings. While this would not preclude a reasonably detailed summary being provided to complainants, instead bland uninformative statements are provided, creating the dissatisfaction noted earlier.[13]

The Government Consultation Paper was issued at the same time in mid-2000 as a report by Liberty[14] and a government-commissioned management consultants' (KPMG) report.[15] Perhaps the most constructive immediate reforms which can be currently envisaged, all advocated in one way or another in one or more of those documents, would be:

- To give potential complainants a choice of places at which to make a complaint (such as the Criminal Defence Service, CABx and so forth), and for their first interview to be conducted by a civilian member of an IPCC (Independent Police Complaints Commission).

- Expansion of conciliation procedures in order to increase understanding on both sides. This does, however, presuppose that there is common ground to be occupied and that policing really is 'for' the whole community and not against parts of it.[16]

- Access for complainants to investigation files for the purposes of civil actions and challenges to PCA and DPP decisions should be improved, something which the courts' interpretation of s 98 currently prohibits.[17]

---

12   Goldsmith (ed) (1991). Disputed by Bayley (1995).
13   See Maguire and Corbett (1991); Loveday (1989), and Home Affairs Select Committee (1998). The PCA itself is unhappy about this, to some extent self-imposed, restriction: see its Triennial Review 1985-88 (HC 466) (1988).
14   Harrison and Cuneen (2000). This is a good general discussion of most of the problems, with suggested solutions.
15   KPMG, Feasibility of an Independent System for Investigating Complaints Against the Police (Police Research Series no 124) (London: Home Office, 2000).
16   See ch 2, particularly section 5, for consideration of this point.
17   Following the recommendation to this effect from Macpherson (1999), the Government has accepted this in principle.

Access to the hearing itself should also be improved. The problem is encapsulated by this statement from the Home Affairs Committee: 'The PCA did advocate that complainants should be allowed to be accompanied by a personal friend or relative at a hearing; but they disagreed with Liberty's call for a complainant to have a right of legal representation, because the complainant was not actually a party to the case.'[18] The fact that the complainant is not a 'party' is, of course, a key facet of the whole problem, as is the PCA's (and Home Affairs Committee's) complacency about this.

- For some allegations, genuinely independent investigators are needed. Liberty suggests about 25%, but the figure will always be arbitrary. For what is 'serious' depends on how one views different factors. Whether racist taunts are serious will depend not only on their ferocity but also on how often the complainant has suffered in those ways before. Whether rough handling is serious will depend in part on how far it was provoked and how sensitive the complainant is.

- The IPCC, which would carry out investigations and (as the PCA does now) supervise and vet investigations carried out by the police, would have to consist of civilians and seconded police officers, in order to overcome the 'insider/outsider' problems identified earlier.

None of these should be seen as 'quick-fix' solutions to complex policing and investigatory processes.[19] For example, none of the reports address the problem of withdrawals of complaints. Perhaps this is because it is assumed that under a new system this problem would be reduced because of less police pressure to withdraw. If so, this is probably over-optimistic. The fear, intimidation or deals offered which lead to many withdrawals will not necessarily disappear just because some complaints investigation is done by another body. However, if complainants who seek to withdraw are interviewed again by the IPCC before withdrawal is agreed, the problem might be somewhat alleviated, or at least its magnitude and character better understood.

Another issue is what body should decide on prosecutions following an investigation. Liberty suggests that thought be given to the IPCC doing this. This may have the merit of increasing public confidence, but it is unlikely to make any substantive difference. Whatever body makes decisions on the basis of reports and investigations by another body will be dependent on that other body in the sense that it is led by that body's often hidden working rules and cultural norms. On the other hand, retaining the power within the CPS has an advantage. At present the DPP's decisions regarding police officers can be contrasted unfavourably with those of civilians when the criteria regarding both should be the same. If

18   Home Affairs Select Committee (1998) para 177 and see generally, paras 172-180.
19   McMahon (1988).

Complaints against the police

prosecutions of officers were hived off to the IPCC, there is the danger that, like prosecution decisions by non-police agencies in 'regulatory crimes' (discussed in chapter 6), they would come to be seen as 'different'. The best way of ensuring that prosecution decisions are taken in the way that other decisions are taken is by the application and development of ECHR case law. If this is to be effective, far more openness in relation to prosecution and adjudication decisions will be needed.

The main value of reforms such as these would lie less in establishing the 'truth' or in securing more 'successes' for complainants than in opening up investigation and police processes to public scrutiny. Such a reform programme may not succeed in making the complaints system conform to due process values, but at least the limitations of the system would become more widely recognised. Less would be claimed for the system and less expected of it. At present, it is as though the police complaints procedure does not exist for those who set it in motion—complainants—but is essentially an internal matter for the police and the PCA. For example, the detective superintendent in charge of the inquiry into the murder of PC Blakelock (which led to the wrongful conviction of the 'Tottenham Three') was put before a disciplinary tribunal by the Police Complaints Authority (PCA). The assistant commissioner of the Metropolitan Police is reported to have urged the PCA to drop proceedings 'on grounds including the damage which substantiation of the allegations would do to force morale.'[20]

The complaints procedure has been grafted onto the police disciplinary procedure and the PCA has been grafted onto that. If the current system allows a degree of latitude for police working rules by prioritising morale, efficiency and cost considerations, this is because it is not intended to punish and deter most breaches of the legal rules or to protect suspects and defendants. It is not intended to expose police procedures and practices for the public to see. One way in which this is evident is the fact that investigation of, and discipline for, malpractice overlaps with procedures for dealing with poor performance, inefficiency and so forth. These two distinct problems need to be separated. One is for the police themselves to deal with, while the other is a public matter (albeit requiring the police to co-operate).[1]

The current system facilitates crime control and neither due process nor freedom. However, the due process demand for punishment for all malpractice is not identical to a freedom approach. Our approach is restorative and preventive in aim. Complainants generally seek a restoration of respect, an apology and an assurance that the police will alter their

---

20   *The Guardian*, 12 May 1990.

1   See Home Affairs Select Committee (1998). The Police (Conduct) Regulations 1999, pursuant to Police Act 1996, ss 83, 87 (discussed in Legal Action, Dec 1999, p 8) have dealt with this problem to some extent, but the fundamental problem of the same system for two different types of problem remains.

practices and attitudes. They do not generally seek punishment except in very serious cases. The freedom approach would seek to facilitate the outcomes that most complainants most often seek, whilst not overlooking the need for a more punitive approach where that is required for full restoration.[2] This enhanced conciliation approach would be more freedom-enhancing than a due process-oriented punitive approach. It would also seek to further a preventive programme to reduce future malpractice. As well as being of general social benefit it would also benefit current complainants. For people who complain about the police are generally those who come into repeated, and repeatedly adversarial, contact with the police. This approach would also be more facilitative in the sense of educating the police to be honest about malpractice and open to ways of reducing it. As we stated earlier in this chapter, the current system deals with complaints individually, failing to see malpractice as a process. Since it is a process it can only be effectively tackled at the level of the system as a whole, eradicating the systemic causes of malpractice instead of picking out the allegedly few 'bad apples'.[3] Thus even commentators who argue against civilian investigators or PCA-style civilian review boards often argue *for* civilian oversight of police management, with particular emphasis on those aspects of management related to malpractice. Civilians, in other words, can help to pressure police management to tackle malpractice at all levels, including that of system incentives and system obstacles, and public confidence will remain low, whatever the reality, unless this is done.[4]

5. TRIAL REMEDIES: EXCLUSION OF EVIDENCE AND HALTING PROSECUTIONS[5]

One of the great dilemmas of any system of criminal justice is what to do about evidence obtained in the course of rule breaking by police and other

---

2   We thus support the current experiment by Thames Valley Police which involves introducing principles of restorative justice into its complaint procedures: C Pollard and J Keyser, 'Restorative Justice in the Thames Valley Police', keynote speech delivered at Toronto International Conference on Restorative Justice, August 2000.

3   A Goldsmith, 'Necessary but not sufficient: the role of public complaints procedures in police accountability' in Stenning (1995).

4   Bayley (1995).

5   The literature on this topic is enormous and only a brief outline is given here. For detailed discussions see, for instance: J McEwan, *Evidence and the Adversarial Process* 2nd ed (Oxford: Hart, 1998) ch 6; P Mirfield, *Silence, Confessions and Improperly Obtained Evidence* (Oxford: OUP, 1997); K Grevling, 'Fairness and the exclusion of evidence' (1997) 113 LQR 667; A Choo, 'Halting criminal prosecutions: the abuse of process doctrine re-visited' [1995] Crim LR 864, and S Sharpe, *Judicial Discretion and Criminal Investigation* (London: Sweet & Maxwell, 1998).

officials. The crime control position is that the only sensible test of evidence is its probative value—ie its reliability. If evidence is obtained wrongly, the officials responsible should be dealt with and the wronged defendant should be compensated, in proceedings designed for those purposes. The remedies and complaints procedures discussed above should therefore compensate, punish and deter. Excluding reliable evidence at trial (that is, the use of an 'exclusionary rule') - or, worse, halting the trial altogether - so that a guilty person walks free, punishes the innocent public along with the guilty police. The purpose of the criminal trial is to establish guilt or innocence, not to provide a system of 'trial remedies', so legal niceties should not obstruct the search for the truth.

The due process position is that the best way of deterring future breaches of the rules is by preventing the police from benefiting from them. Moreover, in so far as due process protections have value in themselves as ethical standards, a system which accepts evidence secured in breach of those standards is tainted. If citizens are to respect the law, the criminal justice system has to set an example. The crime control adherent argues that the ends justify the means. The due process adherent argues that the means themselves must have moral integrity, regardless of what ends are being pursued, and that trial remedies are one way of securing that.

There are a number of problems with both positions. For instance, both make assumptions about the value of all these remedies and controls without a firm factual basis for those assumptions. What discredits the criminal justice system more: ignoring apparently reliable evidence and allowing the apparently guilty to go free, or using illegally obtained evidence and, by doing so, condoning illegal police behaviour which may not be subject to any other sanction? What is the best way of controlling police illegality? Is it the threat of civil or disciplinary sanctions, given what we have said about them earlier in this chapter? Is halting the whole trial using a sledgehammer to crack a nut? Does the exclusion of illegally obtained evidence operate equally quixotically, 'punishing' police officers only when illegal behaviour occurs in cases with not enough lawfully obtained evidence to support a conviction? And how valuable are trial remedies as protections? They provide no comfort for suspects who are not tried; that is, who are not charged or who plead guilty or who may have suffered greatly through having had their home unlawfully searched, being interrogated roughly or being denied access to legal advice.[6]

Advocates of crime control and due process do share some common ground. No civilised systems would countenance the use of evidence secured through torture, no matter how reliable it might be, and if a minor rule were breached (for example, refreshments to a suspect held in cells being provided 10 minutes late) it would be difficult for the most ardent

6   Many of the arguments were canvassed by the RCCP (1981) pp 110-118.

due process advocate to argue for all evidence secured thereafter being excluded. There are no systems in democratic societies which use absolute all-embracing inclusionary or exclusionary rules. It is usually therefore said that a compromise is needed. However, the freedom perspective offers a way of avoiding the logical absurdities of either pure due process or pure crime control without resorting to an unprincipled compromise.

Since minor breaches reduce freedom insignificantly, reliable evidence obtained following them would not be excluded. The point at which a minor breach became, for this purpose, a major breach, would depend on the loss of freedom created by such breaches in comparison with the loss of freedom that occurred as a result of exclusion. In weighing up the former, the value or otherwise of the other remedies discussed in this chapter would be assessed, as would the loss of confidence people would have in the system in the event either of condoning police rule-breaking or of acquittals stemming from the rejection of reliable evidence. Weight would also have to be given to the nature of the suspects' rights that the police had infringed, since some rights (such as the right of access to a lawyer) are properly regarded as so fundamental that even relatively minor infringements of them should be seen as posing a fundamental threat to freedom. This would be so even if the general populace would prefer evidence obtained through such an infringement to be admitted at trial, since one of the purpose of a system of democratically established rights is to defend the interests of unpopular minorities against the preferences of the majority.

Historically, the common law position on exclusion was at the crime control end of the spectrum. In *Sang*[7] (where evidence was obtained by an agent provocateur) it was held that judges had no general discretion to exclude evidence simply because of the duplicitous or oppressive way in which it was obtained. However, there were various common law exceptions to this, particularly in relation to confession evidence. This has always been treated differently, because of the peculiar difficulty of reconciling police questioning which produces confessions with the right of silence. The Judges' Rules, which codified the common law, stated that 'it is a fundamental condition of the admissibility in evidence' of a confession that 'it shall have been voluntary' and not secured 'by oppression'.[8] The preamble also stated that non-conformity with the rules (for example, the requirement to caution suspects) 'may render answers and statements liable to be excluded.' Confessions obtained involuntarily, through oppression or through inducements had therefore to be excluded. Confessions obtained in breach of other of the Judges' Rules could be excluded in certain

7   [1980] AC 402.
8   See ch 5 above.

circumstances.[9] Most non-confession evidence (for example, fingerprints, blood or clothing) would not generally be excluded, however it was obtained.[10]

When PACE was drafted, the government intended largely to re-enact these common law rules. What is now s 76 provides for the exclusion of confession evidence obtained oppressively or in conditions making it likely to be unreliable.[11] And what is now s 82(3) provides that nothing '. . . in this Part of this Act shall prejudice any power of a court to exclude evidence . . . at its discretion', allowing the judges to apply the common law as it had been developing. Amendments were put forward, however, which would have introduced a powerful exclusionary rule. As a compromise, the government introduced what is now s 78, allowing judges to exclude, at their discretion, any evidence obtained 'unfairly'.[12] This criterion need not relate to reliability at all. Thus it covers most situations covered by s 82(3), but not all.[13] Section 78 also covers some situations covered by s 76, and many other situations not previously covered by the common law.[14] In addition we have to consider the common law abuse of process doctrine under which prosecutions can be halted entirely.

(a)   Principles underlying trial remedies

PACE, s 78 clearly represents a movement towards due process. The extent of that movement has depended, and will continue to depend, on the way 'unfairness' is interpreted by the judges and how they use their discretion. As in other areas of law we have examined, the judicial role is of utmost importance. This is equally true in relation to judicial interpretation of s 76

---

9   See generally Sharpe (1998) ch 2 (the common law position) and 3 (the legislative and policy background to the current law).

10   See eg *Jeffrey v Black* [1978] QB 490, in which evidence of theft, obtained after an unlawful search, was held to be admissible.

11   There is, significantly, no mention of 'voluntariness'. The Philips Commission drew on research showing that 'voluntariness' was a meaningless concept in the context of involuntary police station detention and recommended that it be abandoned: see ch 5, section 4(a)(iii).

12   For the legislative history of s 78 see Sharpe (1998) pp 109-114

13   In *Howden-Simpson* [1991] Crim LR 49, the Court of Appeal ruled that confession evidence obtained through an inducement (not interviewing choristers about the defendant's alleged dishonesty if he confessed) should have been excluded. The Court of Appeal appeared to think that s 82(3) should have been applied by the trial judge, but this is not clear from the report. The trial judge in fact took a decision under s 76 not to exclude. Section 78 might also have provided a basis for exclusion. The overlap between these provisions has contributed to a lack of clear jurisprudence on how each should be applied.

14   See D Birch, 'The PACE Hots Up: Confessions and Confusions Under the 1984 Act' [1989] Crim LR 95.

and the abuse of process doctrine. Interpretation now has to comply with the ECHR. The main relevant provision is Art 6, the right to a fair trial, but Art 6 and the jurisprudence of the ECHR is no more precise about what 'fairness' means than is PACE. We shall see that other human rights, such as to privacy (Art 8), also come into play, but not in a way that actually makes any difference to the way trial remedies are (or are not) applied. Various different principles, which are to varying degrees incompatible with each other, underlie judicial decision-making here. Sometimes they are explicitly stated in judgments, but often not, and predicting which will be prominent in any one case is impossible. These principles are:[15]

Reliability: Evidence which is unreliable will be excluded. This hardly needs stating as a matter of principle, and is enshrined (in relation to confessions) in s 76. What is, or is not, regarded as reliable is, however, not at all straightforward, and some commentators argue that court evaluations here are based implicitly on the other principles set out below.[16] A pure crime control approach would adopt this principle alone.

Disciplinary: Sometimes evidence is excluded to discipline the police if the court considered that the police behaved especially badly or oppressively. Use of this principle in relation to all rule breaking would be a hallmark of a pure due process approach.

Voluntarism: As an illustration of the due process origins of English law (in principle, although not in practice), it used to be a principle that evidence obtained through compulsion should be excluded. As we saw in chapter 5, however, this idea has long been abandoned. For example, bodily samples may in some circumstances be taken forcibly, and interrogation is imposed, not requested. The courts and legislature have attempted to put broad limits on the compulsion that can be adopted (banning violence, oppression, and so forth), but otherwise this principle is rarely referred to, and it appears to be even more rarely relied upon even implicitly.

Judicial integrity: Although there are various formulations articulated in different cases and by different writers, the essence of this principle is that evidence should be excluded if this best preserves the moral integrity of the legal system and/or public confidence in it, and included if this best fulfils that aim. This effects some kind of compromise between due process and crime control positions, but such compromises, as we suggested earlier, tend to be based on unarticulated assumptions (about, for example, what may or may not erode public confidence), lack of principle and

15 These principles are set out in Sharpe (1998) ch 2, and in Mirfield (1997) ch 2.
16 Eg Sharpe (1998).

inconsistency from case to case. Thus is integrity eroded more by a minor deviation from the rules which was motivated by dishonesty on the part of the police, or by a major deviation from the rules which was the result of honest error by the police? What relevance, if any, is the effect on the defendant of the breach? We shall see that this principle is articulated usually in relation to abuse of process.

Protective: The essence of this principle is that where a defendant has been disadvantaged by a breach of the rules, the evidence obtained should be excluded. This could be seen as a variant on the 'judicial integrity' principle, in that it preserves moral integrity by preventing the system from profiting from a breach. Where a breach does not lead to a profit for the system (for example, if a detention review is late but would have led to continued detention had it been at the right time), the evidence obtained thereafter is useable. This principle has the merit of effecting a principled compromise between due process and crime control positions, although as we shall see, in practice it has been misused by the courts.

(b)　PACE, s 76: oppression and reliability

Confession evidence cannot be presented in court unless the prosecution proves that it was not obtained:

'(a)　by oppression of the person who made it; or
(b)　in consequence of anything said or done which was likely, in the circumstances existing at the time, to render [it] unreliable …' (s 76(2)).

We saw in chapter five that 'oppression' is not defined in PACE or elsewhere. It includes 'torture, inhuman or degrading treatment, and the use or threat of violence . . .' (s 76(8)) but is not confined to such extreme circumstances.[17] In *Fulling*, it was stated, obiter, that oppression must almost necessarily 'entail some impropriety'.[18] However, not all law-breaking, such as denial of access to legal advice, is oppressive.[19] Not knowing just what behaviour will, and will not, be excluded under this

---

17　In *Davison* [1988] Crim LR 442, where the police breached many rules and detained the defendant unlawfully, the confession was held by the Crown Court judge to have been obtained by oppression. However, this appears to be a 'rogue' case, both in terms of the way the words of s 76 were interpreted (see, for example, criticism by Birch [1989]) and in terms of subsequent case law (eg *Parker* [1995] Crim LR 233). See generally, Sharpe (1998) pp 114-9.

18　[1987] QB 426. The case is more fully discussed in ch 5, section 4(a)(iii). See, similarly, *Heaton* [1993] Crim LR 593.

19　*Parker* [1995] Crim LR 233.

heading means its value as a deterrent to malpractice is limited. Circumstances 'likely' to render confession evidence 'unreliable' is similarly vague, and of similarly limited value as a deterrent. In *W*, for example, a confession made by a 13-year-old was held to be 'reliable'. Yet her 'appropriate adult' was her mother, who was psychotic at the time and therefore not capable of protecting or supporting her daughter.[20] Since anything which is excludable under s 76 is also, as we shall see, excludable under s 78, most defence lawyers argue under the latter. There is therefore little case law to clarify the scope of s 76.

Whilst this section seems to be intended to protect suspects, the focus of the courts in interpreting it has been on examining police intentions rather than the effects of their behaviour on suspects. In *Miller*,[1] a paranoid schizophrenic was questioned at length. This produced hallucinations and delusions, along with a confession. The Court of Appeal held that the fact that the defendant experienced the interrogation as oppressive did not make it so in law, for this was not the intention of the police and would not have been the result in normal circumstances. This was small comfort to Miller. The decision ignored the fact that few suspects experience custodial interrogation as normal, that the application of pressure is a natural police interrogation tactic, and that many more suspects are 'vulnerable' than are ever officially recognised as such, as we saw in chapter 5. However, the 'reliability' rule should cater for such cases, and the Court of Appeal has held on a number of occasions that confessions by vulnerable suspects with very low IQs should have been excluded on this basis.[2] Section 77 of PACE requires a special warning to be given to juries if a prosecution case relies wholly or largely on a confession by a 'mentally handicapped' person where the confession is not made in the presence of an independent party. These circumstances should not, of course, ever occur, but Parliament and the courts have had to accept that occur they do. What they do not have to accept is that confessions made in such circumstances be used against the vulnerable person in question - people like Stefan Kiszko and the defendants in the 'Cardiff Three' case discussed in chapter 5.

One problem for which there is no easy solution is what happens when there is a series of interviews which begin oppressively. Should confession evidence from the later interviews be excluded on the grounds that they are 'tainted' by the earlier oppression? The courts have adopted a case-by-case approach here: in *Glaves*,[3] interviews separated by eight days

20   [1994] Crim LR 130. See ch 4, section 2(c) for discussion of vulnerable suspects and the 'appropriate adult'.
1   [1986] 1 WLR 1191.
2   See eg *Everett* [1988] Crim LR 826; *Delaney* (1988) 88 Cr App Rep 338; and the 'Tottenham Three' case: *Re Raghip, Silcott and Braithwaite* (1991) Times, 9 December. Also see *Mackenzie* (1992) 96 Cr App Rep 98.
3   [1993] Crim LR 685.

were held to be tainted in this way, as separate interviews were in *Canale*[4] (a s 78 case). However, in *Gillard and Barrett*[5] (another s 78 case) later interviews were held not to be tainted in this way because the earlier improprieties were no longer operative.

Section 76 does not take the due process route very far. The idea of excluding evidence on the basis of 'oppression' allows the disciplinary and voluntarism principles to operate. But because 'oppression' is interpreted so narrowly, only the most gross malpractice leads to exclusion. In particular, s 76 does not take the due process route adopted for a while in the United States. The 'fruit of the poisoned tree' doctrine used in some American cases would mean that evidence obtained as a result of oppressively obtained confessions is no more admissible than the confessions themselves.[6] Section 76(4)(a), however, provides that exclusion does not affect the admissibility 'of any facts discovered as a result of the confession.' Such facts might be the hidden proceeds of a robbery, or blood-stained clothes worn by the suspect at the time of an assault and then discarded. Where suspects are likely to both confess and tell the police where to find evidence of this kind, the exclusionary rule may not deter the police from oppressive questioning.[7] Sharpe concludes, in relation to s 76, that 'where reliability is adverted to . . . it is more often than not used to support a decision which upholds crime control values . . .'[8]

(c) PACE, s 78: fairness

Section 78(1) provides that:

> '. . . the court may refuse to allow evidence . . . if it appears to the court that, having regard to all the circumstances in which the evidence was obtained, the admission of the evidence would have such an adverse effect on the fairness of the proceedings that the court ought not to admit it.'

---

4   [1990] 2 All ER 187.
5   [1991] Crim LR 280.
6   There has been a retreat from this doctrine: J Driscoll, 'Excluding Illegally Obtained Evidence in the United States' [1987] Crim LR 553 and Mirfield (1997) pp 319-339.
7   On s 76(4) see Mirfield (1997) pp 221-5. Also P Mirfield, 'Successive Confessions and the Poisonous Tree' [1996] Crim LR 554. Note that exclusion of collateral evidence can always be considered under s 78.
8   Sharpe (1998) p 132. Sharpe argues that the Court of Appeal is not always crime control oriented. See her discussion of *Delaney* (1988) 88 Cr App Rep 338 and other cases, pp 125-132.

Whereas s 76 applies to confession evidence alone, s 78 applies to all evidence, including confession evidence. Unlike in s 76, the burden of proof in s 78 is on the defence.[9] The test is one of 'fairness' and if the court is satisfied on this it must then exercise a discretion (unlike s 76 where exclusion is mandatory if the 'oppression' or 'reliability' tests are satisfied). The decision not to adopt a hard and fast rule, combined with the sheer volume of unfair police practices, has resulted in a flood of reported appellate cases on exclusion (s 78 is said to be the most cited provision of PACE).[10] As Zuckerman puts it:

'The notion of fairness . . . can refer to a multitude of aspects and merely furnishes an excuse for achieving whatever result is wanted without rigorous justification.'[11]

The changes to the right of silence in the mid-1990s stimulated this flow yet further. These appellate decisions must form only a small fraction of the cases on which judges rule in the Crown Court. We have little idea of how Crown Court judges exercise their discretion, although in a small interview study most said that they decided on the basis of 'fairness' - which, in the light of Zuckerman's comment, tells us nothing. Few, if any, of the judges interviewed articulated the principles discussed earlier. One said that if his colleagues 'were asked about these principles they would not know what you were talking about'.[12] This confirms what we would have expected, given the generally pragmatic nature of most judges - that is, anti-principle and anti-theory - and their lack of experience in criminal matters. This latter point is especially true of High Court judges, from the ranks of which virtually all appellate judges are chosen. Asked by one of the authors how he decided s 78 cases, one (who is now a Court of Appeal judge with a commercial law background) replied, 'by the seat of my pants'.

It is not surprising to find that there is little consistent pattern in the appellate decisions. No criteria are provided either for recognising 'unfairness' or on exercising the discretion. All that is clear is that a pure 'disciplinary' rule is disallowed, for a court which automatically excluded evidence obtained in breach of legal rules would not be exercising discretion properly;[13] but that something more than the 'reliability' principle must be

9   See the commentary on *Keenan* [1989] Crim LR 720.
10 Grevling (1997).
11 A Zuckerman, 'Illegally Obtained Evidence: Discretion as a Guardian of Legitimacy' [1987] CLP 55.
12 M Hunter, 'Judicial discretion: s 78 in practice' [1994] Crim LR 558 at 562.
13 As if there were any doubt, consider this rejection of the due process position by the then Lord Chief Justice: '... the object of a judge in considering the application of s 78 is not to discipline or punish police officers or custom officers ...' (*Hughes* [1994] 1 WLR 876 at 879). Similarly strong statements were made by the Court of Appeal in *Chalkley and Jeffries* [1998] 2 All ER 155, discussed in subsection (e) below and in ch 3, section 4(b)(ii).

applied, for 'unfairness' does not necessarily imply a lack of probative value. Of the other principles outlined in (a) above, 'judicial integrity' is simply an apparently more sophisticated formulation of 'fairness'. We are left, then, with the 'voluntarism' principle (which is rarely referred to) and the 'protective' principle. Where legal rules and provisions of the PACE Codes are breached, two other broad—but conflicting—principles can be discerned, which we will now briefly discuss in relation to confession evidence.

(i)   Bad faith

In *Matto v Wolverhampton Crown Court*,[14] the police pursued a speeding driver. He stopped his car on his driveway and the police asked him to take a breath test. He protested that they were on his private property. They replied that if they wrongly arrested him he could sue. He was convicted of driving with excess alcohol. It was held on appeal that the evidence of intoxication obtained as a result of the wrongful arrest should have been excluded because of the bad faith of the police. Had the wrongful arrest been an honest mistake, as in a later case,[15] the evidence would have been admissible.[16] In *Alladice*,[17] the police delayed access to legal advice under s 58. They thought that they were entitled to do this but the Court of Appeal decision in *Samuel*[18] intervened, making what they thought was lawful into an unlawful act. The confession evidence secured in the absence of a solicitor was held admissible due, in part, to what the Court of Appeal regarded as their good faith.

Section 78 does not require that there be a breach of the law or of PACE Code C. In *Brine*,[19] the defendant suffered from stress and mental illness. His confession under normal interrogation conditions was thought to be unreliable because of this. The Court of Appeal held that s 78 should be applied even though the police behaviour remained within the law. And in *Mason*,[20] the police deliberately deceived the defendant (D) and his solicitor, saying that they had found D's fingerprints on an item when in fact they had not. D confessed. It was held that the confession should have been excluded, even though the police lies were not characterised as unlawful. However, only rarely is it held that behaviour which does not breach PACE

14   [1987] RTR 337.
15   *Thomas v DPP* (1989) Times, 17 October, where the facts were otherwise similar and the evidence was not excluded.
16   See also *Quinn* [1990] Crim LR 581.
17   (1988) 87 Cr App Rep 380.
18   [1988] QB 615.
19   [1992] Crim LR 122.
20   [1987] 3 All ER 481.

should be excluded, and trickery which does not involve lying is not regarded as per se unfair.[1]

As with the case law on oppression, the court is looking at the issue of exclusion and fairness from the point of view of the police rather than the defendant. Alladice suffered no less through the police making an honest mistake than he would have done if they had acted out of malice. Good or bad faith is, in any case, difficult to ascertain. With no solicitor present, and no other independent witness, it was the officers' word against that of Alladice. It is also questionable whether good and bad faith are meaningful concepts in the context of police interrogation. After all, if suspects do not wish to speak, it is the job of the police to persuade them to do so. Like inducements, 'bad faith' is part of the game.

Most important of all, in Alladice, as in many of these cases,[2] the defendant not only disputed the offence, but also disputed making the alleged confession to it. One of the purposes of having a right to a solicitor is to have a witness to the interrogation precisely to avoid such disputes.[3] Unlawful denial of the right to a solicitor deprives suspects of the chance of calling independent evidence to corroborate their claims that they did not make the confessions attributed to them. The most powerful argument for excluding evidence in such circumstances, whatever the motives of the police, is that this is the only way of ensuring that suspects do not suffer from the wrongs done to them by the police.

(ii) Protective

This principle is attractive, for it allows evidence to be excluded where there are serious breaches of propriety but only where the defendant would be prejudiced if the evidence was admitted. It is consistent with the freedom approach. The problem is the evaluation of whether or not there would be such prejudice. In Samuel,[4] the defendant was thought to have suffered through the admission at trial of illegally obtained evidence. While similar decisions have been made in several other 'access to solicitor' cases,[5] some decisions on this point have gone the other way. In Alladice,[6] the Court of Appeal considered that, leaving aside the issue of good faith, the confession was rightly admitted. Its reasoning was that, had Alladice seen

---

1   See eg Maclean and Kosten [1993] Crim LR 687 and Bailey and Smith (1993) 97 Cr App Rep 365, both discussed in subsection (d) below.
2   For example, Samuel [1988] QB 615. See ch 5, sections 4-5, for discussion of interrogation and confession problems.
3   Dunn (1990) 91 Cr App Rep 237.
4   [1988] QB 615.
5   See eg Parris [1989] Crim LR 214.
6   (1988) 87 Cr App Rep 380.

a solicitor, the solicitor would only have told him of the rights of which he was already aware. No consideration was given to whether Alladice would have been better able to exercise his rights (particularly to silence) had his lawyer been present or, of course, to Alladice's 'right' to have a witness to what he did say to the police. As is clear from chapter five, knowing one's rights and having the resilience to exercise them when under pressure to speak are entirely different things. If the protective principle is to afford any real protection to suspects, the courts must take into account the realities of police interrogation rather than make the glib assumption that knowledge of one's rights puts one on an even par with the police.

The protective principle has formed the basis of many Court of Appeal decisions. It was reiterated in relation to access to legal advice in, for instance, *Dunford*[7] and *Oliphant*.[8] In *Dunn*,[9] it was employed following a failure to take contemporaneous notes in an 'informal interview' conducted after the tape recording of a formal interview ended. It was applied in *Quinn*[10] in relation to improperly obtained identification evidence. In *Taylor*,[11] it was utilised in relation to breach of the requirement to review the detention of a suspect in the police station at periodic intervals. And in *Aspinall* it was used for a schizophrenic man who had no lawyer or 'appropriate adult'.[12]

As a result of the CJPO 1994, courts now have to decide whether to admit evidence of interviews where defendants did not answer questions. This can be a question decided under s 78 as judges may exclude such interviews if inclusion would be 'unfair'. This might happen if, at the time of the interview, the suspect was mentally ill or otherwise particularly vulnerable (such as drunk or suffering from the symptoms of drug withdrawal). If the suspect was not able to think rationally, no reasonable inference could be drawn from a failure to speak. Although this is accepted, in principle, by the Court of Appeal as well as academic commentators,[13] it does not seem to be acted upon. In *Condron*, discussed in chapter 5, the defendants, suffering from heroin withdrawal were in precisely this position. They argued that their silence in police interviews was the result of bona fide advice from their solicitors, and that it was therefore unfair to allow the jury to draw adverse inferences from that silence. This argument was

---

7   (1990) 91 Cr App Rep 150. Discussed by A Sanders, 'Access to a Solicitor and s 78 PACE' (1990) LS Gaz 31 October p 17 and J Hodgson, 'Tipping the Scales of Justice: The Suspect's Right to Legal Advice' [1992] Crim LR 854.
8   [1992] Crim LR 40.
9   (1990) 91 Cr App Rep 237. Discussed in ch 5, section 3(c).
10   [1990] Crim LR 581.
11   [1991] Crim LR 541.
12   [1999] Crim LR 741. Discussed in ch 4, section 2(c).
13   See, for example, the discussion of *Condron* [1997] 1 WLR 827 and *Argent* [1997] 2 Cr App Rep 27 by Mirfield (1997) ch 9.

rejected on the grounds that silence was *their* choice. In other words, none of their rights were in need of protection.

(iii) Significant breach

Several s 78 cases have held that some breaches of PACE or the codes of practice are so serious that exclusion of evidence is justified regardless of what the intentions of the police or the consequences of that breach might have been. One such case was *Keenan*,[14] where contemporaneous notes were not taken. Others include *Canale*[15] and *Oransaye*,[16] in each of which the police blatantly breached the rules on, among other things, contemporaneous recording,[17] and *Weekes*,[18] where a 'conversation' was said by the Court of Appeal to be an 'interview'. The defendant was a juvenile at the time, so not only did the interview wrongly take place outside the station, but an appropriate adult should have been present.

However, the principle was diluted somewhat in *Walsh*[19] where the Court of Appeal held that it was not enough that there be a substantial breach; there must also be 'such an adverse effect that justice requires the evidence to be excluded'. This seems to be a move towards the protective element in the 'judicial integrity' principle. It suggests that the interests of the defence and prosecution must be weighed and balanced in what can only be a highly subjective exercise, which is a problem with the 'judicial integrity' principle. The result is a case like *Dunn*[20] where the failure to record the informal interview was, by any standards, a substantial breach. Despite this breach of Code of Practice C, the Court of Appeal held that the evidence was rightly admitted.[1] The court justified its stance by arguing that the safeguard that contemporaneous recording would have provided was rendered redundant because Dunn's solicitor was present to witness

---

14 [1989] 3 All ER 598.
15 [1990] 2 All ER 187.
16 [1993] Crim LR 772.
17 Doubtless the 'good faith' principle also operated in these cases.
18 [1993] Crim LR 211. Discussed in ch 5, section 3(b) above.
19 [1989] Crim LR 822. It is hard to discern consistency. In the later case of *Raphaie* [1996] Crim LR 812 a straightforward 'substantial breach' test was adopted.
20 (1990) 91 Cr App Rep 237. Discussed earlier in this chapter, and in ch 5, section 3(c) and in subsection (c)(ii) above.
1 'Contemporaneous recording' cases like this will be of continued relevance, despite tape recording requirements, for as long as alleged confessions made informally are allowed. See ch 5, section 4(e) above. *Okafor* (1994) 99 Cr App Rep 97 and *Heslop* [1996] Crim LR 730 are examples, and the Court of Appeal held in both cases that the evidence was rightly allowed.

the informal interview. On this reasoning the defence argument for exclusion under the protective principle also failed.[2]

The merit of the undiluted 'significant breach' test is that it enables judges to exercise discretion on the basis of the objective significance of the law in question. This is more certain and fairer than the other two tests which require subjective judgments and, in the case of the protective principle, a guess as to what defendants would have done had they been allowed by the police to exercise their rights. However, what is a substantial breach is itself a matter of subjective interpretation. The factors that might be considered in making such a judgment were alluded to in *Marsh*. The officers in this case did not caution the suspect as they did not regard their conversation as an 'interview'. The Court of Appeal held that this was not a substantial breach. Bingham LJ said:

> 'There has to be a reasonable common-sense approach to the matter such that police officers confronted with unexpected situations, and doing their best to be fair and to comply with the Codes, do not fall foul on some technicality of authority or construction.'[3]

This appears to dilute the substantial breach test by incorporating into it the additional test of whether the police officers acted in good faith. The danger in this approach is that the courts, lacking insight into the realities of police practices, may take too charitable a view of whether police officers in any given case were 'doing their best to be fair and to comply with the Codes.'

One of the major sources of miscarriages of justice concerns confession evidence: what was said and whether what may have been said was true. Adherence to PACE and the codes of practice would not completely eliminate disputes over these issues, but it would substantially reduce the use of 'informal' and therefore unverifiable statements and unlawful pressure. Thus in *Scott*,[4] the defendant allegedly made an incriminating remark after the end of the interview. It was not tape recorded and no note of it was taken contemporaneously. He was convicted after the judge allowed it to be used in evidence. The Court of Appeal held that this was a substantial breach and the alleged comment should have been excluded

---

2   Had the argument used in *Dunn*, that a major purpose of a legal advisor is to act as a witness, been accepted in *Alladice* and *Dunford*, the rights of, and protections for, the suspects in those cases would have been regarded as significantly violated. This would have justified exclusion of the evidence in those cases. It seems that the Court of Appeal is being selective about the purposes it attributes to government legislation, as well as the principles it uses in reviewing the application of it by trial judges.

3   [1991] Crim LR 455 at 456.

4   [1991] Crim LR 56.

because he had not been given the opportunity to deny making the comment at the time he was alleged to have made it.

The application of the significant breach principle is the most effective way of reducing miscarriages of justice, given the disadvantages of a complete exclusion rule, in the light of the unwillingness or inability of Court of Appeal to apply the protective principle in a way that is genuinely intended to protect defendants. As one of us has argued elsewhere, the systemic nature of police malpractice calls for a systemic exclusionary rule.[5] If the police are shown to have acted in bad faith, or if a suspect has been prejudiced by a failure to protect rights, then evidence should certainly be excluded. But even if neither of these things can be shown to be true, evidence must be excluded whenever there has been a significant breach of a significant right or rule. Otherwise implicit encouragement will be given to the current culture of police malpractice.

(d) Halting criminal prosecutions: the abuse of process doctrine

It has long been a principle of common law that trials could be halted by the judge if malpractice by police officers or prosecutors made the trial an 'abuse of process'.[6] It was rarely used, being reserved for the most deplorable behaviour. However, in two major cases in the 1990s, where the defendants were effectively kidnapped unlawfully by the police and security services and brought to the UK against their will, the doctrine was invoked and charges were dismissed on appeal.[7] This was despite the *reliability* of the evidence against them not being in doubt. In *Mullen* the Court of Appeal said that the unlawful deportation of the defendant was:

'a blatant and extremely serious failure to adhere to the rule of law . . . the need to discourage such conduct on the part of those who are responsible for criminal prosecutions is a matter of public policy to which . . . very considerable weight must be attached.'[8]

5   A Hunt and R Young, 'Criminal Justice and Academics: Publish and Be Ignored?' (1995) 17 Holdsworth LR 193.
6   For the background, see A Choo, 'Halting criminal prosecutions: the abuse of process doctrine re-visited' [1995] Crim LR 864.
7   *Horseferry Road Magistrates Court, ex p Bennett* [1994] AC 42; *Mullen* [1999] 2 Cr App Rep 143.
8   [1999] 2 Cr App R 143 at 157. The invocation of the 'rule of law' here follows the House of Lords' judgment in *Horseferry Road Magistrates Court, ex p Bennett* [1994] AC 42; *Mullen* [1999] 2 Cr App Rep 143. For discussion of the rule of law in this context see A Sanders and R Young, 'The Rule of Law, Due Process and Pre-Trial Criminal Justice' (1994) 47 CLP 125.

The invocation of the 'disciplinary' principle in this judgment is more apparent than real, as the Court held that judges must exercise a 'discretionary balance' (as with PACE, s 78). The 'judicial integrity' principle is being invoked here, with all the vagueness and unpredictability that entails. Thus although in these two cases it was eventually decided that the 'balance' should be exercised in the defendants' favour, in cases where - in our opinion - officials behaved equally reprehensibly, the 'balance' has been held to come down against them.[9] In other words, public policy, in the hands of the judiciary, does not always accept the need to discourage blatant and extremely serious failures to adhere to the rule of law. This raises some stark questions for you to consider. Is it right to convict citizens following trials tainted by such gross failures? Has not the verdict been deprived of all moral and condemnatory force by the illegal behaviour of the very officials charged with upholding the law?

(e)   Are there any principles underlying trial remedies?

Although many s 76 and s 78 cases concern interrogation, the discussion of abuse of process shows that there are also cases concerning other evidence obtained following some form of malpractice. Identification evidence, entry search and seizure, and evidence obtained through covert methods such as informers, bugging and entrapment all give rise to similar problems. Court of Appeal decisions on these points are, in Sharpe's view,[10] crime control-based in general, the reliability principle usually outweighing the other principles. Thus, convictions in many identification cases are quashed because breach of PACE Code D (the code governing identification evidence) often entails that identification evidence is less reliable than it would otherwise be. When that is (in the view of the courts) not so, inclusion of the evidence is generally endorsed.[11]

Restrictions on the power of the police and similar bodies (eg Customs and Excise) to search, bug, tap and engage in surveillance are generally based on the desire to protect privacy. Taped incriminating statements made under such conditions are not generally unreliable, and the argument for exclusion is usually one of fairness when privacy is unlawfully invaded. This argument is usually rejected by the courts, the reliability principle again predominating over 'judicial integrity' and 'discipline'. The protective principle is sometimes implicitly invoked, but - echoing police working rules

9   See discussion in subsection (e) below of *Latif and Shazad* [1996] 1 All ER 353.
10   Sharpe (1998) ch 5. A similar point is made by A Choo and S Nash, 'What's the matter with s 78?' [1999] Crim LR 929.
11   See eg *Penny* (1991) 94 Cr App Rep 345; *Tiplady* [1995] Crim LR 651, and *Popat (No 2)* [2000] Crim LR 54.

and the very processes of stereotyping and suspicion that lead to such people being 'targeted' in the first place - largely to protect defendants with no relevant criminal record.[12] In *Bailey and Smith* the police adopted the deceptive tactic of pretending that they did not want two robbery suspects to share a cell. Put together nonetheless, the two suspects made incriminating statements in the course of a conversation with each other. Unknown to them, the cell was bugged. They argued that the evidence should be excluded because they did not know of the bugging, the police tricked them, and this took place after charge so the evidence could not have been obtained by questioning without breaching Code C. All these arguments were rejected: 'very serious crimes have been committed - and committed by men who have not themselves shrunk from trickery and a good deal worse.'[13] Anything the villains can do, it seems, the police can do too. Even overt deception is endorsed. Thus in *Maclean and Kosten* a suspected drugs importer (K) was tricked by customs officers into believing that a drugs courier (C) had been involved in a car accident when transporting drugs. An officer masqueraded as a car salvage operator and thereby successfully trapped K in incriminating circumstances. This subterfuge was ruled by the Court of Appeal to be acceptable.[14]

The leading cases are now *Chalkley and Jeffries*[15] and *Khan*.[16] In both cases the police entered and bugged the homes of suspected criminals. Incriminating statements were thereby electronically recorded. The defendant argued that this evidence should be excluded, but this was rejected by the English courts. Choo and Nash make a lot out of the difference in the reasoning in the judgments in these two cases, for the Court of Appeal in *Chalkley* held that exclusion of non-confession evidence could only take place in certain restricted circumstances, while the House of Lords in *Khan* indicated that broader circumstances (such as breach of the ECHR) could be taken into account. However, the remarks in both cases are obiter, and in our view the difference is in the rhetoric alone. Moreover, *Chalkley's* endorsement of the reliability principle has

---

12 S Sharpe, 'Judicial Discretion and Investigative Impropriety' (1997) 1 Int J Ev and Proof 149.
13 (1993) 97 Cr App Rep 365 at 375. In similar circumstances the accused in *Roberts* [1997] Crim LR 222 had not confessed during formal questioning but then did so in his secretly bugged cell. The tactic of trickery and the question of when questioning must cease is discussed in ch 5 above, sections 4(b)(vi) and 3(e) respectively.
14 [1993] Crim LR 687.
15 [1998] 2 All ER 155. Discussed in ch 3, section 4(b)(ii).
16 [1995] 1 Cr App Rep 242. Similarly, see *Stewart* [1995] Crim LR 500, where illegal tampering with gas and electricity supplies was discovered only as a result of unlawful entry. The illegality was held not to render the evidence inadmissible.

been approved as follows: 'Here the quality of the evidence is simply unaffected by the . . . illegality and in our judgment the decision under s 78 therefore *had to go in favour of the prosecution.*'[17]

Khan took his case to the ECtHR, which subsequently agreed with him that his privacy had been violated (Art 8 ECHR), but did not agree that it automatically followed from this that the evidence should have been excluded or that the general approach of the English courts on trial remedies was wrong.[18] The crime control approach of the English courts was, in other words, endorsed by the ECtHR. As we have seen in relation to most of the topics covered in this book, the ECHR, and human rights perspective in general, does little to push criminal justice in a more due process or freedom-oriented direction.[19]

A similar approach is taken in 'sting' cases where traps for criminally-minded people are baited. The range of such traps include police officers masquerading as contract killers[20] or, more prosaically, as cab customers,[1] cars which lock on entry and cannot be driven away,[2] and second-hand shops manned by undercover officers posing as 'fences' for stolen goods.[3] The use of evidence in all these cases has been endorsed as fair. Two issues in particular can arise in cases such as these. First, there is the question of whether the defendants are induced into committing crime that they would not have thought of had the police not been involved - in other words, where the police act as *agents provocateurs*. There are fine lines between creating circumstances conducive to crime, inciting crime, and participating in crime. Despite due process rhetoric endorsing exclusion if the latter two categories apply,[4] the reality is that English courts stretch categories to allow evidence in as many dubious circumstances as possible. Thus in *Latif and Shazad* a customs officer acted as a go-between who encouraged one of the defendants to come to England and take part in the conspiracy. The argument that evidence should be excluded because of the unfairness of this was rejected by the House of Lords largely on the grounds of

---

17 *Bray* (31 July 1998, unreported), CA emphasis added. Cited by Choo and Nash [1999].

18 *Khan (Sultan) v United Kingdom* [2000] Crim LR 684.

19 Although it was in this case that the ECHR condemned the lack of independence of the English complaints investigation system (see section 4 above), it is likely that any change that there will be to that system will be more the result of political pressures.

20 *Smurthwaite and Gill* [1994] 1 All ER 898.

1 *Nottingham City Council v Amin* [2000] Crim LR 174.

2 *Williams v DPP* (1993) 98 Cr App Rep 209.

3 *Christou and Wright* [1992] 4 All ER 559.

4 See for example *obiter* remarks in *Smurthwaite and Gill* [1994] 1 All ER 898 at 903. It was not suggested that the police in *Smurthwaite, Christou,* or *Williams* were *agents provocateurs*.

Shazad's general criminality.[5] Second, in some of these cases, such as *Christou*[6] and *Maclean and Kosten*,[7] there were arguably breaches of PACE Code C, as the suspects were 'interviewed' without being cautioned. The view of the Court of Appeal is that cautioning would blow the officers' cover, and so it is not required. When crime control concerns come into conflict with judicial integrity the latter, it seems, is expendable.

What about when evidence whose reliability is not in doubt is obtained unlawfully? In *Cooke*[8] the defendant was 'persuaded' by several officers in riot gear to allow a hair to be taken for DNA analysis, and this was the basis of his conviction. As one would expect from the majority of s 78 decisions, the Court of Appeal held that, whether or not the police behaved unlawfully, any taint of unfairness affecting the evidence did not outweigh its probative value. An exception to this general trend can be seen in *Nathaniel*.[9] The defendant had been suspected of two rapes and so was asked for a blood sample for DNA testing. The law provided for the destruction of the sample in the event of him not being convicted of those rapes, and he had been promised this when the sample was requested. In fact the sample was not destroyed. It was later matched with an entirely different rape, and he was convicted. On appeal the conviction was quashed on the ground that the DNA evidence should have been excluded because of the breach of the law and the deception. The only difference between the two cases is that Nathaniel was deceived by the police (and not deliberately so) into giving permission for the sample to be used, whereas Cooke's 'permission' was coerced. If the police's action in taking Cooke's hair was unlawful it would have amounted to assault.[10] Is it really more acceptable to have evidence used against you which was taken from you by force rather than by request? Whereas the general judicial trend is contrary to the freedom perspective in overly embracing crime control concerns, one could argue that *Nathaniel* is contrary to the freedom perspective in embracing an overly rigid due process version of 'judicial integrity'. A rational weighing up of the gains and losses of freedom involved in the inclusion/exclusion decision in that case might have indicated that the breach of the law by the police was not in bad faith, did

5   [1996] 1 All ER 353. This crime control-oriented approach is similar to that taken in many US States but not in other Common Law jurisdictions: S Sharpe, 'Covert policing: A comparative view' (1996) 25 Anglo-Am LR 163.
6   *Christou and Wright* [1992] 4 All ER 559.
7   [1993] Crim LR 687.
8   [1995] 1 Cr App Rep 318.
9   [1995] 2 Cr App Rep 565.
10 Both cases are discussed by Mirfield (1997) pp 135-7 (*Nathaniel*) and 209-10, 213 (*Cooke*). Strangely, Mirfield does not compare the reasoning behind these two cases. Grevling (1997) p 683 does compare them but comments cryptically, while commending the decision in *Nathaniel*, that here there '. . . was an element of conscription that is absent where the sample is obtained by assault.'

not infringe a fundamental right of the suspect, and was not substantial enough to outweigh the value of convicting a rapist.

Although this chapter has done no more than scratch the surface of the problem of when trial remedies should or should not be applied in relation to 'unfair' evidence, it should be clear by now that there are a multitude of potentially relevant considerations involved. The courts take all of them into account at one time or another but not in a rational or principled manner. This is most apparent when the most crime control-oriented s 78 cases are compared with the abuse of process cases. In *Chalkley* it was said that:

> 'The determination of the fairness or otherwise of admitting evidence under s 78 is distinct from the exercise of discretion in determining whether to stay criminal proceedings as an abuse of process.'[11]

The balancing approach used in the latter was not to be used in the former. As Choo and Nash point out, this leads to the ludicrous position that in some circumstances, judges would be able to halt proceedings entirely even though they would not be able to take the less drastic action of excluding the offending evidence: 'What is at stake is surely the same fundamental question: should the prosecution be deprived of the fruits of the pre-trial police impropriety?'[12]

Unfortunately the Runciman Commission's evaluation of trial remedies was less than profound. Its complacent contribution to this much-debated topic amounted to a single sentence: 'We are satisfied generally with the way in which section 78 has worked in practice and propose no changes to it.'[13] It is impossible to understand how anyone could be satisfied with such confusion and contradiction unless an underlying rationality is perceived and accepted. There is a kind of rationality to many of these decisions, which is that if an appropriate adult and/or legal advisor is present during interrogation, exclusion rarely follows. This is on the ground that suspects have been protected.[14] Thus even when advisors or appropriate adults do their jobs badly,[15] or when breaches of Code C take place in front of them,[16] the evidence is allowed. Paradoxically, the protections which PACE and its Code provide to give some effect to due process values

11 [1998] 2 All ER 155 at 178.
12 [1999] 937. Also see, for a similar argument, G Robertson, 'Entrapment evidence: manna from heaven, or fruit of the poisoned tree?' [1994] Crim LR 805.
13 RCCJ (1993) p 58.
14 One of many examples of this is the identification case of *Ryan* [1992] Crim LR 187.
15 *W* [1994] Crim LR 130.
16 *Dunn* (1990) 91 Cr App Rep 237.

are used to justify the application of crime control values at the trial and appeal stages.

Runciman's acceptance of s 78 also sits oddly with the majority's recommendations on removing the power of the Court of Appeal to quash convictions where malpractice has occurred but the evidence against a defendant is none the less reliable.[17] If the crime control 'reliability principle' is to govern the Court of Appeal's powers to quash convictions, then why not also the trial judge's powers to exclude evidence? As Zander points out in his dissent to the Runciman Commission's report, the stance of the majority risks:

'... undermining the principle at the heart of section 78 ... the majority would in effect be encouraging the Court of Appeal to undercut a part of its moral force by saying that the issue of "unfairness" can be ignored where there is sufficient evidence to show that the defendant is actually guilty.'[18]

The inadequate and incoherent treatment of s 78 by the Runciman Commission is revealing as to that body's priorities. Whereas pages and pages of its report were devoted to numbingly tedious managerial concerns—how to process cases more cheaply and efficiently—s 78 was afforded the most cursory of nods.

Since Runciman reported, the situation has become more complicated. The changes to the right of silence introduced in the Criminal Justice and Public Order Act 1994, in particular, has caused immense problems for the courts as well as for defendants, defence lawyers and prosecutors. Speaking of s 76, for example, Sharpe comments that the 'generous interpretation' of PACE sometimes adopted by the Court of Appeal 'does not apply where the defendant is not perceived as deserving of protection'.[19] This fits with the broadly crime control approach which most commentators attribute to the Court of Appeal. Doubtless it is the adoption of this approach which Runciman found satisfactory. We can accept that there is scope for a difference of opinion here, although not when it extends to remarkably generous treatment for drink-drivers.[20] What is not forgivable is the attempt to hide the reality behind the facade of legal reasoning.

17 See ch 10 above, section 3(e).
18 RCCJ (1993) pp 234-235. One other member of the Runciman Commission supported Zander in this part of his dissent. There were 11 members of the Runciman Commission in total.
19 (1998) p 113.
20 See M Hirst, 'Excess alcohol, incorrect procedures and inadmissible evidence' (1995) 54 CLJ 600. Perhaps this reflects the courts' greater readiness to exclude evidence in less serious cases. Offence seriousness is something the freedom approach would take into account although it would not class drink-driving as trivial in the way the courts appear to.

This discussion gives rise to a final point which we shall pick up again in chapter 12. Section 78 cases increasingly concern covert operations, surveillance, bugging, the use of informers, and so forth. This reflects a shift in policing tactics from reactive to proactive policing. We have seen that the courts do not impose the same level of protections for suspects in these cases as with police interrogation. Yet many of the people involved in these cases, such as informers, are even less trustworthy than the police, and when the police are under-cover the scope for malpractice is at its height. When protection and control is most needed the courts fail to provide it.[1] At worst, major corruption and malpractice has been encouraged and now flourishes; at best, it is a crisis waiting to happen.

6.   MALPRACTICE: INDIVIDUAL FAULT OR THE SYSTEM AT WORK?

Like most sets of facts amounting to possible crimes, most statistics can be presented in two or more ways. This chapter has made a lot out of the hundreds of substantiated complaints, millions of pounds in damages and hundreds of excluded confessions that every year point to widespread police malpractice and error. And that is not including the malpractice and error that is not proven or even challenged. But another way of looking at this dismal picture is to observe that, in a country with over 100,000 police officers, who arrest one million suspects each year, a few hundred (or even a few thousand) mistakes per year are only to be expected, especially as so many are fairly trivial. Both views are plausible until one looks at the source and nature of malpractice and error. In reality, there is so much that the police can do in furtherance of their goals within the rules that there is rarely much need to breach them. In low visibility situations, police officers may none the less break the rules on a systematic basis when going 'by the book' is either inefficient or completely obstructs policing. In other words, just because malpractice and rule breaking is (relatively) rare, it does not follow that it is aberrant. Instead of malpractice being different in nature from normal policing, it may just be one end of the spectrum of normal policing; and instead of rule-breaking officers being unusually incompetent, unethical or corrupt, it may be that *most* officers break rules for *normal* policing purposes some of the time.

If it is true that rule-breaking is systemic, then it should be tackled at the level of the criminal justice system through structural reform. However, all the remedies discussed in this chapter are individualistic, that is, they

---

1   See S Sharpe, 'Covert police operations and the discretionary exclusion of evidence' [1994] Crim LR 793. For a different view, see D Birch, 'Excluding evidence from entrapment: What is a fair cop?' [1994] CLP 73.

all treat alleged wrongs and errors as individual problems arising from individual mistakes. Although legal processes usually individualise conflict, the structural nature of some problems are glaringly obvious. Thus, when the Police Complaints Authority belatedly launched an inquiry into the West Midlands Police Serious Crime Squad, this took the form of pursuing individual malpractices, rather than investigating the squad and its working practices as a whole. But the response need not be individualistic. In *Edwards*,[2] the Court of Appeal has accepted that some police officers break the law on a systematic basis and that defence lawyers should be able to discredit them by referring to their past deeds. Similarly, in *Judith Ward*,[3] the Court of Appeal responded to evidence of the systematic non-disclosure of evidence by the police, government forensic scientists, the Director of Public Prosecutions and prosecuting counsel by laying down, for the first time, a systematic statement of the common law requirements on disclosure.[4] And wide-ranging inquiries into policing, its context and its consequences are possible, as Lord Scarman's inquiry into the Brixton disorders of 1981 demonstrates.[5] But the Scarman inquiry was virtually unique, and the government did not repeat the experiment until it established the Macpherson inquiry into the Stephen Lawrence affair in the late 1990s.[6]

It is one thing to point to systemic malpractice by one squad, or to finally accept that there is institutionalised racism in the police (as the Macpherson inquiry did), and another to claim that the great bulk of police malpractice is systemic (ie a natural product of the criminal justice system). There are several possible explanations for police malpractice; they are not mutually exclusive.

Firstly, there is the 'rotten apple' theory, beloved of senior police officers and politicians, whereby a few unscrupulous or incompetent officers commit all the wrongs. Such rotten officers will be detected and removed from the barrel before the great mass of law-abiding police officers become infected through contact. This ignores the evidence of widespread rule breaking uncovered by research; the 'code of silence' operated by senior as well as junior officers to cover it up; and the failure to discipline adequately most of those few officers who are found to have broken the rules. If malpractice is a result of rotten apples, they must have infected the barrel as well as its contents.

Secondly, there is the 'technical failure' theory. We all make mistakes, rules are misunderstood, training needs improvement, technology needs

---

2   [1991] 2 All ER 266.
3   [1993] 1 WLR 619. See further ch 6, section 3(c)(v).
4   The requirements laid down in this case were quickly watered down by the Criminal Procedure and Investigations Act 1996, discussed in ch 6, section 3(c)(v).
5   Scarman (1981) discussed in ch 2, section 2.
6   Macpherson (1999).

development. That there is some truth in this is undeniable. But for it to be generally true we would expect many more even-handed 'errors': as many summaries of interrogation which wrongly suggest that no incriminating statements were made as suggest the opposite; non-authorisation of detention when it is necessary, as well as authorisation when it is not; police contact with solicitors, friends or family when it was not clear that this was the wish of the suspect, as well as non-contact in these circumstances; and contact with a psychologist or social worker when a suspect might be, but probably is not, vulnerable, as well as non-contact when suspects might not be, but probably are, vulnerable. The 'errors' we detected as we have examined each stage of the criminal process in turn can scarcely be described as even-handed.

These two theories are primarily individualistic. The remedies we have discussed are directed at 'the problems' as conceived by these theories. They are individualistic remedies for individualistic problems. They seem to us to be inadequate in the light of the evidence discussed in this book. The final two theories are systemic. Irving and Dunnighan apply a systems approach to police work similar to that applied by social psychologists in other fields of work.[7] This approach assumes that humans naturally err and that the best systems are those that accept this as inevitable but which also work on the basis that this is undesirable. Prevention and correction of error should therefore be designed into the system through quality control procedures as with factories and other production systems. Irving and Dunnighan found that the CID has no systems for identifying the sources of error, that training does not direct itself to sources of error, and that there is little, if any, supervision which aims to identify error.[8]

The implications of Irving and Dunnighan's theory are that individualistic remedies will be far less effective as preventive measures than will training and supervision which focuses on error combined with a complete redesign of police structures. But they seem to assume that systemic error in legal terms is also systemic error in terms of the organisation and production of criminal justice. The evidence discussed in this book suggests that this is rarely so. Arrest without reasonable suspicion is often functional for the system, so is unnecessary detention and informal interviews. And the issue goes beyond the police. Prosecutors prosecute in breach of prosecution guidelines, judges engage in plea

---

7   B Irving and C Dunnighan, Human Factors in the Quality Control of CID Investigations (Royal Commission on Criminal Justice, Research Study no 21) (London: HMSO, 1993).

8   On the inadequacy of supervision, see also the similar conclusions of J Baldwin and T Moloney, Supervision of Police Investigation in Serious Criminal Cases (Royal Commission on Criminal Justice Research Study no 4) (London: HMSO, 1992) and M Maguire and C Norris, The Conduct and Supervision of Criminal Investigations (Royal Commission on Criminal Justice, Research Study no 5) (London: HMSO, 1992).

bargaining and defence lawyers do little by way of defence, even if these things are not always and everywhere the same. Much of this behaviour involves rule breaking but it is all grist to the crime control mill. Systemic rule breaking, on this theory, then, is a product of the lack of fit between due process rules (to the extent that they are due process in content) and crime control roles, objectives and working rules. On this theory, unlike in Irving and Dunnighan's, it is not in the interest of the organisation to discover and correct most rule breaking because rule breaking is, from its perspective, almost always functional. This could explain why there are no quality control systems, why complaints procedures 'fail' to uncover malpractice, and why court-based remedies are so inadequate. There are only two ways to eradicate malpractice: either eradicate the whole crime control environment so that roles, objectives and working rules are transformed and infused with due process values (unrealistic in the current political climate) or eradicate the due process rules so that practices are no longer *mal*practices.

However, to the extent that some malpractice is attributable to the first three theories we examined, malpractice can be reduced without such drastic change. To correct and prevent error, the fullest information is needed. To secure this, especially in a low visibility occupation like the police, the co-operation is needed of those who know what is happening. If either of the two individualistic theories (especially the 'rotten apple' theory) are valid, co-operation would be expected: information would be provided by the 'good' officers against the 'bad'. This rarely seems to happen, indicating that only a small amount of malpractice can be explained using those two theories. If most malpractice cannot be explained individualistically, information and co-operation will not generally be provided willingly. For everyone will be protected by the silence of the others, and it will be perceived as unfair to punish one person for something that is routine and condoned by senior officers. The protection of colleagues, oneself and one's organisation is a natural response if discovery of malpractice is likely to lead to adverse consequences for those 'found out' or for organisational morale. On the other hand, if information and co-operation are required only to correct and prevent error, with no disciplinary or punitive consequences, co-operation and information are much more likely to be forthcoming. As Irving and Dunnighan say:

'Where systems of discipline . . . exist against operatives, accurate data about system malfunction, human factors phenomena, etc can only be obtained by offering informants generous protection and by keeping the de-briefing procedures as far as possible inside the work group.'[9]

9   (1993) p 5.

It is for this reason that analysts such as Bayley argue against independent police complaints investigation systems.[10] In other words, systems of discipline are incompatible with systems of diagnosis and prevention. Even the brutality of the Holloway Road scandal—which could well have had a 'bad apple' element to it—was opened up only after limited immunity was offered.[11]

Irving and Dunnighan's analysis applies equally to our systemic theory of rule breaking. If it is right, it means that the only way malpractice can be tackled systematically, if at all, whilst retaining a genuine system of remedies (ie which punish and/or compensate), is by having two systems working in parallel: a management information system and a complaints and remedies investigation system, whereby no 'leakage' would be allowed from the former to the latter.[12] At present there is no 'leakage' allowed from complaints investigation to civil actions, although the discipline and criminal prosecution processes do share the same information. It seems that if we want to alter police practices systematically we not only have to accept Irving and Dunnighan's optimistic theory of malpractice, we also have to abandon the idea that complaints files be made available to civil litigants, and agree to keep separate investigations into error from investigations into possible criminal acts by officers. This might be too high a price to pay for the hope of improving police practices in general. If we abandon that goal, we could instead try to make investigation procedures work against a 'wall of silence', but this would be an enormous undertaking. Only one thing is reasonably certain: if we stick with our current messy compromise, we will satisfy few wronged individuals and change few systemic malpractices.

This might seem an unduly negative and cynical conclusion. We seem to be stuck with accepting a crime control culture, where a fairly high level of wrongful convictions are inevitable and many more suspects suffer indignity and deprivation. But scepticism about the way systems work need not be cynical. Irving and Dunnighan's work in effect applies to the police the sceptical model of analysis which sociologists have long applied to all occupations. Their aim, like ours, is to improve the police system, not to undermine it. The first step to successful reform is accurate identification

10   Bayley (1995).
11   A similar problem dogged the Sir John May inquiry into the 'Guildford Four' case. In November 1989, he said he wanted to receive factual evidence, but could not do so until the prosecution of the police officers allegedly involved in malpractice was completed. He thought this would take two or three months. It in fact took four years. See Rozenberg (1992) pp 95-97.
12   This problem arises in all occupational settings. Academics, for example, are fighting to keep the system of personal appraisal (in which an individual's weaknesses are meant to be identified, discussed and remedied) separate from the system of determining pay and promotion. If they are not kept so separate, the prospects for frank discussion during appraisal are, for obvious reasons, poor.

of the problem to be addressed. Reforms are doomed to failure if the system they are applied to is not understood in the first place. The second step is to encourage a frank debate in which the police are open about what they do, lawfully and unlawfully, and what they can deliver without rule-breaking. If what can be delivered legally is not enough, then we have to consider such options as legitimising their currently illegal practices, reducing or changing our expectations of the police, or tackling crime in some other way, as by alleviating the conditions which are associated with violence, theft and so forth.

7. CONCLUSION

In this chapter, we have examined the response of the system to error and malpractice. One response is the exclusion of evidence or halting of prosecutions obtained through, or in the course of, rule breaking. This approach has several potential rationales:

(a) to prevent the conviction of the factually innocent (the reliability rule);
(b) to compensate (the protective principle);
(c) to punish and deter malpractice (the rules on oppression and inducements, and the 'bad faith' and 'substantial breach' principles); and
(d) to maintain the moral integrity of the trial process and ensure a fair trial (the judicial integrity principle).

Due process theorists would advocate all four rationales. The system in England and Wales is driven much more by the first than the others. For the crime control theorist only the first is valid: punishment, compensation and deterrence are all laudable objectives of the system but should be pursued through other mechanisms. Those mechanisms are civil, criminal and disciplinary proceedings. Evaluation of the due process and crime control models and the current system's position between them should depend, in part, on the effectiveness of those alternative mechanisms.

Civil procedures seek mainly to compensate, although punishment and deterrence are secondary rationales. They are necessary because trial remedies cater only for those who are prosecuted and who plead not guilty. However, we saw that there are many obstacles in the path of successful civil actions, which were, after all, designed to allow propertied individuals to assert their rights against other individuals, not to remedy criminal injustice.

The complaints and discipline system, like recourse to the civil courts, is in theory open to all. One might think that this system would be geared towards punishing malpractice and deterring it in future. It too, however, was designed for something else—to discipline officers breaking the rules of the police organisation—and this is reflected in the operation of the system. Unlike the other remedies, this one is largely controlled by the police themselves. Complainants find themselves complaining to the police about the police, and initiating a process in which the police investigate the police, the police adjudicate on the police and the police decide on the punishment for the police. That this system is put to police purposes (improving efficiency and defusing and deflecting criticism) rather than being operated for the benefit of complainants is hardly surprising. The same is true, but even more so, in relation to prosecutions. In low visibility situations the police break the rules when they wish to for there is little risk of any sanctions being applied as a result. In higher visibility situations, perhaps where a middle class suspect is being interrogated with a competent solicitor present, the police usually revert to 'doing it by the book'. This may be relatively inefficient, but it avoids the risk of sanctions, and the rule-book gives plenty of scope for dragging confessions out of people. Our system of remedies is primarily enabling, legitimising and presentational in relation to police working rules. This is not to say that the police do not fear losing cases or being sued, sacked or prosecuted. But it is to say that they so rarely do lose cases and so rarely are sued, sacked or prosecuted that this fear is relatively slight.

Remedial procedures exist in order that abuse of power by officials (the police, prosecutors and trial judges) acting for, or in tandem with, the Executive may be checked and redressed. Yet it is the Executive which determines how well resourced these procedures shall be. There is a conflict of interest here. In practice, remedial procedures are starved of the necessary resources. Legal aid is being cut for civil actions, is not available for police complaints and does not get through to convicted people who might have grounds for appeal. Like the Criminal Cases Review Commission (see chapter 10), the Police Complaints Authority does not have the resources needed to assert true independence from the Executive, and the same is increasingly true of defence lawyers. The former two bodies are forced into deterring, sifting out and not acting upon the majority of cases which potentially fall within their jurisdictions, whilst the most important decision most of the latter have to make is the precise level of poor practice at which they will operate. But the problems run deeper, much deeper, than a lack of resources.

None of the remedies we have discussed provides adequate protection for some of the most central 'rights' in the criminal justice system. Rules restricting stop-search, roadblocks and unsuitable identification procedures, and rights, for instance, to a lawyer, to silence, and to be treated with respect when in police custody, are not catered for at all by civil and criminal remedies; equivocally by exclusionary rules; and only half-heartedly by appeal procedures. These rights have no effective remedies.

This should be troubling for legal theorists of various persuasions.[13] 'Realists' argue that 'real' law is the 'law in action' but there is little action available to remedy abuse of rights. Here, the law in action is the law of inaction. Positivists argue that laws are commands backed by sanctions. A right without a remedy is a command without a sanction. Thus Lawson and Rudden say that: 'English lawyers ... think of legal relations as directly or indirectly giving a specific plaintiff an action against a specific defendant.'[14] And Lawson says that '... a wrong which cannot give rise to a remedy is not properly speaking a wrong.'[15] Whichever school of jurisprudential thought one subscribes to, it seems that many police actions take place in a legal wilderness, such that they can roam at will without the restraint of the rule of law.

13   See ch 2, section 3(a), above, for related discussion of the various theoretical approaches to law.
14   F Lawson and B Rudden, *Law of Property* (Oxford: OUP, 1982) p 2.
15   F Lawson, *Remedies of English Law* (Oxford: OUP, 1980) p 2.

Conclusion

Victims, the accused and the future of criminal justice

A shop assistant who was hurt apprehending a shoplifter wrote the following in her victim impact statement (for use by the prosecution and the courts): '. . .continuously feeling sick whenever I have to go to work . . . cannot walk through shops to take children to their grandma's . . . if I walk outside at night I break out in a hot sweat.'[1]

A magistrate, answering a question about victim impact statements: 'The more information the better . . . We should be seen to be listening to victims more than we do.'[2]

A judge: 'Victim impact statements have PR value and may be favoured by victims - to the extent that they do, they should be retained.'[3]

A victim at the end of his case, having made a statement at the start: 'the police were great at first, then they left us to it. No phone calls, nothing.'[4]

Another victim: 'I think it's all a gimmick. It achieves nothing. I took the victim impact statement very seriously and I'd suffered a very serious attack but I doubt that anyone even looked at it. It clearly didn't influence anything . . . a totally useless outcome.'[5]

1   R Morgan and A. Sanders, The Uses of Victim Statements (London: Home Office, 1999) p 10.
2   Morgan and Sanders (1999) p 6.
3   Morgan and Sanders (1999) p 7.
4   C Hoyle, E Cape, R Morgan and A Sanders, Evaluation of the 'One Stop Shop' and Victim Statement Pilot Projects (London: Home Office, 1998) p 32.
5   Hoyle et al (1998) p 32.

A prosecutor: 'You don't see impact statements having much of an impact.'[6]

I. INTRODUCTION

In this book, we have tried to show that in criminal justice, as in the rest of life, you cannot have everything. Trade offs cannot be avoided. In criminal justice, one of the main trade offs is that in the course of catching and convicting more criminals, one will catch and convict more innocent people too. Another is that the system cannot always do what victims want, especially if different victims ask for different things, without prejudicing other important values, such as equality of treatment. Criminal justice rules and policies reflect the natural ambivalence most of us feel when faced with uncomfortable reality, but unwillingness to accept this lesson fully has led to many rules and policies—not only those with most due process content, but also those concerning victims—being unworkable.

This is not to say that due process-based rules, for example, are necessarily unworkable, nor that they are continually broken. The police probably stick to most of the rules most of the time. However, most of the time, the rules enable the police to do their job without difficulty. The problem arises when they get in the way. Due process rules are unworkable in the sense that, in those circumstances, the police have the incentive and the opportunity to break them with little fear of negative consequences. The same is true of procedures for taking account of victims.

The working rules of the law enforcement bureaucracies are not in harmony either with those legal rules which are due process-based or with those which seek to give effect to the interests of victims. And so we have a significant (but unquantifiable) level of rule breaking by law enforcement agencies, some of which leads to wrongful conviction, and much of which leads to unnecessary and unpleasant pre-charge detention. But many legal rules are inspired by crime control ideology, so we also have a significant (and also unquantifiable) level of wrongful conviction which is a product of the police following the legal rules, just as much unpleasant pre-charge detention is perfectly lawful. The same is true of victims - sometimes what they want is ignored, in defiance of applicable policies, and sometimes what they want is ignored in accordance with applicable policies. The criminal justice system encompasses largely crime control-oriented rules and even more profoundly crime control-oriented policies and practices.

One conclusion which flows from the analysis in this book is that the criminal justice system is not due process or freedom oriented. Several

6   Morgan and Sanders (1999) p 22.

important consequences flow from this, which we shall briefly survey in this final chapter.

2. THE PACE-BASED DETENTION REGIME

We saw in chapters 3-5 that, over the course of the 20th century, police investigation has increasingly centred on the police station. Not only have interrogation-based confessions become steadily more central to the prosecution case, but other investigative procedures take place in, begin from, or are authorised in the police station. For example, intimate and non-intimate samples are taken there, for later analysis, and suspects are held there while ID parades and searches of premises are organised. What PACE did was, in part, to *legitimise* this evolving process. It also assisted its intensification. Take the initiation of prosecutions; arrest and charge (which entails initial detention) have now almost entirely supplanted the use of report and summons (which does not) for arrestable offences. Furthermore, much police power is used to further policies and strategies such as gathering information, disciplining 'suspect populations' and so forth, whereby there is no intention of prosecuting. There is nothing new in this, nor in police station detention being used as part of these tactics, but the legitimisation of this has probably increased its scale, such that around half of all arrests are now NFAd, ie, do not result in any further action. A core crime control value is trust in the police, and trends in criminal justice show that policy makers do indeed have blind faith in these officials.

Against our argument, other commentators contend that the police are closely regulated and that the system is 'in balance'. Everything that takes place in the station is regulated by custody officers, records, time limits, tape-recordings (in the case of interrogations), special safeguards where suspects are vulnerable (such as appropriate adults, doctors and so forth) and access to free legal advice for all. There are guarantees of proper treatment and freedom from coercion and violence. Questioning used to take place outside the station where suspects were 'verballed' and sometimes assaulted and intimidated.[7] Also the CPS holds out the promise of some protection for defendants' rights. It must decide whether or not to continue prosecutions, and it decides not to do so in a significant minority of cases. Although we saw that none of these protections work perfectly, and that legal advice, for example, is secured by only around one third of suspects, the 'balanced' response of our critics is that these protections do operate satisfactorily most of the time. Most suspects who do not secure legal advice, for example, choose not to seek it and come to no harm as a result of not securing it.

7   See, for example, D Dixon, *Law in Policing* (Oxford: Clarendon, 1997).

There is some truth in this. It is better to have these protections than not, and it is better that police power is exercised in the station, where it is regulated, than outside, where it is not. But all that proves is that it is possible to envisage an even more crime control oriented system than the PACE-based one. As for the CPS acting as a safeguard, if the objective is to protect suspects and defendants would it not be better to put more resources into funding defence lawyers, into strengthening the defence side of the adversarial system? Further, we saw in chapters 2 and 5, in particular, that PACE's detention-based system does not operate exclusively in the police station. PACE has led to a vast increase in stop-search (including questioning) outside the station, and 'informal interviewing' (both inside and outside the station) is rife. Even when it is unlawful its products are often useable, and used, at trial. And we know from chapters 7-9 that trials are rare anyway, for a host of reasons that have only a tenuous link with factual guilt and innocence. Further, the main reason why so many people refuse legal advice and confess or make incriminating statements is that they experience the police station as coercive, frightening and humiliating. Suspects make coerced choices without the police having to be overtly threatening or hostile. There are no remedies available to suspects who suffer from many of these rules being broken, and the remedies that are available are without exception deeply flawed. Not only is this a crime control-based system, it is one which subjects the police to the rule of law (and human rights standards) only in a minimalist and largely rhetorical manner.[8]

It is possible to envisage a different kind of system altogether, based on our freedom perspective. Without compulsory detention for all suspected offences except the most serious, the police would have to investigate more thoroughly before arrest. This would be less intrusive and therefore less eroding of freedom. Interviews could be conducted at home, work or anywhere suspects felt most comfortable. Most suspects would be happy to wait for a legal advisor or supporter to arrive in those circumstances. The police could be obliged to disclose their case to suspects and their advisors so that they knew what allegations they were answering and so that advisors did not have to barter their clients' rights. Of course this system would lead to fewer confessions, fewer convictions and, on the face of it, greater expenditure of police resources (although the improvement in police-community relations it could lead to would increase public co-operation which should counter-balance, to an unknown extent, what the police lose in effectiveness). It is true that there would be fewer convictions of the guilty. But there would also be fewer convictions of the

8   We make this argument at length in A Sanders and R Young, 'The Rule of Law, Due Process and Pre-Trial Criminal Justice' (1994) 47 Current Legal Problems 125.

innocent, as well as less coercion of all suspects, whether guilty or not. Also, the latitude currently given to the police allows discretion to be exercised in unfairly discriminatory ways in terms of ethnic group, socio-economic group, age and gender. Our ideal system may not be the value-choice of all, or even of many, but it is the value choice which prioritises due process and, more important, freedom. The current system does not and cannot. To pretend otherwise is to delude ourselves.

3. TOWARDS PROACTIVE POLICING?

We should recognise that, in the years since PACE was enacted in 1984, the proportion of suspects who secure legal advice has gone up markedly. This undoubtedly has given suspects more protection than if they were left to the meat-tendering mercies of the police with no support at all. Further, the quality of that advice has improved, and in particular, by the early-1990s, more lawyers were sufficiently confident to intervene when questioning became rough. This, combined with the courts' intolerance of oppressive questioning tactics, probably reduced the effectiveness of police questioning. We saw in chapter 5 that the proportion of suspects remaining silent increased in the early 1990s. To this extent, some of the controls on the police were working and the wilder excesses of crime control practices were curbed.

It is no coincidence that in the early-1990s the police were being increasingly urged to move away from 'reactive' policing. This pressure was fuelled by research findings. A study in the early 1990s found that in nearly half of the detected cases in a typical police area, police questioning was cited by officers as the 'key factor' in detection. Being caught in the act or identified by the victim or other civilian accounted for most of the rest. In less than 10% of cases were methods such as surveillance and crime intelligence cited.[9] As we saw in the first part of chapter 2, the police were encouraged to develop 'proactive policing' techniques, including the use of informers, undercover police operations, targeting and surveillance. In other words, the police were being exhorted to return to the old ways, seemingly more consistent with the freedom model, of investigating first, then arresting. These investigative methods rely far less on questioning than does the practice of 'rounding up the usual suspects'. Alternative forms of evidence, often gathered by specialist squads, include:
- systematic records of targeted suspects' movements;
- financial dealings and associations with other suspects;

9   M Maguire and T John, Intelligence, Surveillance and Informants (Police Research Group Paper No 64) (London: Home Office, 1995) Table 3.

- information from informants about the location of stolen property or 'tools of the trade';
- information from informants about planned offences;
- police observation or 'bugging' of criminal planning or actual offences (including 'stings');
- information from undercover officers.[10]

We saw in chapter 11 that applications to exclude evidence shifted gradually throughout the 1990s from malpractice regarding interrogation to malpractice regarding bugging and 'agents provocateurs'. Covert policing is more extensive than has generally been realised. In 1998, for example, it emerged that 50,000 informers were officially registered with the police,[11] leaving aside an unknown number of occasional and 'unofficial' informers. Supervision of informers and the use of other covert methods is minimal, creating enormous scope for corruption, fabrication of evidence and other malpractice.[12] But as with interrogation, the problem with proactive policing lies not just in the scope for malpractice, which is vast, but with what the rules allow the police to do.

One problem is that some types of proactive policing lead to mass arrests (on the basis of prior information, surveillance and so forth), such as 'Operation Bumblebee' in London, which targeted burglary and car crime. Inevitably, a mass arrest operation does not follow the 'reasonable suspicion' rules discussed in chapter 3, and many innocent people get caught up in the net.[13]

We saw in chapters 4-6 that effective defence against criminal charges requires full disclosure of the evidence on which the prosecution case is based. Covert police investigation creates a problem here. If, for example, the identities of informers and undercover officers become known, their lives could sometimes be endangered. Further, as we saw in chapter 11, many PACE protections - such as issuing a caution to a suspect - are impractical in these situations. Sometimes the methods do not need to be exposed if, for example, they led to offenders being caught red-handed. But at other times only by revelation of names, methods and sources - which may be out of the question - is it possible to be fair to both the prosecution and defence case.[14] Information derived from 'bugging' and

---

10   This list is derived from Maguire and John (1995).
11   *The Guardian*, 12 October 1998.
12   C Dunnighan and C Norris, The role of the informer in the criminal justice system (unpublished report, 1995).
13   See, for example, 'Operation Major', discussed in ch 3, section 4(d). 'Operation Bumblebee' and similar operations are discussed in the Introduction to S Field and C Pelser (eds), *Invading the Private: State Accountability and New Investigative Methods in Europe* (Aldershot: Dartmouth, 1998).
14   E Cape and T Spronken, 'Proactive policing: limiting the role of the defence lawyer', in Field and Pelser (1998).

telephone tapping is another example of information the defence may need to scrutinise (for example, to check that what is claimed the 'bugs' reveal really do so), but defendants often do not know that they have been bugged. It may be that a more active pre-trial role for judges could alleviate these difficulties, but that would be difficult to graft onto the relatively passive role of judges in adversary systems such as ours.[15] As it is, the courts have to operate a policy when, for example, the prosecution request that a name is withheld, of 'balancing' the interests of prosecution and defence - ie being unfair to one or the other.[16]

One common line of argument deployed by defence lawyers is that an undercover officer or informer crossed the line to become an *agent provocateur*. If so, evidence obtained as a result, and arguably the whole case, should be dropped since, the defence could argue, the crime would not have occurred had they not incited it. As we saw in chapter 11, this argument is not successful with courts if the defendant had a 'previous disposition' to the type of crime involved, if the informant or officer played only a minor part, the 'sting' was not an attempt to by-pass PACE protections, and if the evidence is reliable. Due process protections are thus eroded in favour of crime control. However, because here, as so often in police work, the police control information making up 'the case' the CPS, defence and courts may never know *what* the involvement of the informer or undercover officer was. The fact that there was such involvement (or bugging or tapping and so forth) can be concealed.[17]

This is only one of many problems of ensuring accountability and lack of corruption when dealing with necessarily 'hidden' activities such as the handling of informants. Another problem is that many informants act in their self-interest: for financial gain or to get charges dropped or bail granted, to take a few examples. The desire to say what they think the police want to hear must be very powerful.[18] Thus when, in the mid-1990s, the police began to pay informers for 'results' (£70 per arrest) arrests rose. This led, police claim, to a drop in burglary.[19] But at what cost? Sometimes the police have to turn a blind eye to an informant's criminal activities -

---

15 S Field and N Jorg, 'Judicial regulation of covert and proactive policing in the Netherlands and England and Wales' in Field and Pelser (1998).

16 Guidelines, emphasising that identity is to be withheld only in rare and exceptional circumstances, are set out in *Taylor* [1995] Crim LR 253. Nonetheless, anonymity could still violate Art 6 of the European Convention on Human Rights (right to a fair trial). See the discussion in ch 7, section 5(b) of recent European Court of Human Rights (ECtHR) decisions on the disclosure of sensitive information.

17 C Dunnighan and C Norris, 'The nark's game' (1996) 146 NLJ 456.

18 For a general discussion see S Greer, 'Towards a sociological model of the police informant' (1995) 46 BJ Sociology 509.

19 *The Guardian*, 5 September 1996.

allowing a hopefully minor crime to occur in the hope of preventing or detecting a more serious crime.[20]

Finally there is the question of controls over proactive policing. These are inevitably inadequate because the idea of public accountability is completely incompatible with covert operations. For example, informants should be officially registered and their use monitored, but this is done by the police themselves and the rules are frequently breached. Regarding the entry and bugging of private premises, authorisation is supposed to be given only by very senior police officers or, in some cases, a specially appointed Commissioner (a public official). But this does not apply in cases of 'urgency', senior officers and Commissioners are not genuinely independent, the information on which their decisions are based is provided by the officers seeking permission, the rules are frequently breached, and evidence is not necessarily excluded even if breaches become known. Further, complaints from aggrieved citizens in relation to many bugs and taps have to be made to a Commissioner (the official who authorises them in the first place), not to a court or tribunal.[1] As John and Maguire conclude, 'while the use of surveillance has expanded enormously in both degree and diversity, mechanisms for its regulation have remained weak, unco-ordinated and unable to keep up with the pace of change.'[2] There has been what Marx calls, in the similar US context, 'surveillance creep'.[3] One might have thought that the right to privacy in the European Convention on Human Rights (ECHR) (Art 8) would provide some protection, but this is unlikely in the light of *Lüdi v Switzerland*. Here it was held by the ECtHR that a person who used his home to plan major drugs offences had no 'reasonable expectation of privacy' and hence could not object to being bugged.[4]

The move to proactive policing is a response to the (limited) obstruction to police crime control policies which the legal advice provisions of PACE belatedly created. This shows the resourcefulness of the government and its agencies to achieve the same goals as before but to find new ways of doing so when legal rules get in the way. The use of these novel methods,

20 M Colvin, Under surveillance - covert policing and human rights standards, (London: JUSTICE, 1998) ch 2.

1 Colvin (1998). As Colvin shows, the applicable legislation (mainly the Police Act 1997) has many gaps, such as when people are 'wired'.

2 T John and M Maguire (1998) 'Police surveillance and its regulation in England and Wales' in Field and Pelser (1998) p 61. Also see the concluding chapter to Field and Pelser (1998) by Field.

3 G Marx, *Undercover: Police surveillance in America* (Berkeley: U of Calif Press, 1988).

4 15 June 1992 Series A Vol 238. A similar sentiment was expressed in *Khan* [1996] 3 All ER 289, discussed in ch 11, sections 4(e) and 5(e). See generally, S Uglow, 'Covert surveillance and the European Convention on Human Rights' [1999] Crim LR 287.

in many respects, makes the police even less subject to the rule of law than when they rely on interrogation-based strategies. However, proactive policing can only supplement, not supplant, reactive policing. It does not successfully 'bolt-on' to police forces organised in a reactive fashion, yet to organise a police force solely around 'targeted' crime and not to react to serious 'non-targeted' offending is unthinkable. Although a survey found that most forces claim to achieve a 'balance' between the two approaches,[5] police forces have difficulty in handling both approaches without marginalising one or the other.[6]

Serious crimes will always be committed without the police's prior knowledge, thus calling for an investigative reaction. The police have to have some powers if there is to be a reasonable conviction rate without unreasonable expenditure of resources. Thus, at the same time as proactive policing was developing in order to counteract the effect of PACE on police 'success' rates, the government was planning a further move to achieve the same objective but in a different way. This was the virtual abolition of the right of silence achieved by the Criminal Justice and Public Order Act 1994 (CJPO), discussed in chapter 5. The result, by the late-1990s, was plain to see. The police no longer have to intimidate to secure confessions, because silence is equally incriminating. All the police have to do is to ask the right questions. The rate at which suspects remain silent has fallen back to the level, as far as can be determined, of the mid-late 1980s. Legal advice is largely sidelined. In other words, the main plank holding up the 'PACE is nicely balanced' school has been removed. From the suspect's point of view, PACE is now icily unbalanced.

4. TAKING VICTIMS' RIGHTS SERIOUSLY

This chapter has been concerned so far with the erosion of the freedom of suspects and defendants. We should be equally concerned with the freedom of victims. It is justifiable to reduce freedom for suspects if this leads to more freedom for victims, to the extent of a net gain in freedom.[7] It is not possible to be sure about whether this has happened, but it seems unlikely. As we saw in chapter 1, section 11, victims and offenders are not distinct groups. There is considerable overlap between them. Further, what victims want most is not increased punishment or even detection, but some

---

5   J Stockdale, C Whitehead, P Gresham, Applying economic evaluation to policing activity (Police Research Series Paper No 103) (London: Home Office, 1999).
6   Maguire and John (1995); A Barton and R Evans, Proactive Policing on Merseyside (Police Research Series Paper No 105) (London: Home Office, 1999).
7   Whilst this sounds like a form of utilitarianism we show in ch 1, section 11, that this perspective can accommodate giving special weight to human rights, fundamental democratic values, and legal principles such as the rule of law.

confidence that it will not happen again.[8] The kind of detection, prosecution and conviction methods detailed in this book create resentment and marginalisation on the part of suspects, offenders, their families and their communities. One result is stigmatisation and the enhancement of anti-authority attitudes which de-integrate rather than re-integrate, and which leads to more crime, not less. The re-conviction rate is very high. In other words, taking freedom away from suspects and offenders in order to increase conviction rates does little to increase the freedom of victims. It is true that restorative processes, which are less coercive and aim to reintegrate, are important features of some late 1990s legislation. But they currently only nibble away at the edges of conventional justice processes, and their effect on re-conviction rates is likely to be small.[9]

It could be argued that crime control methods do at least lead to relatively high arrest and prosecution rates, without which people would commit even more offences. Indeed one of the (unlawful) reasons for mass stop-search is precisely to intimidate suspect populations and deter them from offending. But this argument also ignores the research outlined in chapter 2 showing that members of the public (especially victims) are the main sources of information about the identity of offenders. In other words, crime control methods lead to only a few extra arrests at the margin, and only a few extra prosecutions of those who would anyway be arrested. What are the most upsetting offences that occur frequently? There are sex offences, which have particular detection and conviction difficulties which no amount of police powers will ever be able to do much about (see section 3(b) below); street robberies, where victims can often give descriptions and where the detection rate is reasonably high; and burglaries, where offenders are rarely seen in the act, and which usually remain undetected. Changes to police powers make very little difference to the detection and conviction rates of any of these offences.

It could also be argued that even if crime control methods do not reduce crime, at least that is one of their objectives. Another, related, objective is to ease the fears and assuage the anger of victims. Even though reducing police powers may not reduce detection rates much, it may be thought that this would upset victims. Again, however, this wrongly assumes that victims and offenders are different people. Time after time, newspaper stories report victims of wrongful arrest, for example, who say that they

8   On victims of domestic violence, for example, see C Hoyle and A Sanders, 'Domestic violence: From victim choice to victim empowerment' (2000) 40 BJ Crim 14.

9   See ch 6, section 4(a)(iv) on restorative cautioning and forms of reparative sentencing (Crime and Disorder Act 1998) and ch 7, section 3(a) on the restorative sentencing of youth offenders (Youth Justice and Criminal Evidence Act (YJCE) 1999).

had not been in trouble before and had always respected the police, but do so no longer.

What about the more general argument that crime control systems have the interests of victims at heart? We cast doubt on this in chapter 1, because in an adversarial system the two parties are the state and the suspect/ defendant. The interests of the state and those of victims do not always coincide. Take plea bargaining. This is a key feature of the crime control model and, as we saw in chapter 7, of the Anglo-American system in practice. It has become even more entrenched in recent years as a result of the sentence discount requirements of the CJPO 1994 and the Narey reforms to the magistrates courts discussed in chapter 8. These developments are driven by the desire to conserve resources and to secure convictions in what might be weak cases. It is true that plea bargaining is in the interests of some victims, who are saved from giving evidence and to whom this guarantees at least some kind of 'result'. But few victims see it this way. In some of the most distressing and dangerous offences of all, that is, domestic violence and sexual offences, plea bargaining is both most rife and most upsetting to victims. We should also remember that some weak (and indeed some strong) cases are mounted against innocent people. Just as due process-oriented systems do not help victims when guilty people are acquitted, equally, crime control-oriented systems do not help victims when innocent people are convicted.[10] Pressure to plea bargain reduces the capacity of innocent (as well as guilty) people to contest guilt.

Victims have no right to be involved in, or even consulted about, plea bargaining. For victims have no rights over 'their' cases, which are technically not theirs at all. As we saw in chapter 6, victims have a right to privately prosecute 'normal', but not most 'corporate', offences. But this right is largely theoretical because of the cost involved, and even then the CPS is entitled to take the case over and then plea bargain or drop it. The powers of police and prosecution are therefore available to be used both for and against both suspects/defendants and victims - or without a care for either group. In recent years, however, the 'victim movement' has become politically influential. The political parties now compete with each other for the mythical 'victims' vote', and heed must also be paid to various international obligations.[11] The idea of 'victims' rights' has taken centre stage after years of skulking in the wings. Some of the most important

10 In September 2000 Stuart Gair was released from prison on bail, pending a hearing of his appeal, by a Scottish court after serving 12 years for murder. This indicated that the court expects his appeal to be successful. Even the victim's sister is convinced that he is innocent. She said, 'I am glad to see Stuart go free, but I am angry justice has not been done for my brother. Hopefully the truth will come out. The trial was a farce.' *The Guardian*, 30 September 2000.

11 United Nations, Declaration on Basic Principles of Justice for Victims of Crime and Abuse of Power (UN, 1985) and Council of Europe, The Position of the

Chapter 12 The future of criminal justice

changes in the criminal justice system in the first decade of the new millennium will concern victims, and it is to these new developments that we now briefly turn.

(a) The Victims' Charter

Ashworth distinguishes between two types of 'right' for victims.[12] First there are 'service' rights - that is, rights to be treated with dignity and respect - which, in principle, everyone agrees with, although in practice are not easy to deliver. Second, there are 'procedural' rights - that is, rights to have some involvement in the criminal justice process - which are far more controversial. For many years victims were ignored and 'invisible' as they had neither type of 'right'. These are not rights in any real sense, because they are not enforceable. Like many rights of suspects, there is no remedy for people who are deprived of these entitlements.[13] In the case of C, prosecutions were initiated after a teenager was allegedly sexually assaulted by a group of young people. All charges were later dropped, but C only discovered this when she bumped into one of the accused near her home (his bail conditions had originally kept him away from the area). She challenged the failure of the police and CPS to inform her of their decisions. The court criticised those agencies but said that there was no remedy available to C.[14]

(i) Service rights

Service rights include victims being given appropriate facilities in court[15] and being given information about their cases by agencies such as police and CPS. Because victims have no standing, they have traditionally had no right to know what was happening in 'their' cases. Some victims, such as 'C', discussed above, suddenly find themselves bumping into the alleged

Victim in the Framework of Criminal Law and Procedure (Council of Europe, 1985) both discussed in A Sanders, Taking Account of Victims in the Criminal Justice System (Edinburgh: Scottish Office, 1999).

12 A Ashworth, 'Victim impact statements and sentencing' [1993] Crim LR 498.
13 The lack of remedies for many 'rights' is discussed in ch 11. See also H Fenwick, 'Rights of victims in the criminal justice system' [1995] Crim LR 843.
14 *The Guardian*, 9 March 2000.
15 Improvements have been made in recent years but there is still some way to go: J Shapland and E Bell, 'Victims in the Magistrates' Courts and Crown Court' [1998] Crim LR 537; J Plotnikoff and R Woolfson, Witness Care in Magistrates' Courts and the Youth Court (Home Office Research Findings no 68) (London: Home Office, 1998).

offender because the latter is let out on bail, has the case dropped or is given a non-custodial sentence. The shock caused by being kept in the dark can exacerbate the encounter itself.

The Victims' Charter, first introduced in 1990, and revised in 1996, told victims that they are entitled to 'proper' services. In the mid-1990s the government established some experiments whereby, in selected police areas, victims where someone had been charged would be asked whether they wanted information about 'their' cases. If they did, they would be told about: the first hearing; the plea and directions hearing (if applicable); trial (if there was one); verdict, and sentence. The information would all be provided from victim liaison units within police forces so that a victim had only one point of contact (a 'One Stop Shop' or OSS) regarding information about the stages of the process covered by this service. About two thirds of victims did seek this information, but many were disappointed.

Many victims did not get all the information they wanted (for example, about bail), and many wanted to know not just *what* happened, but *why*. This information was usually not forthcoming, partly because it is often only the decision-maker who can provide it - which is rarely practical without using considerable resources. If a decision is unpalatable, the more that one is told, the more one wants to discuss and challenge it. Again, this is rarely practical except at a high financial cost, but it leaves victims feeling as frustrated and 'forgotten' as ever. In other words, giving victims a 'right to know' raises expectations which, in many cases, are dashed.[16] Nonetheless, in serious cases in particular, keeping information from victims cannot be justified from a freedom perspective, as this is a form of 'secondary victimisation' which erodes freedom.[17] A classic case was that of the Stephen Lawrence family who were denied information, given misinformation, and then unhelpful information about the investigation into the murder of their son.[18] Ironically, the police decisions which people want to know about in cases like that of Stephen Lawrence are not covered by OSS, which only begins providing information if someone is charged.

The Macpherson report recommended that the CPS communicate directly with victims in serious cases like this (that is, not using an OSS-style system). Similarly, it was held in *DPP, ex p Manning*[19] that when the DPP decided not to prosecute following deaths in custody, detailed reasons should be given to the family. In 1999 the CPS announced that it would

---

16　Hoyle et al (1998). Summarised by the same authors in Home Office Research Findings No 108 (London: Home Office, 1999).

17　On 'secondary victimisation' see S Walklate, *Victimology: The Victim and the Criminal Justice Process* (London: Unwin Hyam, 1989). Also see L Sebba, *Third parties: victims and the criminal justice system* (Columbus: Ohio State UP, 1996).

18　Sir William Macpherson of Cluny, The Stephen Lawrence Inquiry (Cm 4262-I) (London: SO, 1999).

19　[2000] 3 WLR 463.

Taking victims' rights seriously

experiment with the best procedures for doing this, but early in 2000 the experiment was put on indefinite hold because of lack of resources. More and more money is pumped into the police and prisons, largely in the name of victims. If this were the real motivation, would not some of this money be diverted into giving these victims' rights some real substance, to make an OSS-style system work properly and to enable decision-makers in serious cases to communicate directly with victims and their families? Not if the system is crime control based, for victims' rights are not central to that model.

(ii) Procedural rights

These are rights to be *involved* in one's case. As with OSS, the freedom perspective is concerned to reduce secondary victimisation. So if being involved achieves this, without any loss of freedom to suspects or defendants, it is to be encouraged. Different legal systems provide a variety of ways of being involved - by providing information to the prosecutor or court through a 'victim impact statement' (VIS) as in some common law systems; by being a secondary party of some kind to the case as in many civil law systems;[20] or by being fully involved as in restorative processes.[1] This chapter will be concerned only with 'mainstream' Anglo-American criminal justice where, traditionally, victims have not been involved at all, leading to their 'invisibility' mentioned earlier.

Involvement can, in principle, take various forms - an opportunity to discuss, to be consulted, or to actually participate in decision-making. We shall see that the problem with the VIS initiative is that it is a *statement* scheme that has been grafted on to the existing adversarial framework. It does not, therefore, facilitate discussion. Whatever type of involvement is provided, it can take place at one or more of five stages of the criminal process: the decision to prosecute, bail/remand decisions, decisions to reduce or drop charges, sentencing, and early release from prison.

In the USA, where the victims' movement took off earlier than in the UK, involvement began to take the form of making a VIS to police or probation officers, who relayed the information provided by the victim to the court and/or the prosecutor. The 1996 Victims' Charter included a requirement that the police and CPS take the interests of victims 'into account', and announced experimental VIS schemes. These took place in

---

20 See M Joutsen, 'Victim participation in proceedings and sentencing in Europe' (1994) 3 Int Rev Victimology 57; Sanders (1999).

1 For a proselytising discussion (from a Chief Constable), see C Pollard, 'Victims and the criminal justice system' [2000] Crim LR 5. For a more measured evaluation see R Young and B Goold, 'Restorative Police Cautioning in Aylesbury' [1999] Crim LR 126.

the same areas as the OSS 'right to know' schemes. Again, victims were asked, following charge, if they wanted to participate by making a statement. The VIS supplements the original witness statement with another written statement detailing the medical, psychological, financial and emotional harm caused by the crime. Unlike in some American states,[2] only facts are sought, not opinions about what victims think should happen to the offender.[3] This is, in other words, not a consultative process. Victims' interests are to be taken into account but not, it seems, their views about what is in their interests.

Victims are invited to make a VIS only after someone has been charged with the offence despite the fact that charge decision-making is the stage in which the victim has most legitimate interest. Compensation is most easily secured, for example, as a result of an order by a sentencing court. If no charge is made, the case will never get to court and the victim will lose out. The fact that a VIS is not asked for at the point of considering charge might be thought not to matter because under the police cautioning guidelines, victims are *supposed* to be consulted about prosecution decisions. As we saw in chapter 6, this guidance is sometimes abused and manipulated by the police. From the point of view of principle, however, it is paradoxical that victims are meant (under the cautioning guidelines) to be *consulted* about their views on prosecution, yet are only asked (under the VIS scheme) for *information* at other stages.

In the evaluation of the Victims' Charter VIS scheme by Hoyle et al, one third of victims opted to make an impact statement. As with OSS, a large minority who did so were disappointed. Many who said, at the start of their case, that they were pleased that they made a VIS, said at the end that they no longer felt this way. Like OSS, VIS raised expectations and then dashed them.[4] But Erez claims on the basis of her research that VIS is good for victims, because it 'empowers' them by making them visible to criminal justice officials who can thus no longer ignore their interests.[5] She argues that this has two beneficial consequences. First, she claims that making the VIS is cathartic. Her findings and those of Hoyle et al are reconcilable in that for some victims they are cathartic at first, but not by the end of the

2   For an example of the way this works even in capital punishment cases where juries, who in some states decide whether to order the death penalty, can be influenced by emotive appeals from victims' families, see L Sebba, 'Sentencing and the victim: the aftermath of *Payne*' (1994) 3 Int Rev Victimology 141. For a general survey of the use of VIS in the USA, see E Erez, 'Victim participation in sentencing: and the debate goes on' (1994) 3 Int Rev Victimology 17.

3   *Perks* [2000] Crim LR 606.

4   Hoyle et al (1998).

5   E Erez, 'Who's Afraid of the Big Bad Victim? Victim Impact Statements as Victim Empowerment *and* Enhancement of Justice' [1999] Crim LR 545. Also see E Erez and L Rogers, 'The Effects of Victim Impact Statements on Criminal Justice Outcomes' (1999) 39 BJ Crim 216.

case. As one victim put it: 'It was worthwhile at the time because it made me feel better but it was obviously ignored so it was a waste of time.'[6] For others they are not cathartic at all. Whether, on balance, they produce a net cathartic benefit is hard to say. The important question, though, is to discover why they do not work for many victims so that a better scheme can be devised.

The second beneficial consequence claimed by Erez is that VIS can influence decisions.[7] She is here referring to sentencing only. In a further evaluation, Morgan and Sanders found that VIS, in the Victims' Charter schemes at any rate, had virtually no effect on sentencing or on any of the pre-trial stages.[8] Again, there is little contradiction here, as Erez concedes that most research, including her own, found the effect to be slight. This partly explains why VIS is so unsatisfactory for so many victims. They expect VIS to make a difference, and when it does not they are disappointed. Again, expectations are raised and then dashed. Victims remain ignored even if not forgotten. Morgan and Sanders found that few prosecutors, judges or magistrates were willing to take any notice of VISs even though they almost universally subscribed to the rhetoric of victims' rights. And in the USA it was found that in one area a large number of impact statements were neither read nor, if read, put in the prosecution file.[9] Being treated like this hardly restores the self-respect of victims or reduces their secondary victimisation. The victims' movement complaint was that victims are used by the system: their witness statements were taken and then they were ignored. And now under the VIS scheme? Two statements are taken (witness and impact), and then they are both ignored. Hardly a revolutionary change. As Erez herself complains, the limited use of VIS represents a compromise between supporters and opponents of victims' rights, 'maintaining the time-honoured tradition of excluding victims from criminal justice with a thin veneer of being part of it'.[10] We do not regard this as empowerment.

Despite these findings, the Home Office decided in 2000 to introduce VIS schemes nationwide, although the impact statement will be taken at the same time as the witness statement.[11] In one sense there is no stopping the trend towards the provision of victim information to criminal justice

6   Morgan and Sanders (1999) p 32.
7   Many writers object to VIS precisely for this reason. See, for example, A Ashworth, 'Victim's rights, defendant's rights, and criminal procedure' in A Crawford and J Goodey (eds), *Integrating a Victim Perspective within Criminal Justice* (Aldershot: Ashgate, 2000); A Sarat, 'Vengeance, Victims and the Identities of Law' (1997) 6 Social and Legal Studies 163.
8   Morgan and Sanders (1999).
9   M Henley, R Davis and B Smith, 'The reactions of prosecutors and judges to victim impact statements' (1994) 3 Int Rev Victimology 83.
10   Erez and Rogers (1999) pp 234-235.
11   *The Guardian*, 27 May 2000.

officials and the courts. This is partly because, in the political sphere, no-one dares argue against 'victims' rights'. It is also because sentencing legitimately takes account of harm done (including emotional and psychological harm). Many courts (especially the Crown Court) have been receiving, and sometimes even seeking,[12] such information in cases concerning serious sexual offences, robbery and violence for some years.[13] However, statement schemes are not the best way of involving victims and of ensuring that relevant information is transmitted.[14] Nor are court actions, such as those brought (sometimes successfully in recent years) against the DPP following deaths in custody and at work. We saw in chapters 6 and 11 that in these actions the DPP is sometimes forced to reconsider not prosecuting, but these are expensive, lengthy and distressing strategies, to be reserved for the worst cases only.[15] More effective ways of taking account of victims' interests and reducing secondary victimisation, modelled on civil law or restorative procedures, are more expensive than statement schemes. They would also require us to re-think the role of victims in adversary processes.[16] For a crime control system which only pays lip service to the interests of victims, this is not even on the agenda. The penalty which will be paid is that, as victims continue to be dissatisfied, their concerns will be hijacked by populist politicians to justify ever greater incursions on the liberties and rights of suspects, defendants and prisoners.[17]

(b) Vulnerable victims

Some years ago it was recognised that child victims of crime were less likely to have 'their' cases prosecuted, and more likely to suffer secondary victimisation, than adult victims. Children were often afraid to report crimes, were frequently not believed, had difficulty explaining or remembering

12 Morgan and Sanders (1999).
13 See, for example, *Perks* [2000] Crim LR 606, in which, following a review of several cases in which victim impact statements were considered, the relevant principles of sentencing are set out.
14 There are far more effective ways of enhancing their freedom: A Sanders, C Hoyle, R Morgan, E Cape, 'Victim Statements: can't work, don't work' [2001] Crim LR (forthcoming).
15 See, for example, *DPP, ex p Manning* [2000] 3 WLR 463. But note the failure of the victim in *C* (*The Guardian*, 9 March 2000) to secure a ruling that the police and DPP should consult with her before dropping 'her' case.
16 For a radical victim-centred model, see J Dignan and M Cavadino, 'Towards a framework for conceptualising and evaluating models of criminal justice from a victim's perspective' (1996) 4 Int Rev Victimology 153. For less radical proposals see Sanders et al [2001].
17 See R Elias, *Victims Still: The Political Manipulation of Crime Victims* (London: Sage, 1993) and Sarat (1997). See also Roach (1999) for an insightful analysis of punitive and non-punitive (ie restorative) victims' rights models.

exactly what happened, and could be made to appear untruthful or confused in court. Police officers and prosecutors were therefore reluctant to prosecute, and these children suffered greatly under cross-examination if there was a prosecution.[18] Once this was documented by research, and became a matter of public scandal because of revelations of widespread sexual abuse, court procedures were amended to facilitate prosecutions. The government established the Pigot Committee in 1988 and, as an interim measure, enacted the Criminal Justice Act 1988, which permitted child witnesses to give evidence via CCTV.[19] Pigot recommended that child witnesses should be allowed to give all their evidence via pre-recorded video tape,[20] but this recommendation was only half-implemented.[1]

It was recognised that child victims are only one group of vulnerable victims who traditionally lack credibility and have difficulty coping with criminal justice processes (along with all official processes). People who are learning disabled or mentally ill suffer from similar problems, so it made no sense to prevent them from being helped in the way children were helped.[2] In some ways the victims of sexual offences were in a similar position. Sadly, what makes these groups of people vulnerable in the criminal justice system also makes them especially vulnerable to crime.[3] Some of the most exploited groups in society were receiving less protection than 'normal' victims. At the same time, concern was developing about witnesses being intimidated by defendants and their friends or family in some cases. A Home Office working party therefore made wide-ranging proposals to support all these vulnerable groups of witnesses,[4] many of which were enacted in the Youth Justice and Criminal Evidence Act (YJCE) 1999 (Part II). Not all the problems which have been identified require legislation. Many police, prosecution and court procedures (and the attitudes and culture which lie behind them) which are not laid down in the law are as important as those which are. We do not attempt here to discuss in detail the legislative and other changes which are planned, as at the time

---

18   J Morgan and L Zedner, *Child Victims* (Oxford: Clarendon, 1992).

19   Criminal Justice Act (CJA) 1988, s 32

20   Judge Thomas Pigot, Report of the Advisory Group on Video-Recorded Evidence, (London: HMSO, 1989).

1   CJA 1991, amending CJA 1988.

2   This was noted by Pigot (1989). Research on this is reported by A Sanders, J Creaton, S Bird, L Weber, Victims with Learning Disabilities (Oxford: Centre for Criminological Research, 1997). Summarised in Home Office Research Findings no 44 (London: Home Office, 1997).

3   Again noted by Pigot (1989). Also see C Williams, *Invisible Victims: Crime and Abuse Against People with Learning Disabilities* (Bristol: Norah Fry Research Centre, 1995).

4   Home Office, Speaking up for Justice (London: Home Office, 1998).

of writing they have not yet been implemented, but it is important to provide a brief overview.[5]

The first problem which vulnerable victims face is whether or not to report the offence. Sometimes reluctance to report stems from the fact that their 'authority figures' (parents, teachers, carers) are the abusers or close to the abusers. This is a structural feature of vulnerability about which little, regrettably, can be done. But traditionally some reluctance has been because of fear at how the police and courts would treat their complaint. This fear used to be justified in many cases. Sanders et al found that, even in the mid-1990s, the police were often dismissive of crimes against the learning disabled which may have been objectively minor but which, to the victims, were traumatic.[6] At least the police have, for many years now, treated rape and domestic violence complainants with a measure of care and respect. The same cannot be said of the courts. No matter how caring the police are, if a victim fears being humiliated in court they will frequently not report. And even when they do, they often seek to withdraw their complaint or choose not to give evidence in court, usually causing the case to collapse.

It is not enough to be caring. The police need to interview vulnerable witnesses in ways which elicit the best evidence without distorting the witnesses' recollections or intimidating them. Further, compared with 'normal witnesses', vulnerable witnesses tend to have greater difficulties in telling a traumatic story of victimisation several times. Once the Pigot proposals were (half) implemented for children, the police were encouraged to adopt 'cognitive interviewing' techniques which are recorded for later use in court.[7] Skill is needed in the use of these techniques and there have been problems in the interviews carried out to date.[8] A test of the government's commitment to victims will be whether or not it commits the resources needed to train personnel properly and provide the necessary equipment now that pre-recorded interviews can be made with a wider range of vulnerable witnesses.

The next stage is the prosecution decision. The two tests discussed in chapter 6 are applied here as in all cases. Because of the difficulties of these

5   Much of this legislation is exceptionally and unnecessarily complex. The April 2000 issue of the Criminal Law Review contains several articles which dissect the Act in detail, and comment critically on it, drawing on the relevant research. For a review of the research see the Appendix to Home Office, Speaking up for Justice (1998).

6   Sanders et al (1997).

7   These techniques are briefly discussed in ch 5, section 4(c) in the context of questioning suspects.

8   See C Keenan, G Davis, L Hoyano and L Maitland, 'Interviewing Allegedly Abused Children with a View to Criminal Prosecution' [1999] Crim LR 863. Interviewing is guided by Home Office, Memorandum of Good Practice (1992), which is being re-drafted.

cases, many fall at the 'evidential' hurdle. It is not suggested by government (or us) that the tests should change. Instead, full and prompt investigation by the police is needed so that fewer cases are evidentially weak, and the police need to inform the CPS of the problems which the vulnerability in question could cause. For there are ways of mitigating vulnerabilities so that evidence can be better presented in court (if there is no pre-recording of evidence), reducing the prospects of acquittal and thus feeding back to the prosecution decision, making a negative decision both less justifiable and less likely.

One way of helping witnesses is to prepare them for court. Familiarisation with court procedures, practice in giving evidence, and so on, can do a lot to reduce fear and help witnesses cope.[9] Another way is to provide 'special measures' in court. These include judges and barristers removing wigs and gowns, screening off the defendant from the sight of the witness, providing interpreters and communication aids (important not only for people who have difficulty with English but also for some learning disabled people who have difficulty speaking at all), and giving evidence via CCTV from a room outside the courtroom. Assessments will be made in each case of which, if any, of these special measures would help the particular witness (because each vulnerability and every way of alleviating it is different) so that preparation and, where necessary, application to the court can be made in good time. Where appropriate, interviews and cross-examination will be video-taped in advance and played in court (the full Pigot proposals). Apart from full implementation of Pigot, all these measures have been available for children for some time, and the Act extends them to other vulnerable witnesses.[10]

Finally, there are the actual procedures in court. There is the potential in all types of case for witnesses to find cross-examination, and sometimes questioning from the judge, upsetting and challenging. This can ruin an otherwise strong case as well as weak cases. It is sometimes hard to know whether testimony lacks credibility because it really is untrue or mistaken, or because questioning unfairly tripped up or confused the witness. In an adversarial system it is essential that the defence be allowed to test prosecution evidence, and if there is reasonable doubt about its strength, there should be an acquittal. Drawing the line between what is robustly fair and what is viciously destructive of the character of the witness is often difficult. Judges have the power to stop oppressive cross-

9 Sanders et al (1997).
10 Sections 23-30. Not all these special measures are available to all types of vulnerable witness, and for some a special case has to be made by the CPS to a judge at a pre-trial hearing (sections 16-22). See D Birch, 'A better deal for vulnerable witnesses?' [2000] Crim LR 223 and L Hoyano, 'Variations on a theme by Pigot: special measures directions for child witnesses' [2000] Crim LR 250.

examination,[11] but they dare do this only in the most extreme circumstances. For victims will not be helped if convictions are quashed on the ground that judges did not give defence counsel full opportunities to cross examine. One possibility is for judges to 'translate' intimidating or convoluted questioning for witnesses, but the problem can only really be alleviated through changing the culture of the Bar, which is a long-term and indeterminate prospect.[12]

The nature of the adversary system puts limits on how far secondary victimisation of victims in the witness box can be reduced, as trashing, trapping and tripping is all part of proving and disproving cases.[13] Further, there remains too little understanding of the variety of types of vulnerability and the ways in which vulnerabilities are manifested, especially when the problem is learning disability. This means that often witnesses are thought, wrongly, to lack credibility[14] but there is little in this programme of action to deal with this problem in court.

For victims of sexual offences, in particular, aggressive and humiliating questioning in court has been a major cause of attrition - that is, acquittals and, further back down the line, withdrawals and decisions not to report. For these victims, and those of certain other crimes, there are provisions to prevent defendants cross-examining in person[15] and to prevent certain types of evidence (on the witnesses' sexual history in particular) being elicited.[16] But while alleged consent, which is often impossible to disprove,[17] remains a defence to most sexual offences, the rate of acquittals and secondary victimisation of witnesses in court will be higher than in most other offences. As Birch points out, changes to the substantive law, for example on consent, is needed if these provisions of the Act are to be effective.[18]

We should not fool ourselves into thinking that these measures will solve the problems that vulnerable victims have with the criminal justice

11 *Milton Brown* [1998] 2 Cr App Rep 364. They rarely do this. See for example, G Davis, L Hoyano, C Keenan, L Maitland and R Morgan, An assessment of the admissibility and sufficiency of evidence in child abuse prosecutions (London: Home Office, 1999).
12 M Blake and A Ashworth, 'Some Ethical Issues in Prosecuting and Defending Criminal Cases' [1998] Crim LR 16 at pp 25-26.
13 D McBarnet, 'Victim in the witness box - confronting victimology's stereotype' (1983) 7 Contemporary Crises 293.
14 Sanders et al (1997).
15 Section 35. There are also provisions giving judges discretion to prohibit cross-examination in person in any other case: ss 36 and 37.
16 Section 41. See N Kibble, 'The sexual history provisions' [2000] Crim LR 274.
17 J Harris and S Grace, *A question of evidence? Investigating and prosecuting rape in the 1990s* (Home Office Research Study no 196) (London: Home Office, 1999).
18 Birch [2000]. As she points out, the same is true in relation to some types of offence such as 'intercourse with a mental defective' which involve the exploitation of mentally vulnerable people.

system. That is not because of a lack of will on the part of government or criminal justice agencies, or (we hope) a lack of resources. The fact is that vulnerable victims are in structurally weak positions in society. That is what makes them vulnerable. Social and cultural change might alleviate this for the victims of sexual offences and domestic violence, but not for the aged and mentally vulnerable. Legal solutions to social problems can only ever be partial solutions.

It is important to remember that these problems are not completely solvable. Otherwise we will go to more and more extreme lengths with harmful consequences to try to solve them. People with very low actual or mental ages, for example, simply have less comprehension than other people. There comes a point when a witness has to be regarded as not competent to give evidence or, in some cases, not competent to give evidence on matters of detail or in relation to forgotten events. The Act tries to deal with this problem more intelligently than the law used to do, by providing for 'intermediaries' to 'translate' questioning for witnesses who cannot cope, and by a new 'competence' test of 'understanding'.[19] However, this test may not be adequate in practice.[20] It may be tempting in future to allow witnesses who understand very little of what is happening to give evidence, but this would be a further attenuation of the already-eroded rights of suspects and defendants. Along with further restrictions on cross-examination and the method of cross-examination to help vulnerable witnesses, this would harm the prospects of acquittal of innocent defendants. It hardly needs to be said that not all alleged victims and witnesses, whether vulnerable or not, tell the truth;[1] not all are correct in their beliefs and recollections; and some defendants are innocent even when victims tell the truth if, for example, a defence is proved or there is a lack of mens rea. But in an era of crime control-mindedness this could all be forgotten or brushed aside.

---

19 Section 29 provides for intermediaries, and s 53 creates the new test of competence. The suggestion that judges could act as intermediaries when witnesses are confused or intimidated by questioning is that of Birch [2000]. The use of intermediaries will present formidable problems: Hoyano [2000].

20 Birch [2000].

1   An unusual example was that of a teenager who claimed that she had been raped in a park by a tramp. A young man was later arrested on a minor charge and his DNA sample matched the one taken from the young woman. When the police questioned her again, because the man's description did not match that of the 'tramp', she admitted that she had had consensual sex with him. She was later jailed for six months: *The Guardian*, 27 September 2000. In Stuart Gair's case (*The Guardian*, 30 September 2000) three gay witnesses were intimidated by police into lying: one was told that charges against him would be dropped if he 'fingered' Gair, and another was shown a photo of Gair before the ID parade in which he picked Gair out.

There would be no need for trials at all if we automatically accepted what victims and other witnesses said. We may soon reach the point when vindication of more victims' cases will only be achievable by failing to vindicate defence cases. This is the classic dilemma running through this book. The Government deserves to be congratulated, in this respect at least, for not falling into this trap in the main. Most of these measures for vulnerable witnesses, legislative and otherwise, attempt to put vulnerable witnesses on a level playing field with other witnesses without eroding significant rights of defendants.[2] There is a cost in resources, but not in other aspects of freedom. But there are two major points of criticism. First, the restrictiveness of the provisions on sexual history may be an over-reaction to the way in which many judges previously allowed irrelevant sexual history to be used in trials. The fear is that relevant sexual history will now be excluded, putting defendants at an unfair disadvantage.[3] Second, 'special measures' are not available for defendants. This omission may fall foul of the ECHR, and rightly so. Witnesses on both sides are entitled to as fair a trial as is reasonably possible, and such discrimination is only acceptable if one accepts the crime control agenda.

5. RHETORIC AND REALITY: MANAGING THE GAP

In chapter 1 we reminded readers of the famous tenet of Hobson J that 'ten guilty men should escape rather than one innocent man' be wrongly convicted. In addition to proclaiming the greater importance of acquitting the innocent than convicting the guilty, and recognising the trade-off between the two, this also recognises that, at some point, there may be doubt about someone's guilt but if that doubt is insubstantial, conviction should follow. Statistically, occasionally the convicted defendant will be innocent, but that is a price worth paying for the freedom as well as for the crime control model. Hobson's choice words recognise that the system is not, and never will be, perfect. The real problem with this rhetoric is that it does not adequately characterise the reality, or indeed the rules, of the criminal justice system. There is a gap between the rhetoric of the system as a whole (largely due process), the rules (displaying a mixture of values) and the reality (largely crime control). We say that the rhetoric is *largely* due process-oriented, for governments have for more than a decade

---

2   Whether these measures actually succeed in making major changes for vulnerable witnesses remains to be seen, especially as implementation of special measures in magistrates' courts (and it will only apply to the largest ones) will take years. Further, there are doubts about how, in practice, vulnerable defence witnesses will have access to the help that prosecution witnesses will get.

3   The issues and dilemmas are brought out well by Kibble [2000].

expressed crime control rhetoric too.[4] This has increased in recent years as the rhetoric of the rights of victims and 'the community' are called on in contrast to those of suspects and defendants.[5]

The shift in rules, as well as practices, towards crime control is nonetheless faster than that of the rhetoric. How likely is it that this process will continue until we have a totalitarian 'police state'? It seems to us unlikely as it would simply be too politically dangerous. Within all the major political parties, there is sufficient attachment to the rhetoric and substance of due process to rule out the possibility of introducing an undiluted and naked system of crime control. There is also an ideological reason. By arguing that the criminal justice system has become too heavily tipped towards the interests of suspects, the government has chosen to lock itself into the discourse of 'balance' in which more crime control can be justified by reference to bits and pieces of due process. In this sense, rather than in the crude sense implied by McBarnet,[6] due process is for crime control. But it also means that some genuine due process safeguards are sure to be retained, since one cannot create the appearance of due process if there is no substance to such safeguards.[7] Finally, the Human Rights Act 1998 and ECHR will ensure that there is an irreducible minimum of due process safeguards, although we must note that this safety net is threadbare in many areas.[8]

We have seen that the gap between rhetoric and reality is no smaller when we consider the plight of victims. For vulnerable victims, real improvements are in sight. But most victims will have 'rights' which are totally unenforceable, and are therefore even less substantial than many of the rights of suspects and defendants. Indeed, Government decided to expand the Victims' Charter provisions despite research evidence showing

4   See M McConville, A Sanders and R Leng, *Case for the Prosecution* (London: Routledge, 1991) which challenges the view expressed by D McBarnet *Conviction* (London: Macmillan, 1981) that criminal justice rhetoric is wholly due process.

5   See, for example, Lord Williams, for the government, trying to justify the sexual history provisions of the YJCE 1999 in this way, discussed by Kibble [2000] p 290.

6   McBarnet p 156: 'the law on criminal procedure in its current form does not so much set a standard of legality from which the police deviate as provide a licence to ignore it. If we bring due process down from the dizzy heights of abstraction and subject it to empirical scrutiny, the conclusion must be that due process is for crime control.' This argument assumes that we must characterise rules of procedure as due process even when they served the goals of crime control. This is mistaken, in our view. Rules of procedure can be either due process or crime control in orientation as H L Packer, *The Limits of the Criminal Sanction* (Stanford: Stanford UP, 1968) himself pointed out.

7   In this, we follow E P Thompson, *Whigs and Hunters* (London: Allen Lane, 1975) pp 259-265.

8   See, for example, the discussion by Kibble [2000] (pp 290-291) of the (lack of) ECHR relevance in relation to the sexual history provisions of the YJCE 1999.

that they are useless or even unhelpful to as many victims as they are helpful. Judges are happy to endorse victim impact statements (for 'PR purposes') as long as they can ignore them. Crime control systems make use of the rhetoric of the rights of the victim, but not the reality, for the rights of victims get in the way almost as much as the rights of defendants. For victims, just as much as innocent suspects and defendants, want the *right people* to be convicted. This is not the same as wanting the *criminal population* to be controlled (the crime control objective).

It may appear surprising that the crime control system serves victims as badly as it serves defendants until we remember that prosecution (in the minority of cases that get that far) requires the presentation of a *case*. All cases are constructions, and become the property of the side which built it. Cases often become far removed from the facts which provided their initial impetus and therefore, not infrequently, as far removed from anything the victim recognises as from anything the defendant recognises. As McBarnet says:

'In a legal system based on adversarial advocacy a case is not "the whole truth" but a partial account (in both senses) limited to "the facts of the case" as defined by law and strategy rather than by the victim's perception of his or her experience.'[9]

According to official rhetoric, suspects/defendants and their interests are prioritised at the expense of victims. On the other hand, one might think, in the light of the 11 preceding chapters, that the reverse is true - that victims and their interests are prioritised. In reality, suspects/defendants and victims are in a similar position, because the search for truth (whoever's version that might be) is subordinated to other priorities. Neither victims nor suspects/defendants have any significant leverage on the agencies and officials about what should happen, when, and to whom.

The criminal justice system will continue to represent a site of struggle and conflict. Many skirmishes will result in victories for due process (as where evidence is excluded on the grounds of unfairness), even some battles may be temporarily won (as with the creation of court and police station duty solicitor schemes), only for ground to be taken back again (the right of silence sidelining legal advice in many cases). The Court of Appeal sometimes quashes convictions to express its disapproval of police malpractice even though there is reliable evidence of guilt, some police officers behave ethically and advocate progressive reforms, and some defence lawyers provide an outstanding service to their clients, often at great emotional and financial cost to themselves. But these events and people are exceptional, tending to occur in high-profile contexts (as with

9   McBarnet (1983).

the dramatic freeing of the 'Birmingham Six'), creating an appearance of far more due process than is really the case. So the war will continue. Crime control cannot be imposed by an open show of naked force, since its ideological justification is that it increases real freedom and liberty, but nor are we asked to consent to it. Instead we are presented with a picture of a system—neatly balancing due process rights, crime control powers and the rights of victims—which is a gross distortion of reality.

Part of this distortion is achieved by judges and legislators proclaiming the virtues of due process at the same time as they are acting on crime control instincts. For example, the case law on exclusion provides the judges with a wide scope as to which precedents to follow, which tests to apply and which decisions to reach. The open texture of the law means that, and on this point we follow McBarnet, 'judges can both uphold, even eulogise, the rhetoric yet simultaneously deny its applicability ...'.[10] Thus in *Fulling*,[11] we saw the Court of Appeal adopt a broad definition of oppression, which clearly covered the case in question, yet the appellant still lost. The protections introduced by PACE and the Codes of Practice are used against suspects, so that when a solicitor is present, this is usually judged to be sufficient protection to condone rule breaking such as failure to caution, record questioning properly, and so forth. Similarly, in examining the Court of Appeal's powers, we saw how malpractice by police or prosecution agencies might be condemned but the conviction upheld. And, at other times, such as when informers or undercover officers are involved, the courts are happy to admit to discarding due process protections in favour of crime control.

The use of rhetoric bearing little relation to reality is not confined to English governments and courts. The ECtHR is equally guilty. For example, we saw in chapter 8 that according to the ECtHR the bail decision has to be based on evidence (not speculation) and it has to be proven beyond reasonable doubt that someone is likely to breach bail. This is plainly ridiculous. Bail decisions in reality have to be based on risk and prediction (that is, *intelligent* speculation). This is a probabilistic, and not evidence-based, process and we doubt that anyone in the ECtHR believes otherwise.

The uneven distribution of due process protections across society is as worrying as their general erosion. At various points in this book, we have seen that disadvantaged sections of society are disproportionately at the receiving end of state power. 'We' are taken in by the ideological self-portrait of criminal justice because we have so little experience of the system and have no incentive to question its operation. It does not threaten 'our' interests, but appears to serve them. Ask people who regularly come into contact with the system, whether as victims or offenders, and they

10   McBarnet (1981).
11   [1987] QB 426, discussed in ch 5, section 4(a)(iii).

will have a different story to tell. We saw that this has led to so much dissatisfaction with the police complaints system that change is now likely, but this disaffection—bordering on disbelief in the rule of law—can be seen in many other criminal justice contexts (such as stop-search) where no change is on the cards.

Widespread disbelief in the rule of law is hardly surprising, for when we look at the rule of law another gap between rhetoric and reality is revealed. As we argue elsewhere,[12] two vital elements of the rule of law are equality before the law (as between citizens in different communities and as between citizens and officials) and the accountability of state officials to the courts. We have seen that, despite the rhetoric, neither of these conditions apply in many situations. The gap is managed, however, because they *appear* to apply. For example, anyone can ask anyone else a question without requiring an answer. Whether on the street or in the station, this is held to apply equally to police officers as to citizens. But treating people *the same* in this way is not treating them *equally*. By ignoring the power which police officers exert over citizens, whether unstated (as often happens on the street) or overt (as in the station), the citizen is not treated equally and the police are not made subject to legal control - 'consent' searches, for example, are not subject to the restrictions, such as they are, of PACE. Moreover, because some communities are disadvantaged by comparison with others in the way this type of power is exercised, people are treated unequally in an *institutionalised* manner, thus further violating the rule of law. And the lack of accountability of enforcement agencies - police, CPS and non-police agencies - means that they never have to account for this or its effects, violating the rule of law yet further.

We cannot expect, and nor would we advocate, the adoption of either a consistent crime control philosophy and all that goes with it, nor the adoption of the due process model and all that that would imply. Unfortunately, the freedom approach which we advocate is also unlikely to materialise unless politicians decide to take a lead in raising the debate as distinct from raising their opinion poll ratings. Looked at in this way, the prospects for an open, rational and coherent system of justice are bleak.

Our negative tone might be criticised on the grounds that the English system is, for all its faults, the best in the world. It is probably true that it is better than most, and undoubtedly true that it is better than some. This is as it should be, as we are still one of the wealthiest societies in the world. We ought to be able to afford the best justice. And if we are as civilised as we would like to think, we should aspire to have the best system. The argument of this book is that the system neither achieves, nor aspires to achieve, such a high standard. The due process and crime control models

12   Sanders and Young (1994) 'The Rule of Law ...'.

help us understand the tensions within the system as it stands. But they cannot help us make out a persuasive argument for a transformation of that system. We need a new language in which to express our aspirations, and the language of freedom seems to us to provide a vocabulary most likely to persuade the various entrenched interest groups of the need for change. It is time to set the primary goal of the criminal justice system as the promotion of freedom of all citizens and social groups alike.

Bibliography

Adams, C, *Balance in Pre-Trial Criminal Justice* (Unpublished PhD thesis, LSE).

Alderson, J, *Policing Freedom* (Plymouth, Macdonald and Evans, 1979).

Alschuler, A, 'The all-white American jury' (1995) 145 NLJ 1005.

Amnesty International, Deaths in Police Custody: Lack of Police Accountability (London: AI, 2000).

Aranella, P, 'Rethinking the Functions of Criminal Procedure' reprinted in Wasserstrom, S, and Snyder, C, *A Criminal Procedure Anthology* (Cincinnati: Anderson, 1996).

Ashworth, A, 'A threadbare principle' [1978] Crim LR 385.

Ashworth, A, 'Prosecution and Procedure in Criminal Justice' [1979] Crim LR 490.

Ashworth, A, 'Concepts of Criminal Justice' [1979] Crim LR 412.

Ashworth, A, 'The "Public Interest" Element in Prosecutions' [1987] Crim LR 595.

Ashworth, A, 'Defining Offences Without Harm' in P Smith (ed), *Criminal Law: Essays in Honour of JC Smith* (London: Butterworths, 1987).

Ashworth, A, 'Public Order and the Principles of English Criminal Law' [1987] Crim LR 153.

Ashworth, A, 'Criminal Justice and the Criminal Process' (1988) 28 BJ Crim 111.

Ashworth, A, 'Plea, Venue and Discontinuance' [1993] Crim LR 830.

Ashworth, A, 'Some doubts about restorative justice' (1993) 4 Criminal Law Forum 277.

Ashworth, A, 'Victim impact statements and sentencing' [1993] Crim LR 498.

Ashworth, A, 'Human Rights, Legal Aid and Criminal Justice' in R Young and D Wall (eds), *Access to Criminal Justice* (London: Blackstone, 1996).

Ashworth, A, 'Crime, Community and Creeping Consequentialism' [1996] Crim LR 220.

Bibliography

Ashworth, A, 'Sentencing' in M Maguire, R Morgan and R Reiner (eds), *The Oxford Handbook of Criminology* 2nd edn (Oxford: Clarendon Press, 1997).

Ashworth, A, *The Criminal Process* 2nd edn (Oxford: OUP, 1998).

Ashworth, A, 'Article 6 and the Fairness of Trials' [1999] Crim LR 261.

Ashworth, A, 'The Human Rights Act and the Substantive Criminal Law: A Non-Minimalist View' [2000] Crim LR 564.

Ashworth, A, 'Victims' Rights, Defendants' Rights and Criminal Procedure' in A Crawford and J Goodey (eds), *Integrating a Victim Perspective within Criminal Justice: International Debates* (Aldershot: Dartmouth, 2000).

Ashworth, A, 'Should the police be allowed to use deceptive practices?' (1998) 114 LQR 108.

Ashworth, A, and Blake, M, 'The Presumption of Innocence in English Criminal Law' [1996] Crim LR 306.

Ashworth, A, and Fionda, J, 'The New Code for Crown Prosecutors: Prosecution, Accountability and the Public Interest' [1994] Crim LR 894.

Ashworth, A, Genders, E, Mansfield, G, Peay, J, and Player, E, Sentencing in the Crown Court (Occasional Paper no 10) (Oxford Centre for Criminological Research, 1984).

Astor, H, 'The Unrepresented Defendant Revisited: A Consideration of the Role of the Clerk in Magistrates' Courts' (1986) 13 JLS 225.

Audit Commission, Helping with enquiries: tackling crime effectively (London: Audit Commission, 1993).

Audit Commission, Tackling Crime Effectively, vol 2 (London: Audit Commission, 1996).

Aye Maung, N, Young people, victimisation and the police (Home Office Research Study no 140) (London: HMSO, 1995).

Ayres, I, and Braithwaite, J, *Responsive regulation: Transcending the deregulation debate* (New York: OUP, 1992).

Backhouse, J, 'Rights of Appeal by Way of Case Stated – Should it be Simplified?' (1992) JPN 310.

Bailey, S H, and Birch, D, 'Recent Developments in the Law of Police Powers' [1982] Crim LR 475.

Bailey, S H, and Gunn, M J, *Smith and Bailey on the English Legal System* 3rd edn (London: Sweet & Maxwell, 1996).

Baker, E, 'Taking European Criminal Law Seriously' [1998] Crim LR 361.

Balbus, I, *The Dialectics of Legal Repression* (New York: Russell Sage, 1973).

Baldwin, J, 'The Social Composition of the Magistracy' (1975) 16 BJ Crim 171.

Baldwin, J, 'Pre-Trial Settlement in the Magistrates' Courts' (1985) 24 Howard JCJ 108.

Baldwin, J, *Pre-Trial Justice* (Oxford: Basil Blackwell, 1985).

Baldwin, J, 'The Green Form: Use or Abuse?' (1988) 138 NLJ 631.

Baldwin, J, Preparing the Record of Taped Interview (Royal Commission on Criminal Justice Research Study no 2) (London: HMSO, 1992).

Baldwin, J, 'Power and Police Interviews' (1993) 143 NLJ 1194.

Baldwin, J, The Role of Legal Representatives at the Police Station (Royal Commission on Criminal Justice Research Study no 3) (London: HMSO, 1993).

Baldwin, J, 'Police Interview Techniques: Establishing Truth or Proof?' (1993) 33 BJ Crim 325.

Baldwin, J, 'Understanding Judge Ordered and Directed Acquittals in the Crown Court' [1997] Crim LR 536.

Baldwin, J, and Bedward, J, 'Summarising Tape Recordings of Police Interviews' [1991] Crim LR 671.

Baldwin, J, and Feeney, F, 'Defence Disclosure in the Magistrates' Courts' (1986) 49 MLR 593.

Baldwin, J, and Hill, S, The Operation of the Green Form Scheme in England and Wales (London: Lord Chancellor's Department, 1988).

Baldwin, J, and Hunt, A, 'Prosecutors Advising in Police Stations' [1998] Crim LR 521.

Baldwin, J, and McConville, M, *Negotiated Justice* (London: Martin Robertson, 1977).

Baldwin, J, and McConville, M, 'Allegations Against Lawyers' [1978] Crim LR 744.

Baldwin, J, and McConville, M, 'The Influence of the Sentencing Discount in Inducing Guilty Pleas' in J Baldwin and A Bottomley (eds), *Criminal Justice: Selected Readings* (Oxford: Martin Robertson, 1978).

Baldwin, J, and McConville, M, *Jury Trials* (Oxford: OUP, 1979).

Baldwin, J, and Moloney, T, Supervision of Police Investigation in Serious Criminal Cases (Royal Commission on Criminal Justice Research Study no 4) (London: HMSO, 1992).

Baldwin, J, and Mulvaney, A, 'Advance Disclosure in Magistrates' Courts: The Workings of Section 48' (1987) 151 JP 409.

Baldwin, J, and Mulvaney, A, 'Advance Disclosure in the Magistrates' Courts: How useful are the Prosecution summaries?' [1987] Crim LR 805.

Baldwin, J, and Mulvaney, A, *Pre-Trial Settlement of Criminal Cases in Magistrates' Courts* (Birmingham: University of Birmingham, 1987).

Baldwin, J, and Mulvaney, A 'Advance Disclosure in the Magistrates' Courts: Two Cheers for Section 48' [1987] Crim LR 315.

Baldwin, R, *Regulation in Question* (London: LSE, 1995).

Ball, C, 'The Youth Justice and Criminal Evidence Act 1999: A significant move towards restorative justice, or a recipe for unintended consequences?' [2000] Crim LR 211.

Bibliography

Ball, C, McCormac, K, and Stone, N, *Young Offenders* (London: Sweet & Maxwell, 1995).

Bankowski, Z, Hutton, N, and McManus, J, *Lay Justice?* (Edinburgh: T & T Clark, 1987).

Banton, M, *The Policeman in the Community* (London: Tavistock, 1964).

Barclay, G, and Tavares, C, Information on the Criminal Justice System in England and Wales: Digest 4 (London: Home Office, 1999).

Barnard, C, and Hare, I, 'Police Discretion and the Rule of Law: European Community Rights Versus Civil Rights' (2000) 63 MLR 581.

Barton, A, and Evans, R, Proactive Policing on Merseyside (Police Research Series Paper no 105) (London: Home Office, 1999).

Bases, N, and Smith, M, 'A Study of Bail Applications Through the Official Solicitor to the Judge in Chambers by Brixton Prisoners in 1974' [1976] Crim LR 541.

Baxter, J, and Koffman, L, 'The Confait Inheritance – Forgotten Lessons?' [1983] Cambrian LR 14.

Bayley, D, *Police for the Future* (Oxford: OUP, 1994).

Bayley, D, 'Getting serious about police brutality' in P Stenning (ed), *Accountability for Criminal Justice* (Toronto: University of Toronto Press, 1995).

Bevan, G, Holland, T, and Partington, M, Organising Cost-Effective Access to Justice (London: Social Market Foundation, 1994).

Bevan, V, and Lidstone, K, *The Investigation of Crime* 2nd edn (London: Butterworths, 1996).

Bing, I, 'Curing Bias in Criminal Trials – the consequences of R v Gough' [1998] Crim LR 148.

Birch, D, 'The PACE Hots Up: Confessions and Confusion Under the 1984 Act' [1989] Crim LR 95.

Birch, D, 'Excluding evidence from entrapment: What is a fair cop?' [1994] CLP 73.

Birch, D, 'Suffering in Silence?' [1999] Crim LR 769.

Birch, D, 'A Better Deal for Vulnerable Witnesses?' [2000] Crim LR 223.

Blake, C, 'Legal Aid: Past, Present and Future' (2000) Legal Action, Jan, p 6.

Blake, M, and Ashworth, A, 'Some Ethical Issues in Prosecuting and Defending Criminal Cases' [1998] Crim LR 16.

Blake, N, 'Picketing, Justice and the Law' in B Fine and R Millar (eds), *Policing the Miners' Strike* (London: Lawrence and Wishart, 1985).

Block, B, Corbett, C, and Peay, J, 'Ordered and Directed Acquittals in the Crown Court: A Time of Change?' [1993] Crim LR 95.

Block, B, Corbett, C, and Peay, J, Ordered and Directed Acquittals in the Crown Court (Royal Commission on Criminal Justice, Research Study no 15) (London: HMSO, 1993).

Bohlander, M, '"... By a jury of his peers" – The issue of multi-racial juries in a poly-ethnic society' [1992] XIV(1) Liverpool Law Review 67.

Bottomley, A, *Decisions in the Penal Process* (London: Martin Robertson, 1973).

Bottomley, A, 'Sentencing reform and the structuring of pre-trial discretion' in M Wasik and K Pease (eds), *Sentencing Reform* (Manchester: MUP, 1987).

Bottomley, A, and Pease, K, *Crime and Punishment: Interpreting the Data* (Milton Keynes: Open UP, 1986).

Bottoms, A E, and McClean, J D, *Defendants in the Criminal Process* (London: Routledge & Kegan Paul, 1976).

Bowling, B, *Violent Racism* (Oxford: Clarendon, 1998).

Box, S, *Power, Crime and Mystification* (London: Tavistock, 1983).

Box, S, and Russell, K, 'The Politics of Discreditability: Disarming Complaints Against the Police' (1975) 23 Soc Rev 315.

Braithwaite, J, *Crime, Shame and Reintegration* (Cambridge, CUP, 1989).

Braithwaite, J, 'Restorative Justice: Assessing Optimistic and Pessimistic Accounts' (1999) 25 Crime and Justice: A Review of Research 1.

Braithwaite, J, 'The New Regulatory State and the Transformation of Criminology' (2000) 40 BJ Crim 222.

Brake, M, and Hale, C, *Public Order and Private Lives* (London: Routledge, 1992).

Brants, C, and Field, S, 'Discretion and Accountability in Prosecution', in P Fennell, C Harding, N Jorg and B Swart (eds), *Criminal Justice in Europe: A Comparative Study* (Oxford: Clarendon, 1995).

Bredar, J, 'Moving Up the Day of Reckoning: strategies for attacking the "cracked trials" problem' [1992] Crim LR 153.

Brereton, D, 'How Different are Rape Trials? A Comparison of the Cross-Examination of Complainants in Rape and Assault Trials' (1997) 37 BJ Crim 242.

Bridges, L, 'The Fixed Fees Battle' (1992) Legal Action, November, p 7.

Bridges, L, 'The professionalisation of criminal justice' (1992) Legal Action, August p 7.

Bridges, L, 'The Right to Jury Trial: How the Royal Commission Got it Wrong' (1993) 143 NLJ 1542.

Bridges, L, 'The Reform of Criminal Legal Aid' in R Young and D Wall (eds), *Access to Criminal Justice* (London: Blackstone, 1996).

Bridges, L, 'False starts and unrealistic expectations' (1999) Legal Action, 6 October, p 6.

Bridges, L, 'The Lawrence Inquiry – Incompetence, Corruption and Institutional Racism' (1999) 26 JLS 298.

Bridges, L, 'Taking Liberties' (2000) Legal Action, 6 July, p 8.

Bridges, L, and Bunyan, T, 'Britain's new urban policing strategy – the Police and Criminal Evidence Bill in Context' (1983) 10 JLS 85.

Bridges, L, Cape, E, Abubaker, A, and Bennett, C, Quality in Criminal Defence Services (London: Legal Aid Board, 2000).

Bibliography

Bridges, L, Carter, J, and Gorbing, S, 'The Impact of Duty Solicitor Schemes in Six Magistrates' Courts' (1992) LAG Bull, July, p 14.

Bridges, L, and Choongh, S, Improving Police Station Legal Advice (London: Law Society, 1998).

Bridges, L, Choongh, S, and McConville, M, Ethnic Minority Defendants and the Right to Elect Jury Trial (London: Commission for Racial Equality, 2000).

Brodgen, A, 'Sus is dead: what about "SaS"?' (1981) 9 New Community 44.

Brodgen, M, 'Stopping the People' in J Baxter and L Koffman (eds), *Police: The Constitution and the Community* (Abingdon: Professional Books, 1985).

Brodgen, M, *On the Mersey Beat* (Oxford: OUP, 1991).

Brodgen, M, and Brodgen, A, 'From Henry III to Liverpool 8' (1984) 12 IJ Sociology of Law 37.

Brown, D, Police Complaints Procedure (Home Office Research Study no 93) (London: HMSO, 1987).

Brown, D, Invesitgating Burglary (Home Office Research Study no 123) (London: HMSO, 1991).

Brown, D, Detention at the Police Station under the Police and Criminal Evidence Act 1984 (Home Office Research Study no 104) (London: HMSO, 1989).

Brown, D, PACE Ten Years On (Home Office Research Study no 155) (London, Home Office 1997).

Brown, D, Offending on Bail and Police Use of Conditional Bail (Home Office Research Findings no 72) (London: Home Office, 1998).

Brown, D, and Ellis, T, Policing low level disorder: police use of section 5 of the Public Order Act 1986 (Home Office Research Study no 135) (London: Home Office, 1994).

Brown, D, Ellis, T, and Larcombe, K, Changing the Code: Police Detention under the Revised PACE Codes of Practice (Home Office Research Study no 129) (London: HMSO, 1992).

Brown, S, *Magistrates at Work* (Buckingham: Open UP, 1991).

Bryan, I, *Interrogation and Confession* (Aldershot: Dartmouth, 1997).

Bucke, T, Policing and the Public: Findings From the 1994 British Crime Survey (Home Office Research Findings no 28) (London: Home Office, 1995).

Bucke, T, Ethnicity and Contacts with the Police: Latest Findings from the British Crime Survey (Home Office Research Findings no 59) (London: Home Office, 1997).

Bucke, T, and Brown, D, In Police Custody: Police Powers and Suspects' Rights Under the Revised Pace Codes of Practice (Home Office Research Study no 174) (London: Home Office, 1997).

Bucke, T, and Brown, D, The Right of Silence: The Impact of the CJPO 1994 (Home Office Research Study no 199) (London: Home Office, 2000).

Bucke, T, and James, Z, Trespass and Protest: Policing under the Criminal Justice and Public Order Act 1994 (London: Home Office, 1998).

Burney, E, *Magistrate, Court and Community* (London: Hutchinson, 1979).

Burrow, J, 'Bail and the Human Rights Act 1998' (2000) 150 NLJ 677.

Burrow, J, and Tarling, R, Clearing Up Crime (Home Office Research Study no 73) (London: HMSO, 1982).

Burrows, J, Henderson, P, and Morgan, P, Improving Bail Decisions: the bail process project, phase 1 (Research and Planning Unit Paper 90) (London: Home Office, 1994).

Burton, M, 'Reviewing CPS decisions not to prosecute' [2001] Crim LR (forthcoming).

Butler, G, Inquiry into CPS Decision Making in relation to Deaths in Custody and Related Matters (London: SO, 1999).

Butler, S, Acquittal Rates (Home Office Research and Planning Unit Paper 16) (London: HMSO, 1983).

Buxton, R, 'Challenging and Discharging Jurors' [1990] Crim LR 225.

Buxton, R, 'The Human Rights Act and the Substantive Criminal Law' [2000] Crim LR 331.

Buzawa, E, and Buzawa, C, 'The Impact of Arrest on Domestic Assault' (1993) 36 American Behavioural Scientist 558.

Cameron, N, 'Bail Act 1976: Two Inconsistencies and an Imaginary Offence' (1980) 130 NLJ 382.

Cane, P, *Tort Law and Economic Interests* (Oxford: OUP, 1996).

Cape, E, 'Sidelining Defence Lawyers: Police Station Advice After *Condron*' (1997) 1 IJ Evid and Proof 386.

Cape, E, *Defending Suspects at Police Stations* 3rd edn (London: Legal Action Group, 1999).

Cape, E, 'Detention Without Charge: What Does "Sufficient Evidence To Charge" Mean?' [1999] Crim LR 874.

Cape, E, 'New Labour: New Criminal Justice?' (2000) February, Legal Action p 6.

Cape, E, and Spronken, T, 'Proactive policing: limiting the role of the defence lawyer', in S Field and C Pelser (eds), *Invading the Private: State Accountability and New Investigative Methods in Europe* (Aldershot: Dartmouth, 1998).

Caplan, J, 'The Criminal Bar' in R Hazell (ed), *The Bar on Trial* (London: Quartet, 1978).

Carlen, P, 'Remedial Routines for the Maintenance of Control in Magistrates' Courts' (1974) 1 BJ Law & Soc 101.

Carlen, P (ed), *The Sociology of Law* (Keele: University of Keele, 1976).

Bibliography

Carlen, P, *Magistrates' Justice* (London: Martin Robertson, 1976).

Carns, T W, and Kruse, J, 'A Re-Evaluation of Alaska's Plea Bargaining Ban' 8 Alaska Law Review 27.

Carson, W, 'White-Collar Crime and the Enforcement of Factory Legislation' (1970) 10 BJ Crim 383.

Cashmere, E, and McLaughlin, E, (eds), *Out of Order?* (London: Routledge, 1991).

Cavadino, M, 'A Vindication of the Rights of Psychiatric Patients' (1997) 24 J LS 235.

Cavadino, M, and Dignan, J, 'Reparation, Retribution and Rights' (1997) 4 Int Rev Victimology 233.

Cavadino, P, and Gibson, B, *Bail: The Law, Best Practice and the Debate* (Winchester: Waterside, 1993).

Cavadino, M, Crow, I, and Dignan, J, *Criminal Justice* 2000 (Winchester: Waterside, 1999).

Chan, J, 'Changing Police Culture' (1996) 36 BJ Crim 109.

Chatterton, M, 'Police in Social Control' in J King (ed), *Control Without Custody* (Cambridge: Univerity of Cambridge, 1996).

Cherryman, J, and Bull, R, 'Investigative Interviewing' in F Leishman, B Loveday and S Savage (eds), *Core Issues in Policing* (Harlow: Longman, 1996).

Childs, M, 'Medical Manslaughter and Corporate Liability' (1999) 19 Legal Studies 316.

Choo, A, 'Halting criminal prosecutions: the abuse of process doctrine re-visited' [1995] Crim LR 864.

Choo, A, and Nash, S, 'What's the matter with s 78?' [1999] Crim LR 929.

Choongh, S, *Policing as Social Discipline* (Oxford: Clarendon, 1997).

Choongh, S, 'Policing the Dross: A Social Disciplinary Model of Policing' (1998) 38 BJ Crim 623.

Christian, L, 'Restriction without Conviction' in B Fine and R Millar (eds), *Policing the Miners' Strike* (London: Lawrence and Wishart, 1985).

Christian, L, 'Let down by Lawyers', *The Guardian*, 15 May 2000.

Cicourel, A, *The Social Organisation of Juvenile Justice* (London: Heinemann, 1976).

Clare, I, and Gudjonsson, G, Devising and Piloting an Experimental Version of the Notice to Detained Persons (Royal Commission on Criminal Justice, Research Study no 7) (London: HMSO, 1993).

Clarke, A, 'Safety or Supervision? The Unified Ground of Appeal and its Consequences in the Law of Abuse of Process and Exclusion of Evidence' [1999] Crim LR 108.

Clarke, R, and Hough, M, Crime and Police Effectiveness (Home Office Research Study no 79)(London: HMSO, 1984).

Clarkson, C, 'Kicking corporate bodies and damning their souls' (1996) 59 MLR 557.

Clarkson, C, Cretney, A, Davis, G, and Shepherd, J, 'Assaults: the relationship between seriousness, criminalisation and punishment' [1994] Crim LR 4.

Clayton, R, and Tomlinson, H, 'Arrest and Reasonable Grounds for Suspicion' (1988) LS Gaz, 7 September 22.

Clayton, R, and Tomlinson, H, *Civil Actions Against the Police* 2nd edn (London: Sweet & Maxwell, 1992).

Clayton, R, and Tomlinson, H, *Civil Actions Against the Police* 3rd edn (London: Sweet & Maxwell, 1999).

Coles, D, and Murphy, F, 'O'Brien: Another Death in Police Custody' (1999) Legal Action, Nov, p 6.

Colvin, M, Under surveillance – covert policing and human rights standards, (London: JUSTICE, 1998).

Conlon, G, *Proved Innocent* (London: Penguin, 1990).

Cook, D, *Rich Law, Poor Law* (Milton Keynes: Open UP, 1989).

Cook, D, *Poverty, Crime and Punishment* (London: CPAG, 1997).

Corbett, C, 'Complaints Against the Police: The New Procedure of Informal Resolution' (1991) 2 Policing and Society 47.

Cornish, W, *The Jury* (London: Penguin, 1968).

Corre, N, 'Three Frequent Questions on the Bail Act' [1989] Crim LR 493.

Cotterrell, R, *The Politics of Jurispriudence* (London: Butterworths, 1989).

Cotton, J, and Povey, D, Police Complaints and Discipline, 1998-9 (Statistical Bulletin 17/99) (London: Home Office 1999).

Council of Europe, The Position of the Victim in the Framework of Criminal Law and Procedure (Council of Europe, 1985).

Cowan, D, and Marsh, A, 'There's Regulatory Crime and then there's Landlord Crime: From Rachmanites to Partners' (2000) (unpublished).

Cox, B, *Civil Liberties in Britain* (Harmondsworth: Penguin, 1975).

Craig, P, 'Formal and Substantive Conceptions of the Rule of Law: An Analytical Framework' (1997) PL 467.

Crawford, A, *The Local Governance of Crime* (Oxford: Clarendon, 1997).

Crawford A, and Goodey, J, (eds) *Integrating a Victim Persective Within Criminal Justice: International Debates* (Aldershot: Dartmouth, 2000).

Crawford A, Jones, T, Woodhouse, T, and Young, J, The Second Islington Crime Survey (Enfield: Centre for Criminology, Middlesex University, 1990).

Cretney, A, and Davis, G, *Punishing Violence* (London: Routledge, 1995).

Cretney, A, and Davis, G, 'Prosecuting "Domestic" Assault' [1996] Crim LR 162.

Cretney, A, and Davis, G, 'Prosecuting Domestic Assault: Victims Failing Courts or Courts Failing Victims?' (1997) 36 Howard JCJ 146.

Cretney, A, Davis, G, Clarkson, C, and Shepherd, J, 'Criminalising assault: the failure of the "offence against society" model' (1994) 34 BJ Crim 15.

Criminal Appeals Office, A Guide to Proceedings in the Court of Appeal Criminal Division, (Criminal Appeals Office, 1990).

Crisp, D, 'Standardising Prosecutions' (1993) 34 Home Office Research Bulletin 13.

Crisp, D, and Moxon, D, Case Screening by the CPS (Home Office Research Study no 137) (London: Home Office, 1994).

Crisp, D, Whittaker, C, and Harris, J, Public Interest Case Assessment Schemes, (Home Office Research Study no 138) (London: Home Office, 1995).

Croall, H, 'Mistakes, Accidents and Someone Else's Fault: The Trading Offender in Court' (1988) 15 JLS 293.

Crown Prosecution Service, Annual Report 1990-1991 (London: HMSO, 1991).

Crown Prosecution Service, Annual Report 1992-1993 (London: HMSO, 1993).

Crown Prosecution Service, Discontinuance Survey (November 1993) (unpublished).

Crown Prosecution Service, Code for Crown Prosecutors (London: CPS, 1994).

Crown Prosecution Service, Offences Against the Person Charging Standard Agreed by the Police and Crown Prosecution Service (London: CPS, 1996).

Curran, J, and Garnie, J, Detention or Voluntary Attendance?: Police Use of Detention under section 2 of the Criminal Justice (Scotland) Act 1980 (Scottish Office) (Edinburgh: HMSO, 1986).

Damaska, M, 'Evidentiary Barriers to Conviction and Two Models of Criminal Procedure: A Comparative Study' (1973) 121 U Penn LR 506.

Damaska, M, *The Faces of Justice and State Authority* (New Haven: Yale University Press, 1986).

Darbyshire, P, 'The Role of the Magistrates' Clerk in Summary Proceedings' (1980) 144 JP 186, 201, 219, and 233.

Darbyshire, P, *The Magistrates' Clerk* (Chichester: Barry Rose, 1984).

Darbyshire, P, 'Notes of a Lawyer Juror' (1990) 140 NLJ 1264.

Darbyshire, P, 'The Lamp That Shows That Freedom Lives – Is it Worth the Candle?' [1991] Crim LR 740.

Darbyshire, P, 'An Essay on the Importance and Neglect of the Magistracy' [1997] Crim LR 627.

Darbyshire, P, 'For the New Lord Chancellor: Some Causes for Concern About Magistrates' [1997] Crim LR 861.

Darbyshire, P, 'Previous Misconduct and Magistrates' Courts: Some Tales from the Real World' [1997] Crim LR 105.

Darbyshire, P, 'Strengthening the Argument in Favour of the Defendant's Right to Elect' [1997] Crim LR 911.

Darbyshire, P, 'A Comment on the Powers of Magistrates' Clerks' [1999] Crim LR 377.

Davis, G, Hoyano, L, Keenan, C, Maitland, L, and Morgan, R, An Assessment of the Admissibility and Sufficiency of Evidence in Child Abuse Cases (London: Home Office, 1999).

Daw, R, 'A Response' [1994] Crim LR 904.

Dennis, I, 'Miscarriages of Justice and the Law of Confessions' [1993] PL 291.

Devlin, P, *Trial by Jury* (London: Stevens & Sons, 1956).

Devlin, P, *Criminal Prosecution in England* (Oxford: OUP, 1960).

Devlin, P, 'The Conscience of the Jury' (1991) 107 LQR 398.

Dickson, B, 'Northern Ireland's Emergency Legislation – The Wrong Medicine?' [1992] PL 592.

Di Federico, G, 'Prosecutorial Independence and the democratic requirement of accountability in Italy' (1998) 38 BJ Crim 371.

Dignan, J, 'Repairing the Damage' (1992) 32 BJ Crim 453.

Dignan, J, 'The Crime and Disorder Act and the Prospects for Restorative Justice' [1999] Crim LR 48.

Dignan, J, and Cavadino, M, 'Towards a Framework for Conceptualising and Evaluating Models of Criminal Justice from a Victim's Perspective' (1996) 4 Int R Victimology 153.

Dignan, J, and Whynne, A, 'A Microcosm of the Local Community? Reflections on the Composition of the Magistracy in a Petty Sessional Division in the North Midlands' (1997) 37 BJ Crim 184.

Dine, J, 'European Community Criminal Law?' [1993] Crim LR 246.

Dingwall, G, and Harding, C, *Diversion in the Criminal Process* (London: Sweet & Maxwell, 1998).

Dingwall, G, 'Judicial Review and the DPP' (1995) 54 CLJ 265.

Dingwall, R and Lewis, P (eds), *The Sociology of the Professions* (London: Macmillan, 1983).

Ditchfield, J, Police Cautioning (Home Office Research Study no 37) (London: HMSO, 1976).

Dixon, D, 'Common Sense, Legal Advice, and the Right of Silence' [1991] PL 233.

Dixon, B, and Smith, G, 'Laying Down the Law: The Police, the Courts and Legal Accountability' (1998) 26 IJ Soc of Law 419.

Dixon, D, *Law in Policing* (Oxford: Clarendon, 1997).

Dixon, D, Bottomley, AK, Coleman, C, Gill, M, and Wall, D, 'Reality and Rules in the Construction and Regulation of Police Suspicion' (1989) 17 IJ Sociology of Law 185.

Dixon, D, Bottomley, AK, Coleman, C, Gill, M, and Wall, D, 'Safeguarding the Rights of Suspects in Police Custody' (1990) 1 Policing and Society 115.

Dixon, D, Coleman, C, and Bottomley, AK, 'Consent and the Legal Regulation of Policing' (1990) 17 JLS 345.

Doherty, M J, and East, R, 'Bail Decisions in Magistrates' Courts' (1985) 25 BJ Crim 251

Doran, S, 'Descent to Avernus' (1989) 139 NLJ 1147.

Doran, S, 'Alternative Defences: the "invisible" burden on the trial judge' [1991] Crim LR 878.

Doran, S, and Jackson, J, 'The Case for Jury Waiver' [1997] Crim LR 155.

Doran, S and Glenn, R, Lay Involvement in Adjudication: Review of the Criminal Justice System in Northern Ireland (Criminal Justice Review Research Report no 11) (Belfast: SO, 2000).

Driscoll, J, 'Excluding Illegally Obtained Evidence in the United States' [1987] Crim LR 553.

Driver, E, 'Confessions and the Social Psychology of Coercion' (1968) 82 Harv LR 42.

Duff, A, (ed) *Criminal Law: Principle and Critique* (New York: CUP, 1998)

Duff, A, and Garland, D, (eds) *A Reader on Punishment* (Oxford: OUP, 1994).

Duff, P, 'The Prosecutor Fine and Social Control' (1993) 33 BJ Crim 481.

Duff, P, 'Crime Control, Due Process and "The Case for the Prosecution"' (1998) 38 BJ Crim 611.

Duff, P, 'The Defendant's Right to Trial by Jury: A Neighbour's View' [2000] Crim LR 85.

Duff, P, and Findlay, M, 'Jury vetting – The jury under attack' (1983) 3 LS 159.

Dunnighan, C, and Norris, C, The role of the informer in the criminal justice system (unpublished report, 1995).

Dunnighan, C, and Norris, C, 'The nark's game' (1996) 146 NLJ 456.

Dworkin, R M, *Taking Rights Seriously* (London: Duckworth, 1977).

Dworkin, R M, 'Principle, Policy, Procedure' in C Tapper (ed), *Crime, Proof and Punishment* (London: Butterworths, 1981).

Dyer, C, 'Anyone know what the judge is on about?' *The Guardian*, 17 July 2000.

East, R, 'Jury Packing: A Thing of the Past?' (1985) 48 MLR 518.

East, R, 'Police Brutality: Lessons of the Holloway Road Assault' (1987) 137 NLJ 1010.

East, R, and Thomas, P, 'Freedom of Movement: *Moss v McLachlan*' (1985) 12 LJS 77.

Easton, S, *The Case for the Right to Silence* 2nd edn (Aldershot: Ashgate, 1998).

Easton, S, 'Legal Advice, Common Sense and the Right of Silence' (1998) 2 IJ Evidence and Proof 109.

Eaton, M, 'The Question of Bail' in P Carlen and A Worrall (eds), *Gender, Crime and Justice* (Milton Keynes: Open UP, 1987).

Ecclestone, B, 'Work related deaths' (1998) 148 NLJ 910.

Editorial, 'Bail and Human Rights' [2000] Crim LR 69.

Edwards, J, *The Attorney General, Politics and the Public Interest* (London: Sweet & Maxwell, 1984).

Edwards, S, *Policing Domestic Violence* (London: Sage, 1989).

Ekblom, P, and Heal, K, The police response to calls from the public (Home Office Research and Planning Unit Paper 9) (London: Home Office, 1982).

Elias, R, *Victims Still: The Political Manipulation of Crime Victims* (London: Sage, 1993).

Elliman, S, 'Independent Information for the CPS' (1990) 140 NLJ 812.

Ellison, L, 'Cross-Examination in Rape Trials' [1998] Crim LR 605.

Emmins, C J, 'Why No Advance Information for Summary Offences?' [1987] Crim LR 608.

Erez, E, 'Victim participation in sentencing: and the debate goes on' (1994) 3 Int Rev Victimology 17.

Erez, E, 'Who's Afraid of the Big Bad Victim? Victim Impact Statements as Victim Empowerment *and* Enhancement of Justice' [1999] Crim LR 545.

Erez, E, and Rogers, L, 'The Effects of Victim Impact Statements on Criminal Justice Outcomes' (1999) 39 BJ Crim 216.

Ericson, R, *Making Crime: A Study of Detective Work* (London: Butterworths, 1981).

Ericson, R, *Reproducing Order: A Study of Police Patrol Work* (Toronto: University of Toronto Press, 1982).

Ericson, R, and Haggerty, K, *Policing the Risk Society* (Oxford: Clarendon, 1997).

Evans, R, 'Police Cautioning and the Young Adult Offender' [1991] Crim LR 598.

Evans, R, The Conduct of Police Interviews with Juveniles (Royal Commission on Criminal Justice Research Study no 8) (London: HMSO, 1993).

Evans, R, 'Evaluating Young Adult Diversion Schemes in the Metropolitan Police District' [1993] Crim LR 490.

Evans, R, 'Comparing Young Adult and Juvenile Cautioning in the Metropolitan Police District' [1993] Crim LR 572

Evans, R, 'Cautioning: Counting the cost of retrenchment' [1994] Crim LR 566.

Evans, R, 'Is a police caution amenable to judicial review?' [1996] Crim LR 104.

Evans, R, and Ellis, R, Police Cautioning in the 1990s (Home Office Research Findings no 52) (London: HMSO, 1997).

Evans, R, and Ferguson, T, Comparing Different Juvenile Cautioning Systems in One Police Force Area (Report to the Home Office Research and Planning Unit) (1991).

Evans, M, and Morgan, R, 'The European Convention for the Prevention of Torture: Operational Practice' (1992) 41 ICLQ 590.

Evans, R, and Wilkinson, C, 'Variation in Police Cautioning Policy and Practice in England and Wales' (1990) 29 Howard JCJ 155.

Faulkner, D, Darkness and Light: Justice, Crime and Management for Today (London: Howard League, 1996).

Bibliography

Fennell, P, Harding, C, Jorg, N, and Swart, B, (eds), *Criminal Justice in Europe: A Comparative Study* (Oxford: Clarendon, 1995).

Fenwick, H, 'Confessions, Recording Rules, and Miscarriages of Justice: A Mistaken Emphasis?' [1993] Crim LR 174.

Fenwick, H, 'Rights of victims in the criminal justice system' [1995] Crim LR 843.

Fenwick, H, 'Charge Bargaining and Sentence Discount: the Victim's Perspective' (1997) 5 Int R Victimology 23.

Fenwick, H, 'Procedural "Rights" of Victims of Crime: Public or Private Ordering of the Criminal Justice Process?' (1997) 60 MLR 317.

Ferraro, K, 'Policing Woman Battering' (1989) 36 Social Problems 61.

Field, S, 'Defining Interviews under PACE' (1993) 13 LS 254.

Field, S, 'Discretion and Accountability in Prosecution' in P Fennell, C Harding, N Jorg and B Swart (eds), *Criminal Justice in Europe: A Comparative Study* (Oxford: Clarendon, 1995).

Field, S and Jorg, N, 'Corporate Liability and Manslaughter: Should we be going Dutch?' [1991] Crim LR 156.

Field, S, and Jorg, N, 'Judicial regulation of covert and proactive policing in the Netherlands and England and Wales' in S Field and C Pelser (eds), *Invading the Private: State Accountability and New Investigative Methods in Europe* (Aldershot: Dartmouth, 1998).

Field, S, and Pelser, C (eds), *Invading the Private: State Accountability and New Investigative Methods in Europe* (Aldershot: Dartmouth, 1998).

Field, S, and Thomas, P, (eds), *Justice and Efficiency? The Royal Commission on Criminal Justice* (London: Blackwell, 1994) (also published as (1994) 21 JLS no 1).

Fielding, N, *Joining Forces* (London: Routledge, 1988).

Fielding, N, *Community Policing* (Oxford: Clarendon, 1995).

Fine, B, and Millar, R, *Policing the Miners' Strike* (London: Lawrence and Wishart, 1985).

Fionda, J, 'New Labour, Old Hat: Youth Justice and the Crime and Disorder Act 1998' [1999] Crim LR 36.

Fisher, G, 'Plea Bargaining's Triumph' (2000) 109 Yale LJ 857.

Fisher, Sir Henry, Report of an Inquiry into the Circumstances leading to the Trial of Three Persons on Charges arising out of the Death of Maxwell Confait and the Fire at 27 Doggett Road, London SE6 (HCP 90) (London: HMSO, 1977).

Fitzgerald, M, Ethnic Minorities and the Criminal Justice System (Royal Commission on Criminal Justice, Research Study no 20) (London: HMSO, 1993).

Fitzgerald, M, and Sibbitt, R, Ethnic Monitoring in Police Forces (Home Office Research Study no 173) (London: Home Office, 1997).

Fitzpatrick, B, 'Disclosure: Principles, Processes and Politics' in C Walker and K Starmer (eds), *Miscarriages of Justice* (London: Blackstone, 1999).

Flood-Page, C, and Mackie, A, Sentencing Practice: an examination of decisions in magistrates' courts and the Crown Court in the mid-1990s (Home Office Research Study no 180) (London: Home Office, 1998).

Foucault, M, *Discipline and Punish* (London: Allen Lane, 1977).

Foucault, M, *The History of Sexuality* vol 1 (London: Allen Lane, 1979).

Franey, R, Poor Law: The Mass Arrests of Homeless Claimants in Oxford (London: CPAG, 1983).

Frank, N, and Lombness, M, *Controlling Corporate Illegality* (Cincinnati: Anderson, 1988)

Frankel, M E, 'The Search for the Truth: An Umpireal View' (1975) 123 U Penn LR 1031.

Freeman, M, 'The Jury on Trial' (1981) CLP 65.

Fuller, L L, 'The Forms and Limits of Adjudication' (1978) 92 Harv LR 353.

Galanter, M, 'Mega-Law and Mega-Lawyering in the Contemporary United States' in R Dingwall and P Lewis (eds), *The Sociology of the Professions* (London: Macmillan, 1983).

Galligan, D, 'Regulating Pre-Trial Decisions', in I Dennis (ed), *Criminal Law and Justice* (London: Sweet & Maxwell, 1987).

Gardner, S, 'Recklessness refined' (1993) 109 LQR 21.

Garland, D, *Punishment and Modern Society* (Oxford: Clarendon Press, 1990).

Garland, D, 'The Limits of the Sovereign State: Strategies of Crime Control in Contemporary Society' (1996) 36 BJ Crim 445.

Gaskell, G, 'Black Youths and the Police' (1986) 2 Policing 26.

Gelsthorpe, L, and Giller, H, 'More Justice for Juveniles' [1990] Crim LR 153.

Gemmill, R, and Morgan-Giles, R, Arrest, Charge and Summons (Royal Commission on Criminal Procedure, Research Study no 9) (London: HMSO, 1981).

Genders, E, 'Reform of the Offences Against the Person Act: Lessons from the Law in Action' [1999] Crim LR 689.

General Council of the Bar, Code of Conduct for Barristers (1990).

Gill, O, 'Urban Stereotypes and Delinquent Incidents' (1976) 16 BJ Crim 312.

Gillespie, A, 'Practice direction on child defendants and the case of T v UK' (2000) 150 NLJ 320.

Glidewell, Sir I, The Review of the Crown Prosecution Service: A Report (Cmnd 3960) (London: HMSO, 1998).

Gobert, J, 'The Peremptory Challenge – An Obituary' [1989] Crim LR 528.

Gobert, J, *Justice, Democracy and the Jury* (Aldershot: Dartmouth, 1997).

Goldsmith, A, 'Taking Police Culture Seriously: Police Discretion and the Limits of the Law' (1990) 1 Policing and Society 91.

Goldsmith, A, 'External Review and Self-regulation' in A Goldsmith (ed), *Complaints Against the Police: the Trend to External Review* (Oxford: OUP, 1991).

Goldsmith, A, and Farson, S, 'Complaints against the Police in Canada: A New Approach' [1987] Crim LR 615.

Gordon, J, 'Juries as Judges of the Law' (1992) 108 LQR 272.

Gordon, P, 'Community Policing: Towards the Local Police State' in P Scraton (ed), *Law, Order and the Authoritarian State* (Milton Keynes: Open UP, 1987).

Goriely, T, 'The Development of Criminal Legal Aid in England and Wales' in R Young and D Wall (eds), *Access to Criminal Justice* (London: Blackstone, 1996).

Grace, S, Policing Domestic Violence in the 1990s (Home Office Research Study no 139) (London: Home Office, 1995).

Grace, S, Lloyd, C, and Smith, L, Rape: from Recording to Conviction (Research and Planning Unit Paper 71) (London: Home Office, 1992).

Graef, R, 'A Spiral of Mutual Mistrust' The Independent, 12 May 1989.

Gray, A, Fenn, P, and Rickman, N, 'Controlling Lawyers' Costs through Standard Fees: An Economic Analysis' in R Young and D Wall (eds), *Access to Criminal Justice* (London: Blackstone, 1996).

Green, P, *The Enemy Without: Policing and Class Consciousness in the Miners' Strike* (Milton Keynes: Open UP, 1990).

Greer, S, 'The Right to Silence: A Review of the Current Debate' (1990) 53 MLR 58.

Greer, S, 'Miscarriages of Justice Reconsidered' (1994) 57 MLR 58.

Greer, S, 'Towards a sociological model of the police informant' (1995) 46 BJ Sociology 509.

Gregory, J, Crown Court or Magistrates' Court? (Office of Population Censuses and Surveys) (London: HMSO, 1976).

Gregory, J, and Lees, S, 'Attrition in Rape and Sexual Assault Cases' (1996) 36 B J Crim 1.

Grevling, K, 'Fairness and the exclusion of evidence' (1997) 113 LQR 667.

Griffith, J, 'Ideology in Criminal Procedure or a Third "Model" of the Criminal Process' (1970) 79 Yale LJ 359.

Griffith, J, *The Politics of the Judiciary* 5th edn (London: Fontana, 1997).

Griffiths, J, and Ayres, R, 'A postscript to the Miranda Project: Interrogation of Draft Protestors' (1967) 77 Yale LJ 300.

Grosskurth, A, 'With Science on their Side' (1992) May, Legal Action 7.

Gudjonsson, G, *The Psychology of Interrogations, Confessions, and Testimony* (Chichester: Wiley, 1992).

Gudjonsson, G, and Mackeith, J, 'A Proven Case of False Confession: Psychological Aspects of the Coerced-compliant Type' (1990) 30 Med Sci Law 187.

Hain, P, 'Regulating for the common good' (1994) Utilities Law Review 90.

Haines, F, *Corporate Regulation: Beyond 'Punish or Persuade'* (Oxford: Clarendon, 1997).

Hall, A, 'Bail: Appeals' (1984) December, LAG Bull 145.

Hall, A, 'Police Complaints: Time for a Change' (1990) Legal Action, August, p 7.

Hall, S, Critcher, C, Jefferson, T, Clarke, J, and Roberts, B, *Policing the Crisis* (London: Macmillan, 1978).

Hansen, O, 'A Future for Legal Aid?' (1992) 19 JLS 85.

Harlow, C, and Rawlings, R, *Law and Administration* 2nd edn (London: Butterworths, 1997).

Harris, D, O'Boyle, M, and Warbrick, C, *Law of the European Convention on Human Rights* (London: Butterworths, 1995).

Harris, J, and Grace, S A question of evidence? Investigating and prosecuting rape in the 1990s (Home Office Research Study no 196) (London: Home Office, 1999).

Harrison, J, and Cragg, S, *Police Misconduct: Legal Remedies*, 3rd edn (London: LAG, 1995).

Harrison, J, and Cuneen, M, An Independent Police Complaints Commission (London: Liberty, 2000).

Hart, HLA, *The Concept of Law* (Oxford: Clarendon, 1961).

Hart, HLA, *Punishment and Responsibility* (Oxford: Clarendon Press, 1968).

Hartless, J, Ditton, J, Nair, G, and Phillips, S, 'More Sinned Against than Sinning: A Study of Young Teenagers' Experience of Crime' (1995) 35 BJ Crim 114.

Hawkins, K, 'Bargain and Bluff' (1983) 5 L Pol Q 8.

Hawkins, K, *Environment and Enforcement* (Oxford: OUP, 1984).

Hawkins, K, 'Compliance Strategy, Prosecution Policy, and Aunt Sally: A Comment on Pearce and Tombs' (1990) 30 BJ Crim 444.

Hayes, M, 'Where Now the Right to Bail?' [1981] Crim LR 20.

Health and Safety Executive, Statement on Enforcement Policy (1995).

Health and Safety Executive, Work-related Deaths: A Protocol for Liaison (HSE, 1998).

Heaton-Armstrong, I A, 'The Verdict of the Court ... and its Clerk?' (1986) 150 JP 340, 342.

Heberling, J, 'Plea Negotiation in England' in J Baldwin and A Bottomley (eds), *Criminal Justice: Selected Readings* (London: Martin Robertson, 1978).

Hedderman, C, and Moxon, D, Magistrates' Court or Crown Court?: Mode of Trial Decisions and Sentencing (Home Office Research Study, no 125) (London: HMSO, 1992).

Henham, R, *Sentencing Principles and Magistrates' Sentencing Behaviour* (Aldershot: Avebury, 1990).

Henham, R, 'Bargain Justice or Justice Denied? Sentence Discounts and the Criminal Process' (1999) 63 MLR 515.

Bibliography

Henham, R, 'Reconciling Process and Policy: Sentence Discounts in the Magistrates' Courts' [2000] Crim LR 436.

Henley, M, Davis, R, and Smith, B, 'The reactions of prosecutors and judges to victim impact statements' (1994) 3 Int Rev Victimology 83.

Herbert, P, 'Racism, impartiality and juries' (1995) 145 NLJ 1138.

Hilliard, B, 'Holloway Road – Unfinished Business' (1987) 137 NLJ 1035.

Hillyard, P, 'The Normalization of Special Powers: from Northern Ireland to Britain' in P Scraton (ed), *Law, Order and the Authoritarian State* (Milton Keynes: Open UP, 1987).

Hillyard, P, *Suspect Community* (London: Pluto Press, 1993).

Hillyard, P, and Gordon, D, 'Arresting Statistics: the drift to informal justice in England and Wales' (1999) 26 JLS 502.

Hilson, C, 'Discretion to Prosecute and Judicial Review' [1993] Crim LR 739.

Hinchcliffe, M, 'Beating the Bail Bandits' (1992) LS Gaz 1 July 19, p 20.

Hirst, M, 'Excess alcohol, incorrect procedures and inadmissible evidence' (1995) 54 CLJ 600.

Hobbs, D, *Doing the Business* (Oxford: OUP, 1988).

Hodgson, J, 'Tipping the Scales of Justice: The Suspect's Right to Legal Advice' [1992] Crim LR 854.

Hodgson, J, 'Adding Injury to Injustice: the Suspect at the Police Station' (1994) 21 JLS 85.

Hodgson, J, 'Vulnerable Suspects and the Appropriate Adult' [1997] Crim LR 785.

Holdaway, S, *Inside the British Police* (Oxford: Blackwell, 1983).

Holdaway, S, *The Racialisation of British Policing* (Houndmills: Macmillan, 1996).

Home Affairs Select Committee, Police Disciplinary and Complaints Procedures, 1st Report (HC 258-I) (London: SO, 1998).

Home Affairs Select Committee, Police Discipline and Complaints Procedures, 2nd Special Report (HC 683) (London: SO, 1998).

Home Affairs Select Committee, The Work of the Criminal Cases Review Commission, 1998-99 (HC 569) (London: SO 1999).

Home Office, Criminal Justice, Plans for Legislation (Cmnd 9658) (London: Home Office, 1986).

Home Office, The cautioning of offenders (Home Office Circular 59/1990).

Home Office, Costs of the Criminal Justice System 1992, vol 1 (London: Home Office, 1992).

Home Office, Memorandum of Good Practice (1992).

Home Office, Central Planning and Training Unit, *Guide to Interviewing* (London: HMSO, 1992).

Home Office, Criminal Statistics England and Wales 1992 (Cm 2410) (London: HMSO, 1993).

Home Office, Police Reform (Cm 2281) (London: HMSO, 1993).

Home Office (Narey Report), Review of Delay in the Criminal Justice System (London: Home Office, 1997).

Home Office, Statistics on the Operation of Prevention of Terrorism Legislation, (HO Stat Bull, 4/97) (London: Home Office, 1997).

Home Office, Juries in Serious Fraud Trials (London: Home Office Communication Directorate, 1998).

Home Office, Speaking up for Justice, Report of the Interdepartmental Working Group on the treatment of Vulnerable or Intimidated Witnesses in the Criminal Justice System, (London: Home Office, 1998).

Home Office, Police Complaints and Discipline, Statistical Bulletin, 1998-9 (London: Home Office, 1999).

Home Office, Statistics on Race and the Criminal Justice System (London: Home Office Research and Statistics Department, 1999).

Home Office, Criminal Statistics England and Wales 1998 (Cm 4649) (London: SO, 2000).

Home Office, Reforming the Law on Involuntary Manslaughter (London: Home Office, 2000).

Home Office, Complaints against the Police: A Consultation Paper (London: Home Office, 2000).

Honess, T M, Levi, M, and Charman, E A, 'Juror Competence in Processing Complex Information: Implications from a Simulation of the Maxwell Trial' [1998] Crim LR 763.

Hood, C, James, O, Jones, G, Scott, C, and Travers, T, *Regulation Inside Government* (Oxford: OUP, 1999).

Hood, R, *Race and Sentencing* (Oxford: Clarendon, 1992).

Hood, R, and Shute, S, The Parole System at Work (Home Office Research Study no 202) (London: Home Office, 2000).

Hough, M, and Mayhew, P, Taking Account of Crime (Home Office Research Study no 111) (London: HMSO, 1985).

Howard League, The Dynamics of Justice (Report of the Working Party on Criminal Justice Administration) (London: Howard League, 1993).

Hoyano, A, Hoyano, L, Davis, G, and Goldie, S, 'A Study of the Impact of the Revised Code for Crown Prosecutors' [1997] Crim LR 556.

Hoyano, L, 'Variations on a theme by Pigot: special measures directions for child witnesses' [2000] Crim LR 250.

Hoyle, C, *Negotiating Domestic Violence* (Oxford: Clarendon, 1998).

Hoyle, C, Cape, E, Morgan, R, and Sanders, A, Evaluation of the 'One Stop Shop' and Victim Statement Pilot Projects (London: Home Office, 1998).

Hoyle, C, Morgan, R, and Sanders, A, The Victim's Charter: An Evaluation of Pilot Projects (Home Office Research Findings no 108) (London: Home Office, 1999).

Hoyle, C, and Sanders, A, 'Police Response to Domestic Violence: From Victim Choice to Victim Empowerment' (2000) BJ Crim 40.

Hueklesby, A, 'The Problem with Bail Bandits' (1992) 142 NLJ 558.

Hueklesby, A, 'The Use and Abuse of Conditional Bail' (1994) 33 Howard JCJ 258.

Hueklesby, A, 'Bail or Jail? The Practical Operation of the Bail Act 1976' (1996) 23 JLS 213.

Hueklesby, A, 'Court Culture: An Explanation of Variations in the Use of Bail by Magistrates Courts' (1997) 36 Howard JCJ 129.

Hueklesby, A, 'Remand Decision Makers' [1997] Crim LR 269.

Hueklesby, A, and Marshall, E, 'Tackling Offending on Bail' (2000) 39 Howard JCJ 150.

Hughes, G, Pilkington, A, and Leistan, R, 'Diversion in a Culture of Severity' 37 (1998) Howard JCJ 16.

Hunt, A, 'Unravelling the golden thread – the prevention of terrorism and the presumption of innocence' (1994) Criminal Lawyer 4.

Hunt, A, and Young, R, 'Criminal Justice and Academics: Publish and Be Ignored?' (1995) 17 Holds LR 193.

Hunter, M, 'Judicial discretion: s 78 in practice' [1994] Crim LR 558.

Hutter, B, *The Reasonable Arm of the Law?* (Oxford: Clarendon, 1988).

Hyder, K, 'Cause for Complaint' (1990) New Statesman and Society, 12 January.

Imbert, Sir P, *The Times*, 17 May 1994.

Institute of Race Relations, *Policing against Black People* (London: IRR, 1987).

Irving, B, Police Interrogation: A Study of Current Practice (Royal Commission on Criminal Procedure Research Paper No 2) (London: HMSO, 1980).

Irving, B, and Dunnighan, C, Human Factors in the Quality Control of CID Investigations (Royal Commission on Criminal Justice, Research Study no 21) (London: HMSO, 1993).

Irving, B, and McKenzie, I, Police Interrogation: The Effects of the Police and Criminal Evidence Act 1984 (London: Police Foundation, 1989).

Jackson, J, 'The Insufficiency of Identification Evidence Based on Personal Impression' [1986] Crim LR 203.

Jackson, J, 'The Royal Commission on Criminal Justice: (2) The Evidence Recommendations' [1993] Crim LR 817.

Jackson, J, 'Evidence: Legal Perspective' in R Bull and D Carson (eds), *Handbook of Psychology in Legal Contexts* (Chichester: Wiley: 1995).

Jackson, J, 'Trial Procedures' in C Walker and K Starmer (eds), *Miscarriages of Justice* (London: Blackstone, 1999).

Jackson, J, and Doran, S, 'Diplock and the Presumption Against Jury Trial: a critique' [1992] Crim LR 755.

Jackson, J, and Doran, S, *Judge Without Jury* (Oxford: Clarendon, 1995).

Jackson, J, and Doran, S, 'Judge and Jury: Towards a New Division of Labour in Criminal Trials' (1997) 60 MLR 759.

Bibliography

Jaconelli, J, 'Some thoughts on jury secrecy' (1990) 10 LS 91.

James, A, Taylor, N, and Walker, C, 'The Criminal Cases Review Commission: Economy, Effectiveness and Justice' [2000] Crim LR 140.

Jefferson, T, 'Race, Crime and Policing' (1988) 16 IJ Soc of Law 521.

Jefferson, T, and Grimshaw, R, *Controlling the Constable: Police Accountability in England and Wales* (London: Muller, 1984).

Jefferson, T, and Walker, M, 'Ethnic Minorities in the Criminal Justice System' [1992] Crim LR 83.

Jefferson, T, Walker, M, and Seneviratne, M, 'Ethnic Minorities and Criminal Justice' in D Downes (ed), *Unravelling Criminal Justice* (London: Routledge, 1992).

Jennings, A, 'Is Silence Still Golden?' Archbold News, 14 June 2000, p 5.

John, T, and Maguire, M, 'Police surveillance and its regulation in England and Wales' in S Field and C Pelser (eds), *Invading the Private: State Accountability and New Investigative Methods in Europe* (Aldershot: Dartmouth, 1998).

Johnson, H, 'Court Duty Solicitors' (1992) Legal Action, May p 11.

Johnston, C, 'Trial by dossier' (1992) 142 NLJ 249.

Jones, C, 'Auditing Criminal Justice' (1993) 33 BJ Crim 187.

Jones, C, *Expert Witnesses* (Oxford: OUP, 1994).

Jones, T, McLean, B, and Young, J, *The Islington Crime Survey* (Aldershot: Gower, 1986).

Jones, T, Newburn, T, and Smith, D, 'Policing and the Idea of Democracy' (1996) 36 BJ Crim 182.

Jorg, N, Field S, and Brants, C, 'Are Inquisitorial and Adversarial Systems Converging?' in P Fennell, C Harding, N Jorg and B Swart (eds), *Criminal Justice in Europe* (Oxford: Clarendon, 1995).

Joutsen, M, 'Victim participation in proceedings and sentencing in Europe' (1994) 3 Int Rev Victimology 57.

JUSTICE, Unreliable Evidence? Confessions and the Safety of Convictions (London: JUSTICE, 1994).

JUSTICE Victims in Criminal Justice (London: JUSTICE, 1998).

Kalunta-Krumpton, A, 'The Prosecution and Defence of Black Defendants in Drug Trials' (1998) 38 BJ Crim 561.

Kalven, H, and Zeisel, H, *The American Jury* (Boston: Little Brown, 1966).

Kaye, T, "Unsafe and Unsatisfactory"? Report of the Independent Inquiry into the working practices of the West Midlands Police Serious Crime Squad (London: Civil Liberties Trust, 1991).

Keenan, C, Davis, G, Hoyano, L, and Maitland, L, 'Interviewing Allegedly Abused Children with a View to Criminal Prosecution' [1999] Crim LR 863.

Keith, M, 'The Criminal Histories of those cautioned in 1985 and 1988' (1992) 32 Home Office Research Bulletin 44.

Keith, M, *Race Riots and Policing* (London: UCL Press, 1993).

Kemp, C, Norris, C, and Fielding, N, 'Legal Manoeuvres in Police Handling of Disputes' in D Farrington and S Walklate (eds), *Offenders and Victims: Theory and Policy* (London: British Society of Criminology, 1992).

Kerrigan, K, 'Unlocking the Human Rights Floodgates' [2000] Crim LR 71.

Kibble, N, 'The sexual history provisions' [2000] Crim LR 274.

King, M, *The Effects of a Duty Solicitor Scheme: An Assessment of the Impact upon a Magistrates' Court* (London: Cobden Trust, 1977).

King, M, *The Framework of Criminal Justice* (London: Croom Helm, 1981).

King, M, and May, C, *Black Magistrates* (London: Cobden Trust, 1985).

Knight, M, *Criminal Appeals* (London: Stevens & Sons, 1970).

KPMG, Feasibility of an Independent System for Investigating Complaints Against the Police (Police Research Series no 124) (London: Home Office, 2000).

Lacey, N, (ed), *A Reader on Criminal Justice* (Oxford: OUP, 1994).

Lacey, N, 'Introduction: Making Sense of Criminal Justice' in N Lacey (ed), *A Reader on Criminal Justice* (Oxford: OUP, 1994).

Lacey, N, 'Community in Legal Theory: Idea, Ideal or Ideology' (1996) 15 Studies in Law, Politics and Society 105.

Lacey, N, 'Government as Manager, Citizen as Consumer: The Case of the Criminal Justice Act 1991' (1994) 57 MLR 534.

Lacey, N, 'Criminology, Criminal Law and Criminalization' in M Maguire, R Morgan and R Reiner (eds), *Oxford Handbook of Criminology* 2nd edn (Oxford: Clarendon, 1997).

Laing, J, 'The Mentally Disordered Suspect at the Police Station' [1995] Crim LR 371.

Langbein, J, 'The Criminal Trial Before Lawyers' (1978) 45 U Ch LR 263.

Law Commission, Involuntary Manslaughter (Report no 135) (London: HMSO, 1994).

Law Commission, Involuntary Manslaughter (Report no 237) (London: HMSO, 1996).

Law Commission, Evidence in Criminal Proceedings: Previous Misconduct of a Defendant, Consultation Paper no 141 (London: HMSO, 1996).

Law Commission, Consents to Prosecution (HC 1085) (Report no 255) (London: SO, 1998).

Law Commission, Prosecution Appeals Against Judges' Rulings (Consultation Paper 158) (July 2000).

Lawson, A, 'Whither the "General Arrest Condition"?' [1993] Crim LR 567.

Lawson, F, *Remedies of English Law* (Oxford: OUP, 1980).

Lawson, F, and Rudden, B, *Law of Property* (Oxford: OUP, 1982).

Laycock, G, and Tarling, R, 'Police Force Cautioning: Policy and Practice' (1985) 24 Howard JCJ 81.

Le Sueur, A, and Sunkin, M, 'Applications for Judicial Review: The Requirement of Leave' [1992] PL 102.

Leach, P, 'Automatic Denial of Bail and the European Convention' [1999] Crim LR 300.

Lee, M, *Youth, Crime, and Police Work* (Basingstoke: Macmillan, 1998).

Legal Action Group, Preventing Miscarriages of Justice (London: LAG Education and Service Trust Ltd, 1993).

Legal Aid Board 'Legal Advice and Assistance at Police Stations Register Arrangements 1995'.

Legal Aid Board, Annual Reports 1998-99 (HC 537) (London: SO, 1999).

Leigh H L, and Zedner, L, A Report on the Administration of Criminal Justice in the Pre-Trial Phase in England and Germany (Royal Commission on Criminal Justice, Research Study no 1) (London: HMSO, 1992).

Leishman, F, Loveday B, and Savage, S (eds), *Core Issues in Policing* (Harlow: Longman, 1996).

Leng, R, The Right to Silence in Police Interrogation: A Study of Some of the Issues Underlying the Debate (Royal Commission on Criminal Justice Research Study no 13) (London: HMSO, 1993).

Leng, R, and Sanders, A, 'The Criminal Law Revision Committee Report on Prostitution' [1983] Crim LR 644.

Leng, R, and Taylor, R, *Blackstone's Guide to the Criminal Procedure and Investigations Act 1996* (London: Blackstone, 1996).

Leng, R, Taylor, R, and Wasik, M, *Blackstone's Guide to the Crime and Disorder Act 1998* (London: Blackstone, 1998).

Leo, R, 'Police Interrogation and Social Control' (1994) 3 SLS 93.

Levenson, H, and Fairweather, F, *Police Powers, A Practitioner's Guide* (London: LAG, 1990).

Levi, M, The Investigation, Prosecution and Trial of Serious Fraud (Royal Commission on Criminal Justice Research Study no 14) (London: HMSO, 1993).

Lewis, H, and Mair, G, Bail and Probation Work II: the use of London Bail Hostels for Bailees (Home Office Research and Planning Unit Paper no 50) (London: Home Office, 1989).

Lewis, G, Gewirtz, S, and Clarke, J (eds), *Rethinking social policy* (Milton Keynes: Open UP, 2000).

Lewis, P, 'The CPS and Acquittals by Judge: Finding the Balance' [1997] Crim LR 653.

Lewis, P, 'The Human Rights Act 1998: Shifting the Burden' [2000] Crim LR 667.

Lidstone, K, Hogg, R, and Sutcliffe, F, Prosecution by Private Individuals and Non-Police Agencies (Royal Commission on Criminal Procedure Research Study no 10) (London: HMSO, 1981).

Lidstone, K and Palmer, C *Bevan and Lidstone's The Investigation of Crime* 2nd edn (London: Butterworths, 1996).

Littlechild, B, 'Reassessing the Role of the "Appropriate Adult"' [1995] Crim LR 540.

Lloyd-Bostock, S, 'The Effects on Juries of Hearing About the Defendant's Previous Criminal Record: A Simulation Study' [2000] Crim LR 734.

Lord Chancellor's Department, Legal Aid in England and Wales: A New Framework (Cm 118) (London: Lord Chancellor's Department, 1987).

Lord Chancellor's Department, A New Framework for Local Justice (Cm 1829) (London: LCD, 1992).

Lord Chancellor's Department, Judicial Statistics 1992 (Cm 2268) (London: HMSO, 1993).

Lord Chancellor's Department, Legal Aid – Targeting Need: The Future of Publicly Funded Help in Solving Legal Problems and Disputes in England and Wales (Cm 2854) (London: HMSO, 1995).

Lord Chancellor's Department, Modernising Justice: the Government's Plans for Reforming Legal Services and the Courts (Cm 4155) (London: SO, 1998).

Lord Chancellor's Department, The Future Role of the Justices' Clerk: A Strategic Steer (London: LCD, 2000).

Lord Chancellor's Department, Judicial Statistics 1999 (Cm 4786) (London: SO, 2000).

Loveday, B, 'Recent Developments in Police Complaints Procedure' (1989) Local Gov Studies, May/June, p 25.

Loveday, B, 'The impact of performance culture on criminal justice agencies in England and Wales' (1999) IJ Soc of Law 351.

Lustgarten, L, *The Governance of Police* (London: Sweet & Maxwell, 1986).

Mack, J A, 'Full-time Major Criminals and the Courts' (1976) 39 MLR 241.

Macphail, I D, 'Safeguards in the Scottish Criminal Justice System' [1992] Crim LR 144.

Macpherson, Sir W, The Stephen Lawrence Inquiry (Cm 4262-I) (London: SO, 1999).

Magistrates' Association, Sentencing Guidelines (London: Magistrates' Association, 1993).

Magistrates' Association, Sentencing Guidelines (London: Magistrates' Association, 1997).

Maguire, M, 'Effects of the PACE Provisions on Detention and Questioning' (1988) 28 BJ Crim 19.

Maguire, M, 'The Wrong Message at the Wrong Time?' in D Morgan and G Stephenson (eds), *Suspicion and Silence: The Right to Silence in Criminal Investigations* (London: Blackstone, 1994).

Maguire, M, 'Complaints against the Police: Where Now?' (Unpublished manuscript).

Maguire, M, 'Crime Statistics, Patterns and Trends' in M Maguire, R Morgan and R Reiner (eds), *Oxford Handbook of Criminology* 2nd edn (Oxford: Clarendon, 1997).

Maguire, M, and Corbett, C, A Study of the Police Complaints System (London: HMSO, 1991).

Maguire, M, and John, T, Intelligence, Surveillance and Informants (Police Research Group Paper no 64) (London: Home Office, 1995).

Maguire, M, and Norris, C, The Conduct and Supervision of Criminal Investigations (Royal Commission on Criminal Justice, Research Study no 5) (London: HMSO, 1992).

Maguire, M, and Pointing, J (eds), *Victims of Crime: A New Deal?* (Milton Keynes: Open UP, 1988)

Maher, G, 'Jury verdicts and the presumption of innocence' (1983) 3 LS 146.

Mair, G, and Lloyd, C, 'Policy and Progress in the Development of Bail Schemes in England and Wales' in F Paterson (ed), Understanding Bail in Britain (Edinburgh: Scottish Office, 1996).

Malleson, K, 'Miscarriages of Justice and the Accessibility of the Court of Appeal' [1991] Crim LR 323.

Malleson, K, 'Appeals against Conviction and the Principle of Finality' (1994) 21 JLS 151.

Malleson, K, 'The Criminal Cases Review Commission: How Will It Work?' [1995] Crim LR 929.

Malleson, K, Review of the Appeal Process (Royal Commission on Criminal Justice, Research Study no 17) (London: HMSO, 1993).

Mansfield, G, and Peay, J, *The Director of Public Prosecutions* (London: Tavistock, 1987).

Mansfield, M, and Taylor, N, 'Post-Conviction Procedures' in C Walker and K Starmer (eds), *Justice in Error* (London: Blackstone, 1993).

Mark, R, *Minority Verdict* The 1973 Dimbleby Lecture (London: BBC, 1973).

Marks, S, 'Civil Liberties at the Margin: the UK Derogation and the European Court of Human Rights' (1995) 15 OJLS 68.

Marx, G, *Undercover: Police surveillance in America* (Berkeley: U of Calif Press, 1988).

Matheson, D, *Legal Aid: The New Framework* (London: Butterworths, 1988).

Matravers, M, (ed) *Punishment and Political Theory* (Oxford: Hart, 1999).

Mattinson, J, Criminal Appeals England and Wales, 1995 and 1996 (Research and Statistical Bulletin 3/98) (London: Home Office, 1998).

May, Sir J, Report of the Inquiry into the Circumstances Surrounding the Convictions arising out of the bomb attacks in Guildford and Woolwich in 1974, 2nd Report (1992-3 HC 296).

May, R, 'Jury Selection in the United States: Are there lessons to be learned?' [1998] Crim LR 270.

Mayhew, P, Elliott, D, and Dowds, L, The 1988 British Crime Survey (Home Office Research Study no 111) (London: HMSO, 1989).

McBarnet, D, *Conviction* (London: Macmillan, 1983).

McBarnet, D, 'Victim in the witness box – confronting victimology's stereotype' (1983) 7 Contemporary Crises 293.

McCabe, S, and Purves, R, *By-passing the Jury* (Oxford: Basil Blackwell, 1972).

McCabe, S, and Purves, R, *The Jury at Work* (Oxford: Basil Blackwell, 1972).

McCabe, S, and Purves, R, *The Shadow Jury at Work* (Oxford: Basil Blackwell, 1974).

McConville, M, 'Search of Persons and Premises: New Data from London' [1983] Crim LR 605.

McConville, M, 'Shadowing the jury' (1991) 141 NLJ 1588.

McConville, M, 'Videotaping Interrogations: Police behaviour on and off camera' [1992] Crim LR 532.

McConville, M, Corroboration and Confessions: The Impact of a Rule that no Conviction can be Sustained on the Basis of Confession Evidence Alone (Royal Commission on Criminal Justice Research Study no 13) (London: HMSO, 1993).

McConville, M, 'Plea Bargaining: Ethics and Politics' (1998) 25 JLS 562.

McConville, M, and Baldwin, J, *Courts, Prosecution and Conviction* (Oxford: OUP, 1981).

McConville, M, and Baldwin, J, 'The Role of Interrogation in Crime Discovery and Conviction' (1982) 22 BJ Crim 165.

McConville, M, and Bridges, L, 'Pleading guilty whilst maintaining innocence' (1993) 143 NLJ 160.

McConville, M, and Bridges, L (eds), *Criminal Justice in Crisis* (Aldershot: Edward Elgar, 1994).

McConville, M, and J Hodgson, J, Custodial Legal Advice and the Right to Silence (Royal Commission on Criminal Justice Research Study no 16) (London: HMSO, 1993).

McConville, M, Hodgson, J, Bridges, L, and Pavlovic, A, *Standing Accused* (Oxford: Clarendon, 1994).

McConville, M, and Mirsky, C, 'The State, the Legal Profession, and the Defence of the Poor' (1988) 15 JLS 342.

McConville, M, and Morrell, P, 'Recording the Interrogation: Have the Police got it Taped?' [1983] Crim LR 158.

McConville, M, and Sanders, A, 'Fairness and the CPS' (1992) 142 NLJ 120.

McConville, M, and Sanders, A, 'Weak Cases and the CPS' (1992) LS Gaz, 12 February, p 24.

McConville, M, Sanders, A, and Leng, R, *The Case for the Prosecution* (London: Routledge, 1991).

McConville, M, Sanders, A, and Leng, R, 'Descriptive or Critical Sociology: The Choice is Yours' (1997) 37 BJ Crim 347.

McConville, M, and Shepherd, D, *Watching Police, Watching Communities* (London: Routledge, 1992).

McEldowney, J, 'Stand by for the Crown – An Historical Analysis' [1979] Crim LR 272.

McEwan, J, 'Documentary Hearsay Evidence – Refuge for the Vulnerable Witness?' [1989] Crim LR 629.

McEwan, J, 'Adversarial and Inquisitorial Proceedings' in R Bull and D Carson (eds), *Handbook of Psychology in Legal Contexts* (Chichester: Wiley, 1995).

McEwan, J, 'Law Commission Dodges the Nettles in Consultation Paper no 141' [1997] Crim LR 93.

McEwan, J, *Evidence and the Adversarial Process* 2nd edn (Oxford: Hart, 1998).

McIvor, G, 'The Impact of Bail Services in Scotland' in F Paterson (ed), Understanding Bail in Britain (Edinburgh: Scottish Office, 1996).

McKenzie, I, 'Regulating Custodial Interviews: A Comparative Study' (1994) 22 IJ Sociology of Law 239.

McKenzie, J, Morgan, R, and Reiner, R, 'Helping the Police with their Enquiries' [1990] Crim LR 22.

McLaughlin, E, and Murji, K, 'The end of public policing? Police reform and "the new managerialism"' in L Noaks, M Levi and M Maguire (eds), *Contemporary Issues in Criminology* (Cardiff: University of Wales Press, 1995).

McLaughlin, H, 'Court Clerks: Advisers or Decision-Makers' (1990) 30 BJ Crim 358.

McMahon, M, 'Police Accountability: the Situation of Complaints in Toronto' (1988) 12 Contemporary Crises 301.

Meehan, A, 'Internal Police Records and the Control of Juveniles' (1993) 33 BJ Crim 504.

Memon, A, et al, 'Improving the Quality of the Police Interview: Can Training in the Use of Cognitive Techniques help?' (1995) 5 Policing and Society 53.

Metropolitan Police Commisioner, Annual Reports, 1991-1998.

Mhlanga, B, Race and the CPS (London, SO, 1999).

Miers, D, 'The Responsibilities and the Rights of Victims of Crime' (1992) 55 MLR 482.

Mirfield, P, 'Successive Confessions and the Poisonous Tree' [1996] Crim LR 554.

Mirfield, P, *Silence, Confessions and Improperly Obtained Evidence* (Oxford: Clarendon, 1997).

Mirrlees-Black, C, and Budd, T, Policing and the Public: Findings from the 1996 British Crime Survey (Home Office Research Findings no 60) (London: HMSO, 1997).

Mirrlees-Black, C, Budd, T, Partridge, S, and Mayhew, P, The 1998 British Crime Survey (Home Office Statistical Bulletin 21/98) (London: Home Office, 1998).

Moody, S, and Tombs, J, *Prosecution in the Public Interest* (Edinburgh: Scottish Academic Press, 1982).

Moody, S, and Tombs, J, 'Plea negotiations in Scotland' [1983] Crim LR 297.

Morgan, D, and Stephenson, G (eds), *Suspicion and Silence: The Right to Silence in Criminal Investigations* (London: Blackstone, 1994).

Morgan, J, and Zedner, L, *Child Victims* (Oxford: Clarendon, 1992).

Morgan, P, and Henderson, P, Remand Decisions and Offending on Bail (Home Office Research Study no 184) (London: Home Office, 1998).

Morgan, R, 'The Process is the Rule and the Punishment is the Process' (1996) 59 MLR 306.

Morgan, R, and Jones, S, 'Bail or Jail?' in E Stockdale and S Casale (eds), *Criminal Justice Under Stress* (London: Blackstone, 1992).

Morgan, R, and Newburn, T, *The Future of Policing* (Oxford: Clarendon, 1997).

Morgan, R, and Sanders, A, The Uses of Victim Statements (London: Home Office, 1999).

Morgan, R, Reiner, R, and McKenzie, I, Police Powers and Policy: A Study of the Work of Custody Officers (report to ESRC) (unpublished).

Morison, J, and Leith, P, *The Barrister's World* (Milton Keynes: Open UP, 1992).

Morley, R, and Mullender, A, 'Hype of Hope? The Importation of Pro-Arrest Policies and Batterer's Programmes from North America to Britain as Key Measures for Preventing Violence against Women in the Home' (1992) 6 IJLF 265.

Morris, A, and Gelsthorpe, L, 'Something Old, Something Borrowed, Something Blue, But Something New? A Comment on the Prospects for Restorative Justice under the Crime and Disorder Act 1999' [2000] Crim LR 18.

Morris, P, and Heal, K, Crime Control and the Γ⸌ ⸌ce (Home Office Research Study no 67) (London: HMSO, 1981).

Moston, S, and Engelberg, T, 'Police Questioning Techniques in Tape Recorded Interviews with Criminal Suspects' (1993) 3 Policing and Society 223.

Moston, S, and Stephenson, G, The Questioning and Interviewing of Suspects Outside the Police Station (Royal Commission on Criminal Justice Research Study no 22) (London: HMSO, 1993).

Moston, S, and Williamson, T, 'The Extent of Silence in Police Stations' in S Greer and R Morgan (eds), *The Right to Silence Debate: Proceedings of a Conference at the University of Bristol in March 1990* (Bristol: University of Bristol, 1990).

Moxon, D, Sentencing Practice in the Crown Court (Home Office Research Study no 103) (London: HMSO, 1988).

Mulcahy, A, 'The Justifications of Justice: Legal Practitioners' Accounts of Negotiated Case Settlements in Magistrates' Courts' (1994) 34 BJ Crim 411.

Mulcahy, A, Brownlee, I, and Walker, C, 'An Evaluation of Pre-Trial Reviews in Leeds and Bradford Magistrates' Courts' (1993) 33 Home Office Research Bulletin 10.

Mulhal, S, and Swift, A, *Liberals and Communitarians* 2nd edn (Oxford: Basil Blackwell, 1996).

Munday, R, 'The Wilder Permutations of s 1(f) of the Criminal Evidence Act 1898'(1987) 7 LS 137.

Munday, R, 'Jury trial, continental style' (1993) 13 LS 204.

Munday, R, 'What do the French think of their jury?' (1995) 15 LS 65.

Munday, R, 'Inferences from Silence and European Human Rights Law' [1996] Crim LR 370.

Mungham, G, and Bankowski, Z, 'The jury in the legal system' in P Carlen (ed), *The Sociology of Law* (Keele: University of Keele, 1976).

Mungham, G, and Thomas, P, 'Solicitors and Clients: Altruism of Self-interest?' in R Dingwall and P Lewis (eds), *The Sociology of the Professions* (London: Macmillan, 1983).

NACRO 'Policing Local Communities – The Tottenham Experiment' (London: NACRO, 1997).

Narey, M, Review of Delay in the Criminal Justice System (London: Home Office, 1997).

Nation, D, 'He can always appeal' (1992) 156 JP 521.

Nelken, D, *The Limits of the Legal Process* (London: Academic Press, 1983).

Nemitz, T, and Bean, P, 'The Use of the Appropriate Adult Scheme' (1994) 34 Med Sci and the Law 161.

Newton, T, 'The Place of Ethics in Investigative Interviewing by Police Officers' (1998) Howard JCJ 52.

Niblett, J, *Disclosure in Criminal Proceedings*, (London: Blackstone, 1997).

Nicolson, D, and Reid, K, 'Arrest for Breach of the Peace and the European Convention on Human Rights' [1996] Crim LR 764.

Noaks, L, Levi, M, and Maguire, M, (eds), *Contemporary Issues in Criminology* (Cardiff: University of Wales Press, 1995).

Nobles, R, and Schiff, D, 'Miscarriages of Justice: A Systems Approach' (1995) 58 MLR 299.

Nobles, R, and Schiff, D, 'Criminal Appeal Act 1995: The Semantics of Jurisdiction' (1996) 59 MLR 573.

Nobles, R, and Schiff, D, 'The Never Ending Story: Disguising Tragic Choices in Criminal Justice' (1997) 60 MLR 293.

Nobles, R, and Schiff, D, *Understanding Miscarriages of Justice* (Oxford: OUP, 2000).

Norrie, A, *Crime, Reason and History* (London: Weidenfeld and Nicolson, 1993).

Norrie, A, 'The Limits of Justice: Finding Fault in the Criminal Law' (1996) 59 MLR 540.

Norrie, A, 'Simulacra of Morality? Beyond the Ideal/Actual Antinomies of Criminal Justice' in A Duff (ed), *Criminal Law: Principle and Critique* (New York: CUP, 1998).

Norris, C, Fielding, N, Kemp, C, and Fielding, J, 'Black and Blue: An Analysis of the Influence of Race on being Stopped by the Police' (1992) 43 BJ Soc 207.

O'Brien, D, and Epp, J A, 'Salaried Defenders and the Access to Justice Act 1999' (2000) 63 MLR 394.

O'Connor, P, 'Prosecution Disclosure: Principle, Practice and Justice' in C Walker and K Starmer (eds), *Justice in Error* (London: Blackstone, 1993).

O'Connor, P, 'The Court of Appeal: Re-Trials and Tribulations' [1990] Crim LR 615.

O'Donnell, I, and Edgar, K, 'Routine Victimisation in Prisons' (1998) 37 Howard JCJ 266.

O'Mahony, P, 'The Kerry babies case: Towards a Social Psychological Analysis' [1992] 13 Irish Jo Psychology 223.

Ovey, C, 'The European Convention on Human Rights and the Criminal Lawyer: An Introduction' [1998] Crim LR 4.

Packer, H L, *The Limits of the Criminal Sanction* (Stanford: Stanford UP, 1968).

Padfield, N, 'The Right to Bail: a Canadian Perspective' [1993] Crim LR 510.

Padfield, N, 'Bailing and Sentencing the Dangerous' in N Walker (ed), *Dangerous People* (London: Blackstone, 1996).

Painter, K, et al, The Hammersmith Crime Survey (Enfield: Centre for Criminology, Middlesex University, 1989).

Palmer, C, 'Still Vulnerable After All These Years' [1996] Crim LR 633.

Parker, H, Casburn M, and Turnbull, D, *Receiving Juvenile Justice* (Oxford: Basil Blackwell, 1981).

Parker, H, Sumner, M, and Jarvis, G, *Unmasking the Magistrates* (Milton Keynes: Open UP, 1989).

Panatzis, C, and Gordon, D, 'Television Licence Evasion and the Criminalisation of Female Poverty' (1997) 36 Howard JCJ 170.

Paterson, F, (ed), *Understanding Bail in Britain* (Edinburgh: Scottish Office, 1996).

Paterson, F, and Whittaker, C, *Operating Bail* (Edinburgh: Scottish Office, 1994).

Pattenden, R, 'Should Confessions be Corroborated?' (1991) 107 LQR 319.

Pattenden, R, 'Evidence of Previous Malpractice by Police Witnesses and *Edwards*' [1992] Crim LR 549.

Pattenden, R, *English Criminal Appeals 1844-1994* (Oxford: Clarendon Press, 1996).

Pattenden, R, 'Silence: Lord Taylor's Legacy' (1998) 2 IJ Evidence and Proof 141.

Pearce, F, and Tombs, S, 'Ideology, Hegemony and Empiricism: Compliance Theories of Regulation' (1990) 30 BJ Crim 423.

Pearce, F, and Tombs, S, 'Hazards, Law and Class: Contextualising the regulation of corporate crime' (1997) 6 Social and Legal Studies 79.

Percy-Smith, J, and Hillyard, P, 'Miners in the Arms of the Law: A Statistical Analysis' (1985) 12 JLS 345.

Phillips, C, and Brown, D, Entry into the Criminal Justice System: a Survey of Police Arrests and their Outcomes (Home Office Research Study no 185) (London: Home Office, 1998).

Pigot, Judge Thomas, Report of the Advisory Group on Video-Recorded Evidence, (London: HMSO, 1989).

Piliavin, I, and Briar, S, 'Police Encounters with Juveniles' (1964) 70 AJS 206.

Plotnikoff, J, and Woolfson, R, Information and Advice for Prisoners about Grounds for Appeal and the Appeals Process (Royal Commission on Criminal Justice, Research Study no 18) (HMSO, 1993).

Plotnikoff, J, and Woolfson, R, *From Committal to Trial: Delay at the Crown Court* (London: Law Society, 1993).

Plotnikoff, J, and Woolfson, R, Witness Care in Magistrates' Courts and the Youth Court (Home Office Research Findings no 68) (London: Home Office , 1998).

Police Complaints Authority, Annual Report, 1995/6 (London: SO, 1996).

Police Complaints Board, Triennial Report (London: HMSO, 1980).

Pollard, C, 'A Case for Disclosure' [1994] Crim LR 42.

Pollard, C, 'Public Safety, Accountability and the Courts' [1996] Crim LR 152.

Pollard, C, 'Victims and the criminal justice system' [2000] Crim LR 5.

Pollard, C, and Keyser, J, 'Restorative Justice in the Thames Valley Police', keynote speech delivered at Toronto International Conference on Restorative Justice, August 2000.

Ponting, C, *The Right to Know, The Inside Story of the Belgrano Affair* (London: Sphere, 1985).

Povey, D, and Prime, J, Recorded Crime Statistics, England and Wales, April 1998 – March 1999 (Home Office Statistical Bulletin 21/98) (London: Home Office, 1998).

Powis, D, *The Signs of Crime* (London: McGraw-Hill, 1977).

Pratt, J, 'Diversion from the Juvenile Court' (1986) 26 B J Crim 212.

Pratt, J, and Bray, K, 'Bail Hostels – Alternatives to Custody?' (1985) 25 BJ Crim 160.

Raifeartaigh, U N, 'Reconciling Bail Law with the Presumption of Innocence' (1997) 17 Ox JLS 1.

Raine, J, and Willson, M, 'Just Bail at the Police Station?' (1995) 22 JLS 571.

Raine, J, and Willson, M, 'The Imposition of Conditions in Bail Decisions' (1996) 35 Howard JCJ 256.

Raine, J, and Willson, M, 'Police Bail with Conditions' (1997) 37 BJ Crim 593.

Redmayne, M, 'Doubts and Burdens: DNA Evidence, Probability and the Courts' [1995] Crim LR 464.

Redmayne, M, 'Process Gains and Process Values: the CPIA 1996' (1997) 60 MLR 79.

Redmayne, M, 'The DNA Database: Civil Liberty and Evidentiary Issues' [1998] Crim LR 437.

Regan, F, Paterson, A, Goriely, T, and Fleming, D, (eds), *The Transformation of Legal Aid* (Oxford: OUP, 1999).

Reiner, R, *Chief Constables* (Oxford: OUP, 1991).

Reiner, R, *The Politics of the Police* (London: Harvester, Wheatsheaf, 1992).

Reiner, R, 'Policing and the Police' in M Maguire, R Morgan and R Reiner (eds), *Oxford Handbook of Criminology* (Oxford: OUP, 1997).

Reiner R, and Spencer, S, (eds), *Accountable Policing* (London: IPPR, 1993).

Rex, J, *The Ghetto and the Underclass* (Aldershot: Avebury, 1998).

Richardson, G, with Ogus, A, and Burrows, P, *Policing Pollution: A Study of Regulation and Enforcement* (Oxford: Clarendon, 1983).

Ridley, A, and Dunford, L, 'No Soul to be damned, no body to be kicked: responsibility, blame, and corporate punishment' (1996) 24 IJ Soc of Law 1.

Riley, D, and Vennard, J, Triable-Either-Way Cases: Crown Court or Magistrates' Court? (Home Office Research Study, no 98) (London: HMSO, 1988).

Roach, K, 'Four Models of the Criminal Process' (1999) 89 J Criminal Law and Criminology 671.

Robbilliard, J, and McEwan, J, *Police Powers and the Individual* (Oxford: Basil Blackwell, 1986).

Robbins, J, 'Who said anything about law?' (1990) 140 NLJ 1275.

Roberts, D, 'Questioning the Suspect: the Solicitor's Role' [1993] Crim LR 369.

Roberts, P, 'Science in the Criminal Process' (1994) 14 OJLS 469.

Roberts, P, 'What Price a Free Market in Forensic Science?' (1996) 36 BJ Crim 37.

Roberts, P, 'All the Usual Suspects: A Critical Appraisal of Law Commission Consultation Paper no 141' [1997] Crim LR 75.

Roberts, P, and Willmore, C, The Role of Forensic Science Evidence in Criminal Proceedings (Royal Commission on Criminal Justice Research Study no 11) (London: HMSO, 1993).

Robertshaw, P, Cox, S, and Van Hoen, N, 'Jury Populations and Jury Verdicts' (1992) 20 IJ Sociology of Law 271.

Robertshaw, P, *Summary Justice* (London: Cassell, 1998).

Robertson, G, 'Entrapment evidence: manna from heaven, or fruit of the poisoned tree?' [1994] Crim LR 805.

Rock, P, *The Social World of an English Crown Court* (Oxford: Clarendon, 1993).

Rose, D, *In the Name of the Law: The Collapse of Criminal Justice* (London: Jonathan Cape, 1996).

Royal Commission on Criminal Justice (RCCJ), Report (Cm 2263) (London: HMSO, 1993).

Royal Commission on Criminal Procedure, The Investigation and Prosecution of Criminal Offences in England and Wales: The Law and Procedure (Cmnd 8092-1) (London: HMSO, 1981).

Rozenberg, J, *The Case for the Crown* (Wellingborough: Equation, 1987).

Rozenberg, J, 'Miscarriages of Justice' in E Stockdale and S Casale (eds), *Criminal Justice Under Stress* (London: Blackstone, 1992).

Rozenberg, J, *The Search for Justice* (London: Hodder & Stoughton, 1994).

Samuels, A, 'Custody Time Limits' [1997] Crim LR 260.

Sandel, M, (ed), *Liberalism and its Critics* (New York: New York UP, 1984).

Sanders, A, 'Does Professional Crime Pay?: A Critical Comment on Mack' (1977) 40 MLR 553.

Sanders, A, 'The Erosion of Jury Trial' (1980) 5 Holds LR 21.

Sanders, A, 'Prosecution Decisions and the 'Attorney-General's Guidelines' [1985] Crim LR 4.

Sanders, A, 'Class Bias in Prosecutions' (1985) 24 Howard JCJ 76.

Sanders, A, 'Diverting Offenders from Prosecution: Can we learn from other Countries?' (1986) 150 JP 614.

Sanders, A, 'Arrest, Charge and Prosecution' (1986) 6 LS 257.

Sanders, A, 'Constructing the Case for the Prosecution' (1987) 14 JLS 229.

Sanders, A, 'Personal Violence and Pubic Order' (1988) 16 IJ Soc L 359.

Sanders, A, 'Rights, Remedies and the Police and Criminal Evidence Act' [1988] Crim LR 802.

Sanders, A, 'The Limits to Diversion from Prosecution' (1988) 28 BJ Crim 513.

Sanders, A, 'Access to a Solicitor and s 78 PACE' (1990) LS Gaz 31 October p 17.

Sanders, A, 'The Silent Code' (1994) 144 NLJ 946.

Sanders, A, 'Access to Justice in the Police Station: An Elusive Dream?' in R Young and D Wall (eds), *Access to Criminal Justice* (London: Blackstone, 1996).

Sanders, A, 'What Principles Underlie Criminal Justice Policy in the 1990s?' (1998) 18 OJLS 533.

Sanders, A, Taking Account of Victims in the Criminal Justice System (Edinburgh: Scottish Office, 1999).

Sanders, A, *The Future of Magistrates' Courts and the Magistracy in England and Wales* (London: IPPR, 2000).

Sanders, A, and Bridges, L, 'Access to Legal Advice and Police Malpractice' [1990] Crim LR 494.

Sanders, A, and Bridges, L, 'The right to legal advice', in C Walker and K Starmer (eds), *Miscarriages of Justice* (London: Blackstone, 1999).

Sanders, A, Bridges, L, Mulvaney, A, and Crozier, G, *Advice and Assistance at Police Stations and the 24 Hour Duty Solicitor Scheme* (London: Lord Chancellor's Department, 1989).

Sanders, A, Creaton, J, Bird, S, and Weber, L, *Victims with Learning Disabilities* (Oxford: Centre for Criminological Research, 1997).

Sanders, A, Hoyle, C, Morgan, R, Cape, E, 'Victim Statements: can't work, don't work' [2001] Crim LR (forthcoming).

Sanders, A, and Young, R, *Criminal Justice* (London: Butterworths, 1994).

Sanders, A, and Young, R, 'The Rule of Law, Due Process, and Pre-Trial Criminal Justice' (1994) 47 CLP 125.

Sanders, A, and Young, R, 'The Legal Wilderness of Police Interrogation' in (1994) The Tom Sargant Memorial Lecture, 20.

Sarat, A, 'Vengeance, Victims and the Identities of Law' (1997) 6 Social and Legal Studies 163.

Savage, S, and Charman, S, 'Managing Change', in F Leishman, B Loveday and S Savage (eds), *Core Issues in Policing* (Harlow: Longman, 1996).

Scarman, Sir L, The Brixton Disorders: 10-12 Apil 1981 (Cmnd 8427) (London: HMSO, 1981).

Schulhofer, S, 'Plea Bargaining as Disaster' (1992) 101 Yale LJ 1979.

Schwartz, J, 'Relativism, reflective equilibrium, and justice' (1997) 17 LS 128.

Scott, I, 'Appeals to the Crown Court following Summary Conviction' (paper delivered to SPTL Criminal Law Group) (1977).

Scott, I, 'Criminal Procedure: Appeals to Quarter Sessions' (1970) 134 JP and G Rev 843.

Scott, R, and Stuntz, W J, 'A Reply: Imperfect Bargains, Imperfect Trials and Innocent Defendants' (1992) 101 YLJ 2011.

Scraton, R, and Chadwick, K, *In the Arms of the Law: Coroners Inquests and Deaths in Custody* (London: Pluto Press, 1987).

Seabrooke, S, and Sprack, J, *Criminal Evidence and Procedure* 2nd edn (London: Blackstone: 1999).

Seago, P, Walker, C, and Wall, D, 'The Development of the Professional Magistracy in England and Wales' [2000] Crim LR 631.

Sealy, L, and Cornish, W, 'Juries and the Rules of Evidence' [1973] Crim LR 208.

Sebba, L, *Third parties: victims and the criminal justice system* (Columbus: Ohio State UP, 1996).

Sebba, L, 'Sentencing and the victim: the aftermath of *Payne*' (1994) 3 Int Rev Victimology 141.

Shapland, J, 'Fiefs and Peasants: Accomplishing Change for Victims in the Criminal Justice System' in M Maguire and J Pointing (eds), *Victims of Crime: A New Deal?* (Milton Keynes: Open UP, 1988).

Shapland, J, and Bell, E, 'Victims in the Magistrates' Courts and Crown Court' [1998] Crim LR 537.

Shapland, J, Hibbert, J, l'Anson, J, Sorsby, A, and Wild, R, Milton Keynes Criminal Justice Audit: Summary and Implications (Sheffield: University of Sheffield Institute for the Study of the Legal Profession, 1995).

Shapland, J, and Hobbs, R, 'Policing Priorities on the Ground' in R Morgan and D Smith (eds), *Coming to Terms with Policing* (London: Routledge, 1999).

Shapland, J, and Vagg, J, *Policing by the Public* (London: Routledge, 1988).

Shapland, J, Willmore, J, and Duff, P, *Victims in the Criminal Justice System* (Aldershot: Gower, 1985).

Sharpe, S, 'Covert police operations and the discretionary exclusion of evidence' [1994] Crim LR 793.

Sharpe, S, 'Covert policing: A comparative view', (1996) 25 Anglo-Am LR 163.

Sharpe, S, Judicial Discretion and Investigative Impropriety' (1997) 1 Int J Ev and Proof 149.

Sharpe, S, *Judicial Discretion and Criminal Investigation* (London: Sweet & Maxwell, 1998).

Sharpe, S, 'HRA 1998: Article 6 and the Disclosure of Evidence in Criminal Trials' [1999] Crim LR 273.

Sigler, J, 'Public Prosecution in England and Wales' [1974] Crim LR 642.

Simon, D, *Homicide: A Year on the Killing Streets* (London: Hodder & Stoughton, 1992).

Singh, R, *The Future of Human Rights in the United Kingdom* (Oxford: Hart, 1997).

Singh, S, 'Understanding the long-term relationship between Police and Policed' in M McConville and L Bridges (eds), *Criminal Justice in Crisis* (Aldershot: Edward Elgar, 1994).

Skogan, W, Contacts between Police and Public – Findings from the 1992 British Crime Survey (Home Office Research Study no 134) (London: Home Office, 1994).

Skogan, W, The Police and Public in England and Wales (London: HMSO, 1990).

Skyrme, Sir T, *History of the Justices of the Peace* (Chichester: Barry Rose, 1994).

Slapper, G, 'Corporate Manslaughter' (1993) 2 Social and Legal Studies 423.

Slapper, G, and Tombs, S, *Corporate Crime* (Harlow: Longman, 1999).

Smith, D, 'Origins of Black Hostility to the Police' (1991) 2 Policing and Society 6.

Smith, D, 'Ethnic Origins, Crime and Criminal Justice' in M Maguire, R Morgan and R Reiner (eds), *Oxford Handbook of Criminology* 2nd edn (Oxford: Clarendon, 1997).

Smith, D, 'Case Construction and the Goals of Criminal Process' (1998) 37 BJ Crim 319.

Smith, D, 'Reform or Moral Outrage-The Choice is Yours' (1998) 38 BJ Crim 616.

Smith, D, and Gray, J, *Police and People in London* vol 4 (Aldershot: Gower, 1983).

Smith, G, 'The DPP and prosecutions of police officers' (1997) 147 NLJ, 8 August.

Smith, G, 'The Butler Report: an opportunity missed?' (1999) 149 NLJ 20 August.

Smith, G, 'Double Trouble' (1999) 149 NLJ 1223.

Smith, G, 'Police complaints and criminal prosecutions', paper presented to SPTL Annual Conference, 19 September 2000 (cited with the permission of the author).

Smith, J, 'Criminal Appeals and the Criminal Cases Review Commission – 2' (1995) NLJ 572.

Smith, J, 'The Criminal Appeal Act 1995: (1) Appeals Against Conviction' [1995] Crim LR 920.

Smith, J, 'Is Ignorance Bliss? Could Jury Trials Survive Investigation?' (1998) 38 *Med. Sci Law* 98.

Smith, R, 'Resolving the Legal Aid Crisis' (1991) LS Gaz, 27 February, p 17.

Snider, L, 'The regulatory dance: understanding reform process in corporate crime' (1991) 19 IJ Soc of Law 209.

Snider, L, *Bad Business: Corporate Crime in Canada* (Toronto: University of Toronto Press, 1993).

Softley, P, Police Interrogation: An Observational Study in Four Police Stations (Royal Commission on Criminal Procedure Research Study no 4) (London: HMSO, 1980).

Sommerlad, H, 'Criminal Legal Aid Reforms and the Restructuring of Legal Professionalism' in R Young and D Wall (eds), *Access to Criminal Justice* (London: Blackstone, 1996).

Southgate, P, Police–Public Encounters (Home Office Reseach Study no 90) (London: HMSO, 1986).

Southgate, P, and Crisp, D, Public Satisfaction with Police Services (Home Office Research and Planning Unit Paper no 73) (London: Home Office, 1993).

Southgate, P, and Ekblom, P, Contacts between Police and Public (Home Office Research Study no 77) (London: HMSO, 1984).

Spencer, J, 'Judicial Review of Criminal Proceedings' [1991] Crim LR 259.

Sprack, J, 'The Trial Process' in E Stockdale and S Casale (eds), *Criminal Justice Under Stress* (London: Blackstone, 1992).

Sprack, J, 'The Criminal Procedure and Investigations Act 1996: The Duty of Disclosure' [1997] Crim LR 308.

Sprack, J, *Emmins on Criminal Procedure* (London: Blackstone, 2000).

Starmer, K, and Woolf, M, 'The Right to Silence' in C Walker and K Starmer (eds), *Miscarriages of Justice* (London: Blackstone, 1999).

Stephenson, G, 'Should Collaborative Testimony be Permitted in Courts of Law?' [1990] Crim LR 302.

Stephenson, G, *The Psychology of Criminal Justice* (Oxford: Basil Blackwell, 1992).

Steer, D, Uncovering Crime: The Police Role (Royal Commission on Criminal Procedure Research Study no 7) (London: HMSO, 1980).

Stenson, K, 'Crime Control, Social Policy and Liberalism' in G Lewis, S Gewirtz and J Clarke (eds), *Rethinking social policy* (Milton Keynes, Open UP, 2000).

Stevens, P, and Willis, C, Race, Crime and Arrests (Home Office Research Study no 58) (London: HMSO, 1979).

Steventon, B, The Ability to Challenge DNA Evidence (Royal Commission on Criminal Justice Research Study no 9) (London: HMSO, 1993).

Stockdale, E, and Casale, S (eds), *Criminal Justice Under Stress* (London: Blackstone, 1992).

Stockdale, E, and Devlin, K, *Sentencing* (London: Waterlow, 1987).

Stockdale, R, and Walker, C, 'Forensic Evidence' in C Walker and K Starmer (eds), *Miscarriages of Justice* (London: Blackstone, 1999).

Stockdale, J, Whitehead, C, Gresham, P, Applying economic evaluation to policing activity (Police Research Series Paper no 103) (London: Home Office, 1999).

Stone, C, *Bail Information for the Crown Prosecution Service* (New York: VERA Institute of Justice, 1988).

Stone, C, *Public Interest Case Assessment* (London: Inner London Probation Service, 1989).

Sunman, D, 'Advancing Disclosure: Can the Rules for Advance Information in the Magistrates' Courts be Improved?' [1998] Crim LR 798.

Sward, E, 'Values, Ideology, and the Evolution of the Adversary System' (1989) 64 Indiana LJ 301.

Tarling, R, Sentencing Practice in Magistrates' Courts (Home Office Research Study no 56) (London: HMSO, 1979).

Tata, C, 'Comparing Legal Aid Spending' in Regan, F, Paterson, A, Goriely, T, and Fleming, D (eds), *The Transformation of Legal Aid* (Oxford: OUP, 1999).

Taylor, N, with Mansfield, M, 'Post-conviction procedures' in C Walker and K Starmer (eds), *Miscarriages of Justice* (London: Blackstone, 1999).

Temkin, J, 'Sexual History Evidence – the Ravishment of Section 2' [1993] Crim LR 3.

Thomas, D A, 'The Crime (Sentences) Act 1997' [1998] Crim LR 83.

Thompson, E P, *Whigs and Hunters* (London: Allen Lane, 1975).

Thornton, P, 'Miscarriages of Justice: A Lost Opportunity' [1993] Crim LR 926.

Tombs, J, and Moody, S, 'Alternatives to Prosecution: The Public Interest Redefined' [1993] Crim LR 357.

Townshend, C, *Making the Peace: Public Order and Public Security in Modern Britain* (Oxford: OUP, 1993).

Tombs, S, 'Law, resistance and reform: Regulating Safety Crimes in the UK' (1995) 4 Social and Legal Studies 343.

Tregilgas-Davey, M, 'The Police and Accountability' (1990) 140 NLJ 697.

Trouille, H, 'A Look at French Criminal Procedure' [1994] Crim LR 735.

Tuck, M, and Southgate, P, Ethnic Minorities Crime and Policing (Home Office Research Study no 70) (London: HMSO, 1981).

Tucker, D, 'The Prosecutor on the Starting Block: The Mechanics of the Bail (Amendment) Act 1993' [1998] Crim LR 728.

Tully, B, and Morgan, D, 'Fair warning' (1997) Police Review 24.

Tyler, T, *Why People Obey the Law* (New Haven: Yale University Press, 1990).

Uglow, S, 'Covert surveillance and the European Convention on Human Rights' [1999] Crim LR 287.

Uglow, S, Dart, A, Bottomley, A, and Hale, C, 'Cautioning Juveniles – Multi-Agency Impotence' [1992] Crim LR 632.

United Nations, Declaration on Basic Principles of Justice for Victims of Crime and Abuse of Power (UN, 1985).

van Dijk, J, 'Implications of the International Crime Victims Survey for a Victim Perspective' in A Crawford and J Goodey (eds), *Integrating a Victim Perspective Within Criminal Justice: International Debates* (Aldershot: Dartmouth, 2000).

Vander Becken, T, (ed), *Prosecution Discretion in European Criminal Justice Systems* (forthcoming).

Veljanovski, C, *The Future of Industry Regulation in the UK* (London: European Policy Forum, 1993).

Vennard, J, Contested Trials in Magistrates' Courts (Home Office Research Study no 71) (London: HMSO, 1981).

Vennard, J, 'The Outcome of Contested Trials' in D Moxon (ed), *Managing Criminal Justice* (London: HMSO, 1985).

Vennard, J, and Riley, D, 'The Use of Peremptory Challenge and Stand By of Jurors and Their Relationship to Final Outcome' [1988] Crim LR 731.

Vogler, R, 'Magistrates and Civil Disorder' (November 1982) LAG Bull, 12.

Vogler, R, *Reading the Riot Act* (Milton Keynes: Open UP, 1991).

von Hirsch A, et al, 'Overtaking on the right' (1995) 145 NLJ 1501.

von Hirsch, A, Bottoms, A, Burney, E, and Wilkstrom, P-O, *Criminal Deterrence and Sentence Severity* (Oxford: Hart, 1999).

Waddington, P, *The Strong Arm of the Law* (Oxford: Clarendon, 1991).

Waddington, P, *Liberty and Order* (London: UCL Press, 1994).

Waddington, P, 'Police (Canteen) Sub-Culture: An Appreciation' (1999) 39 BJ Crim 286.

Waddington, P, *Policing Citizens* (London: UCL Press, 1999).

Wadham, J, and Mountfield, H, *Blackstone's Guide to the Human Rights Act 1998* (London: Blackstone, 1999).

Walker, C, *The Prevention of Terrorism in British Law* 2nd edn (Manchester: MUP, 1992).

Walker, C, 'The Agenda of Miscarriages of Justice' in C Walker and K Starmer (eds), *Miscarriages of Justice* (London: Blackstone, 1999).

Walker, C, 'Miscarriages of Justice in Principle and Practice' in C Walker and K Starmer, (eds), *Miscarriages of Justice* (London: Blackstone, 1999).

Walker, C, 'The Judiciary' in C Walker and K Starmer, (eds), *Miscarriages of Justice* (London: Blackstone, 1999).

Walker, C, and Starmer, K (eds), *Justice in Error* (London: Blackstone, 1993).

Walker, C, and Starmer, K (eds), *Miscarriages of Justice* (London: Blackstone, 1999).

Walker, C, and Stockdale, E, 'Forensic Science and Miscarriages of Justice' (1995) 54 Camb LJ 69.

Walker, C, and Wall, D, 'Imprisoning the Poor: TV Licence Evaders and the Criminal Justice System' [1997] Crim LR 173.

Walklate, S, *Victimology: The Victim and the Criminal justice Process* (London: Unwin Hyam, 1989).

Walkley, J, Police Interrogation (1988).

Walker, N, (ed), *Dangerous People* (London: Blackstone, 1996).

Wall, D, 'Keyholders to Criminal Justice' in R Young and D Wall (eds), *Access to Criminal Justice* (London: Blackstone, 1996).

Walmsley, R, 'Indecencies Between Males' [1978] Crim LR 400.

Wasik, M, 'Sentencing: A Fresh Look at Aims and Objectives', in E Stockdale and S Casale (eds), *Criminal Justice Under Stress* (London: Blackstone, 1992).

Wasik, M, 'Magistrates' Knowledge of Previous Convictions' [1996] Crim LR 851.

Wasik, M, Gibbons, T, and Redmayne, M, *Criminal Justice: Text and Materials* (Harlow: Longman, 1999).

Wasik, M, and Taylor, R, *Blackstone's Guide to the Criminal Justice and Public Order Act 1994* (London: Blackstone, 1995).

Wasik, M, and Turner, A, 'Sentencing Guidelines for the Magistrates' Courts' [1993] Crim LR 345.

Wasserstrom, S, and Snyder, C, (eds), *A Criminal Procedure Anthology* (Cincinnati: Anderson, 1996).

Watson, S, 'Foucault and Social Policy' in G Lewis, S Gewirtz and J Clarke (eds), *Rethinking social policy* (Milton Keynes, Open UP, 2000).

Weatheritt, M, The Prosecution System: Survey of Prosecuting Solicitors' Departments (Royal Commission on Criminal Procedure, Research Study no 11) (London: HMSO, 1980).

Weatheritt, M, 'Measuring Police Performance: Accounting or Accountability' in R Reiner and S Spencer (eds), *Accountable Policing* (London: IPPR, 1993).

Wells, C, *Corporations and Criminal Responsibility* (Oxford: OUP, 1993).

Wells, C, 'Corporate killing' (1997) 148 NLJ 1467.

Wells, C, 'Work related deaths' (1998) 148 NLJ 1007.

White, K, and Brody, S, 'The Use of Bail Hostels' [1980] Crim LR 420.

White, R, *The Administration of Justice* (Oxford: Basil Blackwell, 1985).

White, R, *The Administration of Justice* 2nd edn (Oxford: Basil Blackwell, 1991).

White, S, 'The Antecedents of the Mode of Trial Guidelines' [1996] Crim LR 471.

Wilkins, G, and Addicott, C, Operation of Certain Police Powers under PACE, 1997/8 (Home Office Statistical Bulletin 2/99) (London: HMSO, 1999).

Williams, C, *Invisible Victims: Crime and Abuse Against People with Learning Disabilities* (Bristol: Norah Fry Research Centre, 1995).

Williams, G, 'Letting off the Guilty and Prosecuting the Innocent' [1985] Crim LR 115.

Williams, G, 'The Authentication of Statements to the Police' [1979] Crim LR 6.

Williamson, T, 'Reflections on Current Police Practice' in D Morgan and G Stephenson (eds), *Suspicion and Silence* (London: Blackstone, 1994).

Willis, C, The Use, Effectivenesss and Impact of Police Stop and Search Powers (Home Office Research and Planning Unit Paper no 15) (London: Home Office, 1983).

Windlesham, Lord, 'Punishment and Prevention: The Inappropriate Prisoners' [1988] Crim LR 140.

Wolchover, D, 'Should Judges Sum up on the Facts?' [1989] Crim LR 781.

Wonnacott, C, 'The counterfeit contract – reform, pretence and muddled principles in the new referral order' (1999) 11 Child and Fam LQ 209.

Wood, A, 'Administrative Justice Within the Legal Aid Board', in R Young and D Wall (eds), *Access to Criminal Justice* (London: Blackstone, 1996).

Wood, J, 'Appendix – Extracts from the Transcript of the Trial of the Birmingham Six, Lancaster, June 1975' in C Walker and K Starmer (eds), *Miscarriages of Justice* (London: Blackstone, 1999).

Woolf, Lord and Tumin, S, Prison Disturbances April 1990, Report of an Inquiry by The Rt Hon Lord Justice Woolf (Parts I and II) and His Honour Judge Stephen Tumim (Part II) (Cm 1456) (HMSO, 1991).

Wright, J, 'Policing Domestic Violence: A Nottingham Case Study' (1998) 20 JSWFL 397.

Young, J, Policing the Streets – Stops and Search in North London (London: Islington Council, 1994).

Young, M, *An Inside Job* (Oxford: Clarendon, 1991).

Young, R, *The Sandwell Mediation and Reparation Scheme* (Birmingham: West Midlands Probation Service, 1987).

Young, R, 'The Merits of Legal Aid in the Magistrates' Courts' [1993] Crim LR 336.

Young, R, 'Will Widgery Do?: Court Clerks, Discretion, and the Determination of Legal Aid Applications' in R Young and D Wall (eds), *Access to Criminal Justice* (London: Blackstone, 1996).

Young, R, 'Integrating a Multi-Victim Perspective into Criminal Justice Through Restorative Justice Conferences' in A Crawford and J Goodey (eds), *Integrating a Victim Persective Within Criminal Justice: International Debates* (Aldershot: Dartmouth, 2000).

Young, R and Goold, B, 'Restorative Police Cautioning in Aylesbury: From Degrading to Reintegrative Shaming Ceremonies?' [1999] Crim LR 126.

Young, R, and Sanders, A, 'The Royal Commission on Criminal Justice: A Confidence Trick?' (1994) 15 OJLS 435.

Young, R, and Wall, D, 'Criminal Justice, Legal Aid and the Defence of Liberty' in R Young and D Wall (eds), *Access to Criminal Justice: Lawyers, Legal Aid and the Defence of Liberty* (London: Blackstone, 1996).

Young, R, Moloney, T, and Sanders, A, In the Interests of Justice?: The Determination of Criminal Legal Aid Applications by Magistrates' Courts in England and Wales (London: Legal Aid Board, 1992).

Zander, M, 'Legal Advice and Criminal Appeals: A Survey of Prisoners, Prisons and Lawyers' [1972] Crim LR 132.

Zander, M, 'Are Too Many Professional Criminals Avoiding Conviction?' (1974) 37 MLR 28.

Zander, M, 'What the Annual Statistics Tell Us About Pleas and Acquittals' [1991] Crim LR 252.

Zander, M, *Cases and Materials on the English Legal System* (London: Weidenfeld and Nicolson, 1992).

Zander, M, 'The "innocent" (?) who plead guilty' (1993) 143 NLJ 85.

Zander, M, *Cases and Materials on the English Legal System*, 8th edn (London: Butterworths, 1999).

Zander, M, 'What on Earth is Lord Justice Auld Supposed to Do?' [2000] Crim LR 419.

Zander, M, and Henderson, P, Crown Court Study (Royal Commission on Criminal Justice, Research Study no19) (London: HMSO, 1993).

Zedner, L, 'Reparation and Retribution: are they reconcilable?' (1994) 57 MLR 228.

Zuckerman, A, 'Similar Fact Evidence: The Unobservable Rule' (1987) 104 LQR 187.

Zuckerman, A, 'Illegally Obtained Evidence: Discretion as a Guardian of Legitimacy' [1987] CLP 55.

Index

Index

Index

Index

Index